READING
IN INDUS BASIN DISPUTES BETWEEN INDIA AND PAKISTAN

AN ACADEMIC SELECTION OF ARTICLES, COMMENTARIES, NEWSPAPER REPORTS, LEGAL TEXTS AND ARBITRAL AWARDS

(1948-2018)

EDITOR

NASEEM AHMED BAJWA
M.A., LL.M., BAR-AT-LAW

ASSISTANT EDITORS

MARYUM AMIR
M.B.A

OZAIR ASHRAF
LL.M

GHP

IN ASSOCIATION WITH

PAKISTAN ACADEMY OF INTERNATIONAL LAW AND POLITICS

Grosvenor House Publishing Limited

All rights reserved
Copyright © Naseem Ahmed Bajwa, Aasya Ismail & Faisal Bajwa, 2023

The right of Naseem Ahmed Bajwa to be identified as the author of this
work has been asserted in accordance with Section 78
of the Copyright, Designs and Patents Act 1988

The book cover is copyright to Naseem Ahmed Bajwa

This book is published by
Grosvenor House Publishing Ltd
Link House
140 The Broadway, Tolworth, Surrey, KT6 7HT.
www.grosvenorhousepublishing.co.uk

This book is sold subject to the conditions that it shall not, by way of
trade or otherwise, be lent, resold, hired out or otherwise circulated
without the author's or publisher's prior consent in any form of binding or
cover other than that in which it is published and
without a similar condition including this condition being imposed
on the subsequent purchaser.

A CIP record for this book
is available from the British Library

ISBN 978-1-78623-554-1

DEDICATION

This book is dedicated to the prosperity and the happiness of 1.5 billion brave, resilient and long suffering people living in Kashmir, India and Pakistan whose destiny is closely intertwined with River Indus, its five tributaries and those mighty glaciers in the Holy Himalayas from which these rivers flow.

FOREWORD

We must begin the writing of this foreword by putting on record our highest appreciation and deepest gratitude to the following six stalwarts of great moral courage in India and Pakistan. They were engaged in life long struggle, against heavy odds for fraternal relations between the two neighbours who have not been on the best of terms with each other since 1947 – the year of their birth.

(LATE) ATAL BIHARI VAJPAYEE (ex-INDIAN PRIME MINISTER)

(LATE) KULDEEP NAYYAR (INDIAN JOURNALIST)

ARUNDHATI ROY (INDIAN AUTHOR)

(LATE) M. MASUD (CIVIL SERVANT / PAKISTAN)

(LATE) ASMA JAHANGIR (PAKISTAN / LAWYER)

(LATE) DR. MUBASHIR HASSAN (ex-FEDERAL MINISTER / PAKISTAN)

The editors of this book need not apologise for having merely and simply just edited a book comprising of second-hand material. We know that it is not half as good as writing an original book on the subject in hand. We believe that this book, in its modest way, would serve an academic need in the Indian sub-continent and beyond. It has taken us three years to complete this project. Therefore, understandably, we heaved a sigh of relief when we handed over the manuscript to the publishers. The task of collection all the relevant material, new and old, on the subject of water dispute between India and Pakistan in general and Indus Water Treaty in particular and to exercise our editorial discretion in choosing the most useful and relevant material was not as easy as it looked at the first sight. How we wished we had sufficient expertise to write an original book as so many distinguished scholars have done!

As we raise our hats to them, we believe that we have faithfully followed a strong academic tradition of collecting and editing writings of experts, engineers and well-informed journalists. We are happy that we have managed to get it published, against heavy odds, in order to make it available to the students of international water disputes in general and Indus Water Treaty in particular. The whole business of editing a book means that we had to make some tough decisions, e.g. the full text of Indus Water Treaty had to be excluded. It was done most reluctantly, simply because of constraints of space. We should be forgiven for having made a deliberate decision to include three summaries of Indus Water Treaty and one of outstanding dispute {Kishenganga} to make this book less sleep-inducing that what might have been the case otherwise. It is not easy to give a balanced view of a controversial water treaty and its troubled history we have honestly and to the best of our ability and intellectual honesty, strived to make the contents of this book as objective, impartial, balanced, informative and interesting as possible.

We owe a great debt of gratitude to all the authors whose articles were selected by us and included in this book and, also to the publishers of Journals where these articles first appeared. We must thank the past Pakistan Indus Water Treaty Commissioner (Mirza Asif Ali Baig) and his predecessor (Syed Jamat Ali Shah), three experts of international renown (Dr. Zaigham Habib, Arshad H. Abbasi, Dr. Abid Sulehri, Executive Director of SDPI in Islamabad) and all others who gave us, in the past three years, good advice, useful guidance and much needed encouragement. If this book deserves some credit then it must go to them and if there are shortcomings or omissions or mistake, and there must be many, then we the Editors must assume full responsibility and take the blame. We promise to make amends and to produce a better quality second edition of this book minus the shortcoming and the mistakes made in the first edition. We would greatly appreciate for any feedback, comments and criticism from the readers of this book.

This is the fourth book which has been co-published by Pakistan Academy of International Law and Politics with Grosvenor House Publishing Ltd, London. It must be made clear that it is a non-profit organization and we plan to run it as a charitable trust. The Indian sub-continent is a region which stands on precipice. It is volatile in a unique and represents a critical mass. Notwithstanding its less than happy past, it has undoubtedly a bright future. Countless millions of people, shackled for centuries to the heavy chain of grinding poverty, deprivation and suffering of all sorts have got to break their chains and liberate themselves. They have to make themselves free in the true sense, not superficially and artificially as they did in 1947. This means free from oppression, free from poverty, free from ignorance, free from illiteracy, free from disease, free from subhuman existence, free from scourge of sectarianism and free from the wickedness of fascism and populism.

This book has been thoughtfully and purposefully dedicated to 1.5 billion people living in South Asia. We are proud of their fortitude, resilience and great sacrifices made in the past 3000 years. What unites them is more formidable, more meaningful, and more enduring than what divides them. Let River Indus brings them closer. Let us join hands to save the glaciers in the Himalayas from which this mighty and scared river flows. Let us not jeopardize the well being of our future generations by refusing to resolve our differences using our good sense.

UNITED WE STAND, DIVIDED WE FALL

UZAIR ASHRAF – MARYUM AMIR
LONDON – SUMMER, 2019

PREFACE

Indus basin dispute between India and Pakistan, literally and metaphorically, flows from the way the state (Province) of Punjab was partitioned in August 1947. The seeds of great mischief were sown in the scheme of partition. The fact that the two neighbours in British India (India and Pakistan) have been on unfriendly terms, to say the least, for the last 72 years has not helped matters. The possibility of amicable, if not ideal, relations between the two neighbours remains a remote possibility. Still a hope unfulfilled and a dream yet to be realised. The ongoing Kashmir dispute between India and Pakistan and the desperation of the United States (on which Pakistan had come to rely heavily for economic, military and diplomatic aid and assistance bordering on patronage) to find some practicable and operational solution at the earliest possible date is the main reason why Indus Basin Treaty was signed in 1960. In the terms it was drafted, to put it in blunt words, was to take the sting out of Pakistan festering grievance against India who in the context of Kashmir dispute, controlled most of Kashmir and was in a strong bargaining position being an upper riparian state. To make matters worse for Pakistan, it had the misfortune of being ruled by a military dictator from 1958 until 1970 who was accountable to no one. In the final two years, before the protracted negotiations led to the signing of the Treaty in 1960, the autocratic rule was at its peak in Pakistan. It was an arbitrary decision made by the military dictator, masquerading as a civilian president, which was not discussed, debated or scrutinised by any independent forum of engineers or statesmen or journalists in Pakistan. It could not be rubber stamped by a parliament, since none existed at the time. Lawyers, politicians (who were then in hibernation), journalists and all sections of the nascent civil society were immature and looked the other way. Even if they appreciated the impact of the fateful proceedings, either no one understood what the treaty meant or no one cared or no one dared to tell the truth. The only voice of dissent was that of one senior, and legendry, civil servant and iconoclast, Mr M. Masud (popularly known as KHADDAR POSH) about whom we shall talk later on.

Distinguished scholars, like Qaiser Bengali, tell us that since 1919, the distribution of the waters of river Indus had been a source of controversy between various riparian provinces. The emergence of the two independent states in 1947 divided the Indus river system and internationalised the dispute. India's geographical position (due to its control over most of Kashmir) placed it as the upper riparian with respect to all the rivers flowing into Pakistan. The boundary between the two states (as Punjab got divided almost in the middle) was also drawn in such crude but wicked manner that many of the canal headworks (in undivided Punjab) remained with India. Using this advantage India halted water flow to Pakistan on 1st April, 1948. In the negotiation that followed an interim agreement was reached on the resumption of flow of water. Negotiation for a permanent settlement continued bilaterally at first and through the World Bank, discussed later on, at the second stage, covering 1951 to 1960. It needs to be highlighted that initial efforts to avoid a physical separation of the Indus basin and arrive at an integrated management of the river system were soon abandoned. The reason for this all-important decision also needs to be looked at some stage.

To summarise the position of the two parties, it can be stated that Pakistan was given all the three western rivers (Indus, Jhelum and Chenab) while India was given all the three eastern rivers (Ravi, Biaj and Sutlej)

Before we proceed further Shahid Javed Burki (another renowned Pakistani scholar and an international banker) must be quoted. He makes an interesting point in the context of water dispute, between India and Pakistan, while arguing his case in an article called "The management of Crisis".

"Stoppage by India of the water flowing into the canals that irrigated parts of Pakistan's Punjab provided the civil servants an opportunity to add another facet to their model of economic management. Rather than work toward a more lasting arrangement the civil servants chose a temporary solution which was the construction of a 'link canal' to bring water from a river that flowed through Pakistan. The only viable solution to the canal water crises was political accommodation between Pakistan and India, but the Pakistani politicians eschewed that option. Prime Minister Liaqat Ali Khan appeared in the balcony of his Karachi residence and raised his fist against India. The gesture won him immense political popularity but it also set back, by several years, the search for a lasting solution to the question of an equitable distribution of the water flowing through the Indus river system. Having threatened war with India to obtain what Pakistan considered its legitimate share in the river waters, the then Prime Minister turned to civil servants to find a solution. The civil service came up with a temporary answer: a link canal to bring water from the Ravi into the canals that had been fed from the Beas River. After receiving political blessings for the preferred solution, the bureaucracy displayed its extraordinary capacity for organization of large civil works. The link was completed in 20 months. Such a link was never contemplated prior to partition and therefore was not a part of Punjab's irrigation system. Its construction was an emergency measure and a considerable budgetary burden to the West Punjab".

In April 1948 India stopped water flowing into Pakistan for only five weeks; 1.5 million acres of agricultural land went dry which made cultivation impossible in Pakistan. Bilateral talks between two neighbours kept stumbling along but so shakily and turbulently that world Bank seized initiative in September 1951.The history of negotiations for the next 9 years, under the aegis of World Bank, make worthwhile reading. One senior bureaucrat Mr M Masood (Secretary, Pakistan Ministry of Food and Agriculture) wrote an angry note to the President General Ayub Khan which was submitted on 10th September 1960. Obvisoly it was the case of doing something too little too late .The recipient of this note, based on writer's protestation at the suicidal nature of IWT from Pakistan's point of view, was the military dictator who, unhesitatingly, threw it in the dustbin. One wonders whether he cared to read it at all.

According to Masud's biographers, Ahmad Saleem and Abdullah Malik (authorised by Masood's daughters) Ayub Khan did grant Masood an interview but only to warn him that if he did not keep his mouth shut and continued to express his hostility to IWT, he would personally execute him by shooting him down (page 208).If the reader of these lines is sceptical about the intensity of Ayub's furious reaction then we must invite him/her to read Ayub's autobiography (FRIENDS NOT MASTERS). Ayub wrote couple of pages to justify why he signed IWT. He was convinced that it was in the best interest of Pakistan which could not afford to fight a war with India over water dispute. Ayub's argument was that Pakistan had no choices but to sign IWT even if it meant that Pakistan suffers loss. The alternative, in his view, was to lose all in conflict with India. Half way through this apologetic explanation, Ayub did one decent thing. He did tell us truthfully that while addressing 30/40 government officials, reportedly critical of IWT, in Government House (Governor's House) in Lahore he made it bluntly clear that he alone is responsible for guiding Pakistani destiny and, that being so, if any one dares to criticise his signing of IWT then he would personally sort him out. Ayub cheerfully tells us that no one did so, except our hero Masood, of course. The official handout of Government of Pakistan stated that IWT would affect only 1.6 million acres of agriculture land in Pakistan but Masood insisted that it would be as high as 7 million acres. Ayub put forward various salient feature of IWT, e.g. Pakistan would get 80% of the total water supply of Indus basin system while India would get around 20%. Whatever the strength, or otherwise, of Ayub's argument in favour of IWT, it is certain that no political leader in Pakistan, however weak or imbecile, could have forced himself to sign it, not with-standing international pressure to do so. Only a military dictator (who had no qualms about signing a treaty with China and Iran which allowed him to cede a part of Kashmir's territory to China and cede a part of Baluchistan to Iran) could bulldoze it in a rough and draconian manner. There could be no better illustration of the expression "riding rough shod" over reservations in the minds of countless people, popularly called silent majority, who remained silent as if they were deaf and dumb.

We have reached the stage when the issue of water availability in Pakistan ought to be looked at. Here we can do no better than to rely on Dr. Muneer Gazanfar's contribution appearing in Lahore Journal of Policy studies (LJPS September, 2008)

First the three eastern rivers:

"Let's consider the issue of eastern rivers contribution to the water availability in Pakistan. Let us assume that on average, some 145 MAF (144 MAF, Government of Pakistani, National Water Policy, 2004) water annually arrives in Pakistan. But before we plan any storage we should look at how much of it is already being used and how much will be available on a suitable basis.

As all of us know after the Indus Water Treaty, (IWT, 1960), Pakistan is entitled only to the water flows from the three western rivers, Indus, Jhelum and Chenab. The three eastern rivers, Ravi, Sutlej and Beas now belong only and entirely to India. However, some water does enter Pakistan through the eastern rivers. The first question is: can this water be counted towards water availability in Pakistan on a suitable basis or not? Obviously according to IWT it belongs to India, which is legally entitled to it and will use it without sharing with anybody.

The second question is how much is this water? WAPDA adopted figure of 2 MAF (million acre feet) and 1.5 MAF (million acre feet) as the eastern rivers contributions for the mean year and 4 out of 5 years respectively in its computation of 1987. In the 1994 computation WAPDA raised the average annual eastern river contribution from 2 to 4 MAF and referred to it as the flow generated within Pakistan i.e. between Madhopur and Ferozpur headworks in India and Balloki and Sulemanki headworks in Pakistan. However, water related data issued as part of the Accord Documents by WAPDA in 1994 tell a different story. Page 3 and 4 sheet III (1) b (WAPDA 1994) tell us the average annual flow data between 1976 and 1994, as received from India, was 3.00 MAF for Sutlej below Ferozpur and 1.5 MAF for Ravi below Madhopur.

According to the IWT (1960) this 4.5 MAF addition to the water availability in Pakistan actually belongs to India which country will use it sooner or later. It is for the reader to decide whether this 4.5 MAF can be counted towards sustainable water availability in Pakistan or not? In addition it has been pointed out, that a number of link canals join Ravi and Sutlej rivers upstream of rim stations at Balloki and Sulemanki and transfer water to these barrages from the western rivers".

Dr. Muneer Ghazanfar continues his scholarly exposition by turning to western rivers:

"It has been estimated that for the development of the remaining 557,678 acres, India will require 4.76 MAF more on pro-rota basis (Abbas and Kazi, 2000). They can use more water if they like as there is no such restriction on them about the quantity of water or the time period in which area is developed. Therefore, for the future, authorized use by India from the Western rivers a figure of 4.79 MAF or at the minimum 4.0 MAF should be adopted instead of 2.0 MAF.

Discussing the World Bank expert's verdict on Bglihar Dam, Pakistan's Federal Government told the members of National Assembly that India could store 1.5 million acre feet (MAF) water in addition to 0.6 MAF storage India needs for Baglihar Dam under the Indus Water Treaty (IWT,1960). The Federal Secretary for Water and Power said on 22nd February 2007, "we cannot stop India to go for hydropower generation projects and we have information that it plans eight power projects at Chenab Rivers tributary namely Davi". The Secretary disclosed that India can store water up to 0.5 MAF for each of its planned eight projects on Chenab".

ix

Way back in 2005, Afzal Mehmood wrote an excellent article in "Dawn" in one of the Pakistan's daily paper on 16th July, 2005 under the title "Diffusing the water bomb". The failure of the talks to resolve any of the river-water disputes with India (Baglihar, Kishenganga, or Wullar), followed by the recent flooding of vast areas in Punjab and Sindh, caused by the Indian decision to put 566,200 cusecs of water in the Chenab, has increased Pakistan's concern about its rights as a lower riparian country granted by the 1960 Indus Water Treaty.

A part of this article is being reproduced below: -

- Federal Minister for Water and Power Liaquat Jatoi has disclosed that India informed Pakistan of its intention eight hours before releasing water into river Chenab which enabled the government to evacuate people from river and canal embankments. However, the flood water has caused breaches in protective 'bunds' [Embankment] and huge damage to the rural economy in the affected areas in Punjab and Sindh. Pakistan and India should give top priority to amicably resolving their water disputes because they contain germs of a future conflict.

- According to a recent report of the Geneva-based WorldWide Fund for Nature's Global Climate (WWF), global warming is causing Himalayan glaciers to rapidly retreat, threatening to cause water shortages for hundreds of millions of people who rely on glacier-fed rivers in Western China, North-Western India and the neighbouring Pakistan. The report indicates that glaciers in the region are receding at an alarming average rate of 10 to 15 meters per year.

- The Indus Water Treaty has put out of bounds the ability to store, divert and regulate water of the rivers covered by it. While allocating the western rivers to Pakistan, IWT did allow India some limited use of them. Under the Treaty, if India wants to build a project on the western rivers, it will have to give Pakistan the plan and designs in advance to enable Pakistan to satisfy itself that it is conformity with the treaty conditions. Pakistan is given an opportunity to raise objections, if any, and that is how differences have arisen. Fortunately, in one such case, the Salal hydro-electric projects, the governments of the two countries were able to resolve the issue. However, in other cases like Baglihar, Kishenganga and Wullar or Tulbul, the two sides have so far failed to settle their differences .The Baglihar dispute was referred by Pakistan to the World Bank for arbitration. The World Bank appointed Professor Raymond Lafitte neutral expert (NE) under the arbitration provisions of the Indus Treaty to deal with differences that have arisen over the Baglihar Power project on the Chenab River. It may be added that the arbitration clause has been invoked for the first time in the 45 years history of Indus Treaty.

- Since differences over the Kishenganga project on the river Jhelum have remained unresolved, Pakistan was obliged to refer this project too to the World Bank. The Neutral Expert's findings will be final and binding on both the parties. However, if the NE feels that the points referred to him are beyond his purview or that there is a 'dispute' the matter will have to go to a court of arbitration? Let us hope the problem relating to Baglihar will not reach the 'dispute' stage and will be decided by the Neutral Experts (in fact contrary to the hope expressed here it did go to the Neutral Experts).

- The SFG (Mumbai-Based Storage Foresight Group) report further states that both Pakistan and India have reached the conclusion that the meandering route of the Chenab River on the Indian side of Kashmir is becoming a determining factor in any settlement. Although most of the Chenab River lies in Pakistan, its headwaters are in India's portion of Kashmir. It is now obvious that India has designs on the River Chenab because it has identified no less than nine sites on the river for what it calls 'hydro-electric' projects which are likely to become controversial like the Baglihar dam.

- The truth of the matter is that underlying the technical disagreements over Baglihar, Kishenganga or Wullar are much deeper issues and concerns. Pakistan is justifiably worried about the powers of control that any structure on the western rivers may give the upper riparian country (India). It is apprehensive of the possibilities of a reductions of flows downstream in dry season or alternatively, of flooding in the rainy season. Pakistan is naturally concerned about the possible use of the river water as a weapon of war.

- Pakistan's anxiety over the security of its rights as a lower riparian country granted by the Indus Water Treaty, is not, therefore, uncalled for. The situation has been complicated by New Delhi's plan to build nine 'hydro-electric' projects on the river Chenab. One of them, the Baglihar dam, has already become controversial.

- No one country has the right to deprive another of a shared resource which thanks to geographic design collects in a basin within its borders. The Indus Water Treaty about water sharing between Pakistan and India survived the 1965 and 1971 wars between the two neighbours and water flowed uninterruptedly during both conflicts. It will be a tragedy of immense magnitude if the sanctity of the treaty is now violated by either Pakistan or India because that is bound to lead to disastrous consequences. There can be no greater confidence building measure (CBM) than the resolution of differences over sharing of water under the 1960 treaty. Since the breadbaskets of both the countries will be facing shortage of water in the coming years, the two neighbours must act quickly to defuse the water bomb by implementing the Indus Water Treaty in letter and spirit. For that it will be necessary for them to get out of the prison of the past".

Now we have reached a point where a world-renowned expert must be quoted:

Prof. John Briscoe, a senior advisor of World Bank has written in detail on the Indus Water conflict between the two countries. Part of one of his article reads as follow: "I have deep affection for the people of both India and Pakistan and I see a looming train wreck on the Indus, with disastrous consequences for both countries. Is there an inherent conflict between India and Pakistan? The answer is no, The Indus water Treaty allocates the water of three western rivers to Pakistan, but India to tap considerable hydropower potential of the Chenab and Jhelum rivers before they enter Pakistan."

"The qualification is that this use of hydropower is not to affect either the quality of water reaching Pakistan or to interfere with the natural timing of those flows. Since hydropower does not consume water, the only issue is timing. And timing is a very big issue, because agriculture in the Pakistani plains depend not only on how much water comes, but that it comes in critical periods during the planting season."

"If Pakistan and India had normal, trustful relations, there would be mutually-verified monitoring process which would assure that there is no change in the flow going to Pakistan. In an even more ideal world, India could increase low-flows during critical planting seasons with significant benefit to Pakistani farmers and with very small impact on power generation in India. Because the relationship was not normal when the treaty was negotiated, Pakistan would agree only if limitation on India's capacity to manipulate the timing of flow was hard-wired into the treaty. This was done by limiting the amount of live storage in each and every hydropower dam that India would construct on the two rivers."

Muhammad Suleman Khan of Indus Basin Water Council is not alone in Pakistan who continues to ring danger bells about problems arising out of issues relating to IWT. He has not forgiven India for having shown no respect to Pennsylvania Convention from 1948 to 1959 and he quoted a part of the said convention.

Muhammad Suleman Khan does not mince his words. He keeps writing regularly in Pakistan's (right-wing, nationalist) papers and so do others. There are quite few who share his view point in denouncing India's alleged water aggression. Suleman illustrates his point by giving two concrete examples. First it is alleged by him that India, contrary to IWT, built BAGHLIAR Dam and built a big water reservoir but the decision of the neutral expert, by and large, upheld India's interpretation of the Treaty and, most surprisingly,

Pakistan did not challenge it in the International Court of Arbitration. Critics like him got much needed support from Professor John Briscoe objective assessment (quoted above).

In this case, M.S.Khan uses harsh words to criticise of Government of Pakistan who firstly took six long months before applying for a stay order and then chose, for reason best known to it, to remain quiet about the digging up underground tunnels by India to divert the waters of River Jhelum.

The finding of the Neutral Expert was essentially a reinterpretation of the Treaty saying, saying that the physical limitation no longer made sense. The Neutral Experts finding in Baglihar, left Pakistan without the mechanism-limited live storage which was only (albeit weak) protection against upstream manipulation of flow in India.

India was put in a position of strength. India could deflect Bias River into Satluj River above Bhakra or divert the Ravi into the Beas at Madhopure. It could construct a dam on Wullar Lake in the Kashmir valley and dry up the river Jhelum. A headwork at Chenab at Dhiangarh, north of Jammu (in Indian controlled Kashmir) could deflect the Chenab from its natural course into Pakistan".

Let us now move from Mr.M.S.Khan to Mr. Abdul Sattar.

Nobody has been in a better position to write about Indus Water Treaty, from Pakistan's view-point than him. He was member of Pakistan Foreign Services for 39 years and it is Foreign Minister from 1999 to 2002. We quote at length from his authoritative book "Pakistan Foreign Policy".

"In the last week of 2001, the Indian government leaked a list of options under its consideration. One of them was abrogation of the Indus Water Treaty which India had concluded with Pakistan 1960. 'When Pakistan cannot honour the Simla Agreement and the Lahore Declaration, then why should we honour the Indus Water Treaty?" Union Minister of India said.

Former Indian High Commissioner to Pakistan, G. Parthasarathy, went one step better;

"Should we not consider measure to deprive the Pakistan of the water they need to quench their thirst and grow their crops? Should we not seriously consider whether it is necessary for us to adhere to provisions of the Indus Water Treaty. Extraordinary circumstances demand extraordinary responses".

An Indian writer on strategic affairs, Jasjit Singh, was as ill-informed, as bigoted. He urged that;

"The option of abrogating or withdrawal from the Indus Waters Treaty brokered by the United Nations in the late 1950s exists and Pakistan's reneging from its treaty agreements with India provide enough reasons to do so. Its follow-on steps could have negative impact on Pakistan's economy and food security".

The treaty was not 'brokered' by the United Nations (UN), but by a more potent body-the World Bank. The Indian diplomat directly targeted the people ('Pakistan') and wished to deprive them of water 'to quench their thirst' and to 'grow their crop'. The writer was indirect ('economy and food security'). But the objective was made plain-to starve 'Pakistan' into submission.

It reveals at once in a flash, as it were, barbaric inhumanity, emotional immaturity, intellectual incompetence, great-power arrogance and political ineptness. Water was used as a weapon of war in ages bygone. Article 54 of protocol I (1977) to the Geneva Conventions of 1949 says;

"Starvation of civilians as a method of warfare is prohibited".

It specifically mentions 'drinking water installations and supplies and irrigation works.'

Article 8 (b) (xxv) of the Rome Statue of International Criminal Court lists as a war crime "Intentionally using starvation of civilians as a method of warfare by depriving them (people) of objects indispensable to their survival, including wilfully impeding relief supplies."

Forbidden even during armed conflict, use of water as weapon in diplomacy is a far graver offence.

Nor does International law permit the abrogation of one treaty because another has been broken. Even the unilateralist US gave notice, under Article 15 (2) of the Anti-Ballistic Missile Treaty (1972), before withdrawing from it. The Indus Water Treaty has no such provision. Apart from the World Bank, it involved Australia, Canada, Germany, New Zealand, Britain and the US in collateral Indus Basin Development Fund Agreement signed on 19 September 1960 with Pakistan-the day Jawaharlal Nehru and Ayub Khan signed the Treaty at Karachi.

However, right from Partition in 1947 till 1960 and, in some respects, even thereafter, India swore by the Harmon's opinion for what it was: a piece of advocacy that might be useful as a negotiating device but hardly one that provided a basis for resolving concrete controversies.

In 2002 it is not untenable but barbaric to assert a right 'to cut off all the waters within its jurisdiction' and deprive the lower riparian of 'a necessity of life'. This is now a recognized rule of international law, irrespective of this.

It is also followed by tribunals in inter-states dispute within federations. A water-course system is a natural phenomenon. It becomes 'international' when international political boundaries are superimposed on it as and when new states are created by partition. This is true not only of surface water but also of ground water. Modern international water-course law covers both. 'The constant movement of the earth's water through the hydrologic cycle means that it would be futile for any one state to attempt to subject freshwater within its borders to absolute control. It also means however that the international community has a strong interest in this resource, including its protection and equitable apportionment.' It is certainly not a domestic affair.

When Pandit Nehru visited Pakistan to sign the Indus Water Treaty with the President at Karachi on 19 September 1960, Ayub's focus was on Kashmir. In an address to the Pakistan Institute of International Affairs, he said that "if somebody has a solution other than ours, let him suggest it. We can at least start thinking about it." It serves to tabulate the statements for they reveal a line which is of the utmost significance in the present context.

From 30 June 1960, after meeting President Ayub in Karachi, Member of Indian Parliment, Dr Raghu Vira, said at New Delhi that the Pakistani President no longer insisted on Indian plebiscite as the only solution. Some other 'mutually acceptable' way could be found which could 'save the face' of both countries. On 22nd March 1961, President Ayub said, 'If there is any other reasonable solution as would satisfy the people of Kashmir we should be prepared to listen'.

From 26th March 1961, Foreign Minister Manzur Qadir said in Calcutta that, 'In a mood of conciliation and for the sake of settlement' Pakistan was willing to consider fresh proposals acceptable to all the three parties".

For a different, and perhaps more objective assessment of IWT we must now turn to MR.A.G. Noorani who is a distinguished Indian lawyer. He writes on IWT in his excellent book (The Kashmir Dispute 1947-2012) and we quote.

A Pakistani official familiar with the Treaty said on 23 December 2001 that India had no storages on the rivers flowing into Pakistan and was, thus, in no position to withhold their waters. It would have to first set up storages on the rivers, which would take years to complete. Dr. Mubashir Hasan, a staunch advocate of conciliation with India, said that if the waters from the Indus system to Pakistan are reduced by one percent it would amount to starvation threat for a population of 140 million people. 'No government of Pakistan can take such a measure lying down'.

In 1947, Sir Cyril Radcliffe's Report on the boundary between East and West Punjab reckoned with the problems that would arise. He was asked to apply both the communal composition of the area and 'other factors'. The Upper Bari Doab (UBD) Canal System watered more lands in Lahore district than in Gurdaspur and Amristar districts. The headworks of the UBD Canal were in Gurdaspur district which was assigned to India, as were also the Ferozepur headworks.

The boundary line was ascertained to cut across the Indus basin and canal systems. On 30 December 1947 Sarup Singh and Mohammed Abdul Hamid, the Chief Engineers of both sides in Punjab, hurriedly agreed to a 'standstill agreement' on the UBD Canal and the Ferozepur head works till 31 March 1948. It was approved by the Punjab Partition Committee. On 1 April 1948 East Punjab discontinued delivery of waters from the UBD to the lower part of the canal. Gulhati writes: 'There is no question but that, under the conditions then prevailing, the action then taken by East Punjab could not but be regarded by the West Punjab and Pakistan as provocative.' The Indo Pakistan Indus Waters dispute had begun in a stark form. As it happened, the Indo-Pakistan Arbitral Tribunal also died on 31 March 1948. East Punjab had sought to assert a right. It refused to restore the flow of water in the canals "unless West Punjab recognized that it had no right to the water".

An agreement was signed on 4 May 1948. Supplies of water were resumed. Differences on the law were reserved. West Punjab 'agreed to deposit immediately in the Reserve Bank such ad hoc sum as may be specified by the Prime Minister of India.'

The course of the dispute until its resolution by means of the Treaty of 1960, which McCaffrey traces, is instructive. After a visit to the subcontinent, David Lilienthal, head of the seven states Tennessee Valley Authority (TVA), wrote an article in which he suggested that, 'the whole Indus System must be developed as a unit designed, built and operated as a unit'. Like the TVA, 'jointly financed (perhaps with World Bank help'. The World Bank President, Eugene R. Black, wrote to the Prime Ministers of India and Pakistan on 6 September 1951 to enquire whether they "are disposed to look with favour upon Mr Lilienthal's proposal." If so, he added, 'I should be most happy to recommend that the Bank lend its good offices.' Both Prime Ministers accepted the proposal, as Black confirmed in the letters to them on 13 March 1952. After prolonged discussions, the Bank put forth on 5 February 1954 a twelve-page, 'Proposal for a plan for the Development and Use of the Indus Basin Waters.'

It was after sustained and hard bargaining that the Indus Waters Treaty was signed in 1960. It allocated the waters of the 'eastern rivers of the Indus basin'-the Sutlej, the Beas, and the Ravi-to India and those of its 'western rivers'- the Indus, the Jhelum, and the Chenab-to Pakistan. Pakistan would construct link canals on the western rivers to replace its sources of water from the eastern rivers, and India would supply water from the eastern rivers to Pakistan during a ten-year transition period while the construction went on. The Treaty obligates each country to refrain from any interference with the rivers allocated to the other, with specified exceptions for certain domestic, non-consumptive, agricultural, and hydroelectric uses.

'The Bank's settlement efforts succeeded in part because it was in fact possible to increase the amount of a available water by the construction of works and in part because the Bank was able to secure the participation of various other countries in arrangements to fund those works.' Denunciation of the Treaty cannot fail to incite reaction from the World Bank as well as the countries which provided the money. In Article VII 'the two parties recognize that they have a common interest in the optimum development of the Rivers, and, to that end, they declare their intention to cooperate, by mutual agreement, to the fullest possible extent.'

A permanent Indus Commission was set up comprising a commission for the Indus Waters from each side (Article VIII). 'The Commission shall meet regularly at least once a year, alternatively in India and Pakistan.' The annual meeting must be held in November. The Commission reports to both governments every year before 1 June. Article XI contains detailed provisions for the resolution of disputes by 'a neutral expert' or by 'a court of arbitration'. Article XI reserves the legal rights and contentions of both. 'Nothing in this treaty shall be constructed by the parties as in any way establishing any general principle of law or any precedent.' India chanted a hymn of praise to the Harmon Doctrine while burying it. The Treaty can be terminated only by another treaty 'concluded for that purpose between the two governments' (Article XII [4]).

On 16 February 2002, Pakistan alleged a 'virtual suspension' of the Treaty by India on 24 December 2001, when it suspended inspection by Pakistan's engineers of India's 450MW Baghlihar hydro-electric project on the Chenab. India denied the charge. But a crisis of sorts loom while the inspections remains suspended. It is vital right under the Treaty.

Compulsions of geography persuaded India to retain the Punjab rivers and consent to Pakistan's 'unrestricted use' of the three western rivers which flow from Kashmir. The State is rich in water but deficient in power, eighty percent of it comes from outside. The State produces only 870 million units and it seeks 6000 million units. The Indus Water Treaty grants India limited rights for the construction of power projects on the western rivers. Hence the Wular Lake dispute (Annexure D of the Treaty). Storage rights are even more restricted (Annexure E of the Treaty). The fact that that state of Kashmir was not consulted when the Treaty was signed does not affect its validity, it only makes Chief Minister Farooq Abdullah's periodic, if contrived, tantrums understandable. The great loss has been to agriculture in a drought-prone state.

"Apart from the major rivers, even rivulets like Erin, Madhumati, and Vishev have the potential for hydel generations".

The Editor this book had an opportunity to meet late Mr. Sattar while he was still in office but he definitely looked uneasy when answering sharp questions. The point that I made before him vigorously but politely was that Pakistan's vital national interests, particularly in the field of water dispute in India, were seriously jeopardized by the first military autocrat and it is generally feared that they are not in safe hand, in the hand of Pakistan's third military autocrat (General Zia Ul Haq) whom my host was serving in a very serious position.

The Times of London carried an interesting report from its correspondent (Stephan Farrice) in Islamabad on May 2012 which started with a sensational statement "India may be threatening Pakistan with nuclear strikes but it is keeping its ultimate weapons in reserve. It could, in *extremis* us, cut off Pakistan's water supply .In 1960 the two countries signed a treaty that divides the distribution of water of six rivers that run down through India (actually Indian held Kashmir) to the shred Indus Basin. The Indus Treaty is considered so sacrosanct that India honoured it during both its 1965 and 1971 wars with Pakistan. Delhi is refusing to bow to demands from hardliners that it revoke the accord. Senior Officials from India and Pakistan continue to attend annual meetings of Permanent Indus Commission as if relations between their two countries were perfectly normal .Legislature in India administered Kashmir passed resolution recently (early 2012) demanding that the Treaty be scrapped. Ministers have publicly hinted at just doing that .But India knows that an attempt to interfere with water rights would threaten millions of Pakistani farmers, destroy Pakistan agriculture and attract international opprobrium as well as causing serious harm Bangladesh and Nepal, India's other water sharing neighbours .The Treaty was signed after nine years of negotiation and it says that although the waters of Pakistan's rivers can be used by India, it is not allowed to build storage facilities or to divert their-case .Even if India did derogate from the Treaty, experts estimate that it would take between ten years and 15 years for India to build dams to affect the flow. It is not as if India can turn off the tap in an hour." "It is noteworthy that the caption of the said story was "Indian keep their water weapon at bay."

On 22 February, 2010, Dawn (a Pakistan Daily) reported that Pakistan was still undecided when to formally seek intervention of the International Court of Arbitration against controversial construction of Kishanganga hydropower project by India in violation of the 1960 Indus Waters Treaty, New Delhi has started preparation to build another big dam on the river Chenab. Documents available with Dawn suggest that the government of Indian-occupied Kashmir has invited bids for a topographical survey of Bursar Dam on Chenab for acquisition of land and property. New Delhi plans to begin construction by the end of year. Bursar Dam is considered as the biggest project, among a host of others being built by India on two major rivers-Jehlum and Chenab- flowing through the state of Jammu &Kashmir into Pakistan and assigned to Pakistan under the 1960 Indus Water Treaty. The proposed dam would not only violate the Treaty, international environment conventions and cause water scarcity in Pakistan but would also contribution towards melting of Himalayan glaciers".

Pakistan's permanent Indus commissioner Syed Jamaat Ali Shah in 2010 publicly stated that he had repeatedly asked his Indian counterpart to provide details of the proposed water storage and hydropower projects, including Bursar dam. However, India has taken the stand that it was aware of its legal obligations and it would let Pakistan know about the project details and relevant data six months before construction activities as required under the bilateral treaty, he said, adding the Pakistan could do nothing more when such projects were in the planning and investigation stage.

According to Dawn's report, responding to another question about Kishanganga hydropower project, he said he had already requested to government to move quickly for constitution of an International Court of Arbitration to stop construction of the controversial project. Pakistan, he said, already nominated two members of the Court of Arbitration and had asked India to do the same. He said the procedure laid down in the waters treaty required the two nations to nominate three members to complete the composition of a seven member Court of Arbitration.

He said the procedure also required that in case of a disagreement over three adjudicators, the complainant nation should ask the World Bank to nominate these three members and start formal proceedings. Pakistan, he said, had even prepared the list of three joint adjudicators since India had not yet fulfilled its obligations to nominate its two members and three joint members of the court." We have completed the entire process, it was only a matter of formal launching and only the government could do that," he said, adding that perhaps Islamabad intended to wait for the upcoming Federal Secretary level talks before triggering the legal process. He, however, believed that these issues were of technical nature and should be processed accordingly as provided under the Treaty".

According to Informed source in Pakistan, India had not only started building three other dams namely Sawalkot, Pakal-Dul and Kirthi on Chenab River, it has also completed the detail project report of Bursar Dam site. The proposed dam would have 829 feet height, storage capacity of more than two million acres feet and power generation capacity of 1200MW. It should be noted that the height of Baglihar, Terbela and Mangla Dam is 474, 485 and 453 feet, respectively.

Bursar Dam would be constructed near Hanzal Village (near Kishtwar) in Doda District of Jammu &Kashmir on the 133-kilometre-long Marusudar River which is, the main right bank tributary of the Chenab river. Its construction would be serious violation of the treaty as its storage was much behind the permissible limits. More than 4900 acres of thick forest would be submerged and the whole population of Hanzal village would be displaced.

Arshad H. Abbasi, (Research Fellow at the Sustainable Development Policy Institute Islamabad), was of the view that the project area fell in Seismic Zone V and hence most vulnerable to earthquake. Two active geological faults lines----- Himalayan thrust and the Kishtwar fault----- were passing through the projects area, he said, adding that the worst impact of dam would be on glaciers of Marusudar river basin covering an area of 225.35 sq km and massive construction activities in basin would further aggravate the melting of glaciers. He said the project was located in Kishtwar High Altitude National Park which was an environment-protected area. Spreading over an area of 400 Kilometres, the park contained 15 mammal species including the musk deer and Himalayan black and brown bear and some rare birds for which an environment impact assessment study was necessary.

The News (Pakistan) reported on 10th July 2013 that in an another blow to Pakistan's water interests, India has started constructing the Ratle Hydropower Dam project with a capacity to generate 850MWs of electricity on Pakistan's Chenab River, in violation of the Indus waters Treaty. Pakistan has already objected to this dam, which will be three times larger than the Baglihar Hydropower Dam. Mirza Asif Baig, (Pakistan Commissioner for Indus Water), confirmed that India had planned to construct the Ratle Hydropower project on Chenab and Pakistan's side had objected to the project saying it was s sheer violation of the provisions of Indus water Treaty 1960.

"We have come up with strong objections to the design of the said project in a meeting with India at the permanent Commission of Indus Water (PCIW) level," Baig said and vowed that in the future meeting at PCIW level, he would continue to oppose the said project as its design violated the Indus Water Treaty".

The current position accordingly to expert is that India has already carved out a plan to generate 32,000MWs of electricity on Pakistani rivers and will be having the capacity to regulate the water flows that are destined to reach Pakistan. So far India has built Dalhasti hydropower project of 330MWs, Baglihar of 450MWs and now it has started a new project (Ratle Hydropower project).

On the Neelum River that joints the Jhelum River in Pakistan, India has already completed Uri-1 and Uri-2 Hydropower project and is also close to completing in Kishenganga Hydropower project. So much so, it has also built two hydropower projects on the Indus River that include Nimmo Bazgo and Chattak Hydropower project. The foundation stone of the 850MWs Hydroelectric Project on the Chenab River in the Kishtwar has been laid.

In the expert opinion of Shamsul Mulk (Former Chairman of Water and Power Development Authority), Pakistan needs to develop water uses in its all rivers by building water reservoirs to prevent India from constructing the hydropower project. Once Pakistan develops its water uses, then it can argue at any international court that India cannot build its project by injuring committed flow of Pakistan.

The most notable book which gives us an authentic and firsthand account of recent diplomacy between India and Pakistan, focusing on dispute relating to Indus water treaty was written by Mr. Kurshid Mehmood Kasuri who has been Pakistan Foreign Minister in General Musharraf's time. The book is called "Neither a Hawk nor a Dove" and is published by Oxford University Press, Pakistan. On pages 2001 & 2002, the visit of Indian foreign minister (Natwar Singh) to Pakistan in February 2005 is mentioned. There was a five point agenda of discussion between two foreign ministers and item number three of this agenda was as follow:

"Pakistan's strong reaction to the Baglihar dam issue, based on the fact that installed in the dam were in breach of Indus Water Treaty; moveover, Pakistan felt vulnerable since India could chose to fill the dam exactly when Pakistani farmers downstream would be harmed by this".

Unsurprisingly, both the President and Prime Minister of Pakistan expressed serious concerns to Indian Foreign Minister about the non-resolution of the Baglihar dispute and stressed that Pakistan has no choice but to approach the World Bank for an appointment of Neutral Expert as provided in the Indus Water Treaty. Mr. Kasuri goes on to tell us that Pakistan's reservation over Kishanganga Hydroelectric Project was also conveyed, in the words of Mr. Kasuri, "Urgent need to resolve the water issue equitably and in accordance with not just the letter but spirit of the Indus Water Treaty was emphasised".

Indian Foreign Minister's response was not very helpful and all that he could tell his counterpart that "Pakistanis was over reacting to the construction of Baglihar's dam". Following these sterile negotiations, Mr. Kasuri had no difficulty in reaching the conclusion that "the real issue dividing the two countries over water was a lack of trust between the two uneasy neighbours". Mr. Kasuri found it useful to quote at some length from an article written by John Briscoe (War or peace on Indus) which first appeared in the NEWS (Pakistan) on 3 April 2010. It is interesting to note that the writings of John Briscoe on the topic of water dispute between the two neighbours strike a more friendly chord in Pakistan than India where he is quoted, for obvious reason, more often than the other side of the border. Mr. Kasuri did the right thing to put on record the serious worry of his Government since Baglihar's dam (a450MW Hydroelectric Power) started in the 1990s was completed on 10th October 2008. As if this was not bad enough, as far as Pakistan was concerned, Indian Prime Minister publically expressed his satisfaction that the reconstruction program entailing 67 projects is well underway with 90 projects completed and Baglihar's being only of them. Mr. Kasuri needs to be complimented that he summarised the determination made by the Neutral Expert (Professor Raymon Lafitte) on one page (245) only. The verdict was announced on 12 February 2007, Pakistan claims that three out of the four points referred to the Neutral Expert where decided in its favour. They are as follow:

a. India was required to reduce the free board; the height of the dam above the maximum storage line to be 3 meters from the 4.5 meters set in the original design.

b. Peg the poundage at 32.58 million cubic meters instead of the desired 37.5 million cubic meters;

c. Raised the level of the power intake turbines that control the run-off by 3 meters.

But it must be said, that in all fairness, the verdict of the Neutral Expert was unmistakably vindication of India's position since the World Bank had turned out, Pakistan contention that the construction of the Baglihar dam violated the Indus Water Treaty. Mr. Kasuri deems it fit to quote yet another excellent article by John Briscoe (Professor of Environmental Engineering at Harvard University) which was published in The Economic and Political Weekly (India) on 11 December 2010. A well known report by US Senate Foreign Relations Committee titled "Avoiding water wars in South and Central Asia" was made public on 22 February 2011. Mr. Kasuri did well to quote briefly from this report in his book with a wise piece of advice at the end. Mr. Kasuri is absolutely right when he advises both India and Pakistan that the said report shouldn't not be taken lightly by the two countries. The brief summary of this report, as appearing on page 249 of Mr. Kasuri's book reads as follows:

"The Report cautions that breakdown in IWTs utility in resolving water conflict could have serious ramification for regional stability. Further, the report warns that no single dam along the water controlled by the IWT would affect Pakistan's access to water but the cumulative effect of multiple projects could give India the ability to store enough water to limit the supply to Pakistan at crucial moments in the growing season".

It is ironic that startling disclosure made by Wiki Leaks (no. 25273, 2767796616172003 & 176424) published by Dawn (A Daily newspaper in Pakistan) on 22nd June 2011 carry so much weight and bear so much relevance to the burning issue such as water dispute between India and Pakistan that an ex Foreign Minister of Pakistan felt obliged to reproduce parts of the confidential cable dated 25 February 2011, US Ambassadors in India (David Mulford) in his email to U.S. Ambassador in Pakistan states as follows:

"Even if India and Pakistan could resolve the Baglihar and Kishanganga projects, there are several more hydroelectric dams plan for Indian Kashmir that might be questioned under IWT. Both Baglihar and Kishanganga projects on the Chenab River, one of the three 'western rivers' to those waters Pakistan has exclusive 'consumptive' rights under the IWT in which have been the source of long festering disagreement between the two neighbours".

The leaked cable made particular reference to the Dul Hasti Dam (then under construction but now completed) and the proposed Burser, Pakul Dul and Sawal Kote projects on the Indian site which were all on the order of 1000MW each. In a cable sent out on a 3 November 2008, US Ambassador in Pakistan points out that Pakistan was facing a 34% of water shortage at that year because of reduction in water flow of

Chenab. Ambassador Peterson also revealed that official India dispelled Pakistani's claim but unofficially the Indian side admitted that weather and structural constraint of Baglihar dam had resulted in reduction of Pakistan's share in water. Mr. Kasuri understandably asked the printer of his book to publish the last bit of the disclosure made in the leaked cable in italics in order to emphasis the contents of this disclosure. Before we stop making repeated references to Mr. Kasuri's extremely useful and recommendable book, it would be appropriate to quote the contents of page 268/269 under the title of Wullar Barrage/Tulbul project.

"The Tulbul Project is a navigation lock-cum-control structure at the mouth of Wullar Lake. The original Indian plan envisaged the construction of a barrage, 439 feet long and 40 feet wide, with a maximum storage capacity of 0.30 million acre-feet of water. Indian proposed building the barrage in 1984 on River Jhelum, at the mouth of Wullar Lake, Kashmir's largest fresh-water lake located near Sopore town in the Kashmir Valley. The purpose of this project was to regulate the release of water from the natural storage in the lake to maintain a minimum draught of 4.5 feet in the river up to Baramaulla during the lean winter months. Aimed at making the river navigable, the project was conceived in the early 1980s and work on it began in 1984.

According to Pakistan, construction of Wullar Barrage violates the IWT (Indus Water Treaty) which forbids construction of any storage project on River Jhelum in Jammu & Kashmir. Pakistan contends that its agriculture and hydroelectric uses would be negatively affected and that the use of the western rivers cannot be made subservient to the navigational needs of India which would require restricting the flow pattern of water of the three western rivers in breach of the provisions of the IWT. Pakistan fears that India could use the barrage as a geostrategic weapon by controlling the flow of the river. The barrage could also potentially disrupt Pakistan's Upper Jhelum Canal Project, Upper Chenab Canal Project, and lower Bari Doab Canal Project.

Indian maintains that the Tulbul Project is meant for non-consumptive used and navigational purposes. Further, India holds that there is no man-made storage involved as the lake would naturally fill and that the control gates would only be used during times of water scarcity or depletion. On the issue of Wullar Barrage/Tulbul Project, Pakistan and India held several discussions without any meaningful in 2007 upon Pakistan's objection. The stalemate between the two countries over this issue continues."

Yasmeen Aftab Ali (a lawyer in Pakistan) wrote an article in a newspaper in a memory of Naveed Tajammal who was a Commission Officer in Pakistan Army and was apprehended by a military dictator in Pakistan, General Zia Ul Haq in 1980 for attempting a coup against him with many other Army officers and masterminded by Naveed's father, Major General Tajammal Hussain Malik. In this article Yasmeen quoted from an article written by late Captain Naveed on the topic of the Indus Accord (1960), and that quotation is reproduced as below:

"Two sets of laws govern the water disputes: first is the Harmon Doctrine, named after a Judson Harmon, who was the Attorney General of USA in 1895, when arose a dispute between Mexico and USA over the usage of Rio Grande waters. Mexico was lower riparian, the doctrine above citied gives "absolute territorial sovereignty" to the upper riparian as goes the usage of water resources passing through its lands, though the matter was resolved by a convention held between USA and Mexico on May 21, 1906, by which Mexico got its share of waters".

Indus valley river system is an "international drainage basin", as the geographical area extends and covers the administrative boundaries of more than two states, from Afghanistan to Chinese administered Tibet in the north east, and to Indian Occupied Kashmir.

"A set of rules drafted in 1966 by (International Law Association), a set of rules, drafted in 1966, called "The Helsinki Rules" define the perimeters in case of water related disputes in the cases where the drainage of a basin is international, as stated above. There are 11 main points/clauses that govern the rights of a lower riparian. They are briefly all about the geography of the basin, extent of drainage and area in the territory of each basin state, the hydrology of the basin, past history of water flow, population dependent on the waters, economic and social needs of each basin state may be satisfied without causing injury to a co-basin state. India, it seems, follows the Harmon Doctrine while we twiddle our thumbs".

In Pakistan, the Neelum-Jhelum Hydropower Project was first conceived in 1989 and meant to produce 1000MW. Since then it has been victim at financial woes and corruption in the awarding of contracts, as stated editorially by one of Pakistan's leading newspaper, The News. In 2014, Nawaz Sharif (Pakistan's Prime Minister) finally decided the project had to be operational by the end of 2015 and completed a year after that. To that end he secured $448 million of funding from China's Import-Export Bank. This money was badly needed as Chinese contractors had threatened to stop working because they were owed Rs. 4 billion in unpaid dues. Now that money too has run out and the project is still nowhere near completion.

"The endless delays in the project have added effect of worsening Pakistan's water problems with India. The popular belief of water experts is the only reason India completed the Kishanganga Project is because Pakistan had not finished Neelum-Jhelum Hydropower Project. Under the Indus Water Treaty, India is allowed to divert water which would otherwise reach Pakistan for its energy needs. Had we completed work that water would not have been available for India. The International Court of Arbitration ruled against Pakistan on the Kishanganga project mainly because Pakistan had not demonstrated the ability to use the water for our own energy needs. The longer this project is delayed-and right now there is no end in sight the more opportunity it gives to India to build more dams and diverts more water."

Any avid reader of Pakistani newspaper is regularly comes across news, always startling and occasionally sensational, about building of new hydroelectric projects on rivers Chenab and Jhelum, since these are two of three rivers (the third being Indus) which are generically described as western rivers and allotted to Pakistan as a result of the division of 6 rivers flowing from Kashmir to Pakistan. The list of such projects is fairly long. It includes Jaspa, Karthai and few other names which are equally hard to pronounce.

Almost all water experts in Pakistan agree that Pakistan may lose up to 13% of water to Neelum-Jhelum River as a result of India having built Kishanganga dam which would produce electricity of 333MW and is only 160KM away from Muzzafarabad (the capital of Pakistan controlled Kashmir.) Indian engineers used stream of water (Banar Madh Matti) to connect river Neelum and Jhelum. The length of the tunnel used for diversion of water is 22KM and Wullar Lake would be used to put the diverted water back into River Jhelum. It is a point called Domail near Muzzafarabad where River Neelum and Jhelum merge into each other. It is alleged by the Pakistani's expert that diversion of river Neelum would make Neelum valley barren and significantly reduce the volume of water flowing into Pakistan. Similarly Pakistan apprehension is that Kishanganga would be as detrimental to the volume of water flowing in River Jhelum as Baglihar dam would be to River Chenab.

Shabina Faraz wrote a well researched article in a leading newspaper of Pakistan on 19 January 2014 and used very strident language against the team of legal experts who represented Pakistan before the court of arbitration dealing with Kishanganga dispute. In fact the grounds for the indictment of Pakistani legal team is to be found in the award itself which says that Pakistani team failed to produce the relevant data, in spite of being clearly advised to do so relating to actual and potential use of Kishanganga water and the repercussion of this dam and paucity of the information relevant to Pakistan case. Shabina rightly describes the said critical remarks to be a charged sheet against the Pakistani representatives to be found on pages 93 and 94 of the Courts Award. Pakistani authorities were criticised by the court that they have made no effort at all to exchange hydrological data with India. Shabina is happy to rely on the views of Arshad Abbasi (Pakistani leading water expert) that investigation should be conducted against Pakistani legal team for its dismal failure to present Pakistan case with mathematical accuracy. Annually Pakistani rivers bring to it 2.4 million MAF. Mr. Abbasi expresses his well founded fear that in years to come, the total volume would be reduced by 45%. The charge sheet against Pakistani officials and the authorities responsible for national security is that India was not asked to submit details of the engineering design of Baglihar dam. Pakistan took his case to international forum at very late hour when the construction work on the dam was almost finished. The court thought it pertinent to put it on record that it was the request of Pakistani delegation that court of Arbitration held his meeting in Paris, Washington, Geneva and London. The reason for doing so could safely be left to the reader's common sense. Shabina is not only the first person who expressed her opinion publicly that because of the inherent fault lines in IWT, it should be re-negotiated to enable Pakistan to get more fair and equitable deal. According to report released by Woodrow Wilson International Centre of Scholars in 2009, the availability of water per head in Pakistan has gone down by 70%. In 1947, it was 5000 cubic feet per person but in 2009, it went down to 1000 cubic feet per person. According to Indus Water Treaty, Pakistan was to receive 55000 cusec of water but in 2008 and 2009, Pakistan received only 13000 in water (Rabi season in Pakistan revenue terminology) and 29000 in summer (Kharif season in Pakistan revenue terminology).

Indian engineers deserve to praise on their ability to build big and small dams. By Building 4079 dams in total, India gained the distinction of being third in the world in the list of dam building countries.

It is appropriate to highlight one interesting fact that almost all the hostile criticism of the problem arsing from Indus Water Treaty (such as Baglihar and Kishanganga disputes) appear in Pakistan's newspaper, forums and think tanks. We have dealt with the popular perception in Pakistan relating to Kishanganga dam and now we must briefly deal with the comments focused on the Baglihar dam. The general consensus of Pakistani newspaper could be summarised as follow:

a. The total agricultural land in Punjab which would be adversely affected in terms of irrigation by the building of Baglihar dam would be in the region of 10 million acres.

b. The Indian government repeatedly and maliciously releases vast quantity of water, stored in the dam in order to cause serious floods in Pakistan and make great reduction in flow of waters in the river flowing into Pakistan during the sowing season.

c. As a result of Indian water policy, unfriendly as it is, Pakistan rice production has fallen from 5.7 million tons to 4.7 million tons.

d. Late General Hameed Gul who had been the head of Inter-services Intelligence (ISI) (Pakistan foremost intelligence agency), once invited the Editor of this book to a nice lunch at Islamabad Club in order to hammer his view point that building of 62 dams by Indian on Pakistani rivers poses an existential threat and this view of the late General was treated as gospel in Pakistan. He was very contemptuous of the role played by the World Bank and had serious doubts on the impartiality of the Neutral Experts who ordered the reduction of flow of water by 13.5% and reduced the height of dam by 1.5 meters and to reduce the length of canal by 3KM.

e. The spill way gate of Baglihar dam has been designed in such a way that they would be 27 meters lower than the minimum level (dead level) of the water and this would vastly increase the ability of Indian engineers to control the volume of water flowing into Pakistan.

f. The total volume of water flowing annually into River Chenab between 20 and 22 MAF (million acre feet). Bagalihar dam would enable India to control the flow of half of this water.

g. On 30 December 2008, a delegation of Indian's Indus Basin commission visited Head Maralla an important hydal station on River Chenab in the North of Pakistan and closest point to Kashmir in order to look at the system and the equipment in place to gauge the volume of water. This was at one time the invitation of Syed Jamaat Ali Shah who was the Head of Pakistan Indus Basin Commission. This initiative of Mr. Shah proved useful.

h. According to an International Water Law, India is obliged to give Pakistan notice in good time about the exceptional volume of water to be released flowing into its rivers but this rule has been repeatedly violated. For example in 2014, Pakistan was informed at the eleventh hour that on 5th September 2014 that 3,50,000 cusecs would flow from a border town of Akhonr but next day Pakistan founds to its horror that volume of water is twice more (700,000 cusecs). Sallar and Baglihar dam have the capacity to hold 200,000 cusecs each. When 2, 50,000 cusecs water was added by heavy rains, the total volume of water suddenly released into River Chenab was 600,000 cusecs which obviously caused tremendous devastation in Pakistan.

i. Indian's literally opened the floodgates into 2010 and 2012 to cause devastating floods in Pakistan but reduce the supply of water in 2011 and 2013 to make it impossible for farmers in Pakistan to have sufficient water to irrigate their farms.

Dr. F.J.Berber who studied the treaties, disputes involving international and interstate rivers between 1950-1954 explains in his book "Rivers in International Law" (Stevens & sons Limited, London 1959) the meaning of the riparian right in intelligible terms;

"(It is) the principle of community in the waters by virtue of which the rights in waters are either vested in the collective body of riparians or are divided proportionally; no one state can dispose of the waters without the positive cooperation of the others".

The case of the Jordon River dispute is a good practical example of the riparian law in application. The dispute involved Lebanon, Syria, Jordon and Israel. Israel which is a riparian state in relation to the Jordon river prepared a scheme of irrigation from its own share of the river waters contemplating diversification outside the watershed area of the river. Other riparian States raised objections and the United Nations intervened to stop Israel from implementing its scheme. This was in 1953. The UN then requested the Tennessee Valley Authority to prepare a scheme which would ensure the most efficient method of utilising the whole of the watershed in the best interest of the area disregarding the political boundaries. The TVA prepared a scheme which was based on the following principle explained in the introductory note of its report:

"A quality of water is suggested for each area of use within gravity reach of the supply made available and at the lowest cost....The reasonable needs of all in basin-users in the riparian states must be provided for before out of basin users can be considered..."

Dr. Zaigham Habib, one of the leading experts on water issues in Pakistan, is absolutely right when she rang the danger bell in 2011. She made the following points:

1. If in the context of IWT public sector in Pakistan proves unable or incapable of making correct and timely decisions. It is bound to cause serious domestic tensions between upper and lower riparian provinces in Pakistan.

2. She puts her apprehensions on record that India might be tempted to undertake such engineering activity in (Indian controlled) Kashmir which might be consistent with the letter of IWT but unmistakeably contrary to its spirit.

3. In her view, IWT turned a blind eye to vital issues like the quality of water and environmental flow and other environmental factors, which were obscure in or around 1960 when IWT was given its final shape.

4. She does not hesitate to put most of its blame at the door step of successive regimes in Pakistan who allowed themselves to be paralysed into in action by internal squabbles. All they did was to condemn India for building 130 dams (planning over 150) on the three eastern rivers (allocated to India) and doing the same on the three western rivers (allocated to Pakistan).

5. She believes that Kishanganga project in Kashmir (Indian controlled) could affects the flow of water in River Jhelum for up to 100 miles downstream. Change in the course of river could cause reduction in the number of fountain heads feeding the river. It could be detrimental to ground water re-charge.

6. It is unfortunate that, since 1960, India and Pakistan have not worked at a reliable system of exchange of water flow data between two of them.

7. She strongly advises Pakistan to enter into negotiation with Afghanistan to chalk out a good arrangement for the use of waters of River Kabul by adopting basic level approach.

8. According to her calculation, 5000 cubic feet of water per head was available to every person in Pakistan in 1951 which has now has dropped down to 1000 cubic feet.

It is remarkable that there has been a regular outcry in the newspapers in Pakistan since 2000, against hydro-electric projects, planned and executed in Kashmir (India-controlled), e.g. Karthai and Jespa on River Chenab. A letter written by Farah Naz (Researcher in water conservation) to Pakistan Prime Minister, was given prominent coverage in Pakistani media. She stated that the catchment area of Jespa Hydro-electric project would be 1295 squares Kilometer which means that its capacity is 100 times bigger than that of Baglihar Project. Similarly, Kerthai is designed to be five times bigger than Baglihar. According to a newspaper report, Mirza Asif Baig (Indus Water Commissioner for Pakistan), India did not communicate with him in the first year and a half of his tenure although IWT requires India to give full technical details of its hydro-electric projects, at least 6 months before its implementation. Three rivers (Sutlaj, Indus and Brahmaputra) flow from the massive glaciers in Tibet. The first two flow into Pakistan and the last into India where its name mean 'son of god'. It is 1800 miles long and joins the river holy Ganges (Ganga), at a vast delta in Bay of Bengal in Bangladesh (And that is the habitat of all those wonderful tigers). Unlike the Ganges, only the lower course of Brahmaputra is scared to Hindus. To make a small point, Indus is 100 miles longer than Brahmaputra. Rising in Tibet, it flows west across Kashmir, then southwest through Pakistan where it receives the 'five waters' of the Punjab. This mighty river, which surely deserves to be treated as scared in Pakistan as the Ganges in India, is harnessed for irrigation and hydroelectricity only by two dam's — Sukhur and Kotril in Sindh (Pakistan). In August 1998, a report by Phil Reeves, (Dehli Correspondence of the Times of London) was published with the eye-catching caption "India dusts grandiose plans to link its great rivers to combat drought and floods". A map appearing with this report informed the readers of the Times, that nearly two third of India's water resources flow down from Himalayas.

It would take the readers of this book only few hours to read the confidential letters written by the World Bank officials in 1959 and 1960 during the build up to signing of IWT but it took the two Assistant Editors many months to go through the, vast confidential archival material held at the Public Record Office in Kew, West London. These letters are so important that they must take pride of place in the appendices.

Before this preface is brought to its much needed end, it would be appropriate for the Editor to thank his two assistants, (Uzair and Maryum) for their diligence in doing editorial work and research over a period of two years and to thanks Salal Bajwa and Muhammad Imran Khan for spending many hours on doing good typing; to thanks those members of my family who live with me: my daughter (Ayesha), my granddaughters (Hajira and Zohra), my son (Faisal), and above all my long suffering wife (Yasmeen) who kindly allowed me to spend so many lonely hours in my study.

How two my colleagues and myself wish that readers of this book find it a worth-while exercise. Their suggestion and criticism would enable us to bring our much better revised edition.

Naseem Ahmed Bajwa
London, Summer 2019

CONTENTS

1. The Indus Waters Treaty between Pakistan and India
   By Arshad H. Abbasi 1

2. Indo-Pak Trans-Boundary Water Issues
   By Arshad H. Abbasi 10

3. The Indus Waters Kishenganga Arbitration Award (1 September, 2012)
   PCA Press Release 12

4. The Indus Waters Kishenganga Arbitration Partial Award (19 February, 2013)
   PCA Press Release 19

5. Baglihar Decision - An End To The Dispute?
   By I.M. Sahil 25

6. Transboundary Disputes: Two Neighbours and a Treaty Baglihar Project in Hot Waters
   By Rajesh Sinha 30

7. Unchartered Waters : The Kishenganga River Project Dispute And Arbitration Under The Indus Waters Treaty
   By Omar K. Ibrahim 34

8. The Security Implications of Water Prospects for Instability or Cooperation in South and Central Asia
   By Adam Radin 38

9. Hydropolitics in Pakistan's Indus Basin
   By Daanish Mustafa 48

10. Beyond Indus Water Treaty Ground Water and Environment Management – Policy issues and Options
    IUCN Report 62

11. The Politics Of Water In South Asia: The Case Of The Indus Waters Treaty
    By Hamir K. Sahni 71

12. Conflict and Cooperation on South Asia's International Rivers
    By Salman M.A. Salma & Kishor Uprety 81

13. Margalla Papers (2011)
    Pakistan's Water Security Dilemma: Re- Visiting the Efficacy of Indus Waters Treaty
    National Defence University, Islamabad, Pakistan 99

    A. The Indus Waters Treaty Under Stress: Imperatives Of Climatic Change Or Political Manipulation
       By Engineer Syed Jamait Ali Shah
    B. A Quest For Re-Interpreting The Indus Waters Treaty: Pakistan's Dilemma
       By Dr. Shaheen Akhtar

C. Pakistan Water Security Dilemma – Approaches to Rejuvenating the Indus Waters Treaty
By Sardar Muhammad Tariq
D. Sustaining The Water Division And/Or Sharing The Benefits: A Conflict-Management perspective
By Dr. Zaigham Habib

14. Convention on the Law of the Non-navigational uses of International Watercourses
United Nations 149

15. Pakistan's Water Concerns
By Dr Noor ul Haq and Muhammad Nawaz Khan (Editors) 163

    A. Water Disputes Between India and Pakistan - A Potential Casus Belli
By Tufail Ahmad (31 July, 2009)
    B. Water Scarcity And Riparian Rights
By Ashfak Bokhari (14 February, 2010)
    C. The Indus Waters Treaty - Its Dynamics And Reverberations
By Dr. S. Chandrasekharan (19 February, 2010)
    D. Water War With India?
By Ahmer Bilal Soofi (20 February, 2010)
    E. Interview: Distrust Complicates India-Pakistan River Disputes
By Kamran Haider (24 February 2010)
    F. India's Dam On Chenab Exacerbates Water Wars
By Pakistan Daily (24 February, 2010)
    G. India's Silent Aggression
Editorial, Daily Mail (26 February, 2010)
    H. Looming Threat Of Water Wars
By Nazia Nazar (1 March, 2010)
    I. We Will Have To Look Beyond The Indus Waters Treaty
By Amber Rahim Shamsi (3 March, 2010)
    J. Future Laden With Hydrological Warfare
Gauhar Zahid Malik (4 March, 2010)
    K. Is Pakistan Ready For Water War?
By Zahid Malik (15 March, 2010)
    L. The Water Crisis
Editorial, The Nation (24 March, 2010)
    M. India Plans 52 Projects To Control Pakistan's Water
Nation (Islamabad), (30 March, 2010)
    N. India And Pakistan Feud Over Indus Waters
By Amol Sharma & Tom Wright (30 March, 2010)
    O. Water Talks Run Dry
Editorial, Daily Times (Lahore), (1 April, 2010)
    P. Inconclusive Water Talks
Editorial, Daily Mail (Islamabad), (5 April, 2010)
    Q. The Threat Of Water Wars
By I A. Pansohta, The Nation (Islamabad), (6 April, 2010)
    R. Natural Security And Water
By Kashif Hasnie (13 April, 2010)
    S. Waters Dispute
By Swaminathan S Anklesaria Aiyar (13 April, 2010)

T. War Or Peace On The Indus?
   By John Briscoe (18 April, 2010)
U. Indus Treaty: Pakistan's Options
   By Ahmer Bilal Soofi (18 April, 2010)
V. Water Row
   Editorial (4 May, 2010)
W. The Water Factor
   Amitabh Mattoo (11 May, 2010)
X. Pak – India Moot On Kishenganga
   Post (Lahore), (13 July, 2010)
Y. Pakistan And India Agree To Install Telemetry System
   Dawn (Islamabad), (22 July, 2010)
Z. Pakistan-India Water Talks Conclude
   Dawn (Islamabad), 23 July, 2010
AA. Pakistan Initiates Process To Resolve Kishanganga Issue With India
    Times of India (New Dehli), (9 October, 2010)
BB. Accord On Roadmap To Settle Pak-India Water Dispute
    Dawn (Islamabad), (11 October, 2010)
CC. Pakistan: Nature Of Water Crisis
DD. A Potential Way Out
    By Barrister Mansur Sarwar Khan (17 May, 2010)

16. South Asia's Water: Unquenchable Thirst
    The Economist London (19 November, 2011) 225

17. Water Politics In South Asia: Technocratic Cooperation And Lasting Security In The Indus Basin And Beyond
    By Saleem H. Ali 230

18. Indus Waters Treaty
    By Ashis Ray (The Times of India), (18 March, 2010) 241

19. Pakistan: Indus Basin Water Strategy – Past, Present And Future
    By Shahid Amjad Chaudhry 247

20. Sustaining Energy And Food Security In Trans-Boundary River System: Case Of Indus Basin
    By Professors: F.A Shaheen, M. H.Wani, S.A Saraf 264

21. The Baglihar Difference And Its Resolution Process - A Triumph For The Indus Waters Treaty?
    By Salman M. A. Salman 275

22. Trans-Boundary Water Politics And Conflicts In South Asia: Towards Water For Peace.
    By Richa Singh (1 December 2008) 287

23. History, Ruptures And Water: Socio-Political Sites Of Water Conflicts In South Asia 293

24. Governance Of Trans-Boundary Water In South Asia: Disquiet Over Treaties 306

25. South Asian Rivers And Climate Change: Future Conflict or Cooperation 316

26. Executive Summary (2007) Expert Determination
    Baglihar Hydroelectric Plant
    By Prof. Raymond Lafitte (12 February, 2007) 322

27. Connecting the Drops
    Research papers of Pakistani experts 337

    A. The Indus River Basin Under Pressure
    B. Policy And Research Recommendations:
       Agriculture And Food Security
       Energy And Economic Development
       Climate Change And Environmental Pressures
       Glaciology
       Institutions, Governance, And Diplomacy

28. Case Study Of Transboundary Dispute Resolution: The Indus Water Treaty
    By Aaron T. Wolf and Joshua T. Newton 379

29. Indus Waters Treaty 1960: An Indian Perspective
    By Ramaswamy R Iyer 389

30. Water Wars and Navigating Peace over Indus River Basin
    By Abdul Rauif Iqbal.. 392

31. Pakistan's Relations with India: Beyond Kashmir
    Asia report No. 224 (3 May, 2012) 403

32. Water And Human Security
    By Aaron T. Wolf, Ph.D.. 405

33. Indus Waters Treaty (3 summarised texts) 418

34. The Baglihar Dispute
    International Water Power 439

35. Comparative Analysis of Indus Waters Treaty Drafts of
    9 December 1959 ; 20 April, 1960 and 19 September, 1960.. 446

36. Indus Water Treaty: Pakistan Water Gateway.. 457

37. Mechanism of the Indus Waters Treaty
    By Mirza Asif Baig 463

38. Indian Power Plants on River Chenab 474

39. It's Kashmir's Rivers that Pakistan Really Wants
    The Economic Times (India).. 478

40. Misusing the Indus treaty
    By Asif H. Kazi... 480

41. Briscoe On The Indus Treaty: A Response
    By Ramaswamy R Iyer 482

42. Indus Waters: Treaty And Conflicts
    By Lt. Gen. (R) Pramod Grover... 488

43. Revisiting the Indus Water Treaty and Arbitration of Interstate Water Disputes
    By Tamar Meshel 490

44. Defining the Geopolitics of a Thirsty world – The Parched Tiger: Indus Waters Treaty – An Unjustified Resentment Or Time To Bridge A River Divide?
Water Politics 493

45. Justice Fazal-e-Akbar Report: Indo-Pakistan Water Dispute (1946-60) and
Indus Water Treaty 1960 498

46. Consequences Of Indus Waters Treaty 1960 512

47. Indus Water Treaty
By Ahmed Rafay Alam 516

48. Poverty Issues In Displacement: A Sociological Study of Baglihar Project in
Jammu And Kashmir
By Sudesh Kumar 518

49. Hydro-Politics, The Indus Waters Treaty and Climate Change
By Rohan D'Souza 524

50. Indus Water Treaty: Need For Review
By Rizwan Ullah Kokab and Adnan Nawaz 529

51. Reviving The Indus Treaty: The Kishenganga Arbitral Award
By Dr. K. Uprety 537

52. Indus Waters Treaty and Resolution of Water Conflicts between
Two Nuclear Nations 541

APPENDICES PART ONE CONTENTS

App-1	Water Wager: Kishanganga Dam And Indus Water Treaty By Athar Parvaiz	569
App-2	Wanted: Bridges over Troubled Waters By Joy Deep Gupta	572
App-3	Climate Change: Melting Glaciers Bring Energy Uncertainty By Javaid Laghari	574
App-4	War over Water By William Wheeler	577
App-5	India Re-Thinking Indus Water Treaty By Khalid Chandyo	582
App-6	Reconsidering the Indus Waters Treaty: The Baglihar Dam Dispute	586
App-7	Academic Study of Indus Water Treaty And It's Impact By Parsad M. Chikshe	590
App-8	Violation Of Indus Water Treaty By Malik Muhammad Ashraf	608
App-9	Baglihar Dam By Usman Ahmad	610

App-10	Crucial Water Issues Between Pakistan And India: Confidence Building Measures And The Role Of Media By Muhammad Rashid Khan	616
App-11	Indus Water Treaty & Emerging Water Issues By Nosheen and Toheeda Begum	623
App-12	Pakistan's Water Crisis By Dr. Akmal Hussain	634
App-13	Vicious Anti-India Propaganda In Pakistan On Water By Trithesh Nandan	636
App-14	Harnessing The Indus Waters: Perspectives From India (IPCS)	641
App-15	Glossary and Map of Indus River Basin	647
App-16	Confidential Correspondence between The World Bank and the British Government Relating to Indus Water Treaty	649
App-17	Baglihar and Kishanganga: Problems of Trust By Alok Bansal	666
App-18	Baglihar Hydro Electric Project South Asia Network	668
App-19	Pakistan Asks World Bank to Appoint Neutrai Expert Under Indus Waters Treaty By Grish Kuber	671
App-20	Baglihar Cleared, India Has Its Way Times of India	672
App-21	India to Make Pakistan Barren by 2014 The News	674
App-22	India Violating Indus Water Treaty by Building Dams Daily Times	675
App-23	Noor Aftab The News	677
App-24	India Plans Dam on River Chenab Dawn, 22 February 2010	678
App-25	Another Blow to Pakistan's Water Interests: India starts building 850ms Ratle Dam on Chenab The News	680
App-26	Water as the Carrier of Concord with Pakistan S.V.	683
App-27	Pakistan Steps Up Water Dispute By James Lamont	686
App-28	India Not Stealing Pakistan's Share of River Waters Indian Express	688

App-29	Is India Stealing Pakistan's Water? Indian Express	689
App-30	Piped Irrigation to Check Indus Waters Dispute By Swaminathan S Anklesaria Aiyar	691
App-31	A South Asian Tri-Axis: The Indus Waters Treaty	693
App-32	Pakistan Seeks Resolution of India Water Dispute By Tom Wright and Amol Sharma	697
App-33	Rhetoric Grows Heated in Water Dispute between India and Pakistan By Karin Brulliard	699
App-34	Whose Water Is It Anyway? By Udit Mira and Cuckoo Paul	701
App-35	Indus Water Treaty And Jammu & Kashmir State By Suresh Thukral	703
App-36	Misusing The Indus Treaty By Asif H. Kazi	705
App-37	Neutral Expert Gives Judgement on Baglihar Dam	707
App-38	Going Beyond The Indus Waters Treaty By Maaz Gardezi	709
App-39	Kishanganga – The New Arbitration Between India and Pakistan	711
App-40	Water Treaties & Diplomacy: India Faces Difficult Choices on Water By Brahma Chellaney	714
App-41	Pakistan Gives India 'Non Papers' On Indus Treaty Breach By Muhammad Saleh Zaafir	715
App-42	Indo-Pak Dispute over Kishanganga Project By Zaheer-ul-Hassan	716
App-43	The News By Khalid Mustafa	719
App-44	India and The Indus Waters Treaty By Dr. Ijaz Hussain	721
App-45	Review of Indus Water Treaty (2013)	724
App-46	Winners Are Losers, And Vice Versa, In Indus Water Battle By Shaukat Qadir	725
App-47	Water Sharing between India and Pakistan: An Opportunity For Cooperation By Andrew Holland	727
App-48	The Great Indian Water Folly By Brahma Chellaney	729
App-49	The News (Pakistan) By Muhammad Saleh Zaafir	731

App-50	The Express Tribune (Pakistan)	733
App-51	The News By Khalid Mustafa	734
App-52	Dams Over Troubled Waters For Pakistan And India: Violating The Indus Water Treaty By Grant Atkins	736
App-53	Pakistan's Water Woes and India Bashing By Dr. S. Chandrasekharan	738
App-54	The Express Tribune	740
App-55	Indus Treaty: A Good Model Of Indo-Pak Conflict Resolution	741
App-56	India Accused Of Violating Indus Water Treaty	742
App-57	Kishanganga Dam To Affect Ecosystem By Tariq Naqash	743
App-58	Indus Water Talks: Pakistan to Seek ICJ Intervention If Talks Fail	745
App-59	India Agrees to Re-Examine Objections to Kishanganga Dam Design By Khalid Hasnain	746
App-60	Pakistan Accuses India of Violating Indus Water Treaty Agreement	747
App-61	India's Water Aggression Against Pakistan By Sajjad Shaukat	749
App-62	Pakistan Asks India to Honour Indus Waters Treaty	752
App-63	Water and Power Ministry Non-Serious Over Looming Indian Water Aggression By Zeeshan Javaid	753
App-64	'The Indus Commission Has Not Played an Effective Role' By Shafqat Kakakhel	755
App-65	Water Solutions By Javed Majid	757
App-66	India Not Responsible For Water Shortage In Pakistan	760
App-67	India for Resolving Ratle Hydro Plant Issue With Pakistan Through Talks	761
App-68	India Has Right to Build Wullar Barrage	762
App-69	Report of the Permanent Indus Commission	763

APPENDICES PART TWO CONTENTS

App-1	Recalling the Indus Water Treaty By Mushtaq Ahmed	769
App-2	India's Revocation of Indus Water Treaty Will Be Considered An Act of War By Riazul Haq	771

App-3	Modi stops Short Of Abrogating Indus Water Treaty By Mariana Baabar	773
App-4	Desperate Modi now Plots To Run Pakistan Dry By Zafar Bhutta	776
App-5	Indus Waters Treaty Rides Out Latest Crisis By Athar Parvaiz	778
App-6	World Bank Not Guarantor of Indus Water Treaty By Fawad Yousafzai	780
App-7	Treaty in Trouble By Sikander Ahmed Shah and Uzair J. Kayani	782
App-8	Indus Waters Treaty Model of Peaceful Cooperation By Anwar Iqbal	784
App-9	Implications of the Latest Indian Moves on the Indus Waters By Shafqat Kakakhel	786
App-10	River Diplomacy on Test By Nimmi Kurian	788
App-11	When Modi Proposed And Vajpayee Disposed By Charu Sudan Kasturi	790
App-12	Challenges Before India By Syamal Kumar Sarkar	792
App-13	India Completes Kishanganga Hydropower Project without Resolving Differences By Munawar Hasan	794
App-14	The Indus Waters Treaty By Hussain H. Zaidi	796
App-15	The Indus Waters Treaty Is Here To Stay By Rajeshwari Krishnamurthy	798
App-16	Law of the Indus By A.G. Noorani	801
App-17	Assessing India's Water Threat By Fahim Zaman and Syed Muhammad Abubakar	803
App-18	Review Indus Waters Treaty By Priyanka Mallick	808
App-19	Pakistan Warns India Against Breach of Indus Water Treaty By Zafar Bhutta	810
App-20	Farmers Will Get Every Drop (P.M. Modi)	811
App-21	Pakistan Pre-Empts Indian Water Threats By Mariana Baabar	812

App-22	The Great Water Folly By Brahma Chellaney	814
App-23	World Bank Declares Pause To Protect Indus Waters Treaty By Shahbaz Rana	816
App-24	Water Disputes: World Bank Halts Indo-Pak Arbitration By Shahbaz Rana	817
App-25	Pakistan And India To Consider Alternative Ways On Dispute By Munawar Hasan	819
App-26	Indus Water Treaty: Government Sets Up Task Force to Look At Full Use Of Water Share By Amitabh Sinha	820
App-27	India Signals Peace On Indus Water Issue By Suhasini Haider	822
App-28	Pakistan Not To Accept Alteration In Indus Waters Treaty By Anwar Iqbal	824
App-29	Pakistan Has Itself To Blame For World Bank Decision By Zafar Bhutta	826
App-30	India and Pakistan nurse myths on Indus Treaty By Peerzada Ashiq	828
App-31	World Bank Move Jeopardises Pakistan's Water Rights By Shahbaz Rana	830
App-32	The Indus Water Treaty And The World Bank By Malik Muhammad Ashraf	831
App-33	Pakistan's Water Security Made Part Of CPEC Framework By Shahbaz Rana	833
App-34	Pakistan Seeks U.S. Backing On Water Row With India By Shahbaz Rana	835
App-35	Pakistan, India and The Indus Water Treaty By Kuldip Nayyar	837
App-36	Violation Of Indus Water Treaty? By Babar Khan Bozdar	839
App-37	Pakistan's Neglect Behind Lingering Of Water Dispute - With India: UNDP By Amin Ahmed	841
App-38	Survival of Indus Waters Pact Weak: UN Report By Press Trust Of India	843
App-39	India to lose if it breaches Water Treaty By Sehrish Wasif	844
App-40	India To Attend Lahore Meeting On Indus Waters Treaty By Suasini Haidar	845

App-41	India softens stance on Indus Water Treaty and agrees to meeting By Nayanima Basu 847
App-42	India agrees to revive Indus Waters Commission level talks By Munawar Hasan 848
App-43	Pakistan and India To Discuss Indus Waters Treaty By Munawar Hasan 850
App-44	Revisiting the Treaty By Tariq Husain 851
App-45	India Wants To By Pass World Bank in Water Talks By Munawar Hasan 854
App-46	Pakistan Keen To Set Up Climate Change Monitoring System - For Indus Rivers By Munawar Hasan 855
App-47	Pak-India Water Talks Resume By Muhammad Saleh Zaafir 857
App-48	Dam Issue Likely To Figure In India – Pak Talks By Moushumi Das Gupta and Jayanth Jacob 859
App-49	Indian Team Arrives to Discuss Water Projects By Khaleeq Kiani and Khalid Hasan 860
App-50	Indus Commissioners Talks: First Step To Composite Dialogue? By Mirza Khurram Shahzad 862
App-51	Pak-India Indus Waters Treaty Talks 864
App-52	Shed The Indus Albatross: Indus Waters Treaty Offers One-Sided Benefits To Pakistan By Brahma Chellaney 866
App-53	What Is Indus Water Treaty? By Adrija Roy Chowdhury 868
App-54	Press Release by Pakistan Indus Water Commission About PIC's 113th Meeting Held on 20th – 21st March, 2017 870
App-55	High Level 'Water Talks' With India By Khaleeq Kiani 871
App-56	India Yet To Decide On World Bank Proposed Water Talks With Pakistan By Moushumi Das Gupta and Imtiaz Ahmed 873
App-57	No Indian Word to Halt Work on Controversial Water Projects By Khaleeq Kiani 874
App-58	India Denies Report on Miyar Power Project By Mariana Babar 876
App-59	India May Walk Out Of Indus Water Talks With Pakistan By Jayanth Jacob and Moushumi Das Gupta 878

App-60	Next Round of Water Talks with India in Jeopardy By Anwar Iqbal	880
App-61	Islamabad Believes In peaceful Resolution By Mian Saifur Rehman	882
App-62	Pak-India Showdown over Indus Treaty Likely By Monitoring Desk of The News International	884
App-63	Indian Government to Change it's Stand On Indus Water Treaty	886
App-64	Five Hydel Projects Underway Despite Pakistan's Objections	887
App-65	Pakistan's Water Diplomacy By Ali Tauqeer Sheikh	888
App-66	India Can't Skip World Bank – Mediated Process On Water Issue By Munawar Hasan	890

APPENDICES PART THREE CONTENTS

App-1	Legal Bindings: 'Prior Dispute Resolution Key to all Indus Projects' I.C.A. (Express Tribune)	895
App-2	Pak-India Secretary-Level Talks Likely in US by end of April By Khalid Mustafa	896
App-3	Pakistan's India Obsession Hides it's Real Water Challenges By Hassaan F Khan	897
App-4	World Bank Official In Delhi To Break Water Treaty Stalemate By Anwar Iqbal	898
App-5	Indus Water Treaty: Farmers say Indian Policies Leaving Pakistan High and Dry By (Express Tribune)	899
App-6	Pak - India Deadlock on Ratle, Kishenganga Projects Persists By Khalid Mustafa / News	900
App-7	IWT Violation: India not Sharing Flood Information With Pakistan Since 1999 By Sehrish Wasif / Express Tribune	902
App-8	Pakistan-India Water Talks Next Week By Anwar Iqbal / Dawn	903
App-9	Pakistan, India Conclude Water Talks in Washington By Anwar Iqbal / Dawn	904
App-10	Indus Water Treaty: India - Pakistan Talks Held in Spirit of Goodwill, Cooperation, says World Bank (Indian Express)	905
App-11	Pakistan, India to Meet Again Next Month for Water Talks: World Bank By Anwar Iqbal / Dawn	906

App-12	Positive Attitude Raises Hopes for Resolution of Pakistan-India Water Dispute By Anwar Iqbal / Dawn	907
App-13	Khawaja Asif Accuses India of Violating Indus Waters Treaty, Urges World Bank To Intervene By Naveed Siddiqui / Dawn	909
App-14	India, Pakistan Resume Talks to Resolve Water Dispute By Anwar Iqbal / Dawn	910
App-15	Pakistan's Water Talks with India in Washington By Anwar Iqbal / Dawn	911
App-16	India Pakistan Begin High-Level Talks on Indus Water Treaty in Washington (Hindustan Times)	912
App-17	No Agreement Reached at Indus Water Treaty Talks (The Times of India)	913
App-18	Indo-Pak Talks to Safeguard Benefits of Indus Waters Treaty, says World Bank By Anwar Iqbal / Dawn	914
App-19	Pak India Secretary Level Talks on Indus Water Treaty End Without Agreement (The News)	915
App-20	Talks on Indus Water Treaty End Without Agreement (The Nation)	916
App-21	Pakistan Seeks Arbitration Court as Water Talks Fail By Anwar Iqbal / Dawn	917
App-22	Pakistan Needs to Pursue IWT at World Forums More Vehemently By Rayyan Baig / Pakistan Observer	918
App-23	India Completes Kishenganga Project With Faulty Design By Khalid Mustafa / The News	920
App-24	Indian Government Moves to Tap Share of Indus to Strike Back at Pakistan By Vishwa Mohan / The Times of India	921
App-25	Indus Waters Treaty: Don't Lose the Game By Ahmad Rafay Alam / The News	922
App-26	Jhelum Water Inflow Declines Alarmingly By Khalid Mustafa / The News	924
App-27	India Plans Six New 6,322mw Projects on Chenab River By Khalid Mustafa / The News	925
App-28	Irsa Asks PCIW to Take Up Issue of Reduced Jhelum Water Inflows With India By Khalid Mustafa / The News	926
App-29	Water Shortage Swells to 60PC By Khalid Mustafa / The News	927
App-30	Water Policy Draft to be Tabled In CCI By Khalid Mustafa / The News	928

App-31	India, Pakistan to Hold Permanent Indus Commission Meet From March 29 (The Times of India)	929
App-32	India, Pakistan to Discuss Indus Waters Treaty Issues During 2-Day Meet in Delhi (Hindustan Times)	930
App-33	Pakistan to Double its Water Storage Capacity By Khalid Mustafa / The News	931
App-34	Permanent Indus Commission Meet Begins in Delhi (The Hindu)	932
App-35	Indus Water Talks Begin Amid Political Tensions (The Dawn)	933
App-36	Pakistan Approaches World Bank After India Builds Kishanganga on Neelum By / Khaleeq Kiani / Dawn	934
App-37	Working With India, Pakistan to Settle Dam Controversy, Says World Bank By Anwar Iqbal / Dawn	936
App-38	Non-Fiction: Revisiting The Indus Waters Treaty By Erum Sattar / Dawn	937
App-39	World Bank Urged to Schedule Talks on Water Dispute With India By Anwar Iqbal / Dawn	939
App-40	Pakistan to Pursue with World Bank 'Violations' of Indus Waters Treaty By India By Imtiaz Ahmad / Hindustan Times	940
App-41	Pakistan Expresses Concerns Over Inauguration of Kishanganga Dam Project By India By Naveed Siddiqui / Dawn	941
App-42	Pakistan to Discuss India's Violation of Indus Water Treaty With World Bank President (The Express Tribune)	942
App-43	What Is The Kishanganga Water Dispute By Anwar Iqbal / Dawn	943
App-44	World Bank Listens to Pakistan's Grievances on Indus Waters Treaty (The Hindu)	945
App-45	World Bank says it's Seeking Amicable Solution to Pakistan-India Water Dispute By Anwar Iqbal / Dawn	946
App-46	Water Talks Failed to Produce Agreement in Pakistan's Water Dispute With India: World Bank By Anwar Iqbal / Dawn	947
App-47	Indus Treaty in Jeopardy By Shamila Mahmood / Dawn	948
App-48	Tarbela, Mangla Dams Face 45PC Water Storing Deficit By Khalid Mustafa / The News	950
App-49	Minister Suspects Foreign Involvement in Opposition to Kalabagh Dam By Khaleeq Kiani / Dawn	951

App-50	India, Pakistan to Resume Talks on Indus Waters Treaty in Lahore on Wednesday (The Hindu)	952
App-51	Indian Delegation to Arrive On Aug 28 for Water Talks By Asif Mehmood / The Express Tribune	953
App-52	9-Member Indian Delegation Reaches Lahore for Two-Day Water Talks With Pakistan By Ali Waqar / Dawn	954
App-53	Indus Water Treaty Provided Framework for Resolving Disputes on Water Use: UN (Indian Express)	956
App-54	Indian Delegation Discussing Indus Water Treaty to Arrive in Lahore Today (The News)	957
App-55	Pak-India Water Talks Commence in Islamabad By Asif Mehmood / Express Tribune	958
App-56	Indo-Pak Talks on Indus Waters Treaty Commence, Joint Notification Likely (Hindustan Times)	959
App-57	Pakistani Experts to Inspect Two Indian Hydropower Project Sites By Khalid Hasnain / Dawn	960
App-58	India Agrees to Allow Pakistan to Inspect Kishanganga Project By Khalid Hasnain / Dawn	962
App-59	Pakistan asks India to Share Kishanganga Water Data By Khalid Hasnain / Dawn	964
App-60	World Bank may be Approached over Indian Hydel Projects By Khalid Hasnain / Dawn	966
App-61	Post Script	967
App-62	Introduction to the Editors and Pakistan Academy of Law and Social Sciences	968

CHAPTER - 1

The Indus Waters Treaty between Pakistan and India

Arshad H. Abbasi

Introduction

The Position Paper on **Indus Waters treaty between Pakistan and India** has been authored by **Mr. Arshad H. Abbasi**, for the benefit of Pakistani and Indian Parliamentarians joining the Pakistan-India Parliamentarians Dialogue-Ill, being facilitated by PILDAT.

The paper aims to explore various prospects of the Indus Waters treaty between India and Pakistan, its implications and a 'possible way forward. There should be a better political will for normalising India-Pak water disputes but to enhance it for the benefit of public of both sides, and promote peaceful relations.

As an independent Pakistani think-tank, PILDAT believes that while diplomatic channels for Dialogue must continue, Parliamentarians from both countries should be facilitated on both sides for a greater interaction and developing a better understanding tor resolving issues that should lead diplomatic initiatives. It is for this objective that PILDAT has been facilitating Parliamentarians Dialogues.

Disclaimer

The views expressed in the paper belong to the author and are not necessarily shared by PILDAT.

Islamabad
January 2012

PROFILE OF THE AUTHOR

Arshad H Abbasi is a Water and Energy specialist. He holds a B.S. in Engineering from Engineering University, Lahore and Masters in Engineering Management from the Center for Advanced Studies in Engineering. Mr. Abbasi served in various public sector organizations including the Planning Commission of Pakistan. He has served in various International Organizations such as ILO, WWF, USAID, IUCN and USAID as a consultant. Transboundary Water Governance and Energy management are his major areas of interest. He is currently associated with Sustainable Development Policy Institute (Islamabad/Pakistan), a world renowned think tank, as a senior adviser.

Abbreviation and Acronyms

Introduction

Interpretation of Treaty after Baglihar Dam Judgement

Water Situation and Hydropower Development in Pakistan

Recent Controversies

Illegal Carbon Credits for Nimoo-Bazgo and Chutak HEP Projects

New Multipurpose Hydropower Projects in IHK

Cumulative Impact of Live Storages

Wullar Barrage/Tulbul Navigation Project

Way Forward

Figures:

Figure 1: Water Distribution Chart

Figure 2: Comparison of Live Storage of Pakistan and India

Tables:

Table 1: Water Storage Capacity of Pakistan

Table 2: Electricity Demand

Table 3: Estimated Capacity of Projects

Abbreviations and Acronyms

CBM	Confidence Building Measures
EIA	Environmental Impact Assessment
EU	European Union
HPP	Hydroelectric Power Plant
ICJ	International Court of Justice
ICOLD	International Commission on Large Dams
IHK	Indian Held Kashmir
KHEP	Kishanganga Hydroelectric Power Plant
LOC	Line of Control
MAF	Million Acre-Feet
MW	Mega Watt
TEIA	Transboundary Environmental Information Agency
UNFCCC	United Nations Framework Convention on Climate Change
UNEP	United Nations Environment Programme

Introduction

The Indus river system, which is the lifeline of Pakistan and western India, comprises the river Indus and its five (5) main tributaries namely Jhelum, Chenab, Ravi, Beas and Sutlej. Division of the subcontinent in 1947 created a new international boundary, which cut across the Indus river system unevenly between India and Pakistan.

After years of mounting tension, India and Pakistan signed the *Indus Waters treaty on* September 19, 1960 which consists of 12 articles and 8 appendices. The Treaty defines the principles for sharing water of the Indus river system between the two countries.

Table 1: Water Storage Capacity of Pakistan

Storage Capacity	Indus	Jhelum	Chenab
MAF	0.35	1.5	1.7

The text of the Treaty very clearly defines the level and extent of water sharing for efficient use of the water from Indus river system. Further, the Treaty clearly indicates the rights and obligations of both Pakistan and India. According to the Treaty, the waters of the western rivers (Indus, Jhelum and Chenab) are available to Pakistan, while that of the eastern river (Sutlej, Ravi and Beas) are available for unrestricted use by India.

In the treaty, India has permitted Pakistan to create storages up to the limits shown in Table 1 on the Western Rivers for hydropower generation and flood storages which amount to total permissible storage of 3.6 MAF for non-consumptive use.

The conditions have been illustrated in Annexure 'D' and 'E' of the Treaty. The design of the hydropower plants and the maximum reservoir capacity for firm power is explicitly defined in sub-clauses (a), (c), (e) and (f) of Paragraph 8 of Annexure D of the Treaty. Annexure V of the Treaty also allows India to irrigate a crop area of 13,43,477 acres using waters of western rivers. So far, it has only been irrigating 7,92,426 acres of the land.[1]

The well defined characteristics of the Treaty set a precedent of cooperation between the two countries. It is an emblem of confidence building measure as it is the only treaty to have survived three wars and other hostilities between the two countries. India developed different Hydroelectric Power Projects (HPP), with the gross installed capacity of 2456.20[2] MW, after signing the Indus treaty;[3] however, the total electricity demand of IHK[4] is 1589[5] MW, as shown in Table 2.

India has also developed several run-of-the-river projects. Moreover, other four projects, MW **Uri-II,** 120 Sewa-ll, 45 MW Nimo Bazgo and 44 MW Chutak Hydroelectric Project are likely to be completed in early 2012.

To date, Pakistan has only raised objections on the construction of Baglihar HPP. Baglihar HPP is a run-of-the-river power project on the Chenab and was conceived in 1992. After construction began in 1999, Pakistan claimed that some of the design parameters were too lax than were needed for feasible power generation hence enabling India to accelerate, decelerate or block the flow of the river. This gives India a strategic leverage in times of political tension or war.

---
[1] Ministry of Water, Government of India.
[2] SK Government Order NQ.205 (Power Development Department) DATED 07.07.2011
[3] Before the treaty, only Ganderbal HEP was developed in 1955; all others were completed after the signing of the treaty in 1960.
[4] Indian Held Kashmir.
[5] J & K Electricity Statistics.

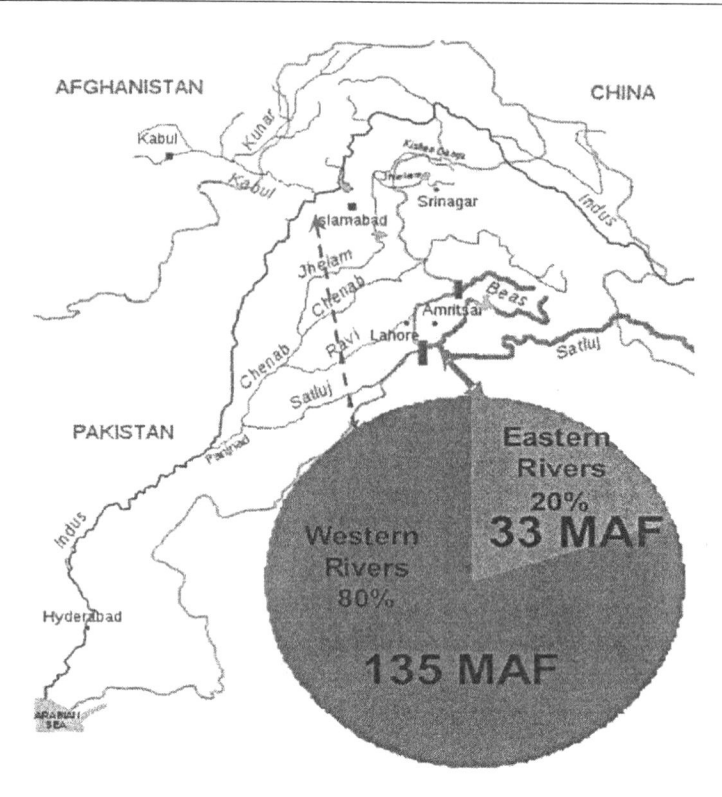

Figure 1: Water Distribution chart

During 1999-2004, India and Pakistan held several rounds of talks on the design of the project but could not reach an agreement. After failure of the talks on January 18, 2005, Pakistan raised six objections to the World Bank (a broker and signatory of the Indus Waters Treaty). India continuously denied the objections of Pakistan and claimed that the design was in line with the provisions of the Treaty. To solve this controversy, Pakistan sent a formal request to the Wold Bank in April 2005 to appoint a Neutral Expert in order to peacefully resolve the differences arising between India and Pakistan under Article IX (2) of the Treaty, in relevance to the Baglihar Project. The World Bank constituted a technical and legal team, headed by an expert, Raymond Lafitte, on May 12, 2005 for adjudication. The expert delivered his final judgment on February 12, 2007, upholding India's stance regarding design of the dam, with minor modifications.

Interpretation of Treaty after Baglihar Dam Judgement:

This judgment set a precedence to be followed in future if the need for the interpretation of the treaty arises. Raymond Lafitte applied the Vienna Convention on the laws of treatises (1969) and referred to the latest bulletins of ICOLD[6] rules of science and the state of the art practices. The need to incorporate state of the art knowledge of science in the interpretation of the treaty was emphasized by Raymond. The verdict of the court was made while using emerging knowledge of hydraulic, environmental science, climate change and contemporary research on dams. The judgment of the court, which is now set as a precedent and an integral part of the treaty, had indubitably said that rights and obligations of both the countries should be read in the light of new technical norms and new standards as provided for by the Treaty.

During the two years of hearing, India, in its counter memorial[7], appended the verdict of the International Court of Justice (1CJ)[8] in the case of Gabcikovo- Nagymaros dam dispute between Slovakia and Hungary

---

[6] The International Commission on Large Dams, or ICOLD, founded in 1928. Pakistan and India both are members of ICOLD.
[7] A legal document based on an answer admitting, denying, or commenting on charges in international court of law.
[8] ICJ Case-1997.

on the Danube River. In this case, the ICJ declared that new norms of international environmental law are relevant for implementation of any Water sharing Treaty.

Water Situation and Hydropower Development in Pakistan

Pakistan is at the brink of water stress level and it is feared that by 2020, per capita water availability may fall to 800 cubic meters. Pakistan has a capacity to store water for 30 days as compared to India's capacity of 120-200 days of water storage. India has utilized 33 MAF of the allocated share of the Indus basin wisely for irrigation and power-generation purposes. Moreover, India has also successfully developed Dams with gross storage capacity of 17 MAF and power generation of 12700 MW on eastern rivers but unfortunately Pakistan has only been able to install 6717 MW of hydropower so far.

Basin	Jhelum River Basin								Chenab Basin						Indus Basin
Name & Location HE-Plants	Lower Jhelum	Upper Sindh–1	Ganderbal	Upper Sindh–II	Pahalgam	Karnah	Uri – I	Chenani – I	Chenani – II	Chenani – III	Bhaderwah	Baglihar	Salal HEP	Dul-Hasti	Nine HEP
Capacity (MW)	105	23	15	105	3	2	480	23	2	7.5	1	450	690	390	13.3

Recent Controversies

The 330 MW Kishanganga HEP is a run-of-the-river hydroelectric scheme that is designed to divert water from the Kishanganga River - known as Neelum River in Pakistan-to a power plant in the Jhelum River basin. Construction on the project began in 2007 and is expected to be complete in 2016.

The waters of the Kishanganga River are to be diverted through a 24-kilometre-long tunnel for power production. The remaining water flow will join the Wullar Lake and ultimately run through Jhelum to Muzaffarabad, evading 213 km long Neelum River.

The Kishanganga HEP is another example of serious violation of Article - IV (3), C of the Treaty and especially Paragraph (5) and Article VII (1) (b). The provision of these articles clearly restrict India to increase the catchment area of any natural or artificial drainage and drain, beyond the area on the Effective Date. The diversion will increase the catchment area, hence resulting into a violation of the Treaty under the above mentioned articles:

i. By diverting the flow of Kishanganga River, upstream at Gurez, the catchment area of River Jhelum (tributary of main Jhelum) will be increased, which will cause enormous material damage in Neelum Valley due to adverse effects of nonavailability/reduction of water.

ii. The catchment area of River Jhelum tributary will increase the flow in the tributary that will cause material damage and will increase the likelihood of floods resulting in the erosion of agricultured land along both sides of the River Jheium tributary.

If KHEP is successfully implemented, it will result in a shortfall of almost 61 % of Neelum River at LoC and inflow for the NHJER. This will reduce the project's much needed energy generation by 35% in winter season. Consequently, Pakistan will be left to suffer over 141.3 million USD annually. This will also jeopardise the execution of already planned agricultural development activities in the area with a loss of 421 million rupees. Owing to the protest by Pakistan against the resultant multifarious effects of the construction of the dam, the construction was halted by the Hague's Permanent Court of Arbitration in October 2011.

Illegal Carbon Credits for Nimoo-Bazgo and Chutak HEP Projects

As per 37 clause (b) of the United Nations Framework Convention on Climate Change (UNFCCC) rules of business,[9] it was mandatory for India to ratify the Environmental Assessment Report (EIA) of both the aforementioned projects from Pakistan to earn carbon credits. India was awarded carbon credits for the above mentioned projects by UNFCCC on August 11, 2008, *These carbon credits were illegally won by India with the connivance of some officials of the Ministry of Water & Power (GOP).*

New Multipurpose Hydropower Projects in IHK

India has announced hydro development plan under the 12th five year plan (2012-2017) in which 74 dams with a capacity of 15208 MW are planned. Work on some of these Dams has already started. India's main argument for the construction of these hydro projects is power generation. These Dams have been repeatedly questioned, especially dams on the Chenab River such as:

i. The Bursar Hydroelectric Project is a storage project in which the flow of water can be regulated not only to benefit this project but all downstream projects, i.e., Pakal Dul, Dul Hasti, Rattle, Baglihar, Sawaikot and Salal Hydroelectric Projects. These projects will enhance the potential of all downstream schemes. The storage provided is intended to be used for additional power generation during lean flow months and releasing regulated flow in the downstream. The storage capacity of the dam will be around 2.2 MAF, while the permissible limit on the Chenab River is only 1.7 MAF.

ii. The detailed engineering design of all projects, especially mega power projects such as 1000 MW Pakaidul, 780 MW Rattle, 990 MW Kirthal and 715 MW Seli 1020 MW of Sawaikot HP, have not been shared with Pakistan.[10]

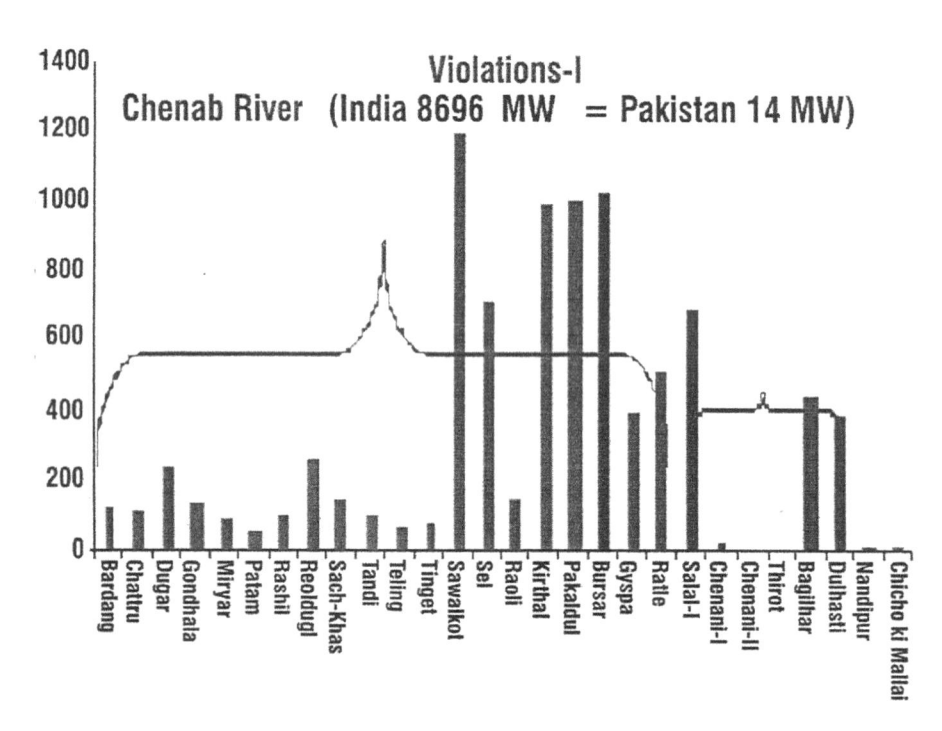

Figure 2: Comparison of Live Storage of Pakistan and India

Source: Detail Design and Tender documents

---

[9] (FCCC/KP/CMP/2005/8/Add.1 dated 30 March 2005)
[10] The details of these nine projects, having an estimated capacity of 1055 MW is given in Table 3 14.

iii. The Government of Jammu & Kashmir has announced to develop another seven dams for hydro electricity on the main Indus River and two projects on Sum and Drass rivers having an estimated capacity of 1055 MW.

iv. Article VI of the treaty explicitly elaborates the need and compulsion to exchange information and data related to the projects to be installed on the Indus River. Besides the parameters defined in the Treaty, India and Pakistan are bound to exchange such information/data under the obligation of the Commission on Large Dams (ICOLD) as members of the ICOLD. According to the ICOLD, dams having height more than 15 metres are defined as Large Dam; therefore, all such dams are to be registered with the commission for dam safety. The judgment passed over Baglihar dam was based on the latest ICOLD bulletin of the Commission on Large Dams (ICOLD) while deciding the design of the spillways.

v. India has been planning to start more than 67 Dams for hydropower generation since long and all these Dams fall under the category of large dams. Unfortunately, India's dam-failure record has been worse as nine of its dams have so far collapsed. J&K area is earthquake prone; hence, a minor failure can result into a catastrophe for the downstream areas. Therefore it is mandatory and important to set up dam safety measures in consultation with Pakistan.

vi. After this decision, India is obligated to design all large dams in line with ICOLD bulletins, No. 120,121 and 123. Being Lower riparian area of the Indus Basin, this is highly important for the safety of infrastructure in Pakistan.

vii. The decision of Bagilhar dam legally dictates the obligation to environmental laws and CJ decisions. Although it is mandatory to share Environmental Impact Assessment (EIA) report of all dams in succession with ICJ decisions and ICOLD Bulletins, India has not shared EIA report of any dam with Pakistan to evaluate transboundary impacts.

Table 3: Estimated Capacity of Projects

Project On Indus	Height of Dam (Feet)	River	Capacity MW
Ulitopp HEP	131	Indus	85
Khaltsi HEP	66	Indus	90
Dumkhar HEP	66	Indus	70
Achinathang – Sanjak HEP	132	Indus	220
Sunit HEP	66	Indus	295
Parkachik-Panikher HEP	198	Drass – Suru	100
Kirkit	99	Drass – Suru	100
Drass – Suru HEP – I	82	Drass – Suru	35
Drass – Suru HEP – II	66	Drass – Suru	60

Source-the office of the Indus Water Commissioner-Pakistan

Cumulative Impact of Live Storages

Pakistan's dispute with India over the construction of an array of hydro-electric projects on the Chenab and the Jhelum rivers is turning into a source of serious tension between the two countries. Almost all Indian projects on Jhelum, Chenab and Indus are classified as run-of- the river projects but they will entail serious consequences for downstream areas both individually and accumulatively if treaty will not be followed in letter and spirit. Pakistan fears that accumulative live storage of these projects will have an adverse impact both in terms of causing floods and running Chenab and Jhelum Rivers dry in the lean period, when Pakistan meets the demand of water from these rivers.

Bangladesh is already experiencing similar tensions with India regarding the sharing of Ganges waters. India has built Farrakha barrage, by diverting waters, causing serious problems in Bangladesh, including 85% groundwater contamination annually causing financial loss of more than 500 Million USD to country's economy, other than enormous flooding in the monsoon season and drought in the dry season.

Wullar Barrage/Tulbul Navigation Project

Wullar Barrage, referred to as the Tulbul Navigation project by India, was the second Indian project that became controversial and still remains unresolved. Wullar Barrage is located on the Jhelum River some 30 km north of Srinagar. India wants to build a barrage on the mouth of the Wullar Lake where it meets the Jhelum River in Jammu and Kashmir with a storage capacity of 300,000 acres feet.[11] The storage capacity of the project would surpass the permissible limit, specified in the annexure "D" of the treaty.

Way Forward

The Article VII of the treaty focuses on future co-operation between the two countries by mutual agreement to the fullest possible extent. To further translate this into action the best practices in managing shared water and the Baglihar Dam Judgment are the guiding principles for the author to develop consensus to make treaty 100% transparent in order to avert any potential conflict and pitch a win-win solution for both countries.

In this regards, after efforts of three years and in-depth discussion and deliberations with Indian water and energy experts, intelligentsia, environmentalists and other experts during series of various dialogues held at New Delhi, Islamabad, Bangkok and Dubai, following recommendations have been unanimously reached that offer win-win, doable, and practical solutions, already replicated in Nile and Danube River Basins:

1. Recognizing that the Indus Waters Treaty is evidently the most successful Confidence Building Measure (CBM) between the two countries, India has the right to use provisions granted in annexures 'D' and 'E'; nevertheless, there is a need to make treaty more transparent by using state-of-the art information communication technology tools.

2. To remove mistrust on data exchange, install the satellite based, real-time telemetry system in IHK Kashmir at a minimum 100 locations for monitoring water quality and quantity.

3. There is a need to set up an independent office of Indus Water Commission (WC) comprising neutral experts outside of the South Asian region, having an unblemished record and integrity. This may also include experts from various international agencies such as the World Bank, the UNEP and the EU, etc. This independent commission of experts shall work directly under the UN to monitor and promote sustainable development in Kashmir and HP.

4. The Independent IWC will also arrange real time data of minor, major tributaries and at all head-works, dams, etc. by website including three dimensional models of dams, three-dimensional models to represent the geometric data of dams (flood storage + Run-of-the River Hydropower projects) for clarity of the global community.

5. It was agreed that environmental threats do not respect national borders. During the last three decades, the watershed in IHK has been badly degraded. To rehabilitate watershed in IHK and Himachal Pradesh (HP), both countries are to take initiatives for joint watershed management in these two states.

6. To rehabilitate watershed in IHK and HP, an environmental impact assessment is the best instrument to assess the possible negative impact that a proposed project may have on the indigenous environment, together with water flow in rivers. The United Nations Economic Commission for Europe's Convention on Environmental Impact Assessment in a Transboundary Context provides the best legal framework for Transboundary EIA for sustainable flow in the Indus Rivers System, so that India should share the TEIA before the physical execution of any project including hydropower.

7. Glaciers are an important and major source of the Indus River System. To preserve these glaciers, there is an immediate need to declare all Himalayan Glaciers as "Protected Area" including immediate demilitarization from Siachen to preserve this second longest glacier of the planet to fall in the watershed of the Indus River.

CHAPTER – 2

Indo-Pak Trans-Boundary Water Issues

Arshad H Abbasi (2009)

The Indus Waters Treaty (IWT) was signed in 1960 and made effective from April 1 of the same year. At the time of independence, the boundary line between Pakistan and India, the two new sovereign states, was drawn right across the Indus Basin, leaving Pakistan as the lower riparian. Moreover, two important irrigation headworks, one at Madhopur on Ravi River and the other at Ferozepur on Sutlej River, on which the irrigation canal supplies in Punjab (Pakistan) had been completely dependent, were left in the Indian territory. A dispute thus arose between the two countries regarding the utilisation of irrigation water from existing facilities. At this crucial stage, the World Bank played a vital role and facilitated diplomatic negotiations between India and Pakistan backed with technical expertise. Under this Treaty, Pakistan obtained exclusive rights to use 135 million acre-feet (MAF) water of the three western rivers: Indus, Jheium, and Chrnab. India retained the rights to use 33MAF of the three eastern rivers: Ravi, Beas, and Sutlej. Here we show how the two countries have performed in the wake of the IWT.

The Indian Planning Commission prepared a master plan to utilize the allocated share of 33 MAF for irrigation and power-generation in an integrated method. Dams having a gross storage capacity 17 MAF were constructed, coupled with an Irrigation system, which helped to achieve 97 percent water utilization efficiency. A canal irrigation system was supplemented with simultaneous installation of tube wells to provide adequate, equitable, and reliable water supplies along with institutional, reforms which resulted in increase in 54 percent sown area in the Eastern Punjab alone that enhanced agricultural productivity at accelerated rate. Within few years Eastern Punjab and Haryana once known for grain deficit areas in the 60,s emerged as India's "bread basket".

Contrary to this, in Pakistan, only three major reservoirs were developed on the western rivers. The accumulative storage capacity of Tarbela, Chashma reservoirs was 18.37 million feet MAF which was reduced to 13.22 IMAF due to sedimentation, resulting in 28 percent loss of capacity. This capacity is only nine percent of the annual flow of the Western rivers and resultantly more that 35 MAF water escape to the sea annually. In this situation, Pakistan would be a water deficient country by 2012 if the water storage capacity is not increased immediately. Besides having abundance of water, crop yields per acre and per acre-feet of water are much lower than international benchmarks and the Eastern Punjab.

India has a hydropower potential of 150,000 megawatt (MW) and is fifth in the world in ranking. The share of the eastern rivers of the Indus basin is only 10 percent but the focus of the Indian hydel policy has remained on the Indus basin. Hydropower projects having on installed capacity of 12500 MW are in operation and having an installed capacity of 8700 MW are under construction on Beas, Ravi and Sutlej rivers. These projects are mostly located in Himachal Pradesh and now it is one of the richest states of India by virtue of exporting cheap hydel power to other states. India has set an unprecedented record in hydropower by developing projects having a capacity of more that 4100 MW on the 470 kilometers long Beas River.

Comparing it with the mighty 3800 km long Indus, the latter has 10 times more annual flow. Pakistan has installed only 4,400 MW. India can irrigate 70,000 acres from Indus, 150 from Jhelum and only 50,000 acres from Chenab. After 1960 India has developed three major canal systems, The Kashmir canal system, The High canal system in Jammu and Ravi-Tawi system which is interlinking system of western river, Chenab, with eastern rivers. It is a severe violation of treaty unnoticed by Indus Commissioner. Similarly, Igo-phey canal and Kurbathang canals have been completed for irrigation in Leah and Kargil. A few more canals under construction in the Ladakh region would surrender the right of India to build dams on the Indus. As per the treaty, only 0.15 million-acre feet can be used for hydropower in Indus and 0.35 MAF for irrigation; with completion of these canals, India cannot build any dams on Indus at all. However, most recently, India has started construction of three dams on the Indus River, Nimoo Bazgo Dumkhar and "Chutak", to harness 213 megawatts of hydropower. As per the treaty, only 0.15 MAF water can be used for hydropower on The Indus River and 0.35 MAF for irrigation. In fact, India reaches its allowable limit on the Indus River after completion of the canals; thus the construction of dams is a violation of the treaty.

To settle all such disputes promptly, with meticulous technical details with data, the Indus Water Commission (IWC) was established in both countries to enforce the treaty in its true spirit. The objective of the Commission is to provide a platform for better co-ordination and exchange of all hydrological data. The commission has been given the right to determine its own procedures for building trust Unfortunately, even after 49 years this institution has failed to build the capacity to settle the disputes and to develop a fair, and transparent mechanism for the enforcement of the treaty.

The IWT is a success, despite the ongoing rivalry between India and Pakistan. With water becoming increasingly scarce, it is essential to transform the Commission into a well-endowed, effective technocratic body.

CHAPTER – 3

PCA PRESS RELEASE

The Indus Waters Kishenganga Arbitration (Pakistan v. India)

The Court of Arbitration Concludes Hearing on the Merits
The Hague, September 1, 2012.

The Court of Arbitration constituted in the matter of the *Indus Waters Kishenganga Arbitration (Pakistan v. India)* has concluded a two-week hearing on the merits at the Peace Palace in The Hague.

Pakistan initiated this arbitration with India under Article IX and Annexure G of the Indus Waters Treaty, an international agreement concluded by India and Pakistan in 1960 which regulates the use by the two States of the Indus system of rivers.

In these proceedings, Pakistan places two matters for determination by the Court of Arbitration:

1. Whether India's proposed diversion of the river Kishenganga (Neelum) into another Tributary, i.e. the Bonar Madmati Nallah, being one central element of the Kishenganga Project, breaches India's legal obligations owed to Pakistan under the Treaty, as interpreted and applied in accordance with the international law, including India's obligations under Article III(2) (let flow all the waters of the Western rivers and not permit any interference with those waters) and Article IV(6) (maintenance of natural channels)? [the "First Dispute"]

2. Whether, under the Treaty, India may deplete or bring the reservoir level of a run-of-the-river Plant below the Dead Storage Level (DSL) in any circumstances except in the case of an unforeseen emergency? [the "Second Dispute"]

The primary subject of the arbitration is the Kishenganga Hydro-Electric Project (the "KHEP") currently under construction by India on the Kishenganga/Neelum River, a tributary of the Jhelum River. The KHEP is designed to generate power by diverting water from a dam site on the Kishenganga/Neelum (within the Gurez valley, an area of higher elevation) to the Bonar Madmati Nallah, another tributary of the Jhelum (lower in elevation and closely located to the Wular Lake) through a system of tunnels, with the moving water powering turbines having a capacity of 330 megawatts. For the management of sedimentation in the reservoir, India intends to employ drawdown flushing, a technique requiring the depletion of the level in the KHEP reservoir below the Dead Storage Level (the Treaty's definition of this term is reproduced in the annex. to this press release). Pakistan contends that the KHEP's planned diversion of the waters of the Kishenganga/Neelum, as well as the use of the drawdown flushing technique, both at the KHEP or at other Indian hydro-electric projects that the Treaty regulates, are impermissible under the Indus Waters Treaty. India maintains that both the design and planned mode of operation of the KHEP are fully in conformity with the Treaty.

* * *

Judge Stephen M. Schwebel, Chairman of the Court of Arbitration, opened the hearing on August 20, 2012 by noting on the historic importance of the *Indus Waters Kishenganga Arbitration* for inter-State arbitration and the Permanent Court of Arbitration and observing that "the Indus Waters Treaty was a great achievement of Pakistan and India and of the World Bank, and it remains so; . . . and these proceedings are an illustration of its continuing vitality."

Opening Statements

The Agent of Pakistan, Mr. Kamal Majidulla (Special Assistant to the Prime Minister for Water Resources and Agriculture), spoke first on behalf of Pakistan. Mr. Majidulla recalled the "existential importance" of the waters of the Indus system of rivers to the people and agriculture of the Indus valley. He described the "Solomonic solution" adopted by India and Pakistan in the Indus Waters Treaty – the apportionment of the rivers of the Indus system between the two States. Mr. Majidulla emphasized the fundamental principle of the Treaty in Pakistan's view: that India should not interfere with the flow of the waters of the "Western Rivers" allocated to Pakistan, including the Jhelum River and its tributaries. Pakistan maintained that India's plan to construct the KHEP on the Kishenganga/Neelum River, which includes the diversion of its waters, is in breach of India's obligations under the Treaty. After Mr. Majidulla's address, Professor James Crawford introduced Pakistan's legal arguments.

The Agent of India, Mr. Dhruv Vijay Singh (Secretary to the Government of India, Ministry of Water Resources), made opening remarks on behalf of India. Mr. Singh stressed the crucial role of hydroelectric projects such as the KHEP in alleviating poverty and improving quality of life across India. He emphasized that under the Indus Waters Treaty, both Pakistan and India have rights to the use of all the rivers of the Indus system for certain purposes, even when particular rivers are, in principle, allocated to the other State. These rights, Mr. Singh maintained, include India's right to hydro-electric uses on the Kishenganga/Neelum River. Mr. Singh also argued that the Treaty's negotiating history shows that hydro-electric power generation was in the Parties' minds from the beginning of the World Bank's involvement in the negotiations, and that the Treaty authorizes certain inter-tributary transfers by India for the purpose of generating hydro-electric power, including, in India's view, the KHEP. Mr. Fali S. Nariman spoke next, introducing India's legal arguments.

Hearing of Expert Witnesses

Following the opening statements, the Chairman called upon the Parties to present their expert witnesses. The experts were cross-examined on matters within their scientific and technical expertise.

Pakistan first presented Mr. Syed Muhammad Mehr Ali Shah for cross-examination regarding the potential hydrological impact of the KHEP on the reach of the Kishenganga/Neelum River downstream, as well as the anticipated impact of the KHEP on the production of electricity by the Neelum-Jhelum Hydro-Electric Project (the "N-JHEP") Pakistan is constructing downstream on the same river. Pakistan then presented Dr. Jackie King and Mr. Vaqar Zakaria for cross-examination with respect to the expected environmental impact downstream of the KHEP. Finally, Pakistan presented Dr. Gregory Morris for cross-examination on sediment management in relation to hydroelectric plants, including the KHEP.

India then presented its experts. Mr. Jesper Goodley Dannisøe and Dr. Niels Jepsen were called to testify with respect to the potential environmental impact of the KHEP. Dr. K.G. Rangaraju was presented for cross-examination regarding sediment control in response to Dr. Morris' views.

The expert examinations concluded mid-day on August 22, 2012.

The Parties' Oral Arguments

The Counsel for both Parties next delivered two rounds of oral arguments. Ms. Shamila Mahmood, Professor James Crawford, Professor Vaughan Lowe, and Mr. Samuel Wordsworth argued on behalf of Pakistan. Dr. Neeru Chadha, Mr. Fali Nariman, Professor Stephen McCaffrey, Mr. RKP Shankardass, Mr. Rodman Bundy, and Professor Daniel Magraw argued on behalf of India. Over the course of pleading, the Members of the Court of Arbitration asked questions and sought clarifications from the counsel.

Pakistan's Arguments

Pakistan maintains that the planned diversion of the waters of the Kishenganga/Neelum River by the KHEP is prohibited by the Indus Waters Treaty.

During the hearing, Pakistan first recalled the ten-year history of painstaking negotiations between the Parties, facilitated through the good offices of the World Bank, which resulted in the conclusion of the Treaty in September 1960. According to Pakistan, the Treaty, drafted at a time when cooperation between the Parties for the joint development of the Indus river system did not seem possible, was written so as to allow each Party to develop water resources in an independent manner. To this end, Pakistan argued that the Treaty apportions the rivers of the Indus river system between the Parties, strictly fixing and delimiting the Parties' rights and obligations with regard to these rivers. Noting the Treaty's careful and nuanced drafting, Pakistan argued that the Treaty terms should be interpreted according to their ordinary meaning and in case of doubt in such a way as to reinforce the Treaty's precise delimitation of the Parties' respective rights.

Pakistan emphasized India's obligation under Article III of the Treaty (see the annex.) to "let flow" and "not permit any interference with" the waters of the Western Rivers (the Indus, the Chenab, the Jhelum and their tributaries, including the Kishenganga/Neelum) before they flow into Pakistan. According to Pakistan, this obligation constitutes an essential element of the compromise reached by the Parties in the Treaty, serving to prevent India from "manipulating" the flow of the waters of the Western Rivers to Pakistan's detriment.

Pakistan recognized that, as a matter of exception, Article III(2) of the Treaty allows India to make use of the waters of the Western Rivers on their upstream stretches for certain purposes, including the generation of hydro-electricity through the "run-of-the-river" plants. However, Pakistan pointed out that the Treaty strictly regulates India's rights on the Western Rivers, for instance through Annexure D, which sets forth the restrictions on Indian hydro-electric power generation.

In particular, Pakistan argued that the Treaty does not establish a general right for India to deliver water from one Western River tributary into another for the generation of hydro-electric power. Such inter-tributary transfers are contrary both to India's general obligation to "let flow" the waters of the Western Rivers under Article III as well as India's specific obligation spelled out in the chapeau of Paragraph 15 of Annexure D (see the annex.) to deliver into the river below the hydro-electric plant the same volume of water that is received in the river above the plant within any given 24-hour period.

Pakistan argued that Paragraph 15(iii) of Annexure D to the Treaty is an operational provision that allows, in specific cases, for the waters of a tributary of the Jhelum (such as the Kishenganga/Neelum) to be delivered into another tributary. However, Pakistan argued that the KHEP's planned diversion cannot be justified by reference to this exception. In Pakistan's view, the Treaty does not allow India to permanently divert all of the waters of one tributary of the Jhelum into another in order to create a potential for the generation of hydro-electric power that does not naturally arise from the flow of the river within its course, as India proposes to do with the KHEP. Pakistan argued that the Treaty solely permits a diversion of the waters of a tributary of the Jhelum when "necessary" – that is, diversion can only be done from time to time as an "emergency exit."

Further, in Pakistan's view, the Treaty gives Pakistan's downstream agricultural and hydro-electric uses on the tributaries of the Jhelum priority, requiring India to adjust its uses so as not to affect Pakistan's uses either now or as they develop in the future. Pakistan contended that selecting a cut-off date at which Pakistan's uses would be evaluated once and for all by India would "freeze" Pakistani development and undermine the bargain struck by the Parties in dividing the Indus system of rivers between them. Pakistan argued that the Treaty protects Pakistan's downstream uses as they exist from time-to-time, at the moment of delivery of the diverted waters.

Pakistan further argued that as a matter of fact, its agricultural and hydro-electric uses will be adversely affected by the KHEP. Specifically, Pakistan argued that the KHEP, under its planned mode of operation, would divert the entirety of the waters of the Kishenganga/Neelum during the lean season and up to its design capacity of 58.4 m^3/s during the high flow season. This would result in a significant loss in power generation and revenue for the downstream N-JHEP and any other hydroelectric projects Pakistan may choose to construct on the Kishenganga/Neelum in the future. Pakistan maintained that it informed India of the anticipated adverse impact on its downstream uses over two decades before construction of the KHEP was commenced. With regard to the N-JHEP, Pakistan asserted that it has continuously reaffirmed its commitment to the project since 1989.

In addition, Pakistan argued that there arises out of Article IV(6) of the Treaty (reproduced in annex.) an obligation for India to carry out a good faith assessment of the environmental downstream impacts of the KHEP. This, in Pakistan's submission, India did not do. Relying on its own expert reports, Pakistan argued that a reduced flow in the Kishenganga/Neelum would have an adverse environmental impact on its downstream reaches.

With regard to the Second Dispute, Pakistan submitted that drawdown flushing, the technique India proposes to use for the management of sedimentation in the KHEP reservoir, is prohibited by the provisions of the Treaty. Drawdown flushing consists of drawing down the level of the water in the reservoir close to the river bed by releasing it through low level outlets in the dam, in order to expel sediments from the reservoir. Pakistan argued that the use of drawdown flushing would give India an impermissible control over the timing and volume of the flow of water downstream of the dam, as well as have an adverse environmental impact downstream. Pakistan argued that India is obligated to employ alternative sediment management methods.

India's Arguments

India contends that the planned diversion of the waters of the Kishenganga/Neelum by the KHEP is in compliance with the Indus Waters Treaty.

During the hearing, India submitted that all the provisions of the Treaty must be interpreted in the light of its object and purpose as it is set forth in the Treaty's preamble. In India's view, the preamble spells out the Parties' desire in signing the Treaty to "attain the most complete and satisfactory utilisation of the waters of the Indus system of rivers." According to India, this object will be served by the planned diversion of the Kishenganga/Neelum waters, as this design will allow India to realize the full power generating potential of the upstream stretch of the Kishenganga/Neelum River, while also benefitting Pakistan's hydro-electric uses (albeit further downstream of the N-JHEP).

India stressed that while the rivers of the Indus system were divided between India and Pakistan, the Treaty also gave each State significant rights in the rivers that were allocated to the other. In particular, India pointed to Article III(2) of the Treaty, which expressly stipulates India's right to use the waters of the Western Rivers to generate hydro-electric power (subject to the provisions of Annexure D to the Treaty) as an exception to India's obligation to "let flow" the waters of these rivers. India argued that the KHEP falls within this exception.

India maintained that it has a right to transfer water between the tributaries of the Jhelum River for the purpose of hydro-electric power generation. Such a right is evident, India argued, given that prior to the Treaty's signature, India was already contemplating the construction of a hydro-electric project at the current location of the KHEP that would include an inter-tributary transfer. In this context, India submitted that it would not have consented to any Treaty provision that would preclude the realization of such a project.

With regard to the stipulation at Paragraph 15(iii) of Annexure D to the Treaty that water from one tributary of the Jhelum may be delivered into another tributary only "if necessary," India submitted that the Treaty allows India to judge what is necessary for the generation of hydro-electric power. In the present case, the KHEP's planned diversion is necessary, being, in light of the area's topography, the only option for significant power generation in the region.

India further recalled that Paragraph 15(iii) of Annexure D to the Treaty only protects Pakistan's "then existing" downstream agricultural and hydro-electric uses, of which, India contends, there are none on the Kishenganga/Neelum. India interpreted "then existing" to mean that India must take into account Pakistan's downstream uses only up to a critical cut-off date, at which point India's hydroelectric design can be finalized. India argued that an interpretation of this provision requiring India to continuously adjust its hydro-electric operations on the Kishenganga/Neelum to Pakistan's downstream uses as they develop would negate India's express right to use the waters of the Western Rivers to generate hydro-electricity, and result in the waste of the vast amount of resources invested in the KHEP.

India submitted that between 1989, when Pakistan was first apprised of the KHEP, and 2006, when the final design of the KHEP was notified to Pakistan, India repeatedly indicated its willingness to take into account Pakistan's downstream uses, urging Pakistan to document them. However, in India's view, Pakistan consistently failed to substantiate its uses within the Neelum valley with verifiable data. With respect to the N-JHEP, for example, India argued that Pakistan relied solely on verbal assurances that the project was "in hand" and "under construction" without demonstrating its commitment to its realization. India also asserted that the agricultural uses of the residents of the Neelum valley are not dependent on the waters of the Kishenganga/Neelum River.

India argued that even if the N-JHEP were a "then existing" use, it would not be adversely affected by the KHEP. India emphasized that the KHEP will divert less than 1% of the total volume of waters of the Western Rivers. Thus, despite operation of the KHEP, during the high flow season, the N-JHEP would receive a volume of water in excess of its maximum discharge capacity. During the lean season, the N-JHEP could be operated by using the water from the numerous tributaries that flow into the Kishenganga/Neelum River between the KHEP and N-JHEP dam sites; in fact, during this period of the year, the N-JHEP would receive more water than the KHEP itself. India added that any adverse effect to hydro-electric power generation by the N-JHEP would be mitigated by the release of water during the lean season from the storage work which Pakistan intends to construct on the Kishenganga/Neelum River at Dudhnial between the KHEP and the N-JHEP. Any adverse effects to the N-JHEP would also be set off, in India's view, by the benefits Pakistan's projected Kohala hydro-electric plant would derive from increased flow in the Jhelum River resulting from the diversion of the Kishenganga/Neelum's waters by the KHEP.

India argued that the provisions of the Treaty, including its Article IV(6), provide no basis for incorporating any international environmental obligations into the Treaty; the alleged breach of such obligations is, therefore, not a proper subject for determination by the Court of Arbitration. In any event, India submitted that it has complied with Article IV(6) of the Treaty, domestic Indian environmental regulations, any environmental customary international law obligations India may have, and the international standards applicable to engineers in the design and operation of hydroelectric projects. India argued that it had commissioned a comprehensive environmental impact assessment in 2000 which has shown that the KHEP will not have any significant adverse environmental impact on the Kishenganga/Neelum. India maintains that a minimum "environmental flow" of at least 3.9 m³/s will be released at all times below the KHEP dam.

With regard to the Second Dispute, at the outset, India disputed its admissibility for determination by the Court of Arbitration, arguing that it should have been referred by Pakistan to a Neutral Expert appointed pursuant to the Treaty. India then urged the Court to follow the decision of the Neutral Expert in the Baglihar case (a proceeding under the Indus Waters Treaty concerning India's Baglihar hydro-electric project), which found that drawdown flushing is permissible under the Treaty. India argued that sediment management is essential to the sustainability of hydro-electric plants and can only be effectively achieved at the KHEP by lowering the water level in the reservoir below the Dead Storage Level – *i.e.* by drawdown flushing. Given that the re-filling of the KHEP reservoir after its depletion is only permitted under the Treaty during a short period in the high flow season, and in light of the relatively small storage capacity of the KHEP, India submitted that the operation will have minimal effect on Pakistan.

Closing Arguments

On August 31, 2012, the Parties gave their closing arguments. Mr. Kamal Majidulla (Agent) and Professor James Crawford (Counsel) completed Pakistan's submissions. On the part of India, Mr. D.V. Singh (Agent) and Mr. Fali Nariman (Counsel) completed India's submissions.

* * *

Under the Court of Arbitration's Rules of Procedure, "[t]he Court shall endeavour to render its Award within 6 months of the close of the hearings."

* * *

The seven-member Court of Arbitration is chaired by Judge Stephen M. Schwebel (United States), former President of the International Court of Justice. The other members of the Court are Sir Franklin Berman KCMG QC (United Kingdom), Professor Howard S. Wheater FREng (United Kingdom), Professor Lucius Caflisch (Switzerland), Professor Jan Paulsson (Sweden), Judge Bruno Simma (Germany), and H.E. Judge Peter Tomka (Slovakia). The Permanent Court of Arbitration in The Hague acts as the Secretariat to the Court of Arbitration.

In June 2011, the Court of Arbitration conducted a site visit to the N-JHEP and KHEP and surrounding areas located on the Kishenganga/Neelum River. In February 2012, a delegation of the Court conducted a second site visit to the Neelum River Valley. The Parties have also exchanged written pleadings.

On September 23, 2011, the Court of Arbitration issued an Order on Interim Measures, which is available on the website of the PCA at http://www.pca-cpa.org/showpage.asp?pag_id=1392.

Other press releases and information relating to this arbitration are available at: http://www.pcacpa.org/showpage.asp?pag_id=1392

Contact: The Permanent Court of Arbitration, E-mail: bureau@pca-cpa.org

Annex: Select Provisions of the Indus Waters Treaty

Article III

(1) Pakistan shall receive for unrestricted use all those waters of the Western Rivers which India is under obligation to let flow under the provisions of Paragraph (2).

(2) India shall be under an obligation to let flow all the waters of the Western Rivers, and shall not permit any interference with these waters, except for the following uses, restricted (except as provided in item (c) (ii) of Paragraph 5 of Annexure C) in the case of each of the rivers, The Indus, The Jhelum and The Chenab, to the drainage basin thereof:

(a) Domestic Use ;

(b) Non-Consumptive Use ;

(c) Agricultural use, as set out in Annexure C ; and

(d) Generation of hydro-electric power, as set out in Annexure D.

(3) Pakistan shall have the unrestricted use of all waters originating from sources other than the Eastern Rivers which are delivered by Pakistan into The Ravi or the Sutlej, and India shall not make use of these waters. Each Party agrees to establish such discharge observation stations and make such observations as may be considered necessary by the Commission for the determination of the component of water available for the use of Pakistan on account of the aforesaid deliveries by Pakistan.

(4) Except as provided in Annexures D and E, India shall not store any water of, or construct any storage works on, the Western Rivers.

Article IV (6)

(6) Each Party will use its best endeavours to maintain the natural channels of the Rivers, as on the Effective Date, in such condition as will avoid, as far as practicable, any obstruction to the flow in these channels likely to cause material damage to the other Party.

Paragraph 15 (iii) of Annexure D

15. Subject to the provisions of Paragraph 17, the works connected with a Plant shall be so operated that (a) the volume of water received in the river upstream of the Plant, during any period of seven consecutive days, shall be delivered into the river below the Plant during the same seven-day period, and (b) in any one period of 24 hours within that seven-day period, the volume delivered into the river below the Plant shall be not less than 30%, and not more than 130%, of the volume received in the river above the Plant during the same 24-hour period : Provided however that:

(iii) where a Plant is located on a Tributary of The Jhelum on which Pakistan has any Agricultural use or hydro-electric use, the water released below the Plant may be delivered, if necessary, into another Tributary but only to the extent that the then existing Agricultural Use or hydro-electric use by Pakistan on the former Tributary would not be adversely affected.

Paragraph 2(a) of Annexure D

"Dead Storage" means that portion of the storage which is not used for operational purposes and the "Dead Storage Level" means the level corresponding to the Dead Storage.

CHAPTER – 4

PCA PRESS RELEASE

The Indus Waters Kishenganga Arbitration (Pakistan v. India)

The Court of Arbitration Issues a Partial Award
in the First Arbitration under the Indus Waters Treaty 1960

The Hague, February 19, 2013.

The Court of Arbitration constituted in the matter of the *Indus Waters Kishenganga Arbitration (Pakistan v. India),* has rendered a Partial Award in respect of the dispute between Pakistan and India under the Indus Waters Treaty concerning (1) the legality of the construction and operation of an Indian hydro-electric project located in India-administered Jammu and Kashmir; and (2) the permissibility under the Treaty of the depletion of the reservoirs of certain Indian hydro-electric plants below, "Dead Storage Level."[1]

In its Partial Award, which is final with respect to the matters decided therein, without appeal and binding on the Parties, the Court of Arbitration unanimously decided:

1. That the Kishenganga Hydro-Electric Project (KHEP) constitutes a Run-of-the-River Plant under the Treaty, and India may accordingly divert water from the Kishenganga/Neelum River for power generation by the KHEP in the manner envisaged.

   However, when operating the KHEP, India is under an obligation to maintain a minimum flow of water in the Kishenganga/Neelum River, at a rate to be determined by the Court in a Final Award.

2. Except in the case of an unforeseen emergency, the Treaty does not permit India's reduction below "Dead Storage Level" of the water level in the reservoirs of Run-of-the-River Plants located on the rivers allocated to Pakistan under the Treaty. This ruling does not apply to Plants already in operation or under construction (whose designs have been communicated by India and not objected to by Pakistan).

The Court expects to be able to render its Final Award, determining the minimum flow of water India would be required to release in the Kishenganga/Neelum River by the end of 2013.

* * *

The Indus Waters Treaty is an international agreement signed by India and Pakistan in 1960 that regulates the use by the two States of the waters of the Indus system of rivers. Pakistan instituted arbitral proceedings against India in 2010, requesting that a court of arbitration determine the permissibility under the Treaty of a hydro-electric project (the Kishenganga Hydro-Electric Project, or KHEP) currently under construction by India on the Kishenganga/Neelum River, a tributary of the Jhelum River. The KHEP is

---

[1] As defined in the Treaty, "dead storage" is "that portion of storage which is not used for operational purposes."

designed to generate power by diverting water from a dam site on the Kishenganga/Neelum (within the Gurez valley, an area of higher elevation) to the Bonar Nallah, another tributary of the Jhelum (lower in elevation and closely located to Wular Lake) through a system of tunnels, with the water powering turbines having a capacity of 330 megawatts.

Pakistan challenges, in particular, the permissibility of the planned diversion by the KHEP of the waters of the Kishenganga/Neelum into the Bonar Nallah, arguing that this inter-tributary transfer will adversely affect the operation of a hydro-electric project—the Neelum-Jhelum Hydro-Electric Project or NJHEP—being built by Pakistan on the Kishenganga/Neelum downstream of the KHEP (the "First Dispute"). The transfer of water contemplated by India may be represented graphically as in the attached diagram (Annex. A). Pakistan has also requested that the Court determine whether the Treaty permits India to deplete or bring the reservoir level of the "run-of-the-river" hydro-electric plants below a level identified as the "Dead Storage Level" in the Treaty (the "Second Dispute"). Pakistan submits that such reservoir depletion would give India impermissibly broad control over the flow of the river waters allocated to Pakistan under the Treaty. For its part, India had stated its intent to use such reservoir depletion to flush sediment out of the KHEP's reservoir. India maintains that both the design and planned mode of operation of the KHEP are fully in conformity with the Treaty.

* * *

In its analysis, the Court emphasized at the outset that its Partial Award, just as the Indus Waters Treaty itself, does not have any bearing on any territorial claims or rights of the Parties over Jammu and Kashmir. The Court's findings pertain solely to the Parties' rights and obligations with respect to the *use* of the waters of the Indus system of rivers, including with respect to the use of the waters of those portions of the rivers that flow through the disputed territory.

THE FIRST DISPUTE

1. The Permissibility of Inter-Tributary Transfers under the Treaty

In the First Dispute, the Court was called upon to determine whether India is permitted under the Treaty to deliver the waters of the Kishenganga/Neelum River into the Bonar Nallah in the course of the operation of the KHEP.

As an initial matter, the Court observed that the Treaty expressly permits the transfer of water by India from one tributary of the Jhelum to another for the purpose of generating hydro-electric power, subject to certain conditions. The Court first found that this right is not circumscribed by the Treaty's restriction of Indian uses on the Western Rivers (which include the Kishenganga/Neelum as a tributary of the Jhelum) to the drainage basin of those rivers. This restriction relates to where water may be used, and is not violated by the use outside of the drainage basin of electricity generated from the water. The Court then examined the Treaty provision requiring the Parties to maintain the natural channels of the rivers and its effect on inter-tributary transfers. The Court found that this obligation involves maintaining the river channels' physical capacity to carry water, and does not require maintaining the timing or volume of the flow in the river. Accordingly, this obligation does not limit India's right to transfer water for the purpose of generating hydro-electricity.

Having established that India's right to inter-tributary transfer is not prohibited by other provisions of the Treaty, the Court considered whether the KHEP meets the express conditions on such transfer. The Court noted that for transfer to be permissible, the KHEP must (1) be a "Run-of-the-River Plant"; (2) be located on a tributary of the Jhelum; and (3) conform to Paragraph 15(iii) of the Treaty Annexure governing hydro-electric power generation. The Court observed that a "Run-of-the-River Plant" is a term of art defined by the Treaty and that the KHEP is a Run-of-the-River Plant within that definition. The Court further decided that on the facts of the case, the KHEP should be regarded as located on the Kishenganga/Neelum notwithstanding that the KHEP's power house is situated at a distance of 23 kilometres from that river. The Court also found that, by releasing water into the Bonar Nallah after it has passed through the power house, the KHEP complies with the requirement that the "water released below the Plant" be delivered "into another Tributary." Finally, the Court found that the KHEP's inter-tributary transfer is "necessary," as required by the Treaty, for the generation of hydroelectric power, as power can be generated on the scale contemplated by India in this location only by using the 665 metre difference in elevation between the dam site on the Kishenganga/Neelum and the place where the water is released into the Bonar Nallah.

2 The Interpretation of the Treaty with Respect to "then existing Agricultural Use or hydro-electric use by Pakistan"

In addition to the requirements described above, the Court recognized that Paragraph 15(iii) requires that "then existing Agricultural Use or hydro-electric use by Pakistan" on the downstream reaches of the Kishenganga/Neelum not be adversely affected by the KHEP's inter-tributary transfer. Pakistan argued that "then existing" uses are to be determined on an ongoing basis, whenever water is transferred from one tributary to another. India, in contrast, argued that such uses must be determined at a fixed point during the design of its hydro-electric project.

In seeking to establish when a "then existing" agricultural or hydro-electric use is to be determined, the Court was guided in the interpretation of the Treaty by Article 31(1) of the Vienna Convention on the Law of Treaties: "[a] treaty shall be interpreted in good faith and in accordance with the ordinary meaning to be given to the terms of the treaty in their context and in light of its object and purpose." The Court first examined the text of Paragraph 15(iii), noting the provision's focus on the operation of hydro-electric plants and the implication that the determination of "then existing" uses should take place on an ongoing basis throughout the operational life of a plant. The Court then considered the context of Paragraph 15(iii) and noted that the provision falls within a continuum of design, construction and operation. The Court observed that the provisions of the Treaty must be interpreted in a mutually reinforcing fashion, as it would make little sense for the Treaty to permit a plant to be designed and built in a certain manner, but then to prohibit the operation of that plant in the very manner for which it was designed. Finally, the Court examined the object and purpose of the Treaty and found that the Treaty both gives Pakistan priority in the use of the waters of the Western Rivers (including the Kishenganga/Neelum) and India a right to generate hydro-electric power on the Western Rivers.

Turning to the application of the Treaty to the KHEP, the Court first considered the implications of the approaches advocated by the Parties. The Court observed that under the "ambulatory" approach advocated by Pakistan, a project's design could be cleared for construction as being consistent with the design specifications of the Treaty, but then be prevented from operating by new uses by Pakistan. In the Court's view, the uncertainty created by this approach, and the potential for wastage, would have a chilling effect on the undertaking of any hydro-electric projects by India on the Western Rivers. With respect to the approach advocated by India, under which Pakistan's uses would be determined at the moment that India communicates a "firm intention" to proceed with a project, the Court observed that identifying a critical date will often be difficult, but that it may be possible to identify a "critical period" in which design, tenders, financing, public consultations, environmental assessments, governmental approvals and construction come together to indicate a firm intention to proceed with a project. Nevertheless, the Court noted that a solely "critical period" approach could result in a "race" in which each Party would seek to create uses that would freeze out future uses by the other, an outcome the Court rejected.

Having considered the approaches advocated by the Parties, the Court concluded that neither the ambulatory nor the critical period approach were fully satisfactory and that the proper interpretation of the Treaty combines elements of both. The Court considered that it must first establish for each of the KHEP and the NJHEP the critical period in which the Parties not only planned the projects, but took concrete steps toward their realization. Reviewing the evidence provided by the Parties, the Court concluded that the KHEP reached this period in 2004–2006. In contrast, the Court found that Pakistan demonstrated a comparable commitment to the NJHEP in 2007 and 2008. Given this timing, the Court decided that India's right to divert the waters of the Kishenganga/Neelum by the KHEP is protected by the Treaty.

However, the Court also decided that India's right to divert the Kishenganga/Neelum is not absolute—it is subject to the constraints specified in the Treaty and, in addition, by the relevant principles of the customary international law. Paragraph 15(iii) gives rise to India's right to construct and operate hydro-electric projects involving inter-tributary transfers, but also obliges India to operate those projects in such a way as to avoid adversely affecting Pakistan's then existing agricultural and hydro-electric uses. Both Parties' entitlements under the Treaty must be made effective so far as possible. The Court therefore, found that Pakistan retains the right to receive a minimum flow of water from India in the Kishenganga/Neelum riverbed at all times. The Court noted that this right also stems from the customary international environmental law, and that it considered that the Treaty must be applied in the light of the contemporary international environmental law principles.

In this context, the Court recalled the commitment made by India's Agent in the course of the hearing that India would ensure a minimum environmental flow downstream of the KHEP at all times.

3. The Court's Request for Further Data

Having concluded that the Treaty requires the preservation of a minimum flow of water downstream of the KHEP, the Court determined that the data provided by the Parties are insufficient to allow it to decide the precise amount of flow to be preserved.

The Court, therefore, deferred its determination of the appropriate minimum flow to a Final Award, and requested the Parties to provide additional data concerning the impacts of a range of minimum flows at the KHEP dam on, (for India), (a) power generation at the KHEP; and (b) environmental concerns from the dam site at Gurez to the Line of Control; and, (for Pakistan), (a) power generation at the NJHEP; (b) agricultural uses of water downstream of the Line of Control to Nauseri; and (c) environmental concerns at, and downstream of, the Line of Control to Nauseri.

THE SECOND DISPUTE

1. The Admissibility of the Dispute over the Depletion of Reservoirs below the "Dead Storage Level"

Insofar as India had raised two objections to the admissibility of the Second Dispute, the Court considered, first, whether Pakistan had followed the Treaty procedure for the submission of disputes to the Court; and second, whether the Second Dispute, given its subject-matter, could properly be heard by the Court. With respect to the first question, the Court observed that the Treaty provides for disagreements between the Parties to be resolved either by a seven-member court of arbitration or by a single, highly-qualified engineer, acting as a neutral expert. The Court concluded that the neutral expert process is given priority only if one or the other Party has, in fact, requested the appointment of a neutral expert. In the present case, neither Party made such a request and the Court was, therefore, not precluded from hearing the Second Dispute. With respect to the second question, the Court found that although the Treaty specifies the technical matters that may be referred to a neutral expert, it does not give the neutral expert exclusive competence over these listed matters. Once constituted, a court of arbitration is empowered to consider any question arising out of the Treaty, including technical questions. Having rejected both objections, the Court found that the Second Dispute is admissible.

2. The Permissibility of the Depletion of Reservoirs for Drawdown Flushing

In approaching the merits of the second dispute, the Court observed that the question of reservoir depletion is linked in the Parties' disagreement with the permissibility of controlling sediment through the procedure of drawing down the reservoir and flushing accumulated sediment downstream. The Court briefly reviewed the process of sedimentation in the reservoirs of hydro-electric plants and the various techniques available for sediment control, including drawdown flushing.

The Court then examined three aspects of the context of the Treaty with respect to drawdown flushing. First, the Court observed that one of the primary objectives of the Treaty was to limit the storage of water by India on the Western Rivers and that the Treaty includes strict restrictions on the volume of storage permitted to India. The Court noted that, in contrast, the volume of Dead Storage is not controlled, suggesting that such storage was not intended to be subject to manipulation. Second, the Court noted that the Treaty includes design restrictions on the low-level outlets that would be required to deplete a reservoir and that these restrictions make sense only if depletion is also restricted. Third, the Court recalled that the Treaty drafters intended for India to have the right to generate hydro-electric power on the Western Rivers, and noted that this right must be given effect by allowing India's hydro-electric development to be sustainable.

Reading the provisions of the Treaty in the light of these contextual aspects, the Court concluded that the Treaty prohibits depletion below the Dead Storage Level of the reservoirs of Run-of-the-River Plants (and, correspondingly, drawdown flushing) through reference to a provision of the Treaty Annexure dedicated to storage works, which states that "the Dead Storage shall not be depleted except in an unforeseen emergency." The Court also noted that the Treaty includes restrictions on the permissible variation in the volume of flow in a river above and below a hydro-electric plant, and that these restrictions may also be incompatible with drawdown flushing in certain reservoirs and in certain flow conditions. To complete its analysis, the Court examined whether the sustainable generation of hydro-electric power on the Western Rivers is possible without drawdown flushing. After reviewing the technical documentation submitted by the Parties and the testimony of the experts presented by them, the Court observed that drawdown flushing is only one means of sediment control and concluded that hydroelectricity may be generated without flushing. Finally, insofar as certain hydro-electric plants are under construction or have been completed by India, the Court stated that its decision on the Second Dispute may not be so interpreted as to cast doubt retrospectively on any Run-of-River Plants already in operation on the Western Rivers, nor as to affect retrospectively any such Plant already under construction the design of which (having already been duly communicated by India under the relevant provisions of the Treaty) has not been objected to by Pakistan as provided for in the Treaty.

* * *

The seven-member Court of Arbitration is chaired by Judge Stephen M. Schwebel (United States), former President of the International Court of Justice. The other members of the Court are Sir Franklin Berman KCMG QC (United Kingdom), Professor Howard S. Wheater FREng (United Kingdom), Professor Lucius Caflisch (Switzerland), Professor Jan Paulsson (Sweden), Judge Bruno Simma (Germany), and H.E. Judge Peter Tomka (Slovakia). The Permanent Court of Arbitration in The Hague acts as Secretariat to the Court of Arbitration.

In June 2011, the Court of Arbitration conducted a site visit to the Neelum/Jhelum and Kishenganga hydro-electric projects and surrounding areas located on the Kishenganga/Neelum river. In February 2012, a delegation of the Court conducted a second site visit to the Neelum river valley. The Parties have also submitted written pleadings. From August 20 to 31, 2012, the Court of Arbitration conducted a two-week hearing on the merits of the dispute between the Parties.

On September 23, 2011, the Court of Arbitration issued an Order on Interim Measures, which is available on the website of the PCA at http://www.pca-cpa.org/showpage.asp?pag_id=1392.

Other press releases and information relating to this arbitration are available at: http://www.pcacpa.org/showpage.asp?pag_id=1392

Contact: Permanent Court of Arbitration
E-mail: bureau@pca-cpa.org

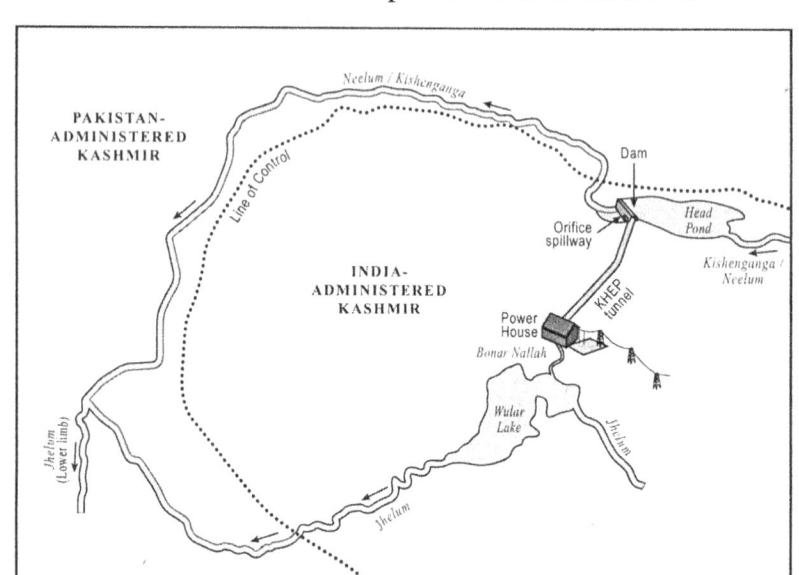

Annex. A: Schematic representation of the KHEP

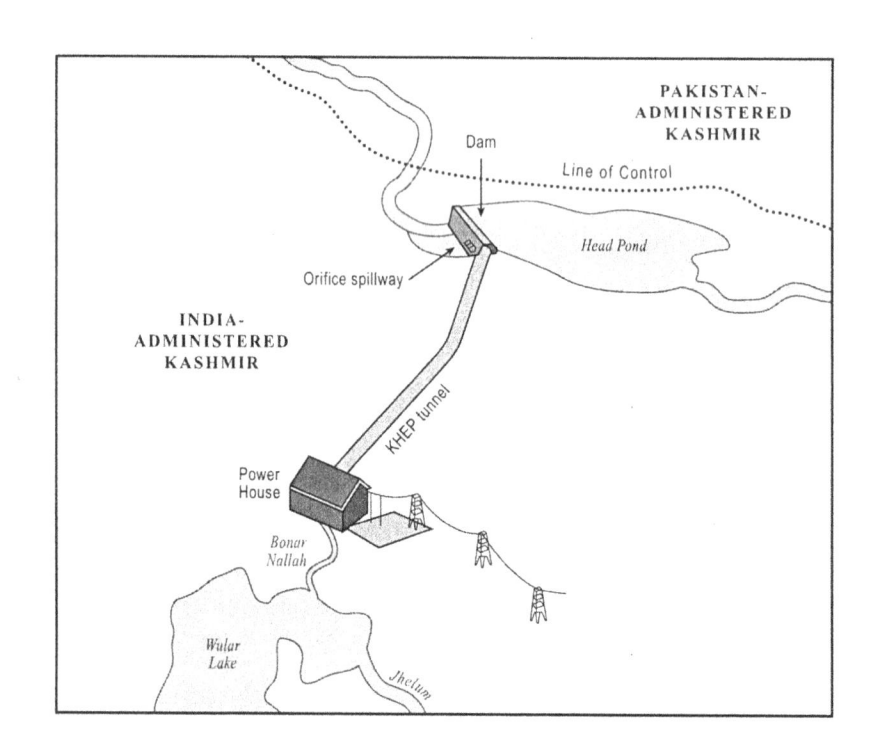

Source: Partial Award, page. 51, reproduced from Pakistan's Memorial.

CHAPTER - 5

Baglihar Decision - An End To The Dispute?

I.M. Sahil (19 March 2007)

I M Sahil asks whether a recent decision by a World Bank appointed expert on the future of the controversial Baglihar dam will bring an end to the 15-year dispute between India and Pakistan.

A 450MW hydroelectric plant proposed to be constructed at Baglihar, and utilising the waters of the river Chenab in India's northern state of Jammu & Kashmir (J&K), had been under dispute between India and Pakistan since 1992, when the former notified its western neighbour of its intentions to develop the project. Pakistan objected on the grounds that the project design was violative of certain key provisions of the Indus Waters Treaty, 1960 (IWT) between the two countries which had governed the use by them of the Indus river system.

With the talks between the two countries in the intervening years having failed to arrive at an agreed solution, Pakistan decided to remit the dispute in 2005 to a Neutral Expert, to be appointed under the provisions of IWT, by the World Bank. The expert, Prof Raymond Lafitte, gave his decision on 12 February this year on the four contentious points that had been referred to him. Under the terms of IWT, his decision is 'final and binding' on both parties. But would it really mark the end of the 15-year dispute between the two neighbouring countries over the Baglihar project?

To appreciate the complexities of the situation, a quick look at the context is necessary. The Indus river system in the sub-continent comprises the main Indus river and its five major tributaries. All of these originate in the Himalayas and pass through Indian territory. After Indus has received the waters of its five tributaries in Pakistan, it flows through the Pak provinces of Punjab and Sind before falling into the Arabian Sea, south of the Pakistan city of Karachi.

Britain granted independence to India in the year 1947 by partitioning it into two countries of India and Pakistan. That led to an arbitrary split in control and usage of the Indus river system. It was only in September 1960 that the two riparian states, through active mediation by the World Bank, signed the IWT. Key provisions of the Treaty included the following:

- The usage of waters of three of the 'Eastern' rivers - Ravi, Beas and Satluj - was given exclusively to India.

- The usage of waters of three 'Western' rivers – Indus itself and its two other tributaries, Jhelum and Chenab – was given exclusively to Pakistan. However, India, as the upper riparian state, was allowed a restrictive use of those waters for domestic, agriculture, non-consumptive and hydro generation purposes.

- To oversee the implementation of IWT, a Permanent Indus Commission was set up, comprising a representative from each of the two countries.

During the 47 years that the Treaty has been in existence, it has served both the countries well. They were able to develop projects to utilise the waters of the respective rivers assigned to them for various purposes. Even on the Western rivers, where India was given a restrictive usage, it developed major hydro projects at Dulhasti and Salal after sorting out points of differences with Pakistan through talks under the ambit of IWT. This was of crucial importance to India as these rivers and their tributaries have nearly all of the estimated 20-GW hydro potential of J&K State. However, until now, only about 8% of the potential has been utilised and India has already identified a number of small and medium-sized projects to be developed in the coming years.

On the Baglihar project, however, both countries found that their differences were irreconcilable. Baglihar is a run-of-the-river scheme, based on a concrete-gravity dam with an original design-height of 144.5m, affording enough live storage to run a 450MW power plant in its first stage, and with gated spillways for flood-control and to reduce sedimentation – both banes of all Himalayan rivers.

Pakistan protested however that certain design features of the Baglihar project were violative of the provisions of IWT :

- The planned pondage of 37.7Mm^3 was excessive and, as per Pakistan's calculations, should only be 6.22Mm^3.

- Similarly, the free board of 4.5m was uncalled for and should be reduced to 3m.

- The water intakes for the power plant, which under IWT had to be located at the 'highest level consistent with satisfactory and economical construction and operation' of the plant, needed to be raised by 7m (from the designed 818m).

- Pakistan objected to the gated spillways in the dam and asked that either ungated or surface-gated spillways be provided, with the bottom-end of gates at the highest level.

Formal talks between the two countries on the dispute began in May 2000 under the Permanent Indus Commission, after India had signed an agreement in the preceding year to execute the project. The level of these talks was raised to that between the senior officials (and later, to the Heads) of the two governments, but no agreement could be reached. In January 2005, Pakistan moved the World Bank to appoint a 'neutral expert' to decide on the 'differences' over the project under the relevant provisions of IWT.

Four months later, in May 2005, the World Bank appointed Prof Raymond Lafitte, a Swiss civil engineer working on the faculty of Federal Institute of Technology at Lausanne.

Lafitte had five rounds of talks with the representatives of both the countries and also visited the project site in their presence. On 12 February 2007, he gave his decision on the questions that had been referred to him. His decision was as follows:

- The planned pondage should be reduced from the designed 37.5Mm^3 to 32.56Mm^3. He did not however, agree with Pakistan's calculations which would have led to a drastic cut to 6.22Mm^3.

- The free board be reduced by 1.5m, to 3m.

- The water intakes be raised by 3m (as opposed to the 7m suggested by Pakistan).

- On the gated spillways, Lafitte held them to be in conformity with international practices and state-of-the-art technology, after studying the database of about 13,000 dams from ICOLD's World Register of Dams. In the existing conditions at Baglihar, he held that the number, size and location of gates as per its design complied with IWT, thus upholding India's stand.

Reactions

In their first reactions, given on the day of Lafitte's decision itself, both India and Pakistan claimed 'victory'. Pakistan's Water and Power Minister L. K. Jatoi justified this by the fact that Lafitte had upheld its objections on three out of four issues, and he asked India to accept the decision as its 'moral, legal and political obligation'.

The Indian reaction, as given by its Water Resources Minister, Prof. S. Soz (who, incidentally, comes from Kashmir), was equally positive. He was happy that the overall design of the project, including the gated spillways, was upheld by Lafitte. On the three issues where Lafitte had asked for variations in design parameters, it was stated that during its negotiations with Pakistan (before Lafitte was appointed), India already 'had offered possible reduction of freeboard' to Pakistan 'in the spirit of good and neighbourly relations'.

The other two variations suggested by Lafitte too were of a minor nature and no difficulty was expected in making the appropriate design changes.

From India's point of view, it could now go full-steam ahead with both stage-I of Baglihar project now planned for commissioning in the coming winter of 2007-08, and with the pre-project work of its stage-II (also 450MW). It also had plans to progressively utilise most of the 20GW hydro potential of J&K state (of which 16.2GW has been identified, but less than 2GW developed). Most of it lay in the waters of the three western rivers and their tributaries. Two projects, Kishenganga and Tulbul (see Table 2) had already remained suspended due to Pakistan's objections. Lafitte's decision was bound to have an effect on settling the differences on these projects too.

Lafitte's approval to India's usage of gated spillways would enable it to deal more effectively with the problems of sedimentation and flood-control in future hydro projects in that state, according to J & K Power Minister Rigzin Jora (as quoted in The Hindustan Times). Pakistan's fears about these spillways being used against its interests, however, remain unallayed. Its Minister Jatoi thus said that the various technical and legal aspects of this particular issue were being studied, and that 'we have the right to take up the spillway issue anytime at an appropriate forum'.

What happens next?

Would Lafitte's decision which, as per the provisions of IWT is 'final and binding' on both the parties, see the end of the dispute over Baglihar project?

India has already accepted the decision and is going ahead with consequential action. For that reason, the award has quickly become a non-issue in India both among the stakeholders and the media. In fact, the media, both in India and Pakistan, had, by and large, taken a balanced and positive view of the situation, and pointed to the peaceful settlement of this dispute under the aegis of a neutral expert as a way out where mutual talks do not lead to a settlement.

Privately, however, fears are expressed whether Pakistan would ultimately accept the finality of the award. It is an accepted fact that there is mistrust in Pakistan over India's plans to utilise the waters of Western rivers purely for developmental needs and in a way that does not damage the interests of the lower riparian State. Water resource is a sensitive issue in both the countries, and Pakistan apprehends that India could regulate the flow of these rivers in a way that goes against both agrarian and geo-strategic requirements of Pakistan.

So, what are the options still open to Pakistan? In the very least, it could seek from India an access to the Baglihar project site from time to time, so as to monitor and satisfy itself that India is complying with the decision of Lafitte on various issues. That itself has the potential to create future discord on the project over technical and other aspects, based on the ground realities.

Then again, on the gated spillways, Pakistan could take a view that a question had arisen out of Lafitte's decision which was beyond his competence to resolve. It could thus invoke the provisions of Article IX (paras 3-5) of IWT and seek reference to a seven-member Court of Arbitration. It could also opt to take that particular issue (or the entire dispute) to the International Court of Justice at the Hague. However, either of that recourse would be a calculated risk, given that Lafitte was a neutral expert.

In the ultimate reckoning, the settlement of Baglihar and other such hydro disputes requires a spirit of goodwill and mutual accommodation between the two countries. The entire Indus Waters treaty 1960 covering such disputes is predicated on that basic premise.

Salient features of the Baglihar hydro project (after Prof Lafitte's decision)

Dam
Concrete gravity
143m high

317m length at the top
Dam pondage : storage capacity of 32.56Mm^3
Intake for power plant : at 821m elevation
Gross head : 130m
Main spillway : six submerged radial gates, 10m wide and 10.5m high
Chute spillway : two crest radial gates, 12m wide and 19m high

Diversion tunnels
Two tunnels, total length 939m, horse-shoe shape

Headrace tunnel
10.15m diameter, circular tunnel, 2070m long

Tailrace tunnel
160m long, 10m wide, 19-27.5m high, D-shape

Power house
Underground cavern, 121m x 24m x 50m.
Three Francis Vertical-axis turbines, each 150MW
Rated discharge per stage: 430m^3/sec
Installed capacity : 450MW in Stage-I
Generation : 2.804B units in a 90% dependable year

Transmission
Underground Transformer Hall having 10 transformers of 11kV/400kV single-phase
Outdoor 400-kV switchyard

Contractors
Jaiprakash Associates of India, for all Civil and H-M works on EPC basis.
Siemens / VA Tech Hydro Vevey for E-M works.
Lahmeyer International for design and contracts review, construction supervision and contract supervision.

Project promotor
J&K Power Development Corporation Ltd., owned by the State Government of Jammu & Kashmir, India.

Location
Over river Chenab in the Doda District in the Indian state of Jammu & Kashmir

Likely total cost
In excess of US$1B

Other projects currently in dispute

Kishenganga project

This comprises a 330MW hydroelectric scheme, utilising the waters of the river Kishenganga, at a total estimated cost of US$500M. Kishenganga is a tributary of river Jhelum (one of the three 'Western' rivers under IWT), of which India is permitted only a restrictive use as the upper riparian State.

The original project, to be executed by India's NHPC, involved construction of a 103m high dam on Kishenganga in the famed Kashmir Valley, which would divert a part of its water to the Wular Lake in the south through a diversion tunnel, and an underground power house with three 110MW Pelton turbines.

However, Pakistan put in objections both to the concept and the design of the project as being violative of IWT. Environmentalists were also concerned that the Indian project could submerge vast tracts of land in the Gurez area and displace local residents. Pakistan also felt that the project would adversely affect its own Neelum-Jhelum hydro project, proposed to be set up downstream of Kishenganga after it enters the Pakistan-occupied Kashmir.

During Indo-Pak talks on the issue, India agreed to take a second look at the design of its project to meet some of the objections raised by Pakistan. This included ensuring that the project remained run-of-the-river and also envisaged non-diversion of water to the Wular Lake. However, no settlement has been reached between the two countries at the time of writing.

Tulbul Navigaton project

This project involves the construction by India of a barrier on the river Jhelum, downstream of the Wular Lake, to make the river navigable during the lean winter months. The structure is to be 134m long and 12.2m wide, with a navigation lock, at a place 40km north of the state capital of Srinagar. It is aimed to improve the lean flow of 2000m^3/sec (with a depth of 0.8m) to above the minimum of 4000m^3/sec (depth of 1.2m) required for navigation in a 20km portion of the river between Sopore and Baramulla.

Work on the project had started in the year 1984, but was stopped in 1987 after Pakistan raised objections on it of being an alleged violation of IWT. It said that the project (which Pakistan has termed as the Wular Barrage) is prohibited by the Treaty which bars India from constructing any storage (except a limited one for flood control) over the Western rivers, or any 'man-made obstruction' which would cause 'change in the volume ... of the daily flow of waters'. Pakistan also felt that the barrage would have the potential to disrupt its own three-canal system downstream.

India's rebuttal is that the Tulbul project is not for storage; that Wular was an existing lake, and that the project amounted to only 'regulating the flow'. It pointed out that augmentation of flow during the lean season would benefit both the countries as the river Jhelum, downstream of the project, entered the Pakistan-occupied portion of the Kashmir State. The project has so far remained unexecuted.

Author Info:

I M Sahal is an independent consultant in hydro power and is based in New Delhi, India.

CHAPTER - 6

Transboundary Disputes

Two Neighbours and a Treaty Baglihar Project in Hot Waters

Rajesh Sinha

Pakistan has objected to several features of the Baglihar hydropower project on the Chenab river in Jammu and Kashmir, contending that it violates the Indus Waters Treaty. The World Bank, which brokered the IWT, has appointed a neutral expert to resolve the differences. Diplomats fear these developments might cast a shadow on the composite dialogue process, as seeking arbitration on the dam means breaking out of the bilateral framework.

This project was conceived in 1992, approved in 1996 and the construction began in 1999. The Baglihar Hydropower Project (BHP) is located on the river Chenab in Ramban tehsil of Doda district, Jammu and Kashmir (J and K). It is about 150 km from the nearest railhead, Jammu, near Batote on the Jammu-Srinagar Highway-1A on the Nasri bypass road. The BHP will have an installed capacity of 450 MW during phase I and 900 MW during phase II. It is a Rs 4,000 crore venture of the government of J and K and about Rs 2,500 crore has already been spent on it. The project is targeted to be completed by 2007.

Pakistan has objected to several features of the project, contending they violate the Indus Waters Treaty (IWT) that lays down the rights and obligations of India and Pakistan for the use of waters of the Indus system of rivers. India disagreed and Pakistan approached the World Bank, which had brokered the IWT to appoint a neutral expert (NE) to resolve the differences.

Drawing Boundaries on Water

When India and Pakistan became independent in 1947, the boundary between the two countries was drawn right across the Indus basin, with Pakistan in the lower riparian region. Two vital irrigation head works – Madhopur on Ravi and Ferozepur on Sutlej – on which the irrigation canals of Pakistan's Punjab had been dependent, were in the Indian territory. The resultant dispute was resolved when negotiations, facilitated by the World Bank, led to the signing of the IWT in 1960 at Karachi. The signatories were Mohammad Ayub Khan for Pakistan, Jawaharlal Nehru for India and W A B Illif of the World Bank.

The treaty has worked well for years. But since the 1980s, the differences that cropped up over several projects have not been sorted out despite protracted talks. Pakistan has not only opposed the BHP on river Chenab, it has also opposed the Wullar Barrage/Tulbul navigation project on the Jhelum, the Swalakote hydroelectric project and Dul Hasti hydroelectric project on the Chenab and the Kishanganga hydroelectric project on the Kishanganga in J and K.

Suspicious Neighbours

The dispute over the BHP centres on the design specifications. Pakistan has raised six objections relating to the project configuration, free board, spillway (ungated or gated), firm power, pondage, level of intake, inspection during plugging of low level intake, and whether the structure is meant to be a low weir or a dam. The argument is based on paragraph 8 of Annexure D to the IWT. India maintains that the conditions at the Baglihar site make a gated spillway necessary but Pakistan insists that an ungated spillway will do just fine and that the plan to provide a gate contravenes the provisions of paragraph 8 (e) of Annexure D to the IWT.

Pakistan also contends that the pondage in the operating pool, at 37.722 mm^3, exceeds the level agreed upon in the treaty and that the intake for the turbine is not located at the highest level as required by the treaty. It believes that the height of the a dam, at 470 feet, is excessive and that the reservoir created at the site will be more than what is required for power generation needs and it might block the flow of the river for a period of 26-28 days during the low season (January-February). This, it is argued, will cause a drop of about 200 cumecs in the river flow during this period at the point of entry into Pakistan.

Based on all these objections, Pakistan insists that India should stop all work on the project till the issue is resolved. India has refused, saying there is no provision in the treaty for the stoppage of work, and that past experiences in trying to find solutions by stopping construction have not been productive.

The IWT gave India exclusive rights over three eastern rivers – Sutlej, Beas and Ravi – leaving Chenab, Jhelum and Indus to Pakistan. But the treaty does allow India limited use of their waters for agriculture, domestic purposes and development projects provided there is no obstruction to the flow of waters into Pakistan.

The Permanent Indus Commission (PIC) set up under the IWT by the two countries has been meeting regularly to sort out any differences that arise. This is the first time the committee has failed to resolve a crisis, forcing Pakistan to invoke the provision to approach the World Bank. The World Bank scrutinised Pakistan's record of actions taken before the request and acknowledged that it has the mandate to appoint a NE but is not a guarantor to the treaty and, therefore, will not directly participate in any discussion or exchange on the subject. And so Raymond Lafitte was appointed as the NE and the arbitration clause is in operation for the first time in the 45-year history of the treaty.

Pakistan's View

Underlying the dispute are suspicions and apprehensions resulting in much rhetoric. Claiming the project will affect the flow of river waters to its territory in violation of the IWT, an upset Pakistan says that India planned the dam and began construction without its approval as mandated by the treaty.

The gates are another big issue. Pakistan feels the closure may adversely affect irrigation in its territory. They argue that 450 megawatts of electricity can be generated even with the gates open. Pakistan fears that tampering with the flow of the river may create floods or drought downstream. The allegation is that India has not been taking it into confidence about the project's technical details and has been adopting evasive tactics right from the beginning. Some sharing of data took place at a pretty late stage of construction (in 2003). Pakistani engineers believe that calling Baglihar a "hydroelectric" project is a misnomer. The structure will create a reservoir at the site and hence should be properly termed a "dam" and a dam is not allowed as per the terms of the treaty. At a briefing after the decision to approach the World Bank was taken, Pakistan's foreign office spokesman Masood Khan said, "Pakistan was left with no choice but to go to the World Bank. Pakistan tried every channel provided by the treaty, but India did not change its stance and refused to meet Pakistan's legitimate concerns."

Pakistan alleged that New Delhi denied Islamabad's repeated demand for an on-site inspection by its members of the Indus Waters Commission for four years. The treaty provides for an inspection tour once every five years or on request. Only when threatened with approaching the World Bank did India allow an on-site inspection in October 2003. Among the reasons given for Pakistan's concern was a drought that had compelled it to economise on water. With insufficient storage capacity and inadequate rainfall, water shortage in Pakistan reached critical proportions and was a major source of inter-provincial disharmony. The Pakistan government's inability to make India bend on the Baglihar dam and the Wullar barrage projects came in for severe criticism not only from the farming community but also from politicians in the ruling coalition.

India claims BHP is a fully legal scheme that involves no water storage. It denies allegations that it violates the IWT or that it will affect the flow in the river since the IWT allows power generation projects to be built on any of the three western rivers of the Indus river system, as long as they benefit the local people and do not interrupt the flow of the river.

India says that reduction in the height of the dam will impact the power generation capacity of the project and render it worthless. India also argues that the statistics provided by Pakistan on decrease in the river water flow are faulty. The rejoinder over the gate issue goes thus: An ungated spillway will require a higher crest and the silting level will also increase. The gates will enable the flushing of silt. India asserts that it made all efforts to dispel Pakistan's apprehensions. It claims to have consistently expressed its willingness to engage its counterpart in technical dis- cussions in PIC meetings; arranged the Pakistani team visits to Baglihar and provided necessary explanations/clarifications to the queries raised by them during the 100th PIC tour.

India claims that information on this project was sent to the Pakistan Commissioner in 1992 as required by the IWT. Since Pakistan feels that the design of this project contravenes the IWT provisions, the matter has been discussed during the 84th, 85th and 86th meetings of the PIC held in 1999, 2000 and 2001. India feels that Pakistan has been taking a rigid stand despite being informed about changes in the design of the plant and that they should have first conveyed their views/observations on these changes to India. Instead they chose to invoke relevant articles in the treaty and sought intervention of a NE.

Meanwhile, India has refused to stop work on the project on the basis of its experience with the Tulbul navigation project (Pakistan calls it Wullar barrage), proposed to be built on the river Jhelum at the mouth of the Wullar lake near Sopore in Kashmir valley. After India stopped construction of the Tulbul project in response to Pakistan's objections a decade ago, it has not been possible to take it up again. India says that Pakistan's objections to BHP are based on apprehensions rather than on technical reality. India's Foreign Secretary Shyam Saran observed that "the 1960 Indus Waters Treaty, under which the reference was made, couldn't deal with suspicions of this nature."

IWT and Jammu and Kashmir

To Kashmiris, the BHP is a project for and by Jammu and Kashmir, a state in dire need of power. They believe Pakistan wants to deny J and K the right to use its own rivers, citing the situation in Pakistan-occupied Kashmir where, they believe, people have no rights over Mangla Dam on Jhelum, built to meet the power and water needs of Punjab and other parts of Pakistan.

London-based moderate separatist leaders Syed Nazir Gilani and Shabir Choudhry reacted sharply to Pakistan's appeal to the World Bank to resolve the controversial Baglihar project and questioned Islamabad's "legal or moral right" over the natural resources of J and K. Gilani even justified chief minister Mufti Mohammed Sayeed's claim that the IWT had greatly harmed the interests of the people of the state. Sayeed had appealed to Pakistan, before the secretary-level meeting between the two countries in New Delhi in the second week of January, to facilitate economic growth in the state by not objecting to projects started on its own water resources. He described the IWT as discriminating against the people of J and K. But, he was quick to add, the BHP had not violated the IWT.

J and K has never been very happy with the IWT. On March 2, 2003, the J and K assembly passed a resolution asking the central government to review the IWT. Public health minister Qazi Mohammed Afzal said that but for the terms of the treaty, over and above the 33,000 ha which was under irrigation before 1960, the state could have increased the area under irrigation by another 40,000 ha.

J and K finance minister, Muzzaffar Hussain Beig, pointed out that the farmers in the state have requested the government to take a strong stand against it. The state has been facing severe water scarcity as a result of a six-year dry spell.

Chronology of Events

2001: Contact between the PIC officials is broken off following tension at the border.

July 12, 2003: PIC meeting between India and Pakistan makes little headway. A follow-up meeting is convened in August to break the logjam. Pakistan serves its first notice threatening to seek intervention.

October 2003: A team of Pakistan's technical experts inspects the project site. Pakistan expresses its objections to the design and India refuses to make any changes. Pakistan serves a second notice on the Indian government to settle the dispute by December 31 that year saying it would otherwise approach the World Bank to appoint a NE.

January 18, 2005: A three-day meeting between the Indus Water Commissioners of Pakistan and India is concluded without finding a solution. Pakistan approaches the World Bank. Kashmir decides to go ahead with the construction of the dam. India terms Pakistan's decision to seek World Bank's arbitration as "premature" and "hasty".

April 2005: World Bank sends a panel of three experts to both countries.

May 10, 2005: World Bank names Swiss national Raymond Lafitte as the NE.

June 9-10, 2005: Lafitte, in the course of his first meeting with Indian and Pakistani delegations, turns down Pakistan's demand that India stop work on the project till he delivers a verdict. It is decided that a Pakistani team would visit the project site in July before submitting its report. India would respond with a "counter report". Lafitte would then visit the site in October.

Fingers Crossed

The issue has gained momentum at a time when India and Pakistan are trying to build mutual understanding and trust. Both countries have made statements, offering full cooperation to the NE and have agreed to abide by his decision. The NE is not concerned with any deeper issues and anxieties underlying Pakistan's technical objections.

The NE has to answer specific questions posed to him, about whether certain features conform to the conditions laid down in the IWT. He is not expected to make any judgment or propose alternatives. Only if either of the two parties put in a request can he suggest measures to compose a difference or to implement his decision. He is also free to conclude that the matters referred to him fall outside his purview or that the differences amount to a dispute, better handled by a court of arbitration. There is also the possibility that the two countries might actually reach a compromise, which makes the NE's job easier.

Diplomats fear that these developments might cast a shadow on the composite dialogue process; seeking arbitration on the Baglihar dam means breaking out of the bilateral framework, even though it will not lead to the collapse of the dialogue process.

Email: rajeshsinha2005@rediffmail.com

CHAPTER – 7

Unchartered Waters: The Kishenganga River Project Dispute and Arbitration Under The Indus Waters Treaty

Omar K Ibrahim

The Indus Waters Treaty (the "Treaty")[1] is regarded as one of the most significant and successful agreements ever executed between India and Pakistan.[2] The Treaty's resilience through multiple wars and political instability between the two parties is in large part due to its well-thought-out, multi-layered, dispute-resolution mechanisms. One of the mechanisms provided for in the Treaty is arbitration under the auspices of a to-be-created court of arbitration.[3] Interestingly, the creation of this unique court of arbitration could involve the President of the World Bank, the Secretary General of the United Nations, the President of the Massachusetts Institute of Technology, the Rector of the Imperial College of Science and Technology in London, the Lord Chief Justice of England, and the Chief Justice of the United Parties Supreme Court.[4]

While other dispute-resolution mechanisms provided for in the Treaty have been utilized, before 2010, in the approximately fifty-year history of the Treaty, the arbitral provisions of the Treaty have never been invoked to resolve a dispute.[5] In June 2010, however, Pakistan, for the first time invoked the arbitral provisions of the Treaty in an action to resolve a dispute regarding India's plans to build a 330-megawatt hydroelectric power plant on the Kishenganga River (the "Kishenganga Project Dispute").[6] This article provides a brief overview of the arbitral provisions of the Treaty and the ongoing arbitration of the Kishenganga Project Dispute.

Background of the Treaty

The Indus waters begin in the Himalayan Mountains of Indian-held Kashmir and flow between Pakistan and India, eventually emptying into the Arabian Sea south of Karachi, Pakistan. Disputes over the Indus waters predate the independence of India and Pakistan from British rule. Prior to 1935, the Indus waters were under the jurisdiction of one political authority, British India, and any disputes regarding the Indus waters were resolved by executive order.[7] In 1935, the Government of India Act put water under provincial jurisdiction and disputes began to arise between the provinces, most notably Punjab and Sindh.[8] The disputes centered around Sindh's concern that the Punjabi irrigation works would disrupt the water flow to the Indus, negatively affecting Sindhi irrigation.[9] In 1935 and 1941, the British government established two dispute-resolution commissions—the Anderson Commission and the Rau Commission—to examine the dispute.[10] Before the provinces could reach a final agreement, however, the subcontinent was partitioned in 1947. The resulting international boundary between India and Pakistan was drawn through the state of Punjab. With the source of the Indus waters in India, Pakistan was left threatened by the prospect of Indian control over the tributaries that fed water into the Pakistani portion of the basin.[11]

Between 1947 through 1951, India and Pakistan engaged in fruitless bilateral negotiations to resolve the disputes over the Indus waters. The impasse was broken when David Lilienthal, the former head of the Tennessee Valley Authority, suggested in a Collier's Magazine article that the dispute over the Indus waters could be resolved better by engineers from the two parties with the World Bank acting as a neutral mediator, rather than by the parties' politicians.[12] The President of the World Bank, David Black, who was a close friend of Lilienthal, acted on this suggestion and offered up the World Bank to serve as a neutral mediator.[13] Both India and Pakistan accepted the World Bank's offer and, after almost a decade of negotiation, the Treaty was born.

Dispute Resolution Under the Treaty

Due to the violent history between the two nations, the Treaty includes a detailed, multi-layered, dispute-resolution mechanism intended to facilitate peaceful resolution.[14] The Treaty identifies three escalating tiers of disputes that may arise concerning the application and interpretation of the Treaty between the parties: "questions," "differences" and "disputes." The Treaty provides a different resolution mechanism for each.

First, the Treaty created a standing Permanent Indus Commission (the "Commission") to examine "questions" concerning the interpretation or application of the Treaty. The Commission is made up of one Commissioner from each State.[15] While, the main goal of the Commission is to operationalize the Treaty and facilitate cooperation between the two parties,[15] Article DC of the Treaty provides that any "question" concerning the interpretation or application of the Treaty is to be first examined by the Commission.[17] If the Commission is unable to resolve such a "question" by agreement, then the "question" escalates into a "difference" between the two parties.

A "difference" is referred to a neutral expert who, ideally, is to be appointed by agreement between the parties.[18] If the parties cannot agree on a neutral expert, or on a third party to appoint a neutral expert, then the neutral expert would be appointed by the World Bank.[19] According to Annexure F of the Treaty, the neutral expert must be an eminent engineer. Thus, the Treaty provides only for a limited set of "differences" that the neutral expert may resolve. The Treaty lists twenty-three types of "differences" that fall under the jurisdiction of the neutral expert, and most of the listed "differences" are technical in nature.[20] "Differences" outside the list in Annexure F do not fall within the authority of the neutral expert and would have to be settled by a "Court of Arbitration," referred to in Article IX and Annexure F of the Treaty but detailed in Annexure G.

If the neutral expert determines that the "difference" (or part of it) referred to him or her does not fall under the expert's jurisdiction as prescribed by the Treaty, then the "difference," or that part, becomes a "dispute" to be resolved by a court of arbitration or by agreement of the parties.[21] Additionally, the Commission, or either party, can unilaterally deem a "difference" a "dispute" and submit the dispute to the court of arbitration.[22] Although the Treaty provides that the decision of the neutral expert is final and binding, it also provides that if any issue not within the competence of the neutral expert should arise out of his or her decision, then that issue should be settled in accordance with the procedures provided for in the Treaty, which would likely involve the court of arbitration.[23]

Notably, although the Treaty identifies three escalating tiers of disputes, the dispute-resolution process in the Treaty is not hierarchical.[24] A "question" referred to the neutral expert is not an appeal of a decision of the Commission – Rather, it is referred to the neutral expert because the Commission cannot resolve it. This is to be expected with complex questions, given that the Commission consists of two persons, each representing one of the two countries. Moreover, the decision of the neutral expert is final and binding and, as such, cannot be appealed to the court of arbitration. Indeed, the Treaty provides that any decision within the competence of the neutral expert is binding not just on the parties, but also on any court of arbitration.[25]

As noted above, should an initial "question" between the parties transform into a "dispute," then the Treaty provides for the "dispute" to be resolved by the court of arbitration. Under the Treaty, courts of arbitration must consist of seven arbitrators, with each party having a right to appoint two.[26] The remaining three arbitrators are referred to as "umpires," and they are selected through a complex and detailed mechanism.

First, according to the Treaty, India and Pakistan agreed to maintain a standing panel of umpires consisting of four people in each of the following three categories: "(i) Persons qualified by status and reputation to be Chairman of the Court of Arbitration who may, but need not, be engineers or lawyers, (ii) Highly qualified engineers, (iii) Persons well versed in international law."[27] If the standing panel has been properly constituted, then the parties must first attempt to reach an agreement on the remaining three arbitrators by choosing one of the four standing panel members from each category. If the parties cannot agree, they are to decide by drawing lots.[23] According to the Appendix to Annexure G of the Treaty, the parties had nominated the following individuals to the standing panel: the Secretary General of the United Nations or the President of the World Sank for category (i), the President of the Massachusetts Institute of Technology or the Rector of the Imperial College of Science and Technology in London for category (ii); and the Chief Justice of the United Parties or the Lord Chief Justice of England for category (iii). Since four members had not been nominated for each category, the standing panel had not, according to the Treaty, been properly nominated.

In the event the standing panel is not properly nominated, the Treaty provides that the parties can agree on the umpires, provided that the umpires are from one of the stated categories. If the parties cannot agree, the parties must then attempt to agree on one or more persons to help them in selecting the remaining three umpires.[29] If the parties cannot agree to one or more persons to assist them, then the parties will draw lots for the names of persons from the categories noted above to make the necessary selection for that category.[30]

The Kishenganga Project Dispute and Arbitration Under the Treaty

As previously noted, in June 2010, Pakistan, for the first time invoked the arbitral provisions of the Treaty to resolve the Kishenganga Project Dispute with India.[31] The essence of the dispute is Pakistan's claim that India, by diverting the course of the river to build the Kishenganga hydroelectric power plant, would reduce Pakistan's water flow by one-third during the winter, thereby constituting a violation of the Treaty.[32] India argues that it is well within its Treaty rights to build the Kishenganga power plant, which it has been planning since the late 1980's.[33] Prior to Pakistan initiating arbitration, Pakistan and India had attempted to reach a resolution for the past two decades but were unable to do so.

As provided for in the Treaty, when Pakistan instituted arbitral proceedings, it nominated Bruno Simma, a German jurist currently serving as a justice on the International Court of Justice, and Jan Paulsson, an internationally recognized attorney and arbitrator, as its party-appointed arbitrators.[35] India, for its appointed arbitrators, selected Peter Tomka, a Slovak national, who, like Bruno Simma, is a justice on the International Court of Justice, and Lucius Caflisch, a professor at the Graduate Institute of International Studies in Geneva.[38]

Because the standing panel called for in the Treaty was not properly constituted, India and Pakistan first attempted to agree on the selection of the remaining three umpires from the categories noted above, but they were unable to do so.[37] The next step was to determine if they could agree on one or more persons to assist them in selecting the three umpires. Again, they were not able to reach an agreement. As a result, in July 2010, they drew lots. The Secretary General of the United Nations was selected to appoint an umpire from category (i) to become the chair of the Court of Arbitration. The Rector of the Imperial College of Science and Technology in London was selected to appoint an umpire from category (ii). And, the Lord Chief Justice of England was selected to appoint the umpire from category (iii).[36]

The Secretary General of the United Nations appointed Stephen Myron Schwebel, an American jurist who previously served on the International Court of Justice.[39] Professor Howard S. Wheater was selected as an umpire by the Rector of the Imperial College of Science and Technology in London. The Lord Chief Justice of England selected Justice Sir Franklin Beman, as the third umpire.[40]

With the Court of Arbitration finally constituted, hearings began in the dispute on 14 January 2011.[41] Although the dispute concerns a public matter—water rights—the Treaty provides that "deliberations" by the members of the court of arbitration are private, and "discussions" in the court of arbitration are private, absent agreement from both the parties and the tribunal. As such, the public will likely not learn much about the arbitration until its ultimate resolution.

Conclusion

In the approximately fifty-year history of the Treaty, its complex and multi-layered dispute-resolution mechanism has effectively functioned to facilitate peaceful outcomes between the two parties. Although not yet resolved, the mere fact that an arbitration panel has been conformed in the Kishenganga Project Dispute is a testament to the success of the Treaty's dispute-resolution mechanism in deftly navigating Indo-Pakistani politics toward the peaceful resolution of potentially explosive issues.

OmarK. Ibrahim, *an attorney in Miami, focuses his practice on commercial litigation and arbitration. He can be reached at Omar@okilaw.com.*

Endnotes:

1. Indus Waters Treaty, India-Pak., Sept. 19,1960, 419 U.N.T.S. 125, *also available at* http://web.worldbank.org/WBSITE/EXTER.-NAL/COUNTTtfES/SOUTHASIAEXT/0, contentMDK:20320047-pagePK:146736-piPK:583444-theSiteFX:223547,0O.htinl (last visited February 6, 2011).
2. Manav Bhatnagar, *Reconsidering the Indus Waters Treaty,* 22 Tul. Envtl. L.J. 271, 278 (Summer 2009).
3. Indus Waters Treaty, *supra* note 1, at art. DC and annex. F.
4. *Id.* at annex. F.
5. Amol Sharma and Tom Wright, *India and Pakistan Feud Over Indus Waters,* Wall St. J., March 30, 2010.
6. Amy Kazim, *India and Pakistan to Arbitrate Water Feud,* Fin. Times (June 18, 2010A *available at* http://www.ft.com/cms/s/0/2587c9b4-7aba-lldf-S549-00144feab-dcO.html#axzalDDGugDBe.
7. Aaron T. Wolf and Joshua T. Newton, Water Conflict Management and Transformation at the Oregon State University, *Case Study of Transboundary Dispute Resolution: the Indus Waters Treaty,* (2008), http://www.transboundarywaters.orst.edu/research/case_ studies/Documents/indus.pdf (last visited Feb. 6, 2010).
8. *Id.; see also,* Bhatnagar, *supra* note 2, at 272-73.
9. *Id.*
10. Bhatnagar, supra note 2, at 272-73.
11. The Henry L. Stimson Center, *The Indus Waters Treaty: A History,* http://www.stimson. org/research-pages/the-indus-waters-treaty-a-history/ (last visited Feb. 6, 2011).
12. Wolf and Newton, *supra* note 7; Colleen P. Graffy, *Water, Water Everywhere, Nor Any Drop To Drink: The Urgency of Transnational Solutions to International Riparian Disputes,* 10 Geo. Int'l Envtl, L.Rev. 399, 426-27 (Winter 1998).
13. Wolf and Newton, *supra* note 7; *see also,* Bhatnagar, *supra* note 2, at 273
14. Indus Waters Treaty, *supra* note 1, at arts. VIII-LX, annex. F and annex. G.
15. Indus Waters Treaty, *supra* note 1, at art. VIII.
16. Sandeep Gopalan, *India-Pakistan Relations: Legalization and Agreement Design,* 40 Vand. J. Traksnat'l L. 687, 699 (May 2007).
17. Indus Waters Treaty, *supra* note 1, at art. IX.
18. Indus Waters Treaty, *supra* note 1, at annex. F.
19. *Id.*
20. *Id.*
21. Indus Waters Treaty, *supra* note 1, at art. LX and annex. F.
22. *Id.*
23. *Id.*
24. Salman M. A.,Salman, *The Eaglikar Difference and its Resolution Process-A Triumph for the Indus Waters Treaty?,* 10 Water Pol'y 105,107 (2008).
25. Indus Waters Treaty, *supra* note 1, at annex. F.

CHAPTER – 8

The Security Implications of Water Prospects for Instability or Cooperation in South and Central Asia

Thesis by Adam Radin, Naval Postgraduate School Monterey, California (March, 2010)

Thesis Advisor: Anne L. Clunan

Co-Advisor: Anshu N. Chatterjee

South Asia

> The water crisis in Pakistan is directly linked to relations with India. Resolution could prevent an environmental catastrophe in South Asia, but failure to do so could fuel the fires of discontent that lead to extremism and terrorism.[1]
>
> —Pakistan President Asif Ali Zardari, 28 January 2009

A. Introduction

India and Pakistan have faced a number of contentious issues since partition in 1947. Territorial disputes over Kashmir, religious and ethnic strife, language conflicts, or asymmetric attacks and retaliation, have constantly fed instability in the region. In each case, defeat, coercion, or deterrence, and in so many cases a blending of all three play a role in eventual resolution of South Asian conflicts.[2] While these conflicts yield short-term resolutions, a shadow of conflict lingers largely due to the symbolic question of control over Kashmir. However, despite multiple conflicts in the region in the past 60 years, water-sharing issues, in comparison, remain a conflict restricted to rhetorical clashes, largely due to the Indus Waters Treaty (IWT) of 1960 and security interdependence that has developed over time. Considering that Indo-Pakistani relations are historically consumed with enmity and paranoia, the stability surrounding this essential resource of such strategic and economic importance is a surprise. However, the pressure to maintain economic development in India and remain fiscally solvent in Pakistan will increasingly test this trend of dormancy. India and Pakistan stand at a crossroads, where the two states will need to build off and evolve from the successes of the IWT and approach water in a regionally cooperative manner.

First, this chapter describes the history of Indo-Pakistani water sharing rights from partition to the eventual signing of the IWT. The second section focuses on recent strains on the IWT, specifically arising out of India's construction of the Baglihar dam in Jammu and Kashmir. The third and fourth section addresses the trends towards marketization of water and future prospects for water issues in South Asia. These sections connect the central argument that while India and Pakistan historically followed and accepted established treaties, development and growth pressures, degradation of fresh water resources, increased Pakistani economic dependence on shared water, and historical enmity will test and strain the IWT. However, due to India and Pakistan's history of reliance on treaties towards resolving water disputes, the region will likely adapt better to interstate water crises because of these lessons learned and the very high cost of cooperation failure—leading to potential armed conflict—for either state.

B. Historic Water Rights Issues And The Indus Waters Treaty Of 1960

Water distribution and allocation rights concerns are not new to South Asia. The British administration from 1860 to 1947 made large investments into the Indus basin irrigation system, making it the largest continuous irrigation system in the world, with a command area of roughly 20 million hectares and an annual irrigation capacity of more than 12 million hectares.[3] The Government of India Act of 1935 placed the distribution and control of water under provincial rule for the first time.[4] Prior to the Act, the central British authority

---

[1] Asif Ali Zardari, "Partnering With Pakistan," The Washington Post, 28 January 2009.
[2] The concept of coercion in South Asian affairs is addressed in, Verghese Koithara, "Coercion and Risk-Taking in Nuclear South Asia," (Stanford: Stanford University Press--CISAC Working Paper, March 2003).
[3] Ashok Swain, "Environmental Cooperation in South Asia," eds. Ken Conca and Geoffrey D. Dabelko (Washington, D.C.: Woodrow Wilson Press, 2002), 66.
[4] "The Indus Waters Treaty," Oregon State University, Department of Geosciences.

settled disputes over water irrigation, but as a precursor to eventual independence, water rights were localized as an element of the Government of India Act. Once water rights became localized, disputes immediately occurred on areas of extensive irrigation, including the provinces of Punjab and Sindh.[5]

After the Radcliffe Lines were hastily drawn in 1947, resulting in the partition of Pakistan and India, much of the region fell into disarray because of the resulting mass cross-border migration. While the British focus was on fair distribution in terms of population, the Radcliffe Lines complicated the distribution of water in the Indus river system. Before partition, as Figure 1 illustrates, "the Indus irrigation system was envisaged to alleviate the water shortage in the Sutlej Valley Project (a primary tributary river for the Indus) by the addition of canals to bring water from the west, together with a dam and a large storage reservoir to be built at Bhakra on the Sutlej. However, partition left Bhakra in India and thus aggravated the problem of shortages in the Sutlej Valley Canals (in West Pakistan)."[6] Due to high agricultural development in the region, the state was forced to look towards the Upper Bari Doab for additional water. It built links of up to 63 miles in order to bring water from the Ravi and Chenab rivers in 1951 and 1954.[7]

The borders—quickly drawn without a genuine understanding over water distribution—led to disputes almost instantly after independence. In 1948, a serious dispute over shared water occurred when India halted water supplies to some Pakistani canals at the start of the summer irrigation season.[8] India halted the water supplies because of the ambiguity surrounding water distribution after partition and to fulfill water needs of the time.[9] Immediate negotiations did not resolve the issue and the action by India led to the deprivation of water from approximately 5.5 percent of Pakistan's agricultural area.[10] While violent confrontation did not ensue, such provincial disputes foreshadowed eventual problems and the need for a binding treaty to settle upstream and downstream water distribution disputes. After the first Kashmir War of 1947, India and Pakistan had set a path towards hostile relations that would not be resolved in the near – term; therefore, a binding water distribution agreement needed to be established to stymie a potential flash point in relations.

The issue of upstream river control versus downstream water usage lies at the heart of the IWT. Once the borders were drawn, West Pakistan found itself in a precarious position of negotiating with an upstream power that needed to look towards its own national interests. As Ken Conca notes,

> Balancing upstream and downstream rights and responsibilities is the most contentious aspect of bargaining over watercourse conventions. As several analysts have pointed out, and as the negotiating parties clearly understood, there are potentially profound tensions between the principle of equitable and reasonable use and the principle of no significant harm to other watercourse states. The principle of no significant harm is generally seen to favor downstream states, in that upstream development of water resources may deny water to human and natural uses downstream, thereby causing significant harm. The principle of equitable use, in contrast, is

---

[5] Ibid.
[6] Pieter Lieftinck, Water and Power Resources of West Pakistan: A Study in Sector Planning (Baltimore: The Johns Hopkins Press, 1968), 10. Before 1971, Pakistan was divided between East Pakistan (modern Bangladesh) and West Pakistan (modern Pakistan). References to West Pakistan refer to modern Pakistan.
[7] Ibid., 10.
[8] G. T. Keith Pitman, "The Role of the World Bank in Enhancing Cooperation and Resolving Conflict on International Watercourses: The Case of the Indus Basin," in M. A. Salman. and Laurence Boisson de Chazournes, eds., International Watercourses: Enhancing Cooperation and Managing Conflict, World Bank technical paper no. 414 (Washington, D.C.: World Bank, June 1998). Cited in Swain, "Environmental Cooperation in South Asia," 66.
[9] Ibid.
[10] Ibid.

generally seen to favor upstream states seeking to develop water resources, in the sense that it gives them a legal basis for claiming and using their fair share of the water.[11]

The IWT, therefore, was an attempt to accommodate the interests of both upstream India and downstream Pakistan.[12] In Article III, Section I of the IWT, the section on "Provisions Regarding Western Rivers" specifically states that, "Pakistan shall receive, for unrestricted use all those waters of the Western Rivers which India is under obligation to let flow…"[13] Furthermore, Article III of the treaty clarifies four conditions in which India can "interfere" with the Indus, the Jhelum and the Chenab: (1) Domestic Use; (2) Non-Consumptive Use; (3) Agricultural Use; and (4) Generation of hydro-electric power.[14] As seen in the treaty, the articles leave room for interpretation in the usage of rivers by the upstream power for its national domestic interests.

International distribution concerns can only exacerbate the domestic pressures within each country. Water distribution arguments are not just an international issue between India and Pakistan but have also become domestic disputes that place pressure on their respective governments. In Pakistan, disputes continuously arise over fair water distribution between the Punjab and Sindh provinces.[15] In January 2010, The Sindh Assembly passed a joint resolution opposing the construction of a proposed power plant at the Chashma-Jhelum Link canal on the grounds that it is likely to compound the water situation in the province and would only add to continuous mistrust between the provinces.[16] In India, inter-state disputes are a routine occurrence and when resolutions cannot be easily resolved, they are then moved to tribunal arbitration according to the Inter-State Water Disputes Act of 1956.[17] Even without international distribution issues, water allocation has a tremendous effect on domestic stability. Especially in Pakistan where the Sindh and Balochistan provinces face multiple water choke points before it reaches their territory, domestic unrest can easily be fomented—whether blame is due to international or domestic reasons.

India faces a growing dilemma regarding its obligations to the IWT and its demographic challenges. India is home to one-sixth of the world's population while only endowed with one-twenty-fifth of the world's available water resources.[18] The language of the IWT calls for "equitable utilization" of the Indus Water System by both sides; however, Pakistan is allocated 75 percent of water distribution; as India continues to develop economically, exploitation of Indian water resources will likely lead to water distribution disputes and heavier reliance on the IWT (through the World Bank) to redefine the term "equitable utilization."[19]

Pakistan already faces a projected water crisis due to overexploitation of its indigenous ground and surface water supplies. According to a World Bank report "Pakistan is close to using all of its available water resources in most years. The bottom line is clear -- Pakistan is currently close to using all of the surface and groundwater that it has available, yet it is projected that over 30 percent more water will be needed over the next 20 years to meet increased agricultural, domestic and industrial demands."[20] As Pakistan continues to struggle through economic hardships, the dependence on water will increase in order to maintain economic sustainability. Any cuts in allocation will likely have significant ramifications for these water dependent sectors. To put in

---

[11] Ken Conca, Governing Water: Contentious Transnational Politics and Global Institution Building (Cambridge: MIT Press, 2006), 100.
[12] While The Indus Waters Treaty refers to water resources of both West and East Pakistan, the paper will only refer to Pakistan in terms of the agreement with Western or present-day Pakistan.
[13] *Op Cite.*, The Indus Waters Treaty, Article III, Section 1.
[14] Ibid., Article III, Section 2.
[15] Cohen, The Idea of Pakistan, 212.
[16] The News, "Sindh Assembly Rejects Punjab Canal Project." 29 January 2010.
[17] Historic and pending water disputes within India can be viewed at http://india.gov.in/sectors/water_resources/river_water.php (accessed on 10 January 2010).
[18] United Nations Environment Programme, "Fresh Water Under Threat: South Asia."
[19] World Bank, "Pakistan: Country Water Research Assistance Strategy," 7, 14 November 2005
[20] World Bank, "Pakistan: Country Water Research Assistance Strategy," 7, 14 November 2005, 26–7.

perspective, Pakistan can only store up to 30 days worth of water (as compared to the 900 days capacity for the United States); therefore, the country is extremely reliant on the output originating from India.[21]

While one of the functions of the IWT is to allow fair distribution of water to include guaranteed downstream access to Pakistan, the presence of four conditions ((1) Domestic Use; (2) Non-Consumptive Use; (3) Agricultural Use; and (4) Generation of hydro-electric power) in the IWT are broad enough to allow reinterpretation.[22] Additionally, Annexe F of the treaty contains conditions under which a neutral representative can be brought in "to determine the component of water availability for the use of Pakistan."[23] Once a neutral representative is brought in by the World Bank to hear testimony and expert opinion, the representative can determine whether the treaty is being adhered to properly. The question rests on whether the decision will be accepted without objection or if future cooperation will be considered more costly than defection from the treaty.

C. The Chenab River And Baglihar Hydroelectric Project

In Indian administered Kashmir, the Chenab River flows downstream from the mountains crossing the border into Pakistani Punjab. In 1999, India initiated the construction of the Baglihar plant in the Doda district of Kashmir and according to Indian officials, the purpose of the project was to supply power (up to 450 MW) to Indian administered Kashmir.[24] The Indian argument is fairly straightforward: India constantly needs energy, and the dam will provide an essential energy supply to Kashmir.[25] In all respects, India is adhering to Article III, Section one of the IWT, under which hydroelectric damming, which restricts water flow, is deemed acceptable under proper guidelines.

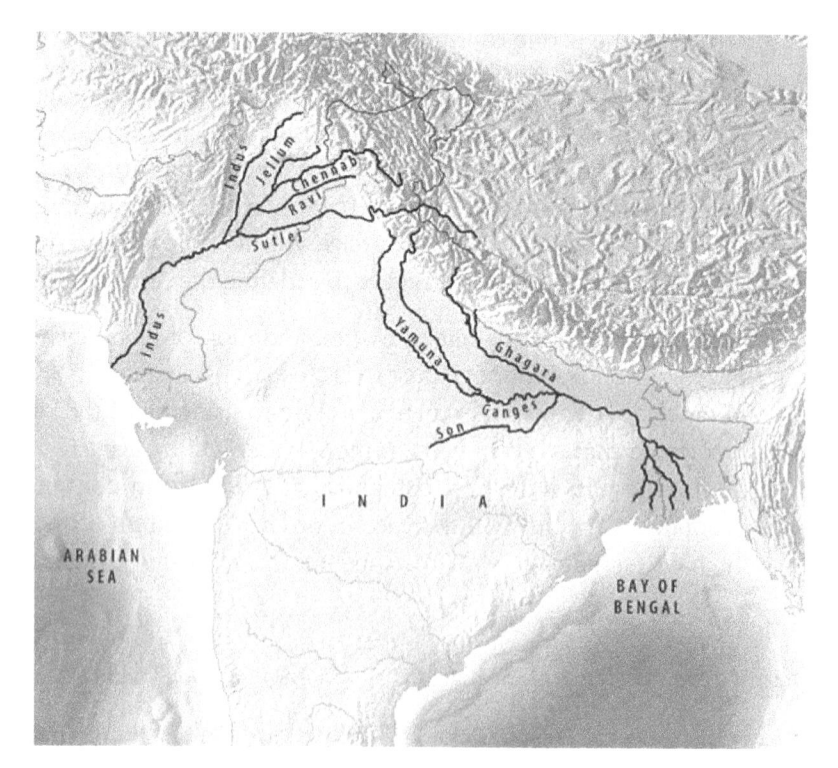

Figure 1. Map of Indus Rivers[26]

---

[21] Ibid., xii.
[22] Ibid. Article III, Section 2.
[23] Ibid. Annexure F, Section 1, Sub-Section 1.
[24] BBC News Online, "Pakistan Team Views Kashmir Dam," July 25, 2005
[25] Ibid.
[26] Figure from Woods Hole Oceanographic Institution.

Pakistan, however, feels threatened by the dam and its potential to significantly reduce the downstream water flow. The Chenab River flows through most of Pakistan and eventually connects with the Indus. The Chenab River is a critical water artery for irrigation and sustains the agricultural industry in western Punjab. In the last several years, the increased draught conditions in both Pakistan and India limit their water supplies. Pakistan claims that the new dam provides India with the ability to restrict the water flow or possibly submerge the area based on the design of the release gates.[27] Whether the claims are valid or not, Pakistan is genuinely concerned about Indian posturing and ability to control a vital component of its agricultural sustainability— making this not only an economic but a security concern.

On 15 January 2005, Pakistan formally requested the World Bank arbitration and for a Neutral Expert (NE) to be appointed according to Article IX of the IWT to resolve its concerns over the Baglihar Plant. The following was one of three claims submitted by the Pakistani government to the World Bank for arbitration. "Pakistan is of the considered view that the design of the Baglihar Plant on Chenab Main does not conform to criteria (e) and (a) specified in Paragraph 8 of Annexure D to the IWT and that the Plant design is not based on correct, rational and realistic estimates of maximum flood discharge at the site."[28] The Indian government formally disagreed with any Pakistani claimed violations. Over the course of two years, the World Bank made multiple visits to the dam site and set about its interpretation of the IWT versus the claims of violation.

In February 2007, after months of delay, the World Bank NE, Mr. Raymond Lafitte, came to a decision over the Baglihar dam in which both India and Pakistan claimed victory.[29] The decision satisfied India because the overall design of the dam remained intact with some minor changes, which would not affect its energy production goals.[30] Pakistan came away with a perceived victory because India was forced to reduce the height of the release gates on the dam, deeming India in violation on certain counts.[31] However, within several months, new contentious issues arouse in which the opposing needs of India and Pakistan once again tested the treaty. The World Bank decision appeased both sides temporarily, but inflammatory rhetoric resurfaced over perceived Indian manipulation.

In October 2008, Pakistan accused India of blocking water flow into the Chenab River, causing significant agricultural damage to the Punjab region.[32] According to Pakistan's Indus Water Commissioner, India completely blocked the supply of regular water (23,000 cubic feet per second (Cusec) a day) to Pakistan from the Chenab River, affecting Pakistan's share of irrigation water.[33] After the allegations in the press, Pakistan confronted India officially over the dispute, demanding compensation for the loss in which India rejected the claim. While Pakistan's request for compensation was denied by India, and the complaint did not move forward to the World Bank, the dispute over water rights reached an argumentative level between the Prime Minister of India and the President of Pakistan. Pakistani President Asif Ali Zardari stated, "Pakistan would be paying a very high price for India's move to block Pakistan's water supply from the Chenab River."[34] President Zardari further noted that any violation of the 1960 IWT by India "would damage the bilateral ties the two countries had built over the years."[35] In contrast, Prime Minister Manmohan Singh refuted any potential IWT violation and noted during the inauguration of the Baglihar project that "electricity is crucial for the development of industry and the project will give a push to the

---

[27] Deutsche Welle, "Baglihar Dam Controversy Further Exasperating Pak-India Ties," 12 January 2005.
[28] World Bank, "Executive Summary: Baglihar Hydroelectric Plant," 12 February 2007.
[29] Ibid.
[30] BBC News Online, World Bank Rules on Kashmir Dam," 13 February 2007
[31] BBC News Online, World Bank Rules on Kashmir Dam," 13 February 2007.
[32] Dawn Online, "Pakistan to seek compensation for Chenab losses," 12 October 2008.
[33] Ibid.
[34] BBC News Online, "Zardari warning over Kashmir dam," 13 October 2008.
[35] Ibid.

industrialization of [Kashmir]."³⁶ This reinforces the evolving divergence of Pakistani concerns over inequitable distribution versus Indian pronouncements of needing to continue its national development.

The statements by the two leaders reveal the divided priorities and evolving stresses on the IWT. Pakistan fears India's control of the water output, while India wants to maintain its progressive developmental stride. With the expanding needs of the Pakistani agricultural industry to consistently deliver, the need for India to generate more energy, and an ever-growing population in the region, fresh water will only become more and more scarce. Compounding this problem, water in South Asia is widely seen as a strategic and "symbolic capital," connected to the larger dispute over Kashmir.³⁷ As recently as June 2009, Pakistani Foreign Minister Shah Mahmood Qureshi accused India of continuous IWT violations that could "lead to heightened tensions between the two countries if ignored."³⁸ Rhetorical jabs are not uncommon between the two states; however, as South Asia continues to develop, the IWT's ability to evolve with and continue to be the primary method towards water dispute resolution will be critical in halting any escalations of tensions over water in the region.

D. Marketization Of Water

While the IWT provides guidelines for water allocation as required during the 1960s, the first glimpses of these evolving problems can be seen through the Baglihar dam dispute and its water marketization value. According to Conca, "When applied to water, structural adjustment conditionality and neoliberal policy reform have produced pressures [towards] the marketization of water. The result is a set of strong pronouncements as to how water should be managed, emphasizing its character as a natural resource good with economic value."³⁹ This is highly relevant when applied to South Asia's allocation of the region's limited resources. Looking at the Baglihar dam, India views the resource as an opportunity to expand its energy production in the area, bolstering industrial capabilities in the region, while Pakistan views the dam as a threat to its already draught ridden agricultural economy.

Applying Conca's terminology to South Asia, India would be a "leader" because of its need to further capitalize on its resource and Pakistan the "laggard" for contesting India's use of water as a market commodity and fearing that any hindrance in existing water supplies will have dire effects on it economic relevancy.⁴⁰ Because of already overstretched water supplies, Pakistan plays the role of the laggard due to its dependency on Indian originated water and sensitivity that any perceived or potential disruption in its flow is a threat to its sustainability. Pakistan, in a sense, has 'failed' due to the inevitability of the Baglihar construction, completion, and potential towards marketization.

The important point of the terminology when applying to South Asia is at what point does the marketization of water elicit a response more than opposition or harsh rhetoric, but conflict or violence? In the case of South Asia, this would be when Pakistan perceives it no longer has control over its own water resource distribution and further feels India is directly responsible for the "strangulation of its economy."⁴¹ Lt. Gen. (ret.) Khalid Kidwai, Director General of Pakistan's Strategic Plans Division, specifically notes that one of Pakistan's potential redlines towards nuclear deployment is the condition of economic strangulation

---

³⁶ Ibid.
³⁷ Uttam Kumar Sinha, "Water Security: A Discursive Analysis," in *Strategic Analysis 29, no. 2* (Institute for Defence Studies and Analysis, April–June 2005), 138.
³⁸ Dawn Online, "Indus Waters Treaty Violations Taken Up With India: Qureshi," 7 June 2009.
³⁹ Conca, *Governing Water*, 29.
⁴⁰ Conca, *Governing Water*, 29.
⁴¹ Quote from Lt. General Khalid Kidwai, Strategic Plans Division, Pakistan Army, in which he describes the possibility of deploying nuclear weapons "when deterrence fails in the event India proceeds to the economic strangling of Pakistan (economic strangling)." See, "Nuclear safety, nuclear stability and nuclear strategy in Pakistan: A concise report of a visit by Landau Network - Centro Volta" (Italy: Landau Network-Centro Volta, 21 January 2002), Section 5.

and specifically "the stopping of the waters of the Indus River."[42] Kidwai's statement is meant as a check against Indian aggression and potential usage of water as a persuasive tool; however, the question that arises from Kidwai's statement is whether Pakistan can differentiate between Indian hostile actions against Pakistan versus decisions aimed towards fulfilling Indian domestic water needs. The prospect of Pakistan defending itself with nuclear assets to stop water manipulation is extremely low, but in tandem with other sources of conflict, water manipulation as a set of persuasive tools could lead to Pakistan perceiving itself as being pushed against the wall.

Until now India and Pakistan have illustrated restraint in terms of water rights and distribution. This stability, however, will be tested as resources begin to become more and more scarce in the region as in the rest of the world. In India, quantitative supply problems are increasing. "India will enter the 'stress zone' by 2025. Water scarcity due to ground water depletion is already a major problem. To complicate matters, water quality is also deteriorating. For example, 80 percent of the fourteen perennial rivers in India are polluted. Organic pollutants from industrial activities are a major cause of degradation of water quality throughout the region. India, for instance, is the third biggest emitter of organic water pollutants with 1,651,250 kilograms per day."[43] With the growing scarcity of water in the region, India will have to apply a conciliatory approach towards its water resources and how it affects its neighbors, including Pakistan. In consideration of how water is distributed through the rivers downstream towards Pakistan, India needs to anticipate that Pakistan (as the laggard) will likely react strongly towards potential manipulation of the rivers. As Peter Gleick notes, "It is very clear that 'water resources have rarely been the sole cause of conflict' but should be viewed as a 'function of the relationships among social, political, and economic factors, including economic development.'"[44] This is increasingly important when viewing the persistently paranoid relationship between India and Pakistan. While violent conflict has not occurred over water, if there comes a time when water resources are stretched thin in conjunction with other conflicts, confrontation may occur with conceivably no way to impede escalation. It is, therefore, a testament to the IWT that, even during violent conflicts and wars between India and Pakistan, the water continued to flow. This reaffirms the necessity of maintaining and strengthening the IWT to keep pace with the continually complex region.

E. Water's Future Implications In South Asia

The premise that water may be used as symbolic or even strategic capital is not a new concept in South Asia. What sets South Asia apart from other regions dealing with water sharing issues is how broader historical conflict between India and Pakistan has allowed the two states to anticipate potential tension over the strategic resource. As seen with the recent arbitration over the Baglihar Dam, contentious rhetoric was the extent of tensions between India and Pakistan. Both the countries largely accepted the IWT ruling. While cooperation is likely to become more difficult as the IWT tries to keep pace with evolving economic, environmental, and security pressures dependent on water usage, the cost of cooperation failure will continue to be too great because of the security interdependence that has developed in the region. Cooperation failure over water has the potential to affect hundreds of millions of Pakistanis and Indians, leaving cooperation the only reasonable approach without risking escalatory conflict.

The pattern of water supplies is one of an unstable and independent physical necessity that is in excess one year and scarce the next. With global climate change, the prospect for vast fluctuations in water supplies will place more pressure on already strained resources. Further, not only is the quantity of water important, but additionally, the quality itself plays a critical role in judging a state's resources, especially for developing states such as Pakistan or India, which do not have advanced water processing facilities for general

---
[42] Ibid.
[43] Sinha, "Water Security," 325.
[44] Ibid., 322.

consumption.[45] Because of these compounding problems, shortfalls in energy production could stymie Indian GDP growth (7.1 percent projected in fiscal year 2009[46]). For Pakistan, a shortfall in water allocation could cripple its already weak GDP growth (2.0 percent projected in fiscal year 2009[47]). One of the few bright spots for Pakistan is its agricultural growth.[48] Therefore, shortfalls in water distribution would have detrimental affects on each state's economies as applied to sustaining GDP growth.

Applying water as a security concern in South Asia, a look at the history of conflicts within the region points to tremendous energy spent by the two countries over patches of land with little physical or strategic value. Specifically, the two nations focused on and sacrificed numerous lives on areas of symbolic importance, such as the Siachen Glacier War in 1984, and the Kargil Conflict in 1999.[49] However, ever since the introduction of nuclear weapons into the region's security posture, armed conflicts have either remained limited in scope (Brasstacks in 1986, Kargil in 1999) or prevented altogether (India Parliament Attack and Military Standoff in 2001-2, Mumbai Terrorist Attack in 2008).[50] A conflict over water has the potential of affecting hundreds of millions of people in the region, while historic conflicts in Kashmir have had limited affects on the region's population. Therefore, if either India or Pakistan chose present day defection over future cooperation, large populations would likely suffer direct consequences and each side would risk conflict difficult to contain.

The Kashmir region has several dimensions keeping the two states at odds, which include Pakistani perception of India as occupying Muslim territory, and India's frustration with Pakistani support of Islamic militants. A long history of low-intensity conflicts and intrusions by both states has not helped—most notably the Kargil War of 1999 that saw Kashmiri militant and Pakistan military incursions into Indian controlled outposts.[51] When these issues are taken into consideration along with the fact that many of the rivers flowing down into Pakistan originate in Kashmir, it is fortunate India and Pakistan have realized the potential dangers of water dispute. The IWT has allowed potential tit-for-tat retaliation to be arbitrated by a third party and thus minimizing the risk of violent conflict.

This foresight on water disputes, however, is being tested as both states strive to maintain and expand their respective wealth and power. Indian construction of the Baglihar dam and Pakistan's response illustrates the problems of realizing common interests in national pursuit of greater wealth and power.[52] Until now, Indian and Pakistani disputes over water involve harsh rhetoric, resolution through the IWT, and eventual cooperation. However, as the variables of resource scarcity and national development continue to grow, stability will continue to depend largely on continual cooperation outweighing the costs of present day defection. According to Axelrod, "A second reason that the future is less important than the present is that individuals typically prefer to get a given benefit today rather than having to wait for the same benefit until tomorrow."[53] As domestic pressures continue to mount, disputes become more complex, and water resources are stretched, the IWT will likely need to take a greater role in resolving present day needs in order to sustain future cooperation. Because cooperation failure would significantly destabilize the region's

---

[45] Jared Diamond, *Collapse: How Societies Choose to Fail or Succeed* (New York: Penguin Group, 2005), 53.
[46] The Times of India, "India's GDP Growth to Stabilize around 7%" 16 March 2009.
[47] Forbes Online, "Pakistan GDP Growth Seen at 2 Percent in 08/09 – Government Official."
[48] Ibid.
[49] Time Magazine Online, "War at the Top of the World," 4 May 2005.
[50] Vipin Narang, "Posturing for Peace? Pakistan's Nuclear Postures and South Asian Stability," *International Security* 43, no. 3 (Winter 2009): 38–64.
[51] Feroz Hassan Khan, "Comparative Strategic Culture: The Case of Pakistan" *Strategic Insights*, Center for Contemporary Conflict (October 2005).
[52] Robert Keohane, After Hegemony: Cooperation and Discord in the World Political Economy (Princeton: Princeton University Press, 2005), 22
[53] Axelrod, The Evolution of Cooperation, 126–127

security interdependence, the cost of conflict would likely be too high not to first exhaust all avenues of cooperation.

F. Conclusion

This above analysis not meant to be a wholly pessimistic vision of India and Pakistan. On the contrary, despite historic violence and hostility, the two countries historically illustrate responsible behavior when it comes to water sharing because of the anticipated disagreements over the resource. Additionally, with the introduction of nuclear weapons into the strategic posture of both states, the costs of non-cooperation and escalatory conflict are too high for either state to risk. The issue now is whether they can adapt this responsible behavior to new stresses on its water supply and maintain the treaty's integrity.

This chapter is an examination of how historic agreements and security interdependence have kept water a cooperative issue between India and Pakistan. Historically, India and Pakistan's mostly non-confrontational behavior in regards to their water issues can be explained by the fact that the issues have been solvable. With the current dam issues at the Chenab River, and the recent decisions by the World Bank expert, it is critical that both sides adhere to the treaty. They also should recognize that the 1960 treaty has been a success in fostering cooperation and in addressing grievances; however, the IWT must adapt in order to anticipate population and economic growth along with environmental stresses in the region.

India and Pakistan have been rife with conflict since partition. However, despite this conflict, the two states were able to anticipate the necessity of cooperation over water because of the heavy costs both populations would incur if they did not. As Axelrod notes, "What makes it possible for cooperation to emerge is the fact the players might meet again. The future can, therefore, cast a shadow back upon the present and, thereby, affect the current strategic situation.[54]" In the early decades of post-British South Asia, India and Pakistan seemed to grasp that while land conflicts could be contained on a limited scope, water is an essential strategic resource that in the short term can cause severe consequences on large populations if not resolved reasonably. Even more importantly, in the past several decades, the security interdependence and integration of nuclear weapons to both countries militaries leaves non-cooperation over an essential resource a costly risk.

India and Pakistan's greatest challenge in the near future is evolving cooperation towards an integrated Indus water system despite other issues that surround them.[55] If India and Pakistan continue to look at water as it relates to the individual state, the movement towards non-cooperation is more plausible. However, if India and Pakistan can add to the historical success of the IWT, continue to restrict hostilities to rhetoric, and move towards a more regional approach towards water, water will remain a dormant issue.

---

[54] Axelrod, The Evolution of Cooperation, 12.
[55] Ashok Swain, "Environmental Cooperation in South Asia," 82.

CHAPTER – 9

Hydropolitics in Pakistan's Indus Basin

Danish Mustafa, United Institute for Peace (special report). November 2010

Summary

- Water problems in Pakistan result largely from poor management, but the consequences of management failures are accentuated, both materially and politically, by international and subnational hydropolitics.

- There is enough water in the Indus basin to provide for the livelihoods of its residents for a long time, provided that the water is managed efficiently and equitably and that additional water is made available not just through storage but, more importantly, through higher efficiency and intersectoral transfers.

- The Indus Waters Treaty (IWT) seems to moderate the worst impulses of India and Pakistan toward each other, and perhaps therein lies IWT's greatest strength.

- Pakistani engineers typically interpret the IWT's extensive technical annexures very literally, whereas the Indian engineers tend to emphasize the treaty's criteria for techno-economically sound project design.

- No single completed or proposed Indian project on the three western rivers of the Indus basin alone has the potential to significantly limit flows of water to Pakistan. But the long list of proposed Indian projects on those rivers will, in the future, give India the cumulative storage capacity to reduce substantively water flows to Pakistan during the low-flow winter months.

- The IWT, by performing an amputation surgery on the basin, made matters simple and allowed India and Pakistan to pursue their nationalist agendas without much need for more sophisticated and involved cooperation in the water field. This lack of cooperative sharing of water leaves the ecological and social consequences of the treaty to be negotiated and contested at the subnational scale.

- The interprovincial conflict over water distribution in Pakistan has potential—albeit entirely avoidable—repercussions for stability, at both the subnational and international levels.

- Instead of constructing very expensive, environmentally damaging, and economically dubious water-storage mega projects in Pakistan, enhancement of the existing infrastructure's efficiency, coupled with better on-farm water management and more appropriate irrigation and farming techniques, would, perhaps, more than make up for any additional water that might be gained from mega projects.

- Since the drought in southern Pakistan in the latter half of the 1990s, the single-minded focus of the Pakistani water bureaucracy on water development has made the issue of the construction of the Kalabagh Dam project a surrogate for a litany of Sindhi grievances against the Punjabi-dominated political, military, and bureaucratic system in Pakistan.

- The emphasis on maximizing water withdrawals and on greater regulation of the Indus river system contributed to accentuating the very high flood peaks in 2010. Although the floods are being used by the pro-dams lobby to call for construction of more storage on the Indus, the tragedy ought to inspire a more nuanced and comprehensive re-evaluation of the water management system in the basin.

- The IWT is a product of its time and could be fruitfully modified and renegotiated to bring it more in line with contemporary international watercourse laws, the Helsinki rules, and emerging concerns with water quality, environmental sustainability, climate change, and principles of equitable sharing. But that renegotiation, if it ever happens, is going to be contingent upon significant improvement in bilateral relations between India and Pakistan.

- India could be more forthcoming with flow data and be more prompt and open in communicating its planned projects on the Indus basin to Pakistan, particularly in the western basin.

- Pakistan can engage with India within the context of the IWT more positively than defensively, and also educate its media and politicians so as not to sensationalize essentially technical arguments by presenting them as existential threats.

Introduction

The semi-arid environment of the Indus basin is home to more than a quarter of a billion people, with some of the lowest human-development indicators in the world. As if the marginal environment and the pervasive poverty were not enough, deep political fissures across international, subnational, and local boundaries characterize the political geography of the basin. Just as Egypt has been described as a gift of the Nile, the bustling ancient cultures of northwestern South Asia and present-day Pakistan and northwestern India can be described as the gift of the Indus. There were, of course, bustling communities of agropastoralists and inundation-irrigation-based agriculture in the basin prior to the construction of the present-day system in the nineteenth century.[1] The present-day agricultural productivity and population densities, however, would not have been possible without the contemporary irrigation system. Given the stakes involved, in terms of the livelihoods of millions of people, the Indus River basin has been a veritable laboratory for international and national research on various problems associated with water distribution, development, and management, especially those problems that pertain to issues of water efficiency, equity, hazards, and environmental quality.[2] More recently, though, what had been a laboratory for devising water management solutions has become an arena of conflict over water both between India and Pakistan and between ethnic groups and provinces in Pakistan.

Nowhere is the need for a focus on the political, economic, and discursive factors driving resource use and distribution more urgent than in the field of water resources. The sterile per capita fresh-water-availability numbers may seem alarming to many observers,[3] but such alarm serves only to divert attention from water's problematic social geography, its extremely skewed distribution across sectors and social groups, and its conceptualization by the power elites as a resource to be deployed toward modernist economic development, in isolation from its ecological and social roles.[4] Surprisingly, even though scholars continue to talk about per capita water-availability numbers, ordinary water users at the local level tend to know that water scarcity is really mediated by social power relations.[5]

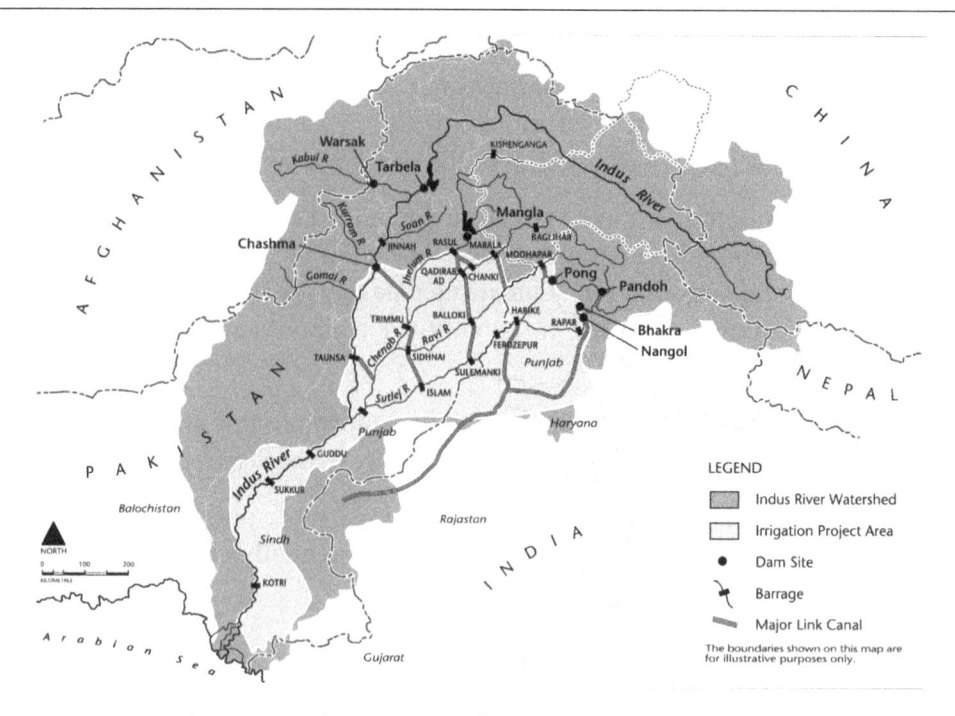

Figure 1. Indus Basin and Its Major Infrastructure

The following analyses of water and security in the Indus basin reject the argument that absolute population growth is responsible for absolute resource scarcity. This report argues instead that environmental degradation, resource scarcity, and resource security are all socially constructed—normative and collective understandings that have consequences for physical and social worlds.[6] Furthermore, the epistemic (knowledge-based experts) and political communities that are most influential in the social construction of environment and security are found at the subnational level, but they have important linkages to international epistemic communities (e.g., the engineering profession). The following survey of the Indus basin concentrates on the geopolitical context that renders Indus basin hydropolitics so riven with conflict and on the perceived limited range of choices of South Asian water managers, which accentuates deeply held sensitivities about water by both the general public and the politicians. The key insight offered by this report is that water problems in Pakistan result largely from poor water management, but that the consequences of management failures are accentuated, both materially and politically, by international and subnational hydropolitics. There is enough water in the basin to provide for the livelihoods of its residents for a long time, provided that the water is managed efficiently and equitably and that additional water is made available not just through storage but, more importantly, also through higher efficiency and intersectoral transfers.

The report builds a narrative of contemporary hydropolitics in the basin at the international level, paying particular attention to the dispute resolution mechanism between India and Pakistan under the rubric of the Indus Waters Treaty (IWT). The report then discusses subnational-scale hydropolitics with reference to the Kalabagh Dam controversy in Pakistan and the water dispute between Punjab and Haryana states in India. The report concludes with identifying possible avenues for the international community's intervention to facilitate cooperation rather than conflict over water in the Indus basin.

International Hydropolitics

In the immediate aftermath of the partition of the subcontinent between the two independent states of Pakistan and India, the issue of water distribution in the Indus basin—now divided—was to gain immediate urgency for the Pakistani government and the populace at large. As a result of the partition on August 15,

1947, the headworks of two important canal systems were left in Indian territory, and the command areas in Pakistani territory. In the absence of any arrangement for the sharing of water in those canal commands, the two countries concluded a "standstill agreement," which provided for the maintenance of existing flows until March 31, 1948, to allow time to reach a longer-term settlement. However, the agreement lapsed without settlement, and the very next day the provincial government of Indian Punjab suspended supplies to Pakistan. This suspension of water was seared into the Pakistani consciousness as evidence of Indian desire to undermine the fragile new dominion of Pakistan.[7] The supplies were restored eighteen days later, and soon after the two countries concluded what came to be known as the Inter-Dominion Agreement, which called for continued negotiations for a final settlement of the water issue. This brief episode of the suspension of water supplies alarmed the Pakistani water bureaucracy into initiating the Bombanwala-Ravi-Bedian-Dipalpur (BRBD) link canal project, which would allow flows from the Ravi River to be diverted to the Sutluj. Significantly, this project demonstrated to Pakistani engineers the viability of compensatory interriver water transfers—a lesson that was to be at the core of Pakistan's postion during the IWT negotiations.[8]

Indus Waters Treaty

Thanks to the active mediation and financial support of the World Bank and the Western powers, led by the United States, India and Pakistan signed the IWT in 1960, allocating the entire flow of the three eastern tributaries of the Indus River—Ravi, Sutluj, and Beas—to India and the three western tributaries—Indus, Jhelum, and Chenab—to Pakistan. The World Bank rewarded both Pakistan and India with massive aid inflows to build storage and conveyance facilities to provide remedial water supplies for the flows that were supposedly lost to the other country.[9]

The resources for water storage and diversion facilities in both countries were made available in the geopolitical context of the Cold War. Pakistan had relatively early on aligned itself with the U.S.-led Western military alliances, such as the Central Treaty Organization (CENTO) and the Southeast Asia Treaty Organization (SEATO). India, on the other hand, was one of the founding members of the Non-Aligned Movement, which sought to chart an independent course between the two superpowers. But despite the trappings of apparent nonalignment, the United States at the time looked upon the Non-Aligned Movement with considerable hostility as a front for pro-Soviet postcolonial states from the global South. Furthermore, the government of India at the time did maintain friendly relations with the Soviet Union and did draw upon the Soviets for military hardware. In that context, then, the Western allies, led by the United States, were willing to make much more resources available to both India and Pakistan to spread their influence in South Asia than would probably have been forthcoming otherwise.

The IWT was a trilateral treaty between, India, Pakistan, and the World Bank. It was concluded in an atmosphere of considerable mutual suspicion, particularly in the context of Pakistan's paranoia about the upper riparian—India's—ability and intentions to deprive Pakistan of water. Nationalist engineers negotiated the IWT, and the treaty did not concern itself with more contemporary principles of equitable sharing of water between riparians.[10] Rather, the treaty mirrored the political landscape of the time by simply dividing the basin between the two countries instead of providing for meaningful cooperative management or sharing. As mentioned, India was given rights to the three eastern rivers of the Indus basin and Pakistan was given full rights to the three western rivers. Pakistan's rights on the three western rivers, however, acknowledged customary use of water in the Indian territory and allowed for limited diversion for agricultural purposes and for run-of-the-river electricity generation projects. It is the IWT provisions allowing India limited use of the three western rivers that has caused the most conflict. The IWT provides for specific coordination mechanisms through the Indus Commission, with dispute resolution to pass in a stepwise fashion from the Indus Commission, which is composed of Indian and Pakistani representatives and administers the IWT,[11] to the governments of India and Pakistan, to a neutral expert, and then to a Court of Arbitration.

The key feature of the IWT was its extensive technical annexures, which are typically interpreted very literally by Pakistani engineers, whereas Indian engineers tend to emphasize the treaty's criteria for techno-economically sound project design.[12] For example, as will be illustrated later, the IWT's technical annexures do not allow for substantial storage projects on the three western rivers upstream of Pakistan. The treaty also puts strong limitations on structures with movable gates that could manipulate the storage upstream of Pakistan in any project on the three western rivers of the basin. But, given the high seasonal flow variability of the Indus basin rivers, which also carry some of the highest silt loads in the world, projects often simply cannot be technically or economically viable without a liberal interpretation of the limitations on those regulating structures, such as movable spillway gates. This issue is further elucidated later in this report, in the context of the first episode of resorting to the neutral expert by India and Pakistan.

The massive water development carried out in both India and Pakistan as part of the Indus Basin Water Development Project in the aftermath of the IWT provided a temporary boon to agricultural water supplies in the basin.[13] But one of the more obvious hydropolitical implications of the IWT was the capacity of the two governments to build infrastructure with more overt security implications. The efficacy of canals as defensive infrastructure that could serve as tank ditches and hinder enemy movement was not lost on the military planners of the two countries. General J. N. Chaudhury, chief of army staff of the Indian Army from 1962 to 1966, commenting on the prospect of an Indian assault on Lahore on the eve of the 1965 India-Pakistan war, proclaimed, "All my experience teaches me never to start an operation with the crossing of an opposed water obstacle; as far as I am concerned, I have ruled out Lahore or a crossing at Dera Baba Nanak."[14] But he was made to go against his better judgment when he was ordered by his civilian bosses to mount precisely such an assault on Lahore. The quote, however, illustrates the recognition of the defensive importance of canals and other water bodies in Indian and Pakistani military thinking. The alignment of the BRBD canal was very much influenced by military considerations, and it served its defensive purpose quite well during the 1965 war. On the Indian side, the importance of defensive considerations cannot be discounted in the alignment and operations of canals—for example, the Indira Gandhi Canal. The 649-kilometer canal serves the dual purpose of irrigation canal and tank ditch. Some have pointed to the ecological and economic pitfalls of the canal, but measures such as encouraging settlement only on its left bank seem to indicate a strong defensive bias in its conception, alignment, and operation.[15] The military functionality of canals is well known on the Pakistani side as well, where canals are often operated to simulate flooding during military exercises to the detriment of their supposed function as irrigation water suppliers.

Dispute Resolution under the IWT Rubric

The IWT has been relatively successful, at the very least by virtue of surviving two and a half wars and frequent military mobilizations by India and Pakistan. But some of the disputes that arose in the context of the treaty are also indicative of the nature of the treaty and the nationalist-driven hydropolitics of the basin, which are further inflected by the supply-side engineering bias of the water managers of the two countries. In this case, supply side means a simplistic equation whereby growing populations must be provided additional water supplies by enhancing the supply of water through storage or more water control structures and not through gains in use efficiency or intersectoral water transfers.

Relatively early on, for example, there was disagreement over Indian plans to build the Salal hydroelectric project on the Chenab River. After negotiations at the governmental level, the Pakistanis accepted the project in the 1970s. Subsequently, the Tulbul/Wullar project on the Jhelum River from the early 1980s and the Baglihar hydroelectric project on the Chenab River from the late 1990s became prolonged sources of disagreement. Because of Pakistani objections, work on the Tulbul/Wullar project was stopped in the 1980s, and the project is still a subject of negotiations between the two governments. On the Baglihar project, however, the government of Pakistan invoked the arbitration clause for the first time in the treaty's history in 2005.[16]

Pakistani objections to the Baglihar regarded primarily the technical specifications of the run-of-the-river project—that is, a river project without dams or storage. Although the project was initiated in 1992, the Pakistanis did not object to it until 1999, when they complained about changes in the design of the project on which they had not been consulted. The Indians protested that the changes were necessary for the techno-economic viability of the project. The public view in Pakistan, however, was that India was somehow trying to dam the Chenab River, which was Pakistan's by virtue of the IWT, whereas Indians viewed Pakistani objections as yet another example of Pakistanis' negativism about any legitimate Indian project on the three western tributaries.[17] The dispute was a manifestation of the different interpretations the two countries' engineers had of the treaty. In the words of a former Indian secretary for water resources, Ramaswamy Iyer,

> Pakistan regards the western rivers as its rivers under the treaty, and tends to look with jaundiced eyes at any attempts by India to build structures on those rivers. Structures give control, and Pakistan is reluctant to agree to India acquiring a measure of control over those rivers, that stand allocated to Pakistan. The treaty gives Pakistan virtually a veto power over Indian projects on the Western rivers, which Pakistan tends to exercise in a stringent rather than accommodating fashion.[18]

Pakistani possessiveness about the western rivers notwithstanding, it is also a fact that much of Pakistan's technical objections to projects such as Baglihar are informed by security oncerns, such as India's potential ability to impound water during low-flow winter months and/or to release excess water during high-flow months to cause flooding in downstream Pakistan. India, of course, protests (1) that it cannot flood Pakistan without flooding itself first, (2) that the water projects are necessary for the development of the disputed state of Jammu and Kashmir, and (3) that the design elements of the Baglihar are necessary for the safety and techno-economic viability of the project. The neutral expert appointed by the World Bank to resolve the dispute gave his binding decision on the Baglihar dispute in 2007, essentially accepting some of the Pakistani concerns by asking India to respond to them but rejecting other concerns. This allowed the project to go forward with some design changes.[19] Both the countries claimed the neutral expert's decision as a victory, though the Indians had more of a cause for such a claim, because the neutral expert conceded the fundamental design issues of the impounding of water and the location of the movable spillway gates for the project.

Overall, Pakistan's perceived negativism might be vexing for India but has not been unreasonable. The Salal Dam was agreed to by Pakistan once Pakistan's concerns were satisfied, and there was no official protest on Baglihar until the design changes that, in Pakistan's view, went against IWT provisions. Pakistan has never opposed an Indian project on the western tributaries in principle. Its objections have always been technical and based upon a literal reading of the IWT. That literal reading is intentional. Indeed, at the time of the treaty signing, extensive technical annexures were added to the treaty and agreed to precisely because such future disputes were anticipated. It should, however, be noted that the Indus Commission is a rather secretive organization and with good reason. News of any Indian projects on the western rivers, once leaked to the Pakistani press, becomes highly emotive and inflames public opinion. In that environment, it becomes virtually impossible for Pakistani engineers to evaluate a project on its technical merits alone and concede Indian projects on the three western rivers without taking public opinion into account. This problem will likely become more pronounced because Pakistan and India have highly diverse and vocal electronic media. The truth is that no single completed or proposed Indian project on the three western rivers of the Indus basin alone has the potential to significantly limit flows of water to Pakistan. But given the long list of proposed Indian projects on the three western rivers, India will, in the future, have the cumulative storage capacity to substantively reduce water flows to Pakistan during the low-flow winter months. It is this potential capacity that Pakistan is ultimately afraid of, but this is a fear that India does not recognize as legitimate.[20]

Besides the Baglihar challenge to the IWT, there was some talk in India in 2002 of rescinding the treaty altogether because of "cross-border terrorism," particularly the attack on the Indian parliament in December 2001, and the ensuing mobilization of the two countries' armed forces. Notwithstanding this talk, the expert view held that the treaty was serving both countries' interests and that rescinding it would open a Pandora's box of bilateral water-sharing issues between India and Pakistan and other South Asian countries—a situation India could ill afford.[21]

More recently, the political temperature in Pakistan again began to rise on account of India's Kishenganga–Jhelum run-of-the-river hydroelectric project. The project, on a tributary of the Jhelum River, proposes to divert water from the Kishenganga River (also called the Neelum River in downstream Pakistan) a few kilometers upstream from where it enters Pakistan across the Line of Control in Kashmir and channel it through a tunnel to a tributary of the Jhelum River to generate electricity. The diverted water does theoretically reenter Pakistan via the Jhelum River. The Pakistani water establishment is irked, because it has a similar planned run-of-the-river project on the Kishenganga River soon after it enters Pakistani-administered Kashmir. Pakistani project's design specifications and economic viability are contingent on the specifications of the Indian project and evaluation of river-flow data supplied by India. According to Pakistani sources, the Indians, when asked for design specifications and flow data, have not been forthcoming.[22] For example, when the upstream low-flow data was requested, the numbers received were much higher than what Pakistan had historically experienced downstream. Pakistanis' suspicions about Indian intentions are further accentuated by the fact that India, in general, holds stream-flow data as a state secret and that there is very little possibility to independently verify the data. In this context, then, data quality and accessibility are at the heart of the brewing conflict between the two countries. The Indus Commission agreed in principle in late July 2010 to install a telemetry system on the Indus River system.[23] One hopes that the installation and judicious use of the system will be an important confidence-building measure between the two countries in the water sector, though the fate of a similar system in Pakistan for interprovincial water distribution—discussed later—is not very encouraging.

To reiterate, the international hydropolitics of surface water between India and Pakistan are delimited within the bounds of the IWT. The treaty is a product of its time and would probably not have been negotiated the same way today. Pakistan's perceived negativism toward Indian projects on the three western tributaries do rankle Indian nationalist elements, just the same as Indian river development arouses Pakistanis' worst fears about India's intentions. Ironically, Pakistan's negativism most rankles the Indian-administered Kashmiri population, which considers such obstructionism as evidence of Pakistan's relative indifference to its well being. The trust deficit between the two countries is played out through the technical negotiations between the two governments and rhetorical posturing in their respective media. All told, though, the IWT does seem to moderate the worst impulses of the two countries vis-à-vis each other, and perhaps therein lies IWT's greatest strength.

The IWT, by performing an amputation surgery on the basin that was much the same as the political bifurcation of the subcontinent, made matters simple and allowed the two countries to pursue their nationalist agendas without much need for more sophisticated and involved cooperation in the water field. This lack of cooperative sharing of water leaves the ecological and social consequences of the treaty to be negotiated and contested at the subnational level, which has considerable negative consequences for the ecology and societies of the Indus basin.

Subnational Hydropolitics

In both India and Pakistan, subnational hydropolitics have been political lightning rods in terms of interprovincial relations. In the case of India, the issue of interstate water distribution between Punjab, Haryana, and Rajastan became one (among many others) of the catalysts for a very destructive separatist insurgency. In the case of Pakistan, however, the conflict over water distribution between the dominant Punjab province and remaining smaller provinces in the federation, particularly Sindh province, has remained peaceful and limited to the political arena, though its wholesale appropriation by Sindhi nationalist elements in their rhetoric bodes ill for the future. The fratricidal insurgency in the Indian Punjab in the 1980s claimed thousands of lives and almost spun into an international conflict between India and Pakistan when the Indian Armed Forces were mobilized in 1987 on the pretext of stopping Pakistan's alleged support to militancy in the Indian Punjab. The insurgency had a number of causes, including water conflict between Punjab and Haryana. Similarly, the ongoing interprovincial argument over water distribution in Pakistan has potential—though entirely avoidable—repercussions for stability, both at the subnational and international levels. It is with the worst-case scenario of the Indian Punjab - style insurgency in mind that this report turns to an analysis of subnational-scale hydropolitics in Pakistan.

Historical Overview of Interprovincial Water Conflict in Pakistan

In Pakistan, the interprovincial conflict over the allocation of the Indus Rivers' water dates to the beginning of the massive canal construction by the British in the Punjab from the mid-nineteenth century onward. The first substantial interprovincial water allocation treaty between the Punjab and the downstream riparian Sindh province dates to 1945. The treaty allocated 75 percent of the waters of the main-stem Indus River to Sindh province, and 25 percent going to Punjab province. The treaty further allocated 94 percent of the water from the five eastern tributaries of the Indus River to Punjab, and 6 percent to Sindh.[24] The partition of the Subcontinent and the subsequent signing of the IWT by India and Pakistan allocated most of what was Punjab's share of the Indus basin waters—according to the 1945 Sindh-Punjab Agreement—to India, and provided for construction of storage and link canals from the western half of the Indus basin to the eastern half to compensate for the water lost to India. The Sindhis widely perceived the compensatory water and the storage on the Indus and Jhelum Rivers to be compensation to Punjab province at the expense of Sindh.[25] The Kalabagh Dam controversy—an argument between the dominant Punjab province and the remaining smaller provinces in Pakistan, especially Sindh, over a proposed storage dam on the main-stem Indus River in Punjab—is perceived by the Sindhis as yet another insult that has been directed at them by the Punjabis in the form of further appropriation of Sindh's rightful share of water.[26]

Although the focus of subnational hydropolitics in Pakistan has been surface water, it would be useful here to point to the significance of groundwater in the basin and related problems of water logging and salinity, which are likely to have much greater impact on water use, agricultural productivity, and hence hydropolitics in the long run. The estimated 0.8 million water pumps in Pakistan supply almost 50 percent of the crop-water requirements in the country.[27] One of the consequences of this major groundwater development has been the secondary salination of 4.5 million hectares of land, half of which affects the Indus basin's irrigated lands. An additional 1 million hectares of the 16 million hectares of irrigated land in the Indus are affected by waterlogging from canal seepage and inappropriate irrigation practices. The problem of salinity is acutest downstream in Sindh province, where 70 to 80 percent of the soils are classified as moderately to severely salinized. This land degradation is severely hurting agricultural productivity, and most remedies have largely been unsuccessful.[28] The simmering ongoing conflict between Sindh and Punjab on surface-water supplies should be viewed in this context, where land degradation and groundwater salinity in the downstream province make its thirst for surface-water supplies much more pronounced. This is apart from the province's pervasive problems of poverty, lost productivity, and consequent social instability, which have not attracted the resources or attention from the country's water managers that they deserve.

The seemingly perpetual water conflict between Sindh and Punjab had a tentative settlement in the form of the interprovincial water accord of 1991, when four provincial governments, all governed by the same political party for the first time in Pakistan's history, agreed to set allocations among the four provinces.

The accord, which was based on the assumed average flow of 114.35 million acre-feet (MAF) of water in the Indus system, allocated 55.94 MAF of water to Punjab and 48.76 MAF to Sindh province, the remaining 9.65 MAF divided between Khyber-Pakhtunkhwa and Balochistan provinces.[29] Although it has been argued that the actual apportionment came closest to what a reasonable apportionment could be, the accord nevertheless suffered a crisis of legitimacy. The legitimacy was in question primarily because the negotiating process leading up to the accord was not transparent and did not include all the stakeholders, particularly from the smaller provinces, and because of the suspect legitimacy of the political setup in Sindh province at the time.[30]

The Dam Controversy

The official figures for average annual flows for the Indus basin used in the interprovincial water accord and subsequent justifications for additional storage on the Indus River, particularly for Kalabagh Dam, on the main-stem Indus River in Punjab province, are suspect. Many have convincingly argued against the official methodology of using the higher number for flows in the Indus system, particularly because it is based on a shorter time frame—that is, since 1977—and because the higher number works to the disadvantage of the downstream riparian.[31] The official argument in favor of the construction of the Kalabagh Dam on the Indus River paints the picture of a scarce water resource, which is being wasted by being allowed to flow out to sea, and outlines a doomsday scenario should additional storage not be built on the Indus River.[32]

On the internal security front, the water scarcity in Sindh, especially in the aftermath of the drought in southern Pakistan in the latter half of the 1990s, coupled with the singleminded focus of the Pakistani water bureaucracy on water development, has made the issue of the construction of the Kalabagh Dam project a surrogate for a litany of Sindhi grievances against the Punjabi-dominated political, military, and bureaucratic system in Pakistan.[33] The controversy is beginning to polarize public opinion in Pakistan, particularly in Sindh province, where more than 80 percent of the groundwater is saline, making the province's farmers exceptionally dependent on surface-water supplies, which itself may be compromised by the upstream dam. Furthermore, the ecology of the Indus Delta and the livelihoods of hundreds of thousands of Sindhi fishermen are also in jeopardy because of reduced fresh water flows to the delta, which are likely to be reduced further if the dam is built. On the other hand, for the Pakistani water managers, Kalabagh Dam has become a metaphor for the persistent meddling of the "untrained" and "nonexpert" politicians in what they perceive to be, or wish to be, a purely engineering issue. All types of appeals to patriotism, science, economics, and neo-Malthusian scenarios are being pressed into service by the Pakistani government and the engineering establishment to make the case for not only Kalabagh Dam but also other storage projects on the Indus. The dam project at the moment is in cold storage, particularly on account of the combined opposition of not just Sindh but also of Khyber-Pakhtunkhwa and Balochistan.[34] Khyber-Pakhtunkhwa is concerned about the potential flooding of rich farmland and Pashtun cultural heartland by the lake that will be created behind the dam. The province is also reluctant to lend its support to the project because of suspicions based on the poor record of the Pakistani government in providing for the rehabilitation of those affected by earlier large-dam projects.

The objections to additional storage on the Indus are not limited to the nationalist politics of smaller provinces. Other convincing arguments have also been made by environmental and citizen groups in Pakistan, pointing out that Pakistan's irrigation sector has some of the lowest conveyance efficiencies in the world. The detractors argue that instead of going for very expensive, environmentally damaging, and economically dubious storage and megaproject solutions to the water issue in Pakistan, enhancement of the existing infrastructure's efficiency, coupled with better on-farm water management and more appropriate irrigation and farming techniques, would perhaps more than make up for any additional water that might be gained from megaprojects.[35] In addition, the lack of sufficient flows in the Indus Delta adversely affects the ecology of the delta, which has a direct effect on the livelihoods of thousands of fishermen and farmers in the lower basin. The interprovincial water debate is a vigorous one and is frequently waged at expert forums in Pakistan. But as far as the Pakistani press and public are concerned, the parameters of the debate are limited to how to build more megaprojects and increase water supplies. A more sensitized and informed media coverage of the debate could go a long way toward lowering the temperature on the issue among politicians and the public.

Recent Developments in the Subnational Water Debate

In 2004, the Indus River System Authority (IRSA), which is the main interprovincial water management body in Pakistan, installed a satellite-based telemetry system on the Indus basin rivers to provide real-time flow data to all the provincial water managers and thereby diffuse the atmosphere of mistrust between the provinces. The system unfortunately has not worked—largely to the disadvantage of Sindh. Some in the government have blamed the faulty design parameters of the system for this, but others have convincingly argued that the faults with the system are not unfixable and that field engineers and their leadership were so disposed that the system could be made functional.[36] In addition, there are perpetual tensions between Sindh and Punjab on the opening or closure of link canals in Punjab and on the whole issue of Sindh's allocated water share not getting to the province because of thefts in Punjab. Again, there could have been a substantive basis for arbitrating those conflicts if the data from the telemetry system were available. This issue is beginning to get considerable attention from the Pakistani press, and there are legitimate concerns that an expensive technology, (it cost US$5.4 million in 2004) that is already in place and has the potential to make water flows between the provinces more transparent, is not working because of incompetence or worse (malice on the part of vested interests).

The Indus waters distribution controversy, at the moment, is limited to sloganeering and street protests by a part of the populace of Sindh and to a lesser extent of Khyber-Pakhtunkhwa, as well as heated debates among the water managers and provincial governments of the Pakistani federation. Incidentally, in the Punjab, the province that stands to benefit the most from the potential construction of the Kalabagh Dam and other water development projects (e.g., the Greater Thal Canal project, which is to supply additional water from the Indus to the arid Thal area of the Punjab),[37] public opinion at the grassroots level is uninterested at best, unlike in the case of Sindh. This is one controversy where the dissonance between the engineers' conceptions of how to manage and develop water seems to be driving the conflict more than any popular demand for additional water projects on the part of the residents of Punjab province. For example, both factions of the ruling Punjabi-dominated Pakistan Muslim Leagues (PML-N and Q) have been at great pains to try to mobilize grassroots public support for the dam, with little evidence of success.[38] This is in stark contrast to the Indian Punjab situation, where public opinion was quite inflamed in support of keeping Punjab's waters from Haryana. Whereas in Sindh, there may have been a fusion of hydropolitics with identity politics of Sindhi nationalists, in the Pakistani Punjab, there do not seem to be any popular passions regarding hydropolitics. Consequently, given the shallowness of popular support for additional water development on the Indus River, there is an opportunity for a more enlightened and multidimensional policy dialogue to resolve the controversy. The specter of an Indian Punjab – style insurgency with hydropolitics as one of the key issues is a nightmarish scenario for Pakistan but is an entirely avoidable one, provided the parameters of the discourse are widened from purely engineering concerns to wider social, cultural, environmental, and equity- and justice-related concerns on water resources.

The subnational water issue in Pakistan took a new twist in 2010 with the worst floods in the country's history. The floods were a consequence of the anomalous intense rains in the western Indus basin, something that was once observed every few decades but that has been experienced more than three times in the past decade alone. The enormity of the disaster and the role played by the highly regulated river channels and the irrigation-system management procedures have drawn renewed scrutiny from the public and the media. There is concern that the single-minded focus on maximizing water withdrawals and on greater regulation of the river system may have contributed to accentuating the already high flood peaks.[39] Furthermore, the issue of deliberate breaching of side levees to protect irrigation infrastructure—something that is routine operating procedure for flood management—drew media attention and accusations of favoritism when it came to protecting some parts of the flood plains at the expense of others. The floods are being used by the pro-dams lobby to call for construction of more storage on the Indus, but the tragedy also ought to inspire a more nuanced and comprehensive reevaluation of the water-management system in the basin. Such a re-evaluation would likely lead to a new balance between the benefits and hazards associated with the river system and more equitable distribution of the same, both spatially and socially.

Moving Ahead: Prospects for Cooperative Hydropolitics

At the bilateral level, the IWT has served an important moderating function in the hydropolitics between India and Pakistan. The treaty is a product of its time and could be fruitfully modified and renegotiated to bring it more in line with contemporary international watercourse laws, the Helsinki rules,[40] and emerging concerns with water quality, environmental sustainability, climate change, and principles of equitable sharing. But that renegotiation, if it ever happens, is going to be contingent on significant improvement in bilateral relations between India and Pakistan. As long as the two countries continue to be hostile and mutually suspicious, the imperfect IWT will have to be the medium for the conduct of hydropolitics between the two countries. In the meantime, however, India could be more forthcoming with flow data and be more prompt and open in communicating its planned projects on the Indus basin to Pakistan, particularly in the western basin. Pakistan, on the other hand, could engage with India within the context of the IWT more positively than defensively, and also educate its media and politicians so as not to sensationalize essentially technical arguments by representing them as existential threats. India, too, will have to be mindful of the fact that although no single Indian project presents a substantial threat to Pakistan's water security, India's planned water development projects on the Indus will have the cumulative capacity to substantially reduce water flows to Pakistan during low-flow months. Pakistan's anxieties about that future capacity are understandable and reasonable, and India must acknowledge and address those anxieties. Claiming compliance with the letter of the IWT will only add to the mistrust between the two countries.

Within Pakistan, considerably greater research needs to be undertaken to establish the relative weight of violence vs. cooperation as a means of conflict resolution over water. The fact that more than 95 percent of water withdrawals in the Indus basin are dedicated to agriculture, where its efficiency does not exceed 36 percent, is a clear indicator that the scarcity of water is institutional rather than absolute.[41] Increased irrigation-water-use efficiency through engineering as well as institutional reforms, coupled with intersectoral water transfers, has the potential to more than make up for any water scarcity. Consequently, the question of whether water shortages and inequities in its distribution will lead to violence or threats to human security also becomes contingent on how water-related institutions behave. This point also relates to the international dimension, whereby a recognition of Pakistan's problems as fundamentally internally driven will provide the necessary perspective to the Pakistani public and media in evaluating the potential threat of Indian projects in the Indus basin. In other words, allowing the experts in the room to negotiate the details of proposed Indian projects in the context of the IWT is the best course of action for Pakistan—short of a future renegotiation of the treaty along the lines mentioned earlier.

The following recommendations to the international community are given with the intent of promoting more cooperative international and interprovincial hydropolitics in Pakistan's Indus basin:

- Provide technical assistance to both India and Pakistan to enable more accurate and timely stream-flow data that is readily accessible to decision makers and the public. This will prevent ignorance, rumors, and emotion from taking hold in the absence of hard data. The provision of more accurate and timely data can be a very important confidence-building measure.

- Encourage the Indian government to take Pakistan's concerns—for example, with regard to data availability or storage capacity in individual projects—more seriously and to address those concerns on merit. Often, with regard to the water sector, the issue is not what the Indian government is doing, it is how it is doing it. Utilize World Bank levers to facilitate greater openness of communication and data sharing within the IWT's Indus Commission and between the commission and the public.

- Facilitate a debate on how a more cooperative tenor, such as through a renegotiated IWT treaty that is in line with the principles of equitable apportionment and other contemporary international legal doctrines, could be beneficial to all relevant parties. A large portion of the subnational problems in Pakistan are partially a function of the treaty, because the Sindhis perceive, with some truth, that Sindh compensates Punjab for water that Pakistan negotiated away to India. The principle of allocating entire rivers may have appeared to be an elegant solution when the IWT was negotiated, but the IWT could be fruitfully renegotiated in the future provided there is sufficient trust between India and Pakistan.

- Provide technical assistance to Pakistan to improve its irrigation-system efficiency. Much more water can be realized from a more efficient distribution system than from any dam.

- Train and sensitize Pakistani water managers to the issue of equity in water distribution. The engineers dominating Pakistan's water bureaucracy do not have the skills to deal with the all-important social-equity aspects of water, which often lie at the heart of water conflict.

- Provide technical assistance to Pakistan so that it can bring its surface and groundwater laws more in line with contemporary developments in water laws.

- Provide training and technical assistance that could address the long-term legitimate storage needs of the country. Groundwater storage capacity and knowledge is extremely underdeveloped in Pakistan.

Notes

1. Indu Agnihotri, "Ecology, Land Use and Colonisation: The Canal Colonies of Punjab," *Indian Economic and Social History Review* 33, no. 1 (1996): 37–58; Imran Ali, The Punjab under Imperialism, 1885–1947 (Princeton, NJ: Princeton University Press, 1988).
2. James L. Wescoat Jr., Sarah J. Halvorson, and Daanish Mustafa, "Water Management in the Indus Basin of Pakistan: A Half-Century Perspective," *International Journal of Water Resources Development* 16, no. 3 (2000): 391–406.
3. See, for example, Peter Gleick, *The World's Water* 2000–2001 (Washington, DC: Island Press, 2000).
4. See, for example, Chris Sneddon and Coleen Fox, "Rethinking Transboundary Waters: A Critical Hydropolitics of the Mekong Basin," *Political Geography* 25, no. 2 (2006): 181–202.
5. Daanish Mustafa, "To Each according to His Power? Access to Irrigation Water and Vulnerability to Flood Hazard in Pakistan," *Environment and Planning D: Society and Space* 20, no. 6 (2002): 737–52.
6. Shlomi Dinar, "Water, Security, Conflict, and Cooperation," *SAIS Review* 22, no. 2002: 229–53.
7. Haris Gazdar, "Baglihar and Politics of Water: A Historical Perspective from Pakistan," *Economic and Political Weekly*, February 26, 2005, 813–17.
8. Ibid.
9. For details of the treaty negotiation process, see Asit K. Biswas, "Indus Waters treaty—the Negotiating Process," *Water International* 17 (1992): 201–09; Aloys Arthur Michel, The *Indus Rivers: A Study of the Effects of Partition* (New Haven, CT: Yale University Press, 1967).
10. Muhammed Siyad, "Indus Waters treaty and Baglihar Project: Relevance of International Watercourse Law," *Economic and Political Weekly*, July 16, 2005, 3145–54.
11. Article VIII of the Indus Waters treaty of 1960 provides for the formation of the permanent Indus Commission. The commission is responsible for facilitating exchange of information and routine treaty-related matters between the two countries.
12. Ramaswamy R. Iyer, "Indus Treaty: A Different View," *Economic and Political Weekly*, July 16, 2005, 3140–44.
13. The Indus Basin Water Development Project comprised World Bank - financed storage, link-canal, and regulatory structure projects to facilitate realization of the water demand in the two signatory countries in order to compensate for the water the two countries had negotiated away to each other in the treaty.

14. Nawaz Sharif, *Crossed Swords: Pakistan, Its Army, and the Wars Within* (Karachi: Oxford University Press, 2008), 209.
15. Rao, "Pitfalls of the Indira Gandhi Canal," *Ambio* 21, no. 6 (1992): 439.
16. Annexure F of the IWT allows for the appointment of a neutral expert for arbitration in case the dispute between the two countries cannot be resolved at the Indus Commission level.
17. Rajesh Sinha, "Two Neighbors and a Treaty: Baglihar Project in Hot Waters," *Economic and Political Weekly*, February 18, 2006, 606–08.
18. Iyer, "Indus Treaty," 3143.
19. Mary Miner, Gauri Patankar, Shama Gamkhar, and David Eaton, "Water Sharing between India and Pakistan: A Critical Evaluation of the Indus Waters treaty," *Water International* 34, no. 2 (2009): 204–16.
20. John Briscoe, "War and Peace on the Indus?" News (Pakistan), April 5, 2010, www.countercurrents.org/briscoe050410.htm.
21. Ramaswamy R. Iyer, "Was the Indus Waters Treaty in Trouble?" *Economic and Political Weekly*, June 22, 2002, 2401–02.
22. Employee of Pakistan's Water and Power Development Authority, personal communication with the author, March 28, 2010.
23. M. S. Shafique, "Telemetry System and Confidence Building," Daily Dawn, August 9, 2010, www.dawn.com/wps/wcm/connect/dawn-content-library/dawn/in-paper-magazine/economic-and-business/telemetry-system-and-confidence-building-980.
24. Michel, *The Indus Rivers*.
25. Mir Atta Muhammad Talpur, "Water Shortage in Sindh: Causes and Consequences," March 2001, www.scribd.com/doc/529124/Water-shortage-in-Sindh.
26. See, for example, www.sindh.ws/indusfarming.
27. A. S. Qureshi, P. G. McCornick, M. Qadir, and Z. Aslam, "Managing Salinity and Waterlogging in the Indus Basin of Pakistan," *Agricultural Water Management* 95, no. 1 (2008): 1–10.
28. Ibid.
29. Simi Kamal, "Pakistan's Water Challenges: Entitlement, Access, Efficiency, and Equity," in *Running on Empty: Pakistan's Water Crisis*, eds. Michael Kugelman and Robert M. Hathaway (Washington, DC: Woodrow Wilson International Center for Scholars, Asia Program, 2009).
30. H. L. Afzal, "Settling Disputes between Ethno-Regional Groups in Young Democracies: Distributing the Indus Waters of Pakistan" (PhD dissertation, University of Michigan, 1995).
31. See, for example, Abdul Majid Kazi and A. N. G. Abbasi, "Kalabagh Dam: Look before You Leap," 2003, www.angelfire.com/az/Sindhi/indus4.html; Shaheen Rafi Khan, "The Kalabagh Controversy," 2003, www.sanalist.org/kalabagh/a-14.htm.
32. Government of Pakistan, "Report of the Technical Committee on Water Resources," August 2005, www.dawn.com/events/tcr_on_wr/text1.htm.
33. Erik Eckholm, "A Province Is Dying of Thirst, and Cries Robbery," *New York Times*, March 17, 2003, www.nytimes.com/2003/03/17/world/gharo-journal-a-province-is-dying-of-thirst-and-cries-robbery.html.
34. Balochistan's own water projects, such as the Pat Feeder canal, are vulnerable to potential water stoppages from the proposed dam.
35. See Daanish Mustafa, "The Dam Dilemma," *Newsline Magazine*, October 2005, 68–70; Khan, "The Kalabagh Controversy."
36. Khaleeq Kiani, "Faulty Telemetry System Leads to Dispute over Water," Daily Dawn, July 9, 2010, www.dawn.com/wps/wcm/connect/dawn-content-library/dawn/the-newspaper/national/19-faulty-telemetry-system-leads-to-dispute-over-water-970-hh-06.
37. See Actionaid, "Greater Thal Canal: A Misadventure," 2009, www.scribd.com/doc/9707184/Greater-Thal-Canal.
38. See "PML-QA to Form KBD Committee," *Daily Times* (Pakistan), September 4, 2003, www.dailytimes.com.pk/default.asp?page=story_4-9-2003_pg7_31. In addition, no political party of any significance in Pakistan in general and in the Punjab in particular has ever passed a resolution in support of Kalabagh Dam, nor is there any evidence of a public rally held in support of the dam in Punjab. The Punjab Assembly in the aftermath of Pakistan's nuclear tests in 1998, did pass a resolution congratulating then prime minister Nawaz Sharif for the nuclear tests and for his announcement on the construction of Kalabagh Dam. There is, however, no resolution of the assembly specifically supporting the construction of the dam.
39. Robert Mackey, "Attempts to Tame Indus River Contributed to Disaster in Pakistan, Expert Says," Lede Blog, August 18, 2010, http://thelede.blogs.nytimes.com/2010/08/18/attempts-to-tame-indus-river-contributed-to-disaster-in-pakistan-expert-says/; Daanish Mustafa, "Pakistan Floods: Living with the Mighty Indus," New Atlanticist Policy and Analysis Blog, August 23, 2010, www.acus.org/new_atlanticist/pakistan-floods-living-mighty-indus.
40. The Helsinki rules, established in 1966, address the principles governing use of international surface waters and aquifers connected to those surface waters. The rules' key overarching principle is of equitable use and apportionment between upstream and downstream riparians in international watercourses. The IWT, however, rather than designating equitable apportionment, designates entire flows of rivers to one or the other riparian.
41. M. A. Kahlown and Abdul Majeed, "Water Resources and Management in Pakistan," in Water and New Technologies, ed. Ishfaq Ahmed, 19–60 (Islamabad: Global Change Studies Center, 2002).

Of Related Interest

- Improving Natural Resource Management in Sudan by Paul J. Sullivan and Natalie Nasrallah (Special Report, June 2010)
- Promoting Cross-LoC Trade in Kashmir: An Analysis of the Joint Chamber by Moeed Yusuf;. (Special Report, August 2009)
- Mapping Peace between Syria and Israel by Fredric C. Hof (Special Report, March 2009)
- Making Borders Irrelevant in Kashmir by P. R. Chari and Hasan Askari Rizvi (Special Report, September 2008)
- My Kashmir: Conflict and the Prospects for Enduring Peace (2008) by Wajahat Habibullah

CHAPTER – 10

IUCN

Beyond Indus water Treaty Ground Water and Envoirment Management – Policy issues and Options

1. THE CONTEXT

1.1. Indo-Gangetic River Basin (IGRB)

Length of the Indus River is 3,199 kms. In the Upper Indus Basin, the principal tributaries are Kabul, Swat and Kurram on the right bank and Jhelum, Chenab, Ravi, Beas, and Satluj on the left bank (Figure 1). The basin extends over an area of 1.166 million km² and its distribution covers: Pakistan 0.693 km²; Afghanistan and China 0.015 km²; and India 0.321 km². The mean annual flow of the Indus Basin is 187 km³ contributed by runoff, snow - and glacier-melt. Catchment area of the Ganga River falls in India, Nepal, China, and Bangladesh and its length is 2,525 kms. Yamuna is the most important tributary that joins it on the right bank at Allahabad. After confluence with Yamuna, the Ganga River flows eastward and is joined by a number of tributaries.

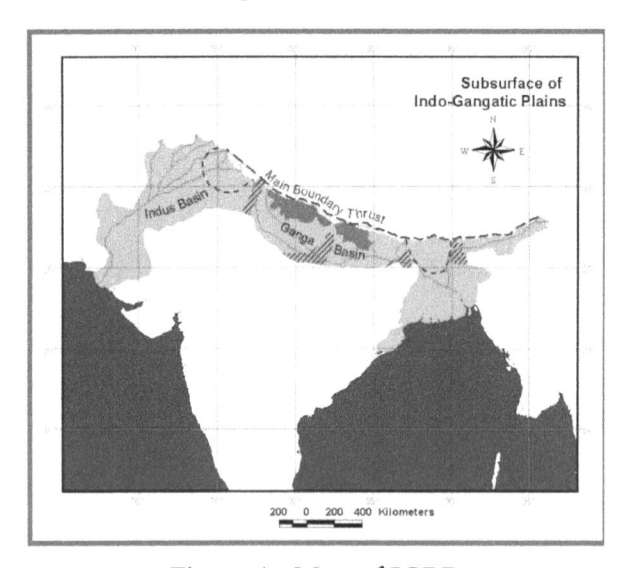

Figure 1. Map of IGBR

1.2. Surface Water Resources in the IGRB

IGRB drains from southern Himalayan and Hindu Kush "Water Tower of Asia" and provides base for economic development for over a billion people. The projected per capita water availability in the Indus-Pakistan and Ganga-India sub-basins by 2025 will be reduced to < 1000 m³ – water scarce subbasins. The Indus-India sub-basin will be a water stress sub-basin by 2030 having per capita water availability of < 1700 m³. Indus-Pakistan is the most water scarce sub-basin in the IGRB (Table 1).

Table 1. Renewable water resources & per capita water availability in IGBR (Sharma et al 2008)[1]

IGRB Basin	Total Renewable Water Resources (km³)	Per Capita Water Availability (m³/person)			
		1990	2000	2025	2050
Indus-India	97	2487	2109	15901	1132
Indus-Pakistan	190	1713	1332	761	545
Ganga-India	663	1831	1490	969	772

1.3. Groundwater Resources in the IGRB

Groundwater in the **IGRB** occurs in porous media below the soil surface and termed as '**aquifer**'. It is well developed in deep alluvium having capacity to retain and transmit water and provides reliable source of water on demand. The canal water diversions in the basin states are still managed in a supply side system. Thus, groundwater is premium water for productive and sustainable agriculture. Groundwater resources can be classified as "**static**" and "**dynamic**". The '**static resource**' is the amount of groundwater available below the zone of water level fluctuations. The '**dynamic resource**' is the amount of groundwater available in the zone of water level fluctuations. **Sustainable groundwater development requires that only dynamic resources are tapped. Abstraction of static groundwater resources could be considered during extreme scarcity, for essential purposes only** (Table 2). Groundwater resources in the Ganga basin are nearly six times that of the Indus basin.

The studies revealed that the number of shallow tubewells in India roughly doubled every 4th year during 1951-91. Groundwater users in poorer provinces tend to rely more on diesel.

Groundwater irrigated crops generally result in higher yields due to availability of water on demand (Shah et al. 2000[2]. Singh and Singh 2002[3]). Overdraft has taken on alarming proportions in several Indian states, and has led to increased competition among water users. Subsidized energy for groundwater pumping is a major contributor to overdraft in Northern India.

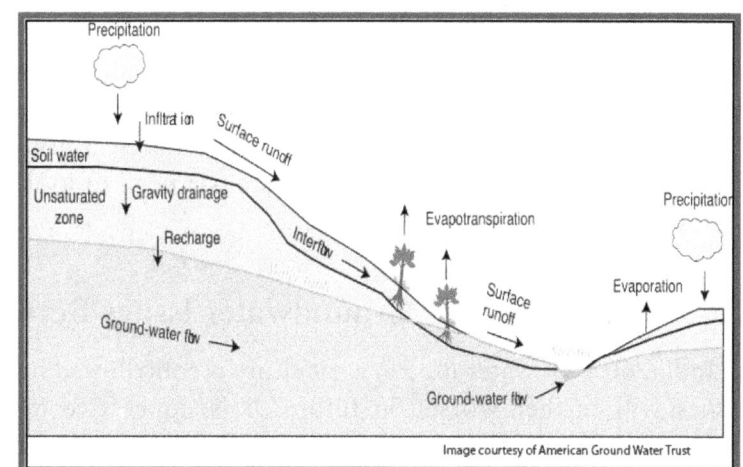

Figure 2. Conceptual framework for groundwater

Table 2. Fresh groundwater resources (km³) in the aquifers of the IGRB[1]

River Basin	Alluvium/ Unconsolidated Rocks	Hard Rocks	Total
Indus	1,334.9	3.3	1,338.2
Ganga	7,769.1	65	7,834.1

---

[1] Sharma, B. R., U. A. Amarasinghe and A. Sikka. 2008. Indo-Gangetic River Basins: Summary Situation Analysis. International Water Management Institute, New Delhi Office, New Delhi, India. 25 July 2008.
[2] Shah, T., D., Molden, R. Sakthivadivel and D. Seckler. 2000. The global groundwater situation: overview of opportunities and challenges. International Water Management Institute, Colombo, Sri Lanka.
[3] Singh, D. K. and A. K. Singh. 2002. Groundwater Situation in India: Problems and Perspectives. International Journal of Water Resources Development 18(4): 563–80.

> *Research conducted by IWMI-TATA revealed that groundwater use has surpassed surface water use in Indian agriculture as the primary source of food production and income generation. The key question for policy makers and planners is how to tap this resource without exhausting the supply. The mind-set and water management skills need to shift from resource development to resource planning and management.*

In **Pakistan**, there are now 1.0 million tubewells energized either with electricity (13%) or by diesel (87%). Growth rate is now stagnant due to the rise in price of energy or due to quality concerns. There is no subsidy on diesel. The subsidy on electricity is only for Balochistan for 15262 tubewells (1.5% of total tubewells[4]) which had serious impacts on the lowering of water table and mining of groundwater; rather, it resulted in wasteful use of water.

1.4. Groundwater and Environmental Management by the Basin States

Over-abstraction of groundwater in Indus-India basin closer to Pakistan's border has serious impacts on the aquifers of Indus-Pakistan – seems an extension of mining of groundwater in Northern India, as rest of the country is not facing groundwater mining. The basic issue is how to address trans-boundary groundwater issues. A Case Study of Excessive Groundwater Abstraction in India conducted by NASA[5]. was analyzed to assess possible impacts on the aquifers of Indus-Pakistan. The Indus Waters Treaty does not clearly articulate the environmental concerns. In the catchment areas of the Indus-India, the effluents are being discharged into the rivers due to rapid urbanization and growth in agriculture. The drains entering into Pakistan are also bringing heavy load of wastes – creating environmental implications for human and livestock health. The surface water scarcity in the basin states would ultimately put more pressure on the depleting aquifers. There is a need to look into options of managing aquifers in the basin states – thinking beyond the Treaty.

2. Trans-Boundary Groundwater Issues Between The Basin States

In India, 60% of water used in agriculture is contributed by groundwater. Groundwater and environmental issues will further worsen in future. It is imperative for the basin states, to envisage comprehensive development and planning for the optimal use of water. A holistic approach of conjunctive use and management of water has to be adopted. Groundwater needs to be managed as a resource as well as a trust. The resource has to be sustained for the future generations so that they also enjoy the opportunity of affordable pumping. It is essential to jointly set up an organisation with representatives from the basin states, whose functions would entail identifying short- and long-term supply capacity of the basin and its integrated development, setting up of infrastructure and coordinating activities within the respective states.

> Integrated development approach is beyond consideration in the current context of relations between the basin states, but all other options will lead to destruction sooner or later. It is only possible with a paradigm shift in the mindset. It will require a complete end to hostilities, both physical and psychological, from both sides.

---

[4] GOP. 2009. Agriculture Statics of Pakistan. Economic Wing, Ministry of Food and Agriculture, Government of Pakistan.
[5] Rodell, M,. I. Velicogna and J. S. Famiglietti. 2009. Satellite-based estimates of groundwater depletion in India. Nature. 08238.

2.1. Groundwater Abstraction in India – Case Study by NASA

The NASA[6] (National Aeronautics and Space Administration) study highlighted that Indian border states with Pakistan are over abstracting groundwater, which might affect aquifers of Pakistan because of depression created by farmers due to subsidized power policy in India (Figure 3). Further, India being located at the upstream may be motivated to exercise environmental management for the movement of effluents into the rivers flowing to Pakistan. There is a need to have clear additions in the Treaty to address the environmental issues more effectively. NASA study revealed that groundwater is vanishing in Northern India[7] as the groundwater levels in Punjab, Rajasthan, Haryana and Delhi are falling by 0.3 m per year — a trend that could lead to "extensive socio-economic stresses" for the region. A staggering 109 km^3 of groundwater has been lost during 2002-08 — a figure twice the capacity of India's largest surface reservoir of Upper Wainganga and "much more" than government's estimation, says the paper published in the international journal Nature by NASA. The study further revealed that the depletion is caused entirely by human activity (irrigation) and not by climatic variability. Groundwater abstraction is more than the recharge. The finding is based on images from NASA's Gravity Recovery and Climate Experiment (GRACE), a pair of satellites that sense changes in Earth's gravity field and associated mass distribution, including water masses stored above or below the Earth's surface. Study also indicated that in India, depletion is likely to continue until effective measures are taken to curb groundwater demand which could propel severe shortages of potable water, reduced agricultural productivity, conflict and suffering. The climate of Rajasthan, Punjab, Haryana and Delhi is classified as semi-arid to arid. The map, showing groundwater withdrawals as a percentage of groundwater recharge, is based on state-level estimates of annual withdrawals and recharge reported by India's Ministry of Water Resources (Figure 4).

The averaging function (spatial weighting) used to estimate terrestrial water storage changes from GRACE data was mapped in the study conducted by Rodell, et al, 2009[8]. Warmer colours indicate greater sensitivity to terrestrial water storage changes (Figure 5). In the larger image beneath northern India's irrigated fields of wheat, rice, and barley – beneath its densely populated cities of Jaipur and New Delhi, the groundwater has been disappearing. The study provided an opportunity to observe groundwater use without any field data. This is critical because in the basin states, hydrological data are sparse and hard to access; space-based methods provide, perhaps, the only opportunity to assess changes in fresh water availability across large regions.

The map shows groundwater changes in India during 2002-08, with losses in red and gains in blue, based on GRACE satellite observations (Figure 6). The estimated rate of depletion of groundwater in north-western India is equivalent to a water table decline of 0.33 m per year.

> There is no excessive abstraction of groundwater in Pakistan, except in a smaller strip along the border, which seems an extended impact of the mining of groundwater in India. Otherwise, there is no region of groundwater depletion in Indus-Pakistan. Even excessive groundwater abstraction in India has affected Nepal from both sides of the Indian border.

Water table does not respond to changes in weather as rapidly as surface water bodies. Therefore, when groundwater is abstracted, recharge to the original water tables can take years. Changes in groundwater masses affect gravity enough to provide a signal, such that changes in gravity can be translated into a

---

[6] NASA Satellites Unlock Secret to Northern India's Vanishing Water 08.12.09 Gretchen Cook-Anderson NASA Earth Science News Team; NASA Study on "Science Serving Society: Water Management.
[7] Groundwater Vanishing in India says NASA. 2009. Online edition of India's National Newspaper, The Daily News Hindu. Banglore, Friday, Aug 14, 2009. ePaper, Mobile/PDA Version.
[8] Rodell, J., T. Schindler, J. Famiglietti and G. C. Anderson. 2009. NASA Satellites Unlock Secret to Northern India's Vanishing Water. NASA Earth Science News Feature, NASA, USA.

measurement of an equivalent change in water. Through the use of GRACE satellite observations, one can observe and monitor water changes in critical areas on temporal and spatial basis without spending time and resources on collection of costly field data.

> The study does not provide information regarding absolute volume of water in the Northern Indian aquifers, but it provides strong evidence that current rates of groundwater abstraction are not sustainable. The region has become dependent on irrigation to maximize agricultural productivity, so the authors predicted water crisis in the near future.

The study further revealed that at its core, this dilemma is an age-old cycle of human need and activity – particularly the need for irrigation to produce food, said Bridget Scanlon, a hydrologist at the Jackson School of Geo-sciences at the University of Texas in Austin. "That cycle is now overwhelming fresh water reserves all over the world. Even one region's water problem has implications beyond its borders."

The study findings raise an issue that how the aquifers of Indus-Pakistan are going to be affected with the excessive abstraction of groundwater on the Indian side. What are the implications on Pakistan side aquifer both in quantity and quality terms is a major question to be addressed? The issue of trans-boundary groundwater with India has to be addressed and an addendum has to be negotiated between basin states for inclusion in the Indus Waters Treaty.

2.2. Pollution of Indian Rivers and Environmental Impacts

Shukla (2009)[9] indicated that most of the Indian rivers are grossly polluted due to the disposal of untreated sewage and industrial effluents into the rivers. It led to environmental disturbance and is a potential source of stress to biotic community. Studies show terrific facts likes death of ghariyals in Chambal sanctuary, pesticide pollution in Yamuna River, etc. He further indicated that though, the CPCB (Central Pollution Control Board) has laid down stringent environmental norms in the form of CREP (Corporate Responsibility for Environmental Protection), but only 45% of the grossly polluting industrial units have installed ETPs (Effluent Treatment Plants). Out of these, over 18% did not function and also did not meet the standards. The NRCD (National River Conservation Directorate) also has no mechanism to ensure that installed ETPs function properly. The contribution to pollution load by various sources was estimated at 75 and 25% for domestic and industrial wastes, respectively. Pratyush (2007)[10] indicated that apart from ensuring proper operationalisation of assets created under different schemes, it is needed to strengthen mechanism and the capacity of institutions for effective control of water pollution and waste from point source by emphasizing socio-economic measures at the same time as using law enforcement measures. Lifelines of India are in dying condition and the threat is coming from the dumping of sewage into freshwater tributaries. Lack of proper sewage system in most of the cities is the main culprit behind the killing of rivers. New Delhi is alone responsible to produces 3.6 billion litres of sewage per day. The city's poor management is unable to treat half of the daily produced sewage. The remaining untreated waste is dumped into the Yamuna River. One can imagine the condition of River Yamuna that is lifeline for Delhiites. This is not the story of Yamuna; only the same thing is being happened with almost every river in India. In India, there are 300 sewage treatment plants and most of them are underutilized and badly located. Most of the sewage treatment plants partially treat the sewage and throw into rivers. India has a badly structured and poorly managed drainage

---

[9] Shukla, K. S. 2009. . Indian river systems and pollution. The Encyclopedia of Earth. //www.eoearth.org/article/ Indian_river _ systems_and_pollution. Last Updated November 12th 2009.
[10] Pratyush. 2007. Poor sewage treatment, drainage system & climate change making Indian rivers 'Dead'. Insta Blogs. Website: http://pratyush.instablogs.com/entry/poor-sewage-treatment-drainage-system-climate-change-making-indian-rivers-dead/. June 15 2007.

system. It is in need of repair as more than half of India's drainage system is virtually outmoded. Situation in Pakistan is relatively better due to less population but rest of the things are almost same like of India.

2.2.2. Pollution of Wular Lake and Seepage Losses

Ready and Char (2004)[11] identified the environmental issues of Wular Lake located in Jammu and Kashmir and comprising of 17,300 ha (**Figures 8 to 11**). Rashid (2009)[12] indicated that shrinkage in Lake's area and rise in the silt and the chloride contents in waters are the major threats for the Wular Lake. The lake has lost its vast area to agriculture, willow plantation and urbanization. The Wular Integrated Conservation and Development Action Plan (2001-2011) indicated that the lake area was reduced to 79 km^2 in 1993 whereas it had 200 km^2 during 1911.

The lake stores excess water during floods in the valley. "Massive willow plantation within and around the lake has been acting as a barrier for heavily silted waters to drain out. The lake is thus fast becoming a huge deposit of silts". The bio-matter from dead plants and decay adds to the organic content of the lake that further deteriorates water quality. The process of agriculture around the lake has eaten away most of the marshy areas that could otherwise act as an absorption area for harmful components entering the lake. About 3,00,000 people are living in floating residences in Baramulla district. Their sewerage and garbage goes directly into the lake and pollutes it. The waste drained directly into the lake has been constantly increasing its chloride content. Any alteration in size, structure and components of the lake body will not only hamper special supplies provided by the lake (fodder, fish, etc.), but also jeopardise livelihood of many fishermen. "Drudging, de-silting and selective de-weeding of channels and nullahs that are connected with Wular can be of great help in restoring its lost glory".

Seepage losses contribute to groundwater and plantations around the Lake are also consuming water. The Wular Lake and Kishenganga Project would further result in feeding the storage, and groundwater recharge will be enhanced, which would also cause serious environmental concerns for surrounding areas of the Lake and it will further reduce the flows of Kishenganga River to Pakistan. The pollutants of the Lake will also pollute the flowing water and there will be more pollutants in the water of the Jhelum River flowing to Pakistan.

2.3. International Water Law on Trans-boundary Aquifers

Article #42 of the International Water Law deals with trans-boundary aquifers and is composed of six points regarding rules and laws applicable to shared waters and apply to aquifers and are relevant to the basin states and may be considered in future while making additions to the Indus Waters Treaty[13]. The Law clearly

---

[11] Ready, M. S. and N. V. V. Char. 2004. Management of Lakes in India. Paper prepared by the Formerly Secretary and Commissioner (Eastern Rivers), Ministry of Water Resources, Government of India.

[12] Rashid, A. 2009. Wular lake faces threat. Report of the J&K Plus On-line Edition. Saturday, July 18th, 2009, Chandigarh, India.

[13] a. The Rules applicable to internationally shared waters apply to an aquifer if: a) It is connected to surface waters that are part of an international drainage basin; or b) It is intersected by the boundaries between two or more States even without a connection to surface waters that form an international drainage basin.
  b. Whenever possible and appropriate, basin States sharing an aquifer referred to in paragraph 1 shall manage an aquifer in its entirety.
  c. In managing the waters of an aquifer referred to in paragraph 1, basin States shall consult and exchange information and data at the request of any one of them and shall cooperate in the collection and analyzing additional needed information pertinent to the obligations under these Rules.
  d. Basin States shall cooperate according to the procedures in Chapter XI to set drawdown rates in order to assure the equitable utilization of the waters of an aquifer referred to in paragraph 1, having due regard for the obligation not to cause significant harm to other basin States and to the obligation to protect the aquifer.
  e. Basin States sharing an aquifer referred to in paragraph 1 shall cooperate in managing the recharge of the aquifer.

states that the basin states sharing an aquifer shall manage it in its entirety and exchange data at the request of any one of them and cooperate in the collection and analysis of additional information, if needed.

The pressure on groundwater will increase in future and there are chances that condition of aquifers will be further aggravated. Pakistan may take up the issue of trans-boundary aquifers with India before it is too late, as in India aquifers are under heavy depletion. There are also chances that due to pressure on groundwater, India may be tempted to divert waters of Western Rivers to recharge depleted aquifers. The extensive development of hydro-power projects in India would also result into heavy seepage of surface water into the groundwater and ultimately reducing the flows to Pakistan.

3. KEY POLICY ISSUES

Water entitlements of India on the western rivers have created a situation where the basin states are facing conflicts in implementing the Treaty. The issues of depleting aquifers could not be given due consideration, but it is expected that in future such issues will be much more serious to address along with environmental issues. The key issues of rapid abstraction of groundwater in Northern India were identified having impacts on sustainability and inter-generational issues of aquifers in basins states.

3.1. Depletion of Aquifers in Northern India and Impact on Pakistan's Aquifers

Lowering of water table due to over-abstraction of groundwater in the Northern India has serious impacts on the depletion of aquifers on the Pakistan's side. Pakistan is not facing acute depletion of groundwater except on the fringe of the border with India, which seems an extended effect of excessive groundwater depletion in India. Rest of the country is either under hydrological equilibrium or receiving higher recharge in the lower Indus basin. With further scarcity of surface water and prolonged droughts, the pressure on groundwater will increase and there are chances that aquifers will be further depleted and this would have negative impacts on aquifers on the Pakistan side, as there is overwhelming evidence generated under the NASA study.

3.2. Entry of Effluents to Western Rivers

Entry of effluents into freshwater rivers and tributaries feeding the Western Rivers on the Indian side is causing serious environmental implications for Indus-Pakistan. The extensive development of agriculture around the Western Rivers in India, with higher use of fertilizers and pesticides, is a concern for Pakistan. The domestic effluent is also a serious issue due to rapid urbanization around water bodies. Furthermore, the drainage channels from India entering into Pakistan are now flowing with effluents having higher concentration of chemicals and causing environmental impacts on the livelihood of rural population, livestock and groundwater quality. Mortality of livestock has been reported due to the use of drainage water as stockwater. The further growth of chemical agriculture in India would further deteriorate the quality of drainage effluents entering into Pakistan.

3.3. Growing Demand of Surface Water to Recharge Aquifers of Indus-India

With the depletion of groundwater in northern India, there will also be additional pressure to construct projects where surface waters can be used either for recharging groundwater or supplementing the

---

f. Basin States sharing an aquifer referred to in paragraph 1 shall refrain from and prevent acts or omissions within their territory that cause significant harm to another basin State, having due regard to the right of each basin State to make equitable and reasonable use of the waters.

groundwater use. Pakistan has to oversee all the river flow projects in Indus-India in terms of seepage losses induced due to heading up of stored water and additional diversions to support the shortages of water in India. There are chances of further aggravating water conflicts in the near future.

3.4. Seepage Losses in Lakes and Reservoirs

India has planned construction of a number of hydro-power and storage projects with creating large heads of water in the reservoirs, which will induce recharge to groundwater and will ultimately reduce the flow of water to Indus-Pakistan. The heading up of water in the hydro-power dams must also be viewed in terms of seepage losses, which might increase by many-fold due to heading up of water in the reservoir. This is also true for the Wular Lake, Kishenganga, Salal and Baglihar dam projects.

4. POTENTIAL OPTIONS

4.1. Dialogues for Addressing Transboundary Aquifer's Management

Emphasis must be placed on the basin aquifer bordering the basin states in future discussions of the Indus Water Commission. With the scarcity of surface water and persistent drought, the pressure on groundwater will increase and there are chances that condition of aquifers will be further aggravated. Pakistan may take up the issue of trans-boundary aquifer with India before it is too late, as in Indus-India aquifer is under heavy depletion.

Initiate dialogues between the basin states for tranboundary aquifer management through: a) sharing information on aquifer abstraction; b) ensuring that electric and diesel fuel policies are not encouraging farmers for over-abstraction of groundwater; c) developing capacity of the basin states for the use of remotely sensed data for the assessment of water table and groundwater abstractions; and d) exchange of knowledge and technologies for efficient use of water to reduce dependence on groundwater through the management of water demand for all sub-sectors of water use.

4.2. Managing Groundwater as a Resource as well as Trust

Manage groundwater as a resource, as it is essential to jointly set up an organisation with representatives from the basin states, whose functions would entail identifying short- and long-term supply capacity of the basin and its integrated development, setting up of infrastructure and coordinating activities of different agencies. Furthermore, groundwater must also be considered as a trust because in the concept of trusteeship, resource is not only depleted but it is also recharged to manage it on sustainable basis. As in the basin states, surface water schemes are largely being managed on *Warabandi* (fixed-rotation) and water allocations are actually based on rationing of water, therefore groundwater provides water on demand basis and hence it has larger impacts on productivity of irrigated agriculture.

4.3. Support Paradigm Shift in the Mindset of People

Support paradigm shift in the mindset of people of the basin states and it would require a complete end to hostilities, both physical and psychological, from both sides. It will have to be a part of the final settlement in letter and spirit. The integrated development approach is beyond consideration in the current context of relations between the basin states, but all other options will lead to destruction sooner or later. Furthermore, trans-boundary water and aquifers have to be seen in terms of opportunities available to manage water (surface, groundwater and wastewater), while developing future plans for the benefits of the basin states.

4.4. Monitoring of Hydro-power Projects on the Wetsern Rivers

Monitor river flow projects in terms of seepage losses due to heading up of water in the reservoir, where seepage is induced by many-fold. This will be a loss to Pakistan but a gain to India. Therefore, water apportionment to India on the western rivers in terms of storage has to be seen in the context of induced seepage losses. Depletion of groundwater in northern India will pose serious implications for India to try to use surface waters from the western rivers over and above the provisions of the Treaty, being an upper riparian. In addition, the seepage of water from the storage projects can be easily estimated by measuring the inflows and outflows from the reservoir. Ultimately, Pakistan has to initiate discussions to include the seepage losses as part of water entitlements for India. In addition, there is an urgent need to exchange the data and information so that experts can formulate options for the benefit of the basin states.

5. Way Forward

Who will be the Champions of creating a shift in the mindset of the experts and people to consider environmental concerns and groundwater issues and to formulate detailed provisions on trans-boundary aquifers and environmental pollution so that dialogues can be initiated to address the emerging issues and formulate plans for the benefits of the basin states – on the Indus?

CHAPTER - 11

The Politics Of Water In South Asia: The Case of The Indus Waters Treaty

Hamir K. Sahni

Because water could be a major source of future conflicts among states (what some have called the coining of the "water wars"), it is extremely important that steps be taken to resolve these issues and ensure greater access to water. Such efforts are especially needed in South Asia. The Indus Waters Treaty (IWT) is an agreement between India and Pakistan to share the waters of the Indus river system that the two countries signed in 1960. The IWT is also one of the few such international agreements on the sharing of river waters that has been a success, despite the ongoing rivalry between India and Pakistan. This paper lays out a role for U.S. policy to help resolve the current dispute between India and Pakistan over the IWT, and explains how it can be used to help achieve larger and broader U.S. policy goals. The lack of sufficient mutual trust among the main partners to the treaty requires the intervention of a third party that is not perceived as biased and yet can be an effective mediator. The paper argues that this policy of intervention is in alignment with U.S. interests and will be a step toward meeting the U.S. goal of stability in this volatile region.

Executive Summary

This paper lays out a case for the United States to intervene in the current Indus Waters Treaty dispute between India and Pakistan. It explains how U.S. mediation and support for Indo-Pak water cooperation is in alignment with achieving current U.S. strategy and policy objectives in the South Asian region. From the U.S. perspective, the main security issues in South Asia are the region's status as the focal point in the war on terrorism and the periodic tensions between the two nuclear rivals India and Pakistan (the two largest countries in the region). Realizing the growing importance of the region, the United States has built up a bilateral relationship with each of the South Asian states. U.S. policy goals also aim to achieve regional stability by encouraging the states to resolve their differences and defuse tensions.

Economic ties are also increasingly important, both between the United States and the region and among regional countries themselves.

Hamir K. Sahni completed her M.A. in International Relations from the Johns Hopkins University School of Advanced International Studies (SAIS) in May 2006. She was born and raised in New Delhi, India. Previously she earned a bachelors degree with honors in Economics from the University of Delhi, and a master's degree in Business Economics from the University of Wales.

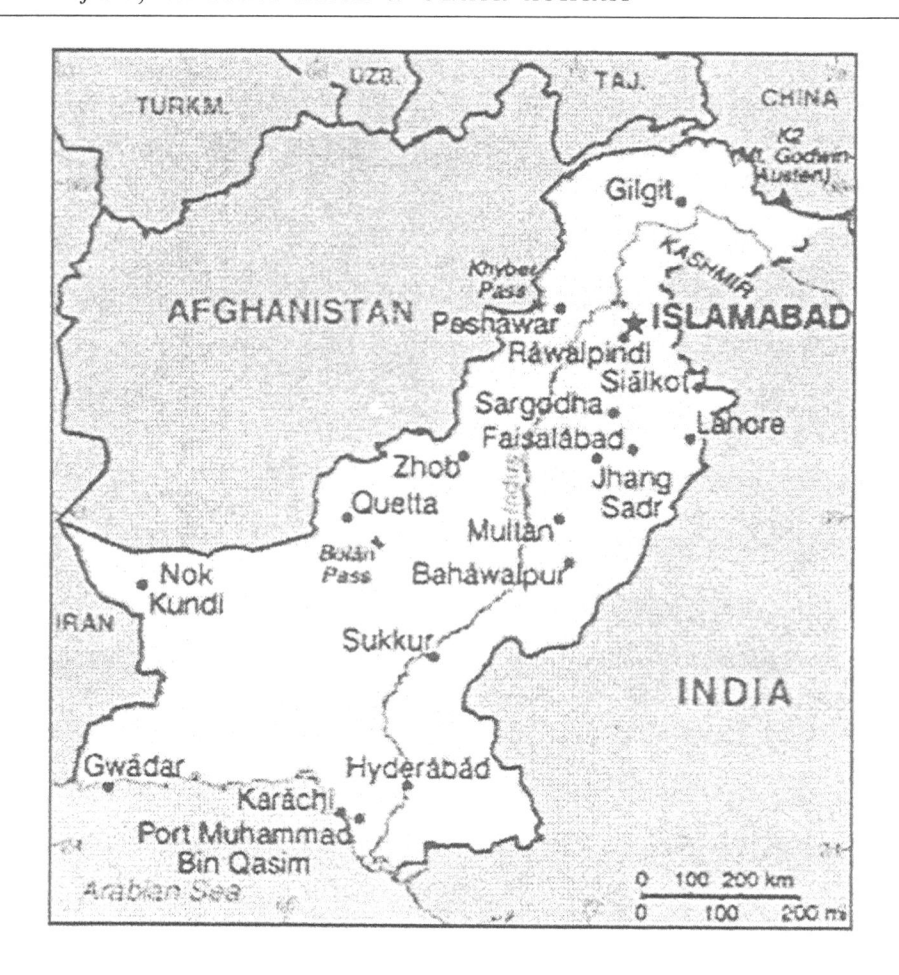

The biggest security threat in the region, and an impediment to regional collaboration, is the territorial dispute over Jammu and Kashmir—the main cause of the conflict between India and Pakistan. The two states have made sustained efforts in recent years to formulate a peace process and to promote goodwill through various confidence-building measures. However, this conflict has become an ideological issue, inextricably linked with the two countries' identities. In order to find a solution, it will be necessary to move away from the political realm—where a tradition of distrust and the desire for prestige complicate matters—into the economic sphere, where immense potential for cooperation exists. Because of the lack of trust among the two main parties, this will require some third-party intervention aiming to depoliticize the issue. The United States can play a direct role here—and, in the process, also achieve its own policy goals.

The Indus Waters Treaty set a precedent of cooperation between India and Pakistan that has survived three wars and other hostilities between the two nations. It is important, therefore, that the current disagreement over the violation of the treaty is resolved quickly so that it serves as a model for peaceful relations rather than an obstacle to cooperation. As Stephen P. Cohen has observed, "The Indus Waters Treaty is a model for future regional cooperation, especially on energy, environmental concerns, and even the management of the region's impressive water resources."[1] The United States can intervene by providing technical expertise, directing multilateral institutions and aid agencies to invest in projects to increase water efficiency in the region, involving its allies and private parties in efforts to promote economic cooperation, and encouraging India and Pakistan to talk about a long-term outlook on water supply issues and move toward joint management of these challenges.

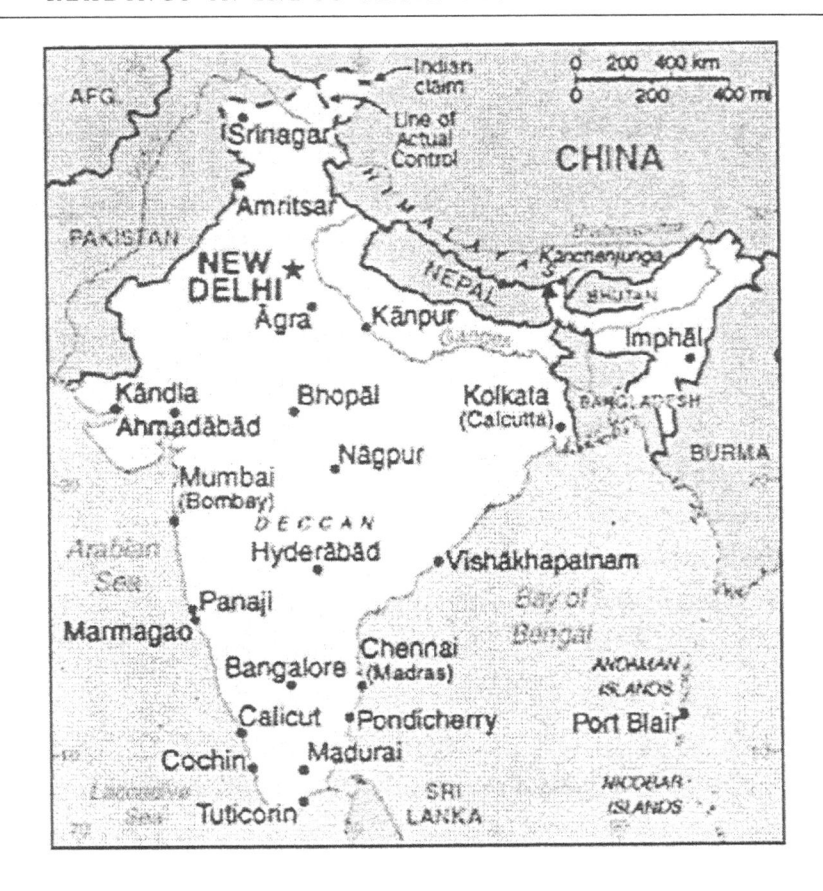

Introduction

South Asia is a region that stretches from Afghanistan in the West across to Bangladesh and Bhutan to the East. The region is home to more than one-sixth of the world's population. It is an area of varied geography and endowed with diverse natural resources. The countries in the region still depend heavily on agriculture, with the majority of their populations relying on it for their livelihood. As a result, water is not only vital for everyday needs, but a critical resource for economic development. Water is a resource on which there is complete dependency and for which there is no substitute. As the demand for water has surpassed supply, with rival demands by various economic sectors, provinces, and sovereign states, this has led to increased competition, tension, and disputes.[2]

Through most of the 18th and 19th centuries, most of South Asia was under the British colonial rule. The new boundaries drawn after the British departure in the 20th century have led to complex inter-state relationships in the region. As a result of these artificial boundaries, many "international rivers" have been created—that is, rivers that begin in one country and end in another. This has led to inefficient and inequitable water distribution, in turn leading to disputes, not only among sovereign states, but also among provinces within countries. There are many great rivers flowing in the region, with multidimensional uses and an immense potential to facilitate economic development.

The politics of water-sharing arrangements have further complicated inter-state relationships.[3] As Peter Gleick has written in a report, ". . . one factor remains constant: the importance of water to life means that providing for water needs and demands will never be free of politics."[4] Because water could be a major source of future conflicts among states (what some writers have called the coming of the "water wars"), it will be extremely important to find ways to resolve these issues and ensure that all of the people in the region have reliable access to water.

India and Pakistan, the two largest countries in the region, have been rivals since their partition and independence from British rule in 1947. The two countries have fought three major wars and have an ongoing conflict over the disputed northern territory of Jammu and Kashmir. This has made the region one of the most volatile in the world, even more so after both India and Pakistan tested nuclear weapons in 1998. Generally speaking, India has insisted on a bilateral approach for the resolution of its disputes with other nations, while Pakistan favors intervention by third parties. This has changed over the last decade with a shift in India's foreign policy and its adaptation to the post-Cold War international order. The change in India's policy was apparent at the time of the Kargil crisis[5] in 1999, when it did not object to U.S. intervention to help calm the situation.

Given the rivalry between India and Pakistan, the only successful agreement between them that has survived despite continued hostilities is the Indus Waters Treaty (IWT). The IWT, which the two countries signed in 1960, is an agreement to share the waters of the Indus river system. The IWT is one of the few such international agreements on the sharing of river waters that has been a success. This paper lays out a role for U.S. policy to help resolve the current dispute between India and Pakistan over the IWT. It also argues that engagement by Washington can be used to help achieve larger and broader U.S. policy goals. The next section lays out a brief overview of the politics of water in South Asia, followed by a summary of the Indus Waters Treaty—its genesis, main provisions, and the current dispute between the parties. The subsequent section then outlines the relationship between India and Pakistan and explains how the IWT has survived despite the hostilities between the two nations. The paper concludes by discussing the potential role for U.S. mediation and the way such a role could promote regional stability and the achievement of U.S. policy goals.

THE POLITICS OF WATER IN SOUTH ASIA

Water Resources in South Asia

South Asia has a vast network of rivers. The main river systems in the region are the Indus, the Ganges, and the Brahmaputra.[6] Most of these watercourses have their source in the Himalayan mountains and flow through more than one country in the region.

Regional Cooperation

Recently, the countries in the region have achieved increasing cooperation, having negotiated various bilateral agreements. In addition to the IWT between India and Pakistan, India and Bangladesh have cooperated to share water from the Ganges, and India and Nepal have shared water according to the principles of the Mahakali River Treaty. South Asian states successfully negotiated five water-sharing treaties in 1996 and 1997. Although obstacles still exist, the region has the potential to achieve greater cooperation. Innovations in negotiating processes have led to greater success in concluding international agreements. These innovations include third-party involvement and actors from the private sector.[7]

Main Conflicts

Despite the existence of a number of agreements, disputes and conflicts have arisen time and again over the distribution of water—not only among countries, but regarding water-sharing agreements even within provinces inside a country. There are illustrations of this in the state of Punjab in India, among the southern Indian states of Karnataka and Tamil Nadu, and the Sindh and Punjab provinces in Pakistan. Due to the significance of water resources, these disputes become politicized. This results in irrational actions by national governments due to domestic political pressures, which in turn may have an adverse impact on international water-sharing agreements and their resolution.

CONFLICT TO COOPERATION

Indo-Pak Relations/Politics

India and Pakistan have had a history of persistent distrust since both gained independence in 1947. The two countries have had an ongoing conflict over the disputed northern territory of Kashmir, and have fought three full-scale wars in the last half-century.

The two countries now are engaged in an ongoing dialogue, seeking to overcome their frozen positions. Pakistan generally has argued that Kashmir is the core issue in the dispute, while India considers it just one part of the overall relationship. The two countries have sought to overcome the lack of trust through various confidence-building measures (CBMs) that can be avenues of cooperation, such as the opening of direct transport links and growth in trade.

Potential Payoffs/Externalities

Active cooperation has great payoffs for both sides. This is the main reason the IWT has survived despite the ongoing conflict between the two countries. For Pakistan, the treaty's direct benefits include greater irrigation potential and more accessible drinking water. India's gains include access to hydroelectric power and navigable rivers. This type of cooperation could have other positive externalities. It could provide the basis for continuing engagement that eventually could help resolve the Kashmir issue. Successful cooperation in this area could serve as a model for emulation in the region and across other sectors, such as trade and exploration for energy resources.

THE INDUS WATERS TREATY

India and Pakistan signed the Indus Waters Treaty on Sept. 19, 1960, after a long dispute over the distribution of the Indus river system's water resources.[8]

Genesis/Rationale

India gained independence from the British in 1947 and was partitioned into two nation-states—India and Pakistan. However, at the time the two new countries drew their borders, they paid no attention to existing irrigation works. In 1948, a bilateral dispute led India to cut off the irrigation waters in canals along the Indo-Pak boundary. This demonstrated the urgent need to formulate an agreement between the two countries on the distribution and use of the waters. Negotiations continued throughout the 1950s, with the World Bank playing a pivotal role in overseeing, designing, and guiding the process.[9] This culminated in the signing of the *Indus Waters Treaty in 1960*.

Main Provisions/Mechanisms

The treaty's main provisions stipulated that all the eastern river waters (the Ravi, Beas, and Sutlej rivers) were solely for India's use, while only Pakistan was to use the western river waters (the Indus, Jhelum, and Chenab rivers). A permanent Indus Commission was appointed to look into any matters concerning the sharing of the river waters and also to serve as a dispute settlement and resolution mechanism. The treaty states that if the commission fails to resolve the matter, it is officially considered a "difference," and a neutral expert is appointed to examine it. In case the neutral expert rules that the difference should be treated as a dispute, or the difference does not fall under the expert's mandate, a Court of Arbitration is established.[10]

With the negotiation of the IWT, each country became independent of the other in the use of its water supplies.[11] The intention was to create strong incentives for each party to make the most efficient use of its own water, as the benefits would directly accrue to it, and not the other party to the treaty.

Current Impasse

The IWT is considered one of the few examples of successful implementation of such an agreement. The treaty has survived continued regional hostility, including three wars between India and Pakistan.

In the 1980s, a dispute arose over India's plans to build a barrage on the Jhelum river, below the Wular lake near Srinagar. Pakistan protested against this project, claiming that it violated the IWT, and referred the case to the Indus Water Commission in 1986. The Commission recorded its failure to resolve the dispute in 1987, and the project was suspended. The matter has been raised and discussed several times during bilateral talks.[12]

More recently, controversy has arisen over the building of the Bagli-har hydropower project by India. Pakistan involved the World Bank as a referee in 2005, alleging violation of the treaty by India, after talks between officials of the two countries in January 2005 were not successful.[13] India has promised to re-examine the objections to the project, but Pakistan has persisted with its complaints. As a result, at the request of the Government of Pakistan, the World Bank has appointed a neutral expert approved by both parties to look into the differences.[14]

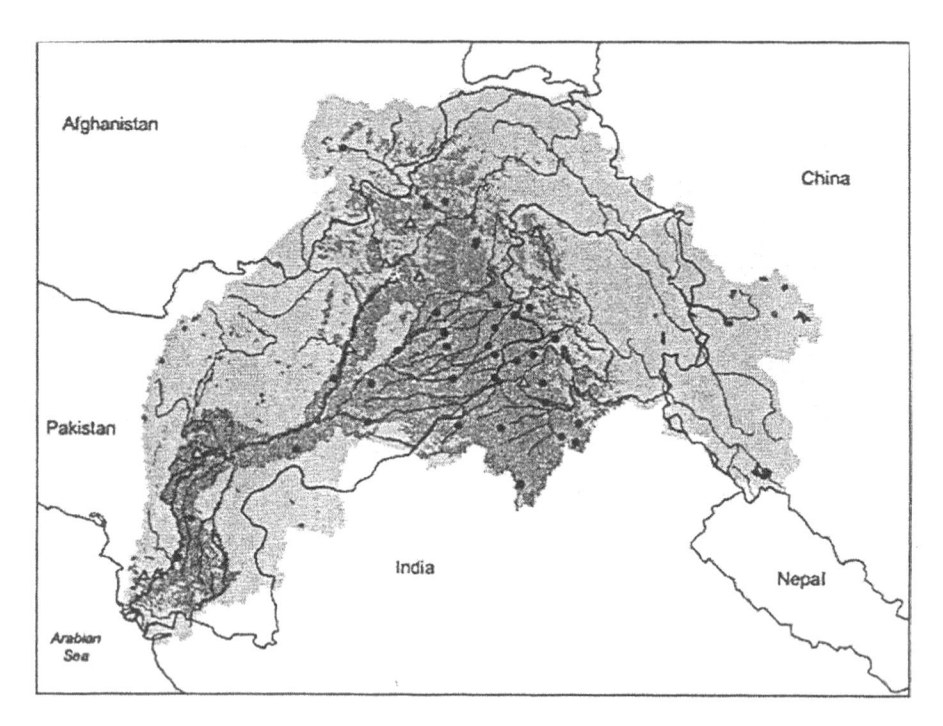

World Resources Institute. 2006. Earth Trends: Environmental Information. Available at http://earthtrends.wri.org <http://earthtrends.vvri.org/> . Washington DC: World Resources Institute. Revenga, C, S. Murray, J. Abramovitz, and A. Hammond, 1998. Watersheds of the World: Ecological Value and Vulnerability. Washington, DC: World Resources Institute.

POTENTIAL U.S. ROLE

Why?

As stared by a U.S. State Department official, "The future of this region is simply vital to the future of the U.S"[15] The United States has strategic interests in the region. It seeks both to achieve stability and to advance its economic interests. Maintaining stability in South Asia is one of the current U.S. administration's main policy objectives.

The main risk to stability in the region is the Indo-Pak dispute over Jammu and Kashmir. Increased cooperation between India and Pakistan would promote regional stability, help control the nuclear arms race, and make an end to the Kashmir conflict more likely. The two countries already have fought three major wars, as well as a smaller one in 1999, since their independence. Since 1989, the Indian part of Kashmir has suffered ongoing civil strife, which Pakistan has fomented, both overtly and covertly. India accuses Pakistan of training insurgents, arming militants, and exporting terrorism to the state of Jammu and Kashmir (J&K). Pakistan has openly extended its support to the people of Kashmir, backing their right to self-determination and alleging that Indian troops have violated human rights in this region.

The standoff attained an even more prominent role in the international arena after India and Pakistan tested nuclear weapons in 1998. The conflict has become a nuclear flashpoint since then, all the more dangerous because no framework of mutual deterrence exists between the two nuclear rivals, as the United States and the Soviet Union had worked out during the Cold War.

Changes in the international order following the 9/11 terrorist attacks led to changes in U.S. policy toward South Asia. Historically, the United States and Pakistan have cooperated closely, especially in the 1980s, following the Soviet invasion of Afghanistan. This was consistent with the U.S. policy of containing the Soviet Union. Following the Soviet withdrawal from Afghanistan in 1989, the United States had lost interest in that country. The 9/11 attacks forced the United States to renew its interest in Afghanistan, which had been a prime breeding ground for terrorist acts against the United States. India has been a staunch ally of the United States in the war on terror.

Another stated U.S. objective now is to support India and build it up as a counter-weight to China as part of a balance-of-power strategy in the region. This is illustrated by growing Indo-U.S. ties and the recent, much-discussed agreements between the two countries on civilian nuclear cooperation. Stability in the region will help solidify stronger Indo-U.S. ties, and the resolution of inter-state disputes can help lay the groundwork for closer regional economic links.

U.S. policy toward Pakistan can help to achieve these objectives. Financial assistance, which has been generous, should not take the form of no-strings-attached cash payments that can be abused. Rather, this assistance must be tied to specific reforms, including economic reforms, that aim to create a long-term, viable institutional structure that does not rely on individual leaders or the military to maintain a semblance of stability. The ultimate goal is to establish democracy in Pakistan.[16]

At a time when India and Pakistan are seeking to improve relations through an ongoing, active dialogue and through various confidence-building measures, it is critically important to ensure that the current dispute over the IWT does not produce a rupture, especially because this treaty has been one of the rare examples of successful cooperation.[17] The actual negotiation of the IWT required a third party, the World Bank, to mediate. At the time the IWT was formulated, the Western powers were highly motivated to help settle disputes among neighbors in South Asia because this clearly suited their interests. Now, once again, such efforts would be in alignment with U.S. interests because maintaining security in the region is an important component of U.S. strategy and policy. This objective serves the U.S. goals of achieving stability in the neighborhood, building India up as a world power to balance China in the region, and building a sustainable, democratic Pakistan.

Because the two main parties to the treaty lack sufficient mutual trust, third-party intervention is necessary. This third party must be perceived as unbiased and capable of being an effective mediator. The South Asian Association for Regional Cooperation (SAARC), formed in 1985, is the main regional body that seems suitable for this role. However, it has not been very effective in promoting regional integration and does not deal with bilateral disputes, such as disagreements on water-sharing arrangements.

Why Will it Work?

There are clear indicators that U.S. intervention at this stage will work. The successful U.S. intervention in the recent Kargil conflict serves as a valuable precedent. The United States played an active role in mediation to defuse the crisis, and India raised no objections to third-party intervention in this case.

The long-standing U.S. relationship with Pakistan has led India to worry about a pro-Pakistan bias by the United States. Moreover, there has been a history of distrust between the United States and India. Pakistan has been a recipient of U.S. aid, particularly in the form of arms supplies, and is classified as a major non-NATO ally of the United States.

The United States continues to provide Pakistan with large amounts of aid, and Pakistan is greatly dependent on this assistance to sustain its economy. There is a growing realization, however, that the U.S. strategy toward Pakistan needs to be broadened, even to be able to meet the primary U.S. objective of countering terrorism. A long-term outlook and aid policy for the economic and institutional rebuilding of Pakistan is needed.[18]

Meanwhile, the relationship between the United States and India has changed in recent years. These two countries have built ever-closer ties in the post Cold-War international system. The United States has increased leverage in India now, with cooperation in various spheres, ranging from a growth in trade to collaboration in strategic areas such as defense and technology. There has been an ongoing dialogue, as with the High Technology Cooperation Group, formed in 2002, to provide a framework for discussing high-technology issues of mutual concern.[19] The advancement in the Indo-U.S. relationship was clear during the July 18, 2005 meeting of U.S. President George W. Bush and Indian Prime Minister Manmohan Singh. The two leaders pledged to further strengthen the relationship, with cooperation in critical areas such as the civil-nuclear sector.

Recommendations

The United States has several policy options for addressing this issue. It could choose not to interfere and keep itself uninvolved, as its resources already are stretched with its engagements in Iraq and Afghanistan. It could focus on helping India and Pakistan resolve the issue of Kashmir, so as to remove the trigger for nuclear conflict in South Asia. Or it could use the IWT as a model of successful cooperation along with the current Indo-Pak framework of confidence-building measures. Given U.S. strategy and policy, the last option would seem to be the best, as it has the potential to help achieve long-term U.S. goals in the region. The previous sections laid out a strong case that justifies the time and expenditure that a U.S. role in the matter would involve.

"Mediation by a third party which is seen as an honest broker by both disputants, and which can assist in implementing the outcome of the mediation, has been the main reason for the success of the World Bank's efforts in the Indus Basin dispute between India and Pakistan."[20] By mediating, the United States can help to resolve the issue. U.S. involvement is especially desirable considering the trust deficit that exists between the two parties to the treaty.

A recent report on U.S. policy options for influencing Pakistan's future outlines the importance of addressing imminent water issues, as well as the political complications that will be involved.[21] The United States can push for a cooperative outcome by using its influence with both parties to help achieve this. As outlined above, the United States has maintained a long-term relationship with Pakistan and recently has built closer ties with India. Its cooperation with both countries continues to increase across diverse areas. The United States can play a direct role by encouraging India and Pakistan to have a dialogue on the long-term view for water supply in the region. The United States also can direct bilateral and multilateral funding through donor agencies such as the World Bank and USAID for linked sectors such as power, irrigation, and infrastructure. For the IWT to survive and help meet increasing demands, it is crucial that both India and Pakistan use water more efficiently.

There is a growing realization that the economic dimension is a crucial element in reaching a resolution in Kashmir, which would lead in turn to a more open and stable South Asia.[22] Addressing water and power limitations will be an important element of economic development in the state of J&K. With this in mind, the United States can direct its aid and other investment toward projects that encourage small-scale irrigation and power generation, within the limitations of the IWT. The waters of the Indus river system have a direct impact on the state of J&K and are therefore crucial to its economic prospects. The Kashmir Valley, which is the main source of the dispute between India and Pakistan, has been affected by the IWT. The western rivers of the Indus river system, which according to the treaty are for Pakistan's exclusive use, flow through J&K. As a result, these waters cannot be used for irrigation and power generation. The Baglihar project, which is the cause of the current dispute, has great potential for energy creation on both sides of the border. In the longer term, the United States can help India and Pakistan develop new resources that would benefit both parties and J&K directly, even if these may require minor adjustments to the IWT. The IWT can serve as a model to encourage joint projects that can harness more resources and use them more effectively. The United States can facilitate this by allowing the private sector to play a greater role in developing these resources. "The inclusion of private parties in negotiations over water development and use not only changes objectives, but makes them generally more transparent."[23]

In their paper, Ben Crow and Nirvikar Singh apply game theory and write that outside efforts to facilitate cooperation often are necessary even though the parties would stand to benefit from cooperation.[24] In many cases, due to obstacles such as uncertainty and differences in the information available to each side, mutual benefits alone are not sufficient to encourage parties to cooperate. In these situations, Crow and Singh write, a third party or mediator can play a role by "sweetening the deal"[25] as in the original IWT negotiations.

Conclusion

Given the central role that South Asia now plays in U.S. foreign policy, it is clear that stability in the region is of critical importance, both for the United States and in the larger international context. As a result, U.S. policy goals aim to facilitate regional cooperation in the region. With the increasing impact of non-traditional areas such as the environment on security, it is going to be essential that nations cooperate in sharing and jointly managing resources. Agreements on sharing these resources often involve transboundary issues and can result in conflicts, as in the case of water resources. This is true in South Asia, where an extensive network of rivers cuts across national boundaries. Because the region's water issues have been highly politicized, compounding the complicated inter-state conflicts that already exist, cooperation has been limited and disputes have gone unresolved. This is why the IWT is such a significant agreement. Despite the long-running rivalry between two South Asian adversaries, the treaty has survived. It can serve as a model for building trust between the two nations as they move toward normalizing relations. The treaty also can be a foot in the door for furthering cooperation in other spheres. Ongoing, successful implementation of the IWT also can serve as an example and provide lessons for settling transboundary water disputes in other parts of the world.

However, as seen with the initial IWT negotiations, third-party intervention and continuous diplomatic efforts by the World Bank (supported by the main Western powers) were required for both parties to reach an agreement. The major powers invested the necessary time and resources because they realized that the water dispute between India and Pakistan could lead to a war, destabilizing the whole region. The lack of trust between the two main parties and an inability to commit to an agreement made outside mediation essential.

For these reasons, the United States should mediate in the current impasse between India and Pakistan over the IWT, extending its effort and resources to help achieve a quick resolution to the dispute. This policy aligns with U.S. interests in South Asia and will be a step toward meeting the U.S. goal of stability in this volatile region.

Notes

1. Stephen P. Cohen, "The US and South Asia," *Seminar*, No. 545 (January 2005): 6.
2. Salman M.A. Salman and Laurence Boisson de Chazournes, *International Watercourses: Enhancing Cooperation and Managing Conflict* in International Watercourses: Enhancing Cooperation and Managing Conflict, Proceedings of a World Bank Seminar, World Bank Technical Paper No. 414, ed. Salman M.A. Salman and Laurence Boisson de Chazournes (1998): 167.
3. B.C. Upreti, *Politics of Himalayan Rivers Waters: An Analysis of the River Water Issues of Nepal, India and Bangladesh* (Jaipur, New Delhi: Nirala Publications, 1993): Foreword.
4. *Water Conflict Chronology*, compiled by Peter H. Gleick (Pacific Institute, December 2004), *http://www.worldwa.Ur.org/chronologyMtrnl*.
5. The Kargil crisis was an armed conflict that took place between India and Pakistan (the first ground war between two declared nuclear powers) in the summer of 1999. Pakistani troops were found to have infiltrated into the Indian side of the state of Jammu and Kashmir, leading to a response by the Indian military and government. The crisis was resolved when Pakistan withdrew its forces, due in part to international pressure, especially by the United States.
5. B.C. Upreti, *Politics of Himalayan River Waters: An Analysis of the River Water Issues of Nepal, India and Bangladesh* Jaipur, New Delhi: Nirala Publications, 1993): 39-40.
7. Ben Crow and Nirvikar Singh, "Impediments and Innovation in International Rivers: The Waters of South Asia." *World Development*, 28, no. 11 (2000): 1909.
8. *Indus Waters Treaty* (The Pakistan Water Gateway) *http://www.waterinfo.net.pk/pdf/iwt.pdf*, 2.
9. G.T. Keith Pitman, *The Role of the World Bank in Enhancing Cooperation and Resolving Conflict on International Watercourses: The Case of the Indus Basin*, in International Watercourses: Enhancing Cooperation and Managing Conflict, Proceedings of a World Bank Seminar, World Bank Technical Paper No. 414, ed. Salman M.A. Salman and Laurence Boisson de Chazournes (1998): 155.
10. **Indus Waters Treaty**: *World Bank Names Neutral Expert on Baglihar* (World Bank Press Release, 10 May 2005).
11. *Indus Waters Treaty* (The Pakistan Water Gateway) *http://www.waterinfo.net.pk/pdf/iwt.pdf* 2.
13. Farzana Noshab and Nadia Mushtaq, *Water Disputes in South Asia*, (Islamabad: Institute of Strategic Studies, 2001), *http://www.issi.org.pk/strategic_studies__bt?n/ 200I/no_3/article/ 4a.htm*.
13. *Reconsidering the Indus Waters Treaty: The Baglihar Dam Dispute* (Jammu and Kashmir Insight, 31 January 2005), *http://www.jammu-kash7nir.com/insights/ insights.html*.
14. *Indus Waters Treaty: World Bank Names Neutral Expert on Baglihar* (World Bank Press Release, 10 May 2005) *http://web.worldbank.org/ WBSITE/EXTERNAL/COUNTRIES/ SOUTHASIAEXT/0content MDK: 20320047 ~pagePK:146736~piPK:583444~theSitePK:223S47₁00.html*.
15. R. Ramachandran, "Changing Equations," *Frontline*, 22, Issue 8 (12-25 March 2005), *http:// www. hinduonnet.com/thehindu/tbscrip/print.pl?file=20050422 00601300 .btm&date=fl 22Q8/&prd=fline&*.
16. Teresita C. Schaffer, "U.S. Strategy in Pakistan: High Stakes, Heavy Agenda," Testimony before the Senate Foreign Relations Committee (Washington: Center for Strategic and International Studies, July 2004).
17. Stephen Brichieri-Colombi and Robert W. Bradnock, "Geopolitics, water and development in South Asia: cooperative development in the Ganges-Brahmaputra delta," *The Geographical Journal*, 169, no. 1 (March 2003): 49.
18. Schaffer, 2004.
19. David H. McCormick, *India and the United States: An Emerging Global Partnership*, (5 December 2005) *http://www.rediff.com/news/2005/dec/05 guestl.htm*.
20. Salman M.A. Salman and Laurence Bcisson de Chazournes, *International Watercourses: Enhancing Cooperation and Managing Conflict* in International Watercourses: Enhancing Cooperation and Managing Conflict, Proceedings of a World Bank Seminar, World Bank Technical Paper No.414, ed. Salman M.A. Salman and Laurence Boisson de Chazournss (1998): 170.
21. Teresita C. Schaffer, Mandavi Mehta, Amir Ahmad, *Regional Economic Relationships: Trade, Energy and Water* (Washington: Center for Strategic and International Studies, April 2003).
22. Schaffer, et al., 2003.
23. Crow and Singh, 1915.
24. Ibid, 1913.
25. Ibid.

CHAPTER – 12

Conflict and Cooperation on South Asia's International Rivers

A Legal Perspective

Salman M. A. Salman
Lead Counsel
Environmentally and Socially Sustainable Development and
International Law Group Legal Vice Presidency
The World Bank

Kishor Uprety
Senior Counsel
Middle East, North Africa, and South Asia Law Group
Legal Vice Presidency
The World Bank

THE WORLD BANK
Washington, D.C.

The Indus River

I. Introduction and History of the Indus Dispute

The conclusion in 1960 of the Indus Waters Treaty between India and Pakistan was, no doubt, a remarkable achievement.[1] After a long period of negotiations carried out under the auspices and mediation of the World Bank, the Indus Waters Treaty brought to an end the long-standing dispute between India and Pakistan on the use of the waters of the Indus river system for irrigation and hydropower.[2] This chapter briefly discusses the history and politics surrounding the dispute as well as the present treaty regime applicable to the waters of the Indus river system.

The Indus is located in Northwest India and Pakistan and is one of the most important rivers in the world. The main river Indus is about 2,000 miles long. Its two principal tributaries from the West, the Kabul River and the Kurram River, together are more than 700 miles long. The five main tributaries from the East, the Jhelum, the Chenab, the Ravi, the Beas and the Sutlej, have an aggregate length of more than 2,800 miles.[3] From their origin in the Himalayan Snow Belt to their end into the Arabian Sea, the Indus Rivers carry 90 x 106 acre-feet of water and cover a drainage area of 450,000 square miles. The Indus and the eastern-most tributary, the Sutlej, both rise in the Tibetan plateau. The Kabul and the Kurram rise in Afghanistan. Most of the Indus Basin lies in Pakistan and India, with about 13 per-cent of the total catchment area of the basin situated in Tibet and Afghanistan.[4]

The Indus system comprises the main river Indus and its major tributaries: the Kabul, the Swat and the KulTam from the West; and the Jhelum, the Chenab, the Ravi, the Beas and the Sutlej from the East. The main river of the system, the Indus, rises north of the Himalayas. Originating near Lake Mansarovar, the Indus flows in Tibet for about 200 miles before it enters the southeastern corner of Kashmir at about 14,000 feet. Skirting Leh in Ladakh (India), the river flows on toward Gilgit and after 35 miles toward the southwest enters Pakistan, long before it emerges out of the hills near Attock (at 1,100 feet), where it receives the waters of the Kabul-Swat system. For several miles after this, the Indus assumes the character of a many-channeled, braided river rather than a meandering, volume-variable one, before it falls into the Arabian Sea near Karachi.[5]

The Indus system of rivers had been used for irrigation since civilization began in the area.[6] Sporadic conflicts were not uncommon, but were resolved through locally available means.[7] Things started to change

---

[1] The Treaty was signed at Karachi, Pakistan, September 19, 1960; see, 419 U.N.T.S. 126.
[2] See Foreword by Sir William uliff, in Niranjan D. Gulhati, Indus Waters Treaty. An Exercise in International Mediation (Bombay: Allied Publishers, 1973); for discussions on the role of the World Bank, see generally, Edward S.Mason and Robert E. Asher, The World Bank Since Bretton Woods (Washington, DC: Brookings Institution, 1973), at 610-627.
[3] See Gulhati, supra note 2, at 18.
[4] See Gulhati, supranote 2, at 18; for detail on the physical geography of the Indus Basin, see generally, Undala Z. Alam, "Water Rationality: Mediating the Indus Waters Treaty," unpublished Ph.D. Thesis, (University of Durham, U. K., 1998), at 42-49.
[5] *See* Gulhati, supra note 2, at 25. It is also worth noting that the Governor General of India, on March 13, 1843, had declared the navigation of the Indus free for the vessels of all nations. See Bela Vitanyi, The International Regime of River Navigation (Alphen aan den Rijn, The Netherlands: Sijthoff and Noordhoff, 1979), at 99.
[6] However, several small-scale projects irrigated only a relatively limited land area. This situation started to change from the middle of the nineteenth century when, in 1859, the Upper Bari Doab Canal was completed. It was meant to irrigate about one million acres of land between the Ravi and the Beas Rivers with the water from the Ravi. See Asit K. Biswas, "Indus Waters Treaty: The Negotiating Process," in Water International 17 (1992), at 202.
[7] Indeed while disputes over sharing of water were not uncommon, the then central government of India acted as a neutral third party to facilitate resolution through negotiations and, if the negotiations failed, appointed independent commissions to arbitrate. The first major dispute was settled through arbitration by the Anderson Commission in 1935, the second through arbitration by the Rau Commission in 1942, and the third through negotiations between the provinces in 1945. The Indus system, as such, had a sound system to address water disputes and establish and protect rights of all canal systems of the basin. See Syed Kirmani and

in the middle of the nineteenth century due to sizable works on the waters of the Indus system. The dispute on the Indus waters began long before the independence of India and Pakistan.[8] The dispute started in the form of inter-state differences between the Punjab, Sind, Bahawalpur and Bikaner.[9]

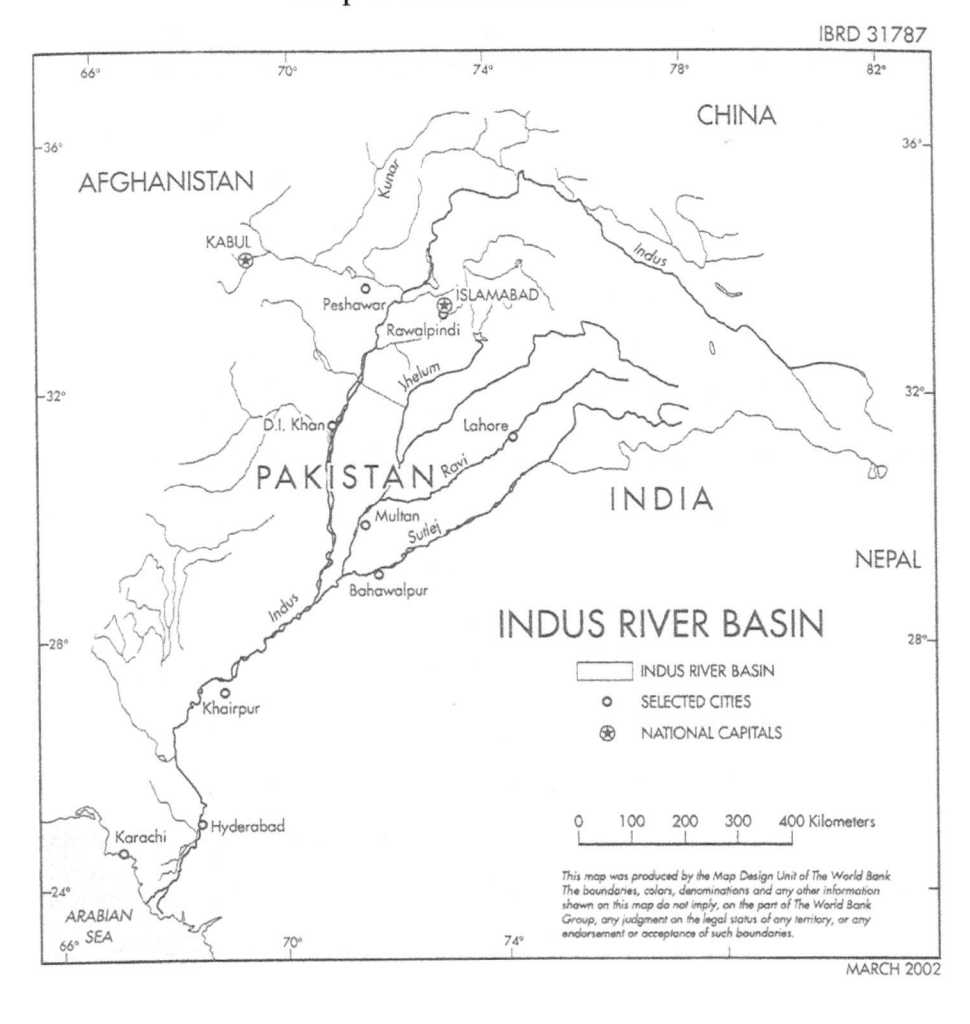

Map 1: The Indus River Basin

Guy Le Moigne, Fostering Riparian Cooperation in International River Basins. The World Bank at its Best in Development Diplomacy, World Bank Technical Paper No. 335 (Washington, DC, 1997) at 3; see also, Biswas, supra note 6, at 201-202; see also, Patricia Wouters, ed., International Water Law: Selected Writings of Professor Charles B. Bourne (London: Kluwer Law International, 1997), at 46.

[8] In October 1939, for instance, Sind had formally complained to the Governor-General about a project initiated by Punjab (the Bhakra Project). As the provinces were now separate and irrigation was a provincial matter, a special commission (Indus Commission) with quasi-judicial powers was appointed by the government of India in September 1941. The Commission comprised two engineers and was headed by Justice B. N. Rau. A report was presented by the Commission in July 1942. See Alam, supra note 4. The central government, after appointing the Commission, made no representations to it, and left Sind and Punjab to discuss their claims to the waters of the Sutlej. Sind tried to use the Commission as a forum in which to have Punjab prevented from encroaching on what Sind regarded as its share of the river. Thus Sind not only complained about projects that had already been built or were being considered, but also tried to guess which projects the Punjab might try to build in the future. Punjab admitted to having further plans for using the Sutlej, but on a much smaller scale than Sind had suggested. See Alam, supra note 4. The Indus Commission's findings essentially acknowledged the damage that would occur to Sind's inundation canals if the Bhakra Dam were constructed. To protect these canals, the Commission recommended the construction of two barrages across the river Indus flowing through Sind (the Gudu and the Hajipur barrages), and suggested that Punjab contribute to the costs of these works. But neither Punjab nor Sind accepted the Indus Commission's findings, and both appealed to the central government. Some informal meetings were held under the auspices of the central government officials, without reaching any final accord. In 1947, the Government of India referred the case to the Secretary of State for India in Whitehall. However, the events of partition overwhelmed the dispute momentarily. It was re-opened later as an international conflict between India and Pakistan.

Bikaner.[9] After the creation of Pakistan in 1947, the dispute became an international issue between East Punjab (in India) and West Punjab (in Pakistan),[10] and was exacerbated by the fact that the political boundary between the two countries was drawn right across the Indus Basin, leaving India the upstream and Pakistan the downstream riparian on five of the six rivers in the Indus system.[11] Most of the water-rich headwater went to India, and Pakistan was left as the water-short lower riparian.[12] Moreover, two important irrigation headworks, one in Madhopur on the river Ravi and one at Ferozepur on the river Sutlej, on which two irrigation canals in West Punjab had been completely dependent for their supplies, were left in Indian territory. India was therefore given the physical capacity to cut off vital irrigation water from large and valuable tracts of agricultural land in West Pakistan.[13] India, which had large areas that needed irrigation, claimed the right to devote to its own use the waters from all six of the rivers as long as they were flowing outside Pakistan territory. Even if India's claim were not to be enforced to the prejudice of Pakistan's historic use, the quantum of water available to Pakistan for the development of new uses would be substantially curtailed.[14]

The partition of India and Pakistan had not dealt with the waters of the Indus. Indeed, when the British Act of Parliament was passed on July 18, 1947, the boundary between the two new dominions was not demarcated[15] and so it was impractical to deal with the allocation of waters. To remedy the legal vacuum created by the partition, the chief engineers of East Punjab (India) and West Punjab (Pakistan) signed a Standstill Agreement on December 20, 1947 providing, inter alia, that until the end of the current rabi crop, on March 31, 1948, the status quo would be maintained with regard to water allocation in the Indus Basin irrigation system.[16] The authorities in East Punjab refused the renewal of the agreements upon expiration

---

[9] As early as 1919, a tripartite agreement between Punjab, Bikaner and Bahawalpur was signed and had paved the way for sanction and construction of the Sutlej Valley Project. However, the Agreement did not specify any right of the downstream Indus riparians: Kharipur State and Sind. See Aloys Arthur Michel, The Indus Rivers: A Study of the Effects of Partition(New Haven: Yale University Press, 1967), at 99; see also Gulhati, supra note 2, at 1.

[10] Following partition, the State of Punjab was divided between India and Pakistan, as per the decision dated August 1947, of the Arbitral Commission presided over by Lord Radcliffe. See Georges Fischer, "La Banque Internationale pour la Reconstruction et le Developpement et l'Utilisation des eaux du Bassin de l'Indus," in Annuaire Francaisde Droit International (1960), at 43. Clearly, the Arbitral Commission handed down decisions predicated on continued supplies of water for irrigation. For detail on the partition and the different alternatives contemplated, see Michel, supra note 9, at 134-194.

[11] However, technically, the Indus dispute started as a dispute on the river Sutlej when the East Punjab government stopped the supply of water to West Punjab on April 1, 1948 (see infra). The action was meant to establish legal right to the water flowing through its territory in the absence of an agreement with West Punjab. This dispute technically needs to be treated as separate from the pre-partition provincial dispute between undivided Punjab and Sind, even though this too was based upon Sutlej.

[12] See G. T. Keith Pitman, "The Role of the World Bank in Enhancing Cooperation and Resolving Conflict in International Watercourses: The Case of the Indus Basin," in International Watercourses: Enhancing Cooperation and Managing Conflict, Salman M. A. Salman and Laurence Boisson de Chazournes, eds. (1998), at 155. In terms of the annual availability of water, however, a clarification is needed. The Indus and the Sutlej both rise in the Tibet within 80 km of each other but do not meet until they reach Pakistan. The three Eastern Rivers (Sutlej, Beas and Ravi) carry approximately 20 percent of the water of the basin, and the three Western Rivers (Indus, Jhelum and Chenab) carry approximately 80 percent.

[13] See Chaudhri Muhammad Ali, The Emergence of Pakistan (New York: Columbia University Press, 1967), at 318-319.

[14] See Foreword by Sir William Iliff, in Gulhati, supra note 2.

[15] See for detail, R. R Baxter, "The Indus Basin," in The Law of International Drainage Basins (Garretson et al, eds. 1967), at 449-457. It should be noted that Radcliffe, in his deliberations, did acknowledge the importance of the Indus system to both the countries, but did not make any explicit recommendation other than to hope that they would work together in finding a solution.

[16] In the effort to solve the problem and at the invitation of the East Punjab government, engineers from the West Punjab had met their counterparts at Simla in April 1948. As a result of the meeting, two Standstill Agreements were signed on April 18, 1948 (also referred to as the Simla Agreements), in connection with the Central Bari Doab canal and the Dipalpur canal, to take effect upon ratification by India and Pakistan. But the West Punjab government refused to ratify them. If the agreements had been ratified, they would have provided an immediate supply of water. The first Standstill Agreement, which dealt with the Central Bari Doab canal, restored the status quo until September 30, 1948. The second Standstill Agreement, which related to the non-perennial Dipalpur canal's supplies from the Ferozepur headworks and other canals in the West Punjab and Bahawalpur offtaking from the Sutlej, was to expire on October 15, 1948. However, in the absence of ratification, none of the agreements became applicable. See Alam, supra note 4, at 57.

and on April 1, 1948, halted the supply of water to several canals in the Pakistan territory.[17] The real reason for the misunderstanding is hard to determine, but deliberately or inadvertently, the West Punjab, until the expiry date of the agreement on March 31, 1948, had not taken the initiative to negotiate any further agreement.[18] On April 1, India discontinued the delivery of water from the Ferozepur headworks to Dipalpur Canal and to the main branches of the Upper Bari Doab Canal.[19] While Pakistan criticized the incident and called India's action "Machiavellian duplicity," India relied on the fact that the agreements had simply lapsed[20] and stated that the proprietary rights in the waters of the rivers in East Punjab continued to be vested in the East Punjab (India), and that the West Punjab (Pakistan) could not claim rights to any share of those waters.[21] In this situation, one option for Pakistan was war, and there were many who advocated for it, but it would have been an error for Pakistan because it could hardly use the Bari Doab, where all the strategic advantages were held by India. Authors have noted that a declaration of war by India might have led to the extinction of the new State. Pakistan could not face the kharif season without water for 5.5 percent of its cropland. So Pakistan opted for negotiations and decided to send its delegation to New Delhi to negotiate for the restoration of the canal waters. India remained firm and wanted recognition of their rights to all of the waters in the Eastern Rivers (Sutlej, Beas and Ravi) and they wanted Pakistan to pay for such water supplied by the Indians until such time as Pakistan could find replacement. India proclaimed its purpose to use all the water in the Eastern Rivers, but because this was not immediately possible, Pakistan would have time to develop alternative supplies. Moreover, India claimed that Pakistan's agreement to pay water dues in the Standstill Agreement of December 1947 was tantamount to recognition by Pakistan of India's proprietary rights. Pakistan, on the other hand, insisted that these payments had been for the costs of operating and maintaining the irrigation works, not payment for water that belonged to Pakistan by right of prior allocation.[22]

Following extensive discussions in an Inter-Dominion conference held in New Delhi on May 3-4, 1948, a new agreement was signed (commonly called the Delhi Agreement) on May 4, 1948. Under the terms of that Agreement, the East and the West Punjab recognized the necessity to resolve the issues in the spirit of goodwill and friendship. Without prejudice to its own rights, the government of the East Punjab granted to

---

[17] The East Punjab declared that it would not restore the flow of water in these canals, "unless the West Punjab recognized that it had no right to the water." See Stephen C. McCaffrey, "Water, Politics and the International Law," in Water in Crisis: A Guide to the World's Fresh Water Resources, Peter H. Gleick, ed. (Oxford University Press, 1993), at 95; see also, F. J. Fowler, "The Indo-Pakistan Water Dispute," in the Yearbook of World Affairs Vol. IX (London: 1955), at 101. The legal rationale, typical of an upper riparian, was to try to establish a claim over waters that flow through one's territory before downstream utilization became a prescriptive right. See Jagat S. Mehta, "The Indus Waters Treaty: A Case Study in the Resolution of an International River Basin Conflict," Natural Resources Forum 12 (1988), at 72. However, it should also be noted that the decision was that of the East Punjab government, made without official knowledge of the Central government. Prime Minister Nehru, who was sensitive to the moral and international implications, is recorded as having chastised the government of East Punjab for its action. See Jagat Mehta, supra at 72.

[18] As a result of India's action, about 5.5 percent of the sown area (and almost 8 percent of the culturable commanded area) in the West Pakistan was without water at the beginning of the critical kharif-sowing phase. The city of Lahore was simultaneously deprived of the main source of municipal water, and incidentally, distribution to the West Pakistan of power from the Mandi Hydroelectric Scheme was also cut off. See Michel, supra note 9, at 196.

[19] See Ali, supra note 13, at 319-320.

[20] Some scholars have noted that India had other politico-economic motives for discontinuing the delivery of water. The motives were: (i) to put pressure on Pakistan to withdraw the "volunteers" from Kashmir; (ii) to use every means at its disposal to wreck Pakistan's economy and demonstrate that it could not succeed as its own nation, therefore bringing it back to India; (iii) and to retaliate for Pakistan's imposition of an export duty on raw jute, leaving the East Bengal for processing in the jute mills of the West Bengal. For detail, see Biswas, supranote 6, at 203; see also Michel, supra note 9, at 196-197.

[21] See Pitman, supra, note 11, at 158. In its arguments, India was asserting, at least by implication, the doctrine of "upstream riparian proprietary rights," which had no historical basis. In effect, India was saying that partition and independence had created a new situation, and that it could proceed from any a priori basis it chose. It could, on the one hand, maintain that it had succeeded to the rights of the British India as a sovereign state. On the other hand, India could assert that because there was no sovereign Pakistan before 1947, there could be no responsibilities of a successor state toward Pakistan. For details, see Michel, supra note 9, at 200.

[22] See Michel, supra note 9, at 202; see also, Mlason and Asher, The World Bank Since Bretton Woods, supra note 2, at 611.

the West Punjab the assurance that it would not suddenly withhold the supply of water without providing sufficient time for the West Punjab to develop alternate sources.[23] The agreement also provided for the gradual diminishing of supply of water to Pakistan, and for Pakistan to tap alternative resources.[24] The West Punjab continued to stress the need for reasonable time to develop alternative resources. Contrary to the expectation, the agreement could not stay intact for long and on issues relating to the interpretation of the agreement, the dispute continued.[25] Although the Inter-Dominion Agreement did not settle many of the issues, it at least blocked out the arguments and provided a modus vivendi until 1960, when it was formally superseded by the Indus Waters Treaty.[26]

Consistent with the conflicting rationales of the two countries, the combination of a series of decisions and actions by India and Pakistan precipitated a dispute that led to Pakistan's formal denouncement of the agreement in 1950. Pakistan proposed that the issue be submitted to the International Court of Justice or the UN Security Council,[27] but India categorically rejected third-party involvement in dispute resolution and urged that the Inter-Dominion Agreement be made permanent.[28]

The stalemate in negotiations was reversed by the visit of David Lilienthal, former Chairman of the Tennessee Valley Authority, and of the United States Atomic Energy Commission, to India and Pakistan in February 1951. Following his visit, Lilienthal wrote an article in which he made a series of recommendations pertaining to the Indus system of rivers. Among others, the recommendations included that the Indus Basin be treated, exploited, and developed as a single unit[29]; that financing be provided by India, Pakistan and the World Bank; and that the Indus be administered by an Indo-Pakistan mixed body or a multinational body.[30] In fact, Lilienthal's proposal was based on a return to a pre-partition premise for the Indus Basin irrigation system. At that time, Mr. Lilienthal believed that the waters from the basin were sufficient to support the needs of the two countries, a belief that would not be confirmed by later studies. But regardless of future studies, Lilienthal's proposal had two notable advantages. It provided a new avenue of negotiations that could be based on technical and engineering data, and it introduced a third party in the negotiations process that was also a potential source of financial assistance.

Eugene Black, the President of the World Bank at the time, acquiesced to Lilienthal's recommendations and decided to react positively to the opportunity.[31] Upon his decision, the World Bank offered its good

---

[23] The Inter-Dominion Agreement between the Government of India and the Government of Pakistan

[24] The Inter-Dominion Agreement between the Government of India and the Government of Pakistan on the canal water dispute between the East and the West Punjab, signed at New Delhi, May 4, 1948, 54 U.N.T.S 45; see also B.C. Upreti, Politics of the Himalayan River Waters: An Analysis of the River Water issues of Nepal, India and Bangladesh (Delhi: Nirala Publication, 1993), at 86-87.

[25] See Fischer, supra note 10, at 671; see also for detail, Gulhati, supra note 2, which deals with the issue in a comprehensive fashion.

[26] See Michel, supra note 9, at 205.

[27] See Fischer supra note 10, at 671. On Pakistan's proposal for submission of the Indus problem to the International Court of Justice, two years later Lihenthal (see infra) had commented that even though the legal position of Pakistan might bring a decision in Pakistan's favor (if India agreed to submit the case), it would be inadequate for the great issues of maintaining peace and providing sufficient food for the people of the Indus Basin. According to Lilienthal, such a decision would antagonize India and certainly would not facilitate active partnership between the two countries in developing their common resource on the six rivers. See for detail, Michel, supra note 9, at 221.

[28] See Michel, supra note 9, at 219.

[29] The problem of Indus, according to Lilienthal, was not a religious or political problem, but a feasible engineering and business problem for which there were plenty of precedents and experiences. But this objective could not be met by the countries working separately. See Michel, supra note 9, at 222.

[30] See Fischer, supra note 10, at 672; see also, for detail, Biswas, supra note 6, at 205; see also, Ali, supra note 13, at 326; it should also be noted that the Indus Basin irrigation system that irrigated some 37 million acres of land was conceived originally as a unified system and considered one of the most extensive and highly developed irrigation systems of the world. See Yunus Khan, "Boundary Conflict Between India and Pakistan,"' Water International 15 (1990), at 195.

[31] See for detail, Wouters, ed., supra note 7, at 16-17. In this context it is also important to note that in 1949, when matters were still undecided between India and Pakistan, India had approached the World Bank for loans for the construction of the Bhakra-

offices for a discussion of the dispute and the negotiation of a settlement, and proposed that a solution to the problem be looked for based purely on technical and engineering grounds. On November 18, 1951, the President of the World Bank proposed the establishment of a working group of engineers which, building on Mr. Lilienthal's recommendations, would deal with the problem of Indus as a single unit without taking into account any past negotiations or political considerations. The World Bank made a clear distinction between the "functional" and "political" aspects of the Indus dispute and asserted that it could most realistically be solved if the functional aspects of disagreement were negotiated apart from political considerations. The World Bank noted that it was important to assess how best to utilize the waters of the Indus Basin while leaving aside questions of historic rights or allocations. India's previous objections to third-party arbitration were remedied by the World Bank's insistence that it would not adjudicate the conflict, but instead work as a conduit for agreement.

Through an understanding dated March 10, 1952, India and Pakistan welcomed the good offices of the World Bank and committed that they would not reduce the supply of water for the other country's actual use until mediation was carried out.[32] While at times both parties failed to comply with their commitments, provisional understandings made it possible to contain the conflict. Each party appointed a Special Commissioner to follow up the implementation of the provisional understandings and to settle any differences. In case a settlement was impossible, negotiations would resume in Washington and each of the two governments could call upon the World Bank to intervene.

The World Bank proposed a comprehensive plan for a joint development of the waters of the basin, but the plan failed to take into account all the sensitive issues and was not endorsed by either party.[33] The World Bank's expectation for a quick resolution to the Indus dispute was premature. Although the Bank had expected that the two sides would come to an agreement on the allocation of waters, neither India nor Pakistan seemed willing to compromise their positions. While Pakistan insisted on its historical right to waters of all the Indus tributaries, India argued that the previous distribution of waters should not determine future allocation. Instead, India set up a new basis of distribution, with the waters of the western tributaries of the Indus allocated to Pakistan and the eastern tributaries allocated to India. The substantive technical discussions that were hoped for were stymied by political considerations.

In the meetings in Karachi in November 1952 and in Delhi in January 1953, the two countries could not agree on a common approach to developing the waters of the Indus system. The World Bank suggested that both countries prepare their own plans. The two countries' water use and allocation plans were submitted to the World Bank on October 6, 1953.[34] They differed significantly. According to the Indian plan, of the 119 million acre-feet (MAF) of total usable water, 29 MAF would be allocated to India and 90 MAF to Pakistan. But according to the Pakistan plan, which estimated 118 MAF of the total usable water, 15.5 MAF would be allocated to India and 102.5 MAF to Pakistan.

Obviously, it was difficult to reconcile the two plans. After some discussions and concessions from both parties, the plans were modified. According to the modified Indian proposal, 7 percent of the waters of the Western Rivers and all waters of the Eastern Rivers were to be allocated to India, whereas 93 percent of the

---

Nangal Multipurpose Project on the Sutlej and the Damodar Valley Project in the State of Bihar. Pakistan had cited the water controversy in its objections to the Indian Bhakra-Nangal Project proposal to the Bank. Only a few weeks before the Lilienthal article appeared, India had also objected to a Pakistani request for financing a barrage at Kotri on the Indus. The Bank was aware of the already strained relations between India and Pakistan and was reluctant to make loans for projects that involved any unresolved disputes, not only because the investment was risky, but also because once built, these projects could exacerbate the existing dispute. See Alam, supra note 4, at 97; see also, Mason and Asher, The World Bank Since Bretton Woods, supranote 2, at 612.

[32] See Michel, supra note 9, at 227.
[33] See generally for detail, Gulhati, supra note 2.
[34] See Biswas, supra note 6, at 206.

waters of the Western Rivers and no water from the Eastern Rivers were to be allocated to Pakistan. But Pakistan's modified proposal was different. It allocated 30 percent of the waters of the Eastern Rivers and none of the Western Rivers to India, and 70 percent of the Eastern Rivers and all of the Western Rivers to Pakistan.[35]

From the proposals and the counter-proposals, it became apparent that political sovereignty and joint development and the use of water resources of a river basin as a single unit were not compatible at all.[36] The only formula that was likely to provide an acceptable basis for settlement was the quantitative division of waters between the two countries, leaving each of the two countries free to carry out its own development independently of the other, and in accordance with its own plans. Indeed, this was the basis for the Bank's revised proposal. It is interesting to note that the Bank's revised proposal signified a complete departure from Lilienthal's proposal to develop the water resources of the Indus Basin as a single unit through the construction of storage dams and other facilities. In fact, the Bank went in the opposite direction in its proposal to divide the water resources of the basin between the two countries on the basis of political boundaries. The Bank envisaged no cooperative development. The justification for this approach was that after transfer works were completed, each country would be independent in the operation of its supplies and avoid the complexities that would arise if the supplies from particular rivers were shared by the two countries.[37] The Bank also explained that its formula of sharing the waters was no mere averaging of the demands of each party, but rather resulted from the Bank's engineers' analysis of the usable supplies on each of the six Indus Rivers.[38]

This new formula, proposed by the World Bank on February 5, 1954, was in principle endorsed, albeit with a few reservations.[39] In fact, India accepted the proposal on March 25, 1954, but Pakistan questioned the proposal's premise that there was enough surplus water in the Western Rivers to replace its irrigation uses on the Eastern Rivers. Pakistan contended that a system of link canals would not be adequate to meet all uses without including storage reservoirs in the replacement works. The Bank agreed to examine Pakistan's contention, and carried out its own independent studies to examine the issues in dispute and to prepare an adequate system of works to replace Pakistan's uses on the Eastern Rivers.[40] The studies confirmed that there was not enough surplus water in the Western Rivers, particularly in the critical crop periods, to replace Pakistan's uses and that storage reservoirs were necessary to meet the shortages. At this juncture, the Bank issued an aide memoire on May 21, 1956 that modified its original proposal and included storage dams in the system of replacement works.[41] Pakistan accepted the modified proposal in 1958, but India disputed the need for storage dams and insisted that its liability should be limited to the original Bank proposal. Recognizing the impossibility of resolving the dispute without additional financing for the huge cost of replacement works, and the fact that neither India nor Pakistan were in a position to bear the costs of the replacement works, the Bank decided to mobilize funds from bilateral donors.[42] At this point, the issue pending in the dispute was practically resolved.

---

[35] See Biswas, supra note 6, at 206.
[36] See Kirmani and Le Moigne, supra note 7, at 4.
[37] See for detail, Ali, supra note 13, at 328. However, one should also note that in terms of the treatment of a river basin as an integrated whole, the Indus Treaty is a success. It embraces to a greater degree the waters falling within the basins of the Indus River and has been successful in providing exact definitions of the notions employed. See Vitanyi, supranote 5, at 208.
[38] See Michel, supra note 9, at 239.
[39] Pakistan's acceptance seems to have been possible particularly because of the coup d'etat that had recently occurred in Pakistan. For detail of the Bank plan, see Alam, supra note 4, at Appendix 5; see also Michel supra note 9, at 235.
[40] See Kirmani and Le Moigne, supranote 7, at 4.
[41] The Aide Memoire recognized that the flow surpluses in the Western Rivers would not be sufficient to meet even the replacement needs in early and late kharif, unless storage was provided. See generally Michel, supra note 9, at 244. The text of the Aide Memoire reproduced in Alam, supranote 4, at Appendix 6; see also, Mason and Asher, supra note 2, at 619.
[42] See infra, Section 11, Part 4 of this chapter.

After almost two years of negotiations on many complex technical, operational and legal issues - the complexity of which are exemplified by the eight annexure the Treaty required - an agreement was finally reached between the parties. On September 19, 1960, the Indus Waters Treaty was signed at Karachi by Field Marshall Mohammad Ayub Khan, then President of Pakistan, and Mr. Jawaharlal Nehru, the then Prime Minister of India. For the purpose of some specific articles, Sir W. A. B. Iliff of the World Bank also became a signatory.[43] As noted by some purists, the legal status of the World Bank as a party to the Indus Treaty is not equal to that of India and Pakistan.[44] However, the World Bank, as shall be discussed later, played a crucial role in the Treaty, much more from a functional rather than a normative perspective.

II. The Indus Treaty Regime

The Indus Treaty is a complex instrument whose basic approach was to increase the amount of water available to the two parties and to apportion the water resources of the Indus equitably between them.[45] It is indeed a complete Treaty in view of its objectives. It has normative as well as functional values as it contains, in addition to the substantive rules regarding the regime of the Indus system of rivers, provisions regarding the implementation of an administrative and institutional mechanism and the management of the basin resources. These two categories of rules aim at resolving the dispute and maintaining peace between the two countries through contributing to their development.

The Governments of India and Pakistan desired the most complete and satisfactory utilization of the waters of the Indus system of rivers.[46] The primary objective was to fix and delimit the rights and obligations of each country's use of the waters in relation to the other. With its preamble, followed by 12 articles and eight annexures (including appendices), the Indus Treaty attempts comprehensively to deal with the issues of water allocation and the flow of water. Crafted by technicians and engineers rather than lawyers and diplomats, the Indus Treaty is complex and prolix, despite its apparent brevity. The complexity was, perhaps, inevitable, but some articles are of unusual length.[47]

The eight Annexures are quite elaborate and deal with issues that are technical in nature. While Annexure A, written in the form of exchange of notes, specifies the extinction, on April 1, 1960, of the May 4, 1948 Agreement, Annexure B deals with the use of certain tributaries of the Ravi by Pakistan for agricultural purposes. Similarly, while Annexure C provides details regarding the use of the Western Rivers by India, Annexures D and E respectively deal with the supply by India of hydropower from some Western Rivers and with the stocking by India of water from such Western Rivers. Annexures F and G of the Treaty deal respectively with the appointment of neutral experts and the constitution of an arbitral tribunal. Finally, Annexure H provides details on specific transitional measures.

---

[43] Along with the Indus Waters Treaty, on September 19, 1960, two other agreements were concluded. The first agreement, the Indus Basin Development Fund Agreement, was between Australia, Canada, The Federal Republic of Germany, New Zealand, Pakistan, the United Kingdom and the United States of America, and the International Bank for Reconstruction and Development. The second one, pertaining to the implementation of the Indus Basin Project, was a Loan Agreement between The Republic of Pakistan and the International Bank For Reconstruction and Development (Loan No 266 PAK); see also, Mason and Asher, supra note 2, at 626.

[44] See Fischer, supra note 10, at 675; see also Yvon-Claude Accariez, "Le Regime Juridique de l'Indus," in The Legal Regime of International Rivers and Lakes, Ralph Zacklin and Lucius Caflisch, eds. (The Hague: Marinus Nijhoff, 1981), at 61.

[45] See Stephen C. McCaffrey, "Water, Politics and the International Law," supra note 17, at 95. It is also worth noting that one interesting aspect of the Treaty is that it only refers to distribution of waters, but remains silent on the issue of navigation.

[46] See preamble to the Treaty.

[47] For instance, Article 10 on "emergency" consists of two sentences that contain 33 lines. This style of treaty drafting often leads to ambiguity.

1. The Principle of Water Sharing: The Eastern and Western Rivers

Briefly put, the waters of the three Eastern Rivers (the Ravi, Beas, and Sutlej) were allocated to India, subject to a duty during a transition period of 10 years to supply a certain quantum of water to Pakistan while Pakistan was carrying out the necessary construction works on the Western Rivers to replace its Eastern Rivers sources.[48]

Pakistan received the flow of the Western Rivers (the Indus, Jhelum and Chenab), subject to the right of India to use some of the water for irrigation, the generation of hydroelectric power, and other designated purposes before the rivers crossed into Pakistan.[49] Pakistan was to refrain from any interference with the waters of the Sutlej Main and the Ravi Main and of their tributaries until the rivers had finally flowed into Pakistan, but was permitted, by way of exception to take water for domestic use, non-consumptive use and certain limited agricultural use.[50] Similarly, India was to refrain from any interference with the waters of the Indus, the Jhelum and the Chenab, except for domestic use, non-consumptive use, and certain limited agricultural use and power generation.[51]

During the 10-year transitional period,[52] India was to limit its withdrawals for agricultural use, to limit its abstractions for storage, and to make deliveries to Pakistan from the Eastern Rivers.[53] The period of transition could be extended for further periods up to a total of three years if Pakistan required additional time to secure replacement waters, but was in no event to terminate later than March 31, 1973.[54] Elaborate provisions governed the supply of water during the period of transition.[55] Water was to be supplied from the Ravi for the Central Bari Doab Channels, which prior to August 14, 1947, formed a part of the Upper Bari Doab Canal System.[56] India was to limit its withdrawals from the Sutlej Main and the Beas component at Ferozepore in kharif during the first phase of transition, running from 1960 to 1965.[57] From 1965 through the remainder of the period of transition, India had to furnish designated quantities of water in kharif[58]. During rabi, India was likewise under an obligation to provide at Ferozepore water from the Sutlej and Beas, in quantities specified in the Treaty, for use in the Pakistan Sutjej valley canals.[59] Pakistan was to compensate India for its proportionate share of the working expenses for headworks, such as those at Madhopur and Ferozepore, and carrier channels relied upon for the furnishing of waters to Pakistan.[60] But if Pakistan were to request extension, it would have to pay graduated charges for the water itself.

Every conceivable safeguard that Pakistan's engineers and lawyers could suggest was included to prevent India from altering the amount or the timing of its water supplies to Pakistan during the transition period. The portions of the "distributable supply" that India was to furnish to the Central Bari Doab Channels are specified not only for rabi and kharif but for six intervals within these periods. Provisions are made for India to reduce supplies if the "distributable supply" falls below certain levels, if closures are necessary

---

[48] Article II of the Treaty; see also for detail, Baxter, supra note 15, at 467.
[49] Article III
[50] Article 11 (2) through (4).
[51] Article III (2). For detailed mechanism, see Annexures C and D.
[52] Beginning on April 1, 1960 and ending March 31, 1970, or if extended, the date up to which it has been extended, but in any manner not later than March 31, 1973.
[53] Article 11 (5).
[54] Annexures H, part 8, and Article 11 (6).
[55] Annexure H. It should be noted that historically, a supply of 8.27 MAF was being delivered during kharif at Madhopore and Ferozepore for use in Pakistan canals. In Phase 1, this supply was to be reduced by 4.7-5.0 MAF and with the beginning of Phase 11, it was to be reduced further by about 2.5 MAF. See Statement of the Indian Minister of Irrigation and Power, Fortnightly News Digest (New Delhi), 7:No.21:605-6, India, Lok Sabha Secretariat, (November 1-15, 1960), at 606.
[56] Annexure H part 2.
[57] Annexure H part 3.
[58] Annexure H part 4.
[59] Annexure H part 5.
[60] Annexure H part 7.

for safety, operations or maintenance, or if Pakistan has completed the highest links (Rasul-Quadirabad and Quadirabad-Balloki). With regard to the Sutlej Valley canals, the transition period is divided into two phases: Phase I up to a point between March 31, 1965 and March 31, 1966, and Phase II from the end of Phase I to the end of the transition period.[61]

Because Pakistan was no longer to have water from the Eastern Rivers, a system of works was required in order to transfer water from the Western Rivers to the canal system of Pakistan.[62] These works would confer a number of benefits on Pakistan. They would permit substantial additional irrigation development, develop 3,000,000 kW of hydroelectric potential, contribute to soil reclamation and drainage by lowering water levels in water-logged and saline areas, and give some protection from floods[63]. Eight link canals, nearly 400 miles in length, were to be constructed or remodeled in order to transfer 14 million acre-feet of water. An earth-fill storage dam was to be built on the Jhelum River (Mangla Dam) with a live reservoir capacity of 4.75 million-acre feet. On the Indus, another earth-fill dam (Tarbela) would permit live storage of 4.2 million-acre feet. Together, the dams would compensate for seasonal fluctuations in supplies of water and would permit the irrigation of additional areas in Pakistan. Additional works would be needed in order to integrate the existing system with the new link canals that were to be constructed. Three barrages (Qadirabad, the Ravi River, and tje Sutlej River) were designed to carry canals across the rivers. Five existing barrages and eight existing canals were to be modified. At the Jhelum Dam, there was to be a power station with a capacity of more than 300,000 kW.[64] It is interesting to note that the Treaty allows each country to develop hydropower independently. From this angle, the Treaty is an example of water trade-off, rather than water-sharing.[65]

2. The Principle of Cooperation Between the Parties

The Indus Treaty acknowledges that both India and Pakistan have an interest in the optimum development of the rivers, and to that effect provides for cooperation and collaboration between the two countries. At the request of the either party, the two parties may, by mutual agreement, cooperate in undertaking engineering works of the rivers. The formal arrangements, in each case, shall be as agreed upon between the parties. The Treaty also provides for the exchange of data. Both countries agreed to monthly exchanges of data on the subjects of: (i) daily gauge and discharge data relating to flow of the rivers at all observation sites; (ii) daily extractions for or releases from reservoirs; (iii) daily withdrawals at the heads of all canals operated by government or any agency thereof, including link canals; (iv) daily escapages from all canals, including link canals; and (v) daily deliveries from link canals.[66] These data were to be transmitted monthly by each party to the other as soon as the data for a calendar month have been collected and tabulated, but not later than three months after the end of the month to which they relate.[67]

If either party plans to construct any engineering work that would cause interference with the waters of any of the rivers and, in its opinion, that would affect the other party materially, it shall notify the other party of its plans and shall supply such data relating to the work as may be available and as would enable

---

[61] See Michel, supra note 9, at 256.
[62] See generally Baxter, supra note 15, at 468.
[63] Id.
[64] See id.
[65] C. K. Sharma, A Treatise on Water Resources of Nepal (Sangeeta Sharma, 1997), at 436.
[66] See Article VI.
[67] An article by a Pakistani official in the early 1990s pointed out that India has not complied with some of its obligations under the treaty. India has, inter alia, failed to share data, has developed new hydroelectric projects on Western Rivers, has constructed the Wuller Barrage and carried out storage works on the Jhelum Main without informing Pakistan, and created a live storage capacity behind the barrage far in excess of Treaty allowance. See M. Y. Khan, "Boundary Water Conflict between India and Pakistan," 15 Water International, at 195, abstracted in Transboundary Resources Report, 5 (1), Spring 1991, International Transboundary Resource Center.

the other party to inform itself of the nature, magnitude and effect of the work. If a work would cause interference with the waters of any of the rivers but would not, in the opinion of the party planning it, affect the other party materially, the party planning the work shall nevertheless, on request, supply the other party with such data regarding the nature, magnitude and effect of the work as may be available.

In addition to the above details, the Treaty also contains certain technical, procedural and institutional provisions designed to promote cooperation and problem solving. Among others, the provisions specify that the two parties would continue to maintain the equipment so as not to prejudice the other party and that they would avoid polluting the waters of the Indus system of rivers. Also Pakistan was required to maintain the actual capacity of the drainage system, and if India asked for the enlargement or additional digging of the drainage canals, Pakistan would carry out the works with Indian finance. In this connection, a provision of the Treaty recognizes the common interest in the optimum development of the rivers and stresses the intention of the parties to cooperate fully.[68]

3. The Dispute Resolution Mechanism and the Permanent Indus Commission

The Indus Treaty establishes a complex system for dispute settlement. The Permanent Indus Commission examines all disputes, in the first instance. From there onward, two procedures are envisaged depending on the nature of the conflict: disputes that are purely technical in nature, and disputes that are of a grave and serious nature that cannot be examined by a neutral expert.

A Permanent Indus Commission consisting of two Commissioners (one appointed by India and another by Pakistan) was to establish and maintain cooperative arrangements for the implementation of the Indus Treaty. The commission was to promote cooperation between the parties in the development of the waters of the rivers, and in particular to study matters referred to it to help resolve questions conerning the interpretation or application of the Treaty, and to make tours of inspection.[69] It may be noted that the Indus Commission was inspired by the International Joint Commission established by the United States and Canada.[70] The Commissioner, unless either government decides to take up any particular question directly with the other govemment, is the representative of his government for all matters arising out of the Treaty and serves as the regular channel of communication on all matters relating to the implementation of the Treaty.

The Commission is required to meet at least once a year, alternately in India and Pakistan. The Commission shall also meet when requested by either Commissioner.

The programs of meetings are generally finalized in a meeting of the Commission. As the Commission comprises the two commissioners who are the representatives of their governments, the decision on a matter can only be taken by agreement. There is no voting involved as the two commissioners have to agree or disagree in regard to a particular matter after discussion. The two Commissioners are assisted by their advisers. There is no restriction on the number of advisers required to assist a Commissioner in a meeting. No participation by the public at any phase of the decision-making is envisaged in the Treaty. The Treaty also does not provide for any contact of the Commission as a body with governmental authorities, agencies or departments of member countries at the national, regional or local level.[71]

---

[68] For detail on notification, exchange of information, and cooperation, see Article VII.
[69] See for detail Article VIII; see also Baxter, supra note 15, at 471; see also Statement of the Minister of Irrigation and Power, supra note 46, at 605; it should also be noted that the original intent ofthe Bank's plan was to avoid the establishment of any continuing Joint administration of the Indus Basin irrigation system. However, a permanent commission was desired later to oversee the implementation of the Treaty and to settle any questions that might arise thereunder. See Michel, supra note 9, at 260.
[70] See Baxter, supra note 15, at 471.
[71] See generally, the Indus Treaty; see also, Khan, supra note 67, at 196-197.

The Commission as a body does not have funds of its own. The respective governments bear the expenses of the organization headed by its Commissioner and also bear the expenses of the Commission meetings in its country. To enable the Commissioners to perform their functions in the Commission, each government has agreed to accord to the Commissioner of the other government the same privileges and immunities as are accorded to the representatives of the member states to the principal and subsidiary organs of the United Nations.[72] The Commission is required to submit to the two governments, before June 1 every year, a report on its work for the year ending on the preceding March 31, and may submit to the two governments other reports at such times as it may think desirable.[73]

Elaborate provisions concerning the settlement of differences and disputes are included in the Treaty. The task of dealing with disputed questions in the first instance falls to the Permanent Indus Commission.[74] If the Commission cannot agree, either Commissioner may, by certifying that the matter falls within one of 23 designated areas, have the "difference" deferred to a neutral expert who is to be a highly qualified engineer.[75] How the matter is to be laid before the neutral expert and how it is to be resolved by him are the subjects of detailed provision. If the "difference" does not fall under one of the 23 categories or the neutral expert decides that the "difference" should be treated as a "dispute," the governments are to negotiate with the assistance of mediators if they so desire. Finally, the "dispute" may be laid before a Court of Arbitration if the parties agree to do so or at the request of either party if the dispute is not likely to be resolved by negotiation or mediation or one party or the other considers that the other is "unduly delaying the negotiations." A Court of Arbitration is to consist of seven members, two to be designated by each of the parties, and the other three to be selected by agreement of the parties or, failing that, by designated individuals. The three neutral "umpires" are to be respectively a person qualified to be chairman of the Court of Arbitration, an engineer, and an international lawyer.[76] The parties were to endeavor to put together a Standing Panel of Umpires, from whom the selections might be made. The constitution and procedure of the Court of Arbitration were spelled out in an Annexure to the Treaty.[77] It is noteworthy that the applicable law includes the Treaty, and for purposes of the interpretation and application of the Treaty, and in order, (i) the international conventions establishing the rules explicitly recognized by India and Pakistan, and (ii) the customary international law.

4. Principle of Basin Administration: The Indus Basin Development Fund

In the context of maintaining an ever-lasting peace, and in addition to the general scope of responsibilities pertaining to the administration of the Indus Basin assumed by the Permanent Indus Commission, the Indus Treaty also envisages assistance in basin administration from bilateral and multilateral organizations, including, and in particular, the World Bank. In order to carry out a series of works in the basin, and recognizing that the sizable work was not in the capacity of Pakistan to finance, the World Bank had been instrumental in the creation of an Indus Basin Development Fund. Financial contribution for the Fund was provided by several countries, including in addition to the World Bank itself, Australia, Canada, Germany, New Zealand, Pakistan, the United Kingdom and the United States of America. These countries agreed to contribute grant money to the establishment and functioning of the Indus Basin Development Fund.[78]

---

[72] Id., at 197.
[73] Id., at 197.
[74] Article IX (1).
[75] Article IX (2), in conjunction with Annexure F.
[76] See generally Article IX and Annexure G.
[77] Id.
[78] During the negotiations of the Treaty, the World Bank had made a distinction between works needed to replace water when the basin was divided between India and Pakistan, and the development works desired to enhance water use by both countries. In this connection, to address the financial liability question, the World Bank had determined the principle of "beneficiary pays," which meant that works would be paid for by the country that benefited. India was willing to pay for the replacement works in

In consideration of the fact that the purpose of part of the system of works to be constructed was the replacement of supplies that had hitherto come from the Eastern Rivers (allocated to India pursuant to the Treaty), India agreed to pay a fixed contribution of 62,060,000 Sterling Pounds toward the cost of the works.[79] The payment was to be made in 10 equal annual installments on November 1 each year.[80] In addition, two loans to Pakistan (from the United States of America and from the World Bank) were also provided. Pakistan also agreed to provide a contribution to the Indus Basin Development Fund. The World Bank was designated administrator of the Fund.

The Indus Basin Development Fund consisted approximately of 900 million dollars to finance the construction of irrigation and other works in Pakistan, made up of 640 million dollars provided by participating governments, 174 million dollars payable by India and 80 million dollars loan from the World Bank. The program for construction work in Pakistan included, interalia, eight link canals nearly 400 miles long for transferring water from the Western Rivers to areas formerly irrigated by the Eastern Rivers; two storage dams, one on the Jhelum and the other on the Indus; power stations; 2,500 tubewells; and other works to integrate the whole river and canal system.[81]

The Indus settlement also envisaged the construction of a storage dam on the Beas River in India which, together with the Bhakra Dam on the Sutlej and the Rajasthan canal, was to irrigate new areas in India. However, it is appropriate to note that the works to be carried out in India did not come within the scope of the Indus Basin Development Fund.

In the context of the administration of the basin, it is important to stress the role of the World Bank. Indeed, the World Bank played an important role in the resolution of the Indus dispute.[82] As mentioned earlier, the signatories to the Treaty were not only India and Pakistan, but also the World Bank. The World Bank representative signed the Treaty only for the purposes of Article V (Financial Provisions) and Article X (Emergency Provision), and the Annexures F,G and H (on Neutral Expert, Court of Arbitration, and Transitional Arrangements, respectively). The provisions of the Treaty specify the role of the World Bank. For instance, if, at the request of Pakistan, the transition period was extended, the World Bank was required to pay to India, out of the Indus Basin Development Fund, amounts specified in the Agreement.[83]

If at any time the execution of works is unfavorably affected by hostilities beyond Pakistan's control, the World Bank would provide its good offices, with a view to reaching a mutual agreement as to whether any modifications of the provisions of the Treaty are appropriate and advisable under the circumstances.[84] The World Bank is also required to inform India and Pakistan of the eventual completion of the work prior to the end of the transition period.[85] If in the course of the work, the junction canals suffered from damage due to flood, the two permanent Commissioners would consult and would call upon the good offices of the World Bank in order to introduce provisional modifications to the work program.[86] Finally, the World Bank was

---

Pakistan, but not development works. Pakistan, on the other hand, insisted that there was no distinction to be made because the development works were based upon pre-partition plans, and thus it was logical for India to also pay for the development works in Pakistan. By applying the "beneficiary pays" principle and establishing the Indus Basin Development Fund, the World Bank was able to overcome this financial obstacle. See generally, Syed S. Kirmani, "Water, Peace and Conflict Management: The Experience of the Indus and Mekong River Basins," in Water International15 (1990), at 201-202.

[79] Article V (1).
[80] Article V (2).
[81] See Ali, supra note 13, at 330.
[82] Statement of the Minister of Irrigation and Power, supra note 55, at 606
[83] See Article V (5).
[84] See Article X.
[85] See Annexure H, paragraph 66.
[86] See Annexure H, paragraph 65.

also vested with responsibilities to designate the Neutral Expert, fix the remuneration, and to nominate the President of the Court of Arbitration.[87]

The role of the World Bank as Administrator of the Indus Basin Development Fund is also noteworthy. Twice a year, the Bank furnishes the reports to the parties to the Indus Basin Development Fund agreement (which, it needs to be emphasized, excludes India). Also, notification to the parties would be sent by the World Bank if unexpected events affected the completion of the Project by Pakistan, funds were considered insufficient, and Pakistan failed to fulfill its obligations. In case there was breach of obligation by Pakistan, the Bank also reserved the right to suspend all disbursements. In connection with the Indus Basin Development Fund, the disputes were to be settled by a single arbitrator, and in case that became impossible, by the Secretary General of the United Nations.

The establishment of the Indus Basin Development Fund and the role played by the World Bank therein are particularly noteworthy illustrations of the potential role of international financing organizations that are able to mobilize expertise and sizable international financial resources for development.[88] At various stages, the World Bank could politely impose its independent proposals.[89] Pakistan, being a lower riparian, was not prepared to risk the breakdown of negotiations for that reason. India's own second five-year plan depended on massive economic aid from the World Bank and from the developed World Bank member countries. These exogenous factors enhanced the effective role of the World Bank in the negotiations.[90] Indeed, the World Bank did not have political power but its ability to bring together several countries with the financial commitment was a kind of quasi-imperial third-party inducement to the successful resolution of the dispute.[91] The Herculean effort by the World Bank in bringing India and Pakistan to the mediating table and keeping them there until the Treaty was signed is also a testimony to the Bank's commitment to resolving international water disputes.[92] Overall, the role of the World Bank, as noted by some scholars, has been proactive, neutral, pragmatic and fair.[93] The World Bank was pragmatic enough to give up its ideal of the unified development of the basin and propose a workable solution based on the division of rivers.[94]

III. Conclusion

The Indus Treaty is an excellent example of the settlement of riparian issues and one of the few examples of a successful settlement of a major international river basin conflict.[95] Also, it is the first dispute regarding water use in which an international organization played a successful mediating role in resolution. Even if it was far from an optimum economic solution and failed to cover vital drainage issues, the Treaty is regarded as a major achievement as it has been able to divide the Indus and its tributaries unambiguously between the riparians.[96] The fact that there were six rivers in the system offered the simple solution of the three Western Rivers (the Indus, Jhelum and Chenab) being reserved for consumptive use by Pakistan, and the three Eastern Rivers (the Ravi, Beas and Sutlej) being reserved for consumptive use by India. The Treaty's

---

[87] See Article IX, Annexures F and G.
[88] Wolfgang Friedman et al., International Law Cases and Material (St. Paul: West Publishing,1969), at 628.
[89] See Mehta, supra note 17, at 75.
[90] Id.
[91] Id.
[92] See Alam, supra note 4, at 179.
[93] See Kirnani and Le Moigne, supra note 7, at 5
[94] Id.
[95] See Mehta, supranote 17, at 69; see also Alam, supranote 4, at I (Introduction).
[96] Opinions have been expressed that the agreement was a triumph of the lesser evil. In terms of optimum gains that could be derived from the total waters of the Indus Basin, by treating the basin as an ecological and economic unity, one must, at least, hypothetically, recognize the great opportunity costs in repudiating the investment in the existing network of irrigation canals. But in the circumstances in the Sub-continent, the Treaty was the most politically feasible solution. See Mehta, supra note 17, at 69-70.

originality has contributed importantly to its success. The allocation of the waters of the three rivers to India and three to Pakistan is in the nature of a territorial division.[97] Since the Treaty was signed, the two parties have not had to deal jointly with water administration other than to enforce the Treaty's terms and iron out some practical difficulties.[98] The Treaty has also set an optimistic tone. Thanks to protracted negotiations, the dispute that had brought the two countries to the brink of war was resolved with the emergence of an effective Treaty.[99] Also noteworthy is the fact that the critical discussions were taken at a political level, but the protracted and complex negotiations were between senior professional engineers. India's chief negotiator was always an irrigation engineer and Pakistan was represented for some time by an engineer who was replaced by a senior administrative civil servant.[100] It follows, then, that in delicate issues involving rivers shared among nations, the decision-makers at the highest level of government must be brought into the process.

One can also assume that the growing realization of a common and mutual interest in the Indus Basin Project provided the real basis for the agreement.[101] Indeed, some amount of dissatisfaction was noted by the parties. In India, it was widely felt that Pakistan obtained a better position from the Treaty for potential development. Seventy-nine percent of the total volume of waters (the statistical average of the three rivers) was made available to Pakistan, whereas the Eastern Rivers earmarked for India equalled only the balance of 21 percent.[102] On the other hand, Pakistan had its own complaints pertaining to an additional commitment for the storage of water. Pakistan was able to obtain this additional storage, in 1964, through a supplemental agreement on the storage project at Tarbela on the Indus.[103]

From the standpoint of international water law, the finalization of the Treaty confirms the resolution that international disputes are not necessarily a problem linked only with the interpretation of existing rules, but also with the drafting of new rules. To that extent, the dispute often may not necessarily be resolved by the usual judicial or arbitral methods.[104]

The Treaty, in accordance with Article 12, was deemed to have entered into force retroactively on April 1, 1960. This was, it should be emphasized, not only prior to the date of exchange of instruments of ratification (which occurred on January 12, 1961), but prior to the date of the execution of the Treaty. This element should, indeed, be noted because it is a practice rarely found in conventional international law.[105]

The Indus Waters Treaty is one of the most shining examples of dispute resolution because it contributes not only to the solution of an international dispute but also to the development of a scheme. The scheme compensates Pakistan for the diversion to Indian usage of certain river waters that irrigated parts of what is

---

[97] Harald D. Frederiksen et al., Water Resource Management In Asia (Vol. 1), World Bank Technical Paper No. 212 (1993), at 23.
[98] Id.; it should be noted that after almost four decades, the Treaty does not include China and Afghanistan, which also share part of the Indus.
[99] See Jayanta Bandyopadhya and Dipak Gyewali, "Ecological and Political Aspects of Himalayan Water Resource Management," in Water Nepal (Ajaya Dixit, ed. September 1994), Vol 4. No.1, at 20.
[100] See Mehta, supra note 17, at 74.
[101] See New York Times (Editorial), March 2, 1960.
[102] See Mehta, supra note 17, at 73.
[103] In connection with this, some scholars argue that the fact that Pakistan had become a United States ally in the CENTO and SEATO gave Pakistan an intangible political advantage and diplomatic leverage. It is still important to note that the overriding consideration that propelled the World Bank and its developing partners to satisfy the demand of Pakistan was the fear of an Indo-Pakistan war precipitated by non-resolution of the Indus Waters Dispute. See Mehta, supra note 17, at 73.
[104] Charles Rousseau, "Inde et Pakistan: Conclusion du traite du 19 septembre 1960 relatif a' l'utilisation des eaux de l'Indus," in Revue generalede droit internationalpublic (1961), at 376.
[105] Id.. at 375. One reason for parties to agree on a retroactive application of the Treaty (as of April 1, 1960) was that the transition period started on that date, as per Article 11(6) of the Treaty. The retroactive effect of the Treaty was meant to serve this practical purpose. During negotiations, indeed, the 10-year transition period (see supra note 52 and the accompanying text) was already agreed to have begun on April 1, 1960. It was, therefore, important for the Treaty to become applicable as of that date. India, it should be noted, was to continue to supply Pakistan with water in the Central Bari Doab Channels and in the Sutlej Valley systems during the transition period.

now Pakistan prior to partition. In that sense, it is not "development aid" for Pakistan but "replacement aid" following one of the exigencies of partition.[106]

As noted by an eminent scholar, the Indus settlement was reached not merely by agreement on a solution of the dispute but by change in the factual situation that had formed the basis of the dispute.[107] Instead of a limited and insufficient quantity of water to quarrel over, the supply of water would be increased to a level that would permit the needs of both parties to be met sufficiently. From the perspective of international law, there is reason to applaud the novel approach. All the existing rights and obligations were wiped clean to start discussions afresh. The negotiated settlement terminated any claims that India, the upper riparian, had to the waters of the Indus on the basis of prior appropriation.[108]

Several key factors contributed to the successful conclusion of the Indus Treaty. The fact that an international organization got involved as a third party to help resolve the dispute; the fact that a solution based on well known principles of developing water resources of a river basin as a single hydrological unit was dropped, and that a unique solution based on the division of rivers was proposed, and the fact that when the solution proved too costly for India to finance, the third party mobilized the needed resources are the most notable factors.[109] A third party or parties (whether countries or organizations) are often very useful in mediating conflicts or disputes as they influence the belligerent's behavior by exploiting the strength of their own position. The third-party mediators can use their leverage. However, the Indus settlement provides the example of an opposite technique: the rewarding of cooperation. By providing Pakistan with the resources needed to control its own water supply, the World Bank, in effect, bought one party its objective, while relieving the other, India, of the burden of the dispute."[110] Indus was thus a settlement in which both parties were able to realize their goals with the aid of outside intervention.[111]

The brief overview of the treaty regime permits us to draw three instructive conclusions.

The first conclusion relates to the issue of exclusive appropriation of water by one riparian state. Under the theory of exclusive appropriation (more commonly known as the Harmon doctrine), which is based on the notion of absolute territorial sovereignty, an upper riparian, in a successive watercourse, enjoys an

---

[106] See 1. M. D. Little and J. M. Clifford, International Aid: A Discussion of the Flow of Public Resources From Rich to Poor Countries(Chicago: Aldine Publishing, 1968), at 225.
[107] See Baxter, supra note 15, at 476.
[108] While the Treaty has achieved, as expected by the negotiators and the mediator, equitable apportionment of Indus waters, the Treaty itself, in Article II (paragraph 2), expressly provides that nothing it contains is to be construed by the parties as in any way establishing any general principle of law or precedent. Due to this provision, Professor McCaffrey believes that the two countries could presumably revert to their fundamental legal postures in any future water dispute that was not governed by the Indus Treaty. See Stephen C. McCaffrey, Water Politics and International Law, supra note 17, at 95. But Professor Baxter views this provision differently, and thinks that despite the stated intention of the Treaty, a provision of this nature cannot keep others from looking to the settlement as a precedent or from deriving what general principles they choose from the terms agreed upon. See Baxter, supra note 15, at 476. Along those lines, Professor Lipper, citing this attempt "...expressly to negate any precedential value (the Treaty) might otherwise have," commented that "of course, if the general thesis were to be accepted that treaties were mere bargains without international law-making effect, a major source of international law would be eliminated. Fortunately, no such thesis has found its way into international legal practice." See Jerome Lipper, "Equitable Utilization," in The Law of International Drainage Basins (Garretson et al.), at 35. A similar approach was adopted in another Treaty between the United States of America and the United States of Mexico pertaining to the "Distribution of the Water of Rio Grande" dated May 21, 1906. Article IV of the said Treaty states that "the delivery ofwater [as herein] provided is not to be construed as a recognition by the United States of any claim on the part of Mexico to the said waters..." see Treaties and Other International Agreements of the United States of America, 1776-1949 (compiled under the direction of Charles 1.Bevans), 1972.
[109] See Kirmani and Le Moigne, supra note 7, at 5.
[110] This is, however, not to suggest that money was the only problem and reason that allowed the Indus Treaty to be signed. But, with hindsight, one can safely note that in the final stage of the negotiations, when almost everything but the resource issue was settled, it would have been risky to prolong the negotiations by discussing which country should pay for the work. So, clearly, the resource aspect was also one piece of the puzzle, albeit not the most important.
[111] See J. G. Mernls, Internlational Dispute Settlement (Cambridge: Grotius Publication Ltd., 1991), at 37.

exclusive status. In the case of the Indus, India tried its best to use this thesis to support its arguments.[112] In addition to the Harmon doctrine, India also invoked the thesis of its economic development needs to justify its claims on the waters of the Indus. Coupled with the Harmon doctrine, the argument based on economic needs brought a third notion according to which the waters of an international river should be reasonably and equitably utilized. This notion, based on the principle of limited territorial sovereignty, recognizes the existence of reciprocal rights and obligations of riparian states and from that emerged the duty to compensate.

The second conclusion relates to the issue of compensation. The solution proposed in the Indus Treaty recognizes the notion of compensation. In 1947, India had claimed an amount of Rs. 150,000,000 from Pakistan to compensate for the loss of water due to the canals built under the British rule[113]. A year later, India accepted the principle of payment of compensation in favor of Pakistan for the deviation of water in the Indian Territory. Finally, the Treaty provides for a financial contribution of India, for the development of the Indus Basin, which was essentially meant to be for carrying out works in Pakistan territory. India contributed to the investment in Pakistan so that benefit flows could be secured as per schedules.[114] The acceptance of compensation also meant that the country endorsed the notion of limited sovereignty of the riparian state. Acceptance also implied the rejection of the prior use notion, and more importantly meant that in order to serve the reciprocal interests best, it was important to effectively apply the principle of equitable water sharing and the theory of equitable utilization.[115]

The third conclusion, thus, is related to water sharing between riparian states. The fact that the Indus Treaty does not specify the quantity of water allocated has led some scholars to believe that the Treaty effectively provides for a territorial type of sharing.[116] The Treaty merely reaffirms the territorial sovereignty of each state on different watercourses. It does not modify the boundary between the two countries but traces a fictitious line East-West that divides the basin and limits the sovereign rights of use of each state to one half of the river system, and grants quasi-exclusive rights on the other half. In fact, it is neither a territorial nor a quantitative division, but a division that concerns only the use of the water, an excellent example in contemporary international law of rivers. This kind of division is what explains the predominantly political and economic, not legal, reasoning behind the Treaty.

---

[112] Similar efforts were made by several countries in the past, such as Austria in its dispute against Hungary and Bavaria in the beginning of the twentieth century, USA in its dispute against Mexico in connection with the Rio Grande, and Canada against the USA in connection with the North American border waters.

[113] Under the Bntish rule, Bikaner State had to pay seigniorage charges to the Punjab for supplying water, and proportionate maintenance costs for the Ferozepur headwork and the feeder canal located in Punjab territory. The East Punjab, based on this precedent, claimed that the West Punjab must pay similar costs. Whether reluctant or not, West Punjab agreed to pay seigniorage charges, proportionate maintenance costs, and interest on a proportionate amount of capital. However, at the Inter-Dominion conference, Pakistan challenged the calculation by which the seigniorage charges and capital cost of the Upper Bari Doab Canal for interest charges were made. The West Punjab government agreed, in turn, to pay seigniorage charges for the cost of transporting water through canals in East Punjab, and give its share of any maintenance costs. As the dispute over the calculation of seigniorage remained unresolved, the portion that was held in dispute was decided to be held in escrow. This amount would be decided by the Indian Prime Minister. It was also agreed that further talks would be held to achieve a mutually acceptable solution. This issue of disputed seigniorage charges had dominated bilateral discussions between India and Pakistan and had reached an impasse by the time the World Bank came to intervene. In the meantime, both countries continued to construct works that would safeguard their water supply, either existing or planned. The matter of the seigniorage charges was only resolved in 1960, in the final stages of the drafting of the Indus Waters Treaty. See, for detail, Alam, supra note 4, at 63-65.

[114] See Kamala Prasad, "Priority and Institutional Development," in Water Nepal (Ajaya Dixit, ed. September 1994), Vol 4., No.1, at 220.

[115] See Vitanyi, supra note 5, at 346.

[116] 1t6 See Accariez, supra note 44, at 68.

CHAPTER – 13

Margalla Papers

2011

Special Edition

"Pakistan's Water Security Dilemma: Re- Visiting the Efficacy of Indus Waters Treaty"

National Defence University
Sector E-9 Islamabad
Pakistan
www.ndu.edu.pk

Paper One:

The Indus Waters Treaty Under Stress: Imperatives Of Climatic Change Or Political Manipulation

Engineer Syed Jamait Ali Shah

Abstract

At the time of independence, the boundary line between the two newly created independent countries, i.e. Pakistan and India, was drawn right across the Indus Basin, leaving Pakistan as the lower riparian. Dispute thus arose between the two countries regarding the utilization of irrigation waters from existing facilities. The negotiations, held under the World Bank, culminated in the signing of the Indus Waters Treaty in 1960. In view of the intent and the spirit of the treaty, Pakistan expects that Indian projects on the western rivers would fall strictly in accordance with the provisions of the Indus Waters Treaty so that the water rights, as envisaged through the treaty, would appropriately be honoured. Though it is true that climatic factors are becoming important to adjudge their effects on flows in river systems, but it is also pertinent to mention that while such factors are being evaluated, Pakistan should make every effort for optimal development of its water resource available through the western rivers. This is probably the only solution available to Pakistan not only to cope with the risk of water scarcity, but also for the wider water resource management, both in view of the climate change, as well as the likely political manipulation of the Indus Waters Treaty by India.

Introduction

The Indus System of rivers in the Indus Basin comprises of river Indus and its five main tributaries i.e. Jhelum, Chenab, Ravi, Beas and Sutlej. They all combine into one river near Mithan Kot in Pakistan, which outfalls into the Arabian Sea at the south of Karachi. The boundary of the Indus Basin is clearly defined in the west, the north and the northeast by mountain ridges (watersheds).[1]

The total area of the Indus Basin is roughly 350,000 square miles. Most of it lies in Pakistan and the rest in Occupied Jammu and Kashmir, India, China and Afghanistan. The climate in the plains downstream of the rim stations ranges from semi arid to arid. Annual rainfall ranges from about 2 inches to about 30 inches. The total annual average discharge of these rivers at the rim stations is about 170 MAF (Million Acre Feet).

On 14 August 1947, when South Asia was divided into two independent countries, there existed one of the most highly developed irrigation systems in the world and approximately 37 million acres of area use to receive irrigation supplies from the flow of waters of the Indus System of rivers.[2] All of the available water supplies were allocated to the various princely states and provinces in conformity with the principle of equitable apportionment of the waters with preferential rights to existing users. At the time of independence, a major portion of the Indus Basin formed a part of Pakistan and out of 37 million acres, 31 million acres were in Pakistan. The boundary line between the two countries was drawn without any respect to the irrigation works. It was, however, affirmed by the boundary commission and expressly agreed by the representatives of the affected zones before the arbitral tribunal that the authorized shares of the two zones in the common water supply would be continued to be honoured.

The Background

➢ The First Indian Aggression

- The water dispute between Pakistan and India came up soon after the ceasure of the arbitral tribunal on 31st March 1948. On 1st April 1948, India, taking advantage of it being an upper riparian at every river, stopped the waters in all irrigation canals (irrigating about 1.6 million acres in Pakistan), which cross the India-Pakistan border and demanded that Pakistan should recognize that the proprietary rights on the waters of the rivers in Punjab (India) wholly vest in that government and the Punjab in Pakistan could not claim any share of these waters as a right.

- The claim forwarded by Pakistan, however, was based upon the time honoured formula that existing uses are sacrosanct and the excess water, not previously committed, could be divided amongst the riparians according to the area, population, etc. This principle had the support of several treaties between the nations or states, or even the provinces in the same country.

- The Indians put forward a principle under which the upper riparian has an absolute right to the water and the lower riparian can only get it under an agreement or treaty entered into between the riparians.

➢ Road to the Treaty

- India agreed to restore some of the supplies to Pakistan in May 1948, when a very pro-Indian temporary agreement was signed. It was, however, generally realized that Pakistan could not live without a restoration of the full supplies and, on this question, there could be no compromise. Even internationally, there was an awareness that there could be a war on the issue.

- Direct negotiations between the parties failed to resolve the dispute. Negotiations under the World Bank commenced in May 1952. It was agreed that specific engineering measures be worked out by which the supplies effectively available to each country will be increased substantially beyond what they have ever been.

- The working party set up under the Bank, however, failed to agree on a comprehensive plan for the utilization of the waters of the Indus River System. The World Bank, in its proposal of 5th February 1954, listed three basic difficulties (given hereafter), which prevented the working party from reaching the heart of the problem, i.e. a fair diversion of the waters between the two countries.

➢ **Difficulties in Resolution:** The three basic difficulties noted by the Bank in resolution of the dispute were the following:[3]

- The first difficulty lies in the fact that the water supplies and storage potentialities are inadequate to the needs of the basin;

- The second difficulty is that although the working party is planning on the basis of the development of the Indus Basin as an economic unit, two sovereign states are involved, which greatly limit the practical aspects of planning. The countries would be reluctant to have works regulating the water supplies on which they depend constructed in the territory controlled by the other country. The prospects of establishing an efficient and smooth-running joint administration would not be favourable too.

- The third difficulty, and the most serious of all, arose in the course of discussions. The plans put forward by the two sides differed fundamentally in concept. An essential part of Pakistan's concept was that existing uses of water must be continued from existing sources and the corresponding concept of the Indian plan, on the other hand, was that although existing uses (defined to include only actual historic withdrawals) must be continued, they need not necessarily be continued from existing sources.

The Indus Waters Treaty -1960

The bank engineers worked out their initial proposals on averages, ignoring the special needs of the season for sowing and maturing of the crops when the demand of water is maximum and the flows are minimum. It took Pakistan two years to convince the bank that Pakistan's contentions were correct; that the division of the waters as put forward by the bank would not accomplish the result visualized in the actual proposal. After protracted negotiations under the World Bank, when the bank was convinced that the existing uses in Pakistan could not be met by transferring the waters from the western rivers, and that storages on the western rivers would be required for the purpose, the Indus Waters Treaty was signed in 1960.[4] The treaty consists of 12 Articles and 8 Annexures.[5] It is based on the division of the rivers between the two countries. The waters of the Sutlej, Beas and Ravi rivers, named in the treaty as "eastern rivers", are for the unrestricted use for India; and the waters of Indus, Jhelum and Chenab rivers, named in the treaty as "western rivers", are for the exclusive use of Pakistan, except for certain specified uses allowed to India in upper catchments.

Replacement Works

Under the treaty,[6] Pakistan was required to construct and bring into operation a system of works on the western rivers, in order to accomplish the replacement of water supplies for irrigation canals in Pakistan, which at the time of partition were dependent on water supplies from the eastern rivers. The replacement works comprised of two storage dams (one on the Indus river and one on the Jhelum river), six new barrages (diversion dams), remodelling of two existing barrages, seven new inter-rivers link canals and remodelling of two existing link canals. This only became possible through the generous assistance (grants and loans) by friendly countries like USA, Canada, UK, Netherlands, Germany, France, Italy, Australia, Newzealand, etc. The fund was called the Indus Basin Development Fund and was set up and administered by the World Bank with the assistance of the Indus Basin Development Board, constituted by the Government of Pakistan. India made a fixed contribution of £ 62.060 million towards this Fund, which was payable in ten years in equal instalments. Thus India got 24.00 MAF of perpetual flow of the rivers for this amount. The estimated cost of replacement works (1964 estimates) was US $ 1208.50 million. There was a transition period of 10 years during which Pakistan was to receive waters from the "eastern rivers" for use in the aforementioned canals. Such a division of rivers was a distinct departure from the concept of international law of upper and lower riparian rights (protection of existing uses from the same source). In this way, Pakistan had to forgo the entire perpetual flow of fresh waters of the three eastern rivers (24.00 MAF), which it used to historically receive for irrigation.

Institutional Arrangements

Under the provisions of Article VIII (1) of the Indus Waters Treaty 1960,[7] both India and Pakistan appointed Commissioners for Indus Waters. Each commissioner, unless either government decides to take up any particular question directly with the other government, is the representative of his government for all the matters arising out of the treaty and serves as the regular channel of communication on all the matters related to the implementation of the treaty. The two commissioners together form the Permanent Indus Commission. The functions of the Commission are:

- To establish and maintain co-operative arrangements for the implementation of the treaty;
- To promote co-operation between the parties in the development of the waters of the rivers;
- To make every effort to settle promptly any question arising between the Parties; and
- To undertake tours of inspection of the rivers to ascertain facts.

Under the treaty, restrictions have been placed on the design and the operation of hydroelectric plants, storage works and other river works to be constructed by India on the western rivers. India is required to supply to Pakistan certain specified information related to these works at least 6 months in advance of undertaking the river works so as to enable Pakistan to satisfy itself that the design conforms to the criteria set out in the treaty. Within a specified period, ranging from two to three months, Pakistan has the right to communicate to India, in writing, its objections, that it may have regarding the proposed design, on the ground that it does not conform to certain criteria specified in the treaty. Under the treaty, restrictions have also been placed for the irrigated cropped area to be raised by India in the basins of western rivers. The treaty also provides for a regular exchange of the daily hydrological data and other data under Articles VI and VII (2) of the treaty.

The treaty provides for a self-generating procedure for the settlement of differences and disputes. Any question, which arises between the Parties concerning the interpretation of the application of the treaty, or the existence of any fact, which, if established, might constitute a breach of the treaty, is to be first examined by the Commission, which endeavours to resolve the question by agreement.

The Current Stress on the Indus Waters Treaty – Major Ongoing Issues with India

➢ Wullar Barrage and Storage Project

- Under the treaty, India is not allowed to construct any storage on the main stem of river Jhelum. However, 0.75 MAF storage is allowed on the tributaries of river Jhelum.

- The site of the Wullar Barrage is located on Jhelum Main about 40 km upstream of the line of control in District Baramula of Occupied Jammu and Kashmir. India started construction of this barrage in 1985 to convert the natural Wullar Lake into a man-made storage work with a capacity of 0.3 Million Acre Feet (MAF) at the outfall of the Wullar Lake. Pakistan lodged a strong protest with India and the work was ultimately got suspended in 1987. Since then, the dispute is under resolution with India at the level of the two Governments, as the Commission was unable to resolve the matter. India has dubbed their project as Navigational Use allowed to India under the treaty. Pakistan has declared the project as treaty violative & non-feasible and has asked for its abandoning. The project, if allowed to India, will provide them the capability to control the flow of river Jhelum.

- So far, 14 rounds of Secretary Level Talks including 5 rounds of Pakistan-India Composite Dialogue, have been held. The work is suspended at the site. Regular vigilance is being kept through all possible means.

➢ Baglihar Hydroelectric Plant

- Baglihar Hydroelectric plant is located on river Chenab in Occupied Jammu and Kashmir about 147 km upstream of Marala Headworks in Pakistan. 'Difference' on the design of the Plant between the

- Parties was resolved by the Neutral Expert in February 2007. The Neutral Expert reduced the height of the dam by 1.5 meter, reduced the storage by 5 Million Cubic Meter (MCM) and raised the level of power intake by 3 meters. However, the number and the level of gates for the spillway, and undersluices, as proposed by India, were retained by the Neutral Expert[8].

- The changes determined by the Neutral Expert were carried out by India before the completion of the Plant and were inspected at site by Pakistan Indus Commissioner on 30th July 2008. India formally commissioned the Plant on 10th October 2008; however, the testing of turbines was started on 5th September 2008; as reported in the print media.

- For the commissioning of the Plant, India filled the dam for its dead storage in August 2008 and did not abide by the specific provisions of the treaty as to maintain the flow of 55,000 cusecs at Marala Headworks in Pakistan. As per our estimate, there was a reduction of above 200,000 Acre Feet of water during this period.

- In spite of repeated requests by our Indus Commissioner, India did not provide the details of schedule for the initial filling of the Baglihar Plant. The protest on the reduction of flow was accordingly lodged with India at the level of the Permanent Indus Commission and the Foreign Office. Pakistan's concern was also raised by the President of Pakistan with the Prime Minister of India at New York. Similarly, the Prime Minister of Pakistan also apprised the Prime Minister of India on the matter in China and the issue also came under discussion between the Security Advisers of the two countries on 13th October 2008.

- On the intervention by Pakistan at the highest level, a site inspection and a meeting of the Permanent Indus Commission was arranged by India from 18-25 October 2008. After the inspection of the site, the Pakistan Indus Commissioner, in the meeting of the Commission, asked for the compensation of lost water which was reduced due to the violation of the treaty provisions by India. Similarly, hourly data for the operation of initial filling was asked in order to jointly agree on the reduction of flow. India, however, did not cooperate to supply the hourly data and refused the compensation of flow to Pakistan. The Indian Indus Commissioner was of the view that the reduction of flow was due to structural constraints inherent in the dam besides the unsupportive weather conditions. The Pakistan Commissioner, however, maintained his stance in line with the above noted facts. The issue was last debated for resolution at the level of the Commission in the year 2010.

➢ Nimoo-Bazgo Hydroelectric Plant

- Nimoo Bazgo Hydroelectric Plant (45 MW) is located on the main stem of the river Indus. This plant is also a run-of-the river Plant; however, it contains a storage component of about 42,500 acre feet (52.40 MCM).

- Pakistan's question with regard to the free board/parapet wall was addressed by the ICIW during the 105th meeting from 29th May 2010 to 2nd June 2010 by making openings (4" x 4") in the solid parapet wall at the dam crest level. With reference to the pondage and the orifice spillway, however, India was unable to support its design as it lacked the data and the information. The PCIW, therefore, recorded his intention to proceed further for the next step as provided in the treaty for the resolution of the issue. The ICIW however, stated that he would address Pakistan's concern with regard to the pondage as well as the spillway gates and in this regard the Indian Commissioner wanted consultations with the high ups and asked for a time of one week to inform Pakistan. The PCIW agreed to India's request and stated that he will give Pakistan reaction after having received information from India. However, the Indian Commissioner did not agree to make changes in the design of the plant. The next step to resolve the issue under the treaty may be initiated.

➢ Kishenganga Hydroelectric Plant

- The proposed Kishenganga Hydroelectric Project is located in occupied Jammu and Kashmir on the river Neelum. The design envisages the construction of 180.05 meter long and 35.48 meter high concrete dam. The full Pondage capacity is 18.35 MCM (0.0169 MAF) with a dead storage of 10.80 MCM (0.00876 MAF) and an operating pool of 7.55 MCM (0.0061 MAF). The water of the river Kishenganga is to be diverted through a 24 km long tunnel to produce 330 MW power. The water after the production of power will join the Wullar Lake. The scheme, if implemented by India, will result in a shortfall of about 21% in the Neelum inflow for Pakistan's Neelum-Jhelum Hydroelectric Project, thus reducing the energy potential by 16%.

- This project was earlier a Storage-cum-Hydroelectric Project (under the Annexure E of the treaty) with a dam height of 75.48 m and a reservoir of 0.18 MAF. The diversion tunnel and the power producing capacity were same. Pakistan raised objections on the diversion of flow and the design of the project by India. The Commission failed to resolve the issue; however, India reconfigured their Project from Annexure E to Annexure D to the treaty i.e. from Storage Works to the Run-of-the River Plant in April 2006.

- The detailed information about the Run-of-the River project was received from India on 25th June 2006, Pakistan's objections, under the provisions of the Indus Waters Treaty, 1960, were sent to India on 24th August 2006. Pakistan's objections/questions on the proposed Run-of-the River Kishenganga Hydroelectric Plant were discussed during three meetings of the Commission held from 30th May to 4th June 2007, 31st May to 4th June 2008 and 24th to 28th July 2008, without reaching the resolution by agreement. The Pakistan Commissioner, therefore, processed the case to resolve the differences regarding the design of the Kishenganga Hydroelectric Project through a Neutral Expert and for the dispute of the "Diversion of Waters" and the "Draw Down below DSL" by a Court of Arbitration as provided in the Indus Waters Treaty, 1960.

- The Government of Pakistan requested the Government of India on 10th July 2009 to jointly appoint a Neutral Expert for resolving the "differences" and for "negotiations" to resolve the "disputes" by agreement as provided in Article IX of the treaty. Pakistan instituted the proceedings for the establishment of a Court of Arbitration on 17 May 2010. The first meeting of the Court was held in January 2011.

- The Neelum Jhelum Hydroelectric Project, considered to be a counter project of the Indian proposed project, is located in Azad Jammu and Kashmir. The project, with a gross head of 420 meter is to produce 969 MW power through two 15 km and one 17 km long tunnels. The President of Pakistan formally inaugurated the project on 9th February 2008. WAPDA has awarded the contract for the construction of the Neelum Jhelum Hydroelectric Project to M/s. CGGS-CMEC, a Chinese consortium. The completion of the project at the earliest possibility is quite important for Pakistan, in view of its stance against India viz-a-viz the Kishenganga Hydroelectric Project.

Conclusion

The crux of the Indus Waters Treaty 1960, is the division of the rivers of the Indus System between Pakistan and India. The Waters of the western rivers (Indus, Jhelum and Chenab) were allocated to Pakistan with certain restricted uses allowed to India in the Occupied Jammu and Kashmir, whereas the waters of the eastern rivers (Ravi, Beas and Sutlej) were available for unrestricted uses by India. In view of the intent and the spirit of the treaty, Pakistan expects that regarding the projects and the usage from the western rivers, the Indian design of the works would fall strictly in accordance with the provisions of the Indus Waters Treaty, 1960, so that the water rights, as envisaged through the treaty, would appropriately be honoured. Though it is true that climatic factors are becoming important to be considered as assessed so as to adjudge their effects on the flows in our river systems, but it also would be worthwhile to mention that while such factors are being evaluated, Pakistan should make every effort for the optimal development of its water resource available through the western rivers. This is probably the only solution available to Pakistan not only to cope with the risk of water scarcity, but also for the wider water resource management, both in view of the climate change, as well as the likely political manipulation of the Indus Waters Treaty, 1960, by India.

Author

Syed Jamait Ali Shah, until recently the Pakistan's Commissioner for the Indus Waters, is a leading technocrat and exponent of Pakistan's position on various key aspects of the treaty implementation process. He was the mainstay of Pakistan's negotiating process for the settlement of differences and disputes in accordance with the treaty and also for case processing with the World Bank and the Neutral Expert on controversy over the Baglihar Plan. He has also advised the Government on the trends of optimal utilization of water resources, hydroelectric developments, flood control and the adoption of international laws on the utilization of the waters of common rivers and its impact on existing treaties, including the preparation of guidelines for a draft agreement between Pakistan and Afghanistan, and prepared guidelines for the National Technological Policy for research and development in the areas of housing, the water resource management and the infrastructural development.

Notes

1. Usman-e-Ghani, "Transboundry Waters – Perspective of the Indus Waters Treaty -1960", Pakistan Engineering Congress, World Water Day 2009.
2. David E. Lilienthal, The Collier's Magazine, New York, August 4, 1951.
3. Bashir A. Malik, "The Indus Waters Treaty in Retrospect", Lahore, 2005.
4. Mohammad Ayub Khan, "Friends not Masters", OUP, Lahore, 1997.
5. The Indus Waters Treaty 1960, The Printing Corporation of Pakistan, Lahore.
6. Gulhati, N.D "The Indus Waters Treaty", New Delhi, 1973.
7. The Indus Waters Treaty, 1960, Printing Corporation of Pakistan, Lahore.
8. Press Release – Baglihar Hydroelectric Plant, February 12, 2007.

Paper Two:

A Quest For Re-Interpreting The Indus Waters Treaty: Pakistan's Dilemma

Dr. Shaheen Akhtar

Abstract

The Indus waters regime created in 1960 is coming under a lot of stress due to growing water scarcity in India and Pakistan and emerging climatic and environmental threats to the Indus basin rivers system. Being a lower riparian, Pakistan is faced with a dilemma as how to reinterpret the Indus Waters Treaty without giving in on its water rights provided in the treaty. The paper argues that given the constraints of a lower riparian, ruptured basin and loss of leverage (i.e. eastern rivers), Islamabad cannot go for fresh negotiations on the treaty but can adopt a multi-pronged strategy based on water rationale to protect its water rights within the parameters of the treaty. This can be done through effective implementation of Article VI, enhancing transboundary water management under Article VII, constructive multi-track water diplomacy and efficient water uses and sustainable water resource management in Indus-Pakistan.

Introduction

Water is emerging as a critical issue in India-Pakistan relations. The growing water stress in the two countries is likely to deepen with emerging climatic threats to the Indus basin river system. As a result, the Indus water regime, created in 1960, is coming under enormous pressure from a change in the demographic, hydrological, political, economic, and energy environment and Himalayan glaciers melt. This is putting strain on the normative, functional and administrative viability of the Indus Waters Treaty (IWT) signed in 1960. Pakistan, being a lower riparian is on the receiving end of the change which has alarmed the water insecure Islamabad. An intense debate is going on in the Pakistani media, public at large and policy making circles as how to defend Pakistan's water rights under the treaty and thwart any Indian attempt to 'steal Pakistan's water'. The water shortages experienced in the last few years, especially in the wake of filling of Baglihar dam by India in 2008, only accentuated such perceptions. Meanwhile, an intense debate around Indus II is going on in India that suggests renegotiation of the treaty with Delhi seeking water sharing rights on the western rivers. This would give India a position vis-a-vis the western rivers which it does not have at present. The norm of 'benefit sharing' is also being played up to maximize Indian control over the western rivers.

The devastating floods in 2010 brought in a yet another dimension of climate change into play. Scientists across the world indicated that global warming might have caused these floods.[1] It is widely believed that climate change would worsen water stress in the Indus basin which depends on glacial runoffs for 90 percent of its waters. Being a lower riparian, Pakistan is faced with a dilemma as how to reinterpret the IWT that ensures its water security in the coming decades without compromising on its water rights under the treaty, especially on the western rivers. The paper argues that given the constraints of a lower riparian, ruptured basin and loss of leverage (i.e. eastern rivers), Pakistan cannot go for fresh negotiations on the Indus Waters

Treaty but can adopt a multi-pronged strategy based on water rationale to ensure its water security within the broader parameters of the treaty. This may include: One, effective implementation of Article VI on 'exchange of data'; enhancing the scope of the Indus Water Commission and maximum use of the dispute resolution mechanism available in the treaty, especially at bilateral level. Two, utilization of Article VII on 'future cooperation' for initiating transboundary watershed management, sharing of Environment Impact Assessment (EIA) of hydropower projects on the upstream of the western rivers and commissioning of joint environmental studies. Three, an effective international water diplomacy using emerging international water and environmental norms, principles and laws to protect its water rights and urging the World Bank, the Western countries, especially the US, to assist Pakistan in improving the deteriorating water infrastructure of the Indus Basin Irrigation System (IBIS). Finally, Islamabad must adopt an internal water resource management strategy based on a socio-centric approach that focuses on indigenous physical and human resource management and is more resource-efficient and ecologically conducive. The questions raised include:

- What are emerging challenges to Pakistan's waters rights under the Indus Waters Treaty, especially on the western rivers of the Indus basin?
- What are major constraints on Pakistan in renegotiating the IWT?
- What is Indus II debate in India and how Pakistan should respond to it?
- What can be done to ensure better functioning of the treaty; bridging trust deficit in the implementation of the treaty and exploring new areas of cooperation so as to meet the challenges of climate change and environmental degradation in the Indus basin?

Growing Water Scarcity: Water Wars vs Water Rationale

Growing water scarcity in Pakistan and India has led to an intense competition over water resources of the Indus basin and stirred a debate on the possibility of a future Indo-Pak war over the Indus waters. Waters wars rationale forecasts war between countries dependent upon a shared water resource if there is water scarcity, competitive use and countries are enemies due to a wider conflict. On the other hand, Water rationality implies any action taken by a state to secure its water supply in the long-term, both in quantity and quality. In 1960, instead of fighting a war over Indus basin waters, two countries negotiated IWT and through cooperation were able to ensure their long term water supply. Thus, water rationale prevailed over water wars rationale.

Is Indus Water Regime Withering Away?

The Indus river basin comprises Ravi, Beas, Chenab, Jehlum, Sutlij and Indus that originate from glaciers in the Western Himalayas, the Karakoram, and the Hindu Kush. Another two tributaries of Indus, the Kabul and the Kurram rise in Afghanistan. Most of the Indus basin lies in Pakistan 52.48 percent-while India has 33.51 percent, and about 13 percent of the total catchment area of the basin is situated in Tibet (China) and Afghanistan. In Pakistan, the alluvial plains of the Indus basin is spread over approximately 25 percent of the land area while in India it is only 9.8 percent of the total geographical area of the country.[2] Further, Indus River feeds ecosystems of temperate forests, plains and arid countryside in the delta region of Pakistan.

In Indus basin, ecological insecurity contributes most to the water resource vulnerability. The quantum of water flowing in the Indus and its tributaries varies widely from year to year, depending on snowfall in the Himalayan and Karakoram ranges and rainfall in the catchment areas. Super floods occur approximately once every five years, which have raised the average flow to 140 MAF over the past 30 years. In the remaining four years, average water availability has been 135.60 MAF.[3] Besides, there is erratic monsoon pattern. Seasonal flow of waters, not only in Chenab, but Jhelum and Indus also has been depleting year after year for reasons ranging from global warming to deforestation and shrinking of mountain glaciers feeding these rivers.

Pakistan's Vulnerability

Pakistan is one of the world's driest countries with a single basin and its dependence on external water resources is 76 percent while that of India 34 percent. The population and economy are heavily dependent on an annual influx into the Indus river system flowing mainly through the Indian occupied territory of Jammu and Kashmir. The basin accounts for 25 percent of gross domestic product (GDP), 47 percent of total employment, and more than 60 percent of annual national foreign exchange earnings.[4] Various national and international reports indicate that the country is fast moving from water stressed to water scarce. The per capita water availability has fallen from about 5,600 cubic meters available at the time of independence in 1947 to 1,100 cubic meters in 2005. It is projected to hit below 700 cm^3 per capita by 2025.[5]

Indus Rivers Basin Regime

The partition of the subcontinent in 1947 divided the Indus Basin between Pakistan and India with most of the water-rich headwater going to India, and Pakistan becoming water-short lower riparian. The physical control to cut off water supplies to Pakistan coupled with population displacements and unresolved territorial issues exacerbated hostilities over the water dispute. Pakistan's vulnerability was exposed when on 1st April 1948, India stopped water supplies from the Ferozpur headworks to the Dipalpur Canal and to the main branches of the Upper Bari Doab Canal. The shut down, timed with the sowing of the wheat crop, affected 1.7 million acres of cultivable land in Pakistan, threatening the loss of about one million tons of wheat output. The wheat crop was saved only after Pakistan accepted, under duress, India's terms for the resumption of water flow.[6]

Under IWT, signed in 1960 after prostracted negotiations with active mediation by the World Bank, the entire flow of the eastern rivers–the Sutlej, the Beas and the Ravi was allocated to India while full use of the western rivers–the Indus, the Jhelum and the Chenab, barring some qualified exemptions, was given to Pakistan. Pakistan, as the lower riparian state, received about 75 percent of the Indus water while India the remaining 25 percent.

Article III, specifying Pakistan's rights to Indus waters, stated:

➢ Pakistan shall receive "unrestricted use of all waters of western rivers" Article III (1)

➢ India shall be under obligation to let flow all waters of western rivers & shall not permit any interference with these waters, except for restricted uses provided in Annex C & D. Article III (2)[7]

Besides, under Article II on eastern rivers, Pakistan was permitted, by way of exception, to take water for domestic use, non-consumptive use and certain limited agricultural use specified in Annexure B. Annex. B stipulated agriculture use of 45,500 acres from four tributaries of river Ravi–Basantar, Bein, Tarnah and Ujh.[8] IWT has normative as well as functional values as it contains, in addition to the substantive rules regarding the regime of the Indus system of rivers, provisions regarding the implementation of an administrative and institutional mechanism and the management of the basin resources.[9] The treaty worked well for the first four decades despite major wars and spells of high political tensions. However, over the last decade, it began to come under stress.

Looming Normative Stresses

The IWT was not based on any principle of law when it divided the waters of the Indus between the parties. Indeed, the treaty expressly stated that nothing contained in it was to be construed as in anyway establishing a general principle of law or any precedent. The lawyers for the parties disagreed strongly about the applicable principles of international law governing international water resources. There were conflicting principles put on the table; India invoked the principle of "equitable utilization" - the favourite of International Law Association (ILA) while Pakistan stressed on "no appreciable harm" - the favourite of International Law Commission (ILC).[10] In the absence of any consensus on principles of international water law, the treaty was based on a political compromise but having implications for sustainable management of the basin. The division of the rivers gave the two countries an independent control and regulation of supplies within their own territories.

Indus II Debate in India

The existing normative dimension of Indus water regime is coming under new pressures from the emerging norms in the area like 'benefit sharing' entering into the water discourse in India. The debate around Indus II in India suggests renegotiation of the treaty, advocating 'benefit sharing' on western rivers, which will allow it to exploit "potential in the upper catchments of the three western rivers that are allocated to Pakistan but are under Indian control".[11] There are two viewpoints on Indus II debate in India, arguing benefit sharing within or outside the treaty. B. G. Verghese refers to Article VII about 'Future Cooperation' and argues that Indus II can be built on Indus I on the basis of 'benefit sharing' on the western rivers.

> "The potential needs to be thoroughly surveyed and could thereafter be harnessed through joint investment, construction, management and control. Pakistan cannot continue to deny India its limited entitlements in the western rivers and also freeze all further development if it wants to grasp what could be a far larger prize by way of additional storage, flood moderation and hydro power which both could share."[12]

Ramaswamy R. Iyer, on the other hand, argues that the existing Indus Treaty offers no scope for Indus II as Verghese is advocating because Indus I has divided the river system. He suggests India to seek 'water-sharing on western rivers' in a new treaty on Indus. "If we want a new relationship between the two countries on the Indus, a totally new treaty will have to be negotiated; it cannot grow out of the existing treaty; and questions will immediately arise about the coexistence of two divergent treaties."[13] A recent IDSA Task Force Report, Water Security for India: The External dynamics, also calls for a modification of the treaty so as to enhance India's rights to western rivers. It states:

"With Pakistan, given some stringent provisions in the IWT that thwart India's plans of developing projects on the western rivers, 'a modification' of the provisions of the treaty should be called for. Whether this is done through renegotiations or through establishing Indus II Treaty, modifications of the provisions are crucial in the case of western rivers."[14]

The task force has also recommended a shift from 'water sharing' to 'sharing benefit' in the Indus basin.[15] There is a possibility of improving the treaty if the two governments want to do that. Article XII of the treaty provides that its provision may be modified by a duly ratified treaty by the two governments. The big question mark is how co-riparians can find ways and means to accommodate each other's emerging concerns.

Emerging Functional Strains

Under the treaty, India has rights to entire waters of eastern rivers, barring minor exceptions. In addition, it has the right to utilize 3.6 MAF of waters from western rivers subjected to restrictive provisions in the treaty which are now at the centre of functional strains. India can irrigate a maximum crop area of 1.34 million acres and utilize 3.6 MAF for storage projects, including general storage (1.25 MAF), power storage

(1.6 MAF) and flood storage (0.75 MAF). Of this storage, 0.4 MAF is allowed on the Indus, 1.5 MAF on the Jehlum and 1.7 MAF on the Chenab. India can also construct run-of-the river hydroelectric plants on the western rivers. All the technical parameters for each river are specified in Annexure D. Annexure E defines the limits of various storages of water for India on the western rivers.

India's Entitlement of Storage on the Western Rivers (MAF)

River system	General Storage	Power Storage	Flood Storage
Indus	0.25	0.15	Nil
Jhelum (Excluding Jhelum Main)	0.50	0.25	0.75
Jhelum Main	Nil	Nil	As in Paragraph 9, Annexure E
Chenab (Excluding Chenab Main)	0.50	0.60	Nil
Chenab Main	Nil	0.60	Nil

Source: Indus Water Commission

In the past decade or so, India started building an array of hydropower projects on the western rivers which has caused controversies and the IWT regime is increasingly facing strains in its functioning especially regarding the exchange of data and transparency in data sharing on new projects. As a result, dispute resolution at the bilateral level at the Indus Water Commission is becoming difficult leading to recourse to second and third tier of dispute resolution mechanism in the treaty—the Neutral Expert and the Court of Arbitration. This is quite evident in case of Baglihar on Chenab main and Kisheganga on a tributary of the Jelum River.

The interpretation of the permissive and restrictive provisions on the western rivers is the main source of controversies around the Indian hydroprojects. This includes interpretation of the technical design of the dams and hydropower projects and legal interpretation of the diversion of rivers or tributaries of the Indus system. Pakistan uses restrictive clauses of the treaty to protect its exclusive rights to western rivers. Many of its concerns get aggravated by its lower riparian status. Thereby, Islamabad strongly feels that the Indian projects do not follow technical parameters laid in the treaty and that unlimited proliferation of dams and the diversion of water would interfere with the flows of the western rivers into Pakistan. In contrast, India uses permissive clauses to justify its projects on the western rivers and its upper riparian position gives it a certain amount of control over the functioning of the IWT.

The treaty lays down principles of cooperation in Articles VI and VII which relate to "exchange of data" and "future cooperation" respectively. This is intended to ensure cooperation in the implementation of the treaty and future collaboration in optimum development of the Indus rivers. From the Pakistani perspective, Article VI on the exchange of data is faced with a number of problems in its implementation. India is not timely sharing all information regarding the flow data and the construction of its hydropower projects on the western rivers. This has caused lot of distrust and misperception, causing panic reactions in Pakistan. Thus, water debate in Pakistan is dominated by a perception that India is 'stealing water' or indulging in 'water terrorism' against Pakistan. Officially, Islamabad is increasingly resorting to the third party dispute resolution mechanism. The growing recourse to the third party mechanism is not only going to cost the parties in money and time but would also widen distrust, undermine the efficacy of the institution of the Indus Water Commission and politicize the water issue between the two countries.

Impending Management Challenges

The partition of the Indus came only after attempts at basin wide development and planning had failed. The Indus Treaty is considered as a 'suboptimal solution to the management of the Indus.'[16] Water resource management in the basin is adversely affected by the hydrology of the Indus River system which is highly variable, season-wise and year-wise, increasing its vulnerability to the vagaries of climate change. Extreme hydrological events may result into droughts or floods. The flow variation between summer and winter, on average, is about five to one while the demand of agriculture is two to one between summer and winter.[17] The trans-boundary management of the Indus basin is facing new challenges from the climate change and environmental degradation in the catchment areas, over abstraction of ground waters and pollution of water bodies. Some of the major transboundary and internal management challenges are:

➢ **The Climate Change** has added complexity to the transboundary water resource management in the Indus basin. The World Bank Report, Pakistan Water Economy Running Dry, in 2005 identified climate change as one of the sobering facts in the Indus basin. "It is now clear that climate change is already affecting these western glaciers in a dramatic fashion".[18] The International Centre for Integrated Mountain Development (ICIMOD) observes that receding and eventually disappearing high altitude reservoirs of snow and ice will over time reduce downstream runoff, and increase its variability.[19] It is generally believed in the scientific community that the 2010 floods in Pakistan were driven by a 'supercharged jet stream' that had also caused floods in China and a prolonged heatwave in Russia. Experts from the United Nations (UN) and universities around the world said the "extreme weather events" prove global warming is already happening.[20] Dr Peter Stott, head of climate monitoring and attribution at the Met Office, observed, it was impossible to attribute any one of these particular weather events to global warming alone. But there is "clear evidence" of an increase in the frequency of extreme weather events because of climate change.[21]

➢ The melting of the Hindu-Kush-Karakoram-Himalaya glaciers will have serious consequences for the Indus basin. Two thirds of the Himalayan glaciers are reported to be receding while Karakoram glaciers are advancing, both having implications for the management of the basin. The Kolahoi, the biggest glacier in the Indian held Kashmir (IHK) and the source of Jehlum River, is melting faster than other Himalayan glaciers. It has receded from 11 km² to 8.4 km² over the past three decades.[22] Similarly, there are 459 glaciers stretched over 1,414 sq kms (Km²), in Chenab basin, but until 2004, they had retreated to 1,110 km².[23] The 3,600 meter high and 78 km long Siachen glacier, on the other hand, has become the highest battleground on the earth between Indian and Pakistani military since 1984. The glacier is melting faster and has shrunk to half of its size. The Indian military presence on the glacier is considered a major reason behind its speedy melting. The Siachen glacier's melting ice is the main source of the Nubra River in the Indian controlled Ladakh, which drains into the Shyok River. The Shyok in turn, joins the Indus River. Thus, the glacier is a major source of the Indus waters.[24] The fast retreat of the glacier will directly touch lives of millions across Pakistan dependent on the Indus River for their livelihood.

➢ **The Environmental Degradation** in the upper reaches of the western rivers is going to have an adverse impact on the downstream flows of the western rivers. The IHK possesses vast forests, stretching from the lower valleys high up into mountain passes right to the edge of massive glaciers. The Forests in Jammu & Kashmir vary according to both altitude and climatic conditions. The KEWA report on deforestation in J & K shows that in the last 50 years, deforestation has accelerated in the region as a result of poor government control (and in some cases corruption), lack of local awareness, and military conflict.[25] Sustained deforestation has begun to have a severe effect on the entire environment of the region. In both IHK and Azad Kashmir, the cutting down of old alpine forests has occurred at an alarming rate with the full knowledge of both administering governments.

➢ The Wullar Lake is facing environmental degradation. The lake located in the IHK, is Asia's largest fresh water reservoir that feeds the river Jehlum and fills the Mangla dam in Pakistan. It is one of the six Indian wetlands designated as Ramsar sites but is facing environmental threats of converting large parts of the catchment area into agricultural lands, pollution from heavy use of chemical and animal wastes, hunting of birds and infestation of weeds.

- Under the increasing water stress, the continued deforestation in the region is affecting the flows downstream. The variation in the flow in the system over the past decade has been observed to be alarming and unprecedented. According to the Indian Meteorological Department (IMD), the temperature in the IHK has increased by over one degree, and it is now continuously soaring at .05 degree every year. The IMD observes that deforestation has caused 35 percent decrease in monsoons and 10 percent in snow annually in the IHK.[26]

- **Transboundary Impacts of Indian Hydroprojects**: Indian hydroprojects are bound to have devastating local and transboundary environmental impacts. Experts strongly believe that India's Kishenganga Project is going to have an adverse environmental impact on the Gurez Valley in IHK and the Neelum Valley in AJK. It will submerge many parts of the beautiful Gurez Valley and displace more than 25,000 Dard Shin natives from the area.[27] The project would reduce the river's flow into Pakistan by 27 percent[28] which will adversely affect the agriculture usages in the Neelam valley and Muzaffarabad district, besides affecting the power generation capacity of the Neelum-Jehlum by 16 percent. It will affect about 200 kms of river bed in AJK. The river will turn dry over 40 kms, a negation of international environmental laws. Under the law, at least 70 per cent of river flows are to be protected in case any project is taken in hand.[29]

- **Transboundary Impact of Over-Abstraction of Ground Water**: Over-abstraction of groundwater in Indus-India basin closer to Pakistan's border is having serious impacts on the aquifers of Indus-Pakistan.[30] Subsidized energy for groundwater pumping is a major reason behind over abstraction in Northern India-Punjab, Haryana, Delhi and Rajasthan. Consequently, the water table in Pakistan's bordering areas with India is going down alarmingly. A National Aeronautics and Space Administration (NASA) study in 2009 using satellite imagery based on Gravity Recovery and Climate Experiment (GRACE) shows groundwater changes in India during 2002-2008.[31] Satellite observations show that over abstraction of groundwater in bordering Indian states is affecting aquifers of Pakistan. The surface water scarcity in the basin states would ultimately put more pressure on the depleting aquifers. There is a need to look into options of managing aquifers in the basin states.

- **Transboundary Impacts of Drainage and Waste Waters Discharges**: Another management issue arises from the pollution of drainage water and waste water discharge into river bodies in the rivers of Indus basin flowing into Pakistan. In the catchment areas of the Indus India, the effluents are being discharged into the rivers due to rapid urbanization and growth in agriculture. The natural slopes allow flow of untreated effluents from the Indian Punjab to the Pakistani Punjab. The drains entering into Pakistan bring heavy loads of wastes having environmental implications for human and livestock health, besides affecting the health of the water bodies.[32] Pollution in the Wullar Lake, The Dal Lake and the Jehlum River is affecting the health of the water bodies of the Indus river system flowing into Pakistan.

The Internal Water Resource Management in the two countries is deeply shaping the new threats to the quality and quantity of water in the Indus basin. As IWT gave independent control to both sides over their respective segment of the basin, they gave little importance to sustainable management of their water bodies by preserving the socio-ecological systems. Instead, the national water strategies on both sides have focused more on the supply side management than demand management. They have followed a technocratic approach that looks almost exclusively on the supply side hydrology and advocates engineering solutions that are least mindful of the health of the basin or transboundary impacts. Thus, there is little emphasis on a socio-centric approach which lays emphasis on indigenous physical and human resource management and is more resource-efficient and ecologically conducive and strongly suggests an integrated Water Resource Management (IWRM) strategy.

Revisiting The Indus Waters Regime: Options for Pakistan
Options within the Treaty: Effective Implementation of Article VI

A number of steps can be taken to build trust and strengthen the functioning of the treaty by effectively implementing Article VI on the exchange of data, expanding the scope of the Permanent Indus Water Commission (Article VIII) and judicious utilization of Article IX on the settlement of 'differences' and 'disputes'.

- **Trust Building through Timely Data Sharing by Installing a Telemetry System:** As a downstream country and being a party to the IWT, Pakistan has a right to know the gauge level and regular inflow and outflow figures from hydro projects in India. In fact, most of Pakistan-India current water conflict is rooted in trust gap caused by inadequacies and opacity in data sharing regarding the flow data provided to Pakistan. Parties are still relying on an outmoded data sharing mechanism that is unable to ensure transparent and real time water transactions between India and Pakistan. The distrust in sharing of flow data can be bridged by guaranteeing real time data sharing through installation of the telemetry system. Telemetry has become an indispensable tool for water management applications on a real-time basis. The Telemetry system is used globally as an effective real time monitoring mechanism for water quantity, quality, sediment flow, snow and ice melt, weather forecasting and meteorological data for improved decision-making.[33] Timing of flows is also very crucial for Pakistan because agriculture in the Pakistani plains depends not only on how much water comes, but that it comes in critical periods during the planting season. In July 2010, in a meeting of the Indus Water Commission, both sides agreed in principle to put in place a telemetry system on the Indus to record and transfer real-time data. If the proposed telemetry is properly installed and operated, either jointly or by a third party, this will help in restoring trust and minimize uncertainty and confusion over the flow of the western rivers. The telemetry systems should include watershed forecasting and flood warning telemetry systems.

- **Transparency in Data Sharing Regarding the Construction of Indian projects** on western rivers is critical in trust building. Pakistan's concerns are multiplied due to the lack of timely and inadequate data sharing which has greatly politicized the water issue and deepened distrust between the two countries. Delays and inadequate data supply to Pakistan by India on projects like the Wullar Barrage, Baglihar, Dul-Hasti, Uri-II and Kishenganga, Chutak, Nimoo Bazgo hydroprojects have deepened Pakistan's apprehensions. Delayed and incomplete information and engineering details constrain Pakistan's ability to review and adjudge the compatibility of Indian projects with the design criteria provided for in the treaty.[34] Further, the provision of such information is essential for Pakistan to ensure that the run-of-the-river plants are being operated in accordance with the treaty. Another related major concern for Islamabad is that Delhi does not stop work on a project where technical parameters have become controversial between the two countries on the plea that it is not provided in the treaty. Under the IWT, India is required to communicate the details of new projects six months before their commencement, diversion for storage and farm purposes from the western rivers and providing details about ancillary projects.[35] The former Indus Water Commissioner, Jamaat Ali Shah, has pointed out that "the provisions of the treaty imply that any objections must be resolved. If India goes on constructing and we go on objecting without resolution in a time bound manner, then both the letter and the spirit of the treaty are negated."[36] If India supplies timely information on the design of its projects on the western rivers before starting work on them, it would remove Pakistan's apprehensions regarding their incompatibility with the treaty. Being a co-riparian, it is also Pakistan's "right to be acquainted with the civil works projects on the eastern rivers in India"[37] which affect it as a downstream riparian.

- **Expanding Scope/Mandate of the Indus Water Commission:** The functioning of the PIWC set up under Article VIII of the treaty should be strengthened by expanding its scope and mandate. The main task of the Commission is to maintain a co-operative arrangement for the implementation of the treaty; promote co-operation between the parties in the development of the waters of the rivers; meet regularly to review the implementation of the treaty; make every effort to settle promptly any question arising between the parties; and undertake tours of inspection of the rivers to ascertain facts.[38] Although, it has performed its supervisory role quite well but it, mandate is too limited that is putting strain on the very functioning of the institution. The role of the PIWC needs to be in line with the current realities or else it will lose its relevance in implementing the treaty. There is a need to expand the role of the Commission regarding co-operation in harnessing and sustainable management of the Indus waters. An Indus Water Consultative Group comprising India, Pakistan and international water experts can be formed to provide input on the supply capacity of the Indus basin taking into account the issues like climatic changes and environmental degradation. The group can conduct joint studies on the impact of climate change on Himalayan glaciers, joint watershed management and joint studies on environmental impact assessments of the hydro projects, especially on the lower riparian. It can also thrash out a joint watershed management strategy for the catchment areas of the western rivers. India is also in favour of revitalizing the institution of Commission. There is a realization within the Commission that its role should be in consonance with emerging realities in the Indus basin or else it will lose its relevance. The meeting of the Commission, held in New Delhi in June 2010 has decided to strengthen the working of the Commission by setting up a body to oversee it.[39] There is also a need to develop the capacity of the Pakistan chapter of the Indus Water Commission in water diplomacy, water conflict resolution, water entitlements, legal and technical issues so that Pakistan can defend its case soundly based on varied expertise in the field.[40] Expanded scope and mandate of the PIWC and a strong Pakistan Indus Water Commission will help in defending Pakistan's case well, averting frequent recourse to the Court of Arbitration (CoA).

➢ **Judicious Utilization of Article IX:** Article IX of the treaty specifies a three tier dispute resolution mechanisms: bilateral level, Commission under Article IX (1) and the two Governments – IX (3) & (4) as well as through third party involvement / Neutral Expert – IX (2)(a), and Court of Arbitration – IX (5). Since the bilateral level is getting weaker due to new realities, the third party option is becoming more attractive. There is an urgent need to strengthen the bilateral strand.

Reinterpreting IWT: Expanding Cooperation under Article VII on 'Future Cooperation'

The IWT is silent on many emerging threats to the Indus basin that may include climate change, environmental degradation, management of shared aquifers and water quality. These can be addressed by utilizing the so far unutilized Article VII on future cooperation. Since these concerns were not present at the time of the signing of the treaty, they could be covered by this provision. The water rationale demand that both countries broaden the scope of Article VII to develop cooperation in transboundary watershed management, declaring all glaciers protected area, sharing 'Environmental Impact Assessment' of hydro projects in the upstream of the western rivers and maintaining transboundary aquifers and ensuring ecological flows in the eastern rivers.

Article VII lays down the principles of 'future cooperation'. It states:

"The two parties "recognize that they have a common interest in the optimum development of the rivers" and they declare their intention "to cooperate by mutual agreement, to the fullest possible extent."[41]

While they just talked about the installation of hydrological and meteorological observation stations and some drainage or engineering works subjected to mutual agreement. There is a need to use Article VII for a sustainable transboundary management of the Indus basin. This article provides an opportunity to meet the threats emerging from the climate change in the Indus Basin which was not factored in when the treaty was signed in 1960. Some of the cooperative steps are identified as under:

➢ **Study of the Behaviour of Himalayan Glaciers:** Glacial fluctuations and changes in precipitation patterns are expected to alter the hydrology of the river basin, hence jeopardising hydropower generation and agricultural production and consequently altering people's livelihoods.[42] The study of the behaviour of Himalayan glaciers is a must as they are considered quite vulnerable to the adverse impact of climate change. Both sides need to form a group of experts to study the behavior of glaciers whether advancing or decreasing. The largest challenges stem from inadequate information and monitoring, and limited scientific understanding of these high elevation glaciers. Conflicting behaviour of glaciers, such as retreating, advancing, and even surging, within small distances, is posing difficult questions to the scientists.[43] The International Centre for Integrated Mountain Development (ICIMOD) based in Nepal has already taken a lead by organizing a workshop in July 2010 on 'Climate and environmental change impacts on the cryosphere of the Indus basin and its implications for future water scenarios'. Scientists at the workshop included those from India, Pakistan, China and Afghanistan who identified key gaps in knowledge about the Indus basin. They agreed to improve collaboration on scientific and technical research on the impacts of climate change on the cryosphere of the Indus basin. They also proposed a long-term Indus Basin Progamme that can be implemented by local and international agencies with ICIMOD in a strong facilitating role. A combination of bilateral and multilateral approach which includes China and Afghanistan that are not part of the treaty is absolutely necessary to respond to new climatic threats in the HKH region. This will also facilitate sharing of experiences to create an environment of ownership of scientific work among regional government institutions engaged in sustainable water resource management in the Indus basin. Transboundary scientific coordination and collaboration in scientific and technical research is essential in order to obtain a holistic perspective of the existing and anticipated changes in the natural system of transboundary river basins like the Indus. Institutional cooperation is quite possible between the metrological departments of India, Pakistan, China, Nepal and Afghanistan that are important stakeholders in the HKH region.

- **Declaring all Glaciers Protected Area:** India-Pakistan urgently need to declare all Himalayan glaciers as protected areas, as climate change and environmental degradation, aggravated by human activity, are adversely affecting these ice reservoirs. Of particular importance is the Siachen glacier where the continued presence of the armies, especially on the Indian side of the glacier, has accelerated the melting of the glacier. Siachen is under threat of disappearance and must be demilitarized. They dialogue on Siachen has moved slowly but is considered doable. A number of new ideas have come up under discussion in the ongoing composite dialogue which suggest turning it into a 'mountain of peace' or a 'zone of peace'. It simply requires political will to formalize them by settling the issue. This will end drain on the resources wasted- India spends about $2 million a day while Pakistan $ 1 million per day to sustain troops on Siachen.[44] This amount can easily be diverted to the creation of Protection of Himalayan Glaciers Fund that can be spent on the sustainability of the HKH region. China and Afghanistan can join the fund and make their contribution.

- **Cooperation in Transboundary Watershed Management:** Environmental threats recognize no political or geographical borders, but no joint effort is being made in India and Pakistan to meet the challenges of environmental degradation in the Indus watershed and monitor the changing weather pattern. Being the lower riparian, Pakistan has no access to the upper catchments of the western rivers allocated to it as these lie in the Indian controlled territory. The changes in watershed condition and the course of rivers demand better strategies for management.

A joint approach to watershed management is critical to maintain sustainable flows in the upstream region to control floods and soil erosion. The basin watershed area in both parts of Kashmir is facing deforestation and environmental degradation. India has been pursuing the idea of joint water management while Pakistan has proposed joint watershed management which is actually geared to augment supply in the system. This can be done through joint surveys and the development of the upper basins of the western rivers that are facing threats and uncertainties emanating from the gathering climate change. Cooperation in watershed management is deeply linked with the joint response to tje climatic threat to the HKH glaciers. This would not only benefit India and Pakistan in the Indus basin but would also benefit India in Jamuna and Ganga river basins that originate from the same region. Article VII on "Future Cooperation" can be used to enhance the sustainability of water in the Indus system in an optimal manner.

> **Sharing of Transboundary Environment Impact Assessment (TEIA):** Hydropower projects in the upstream of the Indus Basin Rivers have adverse transboundary environmental impacts on the downstream flows and flora and fauna which will be aggravated by climate change. The Treaty permitted India under strict conditions, to construct run-of-the-river hydropower projects but was largely silent on the sharing of the transboundary environmental impact assessment on the downstream state. Being the lower riparian and dependent on a single basin, Pakistan is extremely vulnerable to adverse environmental impacts. India should share the Trans-boundary Environment Impact Assessment (TEIA) of various hydropower projects being planned or built on the western rivers as well as the eastern rivers. This can be done bilaterally or multilaterally. At the bilateral level, cooperation is possible under Article VII, by initiating joint commissioning of environmental studies as proposed by Pakistan that can help in ensuring ecological sustainability of the Indus basin. At the multilateral level, there is an emerging body of transboundary environmental laws that require upstream states to share the environmental impact of their projects with the lower riparian. The European and the North American countries are adopting regional agreements that provide for TEIA. The Espoo (EIA) Convention[45] sets out the obligations of parties to assess the environmental impact of certain activities at an early stage of planning. It also lays down the general obligation of the States to notify and consult each other on all major projects under consideration that are likely to have significant adverse environmental impact across boundaries.[46] Canada, Mexico and the US also have the North American Agreement on Transboundary Environmental Impact Assessment.

There are various international treaties on the management of international watercourses and climate change that call for national measures for the protection and ecologically sustainable management of transboundary surface and ground waters. These include the Helsinki Rules on the uses of International rivers (1966), the UN Convention on the Protection and Use of Transboundary Watercourses and International Lakes (1992), the UN Convention on Non-Navigational Uses of International Watercourses (1997). The United Nations Framework Convention on Climate Change (UNFCCC) 1997 can also be used to this effect. Article 5 of the UN Non-Navigational Uses of International Watercourses requires water courses nations to participate in the use, development and protection of an international water course in an equitable and reasonable manner. India and Pakistan are not party to the Convention. Other concerns relating to ecological flows in eastern rivers and transboundary water pollution also need to be addressed.

> **Ensure Ecological Flows in Eastern Rivers:** The flow of the three eastern rivers allocated to India has declined since the signing of the IWT. The two eastern rivers, Sutlej and Ravi, get flood water but during the lean period, there minimum flow is abysmal. Consequently, Pakistan is facing the problem of maintaining the eastern rivers for flood years without water. Ecological flows are also important to maintain biodiversity and environment in Indus-Pakistan. Also important is the issue of minimum flows in the eastern rivers for domestic purposes, especially in the low flow times. The low minimum flows during 1976-77 to 2009-10 touched the very low minimum average of 0.30 MAF-Ravi 0.29; Sutlej 0.01.[47] India should ensure minimum ecological flows in eastern rivers so as to maintain biodiversity and environment in Indus Pakistan. This can be addressed under Article VII. This can be reinforced by various international water and environmental laws, mentioned above.

> **Addressing Transboundary Water Pollution:** The quality of water is as much an important concern as the quantity of the Indus waters. The issue of pollution of the waters of the rivers and tributaries of the Indus

system was taken up in Article IV (9) of the Treaty. It stated that each party should 'prevent' "undue pollution of the water of the rivers" and take measures to ensure that before any sewage or industrial waste is allowed to flow into the rivers, it will be treated." Lately, the issue has been taken up in the meeting of the Indus Waters Commission held in July 2010. Pakistan asked India to stop the contamination of water in the Hadiara nallah that flows near Lahore and brings industrial waste to Pakistan and pollutes the Ravi and Kasur drains. The issue of Baramulla waste polluting the Jehlum River was also raised with India. New Delhi has agreed to conduct joint inspection to measure pollution levels in the Jehlum River, Hudiara drain and Kasur drain. Both sides have also agreed to conduct a joint survey to monitor river pollution.[48] The International Water Laws, the Helsinki Rules on the uses of International rivers (1966) in particular, emphasize on controlling pollution in the transboundary rivers. Both sides need to cooperate to maintain the quality of water and should not dispose of their waste into the watercourses on the Indus basin. Efforts should be made to invest in water quality conservation and waste water infrastructure.

➢ **Maintenance of Transboundary Aquifers:** Pakistan's water table in Punjab, particularly in the bordering areas with India, has gone down alarmingly because of the over extraction of groundwater in the Indian Punjab. The issue of ground water was not visualized in the Treaty as there was not much reliance on it in the 1950s which has increased massively in the last decade or so; the deep fresh aquifers are fast depleting. This warrants a comprehensive study of the current situation of transboundary aquifers, the water table decline and quality degradation in the Indus basin, especially aquifer bordering the basin states.[49] Collaborative steps are also needed to employ artificial ground recharge (AGWR) techniques to improve the long term sustainability of deep aquifers. The issue can be taken up in the discussion of the Indus Commission under Article VII. There should be sharing of information and best practices for better management of the groundwater resource.

Constructive Multi-Track Water Diplomacy

Since India-Pakistan water issue is not only politicized but also internationalized, it would be important for Pakistan to make use of the emerging international water and environmental norms, principles and laws to protect its water rights in the Indus basin. There are number of international conventions on sustainable management of the shared basins that can be drawn upon in responding to the new threats to the Indus basin.

Regional cooperation in addressing vulnerabilities emerging from climate change is quite possible. In the April 2010 Thimphu statement on climate change, both the countries have agreed to undertake measures, which include: (i) to review the implementation of the Dhaka Declaration and the Saarc Action Plan on Climate Change and ensure its timely implementation; (ii) to establish an Inter-governmental Expert Group on Climate Change to develop a clear policy direction and guidance for regional cooperation as envisaged in the SAARC Plan of Action on Climate Change; study climate risks in the region and related socio-economic and environmental challenges; conservation of biodiversity and mountain ecology covering mountains in the region; and monitoring the monsoon pattern to assess the vulnerability to climate change.[50]

Pakistan should come out of a reactive mould and adopt a more proactive strategy to handle transboundary water issues with India. Pakistan has been quite ineffective in using the growing norms in international water and environment laws to its advantage or support its case based on more scientific facts. In NE verdict in Baglihar, enough weightage is being given to the impact of climate change and new technical norms and new standards provided in the treaty. This gives enough space to Pakistan to reinterpret the treaty in the light of new threats to the Indus basin and look for solutions that address mutual vulnerabilities.

Further, there has been hardly any systematic analysis conducted by Pakistani experts in a scientific manner[51] and a coordinated manner on the transboundary water issues with India. There is a dire need to move away from an emotive discourse to a more informed and scientifically supported discourse that strengthens Pakistan's case more logically. Pakistan also need to pursue multi-track water diplomacy for sustainable management of the Himalayan rivers' basins, especially the Indus basin, and use the platforms of ICIMOD, SAARC, and many other social sector organizations like IUCN, WWF, the Global Environment Facility (GEF) and UNEP to explore innovative areas of cooperation, within and outside the treaty.

Also very important is the fact that Pakistan needs international assistance to fix its fast deteriorating infrastructure. The Indus basin irrigation system (IBIS) is the largest contiguous irrigation network in the world but it is crumbling due to a combination of age, deferred maintenance and neglect. The 2010 floods have exposed the weakness in the Pakistan's water infrastructure. The country needs financial resources to sustain its huge irrigation system as well as build new reservoirs as it has a very low storage capacity. The World Bank, the Asian Development Bank and the US can assist Pakistan in this regard.

Internal Management of Water Resources and Sharing of Best Practices

The Internal water resource management becomes very important given the fact that the physical separation of the Indus tributaries has hampered the possibility of an efficient integrated basin management. In view of the growing water scarcity, it is the responsibility of both the states to ensure internal water resources management by following the principles of Integrated Water Resources Management (IWRM) and share best practices in water conservation techniques in agriculture, industrial and domestic uses.

There is a need for a paradigm shift in water management from a technocratic approach that looks almost exclusively toward engineering solutions to a socio-centric approach which lays emphasis on indigenous physical and human resource management as more resource-efficient and ecologically conducive. A combination of supply-demand management strategies would help in meeting new threats to the Indus basin water resources. On the supply side strategies, efforts are needed to augment the availability of 'usable' water through an extensive recourse to local rainwater harvesting ('catching the raindrop as it falls') and watershed development. Reservoir management is also very important and the emphasis should be on small and medium dams that can meet the local needs of the area. The demand side management strategies may include the practice of the utmost economy and efficiency in water use and of resource-conservation. Better water conservation strategies need to be introduced and the maximum conservation needs to be done in the irrigation sector.[52] A holistic approach to water resources, recognizing the linkages between water, land, users, environment and infrastructure is necessary to evade the crisis of water scarcity in the basin states.[53]

Both sides need to share best practices in water conservation techniques in agriculture, industrial and domestic uses. Changing the mindset of the people on both sides to water conservation, a civil society's stakeholders' dialogue, especially between farmers leaders and associations on both sides can help in bridging the trust gap and raising awareness about the diminishing water resources. Interaction between the water institutions of the two countries is also very critical in sharing vulnerabilities and adopting best practices.

Conclusion

The Indus Waters Treaty considered a model of conflict resolution that withstood wars and volatile spells of Indo-Pak relations is coming under normative and functional stress due to new climatic, demographic, developmental and environmental threats in the basin. The sustainable management of Indus waters resources is emerging as the biggest challenge to the riparian states. Pakistan's dilemma for reinterpreting the IWT stems from inbuilt constraints stemming from its lower riparian status and the fractured character of the Indus basin. Growing water scarcity in India and Pakistan, the stress in the Indus basin and India's ambitious plans to exploit the western rivers is going to increase the strain on the functioning of the Indus waters regime.

Cooperation in harnessing Indus waters is possible within the existing parameters of the Treaty by strengthening the data sharing mechanisms under Article VI and expanding the scope of Article VII on future cooperation. Article VII on the future cooperation of the Treaty largely remains unutilized. Not a single project has been undertaken under this clause. The trust gap in water relations needs to be addressed at the political and diplomatic level by depoliticizing the water discourse in both countries. Practical steps should be taken to ensure the communication of real time flow data by way of installation of telemetry system on the western rivers and India observing transparency in communicating information regarding planned projects to Pakistan. Strengthening of the Indus Water Commission in terms of its mandate, scope and capacity will save Pakistan from frequent recourse to NE or court of arbitration.

A reinterpretation of the Treaty is quite possible under Article VII on future cooperation and it has already entered into the water discourse in India. This article can form a basis of cooperative strategies in responding to the emerging climatic threats, environmental degradation to the Indus basin and coordination in resource management strategies in both countries. Cooperative strategies may include scientific collaboration in the study of behavior of Himalayan glaciers, declaring glaciers protected area, a common approach to transboundary watershed management, the sharing of transboundary impact assessment (TIA) of the Indian hydropower projects, the maintenance of transboundary aquifers, addressing transboundary water pollution and ensuring ecological flows in the eastern rivers. There are key gaps in knowledge about the Indus basin that are causing anxieties in the lower riparian Pakistan and need to be addressed. Both sides need to cooperate to install monitoring and forecasting capabilities for the glacial region and the catchment areas of the upper Indus basin to meet challenge of climate change. Finally, efficient water uses and sustainable water resource management in Indus-Pakistan and Indus-India is critical to emerging concerns regarding water quality and environmental sustainability of the Indus basin. Cooperative approaches at the basin and sub-basin levels can help build trust and improve water relations between the upper-lower riparians and assure a long term access to water both in quality and quantity.

Author

Dr. Shaheen Akhtar is a research fellow at the Institute of Regional Studies, Islamabad, Pakistan. She got her PhD degree in International Relations at the Quaid-i-Azam University, Islamabad, Pakistan. Dr. Akhtar remained a visiting fellow at the Institute of Asia and Pacific Studies, China Academy of Social Science (CASS), research fellow at the Centre for International Studies and at the Stingson Research Centre at Washington.

Notes

1. Louise Gray, "Pakistan floods: Climate change experts say global warming could be the cause", The Telegraph, London, 10 August 2010. http://www.telegraph.co.uk/ news/ worldnews/asia/pakistan/7937269/Pakistan-floods-Climate-change-experts-say-global-warming-could-be-the-cause.html.
2. Douglas Hill, "The regional politics of water sharing", in Kuntala Lahiri-Dutt & Robert J. Wasson, Water First: Issues and Challenges for Nations and Communities in South Asia, Sage Publications, New Delhi, 2008. p. 60.
3. Source: Estimated from the data obtained from the government of Pakistan, Water and Power Development Authority, Lahore. Cited in Kaiser Bengali, "Water Management under Constraints: The Need for a Paradigm Shift", in Michael Kugelman, Robert M. Hathaway, ed, Running on Empty: Pakistan's Water Crisis, the Woodrow Wilson International Center for Scholars, 2009. Washington, D.C. www.wilsoncenter.org p. 47.
4. Shams Ul Mulk, "Pakistan's Water Economy, the Indus River System and its Development Infrastructure, and the Relentless Struggle for Sustainability", in Michael Kugelman, Robert M. Hathaway, ed, Running on Empty: Pakistan's Water Crisis", p. 64.
5. Pakistan Strategic Country Environmental Assessment Report 2006. http://siteresources.worldbank.org/SOUTHASIAEXT/Resources/Publications/448813-1188777211460/pakceavolume1.pdf p.50.

6. Kaiser Bengali, "Water Management under Constraints: The Need for a Paradigm Shift", p.467 See the text of the Indus Waters Treaty.
8. See the text of the Indus Waters Treaty.
9. M. A. Salman and Kishor Uprety, Conflict and Cooperation in South Asia's International Rivers: A Legal Perspective, p. 48.
10. Sardar Muhammad Tariq, "The Indus Waters Treaty and Emerging Water Management Issues in Pakistan", in Problems and Politics of Water Sharing and Management in Pakistan, IPRI, 2007. p.88.
11. B G Verghese, "Political Fuss Over Indus-I", The Tribune, 24, 25 May, 2005 Political Fuss Over Indus-I http://www.bgverghese.com/Indus.htm
12. Ibid.
13. Ramaswamy R. Iyer, "Indus Treaty : A Different View", Economic and Political Weekly, Mumbai, Vol. 40. No.29, 16-22 July 2005.
14. Water Security for India: The External dynamics, IDSA Task Force Report, September 2010. P. 10.
15. Ibid. p. 16.
16. N.Kliot, D Shmueli, U. Shamir, "Institutions for the management of transboundary water resources: Their nature, characteristics and shortcomings", The Water Policy, 20 April 2001. p. 240.
17. The Water Resource Management Directorate, WAPDA. See, Shams Ul Mulk, "Pakistan's Water Economy, the Indus River System and its Development Infrastructure, and the Relentless Struggle for Sustainability", op.cit p. 68.
18. John Briscoe, Usman Qamar, Pakistan's Water Economy Running Dry, The World Bank, OUP, 2005. p. xvii.
19. The International Centre for Integrated Mountain Development (ICIMOD). The Changing Himalayas: The Impact of Climate Change on Water Resources and Livlihoods in the Greater Himalayas, Kathmandu, January 2009. p.6. available at http://books.icimod.org/index.php/ search/publications/593.
20. Louise Gray, "Pakistan floods: Climate change experts say global warming could be the cause", The Telegraph, 10th August 2010.
21. Ibid.
22. Michael Renner, "Water Challenges in Central-South Asia", The Peace building Centre, Noref Policy Brief, No. 4 the December 2009.
23. Pakistan persuades India to install telemetry system on rivers", The News, 14th May 2010. 24 Waheed Hamid, "Melting ice of Siachen Glacier, Daily Times, 2nd January 2010. http://www.dailytimes.com.pk/default.asp?page=2010%5C01%5C02%5Cstory_2-1-2010_pg3_325"End the Deforestation of Jammu and Kashmir", http://www.kewa.org/forest.html
26. Green revival: youth to save Kashmir, 25th May 2010. http://india.carbon-otlok.com/content/kashmir-green-revival also see, Arjimand Hussain Talib, On the Brink: A Report on Climate Change and its Impact in Kashmir, Actionaid, 2007.http: //www.actionaidindia.org/download/On_the_brink.pdf P.4.
27. "The Kishenganga River and Gurez Valley", http://www.kewa.org/project.html
28. Khalid Mustafa, "Pakistan asks India to review the modified design again, The News, 6th September 2006.
29. Khaleeq Kiani, Talks for Kishanganga arbitration court on July 6" Dawn, 3 July 2010.
30. Beyond the Indus Waters Treaty: Ground Water and Environmental Management – Policy Issues and Options. IUCN, 2010. http://cmsdata.iucn.org/downloads/pk_ulr_d2.pdf p. 3.
31. M. Rodell, Isabella Velicogna and James S. Famiglietti, "Satellite-based estimates of groundwater depletion in India", 2009. www.nature.com/nature/journal/v460/n7258/abs/ nature08238.html.
32. Beyond the Indus Waters Treaty: Ground Water and Environmental Management– Policy Issues and Options. IUCN, 2010. http: //cmsdata.iucn.org/downloads/pk_ulr_d2.pdf p. 3.
33. Dr M. S. Shafique, "Telemetry system and confidence building", Dawn, 9th August 2010. http://archives.dawn.com/archives/25250
34. The Indus Water Commission sources.
35. Sandeep Dikshit, "Pakistan for new measures to energize the Indus Treaty", The Hindu, 13th March 2010.
36. Khalid Hussain, Water, war and Peace: the Indus Waters Treaty under Threat –Part III", http://www.amankiasha.com_cat.asp?catId=1&id=50
37. Implementation of the Indus Basin Treaty Stressed, Daily Times 23rd February, 2010.
38. Article VIII of the Indus Waters Treaty.
39. "Is Commission effective in resolving the issues?, Pakistan, India to jointly inspect the pollution of drains", Daily Times, Islamabad, 24th July 2010.
40. The Indus Waters Treaty and Managing Shared Water Resources for the Benefit of Basin States – Policy Issues and Options, IUCN Pakistan, 2010. p.12.
41. Article VII of the Indus Waters Treaty.
42. "Experts agree to collaborate on the Indus Basin Programme" 05th Jul 2010, Kathmandu, http://www.icimod.org/?page=1217
43. Ibid.
44. "Pakistan and India urged to resolve the Siachen dispute", Business Recorder, 18th September 2009. See, http://sdpi.org/sdpiold/SDPI_in_the_press/media%20coverage%20200 9/media_coverage_sept_2009.html
45. The Convention was adopted in 1991 and entered into force in 1997. The Treaty has been ratified by forty countries from Europe and Central Asia as well as Canada and European Community.
46. "Introduction to Espoo Convention", The United Nations Economic Commission for Europe (UNECE), http://live.unece.org/env/eia/eia.html

47 Data provided by the Indus River System Authority (IRSA), January 2011.
48 "India agrees to site inspection of hydropower projects", The News, 24th July 2010.
49 See, Beyond the Indus Waters Treaty: Ground Water and Environmental management –Policy issues and options, IUCN, 2010.
50 Thimphu Statement on Climate Change, Thimphu 28-29 April, 2010. http://www.saarc.org/userfiles/thimphuStatementon ClimateChange 29April2010.pdf
51 The Indus Waters Treaty and Managing Shared Water Resources for the Benefit of Basin States – Policy Issues and Options, IUCN Pakistan, 2010, P.11.
52 Sardar Tariq, "Analyzing Pakistan's Irrigation System", in Pakistan Water Management and Security, A National Seminar organized by the Center for Research and Security Studies, (CRSS), 2008.
53 The Indus Waters Treaty and Managing Shared Water Resources for the Benefit of Basin States – Policy Issues and Options IUCN Pakistan 2010, P.12.

Paper Three:

Pakistan Water Security Dilemma – Approaches to rejuvenating the Indus Waters Treaty

Sardar Muhammad Tariq

Abstract

This paper briefly traces the history of water disputes which emerged immediately after the partition of the sub-continent into two independent and sovereign states of India and Pakistan. It highlights the firm views of India and Pakistan on riparian water rights prior to the signing of the Treaty in 1960. It further mentions the strong reaction of Indian Lok Sabha against the Treaty. Also, India has signed bilateral agreements with Nepal and Bangladesh and this article evaluates the extent to which these treaties have been honoured by India and what lessons can be learnt from those treaties. This research paper also discusses the evolution of the International Water Laws since the signing of the Indus Waters Treaty. At the end, available options are discussed to move forward to rejuvenate the Indus Waters Treaty.

Background

Water disputes between India and Pakistan emerged immediately after the partition of the sub-continent into two independent and sovereign states. This partition unfortunately cut across the already established and well functioning networks of irrigation canals and numerous hydraulic structures with control structures of the eastern rivers falling within the domain of India and the canal network extending into the West Punjab and irrigating some 5 million acres of fertile land. Soon after the partition, India communicated to Pakistan of its intention to divert the waters of the eastern rivers for its own uses. As the control structures were in the Indian Territory, India could do it easily. This meant that the single and the only economic base of Pakistan i.e. irrigated agriculture would be left high and dry. This act of India tantamount to strangulating Pakistan's agro-based economy and igniting the fuse for a major war. The sensitivities of this issue were realized by the international communities as well and with the good offices of the World Bank and over a decade of negotiations, the Indus Waters Treaty was signed in 1960 between India and Pakistan with World Bank as a guarantor and also a signatory to the Treaty. Under this Treaty, the three eastern rivers viz. Ravi, Sutlej and Beas were given to India and the three western rivers namely Indus, Jhelum and Chenab were given to Pakistan with limited uses by India.

Post Treaty Reaction[1]

The Treaty was not the best for either side. There were conflicting principles put on the table by both sides. Indians held their argument on "equitable utilization" – the favourite of the International Law Association and took the position that Pakistan got 75% of the water when represented a violation of the principle of "equitable utilization". The Treaty came under heavy fire in the Indian Parliament and was subjected to trenchant criticism by most of the speakers who participated in the Lok Sabha debate on the subject on 30th November 1960. They blamed the Government of India for a policy of appeasement and surrender to Pakistan and said that the Indian interest had been let down.

From Pakistan side, the fact that they were allocated only 75% of the water when they had 90% of the irrigated land represented a violation of the principle of "appreciable harm" – the favourite of the International Law Commission.

Denial of perennial flows to Pakistan of three eastern rivers created tremendous management problems and resulted in the first "hydrological shock" whereby the vast and the most productive irrigated land was deprived of perennial flows of river waters. The three rivers allocated to Pakistan under the Treaty were in the west whereas the irrigated land was in the east with hundreds of kilometers of distance between them. Pakistan not only had to undertake massive engineering works to transfer the waters of western rivers to east through storage dams, inter-river link canals, barrages, headworks etc, the construction of these infrastructural works were the largest civil engineering works ever undertaken in the history of the world and had to be completed within a record and challenging period of 10 years. Pakistan not only faced the problem of infrastructural development but had to set aside a large sum of money annually to meet the future operation and the maintenance cost of these huge hydraulic structures exposing itself to a very high degree of structural safety hazards. The three eastern rivers allocated to India had a cumulative flows of 33 MAF out of which India was only utilizing 3 MAF and left with 30 MAF for future expansion. Against this, Pakistan did not get any additional water and had to develop storages for its future requirements. It was, therefore, a difficult situation for both India and Pakistan, as both were depending upon position based arguments.

India's Bilateral Treaties with Nepal and Bangladesh
Treaties between India and Nepal[2]

Nepal and India so, far, have entered into agreements on the construction of Joint Projects on three main rivers-Koshi, Gandaki and Mahakali. Among the three Projects, the first two are in operation while the third one on Mahakali River has not yet been started.

The Koshi agreement was signed between the two countries in 1954. This Project was basically aimed at controlling flood in India and providing much needed irrigation to the Indian fields. The Project was constructed in Nepal near the Nepal-India border. A barrage has been constructed with two out-flowing canals. The entire water of Koshi River has, thus, been connected to India, leaving Nepal with some water to irrigate about 15 thousand hectares of land. The irrigation water supplied to India could irrigate about 595,000 hectares of land. The entire cost of the Project was borne by India. A small power house of 20 MW is to be built in India whose 50% power is to be provided to Nepal on a mutually agreed price. The Gandak Project Agreement was concluded in 1959 between Nepal and India on the River Gandak. Like the Koshi Agreement, the Gandak Agreement also is meant to construct a barrage to control the flood downstream in India and irrigate its land, leaving some water to irrigate 39,600 hectares of land in Nepal. The entire flow of the river passes to India which irrigates 920,520 hectares of land in India. A small power house of the size of 15 MW was constructed using the canal water for supplying power free of cost to Nepal. Both these agreements are widely criticized by Nepalese people. As such, they were subsequently amended. However, those amendments did not alter the substance of the agreement, particularly the sharing of benefit between the two countries. They remained heavily imbalanced. As a matter of fact, these were the projects done in Nepalese soil by India for their own uses. Whatever meager benefit was given to Nepal was simply a some fraction as a goodwill gesture. Till to date, in the mind of the general public of Nepal, there is an ill feeling about India due to these projects. In 1996, an agreement was signed into between India and Nepal on the

Integrated Development of the Mahakali River. This agreement combines three different projects – the Sarada Barrage, the Tanakpur Barrage and the Pancheshwar Dam on the river. The Pancheshwar Dam Project is yet to be constructed. Among the three Projects, Pancheshwar is a multipurpose Dam Project generating more than 6000 MW of electricity and irrigation to more than one million hectares of land in India and about 94,000 hectare of land in Nepal. The project benefits also include flood control. The project is to be constructed on the river Mahakali which forms the border between the two countries. This agreement has established following principles:

- Power 50 % to each country.

- Nepal to get 50% of the water of which it shall use for irrigating of 94 thousand hectares of land. The rest shall flow to India. The benefits which India is going to get due to extra water shall be assessed and be charged to India for the construction of the Project.

- India shall pay for the flood control benefit also.

- Mahakali Commission shall be established for the implementation of the Project.

The Project Report has not been completed because of the differences between the countries on the calculation of benefits to India and its share in the cost. Although the agreement was concluded in 1996, detail Project Report for Pancheshwar has not been completed. However, other components of the Agreement like Sarada Barrage and Tanakpur power house are in function and India is getting benefits out of these projects. Nepal's benefits from these projects are meagre. From delayed tactics, it looks as India does not want to construct the Pancheshwar Project. India is already getting almost the entire water of the Mahakali River and using it through Sarada Barrage and Tanakpur power house, the first of which was constructed under agreement and the second was unilaterally constructed by India on the face of Nepalese opposition. Apart from the above three projects, both the countries are in negotiation on water resources for the last 30 years without much success. India keeps on re-interpreting the Treaty clauses to its advantage which are constantly being challenged by Nepal. This Treaty could have formed a good example of benefit-sharing had India stuck to the original clauses and the spirit behind these clauses.

Treaty between India and Bangladesh[3]

India constructed a barrage at Farakka on the upstream of the Ganges and started withdrawal of water on the basis of an ad-hoc agreement signed on 18th April 1975. In this agreement, Bangladesh gave consent for the withdrawal of 11-16 thousands cusecs water from April 21 to May 31, for a limited period of 41 days. In return, India promised that rest of the water will flow through Bangladesh. But after the expiry of 41 days period, India kept on withdrawing water in the lean period of 1975 and 1976. In April 1976, the flow of water at Hardinge point came as low as 23,000 cusecs against 65,000 cusecs of the corresponding time of previous years. India signed a 5-year-water-sharing treaty with Bangladesh on 5th Nov 1977. The Treaty had a Guarantee Clause for getting 80% of the flow during the lean period and an arbitration clause. After the expiry of the Treaty in 1982, India refused to renew/extend the time period.

Then, in October 1982, a two-year mutual agreement followed by another three-years agreement (on Nov 22, 1985) was signed between the two sides. But in these two agreements, the Guarantee and Arbitration clause of 1977 Treaty were withdrawn. After that on 12th Dec 1996, a 30-year Water Treaty was signed between India and Bangladesh. This Treaty was also devoid of the Guarantee and Arbitration clauses. After the 1996 Treaty, during the lean period, for the last few years, the flow of water at Hardinge bridge point comes down to 10,000 cusecs, even sometimes as low as 5,000 cusecs.

Adverse Impacts of Farakka Barrage

The main environmental problems already created due to the withdrawal and diversion of water through Farakka Barrage may be summarized as follows:

- Due to continuous withdrawal of water through Farakka Barrage for the last 31 years, a significant number of rivers in the Padma basin of Bangladesh have already turned into dead rivers. The Garai, a pre-Farakka mighty river now is almost dead. In pre-Farakka days, during the rainy season, the maximum flow of water through the Garai used to be in the range of 142,000 – 328,000 cusecs; now, it has become a memory of the past. According to a report of the Water Development Board, 17 rivers in Bangladesh are already dead. Many rivers are nearly dead.

- During the dry season, when water is much needed in all areas of Bangladesh, in particular for the irrigation of 200,000 hectares of land under the Ganges-Kobotak project, water becomes almost non-available. The Ganges-Kobatak (G.K.) is the largest irrigation project of Bangladesh. It supplies water from the Padma (Ganges) to 300,000 acres of land. The project consists of 120 miles long main canal, 292 miles long branch canals and 62 miles long sub-branch canals. But the scarcity of the Padma water has made the project ineffective. Agriculture in a vast area of Kushtia, Hessore and Faridpur regions comes to a standstill in the dry season. Most of the 113 tributaries of the Padma become dry or have scarce water from November – May. The water sharing of the Teesta River ended without any agreement although many meetings were held. The Teesta River near the Teesta Bridge looks like a part of a desert during the dry season. A vast area of the land, once a grainery of Bangladesh, has become desert and a food-deficient area now.

- When excessive rains in the upper Ganges basin and the ice-melt water create pressure on the barrage due to abnormal rise of water, India opens all the sluice gates. Then the sudden on-rush of water causes floods in Bangladesh or increase, the intensity of the floods.

- During the dry season (water-scarce period) the irrigation system based on shallow-tube wells suffers adversely due to the considerable downward shift of the ground water tables (3-15 meters). On an average, every year the ground water tables are lowered by about 5 meters which is recharged from the rain water and normal flooding.

- As a result of the diminished flow, the intrusion of sea-water in the southern part of the country, particularly through the Rupsa River, on the bank of which is located one of the major industrial cities, Khulna, has become so pronounced that salinity has gone up more than 60 times then the pre-Farakka times. Increase of salinity in such magnitude has significantly altered the ecology of the region.

- As an adverse effect of the Farakka barrage, many places of the Murshidabad District of the West Bengal has been suffering from serious water-logging.

- In the post-Farakka period, the ground water in many places of West Bengal is registering a very high arsenic content; since then, the ground water of the district Rajshahi, which is adjacent to Farakka, is also showing a high arsenic content.

- The interrupted and diminished flow of the Ganges has also caused disturbances in the normal sediment transport. As a consequence, the Ganges flood-plain in Bangladesh is being deprived of the natural supply of micro-nutrients.

- Desertification syndromes have already started in the north-eastern part of Bangladesh as a consequence of the withdrawal of water through the Farakka Barrage.

By the adverse impacts so far created, on the environment and the ecology of Bangladesh by Farakka Barrage, it is logical to term it 'an undeclared environmental war against Bangladesh'. But it is pertinent to note that the very purpose for which this dam was constructed is defeated. The Farakka Barrage is popularly known in Bangladesh as "Death Barrage".

The Inter-basin River Linking Project[4]

India is now implementing a gigantic project, the 'Inter-basin River Linking Project' to divert water from all common rivers. This project has two components i.e. (i) the Himalayan component and (ii) the Peninsular component. In the Himalayan component, 14 link canals and in the Peninsular component 16 link canals, all together 30 link canals, will be excavated within the frame work of the project.

India in its river interlinks project, aims to connect 37 rivers by 30 link canals. The total length of these link canals would be approximately 12 thousand kilometers. The breadth of the link canals have been proposed to be 50-100 meters and the depth to be approximately 6 meters.

The upstream withdrawal of water through the Farakka Barrage has already started the desertification syndrome in Bangladesh, the intrusion of salinity in inland fresh water and created many serious environmental problems including the bio-diversity loss. In addition, if India executes the inter basin river link project, then Bangladesh, known all over the world as a land of rivers, fish and rice, and a beautiful green land, will lose all its present identity. There are international protocols for sharing of common rivers flowing through more than one country. It is mandatory to supply the data of the flow of water through a river, its courses, the environment and the ecology of the river bank and the catchments area and the bio-diversity of the country to the country or countries sharing the same river. But India is not supplying any information about its on-going inter basin river link project to Bangladesh. The rivers included in the inter-basin river link project are all international or common rivers between India and Bangladesh. Therefore, unilateral construction of any barrage on upstream, the withdrawal of upstream water and the change of river course are definitely in violation of international laws.

India's Latest Policy Document[5]

India's latest thinking on transboundary waters is amply reflected in a recent report by the Institute of Defense Studies in India (IDSA 2010) on water security and elaborates the increasing attention to water issues within a broader geographical context.

While reviewing India's bilateral water relations with neighbouring countries, country by country, the report notes that if not managed well, riparian issues will lead to increased conflicts. It calls for a paradigm shift from the historical supply side considerations in domestic and international agreements, and past investments focused on water sharing among competing interests, to one that focuses on benefit-sharing. It stresses that rivers can no longer be viewed as the "soft-component" of a country's foreign policy. Rather, they must be seen as intricately linked to development goals and domestic needs impacting bilateral relations. The report goes on to say that while it is important to adopt sensible riparian policies and 'healthy rivers' schemes, there is a need to sub-continent the existing treaties and reframe them based on the current hydrological knowledge and the future mutual needs. India's geographical contours place multiple upper, middle and lower riparian systems within its borders – thus placing it at the epicenter of riparian politics. Therefore, collaborative riparian management will be crucial for settling many of the water induced conflicts in the region; greater hydro-diplomacy–both internally and across national borders – will need to balance the region's growing water needs with the larger security concerns.

The gist of this policy document is described hereunder:

➢ The Policy while reviewing India's bilateral relations with neighbouring countries, country by country, notes that if not managed well, riparian issues would lead to increased conflicts.

➢ It calls for a paradigm shift from the historical supply-side considerations in domestic and international agreements, and past investments focused on water sharing among competing interests, to one that focuses on benefit-sharing.

➢ It stresses that rivers can no longer be viewed as a "soft component" of the country's foreign policy. Rather, they must be seen as intricately linked to development goals and domestic needs impacting bilateral relations.

➢ The document goes on to say that while it is important to adopt sensible riparian policies and healthy river schemes, there is a need to re-evaluate the existing treaties and reframe them based on the current hydrological knowledge and the future mutual needs.

➢ The policy document places India at the epicenter of riparian politics due to its geographical contours as multiple upper, middle and lower riparian systems lie within its borders.

➢ The document goes on to suggest that collaborative riparian management will be crucial for settling many of the water induced conflicts in the region. It emphasizes greater hydro-diplomacy – both internally and across national borders – that will be essential to balance the region's growing water needs with the larger security concerns.

Evolutions of International Water Laws[6]

The International Water Laws since then, have constantly undergone evolutions to reflect the current understandings, which, recently, are more oriented towards the promotion of cooperation rather than conflict, encouraging interest-based prospects rather than positional discussions and negotiations. The primary role of the Law, in this context, is to enable the determination of each state's equitable and reasonable "entitlements" to the benefits of the use of transboundary waters and to establish certain requirements for the state's behavior while managing and developing the resource. To prove that the benefit-sharing paradigm is really a good idea, it will become incumbent on the water resources' management practitioners to demonstrate the material benefits and the positive sum outcomes to adhere to its principles. This is essential in creating confidence in the stakeholders on both sides of the divide. Commenting on the International Water Laws and the IDSA Task Force Report in the Oct-Nov 2010 publication of "Dams, Rivers and People," New Delhi, the importance of the role of water in national and regional politics is summed up as quote: "Resource nationalism will increasingly dominate the hydrological contours of South Asia and will largely define regional politics."

"The hydrological contours of India, both as an upper riparian and a lower riparian, will be the epicenter of new riparian politics and diplomacy over transboundary rivers – India's riparian relations with its neighbours will become progressively fragile, with Pakistan, Bangladesh and Nepal continuously raising concerns over regulating and sharing of river waters."

"The International Water Laws on allocating water within a river-basin are difficult to implement and often contradictory".

The UN Convention on 'Non-Navigational Uses of International Watercourses', approved in 1997 by a vote of 104 to 3 (but not yet ratified), requires watercourse nations (Article 5) to participate in the use, development and protection of an international watercourse in an equitable and reasonable manner. Burundi, China and Turkey (upper riparians) voted against the Convention. India (middle riparian) abstained. While Bangladesh (lower riparian) voted for; Pakistan abstained. Of the other transboundary South Asian states, Nepal voted for, and Bhutan was absent. The Convention was adopted by a vote of 104 in favour to 3 against and with 27 absentees. From India's acts and approaches, it becomes quite obvious that India would not honour the International Water Laws and would not respect the existing treaties. India, in international forums, have repeatedly indicated that under a water stress situation and climate change impacts, the existing treaties would become irrelevant.

Existing Water Disputes between India and Pakistan

Wular Barrage and Tulbul Hydropower Project

India's projects of Wular Barrage and Tulbul Hydropower on the river Jhelum have been objected by Pakistan as a violation of Article (II) of the Treaty which prohibits both parties from undertaking any man-made obstruction that may cause "change in the volume of the daily flow of waters". Further that Article III (4) specifically barred India from "storing any water of, or construct any storage works on, the western rivers". India is allowed "incidental storage" on western rivers on its side under Article 8(h) of the Treaty only after its design has been scrutinized and approved by Pakistan and its storage capacity does not exceed 10,000 acre feet. Both Wular Barrage and Tulbul Project have implications on Pakistan's water availability during the low water season, when river flows are reduced to one fifth of the summer flows. There are chances of a serious threat to Pakistan, if India decides to withhold water over an extended period during the dry season. It would also multiply the risks of floods and droughts. The Mangla Dam also on river Jhelum, which is a source of irrigation and hydropower for Pakistan, would be adversely affected. Similarly, the Kishenganga Project on river Neelum would also affect the Nelum-Jhelum hydropower Project of Pakistan. The issue of Wular Barrage has been one of the disputes highlighted for India-Pak talks.

Kishenganga Hydropower Project

India plans to construct a 103 meter high dam on the Kishenganga River in the Gurez Valley, creating a large reservoir from a channel and a 27 km tunnel, dug south through the North Kashmir mountain range, will redirect the Kishenganga (Neelum) waters to the Wular Lake at Bandipur. The total distance by which the river will be diverted is 100 km. The project would generate 390 MW of hydropower. India's project being on the upstream of Neelum River will affect the flow of the Neelum River on which Pakistan is also constructing a 696 MW Neelum-Jhelum Hydropower Project with a tunnel of almost 47 km. India on the other hand, claims that it is within its rights to construct the Kishenganga Project and has been working on it since 1980s. According to the Treaty, the country that completes the project first will have priority rights over the water uses. So far, the Indus Commission has had numerous meetings but has been unable to resolve the issue. The opinion of an International Arbitrator and referring it to International Experts are being considered by Pakistan.

Baglihar Dam Project

This project is located at Chander Kot about 160 km north of Jammu on Chenab River. In Pakistan's view, the hydropower plant on Chenab River is a clear violation of the Treaty and a clear violation of the International Water Law. The Baglihar Dam Project was planned in two phases and the first phase was completed in 2005 and the second phase was completed in 2008. As per design, the Baglihar Dam is 143.3 m in height, 317 m in length with a design storage of 30,000 acre feet. According to Pakistan's stand, the design of the Baglihar Dam violates the Treaty, as it will affect the flow of Chenab River that will cause the shortage of water in Pakistan. Pakistan and India held numerous meetings without any outcome and finally Pakistan requested the World Bank for the appointment of a Neutral Expert in May 2005. The expert gave his verdict on February 12, 2007 in which he partially upheld some of the objections of Pakistan. The crucial decision was allowing India storage upto 26,000 acre feet to flush sediments. Since India is planning almost 33 hydropower projects on western rivers and if the decision of the Neutral Expert is applied to all of the future storages by India on the western rivers, it will have catastrophic consequences for Pakistan, as if India resorted to filling these reservoirs during the low water season, the cumulative effect of it could destroy the Rabbi crops in Pakistan.

A Way Forward[7]

Moving forward with a particular thinking or mindset can never see the end of the path. The complexities of the issues, the lack of political wisdom and will, positional based stands, a high level of mistrust, linkages to the Kashmir issue, negative public perceptions and deep buried hostilities offer formidable obstacles to cross. Any move forward will require a deep analysis of the mindsets on both sides. India's past history, its respect for already executed treaties, and its recent thinking have to be taken into consideration. Whereas India suggests to adopt a paradigm shift from conflict to cooperation and from water sharing to benefit-sharing, its hegemony in declaring itself at the epicenter of riparian politics due to its geographical contours tantamounts to a warning to other riparian countries. India is suggesting to re-evaluate the existing treaties and reframe them on the current hydrological knowledge and the future mutual needs. Apparently, one can say, India's thinking is in line with the current concepts on transboundary water issues and in conformity with the International Water Laws but, at this point of time, benefit-sharing has very limited international experiences and is relatively a new approach. It is a complex issue with multiple parameters to be addressed, including economic, social, environmental and political gains. Under these circumstances, the way forward is to honestly implement the existing treaty in its true spirit.

Issue that can be Addressed Bilaterally[8]

➤ To remove mistrust on data exchange, a satellite based data collection system should be installed for real time data information. The cost of such a system should be shared by both the countries.

  ➤ Since storage for flushing sediments has already been allowed to India, its timing is crucial for Pakistan's agriculture. This should be addressed bilaterally and can be resolved amicably once the real-time data becomes available. Otherwise, multiple hydropower stations being constructed by India, numbering 33 on the western rivers with cumulative storage, can impose major reductions on water availability in Pakistan during the critical planting season.

  ➤ Since hydropower does not consume water, the only issue is timing, and timing is a crucial issue because agriculture in Pakistan depends not only on how much water comes but that it comes in critical periods during the planting season. Under normal and trustful relations, India could increase low-flows during the critical planting season with significant benefits to Pakistan and small impacts on power generation in India.

  ➤ Presently, there is a very uneven playing field. The regional hegemon is the upper riparian and has all cards in its hands. The Institute of Defense Studies in India has, clearly and in unambiguous terms, identified India as the "epicenter of riparian politics". This asymmetry means that changes must start in India. India, therefore, would need to have some courageous and open-minded Indians who realize and explain to the public why it is an essential and a vital issue for Pakistan.

  ➤ If there is goodwill, there are multiple ways in which the treaty could be maintained and interpreted so that both countries could win. Otherwise, both countries would be dragged into unending processes of litigations. India looking for grey areas in the treaty and Pakistan on the offensive, with developments on both sides having negative impacts leading towards serious conflicts.

> Discussions on the Indus Waters Treaty should be delinked from both historic grievances and from the other Kashmir related issues; both sides showing a sign of statesmanship, and moving forward, considering water as a catalyst for development and not a resource for conflicts.

> Climate change impacts: Various models indicate that global warming can accelerate the glacier melt with the result that additional water would flow in the rivers originating from the Himalayan ranges. Since the treaty stipulates the average flow to be released to Pakistan, India can easily divert this additional water either for direct uses or filling up the large number of storage dams without letting Pakistan to benefit from this additional water. This issue could be taken up with India with positive suggestions to work out a joint climate change adaptation strategy in combating droughts and floods where water shortages and surpluses are jointly managed with minimum negative impacts on both countries.

Bilateral development of Kabul River: Similarly, Pakistan and Afghanistan should also adopt a strategy in developing the water resources of the Kabul River jointly and protecting Pakistan's historic rights on water uses. This is also a priority area where Pakistan must initiate dialogue with the Afghan Regime as soon as possible.

Issues which can Attract International Support and Understanding[9]

> **Environmental Flows to Maintain River Biodiversity:** India, during low-flows, diverts almost 100 percent of the waters of the three eastern rivers, leaving vast stretches of rivers within Pakistan's boundary completely dry. This violates the International River laws where environmental flows and maintaining rivers' health are mandatory for the riparian states. IUCN, WWF, GEF, UNEP, UNDP and many other organizations are strong advocates of such issues. Pakistan can raise this issue with these organizations and in international forums.

> **Transboundary Aquifers:** Another emerging issue on water and benefit-sharing is the maintenance of transboundary groundwater aquifer. India, with low power tariffs, has encouraged the installation of tube wells in Eastern Punjab and other bordering states with Pakistan with the result that ground water aquifers within Pakistan are over-mined by India. This issue can also be raised in the international forums with favourable reactions. An international conference on transboundary aquifers was recently held in Paris, France from 6-8 Dec 2010 organized by UNESCO to address the issues of shared aquifers.

> **Transboundary Water Pollution:** The natural slopes facilitate the flow of untreated effluent from East Punjab to West Punjab. Under the international water laws, the riparian states are required to ensure that untreated effluent is not discharged into the rivers, natural nullahs etc. This is again a justified issue and that Pakistan can raise in the international forums with favourable reactions.

National Water Management[10]

A point to be noted is that good geopolitical management, however, is only possible when countries successfully manage their myriad domestic water challenges. Currently, complex national level issues of food, water and energy tend to be addressed in a cylindrical fashion by sector focused ministries when cross sectoral analysis and solutions are urgently needed. Pakistan, therefore, needs to address its domestic water challenges seriously in an integrated and coordinated manner. Every drop of water needs to be utilized most judiciously to achieve more food, more value and more jobs. Pakistan needs to correct its direction on a top priority basis in managing national waters; else, its position on transboundary negotiations will remain on a weaker wicket. The dismal water management statistics, such as 132 cubic meter per capita storage against America's 6,150 m^3, Australia's 5,000 m^3; carry-over capacity of only 30 days as against 1000 days of Egypt;

the contribution of 34 cents by one cubic meter of water to the GDP against the developed countries of US$ 30 to 40; and wasting precious water resources to the tune of 1334 billion cubic meter value at US$ 158 billion into the sea over the last 32 years, make Pakistan's case extremely difficult for securing any international support. Pakistan is also one of the few countries in the world which does not have a National Water Policy. Pakistan's total hydro power potential is close to 100,000 MW. Pakistan has developed only 6500 MW i.e. 6 percent only. As against this, India has constructed 4,700 medium to large dams and created a carry-over capacity of 220 days. India's productivity is three time more than Pakistan and a unit of water contributes about US dollar 4 to Indian GDP. The total hydro power potential of India is 148,700 MW out of which India has already developed 31,000 MW and over 50 hydro projects are under different stages of development. India's share of coal in the overall energy production is 69 percent whereas Pakistan's share is only 1 percent in spite of having one of the largest coal deposits in the world. India plans to create an additional 180 BCM of storage volume by constructing some 2,500 dams by the year 2050. Pakistan, therefore, needs to have a paradigm shift in its overall water management strategy.

Author

The author is heading the Global Water Partnership – South Asia (GWP-SAS) as its Regional Chair (2010-2012); on the Board of Directors, Pakistan Water Partnership, the country chapter of the Global Water Partnership (GWP); Advisor to the Government of Khyber Pakhtunkhwa on Hydropower. He is on the panel of experts of the World Bank, the Malaysian Government, DFID and ADB. He has technically reviewed a number of water sector development projects for construction in Northern Areas. A variety of technical papers and publications on engineering, water management and allied areas have been printed in different forums all over the world.

Notes

1. Sardar Muhammad Tariq, Regional Chair, Global Water Partnership –South Asia (GWP-SAS), Islamabad, Pakistan.
2. Surya Nath Upadhyay – Mahakali Treaty: The View from the NegotiatingTable.
3. Professor Dr. Jasim uddin Ahmad, Mostafa Kamal Majumder – Regional Cooperation for Sharing Transboundary River Water. Margalla Papers 2011 – Special Edition 65
4. Sardar Muhammad Tariq, Regional Chair, Global Water Partnership –South Asia (GWP-SAS), Islamabad, Pakistan.
5. The Institute of Defense Studies and Analysis (IDSA) (2010) Water Security for India: The External Dynamics, New Delhi: IDSA.
6. Sardar Muhammad Tariq, Regional Chair, Global Water Partnership –South Asia (GWP-SAS), Islamabad, Pakistan.
7. John Briscoe. Water or Peace on the Indus. The News International. April 03, 2010.
8. Sardar Muhammad Tariq, Regional Chair, Global Water Partnership –South Asia (GWP-SAS), Islamabad, Pakistan.
9. Sardar Muhammad Tariq, Regional Chair, Global Water Partnership –South Asia (GWP-SAS), Islamabad, Pakistan.
10. Sardar Muhammad Tariq, Regional Chair, Global Water Partnership –South Asia (GWP-SAS), Islamabad, Pakistan.

Paper Four:

Sustaining The Water Division And/Or Sharing The Benefits: A Conflict-Management perspective

Dr. Zaigham Habib

ABSTRACT

This paper is written in the context of national water security concerns, obligations of the Indus Waters Treaty (IWT 1960), increasing upstream developments leading to shrinking downstream control on river waters and new challenges faced by Pakistan like higher uncertainty and climate induced changes. In the conflict management perspectives, Pakistan needs to carefully evaluate all possible options to protect and use trans-boundary water resources. The paper briefly reviews the conceptualization of trans-boundary benefit-sharing. Despite much discussion, the concept remains loose (Phillips et al., 2006), procedure intensive and situation specific. The upstream and downstream benefits can be mutually conflicting and competitive. The benefits from the rivers (irrigation, hydropower, etc) and benefits to the rivers (water quality control, environmental flows) are two key categories for trans-boundary collaboration. Their implementation mostly requires tradeoffs between upstream and downstream water users. The potential of sharing water use benefits within a particular basin depends upon physical opportunities, attached costs and the level of cooperation between riparian states. Global examples of benefits and costs sharing are summarized in the paper, highlighting the scope and complimentary mechanisms.

Background and Context

More than 260 river basins are internationally shared. These basins have 60 percent of global freshwater surface flows and are home to some 40 percent of the world's population. As the demand for water grows in all countries, the competition for shared resources increase to meet the needs of billions of people for drinking water, food, energy, and industrial production. A direct consequence is less water available for new uses, deterioration of water quality, a threat to the ecosystems and impeding water security to the lower riparian. Even where historically robust water sharing and river basin management is practiced, the uncertainties of climate change are likely to pose new risks, mostly not understood and quantified yet. The global challenge to enhance cooperation is well understood. However, mechanisms to meet this challenge are subject to a wide range of conditions including existing trans-boundary agreements, nature of the water stress, willingness of the riparian to cooperate and to some extent, the role of the global institutes.

Pakistan and India signed the Indus Waters Treaty in 1960, after 9 years of negotiations mediated by the World Bank. The treaty is exclusive, simple and authoritative. It is the only treaty, which recommends to divide and diverting full rivers away from their more than 80 percent of users to establish sovereign water rights. The implementation of the Treaty resulted into large movement of water: i) a major part of the flows of two rivers transferred outside their natural basin on the Indian side, ii) more than 20 cubic kilometers water transferred from the western to the eastern rivers to ensure irrigation supply to the most fertile land of Punjab. Diversion of the eastern rivers by the upper riparian was easy, because the downstream riparian was totally excluded. However, upstream developments in the western catchments raised issues on downstream impacts in terms of control over water volumes, reduced and modified flow patterns, and environmental degradation of fresh water resource.

During the last twenty years, global institutes have move forward in agreeing on the principles of "fairness, no harm to other riparian and protection of water resources" (Helsinki, UN). The global declarations also acknowledge that a definite set of rules cannot be recommended for all trans-boundary solutions. Collective regional drives are launched to address the environmental and climate change issues (EU, Africa). The "benefit sharing approach as a solution" is presented as a "win-win" alternate, while it is practiced in limited cases.

To evolve a crises management approach, Pakistan should formulate pertinent trans-boundary problems faced as a lower riparian of the Indus Basin, identify possible solutions and procedures, and, then, evaluate the scope of the benefit-sharing and the water-division approaches to improve or add to the existing trans-boundary treaty.

Trans-Boundary Water Sharing Norms

Most of the 240 internationally shared river basins have a series of bi-lateral or multi-lateral treaties, representing the stakeholders' interest, and hydro-development scenarios evolved with time. The trans-boundary contracts have been shifted towards regional commitments for the protection of rivers and watercourses, joint management, and water quality issues. The Oregon State University has compiled a Transboundary Freshwater Dispute Database (TFDD) listing 424 agreements signed between 1820 and 2007. The list includes 36 agreements on Rhine and 19 on Nile Rivers. The majority of the agreements, 91, target water quantity, 67 hydropower, 59 water quality, 44 joint management, 46 border issues and 24 each on flood control and navigation. A major addition in trans-boundary agreements during the last two decades is the regional agreements on water quality and joint management of water-ways. All large basins gradually have more riparians involved in the contracts as more countries started developing water resources (Nile, Rhine and Mekong). A higher spirit of cooperation is shown by the EU and the African nations to protect water ways, joint watershed management and maintenance of surface water quality. In 1997, twenty eight (28) EU states, the Economic Commission of Europe and the USA signed a document "convention on environmental impact assessment in a transboundary context". In 2003, fifty (50) African countries signed the "African convention on the conservation of nature and natural resources". On the other hand, Middle East and South Asia could not progress towards better cooperation. Existing agreements remain subject to the implementation difficulties and water insecurity increased with time.

Water Division Rules and Principles

Extensive work is done by global and local experts and institutes to classify existing trans-boundary agreements, on the one hand, and to formulate generally accepted principles for a fair division of shared water resources on the other. To provide a reference, this section briefly summarizes: i) four famous doctrines, ii) principles for equitable sharing agreed through UN and, iii) actual determinants of water treaties.

Four Doctrines of Water Division

These doctrines try to conceptualize guiding rules of trans-boundary agreements.

> ➤ The doctrine of absolute sovereignty is also called the Harmon doctrine. According to the doctrine, each riparian state has the absolute freedom to utilize water flowing through its territory, regardless

its impact on other riparian states. The "sovereign development" can lead to one-sided programs giving a privilege to the riparian having the technical and the economic potential to "develop first". The international agreements under this doctrine create de-facto sovereign conditions which limit them to a non-integrated development regime with minimum sharing of information and no institutional coordination. "Cooperation in the development and conservation of international watercourses is based on sets of self-limitations to sovereignty (Solanes, 1992)". The doctrine is not accepted by the international water laws.

➢ The doctrine of limited territorial sovereignty evolved as an intermediate approach to resolving the international water disputes. It is a widely accepted principle in treaties and in expert's opinions. It conforms to the general legal obligation to use one's property in a manner which will not cause injury to others. According to Dellapenna (1999) restricted sovereignty leads to "equitable utilization".

➢ The doctrine of absolute riverine integrity expects that a state will not alter the natural flow of waters passing through its territory in any manner which will affect the water in another state, be it upstream or downstream. The doctrine is not considered very practical.

➢ The doctrine of joint basin management assumes a riparian collectivism of interests among the basin states, and treats the total volume of basin water as a shared resource. The theory of joint management stipulates that the entire river basin constitutes a single geographic and economic unit that transcends national boundaries, and, therefore, the basin's waters are either invested in the whole community or shared among the riparians.

Principles for Equitable and Reasonable Sharing

The UN convention (1997) and other International Forums recommend a few basic guiding principles for trans-boundary water sharing.

➢ International drainage basins or international water courses are an aggregate of surface and ground waters flowing into a common terminus (Caponera, 1995; Green Cross, 2000).

➢ The principle of equitable use requires that the interests of all riparian countries should be taken into account when allocating and developing international water courses. The principle has been applied by international and national courts. It was endorsed by the Helsinki Rules and by the UN Convention in 1997. The primacy of the rule of equitable utilization was confirmed by the International Court of Justice in its ruling on the Danube River Case in 1997. The principle of equitable utilization emerged as the central concept in reconciling the various interests of the basin states in the development of their trans-boundary waters (Wouters 1992).

➢ The obligation not to cause harm requires preventive and cooperative actions. The duty to curb adverse effects applies to many aspects of the international water law, but is particularly relevant in relation to water pollution. The 1988 Report to the International Law Commission suggests that appreciable harm resulting from water pollution is a violation of the principle of equitable use. The World Bank statement for projects in international waterways requires the assessment of potential significant harm before approving them (Solanes, 1992; Caponera, 1995; McCaffrey, 1996).

➢ **Joint Development of International Rivers:** Joint development, which is ideal for shared water resources, is difficult to achieve because of the questions of sovereignty, the ownership of waterworks, jurisdiction, financing, the scope of cooperation, etc.

➢ **Protection of Natural Water Bodies:** The principle is not only stressed by all international declarations, it has also become a key point for the regional cooperation.

Actual Determinants of Trans-Boundary Treaties

The trans-boundary water dialogues mostly focus on acquiring higher water shares and development rights by each riparian state. A combination of favorable factors and constraints determines to what extent a doctrine is relevant or to what extent recommended principles are applied.

Basin Hydrology and Geospatial Location of Rivers: The topography and location of the runoff source determine the local potential for development and control over river flows. Distribution of drainage runoff determines the level of physical control a riparian state can exercise. Locations for hydropower generation on the main and tributary rivers mostly provide an edge to the upstream states.

In rare cases, downstream states can have this edge, like Egypt on Nile. "The dynamics between littoral riparians (who reside on the opposite banks of a shared river) are likely to be substantially different from sequential riparians (who reside strictly upstream or downstream from one another) in terms of the way in which they view their interests and their alternatives to cooperative water management.

Already Developed Water Uses: These uses are normally protected by the traditional laws as "historical riparian rights or as prior allocations". Generally, treaties accept these rights. However, allocations of untapped water resources hardly follow previous development pattern. In any large basin, emerging needs and development potential often lead to conflicts between "upstream and downstream" and "indigenous and developed water uses". Solutions are sorted in "equitable distribution".

Urgent Water Needs and High Water Demands: The actual water needs and planned development differently affect trans-boundary conflicts. In case of sufficient water available, treaties are easy and leave a room for future adjustments (Canada, US). While, in a water scarce situation, high water needs can delay the treaties or create implementation problems (Middle East region).

Asymmetry of the Political Power: Political asymmetry is a critical factor in shaping the trans-boundary water agreements. The powerful economy in shared catchments has a higher potential to use and develop water resources, regardless of being upstream or downstream. Water resources developments in shared basins clearly show an influence of the larger economy and politically powerful country. For example, Israel in case of Jordan river catchments, Egypt in Nile basin, China in Mekong Basin and India in case of Indus and Barhamputra. In the context of the Middle East, 'the most powerful riparian state manages to impose its own water policies and an open conflict occurs in the interest of the hegemonic' (Lowi, 1993 Waterbury, 1994).

The Environmental Security

High water scarcity and extreme pollution can lead to a high risk of violent conflicts "which are often accompanied by a high population growth and a socially inequitable distribution of resources" (Homer-Dixon, 1994a). The depletion of water resources because of climate induced changes can increase the environmental stress and water conflicts at the national and regional levels.

Benefits and Loss Sharing in a Basin

The concept of benefit sharing as an alternate to the river water division/sharing emerged only during the last decade. The trans-boundary agreements dealing with water quantity, water quality and joint basin management are not directly based on computed and legally allocated water benefits. The future water uses and benefits are subject to political and economic conditions, regional political harmony and the ability of the riparian states to implement development schemes. The economic benefits of the allocated water shares are mostly realized, sometimes quantified and bargained in trans-boundary agreements. The "side payments" are also involved with water transfers. However, trans-boundary water division and distribution have three weak areas:

- Dis-integrated and inefficient use of water resources,
- Large regional inequalities, and
- Environmental degradation of water bodies and ecosystems.

The IWRM approach, advocated by international research and development organizations, (GWP, WB, ADB, FAO) had severe limitations in providing management solutions for shared basins. The transboundary treaties rarely consider groundwater and local rain runoff on the supply side. Similarly, comprehensive water demands and the future development potential, at best, remain as background information. The water use efficiency within the riparian states could be different depending upon the physical and management factors. Needs for the allocation of the environmental flows are normally not included in the treaties. In case of a long river, the upper riparian is hardly convinced to reconsider the downstream impacts of extensive upstream developments.

The management desires for comprehensive planning and optimizing of water based benefits are reflected from the debate on benefit sharing. Sharing a basket of benefits derived from the basin development and to achieve a win-win situation are projected as achievable goals. Benefit sharing is generally defined as "the process where riparians cooperate in optimizing and equitably dividing the goods, products and services connected directly or indirectly to the watercourse, or arising from the use of its waters (SADC 2010)." The arguments in favor of "benefit sharing" claim:

- Approach is more holistic and allows managing river water resources as a "basin unit", considering benefits, different stakeholders and protection of water resources.
- Approach can "broaden the perspective of basin planners" (Sadoff and Grey, 2002 and 2005) for the management and development of international shared rivers.
- Water can be used with high efficiency, developing optimal water schemes.
- It allows the involvement of communities in the planning and development of water resources,
- To implement the benefit sharing approach, political agreement among the governments and the communities is a prerequisite.

Components of the Benefit Sharing Approach

Most of the international literature refers four types of benefits, which can be addressed by the benefit sharing approach. It will be idealistic for a treaty to address all types. The challenges and opportunities indicate the scope and constraints of the approach.

Table 1. Types of Benefits as Proposed by Sadoff and Grey (2002)

	The Challenge	The Opportunity
Type 1: Providing benefits to the river	Water shed, water quality, wetlands, ENV	Flows, floods, droughts, erosion, sediment, climate
Type 2: Yielding benefits from the river	Water demand, development, sub-optimal use of water resources	Hydropower, agriculture, food security, tourism, ecosystems
Type 3: Reducing costs because of river	Management and operational costs	Cooperation, shift from food/energy self sufficiency to food/energy security
Type 4: Generating benefits beyond the river	Regional fragmentation	Regional integration, investment, trade, industrial development, market access

Type 1 benefits can provide optimal conditions for the management of watershed, water quality, water based environmental protection and biodiversity. To achieve the flood, drought and climate management opportunities, technical and financial inputs are required. Hence, the costs could be attached to these benefits. However, measures to provide benefits to the river (floods, sediment, environmental flows) are not equally relevant to all riparians and the estimation of benefits may become a challenge.

The type 2 benefits are more relevant for the riparian states. However, the accounting of the benefits is not a straightforward and one time exercise. The benefits tend to change with time and the opportunities to develop these benefits are normally highly unequal for the co-sharers of a river basin. The formulation of sustainable modes of sharing benefits is easy at the smaller or a single project level.

Under type 3, two types of costs could be reduced, operational costs (by building joint infrastructure) and conflict resolution costs. The approach assumes that a shift from food/energy self-sufficiency to food/energy security is possible. In an ideal situation, one country can grow food or produce electricity for the other, and at a reduced cost.

The type 4, increasing benefits beyond the river, improves regional-interaction by providing a cooperative environment for trade, markets and investment.

However, the question is, what is required to be in a position of availing the above mentioned potential benefits.

Implementation Conditions

Qaddami (1999 World Bank) identifies six conditions or mechanisms which support benefit sharing. According to him, benefit sharing is ultimately a question of political feasibility.

- **Issue Linkage:** Linking upstream-downstream issues to other issues where the downstream state holds power or control and the upstream state is the requesting party (e.g. Kazakhstan, the Kyrgyz Republic, Uzbekistan, and Tajikistan in the Syr Darya basin).

- **Diffuse Reciprocity / Good Relations:** Accepting an agreement – even, perhaps, on less favorable terms in order to keep good relations and to create a 'reservoir of goodwill' (e.g. South Africa and Lesotho in the Lesotho Highlands Water Project).

- **Large Geographical Scope:** Extending the scope of an agreement, for example, include rivers where the downstream river is upstream, and vice versa (e.g., Mozambique, South Africa and Swaziland on the Incomati River basin and the Maputo River basin).

- **Side Payments:** Providing financial compensation in return for a concession.

- **Slack Cutting:** Making use of the international fora in order to introduce a more ambitious national policy than would otherwise be possible through national channels alone.

- **Exercise of Power:** Possessing other sources of power (economic, military) that compensate for an inferior (downstream) location (Egypt in Nile basin & Israel in Jordan basin).

Practical Examples of Benefit Sharing

Lesotho Highlands Water Project: The project on the Orange River is recognized as a successful example of benefit sharing. The agreement is signed between the upstream water rich Lesotho and the downstream South Africa. The project transfers water from the high land in Lesotho to South Africa for domestic and industrial uses. As benefits for Lesotho, about 200 MW hydropower is provided as royalties. South Africa has preferred the project over a local option because of its lower cost and high technical feasibility. Another similar project is planned on the river downstream between South Africa and Botsawana.

The reduced river flows in Namibia, which is the last country of the Basin, are partly addressed by allocating environmental flows.

The orange basin countries, especially South Africa has a history of agreements with other riparian states. The Orange River Basin Commission (ORASECOM) has been expanded to include all sharing countries (Botswana, Lesotho, Namibia, South Africa). The ORASECOM agreement recognizes the Helsinki Rules, the United Nations Convention on the Non-Navigational Uses of the International Waters. It refers to the key concepts: "equitable and reasonable" and preventing significant harm (Earle et al, 2005). The Commission works as the main advisory body for the planning and development of the basin resources.

The Zambezi Basin: It provides another example of benefit sharing around a hydropower project. The basin is shared by eight countries. Two major water users, Zambia and Zambawi have a history of water sharing agreements signed. The Kariba Dam (1955-1959) of 70 km^3 capacity was jointly constructed across the border of Zambia and Zambawi to produce electricity. The dam displaced large populations in both countries, 57000 people. A joint power company CAPCO is responsible for generating and selling electricity while dividing benefits on a 50:50 basis.

This widely quoted success story on "benefit sharing without water allocations" is an excellent example to analyze possible conflicts. Five trans-boundary agreements have been signed after the construction of Kariba Dam, the last one in 2003, among all basin countries to address three types of issues.

> **Generating and Costing Non-Hydel Benefits:** The original contract not includes the benefits generated by irrigation, fishries, domestic and other uses of water, which are generated downstream.

> **The Economic Disparity is Favoring Zimbabwe for Hydel Power Benefits:** With the two electricity markets being asymmetric, and with Zimbabwe having a higher growth rate, this situation favored Zimbabwe.

> **Impacts of the Reduced Flows on Downstream Countries:** The last basin-level treaty includes a real-time information system, synchronizing of flood control and environmental flows.

There are suggestions for "water allocations" in "Zembezi basin".

The Incomati River Basin: It is shared by three countries (Swaziland, South Africa and Mozambique). An agreement between the three riparians was signed in 2002. Before that, there were many bilateral agreements and an interim tripartite agreement. The agreement upheld rules and obligations for equitable sharing by the Helsinki Rules (1966) and the UN Convention (1997). The basin provides an example of sharing water resources in a heavily used basin. The joint management focuses on the better management of water resources, increasing efficiencies, recycling of waste water and demand management, and new developments. A computer model is used to estimate water needs and evaluate water saving options. The water is allocated for domestic, industrial and irrigation uses. The costs are shared, based on water allocations.

The Mekong Basin Example: The Mekong River has annual average flows of 475 bcm. About 15 percent of the annual flows are currently developed. The members have bilateral agreements and different levels of cooperation. Water sharing is based on quantitative allocations. The basin is shared by eight countries. The Mekong River Commission (MRC) was established with active international support. Two upstream countries, China and Myanmar, are only observers.

The MRC is not an example of sharing benefits from a commercial project, but of cooperation for research, technical and institutional capacity building. The commission provides a platform to the basin states for information collection and sharing, management practices, development of guidelines and operational procedures, capacity building for issues like environmental assessments. For example, the MRC had adopted a wide ranging flood control program, which deals with emergencies as well as preventive measures. Numerous studies have been conducted on river protection and environmental issues. Under the MRC Agreement of 1995, there are three 'core programs', five sector programs and one support program.

The Nile Basin: The Nile basin is shared by ten countries. The Nile Basin Initiative (NBI), a partnership among the Nile riparian states was launched in 1999. The initiative "seeks to develop the river in a cooperative manner, share substantial socioeconomic benefits, and promote regional peace and security". Like the Mekong Commission, the NBI have launched programs to develop common analytical tools, a flood warning system, environmental protection and the protection of water bodies like lakes. The NBI also developed a Benefit Sharing Framework based on the Transboundary Waters Opportunities Analysis (TWO) - identify benefits, costs and development potentials. However, water division remains volumetric.

Historically, Egypt and Sudan heavily depends upon the Nile for agriculture and domestic uses. Two major agreements signed between the two in 1929 and 1959 depend upon estimated water needs, which cover about 90 percent of the Nile water. The NBI has not been able to reach to a new riparian agreement, because an agreed sharing formula could not be devised. In May 2010, the upstream states, Ethiopia, Kenya, Uganda, Rwanda, Burundi and Tanzania, signed a Cooperative Framework Agreement to seek more water from the River Nile – a move strongly opposed by Egypt and Sudan. In 2010, the Tana Beles dam conflict between Ethiopia and Egypt led to moving the "Nile file" from the Water and Power ministry to the National Security Authority. Egypt insists that projects, such as the Tana Beles station, need to be approved by it first.

Key Conclusions from Existing Experiences

- ➢ Exclusive benefit sharing schemes are mostly small projects in hydropower and urban water-use sectors.

- ➢ On a long-term basis, "the basket of benefits" can rarely be separated from the water allocation under specific conditions.

- ➢ There are regional commissions not involved in water allocations, but in the issues like flood protection, knowledge sharing, joint planning and research.

- ➢ The joint projects use inter-dependency for the benefit of the basin states or communities. Good political relations and will of the riparian states is more important than the water division agreements.

- ➢ Bilateral treaty is a preferred mechanism even among the countries which are the members of a "benefits sharing initiative among a group of riparians".

- ➢ Principles of equitable sharing, fairness and no harm to other party by Helsinki and UN conventions are referred to by both types of treaties.

- ➢ Generally, global water and finance institutes are involved in the benefit sharing projects.

The Current Status of the Trans-Boundary Conflict Resolution in the Indus Basin

India and Pakistan share all large rivers of the basin, Indus, and its five tributaries. A well reputed treaty (IWT 1960) exists between Pakistan and India dividing trans-boundary rivers with some exceptions. Disagreements on the implementation of the treaty have become frequent and stronger with time, as upstream developments, high water stress and climate change create serious challenges for Pakistan. Pakistan shares a large tributary river of the Indus with Afghanistan, where there is no water agreement yet. The implementation of the IWT has become a key issue between India and Pakistan. Despite following expensive procedures of hiring independent experts through the World Bank, Pakistan has failed to achieve its objectives. No convergence can be seen from the positions taken by both the countries. Technical aspects of the trans-boundary issues of Pakistan are not discussed and analyzed among the water experts of Pakistan. Similarly, suggestions to adopt a different approach (see the background section) are floated without any proper analysis. Before a discussion on future options, this section briefly describes the relevant features of the IWT, the current Indian approach and the issues Pakistan is facing.

Salient Features of the Indus Waters Treaty

- **Start of the Trans-Boundary Water Conflict:** The Indus water dispute started within a few months of the independence and the partition of the subcontinent. India blocked water to the two key canals of the Punjab from their head-works at the start of the wheat sowing period. These supplies were critical to avoid a famine and support the settlement of the millions of refugees. Ironically, this water had to flow through the 1200 km long river reaches in Pakistan. A stand-still agreement was signed in September 1948. Pakistan agreed to pay the water-cost for a year and construct new structures during this period.

- **Joint Management was Rejected in 1960:** The international boundary drawn in 1947 by the British Government did not consider the location of the rivers and canals system. The upper catchments of all the rivers were on the Indian side (Kashmir territory), while the large agriculture areas using 90 percent of the developed river flows were towards Pakistan side (Kashmir and all the four provinces of Pakistan). A historical conflict about the diversions of waters from the Eastern rivers existed in the basin from 1912. Because of high integrity and high dependency of downstream areas on river flows, joint management of the basin was the first recommendation by the WB president. Both countries rejected the joint management concept, first India then Pakistan.

- **Upstream Versus Downstream Control Disparity:** The upstream topography of the basin provides a large potential of small or big storages and diversion structures on river tributaries. While, the downstream topography has a limited potential for storage the and run-of-the-river projects.

- **An Authoritative Division of River Water without any Specific Standards:** The Indus Waters Treaty divides the five large tributary rivers of the Indus physically, without any obligations for the environment, water resource conservation and the protection of drinking water rights. The major part of the Treaty is about operational procedures and conflict handling. An expensive and lengthy conflict management mechanism was agreed upon. The principles of fairness agreed by the Helsinki Rules and the UN Convention, were not acknowledged by IWT (both countries are not signatory to these declarations). The IWT does not consider:

  - Actual uses of water or population based water needs.
  - Groundwater aquifer and source of recharge.
  - Environmental flows for ecological safeguard.
  - Minimum river flows to keep the eastern water ways operational, which have to carry over the flood flows.
  - Pollution and environmental degradation.
  - Future issues like climate change.

- **Side Payments:** India and the international community contributed for the physical works carried out to build two reservoirs, inter-river link canals and new canal head-works. Out of the total Indus Basin Development Fund (IBDF) which consisted of US $ 900 million, India contributed US $62 million, in ten annual installments during the transition period.

- **Institutional Arrangement for Water Security and Dispute Resolution:** Indus Commissions were formed in both countries to supervise the implementation of the IWT and dispute handling. India is bound to inform Pakistan and get its consent before the start of any project on western rivers. India is bound to provide the upstream flow data, specified --. Both sides will avoid building any man-made structure which can change the natural course of water. Both sides will be responsible for maintaining the Indus basin by adopting the best practices available. If India constructs any work on Western Rivers, it will supply water downstream within 24 hours. In case of disagreements, the two commissioners will work closely to plug in the difference. However, if the difference turns out to be a dispute, the World Bank will appoint a "neutral expert." If the neutral expert fails to resolve the dispute, negotiators can be appointed by each side to meet with one or more mutually agreed-upon mediators. If either side views a mediated agreement unlikely, provisions are included for the convening of a Court of Arbitration.

The Current Approach of India

India has started a substantive campaign to build hydropower projects, develop recreational facilities including water-based tourist points at high altitudes (an artificial lake in Jhelum catchment) and, recently, water-transfer structures (70 km tunnel diverting the flows of the Jhelum tributary for the Kishanganga project) on the western rivers. India's dominant approach is reflective from the recent strategic studies.

- Continue developing diversion structures, small dams and water bodies on western rivers, which could provide higher direct control on river flows. Use the "clean energy" and "local development" arguments. Recent climate-credit on two hydropower projects on the Chenab River without Pakistan's knowledge is an example in point.

- Increase agriculture water uses from the western river's tributaries in all upstream catchments using farm level mini-dams, local flood channels, tube-wells and formal irrigation schemes wherever possible. Subsidized groundwater use in western and eastern watersheds is causing aquifer depletion and stopping the normal recharge downstream.

- Maximize direct water benefits through all types of schemes, which could be designed as "non-consumptive water uses".

- A comprehensive and multi-dimensional approach is adopted by India, to manage trans-boundary conflicts with better technical and legal preparation. Some of the steps include: -

- Interpretations of the IWT in the name of new technologies (dead-storage for the run of the river reservoirs) successfully achieved,

- Clean-energy argument to get international support for new hydropower projects,

- Local developments and water rights for Kashmir are used as key arguments,

- Extreme positions within India are projected like a one sided abolition of the Treaty (the Indian Defense Forum).

- Pakistan's objections on Indian projects are linked with the political tension with Pakistan.

Pakistan's Trans-Boundary Water Case Boundary Conditions

While evaluating future trans-boundary options, Pakistan needs to consider a few boundary conditions that evolved from the existing status of the Indus Basin water resources inside and outside the country. These conditions set constraints for future strategy, negotiations and collaborative arrangements because: -

- ➢ Existing national water scarcity,

- ➢ Already disintegrated Basin of the Indus and its tributaries,

- ➢ Prior allocation of river flows inside the country,

- ➢ Indus tributary rivers facing serious environmental shortages and finally,

- ➢ Pakistan has not developed protections against climate change impacts.

A major part of the country has negative demand-supply balance during whole non-monsoon period. During the draught years of 1999-2002, the annual water availability was 900 cubic meters per capita, 10 percent lower other the water scarcity threshold by the UN (1997). The sensitive water use sectors, like drinking and domestic supply, face serious water shortages.

The Indus Basin is already a disintegrated basin with a substantial transfer of water outside the basin. The 100 percent normal river flows of the eastern rivers and 70 percent flows of the western rivers have been already utilized. At the current implementation level of the IWT, both countries are not in a position to go for a "fresh start". The flows of the Indus and tributary rivers have been divided between the provinces/states within both countries through internal water division agreements.

The period of dry river reaches (Habib 2009) is increasing for all Indus tributaries despite flood and heavy monsoons. The eastern rivers remain dry for more than ten months a year and then could receive heavy floods. The flood damages of 2010 and 2011 strongly suggest the need of minimum (maintenance) flows to keep the river reaches and the flood protection system intact. Lack of appropriate measures to address climate change impacts is another weak area for Pakistan.

Pakistan has sufficient space to straighten its national water scenario at two levels. A persistent delay in the planned development of water resources in the energy sector even at a high and regionally distributed economic cost is a key failure of the sector. The water use efficiency is another area of low performance. Unfortunately, under-reporting of actual water uses have increased due to multiple reasons (Habib ICID 2009) especially the lack of accounting in non-agriculture sector, informal agriculture uses and monitoring inaccuracies. The water allocation procedures have become multilayered and non-transparent with a consistent increase in unaccounted water resources.

Evolving Future Approach

The trans-boundary water challenges faced by Pakistan are not only due to the implementation and the interpretation of IWT but there are typical issues of hydrological water stresses faced by a lower riparian against upstream privileges in a water intensive basin economy. There are wide consequences of adopting a non-basin approach in 1960. There are consequences of providing limited securities downstream and ignoring the groundwater aquifer, environmental river flows and the mechanism for a long-term protection of water resources and their eco-systems. There are consequences of adopting a division of rivers without a mechanism to address consistent or sudden hydrological changes like the climate change, and extreme events of floods and droughts. There are also consequences of adopting a non-consultative, an expensive and a narrow process of dispute resolution.

Hence, Pakistan needs to adopt an inclusive approach to work in three domains: implementing the existing IWT, identifying and proposing solutions to address emerging gaps in the water division mechanism, and pursue collaboration for sharing the benefits of joint research and knowledge generation to address the climate change threats and the environmental degradation of water resources. The recommended steps include: -

- Implementation of IWT as conceived by Pakistan in 1960. The strategy will require addressing the Indian approach of making interventions with new techno-legal interpretations, and seeking a new valid interpretation for Pakistan.

- Addressing negative impacts of the IWT and gaps emerging in the Treaty within the water division approach. A case under clause 7 should be developed

- Developing bilateral and regional collaboration to protect the overall natural water resources of the basin and to manage new hydrological scenarios caused by the climate change and environmental degradations.

Scenario I: Strategy to Implement IWT

Full acceptance of IWT by both countries gives it a strong survival footing. India and Pakistan have not signed declarations of the Helsinki and the UN Convention to remain committed to IWT. Both countries consistently disagree on a few issues:

- Numerous hydropower projects planned by India on western rivers and control potential of these works.

- Technical specification of Indian hydropower projects, especially the legitimacy of the storage component.

- Data sharing and exchange of information.

Pakistan's commitment with the Treaty is obvious from a "letter and spirit" implementation approach. Pakistan never raised any objection during Indian works for the storage and diversion of eastern rivers. Objections on western developments are raised within the framework of IWT. the national water security was the main objective of Pakistan in 1960. Pakistan gave a unique sacrifice of 20 maf (25 bcm) water, the total flows of the two eastern rivers entering into its territory to achieve this security. By signing the IWT, Pakistan believed in securing exclusive rights on 97 percent flows of western rivers, unperturbed and uncontrolled upstream. Pakistan believed in achieving this target untill recently. The Baghlihar Dam decision by India in 2008 was a turning point for Pakistan, which allowed India to enter into the control of western rivers and to develop a potential for direct diversions upstream.

Ther new situation has left Pakistan with the only option to revisit the water division concept adopted in 1960, consequences of the assumptions taken in a narrow perspective and the interpretation issues that emerged with time. Today, Pakistan has to look into a different scenario of upstream control, new needs for correct assessment of water quantities (allocates, used, available for short or long durations) and new monitoring challenges in the watershed and across the basin.

For business as usual, there is a bigger ground for disagreements because of a wider gap in the interpretation of the Treaty clauses and the addition of new climate uncertainties. The frequency to approach the World Bank can increase, though the expensive process of WB mediations has no history of permanently resolving the basic issues regarding the IWT.

Within the scenario of IWT implementation, Pakistan needs to evaluate the following options and formulate its case on a long term basis:-

- Technical studies to simulate the combined impact of all structures on Chenab and Jhelum rivers on flow hydrographs under all possible operational scenarios.

- Estimation of water losses, evaporation, infiltration and operational losses, from the run-of-the-river storages in the western rivers' water sheds. The Indian research also provides a good reference for these estimations.

- Estimation of losses to the rain runoff discharges or drainage-inflows into a river due to the diversion of the water ways, especially the tunneling of the flows.

- A comprehensive methodology to independently estimate upstream water uses from western rivers. Remote sensing can be effectively used to estimate net water losses, cropped areas and actual evapotranspiration for the post treaty period.

- Making a case for "appropriate interpretations of IWT clauses/concepts" on three issues:
  - Upstream storages should include all mini and micro storages for agriculture, domestic or industrial purposes.
  - Water consumed by evaporation and seepage losses from the so called "non-consumptive structures" must be measured (India should provide data for that). These losses should be considered as "water utilized from the river".
  - Definition of "irrigation" needs to be "standardized" to include artificial water use from any source (flood canal, tube-well and water tank).

- Carry out comprehensive case studies of a few prominent trans-boundary cases, considering all techno-legal aspects and work on the gaps and lessons learned from these experiences.

- Identify limitations of IWT to accommodate Pakistan's concerns evaluated above. Develop strategies to address these concerns under both approaches, "water division" and "benefit sharing".

Scenario II: Expanding Water Division to Address Emerging Concerns of Pakistan

Can Pakistan move forward within the existing framework of water division to address emerging gaps and some of the negative impacts of the IWT? There are numerous examples of improvements and additions in water treaties with time. The convergence of interests and the consent of the riparians are determining factors in the improvement or enhancement of the old treaties. A strong and justified case by one of the riparians and the opinion of the international water community help in building a potential case. In continuity of the previous section, Pakistan should build a case to combat new water challenges faced by the downstream. All trans-boundary issues with India need to be evaluated and prioritized under the water division approach. Issues like water quality, groundwater, unaccounted uses upstream and environmental protection are linked with the mechanism adopted to divide the rivers without making sure that no harms are transferred downstream.

Two relatively general clauses can be explored; no harm downstream and clause VII of future cooperation. In the continuity of the IWT, Pakistan needs to start mentioning the general principles of fairness and no harm downstream. Even if the benefits of these concepts for a downstream riparian were not envisaged in 1960.

- The quality of river flows during low flow periods should be monitored and maintained. Upstream water-intensive recreational, commercial and agriculture activities not only "consume water" through increased evapotranspiration, the pollute the river flows as well. The pollution is expected to increase with an increase in population and business. Pakistan needs to work on a monitoring setup, the estimation of costs under the concept of "pollutant should pay he" and the identification of permanent solutions.

- Depletion of groundwater aquifer in eastern catchments is going to seriously affect multiple sectors. Transfer of huge quantities of water outside the Basin has substantially disturbed the groundwater aquifer in eastern sub-basins. The critical issue of drinking water availability to 50 million people is already emerging. Deteriorating groundwater quality has direct health impacts. Pakistan will face high costs to ensure domestic supplies to a large and scattered rural population. Soon, there will be a need to bring more fresh water into the eastern region. The IWT does not include any protection for the groundwater aquifer, but, clearly, a cause of disturbing it.

- Allocation of minimum/environmental river flows to all rivers of the Indus basin including Ravi and Sutlej rivers. The concept of environmental flows did not exist in the basin before 1960, but has been globally accepted today. A recent study by the Federal Flood Commission (Environmental Concerns of All Provinces 2005) has calculated these flows for all five rivers courses. The minimum base flows for Rivers Chenab and Jhelum will be an important safety benchmark for these large rivers. The environmental flows have been estimated for the Indus River, which are not available during low flow periods. These allocations provide an important slot when estimating water demands and existing river water shortages during non-monsoon periods.

- Heavy flood damages during 2010 and 2011 have been the most disastrous events of Pakistan's history. During 2000-01, a large part of the country faced the most extended draught of the history. These patterns are yet not properly understood, but are expected to be repeated. Pakistan needs to build defense against extreme events with multiple actions including better water shed management, better information and research.

Scenario III: Benefit Sharing and Protection of Indus Basin Water Bodies

Despite limited success of the approach in large shared basins, trans-boundary collaboration has its scope. The institutes involved in the climate change research face gaps in information and data from the shared catchments, and stress the benefits of joint research and watershed management. The approach is also attractive because of a higher involvement of stakeholders and the sharing of development responsibility from the beginning.

Pakistan needs to evaluate the scope of the "benefit and the loss sharing approach" in its full context. Such an analysis should consider existing allocations, divisions and diversions of rivers. The nature of water shortage and stress faced in different sectors does not allow Pakistan to compromise on water quantities or on the upstream control on river flows. Pakistan faces planning and management challenges to protect the water bodies and address the climate change issues.

The modes of collaboration for a better understanding and the improved management of the watersheds need to be evolved in a neutral environment. The joint/shared planning can bring forward downstream concerns at an early stage. The global climate research institutes (like ICIMOD) are already carrying out research in shared the current climate change events in the region provide an opportunity for the larger forums. Initiatives to enhance regional cooperation by involving the other riparian are important.

Pakistan's case for benefit sharing must adopt a comprehensive and analytical approach to understand its scope, limitations and constraints. While formulating its own case, proposals by different quarters need to be evaluated. Experiences of the Nile, the Mekong and other basins provide good reference for the Indus Basin. In addition, following may also be considered: -

- The benefit sharing and water division are not alternative of each other, not in any large basin. In majority cases, apportionment/allocation of the river flows provides bases for the computation and sharing of benefits.

- All benefit sharing agreements follow the International Principles (UN 1997) of equity, no harm downstream, protection of water resources and transparent sharing of information. Any proposal without these principles is not acceptable to Pakistan.

- All types of agreements face implementation problems and have to develop operational guidelines and dispute resolution mechanisms. The benefit sharing needs joint working, higher trans-boundary cooperation, mutual trust and fair-play by the riparian isa pre-requisite.

- While developing "benefits from the rivers" schemes, "benefits to the rivers" must be taken care of.

- A joint management of the Indus Basin was technically a better option in 1960 to protect and optimally use the water resources of the Basin. It was more in favor of the lower riparian and communities heavily depending upon river flows for livelihood and drinking. However, even in 1960, it was a difficult development scenario because of conflicting development options. Political relations between India and Pakistan would have not allowed fruitful collaboration just on the water issues.

- Pakistan faces not only demand-supply, but also the allocation-availability gap during the major part of a year and most of the years. The provincial allocations are legally protected, while the draft water policy provides sectoral water demands. Hence, Pakistan cannot commit any further consumptive uses from its share outside its boundary.

- Pakistan needs good quality data and research to protect against climate changes, which could be a major area of transboundary collaboration. The climate induced changes are affecting Pakistan in two distinct manners. As a downstream country, Pakistan has to take a bigger share of the extreme events and hydrological changes, as has already happened during the droughts of 2001 and the floods of 2010. The upstream responses and adaptation measures can further influence the hydrological and the eco-systems downstream. India's carbon credit on two hydropower dams in western catchments without Pakistan's approval is an example in point.

- Good analytical studies are required on the opportunity cost of water in different regions of Pakistan. These studies must use primary data collected through proper monitoring procedures.

Author

Dr. Zaigham Habib has worked in the water sector of Pakistan as a development and planning consultant, a researcher, and an advisor on policy issues. Currently, she is an adviser of the National Disaster Management Authority (NDMA) on livelihood. She is a member of the Think Tank Committee on Water Resources, organized by the Pakistan Engineering Council and has contributed towards the task force on climate change, hosted by the Planning Commission Pakistan. Dr. Habib has participated in many development planning and evaluation studies funded by the Government of Pakistan, ADB, WB and FAO. She has worked with the International Water Management Institute (IWMI), the Planning Commission Pakistan and other National Institutes.

References

- Arjen Y. Hoekstra 2011, The Global Dimension of Water Governance: Why the River Basin Approach Is No Longer Sufficient and Why Cooperative Action at Global Level Is Needed; Water, ISSN 2073-4441.

- Aysegül Kibaroglu, 2004, Transboundary Water Issues In The uphrates-Tigris River Basin: Prospects For Cooperation.

- Jesse H. Hamner and Aaron T. Wolf 1998, Patterns in International Water Resource Treaties: The Transboundary Freshwater Dispute Database, Colorado Journal of International Environmental Law and Policy.

- Phillips, D.J.H., M. Daoudy, J. Öjendal, S. McCaffrey and A.R. Turton. (2006). Transboundary Water Cooperation as a Tool for Conflict Prevention and Broader Benefit-Sharing. Stockholm: the Swedish Ministry for Foreign Affairs. Accessible at: www.egdi.gov.se.

Sadoff, Claudia W. and David Grey. (2002). "Beyond the river: the benefits of cooperation on international rivers" in Water Policy, 4, 5: 389-403.

- Wolf, Aaron T. and Hamner, Jesse H., 2000. 'Trends in transboundary water disputes and dispute resolution', Water for Peace in the Middle East and Southern Africa. Geneva: TheGreen Cross International.

- David Phillips, M. Daoudy and others, 2006, Trans-boundary Water Cooperation as a Tool for Conflict Prevention and for Broader Benefit-sharing, Ministry for Foreign Affairs, Sweden.

- The Indus Waters Treaty, 1960. The Indus Waters Treaty. Signed at Karachi on September 19 1960 (entry into force: April 1 1960). (Source: United Nations 1963). Legislative Texts and Treaty Provisions Concerning the Utilization of International Rivers for Other Purposes than Navigation, pp. 300–65. United Nations Legislative Series, New York.

- Halla Qaddumi, ODI, Practical approaches to transboundary water benefit sharing; Working Paper 292. Results of ODI research presented in a preliminary form for discussion and critical comment.

CHAPTER – 14

Convention on the Law of the Non-navigational Uses of International Watercourses Adopted by the General Assembly of the United Nations on 21 May 1997

Adopted by the General Assembly of the United Nations on 21st May 1997. Not yet in force. See the General Assembly resolution 51/229, annex, Official Records of the General Assembly, Fifty-first Session, Supplement No. 49 (A/51/49).

Copyright © United Nations

2005

The Parties to the present Convention,

Conscious of the importance of international watercourses and the non-navigational uses thereof in many regions of the world,

Having in mind Article 13, paragraph 1 (a), of the Charter of the United Nations, which provides that the General Assembly shall initiate studies and make recommendations for the purpose of encouraging the progressive development of international law and its codification, Considering that successful codification and progressive development of rules of international law regarding non-navigational uses of international watercourses would assist in promoting and implementing the purposes and principles set forth in Articles 1 and 2 of the Charter of the United Nations, Taking into account the problems affecting many international watercourses resulting from, among other things, increasing demands and pollution, Expressing the conviction that a framework convention will ensure the utilization, development, conservation, management and protection of international watercourses and the promotion of the optimal and sustainable utilization thereof for present and future generations,

Affirming the importance of international cooperation and good-neighbourliness in this field, Aware of the special situation and needs of developing countries,

Recalling the principles and recommendations adopted by the United Nations Conference on Environment and Development of 1992 in the Rio Declaration and Agenda 21,

Recalling also the existing bilateral and multilateral agreements regarding the non-navigational uses of international watercourses,

Mindful of the valuable contribution of international organizations, both governmental and non-governmental, to the codification and progressive development of international law in this field, Appreciative of the work carried out by the International Law Commission on the law of the non-navigational uses of international watercourses,

Bearing in mind United Nations General Assembly resolution 49/52 of 9 December 1994,

Have agreed as follows:

PART I
INTRODUCTION

Article 1
Scope of the present Convention

1. The present Convention applies to uses of international watercourses and of their waters for purposes other than navigation and to measures of protection, preservation and management related to the uses of those watercourses and their waters.

2. The uses of international watercourses for navigation is not within the scope of the present Convention except insofar as other uses affect navigation or are affected by navigation.

Article 2
Use of terms

For the purposes of the present Convention:

(a) "Watercourse" means a system of surface waters and groundwaters constituting by virtue of their physical relationship a unitary whole and normally flowing into a common terminus;

(b) "International watercourse" means a watercourse, parts of which are situated in different States;

(c) "Watercourse State" means a State Party to the present Convention in whose territory part of an international watercourse is situated, or a Party that is a regional economic integration organization, in the territory of one or more of whose Member States part of an international watercourse is situated;

(d) "Regional economic integration organization" means an organization constituted by sovereign States of a given region, to which its member States have transferred competence in respect of matters governed by this Convention and which has been duly authorized in accordance with its internal procedures, to sign, ratify, accept, approve or accede to it.

Article 3
Watercourse agreements

1. In the absence of an agreement to the contrary, nothing in the present Convention shall affect the rights or obligations of a watercourse State arising from agreements in force for it on the date on which it became a party to the present Convention.

2. Notwithstanding the provisions of paragraph 1, parties to agreements referred to in paragraph 1 may, where necessary, consider harmonizing such agreements with the basic principles of the present Convention.

3. Watercourse States may enter into one or more agreements, hereinafter referred to as "watercourse agreements", which apply and adjust the provisions of the present Convention to the characteristics and uses of a particular international watercourse or part thereof.

4. Where a watercourse agreement is concluded between two or more watercourse States, it shall define the waters to which it applies. Such an agreement may be entered into with respect to an entire international watercourse or any part thereof or a particular project, programme or use except insofar as the agreement adversely affects, to a significant extent, the use by one or more other watercourse States of the waters of the watercourse, without their express consent.

5. Where a watercourse State considers that adjustment and application of the provisions of the present Convention is required because of the characteristics and uses of a particular international watercourse, watercourse States shall consult with a view to negotiating in good faith for the purpose of concluding a watercourse agreement or agreements.

6. Where some but not all watercourse States to a particular international watercourse are parties to an agreement, nothing in such agreement shall affect the rights or obligations under the present Convention of watercourse States that are not parties to such an agreement.

Article 4
Parties to watercourse agreements

1. Every watercourse State is entitled to participate in the negotiation of and to become a party to any watercourse agreement that applies to the entire international watercourse, as well as to participate in any relevant consultations.

2. A watercourse State whose use of an international watercourse may be affected to a significant extent by the implementation of a proposed watercourse agreement that applies only to a part of the watercourse or to a particular project, programme or use is entitled to participate in consultations on such an agreement

and, where appropriate, in the negotiation thereof in good faith with a view to becoming a party thereto, to the extent that its use is thereby affected.

PART II
GENERAL PRINCIPLES

Article 5
Equitable and reasonable utilization and participation

1. Watercourse States shall in their respective territories utilize an international watercourse in an equitable and reasonable manner. In particular, an international watercourse shall be used and developed by watercourse States with a view to attaining optimal and sustainable utilization thereof and benefits therefrom, taking into account the interests of the watercourse States concerned, consistent with adequate protection of the watercourse.

2. Watercourse States shall participate in the use, development and protection of an international watercourse in an equitable and reasonable manner. Such participation includes both the right to utilize the watercourse and the duty to cooperate in the protection and development thereof, as provided in the present Convention.

Article 6
Factors relevant to equitable and reasonable utilization

1. Utilization of an international watercourse in an equitable and reasonable manner within the meaning of article 5 requires taking into account all relevant factors and circumstances, including:

(a) Geographic, hydrographic, hydrological, climatic, ecological and other factors of a natural character;

(b) The social and economic needs of the watercourse States concerned;

(c) The population dependent on the watercourse in each watercourse State;

(d) The effects of the use or uses of the watercourses in one watercourse State on other watercourse States;

(e) Existing and potential uses of the watercourse;

(f) onservation, protection, development and economy of use of the water resources of the watercourse and the costs of measures taken to that effect;

(g) he availability of alternatives, of comparable value, to a particular planned or existing use.

2. In the application of article 5 or paragraph 1 of this article, watercourse States concerned shall, when the need arises, enter into consultations in a spirit of cooperation.

3. The weight to be given to each factor is to be determined by its importance in comparison with that of other relevant factors. In determining what is a reasonable and quitable use, all relevant factors are to be considered together and a conclusion reached on the basis of the whole.

Article 7
Obligation not to cause significant harm

1. Watercourse States shall, in utilizing an international watercourse in their territories, take all appropriate measures to prevent the causing of significant harm to other watercourse States.

2. Where significant harm nevertheless is caused to another watercourse State, the States whose use causes such harm shall, in the absence of agreement to such use, take all appropriate measures, having due regard for the provisions of articles 5 and 6, in consultation with the affected State, to eliminate or mitigate such harm and, where appropriate, to discuss the question of compensation.

Article 8
General obligation to cooperate

1. Watercourse States shall cooperate on the basis of sovereign equality, territorial integrity, mutual benefit and good faith in order to attain optimal utilization and adequate protection of an international watercourse.

2. n determining the manner of such cooperation, watercourse States may consider the establishment of joint mechanisms or commissions, as deemed necessary by them, to facilitate cooperation on relevant measures and procedures in the light of experience gained through cooperation in existing joint mechanisms and commissions in various regions.

Article 9
Regular exchange of data and information

1. Pursuant to article 8, watercourse States shall on a regular basis exchange readily available data and information on the condition of the watercourse, in particular that of a hydrological, meteorological, hydrogeological and ecological nature and related to the water quality as well as related forecasts.

2. If a watercourse State is requested by another watercourse State to provide data or information that is not readily available, it shall employ its best efforts to comply with the request but may condition its compliance upon payment by the requesting State of the reasonable costs of collecting and, where appropriate, processing such data or information.

3. Watercourse States shall employ their best efforts to collect and, where appropriate, to process data and information in a manner which facilitates its utilization by the other watercourse States to which it is communicated.

Article 10
Relationship between different kinds of uses

1. n the absence of agreement or custom to the contrary, no use of an international watercourse enjoys inherent priority over other uses.

2. n the event of a conflict between uses of an international watercourse, it shall be resolved with reference to articles 5 to 7, with special regard being given to the requirements of vital human needs.

PART III
PLANNED MEASURES

Article 11
Information concerning planned measures

Watercourse States shall exchange information and consult each other and, if necessary, negotiate on the possible effects of planned measures on the condition of an international watercourse.

Article 12
Notification concerning planned measures with possible adverse effects

Before a watercourse State implements or permits the implementation of planned measures which may have a significant adverse effect upon other watercourse States, it shall provide those States with timely notification thereof. Such notification shall be accompanied by available technical data and information, including the results of any environmental impact assessment, in order to enable the notified States to evaluate the possible effects of the planned measures.

Article 13
Period for reply to notification

Unless otherwise agreed:

(a) A watercourse State providing a notification under article 12 shall allow the notified States a period of six months within which to study and evaluate the possible effects of the planned measures and to communicate the findings to it;

(b) This period shall, at the request of a notified State for which the evaluation of the planned measures poses special difficulty, be extended for a period of six months.

Article 14
Obligations of the notifying State during the period for reply

During the period referred to in article 13, the notifying State:

(a) Shall cooperate with the notified States by providing them, on request, with any additional data and information that is available and necessary for an accurate evaluation; and

(b) Shall not implement or permit the implementation of the planned measures without the consent of the notified States.

Article 15
Reply to notification

The notified States shall communicate their findings to the notifying State as early as possible within the period applicable pursuant to article 13. If a notified State finds that implementation of the planned measures would be inconsistent with the provisions of articles 5 or 7, it shall attach to its finding a documented explanation setting forth the reasons for the finding.

Article 16
Absence of reply to notification

1. If, within the period applicable pursuant to article 13, the notifying State receives no communication under article 15, it may, subject to its obligations under articles 5 and 7, proceed with the implementation of the planned measures, in accordance with the notification and any other data and information provided to the notified States.

2. Any claim to compensation by a notified State which has failed to reply within the period applicable pursuant to article 13 may be offset by the costs incurred by the notifying State for action undertaken after the expiration of the time for a reply which would not have been undertaken if the notified State had objected within that period.

Article 17
Consultations and negotiations concerning planned measures

1. If a communication is made under article 15 that implementation of the planned measures would be inconsistent with the provisions of article 5 or 7, the notifying State and the State making the communication shall enter into consultations and, if necessary, negotiations with a view to arriving at an equitable resolution of the situation.

2. The consultations and negotiations shall be conducted on the basis that each State must in good faith, pay reasonable regard to the rights and legitimate interests of the other State.

3. During the course of the consultations and negotiations, the notifying State shall, if so requested by the notified State at the time it makes the communication, refrain from implementing or permitting the implementation of the planned measures for a period of six months unless otherwise agreed.

Article 18
Procedures in the absence of notification

1. If a watercourse State has reasonable grounds to believe that another watercourse State is planning measures that may have a significant adverse effect upon it, the former State may request the latter to apply the provisions of article 12. The request shall be accompanied by a documented explanation setting forth its grounds.

2. In the event that the State planning the measures nevertheless finds that it is not under an obligation to provide a notification under article 12, it shall so inform the other State, providing a documented explanation setting forth the reasons for such finding. If this finding does not satisfy the other State, the two States shall, at the request of that other State, promptly enter into consultations and negotiations in the manner indicated in paragraphs 1 and 2 of article 17.

3. During the course of the consultations and negotiations, the State planning the measures shall, if so requested by the other State at the time it requests the initiation of consultations and negotiations, refrain from implementing or permitting the implementation of those measures for a period of six months unless otherwise agreed.

Article 19
Urgent implementation of planned measures

1. In the event that the implementation of planned measures is of the utmost urgency in order to protect public health, public safety or other equally important interests, the State planning the measures may, subject to articles 5 and 7, immediately proceed to implementation, notwithstanding the provisions of article 14 and paragraph 3 of article 17.

2. In such case, a formal declaration of the urgency of the measures shall be communicated without delay to the other watercourse States referred to in article 12 together with the relevant data and information.

3. The State planning the measures shall, at the request of any of the States referred to in paragraph 2, promptly enter into consultations and negotiations with it in the manner indicated in paragraphs 1 and 2 of article 17.

PART IV
PROTECTION, PRESERVATION AND MANAGEMENT

Article 20
Protection and preservation of ecosystems

Watercourse States shall, individually and, where appropriate, jointly, protect and preserve the ecosystems of international watercourses.

Article 21
Prevention, reduction and control of pollution

1. For the purpose of this article, "pollution of an international watercourse" means any detrimental alteration in the composition or quality of the waters of an international watercourse which results directly or indirectly from human conduct.

2. Watercourse States shall, individually and, where appropriate, jointly, prevent, reduce and control the pollution of an international watercourse that may cause significant harm to other watercourse States or to their environment, including harm to human health or safety, to the use of the waters for any beneficial purpose or to the living resources of the watercourse. Watercourse States shall take steps to harmonize their policies in this connection.

3. Watercourse States shall, at the request of any of them, consult with a view to arriving at mutually agreeable measures and methods to prevent, reduce and control pollution of an international watercourse, such as:

(a) Setting joint water quality objectives and criteria;

(b) Establishing techniques and practices to address pollution from point and non-point sources;

(c) Establishing lists of substances the introduction of which into the waters of an international watercourse is to be prohibited, limited, investigated or monitored.

Article 22
Introduction of alien or new species

Watercourse States shall take all measures necessary to prevent the introduction of species, alien or new, into an international watercourse which may have effects detrimental to the ecosystem of the watercourse resulting in significant harm to other watercourse States.

Article 23
Protection and preservation of the marine environment

Watercourse States shall, individually and, where appropriate, in cooperation with other States, take all measures with respect to an international watercourse that are necessary to protect and preserve the marine environment, including estuaries, taking into account generally accepted international rules and standards.

Article 24
Management

1. Watercourse States shall, at the request of any of them, enter into consultations concerning the management of an international watercourse, which may include the establishment of a joint management mechanism.

2. For the purposes of this article, "management" refers, in particular, to:

(a) Planning the sustainable development of an international watercourse and providing for the implementation of any plans adopted; and

(b) Otherwise promoting the rational and optimal utilization, protection and control of the watercourse.

Article 25
Regulation

1. Watercourse States shall cooperate, where appropriate, to respond to needs or opportunities for regulation of the flow of the waters of an international watercourse.

2. Unless otherwise agreed, watercourse States shall participate on an equitable basis in the construction and maintenance or defrayal of the costs of such regulation works as they may have agreed to undertake.

3. For the purposes of this article, "regulation" means the use of hydraulic works or any other continuing measure to alter, vary or otherwise control the flow of the waters of an international watercourse.

Article 26
Installations

1. Watercourse States shall, within their respective territories, employ their best efforts to maintain and protect installations, facilities and other works related to an international watercourse.

2. Watercourse States shall, at the request of any of them which has reasonable grounds to believe that it may suffer significant adverse effects, enter into consultations with regard to:

(a) The safe operation and maintenance of installations, facilities or other works related to an international watercourse; and

(b) The protection of installations, facilities or other works from wilful or negligent acts or the forces of nature.

PART V
HARMFUL CONDITIONS AND EMERGENCY SITUATIONS

Article 27
Prevention and mitigation of harmful conditions

Watercourse States shall, individually and, where appropriate, jointly, take all appropriate measures to prevent or mitigate conditions related to an international watercourse that may be harmful to other watercourse States, whether resulting from natural causes or human conduct, such as flood or ice conditions, water-borne diseases, siltation, erosion, salt-water intrusion, drought or desertification.

Article 28
Emergency situations

1. For the purposes of this article, "emergency" means a situation that causes, or poses an imminent threat of causing, serious harm to watercourse States or other States and that results suddenly from natural causes, such as floods, the breaking up of ice, landslides or earthquakes, or from human conduct, such as industrial accidents.

2. A watercourse State shall, without delay and by the most expeditious means available, notify other potentially affected States and competent international organizations of any emergency originating within its territory.

3. A watercourse State within whose territory an emergency originates shall, in cooperation with potentially affected States and, where appropriate, competent international organizations, immediately take all practicable measures necessitated by the circumstances to prevent, mitigate and eliminate harmful effects of the emergency.

4. When necessary, watercourse States shall jointly develop contingency plans for responding to emergencies, in cooperation, where appropriate, with other potentially affected States and competent international organizations.

PART VI
MISCELLANEOUS PROVISIONS

Article 29
International watercourses and installations in time of armed conflict

International watercourses and related installations, facilities and other works shall enjoy the protection accorded by the principles and rules of international law applicable in international and non-international armed conflict and shall not be used in violation of those principles and rules.

Article 30
Indirect procedures

In cases where there are serious obstacles to direct contacts between watercourse States, the States concerned shall fulfil their obligations of cooperation provided for in the present Convention, including exchange of data and information, notification, communication, consultations and negotiations, through any indirect procedure accepted by them.

Article 31
Data and information vital to national defence or security

Nothing in the present Convention obliges a watercourse State to provide data or information vital to its national defence or security. Nevertheless, that State shall cooperate in good faith with the other watercourse States with a view to providing as much information as possible under the circumstances.

Article 32
Non-discrimination

Unless the watercourse States concerned have agreed otherwise for the protection of the interests of persons, natural or juridical, who have suffered or are under a serious threat of suffering significant transboundary harm as a result of activities related to an international watercourse, a watercourse State shall not discriminate on the basis of nationality or residence or place where the injury occurred, in granting to such persons, in accordance with its legal system, access to judicial or other procedures, or a right to claim compensation or other relief in respect of significant harm caused by such activities carried on in its territory.

Article 33
Settlement of disputes

1. In the event of a dispute between two or more parties concerning the interpretation or application of the present Convention, the parties concerned shall, in the absence of an applicable agreement between them, seek a settlement of the dispute by peaceful means in accordance with the following provisions.

2. If the parties concerned cannot reach agreement by negotiation requested by one of them, they may jointly seek the good offices of, or request mediation or conciliation by, a third party, or make use, as appropriate, of any joint watercourse institutions that may have been established by them or agree to submit the dispute to arbitration or to the International Court of Justice.

3. Subject to the operation of paragraph 10, if after six months from the time of the request for negotiations referred to in paragraph 2, the parties concerned have not been able to settle their dispute through negotiation or any other means referred to in paragraph 2, the dispute shall be submitted, at the request of any of the parties to the dispute, to impartial fact-finding in accordance with paragraphs 4 to 9, unless the parties otherwise agree.

4. A Fact-finding Commission shall be established, composed of one member nominated by each party concerned and in addition a member not having the nationality of any of the parties concerned chosen by the nominated members who shall serve as Chairman.

5. If the members nominated by the parties are unable to agree on a Chairman within three months of the request for the establishment of the Commission, any party concerned may request the Secretary-General of the United Nations to appoint the Chairman who shall not have the nationality of any of the parties to the dispute or of any riparian State of the watercourse concerned. If one of the parties fails to nominate a member within three months of the initial request pursuant to paragraph 3, any other party concerned may request the Secretary-General of the United Nations to appoint a person who shall not have the nationality of any of the parties to the dispute or of any riparian State of the watercourse concerned. The person so appointed shall constitute a single-member Commission.

6. The Commission shall determine its own procedure.

7. The parties concerned have the obligation to provide the Commission with such information as it may require and, on request, to permit the Commission to have access to their respective territory and to inspect any facilities, plant, equipment, construction or natural feature relevant for the purpose of its inquiry.

8. The Commission shall adopt its report by a majority vote, unless it is a single-member Commission, and shall submit that report to the parties concerned setting forth its findings and the reasons therefor and such recommendations as it deems appropriate for an equitable solution of the dispute, which the parties concerned shall consider in good faith.

9. The expenses of the Commission shall be borne equally by the parties concerned.

10. When ratifying, accepting, approving or acceding to the present Convention, or at any time thereafter, a party which is not a regional economic integration organization may declare in a written instrument submitted to the depositary that, in respect of any dispute not resolved in accordance with paragraph 2, it recognizes as compulsory, ipso facto, and without special agreement in relation to any party accepting the same obligation:

(a) Submission of the dispute to the International Court of Justice; and/or

(b) Arbitration by an arbitral tribunal established and operating, unless the parties to the dispute otherwise agreed, in accordance with the procedure laid down in the annex to the present Convention.

A party which is a regional economic integration organization may make a declaration with like effect in relation to arbitration in accordance with subparagraph (b).

PART VII
FINAL CLAUSES

Article 34
Signature

The present Convention shall be open for signature by all States and by regional economic integration organizations from 21st May 1997 until 20th May 2000 at United Nations Headquarters in New York.

Article 35
Ratification, acceptance, approval or accession

1. The present Convention is subject to ratification, acceptance, approval or accession by States and by regional economic integration organizations. The instruments of ratification, acceptance, approval or accession shall be deposited with the Secretary-General of the United Nations.

2. Any regional economic integration organization which becomes a Party to this Convention without any of its member States being a Party shall be bound by all the obligations under the Convention. In the case of such organizations, one or more of whose member States is a Party to this Convention, the organization and its member States shall decide on their respective responsibilities for the performance of their obligations under the Convention. In such cases, the organization and the member States shall not be entitled to exercise rights under the Convention concurrently.

3. In their instruments of ratification, acceptance, approval or accession, the regional economic integration organizations shall declare the extent of their competence with respect to the matters governed by the Convention. These organizations shall also inform the Secretary-General of the United Nations of any substantial modification in the extent of their competence.

Article 36
Entry into force

1. The present Convention shall enter into force on the ninetieth day following the date of deposit of the thirty-fifth instrument of ratification, acceptance, approval or accession with the Secretary-General of the United Nations.

2. For each State or regional economic integration organization that ratifies, accepts or approves the Convention or accedes thereto after the deposit of the thirty-fifth instrument of ratification, acceptance, approval or accession, the Convention shall enter into force on the ninetieth day after the deposit by such State or regional economic integration organization of its instrument of ratification, acceptance, approval or accession.

3. For the purposes of paragraphs 1 and 2, any instrument deposited by a regional economic integration organization shall not be counted as additional to those deposited by States.

Article 37
Authentic texts

The original of the present Convention, of which the Arabic, Chinese, English, French, Russian and Spanish texts are equally authentic, shall be deposited with the Secretary-General of the United Nations.

IN WITNESS WHEREOF the undersigned Plenipotentiaries, being duly authorized thereto, have signed this Convention.

DONE at New York, this twenty-first day of May one thousand nine hundred and ninety-seven.

ANNEX
ARBITRATION

Article 1

Unless the parties to the dispute otherwise agree, the arbitration pursuant to article 33 of the Convention shall take place in accordance with articles 2 to 14 of the present annex.

Article 2

The claimant party shall notify the respondent party that it is referring a dispute to arbitration pursuant to article 33 of the Convention. The notification shall state the subject matter of arbitration and include, in particular, the articles of the Convention, the interpretation or application of which are at issue. If the parties do not agree on the subject matter of the dispute, the arbitral tribunal shall determine the subject matter.

Article 3

1. In disputes between two parties, the arbitral tribunal shall consist of three members. Each of the parties to the dispute shall appoint an arbitrator and the two arbitrators so appointed shall designate by common agreement the third arbitrator, who shall be the Chairman of the tribunal. The latter shall not be a national of one of the parties to the dispute or of any riparian State of the watercourse concerned, nor have his or her usual place of residence in the territory of one of these parties or such riparian State, nor have dealt with the case in any other capacity.

2. In disputes between more than two parties, parties in the same interest shall appoint one arbitrator jointly by agreement.

3. Any vacancy shall be filled in the manner prescribed for the initial appointment.

Article 4

1. If the Chairman of the arbitral tribunal has not been designated within two months of the appointment of the second arbitrator, the President of the International Court of Justice shall, at the request of a party, designate the Chairman within a further two-month period.

2. If one of the parties to the dispute does not appoint an arbitrator within two months of receipt of the request, the other party may inform the President of the International Court of Justice, who shall make the designation within a further two-month period.

Article 5

The arbitral tribunal shall render its decisions in accordance with the provisions of this Convention and international law.

Article 6

Unless the parties to the dispute otherwise agree, the arbitral tribunal shall determine its own rules of procedure.

Article 7

The arbitral tribunal may, at the request of one of the parties, recommend essential interim measures of protection.

Article 8

1. The parties to the dispute shall facilitate the work of the arbitral tribunal and, in particular, using all means at their disposal, shall:

   (a) Provide it with all relevant documents, information and facilities; and

   (b) Enable it, when necessary, to call witnesses or experts and receive their evidence.

2. The parties and the arbitrators are under an obligation to protect the confidentiality of any information they receive in confidence during the proceedings of the arbitral tribunal.

Article 9

Unless the arbitral tribunal determines otherwise because of the particular circumstances of the case, the costs of the tribunal shall be borne by the parties to the dispute in equal shares. The tribunal shall keep a record of all its costs, and shall furnish a final statement thereof to the parties.

Article 10

Any party that has an interest of a legal nature in the subject matter of the dispute which may be affected by the decision in the case, may intervene in the proceedings with the consent of the tribunal.

Article 11

The tribunal may hear and determine counterclaims arising directly out of the subject matter of the dispute.

Article 12

Decisions both on procedure and substance of the arbitral tribunal shall be taken by a majority vote of its members.

Article 13

If one of the parties to the dispute does not appear before the arbitral tribunal or fails to defend its case, the other party may request the tribunal to continue the proceedings and to make its award. Absence of a party or a failure of a party to defend its case shall not constitute a bar to the proceedings. Before rendering its final decision, the arbitral tribunal must satisfy itself that the claim is well founded in fact and law.

Article 14

1. The tribunal shall render its final decision within five months of the date on which it is fully constituted unless it finds it necessary to extend the time limit for a period which should not exceed five more months.

2. The final decision of the arbitral tribunal shall be confined to the subject matter of the dispute and shall state the reasons on which it is based. It shall contain the names of the members who have participated and the date of the final decision. Any member of the tribunal may attach a separate or dissenting opinion to the final decision.

3. The award shall be binding on the parties to the dispute. It shall be without appeal unless the parties to the dispute have agreed in advance to an appellate procedure.

4. Any controversy which may arise between the parties to the dispute as regards the interpretation or manner of implementation of the final decision may be submitted by either party for decision to the arbitral tribunal which rendered it.

CHAPTER – 15

PAKISTAN'S WATER CONCERNS

EDITOR
DR NOOR UL HAQ

ASSISTANT EDITOR

MUHAMMAD NAWAZ KHAN

The Indus River and its tributaries are the life line of Pakistan. There are, however, Indo-Pakistan water concerns and water distribution complaints within Pakistan. The internal concerns were resolved through the Water Accord 1991 amongst the provinces. Yet, at times, complaints crop up against the Indus River System Authority (IRSA), which is responsible for ensuring an equitable and agreed distribution of water among the provinces. Since water scarcity is growing, Pakistan needs to improve its internal water management to satisfy all areas.

The distribution of water of the Indus River system between Pakistan and India was settled through the Indus Waters Treaty (IWT) of 1960. Ever since, India has been building or planning big and small hydropower projects and reservoirs, numbering as many as 67[1], on the principal rivers – Indus, Jhelum and Chenab – that were allotted to Pakistan under the IWT. For instance, there is the Kishenganga dam, the Tulbul dam (Wullar barrage) and the Uri-II hydroelectric plant on River Jhelum; Baglihar, Salal and Bursar dams on River Chenab; and Kargil dam, Nimmo Bazgo hydroelectric project on River Indus and Chutak hydroelectric plant on a tributary of the Indus. These can cause major water shortages in Pakistan in times to come. Also, these can be used to hold back water in days of scarcity or flood the country during excess flows. The natural flow of water is essential for Pakistan's agricultural economy and a wilful obstruction thereof has the potential for serious conflict between the two states. The IWT does not allow India to obstruct the flow of the run-of-the-river by storing or diverting the water. There is a security dimension as well. For instance, the Chenab canal network in Pakistan is the first-line of defence against India's conventional attack. If these canals are dried up, they would afford easier passage for an infantry-armour assault, adversely affecting the defence of the country.

For these reasons, Pakistan should be taken into confidence when such projects are being planned to ensure that they do not violate the IWT. There is no alternative but to settle mutual concerns through dialogue and consultation with the neighbour. The point to ponder is:

> If Pakistan and India had normal trustful relations, there would be a mutually-verified monitoring process which would assure that there is no change in the flows going to Pakistan. In an even more ideal world, India could increase low-flows during the critical planting season, with significant benefit to Pakistani farmers and with very small impacts on power generation in India.[2]

The IPRI Factfile includes selected articles from national and international media appearing during July 31, 2009 — October 11, 2010.

October 31, 2010   Noor ul Haq

---

[1] I.A. Pansohta, "Threat of Water Wars", Nation (Islamabad), April, 2010.
[2] John Briscoe "War or Peace on the Indus", News International (Islamabad), April 3, 2010; Frontier Post (Peshawar), April; 18, 2010.

Paper One:

Water Disputes Between India and Pakistan- A Potential Casus Belli

Tufail Ahmad, 31 July, 2009

Introduction

Concern is growing in Pakistan that India is pursuing policies in an attempt to strangulate Pakistan by exercising control over the water flow of Pakistan's rivers. The concern is most related to Pakistan's agricultural sector, which would be greatly affected by the building of dams and by the external control of the waters of several rivers that flow into Pakistan. The issue has a layered complexity, as three of the rivers flow into Pakistan through the Indian portion of Jammu & Kashmir, the territory over which the two countries have waged multiple wars.

Pakistani columnists, religious leaders, and policymakers are increasingly articulating their concern over the water dispute in terms of traditional rivalry against India and in terms of anti-Israel sentiment that has been fostered by the country's establishment over the years. In one such recent case, Ayaz Amir, a renowned Pakistani columnist, warned: "Insisting on our water rights with regard to India must be one of the cornerstones of our foreign policy. The disputes of the future will be about water." Hamid Gul, a former chief of Pakistan's Inter-Services Intelligence (ISI), charged: "India has stopped our water." Pakistan's Indus Basin Water Council (IBWC), a pressure group that appears deceivingly authoritative as an organization whose central purpose is to address Pakistani water concerns, currently maintains near hegemony over the public debate of the issue. IBWC Chairman, Zahoorul Hassan Dahir claimed that "India, working in conjunction with the Jewish lobby, is using most of the river waters, causing a shortage of food, water and electricity in Pakistan."

The Pakistani concern involves six rivers that flow into Pakistan through northern India, including the disputed state of Jammu & Kashmir and the state of Punjab, both of which have been ideologically divided between India and Pakistan since 1947. After the creation of Pakistan in 1947, disagreements began to arise over sharing of river waters, leading to the 1960 Indus Waters Treaty, an attempt at resolution brokered by the World Bank. Though the treaty is, perhaps, the most enduring pact between the two nuclear powers, it is coming under increasing strain.

Understanding the Indus River System

The Indus Waters Treaty sets out the legal framework for the sharing of the waters of six rivers: the Indus River and its five tributaries. All six rivers - Indus, Chenab, Jhelum, Sutlej, Beas, and Ravi — flow through northern India into Pakistan. Under the pact, the waters of three rivers - the Indus, the Chenab and the Jhelum, which pass through Jammu & Kashmir — are to be used by Pakistan, while India has rights to the waters of the Sutlej, the Beas and the Ravi before these three enter Pakistani territory. The Chenab is the key tributary, as it carries the waters of the rest of the four rivers into the Indus.

The complicated origins of the Indus river system plays a key role in the water debates, as the rivers originate in and pass through a number of countries. According to the Indus Waters Treaty, the following three rivers are for use by Pakistan:

The Indus River: originates in the Chinese-controlled Tibet and flows through Jammu & Kashmir.

The Chenab: originates in India's Himachal Pradesh state, travels through Jammu & Kashmir.

The Jhelum: rises in Jammu & Kashmir and flows into Pakistan, finally joining Chenab.

The Treaty affords India use of the following three rivers:

The Sutlej: originates in Tibet, flows through Himachal Pradesh and Punjab before joining the Chenab.

The Beas and the Ravi: originate in the Himachal Pradesh state and flow into Pakistan, emptying into the Chenab.

Taking into account the flow of the rivers, the importance of the Chenab and the Indus becomes clear. The Chenab combines the waters of four rivers, the Jhelum, the Sutlej, the Beas and the Ravi, to form a single water system which then joins the Indus in Pakistan. The Indus River is considered to be the lifeline of Pakistani economy and livestock.

Pakistani Concern and Baglihar Dam

The Pakistani concern regarding the waters from the rivers started in the 1990s after India began constructing a hydroelectric power project on the Chenab River in the Doda district of Jammu & Kashmir. Since the Chenab is the key tributary of the Indus, Pakistani policymakers, religious and political parties, and political commentators feared that India could exert control over the waters. Such control could be used to injure the Pakistani economy and livestock, or could be used to cause floods in Pakistan by the release of water during times of war. Discussions of Pakistan's concerns are most often centralized around the Baglihar dam, though it is only one of the several water projects being developed by India in its part of Jammu & Kashmir.

The first phase of the Baglihar dam, a 450-MW hydroelectric power project initiated in the 1990s, was completed on October 10, 2008. Inaugurating the project, the Indian Prime Minister, Manmohan Singh, noted: "It is a matter of satisfaction that the reconstruction program... [entailing] 67 projects is well under way with 19 projects completed, one of which is the Baglihar project that I inaugurated today." The fact that the Baglihar dam is one of 67 development projects underway in Jammu & Kashmir raises further concerns among many Pakistanis who believe that Kashmir, having a Muslim majority, rightfully belongs to the Islamic state of Pakistan. The extensive building of infrastructure by India is therefore a cause of further Pakistani displeasure and contention.

The discussion of water easily ignites popular passion because Pakistan is increasingly confronted by an impending water crisis. In early 2009, it was estimated that Pakistan is on the brink of a water disaster, as the availability of water in Pakistan has been declining over the past few decades, from 5,000 cubic meters per capita 60 years ago to 1,200 cubic meters per capita in 2009. By 2020, the availability of water is estimated to fall to about 800 cubic meters per capita. M. Yusuf Sarwar, a member of the Indus Basin Water Council, has warned that the lessening flows of the waters in the rivers and the shortage of water generally could cause Pakistan to be declared a disaster-affected nation by 2013. Dr. Muhammad Yar Khawar, a scientist at the University of Sindh, released research last year based on sample surveys that warns that less than 20 percent of below-surface water in the Sindh province, previously thought to be a viable water source, is acceptable for drinking.

Amidst this shortage of water, Pakistan is also confronted with a number of internal factors that amount to further strain. One columnist warned that with Pakistan's population set to jump to 250 million in just a few years' time, the shortage of water, along with that of oil, sugar, and wheat, will become a major problem. Pakistan is also estimated to be losing 13 million cusecs [approximately 368,119 cubic meters/second] of water every year from its rivers into the sea, as it does not have enough reservoirs or dams to store water. Further tensions arise from allegations of inequitable distribution of water between various Pakistani provinces. The Indus River System Authority (IRSA), which allocates water to provinces, averted a major political controversy between provinces in June 2009 by declaring that there would be no cuts in their water supply.

While Pakistan's domestic behaviour in terms of water usage is partly responsible for the depletion of the water table, the construction of Baglihar dam by India has multiplied Pakistani concerns. Pakistani writers warn that the dam will deprive Pakistan of 321,000 acres feet of water during the agricultural season, greatly affecting wheat production in the Punjab province and leading to crop failures. There are some warnings that the dam will adversely affect 13 million acres of irrigated land around the Chenab and Ravi rivers, forcing Pakistani farmers to change crops, and in the face of starvation, deepening Pakistan's dependence on food imports and burdening the country's national exchequer. In an editorial published in June 2009, Pakistan's mass-circulation Urdu-language newspaper *Roznama Jang* said that India "is nursing an unpious dream of turning the entirety of Pakistan into a desert."

Pakistan-Indian Talks

Under the 1960 Indus Waters Treaty, India is not permitted to build dams for the purpose of water storage on the Indus, Chenab, and Jhelum rivers, but it is allowed to make limited use of their waters, including developing the run-of-the-river hydroelectric power projects. India is required to provide Pakistan with the technical details of any water project it wants to develop on these rivers before building begins. Pakistan has formally raised objections on the technical specifications of the Baglihar dam, including design, size, gated spillways, and water capacity. Over the past decade, India and Pakistan held a series of talks on the issue of the Baglihar dam but could not resolve the matter within the framework of the 1960 treaty.

In 2003, Pakistan formally served a final notice to the Indian government, urging it to resolve the Baglihar issue by December 31, 2003, a process that failed to yield results. In 2005, Pakistan approached the World Bank for mediation. The World Bank noted that it was "not a guarantor of the treaty," but had the authority to appoint a neutral expert. In 2007, the appointed neutral expert, Professor Raymond Lafitte of Switzerland, delivered a verdict rejecting most of the Pakistani objections. However, Professor Lafitte did require India to make some minor changes, including reducing the dam's height by 1.5m. Significantly, Professor Lafitte's judgment classified Pakistani objections as "differences" and not a serious "dispute," which could have paved the way for the issue to be taken to a Court of Arbitration as envisaged in the treaty.

To this day, Pakistan remains dissatisfied over the Lafitte verdict. Though India has facilitated visits by Pakistani officials to the dam site and Indian delegations have visited Pakistan to examine the Pakistani claims of water shortage in the Chenab river, the countries remain at an impasse. Bilateral talks between the two countries are now increasingly focused on water disputes. Pakistan has accused India several times of completely stopping Pakistan's water from the Chenab River. In March 2008, Hafiz Zahoorul Hassan Dahir, the IBWC chairman, charged that India "completely shut down the Chenab river from the 1st to the 26th of January 2008, with not even a drop of water moving." India was also accused of curtailing the water supply from the Chenab River during September-October 2008. Due to a precedent set in the 1978 case of the Salal dam construction by India in Jammu & Kashmir, Pakistan has requested the payment of compensation for any water shortfall. In June 2009, the Pakistani government declared that India had rejected its demand for monetary compensation for the loss of water from the Chenab River. Pakistan alleged that the waters of the Chenab had been stopped by India during August 2008; however, India refuted these claims, citing unreliable Pakistani statistics regarding water stoppage and loss. In an editorial, the Urdu-language Pakistani newspaper *Roznama Express* noted: "If India continues to build dams on our rivers and stop our water, then the day is not far when our lands will become barren and this nation, that has a spectacular history of agricultural production, will be forced to import food." The daily observed that during a meeting with President Asif Zardari, the Indian Prime Minister, Manmohan Singh, assured the President that he was looking into the matter, but no action was taken. In October 2008, President Zardari took "serious notice" of the issue and warned of "damage to bilateral relations" if Pakistani concerns were not addressed. A few days before President Zardari's statement, Prime Minister Manmohan Singh inaugurated the Baglihar dam project, stating that "Pakistan's concerns about the project had been addressed."

On June 6, 2009, two years after the Lafitte verdict, the Pakistani Foreign Minister, Shah Mahmood Qureshi, accused India of violating the Indus Waters Treaty. Qureshi further warned that any failure to resolve the water disputes "could lead to conflict in the region." Sentiment is now emerging in Pakistan that the 1960 Indus Waters Treaty has proven to function to the sole advantage of India. Ayub Mayo, the president of the farmers' lobby group Pakistan Muttahida Kisan Mahaz, declared that the 1960 pact is simply "a conspiracy to deprive Pakistan of its due share of water." While the talks between the two nations regarding water-related issues are continuing into the second half of 2009, the public debate in Pakistan on the subject continues to be vigorous and sentimental, raising complicated concerns of national security, traditional rivalry with India, as well as historical anti-Semitism.

The Perceived Threat

During the past two years, the debate in Pakistan about the Indian water projects in Jammu & Kashmir has gained a bitter momentum, as Pakistani leaders have begun to describe India as their eternal enemy and accuse India of trying to suffocate the Pakistani economy. Speeches by leaders often carry an element of anti-Semitism, blaming India for acting under an international conspiracy led by Israel, the U.S. and India against the Islamic state of Pakistan.

In early 2008, an editorial in the Urdu-language newspaper, Roznama Ausaf, accused India of planning a "Water Bomb" strategy to strangle Pakistan economically. The article quoted the officials of the IBWC pressure group as saying that India wants to achieve through a "water bomb" what it could not achieve through the three wars waged over the past six decades. Noting that India is planning "50 dams to raid the waters of the rivers" flowing into Pakistan, the IBWC warned: "If this is not foiled, Pakistan will face the worst famine and economic disaster."

In April 2008, the IBWC Chairman, Hafiz Zahoorul Hassan Dahir, stated that India plans to construct 10 more dams on rivers streaming into Pakistan in addition to the ongoing construction of 52 new dams. "We believe that if India succeeded in constructing the proposed dams," Dahir disclosed, "Pakistan would join the list of the countries facing a severe water crisis. If we are to save Pakistan, we have to protect our waters and review our policies in Kashmir."

One month later, Dahir accused India of using 80 percent of the water of the Chenab and Jhelum rivers and 60 percent of the water of the Indus, stating: "We can do nothing about what India is doing but we are concerned about the role of our government. If continued, this distribution of water would not only affect our energy but also agricultural production. We wonder as to why we are leading toward collective suicide." In May 2009, Dahir described "India's water terrorism as a bigger threat than Talibani terrorism," and then added: "The day is not far when circumstances like those in Somalia, Ethiopia and Chad will emerge inside Pakistan... Between India and Pakistan, there is an extremely dreadful dispute. In an aggressive manner, India has readied a weapon for use against Pakistan that is more dangerous and destructive than an atomic bomb." Dahir warned that by 2012, India will acquire the capability to completely stop the waters of the Jhelum and the Chenab.

One month after the inauguration of first phase of the Baglihar project by the Indian Prime Minister, Manmohan Singh, Jamaat Ali Shah, Pakistan's Indus Water Commissioner and liaison between the countries within the framework of the 1960 treaty, warned that India plans to make Pakistan barren by 2014 by stopping its water. At a seminar in Lahore, Shah contended that India is permitted to generate electricity from the waters of the rivers but not to stop Pakistan's water as it has on several occasions, most notably from August 19 to September 5, 2008, a suspension presumably necessary to fill up the Baglihar dam. Pakistani leaders estimate that during the 36-day hiatus from September-October 2008, India deprived Pakistan of more than 1.2 million cusecs of water.

Defense Security Concerns

Within a week of the dam's October 2008 inauguration, Major General Athar Abbas, a spokesman for the Pakistan Army, expressed concern over the Baglihar dam, describing it as a "defense security concern." Abbas stated that a number of canals, drains and artificial distributaries used for irrigation purposes are crucial during times of war. The strategic importance of the Indian water projects in Kashmir is so significant that officials from the Pakistani Army headquarters attended a government meeting on the issue in February 2009 "to discuss the impact of the said dams on Pakistan's water and defense interests... The armed forces became alarmed when they learned the projects could wreak havoc... if the said dams were to collapse or malfunction."

Retired General Zulfiqar Ali, former chairman of Pakistan's Water and Power Development Authority, expressed that by building dams on rivers in Kashmir, India has achieved military, economic and political supremacy vis-a-vis Pakistan. In an editorial, the Urdu-language newspaper, Roznama Khabrain, accused India of using water as a weapon, proclaiming: "In order to establish its hegemony over the region [of South Asia], India is even using water as a weapon." Sheikh Rasheed Ahmad, a senior Pakistani politician and former minister of Railways, has warned that Pakistan and India may go to war on the issue of water, adding: "India wants to make Pakistan a Somalia by stopping its water." Addressing a seminar in late-2008, Javed Iqbal, an eminent retired justice in Pakistan, said, "The government of Pakistan should pressure the Indian government to resolve this issue; and if it does not agree, then a threat be issued that we are ready for war."

A number of Pakistani commentators warned that the water issues may incite a nuclear war between the two countries. At the All Parties Hurriyat conference, a convener of the Pakistani chapter of the Kashmiri secessionist rganizations' alliance, Syed Yousaf Naseem stated that Pakistan is facing a water crisis and that the Indian efforts to effect cuts in its water share from the rivers flowing into Pakistan could compel Pakistan to use unconventional weapons against India. Naseem added that "The Kashmir issue is cardinal to Pakistan-India relations. Unless this issue is resolved, the Damocles' sword of nuclear clash will remain hanging over the region. Kashmir is very important for Pakistan and a delay in the resolution of this issue will jeopardize the peace of the region." The warning of a nuclear war between the two neighbors has been reiterated by multiple sources, including a veteran Pakistani editor, Majeed Nizami. Even a former prime minister, Nawaz Sharif, a center-right politician who was responsible for conducting the 1998 nuclear tests, warned in May 2009 that "the issues of water and Kashmir must be resolved as early as possible so that the clouds of war between Pakistan and India can be eliminated forever." A similar linking between water issues and Kashmiri emancipation has been articulated by Hafiz Muhammad Saeed, the founder ofa jihadist organization, Lashkar-e-Taiba. In an address to a group of farmers in Lahore last year, Hafiz Muhammad Saeed warned that the "water problem cannot be resolved without liberating Kashmir from India." Syed Salahuddin, the chairman of the Muttahida Jihad Council, a network bringing together nearly two dozen Pakistan-based militant organizations, warned in October 2008 that jihad against India in Jammu & Kashmir will continue until the territory is liberated.

The International Conspiracy

In April 2009, a former member of the Pakistani parliament and the Emir of Jamaat-e-Islami in the Sindh province, Maulana Asadullah Bhutto, said: "India is Pakistan's eternal enemy and from day one until now has been engaged in destroying Pakistan. It first occupied Kashmir through a conspiracy, thereafter cut off our eastern arm [creating Bangladesh] and for the past several years now has been stealing Pakistan's share of water... India is using Pakistan's water and is engaged in efforts to make our lands barren." The Pakistan-India water dispute was discussed by the Majlis-e-Shura (executive council) of the Jamaat-e-Islami Pakistan in May 2009. In a resolution adopted at the end of the meeting, the Jamaat-e-Islami condemned "water aggression" by India and described it as "a dreadful international conspiracy to make Pakistan face a situation like [the drought-struck] Ethiopia by making Pakistan's fertile lands barren."

Conclusion

Although bitter feelings and heated public debates are likely to persist in the years ahead, the people and the leadership of Pakistan, generally, accept that there is nothing that Pakistan can do, especially in the light of the judgment delivered in February 2007 by the World Bank-appointed neutral expert, Professor Raymond Lafitte. In an editorial, a Pakistani daily, The News, observed: "The only way to avoid problems arising is for the 1960 accord to be respected. India has, on more than one occasion, attempted to violate its spirit if not its letter, by seeking loopholes and technical flaws that can be used to its advantage. But in all this, there is also another message. The interests of the two countries are so closely linked, that they can be protected only by establishing closer ties. A failure to do so will bring only more episodes of discord, over river water, over dams, over toxic dumping in drains and over illegal border crossings...."

In late June 2009, the Pakistani Water and Power Minister, Raja Parvez Ashraf, observed that India does have a right to build dams, but that it cannot stop the flow of water into Pakistan in order to fill the dams. In fact, Jamaat Ali Shah, Pakistan's Indus Water Commissioner, gave a rare candid interview in April 2008, stating that the Indian water projects currently undertaken do not contravene the provisions of the 1960 Indus Waters Treaty. Noting that India can construct dams within the technical specifications outlined in the treaty, Shah acknowledged: "In compliance with the Indus Waters Treaty, India has so far not constructed any storage dam on the Indus, the Chenab and the Jhelum rivers. The hydroelectric projects India is developing are on the run-of-the-river waters of these rivers, projects which India is permitted to pursue according to the treaty."

Paper Two :

Water Scarcity And Riparian Rights

Ashfak Bokhari, Dawn (Islamabad), 14 February, 2010

Water shortage in the country has assumed alarming proportions following reduced flows in the western rivers from their sources in Indian-held Kashmir and, as a corollary, it is aggravating tension over the sharing of available water among the provinces.

Last week, an Indian delegation was in Pakistan for a routine inspection of water-related sites and the Pakistan's Indus Water commissioner, Syed Jamaat Ali Shah, held talks with its members on the issue of low flows on the sidelines because no meeting was scheduled between the two sides during the inspection visit.

Later, a Pakistan team of inspectors was scheduled to visit water-related projects in the Indian Kashmir.

India is currently constructing three hydropower projects on the River Indus. These include Chutak Dam with 59- meter height, Nimoo Bazgo with 57-metre height and Dumkhar of 42-meter height. These projects are at initial or middle stages of construction. Pakistan has repeatedly sought the river flow data from India to ascertain the actual flow of the western rivers at their source but the latter has cold-shouldered the request. Under the 1960 Indus Waters Treaty, India is bound to share the data with Pakistan. Under the treaty, it cannot interfere with the flow of the western rivers before they enter Pakistan but it does so blatantly.

Other violations are: India is irrigating about 800,000 acres in Chenab area which is not permissible; it has built five more canals in the past 10 years to increase the irrigated area in the region. Pakistan has also asked India to provide details of its agricultural acreage, crops and other projects in Kashmir to enable it to make plans in advance.

Low inflows are in evidence in the Rivers Chenab and Jhelum for the past several months. In particular, the flow of the Chenab has become very low after the construction of the Baglihar Hydropower project. In recent months, flows of the River Jhelum have also not been consistent.

On January 20, the water flow in the Chenab was found to have fallen to about 6,000 from 10,000 cusecs, the average flow during the recent years, mainly because of the on-going construction of over a dozen hydropower projects upstream, unauthorised use of water by farmers in Jammu, poor rainfall because of the El Nino effect and the diversion of river waters, according to a report appearing in this newspaper. This is about a 40 per cent decline.

But three leaders of farmers communities in Punjab and Sindh told the media in Lahore on February 10 that the water flow in the Chenab River suddenly jumped up to 15,000 cusecs during the stay of the Indian water delegation in Pakistan to give an impression to our water ministry and the Indus water commissioner that India was not tampering with the flow. It proved, they said, that India was stealing Pakistan's share of river waters.

They want Pakistan to a seek revision of the 1991 river water distribution agreement with India to get more water from Jhelum, Chenab and Indus rivers.

Current estimates of 104MAF flow in Indus, Jhelum and Chenab rivers during dry weather and 114MAF in the event of rainfall were not realistic and required to be revised.

Although, Pakistan has asked India to proportionately reduce its water use if and when there is an abnormal decline in river water, the latter often ignores it. Many observers are of the view that the low flow in Pakistan's rivers has little to do with the lack of rains. It is primarily because India is controlling the water flow of the western rivers, namely, the Indus, the Chenab and the Jhelum which were given to Pakistan under the Indus treaty and India has nothing to do with them. Pakistan complained to the World Bank (WB) regarding hydro-power projects initiated by India but a neutral expert appointed by the WB rejected most of the objections, especially with regard to the Baglihar Dam on the Chenab River.

It only asked India to make some changes in the dam's height. After Baglihar, it is the Kishanganga project which is creating the same problem. Pakistan tried to resolve the issue at the commissioner level but failed. Syed Jamaat Ali Shah intends to raise the issue with a third party. Islamabad fears that the Kishanganga hydro-power project, being constructed on Ganges River to generate 330MW, which on entry into Pakistan becomes Neelum River, will reduce water levels downstream in the plains of Punjab, and thus threaten irrigation and power projects. The Kishanganga dam is located in the remote area of Gurez in the Himalayas, 123km from Srinagar.

The river water is being diverted, through a long tunnel, into the Wullar lake. This will change the course of the Neelum River by about 200 kilometres and will join the Jhelum River through the Wullar lake in the Baramulla district. As a consequence of this diversion, Pakistan's Neelum valley is likely to dry up and become a desert.

A visiting scholar, Arshad H. Abbasi, while writing on this project in this newspaper, wonders why this has not yet been addressed by the ministry of water and power. Most probably, Pakistan is unaware of the fact that India had already diverted the Ganges river at Farrakka by building a barrage, which has brought environmental and economic disaster to Bangladesh.

According to him, the diversion of Ganges waters was an engineering blunder in the history of water engineering. Arsenic contamination in Bangladesh began after the dam's construction and the diversion of the water in 1975. The lowering of the water table resulted in the exposure to air in the zone of aeration. This exposure resulted in the oxidation of arsenic minerals previously present below the water table.

The diversion of the Neelum river is not only a violation of the Indus Waters Treaty signed in 1960 but also of the Helsinki Rule signed in 1966 regarding water rights pertaining to international rivers.

According to this law, all basin states of an international river have the right to access an equitable and reasonable share of the water flow.

Meanwhile, the Indus River System Authority (Irsa) is making hectic efforts to sort out differences between Sindh and Punjab. There exists a serious feud over how much water should go to Sindh and Punjab. The problem is that water available for the current Rabi crop is already reduced by 34 per cent because of low flow.

An Irsa spokesman describes the situation as persistently drought-like because of continuing water shortage. Meanwhile, water level at Mangla Dam dropped last week below 0.3 MAF, which means that Sindh and Balochistan could get 0.1 MAF water.

The continuing drought in the country has not only made the Rabi rops target doubtful, it is also likely to badly affect the Kharif crop output as the weather forecast says that the El-Nino phenomenon, which reduced Pakistan's monsoon rainfall by about 30 per cent last year, is likely to continue till the next summer. This is an alarming situation because, being an agrarian economy, Pakistan can face a huge food deficit. Sindh wants Punjab to release additional water for it because, as it claims, Punjab had promised to give it surplus water after the reopening of canals after January 31.

Paper Three:

The Indus Waters Treaty- Its Dynamics And Reverberations

Dr. S. Chandrasekharan, 19 February, 2010, South Asia Analysis Group, Paper no. 3676,

As late as February 13 this year, many members of the Pakistan National Assembly expressed great concern over the alleged violation of the Indus waters treaty by India in building dams across the rivers meant for Pakistan and warned of a possible war between the two countries over this issue.

These threats of war are nothing new to India. Even before the treaty of 1960, late Suhrawardy, as the Prime Minister of Pakistan, threatened that Pakistan will go to war on the sharing of waters of the Indus. These threats have been repeated periodically and so regularly by people at the political, military, bureaucratic and technical levels that these threats have lost their meanings now. At one point, one of the influential editors of the Urdu press Majeed Nizami, of Pakistan went one step further and threatened that Pakistan will have to go for a nuclear war over the river waters issue.

It should be conceded that the Indus Waters Treaty has survived despite wars, near wars, acts of terrorism and other conflicts that have bedevilled the relations between India and Pakistan. This has been, as such, acknowledged by many of the saner voices from Pakistan, too.

In April 2008, Pakistan's Indus Water Commissioner, Jamaat Ali Shah, in a frank interview, conceded that the water projects undertaken by India do not contravene the provisions of the Indus Waters Treaty of 1960. He said that "in compliance with IWT, India has not, so far, constructed any storage dam on the Indus, the Chenab and the Jhelum rivers (rivers allotted to Pakistan for full use). The Hydro electric projects India is developing are the run of the river waters, projects which India is permitted to pursue according to the treaty."

Yet, many in Pakistan, at very senior levels, have been whipping up frenzy among the people of Pakistan that "India is stealing the waters of Pakistan".

Since 2004-2005, when the opposition to the Bagilhar Project came out into the open, there has been a continuous attempt on the part of Pakistan to push India to renegotiate the Indus Waters Treaty.

This would mean going back to the sharing of waters during the lean season and other extraneous factors and also to ignore the enormous changes that have taken place on both sides of the border in the last fifty years. This could also mean rewarding Pakistan for its failure to manage its scarce and life iving waters to optimum use.

Unfortunately, some Indian scholars, without understanding the past history of negotiations with Pakistan, have supported the idea. One of the senior analysts of India is said to have opined that "negotiating an Indus Waters Treaty 2 would be a huge Confidence Building Measure as it would engage both countries in a regional economic integration process." A pious hope, but an unrealistic one.

The Indus Waters Treaty is unique in one respect. Unlike many of the International agreements which are based on the equitable distribution of the waters of the rivers along with other conditions, the Indus Waters Treaty is based on the distribution of the rivers and not the waters.

This unique division of rivers rather than the waters has eliminated the ery hassles and conflict that would have followed had the equitable distribution of water been based on current usage, historical use, past and potential use etc. People who advocate a revision of the treaty, including some influential ones in India, should realise the trap that India will be getting into.

Briefly, the Indus Waters treaty, having discarded the joint development plan for developing the Indus Basin as suggested by some international bodies, allotted the three western rivers of the Indus basin—the Indus, the Chenab and the Jhelum to Pakistan and the three eastern rivers—Sutlej, Beas and Ravi to India. The Treaty, in its Annexures, acknowledged certain rights and privileges for the agricultural use of Pakistan drawing waters from the eastern rivers and similarly India drawing waters for similar reasons from the three western rivers.

The treaty permitted India to draw water from the western rivers for irrigation up to 642,000 acres that is in addition to another entitlement to irrigate 701,000 acres. India has so far, not made full use of its rights to draw this quantity of water from the western rivers. These allocations were made based on the water flows and usage as existed in April 1960.

While India is not permitted to build dams for water storage purposes (for consumptive uses) on western rivers passing through India, it is allowed to make a limited use of the waters including run of the river hydroelectric power projects. The Baglihar project, the Kishenganga project, as well as Tulbull (Wular) that come in this category are all being opposed by Pakistan on the narrow definition as to what it means by storage.

Pakistan disputed the Indian contention that the Baglihar project was a run-of-the-river project and that the storage called pondage was necessary to meet the fluctuations in the discharge of the turbines and claimed that the water will ultimately go to Pakistan. Since talks over a long period remained unsuccessful, the World Bank intervened though it made it clear that it was not a guarantor of the treaty.

A neutral expert was appointed by the World Bank. The neutral expert, Professor Lafitte of Switzerland, while delivering the verdict, rejected most of Pakistan's objections but did call for minor design changes including the reduction of the dam's height by 1.5 metres. The expert did not object to the right of India to construct dams for storage purposes purely for technical reasons, for the efficiency of turbines, and did not even call the project as a dispute between the two countries but as "differences."

The Tulbul project similarly envisages a barrage to be built at the mouth of the Wular lake to increase the flow of water in the Jhelum during the dry season to make it navigable. The other disputed project is the dam across the Kishenganga River to the Wular lake for the generation of hydroelectric power. The contention of India has been that in both cases, the waters will ultimately go to Pakistan.

In the case of the Kishenganga Project, Pakistan also has objected to the storage of water on the Neelum river on the principle of "prior appropriation" though the project on the Pakistan side, the Neelum - Jhelum power plant, downstream had not then started.

In all the projects objected to, Pakistan has brought in a new dimension to the dispute on security and strategic considerations which are strictly outside the ambit of the Indus treaty. The reasoning goes thus — by regulating the waters of the Chenab and the Jhelum, India has the capability in times of war, to regulate the flow of the waters to its strategic advantage.

There is no doubt that Pakistan will be facing increasing water shortages in the days to come leading to prolonged drought in many of its regions. The reasons are many but some of these are Pakistan's own doing. The availability of water, even now, has reached critical proportions.

1. Global warming over a period of time has depleted the flow of water in the Indus (the major supplier) which depends mostly on glacial runoffs.

2. As in other Himalayan regions like the Kosi in Nepal, the rivers carry very heavy sediments that result in silting the dams and barrages thus reducing the availability of water for cultivation. Proper and periodic maintenance have been lacking.

3. The canals that feed the irrigated lands are not lined resulting in seepage and loss of water.

4. There is mismanagement in the use of water by using antiquated techniques and heavy cropping of water intensive varieties of farm products. Optimum crop rotations have not been done extensively as it should have been done to save water.

5. No serious effort has been made to improve the storage for intensive seasons like Kharif.

6. Dwindling water flow has also been affecting power generation.

7. The discharge of fresh water into the Arabian sea has dwindled considerably (less than 10 MAF) which has resulted in the sea water pushing further into the estuaries and beyond, making water in those areas unfit for cultivation.

Just as in India, there are many water disputes among the four provinces in Pakistan, but there, it is one — Punjab against the other three and Punjab happens to be the upper riparian.

There is a larger political dimension to the whole problem of the river water distribution between Pakistan and India. To Pakistan, the Kashmir issue is irrevocably linked to the Indus Waters Treaty, as the headwaters of all the rivers of Pakistan and meant for Pakistan flow through Kashmir and India happens to be the upper riparian state. The fear exists that India could manipulate the waters to starve Pakistan.

From the Indian point of view, Pakistan need not fear if the Indus Waters Treaty is implemented both in letter and spirit. What is needed is a constructive approach from Pakistan and India should also respond constructively on a crisis that is reaching a very critical stage in Pakistan. Some analysts feel that the "waters' issue" may take precedence over Kashmir.

If one were to interpret the spirit of the Indus Waters Treaty and not the letter, there has to be some give and take from both sides. It needs a conducive environment and mutual trust that are scarce commodities in the relations between India and Pakistan.

Paper Four:

Water War With India?

Ahmer Bilal Soofi, Dawn (Islamabad)

20 February, 2010

The tension relating to water resources held by India has heated up again and Pakistan has complained that India is holding back the the waters of the rivers flowing from the Indian-administered Kashmir.

Some analysts have termed this a clear violation of the Indus Waters Treaty. In a sense, the availability of less water from the rivers is a security issue for Pakistan as it could put the country's very survival at stake. The media in Pakistan and the general public, too, appear convinced that India is withholding the waters in violation of the Indus Waters Treaty. On the other hand, the Indian perception is that Pakistan is assuming that India had restricted the flow, and that this assumption was incorrect as the water level was low the previous year as well.

From a legal point of view, this argument is interesting as it actually raises the issue of jurisdiction and the scope of the Indus Waters treaty itself. The Indus Waters Treaty does not deal directly with the issue of water scarcity. In fact, when the treaty (signed in 1960) was being negotiated, a future possibility of water scarcity was not a priority or a leading concern for the negotiators.

Hence, we find that there is no provision per se that provides a mechanism to both the countries if climate-based water scarcity occurs. The critical provisions of the Indus Waters treaty simply say that India and Pakistan were obliged to "let flow" the river waters without interfering.

Hence any obstruction by India would be seen as an outright breach of the treaty by Pakistan.

Despite speculations by the Pakistani side, there is no specific evidence brought forth, so far, that India is actually obstructing the flow or is diverting the waters. The Indian argument remains that the reservoirs such as the Wullar Barrage and the others are built within the regulatory framework of the treaty tself. Pakistan, naturally, has a different view and in one case, Pakistan was seeking third-party resolution through a neutral expert who did not support fully the Pakistani version.

If the Indian version is correct, then the issue cannot be addressed within the framework of the Indus Waters treaty and, in that case, Pakistan is pursuing a remedy in the wrong direction.The question remains as to who determines whether the reduced amount of water flowing into the rivers of Pakistan from the Indian side is because of obstructions or on account of climatic water scarcity. For that, both countries would need to agree on an independent and a separate framework or neutral experts' assessment. The determination by such a panel would make matters clearer for Pakistani and Indian policymakers who could then follow a bilateral remedial course of action.

The argument is also advanced that even if the water flowing into the Pakistani rivers is less due to genuine climatic water scarcity, India cannot escape responsibility as a state to maintain and manage the water resources that it exercises control over. India's responsibility comes under the general framework of international law that calls on the upper riparian state to take the necessary measures to minimise water scarcity.

In Europe and elsewhere, water scarcity has promoted trans-boundary water cooperation instead of inciting war over this issue. The UN Convention on Uses of International Water Courses 1997 obliges states to conserve, manage and protect international water courses. Pakistan and India are not party to the said convention but the latter, nevertheless, offers a comprehensive framework for trans-boundary water cooperation.

Likewise, the 1992 Convention on Trans-Boundary Water Courses primarily meant for European countries, offers another legislative model for India and Pakistan for bilateral cooperation on the issue of handling water scarcity. The 1997 convention is widely viewed as a codification of the customary international law with regard to obligations for equitable and legal utilisation, the prevention of significant harm and prior notification of planned measures.

At the moment, India and Pakistan lack a legal medium or forum through which the Indian version of 'genuine water scarcity' could be scrutinised and, if found to be correct, handled and responded to properly through bilateral action.

If this issue is not handled technically without a legal mechanism, then it has the potential to further aggravate tensions between India and Pakistan as it will be clubbed with the Kashmir dispute. Further, a reduced water flow could be perceived as India's ploy to put additional pressure on Pakistan and, in that event, the response would be equally unmeasured and misdirected.

Finally, whether India is actually blocking the water, or the decrease in water flow is due to scarcity and climatic change, needs objective and transparent determination by experts. This determination of the real reason should be agreed to beforehand through a bilateral agreement confined to factfinding.

If the finding is that the reduced flow of water is due to obstructions, then Pakistan could take action under the provisions of the Indus Waters Treaty immediately.

On the other hand, if it is determined that there is genuine water scarcity then the issue is outside the jurisdiction of the Indus Waters treaty and needs to be sorted out by both states on a bilateral basis. India, in that case, should undertake its obligations under international law for proper water conservation and management and share the details with Pakistan through a mutually agreed mechanism.

This point may be considered in the India-Pakistan talks as an urgent item.

Paper Five:

Distrust Complicates India-Pakistan River Disputes

Kamran Haider, Reuters, 24 February, 2010

Distrust between India and Pakistan and a "hawkish" Indian mindset were complicating efforts to resolve disputes over the waters of shared rivers, Pakistan's top river water official said.

Some analysts fear that disputes over water between the old rivals could in future spark conflict as the neighbours compete for dwindling supplies of water from melting Himalayan glaciers.

The foreign secretaries of India and Pakistan, which have fought three wars since 1947, will meet in New Delhi on Thursday marking the resumption of official contacts which India broke off after the militants attacked the Indian city of Mumbai in late 2008.

Pakistan wants to put the dispute over river waters at the top of the agenda along with the core dispute over the divided Kashmir region. But the Indian Foreign Secretary, Nirupama Rao, said on Monday that Indian concerns about militant groups based in Pakistan would form the main focus of the talks with her Pakistani counterpart.

"There's mistrust and a lack of confidence," Syed Jamaat Ali Shah, the Indus Water commissioner of Pakistan, told Reuters in an interview on Tuesday.

"There has been reluctance to share information about the water situation in the rivers, which is sad," he said.

The use of the water flowing down the rivers which rise in the Indian part of Kashmir and the flow into the Indus river basin in Pakistan is governed by the 1960 Indus Waters Treaty.

Under the accord, India has the use of waters from three rivers in the east - the Sutlej, Beas, and Ravi.

Pakistan was awarded the use of the waters of the western rivers – the Indus, Chenab and Jhelum.

Diversionary Tactic

But Pakistan accuses India of violating the treaty by reducing the flow of water down the rivers it was awarded use of.

In particular, Pakistan objects to two planned Indian projects, the Wullar barrage, as it is known in Pakistan, or the Tulbul navigation project, as India calls it, and the Kishan-Ganga hydroelectric and water-diversion project.

Shah said the barrage would reduce water flow in the Jhelum river. The water diversion planned in the Kishan-Ganga dam, on a tributary that flows into the Jhelum, would have a serious impact on the Pakistani side and it would seek international arbitration if the dispute could not be resolved bilaterally, he said.

Pakistan also objects to India's Baglihar hydro-power and water storage project on the Chenab river.

But water is also a divisive issue within Pakistan, with the downstream southern provinces of Sindh and Baluchistan complaining that upstream provinces, in particular Punjab, take more than their fair share.

Indian denies any unfair diversion of Pakistan's water.

Some Indian analysts say Pakistani complaints are aimed at diverting attention within Pakistan from the internal water row.

Indian officials also say Pakistan is raising the issue to counter India's attempts to keep the focus of Thursday's talks on militancy.

"Raising the water issue appears to be a diversionary tactic," said an Indian official who declined to be identified.

But Shah played down analysts' fears of conflict over water.

"I don't think the water dispute would become a flash-point," he said. "We want India to get its rights, but it should also fulfil its obligations."

If disputes were handled properly, according to a mechanism set out in the 1960 treaty, the exploitation of the water could be a factor for cooperation, he said.

"It could be a foundation for good relations between the two countries," he said.

Paper Six:

India's Dam On Chenab Exacerbates Water Wars

Pakistan Daily (Islamabad), 24 February, 2010

India's Aqua Bombs: Draught & floods imposed on Pakistan: The Indus Waters Treaty violations - state terror.

Bharat (aka India) has been unable to resolve any of her boundary disputes with any of her neighbors. Bharat's norhtern border is in a state of constant hot and cold war with China. Her disputes with Bangaldesh pre-date the country. Her issues with Nepal are never ending. The Bharati attempts, to bifurcate Sri Lanka were recently defeated when the RAW agent was killed. China, Pakistan and Lanka cooperated to defeat the designs of Delhi.

Bharat also has water disputes with Bangladesh at the Furrakha Barrage which infringes on the rights of the lower reparian (technical term to designate those living on the receiving end of the water).

Bharat, after illegally occupying Kashmir using a fake article of accession which it now claims is lost, (as if it ever existed) has now built an illegal dam called the Kishanganga dam on the Neelam river which eventually flows down to the Indus in Pakistan.

The Americans forced the Field Marshall, Ayub Khan, to sign the Indus Waters Treaty. They had promised the construction of a dozen dams to alleviate the shortage of water (and electricity). Only the Mangla and Tarbeal [Tarbela] were built. The other dams got delayed due to a myriad of issues–too lengthy to get into.

Islamabad: With Pakistan still undecided when to formally seek intervention of the International Court of Arbitration against the controversial construction of the Kishanganga hydropower project by India in violation of the 1960 Indus Waters Treaty, New Delhi has started preparations to build another big dam on River Chenab.

Documents available with Dawn suggest that the government of the Indian occupied Kashmir has invited bids for a 'topographical survey of the Bursar Dam (on Chenab) for the acquisition of land and property'. New Delhi plans to begin construction by the end of the year.

The Bursar Dam is considered as the biggest project among a host of others being built by India on two major rivers – Jhelum and Chenab – flowing through the state of Jammu & Kashmir into Pakistan and assigned to Islamabad under the 1960 Indus Waters Treaty. The proposed dam would not only violate the Treaty, international environmental conventions and cause water scarcity in Pakistan but would also contribute towards the melting of Himalayan glaciers.

Pakistan's Permanent Indus Commissioner, Syed Jamaat Ali Shah, had repeatedly asked his Indian counterpart to provide details of the proposed water storage and hydropower projects, including the Bursar dam. However, India has taken the stand that it was aware of its legal obligations and it would let Pakistan know about the project details and the relevant data six months before construction activities as required under the bilateral Treaty, he said, adding that Pakistan could do nothing more when such projects were in the planning and investigation stage.

Responding to a question about the Kishanganga hydropower project, he said he had already requested the government to move quickly for the constitution of an International Court of Arbitration to stop the construction of the controversial project. Pakistan, he said, had already nominated two members for the court of arbitration and had asked to do the same. He said the procedure laid down in the waters treaty required the two nations to nominate two adjudicators each of their choice and then jointly nominate three members to complete the composition of a seven-member court of arbitration.

He said the procedure also required that in the case of a disagreement over the three adjudicators, the complainant nation should ask the World Bank to nominate these three members and start formal proceedings. Pakistan, he said, had even prepared the list of the three joint adjudicators since India had not yet fulfilled its obligations to nominate its two members and three joint members of the court. "We have completed the entire process; it was only a matter of formal launching and only the government could do that," he said, adding that perhaps Islamabad intended to wait for the upcoming secretary level talks before triggering the legal process.

He, however, believed that these issues were of technical nature and should be processed accordingly as provided under the treaty.

Informed sources said that India had not only started building three other dams, namely, Sawalkot, Pakal-Dul and Kirthai, on Chenab River, it has also completed the detail project report of the Bursar Dam site. The proposed dam would have 829 feet height, storage capacity of more than two million acres feet and power generation capacity of 1200MW. The height of Baglihar, Tarbela and Mangla Dam is 474, 485 and 453 feet, respectively.

The Bursar Dam would be constructed near Hanzal Village (near Kishtwar) in the Doda District of Jammu & Kashmir on the 133-kilometre-long Marusudar River, the main right bank tributary of the Chenab river. Its construction would be a serious violation of the treaty as its storage was much more than the permissible limits. More than 4900 acres of thick forest would be submerged and the whole population of the Hanzal village would be displaced.

Arshad H. Abbasi, visiting research fellow of the SDPI, said the project area fell in the Seismic Zone V and, hence, most vulnerable to earthquake. Two active geological faults lines — the Himalayan thrust and the Kishtwar fault — were passing through the project area, he said, adding that the worst impact of the dam would be on the glaciers of the Marusudar river basin. He said that deforestation, coupled with high altitude military activities, had already created 48 glacial lakes in the Marusudar river basin covering an area of 225.35 sq km and massive construction activities in the basin would further aggravate the melting of the glaciers.

He said the project was located in Kishtwar High Altitude National Park which was an environmentally-protected area. Spreading over an area of 400 kilometres, the park contained 15 mammal species including the musk deer and Himalayan black and brown bear and some rare birds for which an environmental impact assessment study was necessary.

Bharat has built over 60 dams in the Indian Occupied Kashmir. It uses these dams to prevent the flow of water to Pakistan, or on occasion, it simply floods hundreds of villages. This is a direct violation of the Indus Waters Treaty, the United Nations Resolutions and the International Law on riparian rights. Delhi gets away with these acts of war. Terrorism has many faces. One face of state terrorism is murdering innocent farmers by starving them, or by flooding their fields.

Bharat claims that the Kishanganga dam is for the production of electricity only. This is a fake excuse and does not hold water (pun intended).

NEW DELHI (APP) – India claimed on Thursday that the stage of differences or disputes on the controversial Kishenganga Dam had not arisen and the issue could be further discussed at the Commission level.

Paper Seven:

India's Silent Aggression

Editorial, Daily Mail (Islamabad) 26 February, 2010

India maintains a huge military machine in Occupied Kashmir, much larger than the United States and its allies, put together, have in Iraq and Afghanistan. In there, its three-quarters of a million troops, perhaps, out number any such expeditionary force stationed in an occupied or disputed area since the Second World War. On the face of it, the deployment is tasked to deal with freedom fighters, which, of course, is a daunting challenge, but more importantly, it is there to change the face of the Muslim-majority landscape called Kashmir, its main weapon being brutal use of force against unarmed civilian population. But where its work goes almost unnoticed is the security it provides to Indian engineers, who are planning and working day and night to build dams on rivers that take water to Pakistan. So furiously are they working and in such so-far inaccessible areas that, of late, New Delhi is thinking of bringing these projects under the enhanced protection cover of the Central Industrial Security Force (CISF). All this work falls within the definition of an aqua war India is preparing to foist on Pakistan, courtesy a Chanakiya manoeuvre to 'turn Pakistan into a desert'. Not that Pakistanis are not aware of Indian designs; there is plenty of information how India is trying to dam up rivers Jhelum, Chenab and Indus, whose waters under the Indus Waters Treaty should reach Pakistan uninterrupted. According to reports, India is planning or building some three dozen big and small hydropower projects and reservoirs on the tributaries of these principal rivers, including quite a few mega-projects, keeping Pakistan completely un-informed or misinformed. One of these is Bursar Dam on River Chenab, for which New Delhi has invited bids for a 'topographical survey'. Others in different stages of planning/construction include Kishenganga on River Neelam, Uri Todium on River Pooch, which is ta ributary for River Jhelum, and the Baglihar, Dul Husti and Salal dams on River Chenab. On River Indus, Indian engineers are working to steal water at Kargil and from its 12 distributaries. Not content with depriving Pakistan of its waters from Kashmir, the Indians have recently stepped up their aid-assisted work in Afghanistan on two dams on River Kabul, which is a tributary of River Indus. Yes, Pakistanis know all this – and much more, given the fact that the growing water shortages are causing problems that have begun negatively impacting the provincial harmony, power generation and industrial production. As Irsa stood bitterly divided over the opening of the Chashma-Jhelum and Taunsa-Panjnad link canals last week, the prime minister had to call an urgent meeting of the four chief ministers. But the official state or quality of being pusillanimous is detected in raising the issue of India blocking Pakistani rivers at the concerned international forums. Recent reports suggest that Pakistan is 'still undecided' when to formally seek intervention of the International Court of Arbitration against the controversial construction of the Kishenganga project by India, in violation of Indus Waters Treaty. Of course, the Indus Waters Treaty - under which Pakistan lost waters of its three eastern rivers - Ravi, Sutlej and Beas - hoping its monopoly of Indus, Jhelum and Chenab waters would remain uncontested by India - was badly negotiated and more than required was surrendered. But that Pakistan should not even get its allocated share under the treaty is all the more unacceptable.

We hope and expect that at the forthcoming talks in New Delhi, later this week, Pakistani officials would raise the issue of dams India is building or planning to build in the Occupied Kashmir in violation of Indus Waters Treaty. Under international laws, India cannot carry out any major upstream alterations in a river system, and even minor changes have to be discussed and made only with the formal consent of the downstream riparian. If allowed to go unchecked, what India is doing has the dangerous potential to stop the Himalayan snowmelt reaching Pakistan in the next few years. It is a kind of silent strategic warfare India is waging against Pakistan, by creating conditions of perennial drought for a fundamentally agrarian economy that Pakistan is. It would be resisted resolutely and fought back valiantly; if world's future wars would be fought over water and not oil, the first of these may well be in South Asia where India seeks to starve Pakistan to death.

Paper Eight:

Looming Threat Of Water Wars

Nazia Nazar, Pakistan Observer (Islamabad) 1 March, 2010

Last year, Pakistan suffered a loss exceeding five billion rupees in paddy crop production only in the wake of water shortage after India stopped Chenab water to fill its Baglihar dam during the month of September 2008. But this was not the first instance, as India have violated the Indus Waters Treaty many a time, and the objective seemed to be India's attempt to dry up

Pakistan because India feels that Pakistan is a major obstacle in its hegemonic designs against the countries in the region. India's think-tanks have been working on river diversion plans with a view to creating acute water shortage in Pakistan. The objective is to adversely impact the production of wheat and other crops, and also to stoke inter-provincial conflicts over the distribution of water. In the past, the world has witnessed wars between different countries of the world over religions, usurpation of territories and control of resources including oil. But in view of acute shortages of water in Africa, Middle East, Asia and elsewhere, the future wars could be fought over water.

The Indus River Basin has been an area of conflict between India and Pakistan for about four decades. Spanning 1,800 miles, the river and its tributaries together make up one of the largest irrigation canals in the world. However, the distribution of the river basin water has created friction among India and Pakistan, and also among their states and provinces. Accusations of overdrawing of share of water made by each province in Pakistan have resulted in the lack of water supplies to the coastal regions of Pakistan. India and Bangladesh have also a dispute over the Ganges River water and the former is resorting to water theft there as well. It is too well known that water is life; it is indispensable to agriculture and in fact it is critical input into a country's agriculture especially when it is situated in an arid or a semi-arid zone. When India stopped water to fill the Baglihar dam at the Chenab river, Pakistan had taken up the matter with the World Bank, as Pakistan was getting 7000 to 8000 cusecs less water daily during the Rabi season. By violating "the Indus Waters Treaty", India has reduced Pakistan's share of water through the construction of dams on the Indus, Jhelum and Chenab rivers.

Paper Nine:

We Will Have To Look Beyond The Indus Waters Treaty

Amber Rahim Shamsi, Dawn (Islamabad) 3 March, 2010

At the recent foreign secretary-level talks between India and Pakistan in New Delhi, Pakistan's foreign office team presented a paper on water issues to India prepared by Pakistan's Indus Water Commission. Although water is not a core issue for the resumption of talks between the two nuclear neighbours, differences over the use of rivers assigned according to the 1960 Indus Waters Treaty have undercut peace-making efforts. As Pakistan and India's populations grow, water for agriculture and electricity generation is in short supply. Pakistan's Indus Water Commissioner, Jamaat Ali Shah, talks to Dawn.com about the urgent need to resolve water-sharing disputes.

Q. **India says the Kishenganga project does not violate the Indus Waters Treaty. What is Pakistan's position?**

A. The Kishenganga River runs through Kashmir, and becomes the Neelum River. Water flows through Azad Jammu and Kashmir for 165 km before joining the Jhelum at Muzaffarabad. Now, 70-80 kilometres of this river also run through the Occupied Jammu and Kashmir. So, the water re-routed by the Kishenganga power project reduces the flow of water going to Muzaffarabad. And then, Pakistan also has one project on the Jhelum River – the Neelum-Jhelum hyrdro-electric power project.

What are the adverse impacts of this one project according to the Indus Waters Treaty? One, it reduces our annual energy generation. Two, the Kishenganga project also has an environmental impact because the depth of the water is reduced and this has an impact on the flora and fauna in Azad Jammu and Kashmir through which the Neelum flows. Three, there are technical problems in the design of the Kishenganga project such as the height of the gates and so on.

Q. **But India contends that that it started its Kishenganga project earlier than Pakistan's Neelum-Jhelum project. According to the Indus Waters Treaty, India may construct a power plant on the rivers given to Pakistan provided it does not interfere with existing hydro-electric use by Pakistan. Is this true?**

A. Yes. But the Jhelum waters were given to Pakistan. And going by the spirit of the treaty, while the waters are Pakistan's to use, both countries can accrue benefits. When India made its plans known to Pakistan, that did not mean Pakistan did not have the intention [of constructing a plant]. In 1989, we told India that we are constructing a project there. India wanted to inspect the site. At the time, it was only a small exploration tunnel. Now the intention has been shown, with the Chinese being given the project. So we have a legal case. Moreover, while the total quantity of water has not been changed, there are no guarantees that India will not store or divert water into the Wullar barrage. Certainly, re-routing will impact the flow-time and, therefore, reduce the quantum of water [to Pakistan].

Q. **Where are talks between India and Pakistan on the Kishenganga project now?**

A. In 1988, we came to know about Kishenganga and we asked for details. We were told that India was just conducting investigations. India is obliged by the treaty only to give detailed plans six months prior to construction.

In 1992 or 1993, India asked to conduct its first inspection of the site of the Neelum-Jhleum project in Azad Jammu and Kashmir. That was when there was just an underground tunnel. India told us unofficially that the tunnel was an eye-wash.

Then, in 1994, we were officially informed about Kishenganga, which was to be a 330 watt storage work. Now, in a storage work, there is no mention of diversion.

The commission held five meetings between 1994 and 2006 and the storage height of the dam was ultimately reduced by 40 metres. But by 2006, Kishenganga became a run-off project. Pakistan's position was that this is a new project; the run-off was not in the 1994 project, and the 1994 project should be considered abandoned.

In June 2006, we raised objections. Between 2006 and 2008, the commission held three meetings. In 2008, Pakistan informed India that it intends to seek the opinion of a neutral expert appointed by the World Bank. India said Pakistan has no case and that there is no controversy since the Kishenganga project does not harm Pakistan's usage. India wanted to resolve the issue at the level of the commission. So, the government of Pakistan agreed to meet the representatives of the government of India, but the meeting proved inconclusive.

So, India and Pakistan agreed to negotiations, and in March 2009, Pakistan proposed two names of negotiators. But the Indian stance remained the same. According to the treaty, if negotiations reach a deadlock, then a court of arbitration can be constituted with seven experts: two from the government of Pakistan, two from the government of India and three jointly named umpires. If these names are not jointly agreed upon, then the World Bank would help.

Pakistan's point of view is that the direction of flow and the environmental impact of the dam should be addressed by the court of arbitration, while the matter of design would be decided by the neutral expert.

Now, the Pakistan Indus Water Commission has shortlisted several names and these are with the foreign office and the law and justice ministry who have to finalise Pakistan's two names.

Q. Will Pakistan be taking up other Indian projects with the World Bank?

A. As I said, India is planning two more power projects on the River Indus. But those of concern are the ones on the Chenab because we don't have any storage site there. So, the Chenab is more vulnerable. After constructing three, including Baglihar, India intends to construct 10 to 12 more dams on the Chenab and its tributaries.

Certainly, the treaty gives India the right, but the designs should be compliant. Already, India constructed the Wullar barrage unilaterally without informing Pakistan.

Q. It is said that the Baglihar dam issue was settled by the World Bank in India's favour because Pakistan did not raise the objections in time. Do you agree with that?

A. Both parties had different points of view. When we approached the World Bank, India blocked us because it did not want a neutral expert. So, the fact that a neutral expert was appointed was a small victory. The expert asked for documentation from us, which we provided. India believed that Pakistan was maligning them, but the fact is that the neutral expert settled three points in favour of Pakistan and one in India's favour. And both parties bore the cost of the proceedings. Both India and Pakistan need these waters and there is a need for candidness and transparency. Political considerations should not shadow technical aspects. Unfortunately, the technical side is subordinate to the political side. For example, India did not provide us the updated flow data. In August 2008, India violated the treaty by not providing accurate data on the initial filling of the Baglihar dam. The treaty says the initial filling should not reduce the water flowing into Pakistan. So, the initial filling of the Baglihar reduced Pakistan's water and India should compensate for the lost water.

Q. **What impact has the construction of Indian power projects had on Pakistan's waters? We are, after all, facing shortages for agricultural use and electricity generation.**

A. Apart from the Baglihar dam, neither Pakistan nor India has had problems with the Indus Waters Treaty. But looking to the future, I foresee problems, especially given climate changes. India has already constructed 50-60. medium-sized projects and it plans more than a hundred. One hundred and fifty will be in the small catchment areas in the Occupied Jammu and Kashmir. This is human intervention: imagine how many trees will be cut, and the resulting environmental impact? They will also impact Pakistan's water, given the environmental degradation and increased sediment flow.

I think, we will now have to look beyond the treaty for solutions. India is allowed run-off hydro-electric projects according to the treaty, but two or three is different from more than a hundred.

In 1960, Pakistan did not want to give three of its rivers to India, but it did. But clearly, the World Bank had not factored in climate change and the impact of human intervention. I think the World Bank treaty is likely to be jeopardised. Already, we are facing a shortage in the western rivers; how can we then compensate for the lack of water in the eastern rivers?

Q. **Do you think it is time to expand the scope of the treaty?**

A. There are some issues with that. Right now, we need to protect and implement the treaty in its full spirit without re-visiting it. But both governments should initiate talks along with expert stakeholders.

Q. **Would this be in India's interest?**

A. Yes, because we are neighbours. The Indus Waters treaty was not a happy marriage but we accepted it. But Pakistan should take action at the appropriate time: what happens to the state of Bahawalpur where the rivers Sutlej and Ravi are dry?

Paper Ten:

Future Laden With Hydrological Warfare

Gauhar Zahid Malik, Pakistan Observer(Islamabad) 4 March, 2010

There is a consensus among political experts that the world's future wars will be fought over water, not oil. Experts say it would be the era in which rivers, lakes and aquifers become national security assets to be fought over, or controlled through surrogate armies and client states. Surprisingly, where the whole world is fortunately lagging a bit behind for entering into this ill-fated era of the 'hydrological warfare', the Asian region has surpassed the rest of the world due to the Indian expansionist agenda.

It is a hard fact that water wars remain no more a part of science fiction movies; they are happening now. Pakistan, Nepal and Bangladesh are already a victim of the Indian water thievery. India has plans to construct 62 dams/hydroelectric units on rivers Chenab and Jhelum, thus enabling it to render these rivers dry by 2014. The hydroelectric plants both built or are under construction, will enable India to block the entire water of the Chenab for 20-25 days. India has also started the construction of three dams, Nimoo Bazgo, Dumkhar and Chutak, on the river Indus, which will have a devastating impact on Pakistan's northern areas. Chutak is under construction on River Suru. In case of any of these dams collapse or a large quantity of water is deliberately released, it will not only endanger the Bhasha dam but also submerge the Skardu city and the airport. The Karakorum Highway (KKH) between Besham and Jaglot would also wash away. India has also persuaded Afghanistan to create a water reservoir on the River Kabul, another tributary of the river Indus.

Moreover, India has a dispute with Bangladesh over the Farrakha Barrage, with Nepal over the Mahakali River and with Pakistan over the 1960 Indus Waters Treaty. Without any qualms, India is busy building dams on all rivers flowing into Pakistan from the occupied Kashmir to gain the control of the western rivers in violation of the Indus treaty. This is being deliberately done under a well thought out strategy to render Pakistan's link-canal system redundant, and destroy agriculture of Pakistan, which is its mainstay, thus turning it into a desert.

Unfortunately, after using the waters of Pakistani, Bangladeshi and Nepali rivers, India is escalating its water terrorism to Iran as well. India is building Salma Dam on the Hari Rud river basin in northwest in Afghanistan, which flows into Iran and forms the Sistan delta. Originally, Salma Dam was constructed in 1976 while in 2004. The Water and Power Consultancy Service (India) Ltd (WAPCOS) began the reconstruction of the Salma Dam power project in 2004. The completion of the project has been unnecessarily delayed and it is now expected to be commissioned by 2011 instead of 2009.

The Salma Dam Power project is India's largest project in Afghanistan with a total estimated cost of USD 116 million. This mega project, aimed at generating 42MW of power and involves the erection of 110 KV power transmission lines to the Herat city, conspires to restrict the flow of water to Iran. By doing so, India will not only restrict the river Hari Rud's flow of water to Iran but also barren the Sistan inland delta, inhibiting some 400,000 people whose economy strongly depend on agriculture and the goods and services provided by the wetlands.

The Sistan delta in Iran is located at the end of a closed basin. The entire contributing basin is about 200,000 km and is largely located in Afghanistan. The river system discharges into an inland depression which, when sufficient water is available, forms the Hamoun lakes. These lakes are fresh and one of the main and the most valuable aquatic ecosystems in Iran and are registered wetlands in the Ramsar and the UNESCO Biosphere Reserve conventions. The inflowing rivers from Afghanistan support not only the irrigated agriculture in the Sistan delta but are also the source for the lake system around the delta. And blocking the flow of the Afghan River's water into Iran will mean less water for the hamouns with the resulting lower average water coverage of the lakes. Ultimately, this will not only endanger the ecosystem that the hamouns support but also the livelihoods of its people that depend on the goods and services that the lake provides.

The Water Research Institute of Iran, in cooperation with ITC and Alterra from the Netherlands, carried out a study with an extensive analysis of all existing information on the river basin including the natural resource system and its infrastructure, in Iran as well as in Afghanistan. Analyses showed that the hamouns lakes are under serious risk of losing their ecological value and potential developments will decrease the inflow to the lakes with more than 50%. The government of Iran has stated their concerns to the Afghan authorities, urging them to resolve the water sharing issue between the two countries before the construction of the Salma Dam but to no avail. It is not because of Afghan authorities but due to the Indian interest in building a Dam on the Hari Rud. Isn't it intriguing as to what interests India might have in constructing the Salma Dam? Well, India has deep interests in any such activity, whether economic, political, geographical, religious or cultural, which can help consolidate its hegemonic ambitions.

That the Indian interests lie in the goodwill of the Afghan masses is merely an eyewash. The Indian keenness to reconstruct the Salma Dam is aimed at encouraging the Afghan masses to agitate against the Iranian interference in the construction of the Salma Dam in order to create a rift between Afghanistan and Iran one the one hand and to appease the USA by depriving Iran of the appropriate flow of water, thus harming the agricultural economy on the other hand. India, by and large, has no interest in developing Afghanistan besides keeping it under the thumb. Paradoxically, the Indian pledged huge aid package to Afghanistan has neither been dispensed nor any mega development project for Afghanistan has commenced in time. Instead, in the last 7 years, India remain more committed in buying time for India-owned projects in Afghanistan on one or the other pretext and increasing the number of RAW agents in the garb of security personnel, workers, doctors, engineers etc.

Factually, India needs the Afghanistan link for many reasons i.e. to maintain its links with the Central Asian states, to carry out subversive activities against Pakistan considered its enemy No 1 and to appease the US and western allies. During the Taliban rule, India faced difficulties in maintaining its influence in the Central Asian region, which is not only energy rich but its large consumer market is of geo-strategic importance to India. According to an Indian analyst, Meena Singh Roy,"India, as an extended neighbour of CARs, has major geo-strategic and economic interests in this region". That is why India is investing heavily in building roads and infrastructure, linking Afghanistan with the Central Asian states. Apart from the Salma dam project, the Indian oil companies are active in Kazakhstan and Uzbekistan. Moreover, in March 2007, after completing the refurbishment of a military base at Ayni, India became the fourth country, apart from Russia, the US and Germany to have a base in Central Asia. The base is of strategic importance to India. An Indian analyst, Sudha Ramachandran, observed, "A base at Ayni allows India rapid response to any emerging threat from the volatile Afghanistan-Pakistan arc ... It also gives New Delhi a limited but significant capability to inject special forces into hostile theatres as and when the situation demands ... in the event of a military confrontation with Pakistan, India would be able to strike Pakistan's rear from Tajik soil... Ayni has to do with India's growing interests in Central Asia as well".

Salma Dam like projects is a manifestation of India's dual regional policy according to which neighbours are regarded as enemies and an enemy's immediate neighbour as a friend. Also, all such dams are a clear violation of the rights of the lower riparian according to the international law. Yet, the USA is looking up to India as a central player in resolving the Afghanistan problem. But what can one possibly expect from a country which stoops to the lowest level of immorality by stealing water and blocking rivers to turn the agricultural lands barren? If the US really wants peace and stability in the region, then it should restrict India from making war-ravaged Afghanistan a chessboard to pursue her own agenda. Better it would be for India to refrain from playing foul games, testing the patience of the Afghans and victimizing other regional neighbours through its water terrorism before it is too late. On the other hand, it would be better for Afghan authorities too, that despite playing in the hands of India and relying on alien clutches', they better should struggle themselves to stand on their own feet and realize the Indian conspiracy before time runs out.

Paper Eleven:

Is Pakistan Ready For Water War?

Zahid Malik, Pakistan Observer 15 March, 2010

At the very outset, I wish I am wrong, but the most serious problem that Pakistan could be facing in the next five to ten years would be extreme water scarcity, not only due to global warming caused by changes in weather systems, but due to our own failures and, if I may say, follies and criminal negligence as well.

There is a realization the world over that future wars would be on depleting water resources, and this, I fear, is particularly true in the case of Pakistan. We have miserably failed to build water reservoirs and protect our water rights on three rivers-Indus, Jhelum and Chenab, on which Pakistan has priority rights under the Indus Waters treaty.

It is the apathy on the part of our leadership that they politicized the construction of the Kalabagh Dam, downstream Tarbela, and indulged in an unforgivable delay in building other major reservoirs including Diamer- Bhasha. Construction of such dams involves billions of dollars and will take about a decade to complete and even if we start the construction of Diamer-Bhasha Dam right now, which again is being politicised, it would be too late. People in canal irrigated areas, like southern Punjab, Sindh and Balochistan, do not realize the horrible scenario when there will be no water for crops and, may be, for drinking purposes as well.

We will never know the worth of water till the well is dry, and that is the case in Pakistan, as our neighbour is usurping our water rights and we are fighting among ourselves on petty issues relating to the internal distribution of water.

The world over, water is a single substantial issue that mars bilateral relations among subcontinental countries. The issues of cross-border water distribution, utilization, management and mega irrigation hydro-electric power projects affecting the upper and lower riparian countries are gradually taking center-stage in defining interstate relations as water scarcity increases and both drought and floods make life, too, often miserable.

In December 2007, the UN Secretary General, Ban Ki Moon, while speaking at the first Asia-Pacific water summit, said a struggle by nations to secure sources of clean water would be a "potent fuel" for war and that water crisis in Asia was especially troubling.

The Indus Waters Basin Treaty was signed in 1960 after lengthy interventions of the World Bank. Pakistan had accepted the Treaty at the stake of its very survival and the assurances from India that it would not interfere with the rivers over which Pakistan was given the right. However, India never honoured its promises.

In this scenario, I think, that while Jammu and Kashmir is the core issue, the discord on the waters of Jhelum and Chenab, over Baglihar and several other projects being constructed by India upstream Jhelum, Chenab and Indus have the potential to provoke a war between the two countries. If peace was desired in the area, then water and Kashmir will have to be taken as inextricably interlinked issues and resolved as such.

From the record, I can say with authority that the Indian behaviour has been in violation of international norms, arguing that India utilized its share of the eastern rivers but after the eighties, it started tampering with the Pakistani rivers.

Pakistan has been opposing the setting up of the Kishanganga Hydropower Project on Kishnaganga (known as Neelum in Azad Kashmir) as it involves the diversion of water from Neelum to another tributary of Jhelum, called Bunar Mandhumati near Bandipur in Baramula District which is not allowed under the 1960 Indus Waters Treaty. Consequently, Jhelum will face a 27 per cent water deficit when the project gets completed.

Kashmir is a place where water may not be the worst of the problems, yet it's a growing factor in what is already a conflict situation. Baglihar and Kishanganga with plans to construct 62 dams/hydro-electric units on Rivers Chenab and Jhelum, and the diversion of water from these storages through tunnels to Indian rivers would enable New Delhi to render these rivers dry in the next five years. It is because of our survival resting on rivers that Kashmir has been referred to as Pakistan's jugular vein. That all this is part of the overall water strangulation strategy of India is also borne out by the fact that India, taking advantage of its influence over Afghanistan, has succeeded in convincing the Karzai regime to build a dam on the River Kabul and set up the Kama Hydroelectric Project, using 0.5 MAF of Pakistan water with serious repercussions on the water flow of the River Indus.

According to the Indus Waters Treaty, the projects commissioned first would be accorded top priority. Due to criminal negligence, our leadership failed to start any major project in Azad Kashmir and as such, it is likely that the Neelam-Jhelum project would be of no benefit as the Kishanganga project would leave very little water for use. Currently, India's State-owned National Hydroelectric Power Corporation (NHPC) has set 2016 as its deadline for the completion of the project, while Pakistan plans to complete its project in 2017, if everything goes well. According to reports by the Indian media, the NHPC has been directed to expedite its project and commission it before Pakistan has a chance to complete the Neelum-Jhelum project.

Apart from Kishanganga, India has initiated four other mega projects on the Chenab and Jhelum Rivers in Occupied Kashmir that can result in a major water shortage in Pakistan in due course of time. India has also planned three dams on the River Indus which will have a devastating impact on Pakistan's Northern Areas. These are Nimoo Bazgo, Dumkhar, and Chutak. Work on Nimoo Bazgo hydropower project, 70 km from Leh, is already underway, while Chutak is under construction on River Suru. In case any of these dams collapses or a large quantity of water is deliberately released, it will not only endanger our proposed Bhasha Dam but also submerge the Skardu city and the airport. In that case, the strategic KKH between Besham and Jaglot would also be washed away.

Stopping water by India is the policy of desertification of Pakistan, creating invisible aggression and concomitant serious consequences for the agriculture of the country. It is a hostile and destructive attack on our sovereign rights over waters of three rivers and we must take this battle to international arbitrators. Pakistan has to assert its right over the eastern rivers and must do everything for the strict implementation of the Treaty.

I am of the considered view that in the given and future scenario, water is as much a nuclear flashpoint as is Kashmir. We must make the world realize seriously that if it is interested in peace in this region, it must act urgently to help both countries restart negotiations and resolve the contentious issue of water on an urgent basis.

I say this because in the coming years, Pakistan would be in a very difficult situation. According to a recent United Nations report, Pakistan's water supply has dropped from about 5,000 cubic meters per person in 1950s to 1,420 cubic meters in 2009 — perilously close to the threshold at which water shortage becomes an impediment to economic development and a serious hazard to human health.

As a nation, we have the tendency that we wake up when the water passes over our head. Last year, there were less than normal monsoon rains and this year, the winter rains were much delayed and below normal. So, some attention is being paid by the leadership, at least through statements. However, unfortunately, we have a short memory and forget or overlook this problem when there are normal rains and near normal water is available in our storages.

In the face of worsening water shortages and the ensuing serious crisis, I would caution the political leadership to pay its full attention and make the water issue its single top most priority whether it is dispute with India or building of storages at all the identified sites and allocate at least half of the PSDP under this head. That would also create tens of thousands of jobs for the skilled and unskilled workforce. Let us delay some non-essential projects for a few years for the sake of the country and the future of the coming generations. If we just manage our present resources of water efficiently, I am confident that the vast barren lands could be brought under cultivation, boosting our agricultural production and generating 25,000 MW of electricity through hydel means, thus saving billions of dollars of foreign exchange being spent the on import of furnace oil. That amount could then be diverted to other the sectors for socio-economic development of the country.

The question is will we wake up now or left to cry when the water had already passed over our head. I pray, the leadership would listen and act timely and decisively.

Paper Twelve:

The Water Crisis

Editorial, The Nation (Islamabad) 24 March, 2010

There is no disputing Punjab Chief Minister Mian Shahbaz Sharif's bold assertion that since New Delhi has cut off Pakistan's share of the Indus waters as part of its hegemonic designs, we must talk about the matter eyeball to eyeball. He also rightly stated that our agriculture has suffered greatly on account of this water theft. The CM knows well that the economy and livelihood of thousands of families in Sindh and Punjab, whose only bread and butter is agriculture, are doomed to destruction if New Delhi goes on indefinitely blocking the water flowing into Pakistan. On the other hand, a former head of the ISI, General Hamid Gul, speaking at a seminar organised by the Nazria-i-Pakistan Trust, has shown another motive behind India's machinations. He maintained that water was essential for our economy but stressed that it was equally important for the country's defence as well. He got it right by pointing to the Chenab canal network as the first line of defence, without which the country's conventional defence was impossible. It is really good to know that more and more voices are joining the chorus in blowing the whistle on India. However, the onus lies on the federal government to seriously raise the issue, most of which is about building pressure on New Delhi to behave like a lawful state. The World Bank should also be asked to step in as being the third party in the Indus Waters Treaty. It is its duty to ensure that there is no violation of the accord. The Indian water theft is now turning us into an agricultural wasteland. The phenomenon of desertification has picked up pace and has claimed vast tracts of cultivated lands. Farmers are in a virtual catch-22 situation as they do not know where to get water for their crops. For the past two years, among others, our wheat crop has been the biggest casualty of the Indian diversion of water. What is really chilling is the fact that the glaciers, our main source of fresh water, are melting at an alarmingly fast pace because of the effects of global warming. Consequently, the supply to the domestic sector has been reduced. The tube wells have to be dug much deeper but still the water is brackish. New Delhi is deftly exploiting this situation through scores of dams. Its cunning designs can be gauged from the fact that it has ganged up with the Karzai government and is currently building a dam on the River Kabul as well.

Paper Thirteen:

India Plans 52 Projects To Control Pakistan's Water

Nation (Islamabad), 30 March, 2010,

The Chairman Indus Waters Treaty Council, Hafiz Zahoor-ul-Hassan Dahr, has said that previous 131 rounds of talks between Pakistan and India under the Indus Waters Treaty bore no fruits and the latest dialogue would meet the same result. He also warned that Pakistan could become another Somalia and Ethiopia. Talking to 'The Nation' on Monday, Zahoor pointed to various projects launched by India to divert the water flow of three rivers entering Pakistan from Occupied Kashmir and said these projects were aimed at controlling the water of Chenab, Jhelum and Indus rivers, which were illegal and a clear violation of the Indus Waters Treaty. He said India was constructing 52 illegal dams, including five large ones, of which as many as 32 small dams had already been completed, while 12 others would be finalised in 2014.

Zahoor said New Delhi was also constructing Kargil Dam, the second largest in the world, on Indus, adding that India was getting support from a consortium of nine non-Muslim countries, four multi-national companies, an international donor agency and three intelligence agencies to accomplish 17 mega water projects for controlling Pakistan's water. He said India had seized 70 per cent water of Chenab and Jhelum rivers as a result of which over 0.9 million acres of land, being irrigated through Marala Headworks, was now presenting the view of Thar and Cholistan deserts.

Dahr said the Baglihar Dam was causing an annual loss of Rs140 billion to Pakistan and feared that India would soon stop the entire water flow of Chenab and Jhelum rivers, turning 18 districts of Punjab and six districts of Sindh into a desert. He also accused Israel and the US for backing India, which resulted in bulldozing the Indus Waters Treaty and lamented the fact that the international community was silent over the issue.

He urged the government to take the issue seriously to Indian water aggression. "If the rulers fail to adopt immediate measures, India will turn us into Somalia and Ethiopia," he feared.

According to him, the anti-Pakistan forces have united and evolved a plan to turn the country into a desert and the irrigation system is being given to a Swedish company on contract to forward the vested interests of India. He said India was spending billions of dollars on this project with the financial support of Israel. He said it was very much clear that the Indian and Israeli lobbies were working on long-term projects to harm Pakistan.

Paper Fourteen:

India And Pakistan Feud Over Indus Waters

Amol Sharma & Tom Wright, 30 March, 2010

Wall Street Journal

Fight threatens peace talks as Islamabad requests arbitration over New Delhi's plans for a hydroelectric plant

A feud over water between India and Pakistan is threatening to derail peace talks between the two neighbors.

The countries have harmoniously shared the waters of the Indus River for decades. A 50-year-old treaty, regulating access to water from the river and its tributaries, has been viewed as a bright spot for India and Pakistan, which have gone to war three times since 1947.

Now, the Pakistanis complain that India is hogging water upstream, which is hurting Pakistani farmers downstream. Pakistani officials say they will soon begin formal arbitration over a proposed Indian dam. At a meeting that started Sunday, Pakistan raised objections to new Indian dam projects on the Indus River and asked for satellite monitoring of river flows.

"Water, I see emerging as a very serious source of tension between Pakistan and India," said Shah Mehmood Qureshi, Pakistan's foreign minister, in an interview Friday. He said he has raised the issue with the Indian Prime Minister Manmohan Singh.

A senior Indian government official denied India is violating the treaty. He blamed Pakistan's water shortage on changing weather patterns and the country's poor water management. He called the strident rhetoric from Pakistani officials a "political gimmick...designed to place yet one more agenda item in our already complex relationship." Indian officials declined comment on the record.

The latest dispute revolves around India's plans to build a 330-megawatt hydroelectric power project on the Kishenganga River, a tributary of the Indus. India says it is well within its rights to build the dam. The project has been on the drawing board since the late 1980s and is expected to cost about $800 million.

Pakistan says New Delhi's plans to divert the course of the river will reduce its flow by a third in the winter. That would make it unfeasible for Pakistan to move ahead with its own plans for a hydroelectric dam downstream.

Pakistan wants to put the Kishenganga project before an arbitration panel—the first time that mechanism of the treaty will have been used. If India agrees, a seven-person court of arbitration would include two members appointed by each country, and three outsiders. India hasn't yet responded formally to the proposal, according to the Pakistan delegation to the meeting.

"We're already a water-stressed country," Jamaat Ali Shah, Pakistan's Indus waters commissioner, said ahead of this week's meeting. India's construction of new dams is "aggravating the stresses."

The water dispute comes as the relationship between the nuclear-armed neighbors is at an inflection point. India last month invited Pakistan to discuss the resumption of regular peace talks, and the two countries' foreign secretaries met in Delhi Feb. 25th . A water squabble could upset those peace efforts.

That would deal a major blow to Indian the Prime Minister Manmohan Singh, who views engagement with Pakistan as the best way to contain terrorism. Mr. Singh wants Pakistan's aid in bringing to justice Pakistan-based militants that New Delhi believes carried out the November 2008 attacks in Mumbai, a bloody siege that killed 166 people.

Further deterioration of relations between New Delhi and Islamabad would also be a setback for Washington's efforts to stabilize the region. Pakistan has told the U.S. that tensions with India on its eastern border over the disputed territory of Kashmir have prevented it from cracking down more aggressively on Taliban and al Qaeda leaders directing the insurgency in Afghanistan.

The Islamist groups in Pakistan have taken up the water issue as a new focus. "If our government doesn't act to resolve this issue, then the people will take it into their own hands. If water doesn't flow into these rivers, then blood will," said Hafiz Khalid Waleed, the political affairs chief of Jamaat-ud-Dawah, an Islamic charity. India and others call the charity a front for Lashkar-e-Taiba, the militant group it says orchestrated the Mumbai terrorist attacks in Nov. 2008. Mr. Waleed denies any link to terrorism, calling it "American propaganda."

Water scarcity is a growing political issue across the globe, from the Middle East to the U.S. South Asia's water politics date back to the Britain's partition of the Indian subcontinent in 1947, when the newly created nations, India and Pakistan, wrangled over how to divide resources.

The Indus River, whose waters Britain had harnessed through a vast system of irrigation canals, was a crucial lifeline to the farmers in the Punjab region stretching across both countries. But India and Pakistan were fighting over the control of Kashmir, where several Indus tributaries begin.

After years of tense negotiations, India and Pakistan signed the Indus Waters Treaty in 1960 with the help of the World Bank. As part of the treaty—which is widely viewed by water experts as a model of how water conflicts can be managed—each side got unrestricted use of three rivers and the rights to use the others for nonconsumptive purposes such as flood control, navigation and bathing. India was granted limited agricultural usage of Pakistan's rivers, plus the right to build hydroelectric projects, as long as they don't store or divert large amounts of water.

The treaty provides for bureaucrats appointed by both governments to meet regularly, exchange data, and resolve disputes. Commissioners have held more than 200 site inspections and meetings since 1960, even during times of war.

Yet Pakistan's rows with India have intensified as its water situation has worsened over the years. Water availability in Pakistan has fallen 70% since the early 1950s to 1,500 cubic meters per capita. It is expected to reach the 1,000-cubic-meter level considered officially "scarce" by international standards in 25 years, according to a report last year by the Woodrow Wilson International Center for Scholars.Pakistani officials acknowledge their water woes aren't caused by India's damming of rivers alone. Major reservoirs are filling with sediment picked up by the rivers on their routes to the sea. Canals are aging and breaking down. The World Bank says soil erosion and poor irrigation are sapping roughly 1% from Pakistan's Gross Domestic Product growth.

Skeptics in India say Pakistan is simply looking for a scapegoat as it struggles to manage its internal water politics.

The especially arid province of Sindh, for example, blames the powerful upstream province of Punjab for consuming too much.

"Their water management is in a terrible shape, and it's convenient to put the onus on India," said G. Parthasarathy, a former Indian envoy to Pakistan.

But Pakistani officials say New Delhi's actions are exacerbating a precarious situation.

This year, the Pakistan province of Punjab—the political heartland of the nation and a major producer of wheat, rice, maize and sugar cane—is facing unprecedented water shortages. At harvest time in Mandi Bahauddin, an area in the north of Punjab province of relatively prosperous farmland, the wheat still grows waist-high. But farmers here complain that yields and incomes have dropped by a third in the past five years because of water shortages. In the past, canals used to supply water for irrigation year-round. They are now empty for about four months each year. That forces villagers to pump groundwater, which is fast turning brackish and causing diseases like hepatitis, said Tariq Mehmood Allowana, a local farmer and member of the provincial assembly.

In the past, the area's only problem was regular flooding. India's dams stopped this, causing a dearth of water instead, says Mr. Allowana, who owns 25 acres of wheat fields. The farmer represents the Pakistan Peoples Party of the late former Prime Minister Benazir Bhutto. Farmers say they have stopped cultivating rice—a water-intensive crop—except for personal use. Nearby, more than half of the Chenab river bed has become a dusty plain where children play with the flow reduced to a trickle. "India is engaged in an economic warfare against Pakistan. If the problem persists for another five years, the whole area will become barren," said Mr. Allowana, as a group of farmers nearby filled irrigation channels from groundwater supplies using a diesel-fueled pump. Over the years, tensions have built as Pakistan has objected to the size and technical design of various Indian projects. India says it has 33 Indus-related hydrological projects at various stages of implementation, and all have been contested in one way or another by Pakistan. India also says it has yet to make use of its limited rights to store water on Pakistan's rivers or use it for limited irrigation.

"We've found there's a pattern in Pakistan of raising technical issues, ad nauseam, to stall a project or delay a project indefinitely," a senior Indian official said on Friday.

In 2005, Pakistan raised issues with the Baglihar dam, an Indian power project on the Chenab river—one of those allotted to Pakistan—saying it would store too much water upstream and reduce the downstream flow to Pakistan. The countries agreed in 2007 to let the World Bank appoint an independent expert, who ruled that India had to make minor modifications to the dam, such as lowering its height. Pakistan now contends the dam, which began operations in 2008, is reducing the flow of the Chenab below levels stipulated in the treaty. India denies this.

Pakistan wants Washington to play a mediating role with India—in the water dispute and wider issues like the Kashmir conflict. The U.S. is pushing for tighter relations with Pakistan as it steps up pressure on the Taliban in Afghanistan but has to balance this with its close ties to India. For now, the U.S. is treading carefully, offering Pakistan stepped-up economic aid and military hardware supplies.

Pakistan raised the water issue in Washington during an official visit last week. The Secretary of State, Hillary Clinton, has signaled that Washington isn't interested in mediating on water issues.

A State Department spokesperson pointed to an interview Mrs. Clinton recently did with a Pakistani news channel in which she said it would be "sensible" to stick to the Indus Waters Treaty for resolving disputes.

The Indian projects that Pakistan says are draining its water resources are primarily on Indus tributaries in Kashmir. Some experts say the water issue is a back door way for Islamic militants to push their political agenda regarding Kashmir.

"They're saying, "We must liberate Kashmir to save our water," said B.G. Verghese, a veteran journalist who has studied water issues closely and is a visiting professor at the Center for Policy Research, a New Delhi think tank.

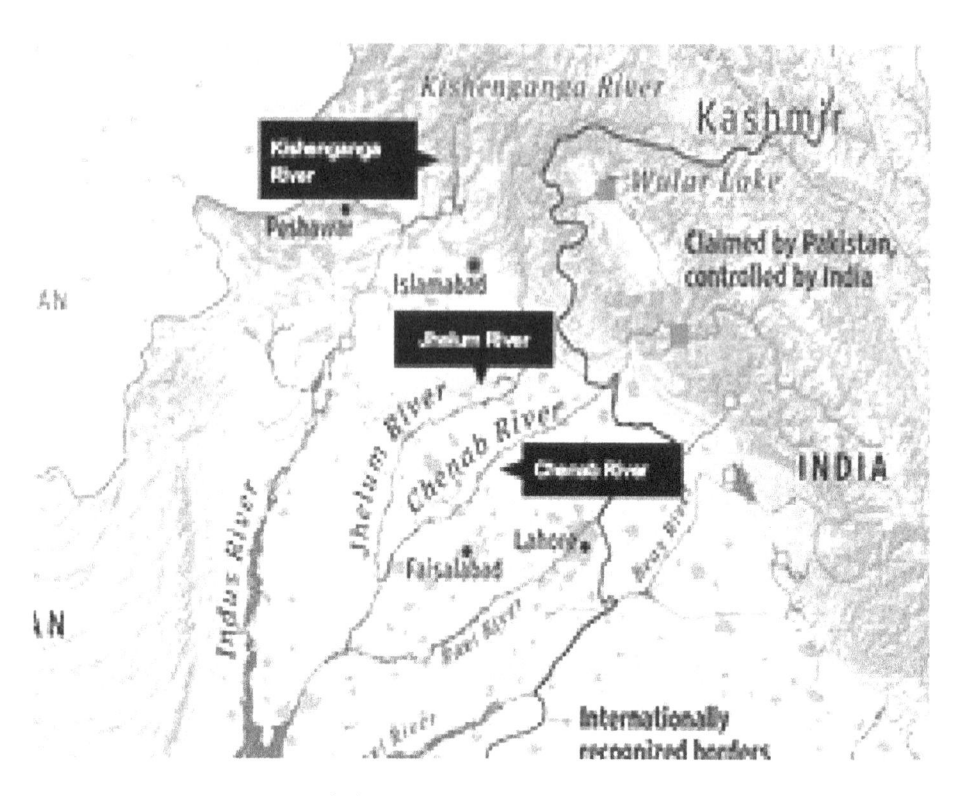

Map of the rivers and dams in dispute.

Paper Fifteen:

Water Talks Run Dry

Editorial, Daily Times (Lahore) 1 April, 2010

Just like the water in the Mangla and Tarbela dams, the recent round of talks between the Indus Water Commissions of Pakistan and India have reached dead level. Aimed at removing the many doubts and reservations of both countries — more so by Pakistan — in respect to water distribution, shortage and the construction of controversial new projects — Nimoo Bazgoo and Chutak — the three-day conference produced no significant breakthrough in dispelling these apprehensions.

An annual deliberation since 1960, when the Indus Waters Treaty (IWT) was signed, the Indus Water Commission met this year to address Pakistan's innate fear that India's end goal was to cordon off water to the country by constructing hydel generation projects on the rivers Chenab and Jehlum in occupied Kashmir. Pakistani reservations extended to the accusation that India had designed these projects along the lines of the maximum allowed figures as stated in the Indus Waters Treaty. This allows the Indians to stay dangerously close to the limits demarcated by the IWT while retaining the potential to manipulate water flows. It is the design of these projects that is proving to be contentious for Pakistan. It is not surprising then that, parallel to these talks, New Delhi has issued a statement confronting Pakistan's claims by saying that any shortage faced by its neighbour was due to the adverse weather conditions and lack of rainfall. Although the emotionally wrought Pakistani psyche may be tempted to discount this argument, it cannot be gainsaid that Nature may very well be to blame for the water crises looming over the nation. India's climate prediction may very well be proved or disproved during further talks scheduled in May of this year in New Delhi, where the advent of summer will bring to light whether the problem has heightened due to the 'facilitated' water shortage or been eased because of the melting snows.

Pakistan is also miffed at the fact that India has, allegedly, violated some of the IWT's fine print by failing to inform Pakistan about the construction of these hydro projects some six months in advance. With India's denial of almost all the points presented by the Pakistani side, the provision of details regarding such projects falls short of being redeemed.

However, Pakistan has made some headway in getting India to agree to the setting up of a telemetry system to ensure the measurement of actual river flows, so as to quell doubts about India's alleged aim to hold back water.

The outcome has come to the sorry stalemate that if, in the proposed May deliberations, Pakistan and India fail to arrive at any conclusions, the World Bank may have to act as a third party arbitrator to sort out the conundrum. Seeing that this guarantor has been the mediator for the occurrence of these talks in the first place, in its presence some sort of reconciliatory possibilities are perceived.

Although the IWT has been getting its undue share of flak from certain elements who accuse it of being a document legitimising the sell-out of Pakistan's eastern rivers, it cannot be stressed enough how defiantly the IWT has stood the test of time. India and Pakistan have engaged in wars and hostilities over the years, but the treaty has consistently remained one of the few common meeting platforms for these traditional enemies.

It must be borne in mind that, at the end of the day, the ecosystem plays by its own rules that transcend political boundaries. Rational solutions ought to be sought instead of playing the blame game. We are living in an era of unpredictable climate change where the only way to battle the elements is to increase cooperation and mutual acknowledgment of a common problem.

Paper Sixteen:

Inconclusive Water Talks

Editorial, Daily Mail (Islamabad) 5 April, 2010

Once again, the Pak-India water talks have remained inconclusive, thanks to India's convoluted interpretation of the Indus Waters Treaty. If there was any tangible outcome of the three days of extensive parleys, it was the promise to meet in New Delhi by the end of May. So sterile were the talks that the thoroughly exasperated Syed Jamat Ali Shah, the Pakistan's commissioner to the water treaty, even threatened to seek intervention of the treaty's guarantor, the World Bank, or third-party arbitration. But his Indian counterpart, Commissioner G. Aranga Nathan, was adamant that the "Indians are living by the treaty and would continue doing so". Every time the Pakistani side produced concrete evidence of some violations of the treaty, the standard response that emanated from the other side of the table was 'back home, we will look into it'. But they wouldn't, and would see to it that Pakistan was presented with a situation of fait accompli. Naturally, there is a growing opinion in Pakistan that it should approach the World Bank to secure New Delhi's faithful implementation of the Indus Waters Treaty. In his words, "We will now have to look beyond the treaty for solutions. India is allowed run-off hydro-electric projects ...but two or three is not the same thing as more than a hundred". But, there does exist also an opposite point of view and that is that Pakistan should persevere in its present mode — because, may be, India's real intention behind its foot-dragging on the treaty is to wriggle out of it. As we know, rivers enhance the lingering phenomenon of water disputes, even water-wars, between the upper riparian and lower riparian states. But there is plenty of history and case law to suggest that such disputes are amenable to peaceful resolutions. The Indus Waters Treaty is one such dispute-resolving mechanism between Pakistan and India, and it is still in the field despite New Delhi's consistent violations. Of course, during the 48-year life of the Indus Waters Treaty, the availability of water has acquired a new, accentuated importance. Not only climate change is drastically affecting the flow of river waters, there is a growing demand for more water to irrigate more land to feed the growing populations.

Then, the water table is lowering, in case of Pakistan, much more rapidly, increasing the dependence on river water. So, instead of scrapping the treaty or rendering it ineffective, it would be in the fitness of things that it is refurbished by enlarging its scope, by re-writing its Addendum. Being the lower riparian, Pakistan suffers at the hands of India's haughtiness. If India insists it is not stealing Pakistan's water, it should readily agree to the proposal made at the recent meeting that the telemetry system should be installed and information on water-flow rate is passed onto Pakistani concerned quarters, on a daily basis. In fact, the theft is on such a large scale that just the Chenab influx is down by 30 percent because of the Baglihar project, built in blatant violation of the Indus Waters Treaty. Pakistan's opposition to the Kishenganga hydro-power project in Occupied Kashmir stems from its fear that the Neelam's water flow would decrease by almost 30 percent, with a concomitant negative effect on the proposed Neelam-Jhelum hydel power station. How India responds to Pakistan's demand for some changes in its designs for the Chutak and Nimoo Bazgo dams is the litmus test for its sincerity in implementing the Indus Waters Treaty, in letter and spirit. May be the rising tide of chauvinistic politics, back home, held back the Indian officials from taking a clear position. Therefore, it may be worthwhile exploring the possibility of introducing the back-channel diplomacy to help a fuller implementation of the Indus Waters Treaty. After all, this is the only way to resolve growing differences on river waters - unless India plans to turn Pakistan into a desert.

Paper Seventeen:

The Threat Of Water Wars

I A. Pansohta, The Nation (Islamabad) 6 April, 2010

The canal system in India was introduced during 1817 by the then Governor General of India, Lord Ellenborough. A mega project, stipulating the construction of 5483 miles of the main channel and 29,282 distributaries, was undertaken. It was first entrusted to Sir Proby Cautley, an English engineer and a palaeontologist. He established his famous training centre at the Gota Canal at Motala Werstad, Sweden, in 1822, that produced many brilliant engineers. His efforts bore fruit for the Indians as well, as a part of the human urge for peaceful co-existence. Then the colonial age in Europe ushered in, resulting in the capture of as many countries as possible. Consequently, the East India Company got its hold on entire India by 1857 AD. However, the partition of India in 1947, which was not anticipated at that time, triggered an array of new problems - water being one of its key issues. In an unprecedented triumph of water diplomacy, the Pakistani engineers together with their Indian counterparts and the World Bank negotiated the Indus Waters Treaty, giving Pakistan the right in perpetuity to the waters of the Indus, Jhelum and Chenab rivers, which accounts for 75 percent of the flow of the whole Indus system. As time passed, the population of India and Pakistan grew. In Pakistan alone, it was estimated around 17 million in 1901 that became around 32 million in 1947. It was around 34 millions at the time of census 1951 and about 140 million during the last decade. India crossed the one billion mark. The first challenge arose because of the 'lines of partition' of the Indo-Pakistan subcontinent that severed the irrigated heartland of Punjab from the life-giving waters of the Ravi, Beas and Sutlej rivers. In Punjab, a densely settled area and a beneficiary of the irrigation system, besides rapid population growth, the need for water has also increased. At present, Pakistan is one of the world's most arid countries with an average rainfall of under 240mm a year. Currently, India has 26 major rivers along with their numerous tributaries, making up the river system of India. All the major rivers of India originate from one of the three main watersheds:

- The Himalayas and the Karakoram ranges

- Vindhya and Satpura ranges and Chotanagpur plateau in central India

- Sahyadri or Western Ghats in western India. The Himalayas serve a very important purpose. The Himalayas, about 2,400 kilometres in length and varying in width from 240 to 330 kilometres, are made up of three parallel ranges — the Greater Himalayas, the Lesser Himalayas and the Outer Himalayas, which is the highest mountain range in the world. It extends along the northern frontiers of Pakistan, India, Nepal, Bhutan, and Burma, having approximately 6,000 meters in average height and containing the highest peaks such as Mount Everest (8,796 meters) on the China-Nepal border. Then K2 (8,611 meters), also known as Mount Godwin-Austen and in China as Qogir Feng, which is located in an area that is claimed by India, Pakistan, and China.

There is yet another mountain known as Kanchenjunga (8,598 meters) located on the India-Nepal border. The snow line average is from 4,500 to 6,000 meters on the southern side of the Greater Himalayas and 5,500 to 6,000 meters on the northern side. Because of climatic conditions, the snow line in the eastern Himalayas averages 4,300 meters, while in the western Himalayas it averages 5,800 meters.

The Lesser Himalayas, located in northwestern India, ranges from 1,500 to 5,000 meters in height. The Outer or Southern Himalayas, averaging 900 to 1,200 meters in elevation, lies between the Lesser Himalayas and the Indo-Gangetic Plain. Although the Trans-Himalaya Range is divided from the Great Himalayan Range for most of its length, it merges with the Great Himalayan Range in the western section — the Karakoram Range — where India, Pakistan, and China meet. Moreover, the southern slopes of each of the Himalayan ranges are too steep to accumulate snow. The northern slopes generally are forested below the snow line. Between the ranges are extensive high plateaus, deep gorges, and fertile valleys, such as the vales of Kashmir and Kulu. They provide a physical screen within which the monsoon system operates and are the source of the great river systems that water the alluvial plains below. As a result of erosion, the rivers coming from the mountains carry vast quantities of silt that enrich the plains.

In Indian Punjab, the only natural resource for water are the three rivers — Ravi, Beas and Sutlej — that flow in its territory. But 75 percent of its water was given to the adjoining non-riparian states of Haryana and Rajasthan. The total estimated water in these three rivers is about 32 million acre feet. Punjab alone needs a total of 52 units and thus is short of 20 million. Pakistan has objected to the construction of 67 projects being undertaken by India on the Indus, besides opposing the construction of Kishanganga Dam, Wullar Barrage Dam on the Jhelum, Baghlihar, Salal and Bursar Dams on the Chenab. If we look at the water stress versus any country's resources, India is in a much better position than Pakistan due to its proximity to Tibet, Kashmir, the Himalayas, and the Bay of Bengal. India at present uses the water of more than 220 rivers; some of its major rivers are Brahmaputra, Dahisar, Damodar, Ganga (with its tributaries) Ghaggar, Godavari, Gomti, the Indus Basin (which includes Sutlej, Jhelum, Beas, Ravi and Chenab), Kaveri (with its main tributaries) Koyna, Krishna, Mandovi, Mhanadi, Mithi, Narmada, Oswiwara, Sabarmati, Tapti (with its main tributaries), Ulhas, Vashishti, Yamuna, and Zuari.

On the other hand, Pakistan has extremely limited water resources. The Indus River, which is regarded the 'life line of Pakistan, and its tributaries are probably the largest water source in this country, as around two-thirds of water supplied for irrigation and in homes comes from the Indus and its associated rivers. However, in case India plans to curtail Pakistan's water supply, the impact on its agriculture and economy would be thoroughly devastating—one could possibly guess.

If the international community does not intervene, a new series of conflicts — Water Wars — could start in the coming years. That would once again change the course of the subcontinent's history. The only ray of hope, for seeking justice, is through the legal battle, as New Delhi's policy of spelling disaster in Pakistan is being pursued on the basis of the view that 'Might is Right'. Technical juggleries are being employed to justify its actions. In this way, it lays a death trap for Pakistan, yet raising a false alarm that it is breeding terrorism in India.

Paper Eighteen:

Natural Security And Water

Kashif Hasnie, Dawn (Islamabad) 13 April, 2010

In one of my earlier commentaries for the Middle East Institute in Washington, D.C., titled, Water Security in Pakistan, I was able to get the attention of the water authorities in Pakistan by explaining to them the grim situation the country is facing with regard to this precious resource.

I wrote that "Islamabad, we have a problem!" Today, I write to attract their attention by saying, "Islamabad, we need a solution!"

In the recently concluded 'strategic dialogue' between Pakistan and the United States, water issues did not get the prominence they deserved. Water became part of the energy dialogue in one of the second-day sessions, giving it less prominence than required.

Given the high population growth rate, growing poverty, religious militancy and natural disasters, it sometimes feels as if matters in Pakistan could not get worse. Pakistan is ranked 125 out of 163 countries in the 2010 Environmental Performance Index (EPI).

The EPI focuses on two overarching environmental objectives: a) reducing environmental stresses to human health; and b) promoting ecosystem vitality and sound natural resource management.

Moreover, since Pakistan is primarily an agrarian country, water becomes the most important of all the natural resources to be secured and managed. Ironically, although the complex Punjab rivers and link canals system could very well be classified as one of the 20th century engineering wonders, today one is left wondering what good the engineering wonder has accomplished in a country where water resource management has failed for all intents and purposes.

To many, water security entails the idea of 'water wars,' which is a plausible scenario in the case of the waters shared by Pakistan and India. A good gauge of the trans-boundary significance of water is the dependency ratio, which is a measure of water resources originating outside the country.

Pakistan has a dependency ratio of 77 per cent, which is one of the highest in Asia. Therefore, we all hear about the classic, model treaty between India and Pakistan, called the Indus Waters Treaty (IWT). So much has been said, written and discussed about the treaty that there might as well be another one by the name of Indus Waters Treaty 2.

Since enough has been said about the trans-boundary water issue between India and Pakistan, I would briefly add that although the treaty is admired for withstanding wars and conflicts between the two countries, it has not been able to play any role in forestalling war. The mechanics of the treaty has survived so far, but the treaty itself has not been able to be part of a solution to animosities.

This is because the institutions, which deal with water and environment, do not work in tandem with the national security agencies. Quite recently, the water issue created friction between the two countries when after the Mumbai attacks of November 2008, Pakistani political commentators started accusing Indian officials of violating the Indus Waters Treaty, suggesting that water was the root cause of the Kashmir issue. Is this the case?

Another external water security issue is with Afghanistan. However, no signs of a serious conflict has arisen regarding the shared waters between the two militancy-infested countries, but the potential is always there. Therefore, as a matter of preventive diplomacy or maybe as a confidence-building measure, both countries should establish a joint multi-disciplinary scientific fact-finding working group to build a mutually agreed-upon hydrological knowledge base on the Kabul river basin.

It is suggested that the two countries should also establish a bilateral water resources commission to review and negotiate hydropower and agricultural development plans affecting the population of both nations. Negotiations are recommended to build a bilateral treaty between Afghanistan and Pakistan on the use and management of the Kabul river water resources. Existing frameworks such as the Economic Cooperation Organisation and the Regional Economic Cooperation Conference on Afghanistan should be used to include effective mechanisms on water-sharing 'Natural security' (natural resources plus national security) is an idea in its infancy. Water security is a subset of 'natural security'. We are taking small steps to inform and advise the movers and shakers of society of the importance of natural security. However, it is clear that the time has come to move swiftly in the right direction and understand the consequences of not doing so.

Water security requires urgent attention. So far, water resource issues have not been adequately addressed, especially when the effects of climate change are growing with each passing day. In most cases, the problems caused by climate change have not been factored into analyses and policy formulation concerning water management. According to many experts, water and its availability and quality constitute the main pressures on societies that are witnessing the effects of climate change. Hence, it is necessary to improve our understanding of the problems involved so that effective action can be taken without delay.

In February 2009, at the launch of The World's Water 2008-2009, Peter H.Gleick of the Pacific Institute with reference to water said that the least we can do is 'educate'. This is the intention here.

The writer is working on a study titled 'Water and Security in South Asia' for the RAND Corporation in Washington, D.C.

Paper Nineteen:

Waters Dispute

Swaminathan S Anklesaria Aiyar, News International(Rawalpindi) 13 April, 2010

Politicians and Islamic outfits in Pakistan accuse India of stealing the upstream Indus system waters, threatening Pakistan's very existence. More sober Pakistanis complain that numerous new Indian projects on the Jhelum and the Chenab will create a substantial live storage even the in the run-of-the-river hydel dams. This will enable India to drastically reduce flows to Pakistan during the crucial sowing season, something that actually happened for a couple of days when the Baglihar reservoir was filled by India after dam completion.

India accuses Pakistan of hysteria, saying there is really no issue, since India has always observed the Indus Waters Treaty, dividing the waters of the Indus and Punjab rivers between the two countries. Pakistan may suffer from water scarcity but so does India.

Inter-state fights over water in India are humungous — Punjab vs Haryana, Karnataka vs Tamil Nadu, and Andhra Pradesh vs Maharashtra. Water raises passions, and farmers in all states claim they are being robbed of water, without going into rather complex facts. Pakistan is no different, say Indian experts, so let's shrug aside Pakistani rhetoric.

What this debate misses is that dam-based canal irrigation is an obsolete, wasteful 19th century technology that cannot meet the 21st century needs. It must be replaced by sprinkler and drip irrigation, distributed through pressurized plastic pipes. This approach has enabled Israel to irrigate the desert. It can enable India and Pakistan to triple the irrigated area with their existing water resources, escaping water scarcity. Drip and sprinkler irrigation systems are expensive. They use a lot of power for pumping. But they greatly improve yields too. Israel's agriculture is highly competitive.

Canals are hugely wasteful of both land and water, something well captured in Tushaar Shah's book 'Taming the Anarchy'. Up to 7 per cent of the command area of a conventional irrigation project is taken up by canals, and this no longer makes sense when land is worth lakhs per acre. In the Narmada command area, farmers have refused to give up their land to build distributaries from the main Narmada canal, so only a small portion of the irrigation potential is actually used today.

Traditionally, the South Asian farmers have levelled their land and flooded it with irrigation water. Rice is typically grown in standing water. This entails enormous water losses through evaporation in canals and flooded fields. This mattered little in the 19th century when land and water were relatively abundant. It matters hugely today. Piped water greatly economises the use of both land and water.

Instead of canals, we can transport water through underground pipes that leave the land above free for cultivation. Indeed, the downhill flow of water through massive pipes can run turbines, generating electricity for pumping the water to the surface where required.

The canal system makes farmers prisoners of water releases decided by canal headquarters. If canal water is released to a village section, say once a month, farmers can grow only those crops suited to this irrigation schedule. This was acceptable in the 19th century when farms were large and grew the same crop, and technology and market for unconventional crops were scarce.

But today, farmers want to diversify into a wide diversity of crops, and for this they need water on demand. This is why they have gone in a huge way for tube well irrigation. This gives them water on demand, enabling them to grow what they like. India's green revolution was based overwhelmingly on tube well irrigation: the Bhakra Dam contributed hardly anything to it, save that Bhakra canal waters leaked into the ground and helped recharge underground aquifers. The same was true of the green revolution in Pakistan too.

This does not cease to make water an emotive issue. Punjab and Haryana fight bitterly over canal water although 80 per cent of their irrigation is based on tube wells. Punjab has refused to let the Sutlej-Yamuna Link be completed. Yet, not even this has saved the state from water scarcity, since excessive tube well pumping is emptying aquifers. The same thing is happening in Punjab.

Gujarat has shown the way out of this water crisis. It has gone in a big way for drip and sprinkler irrigation. It has been rewarded with an astounding agricultural growth rate of 9 per cent despite being a semi-arid state. Jain Irrigation has become one of the biggest producers of drip and sprinkler equipment in the world, and other corporate rivals are coming up fast.

Like Gujarat, India and Pakistan need to replace canal-based irrigation with pipe-based irrigation. India has world-class technology and equipment that it can share with Pakistan. Such co-operation cannot end controversies over Indus water sharing. But it can take the sting out of them.

Paper Twenty:

War Or Peace On The Indus?

John Briscoe, Frontier Post (Peshawar) 18 April, 2010

Anyone foolish enough to write on war or peace in the Indus needs to first banish a set of immediate suspicions. I am neither Indian nor Pakistani. I am a South African who has worked on water issues in the subcontinent for 35 years and who has lived in Bangladesh (in the 1970s) and Delhi (in the 2000s). In 2006, I published, with five Indian colleagues, an Oxford University Press book titled India's Water Economy: Facing a Turbulent Future and, with five Pakistani colleagues, one titled Pakistan's Water Economy: Running Dry. I was the Senior Water Advisor for the World Bank who dealt with the appointment of the Neutral Expert on the Baglihar case. My last assignment at the World Bank was as the Country Director for Brazil. I am now a mere university professor, and speak in the name of no one but myself. I have deep affection for the people of both India and Pakistan, and am dismayed by what I see as a looming train wreck on the Indus, with disastrous consequences for both countries. I will outline why there is no objective conflict of interests between the countries over the waters of the Indus Basin, make some observations of the need for a change in public discourse, and suggest how the drivers of the train can put on the brakes before it is too late. Is there an inherent conflict between India and Pakistan? The simple answer is no. The Indus Waters Treaty allocates the waters of the three western rivers to Pakistan, but allows India to tap the considerable hydropower potential of the Chenab and the Jhelum before the rivers enter Pakistan. The qualification is that this use of hydropower is not to affect either the quantity of water reaching Pakistan or to interfere with the natural timing of those flows. Since hydropower does not consume water, the only issue is timing. And timing is a very big issue, because agriculture in the Pakistani plains depends not only on how much water comes, but that it comes in critical periods during the planting season. The reality is that India could tap virtually all of the available power without negatively affecting the timing of flows to which Pakistan is entitled. Is the Indus Treaty a stable basis for cooperation? If Pakistan and India had normal, trustful relations, there would be a mutually-verified monitoring process which would assure that there is no change in the flows going into Pakistan. (In an even more ideal world, India could increase low-flows during the critical planting season, with significant benefits to Pakistani farmers and with very small impacts on power generation in India.) Because the relationship was not normal when the treaty was negotiated, Pakistan would agree only if limitations on India's capacity to manipulate the timing of flows was hardwired into the treaty. This was done by limiting the amount of "live storage" (the storage that matters for changing the timing of flows) in each and every hydropower dam that India would construct on the two rivers. While this made sense given knowledge in 1960, over time it became clear that this restriction gave rise to a major problem. The physical restrictions meant that gates for flushing silt out of the dams could not be built, thus ensuring that any dam in India would rapidly fill with the silt pouring off the young Himalayas. This was a critical issue at stake in the Baglihar case. Pakistan (reasonably) said that the gates being installed were in violation of the specifications of the treaty. India (equally reasonably) argued that it would be wrong to build a dam knowing it would soon fill with silt. The finding of the Neutral Expert was essentially a reinterpretation of the Treaty, saying that the physical limitations no longer made sense. While the finding was reasonable in the case of Baglihar, it left Pakistan without the mechanism — limited live storage — which was its only (albeit weak) protection against the upstream manipulation of flows in India. This vulnerability was driven home when India chose to fill Baglihar exactly at the time when it would impose maximum harm on farmers in downstream Pakistan. If Baglihar was the only dam being built by India on the Chenab and Jhelum, this would be a limited problem. But following Baglihar is a veritable caravan of Indian projects — Kishanganga, Rawalkot, Pakuldul, Bursar, Dal Huste, Gyspa. The cumulative live storage will be large, giving India an unquestioned capacity to have a major impact on the timing of flows into Pakistan. (Using Baglihar as a reference, simple back-of-the-envelope calculations suggest that once it has constructed all of the planned hydropower plants on the Chenab, India will have an ability to effect major damage on Pakistan. First, there is the one-time effect of filling the new dams. If done during the wet season, this would have little effect on Pakistan. But if done during the critical low-flow period, there would be a large one-time effect (as was the case when India filled Baglihar). Second, there is the permanent threat which would be a consequence of substantial cumulative live storage which could store about one month's worth of low-season flow on the Chenab. If, God forbid, India so chose, it could use this cumulative live storage to impose major reductions on water availability in Pakistan during the critical planting season. Living in Delhi and working in both India and Pakistan, I was struck by a paradox. One country was a vigorous democracy, the other a military regime. But whereas an important part of the Pakistani press regularly reported India's views on the water issue in an objective way, the Indian press never did the same. I never saw a report which gave the Indian readers a factual description of the enormous vulnerability of Pakistan, of the way in which India had socked it to Pakistan when filling Baglihar. How could this be, I asked? Because, a journalist colleague in Delhi told me, "when it comes to Kashmir - and the Indus Treaty is considered an integral part of Kashmir — the Ministry of External Affairs instructs newspapers on what they can and cannot say, and often tells them explicitly what it is they are to say." This, apparently, remains the case. In the context of the recent talks between India and Pakistan, I read, in Boston, the electronic reports on the disagreement about "the water issue" in The Times of India, The Hindustan Times, The Hindu, The Indian Express and The Economic Times. Taken together, these reports make astounding reading. Not only was the message the same in each case ("no real issue, just Pakistani shenanigans"), but the arguments were the same, the numbers were the same and the phrases were the same. And in all cases, the source was "analysts" and "experts" — in not one case was the reader informed that this was reporting an official position of the Government of India. Equally depressing is my repeated experience — most recently at a major international meeting of strategic security institutions in Delhi — that even the most liberal and enlightened of Indian analysts seem constitutionally incapable of seeing the great vulnerability and legitimate concern of Pakistan. This is a very uneven playing field. The regional hegemon is the upper riparian and has all the cards in its hands. This asymmetry means that it is India that is driving the train, and that change must start in India. In my view, four things need to be done. First, there must be some courageous and open-minded Indians — in government or out — who will stand up and explain to the public why this is not just an issue for Pakistan, but why it is an existential issue for Pakistan. Second, there must be leadership from the Government of India. Here, I am struck by the stark difference between the behaviour of India and that of its fellow BRIC — Brazil, the regional hegemon in Latin America. Brazil and Paraguay have a binding agreement on their rights and responsibilities on the massive Itaipu Binacional Hydropower Project. The proceeds, which are of enormous importance to the small Paraguay, played a politicised, polemical, anti-Brazilian part in the recent presidential election in Paraguay. Similarly, Brazil's and Bolivia's binding agreement on gas also became a part of an anti-Brazil presidential campaign theme. The public and press in Brazil bayed for blood and insisted that Bolivia and Paraguay be made to pay. So what did President Luis Inacio Lula da Silva do? "Look," he said to his irate countrymen, "these are poor countries, and these are huge issues for them. They are our brothers. Yes, we are in our legal rights to be harsh with them, but we are going to show understanding and generosity, and so I am unilaterally doubling (in the case of Paraguay) and tripling (in the case of Bolivia) the payments we make to them. Brazil is a big country and a relatively rich one, so this will do a lot for them and won't harm us much." India could, and should, in my view, similarly make the effort to see it from its neighbour's point of view, and should show the generosity of spirit which is an integral part of being a truly great power and good neighbour. Third, this should translate into an invitation to Pakistan to explore ways in which the principles of the Indus Waters Treaty could be respected, while providing a win for Pakistan (assurance on their flows) and a win for India (reducing the chronic legal uncertainty which vexes every Indian project on the Chenab or Jhelum). With goodwill, there are multiple ways in which the treaty could be maintained but reinterpreted so that both countries could win. Fourth, discussions on the Indus waters should be de-linked from both historic grievances and from the other Kashmir-related issues. Again, it is a sign of statesmanship, not weakness, to acknowledge the past and then move beyond it. This is personal for me, as someone of Irish origin. Conor Cruise O'Brien once remarked: "Santayana said that those who did not learn their history would be condemned to repeat it; in the case of Ireland, we have learned our history so well that we are condemned to repeat it, again and again." And finally, as a South African, I am acutely aware that Nelson Mandela, after 27 years in prison, chose not to settle scores but to look forward and construct a better future, for all the people of his country and mine. Who will be the Indian Mandela who will do this — for the benefit of Pakistanis and Indians — on the Indus?

Paper Twenty One:

Indus Treaty: Pakistan's Options

Ahmer Bilal Soofi, Dawn (Islamabad) 18 April, 2010

It is believed that if India starts the construction of any dam or reservoir on the rivers flowing into Pakistan, the only remedy Pakistan has is to resort to the dispute-resolution mechanisms under the Indus Waters Treaty (IWT). Actually, Pakistan has the right to protest outside the IWT whenever it feels that the construction of a dam or reservoir by India will threaten its strategic interests.

The IWT consists of only 12 articles and eight annexes. There is no provision in the treaty which expressly 'authorises' India to construct a certain number of dams. Neither is there one that prohibits India from making dams beyond a certain number. Clearly, therefore, the number of dams that India wishes to construct on the western rivers is an issue outside the scope of the treaty.

This means that the decision of how many dams India will construct is a one taken by India unilaterally, outside the treaty, on the basis of political and strategic considerations, without consulting Pakistan. Once the decision to construct a dam or reservoir has been taken by India, the matter enters the framework of the treaty, which only provides technical specifications for building such a dam or reservoir.

The treaty is a regulatory framework giving technical specifications. It is confined to these technicalities and does not address the substantive decision of the number of dams that the Indian government may wish to construct.

Therefore, Pakistan is free to contest such a political decision of India without entering into the dispute-resolution mechanism of the treaty. Pakistan is entitled to launch a diplomatic offensive outside the treaty if it feels threatened due to the excessive construction of dams, reservoirs etc.

Pakistan is well within its rights to argue before the international community that the construction of too many reservoirs and dams on the western rivers by India constitutes the misuse of the treaty's regulatory framework. Pakistan can raise this issue before any forum in the UN and take this issue to friends such as the US and the European Union. The IWT does not usurp or curtail the right of Pakistan to protest against the construction of too many dams by India.

So far, whenever Pakistan has tried to raise this issue outside the treaty, it has been advised to resort to the mechanism of the treaty. This puts Pakistan on the back foot because the mechanism does not offer the redressal that Pakistan seeks since the neutral expert has no legal competence to stop construction or direct the dismantling of the constructed work.

Whenever India starts construction on the western rivers, Pakistan, instead of protesting diplomatically, invokes the jurisdiction of the neutral expert. After months of neutral experts taking cognisance of the matter, no positive outcome is registered for Pakistan during which time the construction is completed. Pakistan in that sense has 'lost' cases before the neutral experts, whereas the fact is that neutral experts never had the legal competence to grant victory to Pakistan.

In other words, Pakistani officials have been invoking the wrong forum. There was no need to resort to the dispute resolution mechanism under the treaty since the decision being contested — the construction of a dam — was taken outside the treaty mechanism itself. Only when Pakistan has reservations on the technical aspects of a dam's construction should it invoke the IWT's dispute-resolution mechanisms.

Paper Twenty Two:

Water Row

Editorial, Dawn (Islamabad) 4 May, 2010

Unless New Delhi and Islamabad handle the issue with care and within the ambit of the Indus Waters Treaty, the water dispute between Pakistan and India could further sour bilateral ties and hamper peace talks that are likely to be revived. The dispute has already triggered anger among farmers on this side of the border, and provided some groups an opportunity to fuel anti-India emotions. Unfortunately, Indians are doing little to allay Islamabad's concerns regarding their plans to build several dams on the Indus, Jhelum and Chenab. These dams are believed to have the potential to choke off water flows of Pakistani rivers. This attitude has pushed Pakistan to seek international arbitration against the construction of the Kishanganga Hydropower Project in violation of the treaty. Officially, Islamabad has never accused India of stealing its water. Yet, it has time and again complained that India is not providing the information it is bound to supply under the treaty. Even the decision to seek international arbitration in this case has been taken after considerable delay to give the bilateral dispute-resolution mechanism a chance. The issue has been on the agenda of the Permanent Indus Commission for eight years.

Though India has the right to limited use of the rivers allotted to Pakistan for agricultural purposes and to build hydroelectric dams under the water pact, it is not allowed to obstruct the flow of rivers designated to Pakistan by storing or diverting water. India denies cutting off Pakistan's water share. But, in this particular case, Pakistan feels that Indians are trying to divert Jhelum water for storage in Wullar lake. If that happens, it will destroy agriculture in central Punjab and jeopardise Pakistan's food security. Additionally, the diversion of Jhelum water will reduce by 27 per cent the generation capacity of the underconstruction 969MW Neelum-Jhelum hydropower project near Muzaffarabad in Azad Kashmir. There is a sense of frustration in Pakistan and a perception that India is usurping Pakistan's waters. The Indian reluctance to share information about the planned water projects is not helping matters. What we need on the water issue is transparency.

Paper Twenty Three:

The Water Factor

Amitabh Mattoo, News International (Rawalpindi) 11 May, 2010

Water is likely to be the most divisive issue between India and Pakistan in the future. Or water could, with imagination and political will, become the basis for enduring bilateral cooperation. Addressing a gathering at a mosque in the Chowburji area of Lahore in April, Hafiz Muhammad Saeed, the head of the Jamaat-ut-Dawa (and founder of Lashkar-e-Taiba), claimed the next war between India and Pakistan could be fought over water if India did not stop "water terrorism" by building tunnels and dams to turn Pakistan into a desert. Saeed's hysterical claims aside, at almost every official engagement with New Delhi in recent months, Pakistan has raised the issue of water, most recently in Thimphu at the Saarc summit.

The irony is that despite the many wars that India and Pakistan have fought over a variety of issues, water is the one area where the two countries had found accommodation through the Indus Waters Treaty of 1960. The challenge for the two governments, therefore, is to now ensure that cooperation in this respect is not derailed. Rebuilding trust over the sharing of the Indus waters could even become the precursor for generating trust in other areas of conflict.In fact, the "water wars rationale" forecasts war between countries "dependent upon a shared water resource if there is water scarcity, competitive use and the countries are enemies due to a wider conflict." India and Pakistan were, by this logic, prime candidates to go to war. What, then, explains the successful negotiations that translated into the Indus Waters Treaty of 1960? As the academic Undala Z Alam, argues, India and Pakistan cooperated because it was "water-rational." "Cooperation was needed to safeguard the countries' long-term access to shared water," said Alam, who was given a unique access to the World Bank's archives.

What explains this new shrill campaign? Firstly, Pakistan is facing the most severe water crisis in its history. Secondly, in the new Pakistani discourse inspired by military thinking, India's hypothetical plans to construct dams, despite their being within the ambit of the treaty, could potentially create the capability to choke water flow to Pakistan. Here, intentions are not a factor, but just the capability that India may possess in the future. Thirdly, one episode over the filling of the Baglihar water reservoir by India and the alleged "delayed" release of water has been cited as an example of India's mala fide intentions. There are also Pakistani concerns about the Kishanganga project.In any case, none of these issues calls for hysteria, but constructive engagement and bilateral dialogue within the scope of the Permanent Commission or outside it.What is also clear is that while the Indus Waters Treaty is still a vital document, it may be important to think of ways of harnessing the waters of the Indus Basin jointly for a more optimal use of the resources, given new technology, better practices, greater scarcity, and lessons learnt from the past. These could be included though an additional protocol to the treaty.In fact, Article VII of the Treaty on "Future Cooperation" leaves open the possibility of newer avenues of cooperation without the need for the signatories to renegotiate or abandon the treaty. Water is a common, increasingly scarce resource which needs to be shared for mutual benefit.

We have given the world an example in the form of the Indus Waters Treaty. The time is ripe to build on this cooperation.

Paper Twenty Four:

Pak – India Moot On Kishenganga

Post (Lahore), 13 July, 2010,

India and Pakistan will discuss the issue of appointment of umpires for the Kishenganga hydel power project arbitration in Islamabad on Tuesday. Sources in the government said that India has sent a four-member team to Pakistan, comprising officials from the Water Resources Ministry and the Ministry of External Affairs.

The senior-most member of the team AK Bajaj, Chairman of the Central Water Commission. The others are India's Indus Commissioner G Ranganatha, his deputy Darpan Talwar and J N Singh, a Joint Secretary in the MEA.

Pakistan had invited India to discuss the issue of appointment of three neutral umpires. Earlier, India had invited Pakistan to hold consultations here on July 5 and 6 to decide on umpires bilaterally. But Pakistan suggested that the names of the umpires be exchanged between the missions of the two countries.

Last week, India once again invited Pakistan for consultations, saying it was ready to send its representatives to Islamabad to which the latter agreed. If the two countries fail to have a consensus on umpires, then this will be decided by a draw of lots by the World Bank, the United Nations and some other institutions.

The two countries, which have agreed on international arbitration, had been having a dispute over how to finalise the three neutral umpires who will supervise the legal battle between the two sides in a court of arbitration. The two countries have already nominated two legal experts (arbitrators) each to contest their case over the power project being built in Jammu and Kashmir.

Accusing India of breaching the provisions of the 1960 Indus Waters treaty by diverting the water of the Jhelum tributary for its Kishenganga hydel power project, Pakistan sought international arbitration in May this year after the two countries failed to resolve the issue bilaterally for over two decades.

Under the provisions of the treaty, the two countries will have to appoint three umpires, including a Chairman, before the court of arbitration is set up to decide on the issue.

Paper Twenty Five:

Pakistan And India Agree To Install Telemetry System

Dawn (Islamabad), 22 July, 2010

Pakistan and India agreed in principle on Thursday to put in place a telemetry system on the Indus to record and transfer real-time data for the benefit of both countries. The agreement was reached between Indus water commissioners of the two countries on the first day of their two-day meeting after the Indians "conceded to the utility" of the telemetry system in removing the confusion over water flow. However, the visiting delegates maintained that they had to take Indian states (provinces) on board because they controlled water flows and would be providing space for installation of the equipment. The funds needed for installation and running the system was also a matter that would be decided in consultation with the states.

At a media briefing with his Pakistani counterpart Syed Jamaat Ali Shah, Indian Commissioner Aranga Nathan confirmed that the agreement had been reached and promised to take up the matter with the governments of different Indian states where the system could be installed.

According to insiders, both sides also agreed to jointly inspect the flood embankment of River Ravi. India built a number of embankments on Ravi in the year 2001 and Pakistan has since been asking it for permission to inspect them. Instead of agreeing to inspection, India alleged that Pakistan had also built such structures and sought to inspect them.

The dates for joint inspection would be decided through correspondence.

The third issue that came under discussion was about pollution of rivers on both sides, especially in lower riparian Pakistan. The two commissioners agreed that as trustees of waters they must also start talks about the pollution. Pakistan raised the issue of India's Hadiyara drain that flows near Lahore and brings the industrial waste to Pakistan and pollutes Ravi. The issue of Baramulla waste polluting Jhelum river was also brought to the notice of the Indian side.

The Indian officials said that Pakistan's Kasur drain was causing the same damage on their side. The two sides agreed to look into each other's complaints and suggest remedial measures.

Pakistani officials told the visitors that India had not yet responded to technical concerns over different projects which India was building on Pakistani rivers. The Indian side said it would be sending its response to Pakistani objections on the Nimo Bazgo Dam "within days". Pakistan is of the view that Nimo Bazgo Dam and Chutak Power Plant on Indus River would block over 35,000 cusecs and badly hit the river hydrology.

The Indian side agreed to quicken the process.

Paper Twenty Six:

Pakistan-India Water Talks Conclude

Dawn (Islamabad), 23 July, 2010

The Indus Waters treaty (IWT) commissioners of India and Pakistan, Aranga Nathan and Syed Jamaat Ali Shah, held their second round of talks here on Friday, DawnNews reported.

In today's meeting, both sides agreed to jointly inspect the flood embankment of River Ravi.

The commissioners had a five-point agenda for the meeting and discussed a formula for water-sharing, sources said.

Both sides emphasised on continuing dialogue in order to resolve issues.

Speaking to media representatives after the second round of talks, Aranga Nathan said the dialogue took place in a congenial atmosphere.

Earlier, during Thursday's talks, Pakistan and India agreed in principle to put in place a telemetry system on the Indus to record and transfer real-time data for the benefit of both countries.

The agreement was reached on the first day of their two-day meeting after the Indians "conceded to the utility" of the telemetry system in removing the confusion over water flow.

Paper Twenty Seven:

Pakistan Initiates Process To Resolve Kishanganga Issue With India

Times of India (New Dehli), 9 October, 2010

Pakistan has instituted proceedings in the International Court of Arbitration to resolve the issue of the Kishanganga dam, which India is building on the Neelum river in Jammu and Kashmir, a federal minister has said.

Water and Power Minister Raja Pervez Ashraf made the remarks in the National Assembly or lower house of parliament on Friday.

He said the court is likely to take up the matter soon. India had addressed Pakistan's concerns on a parapet of the Nimmo Bazgo hydroelectric project on the Indus river but concerns relating to pondage, spillway and power intake are yet to be resolved, he said.

Issues involving the construction of the Uri-II hydroelectric plant by India on the Jhelum river and the Chutak hydroelectric plant on a tributary of the Indus too have been resolved by the Permanent Indus Waters Commission, Ashraf said. ...

Paper Twenty Eight:

Accord On Roadmap To Settle Pak-India Water Dispute

Dawn (Islamabad), 11 October, 2010

India and Pakistan agreed on Wednesday on a "roadmap for resolving water disputes" and decided to hold two additional meetings, besides a routine meeting due in May, over the next six months. On the last day of a five-day visit, a three-member Indian delegation yielded to a Pakistani demand that all "water disputes must be resolved within an agreed timeframe" because their lingering would create problems for both countries.

Pakistan's Indus Commissioner Syed Jamaat Ali Shah said the two sides had decided to hold one of the additional meetings by the end of March and the other by the end of June to expedite the pace of dispute resolution. "The decision is the biggest achievement made during five days of deliberations," he told Dawn. Pakistan expressed concern over dwindling water supplies in western rivers which were given to Pakistan as a replacement for eastern rivers. Pakistan is supposed to transfer western water to its eastern part.

Shah said the Indians were told that a reduction in supplies was jeopardising the water transfer operation which should be allowed to happen. Pakistan called for an effective flow of information as required under the Indus Basin Water Treaty and said that any obstruction in this regard would create problems for implementing the treaty. Shah said the Indian delegation had agreed that settlement of all water disputes must be time-bound because open-ended talks were counterproductive and bred confusion and frustration. The Indus treaty protects rights of both the upper (India) and lower riparian (Pakistan) states. The two countries needed to stick to their parts of implementation, Mr Shah said, adding that Pakistan had also asked India to take steps if deforestation and environmental impact affected river flows on its side. Talking to reporters at the Lahore airport before leaving for home, Auranga Nathan, India's Indus Commissioner, rejected a perception that the water issue could trigger a war between Pakistan and India.

"After all the two countries have signed an international treaty which includes elaborate dispute resolution mechanism. They not only committed to the treaty provisions but also regularly invoke different provisions to resolve disputes. Under such circumstances, there was hardly any chance of war between Pakistan and India on water issues," he said. Nathan termed his visit a success and reiterated that India was committed to the treaty and ready to resolve all disputes in accordance with the Indus Basin Water Treaty.

The current water reduction, he said, was result of weather variations rather than any activity on the Indian side of the border.

Paper Twenty Nine:

Pakistan: Nature Of Water Crisis A Potential Way Out

Barrister Mansur Sarwar Khan, 17 May, 2010

A. Nature of Water Crisis: Water crisis is a term that refers to the scarcity and quality of available water resources relative to human demand. However, the nature of crisis can change from one context to other. In the global context, according to Wikipedia, the following symptoms are reported for water crisis:

- *Inadequate access to drinking water for 1.1 billion people;*
- *Inadequate access to water for sanitation and wastewater disposal for 2.5 billion people;*
- *Groundwater excessive use leading diminished agricultural yields;*
- *Overuse and pollution of water resources harming biodiversity; and*
- *Regional conflict over scarce water resources sometimes resulting into warfare.*

Internationally, an indicator is devised to see if a certain country can be classified as a water stressed or water scarce country to determine the emerging seriousness of water crisis. This indicator is generally termed as the quantity of water available per year per person. If this per capita annual water availability in a country ranges between 1000-2000 m^3, this status is said to be water stressed and if this amount of water drops below 1000 m^3, the locality in focus is considered to be facing the water scarcity situation.

As far as water availability per capita per year is concerned, sources like Amin Dadbhoy reports huge water distribution distortions in global the context. For example, on the one hand, there are those where water scarcity is too acute like Kuwait, Ghaza and the UAE where the annual per capita water availability is around 10 m^3, 52 m^3 and 58 m^3, respectively. Opposite to such water poor countries, there are some water rich countries, where the annual per capita water availability is very high, for example: French Guiana (812,121 m^3), Iceland (609, 319 m^3), Guyana (316,689 m^3), Surinam (292, 566 m^3), Congo (275,679, m^3), Canada (94,353 m^3) and New Zealand (86,554 m^3).

The reported uneven water availability results because of the nature of the regions. With the ongoing climatic changes, it is predicted that humid regions will receive even more rain and arid and semi arid zones may get lesser and erratic rains in the future. According to an estimate, the climatic change may cause another 20 % water scarcity in drought-prone areas. Because of the population growth and climatic changes, water crisis in many non-humid regions will aggravate.In the case of Pakistan, the water crisis is a much more complex and multi-facet phenomenon. For example, the per capita water availability that was 5, 300 m^3 in 1951 is expected to drop to 850 m^3 in 2013. This is mainly because of the population growth from 34 million in 1951 to 207 million projected in 2013. If Pakistan's population increase in 62 years is six times, the corresponding decrease in the per capita water availability is a natural outcome.This reported water scarcity becomes an even more serious concern when we look at the degree of control of water sources and the percentage of water used in the Pakistani context. As presented in Figure 1, the percentage of water originating outside of Pakistan's territory is 75% or more. When viewing this status in a very hostile environment, this complication becomes even more complex. Added to this very low degree of control, this water crisis takes another boost when we look at the water exploitation index. As shown in Figure 2, Pakistan's use of water as a percentage of the total renewable water resources, it is around 75 % plus. This high water exploitation index puts Pakistan in the category of severe water stressed situation.

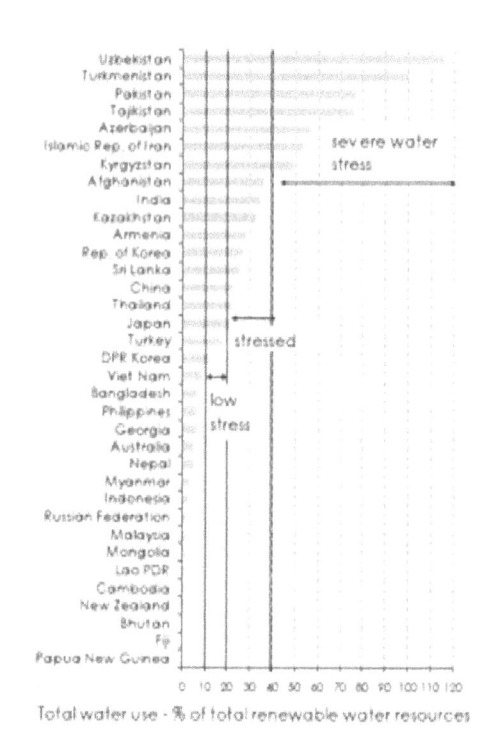

Figure 2: Water stress status in Asia-Pacific

In addition to the above referred indicator of water availability per capita per year, those countries where the overwhelmingly water consuming subsector is agriculture, there is a need to consider the annual irrigation water required or needed versus that is available. In the context of the South Asian sub-continent, the agriculture sector consumes 99%, 97%, 92% and 86% of the total water available in Nepal, Pakistan, India and Bangladesh, respectively. Perhaps, the per capita water available may have to be complemented with additional indicators to identify the real nature of the prevailing water crisis in this region.

For Pakistan, therefore, it is important that we also look at the availability of water for irrigation. We had 9.2 million hectares irrigated land in 1950-53 which has gone up to 18.02 million hectares in 2000 -03; an increase of almost 100 % over a period of 50 years. As shown in Table 2, there has been an increase in water diversions to canals at different stages but not in the same proportion as the horizontal expansion in the irrigated land.

Table 2. Historical Canal Water Diversions in the Indus Basin of Pakistan

Key Influences	Period	Canal Diversions MAF / (billion m³)		
		Kharif	Rabi	Annual
Pre – Partition	1940-1947	47.6/ (58.5)	20.2/ (24.9)	67.8/ (83.4)
Partition	1947-1948	46.3/ (57.0)	22.4/ (27.6)	68.8/ (84.6)
Dispute	1948-1960	51.5/ (63.4)	24.7/ (30.4)	76.3/ (93.8)
Pre – Mangla	1960-1967	60.3/ (74.2)	27.6/ (34.0)	88.0 / (108.2)
Post – Mangla	1967-1975	65.3/ (80.3)	30.2 (37.1)	95.5 (117.4)
Post – Tarbela	1975-1980	68.1/ (83.7)	38.2/ (47.0)	106.3 / (130.7)
Post – Tarbela	1980-1985	68.4/ (84.1)	37.3/ (45.9)	105.7 (130.0)
Post – Tarbela	1985-1990	66.3/ (81.6)	37.7/ (46.4)	104.1/ (128.0)
Post – Tarbela	1990-1995	66.3/ (81.5)	38.5/ (47.3)	104.7/ (128.8)
Post – Tarbela	1975-1995	67.2 (82.7)	38.0 (46.7)	105.2/ (129.4)

Data Source: Water Resources Management Directorate, WAPDA.

Based on meteorological data from 18 stations country-wide, the annual potential evapo-transpiration varies from 1.20 m in Muree to 2.0 m in Jackababad. Similar estimates of irrigation requirements are made for each province of Pakistan. When we compare these annual irrigation requirements, based on areas irrigated, we observe, as shown in Table 3, another dimension of the water crisis. Since water use in the agriculture sector in Pakistan is around 97%, the nature of water crisis becomes very critical for food security and the livelihood of the people. If one province is the dominant source of agricultural production, the overall water deficit per unit area irrigated is going to keep the productivity down and consequently the food security at risk.

Table 3. Comparison of Surface water allocations and Water

Requirements among four Provinces of Pakistan				
Description	Punjab	Sindh	NWFP	Baluchistan
Annual Irrigation Requirements (m)	1.26	1.34	1.16	1.19
Annual Water Allocation as per 1991 Accord in BCM (MAF)	68.81 (55.94)	59.98 (48.76)	10.80 (8.78)	4.76 (3.87)
Canal Irrigated Areas (million hectares) in 2000-03	11.04	1.96	0.77	0.55
Annual water available per unit area irrigated (m)	0.62	3.06	1.40	0.87
Deficit (-) or Surplus (+) in m/ha	−0.64	+ 1.72	+ 0.24	−0.32

Punjab has a canal irrigated area about 11.04 million hectares which constitute 77 % of the entire country. Almost same ratio holds for the cropped areas that are irrigated exclusively either by tube-wells or wells. Shortage of more than half of the irrigation water required has caused deficit irrigation causing productivity concerns. Now, this crisis is not brought either by nature nor by India; it is home-made and we have no option except to find ways and means to face it off.

Because of sever water shortages as presented above, tube-well irrigation got an exponential growth over a period of 50 years. Recent data suggest that over 1.2 million tube-wells are installed in the country and more than one million of these tube-wells are pumping about 35 MAF of groundwater only in Punjab to irrigate 7.17 million hectares conjunctively with canals and 2.74 million hectares exclusively by the tube-wells. Without getting into arguments and counter-arguments, this is a clear and solid ground reality that there is a huge water crisis in the food granary of Pakistan. It is interesting to note that 71.1% irrigated area of Punjab receives either exclusive tube-well water or conjunctively surface and ground water are being used. In contrast to Punjab, the share of tube-well irrigation in other provinces is almost insignificant.

On the one hand, the dependence on groundwater in Punjab is a blessing as the quantity being used is almost three times that of the surface water storage that Pakistan has built. Moreover, this explosion of pumping technology helped to control the twin menace of water-logging and salinity in this region. Imagine the possible severity of water crisis in a scenario where there would have been no use of the groundwater at all. It would have definitely a flabbergasting and horrifying outcome.

On the other hand, this practice of delaying its fatal impact has put the entire sustainability of the irrigation of Punjab at risk. In the insane absence of ian nstitutional support system for groundwater management and due to the shortage of canal water, the farmers of Punjab are forced to use groundwater where almost two-third tube-wells are pumping sodic water for irrigation. As farmers are left on their own to decide about the installation of tube-wells for groundwater extraction, they can only avoid pumping brackish water that gives tastes of excessive salinity but sodic/alkaline waters are, usually, assumed to be alright. This is why that more than two-third tube-wells are adding a slow poison to the irrigated lands and this is becoming a significant factor for low yields in this region. This is another aspect of the seriousness of the emerging colossal water crisis.

At present, on the one hand, our entire focus is confined to either blaming India for stealing water or debating on building the Kala-Bagh Dam. Sure, there is a lot of truth in it, but should we opt for a destructive way of war where there will be no-winners, or look at the options that are still available to overcome such crisis? Obviously, war is NOT an option, period.

CHAPTER – 16

South Asia's Water: Unquenchable Thirst

The Economist (London): 19 November, 2011

A growing rivalry between India, Pakistan and China over the region's great rivers may be threatening South Asia's peace

SONAULLAH PHAPHO has spent half a century picking a living from Wular lake high in Indian-controlled Kashmir. Today he is lucky if he scoops a fish or two out of the soupy mess. Push a boat into the knee-deep lake and the mud raises a stink of sewage. A century ago Wular and its surrounding marshes covered more than 217 square kilometres (84 square miles), making it one of Asia's larger freshwater lakes. Now, thanks to silt and encroachment, the extraction of water by nearby towns and tree planting on the shore, it measures only 87 sq km and is shrinking.

Compared with much of South Asia, Kashmir, a disputed territory in northern India, has many rivers and relatively few people. But even here fresh water is running short. To see how contentious this can be, drive half a day south to where the Baglihar dam (shown above) is rising up. An enormous wall bisects the valley, dressing it in white spray, and three huge jets of water blast from its sluices.

Half complete, the dam is already a local wonder that tourists gape at. It generates 450MW for the starved energy grid of Jammu and Kashmir. Once the scheme fully tames the water, by steering it through a tunnel blasted into the mountain, the grid will gain another 450MW.

The river swirls away, white-crested and silt-laden, racing to the nearby border with Pakistan. But there, Baglihar is a source of bitterness. Pakistanis cite it as typical of an intensifying Indian threat to their existence, a conspiracy to divert, withhold or misuse precious water that is rightfully theirs. Officials in Islamabad and diplomats abroad are primed to grumble about it. Pakistan's most powerful man, the head of the armed forces, General Ashfaq Kayani, cites water to justify his "India-centric" military stance.

Others take it further. "Water is the latest battle cry for *jihadis*," says B.G. Verghese, an Indian writer. "They shout that water must flow, or blood must flow." Lashkar-e-Taiba, a Pakistani terror group, likes to threaten to blow up India's dams. Last year, a Pakistani extremist, Abdur Rehman Makki, told a rally that if India were to "block Pakistan's waters, we will let loose a river of blood."

Assorted hardliners cheer them on. A blood-curdling editorial in *Nawa-i-Waqt*, a Pakistani newspaper, warned in April that "Pakistan should convey to India that a war is possible on the issue of water and this time, war will be a nuclear one."

Upstream, such outbursts are usually dismissed as proof that troubled Pakistan is, as ever, spoiling for a fight. Water is merely the latest excuse. India is not misbehaving, says Mr Verghese placidly. It fails to take all it is entitled to from cross-border rivers in Kashmir. Run-of-the-river dams like Baglihar consume nothing, since water must flow to run turbines. Such a dam, he says, merely briefly delays a river.

Indians point out, too, that Pakistan enjoys a rare guarantee: the Indus Waters Treaty, struck in 1960 by far-sighted engineers and diplomats who saw that after the partition of land, water had to be shared out too.

The treaty, which has survived three wars, details exactly how each side must use cross-border rivers. Mostly this applies to the tributaries that flow from Kashmir to form the massive Indus river, Pakistan's lifeblood.

If Indians abide by the treaty, then in theory, at least, they cannot be misbehaving. They see Baglihar as a proof of co-operation, not a threat. When Pakistan objected to the dam's design, India accepted international arbitration, the first case in the treaty's history. Outside experts studied the dam and ordered small changes. But, in effect, they said, it posed no threat to Pakistan. And last year, the dispute was officially ended by the two governments.

Downstream, however, few sound satisfied. "The Baglihar decision...allowed a reservoir on a river coming into Pakistan, and now a precedent is set," laments John Briscoe, a water expert, formerly of the World Bank, who advises Pakistan. The Pakistanis fear Indian control over the headwaters of the Indus. And Indian bureaucrats fuel these fears with obsessive secrecy about all water data.

Bashir Ahmad, a geologist in Srinagar, Kashmir who studied the Baglihar dam, gives a grim warning about the Indians' future intentions: "They will switch the Indus off to make Pakistan solely dependent on India. It's going to be a water bomb." A less excitable report in February by America's Senate offered a similar assessment: "The cumulative effect of [many dam] projects could give India the ability to store enough water to limit the supply to Pakistan at crucial moments in the growing season." Dams are a source of "significant bilateral tension", the report concludes.

More dams are to come, as India's need to power its economy means it is quietly spending billions on hydropower in Kashmir. The Senate report totted up 33 hydro projects in the border area. The state's chief minister, Omar Abdullah, says dams will add an extra 3,000MW to the grid in the next eight years alone. Some analysts in Srinagar talk of over 60 dam projects, large and small, now on the books.

Any of these could spark a new confrontation. The latest row is over the Kishanganga river (called the Neelum in Pakistan) as each country races to build a hydropower dam either side of Kashmir's line of control. India's dam will divert some of the river down a 22km (14-mile) mountain tunnel to turbines. To Pakistani fury, that will lessen the water flow to the downstream dam, so its capacity will fall short of the planned 960MW.

Pakistan also claims (though the evidence is shaky) that 600,000 people will suffer by getting less water for irrigation. Again, it insisted on international arbitration at The Hague. In September, to Pakistani delight, India was ordered to suspend some of its building for further assessments to be made. But India still looks likelier to come away happy in the end, as the treaty foresaw and permitted the Indian design, and India is likely to finish its dam ahead of Pakistan in any case, by 2016 rather than 2018.

When China's upstream

Countries downstream have genuine reasons to fret. Pakistan is exposed. Like Egypt, it exists around a single great river, though the Indus is nearly twice the Nile's size when it reaches the sea. It waters over 80% of Pakistan's 22m hectares (54m acres) of irrigated land, using canals built by the British. In turn that farming provides 21% of the country's GDP, as well as livelihoods for a big proportion of its 180m people. Many of them are already thirsty.

On average, each Indian gets just 1,730 cubic metres of fresh water a year, less than a quarter of the global average of 8,209 cubic metres. Yet, that looks bountiful compared with each Pakistani's share: a mere 1,000 cubic metres. Worse yet, South Asia's fresh water mostly falls in a few monsoon months. The dreadful floods this year and last showed that untamed and unpredictable rivers can be both resource and threat.

More rows between India and Pakistan are certain. India may keep on dismissing them as Pakistani bluster, an easy thing to do if you are upstream. But India is downstream in another highly tricky area: its border with China.

Tension already exists over the status of India's Arunachal Pradesh state, which China refuses to recognise. A quarrel over rivers in the region could serve as a focus for wider disputes about territory. A measure of the recent slump in relations came when, to the fury of India's authorities, China blocked an attempt by the Asian Development Bank to prepare for a dam project in Arunachal Pradesh. And one of India's largest rivers, the Brahmaputra (Tsangpo in China), flows south from the Tibetan plateau and into Assam not far from the disputed land.

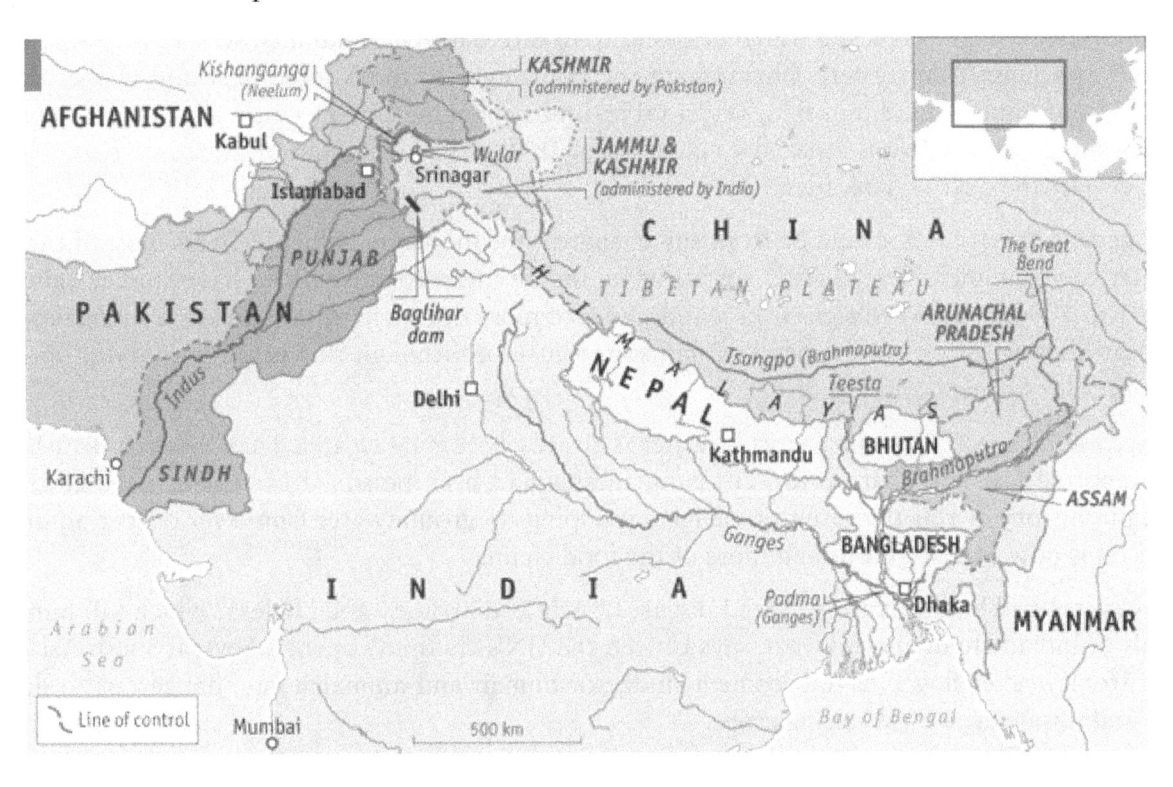

Angry Indian politicians, activists, bloggers and journalists claim that water-starved China (with 8% of the world's fresh water but 20% of its population) has plans to divert the Tsangpo/Brahmaputra to farmers in its central and eastern regions. Feelings are running so high that India's prime minister, Manmohan Singh, felt obliged to issue a statement on August 4th saying that China's leaders had assured him there were no such plans afoot. And though a few run-of-the-river hydroelectric schemes are being built upstream on the Tsangpo, none of these could change the river's course. Cool heads point out that speculation about China channelling the torrent from near the border, at a spot known as the Great Bend, looks fantastical, at least at present.

Chinese engineers would need to use nuclear explosions to have a chance of making tunnels through a series of ridged mountains to get water east from the Great Bend. Although plans have existed since the fourth century to take water from China's west to the east, and the scheme was pushed by Mao Zedong, the engineering, at least for now, appears to be technically impossible. Yet broader Indian strategic fears—the fact that the Chinese control the Tibetan plateau, which is the source of water for parts of the densely populated northern India—will evaporate no more easily than Pakistani fears of India.

An ever-thirstier region

The scarcity of water in South Asia will become harder to manage as demand rises. South Asia's population of 1.5 billion is growing by 1.7% a year, says the World Bank, which means an extra 25m or so mouths to water and feed: imagine dropping North Korea's entire population on the region each year. Greater wealth in South Asia brings with it a soaring demand for food, especially for water-intensive meat and other protein. Industry and energy-producers also use water, though, unlike farms, they return it, eventually, to the rivers.

Worse, overall supply will not only fail to keep up with the rising demand but is likely to fall (unless a cheap way is found to turn the sea water fresh). The Himalayan glaciers are melting. A Dutch study last year of the western Himalayas reckoned that shrunken glaciers will cut the flow of the Indus by some 8% by mid-century. Flows may also get less regular, especially if glacial dams form, withholding water, and then collapse, causing floods.

Others give even scarier predictions. Sundeep Waslekar, who heads a Mumbai think-tank, the Strategic Foresight Group, which has picked water as a long-term threat to Asian stability, sees a "mega-arc of hydro insecurity" emerging from western China along the Himalayas to the Middle East and farther west. The strain of bigger populations, diminishing water tables and a changing climate could all conspire to produce a storm of troubles. South Asia is especially vulnerable: Mr Waslekar sees a cut of 20% in the total available fresh water over the next two decades.

The greatest threat of all would be from any change to the monsoon, which delivers most of the region's fresh water each summer. Here, again, worries arise. Indian meteorologists, who have studied rainfall data from 1901 to 2004, have noted signs in recent decades of more dry spells within the peak monsoon months. If these lead to weaker, or less predictable, monsoons in future (though this year's was about normal) the consequences for farmers could be dire.

In any case, the cost of running short of water is already becoming clearer. The *Lancet*, a British medical journal, reported last year that up to 77m Bangladeshis had been poisoned by arsenic—the largest mass-poisoning in history. It was the result of villagers pumping up groundwater from ever deeper aquifers. The same poison is now entering crops and more of the food chain.

Filthy water and bad sanitation spread diseases, such as diarrhoea and cholera, which kill hundreds of thousands of Indian children every year, says Unicef, the UN's children's agency. Several South Asian rivers, suffering from weaker flows, have become a sludge of human and animal waste, dangerous to drink and wash in, and unsafe even for watering crops.

All over the region water tables are dropping, as bore holes drive deeper. In the dry season, even some of the larger rivers slow to a trickle. Knut Oberhagemann, a water expert in Dhaka, Bangladesh, says that the flow of the mighty Ganges, where it enters Bangladesh, is, at times, a pitiful few hundred cubic metres a second, so low that "you can walk across the river". When the same river, at this point called the Padma, reaches the coast, it is often so feeble that the sea intrudes, poisoning the land with salt.

The same problem curses the delta of the Indus in Pakistan. There, a semi-desert was turned into some of the most fertile land on earth by the British-built irrigation canals. But, as the sea encroaches on the low, flat land, the rivers, at times, are flowing backwards, laments a local environmental activist. Take away the fresh water—around 60% of which is now lost to seepage and evaporation because of the bad management of those canals—and the desert will eventually come back.

Save or snatch

The Governments in South Asia can respond to growing scarcity in one of two ways. The first is to improve the way they use the water they have, both by managing it better and by co-operating with one another. The second is to try to grab as much water as they can from their neighbours.

Better management of irrigation canals and better farming techniques would help hugely to cut waste. In Pakistan, bitter rows between provinces have long scotched coherent planning. Wealthy Punjab, a big farming province, is routinely accused by downstream Sindh (and by others too) of taking an unfair share of the water.

And Pakistan badly needs more dams to control floods, store monsoon water and make electricity (China is said to have offered to help Pakistan build a series of big dams, and has already sent engineers to help speed along the new one on the Neelum/Kishanganga). Only about 10% of the potential hydropower of the Indus has been tapped so far, and only 30 days' average river flow can be stored (by contrast, the Colorado in America has dams to store 1,000 days worth).

Many governments are at least thinking in terms of dams and co-operation. Mr Waslekar reckons that 60-80 big dams (mostly for energy) will be built in South Asia in the next two or three decades, at a cost of hundreds of billions of dollars. In many cases—as for example in mountainous Bhutan, where the economy gets a huge boost from selling hydropower to India—this can foster economic and diplomatic co-operation. India has visions of one day persuading the unstable but the immensely water-rich Nepal to follow suit. The country is the source of more than 40% of the Ganges water, and Indian analysts talk dreamily of 40GW of hydropower potential waiting to be used.

Other cross-border water deals are pending. Cosy ties with Bangladesh's government mean that India can more easily build dams on some of the several dozen rivers that cross their shared frontier. In September, Mr Singh visited Dhaka to sign a deal with Bangladesh to allow the latest hydro dam to go up on the Teesta river. Though the deal was postponed at the last minute by a row with a regional Indian leader, it now looks set to go ahead. However, there are bitter memories in Bangladesh of an earlier deal, on the Ganges, which allowed India to put up a barrage to block the river's flow in the dry season.

Tentative signs of wider co-operation exist. China issues twice-daily reports on the Tsangpo river flow in the flood season, separately to India and to Bangladesh. This could be seen as encouraging, if the two giants of the region wished to consider getting together over water. Indeed, if full-scale friendliness were ever sought, an immense opportunity awaits.

Mr Verghese points out that the Tsangpo/Brahmaputra falls 2,450 metres (8,000 feet) over a few kilometres in China just before it reaches the Indian border. Send it through a 100km tunnel from the Tibetan plateau down to Assam and an enormous 54,000MW could be generated. One day, its power could lightup not only much of north-east India and Bangladesh, but nearby Myanmar and beyond. Such a megastructure would become a keystone for regional co-operation.

It will almost certainly never be built. Analysts have suggested that, given the generally dire relations between South Asian countries, water will provoke clashes rather than co-operation. A 2009 report of the CIA concluded that "the likelihood of conflict between India and Pakistan over shared river resources is expected to increase", though, it added that elsewhere in the region, "the risk of armed interstate conflict is minor". And a Bangladeshi security expert, Major-General Muniruzzaman, predicts that India's "coercive diplomacy", its refusal to negotiate multilaterally on such issues as river-sharing, means that "if ever there were a localised conflict in South Asia, it will be over water."

CHAPTER – 17

Water Politics In South Asia: Technocratic Cooperation And Lasting Security In The Indus Basin And Beyond

Saleem H. Ali

> Water, like religion and ideology, has the power to move millions of people. Since the very birth of human civilization, people have moved to settle close to it. People move when there is too little of it; People move when there is too much of it. People journey down it. People write, sing and dance about it. People fight over it. All people, everywhere and every day, need it.
>
> —Mikhail Gorbachev[1]

The distribution of environmental resources as a potential contributor to conflict has been the subject of considerable research, and these linkages have dominated the post-Cold War interest in environmental security.[2] Within this genre, much attention has been given to water resources, owing to their vital importance for human survival. The distribution of environmental resources may contribute to conflict, but recent scholarship has begun to focus on the potential of environmental threats in stimulating conflict resolution.[3] Uniting around a common aversion to environmental threats, as well as confidence-building through environmental cooperation, potentially hold a great appeal for policy-makers who aim to engage in proactive problem-solving rather than in precise problem identification. What is most significant for government decision-makers to consider is that even if a conflict is not environmental in nature, the remedy may well be achieved through environmental means. Environmental cooperation may offer pathways to confidence-building or peace-building, whether or not the conflict has environmental roots.

This essay explores the potentiality of such instrumental cooperation in the case of South Asia where regional conflict between two nuclear neighbors, India and Pakistan, is predicated in a history of religious rivalries and post-colonial demarcation. Despite inveterate antagonism, the two countries have managed to cooperate over water resources of the Indus River. How was this riparian cooperation, enabled? And can it be reconfigured to provide for lasting peace in the region?

Anatomy of the Indus Waters Treaty

The Indian subcontinent quite literally owes its name to the waters of one river—the Indus. Regional politics are closely tied to the river's history and how different societies have used its waters for livelihood and for consolidating power. Hindu nationalists frequently recount that the very essence of their faith, dating back to the writings of the Rigveda in the second millennium B.C.E., is linked to the flow of the Indus. The name itself is a Latinized version of *Sindhu,* which means river in ancient Sanskrit, and from which the word "Hindu" and its concomitant ethno-religious identity emerged.[4] The partition of the subcontinent by the British in 1947 gave all but the very upper head-waters of the Indus to the newly formed Muslim majority

---

[1] *Journal of International Affairs,* Spring/Summer 2008, vol. 61, no. 2.
167 © The Trustees of Columbia University in the City of New York

country of Pakistan. More significantly, the major tributaries of the Indus that provided irrigation water for the fertile and densely populated region of Punjab on both sides of the border were divided. This was a classic conflict situation between upstream and downstream riparians, exacerbated by a lack of trust and intense territorial animosity between the two sides. This led to a series of disputes related to the Indus and its tributaries. Both countries tried to settle the matter bilaterally several times after partition but no lasting agreement was reached until the World Bank got involved as a mediating entity.

The resulting agreement, known as the Indus Waters Treaty, took nine years to negotiate and was signed in 1960. It is a particularly remarkable treaty since both sides have otherwise had tremendous hostility for one another and have defied efforts at cooperation. It is, therefore, instructive to consider the development and history of the treaty in greater detail as a potential model for regional environmental cooperation. The treaty is often cited as a success story of international riparian engagement, as it has withstood major wars between the two signatories (in 1965 and 1971), several skirmishes over water distribution and derivative territorial concerns.[5] The agreement is also heralded as a triumph for the World Bank, which played an instrumental role in its negotiation during the height of the Cold War. The World Bank's role in this region was particularly unusual because India was a vanguard of the Non aligned. Movement and wanted to disavow any pressure from international institutions or Western nations.

The initiator and technical adviser of the agreement was David Lilienthal, the former head of the United States' Tennessee Valley Authority, who suggested that an engineering perspective could contribute to resolving this political stalemate.[6] After a visit to India and Pakistan in 1951, he advised the two countries to divide the Indus Basin geographically. India would have unrestricted use of the three eastern rivers (the Ravi, Sutlej and Bias), while Pakistan would completely control the three western rivers (the Jhelum, Chenab and Indus). The World Bank played a significant role by providing mediation, support staff, funding and proposals for pushing negotiations forward. Under the leadership of President David Black, the World Bank was able to persuade the international community to contribute nearly $900 million for impoundment construction.[7]

Nine years after Lilienthal's initial visit, both countries were finally convinced to sign the agreement. The Indus Waters Treaty obligated Pakistan to build a canal system, which, by utilizing previously less-developed rivers, decreased Pakistan's dependence on the Indus tributaries the treaty gave to India. The treaty also charged India and Pakistan with exchanging information and establishing joint monitoring mechanisms of river flow to ensure enforcement. The key provisions of the agreement are as follows:

♦ An agreement that Pakistan would receive unrestricted use of the western rivers, which India would allow to flow unimpeded, with minor exceptions;

♦ Provisions for three dams, eight link canals, three barrages and 2,500 tubewells to be built in Pakistan;

♦ A ten-year transition period, from 1st April 1960 to 31st March 1970, during which time water would continue to be supplied to Pakistan according to a detailed schedule;

♦ A schedule for India to provide its fixed financial contribution of $62 million in ten annual installments during the transition period; and,

♦ Additional provisions for data exchange and future cooperation.[8]

As is often the case with riparian agreements, the treaty also established the Permanent Indus Commission, made up of one commissioner of Indus Waters from each country. In the technocratic spirit of the agreement, these representatives are often engineers rather than politicians. The two commissioners meet annually in order to:

♦ Establish and promote cooperative arrangements for implementation of the treaty;

♦ Promote cooperation between India and Pakistan in the development of the waters of the Indus system;

- Examine and resolve by agreement any question that may arise between the two countries concerning interpretation or implementation of the treaty, and,

- Submit an annual report to the two governments.

Both countries have upheld the Indus Basin Commission's information-sharing responsibilities; data on new projects, the water level in rivers and the water discharge of rivers are routinely conveyed to the other parties. If conflicts rise to the level of a dispute, the Indus River Commission will agree to mediation or arbitration, and the World Bank will appoint a neutral expert who is acceptable to both countries to resolve the dispute. Remarkably, although India and Pakistan constructed and carried out this agreement amidst skirmishes, threats and a full-scale war, and even during armed conflict, neither country sabotaged the other's water projects. One of the water negotiators for Pakistan has commented that the role of international institutions is vital in making this enterprise function:

> Both the parties are under the obligation of the Indus Waters Treaty which asked the signatories not to disrupt the functioning of the commission. Any hurdle in the working of the commission is challengeable under the treaty the guarantor of which is the World Bank.[9]

No projects allowed under the treaty's provision of "future cooperation" have been submitted since 1960, nor have any water quality issues.[10] There have, however, been several other disputes that have arisen over the years. The first issues arose from the Indian non-delivery of some waters during 1965 to 1966 that became questions of procedure and of the legality of commission decisions. Negotiators resolved that each commissioner acted as a government representative and had the authority to make legally binding decisions.[11] Another dispute involving the design and construction of the Salal Dam on the Chenab River in Jammu, India was resolved by way of bilateral negotiations.[12]

As noted in a recent World Bank study of Pakistan's water policy, India and Pakistan advocate conflicting principles of management: "equitable utilization" and "no appreciable harm," respectively.[13] Both sides continue to foster misgivings about the treaty but accept it as the best option in a time of conflict. From the Indian perspective, the 75 percent allocation of water to Pakistan represented a fundamental violation of equitable utilization.[14] From the Pakistani perspective, the allocation of only 75 percent of the water when it possessed 90 percent of the irrigated land was a violation of the principle of no appreciable harm.[15] As a mark of how leadership can achieve reconciliation despite high tensions, former Pakistani President Ayub Khan is quoted in the aforementioned study as saying,

> we have been able to get the best that was possible...very often the best is the enemy of the good and in this case we have accepted the good after careful and realistic appreciation of our entire overall situation....The basis of this agreement is realism and pragmatism.[16]

As part of a study of the Tarbela and Mangla dams (the two Pakistani impoundments constructed as a result of the treaty), the World Commission on Dams concluded that:

> The Indus Waters Treaty represents the only ongoing agreement between India and Pakistan that has not been disrupted by wars or periods of high tension. Cooperation that builds on this treaty could not only present opportunities for better water management between those two countries, but also serve as a model for water-sharing arrangements between India, Bangladesh and Nepal.[17]

Beyond Technical Cooperation:
Prospects for Instrumental Peace

Although the Indus Waters Treaty has been able to overcome some minor issues (such as the Salal Dam dispute, which was resolved in 1978 through a new treaty), it has not been able to facilitate the resolution of larger conflicts, like Kashmir. The prospects for using the agreement over riparian issues as a means of conflict resolution more broadly can be traced back to a statement by U.S. Assistant Secretary of State George McGhee, who pointed out in 1951 that,

> a settlement of the canal waters question would signify those basic reversals of policy by the Governments of both India and Pakistan without which there can be no political rapprochement. Thus, the canal waters question is not only a functional problem, but also a political one linked to the Kashmir dispute,[18]

As reported in the World Bank archives on this case, the British Prime Minister Anthony Eden felt that if this linkage were not possible, the resolution of the waters dispute could at least reduce tension over Kashmir.

Interestingly enough, at one time it was argued by Pakistani politicians that the urgency of territorial claims on Kashmir for Pakistan also had a hydrological component. In 1957, the Pakistani prime minister, Hussain Suhrwardy, stated publicly that, "There are, as you know, six rivers (in the Indus Basin). Most of them rise in Kashmir. One of the reasons why, therefore, that Kashmir is so important for us is this water, these waters which irrigate our lands."[19] However, since then, the Pakistani government has de-linked the Kashmir dispute from the reconciliation over water allocation. Commenting on this research, on the potential of using the treaty as a conduit for resolving the Kashmir conflict, the Pakistani government's senior spokesmen on foreign policy, Mohammed Sadiq, stated the following:

> The Indus Waters Treaty has been an important document for the water issue between the two countries. It has also helped in a framework for the resolution of water disputes in the region. Pakistan is fully committed to the treaty in letter and spirit. As far as the Kashmir dispute, this is not a water issue. It relates to the inalienable rights of Kashmiri people to self-determination.[20]

As early as 1951, the Indian government had argued adamantly that: "The Canal Waters dispute between India and Pakistan has nothing to do with the Kashmir issue; it started with and is confined to the irrigation systems of East and West Punjab."[21]

Yet this decision to de-link the two has been made consciously by politicians, despite the ecological reality that Kashmir does indeed lay strategically within the headwaters of the river systems. In fact the Indus flows right through the valley corridor that connects Indian and Pakistani-held Kashmir. One can thus consider the cooperative role of water in this case at two levels. First, as suggested in the aforementioned statement by George McGhee, the resolution of the water dispute was a necessary but perhaps not a sufficient condition for conflict resolution over Kashmir. Second, since that condition for water cooperation has been met, the communication and opportunities for trust-building provided by the treaty continue to act as a potential means of further cooperation at the level of political psychology. Therefore, the Indus Waters Treaty has become the strongest link of cooperation between the two sides and, in times of crisis, it is often referenced as the ultimate cord of engagement that might be cut.

The latter proposition was put to the test in December 2001 following the Kashmiri militants' attack on the Indian Parliament two months prior, when India threatened to unilaterally abrogate the Indus Waters Treaty. However, six months later, the Permanent Indus Commission, which was established as a part of the treaty, still met for the thirty-seventh time in New Delhi and the agreement weathered the storm yet again.

On a technical level, the Indus Waters Treaty was tested again when both India and Pakistan considered new dam projects to meet rising energy demands. India is undertaking the Baglihar Hydropower Project (BHP) on the Chenab River in India, 160 kilometers north of Jammu, under severe opposition from Pakistan.[22] Apart from objecting to the project design of the BHP, Pakistan has expressed opposition to the Tulbul navigation project, the Sawalkote Hydroelectric Project and the Kishanganga Hydroelectric Project, all located in Jammu and Kashmir.[23] The Baglihar dispute was taken to the World Bank, which appointed a neutral technical expert, Swiss engineer Raymond Lafitte, in August 2005 to make a binding decision on the case. Lafitte gave his ruling on the dispute in early 2007 and the matter was amicably settled, with both sides claiming victory.

Table 1. Policy lessons from the Indus Basin case

Key policy issue	Effects thus far	Future prospects
Acceptability of technical solutions	Very effective in providing civil engineering solutions to dam sites and scale issues	Joint hydrological studies between Indian and Pakistani scientists to promote trust
Robustness of agreement, absence of trust	Withstood conflicts through regular mandated meetings and Indus Basin Commission constituted by technical experts and managers	Agreement likely to be a model for other bilateral agreements on fisheries trade, and oil and gas pipelines
Role of external agent. (World Bank)	Continuing support of the dispute resolution system and water resource assistance strategies	Make such agreements part of regional development strategy for South Asia
Peace dividends for existing conflicts	Relatively few visible impacts on peace building; Agreement relegated to mid-level technical exchange and management	Since river headwaters are in Kashmir, the agreement could be used as a conduit for the Kashmir dispute resolution process

So far, the Indus Waters Treaty has served its purpose in de-escalating tensions over riparian water and has provided a direct avenue for regular, if technical, dialogue between the countries. It has not led to greater peacebuilding between the two countries as some of the original motivators of the treaty may have hoped. However, these most recent dam projects in Kashmir raise some potential prospects for using the agreement more instrumentaliy in resolving the Kashmir dispute. Increasingly, Kashmiri politicians are arguing that since the status of the territory is uncertain and so many of the disputes are in Kashmiri territory, they should be a part of the Indus Basin negotiations as well.[24] Whether such integrative solution to the conflict would be found through cooperation on water remains to be seen, and is largely a question of leadership. Even when all the ingredients of rational state behavior are in place, the ultimate action is dependent on individual leaders. Table I summarizes some of the key lessons from this case.

The Indus Waters Treaty may also be relegated to a broad range of confidence-building measures that countries may develop during times of crises. As Shaista Tabassum has argued, the treaty did initially help to build some measure of conciliation between the two countries and was also framed as a "conflict avoidance measure."[25] Soon after the treaty was signed, both countries did agree to negotiate actively on Kashmir and six rounds of talks were held from 1962 to 1964. However, the talks failed because of territorial intransigence on both sides and the escalation of domestic political pressures. It may also be argued that the de-linkage of the substantive issues related to the Indus Waters Treaty and the development of Kashmir as a region might have provided an opening for dialogue which was not availed. India's dominance as a hegemonic power in the region also gave it much more negotiating power that was not effectively countered by international pressure. For efficacy in such asymmetric circumstances, it is also important to consider the regional dynamics of cooperation over water.[26]

Regional South Asian Strategies

South Asia has a remarkable history of cooperation over water-related issues in both maritime and riparian areas. India is South Asia's major littoral state, and shares maritime borders with several other South Asian states; in contrast, none of the other states have maritime borders with each other. India has settled its maritime boundaries with several of its neighbors, signing twelve bilateral agreements, including nine agreements with the Maldives, two each with Sri Lanka, Indonesia and Thailand, and one with Myanmar, as well as three trilateral agreements with Sri Lanka and the Maldives, Indonesia and Thailand, and Myanmar and Thailand.[27] Pakistan has also signed two bilateral agreements to settle its maritime disputes— one with Oman and the other with Iran. However, maritime disputes continue between India, Pakistan and Bangladesh.

In the case of Bangladesh and India, the problem is not the maritime boundary, which can be defined fairly easily, but rather competing sovereignty claims over the island of Talpati.[28] Bangladesh has a concave coast, and maritime boundaries in such geographical structures require integrative solutions and are extremely difficult to draw. Nevertheless, if a comprehensive settlement is reached in such cases, environmental factors can play a pivotal role since they help link various issues such as economic development and security. For example, a joint conservation monitoring arrangement can allow both sides access to areas that would otherwise be off-limits and give both sides an opportunity to cooperate in reducing environmental degradation. In particular, states that are ecologically vulnerable to extreme climatic events, such as Bangladesh, are recognizing that poor environmental planning in coastal areas can have devastating economic impacts. The old environment/economy tradeoff is becoming less relevant as environmental pressures begin to have direct economic impacts. Pakistan's maritime dispute with India over the Sir Creek region could conceivably provide an opportunity to forge such a link between economic development and environmental cooperation.[29]

Jn addition to maritime dispute settlements, several important river-sharing treaties have also been concluded in South Asia. India has agreements with Nepal, Bangladesh and Pakistan over riparian issues that are likely to be expanded in the future. Nepal, a small landlocked neighbor of India, is the upper riparian on the Mahakali River, which flows from Nepal into India. After protracted negotiations, the two states agreed on a treaty for the river in 1996. The importance of water negotiations was highlighted by the fact that the Nepalese parliament passed the treaty with the required two-thirds majority, despite a serious political crisis in Nepal at the time. According to commentator Krishna Rajan:

> The treaty attracted attention in a number of countries as an important indication of the ability of India and Nepal as multi-party democracies to reach an agreement on cooperation on water resources on the basis of equality, transparency and equitable sharing of costs and benefits....it does offer a model for India and Nepal on how to reach important understandings despite the uncertainties of democratic politics and coalition governments.[30]

Also in 1996, India and Bangladesh signed a treaty on India's construction of the Farakkha Barrage, a dam that diverts the flow of the Ganges River into the Hooghly River during the dry season to flush silt from the port of Calcutta. The negotiations were spread over two decades and, after overcoming a number of controversies, finally concluded in the form of a thirty-year Farakkha Barrage Treaty. Regional organizations are often an important mechanism in promoting multilateral peace-building efforts. South Asia, as an example, has the potential to engage in such a process through the South Asian Association for Regional Cooperation (SAARC), which was established in 1985. While bilateral dispute resolution is excluded from SAARC's mandate, there are numerous aspects of bilateral disputes, which can have multilateral, or even global, implications. For example, the Siachen dispute between India and Pakistan has prevented scientists from studying glacial recession, hydrological impacts and climate change that can potentially influence the entire region. Arguments can thus be made that many of the so-called bilateral disputes that involve ecological factors have a salient global purpose.[31]

Despite discouraging signs that both quantitative and qualitative environmental issues (scarcity and pollution, respectively) have historically been relatively low on the priority list of decision-makers in the region, it is important to note the establishment of SAARC was preceded by the formation of a regional environmental organization. At the initiative of the United Nations Development Program, the South Asian countries—including Afghanistan and Iran—came together in 1980 and established the South Asian Cooperative Environmental Program (SACEP). The stated goal of SACEP at the time of establishment was:

> to promote regional co-operation in South Asia in the field of environment—both natural and human—in the context of sustainable development and on issues of economic and social development which also impinge on the environment and vice versa; to support conservation and management of natural resources of the region and to work closely with all national, regional and international institutions, governmental and nongovernmental, as well as experts and groups engaged in such co-operation and conservation efforts.[32]

In its early years, SACEP was able to establish a "Regional Seas" program that had the potential to bring forth the territorial contentions for potential resolution. The interactions at a regional level through SACEP may well have helped to establish SAARC, which has a broader mandate in its charter of regional cooperation, covering a wide range of activities from energy to tourism to environmental protection, as well.

While such instances of regional cooperation are promising, the South Asian case on its own does not provide us with enough structural coherence to develop an effective strategy for moving forward with potential paths to making water an instrumental means of peace-building. Understanding the limitations of the current frames of policy analysis within international relations and considering alternative mechanisms for peace-building are important if we are to move beyond the self-fulfilling prophecy that tends to de-link environmental factors from peace-building.

Exploring Functionality of Water in Peacebuilding

Political geographer Kathryn Furlong has noted that dominant theories in international relations and international organizations tend to have five key flaws: 1) a mis-theorization of hegemonic influences at work; 2) undue pessimism regarding the propensity for multilateral cooperation; 3) an assumption that conflict and cooperation exist along a progressive continuum; 4) a tenet that conflict is restricted to state competition; and 5) a depoliticization of ecological conditions.[33] The Indus Waters Treaty exemplifies these challenges, which need to be addressed by scholars and practitioners alike. Theories of international relations that emphasize interdependence through mediating institutions such as the World Bank or the United Nations are most likely to offer some cooperative mechanisms in such asymmetric cases.[34]

The key to analyzing environmental cooperation as a potential pathway to peacemaking is to dispense with notions of linear causality and instead consider conflict de-escalation processes as nonlinear (not having a simple cause and effect relationship), often constituting a complex series of feedback loops. Positive exchanges and trust-building gestures are a consequence of realizing common environmental threats. Often, a focus on common environmental harms (or aversions) is psychologically more successful in leading to cooperative outcomes than a focus on common benefits, which may lead to competitive behavior over the distribution of the gains.[35] Specific research in game theory and operations research on the potential for cooperation over water is empirically showing that there are clear behavioral responses that suggest that such cooperation is possible.[36]

We also appear to have history on our side in this regard. An important historical study on water conflicts conducted by Oregon State University has noted that "the rate of cooperation overwhelms the incidence of acute conflict."[37] In the last fifty years, only thirty-seven disputes involved violence, and thirty of those occurred between Israel and one of its neighbors. Outside of the Middle East, researchers found only five violent events, while 157 treaties were negotiated and signed.[38] The total number of water-related events between nations also favors cooperation: the 1,228 cooperative events are more than twice the number of 507 conflict-related events.[39] Of these events, 62 percent are verbal, and more than two-thirds of these were not official statements.[40]

Realist scholars argue that cooperation on environmental issues among adversaries merely constitutes "low politics" and does not translate into larger resolutions over high-level national security concerns. In this view, environmental conservation would be at best a means of diplomatic maneuvering between mid-level bureaucrats, and at worst a tool for influential elites to pursue their own narrow interests. Such critics give examples of cooperation on water resources between adversarial states such as India and Pakistan or Jordan and Israel without this cooperation translating into broader reconciliation or peace.[41] Thus, it is presumed by some scholars looking at large historical data sets that environmental issues are not important enough in world politics to play an instrumental role in conflict resolution. Meanwhile, recent research conducted by the International Peace Research Institute in Norway has tried to extricate some of the various geographical aspects of cooperation and the conflict potential of riparian states using regression analyses. The basic conclusion of this study is that a shared river basin tends to accentuate conflict, but a shared river boundary as a border does not.[42] However, such studies cannot provide the granularity of analysis required to understand how cooperative mechanisms might still operate in cases such as the Indus, where the principal cause of the overarching conflict is not water. One of the earliest contributions to the study of environmental peacebuilding was Peter Haas' work in the context of the Mediterranean Action Plan.[43] Haas focused on ways in which knowledge exchange promotes environmental cooperation through the formation of what he termed "epistemic communities," networks of professional experts who arrive at shared views on scientific policy questions. These networks often take the form of civil society groups—sometimes facilitated by development donors—that exchange information on environmental issues. There is also a growing commitment from donors to "bioregionalism," the notion that ecological management must be defined by natural delineations such as watersheds and biomes rather than by national or other borders.[44] Numerous joint environmental commissions between jurisdictions and countries have taken root all over the world, at times with implicit or explicit confidence- or peace-building goals. This evolution has also played out at various international forums in which bioregionalism and common environmental sensitivities have sometimes transcended traditional notions of state sovereignty. An important role for such organizations is to improve an understanding of interconnections between distributive competitive issues of environmental scarcity with the mutual loss of deteriorated quality of the resource in the absence of cooperation. Through such a process, it may be possible to move functionally towards using water as a means of peacebuilding in South Asia and beyond.

Conclusion

The Indus Basin agreement has often been heralded as a success story of riparian cooperation between warring states. The role of the World Bank as the mediating institution in resolving this dispute between India and Pakistan is often cited as a positive intervention that led to a win-win outcome for all sides in the dispute. Yet the cooperation between the two states on this technical matter has not catalyzed the resolution of the overarching conflict over the Kashmir region, giving some credence to realist assumptions about environmental factors being "low politics." A closer examination of the cooperative arrangements reveals that the cooperation may still have played an important role in de-escalating tensions during times of crises. Consequently, it is possible to link such arrangements to larger narratives of conflict over territory that may be deemed "high politics." A more positive framing of the case might reveal that water resources in this context are so important that adversaries must show some semblance of cooperation over them, even when that does not spill over into broader peace. Furthermore, the use of environmental issues in building peace must be considered over longer time horizons and repeated interactions, premised empirically on the following conditions:

- Development of a joint information base on a common environmental threat;
- Recognition that cooperation is essential to alleviate that threat;
- A cognitive connection and trust-building from initial environmental cooperation;
- Continued interactions over time due to environmental necessity;
- Clarification of misunderstandings and de-escalation of related conflicts; and,
- Increased cooperation and resultant peace-building.[45]

These pathways are also considered the most empirically observed mechanisms, following a collective review by policy analysts for the United Nations Environment Program.[46]

The likelihood of environmental resources being used instrumentally in conflict resolution has increased in recent years. Certain environmental resources are now better understood as fundamental to basic economic, environmental and social processes, including sustaining human life. There is a growing realization that environmental issues require integrated solutions across national borders since natural ecosystems do not recognize political boundaries. At the same time, politicians need to acknowledge that natural resources, particularly those as essential as water, can provide an important tool for resolving territorial disputes as well as providing a conduit for confidence-building measures between adversaries. Cooperation over water and the environment is also a potential way of avoiding conflict if we can frame the matter appropriately. While South Asia has exemplified some parts of this framing routine, there is far more which can be accomplished if leaders are more willing to explore inherent ecological linkages between technical collaboration on water and lasting territorial security.

Notes

1. Mikhail Gorbachev, "Out of Water," *Civilization* 7, no. 5 (October-November 2000).
2. For a general review, see Sanjeev Khagram and Saleem H. Ali, "Environment and Security," *Annual Review of Environment and Resources* (2006), 395-411.
3. The first book to propose the concept of environmental peacebuilding is Ken Conca and Geoffrey D. Dabelko, *Environmental Peacemaking* (Baltimore, Md.: Johns Hopkins University Press, 2002); further theoretical and practical development of this concept can also be found in Saleem H. Ali, "Environmental Planning and Cooperative Behavior," *Journal of Planning Education and Research* 23 (2003), 165-176; and Saleem H. Ali, ed.. *Peace Parks: Conservation and Conflict Resolution* (Cambridge, Mass.: MIT Press, 2007).
4. The Nadistuti sukla, "hymn of praise of rivers," is hymn 10.75 of the Rigveda. All of the rivers in this hymn are considered "feminine" except the Indus, which is masculine and hence given a special status second only to the mythical Sarasvati River. Savarkar, among the founders of modern Hindu nationalism, defines a Hindu as "a person who regards this land....from the Indus to the Seas as his fatherland (pitribhumi) as well as his holyland (punyabhumi)." As Ashutosh Varshney has noted, "the definition is thus territorial (land between the Indus and the Seas), genealogical ('fatherland') and religious ('holyland'). Hindus, Sikhs, Jains, Buddhists can be part of this definition for they meet all three criteria. All of these religions were born in India. Christians, Jews, Parsis and Muslims can meet only two, for India is not their holyland." Ashutosh Varshney, "Is Sonia Indian?" *Rediff Online* (21 April 1999).
5. Salman M.A. Salman and Kislior Uprcty, *Conflict and Cooperation on South Asia's Internationa Rivers; A Legal Perspective* (Washington, D.C.: World Bank Publications, 2002).
6. For an account of Lilienthal's career at TVA and beyond, see David Ekbladh, "'Mr. TVA[1]: Grass-Roots Development, David Lilienthal, and the Rise and Fall of the Tennessee Valley Authority as a Symbol for U.S. Overseas Development, 1933-1973," *Diplomatic History* 26, no. 3 (Summer 2002), 335-374.
7. Subrahmanyam Sridhar, "Indus Waters Treaty," *Security Research Review* 1, no. 3 (2005).
8. Descriptive details about the Indus Basin Treaty arc derived from textual information on the Transboundary Freshwater Dispute Database at Oregon State University (http/Avww.transboundarywa-ters.orst.edu/projccts/cascstudies/indus.html); for a detailed written history of the treaty, see Bashir A. Malik, *Indus Waters Treaty in Retrospect* (Lahore, Pakistan: Brite Books, 2005).

9. Capl. CD. Bhatti (Ministry of Defense, Government of Pakistan, Member of the Pakistan delegation in the negotiations on Sir Creek 2000-2007), in discussion with Shaista Tabassum, 1st November 2007.
10. Oregon State University, Department of Geosciences, "Indus Waters Treaty," Transboundary Freshwater Dispute Database, http^/www.transboundary\ vatcrs. orst. edu/ 'projects/ casestudies/indus.html.
11. Ibid.
12. Ibid.
13. For a highly readable introduction to water utilization doctrines, see David H. Getches, *Water Law in a Nutshell* (New York: West Publishing, 1997).
14. Bank, *Pakistan: Country Water Resource Assistance Strategy:* Water *Economy: Running Dry* (Washington D.C.; World Bank, 2005), 7.
15. Ibid., 8.
16. Ibid., 8,
17. Toufiq Siddiqui, "An India-Pakistan Detente: What It Could Mean for Sustainable Development in South Asia and Beyond," *Analysis Report* 75 (Honolulu, Hawaii: East-West Center, 2004).
18. Undala Alam, "Questioning the Water Wars Rationale: A Case Study of the Indus Waters Treaty," *Geographical Journal* 168, no. 4 (2002), 341-353.
19. Ibid., 347.
20. Mohammad Sadiq, in discussion with Shaista Tabassum, 12 November 2007.
21. Alam, 345.
22. "Reconsidering the Indus Waters Treaty: The Baglihar Dam Dispute," *j&K Insights* (31st January 2005), http^/www.jamiriu-kashniir.com/insights/insight20050101a.html.
23. Ibid.
24. Siraj Wahid (Vice Chancellor of the Islamic University of Kashmir), interview with author, 16th May 2006, Toronto, Canada.
25. Shaista Tabassum, "The Role of CBMs in Resolving Non-Military Issues between India and Pakistan: A Case Study of the Indus Waters Treaty," in 77 ie *Challenge of Confidence-Building in South Asia,* ed. Moonis Ahmer (New Delhi, India: Har-Anand Publications, 2001). The incremental role of such efforts in peaccbuilding with an emphasis on psychological and cultural factors in South Asia is provided by Ranabira Samaddara and Helmut Reifdel, cd., *Peace as Process: Reconciliation and Conflict Resolution in South Asia* (New Delhi, India: Manohar Publishers, 2001).
26. The question of how such treaties can address regional disparities is explored by Iftikhar Ahmed Hakim, *The Indus Waters Treaty: An Institutional Mechanism for Addressing Regional Disparity* (Los Angeles, Calif.: Masters dissertation in Urban Planning, UCLA, 2005).
27. Rahul Roy Chaudhry, "Trends in the Delimitation of India's Maritime Boundaries," *Strategic Analvsis* XXII, no. Id (January 1999).
28. The island formed in the estuary of the Haribhanga river on the border between India and Bangladesh, probably after the tidal wave and cyclone of 1970. Each of the states claims ownership of the island. For greater detail on the issue, see Kathryn Jacques, *Bangladesh, India and Pakistan: International Relations and Regional Tensions in South Asia* (New York: St. Martin's Press, 2000), 49-55.
29. For a detailed analysis of linkage of the Sir Creek dispute and its potential for environmental conflict resolution, refer to a forthcoming report by Saleem H. Ali, Shaista Tabussum and Geoffrey Dabclko to the United Nations Environment Program on *Environmental Conflict and Cooperation in South Asia* (available from the author). Some of the narrative presented in this paper is also elaborated in that report.
30. Krishna V Rajan, "Nepal-India Relations," *South Asia Journal* (January-March 2005), 82-87.
31. The U.S. National Science Foundation funded an important effort to engage Pakistani and Indian scientists in joint research in 2005 and 2006 but both sides refused to issue visas for each other's delegates. Science was considered a more politically sensitive issue than exchange of musicians and artists who were routinely granted visas for pcacebuilding activities. The efforts were widely reported in *Science* magazine. See Pallava Bagla, "Pakistan Gives Goology Conference a Cold Shoulder," *Science* 312, 1117 (26 May 2006).
32. SACEP mission statement, http:/Avww.sacep.org.
33. Kathryn Furlong, "Hidden Theories, Troubled Waters: International Relations, the 'Territorial Trap' and the Southern African Development Community's Transboundary Waters," *Political Geography* 25 (2006), 43S-458.
34. It is important to note that much of the recent efforts by international institutions such as the World Bank and the United Nations to provide "water for all" have come under criticism on account of being hegemonic in favoring private interests from the developed world. See Michael Goldman, "How 'Water for All' Policy Became Hegemonic: The Power of the World Bank and its Transnational Policy Networks," *Geofomm* 38 (2006), 786-800.
35. Arthur Stein, *Wy Nations Cooperate: Circumstance and Choice in International Relations* (Ithaca, N.Y.: Cornell University Press, 1993).
36. For an example of how such behavioral models explain potential cooperation in the U.S.-Mexico case, see George B. Frisvold and Margriet F. Caswcll, "Transboundary Water Management: Game Theoretic Lessons for Projects on the U.S.-Mexico Border," *Agricultural Economics* 24, no. I (200), 101-111. More recently, Canadian researchers have also explored prospects internally for dispute resolution; Lizhong Wang, Liping Fang and Keith W. Hipel, "Basin-wide cooperative water resources allocation," *European Journal of Operational Research* (forthcoming 2008). It is also important to note that there have been considerable domestic conflicts over the Indus and its tributaries between Pakistani provinces, and the doctrine of interdependence is most well-

37 suited in addressing those as well. See Toufiq A. Siddiqi and Shirin Tahir-Kheli, eds.. Water *Conflicts in South Asia: Managing Water Resources Disputes within and between Countries of the Region* (New York: Carnegie Corporation of New York, 2004).
37 Shira B. Yoffe, Aaron T Wolf, and Mark Giordano. "Conflict and Cooperation over International Freshwater Resources: Indicators of Basins at Risk," *Journal of the American Water Resources Association* 39, no. 5 (2003), 1109-1126.
38 Ibid.
39 Ibid.
40 Ibid.
41 Miriam Lowri, *Water and Power: The Politics of a Scarce Resource in the Jordan River Basin* (Cambridge, England: Cambridge University Press, 1995).
42 Nils Fetter Gleditsch et al., "Conflicts over Shared Rivers: Resource Scarcity or Fuzzy Boundaries." *Political Geography* 25 (2006), 361-382.
43 Peter Haas, *Saving the Mediterranean: The Politics of International Environmental Cooperation* (New York: Columbia University Press, 1992).
44 Dennis Pirages and Ken Cousins, eds., From *Resource Scarcity to Ecological Security: Exploring New limits to Growth* (Cambridge, Mass.: MIT Press, 2005).
45 The classic works on this matter are those by Robert Axelrod, *The Complexity of Cooperation*, (Princeton, N.J.: Princeton University Press, 1997); and Robert Axelrod, *The Evolution of Cooperation*, (New York: Basic Books, 1985).
46 United Nations Environment Program, *Understanding Environment, Cooperation and Conflict* (Washington, D.C.: Woodrow Wilson Center; and Nairobi, Kenya: UNEP, 2004), http://www.unep.org/pdfy-ECCpdf.

CHAPTER - 18

Indus Waters Treaty

Ashis Ray, The Times of India, 18 March, 2010

1.0 Introduction

The waters of the Indus Basin rivers had been used for irrigation purposes even before the development of the present canal system by British engineers in the early 19th century. There were numerous inundation canals in the Indus Vailey, which diverted supplies directly from the rivers during the high flow periods, without any diversion works across the riverbed. The local community, tribes, or states managed these inundation canals.

From the middle of the 19th century onwards, irrigation was gradually extended through the introduction of improved methods and the construction of diversion works across the rivers. A number of agreements for the sharing of river waters took place. The most significant of these have been the Indus Basin Treaty (1960) between India and Pakistan and the Water Apportionment Accord (1991) between the four provinces of Pakistan. In August 1947, when South Asia was divided into two independent countries, there existed in the area, one of the-most highly developed irrigation systems in the world. The system catered to approximately 37 million acres of land, supplying it with the waters of the Indus rivers. All available water supplies were allocated to various princely States and provinces, in conformity with the principle of equitable apportionment of waters.The Indus System of Rivers in the Indus Basin comprises of the Indus and its five main tributaries i.e. Jhelum, Chenab, Ravi, Beas and Sutlej. They all combine into one river near Mithary Kot in Pakistan and flow into the Arabian Sea, south of Karachi. The total area of the Indus Basin is roughly 365,000 miles^2. Most of it lies in Pakistan and the remaining is part of occupied Jammu and Kashmir, India, China and Afghanistan.

At the time of Independence, 31 out 37 million acres in Pakistan were irrigated. The boundary line between the two countries being partitioned was drawn without any regard to the existing irrigation works. It was, however, affirmed by the Boundary Commission. Representatives of the affected zones expressly agreed before the Arbitral Tribunal that the authorized zones in the common water supply would continue to be respected.

2.0 The Rationale for the Indus Waters Treaty

The water dispute between Pakistan and India began when on April 01, 1948. Immediately after the winding up of the Arbitral Tribunal, India stopped irrigation waters in every irrigation canal which crossed the India-Pakistan boundary. This affected 1.6 million acres of irrigated land in Pakistan.

The abrupt act stressed the urgent need for Pakistan to formulate an agreement between the two countries regarding the future use and distribution of the combined waters.

3.0 Pre-treaty Negotiations

India demanded that Pakistan recognize that the proprietary rights on the waters of the rivers in Indian Punjab were wholly vested in the Indian government and that the Pakistani government could not claim any share of those waters as a right for areas of Punjab in Pakistan. Pakistan's claim was based upon the time honored formula that existing uses were sacrosanct and excess water, not previously committed, could be divided amongst the riparians according to area, population etc. This principle had the support of several treaties, nations or states and provisions in the same country.

The Indians put forward a principle, which had been advanced for some time during international negotiations but had not been accepted anywhere. Under this principle, the upper riparian had absolute right to the Water and the lower riparian could only get it under an agreement or treaty, if the same were entered between the riparians.

India agreed to restore some of the supplies in May 1948, when a very pro-Indian temporary agreement was signed. It was, however, generally realized that Pakistan could not survive without a restoration of the full supplies and on this question there could be no compromise. The controversy was serious enough to provoke an imminent war between the two countries.

Direct negotiations between the two Parties failed to resolve the dispute. Negotiations under the offices of the World Bank commenced in May 1952. It was agreed to work out specific engineering measures by which the supplies effectively available to each country would be increased substantially. The working party set up under the offices of the World Bank however failed to agree on a comprehensive plan for the utilization of the waters of the Indus River System. After eight years of intense negotiation, agreement between the two parties was finally reached in the form of the Indus Waters Treaty in 1960.

4.0 Main Contituents of the Indus Water Tready

The Indus Waters Treaty was signed at Karachi on September 19, 1960. It consists of 12 articles and 8 appendices, which are titled as given below:

CONTENTS OF THE TREATY

Article I	Definitions
Article II	Provisions regarding Eastern Rivers
Article III	Provisions regarding Western Rivers
Article IV	Provisions regarding Eastern Rivers and Western Rivers
Article V	Financial Provisions
Article VI	Exchange of Data
Article VII	Future Cooperation
Article VIII	Permanent Indus Commission
Article IX	Settlement of Differences and Disputes
Article X	Emergency Provisions
Article XI	General Provisions
Article XI	Final Provisions
Annexure A	Exchange of Notes between Government of India and Government of Pakistan
Annexure B	Agricultural Use by Pakistan from certain tributaries of the Ravi
Annexure C	Agricultural Use by India from the Western Rivers

Annexure D	Generation of Hydro-electric Power by India on the Western Rivers
Annexure E	Storage of Waters by India on Western Rivers
Annexure F	Neutral Expert
Annexure G	Court of Arbitration
Annexure H	Transitional Arrangements

5.0 Salient Features Of The Indus Waters Treaty

Provisions regarding the Eastern Rivers:

(i) All the waters of the Eastern Rivers shall be available for the unrestricted use of India.

(ii) Except for domestic and non-consumptive uses, Pakistan shall be under an obligation to let flow, and shall not permit any interference with, the waters of Sutlej Main and the Ravi Main in the reaches where these rivers flow in Pakistan and have not yet finally crossed into Pakistan.

(iii) All the waters, while flowing in Pakistan, of any tributary, which, in its natural course, joins the Sutlej Main or the Ravi Main after these rivers have finally crossed into Pakistan shall be available for the unrestricted use of Pakistan.

Provisions regarding the Western Rivers:

(i) Pakistan shall receive for unrestricted use all the waters of the western rivers.

(ii) India shall be under an obligation to let flow all the waters of the Western rivers, and shall not permit any interference with these waters.

Provisions regarding the Eastern and Western Rivers:

(i) Pakistan shall use its best endeavors to construct and bring into operation a system of works that will accomplish the replacement from the Western rivers (and other sources) of the water supplies for irrigation canals in Pakistan, which, on 15th August, 1947, were dependent on water supplies from the Eastern rivers.

(ii) The use of the natural channels of the rivers for the discharge of flood or other access waters shall be free and not subject, to limitation by either party, or neither party shall have any claim against the other in respect of any damage caused by such use.

(iii) Each party declares its intention to prevent, as far as practicable, undue pollution of the waters and agrees to ensure that, before any sewage or industrial waste is allowed to flow into the rivers, it will be treated, where necessary, in such manners as not materially to affect those use.

6.0 Post-Treaty views

From Pakistan's point of view, the settlement plan, as envisaged under the Indus Waters Treaty 1960, had some advantages as well as certain defects.

Advantages of the settlement plan:

(i) After the completion of the Indus Basin Replacement Plan works, each country became independent of the other in the operation of its supplies.

Each country is responsible for planning, constructing and administering its own facilities in its own interests and free to allocate its supplies within its own territories as it deems fit.This provides strong incentives to each country to make: the most effective use of water, since any efficiency accomplished by works undertaken by either country for storage, transfer, reduction of losses and: the like accrues directly to the benefit of that country. The same is true of efficiency achieved in operations.The independence afforded by the program also brought a benefit of a different kind. The location of works serving each country or territories under its control, and the assurances against interference by either country with the supplies on which the other depends have reduced the chances of disputes and tension.Before the completion of Indus Basin Project works, after the signing of the Treaty, the entire irrigation system in the Indus Basin was based on run-of-the-river supplies. The hydrology of the rivers is such that about 80% of the total water was produced during the monsoon period — July to September–storage projects due to the treaty also increased the canal water diversions.The winter supplies became very critical in drought periods. With supplies made available and the storage of water in the reservoirs, water availability in winter has been assured and so the country is insignificantly affected in drought conditions. Besides total withdrawals and canal heads in Pakistan have increased from about 67 MAF: to 104.5 MAF.

Defects of the settlement plan:

The traditional *sailab* (flood) irrigation, the most ancient way of using river waters, on the Sutlej, Beas and Ravi would disappear, because when these rivers are fully developed by India, the traditional floods would decrease or disappear and the *sailab* areas would not get seasonal water, which permitted cultivation. This area is considerable in extent.

Due to the loss of regular flow in the Eastern Rivers, the channels have become silted up and the floods in the channels cause great havoc in Pakistan, in addition to other environmental effects.The up-keep of the new link canals and storages mean a very heavy additional burden on the cost of maintaining irrigation. Besides, storages are no substitute to the perpetual flow of water as the storages have a limited life.

Changes in River Flows

River	Average Annual Flow (1922-61) MAF	Average Annual Flow (1960-95) MAF
Indus	93.0	60.25
Jhelum	23.0	23.0
Chenab	26.0	25.7
Ravi	7.0	5.8
Sutlej	14.0	5.8
Kabul	26.0	22.3
Total	189.0	142.8

Under the provisions of Article Vlll(1) of the Indus Waters Treaty 1960, both India and Pakistan have appointed a Commissioner for Indus Waters. Unless either Government decides to take up any particular question directly with the other Government, each Commissioner is the representative of his Government for all matters arising out of the Treaty and serves as the regular channel of communication on all matters relating to the implementation of the Treaty.The two Commissioners together form the PERMANENT INDUS COMMISSION whose purpose and functions are (i) to establish and maintain cooperative arrangements for the implementation of the Treaty, (ii) to promote co-operation between the parties in the development of the waters of the Rivers', (iii) to make every effort to settle promptly any question arising between the Parties and (iv) to undertake tours of inspection of the Rivers to ascertain facts. Under the Treaty, restrictions have been placed on the design and operation of Hydroelectric Plants, Storage Works and other river works to be constructed by India on the Western Rivers. India is required to supply Pakistan with certain specified information relating to these works at least 6 months in advance of undertaking the river works, to enable Pakistan to satisfy itself that the design conforms to the criteria set out in the Treaty. Within a specified period, ranging from two to three months of the receipt, Pakistan has the right to communicate its objections in writing to India, if any. Under the Treaty, Pakistan was required to construct and bring into operation a system of works, which could accomplish the replacement of supplies for irrigation canals from the Western Rivers in Pakistan. These included those canals that were dependent on water supplies from the Eastern Rivers on 15th August 1947. These replacement works, comprising two storage dams, six new barrages, remodeling of two existing barrages, seven new inter-rivers link canals and remodeling of two existing link canals, have since been completed.

Replacement Plan Works Constructed As A Result Of Indus Waters Treaty 1960

Storage Reservoir

Storage	River	Gross Storage Capacity (MAF)
Mangla	Jhetum	5.89
Chashma	Indus	0.70
Tarbela	Indus	11.0

Barrages			
Barrage	River	Flood of Record (cusecs)	Design Flood (cusecs)	Length of Barrage (feet)
Sidhnai	Ravi	167,000	167,000	712
Siphon	Sutlej	427,000	429,000	1,601
Qadirabad	Chenab	912,000	900,000	3,373
Rasul	Jhelum	876,000	850,000	3,209
Chashma	Indus	1,176,000	950,000	3,556
Marala	Chenab	1,023,000	1,100,000	4,472

Link Canals			
Link Canals	Capacity (cusecs)	Length (miles)	Excavation (million yds^3)
Trimmu - Sidhnai	11,000	44	21.0
Sidhnai - Mailsi	10,100	62	31.3
Mailsi - Bahawal	3,900	10	2.4
RasuL - Qadirabad	19,000	30	38.3
Qadirabad Baltoki	18,600	80	80.3
L.C.C. Feeder	4,100	20	8.0
Balloki Suleimanki II	6,500	39	20.5
Chashma - Jhelum	21,700	63	118.9
Taunsa - Panjnad	12,000	38	22.5

References

1. Government of Pakistan, "The Indus Waters Treaty 1960".

2. Dr. Bashir A Chandio and Nuzhat Yasmin, "Proceedings of the National Workshop on Water Resources Achievements and Issues in the 20th Century and Challenges for the Next Millennium", Pakistan Council of Research in Water Resources, June 1999.

3. Centre of Excellence in Water Resources Engineering, Lahore, "Proceedings: Water for the 21st Century: Demand, Supply, Development and Socio Environmental Issues", June 1997.

4. Dr. Nazir Ahmad, "Water Resources of Pakistan", Miraj uddin Press, Lahore September 1993.

5. Partial data acquired from Indus River System Authority for flows of rivers in Pakistan.

CHAPTER - 19

Pakistan: Indus Basin Water Strategy – Past, Present And Future

Shahid Amjad Chaudhry[*]

Abstract

This paper looks at the Indus Basin Water Strategy for Pakistan. It begins with a historical overview of the Indus Basin Irrigation System (IBIS), the Indus Basin Replacement Works (1960-1980) and the Indus Basin Salinity Control Efforts (1960-2000). The paper then looks at the IBIS irrigation and salinity control investments that have taken place over the last decade (2000-2010). The paper goes on to look at the present situation of the IBIS as well as discuss an IBIS strategy for the next decade. Finally, the paper discusses supply side and demand management strategies for IBIS. Overall, the paper concludes that Pakistan should focus on (1) Creating additional surface storage, (2) Preserving surface water (particularly through lining canals), (3) Controlling groundwater and controlling salinity (by discouraging excessive tube-well use), (4) Encouraging general efficiency of irrigation water use (through improved land management techniques), (5) Enhancing yields through improved farming practices, and (6) Fully meeting the environmental concerns of the Indus Delta, river systems and wetlands.

Keywords: Indus Basin, water, strategy, irrigation, Pakistan.
JEL Classification: Q15, Q25.

I. Introduction

Pakistan's Indus Basin Irrigation System (IBIS) is the strong heart of the country's economy. Its creation is a tribute to the British irrigation engineers who created the original system (1847-1947) that Pakistan inherited in 1947 and to the Pakistani irrigation engineers and institutions (particularly the Water and Power Development Authority [WAPDA] and the provincial irrigation departments) who have spent the last 60 years adding new dams and barrages, building new link and branch canals, and modernizing and maintaining the world's most complex and extensive irrigation system. From the 1950s onward, the IBIS has also been the product of the generosity and intellectual input of a host of international experts and international institutions, particularly the World Bank. This paper starts with a review of what has been accomplished in order to put the IBIS into perspective and illustrate the magnitude of the effort put into building the present system. The paper's aim is to sketch the task ahead and develop a coherent national strategy for the preservation of the IBIS for the future.

---

[*] Rector, Lahore School of Economics, and Former Deputy Chairman, Planning Commission, Government of Pakistan.

II. The Indus Basin: The First Decade 1947-1957

The Revelle Report[1], commissioned by President Kennedy following a request from President Ayub Khan in 1961, provides a fascinating look at Pakistan in this period. It paints a West Pakistan of 43 million people, malnourished and desperately poor with an average income of less than 20 cents/day, and an average life span of less than 45 years, with a 10% rate of literacy—"industrious, frugal, progressive ... their watch word: 'our sons will have it better'" (Revelle, et al. 1964:35).[1.] Pakistan, at this time, was overwhelmingly rural. There was a magnificent canal irrigation system based on the River Indus and its five tributaries (the Jhelum, Chenab, Ravi, Sutlej, and Beas), but it was plagued by its seasonal nature and lack of surface storage (nearly half the flows went to sea unused in the summer, with less than 2 feet/acre left for the irrigated land). Thirty percent of the cultivated land of 35 million acres was affected by water logging and salinity. Most of all, the report said: "In West Pakistan, we have the wasteful paradox of a great and modern irrigation system pouring its waters onto lands cultivated as they were in the days of Abraham, Isaac and Jacob" (Revelle, et al. 1964:65). The report also presented estimates of irrigation requirements in West Pakistan for various crops: wheat 16"/acre, cotton 28-37"/acre, sugarcane 64-80"/acre, and rice 35"/acre (Revelle, et al. 1964: 213). The irrigation system during the 1950s (largely inherited pre-1947) consisted of 10 barrages (Thal, Jinnah, Taunsa, Guddu, Sukkur, Kotri, Trimmu, Dipalpur, Suleimanke, Islam, and Panjnad) and 35,000 miles of canals. The Indus Basin inflow was 167 million acre feet (MAF) (average 1921-46 and 1952-57) of which 32.7 MAF (average 1921-46) was from the Ravi (6.4 MAF), and Sutlej/Beas (26.3 MAF) (Revelle, et al. 1964: 69). India had started depriving Pakistan of water from the three eastern rivers, i.e., the Ravi, Sutlej, and Beas, from March 1948. This led Pakistan to negotiate and sign the Indus Water Accord (IWA) in 1960, with India giving Pakistan the rights to the Indus, Jhelum, and Chenab, and India the rights to the Ravi, Sutlej, and Beas in perpetuity.[2]

III. The Indus Basin Replacement Works (1960-80) and Salinity Control (1960-2000)

Subsequent to the Indus Waters Treaty, negotiated with India with the help of the World Bank, a massive irrigation river link canal water scheme comprising two large storages, several barrages, and a number of major link canals was undertaken by the newly created WAPDA (under a World Bank umbrella) to transfer 20 MAF of water from the Indus and Jhelum to the Ravi and Sutlej irrigation commands within Pakistan to substitute for the 30 MAF given to India (the Beas merges with the Sutlej in India).[3] Two major dams were constructed, one at Mangla (6 MAF) on the Jhelum, and the second at Tarbela (9 MAF) on the Indus to provide water to the new link canals in the lean winter (kharif) season. Thus, by 1980, Pakistan had two major dams (Mangla and Tarbela), one medium barrage-cum-dam at Chashma (0.8 MAF), 19 barrages, 12 link canals, 43 canal commands covering 90,000 chaks through about 40,000 miles of branch canals, main canals, and distributaries, and water courses, field channels, and field ditches running approximately another 1 million miles.[4] The total replacement cost of the infrastructure is currently estimated at more than $60 billion,[5] and of these, the two major dams (Tarbela and Mangla), a syphon-cum-barrage (Mailsi), five barrages (Chashma, Rasul, Qadirabad, Marala, and Sidnai), and eight major link canals were built under the Indus Basin Replacement Works.[6] A large number of existing canals and their associated irrigation infrastructure were also remodeled to accommodate the increased requirements of the replacement system.

---

[1] Report on Land and Water Development in the Indus Plain, Revelle, Hoffman, Falcon et al. The White House 1964.
[2] "Analysis of Water Accords," Kazi A. in Politics of Managing Water, Oxford University Press 1999 pp.164-169.
[3] Study of the Water Resources of West Pakistan Vol. II, The Lieftinck Report, IBRD 1967 Annex Map.
[4] "Issues in Water Policy Reforms," by Mahmood Ahmed, in The Politics of Managing Water, Edited by Bengali K, Oxford University Press 1999; pp 73-76.
[5] Water Economy Running Dry IBRD 2005, p 58.
[6] "Issues in Water Policy Reforms," by Mahmood Ahmed, in The Politics of Managing Water, Edited by Bengali K, Oxford University Press 1999; pp 73-76.

The World Bank's assistance was invaluable, both on the technical and financial side, as was its role as guarantor of the Indus Basin Water Treaty and its assumption of responsibility for the completion of the replacement works. The role of WAPDA in designing and executing the program was as important. This combination, together with Pakistani and international funding, enabled the entire Indus Basin Replacement Works to be completed by the early 1970s.

Salinity Control (1960-2000)

While covering the entire agriculture sector, Revelle, et al. (1964) also focused on salinity control, this having been President Ayub Khan's original request to President Kennedy during the former's visit to the United States in 1961. At the time of independence (1947), Pakistan's Indus Basin was already affected by water logging and salinity as a result of the massive irrigation canal system having been established on a flat plain with no natural drainage. By the end of the 1950s, almost 30% of the entire Indus Basin command was badly affected while another 30% had high water tables and indicated the adverse effect of salinity. The Revelle Report was bold in its recommendations. It recommended covering 70-80% of the Indus Basin irrigated land or 25 to 30 million acres of the total cultivated area of 35 million acres by dividing it into 25 to 30 project areas of roughly 40 square miles (1,600 square miles) or approximately 1 million acres, with each new project starting every year after a two-year preparatory period and extending over two decades.[7] The projects were to focus on the provision of large public sector tube wells to lower the water table and, as an additional benefit, to provide more irrigation water. As a result of this White House study, the World Bank, in collaboration with the Government of Pakistan and at the urging of the US Government, financed over 40 years (from the 1960s to the end of the 1990s) a large number of salinity controls projects costing more than $1 billion. This effort started with Salinity Control and Reclamation Programs (SCARPs) in the 1960s, focusing on vertical drainage through large capacity public sector tube-wells and vertical drains. These projects were executed by WAPDA over three decades and covered all major salinity-affected areas, proving a great success. However, by the 1970s, it was evident that the private sector had started using Pakistan-made small private tube wells essentially for groundwater extraction but with the same ground table lowering effect; as a result, the SCARPs had become largely superfluous.[8] However, by this time, 16,700 large capacity public tube-wells had been installed: a substantial number still exist today and provide 7.81 MAF of water to the system.[9,11] The Government of Pakistan and the World Bank then shifted their strategy and focused on overall drainage management throughout the Indus Basin including through tile drainage. An innovative salinity drainage project, the Left Bank Outfall Drain (LBOD), was also executed in this period in Sindh to transfer saline water directly to the sea on the left bank of the Indus River. A small Right Bank Outfall Drain Project (RBOD I) was also undertaken to channel saline water from upper Sindh and Balochistan to the Indus River near Manchar Lake in Sindh, but due to general opposition in Sindh to adding saline water to the Indus River, ended up terminating at Manchar Lake with severely adverse consequences for the lake. This problem is now being resolved through RBOD II (discussed later). Today, as a result of these World Bank-financed projects and also as a result of more than 0.8 million private tube-wells providing more than half of Pakistan's total water requirements[10] (or about 50 MAF), Pakistan's salinity problem is confined to about 5 million acres of irrigated areas of which 30% lies in the Punjab and the balance in Sindh. In addition, another 2.44 million acres is waterlogged.[11] This is a vast improvement

---

[7] Lieftinck, op.cit. pp. 130-131.
[8] Pakistan Water Economy Running Dry. World Bank 2005 op cit. pp. 94-99.
[9] Pakistan Agricultural Statistics – 2009, pp. 64.
[10] "Managing Salinity and Water logging in Pakistan": Qureshi A.S. et al. Agriculture Water Management Journal, Volume 95, 2008, pp. 2.
[11] Ibid. pp. 3.

from the 1950s when salinity had rendered 10-12 million acres of land unusable and was, to some extent, estimated to affect a total of about 25-30 million acres by Revelle, et al. (1964).

IV. IBIS Investments in the Last Decade 2000-2010

Irrigation Investments 2000-2010.

The last decade has seen the initiation and completion of a number of important projects relating to the Indus Basin, financed in large part by the Government of Pakistan itself. These include: (i) the Mangla Dam Raising Project 2003-2010 (raising the Mangla Dam 30 feet and thereby adding an additional 2.9 MAF to its existing capacity of 6 MAF at an original cost of Rs 63 billion); (ii) the Greater Thal Canal Project in Punjab 2002-2010 (creating a new culturable command area [CCA] of 1.5 million acres at a cost of Rs 30 billion); (iii) the Kachhi Canal Project for Balochistan, covering Dera Bugti, Naseerabad, and Jhal Magsi 2002-2012 (creating a new CCA of 0.71 million acres at a cost of Rs 31 billion); and (iv) the Rainee Canal Project for Sindh, covering Ghotki, Khairpur, and Sukkur 2002-2012 (creating a new CCA of 0.41 million acres at a cost of Rs 19 billion).[12] In addition, a major effort was made for the first time in Pakistan to start the rehabilitation of the Indus Water Irrigation System by starting the Irrigation System Rehabilitation Project in Sindh in 2002 at a cost of Rs 12 billion.[13] This project is nearly complete. All these projects were financed almost entirely by the Government of Pakistan and executed exclusively by WAPDA, except for the Sindh Irrigation Rehabilitation Project which is being executed by the Government of Sindh and marks for the first time a separation between Government of Pakistan and World Bank projects. As far as the water sector has been concerned in this period, the World Bank has focused almost entirely on institutional development.[14] Except for a barrage rehabilitation project, World Bank irrigation-related projects were only for "institutional development" and represented a continuation of its boycott of irrigation infrastructure investment in Pakistan from 1997 onward and its policy decision to focus on institutional issues and, in the longer term, seek the privatization of Pakistan's irrigation sector. This was similar to its earlier decision not to lend for energy development since 1987 and focus on the privatization of the energy sector. In 1987, the World Bank also stopped the Government through legal covenants from building thermal power plants in the public sector, which is largely responsible for the energy crisis facing Pakistan today. However, there are reports that the World Bank may finance new public sector hydro-electric projects and continue the rehabilitation of barrages.

Salinity Control Investment 2000-2010

On the salinity drainage control front, a large second RBOD project in Sind was undertaken to channel away saline water from Sindh and Balochistan that was previously being disposed of into Manchar Lake (discussed earlier). This project (RBOD II) aims at extending RBOD I from near Manchar to the Arabian Sea, together with additional saline water collected along its length. It is intended both to revive Manchar Lake and also to remove saline water along the entire right bank of the Indus in Sindh. With a capacity of 4,000 cusecs, the project was started in 2002 at a total cost of Rs 10 billion and is nearing completion.[15] This project was financed entirely by the Government of Pakistan and is being executed by the Government of Sindh.

---

[12] Water Resources and Hydro-power Development Vision 2025. WAPDA 2004.
[13] Annual Review (2001-2) of the Ten Year Perspective Plan 2001-11 and Three Year Development Program 2002-05. Planning Commission 2002, pp. 306.
[14] Pakistan Economy Running Dry. World Bank 2005 pp. 113-115.
[15] Annual Review (2001-2) of the Ten Year Perspective Plan. Op. cit. pp. 306 .

V. The Present (2008-10) Situation of the IBIS

Today, the IBIS is relatively stable as a result of investments in the Indus Basin Replacement Works, additional storages built at Mangla and Tarbela, and the large-scale reduction and, in many areas, elimination of water logging and salinity earlier through SCARPs and subsequently through private sector tube-wells. Private sector tube-wells and SCARP tube-wells add an additional 50 MAF to the system (mostly in the Punjab) and lower the water table, thereby reducing salinity in a substantial part in Punjab and to some extent in Sindh. Saline water is also removed by the LBOD and RBOD in Sindh. Table-1 below summarizes the current situation with regard to surface water use and availability. The current situation with regard to water logging and salinity and surface water use is discussed later.

Table-1. IBIS – Canal Withdrawals (Million Acre Feet)

	Average 1952-57[1]		Drought Year 2001-2[2]		5 Years Avg. 2001/2-2004/5[2]		2007-8[2]		1990 Inter-Provincial Accord Indus Basin[3]	
NWFP	2.8	(4%)	4.6	(6%)	4.6	(5%)	5.1	(5%)	8.78	(7%)
Punjab	40.4	(55%)	40.4	(51%)	46.6	(52%)	55.4	(53%)	55.94	(48%)
Sind & Baluchistan (of which Baluchistan)	30.4	(41%)	34.6	(43%)	38.8	(43%)	44.0	(42%)	52.63	(45%)
									(3.87)	(3%)
	73.6		79.6		90.0		104.5		117.35	
Downstream Kotri	68.6		1.9		5.1		15.8		To be determined	

Source: 1 "Report of land and Water Development in the Indus Plain "The Revelle Report. White House, 1964 pp. 69.
2 "Pakistan Statistical Year book 2009" Government of Pakistan pp. 67.
3 Indus Water Accord 1990-91 in Pakistan Water Economy Running Dry. IBRD 2005, p.20. The Accord protects Punjab on the basis of historical use (1977-82) in case of shortages below 117.35 (MAF).

In addition to the need for water storage to provide a regular supply of water downstream Kotri in order to preserve the Indus Basin Delta, the seasonality of the Indus system rivers' flows (with more than 80% of the water flowing in the kharif season (largely in June-August) also requires the storage of summer flows so that an adequate winter crop is cultivable. As Table-2 below indicates, in good river flow years, virtually the entire existing storage capacity at Mangla and Tarbela (13.5 MAF in 1998/99, about 12 MAF in 2007/08) can be used, while in drought years, about 40-50% of the storage capacity can be used to carry water into the next crop.

Table-2. Seasonality in the Indus River System
(Million acre feet)

	1998-99	2001-02	2007-08
Actual Flow Western Rivers[1]			
Kharif	124.97 (84%)	79.88 (82%)	105.89 (84%)
Rabi	24.56 (16%)	17.29 (18%)	20.19 (16%)
	149.53	97.17	126.08
Actual Flows Eastern Rivers	12.26	1.38	1.25
Canal Withdrawals			
Kharif	72.79 (66%)	58.11 (73%)	74.45 (71%)
Rabi	37.91 (34%)	21.50 (27%)	30.08 (29%)

	1998-99	2001-02	2007-08
	110.70	79.61	104.53
Downstream Kotri	35.15	1.93	15.80

1 Actual Flows at Rim Stations – Indus at Tarbela, Jhelum at Mangla, Chenab at Marala for Western Rivers only.
Source: Pakistan Statistical Year book 2009, pp. 66, 67.

Salinity: Current Situation Analysis

The water logging and salinity problems of the Indus System irrigation areas stem from its geography. The Indus Plain is essentially flat, rising gradually at a rate of about 1 foot per mile from the sea in the south to the Kalar Kahar Range in the north near Islamabad. Lahore, at a height of 700 feet, is 700 miles from Karachi. The generally level ground allows canal irrigation but it also means that salts will leach into the soil from the Indus rivers' water that contain salts brought down from the mountains where the rivers originate. In addition, both southern Punjab and Sindh were originally deserts and the present alluvial surfaces of these lands were created by river floods which themselves contained salts.[16] Thus, both the irrigation waters and the soils themselves contain salts, and when the water-table rises to about 10 feet underground, the capillary action of the soil forces the salt-impregnated underground water to the root zone of the crops, damaging plant growth and even killing the plant. As mentioned earlier, at the time of the Revelle Report (1964), while only about 30% of the Indus Basin was affected by water logging and salinity, another 30% had water at least 10 feet near the surface. Revelle, et al. (1964) anticipated that the salinity problem would ultimately affect almost 70-80% of the Indus Basin; hence, the report's ambitious basin-wide proposed projects. Revelle's SCARPs and their subsequent successors – private tube-wells – have largely reversed the problem and today, while there is still a salinity problem because of the nature of the irrigation system and now subsequently through secondary tube-well water-induced salinity, it appears to be more containable. Presently, it is estimated that about 5.4 million acres (of the total of 48.7 million acres under cultivation in the Indus Basin) or about 11% is affected by primary or secondary salinization.[17] One third of the affected area is in Punjab and the remaining in Sindh. In Punjab, salinity is due to both canal water and tube-well irrigation, but the major problem now is secondary or tube-well-related salinity. In Sindh, the problem is overwhelmingly canal water related salinity since the water aquifer is largely saline and tube-well use is relatively limited. Table-3 below summarizes the situation with regard to Indus Basin salt balances. A noteworthy feature is that, in aggregate, the Indus Basin's salt balances retained in the root zone appear to be in balance and may be marginally deceasing.[18] In addition, in Sindh, the LBOD has been remarkably successful and, together with the new RBOD, may actually allow successful management of salt levels in the area.

Table-3. Indus Basin Salt Balances

		2008 Qureshi Estimates Salt Mg[1]			2005 World Bank Estimates Salt Million Tons[2]
		Indus Basin (1) + (2)	Punjab (1)	Sindh (2)	
I.	Total Annual Addition, Net*	52.2	38.3	13.9	68
	Net Indus River System	24.0	13.6	10.4	19
	From T/W	28.2	24.7	3.5	49

---

[16] Revelle, op. cit. pp. 56.
[17] "Managing salinity and water logging in the Indus Basin of Pakistan," Qureshi, A.S etal, Agriculture Water Management Journal, (2008) pp. 3.
[18] "Pakistan: Water Economy Running Dry," op. cit. pp. 48.

		2008 Qureshi Estimates Salt Mg[1]			2005 World Bank Estimates Salt Million Tons[2]
		Indus Basin (1) + (2)	Punjab (1)	Sindh (2)	
II.	Total Annual Disposal, Net*	52.2	38.3	13.9	68
	Retained in Soil (Root Zone) (-3)	50.0	36.1	13.9	57
	Evaporation Ponds	2.2	2.2		
	LBOD directly to sea				4.0
III.	Indus Water to Sea	9.0			10.0
IV	Total Salt / annum	61.2			78.0

* Excluding 9 Mg annual salt flow washed out to Sea (Qureshi etc.) or 10 million tons annual salt flow washed out to sea (World Bank).

Sources: 1 "Managing salinity and water logging in the Indus Basin of Pakistan," Qureshi A.S. et. al. Agriculture Water Management 95 (2008), pp. 4.
2 "Pakistan Water Economy Running Dry," World Bank 2005, pp. 48.

Groundwater: Current Situation Analysis

The increasing use of groundwater extracted through small private tube-wells has changed the nature of the IBIS. Encouraged initially by the example of the massive number of SCARP-imported tube-wells which, as Revelle, et al. (1964) anticipated, added dozens of MAF to the irrigation system, Pakistan's private farmers used local electricians to fabricate small tube-wells running both on electrical and diesel power. This in large part freed farmers from the water shortage experienced in the rabi season and enabled them to balance the system at times of canal closure. In addition, it enabled them to plant more water-intensive crops such as rice in the kharif season by using tube-wells to augment the already plentiful supply of irrigation water in this season (a time when water tables are already high because of monsoon rains). Finally, and most importantly, it enabled Pakistani farmers to counter the approximately 3-5 year drought cycle of the Indus River system (discussed later). There were costs to underground water both in terms of additional salinity (discussed earlier) and the decline in water table levels. However, the overuse of groundwater was mitigated at least to some extent because (unlike India) electricity and diesel for tube-wells was not subsidized. Qureshi (2009) points out that the average cost of tube-well water is about 30 times that of canal water or roughly US$5.5/hectare/year for canal water as compared to US$167/hectare/year for tube-wells.[19] However, as Table 4 below shows, groundwater extracted through tube-wells amounted to about 50 MAF in 2007/08 of which about 40 MAF was from private tube-wells, 7.8 MAF from SCARPs, and 1.73 MAF from public tube-wells. As a result, aquifers are being slowly depleted in Pakistan's Indus Basin (although not as dramatically as in Indian Punjab; this is discussed later). Currently, 80% of Punjab's aquifer recharge is from the irrigation system.[20] The balance is largely from monsoon rainfall and return flow from groundwater. It is estimated that the groundwater level has dropped to inaccessible depths in 5% of Punjab (a sign of groundwater depletion) and this is expected to decline to 15% in the next decade.[21] This implies that, at current rates, Pakistani Punjab aquifers will be completely depleted in 50-100 years. Groundwater prospects are discussed in detail later.

---

[19] "Challenges and Prospects of Sustainable Ground Water Management in the Indus Basin, Pakistan," Qureshi A.S. et al. Water Resources Management Journal, Springer, 2009.
[20] Pakistan Water Economy Running Dry. op. cit. pp. 15.
[21] "Challenges and Prospects of Sustainable Ground Water........" op. cit. pp. 7.

Table-4. Pakistan Overall Water Availability (2007-08)

(Million Acre Feet)

2007-08	Surface Water		Ground Water		(4) Public T/W	(1+2+3+4) Total Water Availability
	at Canal Head	(1) At Farm Gate	(2) Private T/W	(3) SCARP T/W		
Kharif	70.78	61.12	19.70	3.90	0.86	85.58
Rabi	27.94	31.40	20.68	3.91	0.87	56.86
Total	98.72	92.52	40.38	7.81	1.73	142.44

Source: Pakistan Statistical Year Book 2009, pp. 64.

VI. An IBIS Strategy for the Next Decades: The Supply Side

Any analysis of a future IBIS strategy must necessarily begin with the supply side since absolute initial constraints—the flows of the Indus system's three western rivers—limit the total availability of surface water in Pakistan. Secondary constraints relate to the absolute size of groundwater aquifers where more than 80% of the recharge is by the same western rivers. Within these constraints there is annual flexibility in the surface water system determined by storage capacity in dams and multi-year flexibility in the groundwater system with the aquifers acting as huge underground dams. However, before discussing these supply-side constraints and mitigation measures, it is important to examine the Indus Water Accord (IWA) with India and its future prospects.

IWA 196:. Future Prospects

As discussed earlier, the total flow of the entire Indus Water System (the Indus plus its tributaries) is about 180 MAF, which was divided by the IWA by giving the Indus, Jhelum, and Chenab (150 MAF) to Pakistan and the Ravi, Sutlej, and Beas (30 MAF) to India. However, the IWA gave certain rights to India over the western rivers including limited agricultural use (70,000 acres from the Indus, 400,000 acres from the Jhelum, and 225,000 acres from the Chenab—a total of 695,000 acres). The IWA also gave India the right to construct run-off-the-river hydroelectric plants with limited pondage and dead storage.[22] As legally written and if properly enforced, Pakistan would lose only a maximum of 3 to 4 MAF from its western rivers, which would be in conformity with the IWA.

However, in practice, major problems are beginning to average as a result of the construction of new hydro-projects by India. The first of these, Baglihar, completed in 2009, was questioned by Pakistan in that it had live gated storage. This was challenged by Pakistan before the World Bank (the guarantor of the IWA); the World Bank, with the agreement of both India and Pakistan, appointed a "neutral expert" as laid down in the IWA. Unfortunately, the neutral expert "reinterpreted" the treaty to allow limited live storage to allow the flushing out of silt, and this permission allowed India to cause immense damage to Pakistan by completing and filling the Baglihar Dam on the Chenab during the rabi season in 2009/10 when Pakistan received almost no water from the Chenab.[23] John Briscoe, the World Bank Irrigation Advisor at that time and the person responsible for selecting the neutral expert, is now Professor of Environmental Engineering at Harvard and has stated recently that "if Baglihar was the only dam being constructed on the Chenab and Jhelum, this would be a limited problem. But following Baglihar is a veritable caravan of Indian

---

[22] Indus Water Accord 1960, Annexure C and D, Government of Pakistan.
[23] "War or Peace on the Indus?" Briscoe, John, The News, April 3, 2010 pp. 6.

Projects— Kishanganga, Sawalkat, Pukuldul, Bursar, Dal Huste, Gyspa ..... The cumulative live storage will be large, giving India an unquestionable capacity to have a major impact on the timing of flows into Pakistan."[24]

This situation is further complicated by the fact that the Indian Punjab's much vaunted "agricultural miracle" is running out of groundwater. A recent authoritative academic study on the Indian Punjab's groundwater points out that the Indian Punjab's agriculture is overwhelmingly dependant on groundwater which is becoming rapidly depleted. The study states: "The total surface availability at different head works is about 1.80 hectare meter (Mha-m) per annum (Government of Punjab 2005). Out of this, 0.35 Mha-m per annum is lost during conveyance and only 1.45 Mha-m is available at the outlet that irrigates about 1.0 Mha land. The total sustainable availability of ground water is 1.68 Mha-m per annum. The current crop production pattern dominated by paddy wheat crop rotation requires 4.37 Mha-m of irrigation water per annum, against the total supply of 3.13 Mha-m per annum from both surface and annual recharge of groundwater resources, leading to a net deficit of 1.24 Mha-m (Government of Punjab 2005). Consequently the deficit is being met by over exploitation of the groundwater resources. This has played havoc with the groundwater resources of the State."[25] The Columbia Water Centre (the Earth Institute at Columbia University), in a recent concept note on water security in Indian Punjab, states that "In 1985, less than 5% of tube-wells were sustainable. By 2005, that number had increased to over 60%. If these trends of aquifer depletion continue, it is estimated that Punjab's groundwater will be entirely exhausted in 15-20 years.[26]

India is developing the capacity to violate the IWA and has the need for Pakistan's waters as shown above. It is, therefore, imperative that the "Office of the Commissioner Indus Waters Accord" within the Ministry of Water, Government of Pakistan be strengthened and a dialogue with India undertaken to ensure that India does not violate the IWA in letter or spirit. In the meantime, Pakistan should anticipate at a minimum that India will use to the full its allowable water use on the western rivers according to the IWA. This will mean a minimum withdrawal of about 5 MAF of water in flood, normal, and drought years. Thus, if 1998 is considered a flood year with 111 MAF of canal withdrawals, 2007/08 is considered a normal year with 105 MAF withdrawals, and 2001/02 is considered a drought year with 80 MAF of withdrawals; this use of water by India under the IWA would mean a reduction in the Indus system's canal water availability of western rivers' waters to 105 MAF annually in flood years, about 100 MAF in normal years, and about 75 MAF in drought years.

Indus River Seasonality, Drought and Climate Change:

The Requirement for New Storage Dams on the Indus

As shown earlier in this paper, the Indus River system exhibits seasonality within a year, with 80% of its flows occurring in the kharif season when the glaciers melt in the summer in Kashmir (the Western Himalayas). This necessitates having live storage capabilities. A further complicating factor that also requires live storage for mitigation is that the Indus River also seems to have a "3 to 5 year flood and drought cycle" as Figure 1 below indicates.

---

[24] Briscoe, John,. op. cit.
[25] "Concerns of Groundwater Depletion and Irrigation: Efficiency in Punjab Agriculture – A Micro-Level Study," Jeevendas A., Singh RP., and Rumer, B. Agriculture Economics Research Review, Vol. 21, July-December 2008, pp. 195
[26] "Concept Note on Water Security in Punjab, India, Current Scenario." /Water Columbia /edu/..../India. Website dated April 9, 2010.

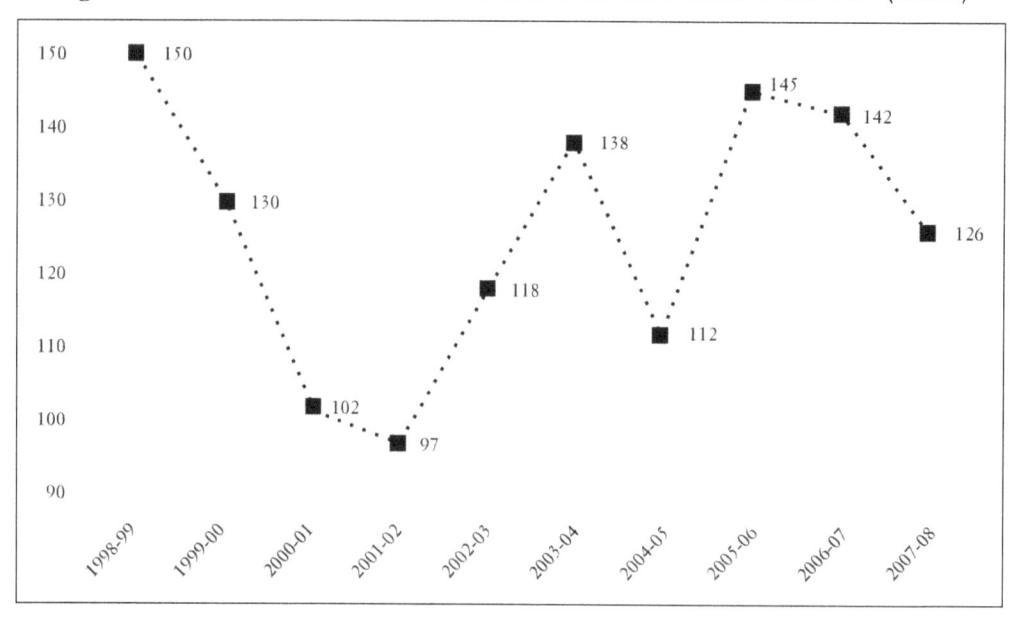

Figure-1: Western Rivers: Inflow at Rim Stations Million Acre Feet (MAF)

Source: Pakistan Statistical Year Book 2009, pp. 66.

In addition to the "flood followed by drought cycle" illustrated above, Pakistan faces the prospects of climate change. Current forecasts (despite their uncertain nature) show the Western Himalayan glaciers melting in the next 50 years which will mean initially massive river flows followed by meltdown and consequent 30 to 40% decreases in river flows. This climate change will be accompanied by increased rainfall which will accentuate flooding problems of the rivers in the first 50 years and subsequently mitigate the low flows in the rivers in the next 50 years.[27] This is a daunting prospect and needs to be managed.

Overall, the implications of the latter three IBIS supply side situations (viz., the kharif-rabi imbalance, the multi-year imbalance, and the climate change imbalance) all require the construction of additional storage on the Indus River. Excluding climate change, requirements for normal Indus River imbalances can be determined on the basis of "yield curves." The Lieftinck Report (1967) calculated a yield curve for storage capacity on the Indus shown in Table-5 below. This seems to indicate that Pakistan optimally requires about 22 MAF of storage on the Indus while the present storage capacity is about 8 MAF at Tarbela and an additional 6 MAF if Basha is constructed as planned. Thus, an additional storage or two after Basha will be required on the Indus to deal with the present situation. The climate change requirement for storage on the Indus will have to be determined after further analysis. The Asian Development Bank has indicated that it will support the construction of Basha on which preconstruction activities (roads, colonies, etc.) have been started by WAPDA and which will cost about $8 billion over the period 2010-2016. The World Bank is still shying away from investing further in Pakistan's water resource development as indicated earlier, but has recently shown interest in a hydro-electric project at Dasu (downstream Basha, upstream Tarbela). The storage capacity at Dasu has not yet been established and it is not yet clear whether this is an optimal second largest new storage dam site. However, if a second storage on the Indus is constructed with a further capacity of 6 MAF, this (together with Basha) should add another 12 MAF of usable canal head availability to the Indus River system in flood and normal years, and about 6 MAF of additional capacity to the system in drought years. Again, applying the same numbers of Indus River system availability and use by India according to the IWA, Pakistan after constructing this additional storage of 12 MAF will have available usable canal head availability of about 117 MAF per annum in flood years, 112 MAF in normal years, and about 87 MAF in drought years.

---

[27] "Pakistan Water Economy Running Dry," IBRD 2005 op. cit. pp. 25.

Table-5. Storage Yield Curve for River Indus

Storage MAF	10	15	20	25	30
Additional Yield in MAF/Yr	10	15	20	22	22.5

Source: Numerical data above estimated from Yield Curve for River Indus presented In Pakistan: Water Resources Running Dry 2005, IBRD, p.xiii based on "Study of Water Resources of West Pakistan" (The Lieftinck Report), IBRD 1967.

Yield curves for the Jhelum River are not available. However, the Jhelum River, with its average flows of 15-23 MAF/ annum (compared to the Indus's average flows of 70-100 MAF/annum), currently has about 9 MAF of storage capacity as a result of the recent raising of the Mangla Dam by an additional 30 feet which increased its storage capacity by 2.9 MAF to the 6 MAF of storage capacity already existing. This capacity now appears adequate for managing the current Jhelum River inter-year and multi-year imbalances. However, additional capacity may have to be added to meet the requirements of climate change. Similarly, while yield curves are not available for the Chenab River and there are no mountainous natural storage sites on the plains where the Chenab enters Pakistan, climate change requirements may require in-line and off-line storage in the future (on/off the rivers and canals).

Ground Water Supply Side Prospects

As discussed earlier, Pakistan's groundwater aquifers are diminishing—although not at the furious pace of Indian Punjab. It is imperative that Pakistan's groundwater aquifers be stabilized (i.e., tube-well withdrawals be equivalent to aquifer recharging by irrigation water leaching, rainfall etc.) Table-6 below presents some estimates (dated almost 10 years) which show that IBIS aquifers were generally in balance during normal years, with about 9 MAF/annum of depletion in drought years, with this depletion being confined entirely to Punjab. This situation must inevitably have worsened in the last decade. Qureshi (2009) estimates that groundwater was inaccessible through small tube-wells (operable at less than 20 m water depth) in 5% of Punjab in 2000 and that this figure was expected to increase to 15% in the next decade.[28] Given this situation, it is clear that Pakistan and particularly Punjab, cannot count on any further increase in groundwater extraction. Regulatory controls have been legislated but it has not proved possible to enforce them. Energy pricing policies with no real subsidy on agricultural tube-wells and the fact that 85% of tube-wells run on market-price diesel have naturally dampened the tube-well demand as compared to the Indian Punjab where electricity for tube-wells is free. Pakistan will need to watch its aquifers carefully and take corrective measures if tube-well extraction soars above current levels. On the supply side, however, it needs to be recognized that an addition to water supply for irrigation from groundwater in the IBIS is not practicable and even minor subsidies, if any, on agriculture tube-well electricity should be withdrawn as soon as possible.

Table-6. IBIS Aquifer Balances 2001-02 (MAF)

	Punjab Normal	Punjab Drought	Sind Normal	NWFP Normal	IBIS Normal	IBIS Drought
Aquifer Balance	0	−8.6	0–0.4	−0.4	−9.0	
Tube wells	−30.8	−33.6	−3.5	−1.8	−36.1	−38.9
Abstractions						
Base Flow to	−2.5	−0.4	−1.2	−1.4	−5.1	−3.0

---

[28] "Challenges and Prospects of Sustainable Groundwater Management in the Indus Basin Pakistan," Qureshi et al, op. cit.

	Punjab Normal	Punjab Drought	Sind Normal	NWFP Normal	IBIS Normal	IBIS Drought
Rivers/Subsurfaces Evapo-Transportation Losses	−1.6	−0.8	−13.8	−0.2	−15.6	−14.8
Recharge from Irrigation System	20.6	15.5	15.4	1.9	37.9	32.8
Recharge from Rivers	3.2	0.8	0.3	0.1	3.6	1.2
Return flow from groundwater	4.6	5.1	0.8	0.1	5.5	6.0
Recharge from Rainfall	6.5	4.8	2.0	0.9	9.4	7.7

Source: "Water Sector Issues with a Focus on Groundwater Management: A Policy Perspective," Qureshi S.K. and Hirashima S. in Problems and Politics of Water sharing and Management in Pakistan, Cheema et. al. Editors, Islamabad Policy Research Institute, 2007.

Increasing Water Supply through Reducing Irrigation Water Transmission Losses

IBIS surface water transmission losses are substantial—25% or a normal 25 MAF in the canal system alone.[29] There is another substantial loss in water course transmissions and there are further losses in field application. However, as Table-6 (above) indicates, the IBIS depends in normal years on about 38 MAF of groundwater recharge from the irrigation system. The only savings that are possible are in saline water areas. In Punjab, poor water quality is found in 23% of the area and this number rises to 78% for Sindh.[30] The lining of canals in saline groundwater areas in Sindh and the saline areas of Punjab is likely to make about 5 MAF of additional irrigation water available in Sind and about 5 MAF additional in Punjab. The WAPDA Chairman has recently stated that WAPDA was studying the possibility of lining the Rohri, Dadu, and Rice canals in Sindh, and if this was undertaken, it would allow an additional 492,000 acres of land to be brought under irrigation in Sind.[31] Another area of savings lies in the lining and rehabilitation of water channels. The Planning Commission estimated that 90,000 water courses (out of a total of 135,000 country-wide) could be improved by lining, rehabilitation, etc., thereby saving about 6 MAF.[32] The total Indus water system farm gate availability cumulatively after adding these water transmission loss savings and savings from additional surface storage and abstracting from Indian IWA uses is therefore likely to be almost 133 MAF in flood years, 128 MAF in normal years, and 103 MAF in drought years.

VII. IBIS Demand Management Prospects

Future Requirements of Agriculture Crops

Pakistan is already a great agricultural country producing about 24 million tons of wheat, 7 million tons of rice, 3.6 million tons of maize, 50 million tons of sugarcane, 12 million tons of vegetables, and 7 million tons of fruits in 2008/09, in addition to an assortment of other crops.[33] The country's cultivated area extended

---

[29] "Issues in Water Policy Reforms," Masood Ahmed, op. cit, pp. 79.
[30] "Sustainable Groundwater Management in the Indus Basin, Pakistan," Qureshi et. al. op. cit.
[31] "WAPDA Reviving Irrigation Network," Durrani, S. Dawn, April 15, 2010, pp. 15.
[32] Ten Year Perspective Plan 2001-11, Planning Commission 2001, pp. 283-288.
[33] Agricultural Statistics of Pakistan, 2008-9, p (xi).

over 52 million acres in 2008/09 (of which 90% is part of the IBIS) and crop production was fairly mechanized with all ploughing done by tractors and a sizeable percentage of wheat and rice crops mechanically harvested. Pakistan itself produced about 65,000 tractors per annum.[34] However, yields are low by international standards and particularly in comparison with Indian Punjab. Thus, recent wheat yields are estimated by the World Bank to be 7 tons/ha or 130 mds/acre in the Imperial Valley, USA, 3.8 tons/ha or 62 mds/acre in Bhakra, India, and 1.8 tons/ha or 31 mds/acre in Punjab, Pakistan. The conclusion drawn by the World Bank is that "attention will have to shift from productivity per unit of land to productivity per unit of water."[35] This is an interesting distinction but not very useful in practice since yield/acre may be significantly different because of the use of high yielding varieties of seed, higher use of fertilizers, etc., while still using the same quantities of water. Data from a recent study that examines irrigation water use in Haryana (India) and Punjab (Pakistan) has estimated water use for wheat in Haryana at 2,200 m³/hectare and in Punjab at 2,500 m³/hectare, while for paddy, the estimated water use was 18,900 m³/hectare for Haryana and 16,000 m³/hectare for Punjab (Table-7).[36] Specifically, Pakistan's Punjab uses water 12% less efficiently than India for wheat production and is 18% more efficient in water use for rice production using the traditional definition of water use per acre. However, both Indian Haryana's and Indian Punjab's wheat and rice productivity is higher than that of Pakistan's Punjab.

Table-7. Comparison of Haryana India and Punjab Pakistan (Per Hectare)

	Haryana India	Punjab Pakistan
Wheat		
Total nutrients ([kg N+P2O5+K2O])ha^{-1}	246	174
Estimated irrigation water use ('000m³ha^{-1})	2.2	2.5
Grain yield (ton ha^{-1})	4.2	3.2
Rice		
Total nutrients ([kg N+P2O5+K2O])ha^{-1}	209	139
Estimated irrigation water use ('000m³ha^{-1})	18.9	16.0
Paddy yield (ton ha^{-1})	4.6	3.6

Source: "Comparing water management in rice-wheat production systems in Haryana, India and Punjab Pakistan", Erenstein, Olaf, Agriculture Water Management 96, 2009, p.1803.

The particularly striking difference in average crop productivity between Indian Punjab and Pakistan's Punjab is sometimes argued in part to be due to the availability of free electricity for tube-wells, which, it is estimated, saves the Indian Punjab farmer about $162/hectare/year for solely tube-well irrigated land as compared to solely canal irrigated land[37] or about Rs 7,000/acre/year for each combined crop cycle of wheat plus rice. This saving, it is argued, is used by the Indian Punjab's farmers to purchase additional fertilizer, pesticides, mechanical land-leveling, mechanical planting, and mechanical harvesting, which contribute to doubling the yield in Indian Punjab as compared to Pakistan's Punjab. This may well be the case. In addition, the Indian Punjab farmer may also have access to cheaper fertilizer, more advanced seeds, and a guaranteed and efficient procurement system. However, it is important to learn from the Indian Punjab's experience in increasing yields. This includes using better land and crop management practices. It has also been estimated that the single most important factor in the efficient use of water in Pakistan's Punjab may be

---

[34] Pakistan Statistical Yearbook 2009, pp. 2, 64.
[35] "Pakistan: Water Economy Running Dry 2005," IBRD, pp. 30.
[36] "Comparing Water Management in Rice-Wheat Production Systems in Haryana, India and Punjab Pakistan," Erenstein, O., Agriculture Water Management 96, 2009, pp.1803.
[37] "Challenges and Proposals of Sustainable Groundwater Management in the Indus Basin," Qureshi et. al. op. cit.

land-leveling—resulting in savings of as much as 20-30% compared to unleveled land.[38] Finally, Pakistan should seriously consider shifting away from water-intensive crops such as rice to alternative efficient water-use crops such as vegetable oils (sunflowers, soya bean), maize, and more cotton.

The future IBIS strategy for meeting additional crop/food requirements over the next decades will therefore require the following: (i) doubling or tripling yields by improving land practices and a greater use of hybrid seeds, fertilizers and pesticides; (ii) using water, both surface and ground water, resources more efficiently, preferably by reducing average surface water requirements for crops through land leveling etc. and reducing, if possible, ground water use. A shift in kharif away from rice to more efficient crops is also required. Total water use in terms of canal withdrawals for crop production should be "frozen" at present "normal year" uses, i.e. about 105 MAF and groundwater withdrawals in IBIS should also be "frozen" at present levels of about 50 MAF.

Environmental Use of IBIS System Waters

A source of contention since the IWA has been the fact that, in drought years, there is almost no water downstream of Kotri, causing immense damage to the Indus Delta. In order to get an agreement on the 1990 Inter Provincial Accord, this issue was deliberately left unaddressed to be determined later by "expert studies." Subsequently, studies were commissioned which came up with the following findings: (i) downstream Kotri requirements and recommended associated environmental flows from the Indus were estimated at 3.60 MAF in dry or average years with 25 MAF additional every five years in times of flood, or alternatively, 8.60 MAF as an average for all years to be provided from the overall share;[39] (ii) the recommended environmental flow allocation for the Indus, Chenab, Ravi, Sutlej, and Jhelum to maintain a minimum water depth of 0.5 to 1 meter were 8.25 MAF to be provided from the overall share; (iii) recommended environmental flows allocation for Punjab's lakes, water bodies, and riverine areas, etc., were 6.22 MAF to be provided from Punjab's share; (iv) recommended environmental flows allocation for Sindh's lakes, water bodies, and riverine areas, etc., were 2.53 MAF to be provided from Sindh's share.[40] Table-8 below summarizes the expert consultants' recommendations.

Table-8. IBIS Environmental Flow Requirements

	Dry Year			Average Year			Every 5 years (Flood Year)		
	Total	Rabi	Kharif	Total	Rabi	Kharif	Total	Rabi	Kharif
Downstream Kotri[1] alt[1]				8.60	1.80	6.80			
(alt 2)	(3.60+)	(1.80)	(1.80+)	(3.60+)	(1.80)	(1.8+)	(25.0)	(0.0)	(25.0)
Indus, Jhelum, Chenab, Ravi, Sutlej[2]				8.25	2.25	6.00			
Punjab Inland Water Bodies[2]				6.22	1.82	4.40			
Sind Inland Water Bodies[2]				2.53	0.43	2.10			
Total Average Year Requirement[2]				25.60	6.30	19.30			

Source: 1 "Study on Water Escapes Below Kotri". 2005, op. cit. p.57.
2 "Environmental Concerns of all Four Provinces, 2005, op.cit. p.1.

---

[38] "Water Saving Technologies: Myths and Realities Revealed in Pakistan's Rice Wheat Systems," Ahmad, M.D, et. al., IWMI Research Report 108, 2007, Colombo, Sri Lanka.
[39] Study on Water Escapes Below Kotri to Check Sea Water Intrusion. Final Report. Montgomery Watson Harza et. al., Ministry of Water and Power, Federal Flood Commission, 2005, pp. 56.
[40] Environmental Concerns of all the Four Provinces: Solutions. Executive Summary, AAB, DHV, ITC, DE, LFT Hydraulics, Ministry of Water and Power, Federal Flood Commission, 2005, pp. 1-8.

The recommendations for the use of net additional water from IBIS storage augmentation (12 MAF), lining of canals (10 MAF), and improvement of water courses (6 MAF), or a total of 28 MAF for the next few decades flow almost naturally from the above. In flood years: (i) the equivalent of additional water to be made available from the new storage at Basha on the Indus plus a large portion of the flood should be used to meet downstream Kotri requirements; (ii) part of the additional flood water plus equivalent additional water to the second storage dam on the Indus (Dasu) should be used to meet the environmental requirements of the Indus, Jhelum, Chenab, Ravi, and Sutlej; (iii) the equivalent of the additional waters to be saved from the lining of canals and water courses in Punjab and Sindh together with a part of the flood waters should be used for reviving the wetlands of Punjab and Sindh. In normal years, half the additional water from additional storage and lining of canal in saltwater areas and water course rehabilitation should be used for irrigation flows and the other half for environmental flows (particularly downstream Kotri). In drought years, three quarters of this additional water should be used to augment irrigation water supplies and the remaining amount for environmental flows (again, with special attention to downstream Kotri). It is not clear whether Pakistan is politically and economically ready to make such an environmental commitment to its IBIS waters. Yet this will have to be done, whether by this or subsequent generations, for Pakistan needs to make its rivers, wetlands, and delta alive again so that Pakistan can revert to being the land of the "Five Rivers" with inland navigation (ultimately) from the Indus Delta to the banks of all the five rivers as was historically the case.

Efficiency in the use of IBIS and Ground Water

If additional water to be made available from the IBIS is recommended for use in a substantial part to meet drought and environmental requirements, then the question arises as to how Pakistan will expand its irrigated areas, particularly in northern Punjab (Thal), southern Punjab (Bahawalpur/Cholistan), Sindh (eastern and western banks), and Balochistan. The sensible answer would be to put a restriction on adding any new command areas to the IBIS. Such a restriction is likely to be unenforceable. Therefore, the many important technologies currently available to preserve water, including precision land-leveling, zero tillage, bed and furrow planting, and drip irrigation together with the adoption of high yielding varieties of genetically modified crops (particularly in maize and cotton) will be useful in both saving water and expanding irrigated areas. The only note of caution that needs to be made is that the current drive by international institutions (particularly the World Bank) to reform the institutional arrangements surrounding the IBIS system is well intentioned but should be handled with sense. The newly created provincial irrigation department authorities (PIDAs) proposed by the World Bank is a good idea especially if it enables the replacements of provincial irrigation departments to retain irrigation revenues (currently these go directly to the provincial government accounts) to be used to rehabilitate the provincial irrigation systems. The creation of farmers' organizations (which now cover 20% of the irrigation areas in the IBIS) also proposed by the World Bank to monitor water supplies from the distributaries (the sequence is rivers to branch canals to main canals to distributaries) to the khalas (watercourses) which each command about 500 acres is also a welcome initiative and has led to improved supplies to tail-enders and some controls over water theft. Farmers also need to pay more for their canal waters to control waste in water use and also to maintain and augment the IBIS. They also need to be not charged if they do not use their assigned water entitlements. However, the current elaborate system of irrigation entitlements throughout the IBIS (i.e., 20 minutes/acre/week for field crops, double for fruit orchards) through a defined capacity and regulated outlet that is uniformly administered should not be touched at any cost since this is the bedrock of the system. No attempt should be made to charge the "full opportunity cost of water" or privatize the system as is the current long-term thrust of the World Bank's recommendations. However, cost recovery for adequate maintenance of the irrigation system by the provincial governments is essential and "abiana" or water rates need to be increased to cover these requirements. Large-scale capital investments in the irrigation system will have to be financed by the federal government although it is tempting to think of some cost recovery from investments in the federal government (WAPDA)-owned and operated storages.

VIII. Conclusions on Future IBIS Strategy

The analysis presented above indicates that Pakistan has come a long way in its development of the IBIS. The first two decades, 1950-1970, were occupied by the urgent need to "re-plumb" the entire system by connecting the western rivers to the eastern rivers to meet the consequences of Pakistan's requirements under the IWA. The next two decades (1970-90), with an overlap between 1965 and 1970, were used primarily to stem the menace of water logging and salinity. The decade 1990-2000 was the "lost decade"—focused on institutional issues, which are important but were used as a means to stop major investments by the public sector in the IBIS. The last decade (2000-2010) has been the first where Pakistan has been able to build and modernize the IBIS and this is expected to be followed by several decades of further enhancement of the system. As the system is modernized, however, it is imperative that Pakistan focus on: (i) creating additional surface storage to offset both intra-year variations in the Indus River system and its three- to five-year flood and drought cycle; (ii) surface water preservation particularly by lining canals in saline areas and watercourse improvement; (iii) groundwater conservation and salinity control by discouraging excessive tube-well use; (iv) encouraging general efficiency of irrigation water use through improved land management techniques including land-leveling and also by changing the kharif cropping pattern away from water-intensive rice to sunflower, soya, maize, and more cotton; (v) yield enhancement through improved farming practices, adopting hybrid seeds, and increased fertilizer and pesticide use; and (vi) fully meeting the environmental concerns of the Indus Delta, river systems, and wetlands. This, together with a clear vision that the IBIS will be publically owned and operated but with sensible institutional reform (including the increased price of canal waters) which would increase water use efficiency without destabilizing the entire system of existing irrigation entitlements, is the recommended strategy for the future.

References

Ahmad, M.D, Turral, H., Masih, I., Giordano, M. and Masood, Z., (2007). Water Saving Technologies: Myths and Realities Revealed in Pakistan's Rice Wheat Systems, IWMI Research Report 108, Colombo, Sri Lanka.

Ahmed, M. (1999). Issues in Water Policy Reforms, The Politics of Managing Water. Edited by Bengali K, Oxford University Press.

Briscoe, J. (2010). War or Peace on the Indus. The News. April 3, 2010.

Durrani, S. (2010). Wapda Reviving Irrigation Network, Dawn, April 15, 2010.

Earth Institute, Columbia University (2010). Concept Note on Water Security in Punjab, India Current Scenario, /Water Columbia /edu/..../India.

Erenstein, O. (2009). Comparing Water Management in Rice Wheat Production Systems in Haryana, India and Punjab Pakistan, Agriculture Water Management, 96.

Federal Flood Commission (2005). Environmental Concerns of all the Four Provinces: Solutions, Executive Summary.

Government of Pakistan (1960). Indus Water Accord (1960).

Government of Pakistan (2009). Pakistan Statistical Year Book.

Government of Pakistan. (2009). Agricultural Statistics of Pakistan (2008-09).

IBRD (2005). Pakistan Water Economy Running Dry.

Jeevendas A., Singh R.P., and Rumer, B. (2008). Concerns of Groundwater Depletion and Irrigation: Efficiency in Punjab Agriculture – A Micro-Level Study, Agriculture Economics Research Review, 21.

Kazi, A. (1999). Analysis of Water Accords in Politics of Managing Water. Oxford University Press.

Lieftinck Report, IBRD (1967). Study of the Water Resources of West Pakistan, II.

Montgomery Watson Harza et al. (2005). Study on Water Escapes below Kotri to Check Sea Water Intrusion. Final Report, Federal Flood Commission.

Planning Commission, Government of Pakistan, (2001). Ten Year Perspective Plan 2001-11.

Planning Commission, Government of Pakistan. (2002). Annual Review (2001-2) of the Ten year Perspective Plan 2001-11 and Three Year Development Program 2002-05.

Qureshi A.S et al, (2009). Challenges and Prospects of Sustainable Ground Water Management in the Indus Basin, Pakistan. Water Resources Management Journal.

Qureshi A.S. et al. (2008). Managing Salinity and Water Logging in Pakistan. Agriculture Water Management Journal.

Qureshi S.K. and Hirashima S. (2007). Water Sector Issues with a Focus on Groundwater Management: A Policy Perspective in Problems and Politics of Water Sharing and Management in Pakistan. Islamabad Policy Research Institute.

Revelle, H., Falcon et al. (1664). Report on Land and Water Development in the Indus Plain. The White House.

WAPDA (2004). Water Resources and Hydro-Power Development Vision 2025.

CHAPTER – 20

Sustaining Energy And Food Security In Trans-Boundary River System: Case Of Indus Basin

Professors: F.A Shaheen, M. H.Wani, S.A Saraf

Sher-e-Kashmir University of Agricultural Sciences and Technology of Kashmir (Srinagar)

Introduction

Growing scarcity of water resources, increasing population and poor water management in developing countries have resulted in an increasing demand for water resources. The increasing scarcity of water leads to the desire for control of water resources, which in turn becomes a ground for breeding conflicts. These conflicts are manifested at interstate and intra-state levels. The conflicts over the use of water between the states become more severe when they are typically agrarian based economies. However, the scarcity of water resources in some cases has been instrumental in developing cooperation among states. The Indus Waters Treaty (1960) between India and Pakistan is one of the few examples in South Asia, of the settlement of a major, international river basin conflict.

At the time of independence (1947), the boundary line between the two newly created independent countries i.e. India and Pakistan was drawn right across the Indus Basin, leaving Pakistan as the lower riparian. Moreover, two important irrigation head works, one at Madhopur on Ravi river and the other at Ferozepur on Sutlej river, on which the irrigation canal supplies in Pakistan Punjab had been completely dependent, were left in the Indian territory. A dispute thus arose between the two countries regarding the utilization of irrigation water from existing facilities. Negotiations held under the good offices of the International Bank for Reconstruction and Development (the World Bank), culminated in the signing of Indus Waters Treaty in 1960. The Treaty fixed and delimited the rights and obligations of India and Pakistan in relation to each other, concerning the use of the waters of the Indus System of Rivers.

The Indus international river basin is the largest, contiguous irrigation system in the world, with a command area of about 20 million hectares and an annual irrigation capacity of over 12 million hectares. The Indus system of rivers comprises three eastern rivers (Sutlej, Beas and Ravi) and three western rivers (Indus, Jhelum and Chenab). Under the Indus Waters Treaty, the waters of the eastern rivers stand allocated to India and those of western rivers largely to Pakistan. The treaty which was carried out in the best interest of the nation has, however, deprived the Jammu and Kashmir (J&K) state to use its own water resources and thereby severely affected the development process of the state.

IWT Vs a Vs J&K state

The recent Punjab Termination of Agreement 2004 cancelled all the agreements of water sharing by which the entire nation was shocked and the Prime Minister had to intervene. And when it comes to the J&K state, nobody cares for this forgotten land. he state government also does not appear to be conscious of its water related issues. The fact is that the controversy over the Sutlej Yamuna Link, popularly called SYL, has for once afforded the J&K a rare opportunity to introspect the grave injustices the state has suffered in terms of its rights over the use of waters from its own rivers. If Punjab could unilaterally terminate its agreement with Harayana and Rajasthan over the sharing of waters from Ravi and Beas and thus, in a way, focus the attention of the whole country on its water problems, why Jammu and Kashmir, with a far more genuine grievance, has never been able to make it an issue. More so, when doing so had far lesser chances of inviting the accusations of politicization of water as in the case of Punjab. At the same time, there was little chance of its opposition within the state itself and that too among the three regions of the state (Jammu, Ladakh and Kashmir) which otherwise find little common ground on most of the issues.

Besides, if Punjab could do it for the agricultural requirements of its farmers in the southern districts of the state, why J&K has accepted, even though grudgingly, the unenviable state of affairs when the Indus Waters Treaty puts the state behind by an estimated Rs 6500 crore annually. The losses are not there in the agricultural sector only but on a much higher scale in the generation of hydropower which has an otherwise legendary estimated potential of 20,000 MW.

Over the years, the fallout has been debilitating for the state's economy. The treaty, while giving exclusive rights to Punjab over the use of waters from the eastern rivers of the Indus system, Ravi, Beas and Satluj, for power generation and irrigation purposes, has permanently restricted the scope of Jammu and Kashmir in the case of western rivers, Indus, Jhelum and Chenab, flowing through its territory. The state's rightful riparian rights have been snatched in the so-called national interest and to benefit Punjab and that, too, without the state being consulted at the time of the signing of the treaty or even compensated for the consequent consistent loss.

Under the treaty, the J&K can use only limited waters of the Indus, Chenab and Jhelum for power generation and lift irrigation. It can't build reservoirs or dams on these rivers to store water for irrigation and power without the prior approval of Pakistan. Nor can it construct any barrage for irrigation. The treaty imposes the limits on the storage capacity that the state can create. That is, it can only store 0.40 million acre feet (MAF) on Indus in Ladakh, 1.50 MAF on Jhelum in Kashmir and 1.70 MAF on Chenab in Jammu.

Table 1. Average annual flow of the rivers of Indus system

Eastern Rivers	Western Rivers	Total
41 BCM (33 MAF)	166 BCM (135 MAF)	207 BCM (168 MAF)

Source: IWT draft

Table 2. Agricultural use permitted to India from western rivers

Name of river	The Indus	The Jhelum	The Chenab	Total
Irrigated Cropped Area (ICA) in acres	70,000	4,00,000	2,31,000	7,01,000

Source: IWT draft

Table 3. Storage permitted to India on Western rivers

	River System	Conservation Storage Capacity		Flood Storage Capacity (MAF)
		General Storage Capacity (MAF)	Power Storage Capacity (MAF)	
1	The Indus	0.25	0.15	Nil
2	The Jhelum (excluding the Jhelum main)	0.50	0.25	0.75
3	The Jhelum Main	Nil	Nil	As provided in Paragraph 9 of Annexure E to the Treaty
4	The Chenab (excluding the Chenab Main)	0.50	0.60	Nil
5	The Chenab Main	Nil	0.60	Nil

Source: IWT draft

The state's agricultural potential has also been worst hit. While in 1950-51, the state could irrigate 1.56 lakh hectares under rice cultivation, today after more than half a century, the irrigation potential has risen by an unremarkable 74 thousand hectare to 2.20 lakh hectares. Similarly, the irrigation for the area under other crops which was about 0.07 hectare in 1950-51 has come down to 0.01 hectare. There has been only a marginal increase in the irrigateion infrastructure. In 1950-51, the state could irrigate 244 thousand hectare through canals, 3000 hectare by tanks and 3000 tube wells and 11,000 hectares by other sources. But in 2000-01, the state irrigated only 284.25 thousand hectare by canals, 2.57 thousand by tanks, 1.42 thousand by wells and 17.73 thousand hectares by other sources. As a result, the state has now a rationed population of 86.14 lakh people dependant on the supply by the consumer affairs and public distribution department which procuress the rice from outside the state. Besides this, a good percentage of the population also purchases rice from private dealers, which forms the staple food of the region.

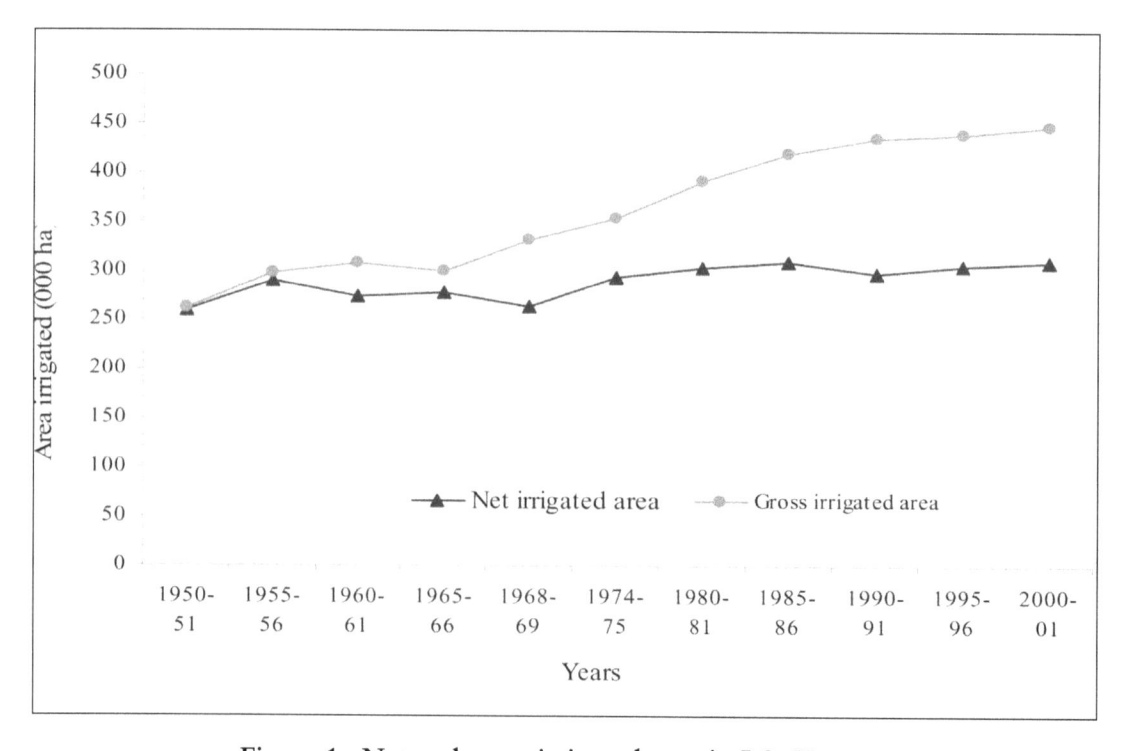

Figure 1. Net and gross irrigated area in J & K state.

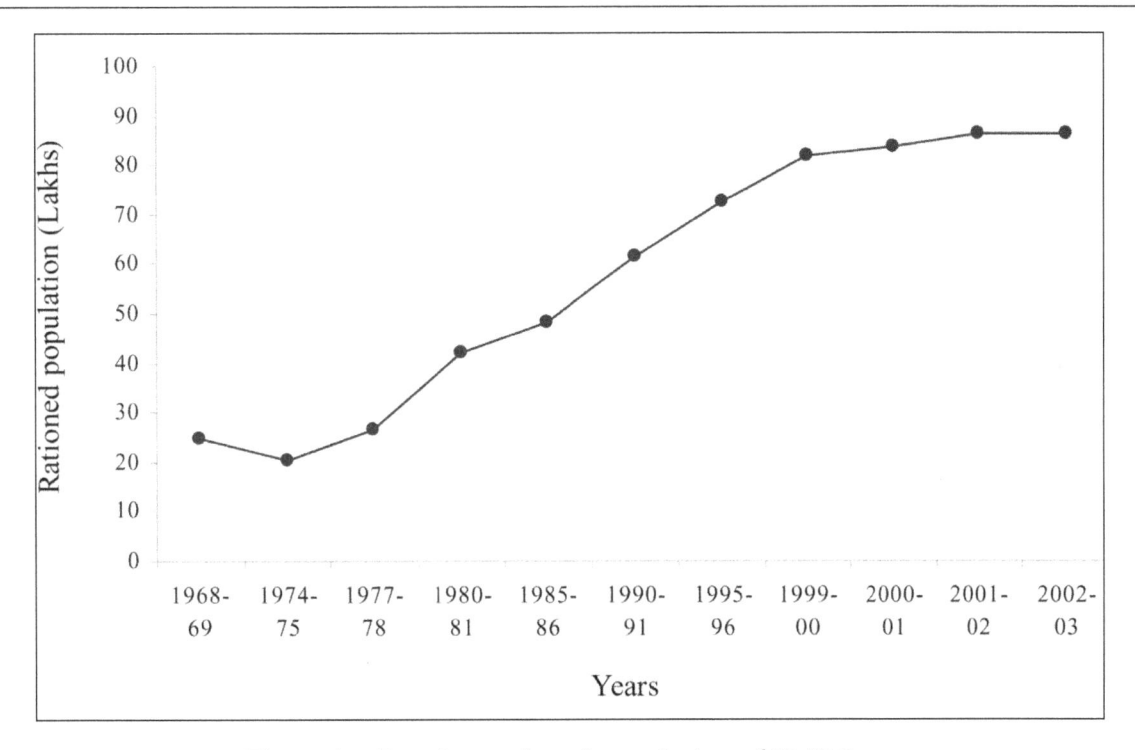

Figure 2. Growing rationed population of J&K State

The J&K, according to an estimate, could have increased its area under irrigation by one lakh acres had the state had the freedom to harness its available water resources. In the case of valley, only 0.5 MAF could be stored under general storage on Jhelum basin and that too not directly on the waters of river but on various streams that form its tributaries. And for every new irrigation scheme, the state has to seek permission from the Indus Commission. The Irrigation and Flood Control Department of the state has proposed 12 new irrigation schemes for Baramulla, Kupwara, Anantnag and Budgam districts on the various streams which are pending approval.

Table 4. Maximum permissible limit for irrigation on Western rivers as per IWT

Basin	ICA as on the effective date (1-4-1960) (Acre)	Additional ICA permissible (Acre)	Net ICA permissible (Acre)	Total ICA achieved in 1999-2000 (Acre)
Indus	42,179	70,000	1,12,179	50,949
Jhelum	5,17,909	1,50,000	6,67,909	6,39,177
Chenab	82,389	50,000	1,32,389	1,15,745
Total			9,12,477	8,05,745

Source: IWT draft

As such the productivity of the agriculture is predominantly at the mercy of rain gods. The fragility of agriculture in the state could be gauged from the fact that a spell of dryness wreaks havoc with the production. For instance, the yield of saffron, the major and exclusive cash crop of the state, that was 2.8 to 3 kg per hectare in early nineties dipped to as low as 500 gm over the past five years. Due to the consequent non-availability of the commodity, it was the cheaper Iranian saffron which claimed the market. Besides, the absence of precipitation also brought pests and diseases to the cultivated fields. As a result, the government has had to shell out Rs 40 crore a month to make purchases under the public distribution system from the Food Corporation of India (FCI). The food-grain import graph of J&K state shows a sharp increase in the overall imports.

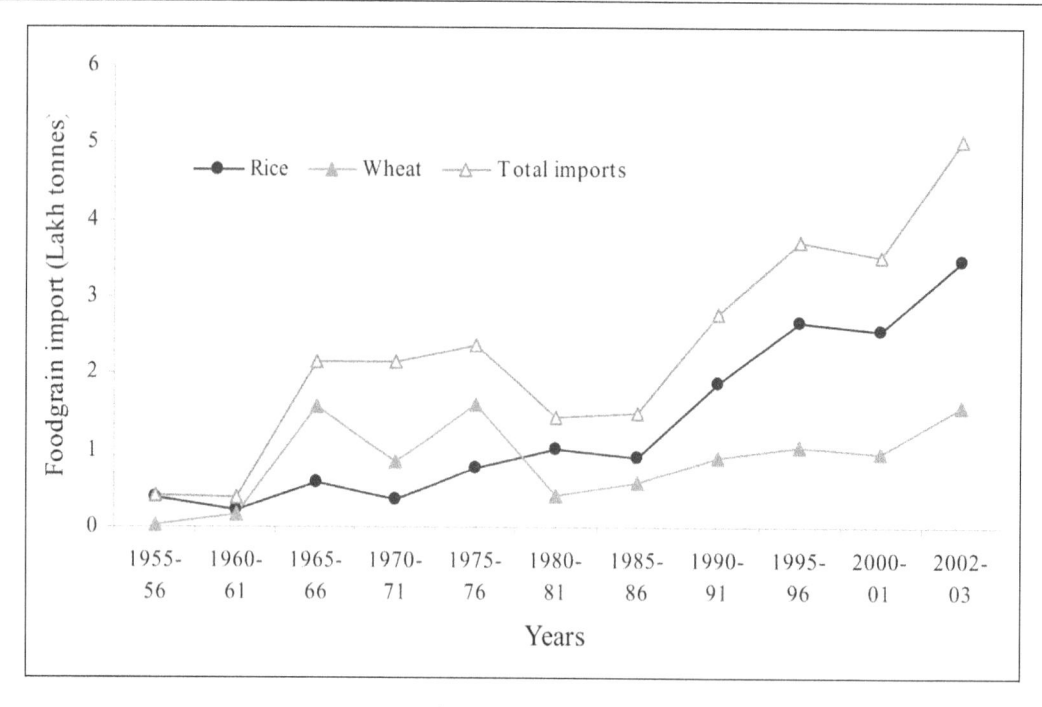

Figure 3. Food-grain imports by J&K state

The existing canal network is very limited in its extent and dates back to the pre-treaty period. This has, in a way, permanently stunted the growth of agriculture and made the J&K dependant on food imports – rice being the major commodity – from other states, particularly Punjab. Interestingly, the productivity level of paddy, at about 40 quintals per hectare in the Kashmir valley, is the highest in the country.

With agricultural land area remaining fixed and not growing due to lack of irrigation, there has also been a steady reduction in the size of landholdings since the time Big Landed Estates Abolition Act was enacted in 1949-50. The Act was a radical land redistribution measure which abolished as many as nine *Jagirs* and *Muafis* and gave these into the ownership of tenants and landless.

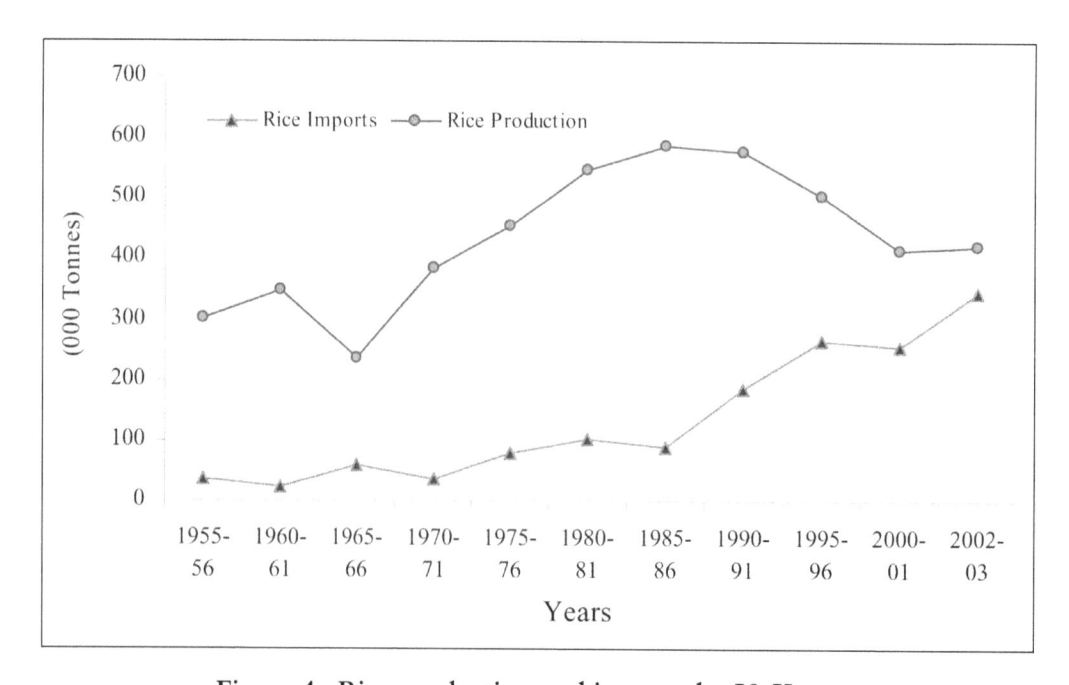

Figure 4. Rice production and imports by J&K state

However, most arable land today is economically unviable. The average size of land holdings has dwindled from 1.7 hectares in 1950 to 0.5 hectares in 1997-98. Almost ninety per cent of arable land, according to a survey, constitutes marginal and sub-marginal holdings. This has reduced the productivity from agriculture to a mere subsistence level.

The existing cultivable land is being further shrunk by the ongoing construction boom in the valley. In the past decade alone, Srinagar has witnessed the growth of as many as five new residential colonies, almost all on what was previously the prime agricultural land dominated by paddy cultivation. Likewise, a similar trend is observed on the conversion of paddy lands into housing colonies and apple orchards in towns and rural areas, respectively.

Being a state with a dearth of plain agricultural land, the state would be enormously benefited by a proper irrigation infrastructure as it would help bring large acres of *Karewa* land (highlands specific to the uneven terrains like that of J&K) across the countryside under cultivation. This has, over the years, given rise to groundswell against the "unjust treaty" which, on the one hand, has made Punjab prosperous by letting the state use freely the water of its rivers for irrigation and power production, has, on the other hand, stagnated these very sectors of J&K. What is regarded as more galling is that though New Delhi did duly compensate Pakistan for the loss of pre-partition canal network of central Bari Doab and Dipalpur, the J&K received nothing. The Nehru dispensation gave a financial aid of Rs 83.3 crore to Pakistan to undertake development works like building storage reservoirs, link canals, tube wells, drainage and hydroelectric installations. Pakistan, in addition, received over Rs 300 crore at the time from the United States, Britian, West Germany, Australia, Canada, New Zealand and the World Bank as aid for the same.

An other way to compensate the J&K state for the losses could be a favorable sharing ratio from the power generated from the centrally funded projects in the state. However, so far the approach of New Delhi on the score has not been encouraging. For example, in case of Salal Project, the experts assert, the central government has recovered its capital cost way back in 1982 but the power sharing continues to be on the existing ratio. That is, the J&K gets a royalty of only 12 per cent from the project which is the same as in case of Uri-Power project. This is despite the fact that against the capital investment of central government, the state has provided the all important water and land resources for the projects. Moreover, in the case of Salal project, one of the provisions agreed upon is that when the capital cost of the project has been recovered, it will be handed over to the state.

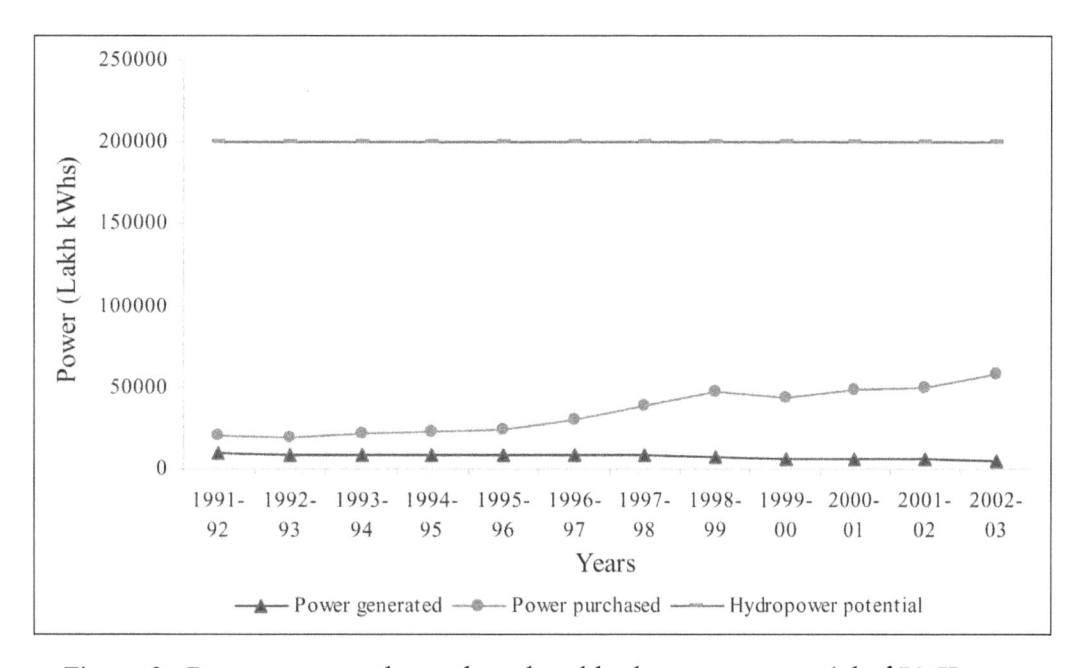

Figure 2. Power generated, purchased and hydropower potential of J&K state

So, there is a case for the transfer of centrally funded power projects, not only on the principle of complete recovery of capital investment but more so as a compensation for the losses incurred by the state as a result of the IWT.

Wullar Barrage Issue

Jammu and Kashmir's attempt to use the water of Wullar Lake for irrigation by building the Tulbul Navigation project, also called Wullar Barrage, soon after the signing of the treaty was frustrated. As a result, the project is stuck up for the past thirty years. The project, according to experts, would in no way have caused damage to Islamabad but, on the contrary, helped regulate the water storage system in Mangla dam. On the other hand, the project would have benefited agriculture in J&K besides stabilizing power generation from the 450 MW Uri project which otherwise slumps to as low as under 100 MW in winter. India and Pakistan are once again discussing a fresh Wullar Barrage or Tulbal Navigation Lock Project. The project on which construction had started in 1980, now stands locked and virtually destroyed. Nothing exists on the ground barring a few shallow waterways and the skeleton of a two storey building. The project was estimated to cost Rs 30 crore, but has already devoured Rs 36 crore.

It was in 1912 that the then Punjab government had approached the Maharaja of Kashmir, seeking permission to construct a major barrage on Wullar Lake. In 1924, the Punjab government renewed the proposal, offering a yearly sum of Rs 1.85 lakh as royalty. The princely state, however, rejected the proposal, apprehending that it might to lead water logging of most of north Kashmir, particularly Sopore and Baramulla.

In 1980, the project was revived and work started at Tulbal, a village at the western tip of Sopore town. However, after a visit by Pakistan Indus Waster Commission authorities, the project was relocated at Ningli, at the eastern tip of Sopore town nearer the Wullar Lake — the site where the river Jhelum outflows from the Wullar Lake. To date, eight rounds of talks have been held on this issue. The two sides almost reached an agreement in October 1991, whereby India would keep 6.2 metres of barrage ungated with a crest level of 1,574.90 metre (5,167 ft), and would forgo the storage capacity of 300,000 acre feet. In return, the water level in the barrage would be allowed to rise to the full operational level of 5,177.90 ft. However, in February 1992, Pakistan added another condition that India should not construct the Kishanganga (390 MW) hydro-power generating unit which India refused to accept and the negotiations were stalled. Till date, nine rounds of talks have been held between the two nations on the Wullar Barrage but no major breakthrough was achieved.

According to the Indian Government, the purpose of the Wullar Barrage was to construct a control structure, with a view to improving the navigation in the River Jhelum during winters, in order to connect Srinagar with Baramula1 for the transportation of fruits and timber as well as to maintain water supply during lean periods for hydropower generation from existing plants and future units proposed downstream. Furthermore, the project would serve to restore the lake ecology. The power generation from the plants banked on the waters of river Jhelum (the Uri-I, Mohra and Lower Jhelum Hydel projects) falls to a mere 30 to 40 MW during four months of winter against their installed capacity of 515 MW. In the autumn, the daily generation from the projects does not exceed 100 to 150 MW. Similarly, the Salal project on river Chenab, which has an installed capacity of 600 MW, has not been able to generate power to its optimum capacity for six months resulting in a rapid fall in the generation thereby affecting drastically the power availability. The state government has to bank on more power imports from the Northern Grid and till date the arrears have touched over Rs 1600 crore. And whenever the state is in a position to meet at least 80 per cent of the demand during the spring season, when the rivers remain gushing, it exports power to reduce the size of the arrears. This question has assumed significance following enormous difficulties being faced by one crore people and several thousand industrialists in the state owing to the acute electricity crisis. The power shortage has been an old phenomenon, but during the past four years, the state government has been forced to resort to 11 to 14 hours power shedding.

India claims that 90 percent of the Wullar Barrage project would be beneficial to Pakistan, as it would regulate the supply to Mangla Dam, which would increase Pakistan's capacity of power generation at Mangla, as well as regulate the irrigation network in the Pakistan Punjab through the triple canal system[2]. India further suggested that Pakistan should bear the greater share of constructing the Barrage, as it would be more beneficial to Pakistan, and would be especially effective in reducing the flow of water during the flood season.

Pakistan, on the other hand, argues that India had violated Article I (11) of the Indus Waters Treaty, which prohibits both parties from undertaking any 'man-made obstruction' that may cause 'change in the volume of the daily flow of waters'. Further that, Article III (4) specifically barred India, from 'storing any water of, or construct any storage works on, the Western Rivers'. According to sub-paragraph 8(h) of the Indus Waters Treaty, India is entitled to construct an 'incidental storage work' on the Western rivers on its side:

a. only after the design has been scrutinized and approved by Pakistan, and

b. its storage capacity should not exceed 10,000 acres feet of water.

Whereas, the Wular Barrage's capacity is 300,000 acres feet, which is thirty times more than the permitted capacity. Regarding the building of a hydroelectric plant, according to the treaty, India is only allowed to construct a small run-off water plant with a maximum discharge of 300 cusecs through the turbines which is insufficient to generate 960 Megawatts of electricity as planned by India.

Bilateral Negotiations

Pakistan referred the Wullar Barrage case to the Indus Waters commission in 1986, which, in 1987, recorded its failure to resolve it. When India suspended the construction work, Pakistan did not take the case in the International Arbitral Court. To date, eight rounds of talks have been held. In 1989, Pakistan agreed to build a barrage conditional to Pakistan's inspection, which India rejected. The two sides almost reached an agreement in October 1991, whereby India would keep 6.2 meters of the barrage ungated with a crest level of 1574.90m (5167 ft), and would forego the storage capacity of 300,000 acre feet. In return, the water level in the Barrage would be allowed to attain the full operational level of 5177.90 ft. However, in February 1992, Pakistan added another condition that India should not construct the Kishenganga (390 MW) hydropower-generating unit. India refused to accept this condition. According to Pakistan, the Kishenganga project on River Neelam affected its own Neelam-Jhelum power-generating project, located in its Punjab province[3]. The issue of Wullar Barrage was one of the disputes on the agenda highlighted for the Indo-Pak talks, both at the Lahore meeting in February 1999, and at the Agra Summit of July 2001.

Pakistan's apprehensions over Wullar Barrage

The control of the River Jhelum by India through a storage work would mean:

- a serious threat to Pakistan should India decide to withhold the water over an extended period, especially during the dry season. It would also multiply and magnify the risks of floods and droughts in Pakistan. The Mangla Dam on River Jhelum, which is a source of irrigation and electricity for Punjab, would be adversely affected.

- a strategic edge India, during a military confrontation, enabling it to control the mobility and retreat of Pakistani troops and enhancing the maneuverability of Indian troops. Closing the Barrage gates would render the Pakistani canal system dry and easy to cross. During the 1965 war, the Indian Army failed to cross the BRB Link Canal, due to its full swing flow. India is already in control of the Chenab River through the Salal Dam constructed in 1976. Many Pakistanis criticise the conceding of the Salal Dam to India.

Present scenario and future confrontations

While the new found bonhomie between India and Pakistan has successfully put the political issues on the backburner, the fight on water rights is set to become acute in the coming years in its gravity. It might even surpass the political disputes between the two neighbors. The main reason for this is growing industrialization in both countries, coupled with depleting water levels and mounting power scarcities.

According to a study report on water and security in the South Asian region, "the water situation in Pakistan is already serious, when compared with other South Asian countries. Although until recently, the Indus Waters Tready allowed both India and Pakistan to act independently in safeguarding issues concerning their water security, they cannot continue to do so in future. This is because Pakistan is already a water-stressed country and requires utilising the full potential of the Indus river system in an integrated basin approach. This cannot take place without further co-operation between India and Pakistan. It is, therefore, necessary to think ahead and conceptualise a follow-up agreement to the 1960 Indus Waters Treaty. One can, for example, envisage storage on the upper Indus, Jhelum and Chenab, over and above what is presently permitted under the current Treaty. Due to the hostility between the two countries, the idea may appear remote at the present time. But the very exercise of looking ahead would reveal the opportunity costs of non-cooperation and confrontation [4]."

During the recent secretary level talks in Islamabad between India and Pakistan on the controversial Wullar Barrage or Tulbal navigation project, political leaders from Pakistan Punjab province have demanded that the government should buy water from India to meet the requirements of the province. They also demanded that the government should scrap the 1960 Indus Waters Treaty. On the other side, there is a growing consensus among the political parties of the J&K state, particularly the National Conference and the People's Democratic Party, to either scrap or abrogate the Indus Waters Treaty as it has, over the period, sounded a death knelt he to the state's economy and is the main impediment to development. During a recent state assembly session, ruling People's Democratic Party (PDP) held a convention and passed a resolution demanding setting up the barrage and sought compensation from the Centre for the losses it suffered by the Indus Waters Treaty. The PDP president also lashed out at Pakistan in the state assembly session for strangulating the Kashmiris by sticking to the Indus Waters treaty which has taken a heavy toll on the J&K's economy. She also asked the Centre to compensate for the losses it suffered due to the treaty.

While Pakistan plans to go ahead with a Hydel project in the Pakistan-occupied Kashmir (PoK), besides starting the construction of the multi billion dollar Kalabagh dam and increasing the height of the Mangla dam, India plans to construct at least 35 power plants over the next decade on the Indus basin. All these factors have led to an increasing desire to do away with the Indus Waters Treaty (IWT) that has distributed six rivers in the Indus basin between India and Pakistan, with the latter getting the three western rivers, Indus, Jhelum and Chenab, and India retained rights to the three eastern rivers, Ravi, Beas and Sutlej.

The Baghliar and Wullar Barrage issues currently being discussed at the expert level are, therefore, just a tip of the iceberg. Islamabad fears the dam could interfere with the flow of water from the Chenab river and deprive it of vital irrigation in Pakistan's wheat growing Punjab province; however, New Delhi says the fears are groundless. The first phase of the Baghliar dam was due to be completed in 2004 but has been delayed by the dispute. Pakistan has now plans to approach the World Bank for the appointment of neutral expert to resolve the Baghliar hydro-electric project issue as it does not conform to the Indus Waters Treaty due to various reasons like design and height of dam. So far, various government agencies in India have identified 25 medium projects, ranging from a one megawatt project in Puga in Leh to a 200 MW project in Naiaguh in Doda district, to be taken up for construction in the coming years. In addition, 10 power projects have been either finalized or are under various stages of construction, including the Bursar project, with an installed capacity of 1020 MW and a dam height of 252 metres.

Recently, the Central Electric Authority (CEA) also gave technical clearance to the controversial 330 MW Kishanganga hydroelectric project and the work has started. According to sources, India is in a hurry to execute the project as Pakistan is also planning to construct a 969 MW hydropower plant worth US$ 1.5 billion downstream on the Kishanganga (known as Neelam in PoK) river across the Line of Control (LoC). Pakistan is also seeking political consensus to build other mega dams. According to IWT, the projects already constructed or in stages of construction shall not be disturbed by the other country. Therefore, India will be bound to release water for the Pakistan projects if they start construction ahead of the Indian ventures.

The Kishanganga project has been stalled since 1996 due to objections filed by the Ministry of Defence and the environmentalists and a lack of funds. Currently, the Kishanganga (Neelam) and Jhelum join each other at Muzaffarabad, the capital of PoK. Through the proposed Wullar Barrage project, India plans to maintain a constant water flow in the Jhelum all the year round. The total distance by which the river will be diverted is around 100 km.

Rejecting Pakistan's opposition to the project, the Indian officials say that as per the IWT, India has been allowed to build a specified storage limited to 3.6 million acre feet (MAF) on the western rivers. They explain that the anuual water flow in the western rivers of the Indus, Jhelum and Chenab have been estimated at 135.6 MAF. Discounting that the proposed Kishanganga project will affect the river Neelam's flow, the officials believe that the stream will be maintained at any cost to Pakistan, since these rivers have been allocated to that country. "We are only diverting the Kishanganga (Neelam) to join the Jhelum at Bandipore near the Wullar lake rather in Muzaffarabad [5]", an official said, adding that the water will ultimately reach Pakistan through the river Jhelum, though not in the shape of the Neelam river.

Conclusion

With water sharing promising to be the new international quarrel area of the 21st century, India and Pakistan have already got a readymade point of friction. Due to growing population, industrial growth and mounting water problems accompanied by an overall fall in the waters of the Indus basin due to climatic change, there is a need for the revision of the old treaty, particularly looking to the current political and economic situation in the Jammu and Kashmir state, which calls for a major review of the Indus Waters Treaty, 1960. The time has come for a fresh look on all the water sharing issues between the two nations for the common benefit and put behind bars all the political issues and do justice to each and every area / region of the Indus basin in terms of its equity in the water resources of the Indus basin. The principle of sharing the costs and benefits of the whole Indus system of rivers may be envisaged rather than a simple division of rivers.

1. India claims to have devised the project to solve the problem of navigation over a distance of 22 km between Lake Wularand Baramula.

2. The triple canal system consists of the Upper Jhelum canal, the Upper Chenab canal and the lower Bari Doab canal.

3. Mallika Joseph, 'Delhi round of Indo-Pak talks-ll; Tulbul navigation project/Wular Barrage', www.ipcs.org/issues/ articles/162-ip-mallika.htm.

4. Study report on "Water and security in South Asian Region", by Carnegie Corporation of Advanced International Studies, Washington, www.expressindia.com/budqet04/index.phD.

5. Kishenganga controversy, News article in 'Greater Kashmir', page 7, dated: 5-07- 04.

References

Jagat Mehta, The Indus Waters Treaty, A case Study in the Resolution of an International River Basin Conflict, National Resources Forum, Vol. 12(1), February 1988. pp. 69-77.

Parul Chandra, The Indus Treaty may be abrogated? The Times of India, December 26, 2001.

Pitman, G.T.Keith. The Role of the World Bank in Enhancing Co-operation and Resolving Conflict on International Watercourses: The Case of the Indus Basin, in Salman M.A. Salman & Laurence Boisson de Chazournes, eds., International Watercourses: Enhancing Co-operation and Managing Conflict, World Bank Technical Paper No. 414, Washington DC, 1998.

Statistical Digest (2003), Directorate of Economics and Statistics, Planning and Development Department, Jammu and Kashmir State.

Syed Naseer A. Gillani & Mohammed Azam, Indus River: Past, Present and Future, in Aly M. Shady & others eds., Management and Development of Major Rivers, Calcutta: Oxford University Press, 1996.

Farzana Noshab and Nadia Mushtaq, Water Disputes in South Asia, Institute of Strategic Studies, Islamabad, 2002.

CHAPTER - 21

The Baglihar Difference And Its Resolution Process - A Triumph For The Indus Waters Treaty?

Salman M. A. Salman*.

Abstract

On January 15, 2005, Pakistan approached the World Bank, asking the Bank to appoint a Neutral Expert to address a "difference" which had arisen with India under the Indus Waters Treaty. The difference related to the Baglihar hydropower plant which was under construction by India. The Bank appointed a Neutral Expert four months later, following lengthy exchanges with the two parties. On February 12, 2007, about 20 months after his appointment, the Neutral Expert issued his decision on the difference. This article reviews the main provisions of the Treaty, examines the process for the appointment and for the decision of the Neutral Expert, and analyzes the decision.

Keywords: Baglihar difference; Indus Waters Treaty; International Centre for Settlement of Investment Disputes; Neutral Expert; The World Bank

1. Introduction: The Indus Waters Treaty

The Indus Waters Treaty, concluded between India and Pakistan in 1960, has a number of unique features. First, rather than dividing the waters of the Indus river system between the two parties, the Treaty divided the six rivers comprising the Indus river system between them. India has been allocated the Eastern rivers (the Sutlej, the Beas and the Ravi), and Pakistan the Western rivers (the Indus, the Jhelum and the Chenab). The initial proposal of the World Bank to have the Indus irrigation scheme administered as one unit by the two parties, irrespective of the new borders drawn as a result of the partitioning of the sub-continent, was turned down by both parties, after a short period of discussion. Similarly, the attempts of the two parties and the Bank to divide the waters of the rivers, rather than the rivers themselves, failed to produce an acceptable formula. After repeated attempts, this approach was also abandoned. The only solution which emerged as viable was the division of the six rivers between the two parties, in addition to assisting Pakistan in the construction of storage reservoirs to make its overall share of water close to the share it had before the rivers were divided (Salman, 2003).

However, despite the specific allocation of the rivers between India and Pakistan, each country has been allowed certain uses in the rivers allocated to the other, subject to certain qualifications. Those uses are detailed in separate annexures to the Treaty. Annexure B deals with the agricultural use by Pakistan from certain tributaries of the Ravi river which has been allocated to India, while Annexure C deals with the agricultural use by India from the Western rivers allocated to Pakistan. Moreover, Annexure D deals with the

---

* Lead Counsel, Legal Vice Presidency, The World Bank, 8448 Clover Leaf Drive, McLean, VA, 22102, USA.

generation of hydro-electric power by India from the Western rivers, while Annexure E deals with the storage of waters by India on the Western rivers. The use by India of the waters of the Western rivers which have been allocated to Pakistan was one of the major issues raised during negotiations of the Treaty in the 1950s. India felt that, as the upper riparian of the Indus river system which runs for large stretches in its territory before entering Pakistan, there would have to be some uses allowed to it. After lengthy and complex negotiations, agreement was reached on some qualified uses for agriculture, hydropower and storage, as discussed above (Salman & Uprety, 2002).

A second unique feature of the Treaty is that it is the only international water treaty co-signed by a third party. This third party is the World Bank, which mediated the original dispute over the Indus basin, and assisted the two parties in reaching an agreement. The process, which led to the conclusion of the Treaty, took almost nine years of intensive negotiations and mediation by the Bank. The result was a lengthy and complex instrument of close to 150 pages. This instrument addresses the various pertinent issues in a general way in 12 articles in the main part of the Treaty, and in a very detailed manner in eight annexures to the Treaty. Some of the annexures have appendices attached thereto.

The World Bank signed the Treaty for certain specified purposes, namely, Articles V and X, and Annexures F, G and H. Article V "Financial Provisions" deals with India's contribution to Pakistan of Pounds Sterling 62,060,000 for the replacement works which Pakistan would construct as a result of the allocation of the Eastern rivers to India, and the termination of Pakistan's water rights on those rivers. The Indian contribution was made to the World Bank in ten equal annual installments, and credited to the Indus Basin Development Fund. Article V also deals with the Bank responsibilities to manage the Indus Basin Development Fund. The Fund consisted of close to 800 million dollars, mostly grant funding from a number of donors, the World Bank loans, in addition to the Indian contribution (Michel, 1967). The Fund was used to finance the replacement works which Pakistan needed to end its reliance on the Eastern rivers, and to augment the flow of the Western rivers. Such works included, inter alia, eight link canals nearly 400 miles long for transferring water from the Western rivers to the areas formerly irrigated from the Eastern rivers; two storage dams, the Tarbela on the Indus and the Mangla on the Jhelum; power stations; 2,500 tubewells; and other works to integrate the whole river and canal system within Pakistan (Ali, 1967). In 1964 it became clear that the original amounts subscribed to the Indus Development Fund would not be sufficient to cover the costs of those works. A supplemental agreement was concluded in that year which provided for the payment of additional contributions by the original participants to the Fund. The World Bank was again instrumental in getting those participants to agree to make such contributions (Baxter, 1967).

Article X deals with "Emergency Provision" and sets forth certain responsibilities for the Bank in case Pakistan was unable to obtain the necessary materials and equipment from abroad prior to March 31, 1965, because of the outbreak of large scale international hostilities. Annexure H deals with "Transitional Arrangements" to be undertaken during the transition period which started in 1960, and ended in 1970, in the course of which Pakistan was to construct the replacement works, and end its reliance on the Eastern rivers. The Bank's role and responsibilities under Articles V and X, and Annexure H were fully completed some time ago. Annexures F and G deal with "Neutral Expert" and "Court of Arbitration", respectively, in connection with the settlement of differences and disputes, where the Bank has, and will continue to have, a limited procedural role (Salman, 2003).

A third unique feature of the Treaty is the varying process for the settlement of issues which may arise between the two parties under the Treaty. According to Article IX of the Treaty on "Settlement of Differences and Disputes" any question concerning the interpretation or application of the Treaty is first examined by the Permanent Indus Commission (The Commission) established under the Treaty, with one commissioner from each country. If the Commission is unable to resolve such a question, then the question becomes a "difference" which shall be dealt with by a Neutral Expert to be appointed by agreement between the two parties. If the parties cannot agree on a Neutral Expert, or on a third party to appoint a Neutral Expert, then, according to the provisions of the Treaty, the Neutral Expert shall be appointed by the World Bank. The World Bank was given the authority also to appoint the Neutral Expert itself during the Transition Period. Detailed provisions on the Neutral Expert are laid down in Annexure F to the Treaty, including the requirement that the Neutral Expert should be an eminent engineer.

The role of the Court of Arbitration is referred to in Article IX and Annexure F of the Treaty, but the details are laid down in Annexure G of the Treaty. Annexure F lays down a list of 23 questions which fall under the mandate of the Neutral Expert. Questions outside this list do not fall within the authority of the Neutral Expert, and would have to be settled by a Court of Arbitration. If the Neutral Expert determines that the difference referred to him, or part of it, does not fall under his mandate as prescribed by the Treaty, then the difference, or that part, becomes a dispute and would be dealt with by a Court of Arbitration. The Commission itself could also deem a difference as a dispute which would be settled by a Court of Arbitration. Although the Treaty states that the decision of the Neutral Expert is final and binding, it also states that if any question which is not within the competence of the Neutral Expert should arise out of his decision, such a question should be settled in accordance with procedures which could involve the Court of Arbitration. The Court of Arbitration consists of seven arbitrators, two of whom would be appointed by each party. The remaining three (also called umpires) would be appointed through a complex process, detailed in Annexure G and its Appendix. That process could involve the World Bank, as well as the United Nations, the President of Massachusetts Institute of Technology, the Rector of the Imperial College of Science and Technology in London, the Chief Justice of the United States, and the Lord Chief Justice of England.

It is worth noting that the process for the settlement of differences and disputes under the Treaty is not a hierarchical one. A question is referred to the Neutral Expert not as an appeal of the decision of the Commission. Rather, it is referred to the Neutral Expert because the Commission cannot resolve it. This is to be expected with complex questions, given that the Commission consists of two persons, each representing one of the two countries. Moreover, the decision of the Neutral Expert is final and binding, and as such, cannot be appealed to the Court of Arbitration. Indeed, the Treaty states that such a decision is binding not just on the parties, but also on any Court of Arbitration to be established.

Closely related to the issue of the settlement of differences and disputes is the concept of notification for planned projects which is widely viewed as a process for the avoidance of disputes. Although negotiated in the 1950s when the international water law was in its infancy, the Treaty includes progressive provisions on notification between the two parties. This is notwithstanding the fact that the Treaty has divided the rivers between the two countries. Article VII of the Treaty on "Future Co-operation" requires the party who plans to construct the engineering works which would cause interference with the waters of any of the rivers and would affect the other party materially, to notify the other party. The notifying party shall supply such data as would enable the other party to inform itself of the nature and magnitude of such work. If such work would cause interference with the waters of any of the rivers but would not affect the other party materially, the party planning such work shall, nevertheless, on request from the other party, supply such data, as may be available.

Another unique feature of the Treaty is that it entered into force and effect retroactively. This is very unusual because treaties are signed, and then ratified, and they enter into force either on the day of ratification, or on a specified date falling thereafter. In this case, the Indus Waters Treaty was signed on September 19, 1960 and the instruments of ratification were exchanged on January 12, 1961. Yet, Article XII (2) of the Treaty stipulated that entry into force of the Treaty would take effect retrospectively from the first of April 1960, more than five months before the Treaty itself was signed. The reason for this unusual arrangement related to the agreements signed by India and Pakistan, starting in 1948, under which India was to supply Pakistan with water from the Central Bari Doab Canal of the Ravi river until March 31, 1960.

Accordingly, it was agreed during the negotiations of the Treaty that the Transition Period would start on April 1, 1960. It was, therefore, necessary for the Treaty to become effective as of that date.

Despite its comprehensiveness, the Indus Waters Treaty is a bilateral treaty which is confined to two of the four riparian states of the Indus basin. In this respect, neither China nor Afghanistan, who are the other two riparians of the Indus river system, is a party to the Treaty. The Indus and the eastern most tributary, the Sutlej, both rise in the Tibetan plateau in China. The Kabul and the Kuram, which are the main tributaries of the Indus river, originate and flow for a while in Afghanistan before crossing into Pakistan and joining the Indus river. In total, about 13 percent of the catchment area of the Indus basin is situated in China and Afghanistan (Gulhati, 1973). No consultations with China or Afghanistan took place during the negotiations of the Treaty. Afghanistan, and to a lesser extent China, are now increasingly asserting their rights to an equitable and, reasonable share of the waters of the tributaries of the Indus river system originating there.

The Bank played a crucial and substantive role in the negotiation and finalization of the Treaty (Kirmani & Le Moigne, 1997). The involvement of the Bank started and continued at the highest level, with the then President of the World Bank, Mr. Eugene Black, personally and directly engaged throughout the process (Salman, 2003). The Bank followed a flexible approach which resulted in abandoning earlier proposals, after it became clear that they would not work (Biswas, 1992). More importantly, the Bank agreed to be a party to the Treaty. Indeed, it was the Bank's acceptance of a major role and of responsibilities in the implementation of the Treaty which facilitated the conclusion of the Treaty (Alam, 2002). It was also the Bank's leverage and convening power which resulted in raising the necessary funds, mostly as grants, to assist in the implementation of the Treaty. As discussed above, the major part of the role and responsibilities of the Bank was completed, and only a procedural role in the settlement of differences and disputes still remains (Salman, 2003). It is this role which has been tested by the recent difference over the Baglihar plant between the two parties, and that brought the Bank again, 45 years later, as a key player in the Indus Waters Treaty.

2. Appointment of the Neutral Expert

Pakistan approached the World Bank on January 15, 2005, stating that a "difference" has arisen with India with regard to the Baglihar hydropower plant which India is constructing on the Chenab river. Although the Chenab river has been allocated by the Treaty to Pakistan as one of the three Western rivers, India has been allowed, as mentioned earlier, certain uses of the Western rivers. Those uses include run-of-river hydropower plants, subject to certain conditions specified in great detail under Annexure D of the Treaty. Pakistan alleged that the design of the Baglihar plant was in violation of a number of those conditions. India, on the other hand, claimed that the Baglihar plant was in conformity with those conditions. Pakistan was concerned that the project would allow India to obstruct and control the flow of the Chenab river which is allocated to Pakistan.

This was the first time since the Treaty was concluded in 1960 that the Bank had been called upon by one of the parties to exercise its role and responsibilities under the Treaty with regard to the settlement of a difference or a dispute. The Treaty states that the appointment of the Neutral Expert would be made jointly by the two parties within one month of the request by one party to the other, or failing that by such person or body as may be agreed upon by them. In the absence of such agreement, the appointment shall be made by the World Bank, after consultation with each of the parties. Thus, the role of the Bank in this respect seems quite a simple administrative process. However, the Baglihar difference proved that the role was not that simple. A number of difficult issues arose as a result of that request, and had to be addressed by the Bank.

The first issue related to the contention by India that the Baglihar plant was still being discussed by the Permanent Indus Commission, and, as such, it was still a "question" and had not yet reached the stage of a "difference" warranting the World Bank's intervention. The Bank asked Pakistan to substantiate its claim that the process had, indeed reached that stage, and Pakistan sent a lengthy report to that effect. India was provided with Pakistan's documentation. In turn, India sent an extensive reply which was also shared with Pakistan who responded to it with an equally voluminous report. The exchange of documentation through the World Bank went on for three rounds. After a thorough analysis of the Treaty and those reports, the Bank concluded that it was required under the Treaty to appoint a Neutral Expert. That process took more than three months to complete. On April 25, 2005, the Bank informed the parties of this conclusion and started its consultation with them on the appointment of the Neutral Expert (World Bank Indus Waters Treaty Website, 2005 – 2007).

The second issue related to what would constitute "consultation" with each of the parties when the Bank is undertaking the appointment of the Neutral Expert. As indicated earlier, the Treaty requires that the Bank appoints the Neutral Expert after consultation with each of the parties. With no precedent under the Indus Waters Treaty to guide it, the Bank had to look for guidance elsewhere, the closest being one of its sister organizations, the International Centre for Settlement of Investment Disputes (ICSID). ICSID is one of the five institutions comprising the "World Bank Group". The other four are the International Bank for Reconstruction and Development (IBRD), the International Development Association (IDA), the International Finance Corporation (IFC), and the Multilateral Investment Guarantee Agency (MIGA). IBRD and IDA are together referred to as the "World Bank". ICSID was established under the "Convention on the Settlement of Investment Disputes between States and Nationals of Other States" which came into force on October 14, 1966. Currently, 143 countries are parties to the ICSID Convention. ICSID assists member countries in settling their investment disputes with private sector corporations or individuals of other states.

The procedures which the Bank conducted in consulting with the two countries in the selection of the Neutral Expert were adopted from the procedures used by ICSID to select arbitrators for the settlement of investment disputes. The ICSID procedures are, in turn, based on Article 6 (3) of the United Nations Commission on International Trade Law (UNCITRAL) Arbitration Rules, adopted by the United Nations General Assembly in 1976. Based on those procedures, the Bank compiled a list of highly qualified and eminent engineers from around the world, as stipulated in the Treaty. Furthermore, the Bank ensured that there was no conflict of interest on the part of any of the nominees. The names and curriculum vitae of three engineers out of this list were sent by the Bank to each of the two parties asking them to indicate, within fifteen days, who of the three engineers was not acceptable to them to serve as the Neutral Expert. The procedures included a second similar round of three names if there was no agreement on one name in the first round. If more than one name was agreed upon by the two parties, then the choice from among them would follow an alphabetical order. If the second round ended without an agreement on a name, then the Bank would appoint the Expert itself without going back to the parties. The person to be appointed by the World Bank in this round would not have been included in the lists of the first and second rounds. However, none of those alternatives were needed because the parties agreed on one name in the first round.

The Bank also developed clear procedures for conducting its role. Those procedures were based on transparency and fairness. All communications from or to the parties would be in writing; every correspondence or document received from one party would be shared with the other party; and no meeting would take place with one party without the presence of the other.

Thus, the simple administrative task for the Bank to appoint a Neutral Expert, if the parties fail to agree on one, and fail to agree on a third party to appoint such an expert, developed into a lengthy quasi-judicial process. Fortunately, the Bank did not have to deal with the situation where India would disagree with the Bank's determination that the issue at hand had indeed reached the status of a "difference" which needed to be referred to a Neutral Expert. Similarly, it was quite fortunate that the two parties agreed in the first round of consultation on a Neutral Expert, and the Bank did not have to appoint the Expert itself in the third round, as mentioned above. As will be discussed in the next part, five months after Pakistan approached the Bank, the Neutral Expert was in place, with full responsibility over the Baglihar difference. Hence, the major and most critical part of the Bank role was successfully completed.

3. The Baglihar difference within the Treaty context

The Baglihar hydropower project is a run-of-the-river plant being constructed by India on the Chenab river in the north eastern state of Jammu and Kashmir. Planning for this project began in the late 1990s, and construction started in 2002. The dam is of concrete gravity type, with a height of 144.5 metres above the deepest foundation. The plant has a capacity of 450 MW in its first stage, with 900 MW on complete design.

As mentioned earlier, the Indus Waters Treaty is a complex instrument, with an intricate process of references and cross references between its articles and paragraphs of the annexures. Although Pakistan claimed that the design of the Baglihar plant does not conform to certain requirements under Annexure D, the context of the Baglihar difference within the Treaty is far more complicated than that, mainly because of such cross-references.

Paragraph (2) (a) of Article IX of the Treaty on the settlement of differences and disputes states that any difference which, in the opinion of either Commissioner, falls within the provisions of Part 1 of Annexure F shall, at the request of either Commissioner, be dealt with by a Neutral Expert in accordance with the provisions of Part 2 of Annexure F. Part 1 of Annexure F specifies 23 questions which fall under the mandate of the Neutral Expert. Those questions include a wide array of issues covered in more details in other annexures to the Treaty. Paragraph 1 (11) of Part 1 of Annexure F deals with questions arising under the provisions of Paragraph 7, Paragraph 11, or Paragraph 21 of Annexure D. Paragraph 11 of Annexure D states that "If a question arises as to whether or not the design of a Plant conforms to the criteria set out in Paragraph 8, then either Party may proceed to have the question resolved in accordance with the provisions of Articles IX (1) and (2)". Paragraph 8 of Annexure D lays down a seven part criteria with which the design of any new run-of-the-river plant shall conform. Part 2 of Annexure F deals with the appointment and procedures concerning the Neutral Expert.

Moreover, paragraph 9 of Annexure D obliges India to communicate to Pakistan, six months before the commencement of construction of any plant referred to in paragraph 8 of Annexure D, certain information, specified in Appendix 2 to the Annexure, concerning such a plant. Paragraphs 10, 11 and 12 of Annexure D detail the procedures concerning the communication between the two parties on the said plant.

Pakistan claimed that the Baglihar plant did not conform to criteria (a), (c), (e) and (f) of paragraph 8 of Annexure D to the Treaty. Criterion (a) states that the works shall not be capable of raising artificially the water level in the operating pool above the full pondage level specified in the design. Pakistan alleged that the Baglihar plant did not meet this requirement. Criterion (c) requires the maximum pondage in the operating pool not to exceed twice the pondage required for firm power. In this connection, Pakistan claimed that the Baglihar pondage exceeded twice the pondage required for firm power. Criterion (e) states that if the conditions at the site of the plant make a gated spillway necessary, the bottom level of the gates in normal closed position shall be located at the highest level consistent with sound and economical design. Pakistan claimed, with regard to this criterion, that the Baglihar plant design was not based on correct, rational and realistic estimates of maximum flood discharge at the site. Criterion (f) requires that the intakes for the turbines shall be located at the highest level consistent with satisfactory and economical construction and operation of the plant as a run-of-the-river plant. Pakistan considered that the intake for the turbines was not located at the highest level as this criterion mandates.

Hence, the Baglihar difference was clearly a complex engineering issue which required an eminent engineer to address it, as the Treaty has rightly required. Indeed, the whole Treaty was a result of the detailed negotiations of engineers, with a limited role for others, including lawyers (Salman & Uprety, 2002).

4. Process for addressing the Baglihar Difference

On May 10, 2005, the World Bank informed the parties, and announced to the world, that it had appointed Mr. Raymond Lafitte, a Swiss national, a highly qualified engineer, and a professor at the Swiss Federal Institute of Technology, as the Neutral Expert to address the Baglihar "difference" (World Bank Indus Waters Treaty Website, 2005 – 2007). This followed the lengthy process described above, and the agreement of Mr. Lafitte to serve as the Neutral Expert for that purpose.

At the request of the Neutral Expert, the World Bank designated ICSID to coordinate the process, including communication with the two parties. Both parties endorsed the designation of ICSID. It is worth adding in this connection that Pakistan became a party to the ICSID Convention in 1966, while India has neither signed, nor acceded to the ICSID Convention. The Neutral Expert appointed an engineer as an assistant, and later, after approval of the two parties, engaged a legal adviser. Indeed, the Treaty itself had envisaged the possibility of the Neutral Expert needing such assistance. Although the designation of ICSID and the appointment of the assistant were both endorsed by the two parties, the Neutral Expert took the prudent step of obtaining the prior approval of the parties for the appointment of the legal adviser.

The Treaty authorizes the Neutral Expert to determine the procedures for addressing the difference, provided that he shall afford to each party an adequate hearing; and in making his decision, he shall be governed by the provisions of the Treaty, and by the compromise, if any, presented to him by the Commission. The procedures adopted by the Neutral Expert replicated those followed earlier by the World Bank of transparency and fairness. All communications from one party would be shared with the other party, and with both parties, if it was originating from the Neutral Expert. Moreover, no meeting would take place with one party without the presence of the other. On the other hand, the Treaty also obliges each of the two governments to extend to the Neutral Expert such facilities as he may require for the discharge of his functions.

Under Annexure F of the Treaty, each of the two parties was required to pay to the Bank, once the Treaty entered into force, the sum of $5,000. The Bank would hold this amount, together with any income therefrom, in a trust to pay the remuneration of the Neutral Expert and any assistance he may need. The $10,000 paid by the two parties in 1960 reached over $100,000 in 2005 when the Neutral Expert was appointed, as a result of the investment of the original amount. This took place despite the fact that the Treaty does not oblige the Bank to invest the contribution of the two parties. The balance in the trust fund provided the initial expenses needed to start the Neutral Expert process. The Treaty authorizes the Bank to ask the parties to pay in equal shares any amount required to cover the cost of the process after depleting the amount held by the Bank in the trust fund.

The Bank handed over the process to Mr. Lafitte on June 9, 2005, following his acceptance to act as the Neutral Expert. The handover took place in the first meeting which was also attended by the representatives of the two parties, and which was held at the World Bank Office in Paris. During that meeting, the basic rules and procedures for the conduct of the process were laid down and agreed upon. The work program was also discussed and agreed upon, keeping in mind the Treaty requirement that the decision by the Neutral Expert should be rendered as soon as possible. A time-table was set, and was adjusted later, which would start with India providing, by July 15, 2005, the information specified in Appendix II to Annexure D, referred to above. Pakistan would provide its memorial by August, and India its counter-memorial by September 2005. Pakistan would file its reply by January 2006, and India its rejoinder by March 2006.

The draft determination of the Neutral Expert would be completed by early October 2006, and the parties' written comments would be submitted by the end of October 2006. In November 2006, the parties would provide additional written comments. The final determination of the Neutral Expert would be rendered by February 2007. It was also agreed that four more meetings would be held before the Neutral Expert would finalize and issue his decision. The sequence of the written procedures was adopted from the ICSID practice which provides for two possible rounds of exchange of documents between the parties, and also provides for following each written procedure by an oral one. It was further agreed that all meetings would be recorded, and that the minutes of each meeting would be prepared, approved by the two parties, and signed by the Neutral Expert and the coordinator.

The first meeting which was held at the World Bank Office in Paris in June 2005, was followed by the submission by India of the basic information on the project, the memorial by Pakistan, and the counter-memorial by India. Subsequent to those submissions, the Neutral Expert, together with delegations from India and Pakistan, visited, in early October 2005, the Baglihar site, as well as the Baglihar hydraulic model. The second meeting of the Neutral Expert with the two parties took place in Geneva from October 19–21, 2005 at the World Meteorological Organization, and was devoted to questions which arose as a result of the Baglihar site visit. The third meeting took place in London from May 25 – 29, 2006, at the International Dispute Resolution Centre, subsequent to the filing of the rejoinder, and was devoted to presentations by the parties.

Five months later, the Neutral Expert finalized his decision and presented his draft determination to the two parties during the fourth meeting which was held at the World Bank Office in Paris from October 2–4, 2006. The practice of presenting a draft determination to the parties is uncommon in international arbitration, but it exists in other fields of dispute settlement. A similar feature can be found in the "Understanding on Rules and Procedures Governing the Settlement of Disputes" of the World Trade Organization (WTO). This feature is called the "Interim Review Stage" and is intended to give the parties an opportunity to review and comment on the draft ruling. After the presentation of the draft decision by the Neutral Expert, the parties were given the opportunity to file written comments on the draft decision, and to further present these comments orally at the fifth meeting. The fifth and last meeting took place in Washington DC at the World Bank Headquarters from November 7 – 9, 2006, where the parties presented their comments on the final draft determination. The parties also filed additional comments on their respective presentations. Thereafter, the Neutral Expert took three months to finalize his determination, keeping in mind those comments. Accordingly, not only did the Neutral Expert give an opportunity to the parties to present their view and comment on his data and findings, he also gave himself the chance to obtain feedback on the basis and strength of his technical data, analysis and decision.

On February 12, 2007, the Neutral Expert delivered, to the ambassadors of India and Pakistan in Bern, Switzerland, signed copies of his final decision on the Baglihar difference (referred to as the Expert Determination by the Neutral Expert). Copies of the decision were also delivered to the World Bank, as required by the Treaty. The decision consisted of a full comprehensive report, and a separate Executive Summary. The two parties agreed that the Neutral Expert and the World Bank could disclose and disseminate the Executive Summary of the Expert Determination. However, the full report of the Determination can only be disclosed and disseminated by the parties themselves, according to their own procedures. Based on this agreement, the World Bank placed the Executive Summary on its Indus Waters Treaty external web site on February 20, 2007 (Executive Summary, 2007).

The Neutral Expert considered his decision as not being rendered against one or the other party. According to the provisions of the Treaty, the decision of the Neutral Expert is final and binding. However, as indicated earlier, paragraph 13 of Annexure F of the Treaty states that without prejudice to the finality of the Neutral Expert's decision, if any question (including a claim to financial compensation) which is not within the competence of the Neutral Expert should arise out of his decision, that question shall, if it cannot be resolved by agreement, be settled in accordance with the provisions of Article XI (3), (4) and (5) of the Treaty. Those provisions call for resolving such an issue by agreement, and failing that, by a Court of Arbitration.

The Neutral Expert, his assistant and legal adviser were financed by the trust fund established under the Treaty in 1960, as discussed earlier. The Neutral Expert is mandated to decide which of the two parties should bear the cost of the process. In this case, he directed that the parties would share the cost equally. This direction underscored his conclusion that his decision was not rendered against one party or the other. The decision of the Neutral Expert with regard to the cost also meant that the parties would reimburse, in equal amounts, the trust fund held by the World Bank of the amounts disbursed by the Bank from the trust fund. As such, the trust fund would revert back to the same amount it had at the start of the process.

The above shows the extensive work undertaken by the Neutral Expert, as well as the two parties, which spanned over a period of more than 20 months. The schedule set by the Neutral Expert and agreed to by the parties was followed, with some adjustments agreed to by both parties. ICSID continued to coordinate the process throughout this period, replicating its experience in handling investment disputes. Only the travel and subsistence expenses of the ICSID staff, in connection with the Baglihar difference, were charged to the trust fund.

5. Decision of the Neutral Expert

The Executive Summary of the decision of the Neutral Expert indicated that in interpreting the Treaty, the Neutral Expert had relied on the rules of the Vienna Convention on the Law of Treaties. This Convention was concluded in 1969, and entered into force in 1980. Neither India nor Pakistan is a party to this Convention. India has not signed the Convention, and Pakistan signed the Convention in 1970, but has not yet ratified it. However, it is widely agreed among experts in this field that the Convention reflects the rules of customary international law with regard to ordinary methods of treaty interpretation. The Executive Summary stated that the Treaty gives a clear indication of the rights and obligations of the parties, and that these rights and obligations should be read in the light of new technical norms and new standards, as provided for by the Treaty. It also stated that the interpretation of the Treaty was guided by the two principles of integration and effectiveness which "provide for the Treaty to find effect in its whole and to ensure that each of the object(s) and purpose(s) of the Treaty is given the fullest weight and effect when interpreting the rights and obligations under the Treaty". Those purposes include attaining the most complete and satisfactory utilization of the waters of the Indus river system, and fixing and delimiting the rights and obligations of each party in relation to the other. The Summary indicates that the rights and obligations contained in Part 3 of Annexure D must be interpreted so as to allow fulfilling the purpose of the Treaty in "a spirit of goodwill and friendship" taking into account the best and latest practices in the field of construction and operation of hydroelectric plants.

The decision of the Neutral Expert on the Baglihar difference dealt with the issues contested under the four criteria of paragraph 8 of Annexure D of the Treaty discussed above, under six headings. Those headings were: (i) maximum design flood, (ii) spillway, ungated or gated, (iii) spillway, level of the gates, (iv) artificial raising of the water level, (v) pondage, and (vi) level of the power intake.

The first issue on the maximum design flood related to the calculation of the maximum amount of water which can arrive at the dam. In view of many uncertainties of flood analysis, the Neutral Expert retained the value proposed by India of 16,500 m^3/s, as opposed to 14,900 m^3/s proposed by Pakistan, for the peak discharge of the design flood. He further stated that climate change, with the possible associated increase in floods, also encourages a prudent approach.

With regard to the second issue of a gated or ungated spillway, Pakistan considered that a gated spillway was not necessary, and would allow India to control the flow of the river. The Neutral Expert determined that the conditions of the site, including hydrology, sediment yield, topography, geology and seismicity, require a gated spillway. He added that the analysis of 13,000 existing spillways in the world demonstrated that the provision of gates on large spillways is common practice. He further indicated that an ungated spillway might create the risk of flooding the upstream shores, and that an elevation of the dam crest, which would prevent such a risk, would be costly.

On the issue of the level of the spillway gates, Pakistan stated that even if it can be assumed (without conceding) that a gated spillway was necessary, the orifice spillway proposed by India is not located at the highest level consistent with the provisions of the Treaty. The position of India was that the design of the chute spillway, sluice spillway and auxiliary spillway were necessary to ensure safe passing of the design flood. The Neutral Expert determined that the gated chute spillway on the left wing planned in India's design is at the highest level consistent with sound and economical design and satisfactory construction and operation of the works. He considered that the outlets composing the sluice spillway, planned by India, should be of the minimum size and located at the highest level consistent with a sound and economical design. However, the Neutral Expert determined that the outlets should preferably be located 8 metres (m) lower to ensure protection against upstream flooding. On this issue, in particular, the Neutral Expert felt the need for the Treaty to be read in the light of new technical norms and standards. He specifically stated. "It appears that the Treaty is not particularly well developed with respect to its provisions on sediment transport. This is not criticism: The Treaty reflects the status of technology on reservoir sedimentation in the 1950s. The consequence is that the provisions of the Treaty which explicitly mention sediment acquire a special significance" (Executive Summary, 2007).

On the fourth issue of the artificial raising of the water level, Pakistan considered that the dam crest elevation proposed by India was exaggerated and could be lower. The Neutral Expert considered that the dam crest elevation should be set at the lowest elevation. He determined that the crest elevation submitted by India at 844.5 m above sea level (asl), resulting from a freeboard above the full pondage level of 4.50 m is not at the lowest elevation, and that the freeboard should be 3.0 m above the full pondage level, leading to a dam crest elevation of 843.0 m asl.

With regard to the volume of the maximum pondage, Pakistan argued that the value of the maximum pondage proposed by India exceeded twice the pondage required for firm power. The Neutral Expert determined that the values for maximum pondage stipulated by India as well as by Pakistan were not in conformity with the criteria laid down in the Treaty, and fixed a lower value.

On the sixth point relating to the level of the power intake, Pakistan considered that the power intake is not located at the highest level as required by the Treaty. The Neutral Expert agreed with this consideration and determined that the intake level should be raised by 3 m and fixed at elevation 821 m asl.

Two observations are worth making with regard to the process and the decision of the Neutral Expert: Firstly, as appeared from the composition of the two delegations, Pakistan seemed to have viewed the difference as largely a legal one, involving the interpretation of the Treaty, while India seemed to have viewed it mainly as an engineering one, regarding hydropower plants (Executive Summary, 2007).

Secondly, the Neutral Expert opined that the rights and obligations of the parties under the Treaty should be read in the light of new technical norms and new standards as provided for by the Treaty. This meant that the Baglihar difference was addressed bearing in mind the technical standards for hydropower plants as they have developed in the first decade of the twenty-first century, and not as perceived and thought of in 1950s when the Treaty was negotiated. The reference to modern technical standards is particularly clear in the discussion and analysis by the Neutral Expert of the issue of gated or ungated spillway summarized earlier. Climate change and its likely effects is another example of contemporary concerns not prevalent or thought about during the 1950s which was taken into account by the Neutral Expert in his decision. It should be added that, along the same lines, the International Court of Justice in the Danube dispute between Hungary and Slovakia (the Gabcikovo-Nagymaros case) required that the current standards must be taken into consideration when evaluating the environmental risks of the project (the International Court of Justice, 1997 p. 66). This manner of interpretation will most likely influence the future interpretations of the Treaty, as well as other international water treaties.

The response from both India and Pakistan to the decision of the Neutral Expert was positive. Both countries claimed victory and highlighted the areas of the decision which they believed responded positively to their claims. The conclusion to be derived from those statements was that both parties have agreed to abide by that decision. This further underscored the successful completion of the Neutral Expert process.

6. Conclusion

The Baglihar difference posed major challenges to India and Pakistan, to the World Bank, as well as to the Indus Waters Treaty itself. This was the first time in 45 years that the Treaty's provisions on the settlement of differences and disputes were tested. Understandably, there were apprehensions in all quarters about how the process might unfold. Questions about whether there would be an agreement that the Baglihar question had indeed reached the stage of a difference, and about whether there would be an agreement on one person to serve as a Neutral Expert, were in the minds of those concerned. Equally concerning was the issue of how the Neutral Expert would handle the difference, and how the parties would deal with him and react to his final decision.

However, the Bank was again able to play a fair, transparent and constructive role which led to the appointment of the Neutral Expert. In turn, the Neutral Expert was able, with the coordinating role of ICSID, and the full cooperation of the two parties, to handle the process in a transparent and fair manner, and to deliver a decision which was accepted by the two parties. ICSID rules and practices provided guidance on a number of procedural decisions taken by the Bank and the Neutral Expert.

Undoubtedly, the process has set precedents in a number of aspects. Transparent and fair procedures for the appointment of the Neutral Expert, and for the conduct of the process, are now firmly in place, if the need were to arise again on another difference. Those procedures drew considerably from the ICSID practice, the UNCITRAL arbitration rules, as well as the WTO disputes settlement rules. The result of this blend is a comprehensive and unique set of rules and procedures. On the substantive side, the notion that the rights and obligations of the parties under the Treaty should be read in the light of new technical norms and new standards, as provided for by the Treaty, will most likely influence any future interpretation of the Indus Waters Treaty. Similarly, interpretation of the Treaty keeping in mind the rules of the Vienna Convention on the Law of Treaties, is likely to reshape many of the understandings about the Treaty. It is worth mentioning in this connection that neither of the two states is a party to the Vienna Convention, and only Pakistan is a party to the ICSID Convention. Nonetheless, both parties endorsed the designation of ICSID as a coordinator, and neither of them raised concerns to the invocation of the rules of the Vienna Convention on the Law of Treaties in connection with the interpretation of the Indus Waters Treaty.

The World Bank, ICSID and the Neutral Expert, no doubt, handled the process in a fair and transparent manner. The cooperation of the two parties and their acceptance of the decision of the Neutral Expert was the ultimate triumph of the process. All in all, the manner in which the process started in January 2005, and ended in February 2007, twenty five months later, attests to the strength and credibility of the Treaty itself, and underscores the notion of the peaceful settlement of international water disputes.

Acknowledgements

The author would like to thank David Freestone, Eloise Obadia and Fuad Bateh for helpful comments on an earlier version of this article. The views expressed in this article are those of the author and do not necessarily reflect the views of the World Bank.

References

Alam, U. (2002). Questioning the water wars rationale: a case study of the Indus Waters Treaty. The Geographical Journal, 168, 341.

Ali, C. M. (1967). The Emergence of Pakistan. Columbia University Press, New York, USA.

Baxter, R. R. (1967). The Indus Basin. In The Law of International Drainage Basins. Garretson, A. H., Hayton, R. D. & Olmstead, C. J. (eds). Oceana Publications, New York, USA.

Biswas, A. (1992). Indus Waters Treaty: The negotiating process. Water International 17, 201.

Executive Summary (2007). Baglihar Hydroelectric Plant, Expert Determination, Executive Summary. available at: http://web. worldbank.org/WBSITE/EXTERNAL/COUNTRIES/SOUTHASIAEXT/0,contentMDK:20320047, pagePK:146736, piPK:146830, theSitePK:223547,00.html.

Gulhati, N. (1973). Indus Waters Treaty – An Exercise in International Mediation. Allied Publishers, Bombay, India.

International Court of Justice (1997). Case concerning the Gabcikova-Nagymaros Project (Hungary/Slovakia). Available at: http://www.icj-cij.org/docket/files/92/7375.pdf.

Kirmani, S. & Le Moigne, G. (1997). Fostering Riparian Cooperation in International River Basins. The World Bank at its Best in Development Diplomacy. World Bank Technical Paper No. 335 at 5.

Michel, A. (1967). The Indus River – A Study of the Effects of Partition. Yale University Press, New Haven, USA.

Salman, S. (2003). Good offices and mediation and international water disputes. In Resolution of International Water Disputes, The Permanent Court of Arbitration. Kluwer Law International, The Hague, The Netherlands.

Salman, S. & Uprety, K. (2002). Conflict and Cooperation on South Asia's International Rivers – A Legal Perspective. Kluwer Law International, The Hague, The Netherlands.

World Bank Indus Waters Treaty Website (2005 – 2007). World Bank Names Neutral Expert on Baglihar. available at: http://web.worldbank.org/WBSITE/EXTERNAL/COUNTRIES/SOUTHASIAEXT/0,contentMDK:20320047, pagePK:146736, piPK:146830, theSitePK:223547,00.html.

CHAPTER – 22

Trans-Boundary Water Politics And Conflicts In South Asia: Towards Water For Peace.

Richa Singh. Centre for Democracy and Social Action (India) 1 December 2008.

INTRODUCTION

1. Locating the Study.

In 2003, the UN Secretary General Kofi Annan stated in a report on the prevention of armed conflict that "….in addressing the root causes of an armed conflict, the United Nations system will need to devote greater attention to the potential threats posed by the environmental problem."In doing so, he was articulating a globally felt need of linking 'security' and the so called 'soft threats' such as environmental degradation and poverty. However, in much of South Asia, the debate on 'security' continues to revolve around national security and high politics. While such a state led discourse has been challenged by feminists and peace activists, a gap remains when it comes to 'environment–security' linkages with much of the debate largely focusing on land issues. The question of 'water conflicts' is an arena that still awaits more attention.

However, 'water' is crucial to life and survival, and concerns of sharing and managing this finite element in South Asia has been generating a lot of heat. At one level are issues that are directly linked to the fact that there is a 'water crisis' looming over the region. It is a reality that the usage of water resources has reached or far exceeded the limits of sustainability in most of the countries in South Asia. Rapid growth of population, urbanisation and mega cities, industries, mining, intensive irrigation and agriculture have combined with an inefficient use of water to ensure that water is fast becoming a scarce resource—both in terms of quantity and quality. This has fuelled conflicts between different uses and users of water, between states within countries, and across countries. With the possibility of devastating impact of climate change, and the severe shortage of freshwater as projected by the Inter-governmental Panel on Climate Change, the situation is likely to take a catastrophic turn. In India alone, the gross per capita water availability is stated to decline from around 1,820 cubic meters a year to as low as around 1,140 cubic meters a year in 2050 (IPCC, 4th Assessment Report).

At another level, water tensions can be seen embedded in South Asia's turbulent history. The region has witnessed wars, and is an area where protracted violent conflicts and border disputes abound. It is argued that many of these conflicts between South Asian countries are also taking environmental forms. Simultaneously, various environmental issues are getting regionalised and politicised. There is thus an 'environmentalisation' of certain conflicts and politicisation of the environment in this region. Against this

---
[1] Kofi Annan, Interim Report of the Secretary-General on the Prevention of Armed Conflict, September, 2003.
[2] Of late, there have been some studies which highlight the environment–conflict link in South Asia, such as C. Gupta and M. Sharma, Contested Coastlines: Fisherfolk, Nations and Borders in South-Asia.
[3] Ibid. p. 5.

broad backdrop, the study attempts to map out the links that underlie water (environment), conflict and peace in South Asia.

2. Why the Study?

To begin with, it must be stated that the purpose of the study is not to give credence to the 'water war' thesis. Indeed, wars continue to be fought over oil and not water. The study is located in the understanding that peace is not simply the absence of war but a value grounded in the issues of human security and the collective well-being of the region. From such a perspective, there have been several reasons as to why this study was undertaken at this juncture in South Asia.

- Water insecurity is all pervasive in the region, visible in conflicts and tensions erupting within and across countries. Hence the need to integrate water security as a key component of human security is crucial.[4]

- The questions of sharing and management of trans-boundary water continues to be an irritant in any attempt to build peace and cooperation in the region. The fact that South Asia lacks a regional framework for ecological/water governance only magnifies these conflict/tension points. As the case stands, the governance of trans-boundary rivers has been carried out through bilateral treaties signed by different countries and India—treaties that themselves have been sites of conflict.

- Of late, our respective governments have been talking about better regional cooperation, and 'peace.' And yet, a closer look reveals that what is being imposed from above as regional 'peace' and 'cooperation' are, in reality attempts to hollow out both these values and give them a minimalist content. At one level, (despite the rhetoric of peace) the dominant discourse in the region remains one of 'security' defined in a narrow militarised term as 'national security,' and as a thing apart from human or resource security. At another level, regional cooperation/peace/integration in South Asia is increasingly getting defined in economic terms, dictated by the neoliberal market agenda. Consequently:

    a) There is a push to perceive water as an 'economic good,' a tradable commodity to be left to the market forces—an approach that then influences how water is to be utilised and shared in the region where India and Indian businesses dominate. Such approach threatens the recognition of water as a common pool resource, as a human right vital for survival, and as an environmental resource to be protected, and treated with the principles of sustainability;

    b) An ascendancy of market discourse has also meant an increased role of business groups (particularly Indian business groups) as legitimate players, and marginalisation of civil society actors at the regional level. Indeed, as the study revealed, South Asian civil society networking and initiatives on water (as well as a host of other issues) have been at an all time low in this phase. Clearly, the battle in much of South Asia to establish a framework for water governance that is fair, equitable, and environmentally sound is far from over.

These various factors form the rationale of this attempt to explore, from the perspective of the people and civil society, the possibility of bringing the question of fair and sustainable trans-boundary water governance right back to questions of peace and cooperation in South Asia. Indeed, the case for South Asian water governance specifically, and the ecological governance, at large, has never been as strong, nor as urgent as now, with the growing impact of global warming. From the Himalayas, which feed water to a billion people, to the coastal areas of Bangladesh, South Asian countries must prepare for the effects of climate change, even as they work to combat its human causes.

---

[4] This got a further fillip post September 11 and one finds an increasing tendency to 'securitising' environment.

3. South Asian Water Profile.

South Asia is a region of both water abundance and scarcity. The Hindu Kush-Himalayan region (HKH) is one of the largest storehouses of fresh water in the world, and its mountains are the source of major river systems. The three Himalayan rivers, the Indus, the Ganga and the Brahmaputra, arise within 300 km from each other in the Himalayan glaciers.[5] While the Ganga originates inside the Himalayas, the Indus and the Brahmaputra originate beyond, in the Trans-Himalayan Tibetan region—the Indus taking a westward course towards the Arabian Sea, and the Ganga and Brahmaputa making the journey towards the Bay of Bengal in the East of the subcontinent.

Individually, each of these main rivers is among the largest rivers in the world, and together they constitute the "Himalayan river system." While the Indus and the Ganga are each principal rivers of two separate river systems, this difference is over-ridden by the over all contiguity of the Indo-Gangetic plains. Together, these three rivers are estimated to carry an average of 1,200 cubic kilometers of water every year. When combined with the Meghna (Barak), a non Himalayan river which has an average annual flow of 100 cubic kilometer, the Ganga-Brahmaputra-Meghna becomes the world's third largest river system. These rivers not only provide water, but are also a major focus of the religious and cultural life in the region.

However, South Asia is inhabited by 1.4 billion people and home to 40 per cent of all those living in poverty worldwide. The IGB basin alone supports over half a billion people (10 percent of the world's population), an area where poverty is endemic and agriculture forms the main basis of livelihood. Hence, though theoretically the availability of water is high, access to water remains one of the major challenges. In addition, water supply remains seasonal in nature. The IGBM river, systems exhibit a remarkable variation in the temporal and spatial availability of water, and the hydrology of the rivers follows the rainfall pattern. About 80% of the total annual flow occurs between June to September, with the remaining 20% occurring during the rest of the months.[8] This results in an alternative cycle of excess and scarcity leading to conflicts over water-sharing. However, to a great extent the crisis is precipitated because of the decreasing water quality and the inefficient and inequitable way the resource is governed and managed. This poses a threat, both to water as an environmental resource, as well as a means of survival.

Socio-Economic Indicators and Projected Water Demand/Availability

Country	Population Density Person Per Km² (2001)	Growth Rate (%) (1990-2001)	Per Capital GDP in 2001 (US$)	Projected Water in BCM Demand upto 2025	Availability	Surplus/ Deficit
Bangladesh	1025	1.8%	370	48	1181	(+) 1133
India	348	1.8%	460	1060	1086	(+) 26
Nepal	165	2.4%	250	40	232	(+) 192
Pakistan	183	2.5%	420	335	236	(+) 102

Source: World Bank (2003) and Reddy et al[9]

---

[5] Bhim Subba, Himalayan Waters, (Kathmandu, Nepal: Panos South Asia), 2001, p. 49.
[6] Ibid. p. 88.
[7] Ibid. p. 52.
[8] "Water Sharing Conflict among Countries and Approaches to Resolving Them," WASSA Project Report, Vol. 3, p. 20.
[9] In Toufiq A. Siddiqi et al, p. 3.
[10] Z.A Bhutto, (the then Prime Minister of Pakistan) while addressing the UN Security Council, 1965 stressed that the main hindrance in resolving Kashmir is water. Also see "India/Pakistan: Water War Warning as Tension Escalates," Daniel Nels, OneWorld.net, 21 May 2002, http://www.corpwatch.org/news/PND.jsp?articleid=2616h
[12] Mallika Joseph, "Delhi round of Indo-Pak talks-II; Tulbul navigation project/Wular Barrage," www.ipcs.org/issues/ articles/162-ip-mallika.htm.

4. Contested Waters in South Asia

Ideally, cooperation based on mutual trust, transparency and information sharing among riparian countries should ensure the best management and sharing of water. However, given the atmosphere of hostility, 'upstream-downstream' syndrome, 'unequal' partnerships, lack of definitive international laws, regional principles or enforceable global conventions, a number of conflicts have erupted in South Asia on trans-border water issues. To understand this, one must begin with a certain geographical reality. India shares contiguous borders with all these South Asian countries, is both an upper and lower riparian, and is a giant in terms of its size (and economy) when compared to Pakistan, Nepal, and Bangladesh. Not surprisingly (and due to a host of other reasons) tensions have arisen between India and most of these countries on cross-border water issues. The atmosphere of mistrust among some of these countries, together with the fact that India is perceived as a 'hegemon' by its neighbours, has not helped the situation. Water has been a serious tension point between India (upper riparian) and Pakistan (lower riparian); between India (upper riparian) and Bangladesh (lower riparian); and between India (lower riparian) and Nepal (upper riparian).

i) India and Pakistan have fought four wars over Kashmir. According to some, the major underlying issue is about water. There is a widespread perception in Pakistan (which heavily relies on the Indus water system) that the Indian control of the Indus water-head can be misused to block water to Pakistan and devastate its economy. India refutes these charges and pledges its commitment to the Indus Waters Treaty (IWT). Indeed, the IWT between the two has survived the ups and downs of Indo-Pak relations, but has lately come under strain with India's plans to construct eleven large hydroelectric projects, including the Baglihar and Kishenganga Hydro Electric projects.

ii) India and Bangladesh are the co-riparian states, with fifty-four rivers crossing their borders, including two large Himalayan river systems, the Ganges and the Brahmaputra. The major issue of dispute between the two countries has been the Ganga, though the Brahmaputra and Teesta are also entering the shadow of conflict. In the past, tensions have peaked when Ganges water have reached extreme low levels in dry seasons causing crop losses in Bangladesh. In 1993, the then Bangladeshi Prime Minister Begum Khaleda Zia accused India's diversion of river water near the border as "a gross violation of human rights and justice." Controversy has raged over the Farrakka Barrage constructed by India on the Ganges near the border with Bangladesh. Attitudes have been rigid on both sides regarding the water dispute. The Indian establishment alleges Bangladesh of being unreasonable as the barrage was crucial to divert water to the Calcutta port, and of greatly over-stating its water needs. Bangladesh contends that such diversion has resulted in falling water tables and greater water salinity downstream for Bangladesh. It is perceived in Bangladesh as typically the case of a more powerful country disregarding the case of a smaller and weaker neighbour. India's proposal of building a number of dams in the North East, and its mega plan of linking its rivers (now under review), has become yet another bone of contention between the two countries.

iii) Between India and Nepal, water has often strained the relatively better relationship between the two countries. Nepal has enormous hydro-electric potential in the Himalayan rivers. The expectation is that a series of projects for the export of power will generate vast financial resources for the country. However, Nepal lacks the capital and technology required for such large projects. Power deficit in northern India is around 9,500 MW, which is expected to rise to 20,000 MW by 2010. Thus, India sees its interest in the utilisation of the Nepal's rivers. This has been the basis of various water-resource development agreements between India and Nepal. All these treaties, including the Mahakali Treaty of 1996, have been criticised in Nepal. The Mahakali treaty faced popular unrest and remains stalled. The dominant feeling in Nepal has been that these treaties have not been equitable and Nepal has been "bulldozed" by India.

Methodology

This is a scoping study, and in that sense, it is aimed to achieve breadth rather than depth of coverage. It has evolved out of the recognition that there is a need to address the issue of politics of water, conflict and peace from a regional perspective, to enable i) the development of effective civil society initiatives on the question of governance of transboundary water at this juncture in the region; ii) to inform and link the question of water security to the ongoing debates of regional peace and global peace.

1. Objectives of the Study

The specific objective of this study is three fold:

1) To understand and bring to the fore issues that plague trans-boundary water disputes in South Asia,

2) To identify initiative or lack of it with regard to water sharing and management from the perspective of peace building in South Asia,

3) To identify alternative approaches, and the possible action points for future intervention.

2. Research Method

Using the scoping study methodology, rather than specific and focused research questions, we began with some broad inquiry on the trans-boundary rivers from three vantage points: 1) common history, 2) ruptures, and 3) people's suffering. These were then used as the axis to probe through a body of literature, develop a more sharpened research design, and conduct field work.

i) Literature review: As a starting point of research, information was collected and analysed using secondary and primary sources. Secondary data was collected from electronic database; using reference lists in libraries as well as manually sifting through key journals; and finally meeting and tapping existing networks, relevant organisations, and individuals who were working on water and conflict issues. This was further supplemented with primary material like government water policy documents, newspaper reports, published and unpublished documents and reports of local NGOs.

ii) Mapping the field: Field work was conducted in three South Asian countries— Nepal, Bangladesh, and India (Kashmir, North East, and Bihar). Aimed at covering a wide gamut of issues, the study used the qualitative interview method with key stake holders such as relevant government officials, NGOs and CBOs, activists, academics working in the field, and media persons. A comprehensive interview guide/probe was prepared, and the questions were kept open ended. Though Pakistan has been a part of the study, given the unstable political situation in the country, we were unable to conduct field work. The dismissal of chief justice Iftikar Chowdhury, followed by the imposition of emergency and later, the assassination of Benazir Bhutto, became grounds for denying visas. The field work was first postponed and finally dropped. Hence, in Pakistan's case, the report relies on secondary sources, media reports, and the internet. Two meetings— GCAP (Global Call to Action against Poverty) in Kathmandu, and another on "South Asian Perspective on Climate Change" in Dhaka—provided an opportunity to meet NGOs and civil society activists from Pakistan. Inputs from these discussions have also been used to supplement the sections on Pakistan.

3. Scope and Limitation of the Study

The study is preliminary in nature. Given the limited time and resources, and the wide range of issues that emerge at the interface of water and border politics, the study confines itself to its objective and to four South Asian countries—India, Pakistan, Nepal and Bangladesh. This was chosen keeping in mind various factors: i) History of these countries both in terms of commonality and differences; ii) History of water dispute/dispute settlement between these countries; iii) Politicisation of water within each country with cross boundary implications; iv) Civil society action within each country with regard to water; v) Accessibility to the region within this limited time and resource.

While we recognise that internally, water conflicts within each country are assuming serious proportion, and externally, the geo-politics of water spill far beyond these four countries to other regions (as in the case of reports concerning the proposed diversion of the water of the Brahmaputra by China), these concerns, though extremely important, remain beyond the limited scope of this work.

4. Problems during the Study

As a South Asian traveling across the region, we make dual journeys. Ordinary people open their homes and hearts, and states and governments shut gates and borders. As faced by most South Asians, entry always remained the biggest problem and visas took days to be received. Nepal was an exception. The other problem we faced had to do with the unstable situation in the region. Each trip had to be meticulously planned weeks in advance only to be cancelled at the last moment. Eventually, field trips to Bangladesh did materialise despite the cyclone and local government instability, and to Nepal amidst the unsure situation and questions as whether the Maoists would pull out of the government and the uneasy peace be broken. Unfortunately, the Pakistan visit did not work out and had to be dropped.

CHAPTER – 23

History, Ruptures And Water
Socio-Political Sites Of Water Conflicts In South Asia

"The Earth is one but the world is not. We all depend on one biosphere for sustaining our lives. Yet each community, each country, strives for survival and prosperity with little regard for its impact on others."

(Brundtland Commission's Report, Our Common Future, 1987.)

1. "Rivers of Collective Belonging"[13]

Rivers, quite literally are life givers, carrying freshwater which is fundamental to life and the very basis of socio-economic wellbeing. In South Asia, rivers are also a deeply ingrained part of cultural and religious life. But rivers know no 'man-made' borders and flow freely across countries, cities, and villages, across fields and industrial belts. In terms of hydrography, one can argue that the states and societies of South Asia share a remarkable unity and its rivers bind the landscape into a composite whole. Nepal and India share the Mahakali-Ganga Basin, India and Pakistan share the Indus Basin, India and Bangladesh share the Ganaga-Brahmaputra-Meghna basin. If one looks at the overall riverscape of these trans-boundary waters, these river systems together cover the vast Indo Gangetic plains—or what constituted the ancient sapt-sindhu (seven rivers) valley and the Gangetic basin.

Not only have these rivers provided a geographical wholeness to South Asia, but they also epitomise a common socio-cultural confluence in the region, synergising varied cultural systems and ways of life, and cradling civilizations such as the ancient Harappa and Mohenjodaro civilization (around 2500 B.C.) that grew on the banks of the river Indus and its five tributaries. Taking the example of the Ganga, Ajaya Dixit points out that:

"….for the present day Bangladeshi, Nepali, Sri Lankan, Pakistani, or Indian, the Ganga is a denominative absolute, be it the Burhi Ganga of Bangladesh, the Trisuli Ganga of Nepal, the Mahaweli Ganga of Sri Lanka, the Sindhu Ganga of Pakistan, or the Cauvery Ganga of peninsular India. The Trisuli Ganga hurtling past the gorge evokes in the Nepali villager the same sentiment as the Ganga entering from upstream to join the Bay of Bengal does in the Bangladeshi farmer."

Undoubtedly, there is a broad "commonness" that untidily spills over the new, neat and not so neat borders that divide South Asia. It was not too long ago that Pakistan, India and Bangladesh were all parts of British India with common political, economic, legal, and administrative structures. There are deep linguistic, cultural, migrational, religious and historical ties that people share across borders. Amidst this, the rivers

---

[13] A phrase used by Ajaya Dixit during the interview on 24.9.2007, Kathmandu, and also the title of his article in Himal South Asian, August 2003.

have been a stream of "collective belonging"—sustaining ecosystems, communities and acting as a unifying force for South Asia's geo-economic and geo-cultural landscape.'[14]

2. Turbulent Past and Present of Frontier Rivers: Partition, Communal Identity and Securitisation of Water

However, these rivers are also embedded in the socio-political context of post colonial, post partition states of South Asia where a number of mental and physical borders are a reality today. Hence flowing water does not purely remain an ecological concern. It gets imbued with notions of security and insecurity; domestic stability and instability; purity and pollution; legitimacy and illegitimacy. Consequently, disputes over control and use of trans-boundary water send ripples across communities, people, and countries in the region. Who has the rights over rivers and their resources? Who can access water? Who can cast their nets into the sea? Competing claims have pitted citizens, communities, states, diverse interest groups against one another—within countries as well across countries in South Asia. Interwoven within these conflicts are other hierarchies of gender and caste which then further work to marginalise women and dalits in the use and management of water.

I) **Partition, Nationalism and Water:** The Partition of the sub-continent into India and Pakistan in 1947 was not just a partition of land and people, but also of its waterways. In the west, the line of partition (Radcliffe line) ran right through Punjab but in effect cut the Indus river system, disrupting ts well integrated irrigation canals. Many of the canals were severed from their headworks. For instance, the existing canal headwork of the Upper Bari Doab canal, and the Sutlej Valley canals fell in India, while the land being irrigated by their water fell in Pakistan, which led to water disputes mmediately after partition. In addition, while the Indus was the main source of water for Pakistan's cultivable land, the source of the rivers of the Indus basin remained with India, adding another dimension of insecurity for Pakistan.

> Partition is simple division, a separation but what happened in 947 was much more than hat....Not only were people separated overnight, homes became trange places, strange places now-a-days to be claimed as home, a line as drawn to be a border, and boundaries began to find reflections n people's lives and minds." **rvashi Butalia**[18]

Similarly, in the East, the Radcliffe line not only partitioned Bengal (into West Bengal and East Pakistan, later to declare independence as Bangladesh), but in effect it divided the delta region of the Ganga basin, severing river etworks of the Ganga, Brahmaputra and Meghna, and severing ports (Calcutta and Chittagong) from their water sources. Hence, East Pakistan, as a lower riparian, was left with little control over the fifty-four of its rivers, including he Ganga and the Brahmaputra. India was left with the only port in the east, the Calcutta port, catering to a vast interland, and inundated by the problem of heavy siltation that was affecting its navigability.[19] In addition, the partition line in Bengal had not factored in two distinct features of the rivers in this region—a) the fact that they tended to be extremely 'wayward' and frequently changed course, and b) they formed chars (strips of land rising from the river bed above the water level). Both these factors then became sources of border disputes between the two nations. Many of these chars,

---
[14] Ajaya Dixit, "Rivers of Collective Belonging," Himal South Asia, August 2003.
[15] Eva Saroch, "Hydro Borders in South Asia: Geopolitical Imagination and Contestations," in Berg, E., and Houtam, ed., Routing Borders between Territories, Discourses and Practices, (England: Ashgate Publishing Limited, 2003), p. 122.
[16] Ibid. p. 120.
[17] K. Warikoo, "Perspective of the Indus Waters Treaty," in Samaddar, R and Reifeld, ed., Peace as Process: Reconciliation and Conflict in South Asia, (New Delhi: Manohar, 2001), p. 283.
[18] Urvashi Butalia, The Other Side of Silence: Voices from the Partition of India, (New Delhi: Viking-Penguin, 1998), p. 271.
[19] The Ganga bifurcated at Farakka into Bhagirathi-Hoogly, with the Calcutta port being fed by the Bhagirathi channel of the Ganga. Complications arose as the Bhagirathi shifted course, thereby creating problems for the Calcutta port.

like the ones on river Padma, are inhabited by people (char dwellers) who have since got caught in these border conflicts and faced untold suffering.[20] It would be worthwhile to mention that while much has, of late, been written on the partition and its impact on land and people, there is relatively less work done from the perspective of water. However, the fact remains that many of the water disputes between these countries today have their genesis in the divisions created herein.

The Partition not only created new borders and three countries out of one in the region, but the unfolding of partition also created mental borders, suspicion and mistrust, which have since been reflected in the water politics of the region. This is evident in the way every water dispute between India-Pakistan (and now India-Bangladesh) takes the form of antagonistic nationalism with overtones of Hindu-Muslim communalised politics. An example of this has been the Sindhu (Indus) Darshan festival in Ladhak, or the Brahmaputra Darshan festival in the North East, organised by the BJP[21] as an assertion of claims on these frontier rivers.[22] In a similar vein, the VHP (Vishwa Hindu Parishad), protesting against the Tehri Dam on the Ganga, sought to collapse the Ganga with (Hindu) nationalism in statements like "Gangatva is Hindutva, Hindutva is Rashtratva" (Ganga = Hindu = Nationalism).[23] Similarly, protests against the Farakka dam, originally rooted in the sufferings of people and the environmental degradation of Bangladesh, took a communal turn among many sections of the population in there.[24]

II) Securitisation of water : If one were to look at the conflict between India and Pakistan through watery frames, there is a view in the region that the dispute on Kashmir between India and Pakistan (over which the two neighbours have already waged four wars), is really about the control of the Indus water heads.[25] Z.A Bhutto, (the then Prime Minister of Pakistan) while addressing the UN Security Council in 1965, stressed that the main hindrance in resolving Kashmir is water. In March 2003, prime minister of the Pakistan-occupied Kashmir Sikandar Hayat, went to the extent of suggesting at a seminar that the "freedom fighters of Kashmir are in reality fighting for Pakistan's water security."[26] How far this is true or not is another matter, but what it does reflect is that there is serious insecurity in Pakistan about India's strategic control over the Indus water systems. At one level, the apprehensions are over India withholding the water for an extended period, especially during the dry season. This carries disastrous implications for Pakistan. For one, the Mangla Dam on the River Jhelum, which is a source of irrigation and electricity for Punjab, would be adversely affected. At another, it is felt that the control of water, through storage and big barrages, provide, India with a strategic edge during a military confrontation. It would enable India to control the mobility and retreat of Pakistani troops and enhance the manoeuverability of Indian troops. Closing the Barrage gates would render the Pakistani canal system dry and easy to cross. India, it is argued, is already in control of the Chenab River through the Salal Dam constructed in 1976, and many in Pakistan criticise the conceding of the Salal Dam to India.[27] Further in this direction came the Kishenganga and the Baglihar projects. Both the projects lie in the state of Jammu and Kashmir and are perceived as being guided more by India's geo-strategic concerns vis-a-vis Pakistan and by its larger geo-political manoeuvers in South Asia, rather than for the development of Jammu & Kashmir as stated by the Indian government.[28] According to

---

[20] See Joya Chatterjee, "The Fashioning of a Frontier: The Radcliffe Line and Bengal's Border Landscape, 1947–52," Modern Asian Studies 33:0101, p. 224.
[21] Bharatiya Janta Party, a Hindu right wing party.
[22] Eva Saroch, n. 10, p. 134.
[23] M. Sharma, "Nature and Nationalism," Frontline, 16th February 2001, p. 17–45.
[24] Interview with Md. Hilal, Dhaka, 11 January 2008.
[25] There have been numerous discussions on this issue on news channels like NDTV. Also see Samuel Baid, "Not Kashmir but Kashmir's water is the core issue for Pakistan," Greater Kashmir, 28th March 2005. Deepak Gyawali also quotes the former Foreign Secretary of India J.N. Dixit, in Gywali, "Pluralistic Politics under Monistic Design."
[26] See Ronojoy Sen, "And a river runs through it," The Times of India, 12th March 2005.
[27] F. Noshab, N. Mushtaq, "Water Disputes in South Asia," see Webpage http://www.issi.org.pk/journal/ 2001_files/no_3/article/4a.htm, 12.10.2007.
[28] Interview with A. Talib, Action Aid Office, Srinagar, Kashmir.

A. Talib, the Tulbul Navigation Project (or Wullar Barrage Project) is a case in point. India has always maintained that the project was meant to improve water navigation on the Jhelum in North Kashmir but water navigation on Jhelum between Sopore and Baramullah or even Uri has never been an issue with the people of these areas.[29] India on its part totally refutes these charges as baseless and commits itself to the IWT.

The situation is similar between India and Bangladesh. A sentiment one often heard in Bangladesh was that the barrage at Farakka was built not so much to flush out the Calcutta port as stated by India, but to give India strategic security vis-à-vis what was then Pakistan, and Bangladesh now. As a respondent stated during the interview (name withheld), "Farakka was built for the purpose of India's security. If it was built to share water, there is very little water at Farakka in the lean season anyway."

Between India and Nepal, despite no overt conflict and a treaty of 'Peace and Friendship' between the two countries, India's "security" concerns have been an irritant in the relationship between the two countries. Problems have erupted over India's insistence to station its troops at Kalapani (a disputed territory) at the headwaters of Mahakali, and its control of the Kosi and Gandak barrages on common rivers in Nepal. In Nepal, the feeling is that this compromises its sovereignty.[30] India, on the other hand, feels that this is a matter of its national security arising out of the use of the Nepalese territory by the ISI agents and other outfits manoeuvered by third countries—a fear that has been aggravated by the hijacking of India Airlines from Kathmandu to Kandhahar.[31]

Another aspect of securitisation of water resources and its management is the classification of hydrological data as "secret" information and its consequent removal from public domain. This is clearly evident in South Asia, and more so with India. In Nepal, in Bangladesh, and in Pakistan, a common complaint has been that India maintains utmost secrecy about any facts/figures/data regarding trans-boundary water. In all these countries, a striking feature was that any project being built on trans-boundary water was known not by open sharing of information, but through newspaper reports. More so, it is a fact that timely and adequate informations are never easily or fully given or shared. For instance, this has been the complaint of Pakistan over the Baglihar and Kishengunga projects, or of Bangladesh over the Tipaimukh or over the now stalled Indian River Linking project. In Nepal, according to Mr. Surya Nath Upadhyay, former Secretary of Water Resources, Nepal and the chief negotiator on the Nepali side on the Mahakali Treaty:

"India treats Nepal as a small and poor country and acts unilaterally. When India was surveying for the Tanakpur barrage, Nepal raised its voice and asked what are you doing? They said no, we are looking at some possibilities of developing water projects and if there will be any possibilities we will certainly consult you. Later, they started construction and Nepal again raised its voice and they said it is not your concern because it is being constructed on Indian territory and continued with the construction work of the Tanakpur barrage well into our territory, for which negotiations were carried out later. There is unrest in the Nepalese mind about the treatment that they are being meted out by India. I think its very unfortunate that this susceptibility has been not really taken into consideration."[32]

India on the other hand feels that it has acted well within the various water treaty provisions it has signed with its neighbours, and that there is little appreciation of the need and energy requirement of a vast country together with a tendency to obstruct any efforts it makes to utilise its 'own' water resources. There is also the feeling that given the disproportionate size and power of India as compared to the rest of the countries, there is a preconceived notion of India as a hegemon.

---

[29] Ibid.
[30] Deepak Gyawali and Ajaya Dixit, "How not to do a South Asian Treaty," in Himal South Asian, April 2001, webpage. 11, 2007.
[31] Dinakar Shukla, "International Relations: India-Nepal Ties," see webpage http://pib.nic.in/feature/feyr2001/fsep2001/f040920011.html. Accessed 8.2.2008.
[32] Interview with Mr. Surya Nath Upadhyay, Kathmandu, now associated with Jalsrot Vikas Sanstha and Global Water Partnership, South Asia, 29.09.07.

However, if one were to unpack the various articulations of disputes over trans-boundary water, the real concern seems to be over water scarcity and availability. Evidently there is a strong tendency in South Asia to turn water into an issue of national pride, and a propensity to place demands as if flowing water is an exclusive property of that country alone, and belongs to no one else. This situation is likely to get worse before it gets better, particularly as water stress grows in the region (to be further discussed under the section on climate change).

3. Reflecting Discrimination: Caste, Gender and Water

Water is not simply a value-neutral physical element but something that percolates into all aspects of our lives, and mirrors the asymmetry of power as it exists in society. Given the widespread gender and caste based discrimination in South Asia, this is also reflected in the way water is perceived (with its accompanying notion of the sacred, purity and pollution), interacted with, accessed, controlled and managed. While of late there has been a growing body of literature on "gender and water," on the ground this has nor translated in women's participation in decision making. The aspect of caste and water remains an issue that is yet to be brought to the fore. In the meanwhile, women and dalits/discriminated communities continue to be invisible, denied a voice, or any say, in decision making, or the management of water. Even in the various initiatives led by the civil society, concerns regarding gender and caste are yet to be effectively registered in terms of action.

I) Gender and Water: An archetyal representation of gender-water metaphor throughout South Asia is that of a poor women, carrying her water burden for miles, standing by a public tap for hours to collect water, struggling on a daily basis with her water chores. The water locations are often feminine spaces and women have been imaged as the 'domestic collectors' of water, as 'domestic consumers', but they have no say in the public/productive role of water uses and participate in its decision making and governance, even as 'commodification' and 'privatisation' of water become the watch words.

Throughout South Asia (and elsewhere), gender is central to social and political power dynamics that shape the use of resources. Critically linked to this are issues of rights, of health and sanitation, of access, of women being 'bearers' of impacts, of women being excluded from the sustainability agenda, of living with decisions imposed from the top. Notably, women are not an undifferentiated category, and gender is often intersected by issues of class, caste, and region. Nevertheless, women and gender perspectives are totally invisible when it comes to water issues across the region, be it over treaties, flood, irrigation projects, dams and displacements. This is all the more stark when it comes to trans-boundary water which is dominated by strategists, bureaucrats, engineers, and is absolutely a male bastion. Women tend to be severely underrepresented in public institutions, at the political and the tech-nobureaucratic level, in the various corporations, though they are among those who are doubly vulnerable when it comes to suffering the impacts. What is required here is the integration of gender concerns and the participatory mechanism of decision making at local, national and regional, and international level, and among the various stake holders.

II) Caste, Discrimination and Water : The question of caste, discrimination and water suffers from double invisibility. Except in India and Nepal where Dalit assertion has brought the issue to the fore, caste or other forms of descent based discriminations that exist underneath the surface of equality often goes unacknowledged even by the civil society at large.

In Pakistan, DAMAN, a development organisation, has highlighted the plight of the indigenous minorities of the Indus basin, such as the Kihals, Musali, and Ode, many of whom have suffered a direct blow to their livelihoods due to water conflict between India and Pakistan, and development activities by the Pakistani state. Allotment of lands to immigrants, development of irrigation systems i.e. canals and dams, clearing of forests and the shift to inorganic farming have a deprived these indigenous minorities of the

The Kihals introduce themselves as Sheikhs. Instead of strictly following one single religion in strict, the Kihals kept to a flexible system of believes. Due to their increasing dependence on neighboring Muslim population however, Kihals are fast converting to Islam and adapting Islamic life styles and traditions. *"We are confirmed Muslims just like you and recite the same Qalma. If you (Sarkar, the government) provide us education, we will recite and understand the Quran. Please provide our women and children with education, and also please don't pollute the river with the city effluent and shift the effluent drains to somewhere else,"* said Sona Kihal during the first ever meeting of Kihals with the concerned councilor. 30.4.2005, Rose Hotel, D.I. Khan (Source: DAMAN Development Organisation, Pakistan).

Indus, their rights and access to water. The fact that many, like the Kihal men and women, do not even have the right to vote and voice their opinion further adds to their invisibility.[33]

In Nepal, Shanta Bahadur Pun, a water activist, pointed out that such discrimination was not practised in all communities, and was not something he had come across within his own community. However, historically in Nepal, there is practised discrimination between "the caste whose water is pure (pani calyna jat)" and "the caste whose water is defiled (pani nacalynâ jat)." As reported by the Human Rights Watch, segregation in neighbourhoods and water wells is a common practice in Nepal.[34] In India, conflicts and discrimination, along caste lines over traditional water bodies like tanks and ponds are widely prevalent. In both India and Nepal, water is treated as a marker of purity, and lower caste groups are often not allowed to touch the water before their high-caste counterparts. The question of access, allocation right to water becomes extremely important here, and increasingly a simmering issue, loaded with tensions. What do these communities on the margins of society and at border-margins of the nation-state lose or gain, what are their needs and suffering, how are their customary water laws being changed or wiped out by what is being imposed from above are other areas on which there has been little documentation.

Dams, Barrages, Diversions as Sites of Conflict in South Asia

The subject of mega projects and dams is one of the better publicised and documented issues in the region, and there is a lot of material existing on it. This is not surprising given the high financial, ecological and human costs these mega projects have entailed, and have been among the most intensely contested sites of conflict within each country and across borders-between dam affected and drought/flood affected areas, between communities and states, between an approach which regards 'dams' as secular 'temples' of modernity, and the other which sees them as giant symbols of destructive development. These studies have highlighted the sufferings of displaced marginal communities, the ills effects of mega projects on the ecology, and the limitation of mega projects in addressing droughts or floods in South Asia.

However, "dam building" seems to have got a new lease of life in the region in the present decade. If in the late 80s/early 90s, various environmental movements in the region had cast doubts on the viability of big dams and barrages, in the present contexts, these projects have acquired a new legitimacy among certain sections of the economic–political elite, and are on their way back in India, and in Pakistan, and with every likelihood of returning to the other countries too.[35] Between India and Pakistan, there is almost a scramble to dam the common rivers, which then has been fuelling discord. Take the case of the Kishenganga or the Neelam in Paksitan. India has started building (330-megawatt) on the river, which Pakistan fears would

---

[33] See http://www.civicus.org/new/media/BriefonIndigenousMinoritiesoffIndus.doc.
[34] See "Discrimination of Dalits in Nepal," Human Rights Watch, website: http://www.hrw.org/english/docs/2004/02/09/nepal/7322.htm
[35] In Pakistan, President Musharraf while announcing an ambitious plan to troops posted in the mountain region, also announced that "all big water reservoirs including the Bhasha Dam at Diamir would be built by 2016." In India, a number of new dams have been announced or are being constructed in the North East and other "newer" areas.

impact its hydro scheme, a 969-MW plant located down-river, directly across the Line of Control in the Neelam Valley. Other cases of tension arising from the daming of frontier or shared rivers are the Indian River Linking Project (IRLP), the Kosi High Dam and Barrage, the Tipaimukh Dam which are among the numerous projects planned or being constructed and which are taking on the form of conflict, not only between the state and communities of people opposed to or affected by them, but also between countries.

Why Dams Now?

The question that becomes relevant here is what is fuelling this 'dam-race' in South Asia at a time when dams are being indicted[36] or decommissioned globally. Prof M. Maniruzzaman Miah feels this has to do with the fact that India is in a hurry for quick 'development' to compete in the world economy, has a huge energy requirement and does not really care about its neighbours.[37] Others point out that in the last decade, across South Asia, there has been a growing control of water resources by giant transnational water companies, and that mega projects and dams are paving the way for the 'merchandising' of water. It is notable that many of these projects today involve high spending, huge loans and involvement of funding consortiums. For instance, the Kishenganga Dam project (KHEP) is to be built at an estimated $500 million, mostly through international funding by the Swedish Consortium Skanska International. Similarly, the Baglihar project is estimated to cost $1 billion. In effect, the cost of electricity will go up substantially for people in the violent affected Kashmir valley who are unable even to pay the Rs. 2 being charged currently.[38]

Mapping Large Dams/Projects and Conflict: Who controls flowing water?

Some of the most contested, old and new mega projects which have troubled hydro relation in South Asia are given below. This is by no means a comprehensive list, but a just few cases among many.

I. Trouble over Dams and Barrages: The case of India and Bangladesh

i) Farakka Barrage: The Farakka Barrage and its impact remains a dominant metaphor of devastation/injustice and is synonymous with anti-India sentiment in all the conversations in Bangladesh, cutting across academics, politicians, NGO persons, and activists. Built to divert water from the Ganga to its tributary Bhaghirathi-Hoogly and to the Calcutta port, it has some how come to embody all that is wrong in water relationship between Bangladesh and India. As people begin talking about the water problem with India, they start with Farakka, about how it totally disregarded Bangladesh's ecology, water needs and the survival of its people. The barrage is, therefore, seen as an unfair treatment meted out, and the disregard shown, to a smaller country by a "boro bhai" (big brother).

Due to silt clogging up rivers, many women have had to give up their traditional roles and take up unwanted ones.

Take the case of Sufia, 35. Sufia use to travel with her family on a boat that they owned, selling pink pearls and medicinal herbs. Sufia's family has had to sell the boat and find a new source of livelihood. Today she smuggles wood and rice into India for survival and brings back saris to sell. *"I often cry for the old gypsy days but the river has got laden with silt and it is impossible now to operate our boats,"* says Sufia. On the other hand, sources in the frontier towns point out that large scale smuggling of firewood was causing rapid deforestation.[39]

---

[36] World Commission on Dams Report 2000.
[37] Interview with Prof. M. Maniruzzaman Miah, TWEDS, Chairman, 11.01.07.
[38] Dams, Rivers & People, May-June 2005, p.7
[39] Tahmina Ahmad, in Rivers of Life, Bangladesh: Journalists take a Critical look at the Flood Action Plan.

There exists a large body of work on the impact of the Farakka project on Eastern India, and on Bangladesh. Some like the SANDRP Report, point out that the interception of the Ganga in its high meandering belt has seriously affected the ecology, agriculture and people's livelihood in West Bengal and Bangladesh. Huge Siltation problem in upstream Malda and downstream Murshidabad has increased flood intensity, limited functioning of the barrage gates and has led to concentrated flow that has caused heavy erosion in these areas.[40] As the river with lower depth meanders, erodes, deposits silt, border disputes have come to the fore, particularly where the river also formed the boundary line between the two counties. Such is the case of border rivers like the Kushiara, Muhuri, Feni, Ichamati and Gumti.[41] In many of the Gangetic districts of West Bengal, water is affected by arsenic toxicity due to lowering of water table.

The Farakka Barrage, according to environmentalists in Bangladesh, has reduced river flows, and led to the problem of saline water intrusion, particularly during the dry months. This has been damaging the Sunderbans, the world's largest Mangrove forest shared by India and Bangladesh, and affected agriculture and fishery. The consequence has been large-scale migration of affected communities within India (from Murshidabad and Malda to places like Gujarat and Maharashtra) and from Bangladesh to India. Ashok Swain makes a link between the diversion of water at Farakka by India and forced migration of Bangladeshi citizens to other parts of the region, including India. These trans-border human-inflicted environmental changes have resulted in the loss of sources of livelihood for a large population in the south-western part of Bangladesh. Absence of alternatives in the other parts of the country has left no other option for these displaced communities but to migrate to India. As his study determines, environmental destruction not only creates resource scarcity conflicts, but these forced migrations further lead to native-migrant conflicts.[42] This can be seen in the way migration from Bangladesh has become a flashpoint in the North East and other parts of India.

ii) *"Fifty-four rivers enter Bangladesh from India. So we have fifty-four problems*[43]*"*

The above statement by Mohammad Hilal captures various small and big conflicts that are brewing on Transboundary Rivers. Though the barrage at Farakka has been the most visible site of conflict, a number of other "development" projects being built in India are also becoming new flashpoints. One such prominent case is the Indian River Linking Project (IRLP)—a massive development project consisting of networks of channels, reservoirs and dams to link all the major rivers in India. On the eastern side, it envisages a large-scale transfer of water from the Brahmaputra and Ganga basin to western and southern rivers in India. The IRLP has met with wide-scale criticism by environmentalists and protests not just within India, but also between India and Nepal, and India and Bangladesh. However, the project stands forestalled for the time being, but a number of other water disputes persist. And such a simmering dispute is over the Tipaimukh Dam. "The Tipaimukh dam will be another Farakka for Eastern Bangladesh," says Mohammad Hilal.[44] The Tipaimukh Dam is being built on the river Barak in the North Eastern state of Manipur, and has been yet another site for anti-dam movement within India. People in Manipur are up in arms against what they see as the destruction of their ecology, livelihoods and possible displacement. On 30/31st December 2005, an

---

[40] Manisha Banerjee, "A Report on the Impact of the Farakka Barrage on the Human Fabric: A Study on the Upstream and DownStream areas of Farakka Barrage," South Asia Network on Dam, Rivers and People, New Delhi, 1999. Webpage http://www.sandrp.in/ dams/impct_frka_wcd.pdf., Accessed 5.12.2007. Also see Dispute over the Ganga, (Kathmandu: Panos Institute, South Asia, 2004).
[41] Narottam Gaan, Environmental Degradation and Conflict, p. 7
[42] Ashok Swain, "Displacing the Conflict: Environmental Destruction in Bangladesh and Ethnic Conflict in India," Journal of Peace Research, Sage, Vol. 33, No. 2. (May, 1996), pp. 189–204, http://links.jstor.org/sici? sici=00223433%28199605%2933%3A2% 3C189%3ADTCEDI%3E2.0.CO%3B2-R
[43] Hilal, 11th January 2008.
[44] Hilal, 11th January 2008.

international conference on the Tipaimukh Dam and its fall-outs was organised in Dhaka with large number of participants from Manipur and Assam. However, sustained coordination between these groups has been difficult.

Explaining the way projects across the border impact people's lives, and in turn Indo-Bangladesh relations, Mohammad Matim, (General Secretary, Bangladesh Poribesh Andolan) stated:

"Bangladesh is a riverine country and we say the river is the mother of this land. The river has created this deltaic region, and nourishes the land, the plants, the ecology including fish and livestock. In one sentence, Bangladeshi people's total life depends on the river because agriculture is a major component. Fifty-four rivers come from India before they end at the Bay of Bengal. Unfortunately, all the rivers have got one or more than one intervention project in India. India has put a dam, a barrage or diverted the water for irrigation purpose, or for power generation, or for making a reservoir. All the fifty-four rivers are affected by the Indian government and these have harmed agriculture, livestock, greenery, fishes and ultimately the total lifestyle of the people of Bangladesh."

According to Mustafa Kamal Mazumdar, "There is the diversion of the river Teesta which despite endless talks between the two countries has yielded little result. During dry season, there is little water for people here from the Teesta. Water is also being diverted from the Mahananda. There are structures on the Gomti and on the western side of Bangladesh. There is yet another structure on the Borai river, the third largest river in Bangladesh, which enters through the Sylhet region.[45]

Much of the apprehension in Bangladesh is about water withdrawal/scarcity and the impact it could have on the lives, livelihood and ecology of Bangladeshis. Environmentalists in Bangladesh express deep reservations and point out that despite the fact that these are shared rivers, there is no environmental assessment in Bangladesh before these projects are sanctioned in India.[46]

II. India-Pakistan: The case of Baghlihar

India-Pakistan relations have been the tensest in the subcontinent, marked by four wars. However, the dispute on the rivers of the Indus has a longer history. Even prior to partition, every major intervention on the rivers of the Indus Basin had been a source of trouble. Under colonial rule, as the British expanded the gigantic irrigation system in this region, a dispute broke out between the two provinces of Punjab and Sindh over the construction of canals on the river Sutlej (1930s).[47] Soon after partition, a conflict emerged between West Punjab (Pakistan) and East Punjab (India) over the Dipalpur and Upper Bari Doab Canal[48] which further escalated to the extent of East Punjab arbitrarily shutting off water supply to the irrigation channels of West Punjab. This became the cause of a lot of damage to the predominantly agricultural economy across the border. A number of squabbles, such as over Pakistan's diversion work on the Sutlej, or India's contraction work on the Bhakra-Nangal continued to mar India-Pakistan's already conflict ridden relationship. Finally in 1960, the Indus Waters Treaty (IWT) was signed, and to some extent worked well till 1980. Thereafter, differences between the two countries on the question of water surfaced once again in the context of several projects, like the Wullar Barrage/Tulbul Navigation project on the Jhelum, Swalakote Hydroelectrical project (HEP), Dal husti HEP on the Chenab. More recently, a controversy has emerged over

---

[45] Interview with Mustafa Kamal Mazumdar, Executive Editor, New Nation, Dhaka, 8.01.08. He writes extensively on rivers, mega projects and environmental issues.
[46] Ibid
[47] In late 19th century, the British undertook a large scale engineering experimentation in the form of irrigation projects and canal networks. For details see, Undala Z. Alam, Water Rationality: Mediating the Indus Waters Treaty, Ph.D thesis, Geography Department, University of Durham, 1998, p. 38 webpage: http://www.transboundarywaters.orst.edu/publications/related_research/Alam1998.pdf, accessed, 30.12. 07.
[48] Ibid.

the Baghlihar HEP on the Chenab and the Kishenganga HEP on the Kishenganga/Neelam river, a sort of hiccup in the cautious peace process the two countries have undertaken since 2004.

Baglihar Project (BHEP):

Located on the Chenab, the BHEP (with power capacity of 450 MW during phase I and 900 MW during phase II) became a point of contention between India and Pakistan.[49] The issue is further complicated by the fact the BHEP is a venture of the state government of J&K—located in a state which is, at one level, a disputed territory between the two countries, and at another, a state which has vehemently opposed the IWT as violating its water rights.

- **Pakistan Government's view:** Pakistan has raised six objections relating to project configuration, free board, spillway, firm power, pondage, level of intake, inspection during plugging of low level intake, and whether the structure is meant to be a low weir or a dam. Based on these objections, Pakistan asked India to stop all work until all issues were resolved and invoked the arbitration clause of the IWT. Subsequently, matters were taken to a Neutral Expert, Professor Raymond Lafitte of Switzerland.

- **The Indian Government's View:** India claims BHEP is a fully legal scheme. It involves no water storage, and therefore does not violate the IWT. India is allowed by the IWT to build power generation projects on any of the three western rivers of the Indus river system, as long as they benefit the local people.[50] India accused Pakistan of trying to prevent it from removing the grievances of the people of J&K.

- **Dominant view in J&K:** BHEP is a project for/by Jammu and Kashmir, a state that had not been taken into account by the IWT, and is in dire need of power. They believe Pakistan wants to deny Jammu and Kashmir the right to use its own rivers, citing the situation in Pakistan occupied Kashmir where, they believe people have no rights over Mangla Dam on the Jhelum, built to meet the power and water needs of Punjab and other parts of Pakistan.[51]

"We used to shift along/across the river Indus, and the Thal desert, but the dams, barrages and canals have locked us in little pockets (areas). Now we can not shift a great deal; instead we usually remain in union council, tehsil council and district council boundaries," said Ghulam Haider Kihals, as Kihal men and women are deprived of their rights in Pakistan. Thala Baloo Ram, D I Khan (Source: DAMAN Development Organisation, Pakistan.

Finally on 12th February 2007 Professor Lafitte, the Neutral Expert, gave his 'determination', suggesting slight changes[52] in the design of the project but allowing the project to proceed. While a number of reports have focused on whether the project violates or does not violate the IWT treaty, a gap remains within the larger debate about the environmental aspects of the dam and its impact on people. On visiting the dam site in Baglihar, one soon discovered why. The dam site had been declared as a "security sensitive zone" and not open to visitors. As an officer at the BHEP (name withheld) told us, "This dam is being targeted by our enemy country and it is high security zone." Any information was difficult to get. Talking to people in the nearby town of Chandrakot (Doda, J&K), we gathered that people/families living where the dam site is being constructed had been moved to Jammu, and about 150 families were still waiting

---

[49] Rajesh Sinha, "Two Neighbours and a Treaty: Baglihar Project in Hot Waters," *Economic and Political Weekly*, 18th February 2006.
[50] Rajesh Sinha, p. 606-607.
[51] Ibid. p. 607.
[52] For details of suggested changes, see Ramaswamy Iyer, *Towards Water Wisdom: Limits, Justice, Harmony*, (Sage: New Delhi, 2007), p. 85.

to be rehabilitated. We were told by government officials who did not want to be named, that "more than 'adequate' compensation was given." According to Arijimand Talib, *"The Chenab river is known to be a heavy silt laden river."*[53] Heavy landslides in the region and the fact that there are already a number of projects existing/being constructed on the same river (like the Salal, Dulhasti and Swalkote) has made the silt situation worse.[54] In addition, the region is in a high seismic zone. The Baglihar clearly leaves many questions unanswered.

III. India-Nepal: Conflict over embankments, barrages and dams

Nepal has three categories of rivers flowing into India: the first are those originating from the Himalayas such as the Koshi, Gandaki, Karnali and Mahakali, which are perennial with a substantial water flow. Mega projects and dams on these rivers have often been at the centre of water tension between India and Nepal. The second set of rivers originates from the Mahabharat, and the third from the Chure range. These rivers have less or no flow in the dry season, but during the monsoons, particularly the rivers from the Chure range, can become turbulent, capable of bringing about massive destructions. Embankments on some of these rivers have been yet another point of dispute.

i) Barrages and Projects on the Himalayan rivers: Large dams and projects on some of the Himalayan rivers have been the most visible and troublesome aspects of the Indo-Nepal water dispute. The case of Tanakpur Barrage on the Mahakali river is but one such example. Problems began at the outset when India began a technical survey for a 120 MW HEP on the Mahakali river near Tanakpur in Uttar Pradesh (now Uttaranchal), 18 km upstream of the Sarada Barrage. Nepal raised objections on grounds that this would affect its Mahakali Irrigation Project. India agreed to redesign its project but continued with construction despite Nepalese discomfort. Indian position throughout was that the barrage was totally on Indian territory and not a matter of Nepal's concern. Problems came to the fore when the project was completed in 1988, but the left afflux bund required to be tied on the high ground on the left bank of Mahakali, i.e., on the Nepalese side of the river. India requested Nepal for 577m of Nepali land for this purpose, which in effect, would also submerge 2.9 ha of land in Nepal. However, given India's unilateral approach earlier, together with the fact that Indo-Nepal relations, in general, had taken a turn for the worse in those years, nothing materialised till 1991. Finally, with a new (democratic) government in place, Nepal agreed to provide the land under an "understanding," that soon became a highly contentious issue in Nepal. The "understanding" was overtaken by the Mahakali Integrated Treaty—a treaty which (discussed in a later section) by itself came under a lot of suspicion and contention.

ii) "Choking the outlets of the water along the border[55]*": Embankments on India-Nepal border.* According to Mr. Ishwar Raj Onta, while large dams and projects often catch media glare, what really escapes policy makers and public attention is a number of smaller barrages and embankments along the Uttar Pradesh and Bihar borders, and the Tarai region of Nepal, which have been causing havoc in the lives of the people living there.

---

[53] A. Talib, Action Aid, Srinanagar.
[54] Dams, Rivers and People, Vol. 3, Issue. 4–5, May 2005, Webpage http://www.narmada.org/sandrp/ MayJune2005.pdf, Accessed 17.7.07.
[55] Mr. Surya Nath Upadhayay of JVS, Kathmandu, 29.09.07.

"Almost 236 rivers cross India-Nepal border. And in all major and medium rivers, India already has barrages, constructed without consulting Nepal. In addition, there are several barrages built by India along the border. Nepal has been losing a lot of land by way of inundation behind these barrages, especially in the monsoons. This has been a problem for the Tarai region of Nepal. At the same time in UP and Bihar, floods have also become a severe problem and very politicised. Much of this could be avoided if there is a proper dialogue. There needs to be a certain give and take in the region."[56]

Explaining these further, Ajaya Dixit states that Tarai is an extension of the Gangetic plains and the region is crisscrossed by several smaller rivers[57] which originate in the southern slopes of the Churia hills and flow southwards into India. All rivers flowing from Nepal join the Ganga or its tributaries in Uttar Pradesh, Bihar and West Bengal. Many of these rivers in the Tarai region have low flow, or are dry during the winters, but with the commencement of the monsoons, the flow increases or a dry river becomes active and acquires a trans-boundary character. The fact that the Churia hills receive some of the heaviest and most intense rainfall in the country makes these rivers fearsome during the monsoons. This region is also densely populated and millions here depend on agriculture based livelihood which has led to the construction of a large number of irrigation canals, roads, railway lines, flood control embankments and urbanisaton—all of which have further constrained drainage and exacerbated the impact of flooding.

How exactly these border obstructions and embankments along the border have affected relations across border communities, there is little research to show. A study by Dinesh Kumar Mishra and Satendra Kumar on one such river, the Bhutahi Balan (a tributary of the Kosi) points out that building of embankments on this river has led to conflicts among various hamlets of the same village because of their locations. This conflict was further deepened as it got politicised by different political parties for votes.[58] Another study by Ram Niwas Pandey provides some idea about the pressure felt by border communities in Nepal because of floods and a large-scale migration of the people from the hill-districts, compelling the landless of the Tarai, particularly the Tharus, to leave their homes and to move into Indian territory for survival.[59] However, there is a gap in terms of research/inclusion of these communities in the larger discourse of people-ecology-border interface. This may have to do with the fact that unlike in the case of Bangladesh or Pakistan, Nepal and India share an open border. However, it is also a reality that there is a growing tendency within the Indian bureaucratic and power circles to "securitise" the India-Nepal border.[60] Moreover, the question of these ephemeral trans-boundary rivers is often left out of the larger discourse of trans-boundary water governance between India and Nepal, and the plight of the communities is not too well documented. Among the few studies that do exist is one by Ajaya Dixit and Madhukar Upadhaya,[61] which, through the vantage point of floods, highlight the vulnerability of some of these communities.

iii) Politics of Flood: A familiar refrain while discussing hydro-politics between India and Nepal is that of floods. There is no doubt that the intensity of floods have increased over the years. This year, in Bihar

---

[56] Interview with Mr. Ishwar Raj Onta, Chairperson, Jal Vikas Shrot (JVS), Nepal, 29.09.07.
[57] Dixit categorises these rivers into six blocks: the Dhangadhi group in the fare west, the Lumbini group, the Birganj group, the Janakput group, the Rajbiraj group and the Biratnagar group. See Ajaya Dixit, Madhukar Upadhaya, Anil Pokhrel, Kanchan Dixit, Deeb Raj Rai and Madhav Devkota, "Flood Disaster Impacts and Responses in Nepal's Tarai's Marginalised Basins," in Moench, Marcus and Ajaya Dixit, (ed.) Working With the Winds of Change: Towards Strategies for Responding to the Risks Associated with Climate Change and Other Hazards, Pro Vention Consortium, Institute for Social Science and Environmntal Transition, Kathmandu, 2007.
[58] "Challenges of Flood Management in the Bhutahi Balan," Water Nepal, Vol. 11, No. 1, Aug 2002–Jan 2004, p. 29.
[59] Ram Niwas Pandey in India-Nepal: Border Relations, Hari Bansh Jha, Kathmandu, Centre for Economics and Technical Studies, 1995.
[60] For instance, a national newspaper report stating that Indo-Nepal border in Bihar "has become a dangerous place to live in," or that "terrorists use Nepal to stage operations in India." See "Breakfast in Nepal, lunch in India, daily," by Manish Tiwari, Hindustan Times, 17 February 2008. See webpage:http://www.hindustantimes.com/storypage/storypage.aspx?id=a7da840f-9aac-4ba5-a725-1102736684cc.
[61] Ajaya Dixit, Madhukar Upadhaya, et al, n. 54.

alone, some 4,822 villages, and 14 million people were affected (as per UN estimates) in one of the worst floods in the last 15 years. With the intensity of floods have emerged shrill political voices for 'daming' rivers in Nepal. According to Dinesh Mishra, who has been working with communities living in these flood prone areas, every monsoon, the Kosi High Dam becomes the flavour of the season among the politicians in Bihar. As the flood water rises, so does the demand for the Kosi High Dam at Barahkshetra in Nepal as the answer to the floods.[62] However, a survey of the flood affected areas of Bihar quickly reveals that the government has done little to put in place an effective flood policy despite recurrent floods. As per the official website of the Eastern Resource ministry, a National Flood Commission was set up in 1976 to draw up a "coordinated" and "scientific" approach to the problem, but adds that "though the report was submitted in 1980 and accepted by the government, not much progress has been made in the implementation of its recommendations."[63] However, in the absence of an effective policy and faced with the annual monsoon public outcry, the issue of dams in Nepal becomes a scape-goat.

The usual strategy of the state governments in both the states of Bihar and Uttar Pradesh has been to blame Nepal for releasing water, and to tell people that even as the state is aware of its obligation, it can do little since the final solution to the flood problem, the construction of dams in Nepal, is an international matter and in the hands of the central government. The central government on its part insists that water, including floods, is a state subject and the sole responsibility of the state.[64]

However, in Nepal, floods in the Tarai are also taking centre stage. The issue of floods has become a sort of a blame game between Nepal and India (states of UP and Bihar). Many environment activists feel that there is a false image being created in people's mind in India by politicians and the media blaming Nepal for floods in Bihar. However, as Mr. Shanta Bahadur Pun points out, *"A number of factors are responsible for flooding, and embankments are an important factor. For instance, the Kosi embankments have worsened the flood situation not just for us in Nepal, but for the people in Bihar, who are caught within these embankments."*[66] This is further supported by Mr. Dinesh Mishra who argues that one of the main causes for the present flooding and water logging in North Bihar is the inability of this water to enter the main river and drain away because of the embankments. A number of studies have highlighted this and have documented the plight of the people caught in between the Kosi embankments. However, the politics of flood remains shrill as ever and continue to sour Indo-Nepal relations.

"In the environmental debates in this region, there is a tendency to externalise the nature of the problem. Indian politicians and media put the blame for the floods on Nepal." Ajaya Dixit[65]

---

[62] Dinesh Mishra, "Bihar: Flooded and Waterlogged," Disputes Over Ganga, p.111.
[63] See Aman Trust's Report on Flood situation in Bihar, http://www.aman panchayat.org/ index.php?option =com_content&task=view&id=181.
[64] Mishra, n. 52
[65] Interview with Dixit.
[66] Interview with Mr. shanta Pun, IIDS, Kathmandu, 27.9.07.

CHAPTER – 24

Governance Of Trans-Boundary Water In South Asia: Disquiet Over Treaties

"There are three issues when it comes to water negotiations between India and Bangladesh. First, the Indian authorities lack basic democratic ideals in dealing with its neighbours. Second, we are not skilled enough in dealing and negotiating with the authorities in India. So, both these worsen the situation. We have a lack of expertise in Bangladesh and they have a lack of democratic approach. Third, water is a common source between us but we don't have water democracy."

Mohammad Hilal, Environmental Activist, Bangladesh.[1]

"We follow a monocentric path that is dominated by the bureaucracy, technicians and the nation-state. This nation has not provided water security to it citizens. The whole conflict over the Mahakali happened because of a unilateral decision-making, hierarchical mind-set based on control. What is required is a more holistic position rather than an anti-India or anti-Nepal approach. We have to critique the basic understanding regarding water."

Ajaya Dixit, Water Nepal, Nepal [2]

"What lies at the heart of water conflict is greed....Agreements, accords and treaties may temporarily bring peace, but conflict will erupt unless we learn to redefine 'development'."

Ramaswaymy Iyer, India[3]

Conflicts on trans-boundary water have been widespread all over the world, plagued by claims and counter-claims by different users and states. Part of the conflict stems from the very nature of water, such as water being divisible and amenable to sharing; it is a common pool resource; one unit of water used by one is a unit denied to others; it has multiple uses and users, and involves resultant trade-offs; the way water is used and managed causes externalities.[4] Others, like Ramaswamy Iyer, point out that water conflicts are about a gross mismanagement of water, and of what he terms as "water-greed" where nobody seems to have enough and there is an unlimited and ever growing demand for more and more water.[5] However, what makes the case particularly fragile in South Asia is not just the existence of these conflicts, but the lack of a democratic framework, or a regional mechanism that involves all the conflicting parties that is perceived to be fair and is rooted in an ecologically sustainable approach. The existing mode for trans-boundary water governance in South Asia is bilateral treaties, signed by Nepal, Bangladesh, Pakistan with India (which is an upper riparian

---

[1] Interview, Dhaka, 11.01.08.
[2] Interviewed in Kathmandu, 24.09.07.
[3] Ramaswamy Iyer, "Trans-boundary Water Conflicts: A Review" In Joy, Gujja, Paranjape, Gould and Vispute, ed., Water Conflicts in India: A Million Revolts in the Making, (Routledge: New Delhi, 2008), p. 375.
[4] Joy, Gujja, Paranjape, Gould and Vispute, in "Million Revolts in the Making," Economic and Political Weekly, Vol. XLI, No. 7, February 2006, p. 570.
[5] Iyer, n. 62.

in most cases, except with Nepal). Some of these treaties have worked, others have not, but each has been surrounded by controversy and misgivings at some point or other.

1. **India-Nepal Treaties:** Since the beginning of the 20th century, a number of agreements have been signed between India and Nepal.

These include:

I. *The Sarada Agreement (1920)* on the Mahakali river, (now encompassed within the Mahakali Integrated Development Treaty). The Sarada Agreement stipulated the following:

- Formed the basis of the Sarada Barrage built to irrigate United Provinces (today's Uttar Pradesh).
- Transferred 4000 acres on the eastern bank of the Mahakali to India to build the Sarada Barrage in exchange for 4000 acres of forested land in areas further to the east as well as Rs. 50,000 compensation for Nepal.
- Out of the annual flow of approximately 650 cumecs (cubic meters per second) Nepal could withdraw 4.25 of water during the dry season and 13 in the wet season, which could be further increased to 28.34 cumecs if water was available. No specification given regarding India's withdrawal amount. In effect, it was limited only by the scale of the technology it was able to employ.

After the treaty, both the left and the right bank of the river near the Sarada Barrage came under India's control.

II. *The Koshi Project Agreement (1954)*

- To build a barrage on the Kosi river to confine the river (which shifts course frequently), prevent floods in Bihar and divert water for irrigation.
- The 1.15 km barrage, completed in 1962, is wholly in Nepal, and the Eastern Main Canal is entirely in India.
- Nepal is allowed to withdraw water from Kosi and its tributaries for irrigation and other purposes.
- India has the right to regulate the 'balance' at the barrage site from time to time for irrigation and to generate hydro power from the eastern main canal.
- With the "Kosi sell-out" furor in Nepal, the Kosi Agreement was revised in 1966.
- The Western Main Canal first passes through a 35 km stretch of Nepal territory. The Western main Canal, completed only in 1982, was designed to irrigate 356,000 hectares as far west as Darbhanga. Nepal was to receive water from the Western Canal to irrigate 11,000 hectares. The other major component of the project was the 220 km of embankment "jacketing" the Kosi on both banks.
- Recently, the two countries have agreed to jointly investigate the Kosi Multi purpose project, which includes a high dam in upstream Nepal near Barakshetra, the details of which are to be prepared under the Indo-Nepal Mahakali Treaty.

III. *The Gandak Irrigation and Power project Agreement or the Gandak Agreement (1959)*

- This Agreement allowed India to construct a barrage on the Gandak (Narayani in Nepal) at its own cost at the India-Nepal border near Bhaisalotan village. The barrage was designed to irrigate 920,000 hectares in western Bihar and 37,000 hectares in western Nepal from the Eastern Main Canal, and 930,000 hectares in the eastern UP and 20,000 hectares in Nepal from the Western Canal.

- Although the treaty specified Nepal's share of water, the quantum of water that could be withdrawn by India was left unspecified. The treaty was subsequently amended in 1964.

IV. *The Mahakali Integrated Treaty (1996)*

Signed between India and Nepal in 1996, the Mahakali Integrated Treaty (referred to as the Mahakali Treaty) looks at the integrated development of the Mahakali River, including the Sarda barrage, Tanakpur barrage and Pancheshwar Project, and tries to develop a principle of sharing costs and benefits, and recognises (for the first time) Nepal's prior water right.

- The treaty recognises the Mahakali as a boundary river on major stretches between the two.
- Sarada Barrage: Nepal to have the right to supply of 1,000 cusecs of water from the Sarada Barrage in the wet season (May 15 to October 15), and 150 cusecs in the dry season (October 16 to May 14). India is required to maintain a flow of no less than 350 cusecs downstream of Sharda Barrage in the Mahakali River to maintain and preserve the river ecosystem.
- Tanakpur Barrage: Nepal to continue having sovereignty over the land (2.9 hectare) needed for building the eastern afflux bund, as well as a hectare of the pondage area. In exchange Nepal to have, free of cost, 1,000 cusecs of water in the wet season and 300 cusecs in the dry season, and 70 million kwhrs of electricity (as against the earlier agreed figure of 20 million kwhrs) from the Tanakpur power station, with the transmission line to its border. Half the incremental power generated at Tanakpur after the augmentation of the river flows with the commissioning of the Pancheswar dam, to be supplied to Nepal at half the operational and any additional cost. India to also construct an all weather road connecting the Tanakpur barrage to Nepal's East-West Highway, including bridges en route. There is a provision for the supply of 350 cusecs of water for the irrigation of Dodhara Chandni area.

Of late, trouble has been brewing on the India-Nepal border points of Gadda Chauki and Brahmadev, in Uttaranchal.

The Young Communist League or the Nepalese Maoistyouth group, carried out a Seema Nirakshan Abhiyan tosurvey the border area from Tanakpur to Banbasa, followedby a huge rally demanding 'return of Nepalese landencroached by India,' and 'scrapping of unfair treaties.' Onthe Indian side, there has been heavy deployment of SeemaSuraksha Bal (SSB), the paramilitary force deployed alongthe Nepal–India border, fearing possible untowardincidents.

Frequent skirmishes in border towns between YCL and the Hindu Jagran Manch (Hindu right-wing group in India) is fast becoming common. Caught in its shadow are Nepalese families living for years in these border towns; wage workers who unmindfully cross-over; trade and friendly neighbourly relations across these very porous Indo-Nepal border.

- Pancheswar Project: A joint Indo-Nepal Hydroelectric project on the Mahakali River on the basis of a 50:50 cost benefit split, which remains the most controversial part of the treaty.
- Setting up of Joint Indo-Nepal Mahakali River Commission However, intricacies of the Mahakali Treaty have been steeped in mistrust and accusations, both in terms of India–Nepal relations, and within Nepal internal politics. A lot of heat has been generated over the interpretation of the treaty, the presence of Indian troops in the disputed upstream territory of Kalapani, the issue of water rights, the selling price of electricity, the environmental impact of the infrastructure project, and the displacement of as many as 65,000 people as a result of the project

The politics of treaties: In the beginning of the last century, irrigation became a high priority in the Gangetic plains of North India. Hence, both the Sarada and the Gandak agreements were guided by the irrigation requirement of North India. The Kosi agreement in contrast, was guided by flood control. All the three agreements have been critiqued for totally disregarding Nepal and being India-centric. Critiquing the Sarada treaty, Ajaya Dixit and Gyawali point out that not only did the treaty under-valuate Sarada Barrage's left (Nepali) bank, there is no evidence of actual transfer of the 4000 acres of land which was meant to be given to Nepal. In fact, each of these treaties evoked strong protests and unrest in Nepal and had to be subsequently amended, but resentment over the treaties, particularly over the Mahakali treaty, persists in Nepal. Mr. Surya Nath Upadhya points out that there is a popular perception in Nepal regarding all water treaties with India, that they are based on the idea where one country is the supplier of water and the other country is the main consumer of the water, and adequate attention is not given to Nepal's water needs.[6]

Finally, the Mahakali treaty, which tried to bring within its fold other treaties and devise a principle of cost benefit sharing, became the most contested, overshadowed by the past, and unable to chalk out a future for equitable and ecologically sound principles of water governance. Nepal, with the aid of the World Bank, began construction of the Mahakali Irrigation project, which became operational in 1975. This project enabled Nepal, for the first time, to utilise its share of water specified in the Sarada Agreement way back in 1920. In 1977, both India and Nepal agreed to jointly investigate the possibility of harnessing the Mahakali water further. Problems began when India unilaterally went ahead and began construction of the Tanakpur barrage in 1983 on land that was transferred to India under the Sarada Agreement. Nepal feared that this would affect the Mahakali Irrigation project, as well as its land and people living across the border river. Some changes were made in the design of the barrage, but (as discussed earlier under mega projects), the Tanakpur barrage became a point of confrontation between India and Nepal, particularly over the issue of the eastern afflux bund that needed to be tied on Nepalese territory.

In 1990, the political situation changed with the restoration of democracy and a new government led by Girija Prasad Koirala. India approached Nepal to overcome the Tanakpur stalemate, and a MOU was signed, but referred by the Nepalese side as an "understanding" subject to parliamentary ratification. However, the MOU was opposed by opposition parties amidst widespread protests in Nepal and the accusation against the government for having sold out to India. The Supreme Court of Nepal intervened to say that the understanding did require parliamentary ratification without specifying the type of majority required to sanction the treaty. In the meanwhile, India agreed that it would double the supply of the hydroelectric energy to Nepal from 10 million kWh to 20 million kWh. This did not help matters as there was a growing demand in Nepal then for principles of equitable sharing of water resources, and India's move was perceived as an ad hoc benefit sharing arrangement. Subsequently, the Mahakali treaty became a rallying point of anti-India sentiment, caught in Nepal's domestic as well as Indo-Nepal imbroglio. Finally, the treaty was signed in February 1995, but remains at an impasse.

Opinions: India-Nepal treaties

In Nepal, there are varying shades of opinion on the Mahakali Treaty. According to Ajaya Dixit and Deepak Gyawali from Water Nepal, the treaty and the manner in which it was signed represent all that is wrong with water treaties in South Asia, of unilateralism and domination by a big neighbour, of failure of senior bureaucrats and politicians within Nepal to stand up vis-à-vis India, of a hierarchical and monistic mindset which dominates water sector in both the countries.[7] For others, like Mr. Upadhyaya, who had been the chief negotiator of the Mahakali Treaty from Nepal's side, *"The Mahakali Treaty was an improvement from the past treaty. The problems have been in the way the treaty is now being interpreted by India to make demands on issues like Pancheshwar which were never discussed."*[8] This is not surprising given that one of

---

[6] Mr. Surya Nath Upadhyay, Kathmandu, 29.09.07.
[7] Gyawali and Dixit, "How not to do a South Asian Treaty," n. 32.
[8] Upadhyay, n. 70.

the biggest problems, and an important cause fueling the long-standing water dispute between India and Nepal, has been the lack of specificity in the provisions of the Mahakali Treaty (as with other treaties). This has left room for ambiguity and controversy in the interpretation and enforcement of the provisions of the water-sharing agreement. In the case of the Mahakali river, the problems of catchment area ratios, land area development ratios, investment ratios and riparian rights are further complicated and intensified because the river also serves as an international border between the two countries in major stretches.[9]

Adding to the roadblock are issues of lack of information sharing, secrecy and closed approach. *"I have been negotiating with the Indian authorities in my capacity as the permanent secretary of Nepal on water resources for many years and I have the feeling that they have got a certain kind of mental barrier which doesn't allow them to come out in a more open way. Take the example of Tanakpur barrage, there is too much secrecy,"* says Mr. Upadhayay.[10]

In India, the dominant view is that the treaty is the outcome of convergence of interests between the two States. Nepal has enormous hydro-electric potential in the Himalayan rivers, which it would like to 'trade,' (many see "water as equivalent to oil for Nepal") and water can be harnessed by the two countries for mutual benefit.[11] For this, it is argued, the Mahakali Treaty provides a comprehensive framework, and offers a fair deal to Nepal. It is stated that the geographical reality is that India has a larger irrigable area and much more water use while Nepal's mountain landscape has limited its irrigable area. Hence, contention at that level, of India using more water, which flows down to it anyway, is 'misplaced.' There is an agreement that the past treaties were not too fair, and hence amendments were made to suit Nepal. The Mahakali Treaty is based on the just principles of cost and benefit sharing but politics in Nepal has allowed past mistrusts to overshadow matters. Issues like Kalapani are separate border disputes, to be dealt separately. The problem over the Pancheshwar project has to do with the site for Nepal's re-regulating dam below Pancheswar being technically unviable, which then is being used to delay the project.[12]

Either way, the fact remains that the issue of water sharing has been volatile, inter-layered with concerns of sovereignty, nationalism, lack of trust and ideological contestation. It has also been pointed out that despite the "much hyped" Mahakali Treaty and substantial investments in building physical infrastructure to provide drinking water, irrigation, and hydropower, citizens in both the countries have not automatically benefited from access to these services—the reason being that institutional questions and issues of governance have been largely neglected.[13] Environmental and human concerns have also been neglected by the treaty. According to Govinda Rajbhandari, *"Nothing is said in the Treaty about the eco-system in and around either the proposed dam or any provision made about relocating more than a thousand families to be displaced. What seems to have been ignored here is that any project to be built should be environmentally safe, economically feasible and acceptable to the people on both sides of the border."*[14]

2. Pakistan, India and the Indus Waters treaty:

Given the history of conflict and wars between the two countries, it is not surprising that the Indus Waters Treaty (IWT) is often hailed as a success and a model of water governance in South Asia's vexed

---

[9] Salman M. A. Salman and Kishor Uprety "Hydro-Politics in South Asia: A Comparative Analysis of the Mahakali and Ganges Treaties," Natural Resources Journal, The University of New Mexico School of Law.
[10] Upadhyay, n. 70.
[11] See in Ramaswamy Iyer, "Delay and drift on the Mahakali," Himal South Asian, webpage file:///C:/Documents%20and%20Settings/Administrator/My%20Documents/water/Himal%20water-200!-ri.htm, Accessed, 7.10.07.
[12] Sidiqqi, Toufiq A. and Shirin Tahir-Kheli, ed., WASSA Project Report, Vol. 3, p. 49.
[13] Ajaya Dixit, Pradeep Adhikari and Rakshya Rajyashwori Thapa, "Nepal: Ground Realities for Himalayan Water Management," in Disputes over the Ganga, (Kathmandu: Panos, October 2004).
[14] Govinda Rajbhandari "Some Remarks on Mahakali Treaty," The Kathmandu Post, 3 October 1996.

trans-boundary rivers. Assisted by the World Bank, India and Pakistan signed the IWT in September 1960, after more than eight years of negotiation to resolve the dispute over the usage for irrigation and hydel power of the Indus water system.[15] Undoubtedly, the treaty has survived four wars between the two neighbours. However, the IWT is a typical case which shows that the absence of war (over water in this case) is not equivalent to an efficient and equitable solution. The IWT water governance mechanism is based on the partition of the Indus River Basin wherein three eastern rivers—the Sutlej, the Beas and the Ravi have been allotted to India; and the three western rivers—Indus, Jhelum and Chenab are allotted to Pakistan. The Indus water head remains in the Indian part of the state of Jammu and Kashmir, and according to some, underlies the conflict over Kashmir. Of late, a series of problems have emerged with regard to water-sharing between the two countries. They include Pakistan's opposition to India's Salal Hydro electrical Project, Tulbul navigation project, Baglihar Hydroelectric project, Sawalkot HEP and Kishanganga HEP, all in the state of Jammu and Kashmir.

Main features of the Treaty are:

- India to have unrestricted use of all the waters of the eastern rivers (the Ravi, Beas and Sutlej).

- Pakistan to have unrestricted use of the western rivers (the Indus, Chenab, and Jhelum). India to let flow all the waters of the western rivers, and shall not permit any interference with these waters. However, India is allowed, under severe restriction, limited use of the western rivers for purposes such as domestic use; non-consumptive use; agricultural use as set out in Annexure C; and generation of hydroelectric power as set out in Annexure D.[16]

- Pakistan may also withdraw water from the Basantsar tributary of the Ravi, as may be available and necessary for irrigation to a maximum limit of 100 acres annually. Pakistan is also allowed to withdraw water from other specified tributaries of the Ravi, under restriction as clearly set out in IWT.

- India to get 33 MAF (million acre feet) of annual flow from the eastern rivers and Pakistan to get 165 MAF from the western rivers.

- Mandates a permanent Indus Commission consisting of a commissioner each from India and Pakistan, and periodical meetings and exchange visits.

- In case of any 'question' that may arise, it is to be resolved within the commission; if an agreement is not reached, the matter is to be referred to the two governments; if still unresolved, the question would become a difference and be referred to a Neutral Expert (NE), whose finding would be binding. If the NE considered the matter to be a dispute, it would have to go to Court of Arbitration.

- Includes provisions of International financial assistance to Pakistan for developing Irrigation works for the utilisation of water allocated to it. India also paid as per treaty requirement.

Opinions on the IWT

There are different opinions regarding the IWT. There is a dominant view that holds that the IWT has been a successful conflict solving mechanism—internationally as well as among some people in India and Pakistan. However, often what is not highlighted is the discontentment with the treaty.

One of the major problems with the IWT has been that it has led to regional disparity and discontent. In the state of Jammu and Kashmir (J&K), the IWT is widely perceived to be discriminatory. According to

---

[15] K. Warikoo, "Perspectives of Indus Waters Treaty," in Samaddar, Ranabir and Helmut Reifeld, ed., Peace as Process: Reconciliation and Conflict Resolution in South Asia, (Delhi: Manohar, 2001), p. 281.
[16] Muhammed Siyad A.C., "Indus Waters Treaty and Baglihar Project," Economic and Political Weekly, 16 July 2005, p.3145.

Arjimand Talib, the IWT was geared more towards safeguarding India's interest in Punjab and the Bhakra-Nangal project, and totally ignored the needs of Kashmiris.[17] Rather than looking at the whole basin, restriction placed on India's use of the western rivers made it virtually impossible for J&K to derive any benefits of irrigation, hydroelectric power, and navigation, from the waters of the Jhelum and Chenab rivers which flow through it. Many people point out that it is ironic that the state, despite being rich in its hydel resources, faces an acute shortage of hydro-electric power, particularly during winter months. It is a reality that J&K accounts for only 0.9 per cent of the hydel power generated in the country. As Biswajeet Saikia states, the IWT made Punjab prosperous by using the three river waters for agriculture and power, but put Jammu and Kashmir behind.[18] On 3rd April 2002, the Jammu and Kashmir Legislative Assembly, cutting across party affiliations, denounced the treaty, calling for its review.

Similarly, in Pakistan, a dispute has simmered between Sindh and Punjab. Matters came to a head in the 1980s, when the military government of General Zia-ul-Haq announced the inception of the Kalabagh dam on the Indus, the third large-scale storage and hydroelectric reservoir, after Mangla and Tarbela. The Kalabagh dam issue became immediately controversial, and led to large-scale protests in Sindh, where it was seen as a further attempt by the Punjab-led military government at encroaching upon the lower riparian water entitlements. Water allocation remains a critical factor in inter-provincial politics in Pakistan.[19]

The treaty also totally neglects environmental concerns and issues of displacement.

Others, like Ramaswamy Iyer, critique the surgical division, but argue that this was the best and the most practical solution given the circumstances of Partition and the difficult relationship between the two newly formed countries.[20] However, as is becoming evident, the IWT is facing far more problems now over dams and water issues than in the past, leading some to call for new visions and possibilities to be explored regarding the IWT.

3. India-Bangladesh and the Ganga Treaty

The Ganga Treaty is the only "water sharing" treaty in South Asia signed on 12th December 1996. The Prime Minister of Bangladesh, Sheikh Hasina Wajed, and the Indian Prime Minister, H. D. Deve Gowda, signed a thirty year long treaty in New Delhi on the sharing of the Ganges water. The Treaty addresses the issue of water allocation between India-Bangladesh which, post Farakka, had strained relations between the two countries. This had become particularly controversial given the sharp seasonal variation of the Ganga which has more than enough during the monsoon, and considerably less water in the dry seasons.

- The treaty guarantees Bangladesh a minimum of 35,000 cusecs in lean season.

- If the Ganga has more than 75,000 cusecs of water, India can divert 40,000 cusec into the Hoogly and allow the rest to flow to Bangladesh.

- If the Ganga flow is between 75,000 and 70,000 cusecs, Bangladesh can withdraw 35,000 cusecs and the rest can be withdrawn by India. If there is 70,000 cusec and less, than the water will be shared equally by the two sides. However, the supply regulation has to ensure that each side gets alternatively 35,000 cusec for 10 days at a stretch from March 1 to May 10, the driest period. In case of an emergency situation, such as the flow at Farakka falling below 50,000 cusec, both sides are required to hold "immediate consultation."

---

[17] A. Talib, Srinagar.
[18] Biswajeet Saikia, "Indus Waters Treaty: Economic Implication to the Jammu and Kashmir," Observer Research Foundation, Delhi.
[19] Haris Gazdar, p. 816.
[20] R. Iyer, "Was the Indus Treaty in Trouble?" Economic and Political Weekly, 22 June 2002, p. 2401.

- Both sides have also agreed to enter into Treaty/Agreement regarding other common rivers.

- Treaty to be implemented by a Joint Committee. Any dispute arising in this is to be referred to the JRC (Joint Rivers Commission). If the dispute remains unresolved, it should be referred to the two governments which would meet immediately at on appropriate level, to resolve issues through discussions.

The thirty year Ganga Treaty was the result of a long phase of turbulent negotiation. As stated earlier, problems over sharing of the Ganga began shortly after partition and took on a confrontational turn over the issue of the Farakka Barrage. With Bangladesh becoming an independent nation in 1971, the initial phase was the "honey-moon period between the two countries,"[21] says Dr. Ainun Nishat. Meanwhile Farakka was nearing completion and the two countries decided to share the water-flow in the lean season, recognizing each other's water shortage in the dry season. Accordingly a friendship treaty was signed under which a Joint Rivers Commission (JRC) was set up to support the two governments. It was a statutory body that would come out with ideas, programs, proposal and projects where the common resources of the two countries could be used for the benefit of people in both countries.[22] However, problems persisted, and with the operationalisation of the Farakka barrage and India's unilateral withdrawal, problems took a turn for the worse. Bangladesh took up the issue with the United Nations, which asked both sides to come to a settlement. In 1977, the first major short term agreement for the sharing of dry season flow at Farakka was signed, for a period of five years. Two more short term MOU's were signed which lapsed by 1988. Between 1988–96, all efforts to reach an understanding failed, in the absence of which India continued to withdraw water. As many activists pointed out in Bangladesh, during the dry season, this meant a crisis in the Ganga Dependent Areas (GDA) of Bangladesh. In 1996, the Ganga Treaty was signed with a new government coming to power in Dhaka.

Opinions on the Ganga Treaty:

According to Prof. Q. K. Ahmad,

"Except for a few problems, the 1996 Ganga Treaty has performed fairly well. The other rivers are the main problem. There has been a discussion for a long time on the Teesta but no agreement has been reached as yet. This is a bilateral problem that needs to be solved. Then there are regional problems. The Ganges treaty sates that both the government will try to augment the flow of the Ganges during the lean season. But that has not been done. It means that some barrages have to be constructed in Nepal to get water during the lean season. But that has not been taken up at all. However India and Nepal have agreed for the Sapta Kosi barrage which is likely to produce 3500 MW energy but all discussion has remained bi-lateral. Bangladesh has proposed that all the three countries should work together. But Bangladesh has not been invited to participate."[23]

It is a fact that the Ganga has very little water during the dry season for both countries to share. "We are not getting water on the barrage point. So what shall we share?" asks Md. Hilal. Over the years, the two countries have floated various proposals to increase the supply, such as the above mentioned dams in Nepal, or diverting the excessive "unused" water from the Brahmaputra, but these proposals have themselves been steeped in controversy. Mustafa Kamal Majumdar points out that the Treaty is not based on sound assumptions of sustainable planning:

"The Treaty cannot guarantee that a certain quantity of water will be available to us. Nor can it guarantee the quality of water that is available. Rivers should be alive if its benefits are to be shared and

---
[21] Interview with Dr. Ainun Nishat, IUCN, 8.01.08.
[22] Ibid.
[23] Interview with Dr. Q. K. Ahmad, Bangladesh Unayan Parishad (BUP), Dhaka, 8.01.08.

water experts on the globe have come to the conclusion that there is a need for the river to have some kind of an ecological flow. In Europe, take the example of the Danube. It had become an extremely polluted river, but with shared responsibility by various stakeholders, it has been cleaned to a tolerable limit. The Ganga Treaty does not address such ecological concerns."[24] Notably, pollution of the Ganga from sewage and chemical discharge in India remains a serious problem despite the Ganga Action Plan initiated in 1985.

There is also a perception in Bangladesh that India secretly diverts a portion of the flow of the Ganges upstream during dry months, causing acute water stress and environmental damage in Bangladesh when the dry-season flow is low.[25] However, the Indian External Ministry states that it releases far more water than is the genuine requirement of Bangladesh. On the contrary, it is felt that Bangladesh exaggerates its needs, and a lot of water is not utilised and "unused" in the Bay of Bengal. Water at Farakka is far more essential to India than Bangladesh for its needs, and for the survival of the Calcutta port.[26] Others, like B.G. Verghese argues that the ecological problem around the Khulna region is caused not so much by Farakka but due to the overall east and north shift of the Ganga river system.

What are the Problems with South Asian Water Treaties?

1. Problem with the dominant paradigm of water in the region: If one were to take an overview from the above discussion to sum up what really have been the problems with South Asian water treaties, a number of discords are evident. According to Ajaya Dixit, the problem with most treaties signed in South Asia is not about blaming one country or another. The fundamental problem is with the dominant paradigm of water in all these countries. Perception of water is guided by a militaristic or a hierarchical view and management of water. This has in practice meant a top-down approach and a preoccupation with seeing flowing as "waste" to justify intervention in its flow. "We follow a monocentric path that is dominated by the bureaucracy, the technicians and the nation-state. This nation has not provided water security to it citizens."

2. Lack of Trust: Given the turbulent history of the region, and of negotiations regarding water projects, there is a lack of trust between the countries, particularly with regard to India. While some of it comes from the sheer geographical and economic facts, a lot of it comes from India playing a dominant role in the region. In Nepal and Bangladesh, it was pointed out that a positive step in building trust was made by the "Gujral Doctrine" which stated that with smaller neighbours, like Bangladesh, Bhutan, Maldives, Nepal and Sri Lanka, India without asking for reciprocity, gives and accommodates what it can in good faith and trust—something that India had later abandoned. The need to have an open sharing of information with regard to water was a fact that was stressed in all the countries.

3. Problem of Bilateralism: Most of these rivers are international rivers, crossing more than two countries. However, the treaties are bilateral. According to Shanta Pun, on the question of whether we should have bilateral or regional treaties, there is a problem. "India would like to be treated bilaterally whereas Nepal and Bangladesh would like a regional approach. That, I think, is the big issue. They think India is a big brother and India thinks that they are ganging up against it." A. N. feels that the "main problem with India is that they will not go for multilateral talks. For instance, if Nepal and Bangladesh have to sign an agreement to use Monglapur, it requires three agreements. Suppose Nepal and Bangladesh agree to certain proposals; before that Bangladesh and India must sign an agreement. And then India and Nepal must sign another agreement. Why can't these three countries sit down for an agreement together?

---

[24] Interview, Mustafa Kamal Majumdar.
[25] Arun P. Elhance, Hydro Politics in the Third World: Conflict and Cooperation in International River Basins, Institute of Peace, Washington, 1999, p. 180.
[26] Indian External Affairs Ministry document, "Sharing of River Water between India and Bangladesh: The Real Story," 1994.

4. Lack of Clarity in the Treaties: The IWT is too technical a treaty, with dense Annexures and Appendices filled with engineering jargons, which then becomes a point of clash between engineers from the two sides over technical details that few understand. The Mahakali, on the other hand, leaves a lot of room for ambiguity and controversies erupt in its interpretation and enforcement.

5. Invisibility of Gender and Environmental Concerns: As Eva Saroch points out, *"No women have ever been involved in treaty-making. Yet they are affected by it."*[27] As in the case of most conflict and peace treaties, water treaties are dominated by men, and the language remains a masculinist domain of military-bureaucratic-engineers and male elites. Similarly, environmental concerns, its impacts on people across borders and their needs, compensation etc have been totally sidelined by the treaties. The Mahakali Treaty has come under flak from environmentalists on grounds of non-viability of large-scale water infrastructure projects. The agreement has failed to address the associated social and environmental factors and has not involved ordinary people in the management of shared water resources, despite being the most affected party. Similarly, under the IWT, the replacement works for diverting water from the western rivers, the resultant water logging and siltation of adjacent areas and its impact on a large section of people who had to give up their traditional rights to water.

6. Nation-State Centric Treaties: Despite the fact that water use and management involve a plurality of players, water treaties remain an 'exclusive business' of nation-states, totally dominated by state machineries. The only other players which seem to get 'legitimate' entry are big corporations and businesses. Civil society, voices of people and other parties living in the basin or affected by these treaties have no voice or space. The governance of water require a far more open and equal interplay between states, markets and civil society in the region.

To conclude, what really emerges is that there has been limited cooperation, in real terms, between these South Asian countries on their rivers. The little progress that has been made has been marred by controversy and simmering resentment. According to some, for instance, Ajaya Dixit and Deepak Gyawali, the problems that have arisen in the course of the framing of troubled treaties, like the Mahakali Treaty, can be lessons in future efforts to jointly govern South Asian water resources.[28] The challenge, then, is to frame what should be the framework for the governance of South Asian trans-boundary water from the point of fairness, and environmental sustainability.

---

[27] Eva Saroch, Second Civil Society Dialogue on Peace: A Report, 2002, website: http://www.mcrg.ac.in/civilsocietydialogue2.htm, Accessed 14.7.2007.
[28] `Gyawali and Dixit, "How not to do a South Asian Treaty."

CHAPTER – 25

South Asian Rivers And Climate Change: Future Conflict or Cooperation

"Muhammad Ali, a wiry 65-year-old, has never driven a car, run an air-conditioner or done much of anything that produces greenhouse gases. But on a warming planet, he is on the verge of becoming a climate refugee. In the past 10 years, the farmer has had to tear down and move his tin-and-bamboo house five times to escape the encroaching waters of the huge Jamuna River, swollen by severe monsoons that scientists believe are caused by global warming and greater glacier melt in the Himalayas. Now that the last of his land is gone, Ali squats on a precarious piece of government-owned riverbank, the only ground available, knowing the river probably will take that as well once the monsoons start this month."

This story, reported by Laurie Goering (Chicago Tribune, 2nd May 2007) is not a unique case nor is it about a calamity confined to a small village in Bangladesh. As the world gets warmer, the IPCC Report on Climate Change projection for South Asia states that the Himalayas are poised to melt, leading to increased flooding, rock avalanches from destabalised slopes, and affect water resources within the next two to three decades. This is expected to be followed by decreased river flows as the glaciers recede. According to ICIMOD (International Centre for Integrated Mountain Development) the temperature of the Himalayas has gone by up to 0.6 degrees Celsius in the past 30 years, and within the next 50 years, the Himalayan glaciers could disappear all together, having far-reaching implications for more than a billion people living in the region.

One can get a peek into the future when one looks at Dhaka, the capital of Bangladesh. The city is daily being flooded by a growing sea of landless rural migrants living in squalid conditions in places like the backwaters of the Turag River. "Climate migrants" are growing by the day and now account for at least a third or perhaps as many as two thirds of rural dwellers coming to Dhaka. Many in Dhaka point out with alarm that if sea level rises by three feet by the turn of the century, as some scientists predict, a fifth of the country will disappear. Meanwhile, land erosion has also led to an escalation of land dispute and litigation in Bangladesh.

Thirty years old Nasima Begum is from Bhola Island and works in a brick kiln. Lying in the southern coast of Bangladesh, half the island has already been lost to the waters. There are many like Nasima Begum who have been forced to flee to the city and make ends meet by working at construction sites, brick kilns, or by pulling rickshaws. However work is becoming difficult to find. Meanwhile, India has started constructing a fence along the border, and within India, anti-Bangladeshi migrants voices are getting shriller. However, though the adverse impact of climate change is becoming visible in a low lying, delta country like Bangladesh, it is not a phenomenon limited to Bangladesh. A small island has already been gulped by the Hoogly River in India, the floods in Bihar, UP are getting worse, glacial lake outbursts are increasing in frequency and affecting thousands in Nepal and Bhutan. Soon the same devastation is likely to spread to other areas, like the coastal areas of India, Pakistan, the Gangetic plains, the Himalayan Hills.

As the IPCC projects, the impact of climate change is going to particularly affect developing countries given their low coping capacity, wide scale poverty, and high density of population. Fresh water shortage is going to be acute and all the progress made in the human development index stands threatened. With increased floods and droughts, endemic morbidity and mortality due to diarrheal diseases primarily, is projected to increase. Rise in coastal water temperature is stated to exacerbate diseases like cholera in South Asia. Crop yields is projected to go up to 20% in East and Southeast Asia while it could decrease up to 30% in Central and South Asia by the mid-21st century. Taken together and considering the influence of rapid population growth and urbanisation, the risk of hunger is projected to remain very high. In short, the future seems ugly unless the South Asian Countries begin to cooperate and do something about it. According to Rehman, the future looks bleak and means "insufficient food, a destabilised government, internal strife that could spread past the country's borders, a massive exodus of climate refugees and more extremism." He further feels that *"a person victimised and displaced will not sit idle. There will be organised climate-displaced groups saying, 'Why should you hang onto your place when I've lost mine and you're the one who did this'."*[2]

"For every hundred thousand tons of carbon you emit, you have to take a Bangladeshi family."

Rehman, Dhaka[1]

Clearly, South Asian cooperation is vital here. Besides coordinating with the UN and international climate regimes, South Asian countries must also establish a coordination that is lacking among them, as well as with neighbouring regions in order to handle the crisis more effectively. Collective monitoring of glaciers, and rivers, sharing and transparency of information is crucial here, along with closer collaboration between scientific, academic, civil society institutions, working on the impact of changing climate in the region.

Conflict of Approaches to Water

In trying to understand the various actors and their approaches on the issue of trans-boundary water, it is important to recognise at the outset that there are plurality of actors in the water sector—the state, which includes governments, bureaucracy and the state machinery, who can also be termed the "managers,"[3] and the market; civil society organisations, activist groups, environmental movements; donors and funding groups; water communities or water users; and knowledge institutions. Each group is characterised with its own strategies and approaches, and within each group there are differences and variations.

1. State/Strategic Approach: The state or the government departments have long been the major actor when it comes to water issues. With regard to trans-boundary rivers, the state approach has been one of strategic and centralised control. In practice, this has meant high-handed approach and securitisation of water. This is quite evident in the way water is 'managed' and hydro politics played out between India-Pakistan, Bangladesh-India, and sometimes between Nepal-India and in the way some of the other conflicts, such as those existing between India and Pakistan, superimpose themselves over watery spaces. One can also draw comparisons of national security and other aspects of high politics getting linked to water management in parts of West Asia.

2. Market/Economic Good Approach: The market approach is based on the understanding that given the problems that nation-states have had in sharing their water resources, the mechanisms for governance of water must be left to the market and economic instruments. It includes a wide range of actors who argue for water markets, privatisation of water, tradable water rights, accounting for the economic value of water,

---

[1] http://www.chicagotribune.com/ news/nationworld /chi-bangldsh070 502, Accessed 8.05.07.
[2] Ibid
[3] A term used by A. Dixit.

public-private partnership. It is supported by Institutions such as the World Bank, Asia Development Bank, UN; International 'Water' Institutions like World Water Council, Global Water Partnership; corporates, some governments; and some NGOs.

This has been facilitated by two trends in the 90s. 1) The growing acceptance of privatisation of public services as a way of dealing with inefficiency, poor delivery and fund shortage. 2) Institutional backing of World Bank (WB) and IMF for water privatisation. Within the governments in the region, given the growing scarcity and increasing demand for water, there are two mindsets. 1) To increase 'production' and bring in more water available in nature to the 'usable' category. 2) To then build water reservoirs and infrastructure to store water that is going "waste" into the environment. Hence water is seen as subject to laws of supply and demand. Such an approach then ties in well with the more blatant market approach propagated by institutions like WB and ADB. The argument here is that effective resource management requires that water is given an economic value. Hence, water rights should be defined and water trading allowed. The underlying premise is that if markets are given a free play, private sector allowed in, the state only plays a facilitating role; the market will ensure that supply side meets the demand. Within this, Public-Private Partnership (PPP) is held as a model for improved services, better efficiency and better investment.

Given that water is fast becoming a scarce resource, there is also a growing trend to merchandise it for profit.[4] In its most blatant forms, giant corporations are rapidly acquiring control of water through the ownership of dams, waterways, water infrastructures, municipal corporations, development of new technologies, such as water desalination and purification, among others.

There have also been attempts to give water both an economic and social content. Significant here is the Integrated Water Resource Management (IRWM) approach which tries to combine the social, environmental and economic approach to water. This IRWM has its intellectual roots in the United Nations Conference on Environment and Development (UNCED) that was held in Mar del Plata in 1977. Important to the emerging discourse of IWRM has been the Dublin Principles which espoused interdependencies within natural systems, as well economic and social systems. However, IWRM has been critiqued for defining the unit of management as the river basin. It is argued that this is based solely on hydrological characteristics and takes no consideration of social, cultural, political or economic characteristics that shape water governance. Dissenting voices question the universal applicability of IWRM with leading water experts calling for a renewed analysis of the relevance of some of its core assumptions (Falkenmark, 1993; Gyawali et al., 2006).

3. Alternative Approach/ Water as a social good and a basic human right: Proponents of this approach include social activists, academics, environmentalists and NGOs who vary widely but share a common position that water is a basic human right, a common pool resource and cannot be reduced to a tradable commodity. These groups have been critiquing the hierarchical approach and privatisation of water that ignores people and community based approaches to water. They argue that water and human rights are interlinked at several levels. Water is essential for life, livelihood and survival; the combination of safe drinking water and hygienic sanitation facilities is a precondition for health, to success in fight against poverty, hunger, child deaths and gender inequality; protection of the rights of the displaced people and their cultures that is caused by mega projects and dams; environmental and ecological concerns.

---

[4] In May 2000, Fortune magazine stated that water in the 21st century would be the best investment to ensure wealth of nations. The World Bank places the value of the current water market at close to $1 trillion. With corporations providing water for only 5 percent of the world's population the profit potential is seen as unlimited.

Organisations Working on Trans-boundary Waters in South Asia: A Selective List[5]

Given the fact that tensions on South Asian trans-boundary water have been so widespread, there have been concerns and initiatives by civil society groups, activists, academics and policy makers to address them. These initiatives are rooted in different perspectives or try to synthesise different approaches such as the socio-economic approach, or environmental and people centred approaches. However, one can broadly identify certain trends to these initiatives.

i. The issue of mega-projects and dams is the most dominant, and initiatives on trans-boundary waters have sprung up in context of specific dams and projects. For instance, the Rivers Interlinking Project or the Tipaimukh Dam or the Pancheshwar among others have largely been the context and focal points for cross border networking on rivers. Here, a number of organisations have made significant contribution.

ii. While the 90s saw a greater effort toward working across border on trans-boundary management, in the present decades, the South Asian civil society solidarity, at large, and water related initiatives, more specifically have suffered. In many countries, internal instability and security issues have come to take the centre stage. For instance, in the democratic Nepal of the 90s, water issues and concerns had unleashed a lot of constructive energy but the massacre of the Royal family and the events that followed, the overall war-like situation, far overtook this space in the following decade. The post September 11 South Asia also came to be dominated by concerns of militarism, war, and (national) security, where issues of ecology and environment took a back seat and movement of people within South Asia became difficult. For instance, a number of activists in Bangladesh mentioned that going to India in the 90s was not a problem, while in the past few years, getting a visa has become very difficult. There has also been an ascendancy of market, and a new legitimacy of dams. As Ajaya Dixit from Water Nepal pointed out, in the "1990s, it was possible for Deepak and myself (Water Nepal), to address and talk to the legislative assembly of Bihar on the issue of floods, but this has become a problem now."

iii. While water concerns in Nepal, Bangladesh, and Pakistan invariably involve India, the tendency in India is to remain more centred around internal water issues and conflicts. It was evident that civil society groups in India working on water paid far less attention to trans-boundary rivers, whereas in the other countries, particularly in Nepal and Bangladesh, there have been greater efforts to address these issues. This definitely needs to change, particularly in the context of global warming. According to some activists in Nepal and Bangladesh, in India some of the efforts that have been undertaken tend to be seen by the others as being within the frame of an "nationalist mindset" rather that a "South-Asian mindset."

Water Nepal Conservation Foundation, formed in 1990 has carried out interdisciplinary research on varied issues that affect the use and management of water, focusing on the Himalaya-Ganga region. NWCF is also involved in building knowledge, raising awareness and disseminating insights through innovative actions carried out in partnership with its field partners. **Panos South Asia focuses** on the Himalayan Ganga Region. It carried out a study on the River Ganga in the three countries of Nepal, Bangladesh and India and brought out a publication on Disputes over the Ganga. While the initial idea was to bring about a dialogue between technocrats, journalists and civil society, the study ultimately focused on the perspective of the civil society and activists. **Jalsrot Vikas Sanstha, Nepal** works as the regional arm of the global water partnership, and seeks to implement plans and programs on IRWM.

— **South Asia Network on Dams, Rivers & People (SANDRP), India,** formed in 1998. It is a loose network of people working on issues related to water. Their main focus is on large dams, mostly in India but also

---

[5] To begin with, it must be stated that this is not a comprehensive list of organization and initiatives working on water. We have confined ourselves by our own objectives and focus as stated in the report.

in other parts of South Asia, from the perspective of people, ecology and democracy. Significant writing and initiatives on South Asian water issues and dialogues have also been taken up by Ramaswamy Iyer, B.G Verhese and other scholars based at **Centre For Policy Research, Delhi,** or other Knowledge Institutions like **Centre for Development & Environment Policy,** IIM. An important new initiative has been **South Asia Consortium for Interdisciplinary Water Resources Studies** (**SACIWATER**), based in India that focuses on transforming water resources knowledge systems. Key ideas are an interdisciplinary approach to understanding water resources issues and collaboration at South Asia level. The longer term aim is to establish a South Asian 'virtual water university.'

— **Bangladesh Poribesh Andolan (BAPA)** has been active on the front against India's Rivers Interlinking Linking project. Their emphasis has been to link an internal environmental approach to external environment approach in management of trans-boundary water. Others like **IUCN Bangladesh, Bangladesh Unnayan Parishad (BUP)** focusing on the Ganga basin have sought to emphasise water as a socio-economic good for regional cooperation.

— A number of initiatives have emerged on the **border regions** in the context of dams/embankments/floods and have also sought to build solidarity. In Manipur, **Action Against Tipaimukh (ACTIP)** and the **Citizens' Concern for Dam and Development** have also taken up the issue of the proposed dams, and formed links with groups like in **Angikar Bangladesh Foundation**. An International Tipaimukh Dam Conference, (ITDC2005) held from 30–31 December, 2005 came up with the **Dhaka Declaration**. The **Barh Mukti Abhiyan** has also taken up issues of floods, embankments and people's suffering across the Indo-Napal Border. In Pakistan, the **DAMAN Development Organisation,** has been working among the marginalised water communities of the Indus which have been affected by dams and projects.

Looking Ahead: Framework for Water Governance as a Space of Inclusion

There is a gap when it comes to linking the various small community/border level initiatives on transboundary rivers to the larger dialogues that take place even at the level of civil society. Baring a few, most initiatives have revolved around mega dams, while some initiatives have not really moved due to internal differences and misgivings. Another problem remains with the extreme polarisation that pervades the issue of water in South Asia. Hence, the challenge is to take a bottom up approach towards evolving a framework for water governance.

- There is an urgent need for a water governance framework in South Asia. This is important if there has to be a meaningful implementation of the SAARC social charter signed by all the South Asian countries, stating the need to "fulfill the responsibility towards present and future generations by ensuring equity among generations, and protecting the integrity and sustainable use of the environment." This is also necessary if we have reach anywhere close to achieving the Millennium Development Goals or talk about peace, cooperation and well being of the region in a maximalist sense.

In different parts of the world, joint Agreements on shared water resources are being put in place.

- The South African Development Commission (SADC) has been able to successfully organise several river basins under the "Protocol of Shared Water Courses"—a joint document stating that the 14 DADC countries will collaborate together in managing their shared rivers.

- The Nile Basin Initiative provides another example of 10 countries (some of them with tense relations) forming a joint dialogue platform.

- In South East Asia, the Mekong River Commission is yet another example of basin wide regional collaboration.

It is high time that South Asian countries began a collaborative effort for joint governance of the transboundary rivers.

- Such a framework must emerge from the recognition that there are pluralities of stakeholders in the contested terrain of water, and among them the civil society is so far excluded when it comes to the issue of trans-boundary water.

- The process of water governance must shift from top-down water management to bottom-up water governance, and should be an open and transparent process. It should look to building decentralised partnerships with non-state institutions. Governance implies open and equal interplay between state–market and civil society. As of now now, the civil society and local communities have been totally excluded from water management. This must change.

- Water security means people have secure rights to use water, including future generations. For poor people, this comes from a fair and adequate representation in the policy making process. Hence 'the bottom-up approach' must be integral to the process and the outcome. For instance, it should be designed through consultations with local communities which are affected, and build upon the strengths of customary laws that are often overlooked. There is a need to improve our understanding of the strengths of customary water arrangements (whilst recognising their weaknesses, such as gender/caste inequality).

- There is also a need to include marginal river ecologies that remain neglected, such as the case of smaller border rivers between India and Nepal. Similarly, the India-Pakistan conflict has cast a 'security' shadow over the Indus basin. While there are a number of studies from varied perspectives on the Ganga basin, most studies on the Indus basin tend to be more from a strategic or nation-state perspective. There is an urgent need to bring forth these varied voices, visions of people and communities of the Indus basin, across borders, to inform the debate on water governance.

- Women play a crucial role in sustainable development, resource governance, and in peace- building. As of now, both at the level of government, policy makers as well as civil society, women actors and gender perspective are both missing. Similarly, the question of discrimination and proactive efforts for 'inclusion' of the voices and visions of dalits and other discriminated communities must also be taken into account.

There is also a need to develop joint information infrastructures and services for river basins, and thereby reducing asymmetric access to information among the countries concerned.

CHAPTER – 26

Baglihar Hydroelectric Plant Expert Determination

on points of difference referred by the Government
of Pakistan under the provisions of the Indus Waters Treaty

Prof. Raymond Lafitte, Lausanne,
12 February 2007

Executive Summary

Contents

1. INTRODUCTION — 324
2. POINTS OF DIFFERENCE REFERRED BY PAKISTAN AND INDIA'S POSITION — 326
3. THE TREATY AND ITS INTERPRETATION — 326
4. TECHNICAL DATA CONCERNING THE BAGLIHAR PROJECT — 327
5. EXPERT DETERMINATION — 329
    5.1. Maximum design flood — 329
    5.2. Spillway, Ungated or gated — 329
    5.3. Spillway, level of the gates — 330
    5.4. Artificial raising of the water level — 332
    5.5. Pondage — 333
    5.6. Level of the power intake — 334

POSTSCRIPT — 336

THE INDUS WATERS TREATY 1960

Government of Pakistan – Government of India

BAGLIHAR HYDROELECTRIC PLANT

Expert Determination

On points of difference referred by the Government of Pakistan under the provisions of the Indus Waters Treaty

EXECUTIVE SUMMARY

1. INTRODUCTION

The water resources development of the Indus system of rivers is governed by the Indus Waters Treaty 1960 (referred to hereafter as the "Treaty") signed by the Government of India and the Government of Pakistan.

The Baglihar hydropower plant, a run-of-river plant with a capacity of 450 MW in its first stage, has been under construction since 2002 on the Chenab River, a tributary of the Indus, in the northern Indian state of Jammu & Kashmir.

On 15 January 2005, the Government of Pakistan sent a request to the World Bank (WB) to appoint a Neutral Expert (NE) stating that a "difference" had arisen between India and Pakistan under Article IX (2) of the Treaty, relating to the Baglihar Project.

After consultation with the Parties under the provisions of the Treaty, on 12 May 2005 the Bank appointed the undersigned, Mr. Raymond Lafitte, Professor at the Federal Institute of Technology of Lausanne, Switzerland.

The NE received the advice, with respect to legal issues, from Professor Laurence Boisson de Chazournes[1], and was assisted by Mr. Laurent Mouvet[2], Senior Civil Engineer.

At the request of the NE, the International Centre for Settlement of Investment Disputes of the World Bank (ICSID) assumed the coordinate on of the process and logistical support. Mrs. Eloïse Obadia, Senior Counsel, and Mrs. Martina Polasek, Counsel acted as coordinators.

The Governmental Delegations of India and Pakistan were composed of eminent personalities: engineers and lawyers. They were led by

- Shri J. Hari Narayan, Secretary, Ministry of Water Resources of India, replaced in the same position since August 2006 by Mrs. Gauri Chatterji, and Shri R. Jeyaseelan, Chairman, Central Water Commission, for India, and by

---

[1] Professor, Faculty of Law, University of Geneva, Switzerland.
[2] Head of Dams Department, Stucky Consulting Engineers Ltd, Renens, Switzerland.

- Mr. Makhdoom Ali Khan, Attorney General for Pakistan, and Mr. Ashfaq Mahmood, Secretary, Ministry of Water Power, for Pakistan.

Meeting No. 1 of the Parties and the NE was organized on 9 and 10 June 2005 in Paris at the World Bank Office. Mr. Roberto Dañino, Senior Vice President and General Counsel of the Bank welcomed the Delegations of the Parties and introduced the NE.

With the agreement of the Parties, the NE's work programme was fixed with the intention to produce his determination within the shortest possible time period. The fact that Baglihar power plant was under construction was certainly an important incentive for this. It was necessary for the NE to be briefed as fully as possible on the respective positions; but it was also essential, in his view, that each Party should have the possibility to present its arguments comprehensively.

The procedure proposed by the Parties, agreed by the NE, was to proceed to an exchange of written instruments. A programme was defined, which was adapted as it progressed, with the following order of events:

- 15 July 2005: Documents sent by India to Pakistan according to Appendix II to *Annexure D, Paragraph* 9 of the Treaty as well as additional and updated documents
- 18 August 2005: Memorial dated 14 August 2005 filed by Pakistan
- 23 September 2005: Counter-Memorial filed by India
- 31 January 2006: Reply dated 25 January 2006 filed by Pakistan
- 20 March 2006: Rejoinder filed by India
- 2 and 3 October 2006: Final Draft Expert Determination
- 26 October 2006: Written comments of the Governments of Pakistan and India on the Final Draft Expert Determination
- 24 November 2006: Written additional comments of the Parties on their respective presentations
- 12 February 2007: Final Determination of the NE.

On 2 and 3 October 2005, a visit to the Baglihar site was organised for the NE and the Delegations of India and Pakistan. Then, on 5 and 6 October 2005, the Baglihar hydraulic model was visited at the Irrigation Research Institute (IRI) in Roorkee, India.

Following Meeting No. 1, in Paris, five subsequent meetings were organized:

- Meeting No. 2, from 19 to 21 October 2005, in Geneva, at the World Meteorological Organisation. This meeting was devoted to additional questions from the NE which had arisen following the site visit to Baglihar.
- Meeting No. 3, from 25 to 29 May 2006, in London, at the International Dispute Resolution Centre Ltd. After the filing of the Rejoinder, this meeting was devoted to oral presentations of the Parties.
- Meeting No. 4, from 2 to 4 October 2006, in Paris, at the World Bank Office. The NE presented his Final Draft Determination.
- Meeting No. 5, from 7 to 9 November 2006, in Washington, D.C. The Parties made their comments on the Final Draft Determination.

On 12 February 2007, in Bern, both Ambassadors of Pakistan and of India received, from the hands of the NE, hard and soft copies of his Determination.

2. POINTS OF DIFFERENCE REFERRED BY PAKISTAN AND INDIA'S POSITION

a. Pakistan is of the considered view that the design of the Baglihar Plant on Chenab Main does not conform to criteria (e) and (a) specified in Paragraph 8 of Annexure D to The Indus Waters Treaty 1960 and that the Plant design is not based on correct, rational and realistic estimates of maximum flood discharge at the site.

The Indian side does not agree with Pakistan's position.

Paragraphs 8 (e) and 8 (a) of Annexure D of the Treaty read as follows:

8 (e) *"If the conditions at the site of a Plant make a gated spillway necessary, the bottom level of the gates in normal closed position shall be located at the highest level consistent with sound and economical design and satisfactory construction and operation of the works."*

8 (a) *"The works themselves shall not be capable of raising artificially the water level in the Operating Pool above the Full Pondage Level specified in the design."*

b. Pakistan is of the considered view that the Pondage of 37.722 MCM exceeds twice the Pondage required for Firm Power in contravention of Paragraph 8 (c) of Annexure D to the Treaty.

The Indian side does not agree with Pakistan's position.

Paragraph 8 (c) of Annexure D of the Treaty reads as follows:

(c) "The maximum Pondage in the Operating Pool shall not exceed twice the Pondage required for Firm Power."

c. Pakistan is of the considered view that the intake for the turbines for the Plant is not located at the highest level consistent with satisfactory and economical construction and operation of the Plant as a Run-of-River Plant and is in contravention of Paragraph 8 (f) of Annexure D to the Treaty.

The Indian side does not agree with Pakistan's position.

Paragraph 8 (f) of Annexure D of the Treaty reads as follows:

(f) "The intakes for the turbines shall be located at the highest level consistent with satisfactory and economical construction and operation of the Plant as a Run-of-River Plant and with customary and accepted practice of design for the designated range of the Plant's operation."

3. The Treaty And Its Interpretation

In Interpreting the Treaty, the NE has relied on the rules of the Vienna Convention on the Law of Treaties which reflect customary international law with regard to ordinary methods of treaty interpretation. The Treaty was negotiated and concluded during a period of tension between India and Pakistan. However, in the view of the NE, because of this tension, those who drafted the Treaty aimed for predictability and legal certainty in its drafting, so as to ensure sound implementation. The Treaty contains clear language and wording on how and to which extent India and Pakistan may be allowed to utilize the waters of the Indus system of rivers. The Treaty also gives a clear indication of the rights and obligations of both Pakistan and India. These rights and obligations should be read in the light of new technical norms and new standards as provided for by the Treaty.

Furthermore, and taking account of the ordinary methods of interpretation, the NE is of the opinion that interpretation of the Treaty must be guided by the principle of integration and the principle of effectiveness.

These two principles provide for the Treaty to find effect in its whole and to ensure that each of the object(s) and purpose(s) of the Treaty is given fullest weight and effect when interpreting the rights and obligations under the Treaty. According to the Preamble of the Treaty, the object(s) and the purpose(s) of this Treaty are to attain the most complete and satisfactory utilisation of the waters of the Indus systems of rivers, to fix and delimit the rights and obligations of each party in relation to the other concerning the use of these waters, and to provide for the settlement of questions arising from the application or the interpretation of the Treaty. The objectives set out in the Preamble cannot be read in isolation from each other. They are all complementary in light of the principles of integration and effectiveness and no hierarchy can be deduced from the wording of the Preamble. The rights and obligations contained in Part 3 of Annexure D must be interpreted so as to allow for the fulfilling of the object(s) and purpose(s) of the Treaty in "a spirit of goodwill and friendship" and in "a co-operative spirit", taking into account the best and latest practices in the field of construction and operation of hydro-electric plants.

4. Technical Data Concerning The Baglihar Project

For clarification, the main characteristics of the project, as presented during the site visit in October 2005 and provided by India, are repeated below. Corresponding plates are also given in Annexes 1 to 5 to the Executive Summary.

DAM BODY

Type	Concrete Gravity
Height above deepest foundation [m]	144.50
Length of dam crest [m]	317
Crest elevation [m asl]	844.50

RESERVOIR CHARACTERISTICS

Full pondage level FPL [m asl]	840
Dead storage level DSL [m asl]	835
Pondage [M.m^3]	37.50
Dead storage capacity [M.m^3]	358.45
Gross storage capacity [M.m^3]	395.95

HYDROLOGY

Catchment area [km^2]	17,325
Mean annual inflow [M.m^3]	25,000
Mean discharge [m^3/s]	790
Median annual discharge [m^3/s]	450
Peak flood discharge [m^3/s]	
1 year return period	2,300
10 year return period	5,100
100 year return period	8,100
1000 year return period	12,100
PMF	16,500

SPILLWAYS

Type	Sluice spillway with 5 openings, and Chute spillway with 3 bays
Maximum discharge capacity [m³/s]	16,500 [peak of PMF flood]

a) **Sluice Spillway**

Type	Submerged orifice with ogee-shaped chute
Type of gates	Radial with hydraulic hoists
Number of gates	5
Size of gates	10 m (W) x 10.50 m (H)
Spillway Sill Elevation [m asl]	808
Head above sill [m]	
Normal conditions	32
Maximum extreme conditions	36.50
Energy dissipation	Splitter and ledge along chute, lined stilling basin
Capacity at FPL [m³/s]	10,772

b) **Chute Spillway**

Type of gates	Radial with hydraulic hoists
Size of gates	12 m (W) x 19 m (H)
Number of gates	3
Spillway sill elevation [m asl]	821
Head above sill [m]	
Normal conditions	19.0
Maximum extreme conditions	23.50
Energy dissipation	Flip bucket and lined plunge pool
Capacity at FPL [m³/s]	5,728

c) **Auxiliary Spillway**

Purpose	Evacuation of floating debris
Type	surface chute
Size of gate	6 m (W) x 3 m (H)
Spillway sill elevation [m asl]	837
Location	Right side of the dam, close to power intakes
Capacity at FPL [m³/s]	53

POWER INTAKE

Stages	Stage I: Right intake
	Stage II: Left intake
Type	Lateral submerged intake
Location	On the right bank, forming an angle of 120° with dam
Sill level [m asl]	818
Size of gated section	2 x 10.0 m (W) x 7.5 m (H) for stage I
Size of headrace tunnel	10.15 m diameter circular
Capacity [m³/s]	430

POWERHOUSE

Location	Underground, on the right bank
Installed capacity [MW]	450
Number of unit	3 (x 150 MW)

5. EXPERT DETERMINATION

5.1. Maximum Design Flood

The design flood, generally accepted in the world, has a probability of occurrence of 1/10,000 per year, or expressed differently, has a return period of 10,000 years. According to India's approach, the design flood is the Probable Maximum Flood, which appears to be identical, in this region, to the 10,000 year return period flood. India has correctly applied the statistical approach, but unfortunately the series of peak annual discharges is limited. The deterministic approach was also applied. Probably, for such a large catchment area, India has developed all possible methods of analysis; the NE thinks especially of both the climatological and geomorphological analyses.

The analysis done by India results in a value of 16,500 m^3/s.

Pakistan has used its own statistical approach with a longer annual peak series of 80 years that it obtained by correlation of the discharge measured at the Marala barrage.

The result of Pakistan's calculation is 14,900 m^3/s. The point of view of the NE is that this value is one value among the others, which is not unreasonable.

But finally the choice of the design flood should be based on an analysis of all the results obtained, and supplemented by a strong engineering judgement.

DETERMINATION D1 relating to the maximum design flood [point (a) of the difference referred by Pakistan]

> In view of all the uncertainties of flood analysis, the NE has decided to retain the value of 16,500 m^3/s for the peak discharge of the design flood. Climate change, with the possible associated increase in floods, also encourages a prudent approach.

5.2. Spillway, Ungated Or Gated

Referring to the Treaty, in *Annexure D - Part 3- New Run-of-River Plant, Paragraph 8 (e)*, Pakistan declared that a gated spillway is not necessary,

The determination of the possible arrangement of spillways must be driven by the general conditions of the site, i.e. hydrology and sediment yield, topography, geology and seismicity.

Based on a statistical analysis of 13,000 existing spillways in the world, it has been demonstrated that the provision of gates on large spillways is common practice. Furthermore, it appears that the sole use of ungated free overflow spillways is marginal when the required capacity for flood releases is higher than 15,000 m^3/s.

Free overflow spillways require a higher dam to be able to release the design flood than is the case with gated spillways. The cost of this dam heightening has been compared with the cost of a corresponding gated spillway. A simplified calculation has demonstrated that, with a dam type and size comparable with Baglihar dam, and considering the same discharge requirements, a purely economic comparison always favours a gated spillway.

The maximum water level of the reservoir cannot exceed el. 840 m asl to avoid flooding of Pul Doda town as well as some infrastructure upstream. The potential head of the site (ca.130 m) should be totally utilized for energy production. The Full Pondage Level (FPL), according to the design submitted by India, is fixed at el. 840 m asl. If the design flood should occur, the spillway gates would be opened and the reservoir level would not rise above FPL. On the contrary, if the spillway were ungated, the level of water on the spillway crest would rise by about 12 m to allow for the discharge of the design flood. The reason is the short length of the dam crest which limits the length of the spillway weir. To avoid flooding of the upstream shores, the crest of an ungated overflow spillway should be fixed at el. 828 m asl. The 130 m head of the power plant will be reduced by 12 m, which would represent a loss of 9% in energy production throughout the life of the plant.

DETERMINATION D 2 relating to the issue of gated or ungated spillway [point (a) of difference referred by Pakistan]

> The Treaty provides in *Paragraph 8 (e) of Part 3 of Annexure D the following:*
>
> *"If the conditions at the site of a Plant make a gated spillway necessary,*[3] *the bottom level of the gates in normal closed position shall be located at the highest level consistent with sound and economical design and satisfactory construction and operation of the works.*
>
> The NE considers, in conformity with the state of the art, that the conditions at the site of the Baglihar plant require a gated spillway. An analysis done by the NE on 13,000 existing spillways in the world shows that 89% of these structures, having a design discharge higher than 14,000 m^3/s, are gated.
>
> This decision is consistent with the provisions of the Treaty, requiring a sound and economical design, and satisfactory construction and operation of the works. It is also in accordance with the Preamble of the Treaty, which provides that "[t]he Government of India and the Government of Pakistan, being equally desirous of attaining the most complete and satisfactory utilization of the waters of the Indus system of rivers (...)."

5.3. Spillway, Level Of The Gates

Referring to the Treaty, in Annexure D - Part 3- New Run-of-River Plants, Paragraph 8 (e), which reads as follows:

> *"If the conditions at the site of a Plant make a gated spillway necessary, the bottom level of the gates in normal closed position shall be located at the highest level consistent with sound and economical design and satisfactory construction and operation of the works."*[4]

Pakistan declared that even if it could be assumed (without conceding) that a gated spillway is necessary, the orifice spillway proposed by India is not located at the highest level consistent with the provisions of the Treaty.

The position of India is that the three-bay design for the chute spillway, the five-bay design for the sluice spillway, and the auxiliary spillway are necessary to ensure safe passing of the design flood, and also a silt-free environment near the intakes for trouble-free operation, by transporting sediments together with flood discharges through the sluice spillway. Consequently, the chosen spillway configuration is at the highest possible level consistent with a sound and economical design and satisfactory construction and operation of the works.

It appears clearly to the NE that the keystone of the design of the appurtenant works of Baglihar is not the problem of the flood discharge, but the flow of sediments which could create the following risks:

---

[3] The underlining is by the NE.
[4] The underlining is by the NE.

- Sedimentation of the operating pool (the pondage).

- Sedimentation of the power intake by bed load sediments.

- Suspended sediment with a high concentration and size entering the power intake and power tunnel, causing erosion of the turbines.

- Heightening of the river bed at the entrance of the reservoir and flooding of the town of Pul Doda.

Referring to Bulletin 115 of the International Commission on Large Dams (ICOLD), "Dealing with reservoir sedimentation" (1999), the state of the art today is that "[b]ottom outlets may be used for under sluicing of floods, emptying of reservoirs, sluicing of sediments and preventing sediment from entering intakes, etc."

For its part, the Treaty in *Annexure D - Part 3 - New Run-of-River Plants, Paragraph 8 d)* reads as follows:

"There shall be no outlets below the Dead Storage Level, unless necessary for sediment control or any other technical purpose; any such outlet shall be of the minimum size, and located at the highest level, consistent with sound and economical design and with satisfactory operation of the works."[5]

The NE considers that the two provisions *8 (e) and 8 (d)* of the Treaty should be applied to the design of the spillway, and especially to the level of the gates, which also plays in part the role of a bottom outlet.

To support his determination, the NE conducted an analysis on some important aspects of reservoir sedimentation, the results of which are given below.

In 1960, when the Treaty was signed, the phenomenon of reservoir sedimentation was not recognized everywhere to its full degree of significance. It was only 20 years later, in 1980, that the concept of an integrated reservoir sedimentation management began to be clear and coherent. This simple principle was announced succinctly by the engineers of China stating: "[s]tore the clear water and discharge the muddy water".

It appears that the Treaty is not particularly well developed with respect to its provisions on sediment transport. This is not a criticism: the Treaty reflects the status of technology on reservoir sedimentation in the 1950s. The consequence is that the provisions of the Treaty which explicitly mention sediment acquire a special significance.

Everybody recognizes the necessity to take into consideration the lessons of the past, in particular the last decades, from the design, construction and operation of dams and hydropower plants on rivers with important sediment transport. We refer to, among others cases, Sanmenxia in China commissioned in 1960, Warsak in Pakistan, 1960, and Salal in India, 1987.

The definition of the Dead Storage given in the Treaty states that it cannot be used for operational purposes. The operational purpose of Baglihar is power generation, and so this purpose is not allowed for the Dead Storage. This is precisely the role of the Live Storage which has the purpose of generating power. But the capacity of the Live Storage should be protected against sedimentation. This is an essential matter of sustainability. To meet this objective, "maintenance" of the Live Storage and of the Dead Storage should be carried out – and this is not excluded by the Treaty – in accordance with the various known processes of sedimentation control, and in particular, drawdown sluicing and flushing.

---

[5] The underlining is by the NE.

DETERMINATION D 3 relating to the level of the spillway gates [point (a) of the difference referred by Pakistan]

Referring to the Treaty in **Annexure D Part 3-New Run-of-River Plants, 8 (e)** provides: "If the conditions at the site of a Plant make a gated spillway necessary, the bottom level of the gates in normal closed position shall be located at the highest level consistent with sound and economical design and satisfactory construction and operation of the works."[6]

The NE considers that the gated chute spillway on the left wing, planned in India's design, which has its sill located at el. 821, is at the highest level consistent with sound and economical design and satisfactory construction and operation of the works.

Annexure D Part 3-New Run-of-River Plants, 8 (d) states: "There shall be no outlets below the Dead Storage Level, unless necessary for sediment control or any other technical purpose; any such outlet shall be of the minimum size, and located at the highest level, consistent with sound and economical design and with satisfactory operation of the works."[7]

The NE considers that the sluice spillway, planned in India's design and composed of five outlets, has two functions: sediment control of the reservoir and evacuation of a large part of the design flood. In conformity with international practice and the state of the art, he considers also that the proposed outlets (five gates of 105 m^2) should be of the minimum size and located at the highest level (808 m asl), consistent with a sound and economical design and satisfactory construction and operation of the works. But to ensure protection against flooding of Pul Doda, the outlets should preferably be located 8 m lower, at about el. 800 m asl.

Sound operation of the outlets will necessitate carrying out maintenance of the reservoir with drawdown sluicing each year during the monsoon season. The reservoir level should be drawn down to a level of about 818 m asl, that is to say 17 m below that of the Dead Storage Level. For this level, the free flow discharge is the annual flood of the order of 2500 m^3/s. This is in conformity with the Treaty, which provides that the "'Dead Storage' means that portion of the storage which is not used for operational purpose" *Operational purpose* means power generation (and this is impossible for the Dead Storage because of the high level of the power intake). The reservoir drawdown below the Dead Storage Level will be done for **maintenance purposes**. It is commonly agreed in practice that maintenance is an absolute necessity, with its ultimate objective of ensuring the **sustainability of the scheme**.

5.4. Artificial Raising Of The Water Level

Paragraph 8 (a) of Annexure D of the Treaty reads as follows:

"The works themselves shall not be capable of raising artificially the water level in the Operating Pool above the Full Pondage Level specified in the design."

The only way to limit the technical possibility of raising the full pondage level is to limit the freeboard to the minimum required. In the case of Baglihar dam, utilizing a gated spillway, the Full Pondage Level is at 840 m

---

[6] The underlining is by the NE.
[7] The underlining is by the NE.

asl, and the total freeboard above Full Pondage Level is 4.5 m. Pakistan considers that this value is exaggerated and that the dam crest elevation could be lowered.

Freeboard is the vertical difference in elevation provided between the maximum reservoir level during a routing of the design flood and the dam crest. Thus the elevation of the dam crest is determined by:

- The full pondage level;
- The raising of the reservoir level required to allow for the release of extreme floods. The outflow discharge depends on the extreme flood hydrograph, the arrangement of spillway weirs and outlets, the operating rules of the spillways and the geometrical characteristics of the reservoir; and
- Safety criteria, which depend on: the dam type (concrete, masonry or embankment), the spillway type (gated or ungated), and local conditions, such as wind conditions.

The analysis carried out by the NE allowed him to define objective criteria, based on ICOLD guidelines and sound engineering. The freeboard is an essential safety element to protect the dam against overtopping. The criteria applied took into account the residual risk of malfunctioning of a gate.

The NE could also determine realistic parameters and coefficients for calculating the spillway discharge rating curves. He admitted that the design could be optimised to achieve these coefficients.

Based on these considerations, the NE determined the minimum required freeboard according to the internationally accepted safety criteria.

DETERMINATION D 4 relating to the artificial raising of the water level [point (a) of difference referred by Pakistan]

> In application of the provisions of the Treaty, the NE considers that the dam crest elevation should be set at the lowest elevation compatible with a sound and safe design based on the state of the art.
>
> The dam crest elevation of the Baglihar dam, fixed in the design submitted by India at el. 844.5 m asl, resulting from a freeboard above the Full Pondage Level of 4.50 m, is not at the lowest elevation.
>
> The Determination of the NE is that the freeboard should be 3.0 m above the Full Pondage Level leading to a dam crest elevation at 843.0 m asl. This is possible if the design of the chute spillway is optimised by minor shape adjustments in order to increase its capacity.

5.5. Pondage

Pakistan is of the considered view that the Pondage (which is the Live Storage for a run-of- river plant) calculated by India, exceeds twice the Pondage required for Firm Power and as a consequence is in contravention of the provisions of the Treaty.

The volumes of Pondage calculated by the Parties are:

- Pakistan: Maximum pondage $P = 6.22$ M.m^3, (2 x 3.11)
- India $P = 37.5$ M.m^3, (2 x 18.75)

The Treaty provides in *Annexure D, Part 1 – Definitions, 2 (c)*:

> *"'Pondage' means Live Storage of only sufficient magnitude to meet the fluctuations in the discharge of the turbines arising from <u>variations in the daily and the weekly loads of the plant.</u>"*[8]

---

[8] The underlining is by the NE.

and in *Annexure D, Part 3 - New Run-of-River Plants, 8 (c)*:

"The maximum Pondage in the Operating Pool shall not exceed twice the Pondage required for Firm Power".[9]

Applying these provisions, and based on the state of the art, the NE considers that the role of the pondage is to regulate the river flow to meet consumer demand. When the pondage is calculated on this basis, it can also be used to regulate fluctuations in the river inflow.

The pondage is the operating volume necessary to produce firm power corresponding to the minimum mean discharge at the site of the plant. The method of calculating this minimum ean discharge is clearly explained in the Treaty, and no difference of opinion has arisen between the Parties concerning the value of this discharge.

The pondage calculation presented by Pakistan has been done with the objective of perating the plant at constant power, while regulating the fluctuations in the river flow. The NE cannot agree to this objective.

The pondage calculation presented by India is done with the objective of operating the plant ith a constant river inflow, while regulating the fluctuations in power. The NE agrees with he principle, but not with the hypothesis concerning the time peak load hours on which the alculation should be based; this is not clearly justified.

Logically, the time of peak load each day should be the result of a forecast of the power emand over 15 or 20 years in the region of Baglihar: the Northern Region. Without these data, the NE has made his estimation only on the basis of the graph of power demand in December 2004 provided by India. He is aware of all the uncertainties of this approach, but it s the best available to him at this time.

The calculations made by the NE give a volume of pondage necessary for operation of 6.28 $M.m^3$. The maximum pondage is double this amount: 32.56 $M.m^3$. This volume would llow, in addition to the operation of the plant during peak load hours, for regulation of the ariations in river flow, if any.

DETERMINATION D 5 relating to the volume of the pondage [point (b) of the difference eferred by Pakistan]

> Applying the provisions of the Treaty and based on the state of the art, the NE considers that the first objective of pondage is to regulate the flow of the river to meet consumer demand.
>
> He considers also that the values for maximum pondage stipulated by India as well as by Pakistan are not in conformity with the criteria laid down in the Treaty.
>
> The Determination of the NE is that the maximum Pondage should be fixed at 32.56 $M.m^3$, and the corresponding Dead Storage Level at el. 836 m asl, one meter higher than the level of the Indian design.

5.6. Level Of The Power Intake

Paragraph 8 (f) of Annexure D of the Treaty reads as follows:

> *"The intakes for the turbines shall be located at the highest level consistent with satisfactory and economical construction and operation of the Plant as a Run-of-River Plant and with customary and accepted practice of design for the designated range of the Plant's operation."*

---

[9] The underlining is by the NE.

Pakistan estimates that the design submitted by India does not conform to this criterion and that the intake for the turbines is not located at the highest level consistent with the Treaty requirements. Pakistan also considers that all design choices related to the level of the power intake should be made so as to minimize the submergence of the power intake.

The design submitted by India considers an intake structure with two openings, as shown in Annex 5. The sill level of the intake is 818.0 m asl, 17.0 m below the Dead Storage Level, while the minimum submergence depth is 9.5 m.

In the design submitted by India, a second intake is shown, for a future extension of the Plant. As this future extension is not actually under discussion, it will not be considered, even if it has an impact on the project layout.

Pakistan has developed and proposed an alternative design, with the purpose of demonstrating that higher intake structure elevations are possible.

The design of a power intake structure must be based on the following objectives:

- to minimize hydraulic head losses,
- to prevent entry of floating material,
- to avoid sediment deposition in the intake structure,
- to minimize sediment suspended load in the diverted flow, and
- to prevent air entrainment to the turbines.

Regarding the last criterion, it is well known that eddies can appear in front of the intake, and that vortices can develop and entrain air into the intake and the turbines when concomitantly the reservoir is at a lower operating level and the diverted discharge is high. This criterion fixes the level of the power intake.

The first remedy is to locate the intake structure at a sufficient depth. Several other constructive or operational measures can be taken to avoid the development of these vortices. Finally, resorting to a specifically designed anti-vortex device may be considered under certain conditions.

In the application of the provisions of the Treaty, and based on the state of the art, the NE considers that the elevation of the power intake should be determined to avoid the development of vortices at the Dead Storage Level and air entrainment to the turbines, without limitation of the operation discharge.

He observes that recourse to anti-vortex devices at the design stage is not common practice, and should be limited to particular cases where other measures cannot be undertaken to provide protection against the development of vortices.

The required minimum submergence depth depends on the inflow approach conditions. The proposed location of the intake structure leads to asymmetrical approach conditions. Another arrangement with more symmetrical approach conditions could reduce the required minimum submergence depth.

The NE found that the alternative design proposed by Pakistan would not give sufficient guarantees for protection against sediment deposition in the intake structure and minimum sediment suspended load in the diverted flow.

DETERMINATION D 6 relating to the level of the power intake [point (c) of the difference referred by Pakistan].

> The NE considers that the elevation of the intake stipulated by India is not at the highest level, as required by the criteria laid down in the Treaty.
>
> The determination of the NE is that the intake level should be raised by 3 m and fixed at el. 821.0 m asl.
>
> The required minimum submergence depth depends on the discharge and the inflow approach conditions. The location of the intake structure proposed by India leads to asymmetrical approach conditions. A different arrangement, with more symmetrical approach conditions could reduce the required minimum submergence depth.
>
> The NE believes that at the design stage the normal practice is to avoid the development of vortices by an appropriate arrangement of the intake structure and sufficient submergence for operating restrictions at the minimum water level. In particular cases where these measures cannot be implemented for technical or economic reasons, then recourse to anti-vortex devices would be the best alternative.
>
> He recommends that all possible structural measures should be taken to limit the circulation of flow within the intake structure and in its vicinity, especially avoiding sharp bends inside the intake structure and in its vicinity.

Postscript

The points of difference referred by Pakistan were not trivial and their complexity required from the claimant Party as well as from the respondent a major work of analysis and of synthesis to present their theses. The exchanges between the Parties were documented with great care; the oral presentations during three meetings, and the visit to the site of Baglihar and to the hydraulic laboratory of Roorkee, were found to be of a high technical, scientific and legal interest. The process lasted one year. The work of the NE, of his assistant and of his legal adviser, was also not easy. These are the reasons why the NE believes that the process was equally fruitful for all the participants.

The NE considers that his decision has not been rendered against one or the other Party.

His opinion is that, in fact, specific Parties emerge successfully from the treatment of this difference: the Authors of the Treaty. The Treaty is the successful document.

Professor Raymond Lafitte
Neutral Expert

With the support of

Professor Laurence Boisson de Chazournes,
Legal adviser,

and of

Mr Laurent Mouvet, Senior engineer,
Assistant.

CHAPTER - 27

CONNECTING THE DROPS

Decision makers in India and Pakistan will have to overcome a host of overlapping socio-economic, environmental, and political pressures as they endeavour to ensure their countries' future water needs and sustainably manage the resources of the Indus River Basin that both nations share. Continuing population growth will significantly reduce per capita water availability over the coming decades. Increasing industrialization and urbanization are driving important shifts in water use. Climate change will exert additional, chronic strains on water resources, potentially shifting the seasonal timing or shuffling the geographical distribution of available supplies. Increasingly subject to soaring demand, unsustainable consumption patterns, and mounting environmental stresses, the Indus is swiftly becoming a "closed" basin; almost all of the river's available renewable water is already allocated for various uses - with little to no spare capacity.

Scientists, policy makers, and the broader public in both Pakistan and India will need to better apprehend, assess, and act on the links between water resources management, global and regional environmental change, sustainable development, and social welfare in the Indus Basin in order to meet these emerging challenges. Existing analyses and projections, however, are often fraught with important uncertainties and unknowns. The dearth of consistent information at the relevant regional, national, and sub-national scales has in turn impeded efforts to conduct integrated evaluations that would better connect "upstream" assessment of environmental and socio-economic impacts on water resources with "downstream" implications for agricultural production and livelihoods, drinking water supplies and sanitation infrastructure, and hydropower development and industry. Coordination and exchange across national and disciplinary boundaries will be essential to overcoming this science/policy gap and to providing decision makers with holistic perspectives on the multiple risks weighing on the Indus Basin and the consequent policy choices and possibilities facing the riparian nations.

To help build mutual awareness and understanding between India and Pakistan of the common water resource challenges they confront in the Indus Basin, the Stimson Center, the Sustainable Development Policy Institute (SDPD, and the Observer Research Foundation (ORF) partnered to assemble an Indus Basin Working Group gathering twenty-five analysts and practitioners from a diverse range of professional and disciplinary backgrounds. Together, the participants sought to collectively distinguish the critical knowledge gaps facing scientists and policy makers. Asking both "What information can science provide?" and "What information do decision makers need?" the Working Group looked to identify priority questions for research and analysis. From this foundation, participants collaborated to formulate a suite of practical approaches for meeting key research needs and develop potential options to pursue these common knowledge and policy objectives.

Over six months in 2012, the Working Group met for two three-day workshops, supplemented by webbased dialogues. The first workshop was held in June 2012 in Kathmandu, Nepal. In addition to the Working Group members, four experts from the Kathmandu-based International Centre for Integrated Mountain Development (ICIMOD) - including Director General David Molden, Rajan Bajracharya, Samjwal Bajracharya, and Basanta Shrestha - also took part in the workshop. Participants first considered the contexts and objectives of water policy in the Indus Basin and analyzed the challenges facing decision makers and 4 | Connecting the Drops stakeholders in various domains dependent on water management, such as agricultural production, power generation, poverty reduction, environmental impact assessment, and disaster planning and response. The Working Group experts also examined the increasing demographic and socio-economic pressures on water demand, as well as the emerging environmental strains potentially impacting water supplies in the basin.

Building on this base, the Working Group members assessed the knowledge needs of policy makers and stakeholders situated in different fields, including scientists, development specialists, civil society, and diplomats. In each case, the participants strove to map out the information resources and data shortfalls over various sectors - such as hydrology, climate change and the environment, economic development and livelihoods, agricultural production and lood security, and diplomacy and international relations - and pinpointed the crucial information that different stakeholders and decision makers require to inform their choices.

The Working Group met for its second session in December 2012 in Bangkok, Thailand. Here, the members turned to crafting strategies and options to enhance the knowledge base for sustainable and integrated water resource management policy in the Indus Basin. The participants considered both research measures and knowledge-building approaches to increase the stock of basic data - such as monitoring and measuring the behavior of glaciers and snowpack - and also developed strategies for capacity building and knowledge management for incorporating sound science into policy formulation and deliberation, including data communication and dissemination, and sharing best practices for adaptation to impending climate changes.

Recognizing that different knowledge-building strategies engage different communities and actors, not all research and policy possibilities can proceed at the same pace. The participants sought to elaborate a coherent array of multiple options from which decision makers can select, ranging from exchanges of data collected nationally, to national research projects developed in parallel, to more comprehensive joint and collaborative programs. In this way, different activities can move forward to the extent possible - ideally building trust and confidence for further steps - without inevitable obstacles in any one area precluding progress in others. The Working Group stressed the need to ensure that national and international institutional architectures and mechanisms that structure and regulate water policy-making within and between India and Pakistan operate as effectively as possible. But stakeholders and decision makers must also develop mechanisms for bringing together appropriate partner institutions on either side of the border, both to perform the necessary studies and to communicate the results to policy makers and the public. Expert scientific organizations must be supplemented and supported by other messengers - especially the media - to reach and sway the larger public. A better informed public ultimately holds the key to better informed policy, as public opinion can generate the political will for policy change.

Connecting the Drops: An Indus Basin Roadmap for Cross-Border Water Research, Data Sharing, and Policy Coordination contains the results of the Working Group's deliberations. In its first section, the Roadmap details the manifold socio-economic and environmental stresses on Indus Basin water resources, tracing their potential ramifications and elucidating the resultant looming policy challenges. In the following sections, the Roadmap presents a menu of practical steps to bolster Indian and Pakistani capacities to measure, evaluate, and address increasing pressures on the Indus Basin waters. It provides specific recommendations for priority research on water resources issues and offers programmatic orientations to guide future analyses and data sharing, technical exchange, and collaborative knowledge-building. As a Roadmap, however, this report does not aim to prescribe one fixed route to reach a predefined destination. Rather, it seeks to illuminate the landscape of policy choices and opportunities and chart many potential pathways forward. By articulating strategies for scientific collaboration and international cooperation to

Preface | 5 meet the region's collective water security, development, and environmental challenges, the Roadmap hopes to aide Indian and Pakistani decision makers in framing water relations in the Indus Basin as a confidence building opportunity for mitigating shared risks and generating mutual benefits.

The text of Connecting the Drops: An Indus Basin Roadmap for Cross-Border Water Research, Data Sharing, and Policy Coordination, was prepared by David Michel and Russell Sticklor, drawing on the workshops in Kathmandu and Bangkok and on input papers prepared by the Working Group participants. As such, the Roadmap represents a collective effort. It should not be taken necessarily to imply strict unanimity among the participants, however, either concerning the content of the Roadmap as a whole or the inclusion of any individual recommendation. Working Group members at times expressed diverging views on certain issues, and further consensus building is ongoing. A11 Working Group participants served in their individual capacities. The Indus Basin Working Group would like to acknowledge the financial support of the US State Department. Any findings, conclusions, or recommendations expressed in this report represent the deliberations of the Working Group members, and do not necessarily reflect the views of the State Department or the US Government. The Working Group also thanks Kerri West, Rebecca Rand, Zachary Weiss, Brendan McGovern, Sreya Panuganti, and Weini Li for their considerable contributions to the project.

David Michel
The Stimson Center
Washington, DC, USA

Lydia Powell
Observer Research Foundation
New Delhi, India

Shakeel Ramay
Sustainable Development Policy Institute
Islamabad, Pakistan

Participants in the seminar

- **Arshad Abbasi** – Sustainable Development Policy Institute (Pakistan)
- **Ghazanfar Ali** – Global Change Impact Studies Centre (Pakistan)
- **Dr. Mahendra Bhutiyani** – Snow and Avalanche Study Establishment (India)
- **Amb. Salman Haidar** – Former Foreign Secretary (India)
- **Syed Iqbal Hasnain** – Stimson Center (United States)
- **Dr. Akmal Hussain** – Forman Christian College University (Pakistan)
- **Muhammad Idrees** – National Disaster Management Authority (Pakistan)
- **Amb. Shafqat Kakakhel** – Former Deputy Executive Director, UNEP (Pakistan)
- **Simi Kamal** – Hisaar Foundation (Pakistan)
- **Dr. Iqrar Ahmad Khan** – University of Agriculture, Faisalabad (Pakistan)
- **Amb. Aziz Khan** – Former High Commissioner to India (Pakistan)
- **Prof. Mahendra P. Lama** – Central University of Sikkim (India)
- **Dr. Chandan Mahanta** – Indian Institute of Technology (India)
- **Samir Mehta** – International Rivers (India)
- **David Michel** – Stimson Center (United States)
- **Sonali Mittra** – Observer Research Foundation (India)
- **Khalid Mohtadullah** – International Water Management Institute (Pakistan)
- **Lydia Powell** – Observer Research Foundation (India)
- **Shakeel Ramay** – Sustainable Development Policy Institute (Pakistan)
- **Ahmad Raza Sarwar** – National Institute of Disaster Management (Pakistan)
- **Akhilesh Sati** – Observer Research Foundation (India)
- **Brig. Gen. (Ret.) Krishnaswamy Srinivasan** – Centre for Security Analysis (India)
- **Russell Sticklor** – Stimson Center (United States)
- **B.G. Verghese** – Centre for Policy Research (India)
- **Dr. Masudul Haq Wani** – S.K. University of Agriculture and Technology (India)

PART ONE:

The Indus River Basin Under Pressure

The Indus River is one of the most important water systems in Asia. The Indus originates in China on the Tibetan Plateau and runs for 3,200 km across northern India and the length of Pakistan before emptying into the Arabian Sea near the port city of Karachi. While the Indus system counts 27 major tributaries, the six most significant branches — the Chenab, Ravi, Sutlej, Jhelum, Beas, and the Indus itself — flow west through India before crossing into Pakistan. A seventh major tributary, the Kabul River, rises in Afghanistan and flows east into Pakistan. All told, the Indus River Basin encompasses 1.12 million square kilometers (km^2), with 47 percent of this area falling in Pakistan, 39 percent in India, eight percent in China, and six percent in Afghanistan. In turn, 65 percent of the total area of Pakistan, 14 percent of the Indian land mass, 11 percent of Afghanistan, and one percent of China's land area lie within the Indus Basin.[1]

Climate and precipitation conditions vary considerably over the basin. The Upper Indus Basin, in the north, covers a high mountain region with alpine and highland climates. Most of the precipitation occurs in winter and spring, much of it falling as snow, particularly at higher elevations. To the south, the Lower Basin extends over plains exhibiting subtropical arid and semi-arid to temperate sub-humid climates. Here, most of the precipitation falls during the monsoon from July to September. Across the entire Indus Basin, annual average precipitation ranges between 100-500 millimeters (mm) in the lowlands to 2,000 mm and above in the Himalayan foothills and the higher mountains.

The contrasting climate and precipitation profiles between the wetter, cooler north and the hotter, drier south create marked differences in the origins of local stream flows. In the upper sub-basins, flows derive largely or solely from local runoff from the surrounding catchment. In the lower sub-basins, discharges descending from upstream catchments increasingly predominate in the local river flow. In the Indus plains, inflows from upstream catchments represent 81 percent or more of discharge in the lower river. On the whole, the high-altitude catchments comprise net contributors to the basin's water supplies and the lowland catchments constitute net consumers. Even so, all the basin catchments show substantial seasonal fluctuations, with river flows peaking during June-September when the monsoon brings intense rainfall to the Lower Basin and higher temperatures increase snow and glacier melt in the Upper Basin. Observed monthly flows in individual sub-basins can be ten times greater at the height of the summer wet season than during the lean winter months. Large year-to-year variations in annual precipitation induce corresponding variability in the Indus' annual flow.[2]

Today, the Indus supplies the needs of some 300 million people living throughout the basin. Together, India and Pakistan represent almost all of the demand on the river's resources, with Pakistan drawing 63 percent of water used in the basin and India drawing 36 percent. Pakistan depends critically on the Indus, as the country's other rivers run only seasonally and their total flows equal less than two percent of the mean annual inflow entering Pakistan through the Indus system. For India, meanwhile, the Indus furnishes about seven percent of the annual utilizable surface water available nationwide. Crucially, the basin's freshwater resources nourish the agricultural breadbaskets of both countries. Agriculture accounts for 93 percent of water withdrawn from the Indus, while industrial and domestic demands combined make up just seven percent of total use. Pakistan annually abstracts three-quarters of the river's flow into canal systems supporting the world's largest contiguous system of irrigated agriculture, and 95 percent of all the country's irrigation occurs within the basin. Farming in turn employs 40 percent of Pakistan's labor force and generates 22 percent of its GDP, while also delivering critical inputs to industry (notably cotton for the textiles sector). In India, the combined Indo-Gangetic Plain constitutes the most intensely irrigated area on Earth, while agriculture comprises 17 percent of GDP and occupies 55 percent of the economically active population. The Indus Basin, in turn, generates a quarter of Indian grain production, supplying substantial surpluses that offset deficits in other regions.[3] In both countries, the Indus waters help feed and employ significant numbers of people beyond the basin boundaries.

In addition to sharing the Indus' surface waters, India and Pakistan also share important — though inadequately mapped and characterized — transboundary aquifers in the basin.[4] Groundwater constitutes an essential additional source of freshwater for the region. Groundwater and surface water resources in the Indus Basin are closely linked both hydrologically and socio-economically. Hydrologically, seepage from surface sources — such as rivers and irrigation canals — contributes to recharging subterranean aquifers, while groundwater flows similarly enter and augment surface streams. By some assessments, 45 percent of Pakistan's renewable groundwater supply originates in leakage from the canal system, 26 percent comes from irrigation return flows, and six percent derives from river recharge. In India, an estimated one-fifth of the surface water withdrawn from the Indus for irrigation subsequently drains into groundwater aquifers as return flow.[5] Socio-economically, many water users in the basin rely on groundwater to supplement or supplant surface water supplies where these prove inadequate, intermittent, or unavailable. Over 40 percent of the irrigated land area in Pakistan, for example, is irrigated from mixed surface water and groundwater.[6]

For many cities in the basin, groundwater is the principal or unique source for municipal water supplies. In India, groundwater abstractions in those states situated wholly or partially within the Indus Basin — Haryana, Himachal Pradesh, Jammu and Kashmir, Punjab, and Rajasthan — amount to 62.7 km^3. Pakistan's annual groundwater withdrawals from the basin totaled 61.6 km^3 in 2008, or one-third of all national water use. Across the Indus Basin, groundwater accounts for 48 percent of total water withdrawals.[7]

Growing populations and increasing development, however, are placing mounting pressures on the Indus Basin's water supplies. In Pakistan, total annual water withdrawals have risen from 153.4 km^3 in 1975 to 183.5 km^3 in 2008, while total annual renewable water resources per capita have plunged from 3,385 cubic meters (m^3) in 1977 to 1,396 m^3 in 2011. Over the same period, total annual water withdrawals in India have doubled, leaping from 380 km^3 in 1975 to 761 km^3 in 2010, while annual renewable water resources per capita have tumbled from 2,930 m^3 in 1977 to 1,539 m^3 in 2011.[8] To place these numbers in perspective, hydrologists commonly consider 1,700 m^3 per year the national threshold for filling each person's water requirements for domestic needs, agriculture, industry, energy, and the environment. Annual availability under 1700 m^3 per capita constitutes conditions of "water stress," and less than 1,000 m^3 per capita represents "water scarcity."[9] For the Indus Basin as a whole, the United Nations Environment Programme (UNEP) calculates that per capita annual renewable water availability stands at 1,329 m^3. Another analysis by the International Centre for Integrated Mountain Development (ICIMOD) estimated yearly water supplies in the basin at 978 m^3 per person. Both figures indicate that the basin's inhabitants face severe water stress.[10]

Figure 2. Renewable Water Resources and Withdrawal Levels in the Indus River Basin

Country	India	Pakistan	Total
Average long-term available renewable water supplies in the IRB	97 km³/year	190 km³/year	287 km³/year
Estimated renewable surface water supplies in the IRB	73 km³/year	160-175 km³/year	239-258 km³/year
Estimated renewable groundwater supplies in the IRB	27 km³/year	63 km³/year	90 km³/year
Estimated total water withdrawals in the IRB	98 km³/year	180-184 km³/year	257-299 km³/year
Estimated total surface water withdrawals in the IRB	39 km³/year	128 km³/year	
Estimated total groundwater withdrawals in the IRB	55 km³/year	52-62 km³/year	

Note: Figures for surface and groundwater supplies may not sum evenly to figures for total renewable water resources because a large fraction of groundwater and surface water resources overlap, so that separate supplies cannot be absolutely distinguished.
Source: Derived from FAO, Irrigation in Southern and Eastern Asia in Figures: AQUASTAT Survey 2011, Karen Frenken ed. Rome: FAO, 2012) A.N. Laghari et al., "The Indus basin in the framework of current and future resources management,"
Hydrology and Earth Systems Sciences 16, no.4 (2012); Bharat R. Sharma et al., "Indo-Gangetic River Basins: Summary Situation nalysis," International Water Management Institute, New Delhi Office, July 2008.

The intensifying strains on the Indus can be read in diminishing river flows and dropping water tables. Water is a renewable resource, but also a finite one. Rainfall, snow and ice melt, seepage between surface waters and groundwater, and return flows from irrigation and other uses ultimately drain to the Indus River and recharge aquifers to varying degrees. For any given source, however, renewals vary over time and place. Natural processes may only recharge underground aquifers over tens, hundreds, or even thousands of years, and the glaciers that nourish many watercourses have accumulated over millennia. Every watershed is only replenished by a certain amount of renewable water every year.

According to various studies, long-term available renewable water supplies in the Indus Basin average 287 km³ per year, representing 190 km³ of annual renewable water resources in Pakistan and 97 km³ in India. Of his total, surface water accounts for around 239-258 km³, comprising 73 km³ from India and 160-175 km³ in Pakistan. Annual renewable groundwater supplies have been estimated at 90 km³, reflecting resources of 27 km³ in India and 63 km³ in Pakistan. (A large fraction of replenishable groundwater reserves and surface water resources overlap, however, so that separate supplies cannot be absolutely distinguished.) Against the basin's renewable freshwater resources, estimates of total annual water demand range from 257-299 km³. India withdraws about 98 km³ yearly, with around 55 km³ of withdrawals coming from groundwater stocks and 39 km³ from surface sources. Pakistan's annual water demands from the Indus add up to 180-184 km³, with 128 km³ from surface water and 52-62 km³ pumped from groundwater aquifers.[11] Annual averages, though, can camouflage important year-to-year fluctuations in water availability. An assessment of supply and demand on the Indus River by experts at the International Water Management Institute (IWMI) helps frame the importance of such variations. In recent decades (1957-1997), annual flow in the Indus ranged from 120-230 km³, with a long-term average of 187 km³. Meanwhile, combined Indian and Pakistani withdrawals from the river now amount to 176.5 km³.[12]

As the riparians' resource requirements have grown, water removals from the Indus are outpacing natural rates of renewal. Total withdrawals nearly equal or even surpass long-term flow balances and ecosystem needs. Increasingly, the Indus is a "closed" basin. A basin is considered closed when all of its water resources are already allocated to meet various societal and environmental needs, with little to no spare capacity leftover, such that supply falls short of demand during part or all of the year.[13] Claims on the Indus have reached the point that some sub-basins, and even the river as a whole, may generate no net runoff (i.e., mean annual discharge from the river is zero percent of mean annual precipitation). In fact, at times the Indus no longer reaches the sea year round.[14]

With human water demands effectively absorbing available supplies, little flow remains to support the natural environment. Hydrologists and environmental scientists recognize that river systems require base "environmental flows" to sustain riverine habitats and ecosystems and maintain ecological functions such as diluting pollution, flushing sediment and nutrients downstream, controlling salinity intrusion, and replenishing wetlands and estuaries. No fixed formula has been found to determine appropriate environmental flows, which will vary from river to river. One preliminary assessment, however, has suggested that environmental water requirements for the Indus River should equal 25 percent of mean annual runoff, or about 46.75 km³ per year based on the reported long-term average annual flow of 187 km³.[15] The Indus is not meeting this target. Within Pakistan, the 1991 Water Apportionment Accord between the provinces committed to ensure that annual environmental flows to the Indus Delta below the Kotri barrage would not descend below 12.3 km³ — so as to check seawater intrusion, maintain the river channel and sediment transport, and support fisheries — but flows since the 1990s indicate the terms of the Accord are not being fulfilled and runoff to the delta has been notably less than 12 km³ per year.[16]

India and Pakistan are likewise rapidly depleting the basin's groundwater resources. Indeed, abstractions from the Indus aquifers reflect both the most intensive and the most unsustainable levels of groundwater exploitation on Earth.[17] Studies in Pakistan reveal water tables plummeting by two to three meters a year, with groundwater levels falling to inaccessible depths in many wells. Because groundwater salinity in these aquifers typically increases with depth, dropping water tables lead farmers to irrigate with ever more saline water, salinizing the soils and degrading their production potential. Salt-affected soils now afflict 4.5 million hectares, amounting to over 22 percent of Pakistan's irrigated lands.[18] Similarly, a review by India's Central Ground Water Board determined that overdrafts exceeded rates of recharge in 59 percent of the administrative units monitored in the Haryana state, 80 percent of units in Punjab, and 69 percent of units in Rajasthan. Around the region, yearly groundwater withdrawals equaled 127 percent of the total renewable supply in Haryana, 170 percent in Punjab, and 135 percent in Rajasthan.[19] As a result, the Indus Basin is literally losing water. Estimates based on satellite data indicate that the basin aquifers lost groundwater at a rate of 10 km³ per year between April 2002 and June 2008, an annual debit representing more than half the combined capacity of India's six large dams in the Indus system, or almost half the available water storage in all the reservoirs of Pakistan.[20]

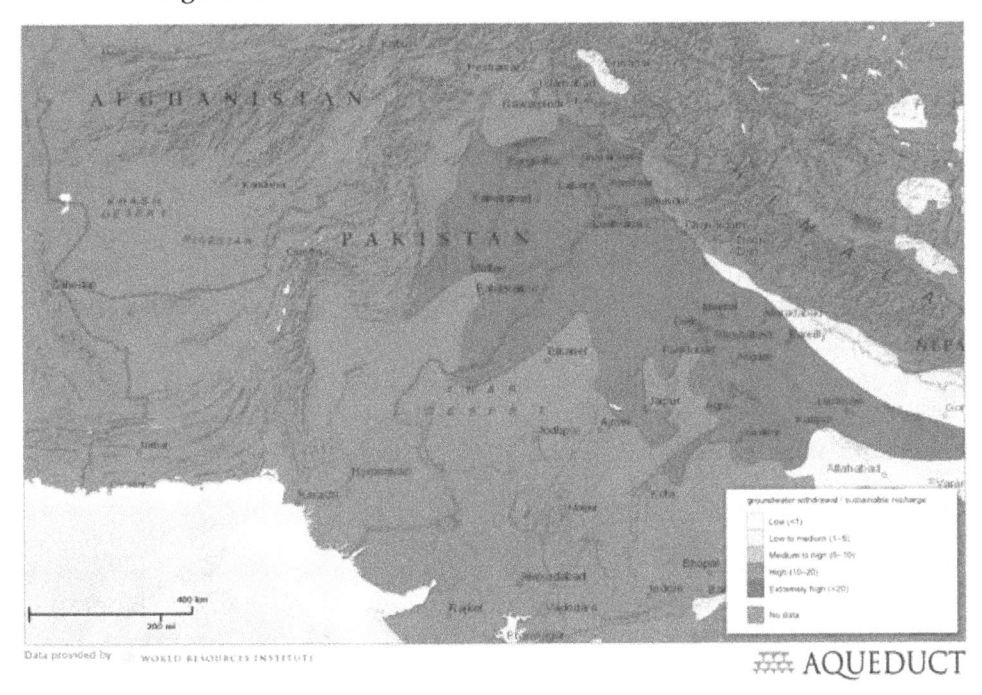

Figure 3. Groundwater Stress in the Indus River Basin

Increasing water pollution also burdens the Indus Basin. Natural processes can contaminate water supplies, but poor water quality more often results from human factors.[21] Agriculture, industry, mining, and other activities charge surface and groundwater resources with synthetic chemicals, fertilizers, pesticides, toxic metals, and microbial pathogens that can compromise human health. Human activities also generate heightened levels of nitrogen, phosphorous, and other nutrients, causing eutrophication that chokes waterways with algal blooms, weeds, and toxic bacteria.

Pressures on water quantity and quality interact. Decreasing water quality ultimately can lower effectively available water quantities, as some sources become too degraded for certain uses. Likewise, diminishing water quantities boost the concentration of any pollutants present, eroding water quality. Water quantity and water quality stresses frequently occur together, as demand centers requiring large withdrawals — such as zones of intensive agriculture, urban agglomerations, and industrial concentrations — also generate substantial pollution.[22]

Surface water quality in the upper Indus is high on certain measures, but progressively deteriorates downstream as farms and towns dump untreated agricultural effluents, human waste, and industrial pollutants into the river, canals, and drains. Nitrogen loading, phosphorous loading, pesticide loading, organic loading, and mercury deposition exhibit alarming levels throughout the river's course, and agricultural and industrial pollutants taint almost all shallow groundwater.[23] According to UNEP, farms, cities, industries, and households pour 54.7 km³ of wastewater into the Indus every year, with 90 percent of these effluents coming from the agricultural sector.[24]

Little of this wastewater is treated. In Indian towns of 50,000 to 100,000 people and cities with populations of 100,000 to one million, wastewater treatment capacities can handle less than one-third of the sewage generated daily. Even in larger metropolitan areas with more than a million inhabitants, installed capacities can treat little more than two-thirds of urban wastewater, and nearly 39 percent of treatment plants tested in 2009 did not conform to discharge standards. A sanitation survey carried out by the Ministry of Urban Development evaluating 423 cities nationwide judged not a single city "healthy," and only four were assessed as "recovering," with none of those four cities in the Indus Basin. Instead, most cities were rated "needing considerable improvements," and 190 were deemed "cities on the brink of public health and environmental emergency."[25] Available data on Pakistan suggest that only about eight percent of urban wastewater is treated in municipal plants and 99 percent of industrial effluents are discharged untreated. One five-year national study found that water quality fell below recommended standards for human consumption in 76-96 percent of the samples tested across the country's four provinces.[26]

The consequences for Pakistani and Indian societies are dire. Inadequate sanitation costs Pakistan 343.7 billion Pakistani rupees (USD$5.7 billion) annually in health damages, productivity losses, and work and school absences, a sum equal to over 3.9 percent of GDP in 2006. Meanwhile, inadequate sanitation costs India 2.4 trillion Indian rupees (USD$53.8 billion) annually, equivalent to 6.4 percent of the national GDP. More troubling than the economic impacts is the human toll. Water-borne diseases account for 20-40 percent of all hospital patients and one-third of all deaths in Pakistan, and an estimated 200-250,000 Pakistani children die from diarrhea and other water-related illnesses each year. Inadequate sanitation is responsible for 10 percent of all deaths in India and causes more than 30 percent of deaths among children under five. Diarrhea alone killed 395,000 Indian children in 2006.[27]

Reshaping the Basin: Population Growth, Urbanization, and Climate Change

Water managers in the Indus Basin will have to overcome a host of overlapping socio-economic, environmental, and policy pressures as they strive to fulfill their countries' future water needs. Historically, demographic pressures constitute the most powerful driver of regional water stress; the influence of population growth on water shortage has proven about four times more important than the effect of long-term shifts in available water resources due to climate factors.[28] Even in the absente of any other stresses, demographic changes alone will significantly trim per capita water availability over the coming decades. As populations expand, renewable water resources remain finite, reducing available shares per person. The UN expects that India's population will increase by almost a quarter in the next 20 years, topping 1.5 billion in 2030 and approaching 1.7 billion by 2050. Pakistan will witness even more spectacular growth. From 174 million inhabitants in 2010, its population will surge to 234 million in 2030 and near 275 million in 2050.[29] Within the confines of the Indus, one assessment projects that 383 million people will be living in the basin — including populations in Afghanistan and China — by 2050. Annual renewable water availability across the basin would then be under 750 m^3 per capita. Another model evaluation by the International Water Management Institute calculates that the total annual availability of renewable water on the Indian portion of the Indus Basin will slip from 2,109 m^3 per capita (in 2000) to 1,732 m^3 in 2050. On the Pakistani portion of the basin, yearly per capita water availability is expected to slide from 1,332 m^3 to 545 m^3.[30]

Economic growth and urbanization will also propel important shifts in water use. The Organisation for Economic Cooperation and Development (OECD) projects that the Indian GDP will rise 5.1 percent per annum on average over the next 50 years — more rapidly than any other major economy—boosting per capita income more than sevenfold in 2060. Pakistan aspires to achieve seven percent annual GDP growth, quadrupling per capita income by 2030.[31] Expanding economies will fuel growing industrial sectors, requiring increasing water inputs. By the same token, the UN anticipates that India's urban population will swell a further 62 percent over the next two decades, and Pakistan's will balloon by 83 percent.[32] City dwellers use more water on average than their compatriots in the countryside, and over the past two decades, municipal water withdrawals have doubled in India and quadrupled in Pakistan. On the Indian side of the Indus, analyses by IWMI conclude that by 2025 both domestic and industrial water withdrawals will double from 2001 levels. Likewise, the municipal and industrial demand in Pakistan is expected to grow more than two-and-a-half times over the current use.[33]

	India	Pakistan
GDP (2011)[i]	4,503,069,382,752	485,136,390,937
GDP per capita (2011)[i]	3,627	2,745
Human Development Index 2011[ii]	0.547	0.504
Population in 2011 (in thousands)[iii]	1,241,492	176,745
Population in 2050 (in thousands)[iv]	1,692,008	274,875
Percentage of total population using improved drinking water sources, 2010[v]	90	89
Percentage of total population using improved sanitation facilities, 2010[v]	23	34
Total annual renewable water resources, 2011 (10^9 m^3/yr)[vi]	1,911	246.8
Total annual water resources per capita, 2011 (in m^3/person/year)[vi]	1,539	1,396
Total annual water withdrawals, 2005 or most recent year (in 10^9 m^3/year)[vi]	761 (in 2010)	183.5 (in 2008)
Total annual water withdrawals per capita (in m^3/person/year)[vi]	613 (in 2010)	1,038 (in 2008)

i   GDP and GDP per capita converted to current international dollars for 2011 using purchasing power parity rates.

Source: World Bank, World Development Indicators, http://databank.worldbank.org/ddp/html

ii   The Human Development Index (HDI) is a summary measure of human development.

Source: UNDP, Human Development Report 2011, http://hdr.undp.org/en/data/map/

iii   *Source:* World Bank, World Development Indicators, http://databank.worldbank.org/ddp/html

iv   Population growth estimates based on the medium-fertility variant.

Source: UN World Population Prospects, the 2010 Revision, http://esa.un.org/wpp/unpp/panel_population.htm

v   *Source:* UN Millenium Development Goals Indicators, 2012 Update, http://mdgs.un.org/unsd/mdg

vi   *Source:* FAO AQUASTAT, http://www.fao.org/nr/water/aquastat/data/factsheets/aquastat_fact_sheet_pak_en.pdf and http://www.fao.org/nr/water/aquastat/data/factsheets/aquastat_fact_sheet_ind_en.pdf

Larger, wealthier, and more urban populations will need sufficient sustainable water supplies to drink, wash, and cook. But it is the water needed to produce the food that they will eat that will challenge policy makers. International norms established by the World Health Organization (WHO) and the United Nations Children's Fund (UNICEF) hold that each person requires a minimum of 20 liters of water a day for drinking and basic hygiene.[34] By contrast, to grow a kilogram of wheat — the primary crop cultivated in the Indus — requires 1,827 liters of water on average, while a kilogram of rice takes 1,673 liters. Producing dairy, meat, poultry, and other animal products can be even more water intensive, necessitating appreciable amounts of freshwater to grow feed, provide drinking water, and care for the animals. Raising a kilogram of lamb, for example, demands 10,412 liters of water; a kilogram of eggs uses 3,265 liters; and a kilogram of milk, 1,020 liters.[35] All freshwater inputs considered, it takes 2,000 to 5,000 liters of water per person per day to grow the food to support diets of 2,800 kilocalories daily that the FAO deems the threshold for ensuring food security.[36]

With rising incomes, urban and rural citizens alike discover different dietary possibilities and preferences, deriving less of their daily caloric intake from food grains and more from non-grain crops (fruits, vegetables, oils, and sugar) and animal products (meat, fish, and dairy). Driven by these socio-demographic pressures, experts calculate that Pakistan will need 250 km³ of water to irrigate its fields in 2025. By the same token, models developed by the International Food Policy Research Institute (IFPRI) anticipate that irrigation water use on the Indian stretches of the Indus will climb some 12 percent above 1995 levels by 2025.[37] (Increased agricultural production and increased irrigation, in turn, suggest that increased amounts of agricultural effluents will drain into Indus water systems. According to models developed by the OECD, as India boosts its crop production by some 50 percent by 2030, annual nitrogen loads in the country's wastewater will soar fivefold and phosphorous loading will more than triple above year 2000 levels.)[38]

Consequently, a growing number of analyses foresee increasing water scarcities striking the Indus Basin. A consortium led by the consulting firm McKinsey & Company and the International Finance Corporation, an arm of the World Bank, recently constructed a baseline for charting emerging global resource challenges by comparing expected future water requirements against actually accessible, reliable, and environmentally sustainable supplies of surface and groundwater. According to this international assessment — assuming that present policy regimes continue and existing levels of efficiency and productivity persist — renewable water supplies will fall 52 percent short of annual demands on the Indian side of the Indus Basin in 2030. The consortium's findings echoed an earlier Indian prognosis concluding that total utilizable freshwater resources in the Indian reaches of the Indus will meet less than half of the basin's requirements in 2050.[39] The situation is equally alarming on the other side of the frontier. There, the World Bank figures that Pakistan has already breached the limit of its available resources. Yet by 2025 the country will require 30 percent more water than today to meet its rising agricultural, domestic, and industrial needs.[40]

The growing danger of climate change compounds the water resource challenges confronting the region. Continuing global warming may shift the seasonal timing or the geographical distribution of water supplies. Extreme weather events are predicted to increase in frequency and degree, with stronger storms, higher floods, and deeper droughts becoming more numerous and severe. Such impacts could significantly alter water availability and damage or degrade the water supply and sanitation infrastructure on which Indians and Pakistanis depend. Regional-scale climate change projections remain clouded by many uncertainties. Nevertheless, ensemble analyses of multiple models suggest that the Indus Basin region will experience increasingly variable precipitation. Winter precipitation is projected to decrease, implying less availability and higher water stress during the lean season. Summer precipitation is expected to increase overall, but with enhanced year-to-year variability in daily rainfall during the monsoon. An anticipated rise in intense precipitation presages more severe monsoon flooding. With more rainwater coming in short sudden downpours, less will be absorbed by saturated soils and more lost as direct runoff, correspondingly reducing the potential for recharging groundwater.[41]

Figure 5. Glaciers in the Major Basins of the Hindu Kush Himalaya Region

Basins	Number	Glaciated area (km²)	Estimated ice reserves (km³)	Average area per glacier (km²)
Amu Darya	3,277	2,566	162.6	0.8
Indus	18,495	21,193	2,696.1	1.2
Ganges	7,963	9,012	793.5	1.1
Brahmaputra	11,497	14,020	1,302.6	1.2
Irrawaddy	133	35	1.3	0.3
Salween	2,113	1,352	87.7	0.6
Mekong	482	235	10.7	0.5
Yangtze	1,661	1,660	121.4	1.0
Yellow	189	137	9.2	0.7
Tarim	1,091	2,310	378.6	2.1
Qinghai-Tibetan Interior	7,351	7,535	563.1	1.0
Total, HKH	54,252	60,055	6,126.8	1.1

Source: Bajracharya, SR (2012) Status of glaciers in the Indus Basin. Kathmandu: ICIMOD
Credit: ICIMOD/Samjwal Ratna Bajracharya

Climate change will exert additional, chronic pressures on key sources of fresh water supplies in the Indus Basin. The headwaters of the Indus rise in the glaciers of the Himalaya Hindu Kush (HKH). Often called the continent's "water towers," the glaciers of the greater Himalayan range constitute the world's largest body of ice outside the polar ice caps. The glaciers act as massive regional freshwater repositories, seasonally accumulating snow and ice at high elevations and releasing melt water that feeds 10 large river systems across Asia. According to a recent inventory undertaken by ICIMOD, the Indus is by far the most heavily glaciated of the region's major basins. It counts 18,495 glaciers covering 21,193 km² and containing an estimated 2,696 km³ of ice, representing 44 percent of the total ice reserves in the entire HKH region. Snow and glacial melt contribute more than 50 percent of the total flow of the Indus, forming an especially critical source of water during the summer shoulder seasons (before and after the rains from the summer monsoon) when melt water comprises 70 percent of the river's summer flow. In years of feeble or failed monsoons, melt water can avert or alleviate the otherwise calamitous drought.[42] As global warming drives up temperatures and shifts precipitation patterns worldwide, however, glaciers in the Himalayas are generally retreating.[43]

Initially, increased glacier melting could boost river flows. This trend could pose risks of its own, however. Rising runoff can heighten the danger of "glacial lake outburst floods" (GLOF) as melt water collects behind natural barriers of ice or debris. Seismic activity, avalanches, landslides, or other triggers can weaken or collapse these retaining barriers, sending sudden waves of water rushing downstream. Historically, some 33 GLOFs have been recorded in Bhutan, Nepal, and the Tibetan Autonomous Republic (China) since the 1930s, some causing loss of life and significant damage to roads, bridges, hydropower plants, and other infrastructure. In some instances, the flooding spread across international borders. ICIMOD has catalogued 16 potentially dangerous glacial lakes just on the Indian tributaries of the Indus in Himachal Pradesh, and a further 52 potentially dangerous lakes in the Pakistani reaches of the basin.[44] As de-glaciation continues, however, melt water flows will subsequently wane, diminishing the downstream supplies available for drinking, sanitation, agriculture, hydropower, industry, and ecosystems. As melt water contributions to the Indus Basin decline, one set of model projections shows mean water supply decreasing by 8.4 percent on the Indus by 2050. When integrated with assessments of projected irrigation requirements and crop yields, these anticipated shifts in water availability imply a drop in the effective population that can be fed by the basin's water resources. By mid-century, such calculations warn, the Indus Basin will be able to feed 26 million fewer people than it currently supports.[45]

The Challenge and the Opportunity

Left unaddressed, such pressures could sow increasing competition over dwindling water supplies, fueling potentially destabilizing international tensions. Historically, the international boundary that set India and Pakistan apart at independence also set them at odds over water. As the downstream neighbor, Pakistan feared Indian withdrawals or diversions could deprive it of its water supply, posing an existential threat to its agriculture and economy, and undermining its food security. As the upper riparian, India worried that according all of the Indus' flow to Pakistan would curtail possibilities for developing the river for its own benefit. Since 1960, the Indus Waters Treaty (IWT) between the two countries has governed water resource development on the river and its main tributaries. Unlike other water agreements that typically distribute water allowances between riparians — either as absolute amounts or percentages of the river flow — the IWT physically divided the river, allocating use of the three western tributaries that contribute to the main river entirely to Pakistan, and allotting the three eastern tributaries to India. The treaty also controls the type and features of projects that India can establish on its portion of the Indus.

Since its inception, the IWT has stood through three wars and countless lesser clashes. But the accord has no provisions for how the parties should respond to the variations in water flow that climate change could engender. Nor does the agreement contain effectively binding provisions to address water quality or pollution. Similarly, while the two countries share transboundary aquifers as well as surface waters, there are no provisions for managing this key resource, or even for sharing data on groundwater supplies. Yet consumers across the Indus Basin rely on groundwater to supplement or substitute for surface water. As pressures on one source of supply grow, users will of necessity turn to the other.[46]

South Asia's earliest civilizations arose on the banks of the Indus, encompassing sites in both modern day Pakistan and India. Recent archaeological evidence suggests that climatic shifts dried the rivers that once watered the irrigated agriculture on which those Bronze Age cities depended, precipitating the ultimate collapse of the Harappan civilization.[47] Today, India and Pakistan again face significant water resource challenges. In 2005, a World Bank assessment judged that India's clashing water supply and demand trajectories offered "a stark and unequivocal portrayal of a country about to enter an era of severe water scarcity." A parallel 2005 World Bank analysis of Pakistan warned that while development of the Indus had transformed one of the world's most arid nations — providing the platform for the country's economy — "the survival of a modern and growing Pakistan is threatened by water."[48] Yet the contemporary Indus civilization is by no means destined to suffer the fate of its Bronze Age predecessors. Effective management of the basin's water resources — built on sound scientific data, guided by an integrated knowledge base, and anchored by capacity building and confidence building measures — can promote a sustainable future for both India and Pakistan in the Indus Basin.

PART TWO:

Policy And Research Recommendations: Agriculture And Food Security

With the introduction of modern irrigation techniques in the mid-19th century, modern-day Indian and Pakistani Punjab transformed themselves into agricultural breadbaskets — a role they continue to fulfill today. Dubbed the "food bowl of India," the Indian Punjab accounts for roughly 12 percent of India's 234 million tons of food grain, making the state critical to the nation's food security, despite the fact that the state accounts for less than 1.6 percent of the country's total land area.[49] Pakistani Punjab, meanwhile — home to nearly 70 percent of the country's total cropped area — produces 80 percent of Pakistan's wheat, 97 percent of its fine aromatic rice, 63 percent of its sugarcane, and 51 percent of its maize, in addition to 83 percent of the country's total cotton.[50]

Vital to the economic stability and food security of both countries, the Punjab region of the Indus Basin, as well as Sindh province in Pakistan and Haryana state in India, face the dual challenges of population growth and climate change. These pressures are taxing soil and water resources in an unprecedented fashion by eroding food security, threatening agricultural livelihoods, and heightening competition among water users for increasingly scarce water resources. Erratic seasonal water supply is particularly problematic for Pakistan, where agriculture generates approximately 22 percent of GDP, employs roughly 40 percent of the country's total workforce, and generates some 80 percent of total Pakistani export revenue.[51] Across the country, some 13 million hectares of arable land now lies untouched due to insufficient water supply, even though Pakistan possesses more than 20 million hectares of arable land.[52] In response to the increased variability of monsoon precipitation across the basin, food producers in both countries frequently resort to groundwater pumping — an almost entirely unregulated practice, which is often encouraged via fuel subsidies — to meet their irrigation needs, resulting in the unsustainable drawdown of vital underground water supplies. Reliance on this resource is driven by the fact that roughly 10 percent of total rainfall within the basin evaporates, while poorly lined canals result in the loss of roughly 41 million acre feet per year due to seepage.[53]

Meanwhile, mounting water scarcity also has long-term implications for food production and livelihoods beyond the two countries' agricultural heartlands. In the mountainous reaches of the Indian and Pakistani portions of the basin, rural communities adjacent to glaciated areas regularly siphon water directly from the glaciers' peripheries to irrigate crops. As climate change accelerates glacial melt rates in the Indus headwater regions, these communities face the potential short-term challenge of increased flooding, and the long-term prospect of depleted melt water flows, which will reduce water supply required for local food production.[54]

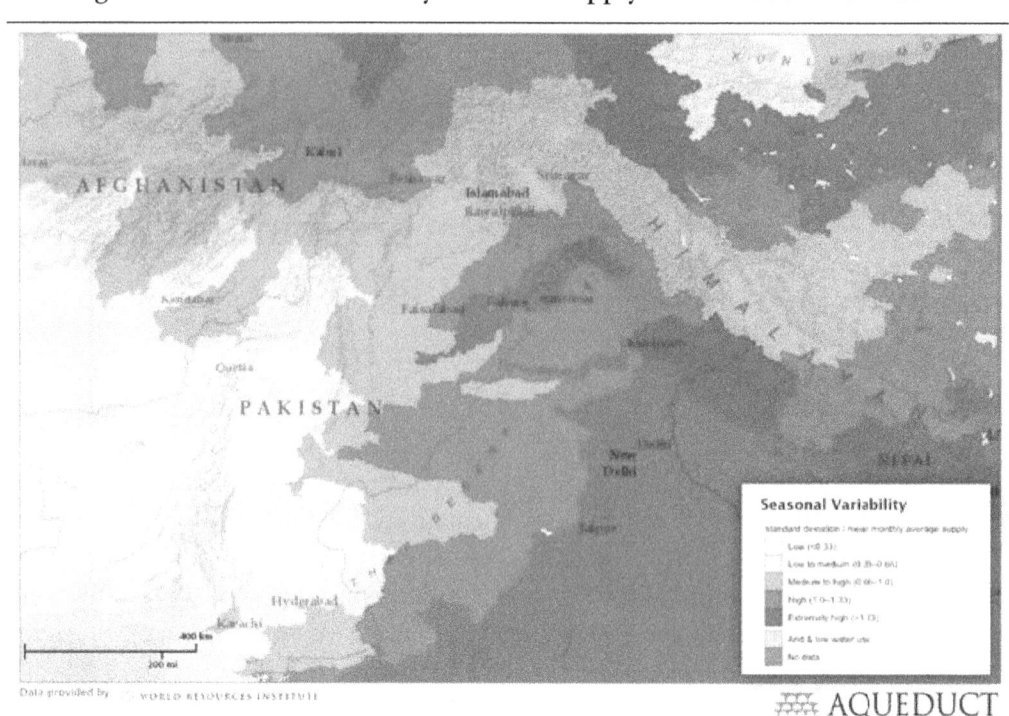

Figure 6. Seasonal Variability of Water Supply in the Indus River Basin

In addition to population growth, changing lifestyles and diets across the region are also driving intensified water demand for food production. In India, in particular, an emerging middle class is showing an increased preference for meat and dairy products, which have a much larger virtual-water footprint than grains and other agricultural produce due to the water resources needed to raise livestock. Shifting dietary preferences and their attendant impact on water resource allocations threaten to increase tensions and heighten competition between water users in the Indus Basin, particularly between stakeholders in the agricultural and livestock sectors.Irrigation efficiency in the Pakistani portion of the Indus Basin Irrigation System (IBIS) is roughly 40 percent, with the situation not appreciably better within the Indian portion of the IBIS.[55] Across India, irrigation efficiency in canal systems is generally between 38-40 percent.[56] Such water-use inefficiency in the agricultural sector jeopardizes short-term and long-term food security in the Indus Basin. For decades, funding the maintenance of the vast irrigation network spanning the India-Pakistan border has remained a low priority for government agencies at the state and federal level in both countries. The resulting deterioration of critical water-transport infrastructure has led to substantial water losses, particularly in the form of leakage from poorly-lined canals. Additionally, the continued reliance on flood-based surface irrigation in an increasingly arid basin climate has resulted in major water losses through evaporation. Even for the water that does make it to the crops, poor drainage infrastructure can result in improper distribution of water across farms, oversaturating some plants while leaving insufficient water for others.

To improve agricultural water-use efficiency and enhance food security in the Indus Basin, the Working Group puts forth the following recommendations:

› Prioritize investment in and institutionalize regular maintenance of canal infrastructure to minimize agricultural water losses. Public works investments aiming to rehabilitate aging canals represent one of the most likely means of improving water-use efficiency in the Indus Basin. In India, poorly maintained canals lose between 10-40 percent of the water they transport due to seepage.[57] In Pakistan, less than 50 percent of water diverted from rivers for irrigation purposes is ultimately available at the farm gate.[58] To date, rehabilitation of the canals has long been avoided because of cost considerations, and the fact that large-scale agricultural interests in both countries have been able to absorb water losses due to an unregulated supply of irrigation water. Population growth and climate change have changed that equation, however, highlighting the need for improved water-transportation infrastructure to ensure that surface-water withdrawals from the Indus and its tributaries reach their target farmland. In particular, a comprehensive canal-lining public-works campaign prioritizing rehabilitation of waterways carrying the greatest volume of diverted river flows would enhance water-use productivity by reducing losses due to seepage and evaporation. While such an initiative would necessitate a major public investment, it would serve as a job-creating engine given the labor force needed to execute such a project, and costs would be recouped in the form of heightened agricultural productivity and augmented water security. Pakistan's Water and Power Development Authority (WAPDA) anticipates that upgrading water courses could reduce 2.36 million acre feet worth of water losses, while upgrading the lining of minor canals throughout the basin could generate savings of five million acre feet.[59] Meanwhile, it is estimated in India that enhancing irrigation water-use efficiency by five percent could boost irrigation potential by 10-15 million hectares.[60]

› Improve cross-border dissemination of hydrological data regarding dry season flow levels and **heavy precipitation events to accommodate downstream agricultural interests.** Changing melt rates in the glaciated regions of the Upper Indus Basin and shifting monsoon patterns are not necessarily leading to a net decrease in water availability throughout the basin. However, these changes are altering the traditional patterns of water delivery throughout the basin, resulting in an uneven distribution of water resources that becomes particularly problematic during the shoulder months of the dry season. Given its lower riparian status, Pakistan is particularly dependent on receiving surface water flows of a certain volume during this time, to ensure sufficient supply for power generation, industrial production, and most crucially, crop growth. To mitigate Pakistan's legitimate sensitivities about water access during such periods, Indian water managers in the higher-elevation portions of the basin could institutionalize a modest exchange of hydrological data on flow levels to better equip Pakistani water managers with the information needed to anticipate future changes in water supply. Disclosing information on abnormally heavy precipitation, prolonged drought, or other major weather-related anomalies in Indian portions of the basin would help Pakistani water managers and farmers plan ahead for reduced water supply, or in the case of pending flooding, allow disaster-management officials lead time to conduct evacuations and mobilize equipment and first responders. If instituted, the sharing of meteorological information could serve as the foundation for greater regional data exchange between water-management agencies at the state/province and federal level in both countries. However, if government involvement proves unfeasible due to bilateral political tensions, third-party meteorological agencies with satellite capability — such as the European Space Agency (ESA), German Aerospace Center (DLR), US National Aeronautics and Space Administration (NASA), or US National Oceanic and Atmospheric Administration (NOAA), among others — could assume the role of primary data provider.

› **Utilize new mapping technologies to build the knowledge base on the status of groundwater supplies in the Indus Basin.** The status and health of groundwater reserves has long been much harder to gauge than surface water supplies, but new technologies are beginning to unearth data on the location and volume of underground aquifers. For example, Interferometric Synthetic Aperture Radar (InSAR) satellite data — which reveals changes in land elevation in areas where aquifers have been heavily depleted — is one of a growing number of tools that can be used to gauge the sustainability of groundwater stocks.[61] Other groundwater mapping practices — such as the Gravity Recovery and Climate Experiment (GRACE), pioneered and implemented by the likes of DLR, NASA, and the University of California Center for Hydrological Modeling — also represent a potential starting point for scientific researchers and water managers in both India and Pakistan to better assess depletion rates of the basin's vulnerable groundwater stocks.

Government investment in such technology could prove expensive, but costs could be reduced by enlisting the assistance of third-party scientific agencies with capacity to monitor the health of groundwater supplies via satellite. Existing domestic capacity for monitoring groundwater reserves could also be augmented by bringing hydrological experts experienced in the use of such technology to the region to discuss with their Indian and Pakistani professional counterparts the equipment and logistical capacities needed to map aquifers, and share best practices for accurately mapping groundwater stocks. Developing local water managers' knowledge base and monitoring capabilities will lead to a more comprehensive understanding of groundwater availability, and provide the data needed to inform more efficient and sustainable usage of this vital resource.

› **Promote use of laser land leveling technology on small (subsistence-level) and mid-sized farms.** Laser land leveling is a land intervention process that allows for significant improvements in agricultural water-use efficiency, reducing the amount of irrigation water needed on farms. Alongside zero tillage for wheat crops, laser land leveling has emerged as one of the basin's most widely adopted interventions for agricultural water savings. To date, the technology has primarily been implemented by large-scale agricultural operations, with the trend becoming more widespread among these stakeholders in the Punjab around 2005.[62]

Studies suggest the technology can greatly enhance water-use productivity for key crops in the basin such as wheat and rice. Recent studies conducted in the Ganges Basin (in Modipuram, India) and the Indus Basin (in Mona, Pakistan) show that laser land leveling increased irrigation water productivity for those staples by more than 50 percent.[63] The technology's overhead costs are prohibitive for many smaller scale farming operations — a laser leveling system costs between USD$3,500 and USD$10,000 — and the actual leveling itself can prove expensive as well, particularly if a tractor is used instead of animal power to redistribute soil. However, facilitating small- and mid-scale farmers' access to such technology through equipment loans or financial assistance would likely accelerate the technology's spread. Further, the equipment would only be needed periodically; if plowed and subsequently maintained correctly, laser leveled fields typically need re-leveling only after eight years, and possibly as long as ten years.[64]

Principal challenges to a wider adoption of laser leveling technology include the absence of broader public awareness, overhead costs, and insufficient training regarding equipment and best practices for land leveling. Expenses typically vary according to the type and amount of soil being leveled, type of equipment, and geographic contours of the farmland. Despite the associated risks, land leveling technology provides a variety of benefits, including: decreasing weed-removal expenses by some 40 percent; fostering uniform crop growth across a farm by reducing pooling of irrigation water; limiting evaporation rates; and improving drainage so as to help farmland better cope with flooding.[65]

› **Develop cross-border research projects between scientific and agricultural agencies exploring the potential for drip irrigation in the basin; establishing best practices for increased water storage; and identifying alternative crops better suited for growth in the basin's arid climate.**

One potential avenue for joint research inquiry might analyze and evaluate the potential impact of drip irrigation in the basin. Despite a relatively high installation cost and unsuitability for certain crops, drip irrigation has shown potential for massive water savings, with some studies documenting water savings of 25-80 percent.[66] The International Water Management Institute further estimates that there exists 0.6 million hectares' worth of cropland suitable for drip irrigation in Indian Punjab, with roughly equivalent areas available in the Pakistani portions of the Indus Basin.[67]

A second joint research study might explore best practices for enhanced water storage in arid environments, a research initiative that would be particularly applicable to Pakistan, which has struggled to cope with both abnormally high and low flow levels in recent years during alternating cycles of severe flooding and drought. Irrigation for the Pakistani portions of the Indus Basin is largely regulated through two major storage dams — the Tarbela Dam on the Indus River, and the Mangla Dam on the Jhelum River, both of which are located in the Upper Indus Basin and fed predominantly by glacier and snowpack melt water. A joint-research initiative on developing additional water storage infrastructure might analyze: best practices for storing excess water during times of abnormally high flow; how to most effectively store water during the shoulder months of the dry season; how to minimize water loss from evaporation in surface reservoirs; and identify effective and sustainable water-storage interventions utilized in other, similarly arid regions of the globe, such as the American Southwest. A third joint research initiative might examine the logistics of planting alternative crops in some portions of the basin, with an emphasis on identifying plants that are economically lucrative and more appropriate for the region's increasingly arid environment in terms of water requirements per unit produced. The recommendations emanating from such a project might encounter significant pushback from entrenched agricultural interests that have traditionally used the basin for growing export oriented, water-intensive cash crops like jasmine rice, which requires fields to be flooded for several months. However, recognizing the increasingly evident truth that some crops irrigated in the basin are ill-suited for the local environment, a transition to new, more heat-resistant and drought-tolerant crop types in certain regions of the Indus Basin Irrigation System could lead to more efficient usage of water resources and bolster food security in the process. One potentially strategic crop worthy of greater research inquiry is moringa, a highly nutritious, antioxidant-saturated plant native to both Africa and Asia that grows rapidly in a variety of environments and boasts high levels of protein and vitamins A, B, and C. Greater reliance on this crop could prove strategically important, as much of it is edible, and the plant can be consumed by livestock and human populations alike.

PART THREE:

Policy And Research Recommendations: Energy And Economic Development

Water is an essential input to economic and social development. All people need clean fresh water for drinking, cooking, and washing, while modern civilization depends on reliable water supplies for agriculture and industry, power production, waste elimination, support of fisheries and forests, and maintenance of essential ecosystems. Insufficient water access and inadequate sanitation impose substantial burdens on society. Scarce water supplies and polluted sources can impair farming and food security, compromise industrial production and power generation, endanger public health, jeopardize livelihoods, and hobble economic growth. Indian and Pakistani policy makers at the highest levels increasingly recognize that rising water stresses risk undermining national welfare. Indian Prime Minister Manmohan Singh has repeatedly singled out water supplies as posing a fundamental challenge to the country's continued economic growth. Similarly, the deputy chairman of India's Planning Commission, referring to the looming shortfall between increasing demand and available water resources, has said, "If we are not able to meet this gap, what this means is that GDP growth cannot take place…We will not be able to achieve the improvements in the levels of living that we want unless we can fill this gap."[68] Likewise, Pakistan's Planning Commission identifies scarce supplies as a significant constraint on national GDP growth.[69]

Even so, despite considerable progress achieved in the past two decades, millions of Indians and Pakistanis lack adequate water services. In India, 97 percent of urbanites and 90 percent of rural residents enjoy access to an improved water source. In Pakistan, the figures are 96 percent and 89 percent, respectively. Sanitation services, however, are less widespread. Some 42 percent of urban Indians and 77 percent of their rural compatriots lack access to improved sanitation. In Pakistan, 28 percent of city dwellers and 66 percent of rural residents live without improved sanitation.[70] The public health consequences — counted in disease, deaths, and days of productivity lost — are severe. Unsafe water and inadequate sanitation cost India 2.4 trillion Indian rupees (USD$53.8 billion) annually — equivalent to 6.4 percent of national GDP in 2006 — while water and sanitation shortfalls cost Pakistan 343.7 billion Pakistani rupees (USD$5.7 billion) annually, or over 3.9 percent of GDP.[71]

Just as insufficient water supplies threaten to curb economic productivity, economic growth is also placing new demands on water resources. Worldwide, cities increasingly constitute critical centers and drivers of growth and innovation, drawing in people and investment in search of economic opportunity. By 2030, for example, Indian cities could generate 70 percent of net new jobs, produce 70 percent of GDP, and fuel a fourfold rise in per capita income. Indeed, recognizing cities as engines of economic expansion, Pakistan's Planning Commission proposes placing dense, multi-function city development at the heart of the nation's growth strategy.[72] Rising urbanization, in turn, and the concomitant concentrations of demographic and economic growth, will shift the locations, intensity, and nature of water demands. Across South Asia, experts project that municipal water demand will surge six-fold and industrial demand will jump sevenfold from 2000 to 2050.

Economic growth will also ripple through water use patterns via rising energy demand. Under the terms of its 12th Plan, India anticipates adding 9,204 megawatts (MW) of hydropower to its generating capacity in the next five years alone. The Central Electricity Authority has identified 33,832 MW of hydropower potential in the Indus Basin, but calculates that only 47 percent of this capacity has been developed or is under construction.[73] Pakistan also nurtures plans for significant additional hydropower development on the Indus. Pakistan's Water and Power Development Authority has identified over 56,000 MW of hydroelectric capacity in various sub-basins of the Indus. With the goal of raising hydro to supply 70 percent of Pakistan's power mix, WAPDA has undertaken studies towards generating an additional 25,000 MW of hydropower by 2020.[74] The amount and type of new hydroelectric infrastructure constructed in both the Indian and Pakistani portions of the basin in the coming years will have major implications for water users throughout the region.

To foster low-impact economic development in the basin, increase water-use efficiency among non-agricultural industries, and improve cross-border communication concerning hydroelectric development, the Working Group puts forth the following recommendations:

Country	Identified capacity as per assessment study Total (MW)	Capacity developed (MW)	Capacity developed (%)	Capacity under construction (MW)	Capacity under construction (%)
India	33,832	11,113.3*	33.65	4,697*	14.22
Pakistan	59,208	6,516.0	11.01	1,628.76	0.03

* Excludes Small Hydropower installations under 25MW
Sources: Government of India, Central Electricity Authority, "Status of H. E. Potential Development – Basinwise," (As of 31/12/2012) at http://www.cea.nic.in/reports/hydro/he_potentialstatus_basin.pdf; Pakistan Power and Water Development
Authority, *Hydro Potential in Pakistan* (Islamabad: Water and Power Develooment Authority, November 2011), pp.3-4, at http://
www.wapda.gov.pk/pdf/brohydpwrpotialapril2011.pdf.

> **Initiate a professional exchange program for hydraulic engineers and water managers from each country to jointly identify and expand upon best practices for sediment flushing, water temperature regulation, maintenance of environmental flows, and pollution control as it pertains to hydroelectric infrastructure.** In the absence of direct government-to-government dialogue, Indian and Pakistani research institutions and universities should consider implementing exchange programs bringing together engineers or water managers from both countries to collaborate on a joint research project on environmentally sustainable hydroelectric development. Such a project could analyze and build knowledge on dams' impact on: sediment distribution throughout downstream portions of the basin; erosion rates and flood plain utilization; water temperature fluctuations; health of fresh water fisheries; and geologic stability in seismically active regions. By considering this full range of issues, joint research initiatives could develop a template for more holistic environmental impact assessments that could be applied to new hydroelectric construction in the basin.

In the event that bilateral political tensions prohibit direct person-to-person exchange, participants could use virtual exchange platforms such as Skype to deepen professional linkages. Relevant and interested institutions might also agree on undertaking separate but coordinated research, with results later integrated and synthesized among the cross-border partner institutions. During periods of greater bilateral cooperation, teams sanctioned by the Indus Waters Commission might even consider joint observations of output flow levels from basin dams during winter months (when flows are typically low) and during the monsoon period (when wider dissemination of flow data can help disaster management planners downstream better anticipate pending flood events). Making institutional arrangements for the timely exchange of information on water flows could build confidence and heighten transparency surrounding hydrological data sharing, and mode and speed of data provision could be set between the two coordinating teams.

› **Deepen public understanding on how climate change and shifting precipitation patterns are influencing water availability and impacting the operation and productivity of hydroelectric infrastructure.** Sustained dam construction in Indian-controlled Kashmir over the past several decades has driven Pakistani perceptions that with each additional project, India heightens its capacity to disrupt or delay flows of the Eastern Rivers into Pakistan in the event of conflict between the two countries. This tactic, which may be technically impossible, would theoretically have a major impact on Pakistanincrop yields and inflict a significant damage on Pakistan's agriculture-dependent economy within weeks. This vulnerability shapes Pakistan's attitudes toward Indian water management in the Indus Basin, but also represents a starting point for building bilateral confidence over both countries' hydroelectric development of the basin.

Indian hydroelectric development — particularly in Kashmir — is one of the most emotive aspects of India-Pakistan water tensions, fueled by misperceptions among downstream water users both about how upstream dams operate on a technical level and how climate change is impacting water inflow rates at the border. The majority of Indian dams are run-of-the-river, meaning they do not feature reservoirs with the capacity to hold back significant volumes of water. However, this is not common knowledge among downstream water stakeholders. Meanwhile, relatively small amounts of water from the Indus, the Jhelum, and Chenab are diverted for local agriculture in Indian-controlled Kashmir. India is required by law to release a certain flow volume to Pakistan throughout the year, an obligation which it honors under the terms set by the Indus Waters Treaty.

Nevertheless, in recent years, India has fed Pakistani threat perceptions by often choosing to initiate dam construction unilaterally, delaying responding to Pakistani objections over projects on the Western Rivers, and providing incomplete data on engineering specifications and the timing and volume of water releases. Civil society actors — chief among them scientific research institutions, universities, and environmental NGOs — in both countries should consider developing joint or coordinated research projects that help dispel misinformation about India's ability to withhold or divert shared basin waters. Joint research initiatives might also analyze the myriad climate change drivers responsible for increasingly erratic precipitation patterns over the basin, highlighting the fact that emerging environmental pressures are largely responsible both for uneven water deliveries from the Indian-controlled parts of the basin into Pakistan and inconsistent hydroelectric production in the two countries' sections of the Indus Basin. Subjecting such research reports to international peer-review would heighten the scientific credibility of the projects, and help insulate them from subsequent politically motivated interference. More generally, civil society actors must use these types of collaborative research efforts to educate decision makers, water managers, journalists, farmers, and the public at large about the science — not the politics — of growing water stress on both sides of the border.

› Recognizing the growing long-term stresses on basin water supplies, heighten the visibility of research on water recycling innovations and promote policies emphasizing demand-side "water consumption management." Twentieth century water resource development in the basin focused almost exclusively on building supply-side capacity, a trend that has continued unabated into the 21st century. Pakistani and Indian NGOs or universities might consider jointly identifying research priorities for improving water recycling as a means to achieve greater water-use efficiency. Such an initiative would first and foremost focus on the agriculture sector — which constitutes the lion's share of total water withdrawals in the basin — but would also focus on best practices for wastewater recycling in key industrial sectors as well, including power generation, textiles, manufacturing, and livestock husbandry. Joint research might draw upon lessons learned and best practices from industrial actors situated in river basins in similarly arid climates — such as the Colorado, Jordan, and Nile — and establish best practices for low-impact economic development in the Indus Basin centered on sustainable land-use and enhanced waste-water treatment.

Raising the profile of waste-water recycling among academic and other civil society actors could allow the practice to eventually gain greater scientific acceptance among policy-making bodies and private water managers in the basin. Indeed, it is in the vested self-interest of all basin water stakeholders to utilize surface and groundwater resources more efficiency via a heightened

Figure 8. Large Dams and Barrages in the Indus River Basin Large Dams in the Indus River Basin (2010)

Country	Name	Nearest city	River	Year	Height (m)	Capacity (million m³)	Main use
India	Bhakra	Nangal	Sutlej	1963	226	9,620	Irrigation, hydropower
	Nangal	Nangal	Sutlej	1954	29	20	Irrigation, hydropower
	Pandoh	Mandi	Beas	1977	76	41	Irrigation, hydropower
	Pong	Mukenan	Beas	1974	133	8,570	Irrigation, hydropower
	Salal	Reasi	Chenab	1986	113	285	Hydropower
	Baglihar		Chenab	2008		33	Hydropower
						Total: 18,589	
Pakistan	Mangla	Mangla	Jhelum	1968	116	10,150*	Irrigation, hydropower
	Tarbela	Ghazi	Indus	1976	137	11,960	Irrigation, hydropower
	Chashma (barrage)	Mianwali	Indus	1971		870	Irrigation
						Total: 22,980	
						Combined Total: 41,569	

Barrages in the Indus River Basin (2010)

Country	Name	River basin	Year	Main use
India	Rupar	Sutlej		Irrigation
	Harike	Sutlej		Irrigation
	Ferozepur	Sutlej		Irrigation
	Madhopur Headwork	Ravi		Irrigation
Pakistan	Sulemanki & Islam	Sutlej		Irrigation
	Balloki & Sidhnai	Ravi	1965	Irrigation
	Marala	Chenab	1968	Irrigation
	Khanki	Chenab		Irrigation
	Qadirabad	Chenab	1967	Irrigation
	Trimmu	Chenab		Irrigation
	Punjnad	Chenab		Irrigation
	Rasul	Jhelum	1967	Irrigation
	Kalabagh	Indus		Irrigation
	Chashma	Indus	1971	Irrigation
	Taunsa	Indus	1958	Irrigation
	Guddu	Indus	1962	Irrigation
	Sukkur	Indus		Irrigation
	Kotri	Indus	1955	Irrigation
	Mailsi (Siphon)	Under Sutlej	1965	Irrigation

* Includes recent raising of 3.58 km³
Source: FAO, "Indus river basin," in *Irrigation in Southern and Eastern Asia in Figures: AQUASTAT Survey 2011*, Karen Frenken ed. (Rome: FAO, 2012), page 139, http://www.fao.org/docrep/016/i2809e/i2809e.pdf

emphasis on water reuse, as institutionalizing the practice would help build water-access resiliency during dry periods. Joint studies on potential applications for recycled water resources could emphasize how to gain the greatest economic benefit from multi-functional water sources, including blue and green water.[75]

Lastly, civil society actors should seek to dialogue with policy makers and members of the media and begin to shift the culture of basin water resource management away from installing massive detention reservoirs and large-scale water diversions as a means to improve water security, and instead focus more intensively on water-use efficiency. Indeed, changing the mindset of water managers from supply-side to demand-side could herald a sea change in the availability of basin water supplies. Research initiatives into demand-side water management should begin with the agriculture sector, but encompass industry and domestic water usage as well. In addition to researching new pathways toward improving demand-side water efficiency — such as developing experimental models for water pricing and creating potential financial incentives for more efficient water resource utilization across industries — joint research efforts might also consider the revival of traditional water storage techniques (including large-scale and smallscale rooftop water harvesting), which improves water users' ability to trap precipitation and distribute it evenly across the drier months to sustain water supply. Looking at water resources from a demandside perspective as opposed to a supply-side perspective is an effort that may ultimately unfold across several generations, but universities, think-tanks, and other NGO actors can begin to lay the foundation for this shift by supplying new research initiatives and building the region's knowledge base.

> Explore the potential for newly established protected wildlife reserves to stimulate the local ecotourism industry on both sides of the border. Cooperative efforts between Indian and Pakistani ecotourism operators could help jumpstart an already rapidly expanding industry, while also raising the public profile of environmental preservation efforts. The Indus and its tributaries support a wide range of habitats, flora, and fauna, all of which have faced progressive degradation over recent decades due to population growth, water diversions, and industrial and agricultural pollution.

To improve the basin's ecological health and spur development of a new set of ecotourism-based livelihoods, state/province or federal agencies in either Pakistan or India might consider environmental restoration efforts in targeted sections of their portion of the basin. Strengthening wetland protections or conducting afforestation campaigns, for example, could boost resiliency against flooding by restoring natural flood barriers and flood plains, while the establishment of new nature reserves dedicated to ecosystem restoration could provide new revenue streams for local entrepreneurs in the ecotourism sector. Whether ad hoc or institutionalized, cross-border exchange between ecotourism operators would represent a confidence-building measure in and of itself, by developing person-to-person connections at the civil society level.

PART FOUR:

Policy And Research Recommendations: Climate Change And Environmental Pressures

Impacts of a changing climate are increasingly evident throughout the Indus Basin. From rising temperatures and accelerating melt rates in the glaciated upper reaches of the basin to intensified cycles of drought and flooding at lower elevations, shifts in the typical rhythms of water delivery into the basin are fundamentally reshaping the basin's hydrology. These changes have major implications for the region's environmental, economic, and human security, with serious implications for the quality of life of the roughly 300 million people that the Indus Basin supports. Population growth rates are soaring throughout the basin and economic and agricultural expansion and increasing urbanization are placing an elevated pressure on available water supplies. India and Pakistan cannot disentangle themselves from one another, and climate change poses a shared and urgent threat to the viability of key agricultural breadbaskets in the Indus Basin, particularly in Sindh province and Punjab province in Pakistan, and Punjab state in India.

One of the most pronounced aspects of climate change across South Asia has been variation in the timing and intensity of monsoon rains, which has significantly impacted agricultural production and weakened food security, often driving tensions between the two countries over water access during the dry periods between rainy seasons. Indeed, leading Indian meteorologists announced at a February 2012 meeting in Pune, Maharashtra state, that monsoon precipitation across the country had fallen 4.5 percent between 1979 and 2009.[76] The health and sustainability of basin water supplies have been further eroded by a variety of human-induced causes including: agricultural and industrial pollution of surface water courses and groundwater stocks; large-scale water withdrawals for irrigation that often leave rivers without the minimal environmental flow volumes needed to provide continuous ecological services; cascades of hydroelectric dams that collectively block sediment flows, degrade freshwater fisheries, and erode rivers' ecological health; and the commercial development and the residential settlement of the vulnerable low-lying flood plains that place human populations at risk and decrease rivers' natural ability to absorb heightened flows during periods of heavy precipitation.

There is a growing consensus within the region that these environmental pressures are contributing to an increased strain on basin water supplies. In India's portion of the Indus Basin, per capita water availability is projected to drop by nearly 50 percent during the first half of the 21st century, falling from 2,109 m^3 in 2000 to 1,132 m^3 in 2050; in Pakistan's portion of the basin, per capita water availability is expected to drop from 1,332 m^3 in 2000 to 545 m^3 in 2050.[77] Public awareness of these critical water security issues must be heightened in order to better understand and cope with these challenges, and address popular perceptions within certain segments of Pakistani society that India is diverting more than its fair share of water from its portion of the Indus Basin. Although a contentious political relationship has prevented a meaningful and progressive dialogue on the shared risk that both countries face from climate change and human-induced environmental pressures, it is in the enlightened self-interest of both India and Pakistan to jointly respond to these issues in the decades ahead.

The basin's hydrology pays no attention to national boundaries. Given that the causes and effects of mounting environmental pressures are interrelated and transcend specific sectors of society and industry, policy makers within India and Pakistan must recognize that only a collaborative, holistic approach to responding to these challenges will bolster the resiliency of the basin's human, environmental, and economic security. The absence of increased cooperation will simply lead to the continuation of the status quo of water management within the basin, a situation that is marked by a highly inefficient usage of available water supplies on both sides of the border, and little to no communication between water managers in the two countries. This situation is becoming more untenable with each passing year in the face of growing population and soaring water demand. In short, the status quo is no longer an option.

Even in light of ongoing bilateral political tensions, several pathways exist for interested parties at the government and civil-society levels to engage with one another to deepen the knowledge base on emerging climate change impacts and environmental pressures, and develop reformed water management policies at the national and basin-wide level that can bolster economic productivity within the basin while institutionalizing greater safeguards for the ecological health of the Indus and its tributaries.

To develop a comprehensive knowledge base on emerging climate change impacts and mounting environmental pressures on the basin's hydrological health, and create a cooperative framework for safeguarding the region's ecological health, the Working Group puts forth the following recommendations:

› **Conduct a joint research study evaluating the cumulative environmental impact of multiple dams on a single waterway and develop the knowledge base on the relationships between dam cascades, river basin hydrology, and climate change.** Dam construction across the Indus Basin over the past 50 years has resulted in fundamental transformations to the hydrology of the Indus and its tributaries. While a new hydroelectric infrastructure is subject to environmental impact assessment, contemporary and past environmental assessments of hydroelectric infrastructure conducted by the Indian government, Pakistani government, or third parties such as the World Bank or the Asian Development Bank, have typically focused on the potential downstream environmental impacts of a single dam project. Rarely have these assessments taken a broader, more holistic approach that analyzes the potential cumulative environmental impact of multiple dam construction on the same river and taken into account the wide sweep of human security impacts that dam cascades entail, and no studies to date have thoroughly evaluated the subject. Given that the net impact of a cascade of dams upon a river's ecological health is far more intensive than the impact of a single dam, the subject deserves greater attention from policy makers, water managers, and energy developers in the Indus Basin.

A joint or coordinated study between Indian and Pakistani universities, NGOs, or scientific bodies might assess the pressures that dam cascades on the Eastern Rivers impose upon the local environment, and highlight the relationship between dam-related ecological degradation, food security, livelihoods, and economic productivity. Such collaboration could establish a mutual methodology for environmental impact assessments and create data sets documenting the impact of dam cascades on: sediment flows and distribution through the Indus Basin; soil fertility in agricultural areas adjacent to rivers; biodiversity conservation; natural flood barriers and wetland preservation; and water quality and water flow volume. Nurturing a cross-border dialogue between civil society actors on this subject will help develop a knowledge base that can eventually provide policy makers and water managers with a better platform to assess the various environmental, economic, and human security impacts that multiple dam construction has upon the basin. These holistic environmental assessments may then enter into the policy-making dialogue, potentially influencing the design of a new hydroelectric infrastructure and informing policy-making decisions regarding dam operation to ensure sufficient water levels within the Indus and its tributaries to maintain minimum environmental flows. Establishing a mutually agreed upon baseline level for minimum flow volume in dammed rivers would need to take into account the shifting volume requirements of the dry and wet seasons, but would ultimately help water managers ensure the continuous delivery of waterways' ecological services.

A subsidiary area for joint research inquiry on the subject might encompass the cumulative impact of multiple hydroelectric projects on freshwater fisheries. Across the Indus Basin, freshwater fisheries constitute a small yet important part of diets and local livelihoods. Heavy development of the basin threatens or destroys spawning grounds and migration routes, endangering fish populations and reducing their role in local economies and diets. Dams' impact on fisheries remains understudied, and represents a common starting point for Indian and Pakistani hydrologists and wildlife management officials to deepen research ties and build knowledge on the subject.

› **Increase the knowledge base on monsoon variability trends to improve outcomes for rainfall-dependent agriculture.** Despite the extensive irrigation network spanning Indian and Pakistani Punjab, a significant portion of arable land in the basin — particularly in Pakistan — is partially or wholly dependent on direct rainfall for irrigation. With climate change driving erratic delivery of monsoon rains, food security and livelihoods in these sections of the basin are jeopardized, particularly among smaller-scale farmers whose land is not linked to broader irrigation networks. Joint research studies might be executed by relevant government agencies, universities, or civil society actors within India and Pakistan to analyze the nature of evolving monsoon trends using available data. Researchers also can draw upon hydrological and meteorological data supplied by third-party scientific agencies such as the NOAA (US) and ICIMOD (Nepal) to deepen the understanding of current and projected future precipitation changes, and analyze how such shifts will impact the hydrological health of the Indus and its tributaries. Based on this data, a range of models illustrating water availability scenarios for rainfall-dependent agriculture can be developed for use within the policy-making community.

A secondary focus of a research initiative on evolving monsoon trends might evaluate the potential human security impacts of precipitation variability, particularly as it pertains to disaster preparedness. Anticipated changes in snowfall include reduced snow and increased winter rain at elevations close to the present winter snowline, with increased snowfall during extreme precipitation events at higher elevations. For populations inhabiting high-altitude regions of the basin, increased frequency of high precipitation events such as cloud bursts can trigger flash flooding and avalanches, which in turn damage or destroy communication and transportation infrastructure.

› **Use multimedia tools to raise public awareness of climate change within India and Pakistan.** Despite mounting evidence that climate change is contributing to water supply issues within the Indus Basin, the causes behind shifting patterns of water availability remain poorly understood within the civil society. In addition to the lack of awareness, a principal driver of misperceptions is inaccurate media coverage of water-related issues, with scientifically inaccurate and often purposefully inflammatory reporting fueling political tensions between the two countries. One approach to combat such media inaccuracies — and to raise awareness and foster an informed public discussion about environmental pressures in the region — would be the creation of a high-impact documentary on climate change in the Indus Basin, produced in the vein of "An Inconvenient Truth," the award-winning 2006 climate change documentary.

Funding such a film project represents one of the principal challenges, although financial backing could be secured from foundations and the private sector, both inside and outside of South Asia. The key towards ensuring maximum public impact for such a documentary would be the presence of prominent Indian and Pakistani scientific and environmental experts on screen — side by side — discussing the shared threat both countries face from climate change, and making clear the likely results for South Asian security if inaction on the issue persists. In addition to crafting a visually arresting case for climate change's impact on food production and water availability, a film would allow for the creation of a narrative on climate change that features informed commentary, which could be used to bolster civil society awareness on key issues including glacial melt trends and monsoon variations. Experts and well-known authoritative figures featured in the film could emphasize the mutual economic and political benefits of taking a joint action on climate change adaption and mitigation, highlighting that it is in the self-interest of both countries to collaborate on such measures instead of remaining mired in a cycle of perpetual conflict over shared water resources. Commenters from both countries could also present scientific evidence illustrating that declining river flows, intensified droughts, and changing rainfall patterns are natural phenomena symptomatic of climate change, and not evidence that evidence that upstream users are unfairly withholding water from downstream consumers.

Without heightened public understanding, there can be no political will at the state/province and federal government levels to implement appropriate policy interventions dealing with climate change. However, using the documentary medium to directly correct misperceptions on water supply variability and educate media consumers on climate change issues would ensure the message is not inappropriately filtered or altered via government channels or biased media coverage. From a practical standpoint, given the growing prevalence of Internet and satellite-television access across the basin, a documentary could reach its target audiences relatively easily, and be rebroadcast indefinitely across traditional media channels as well as social media. Media outlets including the British Broadcasting Corporation, National Geographic, and the Discovery Channel have a track record of developing original, high-quality educational programming on climate change issues and environmental trends, and might be enlisted to participate in the production of the film. The ultimate goal of the project is to help reshape public perceptions of climate change and drive home the message that there must be political will on both sides to jointly address the issue of long-term sustainable water resource management, emphasizing that cooperation on the issue is now a matter of survival for both countries.

› Develop a digitized online model of the Indus Basin to foster regional network building and deepen hydrological modeling capacities. Short of direct and sustained government-to-government collaboration at the state/province and federal levels, continuing to deepen and institutionalize relationships between Indian and Pakistani NGOs, universities, and other relevant civil society actors will prove critical in creating an atmosphere conducive to bilateral cooperation on climate change issues. While travel restrictions and visa issues can and often do prohibit direct meetings between these parties, the growing prevalence of high-speed Internet connectivity allows for a greater interaction between hydrological experts and environmental generalists on both sides of the border via virtual exchange to boost the role of science diplomacy in encouraging joint responses to shifting water availability.

One pathway towards a greater joint analysis of potential climate change impacts on water availability in the Indus and its tributaries would be the development of a digitized, Internet-based model of the basin that utilizes Geographic Information Systems (GIS) data to allow online users to run various hydrological modeling simulations. In recent years, such models have already been developed in other river basins, such as the Yellow River in China, which can provide a useful template for creating an Indus-specific modeling platform. Developing a GIS-based version of the basin would allow scientists, hydrologists, and water managers in both countries to accurately model water flow levels; develop new theoretical scenarios for water availability that incorporate shifting precipitation patterns; and easily share data and models with one another. Further, once the modeling platform has been designed and established online, it can be operated at minimal cost, while providing significant informational benefits to water researchers and other water stakeholders in both countries.[78]

› **Explore pathways for improved data sharing on precipitation trends and meteorological forecasting to better infuse scientific data into the water policy-making process.** Both countries should seek to institutionalize a heightened degree of hydrological data-sharing, with the aim of enhancing policy makers' ability to anticipate future changes in water supply and design appropriate interventions. To advance this exchange of data, parties in both India and Pakistan should jointly categorize the best existing sources — both inside and outside the South Asian region — of satellite photography and remote-sensing data documenting current and projected future environmental and meteorological changes in the Indus Basin. Priority information repositories will include those populated with data on short-term and long-term shifts in the timing, duration, and intensity of monsoon precipitation, as well as those documenting past (or anticipating future) glacial and snowpack melt trends in the two countries' Himalayan headwater regions. Once the information landscape of existing hydrological data in the Indus Basin has been mapped, a joint research project could outline a sequence of concrete measures needed to move this information out of existing online databases and into the hands of Indian and Pakistani water planners, taking into account the realities and nuances of the water policy-making sectors in each country.

Another venue for enhanced bilateral cooperation on climate change research is the Coordinated Regional Downscaling Experiment (CORDEX) program. CORDEX, sponsored by the World Climate Research Program, has a dedicated South Asian program that helps generate multi-model simulations and assessments of regional climate change. These research outputs, which are subsequently archived online, are meant to help develop the capacity of India, Pakistan, and neighboring countries to understand and effectively address climate shifts. Between 2013 and 2015, CORDEX is planning a series of science oriented workshops across South and Southeast Asia to further bolster the region's knowledge base on emerging climate change trends.

> **Conduct joint research to better understand the role agricultural and industrial pollution play in limiting water availability, shaping public health outcomes, and weakening rivers' ability to deliver ecological services.** Improper disposal and insufficient treatment of industrial and agricultural wastewater, coupled with depleted flow volumes, have a major impact on water availability in the Indus and its tributaries, with downstream water users most seriously impacted. Rampant pollution of waterways also erodes biodiversity, threatening fresh water fisheries, and the flora and fauna that drive the economically lucrative ecotourism sector.

A potential joint study on water pollution throughout the basin might examine: best practices for lowtech, low-cost wastewater treatment interventions; the extent to which untreated wastewater impacts agricultural water availability; the interplay between surface pollutants and groundwater contamination; the passage of pollutants throughout the basin system, so as to monitor how hydroelectric infrastructure impacts their movement; and the extent to which pesticide and fertilizer run-off enters municipal and rural drinking water supplies. Developing the region's knowledge base on these issues will help inform more sustainable policies on wastewater treatment and disposal, and allow government officials to better gauge the potential public health threat that contaminated water supplies pose. In executing such research initiatives, particular attention should be paid to pollution of waterways during the dry season, when contaminants' environmental impact is exacerbated due to low flow volumes.

PART FIVE:

Policy and research recommendations: Glaciology

Glaciers of the Hindu Kush Himalayan (HKH) region affect the hydrological regimes of 10 of the largest river systems in Asia. These glaciers help regulate water flows, control the regional and global climate systems on several time and spatial scales, and help sustain the livelihood of more than 1.3 billion people. The Indus Basin is uniquely dependent on these glaciers — snowpack and glacial melt account for more than 50 percent of the Indus' annual average flow volume, and melt waters constitute roughly the same portion of flow volume for the river's primary tributaries. The arrival of snowpack and glacial melt waters is particularly vital to downstream water users during the spring and fall shoulder months that come before or after the westerly monsoons, when these waters account for a significant portion of the base flow volume of the Indus and its tributaries.[79]

Within the Indus Basin portion of the HKH, roughly 3.8 percent of the land is glaciated, covering approximately 21,200 km^2. The vast majority of the 18,495 glaciers in the Indus Basin remain unstudied or understudied. These glaciers collectively hold estimated ice reserves of 2,696 km^3, more than twice the reserves of the next most heavily glaciated river basin, the Yarlung Tsangpo/Brahmaputra.[80] Indus Basin glaciers are understudied in part due to the rough physical topography of the region — much of the glaciated Upper Indus Basin sits 5,000 meters or more above sea level, making glacial monitoring difficult due to the region's inaccessibility. The other primary reason these critical water reserves are understudied is the lack of technical capacity and funding to execute such efforts. Without better data on glacial and snowpack melt trends, policy makers in downstream portions of the Indus Basin are left unequipped to understand the important climate change-driven hydrological changes now taking place in the glaciated regions, and are subsequently unable to design and implement effective measures for coping with the attendant future changes on downstream water availability.

Given the key role of glacial and snowpack melt in the Indus Basin, it is crucial to bolster India and Pakistan's knowledge base on HKH glaciology. Improved understanding of change dynamics in glaciated regions has significant implications for weather forecasting, managing river flows, irrigation, livelihoods, biodiversity conservation, and power generation in downstream portions of the basin. Glaciers are very sensitive to meteorological conditions; study of their mass balance and dynamics yields important data on climate change impacts, such as shifting precipitation patterns and warming temperatures in high-altitude regions. Increased study of the glaciated reaches of the upper Indus Basin would also provide more comprehensive information on the accumulation of black carbon aerosols on glacial surfaces, a byproduct of industrial activity that accelerates melt rates and may influence the timing and volume of water delivery to downstream populations in the long term.

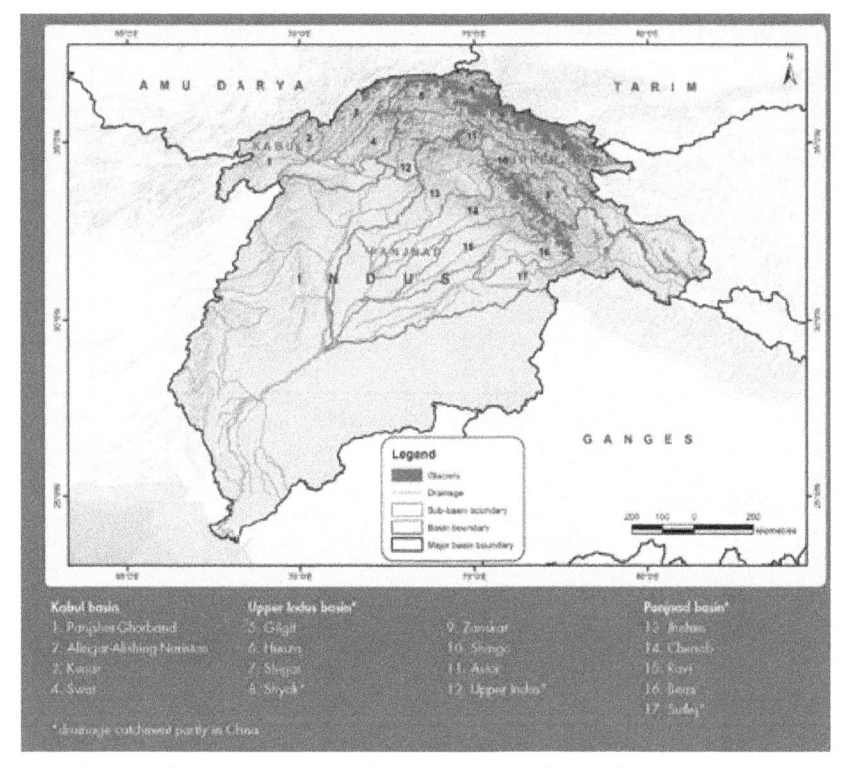

Source: Bajracharya, SR (2012) Status of glaciers in the Indus Basin. Kathmandu: ICIMOD

Various studies have confirmed that the glaciers of the northwestern Himalaya were largely in a state of retreat during the 20th century, with glacial recession rates appearing to have accelerated between 1970 and 2000. Changing snow accumulation and ablation patterns, coupled with ongoing glacial melt trends, may have a significant effect on the hydrology of the Indus. Discharges of water from the glaciated Indus headwater regions are likely to increase in near future as a result of enhanced melting, but on a longer time scale, these discharges are likely to decrease as glaciers' contribution to the waters of the Indus Basin gradually lessens over time. The extent of glacial melt has not been uniform, however. The larger glaciers appear to have receded at a comparatively slower rate than smaller length glaciers, and there are certain transverse or tributary glaciers (also known as 'surging glaciers') in the Karakoram Himalaya showing abnormal rates of advancement. Nevertheless, glaciers in the Indus Basin are generally considered to be in a state of retreat, with variations in glacier length appearing to be influenced by increasing average air temperatures during the 20th century and into the 21st century. Between 1906 and 2005, average air temperatures across the region increased by 0.74°C, with more than half of the increase — 0.44°C — occurring between 1980 and 2005. Temperatures are almost certain to continue increasing in the short term, with an anticipated further increase of 4°C over current average temperatures by 2050.[81]

To deepen knowledge of glacial melt trends and better understand their implications for water stakeholders in the Indus Basin, the Working Group puts forth the following recommendations:

Figure 10. Distribution of Glaciers in the Indus River Basin

Basin	Sub-basin	Number of glaciers	Glacier area (km²)	Estimated ice reserves (km³)	Highest elevation (m a.s.l.)	Lowest elevation (m a.s.l.)	Largest glacier area (km²)
Kabul	Panjsher-Ghorband	88	14.6	0.4	5,242	3,857	2.5
	Alingar-Alishing-Nuristan	37	5.8	0.2	5,284	4,162	1.5
	Kunar	1,149	1,573.9	176.8	7,578	3,114	189.5
	Swat	327	127.4	5.3	5,580	3,772	4.9
	Total	1,601	1,721.7	182.7	7,578	3,114	189.5
Upper Indus	Gilgit	968	938.3	71.3	7,730	2,703	61.8
	Hunza	1,384	2,753.9	310.6	7,749	2,409	345.7
	Shigar	439	2,374.1	601.9	8,566	2,774	631.5
	Shyok	3,357	5,937.7	981.7	7,803	3,231	925.9
	Zanskar	1,197	975.5	82.1	6,368	3,997	62.6
	Shingo	882	612.7	42.9	7,027	3,656	46.3
	Astor	372	239.6	16.9	8,032	2,991	31.0
	Upper Indus	2,814	1,230.0	66.1	7,820	2,760	51.9
	Total	11,413	15,061.7	2,173.5	8,566	2,409	925.9
Panjnad	Jhelum	733	222.8	9.0	6,285	3,404	6.8
	Chenab	2,039	2,341.2	210.7	7,103	3,001	109.3
	Ravi	217	113.6	5.5	5,824	3,276	9.2
	Beas	384	416.6	31.8	6,196	3,079	29.0
	Sutlej	2,108	1,315.0	82.9	6,652	3,606	49.6
	Total	5,481	4,409.2	339.9	7,103	3,001	109.3
	Total	18,495	21,192.6	2,696.1	8,566	2,409	925.9

Source: Bajracharya, SR (2012) Status of glaciers in the Indus Basin. Kathmandu: ICIMOD

› Enlist third-party scientific agencies with satellite-based remote-sensing capacity to disseminate non-politicized, reliable, and timely hydrological data documenting glacial melt trends to water policy-makers and the general public in both countries to enhance transparency. Outlining a consortium of multilateral and nongovernmental bodies with the technological capability to gather (and a willingness to distribute) accurate information on glacial and snowmelt trends in the Indus Basin represents a first step toward heightening transparency between the two countries vis-à-vis transboundary water resource management. Equipping Indian and Pakistani policy-makers with scientific data supplied by neutral third parties — such as the Nepal-based International Centre for Integrated Mountain Development (ICIMOD), the European Space Agency (ESA), or the US National Oceanic and Atmospheric Administration (NOAA) and the US National Aeronautics and Space Administration (NASA) — would establish a baseline for both countries to analyze hydrological changes in the upper Indus Basin and better understand and prepare for evolving climate change impacts in the region. Building the knowledge base of each country via third-party data dissemination will also mitigate suspicions concerning the source and accuracy of the data.

In terms of starting points for such collaboration, ICIMOD — which receives funding from both the Indian and Pakistani governments — has conducted a thorough remote-sensing analysis of the Indus Basin's glaciers in recent years, based on geo-spatial data points including slope, hypsometry, debris cover, elevation range, and latitude/longitude, among others. Similar work has been undertaken by the World Glacier Monitoring Service (WGMS), a multilateral organization that counts both India and Pakistan among its 30+ country membership. Streamlining Indian and Pakistani policy makers' access to the state-of-the-art data from such organizations would provide both countries with the information needed to monitor glaciated areas of the upper Indus Basin, and proactively plan for the looming water supply challenges that shrinking glaciers and snowpack present.

› **Devise joint research projects to increase understanding of emerging climate impacts in the Upper Indus Basin.** While India and Pakistan's political relationship warms and cools in cycles, collaboration on science-based research initiatives at the university or civil society level has the potential to withstand these shifts. Scientific diplomacy in the form of joint glaciology research projects can serve as a foundation for broader bilateral confidence-building, particularly among academic institutions and civil society groups, by allowing these parties to better understand and appreciate the water supply challenges faced by their neighbour.

Projects coordinated between NGO organizations in each country, or between other elements of civil society, could help identify common ground between the two countries based on the shared threat that increased glacial and snowpack melt rates poses to water users in both countries. Initiatives analyzing the anticipated short-term and long-term water supply challenges that climate change will impose on the basin could also draw lessons learned from issues faced in contentious transboundary river basins reliant on glacial and snowpack melt waters, such as the Amu Darya and the Yarlung Tsangpo/Brahmaputra. Research projects could alternatively identify best practices implemented by policy makers in climate change-impacted river basins in other parts of the world, with an emphasis on highlighting policy interventions that bolster resiliency to water supply disruptions, such as enhanced water storage.

› **Improve mutual disaster preparedness regarding the threat posed by glacial lake outburst flooding.** Melting glaciers and snowpack significantly increase the risk of catastrophic flooding in the form of GLOFs, which can be found in the Shyok, Indus, and Yarkhand valleys, among others. These unstable lakes in high-altitude regions can breach their banks with little warning, sending powerful torrents of mud and water downstream that sweep away people and homes, and destroy power and transportation infrastructure. While difficult to predict, the GLOF risk faced by populations in both countries can be mitigated through increased cross-border sharing of data on seismic activity, heavy precipitation events, and the location of potential GLOFs, as well as the development and deployment of early warning systems. Improved monitoring of GLOFs is particularly important as glaciers shrink because remnantal, terminal, and lateral moraines exposed due to glacier recession have led to increased incidences of rock fall, as well as the formation of unstable moraine-dammed lakes in some locations. Enhanced coordination between India and Pakistan in addressing the mutual GLOF threat represents a relatively attainable means of bolstering disaster preparedness in the basin, and offers a strategic opening for institutionalizing a modest exchange of hydrological information between disaster management agencies at the federal and state/province level in each country.

› **Invest in the educational infrastructure needed to train the next generation of Indian and Pakistani glaciologists.** To date, India possesses a more robust academic and professional institutional infrastructure to support the study of glaciology than Pakistan. This imbalance can begin to be corrected through a heightened emphasis within Pakistan's institutes of higher learning on glaciology, in particular, and earth sciences more broadly. Developing specialized curriculum specifically geared toward training glaciologists at the undergraduate and graduate levels would help Pakistan achieve parity with India vis-à-vis glaciology-related academic infrastructure. Such academic programs must secure funding to be sustainable, and young scientists choosing to specialize in glaciology must be reassured that there will be jobs available in research and policy-making circles once they have completed their studies. Nevertheless, bolstering the long-term capacity for each country to provide specialized academic training and heightening the profile of glaciology studies will prove critical in training a new cadre of young Indian and Pakistani science professionals, equipping them with the skills needed to build domestic capacity within their home countries for understanding and addressing the implications of glacial melt trends.

> **Heighten cross-border sharing of best practices and technical resources for on-the-ground glacier monitoring.** Building India and Pakistan's knowledge base on glacial and snowpack melt trends and heightening each country's technical capacity to document such changes from the ground will be crucial during the coming decades. Ground-based measuring equipment — although vulnerable to periodic flash flooding — helps fill in important gaps of data generated via satellite photography or remote-sensing. When combined, ground-based data and aerial imagery provide a more holistic and complete picture of the status of glaciers and snowpack. To date, India also has installed more glacier monitoring stations in its portion of the basin than Pakistan. To rectify this imbalance and help Pakistan achieve a similar capacity, Indian glaciologists could share best practices with their Pakistani counterparts for installing such stations.

The development of joint glacier-monitoring stations in glaciated border regions would also help in this regard, by not only providing water policy makers in both countries with accurate data on melt rates, but also more broadly serving as a means to enhance hydrological information sharing in the basin. Development and installation of a single glacier monitoring station costs roughly USD$100,000, a figure which does not include maintenance costs. Funding such infrastructure represents a principal challenge, but costs could potentially be mitigated through third-party financial assistance. Short of installing joint monitoring stations or having a direct exchange of glaciologists traveling between the two countries, progress could still be made in the form of Indian and Pakistani glaciologists communicating via online channels to either discuss the technology needed to measure glacial movements from ground-based monitoring stations, or devising and executing coordinated research projects on climate change impacts in the two countries' portions of the glaciated Upper Indus Basin.

PART SIX:

Policy And Research Recommendations: Institutions, Governance, And Diplomacy

The international boundary that set India and Pakistan apart at independence also set the two nations at odds over water. The 1947 line of Partition divided the Indus Basin, cutting across long-established irrigations systems, and separating downstream Pakistan from the sources of the water supplies on which it had relied for centuries, which now ran first through Indian territory. Following several years of negotiations brokered by the World Bank, Pakistan and India signed the 1960 Indus Waters Treaty (IWT).[82] Under the provisions of the IWT, Pakistan receives unrestricted use of the waters of the three Western Rivers: the Jhelum, the Chenab, and the Indus itself. India must let these waters flow unhindered, except for restricted uses and defined amounts related to domestic and agricultural uses and for limited hydropower generation. The IWT allots to India the waters of the three Eastern Rivers: the Sutlej, Beas, and Ravi. Pakistan must refrain from impeding the flow of any tributaries of the Ravi and the Sutlej that traverse its territory before the tributaries join these rivers in India. When the Eastern Rivers ultimately enter Pakistan, they become available for Pakistan's unrestricted use.

To oversee the accord, the IWT also established institutional arrangements, creating the Permanent Indus Commission, composed of one Commissioner from each country. The Treaty provides for the two Commissioners to meet annually and for periodic exchanges of visits to ensure cooperative implementation of the Parties' obligations and to resolve differences that may arise. (If the Commissioners cannot reach agreement, the matter may be referred first to the two governments, then to a Neutral Expert, and finally to a Court of Arbitration.) Importantly, the IWT also mandates the regular exchange of data on river flows and water utilization, and calls upon each country to inform the other if it undertakes engineering works on the tributaries that could affect the other party and to provide any requested data. Further, Article VII of the agreement records the Parties' declared intention to potentially undertake future cooperation to install hydrological and meteorological observation stations, carry out drainage works, and collaborate on engineering works.

Since 1960, the IWT has stood through the 1965 and 1971 wars and the 1999 Kargil conflict between the two countries, and survived numerous lesser clashes. Yet marked dissatisfaction with the IWT exists in both India and Pakistan. A significant body of opinion in India regards persistent Pakistani objections to planned Indian infrastructure projects on the Western Rivers as unfairly stalling India's legitimate development programs. Many in Pakistan, in turn, fear that — though individual Indian proposals may abide by the technical letter of the IWT — erecting multiple structures on the rivers may generate substantial cumulative impacts downstream. In the wake of continuing controversies, voices in both countries have suggested revisiting the IWT terms — or even scrapping the accord and starting over. Ultimately, some future mutually agreed alterations to the IWT might improve the scope for effective international cooperation and integrated resource management across the basin. Presently, however, moves to renegotiate the IWT would almost certainly prove more contentious than current confidence levels between the parties could bear.

Nevertheless, despite its historical success at avoiding water conflicts between India and Pakistan, the current treaty alone provides little response to several emerging threats to the Indus Basin's water supplies.

The accord has no provisions for how the parties should respond to variations in water flow that climate change could engender, for instance. Nor does it adequately address water quality — beyond hortatory declarations of intent to prevent pollution where practicable — though deteriorating quality increasingly cuts into available quantities as sources become too degraded for many uses. And while consumers across the basin rely on groundwater to supplement or substitute for surface water, there is no agreement for sharing supply or even sharing data on shared groundwater resources.

India and Pakistan must strive to ensure that the IWT institutions that govern their international water relations operate as effectively as possible. But decision makers and stakeholders at all levels across the basin must also work to strengthen other existing mechanisms and to forge new spaces for collaboration. Successful cross-border cooperation will require not only identifying the right issues for joint knowledge building and research, but also identifying the right actors and institutional arenas amenable to developing and enacting effective collaboration in specific issue areas.

To fully utilize and effectively empower the institutional arenas and governance mechanisms that shape water policy-making within and between India and Pakistan, the Working Group puts forth the following recommendations:

› **Explore potential means to strengthen the Article VI "Exchange of Data" and operationalize the Article VII "Future Cooperation" provisions of the IWT and consider options to enhance the advisory capacities of the Permanent Indus Commission.** Powerful new technologies, such as satellite based remote sensing and GIS mapping, that have been developed since the signing of the IWT in 1960, now enable increasingly comprehensive environmental monitoring and measuring capabilities coupled with possibilities for non-intrusive real-time data collection and exchange. Interpreted together, Articles VI and VII prospectively lay the foundations for joint monitoring stations and telemetry platforms, potentially integrated to form a collective Indus Basin Earth Observation system. Such a system could, in turn, supply data inputs, calibration, and validation for constructing joint hydrological and climate models and scenarios for the basin. On the ground, both India and Pakistan suffer from power shortages and insufficient water storage capacities that might be mutually addressed via agreed activation of Article VII provisions for cooperative engineering works. Joint water resources data and models for the basin could then inform common decisions about optimal siting, construction, and operation of such facilities for storage, hydropower, flood control, habitat maintenance, and environmental flows, as well as trade-offs between these objectives.

The advisory capacities and dispute resolution capabilities of the Commission could be expanded by the addition of Assistant Commissioners or other professional staff so as to endow the Commission with supplementary breadth and depth of expertise. Drawing on the mediating role played by the World Bank in the original drafting of the IWT, the Commission could also be augmented with an independent office of neutral experts from outside South Asia charged to execute transboundary environmental assessments and promote sustainable development and cooperative water management under the IWT. Such an independent office could provide oversight or actively manage the initial establishment of joint monitoring and observation systems so as to defuse mistrust on data exchange.

› **Leverage technical expertise and capitalize on structured forums for policy deliberation, data exchange, collaborative research, and sharing of best practices offered by regional organizations and associations such as the International Centre for Integrated Mountain Development (ICIMOD), the International Water Management Institute (IWMI), the South Asia Association for Regional Cooperation (SAARC), and the Global Water Partnership (GWP).** ICIMOD and IWMI operate as international knowledge hubs. ICIMOD conducts research on mountain climate, environment, and communities, while IWMI conducts research on water resources and management policies. Both generate and distribute data and knowledge resources through training, publications, and web-based portals. Both represent internationally recognized sources of scientific expertise on which Indian and Pakistani decision makers can draw for "neutral" information and analyses. Both additionally represent potential "third party" nodes for implementing data exchanges or cooperative research in settings possibly less susceptible to bilateral secrecy, suspicion, and mistrust.

SAARC, an eight-member intergovernmental organization, offers another possible arena for defusing potentially acrimonious bilateral zero-sum dynamics by embedding consideration of regional, basinwide water resource challenges in a multilateral setting. (Indeed, SAARC's charter precludes treatment of purely bilateral issues among the member states.) Although questions do surround the organization's real efficacy, SAARC has moved to adopt a Convention on Environmental Cooperation, calling for regional policy collaboration and sharing of knowledge and policy experience. It has also established a number of joint research centers — including the SAARC Disaster Management Centre, a SAARC Meteorological Research Center, the South Asia Forum, and the new South Asia University — that could host or carry out collaborative projects linking Pakistani and Indian scientists and students. Beyond supporting such collective scientific efforts, with some investment of political energy, SAARC's ministerial meetings and gatherings of Heads of State could be made a high-level stage for exploring and enacting a degree of policy cooperation.

GWP was founded in 1996 to foster integrated water resources management (IWRM), defined as the coordinated development and management of water, land, and related resources in order to maximize economic and social welfare without compromising the sustainability of vital environmental systems. Pakistan and India are both members of the NGO's South Asia Regional Water Partnerships. The Regional Partnerships especially function to promote water sharing across national boundaries and broad, inclusive stakeholder dialogue. NGOs such as GWP can furnish an alternative forum to official intergovernmental organizations in which to convene potentially different sets of stakeholders. However, at the same time, entities such as GWP — like ICIMOD or IWMI — can prove highly effective at designing solutions tailored to local conditions, and at identifying, collecting, and conveying good practices from one community to others across the network.

› **Recognize and promote possibilities for knowledge building and exchange — and for policy learning and collaboration — between India and Pakistan, and within India and Pakistan at the subnational state/ province, city-to-city, local, and civil society levels.** Many of the sharpest tensions over shared water supplies in the Indus Basin occur at the subnational level, between neighboring states, provinces, and communities. In Pakistan, disputes over the disposition of Indus water resources particularly divide Punjab and Sindh, for example. In India, Punjab and Himachal Pradesh contest the resources of the Ravi. These internal frictions can render local communities all the more sensitive in the face of perceived cross-border threats to shared water supplies. Reducing this domestic strife could simultaneously contribute to alleviating international discord on the Indus.

Between India and Pakistan, cross-border water diplomacy has concentrated at the level of the nation state. But some neighboring jurisdictions in the basin have managed a modicum of local cooperation in other issue areas that might serve as a model for exploring subnational collaboration on the Indus. Cross-border bus service and trade has linked the two sides of Jammu and Kashmir. Pakistani and Indian Punjab have signed a memorandum of understanding to boost trade over the frontier, backed by local business communities who have also pushed the central governments to loosen the visa regime to facilitate economic ties.[83] City governments could also play a significant role paving the route to more international cooperation and exchange. Sharing many of the same water management challenges for providing municipal water and sanitation, city governments on both sides of the border are especially well placed to share best practices and policy lessons, backed by growing support networks for city-to-city initiatives.[84] For example, the multi-city association, Local Governments for Sustainability (ICLEI) links hundreds of cities in 84 countries. ICLEI provides information, delivers training, organizes conferences, facilitates networking and city-to-city exchanges, carries out research and pilot projects, offers technical services, and provides software and tools to help local governments achieve their sustainable development goals regarding climate change, energy, infrastructure, and urban water supply. Over 40 Indian cities are members, although no Pakistani cities currently are.

In addition to such institutional networking opportunities, state/province and municipal governments could supply the structures for organizing joint parliamentary committees, staff studies, and site visits by the legislators whose constituencies are most at risk from water scarcity. City and state/province legislator groups could also constitute important focal points for establishing broad-based local, regional, and national cross-border civil society forums or networks of institutions and individuals from both India and Pakistan, drawing on their collective knowledge and policy assets to promote cooperative initiatives that can be tailored to specific communities and contexts, or adapted and replicated to scale, at the regional or basin level.

Endnotes

1. FAO, "Indus river basin," in Irrigation in Southern and Eastern Asia in Figures: AQUASTAT Survey 2011, Karen Frenken ed. (Rome: FAO, 2012), http://www.fao.org/docrep/016/i2809e/i2809e.pdf. Note that some other studies cited in this report furnish slightly different figures for the total basin area and its distribution between the riparian states.
2. FAO, "Indus river basin"; J. Eastham et al., "Water-use accounts in CPWF basins: Simple water-use accounting of the Indus basin," CPWF Working Paper BFP07 (Colombo, Sri Lanka: CGIAR Challenge Program on Water and Food, 2010), http://cgspace.cgiar.org/handle/10568/4696.
3. FAO, "Indus river basin"; FAO, "Pakistan country profile," in Irrigation in Southern and Eastern Asia in Figures: AQUASTAT Survey 2011, Karen Frenken ed. (Rome: FAO, 2012), http://www.fao.org/docrep/016/i2809e/i2809e. pdf; FAO, "India country profile," in Irrigation in Southern and Eastern Asia in Figures: AQUASTAT Survey 2011, Karen Frenken ed. (Rome: FAO, 2012), http://www.fao.org/docrep/016/i2809e/i2809e.pdf; Bharat R. Sharma et al., "Indo-Gangetic River Basins: Summary Situation Analysis," International Water Management Institute, New Delhi Office, July 2008, http://cpwfbfp.pbworks.com/f/IGB_situation_analysis.PDF.
4. S. Puri and A. Aureli eds., Atlas of Transboundary Aquifers (Paris: UNESCO, 2009), http://www.isarm.org/ publications/324.
5. A.N. Laghari et al., "The Indus basin in the framework of current and future resources management," Hydrology and Earth Systems Sciences 16, no.4 (2012), p.1065; N.K. Garg and Q. Hassan, "Alarming scarcity of water in India," Current Science 93, no.7 (2007), p.940.
6. Tushaar Shah, "The Groundwater Economy in South Asia: An Assessment of Size, Significance and Socioecological Impact," in M. Giordano and K.G. Villholthi eds., The Agricultural Groundwater Revolution: Opportunities and Threats to Development (Wallingford, UK: CABI Publishing, 2007); FAO, "Pakistan country profile", p.384.
7. Central Ground Water Board, Ground Water Year Book India: 2011-12 (Faridabad: Government of India, May 2012), pp.38-39, http://cgwb.gov.in/documents/Ground percent20Water percent20Year percent20Book percent20- percent202011-12.pdf; FAO, "Indus river basin," p.137.
8. FAO, AQUASTAT database, 2012, Food and Agriculture Organization of the United Nations, accessed January 2013. 1 cubic kilometer = 1 billion cubic meters, http://www.fao.org/nr/water/aquastat/main/index.stm.
9. United Nations Development Programme, Human Development Report 2006. Beyond Scarcity: Power, Poverty and the Global Water Crisis (New York: UNDP, 2006), p.135, http://hdr.undp.org/en/media/HDR06-complete.pdf.
10. Mukand S. Babel and Shahriar M. Wahid, Freshwater Under Threat: South Asia (Bangkok/Nairobi: Asian Institute of Technology/UNEP, 2008), p.14, http://www.unep.org/pdf/southasia_report.pdf; Mats Eriksson et al., The Changing Himalayas: Impact of Climate Change on Water Resources and Livelihoods in the Greater Himalayas (Kathmandu: ICIMOD, 2009), p.2, http://books.icimod.org/index.php/search/publication/593.
11. Mukand S. Babel and Shahriar M. Wahid, Freshwater Under Threat: South Asia, p.15; Laghari et al., pp.1064-1066; Sharma et al., p.3; FAO, "Indus river basin," p.137; FAO, "Pakistan country profile," p.381.
12. Sharma et al., "Indo-Gangetic River Basins," p.5; Bharat Sharma et al., "The Indus and the Ganges: river basins under extreme pressure," Water International 35, no.5 (2010), p.496.
13. Vladimir Smakhtin, "Basin Closure and Environmental Flow Requirements," International Journal of Water Resources Development 24, no.2 (2008); Sharma et al., "The Indus and the Ganges: river basins under extreme pressure," Water International 35, no.5 (2010), p.494.
14. Eastham et al., pp.23-24; Asif Inam et al., "The Geographic, Geological and Oceanographic Setting of the Indus River," in Large Rivers: Geomorphology and Management, Avijit Gupta ed. (Chichester, UK: John Wiley & Sons, 2007).

15 Vladimir Smakhtin, Carmen Revenga, and Petra Döll, "A Pilot Global Assessment of Environmental Water Requirements and Scarcity," *Water International* 29, no.3 (2004), p.312; A. Das Gupta, "Implication of environmental flows in river basin management," *Physics and Chemistry of the Earth* 33, no.5 (2008).

16 V.I. Kravtsova et al., "Variations of the Hydrological Regime, Morphological Structure, and Landscapes of the Indus River Delta (Pakistan) under the Effect of Large-Scale Water Management Measures," *Water Resources* 36, no.4 (2009), pp.367, 369; Rafik Hirji and Richard Davis, *Environmental Flows in Water Resources Policies, Plans, and Projects: Findings and Recommendations* (Washington, DC: World Bank, 2009), p.48, http://siteresources.worldbank.org/INTWAT/Resources/Env_Flows_Water_v1.pdf.

17 Yoshihide Wada et al., "Nonsustainable groundwater sustaining irrigation: A global assessment," *Water Resources Research* 48, W00L06 (2012), p.11, http://onlinelibrary.wiley.com/doi/10.1029/2011WR010562/pdf.

18 Asad Sarwar Quereshi et al., "Challenges and Prospects of Sustainable Groundwater Management in the Indus Basin, Pakistan," *Water Resources Management* 24, no.8 (2010); FAO, "Pakistan country profile," p.384.

19 Central Ground Water Board, pp.38-39, 41-42.

20 V.M. Tiwari, J. Wahr, and S. Swenson, "Dwindling groundwater resources in northern India, from satellite gravity observations," *Geophysical Research Letters* 36, L18401 (2009), http://fore.research.yale.edu/information/Yamuna/Tiwari_Wahr_Swenson.pdf; FAO, "Indus river basin," p.139; FAO, "Pakistan country profile," p.380.

21 Geneviève M. Carr et al., *Water Quality for Ecosystem and Human Health*, 2nd ed. (Burlington, Canada: UNEP Global Environmental Monitoring System/Water Programme, 2008).

22 Christer Nilsson and Brigitta Malm Renöfält, "Linking Flow Regime and Water Quality in Rivers: A Challenge to Adaptive Catchment Management," *Ecology and Society* 13, no.2 (2008).

23 FAO, "Indus river basin," p.133; C.J. Vörösmarty et al., "Global threats to human water security and river biodiversity," *Nature* 467, no.7315 (2010), On-line Supplementary Information, doi:10.1038/nature09440.24 Babel and Wahid, pp.17-18.

25 Water and Sanitation Program, *The Economic Impacts of Inadequate Sanitation in India* (New Delhi: Water and Sanitation Program, 2011), p.19; Ministry of Urban Development, *National Rating and Award Scheme for Sanitation for Indian Cities* (New Delhi: Government of India, 2010); Ministry of Urban Development, "Rank of Cities on Sanitation 2009-2010: National Urban Sanitation Policy, New Delhi, Government of India, 2010, at http://urbanindia.nic.in/programme/uwss/slb/SubNUSP.htm.

26 Azizullah et al., "Water pollution in Pakistan and its impact on public health – A review," *Environment International* 37, no.2 (2011), p.493.

27 Water and Sanitation Program, *The Economic Impacts of Inadequate Sanitation in India* (New Delhi: Water and Sanitation Program, 2011), http://www.wsp.org/sites/wsp.org/files/publications/wsp-esi-india.pdf; Azizullah et al., p.493; Water and Sanitation Program, *The Economic Impacts of Inadequate Sanitation in India*, pp.9, 37.

28 Matti Kummu et al., "Is physical water scarcity a new phenomenon? Global assessment of water shortage over the last two millennia," *Environmental Research Letters* 5, 034006 (2010).

29 UN World Population Prospects – 2010 Revision, (medium variant projections), http://esa.un.org/unpd/wpp/unpp/panel_population.htm, accessed January 2013.

30 Laghari et al. p.1069; Sharma et al., "Indo-Gangetic River Basins," p.4.

31 Åsa Johansson et al., *Looking to 2060: Long-term global growth prospects*, OECD Economic Policy Paper No.3 (Paris: OECD, November 2012), http://www.oecd.org/economy/economicoutlookanalysisandforecasts/2060 percent20policy percent20paper percent20FINAL.pdf; Malik Amin Aslam Khan and Amber Pervaiz, *National Sustainable Development Strategy: Pathway to a Sustainable Pakistan* (Islamabad: UNDP Pakistan/Government of Pakistan: May 2012), pp.12-13, http://undp.org.pk/images/documents/NSDS-document.pdf.

32 FAO, AQUASTAT database, 2012, Food and Agriculture Organization of the United Nations, accessed January 2013; UN Habitat, *State of the World's Cities 2012/2013: Prosperity of Cities* (Nairobi: UN Habitat, 2012), p.146, http://www.un.int/wcm/webdav/site/portal/shared/iseek/documents/2012/November/UNhabitat percent 20201213.pdf.

33 Sharma et al., "Indo-Gangetic River Basins," p.3; Asad Sarwar Qureshi, "Water Management in the Indus Basin in Pakistan: Challenges and Opportunities," *Mountain Research and Development* 31, no.3 (2011), http://www.bioone.org/doi/pdf/10.1659/MRD-JOURNAL-D-11-00019.1.

34 United Nations Development Programme, *Human Development Report 2006. Beyond Scarcity: Power, Poverty and the Global Water Crisis* (New York: UNDP, 2006), p.34, http://hdr.undp.org/en/media/HDR06-complete.pdf.

35 M.M. Mekonnen and A.Y. Hoekstra, "The green, blue and grey water footprint of crops and derived crop products," *Hydrology and Earth System Sciences* 15, no.5 (2011), http://www.waterfootprint.org/Reports/Mekonnen-Hoekstra-2011-WaterFootprintCrops.pdf; Mesfin M. Mekonnen and Arjen Y. Hoekstra, "A Global Assessment of the Water Footprint of Farm Animal Products," *Ecosystems* 15, no.3 (2012), http://www.waterfootprint.org/Reports/Mekonnen-Hoekstra-2012-WaterFootprintFarmAnimalProducts.pdf.

36 World Water Assessment Programme, *United Nations World Water Development Report 3: Water in a Changing World* (Paris/London: UNESCO/Earthscan, 2009), p.107, http://www.unesco.org/new/en/natural-sciences/environment/water/wwap/wwdr/wwdr3-2009/downloads-wwdr3/.

37 Qureshi, "Water Management in the Indus Basin in Pakistan," p.254; Claudia Ringler et al., "Water supply and food security: Alternative scenarios for the Indian Indo-Gangetic River Basin," *International Journal of River Basin Management*, 7, no.2 (2009), pp.169-170.

38 OECD, *OECD Environmental Outlook to 2050: The Consequences of Inaction* (Paris: OECD, 2012), pp.225-226.

39 Garg and Hassan; 2030 Water Resources Group, *Charting Our Water Future: Economic Frameworks to Inform Decision-Making* (McKinsey & Company, 2009), http://www.mckinsey.com/App_Media/Reports/Water/ Charting_Our_Water_Future_Full_Report_001.pdf.

40 World Bank, *Pakistan's Water Economy: Running Dry* (Washington, DC: World Bank, 2005).

41 Rex Victor Cruz et al., "Asia," in *Climate Change 2007: Impacts, Adaptation and Vulnerability. Contribution of Working Group II to the Fourth Assessment Report of the Intergovernmental Panel on Climate Change*, M.L. Parry et al. eds. (Cambridge: Cambridge University Press, 2007), http://www.ipcc.ch/publications_and_data/ publications_ipcc_fourth_assessment_report_wg2_report_impacts_adaptation_and_vulnerability.htm; ; Ministry of Environment and Forests, *Climate Change and India: A 4x4 Assessment – A Sectoral and Regional Analysis for 2030s* (New Delhi: Government of India, November 2010), at http://moef.nic.in/downloads/ public-information/fin-rpt-incca.pdf; Planning Commission, *Task Force on Climate Change: Final Report* (Islamabad: Government of Pakistan, February 2010), http://www.pc.gov.pk/usefull%20links/Taskforces/ TFCC%20 Final %20Report.pdf.

42 Jianchu Xu et al., "The Melting Himalayas: Cascading Effects of Climate Change on Water, Biodiversity, and Livelihoods," *Conservation Biology* 23, no.3 (2009), http://academic.regis.edu/ckleier/conservation%20biology/ melting_himalaya.pdf; ICIMOD, *The Status of Glaciers in the Hindu Kush-Himalayan Region* (Kathmandu: ICIMOD, November 2011), http://books.icimod.org/uploads/tmp/icimod-the_status_of_glaciers_in_the_ hindu_kush-himalayan_region.pdf; ICIMOD, *Status of Glaciers in the Indus Basin* (Kathmandu: ICIMOD, March 2012), http://geoportal.icimod.org/MENRISFactSheets/Sheets/2icimod-snow_cover_status_and_trends_ in_the_indus_basin.pdf.

43 ICIMOD, *Climate Change in the Hindu Kush-Himalayas: The State of Knowledge* (Kathmandu: ICIMOD, 2011),http://lib.icimod.org/record/9417/files/icimod-climate_change_in_the_hindu_kush-himalayas.pdf; National Research Council, *Himalayan Glaciers: Climate Change, Water Resources, and Water Security* (Washington, DC: National Academies Press, 2012).

44 ICIMOD, *Formation of Glacial Lakes in the Hindu Kush-Himalayas and GLOF Risk Assessment* (Kathmandu: ICIMOD, May 2010), http://books.icimod.org/demo/uploads/tmp/icimod-formation_of_glacial_lakes_in_the_ hindu_kush-himalayas_and_glof_risk_assessment.pdf.

45 Walter W. Immerzeel, Ludovicus P.H. van Beek, and Marc P.F. Bierkens, "Climate Change Will Affect the Asian Water Towers," *Science* 328, no.5984 (2010), http://1004378.liweb1.pinshosting.net/wp-content/uploads/2011/05/Immerzeel_Science_11June 2010.pdf.

46 Mary Miner et al., "Water sharing between India and Pakistan: a critical evaluation of the Indus Waters Treaty," *Water International* 34, no.2 (2009).

47 Liviu Giosan et al., "Fluvial landscapes of the Harappan civilization," *Proceedings of the National Academy of Sciences*, Early Edition on-line, forthcoming 2013, http://www.pnas.org/content/early/2012/05/24/1112743109. full.pdf.

48 World Bank, *India's Water Economy: Bracing for a Turbulent Future* (Washington, DC: World Bank, 2005), http://www-wds.worldbank.org/external/default/WDSContentServer/WDSP/IB/2008/06/25/000333037_2008 0625020800/Rendered/PDF/443760PUB0IN0W1Box0327398B01PUBLIC1.pdf; World Bank, *Pakistan's Water Economy: Running Dry* (Washington, DC: World Bank, 2005), http://www-wds.worldbank.org/external/default/ WDSContentServer/WDSP/IB/2010/02/01/0003330 37_20100201014523/Rendered/PDF/529140WP0Box341Un iversity0Press2006.pdf.

49 "Punjab, India." Columbia Water Center, Earth Institute, Columbia University, http://water.columbia.edu/ research-projects/india/punjab-india; Polycarpou, Lakis. "'Small Is Also Beautiful' — Appropriate Technology Cuts Rice Farmers' Water Use by 30 Percent in Punjab, India." Columbia Water Center, Earth Institute, Columbia University, 17 November 2010, http://blogs.ei.columbia.edu/2010/11/17/%E2%80%9Csmall-isalso- beautiful%E2%80%9D-%E2%80%93-appropriate-technology-cuts-rice-famers%E2%80%99-water-useby-30percent-in-punjab-india; "Columbia Water Center Released New Whitepaper: 'Restoring Groundwater in Punjab, India's Breadbasket." Columbia Water Center, Earth Institute, Columbia University, 7 March, 2012, http://water.columbia.edu/2012/03/07/columbia-water-center-released-new-whitepaper-restoring-roundwaterin-punjab-indias-breadbasket.

50 "Agriculture in Punjab." Agri Punjab, Agriculture Department, Government of Punjab, Pakistan, April 2010, http://www.agripunjab.gov.pk/index.php?agri=detail&r=0.

51 FAO, "Indus river basin"; FAO, "Pakistan country profile," in *Irrigation in Southern and Eastern Asia in Figures: AQUASTAT Survey 2011*, Karen Frenken ed. (Rome: FAO, 2012), http://www.fao.org/docrep/016/i2809e/i2809e. pdf; "Agriculture in Punjab." Agri Punjab, Agriculture Department, Government of Punjab, Pakistan, April 2010, http://www.agripunjab.gov.pk/index.php?agri=detail&r=0.

52 ICIMOD, *Climate Change Impacts on the Water Resources of the Indus Basin* (Kathmandu: ICIMOD, March 2010), http://books.icimod.org/uploads/tmp/icimod-climate_change_impacts_on_the_water_resources_of_the_ indus_basin:_.pdf; World dataBank, World Development Indicators (WDI), World Bank 2009, http://databank. worldbank.org/ddp/home.do.

53 Antarpreet, Jutla, and Dewayne Wan. "Indus River Basin." Tufts University, February 2009.

54 ICIMOD, *Climate Change Impacts on the Water Resources of the Indus Basin* (Kathmandu: ICIMOD, March 2010), http://books.icimod.org/uploads/tmp/icimod-climate_change_impacts_on_the_water_resources_of_the_ indus_basin:_.pdf.

55 FAO, "Pakistan: Geography, Climate, and Population." *AQUASTAT*, Food and Agriculture Organization of the United Nations, 2010, http://www.fao.org/nr/water/aquastat/countries_regions/PAK/index.stm.

56 FAO, "India: Geography, Climate, and Population." *AQUASTAT*, Food and Agriculture Organization of the United Nations, 2010, http://www.fao.org/nr/water/aquastat/countries_regions/IND/index.stm.

57 Kapadia, Vivek, B.L. Deopura, and B.R. Chahar. "Canal Lining Through Geomembranes: A Case Study of Sardar Sarovar Project," *India Water Week 2012 (New Delhi) – Water, Energy and Food Security: Call for Solutions*, https://indiawaterweek. water.tallyfox.com/documents/canal-lining-through-geomembranes-case-study- sardarsarovar-project.

58 Project Management & Policy Implementation Unit, Ministry of Water & Power, Government of Pakistan. "Irrigation System of Pakistan," 2011, p. 82, http://www.wspakistan.com/Admin/Prerequisite_images/54f29a5. irrigation%20system%20of%20 pak.pdf.

59 Ahmed, Ayaz, Henna Iftikhar and G.M. Chaudhry. "Water Resources and Conservation Strategy of Pakistan." Pakistan Institute of Development Economics, http://www.pide.org.pk/psde23/pdf/Ayaz%20Ahmed.pdf.

60 Brar, MS and SS Mukhopadhyay, eds. "Potassium Role and Benefits in Improving Nutrient Management for Food Production, Quality and Reduced Environmental Damages," *Proceedings of the IPI-OUAT-IPNI International Symposium (Bhubaneswar, Orissa, India, 5-7 November 2009)*, p. 29, http://india.ipni.net/ipniweb/ regions/india/regionalPortalIN.nsf/4d69 fbe2e4abc746852574ce005c0150/2bfb0e869b7db6b4852578c60056f2c2$FILE/IPI-OUAT-IPNI%20K%202010x. pdf#page=9.

61 Young, Susan. "Satellite Data Provide a New Way to Monitor Groundwater Aquifers in Agricultural Regions." *Stanford Report*, 13 December 2010, http://news.stanford.edu/news/2010/december/agu-water-imaging-121310. html.

62 Singh, Karam. "Act to Save Groundwater in Punjab: Its Impact on Water Table, Electricity Subsidy and Environment." *Agricultural Economics Research Review*, Vol. 22, 2009, pp. 365-386, http://ageconsearch.umn. edu/bitstream/57482/2/6-Karam-Singh.pdf.

63 Sharma, Bharat and Upali Amarasinghe (Eds.). "Tackling Water & Food Crisis in South Asia: Insights from the Indo-Gangetic Basin." CPWF Project Report, Project Number PN60, International Water Management Institute, 2009, p. 76, http://www.dfid. gov.uk/r4d/PDF/Outputs/WaterfoodCP/PN60_IWMI_ProjectReport_Mar10_ approved.pdf.

64 "Economics of Land Leveling." International Rice Research Institute, 2009, http://www.knowledgebank.irri.org/ rkb/benefits-of-laser-leveling/why-laser-level-land/economics-of-land-leveling.html.

65 "Economics of Land Leveling." International Rice Research Institute, 2009, http://www.knowledgebank.irri.org/ rkb/benefits-of-laser-leveling/why-laser-level-land/economics-of-land-leveling.html.

66 Sharma, Bharat, Upali Amarasinghe, and Cai Xueliang. "Assessing and Improving Water Productivity in Conservation Agriculture Systems in the Indus-Gangetic Basin." International Water Management Institute, 2009, http://cpwfbfp.pbworks. com/f/WCCA-Paper_BRS_.pdf.

67 Sharma, Bharat, Upali Amarasinghe, and Cai Xueliang. "Assessing and Improving Water Productivity in Conservation Agriculture Systems in the Indus-Gangetic Basin." International Water Management Institute, 2009, http://cpwfbfp.pbworks. com/f/WCCA-Paper_BRS_.pdf.

68 Prime Minister of India, "PM's opening remarks at the National Development Council Meeting," 27 December 2012; Margherita Stancati, "India's Water Waste Could Hurt Growth," *Wall Street Journal India*, 11 April 2012.

69 Planning Commission of Pakistan, *Pakistan: Framework for Economic Growth* (Islamabad: Government of Pakistan, May 2011), pp.41-43, http://202.83.164.29/ministries/planninganddevelopment-ministry/hot%20links/ growth_document_english_ version.pdf.

70 World Bank, *World Development Indicators 2012* (Washington, DC: World Bank, 2012), pp.155, 187.

71 Water and Sanitation Program, *The Economic Impacts of Inadequate Sanitation in Pakistan* (Islamabad: Water and Sanitation Program, 2012), http://water.worldbank.org/sites/water.worldbank.org/files/publication/WSPesi- pakistan.pdf; Water and Sanitation Program, *The Economic Impacts of Inadequate Sanitation in India* (New Delhi: Water and Sanitation Program, 2011), http://www.wsp.org/sites/wsp.org/files/publications/wsp-esiindia. pdf.

72 Shirish Sankhe et al., *India's Urban Awakening: Building Inclusive Cities, Sustaining Economic Growth* (McKinsey Global Institute, April 2010), p.13; Planning Commission of Pakistan, *Pakistan: Framework for Economic Growth* (Islamabad: Government of Pakistan, May 2011), http://202.83.164.29/ministries/planninganddevelopmentministry/ hot%20links/growth_document_english_version.pdf.

73 Working Group on Power, *Report of the Working Group on Power for 12th Plan 2012-2017* (New Delhi: Government of India, January 2012), http://planningcommission.nic.in/aboutus/committee/wrkgrp12/cit/wg_ reppost.pdf; Central Electricity Authority, "Status of H.E. Potential Development – Basinwise," 31 October 2012.

74 Pakistan Water and Power Development Authority, *Hydro Potential in Pakistan* (Islamabad: Government of Pakistan, May 2010).

75 According to the Water Footprint Network, blue water refers to surface and groundwater supplies, while green water refers to precipitation that remains in soil or on vegetation, as opposed to running off into surface waters or recharging groundwater stocks.

76 "Monsoon, Or Later." *Economist*, 28 July 2012, http://www.economist.com/node/21559628.

77 Bharat R. Sharma et al., "Indo-Gangetic River Basins: Summary Situation Analysis," International Water Management Institute, New Delhi Office, July 2008, http://cpwfbfp.pbworks.com/f/IGB_situation_analysis. PDF.

78 ESRI, "The Digital Yellow River Project," Spring 2010, http://www.esri.com/news/arcnews/spring10articles/thedigital-yellow.html.
79 ICIMOD, *Climate Change Impacts on the Water Resources of the Indus Basin* (Kathmandu: ICIMOD, March 2010), http://books.icimod.org/uploads/tmp/icimod-climate_change_impacts_on_the_water_resources_of_the_ indus_basin:_.pdf.
80 ICIMOD, *Status of Glaciers in the Indus Basin* (Kathmandu: ICIMOD, March 2012), http://geoportal.icimod.org/MENRISFactSheets/Sheets/2icimod-snow_cover_status_and_trends_in_the_indus_basin.pdf.
81 ICIMOD, *Climate Change in the Himalayas* (Kathmandu: ICIMOD, May 2009), http://books.icimod.org/ uploads/tmp/icimod-climate_change_in_the_himalayas.pdf.
82 Indus Waters Treaty (1960), http://siteresources.worldbank.org/INTSOUTHASIA/ Resources/223497-1105737253588/IndusWatersTreaty1960.pdf.
83 Tridivesh Singh Maini, "The two Punjabs: one step more toward closer cooperation," *East Asia Forum*, 14 November 2012.

CHAPTER - 28

Case Study Of Transboundary Dispute Resolution: The Indus Water Treaty

Authors: *Aaron T. Wolf and Joshua T. Newton*

Adapted from a larger document, cited below:

Case Summary	
River Basin:	Indus River and tributaries (figure 1 and table 1).
Dates of Negotiation:	1951-1960
Relevant Parties:	India, Pakistan
Flashpoint:	Lack of water-sharing agreement leads India to stem flow of tributaries to Pakistan on 1 April 1948.
Issues:	
Stated Objectives:	Negotiate an equitable allocation of the flow of the Indus River and its tributaries between the riparian states; develop a rational plan for integrated watershed development
Additional Issues:	
Water-related:	Financing for development plans, whether storage facilities are "replacement" or "development" (tied to who is financially responsible).
Non-water:	General India-Pakistan relations.
Excluded issues:	Future opportunities for regional management; Issues concerning drainage.
Criteria for water allocations:	Historic and planned use (for Pakistan) plus geographic allocations (western rivers vs. eastern rivers).
Incentives/Linkage:	Financial: World Bank organized International Fund Agreement; Political: None.
Breakthroughs:	Bank puts own proposal forward after 1953 deadlock; International funding raised for final agreement.
Status:	Ratified in 1960, with provisions for ongoing conflict resolution. Some suggest that recent meetings have been lukewarm. Physical separation of tributaries may preclude efficient integrated basin management. Renewed attempts to resolve Wuller Barrage and Baglihar dam conflicts begin to take place in July 2004.

Background

Irrigation in the Indus River basin dates back centuries; by the late 1940s the irrigation works along the river were the most extensive in the world. These irrigation projects had been developed over the years under one political authority, that of British India, and any water conflict could be resolved by executive order. The Government of India Act of 1935, however, put water under provincial jurisdiction, and some disputes did begin to crop up at the sites of the more extensive works, notably between the provinces of Punjab and Sind.

379

In 1942, a judicial commission was appointed by the British government to study Sind's concern over planned Punjabi development. The Commission recognized the claims of Sind, and called for the integrated management of the basin as a whole. The Commission's report was found unacceptable by both sides, and the chief engineers of the two sides met informally between 1943 and 1945 to try to reconcile their differences. Although a draft agreement was produced, neither of the two provinces accepted the terms, and the dispute was referred to London for a final decision in 1947.

Before a decision could be reached, however, the Indian Independence Act of August 15, 1947 internationalized the dispute between the new states of India and Pakistan. Partition was to be carried out in 73 days, and the full implications of dividing the Indus basin seem not to have been fully considered, although Sir Cyril Radcliffe, who was responsible for the boundary delineation, did express his hope that, "some joint control and management of the irrigation system may be found" (Mehta 1986, p. 4). Heightened political tensions, population displacements, and unresolved territorial issues, all served to exacerbate hostilities over the water dispute.

As the monsoon flows receded in the fall of 1947, the chief engineers of Pakistan and India met and agreed to a "Standstill Agreement," which froze water allocations at two points on the river until March 31, 1948, allowing discharges from headworks in India to continue to flow into Pakistan.

On April 1, 1948, the day that the "Standstill Agreement" expired, in the absence of a new agreement, India discontinued the delivery of water to the Dipalpur Canal and the main branches of the Upper Bari Daab Canal. Several motives have been suggested for India's actions. The first is legalistic–that of an upper riparian establishing its sovereign water rights. Others include an Indian maneuver to pressure Pakistan on the volatile Kashmir issue, to demonstrate Pakistan's dependence on India in the hope of forcing reconciliation, or to retaliate against a Pakistani levy of an export duty on raw jute leaving East Bengal. Another interpretation is that the action was taken by the provincial government of East Punjab, without the approval of the central government.

Table 1. Features of the Indus watershed.

Name	Riparian states (With % of national available water being utilized) b a	Riparian relations (with dates of most recent agreements)	Watershed features a			Special features
			Average annual flow (km^3/yr.) c	Size (km^2)	Climate	
Indus	Afghanistan (47.7), China (19.3), Chinese control, claimed by India (n/a), India (57.1), Indian control, claimed by China (n/a), Nepal (n/a), Pakistan (53.8)	Cool (1960 Indus Water Treaty between India and Pakistan)	238	1,138,800	Dry to humid sub-tropical	Scheduled as case to be "back-modeled"

a *Values for lakes under "Annual Flow" are for storage volumes.*
b *Source: Kulshreshtha (1993)*
c *Sources: Gleick ed. (1993); UN Register of International Rivers (1978). The remaining data in this table is from the TFDD (2007).*

Figure 1. Map of the Indus River Basin.

The problem

Even before the partition of India and Pakistan, the Indus posed problems between the states of British India. The problem became international only after partition, though, and the attendant increased hostility and lack of supra-legal authority only exacerbated the issue. Pakistani territory, which had relied on Indus water for centuries, now found the water sources originating in another country, one with whom geopolitical relations were increasing in hostility.

The question over the flow of the Indus is a classic case of the conflicting claims of up- and down-stream riparians. The conflict can be exemplified in the terms for the resumption of water delivery to Pakistan from the Indian headworks, worked out at an Inter-Dominican conference held in Delhi on 3-4 May 1948. India agreed to the resumption of flow, but maintained that Pakistan could not claim any share of those waters as a matter of right (Caponera, 1987, p. 511). This position was reinforced by the Indian claim that, since Pakistan had agreed to pay for water under the Standstill Agreement of 1947, Pakistan had recognized India 's water rights. Pakistan countered that they had the rights of prior appropriation, and that payments to India were only to cover operation and maintenance costs (Biswas, 1992, p. 204).

While these conflicting claims were not resolved, an agreement was signed, later referred to as the Delhi Agreement, in which India assured Pakistan that India would not withdraw water delivery without allowing time for Pakistan to develop alternate sources. Pakistan later expressed its displeasure with the agreement in a note dated 16 June 1949, calling for the "equitable apportionment of all common waters," and suggesting turning jurisdiction of the case over to the World Court. India suggested rather that a commission of judges from each side try to resolve their differences before turning the problem over to a third party. This stalemate lasted through 1950.

Attempts at conflict management

In 1951, Indian Prime Ministe, Nehru, whose interest in integrated river management along the lines of the Tennessee Valley Authority had been piqued, invited David Lilienthal, former chairman of the TVA, to visit India. Lilienthal also visited Pakistan and, on his return to the US, wrote an article outlining his impressions and recommendations (the trip had been commissioned by Collier's Magazine-international water was not the initial aim of the visit). These included steps from the psychological-a call to allay Pakistani suspicions of Indian intentions for the Indus headwaters, to the practical-a proposal for greater storage facilities and cooperative management. Lilienthal also suggests that international financing be arranged, perhaps by the World Bank, to fund the workings and findings of an "Indus Engineering Corporation," to include representatives from both states, as well as from the World Bank.

The article was read by Lilienthal's friend, David Black, president of the World Bank, who contacted Lilienthal for recommendations on helping to resolve the dispute. As a result, Black contacted the prime ministers of Pakistan and India, inviting both countries to accept the Bank's good offices. In a subsequent letter, Black outlined "essential principles" that might be followed for conflict resolution. These principles included the following: that water resources of the Indus basin should be managed cooperatively; and that problems of the basin should be solved on a functional and not on a political plane, without relation to past negotiations and past claims. Black suggested that India and Pakistan each appoint a senior engineer to work on a plan for development of the Indus basin. A Bank engineer would be made available as an ongoing consultant.

Both sides accepted Black's initiative. The first meeting of the Working Party included Indian and Pakistani engineers, along with a team from the Bank, as envisioned by Black, and met for the first time in Washington in May 1952. The stated agenda was to prepare an outline for a program, including a list of possible technical measures to increase the available supplies of Indus water for economic development. After three weeks of discussions, an outline was agreed to, whose points included

- determination of total water supplies, divided by catchment and use;
- determination of the water requirements of cultivable irrigable areas in each country;
- calculation of data and surveys necessary, as requested by either side;
- preparation of cost estimates and a construction schedule of new engineering works which might be included in a comprehensive plan.

In a creative avoidance of a potential and common conflict, the parties agreed that any data requested by either side would be collected and verified when possible, but that the acceptance of the data, or the inclusion of any topic for study, would not commit either side to its "relevance or materiality."

When the two sides were unable to agree on a common development plan for the basin in subsequent meetings in Karachi, November 1952, and Delhi, January 1953, the Bank suggested that each side submit its own plan. Both sides did submit plans on October 6, 1953, each of which mostly agreed on the supplies available for irrigation, but varied extremely on how these supplies should be allocated (Table 2).The Indian proposal allocated 29 million acre-feet (MAF) per year to India and 90 MAF to Pakistan, totaling 119 MAF (MAF = 1233.48 million cubic meters; since all negotiations were in English units, that is what is reported here). The Pakistani proposal, in contrast, allocated India 15.5 MAF and Pakistan 102.5 MAF, for a total of 118 MAF.

Table 2. Water allocations from Indus negotiations, in MAF/year [1]

Plan	India	Pakistan
Initial Indian	29.0	90.0
Initial Pakistani	15.5	102.5
Revised Indian	All of the eastern rivers and 7% of the western rivers	None of the eastern rivers and 93% of the western rivers
Revised Pakistani	30% of the eastern rivers and none of the western rivers	70% of the eastern rivers and all of the western rivers
World Bank Proposal	Entire flow of the eastern rivers [2]	Entire flow of the western rivers [3]

1 *Initial estimates of supplies available differed only slightly, with the Indian Plan totaling 119 MAF and the Pakistani Plan arriving at 118 MAF. The "eastern rivers" consist of the Ravi, Beas, and Sutlej tributaries; the "western rivers" refer to the Indus, Jhelum, and Chenab.*

2 *India would agree to continue to supply Pakistan with its historic withdrawals from these rivers for a transition period to be agreed upon, which would be based on the time necessary to complete Pakistani link canals to replace supplies from India.*

3 *The only exception would be an "insignificant" amount of flow from the Jhelum, used at the time in Kashmir.*

The two sides were persuaded to adjust somewhat their initial proposals, but the modified proposals of each side still left too much difference to overcome. The modified Indian plan called for all of the eastern rivers (Ravi, Beas, and Sutlej) and 7% of the western rivers (Indus, Jhelum and Chenab) to be allocated to India, while Pakistan would be allocated the remainder, or 93% of the western rivers. The modified Pakistani plan called for 30% of the eastern rivers to be allocated to India, while 70% of the eastern rivers and all of the western rivers would go to Pakistan.

The Bank concluded that not only was the stalemate likely to continue, but that the ideal goal of integrated watershed development for the benefit of both riparians was probably too elusive a goal at this stage of political relations. On February 5, 1954, the Bank issued its own proposal, abandoning the strategy of integrated development in favor of one of separation. The Bank proposal called for the entire flow of the eastern rivers to be allocated to India, and all of the western rivers, with the exception of a small amount from the Jhelum, to be allocated to Pakistan. According to the proposal, the two sides would agree to a transition period while Pakistan would complete link canals dividing the watershed, during which India would continue to allow Pakistan's historic use to continue to flow from the eastern rivers.

The Bank proposal was given to both parties simultaneously. On March 25, 1954, India accepted the proposal as the basis for agreement. Pakistan viewed the proposal with more trepidation, and gave only qualified acceptance on July 28, 1954; they considered the flow of the western rivers to be insufficient to replace their existing supplies from the eastern rivers, particularly given limited available storage capacity. To help facilitate an agreement, the Bank issued an aide memoir, calling for more storage on the western rivers, and suggesting India's financial liability for "replacement facilities"–increased storage facilities and enlarged link canals in Pakistan which could be recognized as the cost replacement of pre-partition canals.

Little progress was made until representatives from the two countries met in May 1958. Main points in contention included whether the main replacement storage facility ought to be on the Jhelum or Indus rivers–Pakistan preferred the latter but the Bank argued that the former was more cost-effective; and what the total cost of new development would be and who would pay for it–India's position was that it would only pay for "replacement" and not "development" facilities.

In 1958, Pakistan proposed a plan including two major storage facilities: one each on the Jhelum and the Indus; three smaller dams on both tributaries; and expanded link canals. India, objecting both to the extent and the cost of the Pakistani proposal, approximately $1.12 billion, proposed an alternative plan which was smaller in scale, but which Pakistan rejected because it necessitated continued reliance on Indian water deliveries.

By 1959, the Bank evaluated the principal issue to be resolved as follows: which works would be considered "replacement" and which "development;" in other words, for which works would India be financially responsible. To circumvent the question, Black suggested an alternative approach in a visit to India and Pakistan in May. Perhaps one might settle on a specific amount for which India is responsible, rather than arguing over individual works. The Bank might then help raise additional funds among the international community development for watershed development. India was offered help with construction of its Beas Dam, and Pakistan's plan, including both the proposed dams would be looked at favorably. With these conditions, both sides agreed to a fixed payment settlement, and to a ten-year transition period during which India would continue to provide Pakistan's historic flows to continue.

In August 1959, Black organized a consortium of donors to support development in the Indus basin, which raised close to $900 million, in addition to India's commitment of $174 million. The Indus Water Treaty was signed in Karachi on September 19, 1960, and government ratifications were exchanged in Delhi in January 1961.

Outcome

The Indus Water Treaty addressed both the technical and financial concerns of each side, and included a timeline for transition. The main points of the treaty included (Alam, 2002):

- an agreement that Pakistan would receive unrestricted use of the western rivers, which India would allow to flow unimpeded, with minor exceptions;

- provisions for three dams, eight link canals, three barrages, and 2500 tube wells to be built in Pakistan;

- a ten-year transition period, from April 1, 1960 to March 31, 1970, during which water would continue to be supplied to Pakistan according to a detailed schedule;

- a schedule for India to provide its fixed financial contribution of $62 million, in ten annual installments during the transition period

- additional provisions for data exchange and future cooperation.

The treaty also established the Permanent Indus Commission, made up of one Commissioner of Indus Waters from each country. The two Commissioners would meet annually in order to establish and promote cooperative arrangements for the treaty implementation; promote cooperation between the Parties in the development of the waters of the Indus system; examine and resolve by agreement any question that may arise between the Parties concerning interpretation or implementation of the Treaty; submit an annual report to the two governments.

In case of a dispute, provisions were made to appoint a "neutral expert." If the neutral expert fails to resolve the dispute, negotiators can be appointed by each side to meet with one or more mutually agreed-upon mediators. If either side (or the mediator) views mediated agreement as unlikely, provisions are included for the convening of a Court of Arbitration. In addition, the treaty calls for either party, if it undertakes any engineering works on any of the tributaries, to notify the other of its plans and to provide any data which may be requested.

Since 1960, no projects have been submitted under the provisions for "future cooperation," nor have any issues of water quality been submitted at all. Other disputes have arisen, and been handled in a variety of ways. The first issues arose from Indian non-delivery of some waters during 1965-66, but became instead a question of procedure and the legality of commission decisions. Negotiators resolved that each commissioner acted as government representatives and that their decisions were legally binding.

One controversy surrounding the design and construction of the Salal Dam was resolved through bilateral negotiations between the two governments. Other disputes, over new hydroelectric projects and the Wuller Barrage on the Jhelum tributary and the Baglihar dam on the Chenab River in Kashmir, have yet to be resolved.

Lessons learned (Alam, 2002)

- *Shifting political boundaries can turn intra-national disputes into international conflicts, exacerbating tensions over existing issues.*

Shifting borders and partition exacerbated what was, initially, an intra-national Indian issue. After partition, political tensions, particularly over Kashmir territory, contributed to tensions of this newly international conflict.

- *Power inequities may delay the pace of negotiations.*

Power inequities may have delayed pace of negotiations. India had both a superior riparian position, as well as a relatively stronger central government, than Pakistan. The combination may have acted as disincentive to reach agreement.

- *Positive, active, and continuous involvement of a third party is vital in helping to overcome conflict.*

The active participation of Eugene Black and the World Bank were crucial to the success of the Indus Water Treaty. The Bank offered not only their good offices, but a strong leadership role as well. The Bank provided support staff, funding, and, perhaps most important, its own proposals when negotiations reached a stalemate.

- *Coming to the table with financial assistance can provide sufficient incentive for a breakthrough in agreement.*

The Bank helped raise almost $900 million from the international community, allowing for Pakistan's final objections to be addressed.

- *Some points may be agreed to more quickly, if it is explicitly agreed that a precedent is not being set.*

In the 1948 agreement, Pakistan agreed to pay India for water deliveries. This point was later used by India to argue that, by paying for the water, Pakistan recognized India's water rights. Pakistan, in contrast, argued that they were paying only for operation and maintenance. In an early meeting (May 1952), both sides agreed that any data may be used *without* committing either side to its "relevance or materiality," thereby precluding delays over data discrepancies.

- *Sensitivity to each party's particular hydrologic concerns is crucial in determining the bargaining mix.*

Early negotiations focused on quantity allocations, while one of Pakistan's main concerns was storage– the timing of the delivery was seen to be as crucial as the amount.

- *In particularly hot conflicts, when political concerns override, a sub-optimal solution may be the best one can achieve.*

The plan pointedly disregards the principle of integrated water management, recognizing that between these particular riparians, the most important issue was control by each state of its own resource. Structural division of the basin, while crucial for political reasons, effectively precludes the possibility of increased integrated management.

Creative outcomes resulting from resolution process

In a creative avoidance of a potential and common conflict, the parties agreed that any data requested by either side would be collected and verified when possible, but that the acceptance of the data, or the inclusion of any topic for study, would not commit either side to its "relevance or materiality."

Water was separated out from other contentious issues between India and Pakistan. This allowed negotiations to continue, even in light of tensions over other topics. Water problems were to be viewed as "functional" rather than political.

When both sides were unable to agree on a common development plan in 1953, the Bank suggested that each prepare its own plan, which the Bank would then inspect for commonalities. This active strategy to breaking impasses is currently being attempted with the riparians of the Jordan River watershed in conjunction with the multilateral working group on water.

Timeline

Pre-1935	British India has authority to resolve interstate water conflicts by executive order.
1935	Government of India Act makes water a subject of provincial jurisdiction, unless asked to intervene by states.
Oct 1939	Province of Sind formally requests Governor-General to review new Punjabi irrigation project and potential detriment to Sind.
Sep 1941	Indus Commission established.
July 1942	Commission submits its report suggesting that withdrawals by Punjab would cause "material injury" to inundation canals in Sind, particularly during the month of September. Incidentally called for management of the river system as a whole. Report found unacceptable to both sides.
1943-5	Chief engineers of both states meet informally, finally producing a draft agreement–provinces refuse to sign. Dispute referred to secretary of state for India in London early 1947.
15 Aug 1947	Independent states of India and Pakistan established. Eastern Punjab becomes part of India, western Punjab and Sind become part of Pakistan. Conflict becomes international, British role now irrelevant. Chair of Punjab Boundary Commission suggests that Punjab water system be run as joint venture–declined by both sides.
10 Dec 1947	"Standstill Agreement" negotiated by chief engineers of west and east Punjab, freezing allocations at two points until 31 Mar 1948.
1 Apr 1948	Without new agreement, India discontinues delivery of water to Dipalpur Canal and main branches of Upper Bari Daab Canal.
30 Apr 1948	India resumes water delivery as negotiations undertaken.
3-4 May 1948	Inter-Dominion conference, and an agreement is signed. India assures Pakistan that India will not withdraw water delivery without allowing time for Pakistan to develop alternate sources. Other issues remain unresolved.
16 June 1949	Pakistan sends a note to India expressing displeasure with agreement. The note calls for a conference to resolve the "equitable apportionment of all common waters," and suggesting giving the World Court jurisdiction on the application of either party. India objects to third party involvement, suggests judges from each side might narrow dispute first. Stalemate results through 1950.
1951	David Lilienthal, past chairman of the Tennessee Valley Authority, invited to India as Prime Minister Nehru's guest. He later publishes an article with his suggestions, which captures the attention of Eugene Black, president of the World Bank.

Aug 1951	Aug 1951
Jan-Feb 1952	Meetings continue, Black finds "common understanding," at least that neither side will diminish supplies for existing uses.
May 1952	First meeting of working party in Washington of engineers from India, Pakistan, and Bank engineers. Agreement to: determine future supply and demand; calculate available and desired data; prepare cost estimates and construction schedule of necessary infrastructure.
Nov 1952 & Jan 1953	Meetings continue in Karachi and Delhi without agreement. Bank suggests each side submit its own plan.
6 Oct 1953	Plans submitted with proposed allocations and sources for each state. Agreement on available supplies, not on allocations.
5 Feb 1954	Bank puts forth own proposal, essentially suggesting dividing the western tributaries to Pakistan, and the eastern tributaries to India. The proposal also provided for continued deliveries to Pakistan during transition period.
25 Mar 1954	India accepts proposal. Pakistan is less enthusiastic–it would have to replace existing facilities.
28 July 1954	Pakistan delivers a qualified acceptance of proposal.
21 May 1956	Bank Aide Memoire suggests that replacement facilities be financed by India.
May- Nov 1958	Disagreements over which storage facilities are "replacement," for which India would pay, and which are "development" for which Pakistan would be responsible.
May 1959	Black visits India and Pakistan. Suggests that India's share be a fixed cost, rather than by facility, and that the Bank would arrange for additional financing. India agrees, and accepts a 10-year transition period.
Sep 1960	Bank arranges an international Indus Basin Development Fund Agreement. Raises $893.5 million.
19 Sep 1960	Indus Water Treaty signed in Karachi. Provisions call for an Indian and Pakistani engineer to constitute the Permanent Indus Commission, which will meet at least once a year to: establish and promote cooperative arrangements.
29 Jul 2004	Talks about the Wuller barrage and Baglihar dam begin in Lahore. Pakistan indicates that it might seek World Bank arbitration if the matter is not sorted out through bilateral talks.

Acknowledgements

The map owes its appeal to the cartographic expertise of Sara Ashley Watterson, currently of Earthjustice, and Gretchen Bracher and Nathan Eidem, of Oregon State University.

References

Alam, U. (2002). Questioning the water wars rationale: a case study of the Indus Waters Treaty. *The Geographical Journal,* **168** (4), pp. 354-64.

Biswas, A. (1992). Indus Water Treaty: The Negotiating Process. *Water International,* **17**, (44), pp. 201- 209.

Caponera, D. (1987). International Water Resources Law in the Indus Basin. In *Water Resources Policy for Asia,* ed. M. Ali. Boston : Balkema (4), pp. 509-515.

Gleick, P.H., ed. *Water in Crisis. A Guide to the World's Fresh Water Resources,* New York : Oxford University Press, pp. 13-24.

Kulshreshtha, S.N. (1993). *World Water Resources and Regional Vulnerability: Impact of Future Changes.* RR-93-10, IIASA, Laxenburg, Austria.

Mehta, J. (1986). The Indus water treaty. In *The Management of International River Basin Conflicts,* ed. E. Vlachos, A. Webb and I. L. Murphy. Washington, DC : Graduate Program in Science, Technology, and Public Policy, George Washington University.

Transboundary Freshwater Dispute Database (TFDD) (2007). Oregon State University. Available on-line at:**http://www.transboundarywaters.orst.edu/**

United Nations. (1978). Register of international rivers, *Water Supply Management,* **2** (1). New York: Pergamon Press.

CHAPTER - 29

Indus Waters Treaty 1960: An Indian Perspective

Ramaswamy R Iyer

The Indus Waters Treaty is regarded internationally to be a successful instance of conflict-resolution between two countries that have otherwise been locked in mutual antagonism. That favorable view of the Treaty is by and large shared in India as well as in Pakistan, but there is a measure of dissatisfaction in both countries regarding matters of water allocation in the Treaty. Furthermore, the operation of the Treaty has been characterized by a series of differences. Should we regard it as a success or a failure?

The Treaty has settled the water-sharing dispute, and it has managed to survive four wars. In that sense it must be regarded as a success. Dividing the river system into two segments was perhaps not the best thing to do; the better course might have been for the two countries jointly to manage the entire system in an integrated and holistic manner. However, given the circumstances of Partition and the difficult relationship between the two newly formed countries, it would have been naïve to expect that such a joint, integrated, cooperative approach would work. If the best course is unavailable, then we have to settle for the second best – that is what the Treaty represents. The Treaty is essentially a partitioning agreement, not a grand instrument of inter-country cooperation. The land was partitioned in 1947, and the waters were partitioned in 1960.

Technical differences over projects

The water-sharing has been settled, but differences have continued to arise about certain design and engineering features of Indian projects on the western rivers. The Treaty allows India limited use of the waters of those rivers, but the use is subject to fairly stringent technical conditions and stipulations to safeguard Pakistan's interests. Thus, the Treaty is both permissive and restrictive toward Indian projects – particularly big projects – on the western rivers. India tries to use the permissive provisions to the fullest, whereas Pakistan tries to apply the restrictive provisions stringently. The two countries are thus pulling in two opposite directions. This leads to a permanent tug of war in the Indus Commission. As the lower riparian on the Indus system, Pakistan tends to look with anxious eyes at any attempts by India to build structures on the western rivers that may enable India either to reduce water flows or to release stored waters and cause floods. Pakistan's objections are thus partly water-related and partly security-related. The Indian position is that the security fears are misconceived because India cannot flood Pakistan without flooding itself first; that its capacity to reduce flows to Pakistan is very limited; and that the record of the last half-century gives no basis for any such apprehensions.

An important political dimension to these differences is that the projects are – or will be – located in Jammu and Kashmir. Pakistan can hardly be enthusiastic about facilitating Indian projects in what it regards as disputed territory.

Where do we go from here?

Abrogation of the Treaty, occasionally advocated by some, does not merit serious discussion. Should there be a renegotiation of the Treaty, as is often urged in both countries? It is difficult to envisage an outcome that would be better than before, from the points of view of both countries. Unfortunately, water-sharing is a zero-sum game: One side cannot increase its share without diminishing that of the other. The best course would perhaps be to leave things as they are and hope that, with improving political relations, a more reasonable and constructive spirit on both sides toward the operation of the Treaty will prevail in the future.

Until a few years ago, while there were arguments about certain Indian projects on the western rivers and their conformity to the provisions of the Indus Treaty, no one in Pakistan talked about water as being a major issue between their country and India. From early 2010 onwards, Pakistan has been projecting water as being a major issue between the two countries, indeed as a new "core issue" that is as important as Kashmir, if not more so.

Why has it decided to do so? We can only guess. Focusing public attention on the water issue may act as a powerful mobilizing factor and rally the people as a whole behind the government and/or the army. The government of Pakistan perhaps hopes to distract attention from bitter inter-provincial water-sharing disputes within its own country. Raising water as a new core issue may also be a counter move in response to the focus that India has been maintaining on terrorism.

The view seems to be widely held that if Pakistan faces a present or imminent water crisis, India is an important factor in that development. This could have a serious impact on India-Pakistan relations, even at the people-to-people level.

Some Pakistani concerns

Leaving aside popular misconceptions in Pakistan, let us take note of some of the concerns expressed in Track II meetings by thoughtful, well-informed members of Pakistani civil society and academia, including those who want good relations with India.

Popular perceptions or misperceptions about the diversion of water by India seem to receive unwitting corroboration in reported findings by Pakistani scholars of a trend of reduction in the flows in the western rivers. The tendency is to assume that the upper riparian must be responsible for that reduction. The only answer to this is to institute a joint study by experts from both countries to determine whether in fact flows in the western rivers have diminished, and if so, to identify the factors responsible.

Other popular beliefs in Pakistan are: that the Indus Waters Treaty never envisaged the construction of a large number of major projects by India on the western rivers; that what was intended to be a minor concession has been stretched by India unduly; and that because of this stretching, every Indian project on the western rivers is in violation of the Treaty. These accusations arise from a misreading of the Treaty, which clearly envisages major Indian projects on the western rivers, as documented by the massive annexes to the Treaty. So long as India conforms to the stringent restrictive provisions of the Treaty, it cannot be charged with stretching or violating the Treaty.

A third point on which much anxiety is expressed is the cumulative impact of a large number of projects on the western rivers. India might argue that if each project conforms to the Treaty, there can be no such thing as the "cumulative impact" of a large number of projects. However, Pakistani apprehensions on this score cannot be lightly dismissed. Many in India have been worried about the cumulative impact of a large number of hydroelectric projects on the Ganges River, and studies have been commissioned to address the issue. What applies to the Ganges applies equally to the Indus system. The issue needs to be carefully considered. Here again, a joint study by experts from both countries seems desirable.

In recent years, pleas have been made for a holistic, integrated management of the entire system, joint watershed management, etc. These are unexceptionable ideas, but a completely different "holistic" Treaty will have to wait for better times. Current concerns such as environmental impacts, minimum or ecological flows, etc., are as applicable to the Indus system as to other systems, and demands for them should not be brushed aside merely because the Indus Treaty did not foresee them. Presumably, environmental impact assessments are being made for each of the hydroelectric projects that are being planned on the western rivers. Environmental impacts do not stop at the border; a project on the Indian side can have impacts across the border, and a project on the Pakistani side – for instance the Neelum Jhelum hydroelectric project that Pakistan is planning – may have impacts on the Indian side of the border.

Conclusion: The Indus Waters Treaty in an age of climate change

Global climate change and its possible impact on water availability in the Indus river system are matters of vital concern, and the two countries must begin immediately to work together on these. There has already been a measure of cooperation between them during international negotiations on climate change, but this must go beyond the limited issue of emission reductions. This cannot be brought within the ambit of the Indus Waters Treaty but must be a separate exercise.

Summing up, agreed solutions can be found for the differences that have arisen during the course of operation of the Treaty, but they become difficult because of fluctuating political relations between the two countries. An improvement in those relations and the harmonious operation of the Treaty are interrelated, and each will facilitate the other. The newer emerging concerns that were not foreseen in 1960 – and in particular climate change and its impact on water resources – call for inter-country cooperation beyond the Treaty.

16 March 2014

CHAPTER - 30

Water Wars and Navigating Peace over Indus River Basin

By Abdul Rauif Iqbal
(National Defence University Islamabad)

Introduction

Water – a source of life - is threatened today because of extensive demographic growth, disordered urbanization, political actions and climatic changes etc. The human actions are, and their unpredictable behaviour is, regarded as water's primary enemy in most of the "hydropolitics" literature. States are confronted with numerous challenges in regard of water; the demand for water is ever-increasing and at the same time, supply of water is decreasing. This disparity in demand and supply of water is now a serious source of concern in the study of International Relations. When it comes to the waters that cross political boundaries, additional complexities arise and strain the relationship of riparian states.[1] Hence, sharing of transboundary water is an extremely difficult task and may create both conflict and cooperation among the states and same is the case with waters of Indus in South Asia.

South Asia –home of more than one-sixth of the world's population,[2] depends heavily on agriculture. Water in South Asia is not only vital for everyday needs, but also a critical resource for economic development.[3] The increasing demand for water has surpassed supply and led to increased competition, tension, and disputes among various economic sectors, provinces, and sovereign states.[4] The politics of water-sharing arrangements have complicated inter-state relationships in the region[5] as Peter Gleick has reported that ". . . one factor remains constant: the importance of water to life means that providing for water needs and demands will never be free of politics."[6]

Addressing the water disputes between Pakistan and India, both countries signed the Indus Waters Treaty (IWT) in 1960 under the mediation of the World Bank, which has survived three wars and other hostilities between the two nations. IWT is regarded as a remarkable example of conflict resolution and sets the path for future cooperation, as Stephen P. Cohen has observed that, "the Indus Waters Treaty is a model for future regional cooperation, especially on energy, environmental concerns, and even the management of the region's impressive water resources."[7] Yet, recent Indian intentions of building a chain of dams on Pakistani (western) rivers have once again brought the prospects of water conflicts among both countries. The recent stress and strain in the observance of the treaty has had many analysts believe that water-sharing will take a politically charged dynamic in the relations of two nuclear states.[8]

Aim of the Study

According to Elhance, hydro-politics is a systematic study of conflict and cooperation between states over water resources that transcend international borders.[9] The Indus water dispute is a burning issue between

Pakistan and India, as Pervaiz Iqbal Cheema concludes that "no dispute generated so much bitterness as did the one over the flow of waters."[10] Starting from the very quotation, this research intends to analyze the future prospects of the Indus by comparing both conflict and cooperation. The paper will start from discussing the importance of the Indus River Basin and will go on by assessing the potential of conflict and evaluates the avenues of cooperation.

Literature Review

The international and transborder characteristics of shared water bodies make them a compelling test case for the analysis of conflict and cooperation.[11] Scholars like Westing, Gleick, Homer- Dixon, Remans, and Samson and Charrier stress the dangers of violence over international waters while others including Libiszewski, Salman and de Chazournes, and Wolf argue more strongly for the possibilities[12] and historical evidences of cooperation between co-riparians.

Water is a resource vital to all aspects of a nation's survival and the scarcity of water leads to forceful political pressures, often referred to as "water stress," a term coined by Falkenmark.[13] Moreover, international law is equally obscure, vague and contradictory in terms of water which is a critical and non- substitutable resource.[14] May be on this premise, Ismail Serageldin, Vice President for Environmental Sustainable Development at the World Bank went on saying that "if the wars of this century were fought over oil, the wars of the next century will be fought over water."[15] Keeping in view the critical importance of water, it is banal to know that water is more often associated with war. Bulk of literature describes water as a future cause of interstate warfare. Westing suggested that "competition for limited fresh water leads to severe political tensions and even to war."[16] Gleick described water resources as military and political goals.[17] Remans used case studies from the Middle East, South America, and South Asia as "well known examples" of water as a cause of armed conflict.[18] Samson and Charrier wrote that "a number of conflicts linked to fresh water are already apparent" and suggested that a "growing conflict looms ahead."[19] Butts suggested that "history is replete with examples of violent conflict over water".[20] Finally, Homer-Dixon, came to the conclusion that "the renewable resource most likely to stimulate interstate resource war is river water."[21]

On the other hand, besides the hue and cry over water wars, there also exists an impressive history of water dispute resolution, in the academic literature. The Food and Agriculture Organization (FAO) of the United Nations has identified more than 3600 treaties relating to international water resources, dating from 1805, and a majority of these treaties deal with navigation.[23] Since 1814 about 300 international treaties have been negotiated to deal with non-navigational issues of water management including flood control, hydropower projects, and allocations for consumptive or non-consumptive uses in international basins. Water as a source of cooperation has been analyzed in a greater detail by Hamner and Wolf.[24]

The waters of the Indus daily find a special place in the leading newspapers of the region because of ongoing water problems. Hundreds of articles have been written on the Indus water issue but the dichotomy with the existing literature is that it is more of diverse in nature. Scholars have touched various aspects of the issue starting from economic importance,[25] technical problems,[26] climate change[27] and violation of the treaty[28] to potential of conflict,[29] legal aspects,[30] management[31] and mediation[32] factor. Contrary to the existing literature, this essay will employ both the theories of conflict and cooperation in order to analyze the future prospects of the Indus and tries to locate the avenues of peace.

Indus Waters – A Lifeline for Pakistan

The northwestern part of South Asia is dominated by the Indus Basin. The Indus River originates near Mount Kailash Range in Tibet and thereafter it flows to the West, eventually running into the Arabian Sea.[33] The total area of the Indus basin, the area draining the Himalayan water into the Arabian Sea, is about

365,000 square miles.[34] With its source at 5,100 metres elevation in south-west of Tibet, it extends to Tibet, Afghanistan and India.[35] Afterwards, it enters into Pakistan in north-western Baltistan, crossing from east to west over Indian Ladakh.

Flowing for about 1,800 miles within Pakistan, Indus could be associated as the life-blood of the country – which could not function without the support of this mighty river.[36] The watershed area of the Indus outside Pakistan is largely in the arid upland cold desert with a sparse human population while the story is quite different within Pakistan territory, where the Indus is known to have given birth to one of the man's earliest recorded civilizations.[37]

The Indus basin mainly involves two countries – Pakistan and India. In Pakistan, the alluvial plains of the Indus basin cover approximately 25 percent of the land area of Pakistan, with Punjab and Sind the most agriculturally important provinces.[38] In India, the basin includes only 9.8 percent of the total geographical area of the country. On the Indian side, the upper part of the basin involves Jammu & Kashmir and Himachel Prdesh, while the lower part covers the area of Punjab, Haryana and Rajasthan.[39]

Dispute over Indus Waters – A Historical Background

Given the territorial limits of the basin, it is unsurprising that the division of this basin has become a source of significant controversy. The dispute over Indus waters started in the form of inter-state differences before the partition of the subcontinent. But after the independence in 1947, the dispute became an international issue between Pakistan and India. In this sense, the region's defining event was a 'hasty, unimaginative and surgical partition' of the British India.[40] After the partition, the political boundary between the two states was drawn right across the Indus Basin. It left Pakistan as the lower riparian while making India as the upper riparian. Adding insult to injury most of the headwaters went to the Indian and thus leaving Pakistan as the more vulnerable state. India was therefore given the physical capacity to cut off vital irrigation water from large and valuable tracts of agriculture land in Pakistan[41].

The water dispute between the newly born states surfaced in April 1948, when India closed the canals on the eastern rivers of Ravi and Sutlej, only agreeing to reopen them after the Inter Dominion Agreement of May 1948, where it claimed the entire water of eastern rivers[42]. This was only a provisional agreement and the Indus Water Treaty (IWT) was finally negotiated between India and Pakistan in 1960 under the mediation of the World Bank. This gave Pakistan the western rivers (Chenab, Jhelum and Indus) and India, the eastern rivers (Beas, Sutlej and Ravi). Some restrictions were also imposed on the Indian capacity to modify the flow of western rivers as she was the upper riparian for even these rivers.

Indus Water Treaty (IWT)

The signing of the Indus Waters Treaty (IWT) in 1960 was no doubt a 'remarkable achievement'.[43] It brought to an end the long standing dispute between India and Pakistan. This treaty was culminated through a long period of negotiation under the mediation of the World Bank. The primary objective of IWT was to fix and delimit the rights and obligations of each country's use of waters in relation to other.[44] The water sharing under this treaty was quite simple:-

- The three western rivers (Chenab, Jhelum and Indus) were allocated to Pakistan, and India was given the full control of three eastern rivers (Beas, Sutlej and Ravi).

- India was not allowed to build storages on the western rivers except to a very limited extent.

- Restrictions were also imposed on the extension of irrigation development in India.

- There were also provisions regarding the exchange of data on project operation, extent of irrigated agriculture, and so on.

The treaty further mandated certain institutional arrangements:-

- There was to be a permanent Indus Commission consisting of a Commissioner each for Pakistan and for India, and there were to be periodical meetings and exchanges of visits.

- Provisions were included for the resolution of the differences that might arise.[45]

- The treaty also included the provision of international financial assistance to Pakistan for the development of irrigation works for utilizing the waters of western rivers.

Recent Stress & Strain in Observance of IWT

IWT survived in the midst of wars and border clashes but at present, a bitter dispute over limited water resources is stimulating Pakistan-India tensions. Water is a longstanding feud that has worsened in recent months as India is planning to build new dams on Pakistani (western) riveres. Under the IWT, India was granted limited use of Pakistan's rivers for agricultural purposes and the right to build hydroelectric dams, provided they don't store or divert large amounts of water. Contrary to it, India is building a chain of dams in clear violation of the treaty with the storage and diversion capability.

The "dams fever" of India has gripped the region with suspicions, trust deficit and hostility as India has a history of water conflicts with almost all its neighbours.[46] Forgoing in view, it is quite obvious that Pakistan is very much concerned with the Indian projects on western rivers. Further, Pakistan has become one of the driest countries in the world because of the recent shortages of water. Islamabad criticizes Indian dams which have enabled India either to reduce water flows to Pakistan or to release stored waters and cause floods. While the Indian officials blame any reduction in water to the climate change and denies any intention to cut off Pakistani waters. The Indian ambassador to Pakistan, Sharat Sabharwal, went on saying that "preposterous and completely unwarranted allegations of stealing water and waging a water war are being made against India."[47] But it is quite obvious that India has gained a somewhat physical capacity of storage and diversion on western rivers.

Pakistani objections are related with the availability and security of the water but the Indian position is different to that of Pakistan, as Shamsul Mulk said that "if he has the capacity to hurt me, the best that can be said about him is that he will use it for blackmailing and the worst is that he will use it to harm me."[48] Whatever the reality is, the recent stress and strain in the observance of IWT have had many analysts believe that water sharing will take a politically charged dynamic in the relations of the two nuclear rival states.[49]

Indian Projects and their Implications for Pakistan

A critical analysis of the Indian measures shows that India's needs for water and yearns for hydro electricity have grown over the period of time. Its greed has reached to an extent that it feels no problem in depriving Pakistan from its due share of water from the western rivers. Although India was granted limited rights over the western rivers yet, unfortunately, it is exceeding from its share in clear violation of the treaty. Also, India has become the third country in the world in dam building, after United States and China and instigated numerous projects on the Pakistani rivers in the Indian Held Kashmir (IHK) including five large ones.[50] India is not only limiting itself to IHK but has also succeeded in constructing a dam on River Kabul, a tributary of River Indus. It is setting up *Kama* hydroelectric project on River Kabul in Afghanistan which will have serious repercussions on the water flow in the Indus. Some Indian projects and their possible implications for Pakistan are discussed below.

- **Wullar Barrage:** In 1984, India started the construction of Tulbul Navigational Project (Wullar Barrage) near *Sopor*, 25 kilometers north of Srinagar in IHK, on the river Jhelum, involving the construction of a barrage with a storage capacity of 0.3 million acre feet (MAF) and planned power generation of 960 Megawatt (MW).[51] After much resistance from Pakistan, it was halted in 1987. Pakistan protested terming it a clear violation of Article 1 (11) and Article 3(8) of IWT. The strategic significance of the site lies in the fact that its possession provides India with the means to intimidate Pakistan, as a dam there has the potential to ruin the entire triple canal project (namely, Upper Jhelum Canal, Upper Chenab Canal and Lower Bari Doab Canal) and also enable India to reduce water inflow in Mangla Dam during dry season.[52] After a series of unsuccessful discussions, Pakistan threatened to take the case to the International Arbitral Court. India stopped the works on the project thereafter and the project is still lying redundant.[53] The barrage is located at the outfall of Wullar Lake, having a length of 439 feet with a gated weir, under-sluices and a 12 meter wide navigation lock.[54] Under the provisions of IWT, India is not allowed to build any storage on the main river (Jhelum) except for 0.75 MAF (Annexure D of IWT) of storage on the tributaries of river Jhelum and 0.01 MAF incidental to a barrage by virtue of paragraph 8(h) of Annexure E which clearly states that "storage incidental to a barrage on the Jhelum Main not exceeding 10,000 acre feet'.[55] By virtue of paragraph 9, India is permitted to construct on the Jhelum Main such works which it deems necessary for flood control of River Jhelum and complete any works which were under construction on the effective Date (date on which IWT took effect). However, such a concession predicated on the condition that no storage is constructed on the Jhelum Main and instead the storage is constructed in side valleys depression and lakes. It is also stipulated that the stored waters would be released and returned to the Jhelum Main lower down soon after the flood recedes with the exception of those waters held in lakes, borrow-pits and natural depressions.

- **Kishanganga Project:** The proposed Kishanganga Project is located in IHK at river Neelum. The original design envisaged the construction of 268 meter long and 75.48 meter high concrete dam with a reservoir capacity of 0.18 MAF and power storage of 0.14 MAF. The stored water of River Kishanganga is to be diverted through a 22 km long tunnel to produce power of 330 MW. The water after the production of power is to join the Wullar Lake. Pakistan has objected to the project terming it a violation of IWT. It has been reported that India has almost completed the 22 km tunnel to divert Kishanganga (Neelum) waters to Wullar Lake in violation of the Indus Waters Treaty and is working to complete the 330 MW project by 2016.[56] If completed, the project would severely affect Pakistan's rights over the river, reduce the river flows into Pakistan and minimize its power generation capacity of the 969 MW Neelum Jhelum Hydropower project near Muzaffarabad in Azad Kashmir. Pakistan raised objections on two accounts; first, the design criteria of the project and secondly, the diversion of flow of one tributary to another is not allowed in IWT. In addition, this is likely to harm Pakistan's power potential, as Pakistan has already started constructing Neelum Jhelum HEP in Azad Kashmir. The issue had been on the agenda of the Permanent Indus Commission for more than eight years and now Pakistan has finally decided to approach the International Court of Arbitration against the construction of the controversial Kishanganga Hydropower Project and has formed a team of legal experts to fight the case.[57]

- **Baglihar Hydropower Project:** Baglihar Hydroelectric Plant is a run-of- the river project being constructed by India on river Chenab. Under the IWT, India is allowed to construct run-of- the river hydroelectric plants on western rivers, subject to the provisions of the treaty. The design of the plant should be in accordance with the criteria provided in paragraph 8 of Annexure D to the treaty. This project involves construction of 144.5 m high concrete gravity dam on Chenab River, 90 km north of Jammu and upstream of Salal Dam, and q power generation capacity of 450 MW in its first stage. Pakistan raised a number of objections on the design parameters of the dam which were found in clear violation of the IWT. The dispute, after years of unsuccessful talks, was referred to the World Bank, which appointed neutral expert, a Swiss civil engineer, Professor Raymond Lafitte, who gave his decision in Feb 2007. The decision asked India to make necessary amendments in design parameter on three out of four major technical objections raised by Pakistan.[58] It is believed that minor changes in design parameters will not make a considerable difference to the initial design, however, will cost India billions of extra rupees and delay in completion of project. Both countries have termed Latiffe's ruling as their victory as *The News* reported that "the common people found it strange as to how a ruling could simultaneously satisfy two conflicting claims".[59] Experts are of the view that the Baglihar dam will have major security and economic implications for Pakistan owing to increased Indian control over its share of water supplies, as the project will tap around 7000 cusecs of water for irrigation purpose in the short term.[60] Further, India can use water as a weapon as she has got the capability to manipulate the flow of water and also, the project can lead to the inundation of the area above the Marala Head Works due to the sudden synchronized releases from Dul-Hasti, Baghlihar and Salal reservoirs.

Reasons of Differences

Differences are arising from different approaches to, and interpretations of, various provisions of the main text of the IWT.[61] The detailed provisions and specifications given in several Annexures and Appendices of the treaty further pave the way of differences. Critical evaluations of the recent tensions show that there are following major problems which pave the way for differences:-

- IWT is a highly technical treaty and dense technical details provide ample opportunities for differences, among both sides of engineers.

- Environmental issues like climate change and global warming have not been covered in the treaty and India links the reduction of water in western rivers with climatic change.

- The treaty has divided eastern and western rivers between India and Pakistan. Although both countries have got exclusive rights on three rivers each, yet Pakistan lost the lower riparian rights on eastern rivers under the treaty.

Hydro-Environment of Pakistan

Pakistan, one of the world's most arid countries, with an average rainfall of under 240 mm a year is heavily dependent on an annual influx into the Indus River system – of which about 180 billion cubic meters of water of the system emanates from the neighboring country and is mostly derived from snow-melt in the Himalayas.[62] This hydraulic economy of Pakistan faced massive challenges right from the independence of the country in 1947. At present, major challenges emanating from the availability of water in Pakistan are:-

- **Water Scarcity.** Pakistan is one of the most water-stressed countries in the world. The situation is going towards the worst water scarcity scenario due to Indian obstruction of the western rivers' water, he population growth and climate change.

- **A high risk water environment.** Pakistan is dependent on a single river basin i.e. Indus River. This dependence on a single river system means it has little of the strength that most countries enjoy by virtue of having a multiplicity of river basins and diversity of water resources.[63]

Prospects of Conflict

The summer's catastrophic floods of 2010 in Pakistan have affected about 20 million of the population and it is constantly inundating into new parts of the country and thus causing a humanitarian disaster.[64] The people living near the banks of the Indus have been seriously affected and the flood has caused deaths, injuries, diseases and displacements in Balochistan, Khyber Pakhtunkhwa, Punjab and Sind. According to the United Nations, the number of people suffering from the massive floods in Pakistan could exceed the combined total in three recent mega disasters: the 2004 Indian Ocean tsunami, the 2005 Kashmir earthquake and the 2010 Haiti earthquake.[65] At this juncture, when a huge area of Pakistan is covered with the flood water, probably it seems very odd to talk about the scarcity of water. But one needs to really understand two important points. Firstly, the flood water is of no use at all; rather, it is a curse which has demolished the prosperous lives of hundreds of families and caused damage to the economy worth billions of dollars. Secondly, when the flood water will eventually fall into the Arabian Sea and the Indus River would calm down, people would be again suffering from the water shortage as it was the situation before the flood.

In fact, water in Pakistan is increasingly becoming a scarce commodity due to Indian hitching of western rivers, increasing population pressures, intensive irrigation and erratic weather patterns. Water scarcity is related with the availability of water, which is measured in cubic meters per capita per year and according to the World Bank, Pakistan became a water-stressed country (1,700 cubic meters per capita per year) around the year 2000.[66] While the government sources project that Pakistan became a water-short country in 1992 (1,700 m^3) and then declined further to 1,500 m^3 in water scarcity (1,000 m^3 per capita per year of renewable supply is expected in about 2035).[68] However, a United Nations Development Programme source gives Pakistan's current water availability as 1,090 m^3 per capita per year.[69] This is because the terms 'water shortage' and 'water scarcity' are often used interchangeably, while both use the 1,000 m^3 per capita per year as a benchmark. It is pertinent to mention that 'shortage' is an absolute term and 'scarcity' is a relative concept.

Given the Indian capacity, water scarcity and the high risk water environment of Pakistan, one can easily conclude that the future wars of South Asia would be on water as numerous scholars have already concluded. Both are nuclear states and possess a rivalry record right from the independence. A US based environmental action group, NRDC (Natural Resources Defense Council) has conducted analysis of the consequences of nuclear war in South Asia and has produced far more horrific results.[70] May be, the water war theorists have no time to go through such reports and also the hawks from both sides find their reports as a holy version for future. They used to project the conflicting news without understanding the dire consequences of conflict between the two states.

Prospects of Cooperation

A critical evaluation of the Indus water dispute reveals that the prospects of conflict are there because both governments seek to control the rivers of their region as tangible solutions to the most of the economic problems.[71] This desire to control the rivers through national visions, covert appropriation and bilateral bargaining is a pathway to conflict. Contrary to this view, a good number of scholars, officials and politicians in South Asia believe that the region's rivers can be better harnessed in support of economic development.[72] As George Verghese has written that "there is no reason why the immiserised population of this resource rich Basin should remain poor and hostage to a recurring cycle of devastating flood and drought."[73] This link between water and development can be fully harnessed by removing conflicts over water. It also shows that cooperation is the only viable option, as water is so important that nations cannot afford to fight over it. Rather, water injects interdependence by joint management of shared water resources; it promotes trust and prevents conflict.[74]

Water war scholars suggest prospects of war on the basis of scarcity but one has to also look upon the other side of the story. It is true that water is increasingly emerging as a scarce commodity and one third of world's population will lack access of water by 2025.[75] But it does not mean that scarcity always leads to conflict. Besides the conflicting patterns, a ray of hope still exists which can lead to the avenues of further cooperation. At the global level, two thirds of the time, cooperation occurs over shared waters and the same can happen over Indus waters. In fact there are solutions for the dispute, but immense resistance to adopting them.[76] One has to understand the fact that no country would run out of water but providing water will have to become a more careful process.[77] When it comes to the shared waters, it is a fact that water itself does not respect political boundaries, but the governments used man-made borders to protect their sovereignty, economies and nationalities.[78] Because of the waters crossing the international borders, unilateral and inefficient management of shared waters often exacerbates tensions.[79] But violence over water, though not uncommon, is not a strategically rational, effective or economically viable option for countries.[80] History bears witness to the fact that cooperation, not conflict, is the most logical response to trans-boundary water management issues.[81] Cooperation over waters starts from acknowledging that water is at the centre of everything and it is not 'lost' from Earth,[82] but it is often moved from where it is needed, as its movement is essential for life.[83] Also, when shortages pinch, states do cooperate and compromise because no one can do anything without water.[84]

Coming over to Indus waters, Pakistan and India possess a long history of rivalry, starting from Kashmir to the present water dispute. And the hawks on both sides are attempting to use water to create an insurmountable impasse in the dispute over Kashmir.[85] Some experts are of the view that water will be the most potent political weapon by which India will 'screw' Pakistan.[86] On the other hand, some also suggest that sharing of waters forms a framework for the two enemies to cooperate.[87] Significance of water resources leads to the politicization of the issue and eventually increases tensions. This results in irrational actions by national governments due to domestic political pressures, which, in turn, may have an adverse impact on international water-sharing agreements and their resolution.[88] But the policy-makers have to understand that they cannot solve a very complex geographical, hydrological, economic and environmental problem through politicizing the issue. It is true that India has brought Pakistan on the brink of mass starvation and the tactic of turning it into a desert has begun by shrinking water availability from 5000 cubic meters per capita in 1950s to 1000 cubic meters in 2010.[89] Meanwhile, India's long term energy requirements are also linked with Pakistan and it cannot fulfill its development goals without having transit facilities through Pakistan for oil and gas pipelines from Iran and Central Asia. As the concept of security now covers assured access to both water and energy resources, this demands a virtual transformation of Pakistan-India relations from one of confrontation to that of cooperation.[90] Increased cooperation between India and Pakistan would promote regional stability, help control the nuclear arms race, and make an end to the Kashmir conflict more likely.

Policy Recommendations

Gaining cooperation is not an easy job. It requires commitments and so many policy decisions from both sides. Some of the policy recommendations for avenues of peace are given below:-

- Cooperation over water is likely to happen when the parties see shared benefits.

- Pakistan should highlight the importance of the issue on various international forums. Merely passing political statements will not resolve the problem.

- Indian intentions and needs should be distinguished on quantitative terms to highlight the real face of India among the international community.

- The treaty does not provide so many important issues like the availability of water, the effects of climate change and proportional increase or decrease of water in quantitative terms. Pakistan should look for a proper strategic forum for deliberative discussions and policy options for these issues.

- At present, renegotiating the treaty seems impossible and Pakistan has to relook its water policy in the given limits of the treaty. Therefore, an effective role of the Indus Water Commissioners is the need of the hour.

- Interstate conflicts can be managed through internal strength and same is the case with water conflicts. Pakistani policy makers should understand the concept of conflict resolution, and initiatives

- must be taken on capacity building, as no one can compel any sovereign state (India or Pakistan) to act on morality alone.
- There is a serious need to work on water management as the available water is being wasted and the groundwater table is going lower and lower.

Conclusion

Pakistan has become a 'water stressed' country and has reached the limit of 1000 cubic meters per person per year. If the situation becomes worse, serious economic and social consequences are likely. Indian's violation of the treaty is not only a security and economic concern for Pakistan but also can pose serious implications on the region's overall security as both states possess nuclear arms. Although, chances of direct violence exist because of the hawkish elements on both sides but it can be avoided through effective implementation of the treaty. Both sides have to understand the fact that cooperation is the only way to survive as water is a necessity for the development of both countries. Further, inability to resolve water issues will limit the ability of both countries to manage and utilize water resources in the most efficient manner. One can hope for peace but unless the basic cause is removed, a nuclear war in South Asia cannot be ruled out.

Notes:

1. Aaron T. Wolf etal., "International River Basins of the World", *International Journal of Water Resources Development*, Vol. 15 No. 4, December 1999.
2. Mukand S. Babel and Shahriar M. Wahid, *Freshwater under Threat: South Asia*, (Nairobi: United Nations Environment Programme, 2008), pp. XI.
3. Hamir K. Sahni, "The Politics of Water in South Asia: The Case of Indus Waters Treaty", *SAIS Review*, vol. XXVI no. 2, (Summer-Fall 2006), pp. 155.
4. Salman M.A. Salman and Laurence Boisson de Chazournes, ed., *International Watercourses: Enhancing Cooperation and Managing Conflict*, Proceedings of a World Bank Seminar, World Bank Technical Paper No. 414,1998, pp. 167.
5. B.C. Upreti, *Politics of Himalayan River Waters: An Analysis of the River. Water Issues of Nepal, India and Bangladesh* (Jaipur, New Delhi: Nirala Publications, 1993), Foreword.
6. Peter H. Gleick, *Water Conflict Chronology*, Pacific Institute, December 2004, available online at *http://www.worldwater.org/chronology.html*.
7. Stephen P. Cohen, "The US and South Asia," *Seminar*, No. 545, January 2005, pp. 6.
8. Pervaiz Iqbal Cheema, "Pak-India Water Disputes", *The Post*, 26 February 2006.
9. A. Elhance, Hydropolitics in the 3rd World: Conflict and Cooperation in International River Basins, (Washington DC: United States Institute of Peace Press), 1999, pp.3.
10. Pervaiz Iqbal Cheema, *Op. cit.*
11. Ariel Dinar, Shlomi Dinar and Stephen McCaffrey, Bridges over Water: Understanding Transboundary Water Conflict, Negotiation and Cooperation, (Singapore: World Scientific Publishing Company, 2007), pp. 153.
12. A. Wolf and J. Hamner, A., "Patterns in International Water Resource Treaties: The Transboundary Freshwater Dispute Database", *Colorado Journal of International Environmental Law and Policy*, 1997 Yearbook.
13. M. Falkenmark, "Fresh waters as a factor in strategic policy and action", in A.H. Westing, ed., *Global Resources and International Conflict: Environmental Factors in Strategic Policy and Action*, (New York: Oxford University Press, 1986) pp. 85–113.
14. As described in more detail in Wolf 1997.
15. "Severe Water Crisis Ahead for Poorest Nations", *The New York Times*, 10 August 1995.
16. M. Falkenmark, "Fresh waters as a factor in strategic policy and action", pp. 85–113.
17. P. Gleick, "Water and Conflict: Fresh Water Resources and International Security", *International Security*, 18(1), 1993, pp.79–112.
18. W. Remans, "Water and War", *Humantares Volkerrecht*, 8(1), 1995.
19. P. Samson and B. Charrier, "International freshwater conflict: issues and prevention strategies", *Green Cross Draft Report*, May 1997.
20. Kent Butts, "The Strategic Importance of Water", *Parameters*, Spring 1997, pp. 65-83.
21. Thomas Homer-Dixon, "Environmental Scarcities and Violent Conflict", *International Security*, Summer 1994.
22. FAO (Food and Agriculture Organization of the United Nations), *Systematic Index of International Water Resources Treaties, Declarations, Acts and Cases, by Basin*, vol. 1, Legislative Study 15, 1978.

23 FAO (Food and Agriculture Organization of the United Nations), *Systematic Index of International Water Resources Treaties, Declarations, Acts and Cases, by Basin*, vol. 2, Legislative Study 34, 1984.
24 A. Wolf and J. Hamner, A., *Op. cit.*
25 Douglas Hill, "The Politics of Water in South Asia", *Transforming Cultures e Journal*, Vol. 1 No. 2, June 2006.
26 Ramaswamy R Iyer, "Indus Treaty: A Different View", *Economic and Political Weekly*, vol. 11, no. 29, 16 July 2005
27 B. G. Verghese, "Talking of Abrogating Indus Water Treaty; Misconceived Facts, Fallacious Arguments", *The Tribune*, 29 April 2002.
28 S. Waslekar, *The Final Settlement: Restructuring India-Pakistan Relations* (Mumbai: Strategic Foresight Group, 2005)
29 Robert G. Wirsing and Christopher Jasparro, "Spotlight on Indus River Diplomacy: India, Pakistan, and the Baglihar dam dispute", *Asia-Pacific Center for Security Studies*, May 2006.
30 Salman M.A. Salman and Kishor Uperty, *Conflict and Cooperation on South Asia's International Rivers: A legal Perspective*, World Bank Report, January 2003.
31 John Briscoe and Usman Qamar, *Pakistan's Water Economy: Running Dry*, (Oxford and The World Bank: November 2005).
32 Hamir K. Sahni, "The Politics of Water in South Asia: The Case of Indus Waters Treaty", *SAIS Review*, vol. XXVI no. 2, Summer-Fall 2006.
33 Douglas Hill, "The Politics of Water in South Asia", *Transforming Cultures e Journal*, Vol. 1 No. 2, June 2006
34 Mohammad Arif Khan, "The Effective Interface of Irrigation Water from the Tarraa Dam Project and the Nature Resources of the Central Indus Watershed", (MS Agricultural Engineering diss., Texas Tech University, Texas, 1972)
35 WWF Pakistan, "Study of Riverine forest upstream Sukkur and downstream Kotri – 2008", (Lahore: WWF, 2008), 24.
36 Government of Pakistan, *Pakistan: An Official Handbook*, (Islamabad: Ministry of Information and Broadcasting), 1988.
37 Tom Roberts, "The Indus – life-blood of Pakistan", *Asian Affairs*, vol. 36, no. I, March 200, pp. 1.
38 Executive Summary, World Commission on Dams, *Pakistan: The Tarbela Dam and Indus River Basin,* November 2000, available at www.dams.org/kbase/studies/pk/pk-exec.htm accessed on 26 May 2010.
39 Douglas Hill, *Op. cit.*
40 Pervaiz Iqbal Cheema, *Op. cit.*
41 Chaudhri Muhammad Ali, *The Emergence of Pakistan*, (New York: Columbia University Press, 1967) pp. 318-319
42 H. Gazdar, "Baglihar and Politics of Water", *Economic and Political Weekly*, 26 February 2005
43 Salman M.A. Salman and Kishor Uperty, *Op. cit.*, pp. 37.
44 Ibid., p. 48.
45 Questions, if any arose, were to be resolved within the commission; if agreement could not be reached at the commission level, the matter was to be referred to the two governments; if they too failed to reach an agreement, the 'question' would become a 'difference' to be referred to a Neutral Expert (NE). The NE's findings on the differences referred to him would be final and binding. If the NE decided that the matter was in fact a 'dispute', it would have to go to a Court of Arbitration.
46 "Indian water aggression: Pakistan on brink of disaster", *The Nation*, 12 February 2010.
47 "Water dispute fuels India-Pakistan tensions", *DAWN*, 30 April 2010.
48 Ibid.
49 Pervaiz Iqbal Cheema, *Op. cit.*
50 Mohammed Arifeen, "Indian dams to spur regional chaos", *The Financial Daily*, 24 Aug 2010.
51 Priyanka Mallik, "Tulbul: The Politics of Water between India and Pakistan", *IPCS Articles # 2055*, (New Delhi: Institute of Peace and Conflict Studies), 30 June 2006.
52 "Wullar Barrage/Tulbul Navigation Project", *The Times of India*, 29 July 2004. 53 Farzana Noshab and Nadia Mushtaq, "Water Disputes In South Asia", The *Institute of Strategic Studies, Islamabad* http://www.issi.org.pk/journal/2001_files/no_3/article/4a.htm (accessed on 15 Aug 10)
54 Engr. Usman-e-Ghani, "Coping with Water Scarcity and the Indus Waters Treaty Vision", *World Water Day March 2007 Report*, pp.51.
55 For details see Annexure D and E of IWT.
56 Khaleeq Kiani, "Pakistan to move arbitration court on Kishanganga project", *DAWN*, 03 May 2010.
57 Ibid.
58 Prof. Raymond Lafitte, "Baglihar Hydroelectric Project Expert Determination – Executive Summary", (Lausanne: World Bank, 2007), pp. 18.
59 Adnan Adil, "A Win-Win Verdict", *The News*, 04 March 2007.
60 Syed Shahid Husain, "Pakistan's Perspective: The Baglihar Project", *South Asian Journal* 8 (April-June 2005), pp. 35.
61 Ramaswamy R Iyer, "Indus Treaty: A Different View", available at http://www.upscportal.com/civilservices/blog/Indus-Treaty-Ramaswamy-R-Iyer accessed on 14 April 2009.
62 John Briscoe and Usman Qamar, *Op. cit.*, pp. xiii.
63 For example, India might be able to muddle through because it has many rivers and if something goes wrong in one place, the effect is cushioned by opportunities in other places; this is a luxury which Pakistan does not have.
64 Griff Witte, "Pakistan floods affecting 20 million; cholera outbreak feared", *The Washington Post*, 15 August 2010.
65 "Pakistan flood crisis bigger than tsunami, Haiti: UN", *Dawn*, 09 August 2010.
66 John Briscoe and Usman Qamar, *Op. cit.*
67 "Population Stabilization, a Priority for Development," United Nations Population Fund/Ministry of Population Welfare, Government of Pakistan, undated.

68 *Pakistan's Water Economy: Running Dry.*
69 *Economic Survey of Pakistan, 2007-2008*, and *Global Human Development Report 2007*, quoted on UNDP website, www.undp.org.pk.
70 "The Consequences of Nuclear Conflict between India and Pakistan", (New York: Natural Resources Defense Council), available online at http://www.nrdc.org/nuclear/southasia.asp (access date 26 August 2010).
71 Ben Crow and Nirvikar Singh, "Impediments and Innovation in International Rivers: The Waters of South Asia", (06 October 1999), pp. 3.
72 Ibid. pp. 3.
73 B.G. Verghese, *Waters of Hope: Himalaya-Ganga Development and Cooperation for a Billion People*, (New Delhi: Oxford and IBH Publishing, 1990).
74 Aaron T. Wolf etal, "Water can be a Pathway to Peace, not War", Navigating Peace, No. 1 July 2006 (Washington: Woodrow Wilson International Centre for Scholars).
75 IWMI, *Water Policy Briefing*, Issue 23, (Colombo: International Water Management Institute, 2006), pp.1.
76 Alexander Bell, "World at War over Water", *The New Statesman*, 28 March 2010.
77 Ibid.
78 United Nations, "Conflicts over water have potential to be catalysts for peace, cooperation", *Press Release*, United Nations, 06 November 2009.
79 Ibid.
80 Dr Summaiya Syed Tariq, "World Water Day: Transboundry Waters", *Dawn*, 23 March 2009.
81 Ibid.
82 Juliette Jowit, "Is Water the New Oil?", *The Guardian*, 02 November 2008.
83 Ibid.
84 Ibid.
85 Jason Overdorf, "The Coming War for Water", *The Global Post*, 21 September 2009.
86 Ibid.
87 Hamir K. Sahni, "The Politics of Water in South Asia: The Case of Indus Waters Treaty", pp. 156.
88 Ibid. pp. 157.
89 "Water Problems: Alliance with friendly countries needed: Shamsul Mulk", *Daily Times*, 26 March 2010.
90 Maqbool Ahmed Bhatty, "Energy, Water issues in South Asia", *Dawn*, 26 February 2007.

CHAPTER - 31

Pakistan's Relations With India: Beyond Kashmir

Asia report No. 224 – 3 May, 2012

Water And Energy

The Indus River Basin consists of six shared rivers: Beas, Chenab, Jhelum, Ravi, Sutlej and the Indus. Water distribution between Pakistan and India through these rivers is governed by the Indus Basin Waters Treaty of 1960 (IWT), which gives control of the Indus, Chenab and Jhelum to Pakistan and the remaining three to India. The lower riparian, Pakistan, has access to 80 per cent of the water in the Indus River system while India can use some of the water for farming, drinking and power generation, provided that this does not reduce or delay Pakistan's supply. While the treaty has survived three wars, it has recently been under strain, because of Pakistan's increased needs for agriculture, which accounts for 23 per cent of its GDP, and India's increasing use of the shared waters. Pursuing hydropower development to meet the demands of a growing economy, a steadily expanding population and mushrooming energy requirements, India is constructing as many as 33 multi-purpose dams in the Indus River Basin. The most contentious include the Wullar Barrage (also known as the Tulbul Navigation Project), the Kishanganga hydroelectric project and the Baglihar dam.

In 1984, India began construction on a barrage on Wullar Lake in J&K's Baramulla district to make the Jhelum River navigable all year. Pakistan complained that any attempt to block the Jhelum would violate the IWT. While India suspended construction in 1987, it still claims the right to build the barrage but is prepared to negotiate with Pakistan on changes to its design and structure. Pakistan, however, continues to oppose the Wullar Barrage and any other project that may result in Indian control over waters allocated to it under the IWT. This includes the Kishanganga hydroelectric project, which, Pakistan alleges, will divert the waters of the Neelum River (where Pakistan is working on the Neelum-Jhelum hydropower project) to the Wullar lake, and the Baglihar dam on the Chenab, whose design Pakistan believes breaches the IWT because it could restrict the Chenab's flow into Pakistan. This disagreement led Pakistan to submit its case to a neutral adjudicator appointed by the World Bank under the IWT, who in 2007 concluded that India's construction of the dam was consistent with the IWT but required minor structural modifications, a ruling that Pakistan accepted. Prime Minister Gilani's government is also considering going to the International Court of Arbitration to prevent India's construction of the Nimoo-Bazgo hydropower project on the Suru River (a tributary of the Indus) in Kargil, because it could curtail Indus River flows to Pakistan. Water from the Indus is more necessary than that of any other river, because of its central role for the agricultural sector, supplying the world's largest contiguous irrigation system, which covers 83 per cent of the country's cultivated land and contributes to almost a quarter of its GDP. Pakistan's concerns about the potential depletion of its lower riparian water resources are justifiable. According to a February 2011 report by the U.S. Senate Foreign Relations Committee, while no single Indian dam would affect Pakistan's IWT-guaranteed access to water, "the cumulative effect of these projects could give India the ability to store enough water to limit the supply to Pakistan at crucial moments in the growing season". The report stressed that any future reductions in water flow would magnify mistrust between Pakistan and India, potentially imperilling the IWT. With India's population expected to reach 1.5 billion by 2035, the demand for water is rising, but management of the resource remains "extremely decentralised and virtually unregulated". In Pakistan, economists and water experts warn that increasing scarcity, stemming in part from "the inherent limitations of water supply in the Indus [R]iver system" and partly from "the growing water demand associated with inefficient water use in the process of economic and population growth", is assuming grave proportions. They believe that water disputes with India could provoke a crisis and even, in the extreme, military conflict.

Indian observers believe that water disputes are rapidly becoming the "core issue" in the "Pakistani establishment's narrative about bilateral problems". Some Pakistanis concur, with a political analyst emphasising that water issues are already becoming "another Kashmir-like rallying point for Pakistani jihadis". There is sufficient evidence for such concern. For instance, LeT/JD has held major rallies countrywide, accusing India of a "water war" against Pakistan and calling upon Islamabad to take "practical steps" to counter its "deep conspiracy of making Pakistan's agricultural lands barren and economically annihilating us". In India, too, according to a senior cabinet member, opponents of peace with Pakistan could use water disputes to disrupt bilateral ties. These spoilers would even want the IWT scrapped altogether, since they contend that 80 per cent of the Indus system has been "given away" to Pakistan.Improved economic ties and the resultant easing of tensions would provide a more conducive environment to work toward resolving water disputes. The IWT's Article VII calls on the signatories to "recognise that they have a common interest in the optimum development of the rivers, and to that extent, they declare their intention to cooperate, by mutual agreement, to the fullest extent". With water emerging as an increasingly emotive issue, Islamabad and New Delhi should build on the momentum of the ongoing dialogue to hold comprehensive talks that go beyond project-related disputes. Along with using the existing IWT mechanisms for dispute resolution, they should abide by their commitments under the treaty to identify "short, medium and long-term steps for the optimum development of the rivers"/ Further cooperation should include joint watershed management, increasing the efficiency of irrigation and water use, joint development of technologies, sustainable agricultural practices and institutional arrangements to manage food shortages and counter natural disasters.

As their energy needs rise, both countries should also identify opportunities to cooperate in developing hydropower. There are other options for energy sharing, some of which are already being explored. These include a power line, on a joint ownership basis, that would transfer 500 megawatts of electricity from Amritsar to Lahore. In the longer term, enlarging a bilateral and a regional energy grid would work in their mutual interest.

CHAPTER – 32

Water And Human Security

Aaron T. Wolf, Ph.D.
Department of Geosciences, Oregon State University

Till taught by pain, men know not water's worth. (Byron)

INTRODUCTION[1]

As human populations and economies grow exponentially, the amount of freshwater in the world remains roughly the same as it has been throughout history. While the total quantity of water in the world is immense, the vast majority is either saltwater (97.5 percent) or locked up in ice caps (1.75 percent). The amount economically available for human use is only 0.007 percent of the total, or about 13,500 km^3. This comes out to only about 2300 m^3 per person – a 37 percent drop since 1970 (United Nations 1997). Adding complexity to this increasing scarcity is the fact that almost half the globe's land surface lies within international watersheds (i.e., that land which contributes to the world's 261 transboundary waterways).

The scarcity of water in an arid and semi-arid environment leads to intense political pressures, often referred to as "water stress." Furthermore, water not only ignores political boundaries; it evades institutional classification and eludes legal generalizations. The 1997 Convention on the Non-Navigational Uses of International Watercourses Commission is vague and occasionally contradictory, and international agencies have historically been limited in coordination or strategy.

While water quantity has been the major issue of this century, water quality has been neglected to the point of catastrophe. The numbers are staggering:

- More than a billion people lack access to safe water supplies;
- Almost three billion do not have access to adequate sanitation;
- Five million people die each year from water-related diseases or inadequate sanitation;
- Twenty percent of the world's irrigated lands are saltladen to the point of affecting production.

Water demands are increasing, groundwater levels are dropping, surface-water supplies are increasingly contaminated, and delivery and treatment infrastructures are aging. The World Bank estimates that it would take $600 billion to repair and improve the world's existing water delivery systems (CAFRW 1997).

When all of these characteristics are put together – water as a critical, non-substitutable resource, which flows and fluctuates across time and space, for which legal principles are vague and contradictory, and which is becoming relatively more scarce and degraded as world populations and standards of living grow – compelling arguments for considering the security implications of water resources management are found.

This paper investigates both the global water crisis – too little clean freshwater for too many people, and global water conflict – the political tensions that result.

Water And International Conflict

An increasingly prevalent viewpoint about water and security is best summed up by Ismail Serageldin, vicepresident of the World Bank: "The wars of the next century will be about water" (quoted in the New York Times 10 August 1995). The view that water will lead to acute international conflict, one that is often tied to causal arguments of environmental security, unfortunately is gaining ground in both academic and popular literature. Some authors assume a natural link between water scarcity and acute conflict, suggesting that "competition for limited . . . freshwater . . . leads to severe political tensions and even to war" (Westing 1986). Others, often citing examples from the arid and hostile Middle East, assume that "history is replete with examples of violent conflict over water" (Butts 1997). Still others, combining this "natural" connection between water and conflict with assumed historic evidence, forecast: "The renewable resource most likely to stimulate interstate resource war is river water" (Homer-Dixon 1994).

There are two major problems with the literature that describes water both as a historic and, by extrapolation, as a future cause of acute international conflict:

1. There is little historic evidence that water has ever been the cause of international warfare; and

2. War over water seems neither strategically rational, hydrographically effective, nor economically viable.

What Is The Evidence Of A Link Between Water And International Conflict?

One component of the Transboundary Freshwater Dispute Database Project[2] at Oregon State University has been an assessment of historic cases of international water conflicts. In order to counter the prevailing anecdotal approach, researchers associated with the project utilized the most systematic collection of international conflict – Brecher and Wilkenfeld's (1997) International Crisis Behavior data set – and supplemented their investigation with available primary and secondary sources. This search revealed a total of seven cases in which armies were mobilized or shots were fired across international boundaries – in every case, the dispute did not degrade into warfare.[3] According to our findings, with one exception (now almost 4,500 years old),[4] *there has not been a war fought over water.*

It is, however, disingenuous to base a discussion about the future solely on history. Part of the basis for predictions of future "water wars," after all, is that we are reaching unprecedented demand on relatively decreasing clean water supplies. But there are other arguments against the possibility of "water wars."[5] They might include:

A Strategic Argument

If one were to launch a war over water, what would be the goal? Presumably, the aggressor would have to be both downstream and the regional hegemony – an upstream riparian nation would have no cause to launch an attack and a weaker nation would be foolhardy to do so. An upstream riparian nation, then, would have to initiate an action, which decreases either quantity or quality, knowing that doing so will antagonize a stronger down-stream neighbour.

The down-stream power would then have to decide whether to launch an attack – if the project were a dam, destroying it would result in a wall of water rushing back on down-stream territory. Were it a

406

quality-related project, either industrial or waste treatment, destroying it would probably result in even worse quality than before. Furthermore, the hegemony would have to weigh not only an invasion, but an occupation and depopulation of the entire watershed in order to forestall any retribution – otherwise, it would be simple to pollute the water source of the invading power. It is unlikely that both countries would be democracies, since the political scientists tell us that democracies do not go to war against each other, and the international community would have to refuse to become involved (this, of course, is the least far-fetched aspect of the scenario). All of this effort would be expended for a resource that costs about one U.S. dollar per cubic meter to create from seawater.

A Shared Interest Argument

What is it about water that tends to induce cooperation even among riparian nations that are hostile over other issues? The treaties negotiated over international waterways offer some insight into this question. Each treaty shows sometimes exquisite sensitivity to the unique setting and needs of each basin, and many detail the shared interests a common waterway will bring. Along larger waterways, for instance, the better dam sites are usually upstream at the headwaters where valley walls are steeper and where, incidentally, the environmental impact of dams is not as great. The prime agricultural land is generally downstream, where the gradient drops off and alluvial deposits enrich the soil. A dam in the headwaters, then, not only provides hydropower and other benefits for the upstream riparian nation, it also can be managed to evenly control the flow for the benefit of downstream agriculture, or to enhance water transportation for the benefit of both riparian nations. Other examples of shared interests abound: the development of a river that acts as a boundary cannot take place without cooperation; farmers, environmentalists, and recreational users all share an interest in seeing a healthy stream-system; and all riparian nations share an interest in high quality water.

An Institutional Resiliency Argument

Another factor adding to the political stability of international watersheds is that once cooperative water regimes are established, they turn out to be tremendously resilient over time, even between otherwise hostile riparian nations, and even as conflict is waged over other issues. For example, the Mekong Committee has functioned since 1957, exchanging data throughout the Vietnam War. Secret "picnic table" talks have been held between Israel and Jordan, since the unsuccessful Johnston negotiations of 1953-55, even as these riparian nations were in a legal state of war until recently. And, the Indus River Commission not only survived through two wars between India and Pakistan, but treaty-related payments continued unabated throughout the hostilities.

Any of these arguments, in and of itself, might not convince one of the unlikelihood of "water wars." The combination of all of these factors, though – a historic lack of evidence combined with strategic, interest-based, and institutional irrationality of acute international hydroconflicts – should help convince us to think of water as a vehicle for reducing tensions and encouraging cooperation even between otherwise hostile co-riparian nations. Undala Alam (1998) has aptly dubbed this concept of water as a resource that transcends traditional thinking about resource-related disputes, "water rationality."

If Not "Water Wars," Then What Are The Security Issues?

The concept of "environmental security" is not restricted to a presumed causal relationship between environmental 31 issues and international warfare. Much of the thinking on the issue has evolved to incorporate a broader sense of "human security" – a much more inclusive concept which stresses the intricate set of relationships between environment and society.[6]

407

Until now it is only the relationship between international armed conflict and water resources as a scarce resource that has been described. Internal disputes, such as those between interests of states/provinces, were excluded, as were those where water was a means, method, or victim of warfare. Also excluded were disputes where water is incidental to the main issue, such as those about fishing rights, access to ports, transportation or river boundaries.

It is important to understand, therefore, that there is history of water-related violence. It is a history of incidents that are at the sub-national level, generally between tribes, water-use sectors, or states/provinces. Examples of internal water conflicts, in fact, are quite prevalent. They range from interstate violence and death along the Cauvery River in India, to California farmers blowing up a pipeline meant for Los Angeles, to much of the violent history in the Americas between indigenous peoples and European settlers. The desert state of Arizona in the United States even commissioned a navy (made up of one ferryboat) and sent its state militia to stop a dam and diversion on the Colorado River in 1934.

While these "flashpoints" can and do occur at the subnational level, the more common security issue is both more subtle and more pervasive. As water quality and/or quantity degrades over time within a local setting, the effect on the stability of a region can be unsettling. Since the degradation generally occurs slowly over time, it is difficult to say precisely where its impact begins and ends; yet the effects can be profound. Take, for example, the case of the Gaza Strip where, over the thirty years the region was under Israeli occupation, water quality steadily deteriorated, saltwater intrusion degraded local wells, and water-related diseases took a rising toll on the population. In 1987, the intifada, or Palestinian uprising, broke out in the Gaza Strip, and quickly spread throughout the West Bank. Was water quality the cause? It would be disingenuous to identify such direct causality. Was it an irritant which exacerbated an already tenuous situation? Undoubtedly.

Moreover, one need look no further than relations between India and Bangladesh to note that these internal instabilities can be both caused and exacerbated by international water disputes. At issue is a barrage that India built at Farakka, which diverts a portion of the Ganges flow away from its course into Bangladesh, and towards Calcutta 100 miles to the south, in order to flush silt away from that city's seaport. Adverse effects in Bangladesh resulting from reduced upstream flow have included degradation of both surface and groundwater, impeded navigation, increased salinity, degraded fisheries, and danger to water supplies and public health. Migration out of affected areas has further compounded the problem. Ironically, many of those displaced in Bangladesh have found refuge in India.

So, while no "water wars" have occurred, there is ample evidence that the lack of clean freshwater has led to occasionally intense political instability, and that on a small scale, acute violence can result. What we seem to be finding, in fact, is that geographic scale and intensity of conflict are inversely related.

Finally, there is the security issue of "simple" human suffering. Again, five million people die each year from water-related diseases or inadequate sanitation. More than half the people in the world lack adequate sanitation. Eighty percent of disease in the developing world is related to water. With a crisis this clearly defined over a resource this vital, the threats to security seem almost self-evident.

How Are We Equipped Institutionally To Handle Water Security?

Resolving the global water crisis, and ameliorating the attendant political stresses, increasingly will involve sophisticated mechanisms for cooperation. Current legal and institutional capacities are limited, but strides are being made slowly. Addressing both the water crisis and water conflict, global institutions both foster good relations among sovereign neighbours and improve capabilities for water resources management.

Legal Principles

Generalized legal principles for the management of transboundary waters are currently defined by the Convention on the Non-Navigational Uses of International Watercourses, ratified by the U.N. General Assembly in 1997. The Convention, which took 27 years to develop, reflects the difficulty of marrying legal and hydrologic intricacies: while the Convention provides many important principles, including responsibility for cooperation and joint management, it is also vague and occasionally contradictory. The Convention also provides few practical guidelines for water allocations – the heart of most water conflict. Neither these principles, nor those of the Convention's precursors – the 1966 Helsinki Rules or subsequent draft articles by international legal bodies – have been explicitly invoked in more than a handful of water negotiations or treaties.

Furthermore, international law only concerns itself with the rights and responsibilities between nations. Some political entities that might claim water rights, therefore, would not be represented, such as the Palestinians along the Jordan River or Kurds along the Euphrates River. In addition, cases are heard by the International Court of Justice (ICJ) only with the consent of the parties involved; and no practical enforcement mechanism exists to back up the Court's findings, except in the most extreme cases. A nation with pressing national interests can, therefore, disclaim entirely the court's jurisdiction or findings. Since its creation in 1945, the ICJ has decided only a single case regarding international waters.

International Institutions

Just as the flow of water totally ignores political boundaries, so too does its management strain the capabilities of institutions. No global institution currently exists for the management of transboundary water resources. Several UN agencies, including UNEP, UNDP, UNESCO, WHO, FAO, and UNIDO, incorporate water related issues in their charter, as does the World Bank. All of these agencies recently collaborated in production of the Comprehensive Assessment of the Freshwater Resources of the World (CAFRW). Many global water-related agencies have also recently cooperated in formation of the Global Water Partnership that aims to coordinate water policy worldwide. The World Water Council was also established recently as a self-described "think tank" for world water resources issues. However, none of these agencies incorporate mechanisms for the resolution of transboundary water resources disputes within their mandates.

Many of the most productive efforts at the international level are brought about by strong personalities within agencies and/or through ad hoc collaborations between agencies. The 1960 Indus Water Treaty owes much to David Black, thenpresident of the World Bank; the Mekong Committee was formed due primarily to an alliance between UNECAFE and the US Bureau of Reclamation; and the 1994 Danube River Protection Convention involved leadership from UNDP, the World Bank, and the Commission of European Communities. Occasionally, initiative is offered through economic and political alliances, as has been the case with the European Union's water quality guidelines, and the Southern African Development Community's protocol on Shared Watercourse Systems.

International Water Treaties

In the absence of detailed water law, adequate institutions, or warfare, the countries that incorporate the world's 261 international waterways have managed to muddle through. The UN Food and Agriculture Organization has identified more than 3,600 treaties relating to international water resources dating between AD 805 and 1984, the majority of which deal with some aspect of navigation. Since 1814, states have negotiated a smaller body of treaties that deal with nonnavigational issues of water management, flood control, hydropower projects, or allocations for consumptive or nonconsumptive uses in international basins. The Transboundary Freshwater Dispute Database project includes an online collection of 145 of these treaties, which include only those dating from 1870 and later which deal with water per se, and exclude those that deal only with boundaries, navigation, or fishing rights.

Table 1. Treaty Statistics Summary Sheet

Signatories Bilateral 124 out of a total 145 treaties, or 86% Multilateral 21/145 (14%)
Principal Focus Water Supply 53/145 (37%) Hydropower 57/145 (39%) Flood Control 13/145 (9%) Industrial Uses 9/145 (6%) Navigation 6/145 (4%) Pollution 6/145 (4%) Fishing 1/145 (0.7%)
Monitoring Provided 78/145 (54%) No/Not Available 67/145 (46%)
Conflict Resolution Council 43/145 (30%) Other Governmental Unit 9/145 (6%) United Nations/Third Party 14/145 (10%) None/Not Available 79/145 (54%)
Enforcement Council 26/145 (18%) Force 2/145 (1%) Economic 1/145 (1/145(<1%) None/Not Available 116/145 (80%)
Unequal Power Relationship Yes 52/145 (36%) No/Unclear 93/145 (64%)
Information Sharing Yes 93/145 (64%) No/Not Available 52/145 (36%)
Water Allocation Equal Portions 15/145 (10%) Complex but Clear 39/145 (27%) Unclear 14/145 (10%) None/Not Available 77/145 (53%)
Non-Water Linkages Money 44/145 (30%) Land 6/145 (4%) Political Concessions 2/145 (1%) Other Linkages 10/145 (7%) No Linkages 83/145 (57%)

Source: Hamner and Wolf (1998).

Despite their number and rich history, these 145 treaties reveal that the legal management of transboundary rivers is still in its conceptual infancy. More than half of these treaties include no monitoring provisions whatsoever, and perhaps as a consequence, two-thirds do not delineate specific allocations and four-fifths have no enforcement mechanism. Moreover, those treaties, which do allocate specific quantities, allocate a fixed amount to all riparian nations but one – that one nation must then accept the balance of the river flow, regardless of fluctuations. Finally, multilateral basins are, almost without exception, governed by bilateral treaties, precluding the integrated basin management long-advocated by water managers.

What Technical/Policy Options Are Available?

The solutions to this crisis are complex and expensive. They range from agricultural to technological to economic and public policies, but they all fall under the same three basic categories as for any resource shortage: increase supply, decrease demand, or improve the quality.

Table 1. Water management options to increase supply, decrease demand, or improve quality

UNILATERAL OPTIONS
DEMAND
• Urban/industrial demand management. • Rationing. • Public awareness. • Allow price of water to reflect true costs. • Efficient agriculture, including drip irrigation, greenhouse technology, and genetic engineering for drought and salinity resistance.
SUPPLY
• Wastewater reclamation. • Increase catchment and storage (including artificial groundwater recharge). • Cloud seeding. • Desalination. • Fossil aquifer development.
QUALITY
• Treat drinking water supplies at its most appropriate level. • Work towards universal sanitation. • Eradicate water-related disease through water treatment and/or vaccination programs.
COOPERATIVE OPTIONS
• Shared information and technology. • International water markets to increase distributive efficiency (where appropriate). • Inter-basin water transfers. • Joint regional planning and coordination.

Some of the current issues include:

Increasing Supply

New Natural Sources. No new rivers are likely to be discovered in the world, but more efficient management of existing sources and greater catchment of floodwaters, perhaps stored underground through artificial groundwater recharge, can add to supplies just as effectively.

New Sources Through Technology. Projects like iceberg towing and cloud-seeding, though appealing to the imagination, do not seem to be the most likely direction for future technology. The two more likely (although more mundane) means to increase water supply for the future are desalination and wastewater reclamation. High costs have precluded both – particularly desalination for most uses, although efforts are being made to lower these costs through multiple use plants (getting desalted water as a byproduct in a plant designed primarily for energy generation), increased energy efficiency in plant design, and by augmenting conventional plant power with solar or other energy sources.

Decreasing Demand

Agricultural Sector. Agriculture is far and away the leading consumer of water resources, taking about 70 percent of withdrawals worldwide. Technological advances like dripirrigation and micro-sprinklers are 20-50 percent more efficient than standard sprinklers and tremendously more so than the open-ditch flood method. Computerized control systems, working in conjunction with direct soil moisture measurements can add even more precision to crop irrigation. Other water savings have come through bioengineered crops that exist on a minimal amount of freshwater, on brackish water, or even on the direct application of saltwater.

Economic Water Efficiency. Water costs worldwide are highly subsidized, especially water earmarked for agriculture. Economic theory argues that only when the price paid for a commodity is a reasonable reflection of the true price can market forces work for efficient distribution of the commodity. Take away subsidies and allow the price to rise, it is argued, and market incentives are created for both greater efficiency on the farm and a natural shift of water resources from the agricultural sector to industry, where contribution to GNP per unit of water is often much higher. These arguments, though, tread through quite sensitive territory, have serious implications for equity, and often overlook other effects of urbanization.

Improving Quality

The strategies for improving quality have long been known: clean water both before and after it is used, and eradicate water-related diseases. The problem has too often been a "simple" lack of funds and/or coordination for this enormous task. The near eradication of dracunculiasis (guinea worm) in this decade provides a good example of a successful focused effort, coordinated between UN agencies and national and local governments, where attention was paid to all aspects of the disease and its transmission, from surveys and education to treatment and containment.[7]

What Are The Major Lessons Learned Which Have Policy Implications?

The most critical security lessons learned from the global experience in water security are as follows:

1. Water that crosses international boundaries can exacerbate relations between nations that share the basin. While the tension is not likely to lead to warfare, early coordination between riparian states can help ameliorate the issue entirely.

2. Once international institutions are in place, they are tremendously resilient over time, even between otherwise hostile riparians, and even as conflict is waged over other issues.

3. More likely than international "flashpoints" is a gradual decreasing of water quantity and/or quality, which over time can affect the internal stability of a nation or region, and act as an irritant between ethnic groups, water sectors, or states/provinces. The resulting instability can spill into the international arena.

4. The greatest human security threat of the global water crisis comes about not from the threat of warfare, or even from political instability, but rather from the simple fact that millions of people lack access to sufficient quantities of this critical resource at sufficient quality for their well being.

WHAT TYPES OF POLICY RECOMMENDATIONS CAN ONE MAKE?

Given these lessons, what can the international community do?

International Institutions:

Water dispute amelioration is as important, more effective, and less costly than conflict resolution. Watershed commissions should be developed for those basins that do not have them, and strengthened for those that do.

Three traits of international waters – the fact that conflict is invariably sub-acute, that dangerous flashpoints can be averted when institutions are established early, and that such institutions are tremendously resilient over time – inform this recommendation. Early intervention is also beneficial to the process of conflict resolution, helping to shift the mode of dispute from costly, impasse oriented dynamics to less costly, problem solving dynamics. In the heat of some flashpoints, such as the Nile, the Indus, and the Jordan, as armed conflict seemed imminent, tremendous energy was spent just getting the parties to talk to each other. In contrast, discussions in the Mekong Committee, the multilateral working group in the Middle East and on the Danube, have all moved beyond the causes of immediate disputes on to actual, practical projects that may be implemented in an integrative framework.

Funding and Aid Agencies:

Water-related aid needs to be coordinated and focused, relating quality, quantity, groundwater, surfacewater, and local socio-political settings in an integrated fashion. Funding should be commensurate with the responsibility these agencies have for alleviating the global water crisis.

Ameliorating the crux of water security – the crisis of human suffering – often rests with these agencies which, given the size of the crisis, are extraordinarily underfunded. One can contrast the resources spent on issues such as global change and arms control in efforts to protect against potential loss of life in the future, while millions die in the present due to a lack of access to clean fresh water. Agencies such as USAID, CIDA, and JICA have the technical expertise and experience to help, yet are hindered by political and budget constraints. Funding agencies often are hamstrung by local politics. A powerful argument might be made for the fact that water-related disease costs the global economy US$125 billion per year, while ameliorating them would "only" cost US$7-50 billion (Gleick, 1998). Projects such as USAID's Project Forward, which integrates water management with conflict resolution training, offer models for the future.

Universities and Research Agencies:

Universities and research agencies can best contribute to the alleviation of the water crisis in three major ways: 1) acquire, analyze, and coordinate the primary data necessary for good empirical work; 2) identify indicators of future water disputes and/or insecurity in regions most at risk; and 3) train tomorrow's water managers in an integrated fashion.

The internet's initial mandate is still one of the best: to allow communication between researchers around the world to exchange information and enhance collaboration. The surfeit of primary data currently threatens an information overload in the developed world, while the most basic information can be lacking in the developing world. University programs such as the Institute of Earth, Oceans, and Space at the University of New Hampshire are working to ferret out useful global hydrological data, while encouraging greater collection and dissemination capabilities where they are lacking. Data availability not only allows for greater understanding of the physical world but, by adding parameters from the socio-political realm, indicators showing regions at risk in the future can be identified. Such projects are taking place for human security at the University of Victoria, and for indicators of water dispute at Oregon State University. Finally, universities are slowly recognizing that water is, by its nature, an exceptionally interdisciplinary resource and that the attendant disputes can only be resolved through active dialog among fields as diverse as science, law, economics, religion, and ethics. It is difficult enough to find university programs at the graduate level which adequately train students in water from a truly interdisciplinary perspective, allowing for exposure to both the science and policy of water resources (there are maybe four such programs in the entire United States) but there is no program which explicitly adds the international component.

Private Industry:

Private industry has historically taken the lead in large development projects. As the emphasis in world water shifts to a smaller scale, and from a focus on supply to one on demand management and improved quality, private industry has much to offer.

Private industry has three traits that can be harnessed to help ameliorate the world water crisis: their reach transcends national boundaries, their resources are generally greater than those of public institutions, and their strategic planning is generally unmatched. Historically, private companies such as Bechtel and Lyonnaise des Eaux have been involved primarily in large development projects, while the smaller scale projects have been left to aid agencies to develop. Recently, a shift in thinking has taken place in some corporate board rooms. Bank of America, for example, was not involved in the Californiawide process of water planning until recently, when its president noticed that practically all of the bank's investments relied on a safe, stable supply of water. This was true whether the investments were in micro-chip manufacturing, mortgages, or the more traditional agriculture. When the bank became involved in the "CalFed Plan," bringing with it its lawyers, planning expertise, and facilitators, not to mention its financial resources, progress was made in several areas which had till then been mired down in impasse.

Civil Society:

Inherent in our recognition that the most serious problems of water security are those at the local level, is the attendant recognition that civil society is among the best suited to address local issues.

One recurrent pattern in water resources development and management has been a series of projects or approaches which are in opposition to local values or customs. These projects can be as large as dams which displace hundreds of thousands of people and wipe out sites of cultural and religious heritage; as heedless as promoting water markets among religious groups for whom the idea is sacrilege; or as seemingly minor as cutting down a tree which is sacred to a village djinn. In recent years, as a consequence, the idea of including those affected by a project into the decisionmaking process has taken hold. Moreover, some aspects of civil society have both local roots and a global reach. Rotary International, for example, was awarded the 1997 Crystal Drop Award, the most prestigious institutional award of the International Water Resources Association, for its coordinated efforts in water supply and sanitation projects throughout the world.

CONCLUSIONS

The global water crisis has led to a large and growing literature warning of future "water wars," and pointing to water not only as a cause of historic armed conflict, but as the resource which will bring combatants to the battlefield in the 21st century. The historic reality has been quite different – we have not, and probably will not, go to war over water. In modern times, only seven minor skirmishes have been waged over international waters. Conversely, over 3,600 treaties have been signed over different aspects of international waters – 145 in this century on water qua water – many showing tremendous elegance and creativity for dealing with this critical resource. This is not to say that armed conflict has not taken place over water, only that such disputes generally are between tribes, water-use sectors, or states/provinces. What we seem to be finding, 36 in fact, is that geographic scale and intensity of conflict are inversely related.

While the patterns described in this paper suggest that the more valuable lesson of international water is as a resource whose characteristics tend to induce cooperation and incite violence only in the exception, one should not lose sight of the truly dire straits that have been brought about by the global water crisis. The critical problems that need addressing are neither of wars nor of politics, but rather of "simply" getting an adequate supply of clean freshwater to the people of the world.

REFERENCES

Alam, U. 1998. "Water Rationality: Meditating the Indus Waters Treaty." Unpublished Ph.D. dissertation, University of Durham.

Brecher, M., and J. Wilkenfeld. 1997. A Study of Crisis. Ann Arbor, MI: University of Michigan Press.

Butts, Kent. 1997 "The Strategic Importance of Water." Parameters. Spring, pp. 65-83.

Cooper, Jerrold. 1983. Reconstructing History from Ancient Inscriptions: The Lagash-Umma Border Conflict. Malibu, Calif.: Undena.

Gleick, P. 1998. The World's Water: The Biennial Report on Freshwater Resources. Washington DC: Island Press.

Hamner, J., and A. Wolf. 1998. "Patterns in International Water Resource Treaties: The Transboundary *Freshwater Dispute Database.*" *Colorado Journal of International Environmental Law and Policy.* 1997 Yearbook.

Homer-Dixon, Thomas. 1994. "Environmental Scarcities and Violent Conflict." International Security. Summer.

Lonergan, S.C. 1997. Global Environmental Change and Human Security. Changes 5. Ottawa: Canadian Global Change Program – The Royal Society of Canada.

Crossette, Barbara. "Severe Water Crisis Ahead for Poorest Nations in Next Two Decades." New York Times, 10 August 1995, p. A-13.

United Nations. 1997. Water in the 21st Century: Comprehensive Assessment of the Freshwater Resources of the World. Geneva: World Meteorological Organization and the Stockholm Environment Institute.

Westing, A. H., ed. 1986. Global Resources and International Conflict: Environmental Factors in Strategic Policy and Action. New York, NY: Oxford University Press.

Wolf, A. 1999. "Water Wars" and Water Reality: Conflict and Cooperation along International Waterways. In S.C. Lonergan (Ed.). Environmental Change, Adaptation and Human Security (forthcoming). Dordrecht: Kluwer.

OTHER SUGGESTED READINGS

Elhance, Arun. 1999. Hydropolitics in the 3rd World: Conflict and Cooperation in International River Basins. Washington, DC: US Institute of Peace.

Gleick, P. 1993. Water and Conflict: Fresh Water Resources and International Security. International Security, 18 (1), 79-112.

Kliot, N., D. Shmueli, D., & U. Shamir. 1997. Institutional Frameworks for the Management of Transboundary Water Resources. (Two volumes.) Haifa, Israel: Water Research Institute.

Postel, S. 1996. Dividing the Waters: Food Security, Ecosystem Health, and the New Politics of Scarcity. Worldwatch Paper 132. Washington, D.C.: Worldwatch Institute.

Wolf, A. 1997. International Water Conflict Resolution: Lessons from Comparative Analysis. International Journal of Water Resources Development, 13 (3), pp. 333-365.

USEFUL WEB ADDRESSES

The International Water Resources Association (IWRA)

IWRA has strived to improve water management worldwide through dialogue, education, and research for over 25 years. Since its official formation in 1972, the organization has actively promoted the sustainable management of water resources around the globe. The world is a much smaller place today than when IWRA began its work due to advancing technologies and global social changes. The belief that sustainability requires interdisciplinary action and international cooperation is a driving force behind the association. IWRA seeks to improve water resource outcomes by improving our collective understanding of the physical, biological, chemical, institutional, and socioeconomic aspects of water.

The Pacific Institute

The Pacific Institute for Studies in Development, Environment, and Security is an independent, non-profit center created in 1987 to conduct research and policy analysis in the areas of environment, sustainable development, and international security. Underlying all of the Institute's work is the recognition that the pressing problems of environmental degradation, regional and global poverty, and political tension and conflict are fundamentally interrelated, and that long-term solutions require an interdisciplinary perspective.

The Transboundary Freshwater Dispute Database

The Transboundary Freshwater Dispute Database, an ongoing research effort at Oregon State University, currently includes a computer compilation of 150 waterrelated treaties and 39 US inter-state compacts, catalogued by basin, countries or states involved, date signed, treaty topic, allocations measure, conflict resolution mechanisms, and non-water linkages. The Database also includes a digitized inventory of international watersheds, negotiating notes and background material on 14 case-studies of conflict resolution, news files on cases of acute waterrelated conflict, and assessments of indigenous/traditional methods of water conflict resolution.

The Water Web

The WaterWeb consortium has been created to promote the sharing of information concerning water and the earth's environment. The organization seeks to create a global community, bringing together educational, governmental, nonprofit, and commercial entities interested in water research, conservation, and management. WaterWeb's goals are to advance water related issues, promote the use of quality information, and share information with water use stakeholders and decisionmakers.

ENDNOTES

1. A shorter version of this paper appeared as, Wolf, A. "Water and Human Security." AVISO: An Information Bulletin on Global Environmental Change and Human Security. Bulletin #3, June 1999.
2. For more information on the Database Project, see A. Wolf. "The Transboundary Freshwater Dispute Database Project." Water International. December 1999 (forthcoming).
3. For a list of conflicts see A. Wolf, 1999. "Water Wars" and Water Reality: Conflict and Cooperation along International Waterways. In S.L. Lonergan (Ed.), Environmental Change, Adaptation and Human Security, (forthcoming). Dordrecht: Kluwer Academic Publishers.
4. The exception is the earliest documented interstate conflict known, a dispute between the Sumerian city-states of Lagash and Umma over the right to exploit boundary channels along the Tigris in 2,500 BCE (Cooper 1983). In other words, the last and only "water war" was 4,500 years ago.

5 These arguments are described in more detail in A. Wolf, 1999. "Water Wars" and Water Reality: Conflict and Cooperation along International Waterways.
6 For a more detailed discussion of these issues see, S. C. Lonergan (1997) Global Environmental Change and Human Security. In Changes 5. Ottawa: Canadian Global Change Program - The Royal Society of Canada.
7 Gleick (1998) provides more detail on this and other water quality examples.

CHAPTER – 33

Indus Waters Treaty 1960 Three Summaries

First Summary

PREAMBLE

The Government of India and the Government of Pakistan, being equally desirous of attaining the most complete and satisfactory utilisation of the waters of the Indus system of rivers and recognising the need, therefore, of fixing and delimiting, in a spirit of goodwill and friendship, the rights and obligations of each in relation to the other concerning the use of these waters and of making provision for the settlement, in a cooperative spirit, of all such questions as may hereafter arise in regard to the interpretation or application of the provisions agreed upon herein, have resolved to conclude a Treaty in furtherance of these objectives, and for this purpose have named as their plenipotentiaries:

The Government of India:
    Shri Jawaharlal Nehru,
        Prime Minister of India,

    and

The Government of Pakistan:
    Field Marshal Mohammad Ayub Khan, HP., H.J.,
        President of Pakistan;

who, having communicated to each other their respective Full Powers and having found them in good and due form, have agreed upon the following Articles and Annexures:—

ARTICLE I

Definitions

As used in this Treaty:

(1) The terms "Article" and "Annexure" mean respectively an Article of, and an Annexure to, this Treaty.Except as otherwise indicated, references to Paragraphs are to the paragraphs in the Article or in the Annexure in which the reference is made.

(2) The term "Tributary" of a river means any surface channel, whether in continuous or intermittent flow and by whatever name called, whose waters in the natural course would fall into that river, e.g. a tributary, a torrent, a natural drainage, an artificial drainage, a vadi, a nallah. A nai, a hhad, a cho. The term also includes any subtributary or branch or subsidiary channel, by whatever name called, whose waters, in the natural course, would directly or otherwise flow into that surface channel.

(3) The term "The Indus," "The Jhelum," "The Chenab," "The Ravi," "The Beas" or "The Sutlej" means the named river (including Connecting Lakes, if any) and all its Tributaries: Provided however that

(i) none of the rivers named above shall be deemed to be a Tributary;

(ii) The Chenab shall be deemed to include the river Panjnad; and

(iii) the river Chandra and the river Bhaga shall be deemed to be Tributaries of The Chenab.

(4) The term "Main" added after Indus, Jhelum, Chenab, Sutlej, Beas or Ravi means the main stem of the named river excluding its Tributaries, but including all channels and creeks of the main stem of that river and such Connecting Lakes as form part of the main stem itself. The Jhelum Main shall be deemed to extend up to Verinag, and the Chenab Main up to the confluence of the river Chandra and the river Bhaga.

(5) The term "Eastern Rivers" means The Sutlej, The Beas and The Ravi taken together.

(6) The term "Western Rivers" means The Indus, The Jhelum and The Chenab taken together.

(7) The term "the Rivers" means all the rivers, The Sutlej, The Beas, The Ravi, The Indus, The Jhelum and The Chenab.

(8) The term "Connecting Lake" means any lake which receives water from, or yields water to, any of the Rivers; but any lake which occasionally and irregularly receives only the spill of any of the Rivers and returns only the whole or part of that spill is not a Connecting Lake.

(9) The term "Agricultural Use" means the use of water for irrigation, except for irrigation of household gardens and public recreational gardens.

(10) The term "Domestic Use" means the use of water for:

(a) drinking, washing, bathing, recreation, sanitation (including the conveyance and dilution of sewage and of industrial and other wastes), stock and poultry, and other like purposes;

(b) household and municipal purposes (including use for household gardens and public recreational gardens); and

(c) industrial purposes (including mining, milling and other like purposes); but the term does not include Agricultural Use or use for the generation of hydro-electric power.

(11) The term "Non-Consumptive Use" means any control or use of water for navigation, floating of timber or other property, flood protection or flood control, fishing or fish culture, wild life or other like beneficial purposes, provided that, exclusive of seepage and evaporation of water incidental to the control or use, the water (undiminished in volume within the practical range of measurement) remains in, or is returned to, the same river or its Tributaries; but the term does not include Agricultural Use or use for the generation of hydro-electric power.

(12) The term "Transition Period" means the period beginning and ending as provided in Article II (6).

(13) The term "Bank" means the International Bank for Reconstruction and Development.

(14) The term "Commissioner" means either of the Commissioners appointed under the provisions of Article VIII(1) and the term "Commission" means the Permanent Indus Commission constituted in accordance with Article.

(15) The term "interference with the waters" means:

(a) Any act of withdrawal therefrom; or

(b) Any man-made obstruction to their flow which causes a change in the volume (within the practical range of measurement) of the daily flow of the waters: Provided however that an obstruction which involves only an insignificant and incidental change in the volume of the daily flow, for example, fluctuations due to afflux caused by bridge piers or a temporary by-pass, etc., shall not be deemed to be an interference with the waters.

(16) The term "Effective Date" means the date on which this Treaty takes effect in accordance with the provisions of Article XII, that is, the first of April 1960.

ARTICLE II

Provisions Regarding Eastern Rivers

(1) All the waters of the Eastern Rivers shall be available for the unrestricted use of India, except as otherwise expressly provided in this Article.

(2) For Domestic Use and Non-Consumptive Use, Pakistan shall be under an obligation to let flow, and shall not permit any interference with, the waters of the Sutlej Main and the Ravi Main in the reaches where these rivers flow in Pakistan and have not yet finally crossed into Pakistan. The points of final crossing are the following: (a) near the new Hasta Bund upstream of Suleimanke in the case of the Sutlej Main, and (b) about one and a half miles upstream of the syphon for the B-R-B-D Link in the case of the Ravi Main.

(3) Except for Domestic Use, Non-Consumptive Use and Agricultural Use (as specified in Annexure B), Pakistan shall be under an obligation to let flow, and shall not permit any interference with, the waters (while flowing in Pakistan) of any Tributary which, in its natural course, joins the Sutlej Main or the Ravi Main before these rivers have finally crossed into Pakistan.

(4) All the waters, while flowing in Pakistan, of any Tributary which, in its natural course, joins the Sutlej Main or the Ravi Main after these rivers have finally crossed into Pakistan shall be available for the unrestricted use of Pakistan: Provided, however, that this provision shall not be construed as giving Pakistan any claim or right to any releases by India in any such Tributary. If Pakistan should deliver any of the waters of any such Tributary, which on the Effective Date joins the Ravi Main after this river has finally crossed into Pakistan, into a reach of the Ravi Main upstream of this crossing, India shall not make use of these waters; each Party agrees to establish such discharge observation stations and make such observations as may be necessary for the determination of the component of water available for the use of Pakistan on account of the aforesaid deliveries by Pakistan, and Pakistan agrees to meet the cost of establishing the aforesaid discharge observation stations and making the aforesaid observations.

(5) There shall be a Transition Period during which, to the extent specified in Annexure H, India shall

  (i) limit, its withdrawals for Agricultural Use,

  (ii) limit, abstractions for storages, and

  (iii) make deliveries to Pakistan from the Eastern Rivers.

(6) The Transition Period shall begin on 1st April 1960 and it shall end on 31st March 1970, or, if extended under the provisions of Part 8 of Annexure H, on the date up to which it has been extended. In any event, whether or not the replacement referred to in Article IV(1) has been accomplished, the Transition Period shall end not later than 31st March 1973.

(7) If the Transition Period is extended beyond 31st March 1970, the provisions of Article V(5) shall apply.

(8) If the Transition Period is extended beyond 31st March 1970, the provisions of Paragraph (5) shall apply during the period of extension beyond 31st March 1970.

(9) During the Transition Period, Pakistan shall receive, for unrestricted use, the waters of the Eastern Rivers which are to be released by India in accordance with the provisions of Annexure H. After the end of

the Transition Period, Pakistan shall have no claim or right to releases by India of any of the waters of the Eastern Rivers. In case there are any releases, Pakistan shall enjoy the unrestricted use of the waters so released after they have finally crossed into Pakistan: Provided that in the event that Pakistan makes any use of these waters, Pakistan shall not acquire any right whatsoever, by prescription or otherwise, to a continuance of such releases or such use.

ARTICLE III

Provisions Regarding Western Rivers

(1) Pakistan shall receive, for unrestricted use all those waters of the "Western Rivers" which India is under obligation to let flow under the provisions of Paragraph (2).

(2) India shall be under an obligation to let flow all the waters of the "Western Rivers", and shall not permit any interference with those waters, except for the following uses, restricted (except as provided in item (c) (ii) of Paragraph 5 of Annexure C) in the case of each of the rivers, The Indus, The Jhelum and The Chenab, to the drainage basin thereof:

    (a) Domestic Use;

    (b) Non-Consumptive Use;

    (c) Agricultural Use, as set out in Annexure C; and

    (d) Generation of hydro-electric power, as set out in Annexure D.

(3) Pakistan shall have the unrestricted use of all waters originating from sources other than the Eastern Rivers which are delivered by Pakistan into The Ravi or The Sutlej, and India shall not make use of these waters. Each Party agrees to establish such discharge observation stations and make such observations as may be considered necessary by the Commission for the determination of the component of water available for the use of Pakistan on account of the aforesaid deliveries by Pakistan.

(4) Except as provided in Annexures D and E, India shall not store any water of, or construct any storage works on, the Western Rivers.

ARTICLE IV

Provisions Regarding Eastern Rivers and Western Rivers

(1) Pakistan shall use its best endeavours to construct and bring into operation, with due regard to expedition and economy, that part of a system of works which will accomplish the replacement, from the Western Rivers and other sources, of water supplies for irrigation canals in Pakistan which, on 15th August 1947, were dependent on water supplies from the Eastern Rivers.

(2) Party agrees that any Non-Consumptive Use made by it shall be so made as not to materially change, on account of such use, the flow in any channel to the prejudice of the uses on that channel by the other Party under the provisions of this Treaty. In executing any scheme of flood protection or flood control, each Party will avoid, as far as practicable, any material damage to the other Party, and any such scheme carried out by India on the Western Rivers shall not involve any use of water or any storage in addition to that provided under Article III.

(3) Nothing in this Treaty shall be construed as having the effect of preventing either Party from undertaking schemes of drainage, river training, conservation of soil against erosion and dredging, or from removal of stones, gravel or sand from the beds of the Rivers: Provided that

    (a) in executing any of the schemes mentioned above, each Party will avoid, as far as practicable, any material damage to the other Party;

(b) any such scheme carried out by India on the "Western Rivers" shall not involve any use of water or any storage in addition to that provided under Article III;

(c) except as provided in Paragraph (5) and Article VII(1) (b), India shall not take any action to increase the catchment area, beyond the area on the Effective Date, of any natural or artificial drainage or drain which crosses into Pakistan, and shall not undertake such construction or remodelling of any drainage or drain which so crosses or falls into a drainage or drain which so crosses as might cause material damage in Pakistan or entail the construction of a new drain or enlargement of an existing drainage or drain in Pakistan; and

(d) should Pakistan desire to increase the catchment area, beyond the area on the Effective Date, of any natural or artificial drainage or drain, which receives drainage waters from India, or, except in an emergency, to pour any waters into it in excess of the quantities received by it as on the Effective Date, Pakistan shall, before undertaking any work for these purposes, increase the capacity of that drainage or drain to the extent necessary so as not to impair its efficacy for dealing with drainage waters received from India as on the Effective Date.

(4) Pakistan shall maintain in good order its portions of the drainages mentioned below with capacities not less than the capacities as on the Effective Date:—

(i) Hudiara Drain

(ii) Kasur Nala

(iii) Salimshah Drain

(iv) Fazilka Drain.

(5) If India finds it necessary that any of the drainages mentioned in Paragraph (4) should be deepened or widened in Pakistan, Pakistan agrees to undertake to do so as a work of public interest, provided India agrees to pay the cost of the deepening or widening.

(6) Party will use its best endeavours to maintain the natural channels of the Rivers, as on the Effective Date, in such condition as will avoid, as far as practicable, any obstruction to the flow in these channels likely to cause material damage to the other Party.

(7) Neither Party will take any action which would have the effect of diverting the Ravi Main between Madhopur and Lahore, or the Sutlej Main between Harike and Suleimanke, from its natural channel between high banks.

(8) The use of the natural channels of the Rivers for the discharge of flood or other excess waters shall be free and not subject to limitation by either Party, and neither Party shall have any claim against the other in respect of any damage caused by such use. Each Party agrees to communicate to the other Party, as far in advance as practicable, any information it may have in regard to such extraordinary discharges of water from reservoirs and flood flows as may affect the other Party.

(9) Each Party declares its intention to operate its storage dams, barrages and irrigation canals in such manner, consistent with the normal operations of its hydraulic systems, as to avoid, as far as feasible, material damage to the other Party.

(10) Party declares its intention to prevent, as far as practicable, undue pollution of the waters of the Rivers which might affect adversely uses similar in nature to those to which the waters were put on the Effective Date, and agrees to take all reasonable measures to ensure that, before any sewage or industrial waste is allowed to flow into the Rivers, it will be treated, where necessary, in such manner as not materially to affect those uses: Provided that the criterion of reasonableness shall be the customary practice in similar situations on the Rivers.

(11) Parties agree to adopt, as far as feasible, appropriate measures for the recovery, and restoration to owners, of timber and other property floated or floating down the Rivers, subject to appropriate charges being paid by the owners.

(12) The use of water for industrial purposes under Articles 11(2), 11(3) and 111(2) shall not exceed:

(a) in the case of an industrial process known on the Effective Date, such quantum of use as was customary in that process on the Effective Date;

(b) in the case of an industrial process not known on the Effective Date:

  (i) such quantum of use as was customary on the Effective Date in similar or in any way comparable industrial processes; or

  (ii) if there was no industrial process on the Effective Date similar or in any way comparable to the new process, such quantum of use as would not have a substantially adverse effect on the other Party.

(13) Such part of any water withdrawn for Domestic Use under the provisions of Articles II (3) and III (2) as is subsequently applied to Agricultural Use shall be accounted for as part of the Agricultural Use specified in Annexure B and Annexure C respectively; each Party will use its best endeavours to return to the same river (directly or through one of its Tributaries) all water withdrawn therefrom for industrial purposes and not consumed either in the industrial processes for which it was withdrawn or in some other Domestic Use.

(14) In the event that cither Party should develop a use of the waters of the Rivers which is not in accordance with the provisions of this Treaty, that Party shall not acquire, by reason of such use any right, by prescription or otherwise, to a continuance of such use.

(lo) Except as otherwise required by the express provisions of this Treaty, nothing in this Treaty shall be construed as affecting existing territorial rights over the waters of any of the Rivers or the beds or banks thereof, or as affecting existing property rights under municipal law over such waters or beds or banks.

ARTICLE V

Financial Provisions

(1) In consideration of the fact that the purpose of part of the system of works referred to in Article IV(1) is the replacement, from the Western Rivers and other sources, of water supplies for irrigation canals in Pakistan which, on 15th August 1947, were dependent on water supplies from the Eastern Rivers, India agrees to make a fixed contribution of Pounds Sterling 62,060,000 towards the costs of these works. The amount in Pounds Sterling of this contribution shall remain unchanged irrespective of any alteration in the par value of any currency.

(2) The sum of Pounds Sterling 62,060,000 specified in Paragraph (1) shall be paid in ten equal annual instalments on the 1st of November of each year. The first of such annual instalments shall be paid on 1st November 1960, or if the Treaty has not entered into force by that date, then within one month after the Treaty enters into force.

(3) Each of the instalments specified in Paragraph (2) shall be paid to the Bank for the credit of the Indus Basin Development Fund to be established and administered by the Bank, and payment shall be made in Pounds Sterling, or in such other currency or currencies as may from time to time be agreed between India and the Bank.

(4) The payments provided for under the provisions of Paragraph (3) shall be made without deduction or set-off on account of any financial claims of India on Pakistan arising otherwise than under the provisions of

this Treaty: Provided that this provision shall in no way absolve Pakistan from the necessity of paying in other ways debts to India which may be outstanding against Pakistan.

(5) If, at the request of Pakistan, the Transition Period is extended in accordance with the provisions of Article II (6) and of Part 8 of Annexure H, the Bank shall thereupon pay to India out of the Indus Basin Development Fund the appropriate amount specified in the Table below:—

Table

Period of Aggregate Extension of Transition Period	*Payment to India*
One year	£ Stg. 3,125,000
Two years	£Stg. 6,406,250
Three years	£ Stg. 9,850,000

(6) The provisions of Article IV(1) and Article V(l) shall not be construed as conferring upon India any right to participate in the decisions as to the system of works which Pakistan constructs pursuant to Article IV(1) or as constituting an assumption of any responsibility by India or as an agreement by India in regard to such works.

(7) Except for such payments as are specifically provided for in this Treaty, neither Party shall be entitled to claim any payment for observance of the provisions of this Treaty or to make any charge for water received from it by the other Party.

ARTICLE VI

Exchange of Data

(1) The following data with respect to the flow in, and utilisation of the waters of, the Rivers shall be exchanged regularly between the Parties:—

(a) Daily (or as observed or estimated less frequently) gauge and discharge data relating to flow of the Rivers at all observation sites.

(b) Daily extractions for or releases from reservoirs.

(c) withdrawals at the heads of all canals operated by government or by a government agency (herein after in this Article called canals), including link canals.

(d) Daily escapages from all canals, including link canals.

(e) Daily deliveries from link canals.

These data shall be transmitted monthly by each Party to the other as soon as the data for a calendar month have been collected and tabulated, but not later than three months after the end of the month to which they relate: Provided that such of the data specified above as are considered by either Party to be necessary for operational purposes shall be supplied daily or at less frequent intervals, as may be requested. Should one Party request the supply of any of these data by telegram, telephone, or wireless, it shall reimburse the other Party for the cost of transmission.

(2) If, in addition to the data specified in Paragraph (1) of this Article, either Party requests the supply of any data relating to the hydrology of the Rivers, or to canal or reservoir operation connected with the Rivers, or to any provision of this Treaty, such data shall be supplied by the other Party to the extent that these are available.

ARTICLE VII

Future Co-operation

(1) The two Parties recognize that they have a common interest in the optimum development of the Rivers, and, to that end, they declare their intention to co-operate, by mutual agreement, to the fullest possible extent. In particular :—

(a) Each Party, to the extent it considers practicable and on agreement by the other Party to pay the costs to be incurred, will, at the request of the other Party, set up or install such hydrologic observation stations within the drainage basins of the Rivers, and set up or install such meteorological observation stations relating thereto and carry out such observations thereat, as may be requested, and will supply the data so obtained.

(b) Each Party, to the extent it considers practicable and on agreement by the other Party to pay the costs to be incurred, will, at the request of the other Party, carry out such new drainage works as may be required in connection with new drainage works of the other Party.

(e) At the request of either Party, the two Parties may, by mutual agreement, co-operate in undertaking engineering works on the Rivers.

The formal arrangements, in each case, shall be as agreed upon between the Parties.

(2) If either Party plans to construct any engineering work which would cause interference with the waters of any of the Rivers and which, in its opinion, would affect the other Party materially, it shall notify the other Party of its plans and shall supply such data relating to the work as may be available and as would enable the other Party to inform itself of the nature, magnitude and effect of the work. If a work would cause interference with the waters of any of the Rivers but would not, in the opinion of the Party planning it, affoct the other Party materially, nevertheless the Party planning- the work shall, on request, supply the other Parly with such data regarding the nature, magnitude and effect, if any, of the work as may be available.

ARTICLE VIII

Permanent Indus Commission

(1) India and Pakistan shall each create a permanent post of Commissioner for Indus Waters, and shall appoint to this post, as often as a vacancy occurs, a person who should ordinarily be a high-ranking engineer competent in the field of hydrology and water-use. Unless either Government should decide to take up any particular question directly with the other Government, each Commissioner will be the representative of his Government for all matters arising out of this Treaty, and will serve as the regular channel of communication on all matters relating to the implementation of the Treaty, and, in particular, with respect to

(a) The furnishing or exchange of information or data provided for in the Treaty; and

(b) The giving of any notice or response to any notice provided for in the Treaty.

(2) The status of each Commissioner and his duties and responsibilities towards his Government will be determined by that Government.

(3) The two Commissioners shall together form the Permanent Indus Commission.

(4) The purpose and functions of the Commission shall be to establish and maintain co-operative arrangements for the implementation of this Treaty, to promote co-operation between the Parties in the development of the waters of the Rivers and, in particular,

(a) to study and report to the two Governments on any problem relating to the development of the waters of the Rivers which may be jointly referred to the Commission by the two Governments; in the event that a reference is made by one Government alone, the Commissioner of the other Government shall obtain the authorization of his Government before he proceeds to act on the reference;

(b) to make every effort to settle promptly, in accordance with the provisions of Article IX (1), any question arising thereunder;

(c) to undertake, once in every five years, a general tour of inspection of the Rivers for ascertaining the facts connected with various developments and works on the Rivers;

(d) to undertake promptly, at the request of either Commissioner, a tour of inspection of such works or sites on the Rivers as may be considered necessary by him for ascertaining the facts connected with those works or sites; and

(e) to take, during the Transition Period, such steps as may be necessary for the implementation of the provisions of Annexure H.

(5) The Commission shall meet regularly at least once a year, alternately in India and Pakistan. This regular annual meeting shall be held in November or in such other month as may be agreed upon between the Commissioners. The Commissionshall also meet when requested by either Commissioner.

(6) To enable the Commissioners to perform their functions in the Commission, each Government agrees to accord to the Commissioner of the other Government the same privileges and immunities as are accorded to representatives of member States to the principal and subsidiary organs of the United Nations under Sections 11, 12 and 13 of Article IV of the Convention on the Privileges and Immunities of the United Nations (dated 13th February, 1946) during the periods specified in those Sections. It is understood and agreed that these privileges and immunities are accorded to the Commissioners not for the personal benefit of the individuals themselves but in order to safeguard the independent exercise of their functions in connection with the Commission; consequently, the Government appointing the Commissioner not only has the right but is under a duty to waive the immunity of its Commissioner in any case where, in the opinion of the appointing Government, the immunity would impede the course of justice and can be waived without prejudice to the purpose for which the immunity is accorded.

(7) For the purposes of the inspections specified in Paragraph (4) (c) and (d), each Commissioner may be accompanied by two advisers or assistants to whom appropriate facilities will be accorded.

(8) The Commission shall submit to the Government of India and to the Government of Pakistan, before the first of June of every year, a report on its work for the year ended on the preceding 31st of March, and may submit to the two Governments other reports at such times as it may think desirable.

(9) Government shall bear the expenses of its Commissioner and his ordinary staff. The cost of any special staff incurred in connection with the work mentioned in Article Vll(l) shall be borne as provided therein.

(10) The Commission shall determine its own procedures.

ARTICLE IX

Settlement of Differences and Disputes

(1) Any question which, arises between the Parties concerning the interpretation or application of this Treaty or the existence of any fact which, if established, might constitute a breach of this Treaty shall first be examined by the Commission, which will endeavour to resolve the question by agreement.

(2) If the Commission does not reach agreement on any of the questions mentioned in Paragraph (1), then a difference will be deemed to have arisen, which shall be dealt with as follows:

(a) Any difference which, in the opinion of either Commissioner, falls within the provisions of Part 1 of Annexure F shall, at the request of either Commissioner, be dealt with by a Neutral Expert in accordance with the provisions of Part 2 of Annexure F;

(b) If the difference does not come within the provisions of Paragraph (2) (a), or if a Neutral Expert, in accordance with the provisions of Paragraph 7 of Annexure F, has informed the Commission that, in his opinion, the difference, or a part thereof, should be treated as a dispute, then a dispute will be deemed to have arisen which shall be settled in accordance with the provisions of Paragraphs (3), (4) and (5):

Provided that, at the discretion of the Commission, any difference may either be dealt with by a Neutral Expert in accordance with the provisions of Part 2 of Annexure F or be deemed to be a dispute to be settled in accordance with the provisions of Paragraphs (3), (4) and (5), or may be settled in any other way agreed upon by the Commission.

(3) As soon as a dispute to be settled in accordance with this and the succeeding paragraphs of this Article has arisen, the Commission shall, at the request of either Commissioner, report the fact to the two Governments, as early as practicable, stating in its report the points on which the Commission is in agreement and the issues in dispute, the views of each Commissioner on these issues and his reasons thereof.

(4) Either Government may, following receipt of the report referred to in Paragraph (3), or if it comes to the conclusion that this report is being unduly delayed in the Commission, invite the other Government to resolve the dispute by agreement. In doing so, it shall state the names of its negotiators and their readiness to meet with the negotiators to be appointed by the other Government at a time and place to be indicated by the other Government. To assist in those negotiations, the two Governments may agree to enlist the services of one or more mediators acceptable to them.

(5) A Court of Arbitration shall be established to resolve the dispute in the manner provided by Annexure G

(a) upon agreement between the Parties to do so; or

(b) at the request of either Party, if, after negotiations have begun pursuant to Paragraph (4), in its opinion the dispute is not likely to be resolved by negotiation or mediation; or

(c) at the request of either Party, if, after the expiry of one month following receipt by the other Government of the invitation referred to in Paragraph (4), that Party comes to the conclusion that the other Government is unduly delaying the negotiations.

(6) The provisions of Paragraphs (3), (4) and (5) shall not apply to any difference while it is being dealt with by a Neutral Expert.

ARTICLE X

Emergency Provision

If, at any time prior to 31st March 1965, Pakistan should represent to the Bank that, because of the outbreak of large-scale international hostilities arising out of causes beyond the control of Pakistan, it is unable to obtain from abroad the materials and equipment necessary for the completion, by 31st March 1973, of that part of the system of works referred to in Article IV(1) which relates to the replacement referred to therein, (hereinafter referred to as the "replacement element") and if, after consideration of this representation in consultation with India, the Bank is of the opinion that

(a) these hostilities are on a scale of which the consequence is that Pakistan is unable to obtain in time such materials and equipment as must be procured from abroad for the completion, by 31st March 1973, of the replacement element, and

(b) since the Effective Date, Pakistan has taken all reasonable steps to obtain the said materials and equipment and, with such resources of materials and equipment as have been available to Pakistan both from within Pakistan and from abroad, has carried forward the construction of the replacement element with due diligence and all reasonable expedition, the Bank shall immediately notify each of the Parties accordingly. The Parties undertake, without prejudice to the provisions of Article XII (3) and (4), that, on being so notified, they will forthwith consult together and enlist the good offices of the Bank in their consultation, with a view to reaching mutual agreement as to whether or not, in the light of all the circumstances then prevailing, any modifications of the provisions of this Treaty are appropriate and advisable and, if so, the nature and the extent of the modifications.

ARTICLE XI

General Provisions

(1) It is expressly understood that

(a) this Treaty governs the rights and obligations of each Party in relation to the other with respect only to the use of the waters of the Rivers and matters incidental thereto; and

(b) nothing contained in this Treaty, and nothing arising out of the execution thereof, shall be construed as constituting a recognition or waiver (whether tacit, by implication or otherwise) of any rights or claims whatsoever of either of the Parties other than those rights or claims which are expressly recognized or waived in this Treaty.

Each of the Parties agrees that it will not invoke this Treaty, anything contained therein, or anything arising out of the execution thereof, in support of any of its own rights or claims whatsoever or in disputing any of the rights or claims whatsoever of the other Party, other than those rights or claims which are expressly recognized or waived in this Treaty.

(2) Nothing in this Treaty shall be construed by the Parties as in any way establishing any general principle of law or any precedent.

(3) The rights and obligations of each Party under this Treaty shall remain unaffected by any provisions contained in, or by anything arising out of the execution of, any agreement establishing the Indus Basin Development Fund.

ARTICLE XII

Final Provisions

(1) This Treaty consists of the Preamble, the Articles hereof and Annexures A to H hereto, and may be cited as "The Indus Waters Treaty 1960".

(2) This Treaty shall be ratified and the ratifications into force upon the exchange of ratifications, and will then take effect retrospectively from the first of April 1960.

(3) The provisions of this Treaty may from time to time be modified by a duly ratified treaty concluded for that purpose between the two Governments.

(4) The provisions of this Treaty, or the provisions of this Treaty as modified under the provisions of Paragraph (3), shall continue in force until terminated by a duly ratified treaty concluded for that purpose between the two Governments.

IN WITNESS WHEREOF the respective Plenipotentiaries have signed this Treaty and have hereunto affixed their seals.

Done in triplicate in English at Karachi on this Nineteenth day of September 1960.

For the Government of India : (Sd) Jawaharlal Nehru

For the Government of Pakistan :

(Sd) Mohammad Ayub Khan
Field Marshal, H.P., H.J.

For the International Bank for Reconstruction and Development

for the purposes specified in Articles V and X and Annexures F, G and H:

(SD) W.A.B. Ilif

Indus Waters Treaty

Second Summary

The **Indus Waters Treaty** is a water-sharing treaty between India and Pakistan, brokered by the World Bank (then the International Bank for Reconstruction and Development).[1] The treaty was signed in Karachi on September 19, 1960 by Indian Prime Minister Jawaharlal Nehru and President of Pakistan Ayub Khan. The treaty was a result of Pakistani fear that since the source rivers of the Indus basin were in India, it could potentially create droughts and famines in Pakistan, especially at times of war.[2] Since the ratification of the treaty in 1960, India and Pakistan have not engaged in any water wars. Disagreements and disputes have been settled via legal procedures, provided for within the framework of the treaty. The treaty is considered to be one of the most successful watersharing endeavours in the world today even though analysts acknowledge the need to update certain technical specifications and expand the scope of the document to include climate change.[3]

The Indus river basin

The Indus System of Rivers comprises three western rivers the Indus, the Jhelum and Chenab and three eastern rivers - the Sutlej, the Beas and the Ravi. The treaty, under Article 5.1, envisages the sharing of waters of the rivers Ravi, Beas, Sutlej, Jhelum and Chenab which join the Indus River on its left bank (eastern side) in Pakistan. According to this treaty, Ravi, Beas and Sutlej, which constitute the eastern rivers, are allocated for exclusive use by India before they enter Pakistan. However, a transition period of 10 years was permitted in which India was bound to supply water to Pakistan from these rivers until Pakistan was able to build the canal system for utilization of waters of Jhelum, Chenab and the Indus itself, allocated to it under the treaty. Similarly, Pakistan has exclusive use of the western rivers Jhelum, Chenab and Indus but with some stipulations for development of projects on these rivers in India. Pakistan also received one-time financial compensation for the loss of water from the eastern rivers. Since March 31, 1970, after the 10-year moratorium, India has secured full rights for use of the waters of the three rivers allocated to it.[7][8] The treaty resulted in partitioning of the rivers rather than sharing of their waters.[9]

The countries agree to exchange data and co-operate in matters related to the treaty. For this purpose, treaty creates the Permanent Indus Commission, with a commissioner appointed by each country.

History and background

The waters of the Indus basin begin in Tibet and the Himalayan mountains in the state of Jammu and Kashmir. They flow from the hills through the arid states of Punjab and Sindh, converging in Pakistan and emptying into the Arabian Sea south of Karachi. Where once there was only a narrow strip of irrigated land along these rivers, developments over the last century have created a large network of canals and storage facilities that provide water for more than 26 million acres (110,000 km^2) - the largest irrigated area of any one river system in the world.

The partition of British India created a conflict over the plentiful waters of the Indus basin. The newly formed states were at odds over how to share and manage what was essentially a cohesive and unitary network of irrigation. Furthermore, the geography of partition was such that the source rivers of the Indus basin were in India. Pakistan felt its livelihood threatened by the prospect of Indian control over the tributaries that fed water into the Pakistani portion of the basin. Where India certainly had its own ambitions for the profitable development of the basin, Pakistan felt acutely threatened by a conflict over the main source of water for its cultivable land.

During the first years of partition the waters of the Indus were apportioned by the Inter-Dominion Accord of May 4, 1948. This accord required India to release sufficient waters to the Pakistani regions of the basin in return for annual payments from the government of Pakistan. The accord was meant to meet immediate requirements and was followed by negotiations for a more permanent solution. Neither side, however, was willing to compromise their respective positions and negotiations reached a stalemate. From the Indian point of view, there was nothing that Pakistan could do to prevent India from any of the schemes to divert the flow of water in the rivers. Pakistan's position was dismal and India could do whatever it wanted.[10] Pakistan wanted to take the matter to the International Court of Justice but India refused, arguing that the conflict required a bilateral resolution.

World Bank involvement

In this same year, David Lilienthal, formerly the chairman of the Tennessee Valley Authority and of the U.S. Atomic Energy Commission, visited the region to write a series of articles for Colliers magazine. Lilienthal had a keen interest in the subcontinent and was welcomed by the highest levels of both Indian and Pakistani governments. Although his visit was sponsored by Colliers, Lilienthal was briefed by state department and executive branch officials, who hoped that Lilienthal could help bridge the gap between India and Pakistan and also gauge hostilities on the subcontinent. During the course of his visit, it became clear to Lilienthal that tensions between India and Pakistan were acute, but also unable to be erased with one sweeping gesture. In his journal he wrote:

"India and Pakistan were on the verge of war over Kashmir. There seemed to be no possibility of negotiating this issue until tensions abated. One way to reduce hostility . . . would be to concentrate on other important issues where cooperation was possible. Progress in these areas would promote a sense of community between the two nations which might, in time, lead to a Kashmir settlement. Accordingly, I proposed that India and Pakistan work out a program jointly to develop and jointly to operate the Indus Basin river system, upon which both nations were dependent for irrigation water. With new dams and irrigation canals, the Indus and its tributaries could be made to yield the additional water each country needed for increased food production. In the article I had suggested that the World Bank might use its good offices to bring the parties to agreement, and help in the financing of an Indus Development program. (Gulhati 93)"

Lilienthal's idea was well received by officials at the World Bank, and, subsequently, by the Indian and Pakistani governments. Eugene R. Black, then president of the World Bank told Lilienthal that his proposal "makes good sense all round". Black wrote that the Bank was interested in the economic progress of the two countries and had been concerned that the Indus dispute could only be a serious handicap to this development. India's previous objections to third party arbitration were remedied by the Bank's insistence that it would not adjudicate the conflict, but, instead, work as a conduit for agreement.[11]

Black also made a distinction between the "functional" and "political" aspects of the Indus dispute. In his correspondence with Indian and Pakistan leaders, Black asserted that the Indus dispute could most realistically be solved if the functional aspects of disagreement were negotiated apart from political considerations. He envisioned a group that tackled the question of how best to utilize the waters of the Indus Basin - leaving aside questions of historic rights or allocations.

Black proposed a Working Party made up of Indian, Pakistani and World Bank engineers. The World Bank delegation would act as a consultative group, charged with offering suggestions and speeding dialogue. In his opening statement to the Working Party, Black spoke of why he was optimistic about the group's success:

One aspect of Mr. Lilienthal's proposal appealed to me from the first. I mean his insistence that the Indus problem is an engineering problem and should be dealt with by engineers. One of the strengths of the engineering profession is that, all over the world, engineers speak the same language and approach problems with common standards of judgment. (Gulhati 110) Black's hopes for a quick resolution to the Indus dispute were premature. While the Bank had expected that the two sides would come to an agreement on the allocation of waters, neither India nor Pakistan seemed willing to compromise their positions. While Pakistan insisted on its historical right to waters of all the Indus tributaries,and that half of West Punjab was under threat of desertification the Indian side argued that the previous distribution of waters should not set future allocation. Instead, the Indian side set up a new basis of distribution, with the waters of the Western tributaries going to Pakistan and the Eastern tributaries to India. The substantive technical discussions that Black had hoped for were stymied by the political considerations he had expected to avoid.

The World Bank soon became frustrated with this lack of progress. What had originally been envisioned as a technical dispute that would quickly untangle itself became an intractable mess. India and Pakistan were unable to agree on the technical aspects of allocation, let alone the implementation of any agreed upon distribution of waters. Finally, in 1954, after nearly two years of negotiation, the World bank offered its own proposal, stepping beyond the limited role it had apportioned for itself and forcing the two sides to consider concrete plans for the future of the basin. The proposal offered India the three eastern tributaries of the basin and Pakistan the three western tributaries. Canals and storage dams were to be constructed to divert waters from the western rivers and replace the eastern river supply lost by Pakistan.

While the Indian side was amenable to the World Bank proposal, Pakistan found it unacceptable. The World Bank allocated the eastern rivers to India and the western rivers to Pakistan. This new distribution did not account for the historical usage of the Indus basin, or the fact that West Punjab's Eastern districts could turn into desert, and repudiated Pakistan's negotiating position. Where India had stood for a new system of allocation, Pakistan felt that its share of waters should be based on pre-partition distribution. The World Bank proposal was more in line with the Indian plan and this angered the Pakistani delegation. They threatened to withdraw from the Working Party and negotiations verged on collapse.

But neither side could afford the dissolution of talks. The Pakistani press met rumors of an end to negotiation with talk of increased hostilities; the government was ill-prepared to forego talks for a violent conflict with India and was forced to reconsider its position. India was also eager to settle the Indus issue; large development projects were put on hold by negotiations and Indian leaders were eager to divert water for irrigation.

In December 1954, the two sides returned to the negotiating table. The World Bank proposal was transformed from a basis of settlement to a basis for negotiation and the talks continued, stop and go, for the next six years.

One of the last stumbling blocks to an agreement concerned financing for the construction of canals and storage facilities that would transfer water from the western rivers to Pakistan. This transfer was necessary to make up for the water Pakistan was giving up by ceding its rights to the eastern rivers. The World Bank initially planned for India to pay for these works, but India refused. The Bank responded with a plan for external financing supplied mainly by the United States and the United Kingdom. This solution cleared the remaining stumbling blocks to agreement and the Treaty was signed by the Prime Ministers of both countries in 1960. [12]

Treaty provisions

The agreement set up a commission to adjudicate any future disputes arising over the allocation of waters. The Permanent Indus Commission has survived three wars and provides an ongoing mechanism for consultation and conflict resolution through inspection, exchange of data and visits. The Commission is required to meet regularly to discuss potential disputes as well as cooperative arrangements for the development of the basin. Either party must notify the other of plans to construct any engineering works which would affect the other party and to provide data about such works. In cases of disagreement, a neutral expert is called in for mediation and arbitration. While neither side has initiated projects that could cause the kind of conflict that the Commission was created to resolve, the annual inspections and exchange of data continue, unperturbed by tensions on the subcontinent.

Sources

- Barrett, Scott, "Conflict and Cooperation in Managing International Water Resources," Policy Research Working Paper 1303, The World Bank, May 1994.
- Gulhati, Niranjan D., The Indus Waters Treaty: An Exercise in International Mediation, Allied Publishers: Bombay, 1973.
- Michel, Aloys Arthur, The Indus Rivers: A Study of the Effects of Partition, Yale University Press: New Haven, 1967.
- Verghese, B.G., Waters of Hope, Oxford and IBH Publishing: New Delhi, 1990.

(Wikipedia)

The Indus Waters Treaty

Third Summary

HISTORICAL CONTEXT

The partition of the Indian subcontinent created a conflict over the waters of the Indus basin. In 1951, David Lilienthal wrote an influential article in Colliers magazine suggesting that the World Bank use its good offices to bring India and Pakistan to an agreement over how to share and manage the river system. The President of the World Bank, Eugene R. Black, agreed to act as a conduit of agreement between the two states. Finally, in 1960, after several years of arduous negotiations did an agreement take form. Even today, the Indus Waters Treaty is the only agreement that has been faithfully implemented and upheld by both India and Pakistan. Following the terrorist attack on the Indian Parliament on December 13, 2001, several high profile commentators in India suggested that the treaty should be scrapped, though the Indian government made no intimations that it was considering such a move.

ABRIDGED TEXT OF INDUS WATERS TREATY (SIGNED IN KARACHI ON SEPTEMBER 19, 1960)

The Government of India and the Government of Pakistan, being equally desirous of attaining the most complete and satisfactory utilisation of the waters of the Indus system of rivers and recognising the need, therefore, of fixing and delineating, in a spirit of goodwill and friendship, the rights and obligations of each in relation to the other concerning the use of these waters and of making provision for the settlement, in a cooperative spirit, of all such questions as may hereafter arise in regard to the interpretation or application of the provisions agreed upon herein, have resolved to conclude a Treaty in furtherance of these objectives, and for this purpose have named as their plenipotentiaries:

The Government of India: Shri Jawaharlal Nehru, Prime Minister of India, and The Government of Pakistan: Field Marshal Mohammad Ayub Khan, H.P., H.J., President of Pakistan, who, having communicated to each other their respective Full Powers and having found them in good and due form, have agreed upon the following Articles and An

ARTICLE II

PROVISIONS REGARDING EASTERN RIVERS

All the waters of the Eastern Rivers shall be available for the unrestricted use of Inida, except as otherwise expressly provided in this Article.

Except for Domestic Use and Non-Consumptive Use, Pakistan shall be under an obligation to let flow, and shall not permit any interference with, the waters of the Sutlej Main and the Ravi Main in the reaches where these rivers flow in Pakistan and have not yet finally crossed into Pakistan. The points of final crossing are the following: (a) near the new Hasta Bund upstream of Suleimanke in the case of the Sutlej Main, and (b) about one and a half miles upstream of the syphon for the B-D Link in the case of the Ravi Main.

Except for Domestic Use, Non-Consumptive Use and Agricultural Use, Pakistan shall be under an obligation to let flow, and shall not permit any interference with, the waters (while flowing in Pakistan) of any Tributary which in its natural course joins the Sutlej Main or the Ravi Main before these rivers have finally crossed into Pakistan.

All the waters, while flowing in Pakistan, of any Tributary which, in its natural course, joins the Sutlej Main or the Ravi Main after these rivers have finally crossed into Pakistan shall be available for the unrestricted use of Pakistan: Provided however that this provision shall not be construed as giving Pakistan any claim or right to any releases by India in any such Tributary.

There shall be a Transition Period during which India shall (i) limit its withdrawals for Agricultural Use, (ii) limit abstractions for storages, and (iii) make deliveries to Pakistan from the Eastern Rivers.

The Transition Period shall begin on 1st April 1960 and it shall end on 31st March 1970, or, if extended under the provisions of Part 8 of Annexure H, on the date up to which it has been extended. In any event, whether the Transition Period shall end not later than 31st March 1973.

During the Transition Period, Pakistan shall receive for unrestricted use the waters of the Eastern Rivers which are to be released by India in accordance with the provisions of Annexure H. After the end of the Transition Period, Pakistan shall have no claim or right to releases by India of any of the waters of the Eastern Rivers. In case there are any releases, Pakistan shall enjoy the unrestricted use of the waters so released after they have finally crossed into Pakistan: Provided that in the event that Pakistan makes any use of these waters, Pakistan shall not acquire any right whatsover, by prescription or otherwise, to a continuance of such releases or such use.

ARTICLE III

PROVISION REGARDING WESTERN RIVERS

Pakistan shall receive for unrestricted use all those waters of the Western Rivers which India is under obligation to let flow under the provisions of Paragraph (2).

India shall be under an obligation to let flow all the waters of the Western Rivers, and shall not permit any interference with these waters, except for the following uses, restricted in the case of each of the rivers, The Indus, The Jhelum and The Chenab, to the drainage basin thereof: (a) Domestic Use; (b) Non-Consumptive Use; (c) Agricultural Use, as set out in Annexure C; and (d) Generation of hydro-electric power, as set out in Annexure D.

Pakistan shall have the unrestricted use of all waters originating from sources other than the Eastern Rivers which are delivered by Pakistan into The Ravi or The Sutlej, and India shall not make use of these waters.

Except as provided in Annexures D and E, India shall not store any water of, or construct any storage works on, the Western Rivers.

ARTICLE IV

Provisions Regarding Eastern Rivers And Western Rivers

Pakistan shall use its best endeavors to construct and bring into operation with due regard to expedition and economy, that part of a system of work which will accomplish the replacement, from the Western Rivers and other sources, of water supplies for irrigation canals in Pakistan which, on 15th August 1947, were dependent on water supplies from the Eastern Rivers.

Each Party agrees that any Non-Consumptive Use made by it shall be made as not to materially change, on account of such use, the flow in any channel to the prejudice of the uses on that channel by the other Party under the provisions of this Treaty.

Nothing in this Treaty shall be construed as having the effect of preventing either Party from undertaking schemes of drainage, river training, conservation of soil against erosion and dredging, or from removal of stones, gravel or sand from the beds of the Rivers: Provided that in executing any of the schemes mentioned above, each Party will avoid, as far as practicable, any material damage to the other Party.

Pakistan shall maintain in good order its portions of the drainages mentioned below with capacities not less than the capacities as on the Effective Date: (i) Hudiara Drain, (ii) Kasur Nala, (iii) Salimshah Drain, (iv) Fazilka Drain.

If Inida finds it necessary that any of the drainages mentioned in Paragraph (4) should be deepened or widened in Pakistan, Pakistan agrees to undertake to do so as a work of public interest, provided India agrees to pay the cost of the deepening or widening.

Each Party will use its best endeavors to maintain the natural channels of the Rivers, as on the Effective Date, in such condition as will avoid, as far as practicable, any obstruction to the flow in these channels likely to cause material damage to the other Party.

Neither Party will take any action which would have the effect of diverting the Ravi Main between Madhopur and Lahore, or the Sutlej Main between Harike and Suleimanke, from its natural channel between high banks.

The use of the natural channels of the Rivers for the discharge of flood or other excess waters shall be free and not subject to limitation by either Party, and neither Party shall have any claim against the other in respect of any damage caused by such use. Each Party agrees to communicate to the other Party, as far in advance as practicable, any information it may have in regard to such extraordinary discharges of water from reservoirs and flood flows as may affect the other Party.

Each Party declares its intention to operate its storage dams, barrages and irrigation canals in such manner, consistent with the normal operations of its hydraulic systems, as to avoid, as far as feasible, material damage to the other Party.

Each Party declares its intention to prevent, as far as practicable, undue pollution of the waters of the Rivers which might affect adversely uses similar in nature to those to which the waters were put on the Effective Date, and agrees to take all reasonable measures to ensure that, before any sewage or industrial waste is allowed to flow into the Rivers, it will be treated, where necessary, in such manner as not materially to affect those uses: Provided that the criterion of reasonableness shall be the customary practice in similar situations on the Rivers.

The Parties agree to adopt, as far as feasible, appropriate measures for recovery, and restoration to owners, of timber and other property floated or floating down the Rivers, subject to appropriate charges being paid by the owners.

Except as otherwise required by the express provisions of this Treaty, nothing in this Treaty shall be construed as affecting existing territorial rights over the waters of any of the Rivers or the beds or banks thereof, or as affecting existing property rights under municipal law over such waters or beds or banks.

ARTICLE V

FINANCIAL PROVISIONS

In consideration of the fact that the purpose of part of the system of works referred to in Article IV (1) is the replacement, from the Western Rivers and other sources, of water supplies for irrigation canals in Pakistan which on 15th August 1947 were dependent on water supplies from the Eastern Rivers, India agrees to make a fixed contribution of Pounds Sterling 62,060,000 towards the costs of these works.

The sum of Pounds Sterling 62,060,000 shall be paid in ten equal installments on the 1st of November of each year.

Each of the instalments shall be paid to the Bank for the credit of the Indus Basin Development Fund to be established and administered by the Bank.

These financial provisions shall not be construed as conferring upon India any right to participate in the decisions as to the system of works which Pakistan constructs or as constituting an assumption of any responsibility by India or as an agreement by India in regard to such works.

Except for such payments as are specifically provided for in this Treaty, neither Party shall be entitled to claim any payment for observance of the provisions of this Treaty or to make any charge for water received from it by the other Party.

ARTICLE VI

EXCHANGE OF DATA

The following data with respect to the flow in, and utilisation of the waters of, the Rivers shall be exchanged regularly between the Parties: (a) Daily guage and discharge data relating to flow of the Rivers at all observation sites. (b) Daily extractions for or releases from reservoirs. (c) Daily withdrawals at the heads of all canals operated by government or by a government agency, including link canals. (d) Daily escapages from all canals, including link canals. (e) Daily deliveries from link canals.

ARTICLE VII

FUTURE CO-OPERATION

The two Parties recognize that they have a common interest in the optimum development of the Rivers, and, to that end, they declare their intention to co-operate, by mutual agreement, to the fullest possible extent.

ARTICLE VIII

PERMANENT INDUS COMMISSION

India and Pakistan shall each create a permanent post of Commissioner for Indus Waters, and shall appoint to this post, as often as a vacancy occurs, a person who should ordinarily be a high-ranking engineer competent in the field of hydrology and water-use. Unless either Government should decide to take up any particular question directly with the other Government, each Commissioner will be the representative of his Government for all matters arising out of this Treaty, and will serve as the regular channel of communication on all matters relating to the implementation of the Treaty, and, in particular, with respect to (a) the furnishing or exchange of information or data provided for in the Treaty; and (b) the giving of any notice or response to any notice provided for in the Treaty.

The status of each Commissioner and his duties and responsibilities towards his Government will be determined by that Government.

The two Commissioners shall together form the Permanent Indus Commission.

The purpose and functions of the Commission shall be to establish and maintain co-operative arrangements for the implementation of this Treaty and to promote co-operation between the Parties in the development of the waters of the Rivers.

The Commission shall determine its own procedures.

ARTICLE IX

Settlement Of Differences And Disputes

Any question which arises between the Parties concerning the interpretation or application of this Treaty or the existence of any fact which, if established, might constitute a breach of this Treaty shall first be examined by the Commission, which will endeavor to resolve the question by agreement.

If the Commission does not reach agreement on any of the questions mentioned in the Paragraph (1), then a difference will be deemed to have arisen, which shall be dealt with by a Neutral Expert. If the Neutral Expert has informed the Commission that, in his opinion, the difference should be treated as a dispute, then a dispute will be deemed to have arisen.

As soon as a dispute to be settled has arisen, the Commission shall, at the request of either Commissioner, report the fact to the two Governments, as early as practicable, stating in its report the points on which the Commisssion is in agreement and the issues in dispute, the views of each Commissioner on these issues and his reasons therefor.

Either Government may, following receipt of the report, or if it comes to the conclusion that this report is being unduly delayed in the Commission, invite the other Government to resolve the dispute by agreement.

A court of Arbitration shall be established to resolve the dispute.

ARTICLE X

Emergency Provisions

If, at any time prior to 31st March 1965, Pakistan should represent to the Bank that, because of the outbreak of large-scale international hostilities arising out of causes beyond the control of Pakistan, it is unable to obtain from abroad the materials and equipment necessary for the completion, by 31st March 1973, of that part of the system of works referred to in Article IV (1) which related to the replacement referred to therein, (hereinafter referred to as the replacement element) and if, after consideration of this representation in consultation with India, the Bank is of the opinion that (a) these hostilities are on a scale of which the consequence is that Pakistan is unable to obtain in time such materials and equipment as must be procured from abroad for the completion, by 31st March 1973, of the replacement element, and (b) since the Effective Date, Pakistan has taken all reasonable steps to obtain the said materials and equipment and has carried forward the construction of the replacement element with due dilligence and all reasonable expedition, the Bank shall immediately notify each of the Parties accordingly. The Parties undertake that in being so notified, they will forthwith consult together and enlist the good offices of the Bank in their consultation, with a view to reaching mutual agreement as to whether or not, in light of all circumstances prevailing, any modifications of the provisions of this Treaty are appropriate and advisable and, if so, the nature and the extent of the modifications.

ARTICLE XII

FINAL PROVISIONS

This Treaty consists of the Preamble, the Articles hereof and Annexures A to H hereto, and may be cited as "The Indus Waters Treaty 1960."

This Treaty shall be ratified and the ratifications therof shall be exchanged in New Delhi. It shall enter into force upon the exchange of ratifications, and will then take effect retrospectively form the first of April 1960.

The provisions of this Treaty may from time to time be modified by a duly ratified treaty concluded for that purpose between the two Governments.

The provisions of this Treaty, or the provisions of this Treaty as modified under the provisions of Paragraph (3), shall continue in force until terminated by a duly ratified treaty concluded for that purpose between the two Governments.

In witness whereof the respective Plenipotentiaries have signed this Treaty and have hereunto affixed their seals.

Done in triplicate in English at Karachi on this Nineteenth day of September 1960.

[Signed:]
For the Government of India:
Jawaharlal Nehru

For the Government of Pakistan:
Mohammad Ayub Khan
Field Marshal, H.P., H.J.

For the International Bank for Reconstruction and Development:
W. A. B. Iliff

CHAPTER – 34

The Baglihar Dispute

International Water Power (16 August, 2006)

India had decided to set up a run-of-river, 450MW hydroelectric plant at Baglihar in its Jammu & Kashmir State, utilizing the waters of river Chenab, a tributary of the mighty Indus. Since the time that India informed Pakistan of that fact in 1992, the two countries had gone through prolonged negotiations, based on Pakistan's objections to the project as the lower riparian state. The talks having not succeeded, a World Bank-appointed 'neutral' expect is currently engaged in the task of finding a solution. His decision is expected in early-November.

To understand the imbroglio, it is necessary to look at the bigger picture. The Indus river system, one of the major systems in the world, comprises the main Indus and its five important tributaries: Jhelum, Chenab, Ravi, Beas and Satluj rivers. For the sake of convenience and geography, Indus, along with Jhelum and Chenab, are referred to as the 'Western rivers', while the other three tributaries are termed 'Eastern rivers'. The common features of all of them is that they originate in the Himalayas, pass through Indian territory and, after Indus has received the waters of its five tributaries in Pakistan, it flows through Pak provinces of Punjab and Sind and falls in the Arabian Sea, south of Karachi.

After the British had colonised India in the 19th century, they built a large network of dams, barrages and canals, over eight decades, utilizing the Indus river system. The command-area so created of about 105M ha was the largest such irrigated tract in the world and turned the Indian province of Punjab (literal meaning Five Waters) and its contiguous areas from a mainly arid zone into a prosperous agrarian state that grew both food grains and cash crops.

Britain granted independence to India in 1947 by partitioning the sub-continent into two separate political entities of India and Pakistan. The process of partition (and its aftermath in Kashmir) led to an arbitrary split of the Indus river system, with its parts divided between the two Countries. The rivers' sources and headworks of some major canals remained in India, and the latter drew plans to further develop the water resources which remained on its side. Pakistan, as the smaller state, located downstream of these rivers, felt threatened that India could well manipulate the flow of those waters to the former's disadvantage.

A temporary accord was signed between the two Countries in 1948 to regulate the usage of the Indus System. This was followed by prolonged negotiations for a more durable settlement. However, by 1951, there was an impasse in those talks. Realising the importance of the matter, the World Bank offered its services, first as facilitator and later as a participant in those talks so as to reach a fair and equitable solution. Still, it was to take another nine years before the Indus Waters Treaty was signed on 19 September 1960. Its signatories were the governments of India and Pakistan and the World Bank. Incidentally, it was the first time that the World Bank had intervened to settle an international river waters dispute.

The Treaty's main provisions included the following:

1. The usage of waters of the three Eastern rivers was given exclusively to India.

2. The usage of waters of the three Western rivers was given exclusively to Pakistan. However India, as the upper riparian state, was allowed a restrictive use of their waters for domestic, agriculture, 'non-consumptive' and hydro generation purposes. One of these three rivers was Chenab.

3. To replace the loss of waters as at (1) above, Pakistan was to construct a system of 'replacement works', to be funded internationally.

4. To oversee implementation of the Treaty, a Permanent Indus Commission was to be set up, to meet periodically. It comprised one Commissioner each from the two countries, appointed by their respective governments.

Conflict resolution under the treaty: role of the World Bank

Under the Treaty, disagreements between India and Pakistan about its provisions have been put under a three-fold classification :

(a) Questions, to be examined by the Commission.

(b) Differences, to be decided by a 'Neutral Expert'.

(c) Disputes, to be decided by a Court of Arbitration (CoA).

Under the Treaty, the first step is for the Commission itself to resolve any 'question' that arises between the two parties. If it were not so resolved, it becomes a 'difference' to be considered and decided by a Neutral Expert. The Expert is to be appointed by the two parties, or a third party (as agreed by the latter), or by World Bank in consultation with the two parties.

If the difference does not fall within the mandate of the Expert (as laid down in detail under the Treaty), on if the Expert treats it as a dispute, it goes before a CoA. Of the seven members of the Court, two each are appointed by either party, while the remaining three (including Chairman) are selected with the assistance of the World Bank, among others.

While the World Bank had been a signatory to the Treaty, it has been making it clear that (a) this was for certain 'specified' purposes, (b) that many of those purposes had since been completed, and (c) that the Bank is not a guarantor of the Treaty.

In its press release relating to the appointment of the Neutral Expert in the Baglihar case, the World Bank reiterated that its 'remaining responsibilities' under the Treaty were only three :

(1) The appointment of a Neutral.

(2) Management of a Trust Fund to meet the Expert's expenses.

(3) A limited role in the constitution of CoA.

Baglihar Project

Located on river Chenab in the north Indian State of Jammu & Kashmir, Baglihar hydroelectric project is based on a 144.5m high concrete gravity dam, affording a live storage capacity of 15Mm^3. In its first stage, the project would have an underground power house with three 150MW Francis turbines, generating around 2.8B units in a 90% dependable year. The salient features of the project are listed in Table 1.

The project promoters, state-owned J&K Power Development Corp. had signed an EPC contract with the Indian construction major, Jaiprakash Associates, in April 1999, giving a completion schedule of five years. The project has however been delayed for more than one reason and the latest date being mentioned for its completion is February 2007.

Pakistan had raised objections to the project after India gave notice of undertaking it way back in 1992. These were raised more vehemently subsequent to the construction contract being signed in 1999. Referring to them, Syed Shahid Husain, a former Secretary in Pakistan's Ministry of Water & Power, explained in an article in South Asian Journal (April- June 2005 issue): "The basic dispute between the two Governments arises more out of mistrust by Pakistan of India's intention because, at some point in future, once it acquires the capacity to store water, India can easily withhold it during shortage and release it during excess, the precise opposite of what the lower riparian state would want. India answers to the Pakistan fears by saying that the first installation which would disappear would be [India's] Salal project, which is downstream [of] the Baglihar project, and if they were to flood Pakistan, they would endanger Salal project".

Husain also quoted India's Foreign Secretary as denying the validity of Pakistan's apprehensions and mentioning that the Treaty had no solution to offer for such fears!

Differences Over The Scheme

Discussions over the last ten years or so between the two sides over Baglihar have led to a crystallisation of their differences. These relate in the main to the design of the project, the extent of pondage to be created by it, and the necessity and placement of the spillway gates on the dam. Pakistan asserts that all the three are in violation of the provisions of the Treaty as given in its Annexure D, Part 3 which deals with new run-of-river power plants to be set up by India on any of the Western rivers. These differences between the two countries are examined as under :

(1) As per the Treaty, the works at such a project shall not be capable of raising the water level in the operating pool artificially above the 'Full Pondage Level' specified in the design. The maximum pondage in the operating pool shall not exceed twice the pondage required for firm power. However, the design shall take due account of the requirements of Surcharge storage and of secondary power. Pakistan feels that the planned pondage of 37.7mcm in the project is violative of the Treaty provisions. India denies this based on its own calculations. Full Pondage Level is defined in the Treaty as the level corresponding to maximum pondage allowed under it. Pakistan asserts that in the Baglihar design, the space between the maximum water-level and top of the dam is unduly large and would enable India to have a greater storage than full pondage level. India says that this space, known as FreeBoard is for safety reasons and any misuse by it to store more water would be against dam safety and thus counter-productive.

(2) The Treaty provisions also regulate the setting up of outlets in the dam. Any such outlet, if considered necessary for technical reason shall be of minimum size and located at the highest level consistent with design and operational parameters. Thus, where gated spillway is considered necessary in the context of the conditions at the plant-site, the bottom level of the gates (in normal closed position) shall be located at the highest level 'consistent with sound and economical design and satisfactory construction and operation of the works'. Baglihar design includes six submerged radial gates on the main spillway and 2 crest radial gates on the chute spillway. Pakistan objects to their number and placement as being violative of the above provisions. India has responded through detailed technical calculations to assert that it is doing what the Treaty allows.

(3) As per the Treaty, the water intakes for the turbines shall be located at the 'highest level consistent with satisfactory and economical construction and operation' of the run-of-river plant and 'with customary and accepted practice of design for the designated range of the Plant's operation'. These being generalised terms, each side has interpreted the existing Baglihar design to suit its own case.

Pakistan had also wanted India to stop further construction on Baglihar project until their differences were finally settled. India declined this for various reasons, including the fact that there was no provisions in the Treaty for such a stoppage. All that was required under the Treaty was for India to intimate to Pakistan, at least six months before beginning its construction, the location of the proposed plant along with a set of technical data specified in the Treaty (Appendix II to Annexure D of the Treaty).

Chronology Of The Dispute

India had given advance notice (with data on the project) to Pakistan back in May 1992 of its intention to take up Baglihar. Following Pakistan's objections in August 1992, the next seven years saw an exchange of letters between the two countries regarding the data etc. to be given by India. In the meantime, in mid-1999, an important step was taken by India with the signing of agreement to construct the project.

Consequently, the first structured discussion between the two countries on Baglihar took place in May 2000 at the 84th meeting of the Permanent Indus Commission. Further discussions and exchange of letters not having yielded results, in May 2003 Pakistan gave notice to move the World Bank for appointment of a neutral expert, as provided under the Treaty. India responded with a request for bilateral discussions. Pakistan put forward three pre-conditions in August 2003 for doing this: (a) stoppage of work at Baglihar, (b) facility to it to make a site-inspection and, (c) a time-bound resolution of the differences between the two sides.

These were discussed in yet another round of meetings, both at technical and official levels. The last such meeting was held in the first week of January 2005 between the two Governments at Secretary-level. While India thought that progress was being made, this view was not shared by its neighbour. Thus on 15 January 2005, Pakistan formally moved the World Bank for the appointment of a 'Neutral Expert' to decide on the differences between the two Countries regarding the Baglihar project.

After examining the previous correspondence on the subject (to satisfy itself that the two sides had taken all preliminary steps) and in consultation with both Governments, the World Bank in May 2005 decided in favour of appointing such an expert. Its choice fell on Prof. Raymond Lafitte, a Swiss Civil Engineer, then working on the faculty of Swiss Federal Institute of Technology at Lausanne.

The procedure to be adopted by the Nuclear Expert is specified in Appendix F (paras 6-13) to the Treaty (Table 2). In October 2005, Lafitte paid a visit to India to view the project site in Baglihar. Apart from the Indian side, a delegation from Pakistan's Ministry of Water & Power accompanied Lafitte. That enabled him to closely question the two parties on the issues raised and to understand them. He also visited the Indian Institute of Technology at Roorkee, north of Delhi, where a live and scale model of Baglihar project had been set up in a laboratory.

Since, then, Lafitte has had more than one round of talks with India and Pakistan. As per the present schedule, a penultimate meeting has been fixed with the two sides in Paris in the first week of October 2006. In that, Lafitte would discuss his draft findings on the Baglihar 'difference' with both the sides. The latter would then have an opportunity to make written submissions relating to those findings to him, during the course of that month.

During 6-8 November 2006, Lafitte will be in Washington, DC, where both the sides would again meet him prior to the finalisation of his report. The report, after being signed by him, would then be delivered to the Commissioners on both the sides and to the World Bank (which had appointed him).

Post-Decision Scenario

So what could happen after Raymond Lafitte gives his decision? There could be varying scenarios. The ideal scenario would be if both the parties agreed to accept the award as 'final and binding', as envisaged under the Treaty, and proceeded to give effect to it.

To help in that process, the Treaty's Appendix F, para 12 allows Lafitte to suggest for the consideration of both the Parties, 'such measures as are, in his opinion, appropriate to compose a difference or to implement his decision'. That could happen if he were asked by the Indus Commission to do so, and the provision appears generally to relate to a situation where his decision may contain any ambiguity or technicality.

What would happen if Lafitte's decision, even though clear-cut, were found not acceptable by one of the two Parties for extraneous reasons ? Such a scenario could well arise from the context in which the Neutral Expert was appointed last year, and the subsequent developments. As it happens, the Treaty does not include any provision to ensure implementation of the Neutral Expert's 'decision'.

The political relations between India and Pakistan in the current millennium have led to both positive and negative results. On one side a series of 'confidence building' measures in the various areas have been put into effect through periodic rounds of official-level talks between the two countries. As stated earlier, even a last-minute agreement on Baglihar was attempted through these talks in early-January 2005, prior to Pakistan approaching the World Bank to appoint a neutral expert under the Treaty.

Water Resource is a live and sensitive issue in Pakistan, both internally between its provinces and externally with India. To add to this, federal elections are due to be held in Pakistan any time over the next twelve months. Thus an adverse finding by Lafitte may be difficult for the Pakistan Government to sell to its people.

In India, the public view on Baglihar issue is related to the perceived intransigence of its neighbour generally in settling most issues between the two countries without seeking third-party intervention. As it happens, the already-delayed project is due for completion in early-2007. Thus, if Lafitte were to uphold any or all of Pakistan's case, it would be very difficult technically - as well as in terms of time and cost - to make consequential modifications in the design and construction of the project, at that stage.

So what could either Party do in the event of its finding Lafitte's decision adverse to it and thus hard to accept? A number of possibilities could arise.

The two parties could return to the negotiating table (as they did prior to Lafitte's appointment). This could be for two reasons. One could be a bona fide desire to finally resolve the 'difference' (hopefully narrowed through Lafitte's decision), in a spirit of mutual goodwill.

The other is if one of the Parties were to assert that a question had arisen out of Lafitte's decision which he could not resolve. That could also happen if Lafitte were to decide that the whole or part of the issues before him was not a 'difference' between the Parties but was in fact a 'dispute', which required settlement under the procedure prescribed in Article IX of the Treaty. Normally, such a determination, if made by the neutral expert, is expected to be done during the early stages. However, there is nothing in the Treaty to bar him from doing so even after he has heard both the parties at length and received their written submissions.

The said Article IX (paras-3-5) requires both the Governments to follow a serialised procedure. The first step is to try and resolve the dispute through a mutual agreement. This is done by nominating negotiators by either side and, if agreed, one or more 'mediators' acceptable to both. If the 'dispute' still continues, then under certain specified conditions, it would need to be referred to a seven member Court of Arbitration appointed to deal with it. The whole process of the creation, deliberations and decision of the Court is likely to be time-consuming, even through at the end of it, the 'award' of the Court (like the neutral expert's decision) is termed as 'final and binding' on both the Parties to the Treaty.

To sum up, therefore, the entire thrust of the Indus Waters Treaty is for India and Pakistan to themselves resolve any differences over the use of those waters in a spirit of mutual goodwill and accommodation. Only in rare cases may a neutral expert or arbitrators be needed to help in the process. It is no surprise that Baglihar was the first case, in over four and half decades since the Treaty was signed, that this had to be done.

Author Info:

I.M. Sahai is an independent consultant in hydro power, and is based in New Delhi, India

Related Articles
World Bank expert clears Baglihar

Table 1. Features of the Baglihar hydro project

Dam
Type: Concrete gravity
Height: 144.5m
Length: 317m long at the top
Main spillway: six submerged radial gates, 10m wide x 10.5m high
Chute spillway: two crest radial gates, 12m wide x 19m high
Reservoir : Live storage capacity of 15Mm^3
Gross head : 130m
Two horseshoe shape diversion tunnels, 939m long
10.15m diameter circular headrace tunnel, 2070m long
Tailrace tunnel - 160m long, 10m wide, 19-27.5m-high, D-shaped
Power house
Underground cavern, 121 m x 24 m x 50 m
3 Francis Vertical axis turbines of 150 MWs each
Rated discharge per stage: 430 cubic metres/sec.
Installed capacity: 450 MWs, in Stage I.
Generation: 2.804 billion units in a 90% dependable year.
Transmission
Underground transformer hall having 10 transformers of 11kV/400kV single-phase.
Outdoor 400kV switchyard.
Contractors
1) Jaiprakash Associates Ltd., for all civil and hydromechanical works, on EPC basis.
2) Siemens/VA Tech Hydro Vevey for Electro-Mechanical works.
3) Lahmeyer International for design and contracts review, construction supervision and contractmanagement.

Source: Jaypee Group / Lahmeyer International

Table 2. Procedure to be adopted by the neutral expert (Extracts from the Indus Water Treaty, 1960 : Annexure F)

6. The procedure with respect to each reference to a Neutral Expert shall be determined by him, provided that :

   (a) He shall afford to each Party an adequate hearing;

   (b) In making his decision, he shall be governed by the provisions of this Treaty and by the Compromise, if any, presented to him by the Commission;

   (c) Without prejudice to the provisions of Paragraph 3, unless both Parties so request, he shall not deal with any issue of financial compensation.

7. Should the Commission be unable to agree that any particular difference falls within Part I of this Annexure, the Neutral Expert shall, after hearing both Parties, decide whether or not it so falls. Should he decide that it so falls, he shall proceed to render a decision on the merits; should he decide otherwise, he shall inform the Commission, that, in his opinion, the difference should be treated as a dispute. Should the Neutral Expert decide that only a part of the difference so falls, he shall at his discretion, either;

   (a) Proceed to render a decision on the part which so falls, and inform the Commission that, in his opinion, the part which does not so fall should be treated as a dispute, or

   (b) Inform the Commission that, in his opinion, the entire difference should be treated as a dispute.

8. Each government agrees to extend to the Neutral Expert such facilities as he may require for the discharge of his functions.

9. The Neutral Expert shall, as soon as possible, render a decision on the question or questions referred to him, giving his reasons. A copy of such decision, duly signed by the Neutral Expert, shall be forwarded by him to each of the Commissioners and to the Bank. .....

11. The decision of the Neutral Expert on all matters within his competence shall be final and binding, in respect of the particular matter on which the decision is made, upon the Parties and upon any Court of Arbitration established under the provisions of Article IX (5).

12. The Neutral Expert may, at the request of the Commission, suggest for the consideration of the Parties such measures as are in his opinion, appropriate to compose a difference or to implement his decision.'

13. Without prejudice to the finality of the Neutral Expert's decision, if any question (including a claim to financial compensation) which is not within the competence of a Neutral Expert should arise out his decision, that question shall if it cannot be resolved by agreement, be settled in accordance with the provisions of Article IX (3), (4) and (5).

Source: Indus Waters Treaty, 1960.

CHAPTER – 35

Comparative Analysis of Indus Water Treaty Drafts of

9 December 1959; 20 April, 1960 and 19 September, 1960

Article 1

Article 1 has 13 points in Doc 1 and 16 points in doc 2 and 3 respectively

1. Point 1 is same in doc 2 and 3 but different in doc 1.

Difference: Except as otherwise indicated, references to Paragraphs are to the paragraphs in the Article or in the Annexure in which the reference is made.

2. Point 2 is different in all three Docs.

(Doc 1): The term Eastern Rivers means the rivers Satluj, Beas and Ravi, including all surface tributaries torrents and natural or artificial drainages falling into any of these channels and including connecting lakes, if any.

(Doc 2): The term The Indus The Jehlum, The Chenab, The Ravi, The Beas, and The Satluj means the named River (including Lakes if any) and all its tributaries: Provided however that none of the rivers named in this paragraph shall be deemed to be a tributary within the meaning of paragraph (7) and the Chenab shall be deemed to include the River Panjanb.

(Doc 3): The term "Tributary" of a river means any surface channel, whether in continuous or intermittent How and by whatever name called, whose waters in the natural course would fall into that river, e.g. tributary, a torrent, a natural drainage, an artificial drainage, a nalla. The term also includes any sub-tributary or branch or subsidiary channel, by whatever name called, whose waters, in the natural course, would directly or otherwise flow into that surface channel.

3. Point 3 is different in all three Docs.

(Doc 1): The term "Western <u>Rivers</u>" means the Rivers Indus, Jhelum and Chenab including the branches of the Chenab called the Chandra and the Bhaga and all surface tributaries torrents and qatural or artificial "drainages falling into any of these channels and including connecting lakes, if any, but excluding the Eastern Rivers.

(Doc 2): The term Main after Indus. Jehlum, Chenab, Satluj. Beas or Ravi means the main stem of named river excluding its tributaries, but including all channels and creeks of the main stem of that river and such connecting lakes as part of the main stem itself. The Jehlum main shall be deemed to extend up to Verinag, and the Chenab main up to the confluence ofthe river Chandra and the river Bhaga.

(Doc 3): The term "TheIndus," "The Jhelum," "The Chenab," "The Ravi," "The Beas" or "The Sutlej" means the amed river (including Connecting Lakes, if any) and all its Tributaries: Provided however that

  (i)   None of the rivers named above shall deemed to be a Tributary;

  (ii) The Chenah shall be deemed to include the river Panjnad; and

  (iii) The river Chandra and the river Bhaga shall be deemed to be Tributaries of The Chenab.

4. **Point 4 is different in ail three Docs.**

(Doc 1): The term River means the both "The Eastern Rivers" and the "Western Rivers".

(Doc 2): The term "Eastern Rivers means The Satluj, The Beas and The Ravi taken together.

(Doc 3): The term " Main" added after Indus, Jhelum, Chenah, Sutlej, Beas or Ravi means the main stem of the named river excluding its Tributaries, but including ail channels and creeks of the main stem of that river and such Connecting Lakes as form part of the main stem itself. The Jhelum Iain shall be deemed to extend up to Verinag. and the Chenab main up to the confluence of the river Chandra and the river Bhaga.

5. **Point 5 is different in All three Docs.**

(Doc 1): The term "Connecting Lakes" means any lake which receives water from, or yields water to any ofthe rivers: but any lake which occasionally or irregularly receives only the spill of the any of the rivers and returns only the whole and part of that spill is not a connecting lake.

(Doc 2): The term "Western Rivers" means The Indus, The Jehlum and the Chenab taken together.

(Doc 3): The term "Eastern Rivers" means The Sutlej, The Beas and The Ravi taken together.

6. **Point 6 is different in all three Docs.**

(Doc 1): The term "Agriculture Use" means the use for water for irrigation, except for irrigation of household gardens and public recreational gardens.

(Doc 2): The term River means the both "The Eastern Rivers" and the "'Western Rivers".

(Doc 3): The term "Western Rivers" means The Indus. The Jehlum and the Chenab taken together.

7. **Point 7 is different in all three Docs.**

(Doc 1): The term "Domestic Use'"' means the use of water for:

  a) Drinking, washing, bathing, recreation, sanitation (includes the conveyance and dilution of sewage and of industrial and other wastes) stock and poultry and other like purposes.

  b) Household and municipal purposes (including household gardens and use of public recreational gardens); and

  c) Industrial purposes (including mining, milling and other like purposes);

  But the term does not include agricultural use or use for the generation of hydroelectric power.

(Doc 2): Subject to the provisions of paragraph 2. the term Tributary of a river means any surface channel, whether continuous or intermittent How and by whatever name called whose water in natural course would fall in to the river, e.g.. a tributary, a torrent, a natural drainage, an artificial drainage, a Nadi, a Nallah, a

Khad, a Cho etc. The term also include any sub tributary or branch or subsidiary channel by whatever name called whose waters, in the natural course would directly or otherwise would flow into the tributary. (The river Chandra and the river Bhaga shall be deemed to the tributaries of the Chenab).

(Doc 3): The term "the Rivers" means all the rivers, The Sutlej, The Beas. The Ravi. The Indus, The Jhelum and The Chenab.

8. Point 8 is same in Doc 2 and 3 but different in Doe 1.

Same in Doc 2 and 3: The term "Connecting Lake" means any lake which receives water from, or yields water to. any of the Rivers; but any lake which occasionally and irregularly receives only the spill of any of the Rivers and returns only the whole or part of that spill is not a Connecting Lake. Difference (Doc 1): The term "Non Consumptive use" means any control or use of water for navigation, floating of timber or other properly flood protection or flood control, fishing or fish center, wild life or other like beneficial purposes, provided that, exclusive of seepage and evaporation of water incidental to the control or use., the water (undiminished in the volume within the practical range of measurement) remains in. or is returned to, the river or its tributaries, without materially changing, on account of any such control or use, the flow in any channel of the western river, as on the effective date, to the prejudice of downstream uses, but the term does not include agricultural use or use of the generation of hydroelectric power.

9. Point 9 is same in Doc 2 and 3 but different in Doc 1.

Same in Doc 2 and 3: The term "Agriculture Use" means the use for water for irrigation, except for irrigation of household gardens and public recreational gardens. Different in Doc 1: The term "Transition Period" means the period beginning and ending as provided in article 2(7).

10. Point 10 is same in Doc 2 and 3 but different in Doc 1.

Same in Doc 2 and 3: The term "Domestic Use" means the use of water for:

a) Drinking, washing, bathing, recreation, sanitation (includes the conveyance and dilution of sewage and of industrial and other wastes) stock and poultry and other like purposes.

b) Household and municipal purposes {including household gardens and use of public recreational gardens): and

c) Industrial purposes (including mining, milling and other like purposes);

But the term does not include agricultural use or use for the generation of hydroelectric power.

Difference in Doc 1: The term Bank means the International Bank of Reconstruction and Development.

11. Point 11 is same in Doe 2 and 3 but different in Doc 1.

Same in doc 2 and 3: The term **Non Consumptive use" means any control or use of water for navigation, floating of timber or other property flood protection or flood control, fishing or fish center, wild life or other like beneficial purposes, provided that, exclusive of seepage and evaporation of water incidental to the control or use,, the water (undiminished in the volume within the practical range of measurement) remains in, or is returned to, the river or its tributaries, without materially changing, on account of any such control or use, the flow in any channel of the western river, as on the effective date, to the prejudice of downstream uses, but the term does not include agricultural use or use of the generation of hydroelectric power.

Difference in doc 1: The term ""Commission" means the permanent Indus Commission established in accordance with article VIII.

12. Point 12 is same in Doc 2 and 3 but different in Doc 1.

Same in Doc 2 and 3: The term "Transition Period" means the period beginning and ending as provided in article 11(7).

Difference in Doc 1: The term "Interference with waters" means any act of with draw therefrom or any man-made obstruction to their flow which causes a change in the volume of the daily flow of waters.

13. Point 13 is same in Doc 2 and 3 but different in Doc 1.

Same in Doe 2 and 3: The term Bank means the International Bank of Reconstruction and Development.

Difference in Doc 1: The term "'Effective Date" means the date on which the treaty takes effect in accordance with provision of article XI.

Following 3 points are available in all three docs but in different order.

- The term "Interference with waters" means any act of with drawl therefrom or any man-made obstruction to their flow which causes a change in the volume of the daily flow of waters.
- The term '"Effective Date" means the date on which the treaty takes effect in accordance with provision of article XI.
- The term "Commissioner" means either of the Commissioners appointed under the provisions of Article VIII (1) and the term "Commission" means the Permanent Indus Commission constituted in accordance with Article VI11(3).

Article 2

1. Same in all 3 docs
2. Same in doc 2 and 3 but different in 1.

Difference: The points of final crossing shall be deemed to the following; (A) Near the new hasta bund upstream of Sulemanki in the case of Satluj Main and. (B) about one and a half mile upstream of the syphon for the B-R-B-D link in the case of Ravi main.

3. Same in all three docs.
4. Point 4 is same in 2 and 3 but different in 1.

Difference: Provided however that this provision shall not be construed as giving Pakistan any claim or right to any releases by India in any such Tributary. If Pakistan should deliver any of the waters of any such Tributary, which on the Effective Date joins the Ravi Main after this river has finally crossed into Pakistan, into a reach of the Ravi Main upstream of this crossing. India shall not make use of these waters; each Party agrees to establish such discharge observation stations and make such observations as may be necessary for the commission of determination of the component of water available for the use of Pakistan on account of the, aforesaid deliveries by Pakistan, and Pakistan agrees to meet the cost of establishing the aforesaid discharge observation stations and making the aforesaid observations.

5. Point 5 is same in doc 1 and 2 but different in 3.

Difference: There shall be a Transition Period during which, to the extent specified in Annexure H, India shall

(i) limit its withdrawals for Agricultural Use.

(ii) limit abstractions for storages, mul

(iii) Make deliveries to Pakistan from the liastern Rivers.

6. **Point 6 is same in doc 1 and 2 but different in 3**

Difference: The Transition Period shall begin on 1st April 1960 and it shall end on 31st March 1970. or, if extended under the provisions of Part 8 of Annexure H, on the date up to which it has been extended. In any event, whether or not the replacement referred to in Article IV(I) has been accomplished, the Transition Period shall end not later than 31st March 1973.

7. **Point 7 is same in doc 1 and 2 but different in 3**

Difference: I f the Transition Period is extended beyond 31st March 1970, the provisions of Article V [5] shall apply.

8. **Point 8 is same in doc 1 and 2 but different in 3.**

Difference: If the Transition Period is extended beyond 31st March 1970, the provisions of Paragraph (5) shall apply during the period of extension beyond 31st March 1970.

9. Point 9 is same in all three docs.

Article 3

1. Point 1 is same in all 3 docs.
2. Point 2 is same in all 3 docs.
3. Point 3 is same in 1 and 3 but different in 2.

Difference: Each Party agrees to establish such discharge observation stations and make such observations, as may be considered necessary by the Commission for the determination of the component of water available for the use of Pakistan on account of the aforesaid deliveries by Pakistan.

4. Point 4 is same in all 3 docs.

Article 4

1. Point 1 is same in doc 1 and 2 but different in 3.

Difference: Pakistan shall use its best endeavors to construct and bring into operation, with due regard to expedition and economy, that part of a system of works which will accomplish the replacement, from the Western Rivers and other sources, of water supplies for irrigation canals in Pakistan which, on 15th August 1947, were dependent on water supplies from the Eastern Rivers.

Point 2 in doc 1 is different from point 3 in doc 2 and 4 in doc 3.

Point 3 in 1, 4 in 2 and 5 in 3 are same.

Point 4 in 1, 5 in 2 and 6 in 3 are same.

Point 5 in 1, 6 in 2 and 7 in 3 are same.

Numbering of points has changed, making a lot of confusion to continue. Also doc 2 fell short in text as compared to 1 and 3.

Article 5 is named as INDUS BASIN DEVELOPMENT FUND in doc 1 but in doc 3 this article 5 is named as FINANCIAL PROVISIONS.

Article 6 is same in both articles.

Exchange of Data

(1) The following data with respect to the flow in, and utilization of the waters of. the Rivers shall be exchanged regularly between the Parties:-

  (a) Daily (or as observed or estimated less frequently) gauge and discharge data relating to flow of the Rivers at all observation sites.

  (b) Daily extractions for releases from reservoirs.

  (c) Daily withdrawals at the funds of all canals operated by the government or by a government agency.

  (d) Daily escapages from all canals, including link canals.

  (e) Daily deliveries from link canals.

These data shall be transmitted monthly by each Party to the other as soon as the data for a calendar month have been collected and tabulated, but not later than three months after the end of the month to which they relates: Provided that such of the data specified above, as are considered by either Party to be necessary for operational purposes, shall be supplied daily or at less frequent intervals as may be requested. Should one Party request the supply of any of these data by telegram, telephone, or wireless, it shall reimburse the other Party for the cost of transmission.

(2) If, in addition to the data specified in Paragraph (1) of this Article, either Party requests the supply of any data relating to the hydrology of the Rivers, or to canal or reservoir operation connected with the Rivers, or to any provision of this Treaty, such data shall be supplied by the other Party to the extent that these are available.

Article 7

In doc 1 article 7 clause (b) is different from doc 3.

Difference: At the request of either party, the two parties may, by mutual agreement, cooperate in undertaking drainage operations and engineering works on the river. The necessary arrangements to be agreed upon in each case shall form the subject of a separate agreement between the parties. (Clause b of doc 1.)

Each Party, to the extent it considers practicable and on agreement by the other Party to pay the costs to be included, will, at the request of the other Party, carry out such new drainage works as may be required in connection with new drainage works of the other Party (Doc 3 Clause b).

Clause c of article 7 in doc 1 is not available. Clause c is available in doc 3.

Difference: (c) At the request of either Party, the two Parties may, by mutual agreement, co-operate in undertaking engineering works on the Rivers. The formal mTml elements, in each case, shall be read upon between the Parties.

Point 2 in article 7 is half missing in doc 1.

Difference: If a work would cause interference with the water of any of the Rivers but would not, in the opinion of the Party planning it, affect the other Party materially, nevertheless the Party planning the work shall, on request, supply the other Party with such data regarding the nature, magnitude and effect, if any, of the work, as may be available.

Article 8

Point 1 is same in doc 1 and 3

Point 2 is same in doc 1 and 3.

Point 3 is same in doc 1 and 3. Point 4 is same in doc 1 and 3.

Point 5 is same in doc 1 and 3.

Point 6 is different in doc 1 from doc 3.

Difference: (Doc I) Each government agrees to accord to the commissioner of the other government, on reciprocal basis, such diplomatic privileges and immunities and such other facilities as may be necessary for the performance by the commission of its functions.

Doc 3 states to the principal and subsidiary organs of the United Nations under Sections 11, 12 and 13 of Article IV of the Convention on the Privileges and Immunities of the United Nations (dated 13th February, H146) during the period specified in those Sections. It is understood and agreed that these privileges and immunities are accorded to both Commissioners not for the personal benefit of the individuals themselves but in order to safeguard the imlepul'nt exercise of their functions in connection with the Commission; consequently, the Government appointing the Commissioner not only has the right but is under duty to waive the immunity of its Commissioner in any case where, in the opinion of the appointing Government; the immunity would impede the course of justice and can be waived without prejudice to the purpose for which the immunity is accorded.

Point 7 is same in Doc 1 and 3.

Same: For the purposes of the inspections specified in Paragraph (4) (c) and (d), each Commissioner may be accompanied by two advisers or assistants to whom appropriate facilities will be accorded.

Point 8 is same in Doc 1 and 3.

Same: The Commission shall submit to the Government of India and to the Government of Pakistan, before the first of June of every year, a report on its work for the year ended on the preceding 31st of March and may submit to the two Governments other reports at such times as it may think desirable.

Point 9 is same in Doc 1 and 3.

Same: Fach Government shall bear the expenses of its Commissioner and his ordinary staff. The cost of any special staff required in connection with the work mentioned in article 7 shall be borne as provided therein.

Point 10 is same in Doc 1 and 3.

Same: The Commission shall determine its own procedures.

Article 9

Point 1 is same in Doc 1 and 3.

Same: Any question which arises between the Parties concerning the interpretation or application of this Treaty or the existence of any fact which, if established, might constitute a breach of this Treaty shall first be examined by the Commission, which will endeavor to resolve the question by agreement.

Point 2 is same in both Doc 1 and 2.

(2) If the Commission does not reach agreement on any of the questions mentioned in Paragraph (1), then a difference will be deemed to have arisen, which shall be dealt with as follows:

(a) Any difference which, in the opinion of either Commissioner, falls within the provisions of Part 1 of Annexure F, shall be dealt with as provided in paragraph 3 of this article.

(b) If the difference does not come within the provisions of Paragraph (2) (a), then a dispute will be deemed to have arisen which shall be settled in accordance with the provisions of paragraphs (3), (4) and (5):

Provided that, at the discretion of the Commission, any difference may either he dealt with by a Neutral Expert in accordance with the provisions of Part 2 of Annexure F or be deemed to be a dispute to be settled in accordance with the provisions of Paragraphs (3), (4) and (5), or may be settled in any other way agreed upon by the Commission.

Point 3 is different in both docs 1 and 3.

(Doc 1) A difference to be dealt under this paragraph shall, at the request of either commissioner, be settled in accordance with the following provisions:

- a) A neutral expert who shall be a highly qualified engineer, shall be appointed and the terms of his retainer shall be fixed as follows:

    I. During the transition period, the bank;

    II. After the expiration of transition period by agreement between the government of India and by the government of Pakistan or failing such agreement within one month after the date of request referred to above then by such other person or body as may have agreed upon between the two governments in advance, on an annual basis, or in the absence of such agreement by the bank

- (b) The neutral expert shall, as promptly as possible, render a decision on the differences giving his reasons.

- (c) The procedure with respect to each reference to the neutral expert shall be determined by him provided that;

    I. He shall afford to each party an adequate hearing. And;

    II. In making his decisions, he shall be governed by the provisions of this treaty and by the compromise, if any, presented to him by the commission.

- (d) Each government agrees to extend to the neutral expert such facilities as he may require for the discharge of his functions.

Should the commission be unable to agree that any particular difference relates to one or more of the subjects specified in annexure F, the neutral expert shall, after hearing both parties, decide whether or not it so relates. Should he decide the difference so relates, he shall proceed to render a decision on the merits; should he decide otherwise, he shall inform the commission accordingly in order that it may proceed as provided under paragraph 4 of this article. Should the neutral expert decide that some of the issues so relate, but some others do not, he shall, at his discretion, either

> I. Proceed to render a decision on the issues which so relate and inform the commission of the issues which do not so relate, in order that the commission may proceed as provided under the paragraph 4 of this article; or
>
> II. Inform the commission that, in his opinion, that the entire difference should be settled in accordance with the provisions of the paragraphs 4, 5 and 6 of this article.

> (f) Each party shall bear its own costs. The remuneration and the expense of the neutral expert and of any assistance he may need shall be borne initially as provided in annexure G and eventually by the party against which his decision is rendered, except as, in special circumstances, he may otherwise direct.

> (g) The decision of the neutral expert on questions of substance, procedure and costs shall be final and binding upon the parties.

(Doc 3) 3rd point. As soon as a dispute to be settled in accordance with this and the succeeding paragraphs of this Article has arisen, the Commission shall, at the request of either Commissioner, report the fact to the two Governments, as early as practicable, stating in its report the points on which the Commission is in agreement and the issues in dispute, the views of each Commissioner on these issues and his reasons therefor.

Point 4 is different in both docs.

(4) (doc. 1): A soon as a dispute to be settled in accordance with this and the succeeding paragraphs of this article has arisen, the commission shall, at the request of either commissioner, report the fact to the two governments, as early as practicable, stating in its report the points on which the commission is in agreement and the issue in dispute, the views of each commissioner on these issues and his reasons therefor.

(Doc. 3) (4) Either Government may, following receipt of the report referred to in Paragraph (3), or if it comes to the conclusion that this report is being unduly delayed in the Commission, invite the other Government to resolve the dispute by agreement. In doing so, it shall state the names of its negotiators and their readiness to meet with the negotiators to be appointed by the other Government at a time and place to be indicated by the other Government. To assist in these negotiations, the two Governments may agree to enlist the services of one or more mediators acceptable to them.

Point 5 is different in both articles.

5. (Doc 1) Either government may, following receipt of the report referred to in paragraph 4 of this article or it comes to the conclusions that any dispute is unduly delayed in the commission, invite the other government to resolve the dispute by agreement. In doing go, it shall state the names of its negotiators or their readiness to meet with the negotiators to be appointed by the other government at a time and place to be indicated by the other government. To assist in these negotiations, the two governments may agree to enlist the services of one or more mediators acceptable to them.

(Doc 3) 5. A Court of arbitration shall be established to resolve the dispute in the manner provided by Annexure H.

(a) Upon agreement between the Parties to do so; or

(b) at the request of either Party, if, after negotiations have begun pursuant to Paragraph (4), in its opinion, the dispute is not likely to be resolved by negotiation or mediation; or

(c) at the request of either Party, if, after the expiry of one month following receipt by the other Government of the imitation referred to in Paragraph (4), that Party comes to the conclusion that the other Government is unduly delaying the negotiations.

Point 6 in doc 1 is point 5 in doc 3.

Point 7 in doc 1 is as follows:

Pending the resolution of any difference or dispute by any of the means specified in this article, each party agrees to abstain from any action which, in its opinion, might aggravate or extend the dispute or difference, or prejudice the final decision thereof.

Point 6 in Doc 3 is as follows:

(6) The provisions of Paragraphs (3), (4) and (5) shall not apply to any difference while it is being dealt with by a Neutral Expert.

Article 10 in doc 1 is different from article 10 in doc 3
Comparison of article 10 in doc 1 and article 11 in doc 3.

1. **Point 1 is not same completely in docs 1 and 3.**
   Difference: Each of the Parties agrees that it will not invoke this Treaty, anything contained therein, or anything arising out of the execution thereof, in support of any of its own rights or claims whatsoever or in disputing any of the rights or claims whatsoever of the other Party, other than those rights or claims which are expressly recognized or waived in this Treaty.

Point 2 is different in docs 1 and 3 in both articles.

Point 2 doc 1 article 10: Except as otherwise required by the express provisions of this treaty, nothing in this treaty shall be constructed as effecting existing territorial rights over the water of any of the rivers of the beds or banks thereof, or as affecting existing property rights under municipal law under such waters or beds or banks.

Point 2 doc 3 article 11. Nothing in this Treaty shall be construed by the Parties as in any way establishing any general principle of law or any precedent.

Point 3 is different in both articles.

Point 3 doc 1 article 10: Nothing in this Treaty shall be construed by the Parties as in any way establishing any general principle of law or any precedent.

Point 3 doc 3 article 11: The rights and obligations of each Party under this Treaty shall remain unaffected by any provisions contained in, or by anything arising out of the execution of any agreement establishing the Indus Basin Development Fund.

Point 4 only in article 10 doc 1 not in article 11 doc 3.

Point 4 Doc. 1 Article 10: Except for such payments as are specifically provided for in this treaty, neither party shall be entitled to claim any payment for observations of the provisions of this treaty or to take any charge for water received from it by the other party.

Article 11 in Doc 1 (Emergency Provisions) is Article 10 in Doc 3.

Comparison of article 11 in docs 1 and 10 in doc 3.

Article 11 in Doc 1 is same as article 10 in Doc 3.

Same Emergency Provisions:

If, at any time prior to 31st March 1963, Pakistan should represent to the Bank that, because of the outbreak of large-scale international hostilities arising out of causes beyond the control of Pakistan, it is unable to obtain from abroad the materials and equipment necessary for the completion, by 31st March 1973, of that part of the system of works referred to in Article IV(1) which relates to the replacement referred to therein, (hereinafter referred to as the "replacement element") and if, after consideration of this representation in consultation with India, the Bank is of the opinion that

(a) these hostilities are on a scale of which the consequence is that Pakistan is unable to obtain in time such materials and equipment as must be procured from abroad for the completion, by 31st March 1973, of the replacement element, and

(b) since the Effective Date, Pakistan has taken all reasonable steps to obtain the said materials and equipment and, with such resources of materials and equipment as have been available to Pakistan both from within Pakistan and from abroad, has carried forward the construction of the replacement element with due diligence and all reasonable expedition, the Bank shall immediately notify each of the Parties accordingly. The Parties undertake, without prejudice to the provisions of Article XII (3) and (4), that, on being so notified, they will forthwith consult together and enlist the good offices of the Bank in their consultation, with a view to reaching mutual agreement as to whether or not, in the light of all the circumstances then prevailing, any modifications of the provisions of this Treaty are appropriate and advisable and, if so, the nature and the extent of the modifications.

Article 12 in Doc. 1 (Final Provisions) is article 13 in Doc 3.

Article 12 in doc 1 is same as article 13 in doc 3.

Same: (1) This Treaty consists of the Preamble, the Articles hereof and Annexure A to H hereto, and may be cited as "The Indus Waters Treaty 1960".

(2) This Treaty shall be ratified and the ratification comes into force upon the exchange of ratifications, and will then take effect retrospectively from the first of April 1960.

(3) The provisions of this Treaty may from time to time be modified by a duly ratified treaty concluded for that purpose between the two Governments.

(4) The provisions of this Treaty, or the provisions of this Treaty as modified under the provisions of Paragraph (3), shall continue in force until terminated by a duly ratified treaty concluded for that purpose between the two Governments

CHAPTER - 36

Indus Water Treaty: Pakistan Water Gateway

1.0 Introduction

The waters of the Indus Basin rivers' had been used for irrigation purposes even before the development of the present canal system by British engineers in the early 19th century. There were numerous inundation canals in the Indus Valley, which diverted supplies directly from the rivers during the high flow periods, without any diversion works across the riverbed. The local community, tribes, or states managed these inundation canals.:

From the middle of the 19th century onwards, irrigation was gradually extended through the introduction of improved methods and the construction of diversion works across the rivers. A number of agreements for the sharing of river waters took place. The most significant of these have been the Indus Basin Treaty (1960) between India and Pakistan and the Water Apportionment Accord (1991) between the four provinces of Pakistan.

In August 1947, when South Asia was divided into two independent countries, there existed in the area, one of the most highly developed irrigation systems in the world. The syste.n catered to approximately 37 million acres of land, supplying it with the waters of the Indus rivers. All available water supplies were allocated to various princely states and provinces, in conformity with the principle of equitable apportionment of waters.

The Indus System of Rivers in the Indus Basin comprises of the Indus and its five main tributaries i.e. Jhelum, Chenab, Ravi, Beas and Sutlej. They all combine into one river near Mithan Kot in Pakistan and flow into the Arabian Sea, south of Karachi. The total area of the Indus Basin is roughly 365,000 miles^2. Most of it lies in Pakistan and the remaining is part of occupied Jammu and Kashmir, India, China and Afghanistan.

At the time of Independence, 31 out 37 million acres in Pakistan were irrigated. The boundary line between the two countries being partitioned was drawn without any regard to the existing irrigation works. It was, however, affirmed by the Boundary Commission. Representatives of the affected zones expressly agreed before the Arbitral Tribunal that the authorized zones in the common water supply would continue to be respected.

2.0 The Rationale For The Indus Waters Treaty

The water dispute between Pakistan and India began when on April 01, 1948, immediately after the winding up of the Arbitral Tribunal, India stopped irrigation waters in every irrigation canal which crossed the India-Pakistan boundary. This affected 1.6 million acres of irrigated land in Pakistan.

The abrupt act stressed the urgent need for Pakistan to formulate an agreement between the two countries regarding the future use and distribution of the combined waters.

3.0 Pre-Treaty Negotiations

India demanded that Pakistan recognize that the proprietary rights on the waters of the rivers in Indian Punjab were wholly vested in the Indian government and that the Pakistani government could not claim any share of those waters as a right for areas of Punjab in Pakistan. Pakistan's claim was based upon the time honored formula that existing uses were sacrosanct and excess water, not previously committed, could be divided amongst the riparians according to area, population etc. This principle had the support of several treaties, nations or states, and provisions in the same country.

The Indians put forward a principle, which had been advanced for some time during international negotiations, but had not been accepted anywhere. Under this principle, the upper riparian had absolute right to the water and the lower riparian could only get it under an agreement or treaty, if the same were entered between the riparians.

India agreed to restore some of the supplies in May 1948, when a very pro-Indian temporary agreement was signed. It was, however, generally realized that Pakistan could not survive without a restoration of the full supplies and on this question there could be no compromise. The controversy was serious enough to provoke an imminent war between the two countries.

Direct negotiations between the two Parties failed to resolve the dispute. Negotiations under the offices of the World Bank commenced in May 1952. It was agreed to work out specific engineering measures by which the supplies effectively available to each country would be increased substantially. The working party set up under the offices of the World Bank however failed to agree on a comprehensive plan for the utilization of the waters of the Indus River System. After eight years of intense negotiations, agreement between the two parties was finally reached in the form of the Jndus Waters Treaty in 1960

4.0 Main Constituents Of The Indus Water Treaty

The Indus Waters Treaty was signed at Karachi on September 19, 1960. It consists of 12 articles and 8 appendices, which are titled as given below:

CONTENTS OF THE TREATY

Article I	Definitions
Article II	Provisions regarding Eastern Rivers
Article III	Provisions regarding Western Rivers
Article IV	Provisions regarding Eastern rivers and Western Rivers
Article V	Financial Provisions
Article VI	Exchange of Data
Article VII	Future cooperation
Article VIII	Permanent Indus Commission
Article IX	Settlementt of Differences and Disputes
Article X	Emergency Provisions
Article XI	General Provisions
Article XII	Final Provisions
Annexure A	Exchange of Notes between the Government of India and the Government of Pakistan
Annexure B	Agricultural Use by Pakistan from certain tributaries of the Ravi
Annexure C	Agricultural Use by India from the Western Rivers

Annexure D	Generation of Hydro-electric Power by India on Western Rivers
Annexure E	Storage of Waters by India on Western Rivers
Annexure F	Neutral Expert
Annexure G	Court of Arbitration
Annexure H	Transitional Arrangements

Salient Features Of The Indus Waters Treaty

Provisions regarding the Eastern Rivers:

(i) All the waters of the Eastern rivers shall be available for the unrestricted use of India.

(ii) Except for domestic and non-consumptive uses, Pakistan shall be under an obligation to let flow, and shall not permit any interference with, the waters of Sutlej Main and the Ravi Main in the reaches where these rivers flow in Pakistan and have not yet finally crossed into Pakistan.

(iii) All the waters, while flowing in Pakistan, of any tributary which, in its natural course joins the Sutlej Main or the Ravi Main, after these rivers have finally crossed into Pakistan shall be available for the unrestricted use of Pakistan.

Provisions regarding the Western Rivers:

(i) Pakistan shall receive, for unrestricted use, all those waters of the Western rivers.

(ii) India shall be under an obligation to let flow all the waters of the Western rivers, and shall not permit any interference with these waters.

Provisions regarding the Eastern and Western Rivers:

(i) Pakistan shall use its best endeavors to construct and bring into operation a system of works that will accomplish the replacement from the Western rivers (and other sources of) the water supplies for irrigation canals in Pakistan, which, on 15th August, 1947, were dependent on water supplies from the Eastern rivers.

(ii) The use of the natural channels of the rivers for the discharge of flood or other access waters shall be free and not subject to limitation by either party, or neither party shall have any claim against the other in respect of any damage caused by such use.

(iii) Each party declares its intention to prevent, as far as practicable, undue pollution of the waters and agrees to ensure that, before any sewage or industrial waste is allowed to flow into the rivers, it will be treated where necessary, in such manners as not materially to affect those use.

6.0 Post-Treaty Views

From Pakistan's point of view, the settlement plan, as envisaged under the Indus Waters Treaty 1960, had some advantages as well as certain defects.

Advantages of the settlement plan:

(i) After the completion of the Indus Basin Replacement Plan works, each country became independent of the other's supplies.

(ii) Each country is responsible for planning, constructing and administering its own facilities in its own interests and free to allocate its supplies within its own territories as it deems fit.

(iii) This provides strong incentives to each country to make the most effective use of water, since any efficiency, accomplished by works undertaken by either country for storage, transfer, reduction of losses and the like, accrues directly to the benefit of that country. The same is true of efficiency achieved in operations.

(iv) The independence afforded by the program also brought a benefit of a different kind. The location of works serving each country, or territories under its control, and the assurances against interference by either country with the supplies on which the other depends has reduced the chances of disputes and tension.

(v) Before the completion of Indus Basin Project works, after the signing of the Treaty, the entire irrigation system in the Indus Basin was based on the run-of-the-river supplies. The hydrology of the rivers is such that about 80% of the total water was produced during the monsoon period - July to September. Storage projects due to the treaty also increased the canal water diversions.

(vi) The winter supplies became very critical in drought periods. With supplies made available and the storage of water in the reservoirs, water availability in winters has been assured and so the country is insignificantly affected in drought conditions. Besides, total withdrawals and canal heads in Pakistan have increased from about 67 MAF to to 4.5 MAF.

Defects of the settlement plan:

(i) The traditional *sailab* (flood) irrigation, the most ancient way of using river water, on the Sutlej, Beas and Ravi would disappear, because when these rivers were fully developed by India, the traditional floods would decrease or disappear and the *sailab* areas would not get seasonal water, which permitted cultivation. This area is considerable in extent.

(i) Due to the loss of regular flow in Eastern Rivers, the channels have become silted up and the floods in the channels cause great havoc in Pakistan, in addition to other environmental effects.

(ii) The up-keep of the new link canals and storages mean a very heavy additional burden on the cost of maintaining irrigation. Besides, storages are no substitute to the perpetual flow of water, as the storages have limited life.

7.0 Changes In River Flows

River	Average Annual Flow (1922-61) MAF	Average Annual Flow (1960-95) MAF
Indus	93.0	60.25
Jhelum	23.0	23.0
Chenab	26.0	25.7
Ravi	7.0	5.8
Sutlej	14.0	5.8
Kabul	26.0	22.3
Total	189.0	142.8

8.0 Discussions And Post-Treaty Works In Pakistan

Under the provisions of Article VIII(1) of the Indus Waters Treaty 1960, both India and Pakistan have appointed a Commissioner for Indus Waters. Unless either Government decides to take up any particular question directly with the other Government, each Commissioner is the representative of his Government for all matters arising out of the Treaty and serves as the regular channel of communication on all matters relating to the implementation of the Treaty.

The two Commissioners together form the PERMANENT INDUS COMMISSION whose purpose and functions are (i) to establish and maintain cooperative arrangements for the implementation of the Treaty, (ii) to promote cooperation between the Parties in the development of the waters of the 'Rivers', (iii) to make every effort to settle promptly any question arising between the Parties and (iv) to undertake tours of inspection of the Rivers to ascertain facts.

Under the Treaty, restrictions have been placed on the design and operation of Hydroelectric Plants, Storage Works and other river works to be constructed by India on Western Rivers. India is required to supply Pakistan with a certain specified information relating to these works at least 6 months in advance of undertaking the river works, to enable Pakistan to satisfy itself that the design conforms to the criteria set out in the Treaty. Within a specified period ranging from two to three months of the receipt, Pakistan has the right to communicate its objections in writing to India, if any.

Under the Treaty, Pakistan was required to construct and bring into operation a system of works, which could accomplish the replacement of supplies for irrigation canals from Western Rivers in Pakistan. These included those canals that were dependent on water supplies from the Eastern Rivers on 15th August 1947. These replacement works, comprising two storage dams, six new barrages, remodeling of two existing barrages, seven new inter-rivers link canals and remodeling of two existing link canals, have since been completed.

Replacement Plan Works Constructed As A Result Of Indus Water Treaty 1960

Storage Reservoir		
Storage	River	Gross Storage Capacity (MAF)
Mangla	Jhelum	5.89
Chashma	Indus	0.70
Tarbela	Indus	11.0

Barrages

Barrage	River	Flood of Record (cusecs)	Design Flood (cusecs)	Length of Barrage (feet)
Sidhnai	Ravi	167,000	167,000	712
Siphon	Sutlej	427,000	429,000	1,601
Qadirabad	Chenab	912,000	900,000	3,373
Rasul	Jhelum	876,000	850,000	3,209
Chashma	Indus	1,176,000	950,000	3,556
Mara la	Chenab	1,023,000	1,100,000	4,472

Link Canals

Link Canals	Capacity (cusecs)	Length (miles)	Excavation (million yds^3)
Trimmu – Sidhnai	11,000	44	21.0
Sidhnai – Mailsi	10,100	62	31.3
Mailsi – Bahawal	3,900	10	2.4
Rasul – Qadirabad	19,000	30	38.3
Qadirabad Balloki	18,600	80	80.3
L.C.C. Feeder	4,100	20	8.0
Balloki Suleimanki II	6,500	39	20.5
Chashma – Jhelum	21,700	63	118.9
Taunsa – Panjnad	12,000	38	22.5

References

1. Government of Pakistan, "The Indus Waters Treaty 1960".

2. Dr. Bashir A Chandio and Ms Nuzhat Yasmin, "Proceedings of the National Workshop on Water Resources: Achievements and Issues in the 20th Century and Challenges for the Next Millennium", Pakistan Council of Research in Water Resources, June 1999.

3. Centre of Excellence in Water Resources Engineering, Lahore, "Proceedings - Water for the 21st Century: Demand, Supply, Development and Socio- Environmental Issues", June 1997.

4. Dr. Nazir Ahmad, "Water Resources of Pakistan", Miraj uddin Press, Lahore September 1993.

5. Partial data acquired from the Indus River System Authority for the flows of rivers in Pakistan.

CHAPTER - 37

Mechanism of the Indus Waters Treaty

Mirza Asif Baig

(Indus Water Commissioner of Pakistan)

Performance of the Dispute Resolution Mechanism of the Indus Waters Treaty is a briefing paper authored by Mr. Asif Baig Mirza, The Indus Water Commissioner of Pakistan, for the fifth round of the Pakistan-India Parliamentarians Dialogue facilitated by PILDAT.

Background

The Indus basin is one of the largest river basins of the world with on areal extent of 450,000 square miles. It has an average annual inflow, including the flow of its tributaries, of 170 MAF (million acre-feet). Ravi, Sutlej and Beas are its Eastern Tributaries while Chenab, Jhelum and Kabul rivers are the Western Tributaries.

The inflows of these rivers at rim stations or the points above which water has not been diverted out of the river for irrigation (except for minor diversions in the mountainous areas) were as given in Table 1 at the time of the signing of the Treaty on the basis of the data available up to 1952.

The map of the basin is shown in Figure 1. It becomes immediately noticeable that the international boundary between the two countries of India and Pakistan cuts across the rivers and canal systems and that the international and basin boundaries are different. Such drawing of the international border between the two countries led to the dispute of distribution of waters of the Indus basin between the two countries.

A closer look on the map shows that Ravi, Sutlej and Beas, the eastern tributaries of the Indus River, travel significant distances in the plains before crossing over to Pakistan where again the Ravi and Sutlej rivers travel long distances before joining the Chenab River near its confluence with the Indus River; the Beas joins the Sutlej River near the point of entry into Pakistan. It is also immediately noticeable that the three Western Rivers, the Chenab, the Jhelum and theSuch arrangement of the international boundary and physiography caused that India would not have much opportunity of tapping the water resources of the Western Rivers, except for hydropower development, as the availability of land for the use of waters in the area under its control was very limited. But India had vast plains to irrigate from the Eastern Rivers and it laid the claim that India has the right to use all the waters of the Eastern Rivers, though at that time the area that was being irrigated in Pakistan's territory from the waters of the Eastern Rivers was higher than the area irrigated of the territory that became part of India.

The dispute between the two countries started in 1948 and after protracted negotiations, utilizing the good offices of the World Bank, the Treaty was signed in 1960.

The Treaty

The main features of the Treaty are:

a) The waters of the three "Eastern Rivers" (Ravi, Beas and Sutlej) would be for exclusive use of India (Article I).

b) A system of Link Canals would be constructed in Pakistan to transfer water from the Western Rivers to those areas of the Eastern Rivers which, before the Treaty, were dependent on the supplies of the Eastern Rivers.

Table 1. *Inflows of the Rivers at the Time of Signing of Indus Water Treaty (1952 Data)*

No.	River at Gauging Station	Average Annual Runoff (MAF)
1	Indus at Kalabagh (incudes flow of Kabul River)	90
2	Jhelum at Mangla	23
3	Chenab at Marala	23
4	Ravi at Madhopur	6.4
5	Beas at Mandi Plain	12.7
6	Sutlej at Rupar	13.5
	Total	**168.6**

Figure-1. Map of Indus Basin

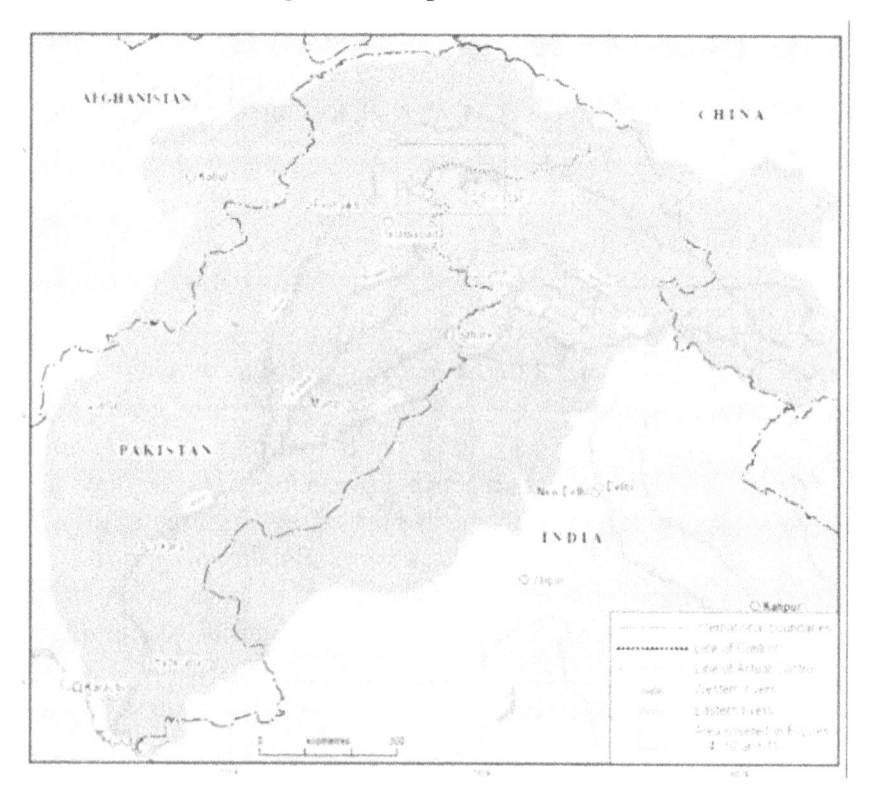

c) The waters of the three "Western Rivers" (Indus, Jhelum and Chenab) are mainly for the use of Pakistan except for certain specified uses by India in the upper areas of the three Western Rivers.

d) India can utilize the waters of the Western Rivers for domestic, non-consumptive, and agricultural uses, and hydropower generation. The agricultural use is limited to 701,000 acres (400,000 acres in the Jhelum basin, 231,000 acres from the Chenab River and 70,000 acres from the Indus River). This includes areas that India can bring under cultivation both from the flow and from the water released from conservation storages (Annexure C).

e) Without the use of storage water, India is allowed to bring under cultivation areas of 150,000 acres from the Jhelum and 50,000 acres from the Chenab, i.e., a total of 200,000 acres (Annexure C).

f) The upper limit of the total storage that India can construct on the Western Rivers is 2.85 MAF. It may be noted that no storage is allowed on the Jhelum Main (Annexure E).

g) India can use storage works for hydropower generation; the filling and release criteria of the storage works are specified in the Treaty in Annexure E; the filling is allowed in the high flow season outside the period in which Kharif sowing is done in Pakistan while the release should be done in a manner that the flow in the river downstream does not fall below the natural flow rate at any point in time.

h) For hydropower generation, India can construct the run-of-the-river projects on the Western Rivers; the design and operational criteria are given in Annexure D. The criteria are oriented towards minimizing the control over the storage. There is no bar on the number or size of the run-of-the-river hydroelectric projects.

i) A Transition Period has been specified in the Treaty for the construction of replacement works and during the transition period, India would limit its withdrawals for Agricultural Use, limit abstractions for storages, and make deliveries to Pakistan from the Eastern Rivers. This period has ended on March 31, 1973.

j) The Treaty provides a dispute resolution mechanism; the issues are discussed first at the level of the Permanent Indus Commission and if these remain unresolved, the Commissioners of the two countries inform their respective Governments and the two Governments can then discuss and resolve the issues at their level. In case the issues still remain unresolved, either Party can take the issue to a Neutral Expert or Court of Arbitration depending upon the nature of the dispute.

k) There are 23 specified technical questions given in Annexure F that are the domain of the Neutral Expert while the disputes related to the interpretation of the Treaty are the domain of the Court of Arbitration.

l) Neutral Expert is required to be a highly qualified engineer in his/her field and is appointed by a consultative process between the Parties or by the World Bank if the two parties do not come to an agreement in this regard.

m) The arbitration proceedings may be instituted by both the parties coming together to the Court of Arbitration or at the request of either Party. Unless otherwise agreed by the Parties, the Court of Arbitration consists of seven arbitrators, the four of which (two each) are nominees of the two Governments while the remaining three, the President, the legal member and the engineer member, are appointed by a process clearly described in Annexure G to the Treaty.

n) Pakistan has built Mangla (5.34 MAF, now about 7.1 MAF), Tarbela (8.1 MAF, now 6.6 MAF), Chashma Barrage (0.5 MAF, now 0.25 MAF) 9 Link Canals and 6 barrages as irrigation and hydropower infrastructure.

o) The Treaty allocates all the waters of the Eastern Rivers (about 33 MAF) to India and 136 MAF (minus water for irrigating additional 0.7 million acres in Jhelum, Chenab and Indus basins) to Pakistan for developing its agriculture.

p) Pakistan has increased its irrigated agricultural area from 21 million acres in 1947 to the present value of 45 million acres while India has increased its irrigated agricultural area from 5 million acres to 21 million acres in the Indus basin, in the same period.

Indian Developments on the Western Rivers
Irrigated Agriculture

It may be noted that India has not constructed any storage dam on the Western Rivers yet and, therefore, as per paragraph 7 of Annexure C to the Treaty, its entitlements of additional area over the area on the effective date are restricted to 150,000 acres in the Jhelum basin and 50,000 acres in the Chenab basin while India has developed 107,265 acres in the Jhelum basin and 28,906 acres in the Chenab basin above the irrigated areas in these basins on the effective date. These figures are based on the data supplied by India under the treaty provisions.

Hydropower Development by India

Thus far, India has constructed 44 hydropower projects with a total generation capacity of 3123 MW while 15 that are under construction would add 2915 MW to the generation capacity.

The names, the location, the type of the structure, and the installed capacity of the projects in each of the Chenab, Jhelum and the Indus are tabulated in Appendix I to this paper. It can be seen that major projects on the Chenab River are Salal, Baglihar, Dul Hasti, Pakal Dul, Ratle, Miyar, and Lower Kalnai. The major projects in the Jhelum Basin are Kishengana, Uri I, Uri-II and Lower Jhelum while the major projects on the Indus River are Chutak and Nimoo-Bazgo.

Table 2. Hydropower Projects of India

Sr. No.	Hydroelectric Projects of India	No. of Projects			Generation Capacity (MW)		
		Completed	Under Construction	Total	Completed	Under-Construction	Total
1	On Chenab River	15	5	20	2,009	2,533	4,542
2	On Jhelum River	17	6	23	1,013	370	1,383
3	On Indus River	12	4	16	101	12	113
	Total	44	15	59	3,123	2,91	6,038

Figure 2. Indus River at Kalabagh

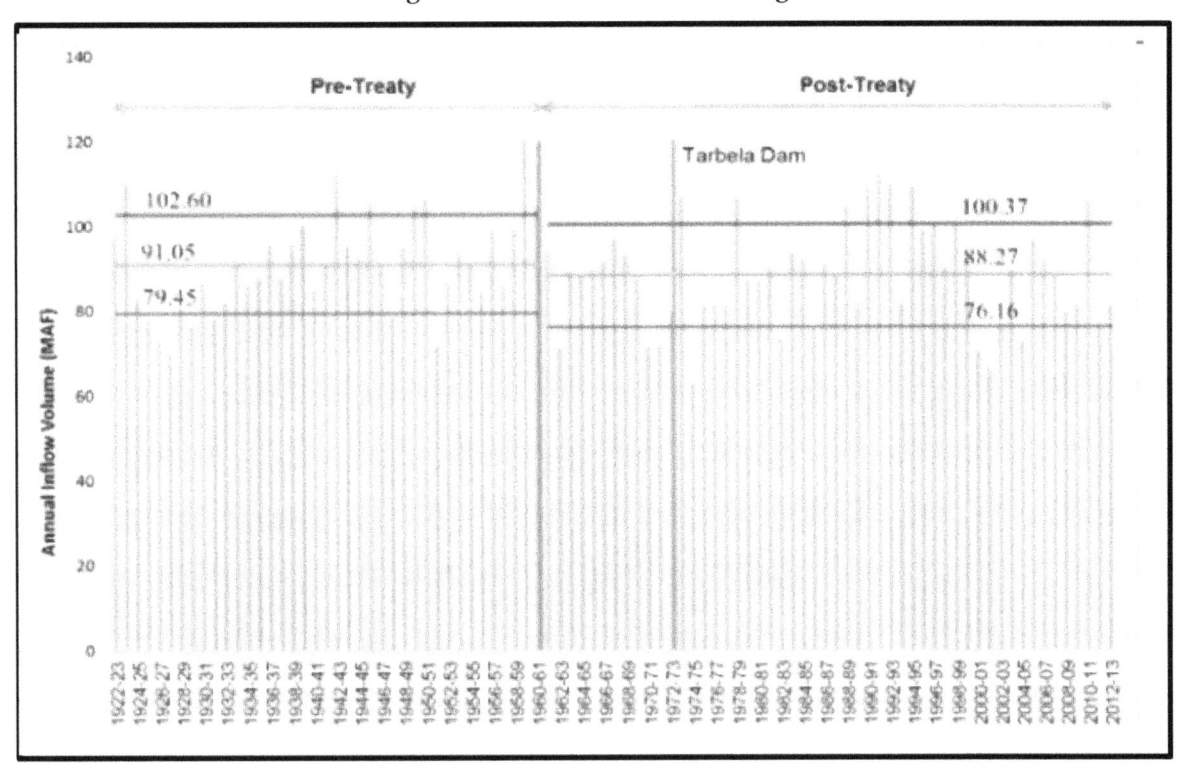

Figure 3. Jhelum River at Mangla

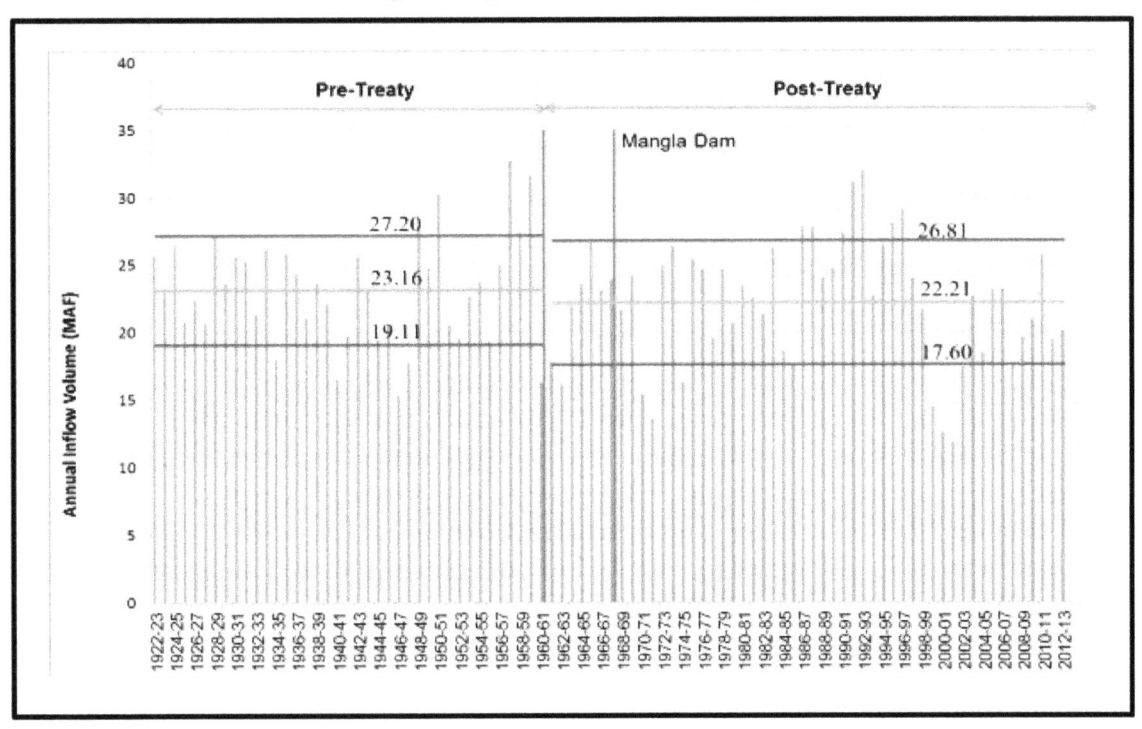

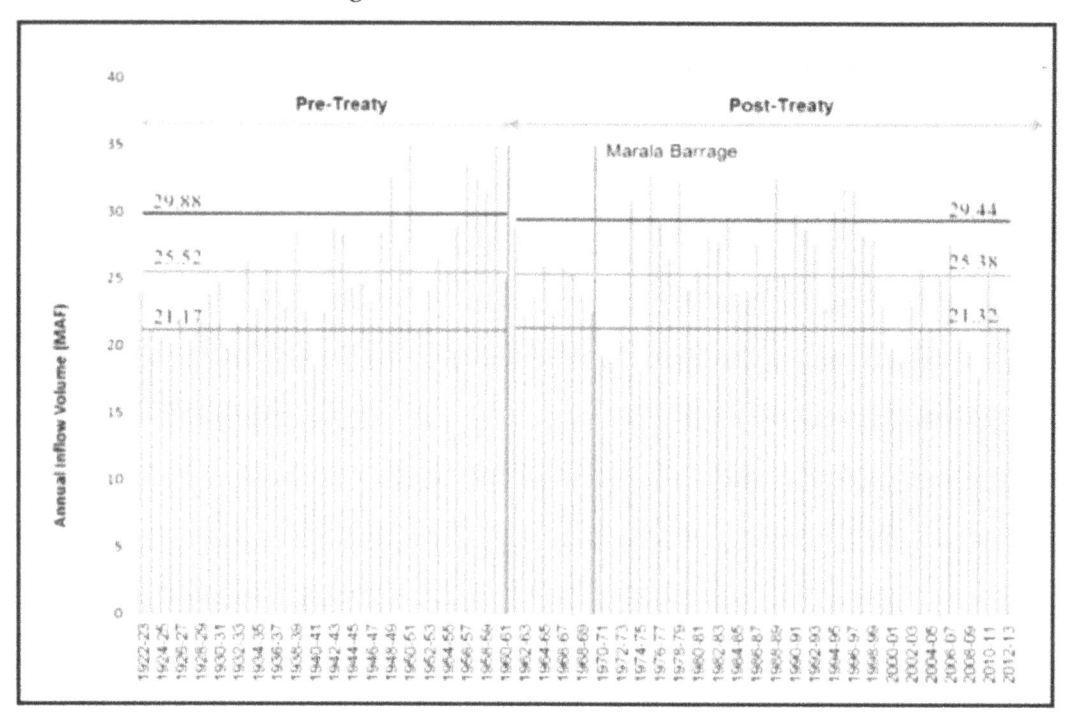

Figure 4. Chenab River at Marala

The Treaty is about 29,000 acres only. The result is logical.

In the case of Jhelum River at Mangla, the reduction for the post Treaty period is about 1 MAF. This, when compared with the increased irrigated area of the Post-Treaty period of 107,000 acres seems excessive. However, a part of it may be due to a change of samples (each sample is different from others) or a change in the measurement of inflows at Mangla. This needs to be further investigated.

The change in inflows of the Indus at Kalabagh is significant but can be attributed to upstream diversions by Warsak canals and increased utilization of water in Swat Basin.

History of Dispute Resolution

Salal Dam (345 MW + 345 MW)

The first run-of-the-river project on which Pakistan had differences with India was Salal Dam on the Chenab River. The design was provided to Pakistan in April 1970 and Pakistan communicated its objections on the design in July 1970. Subsequently, the discussions on the objections started but the dispute could not be resolved at the Commission level and the Indian Commissioner expressed his inability to proceed further in the matter in December 1974. The matter was taken to the Government level in 1975. The issue was resolved at the Government level and India agreed to plug the low level outlets provided in the design and also raised the crest level of the spillway gates by 20 ft by reducing the height of the gates from 50 ft to 30 ft. The discussions started at the Commission level in 1970 and the agreement was reached in 1978 i.e. **it took eight years in resolution.**

Wular Barrage/Tulbul Navigation Project

The second issue on which there was a dispute between the two countries was Wular Barrage/Tulbul Navigation Project, a control structure on the outlet of Wular Lake on the Jhelum River, the structure if built would have a storage capacity of 0.32 million acre-feet. The construction of the project was started without informing

Pakistan in 1985 and on Pakistan's protest, information about the project was provided in 1986. India agreed to suspend and the construction was suspended in 1987. The start of construction without informing Pakistan was in contravention of the Treaty. The Commission could not succeed in resolving the issue and it was taken to the Government level. Up to now, 16 rounds of secretary level talks have taken place on the issue.

Pakistan considers that the structure is in clear violation of the Treaty, as according to Paragraph 7 of Annexure E, dealing with storage works, India is not allowed, except for flood storage, any storage on the Jhelum Main. In case a barrage is to be built on the Jhelum Main, its storage capacity should not exceed beyond 10,000 acre-ft. Pakistan considers that the storage, if constructed, would have a negative impact on the flows coming to Pakistan, particularly during the Kharif sowing period in the drought years. Even in normal years, the demand for water in Pakistan is very high at the time of Kharif sowing and the flows available in the rivers do not match the demand. **Resolution not achieved yet.**

Baglihar Dam (450 MW + 450 MW)

The information on the design aspects of Baglihar dam started in May 1992 and Pakistan communicated its objection in August 1992. The discussions continued at the Commission level up to 2004 and could not succeed. The issue was then taken to the Government level where two rounds of talks were held but convergence could not be achieved. Pakistan then took the case to the Neutral Expert in 2005 who decided on the matter in 2007. **Resolution achieved in 15 years.**

There were five parameters questioned by Pakistan: freeboard, the crest level of the intake, pondage, the crest level of the spillway and design flood. In his decision, the Neutral Expert reduced the freeboard by 1.5 meters, raised the level of the intake by three meters, and reduced the pondage by about 5 Mm.³

The Neutral Expert did not change the design flood nor the crest level of the spillway. The Neutral Expert interpreted that India can lower the water level of a reservoir of a run-of-the-river dam below the dead storage level for sediment flushing which he considered as the 'maintenance' of the reservoir; hence, necessary. The relevant provision of the Treaty reads: *'The dead storage shall not be depleted except in an unforeseen emergency. If so depleted, it will be refilled in accordance of the conditions of its initial filling.'* Pakistan considered this interpretation a great set back as it would allow India to draw down the reservoir for flushing purpose that would adversely affect the flow pattern coming to it and negatively affect the diversions for agriculture from its barrages. Pakistan has asked the Court of Arbitration to provide a clear interpretation of this Treaty clause in Kishenganga Arbitration Case. **The final decision of the Court is expected in December 2013.**

Kishenganga Dam (330 MW)

Pakistan received reports of the construction of a diversion tunnel at the Kishenganga dam site in November 1988 and Pakistan lodged protest in December 1988. India formally supplied information on design aspects of a storage project under Annexure E in June 1994 and Pakistan conveyed its objections in September 1994. Pakistan supplied information about Neelum-Jhelum Hydropower Project and agricultural uses in March 1990. The discussions on the project continued and India informed Pakistan in April 2006 that it is considering revisions in designs. India formally revised its project from storage to run-of-river in June 2006. In 2010, after prolonged discussions in the meetings, Pakistan determined that the Commission has failed to resolve the matter. Pakistan opted for the formation of the Court of Arbitration to get a decision on the legality of the Kishenganga Hydroelectric Project and on the question of the lowering of the water level of the reservoir below the dead storage level. The first meeting of the COA was held in January 2011 and the partial Award was announced in February 2013. The final Award of the case is expected in December 2013. **Resolution achieved in 19 years.**

Chutak Hydro-electric Plant (44 MW)

Pakistan received reports that India had started the construction of the Project in 2004 without informing Pakistan. On repeated reminders, the information was supplied to Pakistan in November 2007 and Pakistan conveyed its objections on the design in February 2008 that the design of the dam did not conform to the design criteria specified in the Treaty. The issue was discussed in the 103rd and 104th meeting of the Permanent Indus Commission in 2009 and 2010. The matter was again discussed in the 105th meeting of the Permanent Indus Commission and settled in 2010.

Resolution achieved in 6 years.
Possible Improvements in the Dispute Resolution Mechanism

From the above history, one infers the following features of the disputes and the dispute resolution mechanism.

1. India starts construction without informing Pakistan.
2. The designs of the works do not conform to the design criteria given in the Treaty.
3. The dispute resolution mechanism is very slow and takes many years in resolving the issues.

Possible improvements in the above are mentioned in three aspects below:

India starts construction without informing Pakistan

Improvements can be brought in by addressing these issues. As regards providing information to Pakistan of the run-of-the-river plants, Paragraph 9 of Annexure D requires India to provide information to Pakistan six months in advance of the start of the construction of river works connected with the Plant. Similar provision exists in Annexure E as well. However, it is important to appreciate that a provision of supply of information to Pakistan also exists in Article VII in its Paragraph 2 which states;

"If either Party plans to construct any engineering work which would cause interference with the waters of any of the Rivers and which, in its opinion, would affect the other Party materially, it would notify the other Party of its plans and shall supply such data relating to the work as may be available and as would enable the other Party to inform itself of the nature, magnitude and effect of the work. If a work would cause interference with the waters of any of the Rivers but would not, in the opinion of the Party planning it, affect the other Party materially, nevertheless the Party planning the work shall, on request, supply the other Party with such data regarding the nature, magnitude and effect, if any, of the work as may be available."

It is clear that this provision is not superfluous in the Treaty and India should supply information to Pakistan at the planning stage. If India supplies information that is available with it at the Feasibility Stage level, it would provide a good basis for Pakistan to review the Project and convey to India its views on the Project. At this stage, the plans are not finalized yet and India, if it considers appropriate, may incorporate the suggestions of Pakistan. This would not only preclude the possibility of starting construction without informing Pakistan but would give the two Parties for exchanging views prior to the finalizations of the designs, after which the inconvenience caused by any changes in designs is rather high and natural.

The designs of the works do not conform to the design criteria given in the Treaty

The design issues are at the root of our differences on the run-of-the-river plants; generally the differences are on freeboard, pondage and on the placement of spillways and intakes. In this context, the following questions are pertinent for the designer. Refer Figure-5.

Is more than the required freeboard really required for the dams? what is the rationale if 1 m freeboard is required and 2m is provided?

Is more than the required pondage beneficial for power generation?

Would deep spillways afford flushing of sediments when the water level cannot be lowered below the DSL? Or are there other alternatives for sediment management?

Whether deep intakes are more beneficial than less deep or surface intakes particularly with reference to the protection of turbines from coarse sediments and overwhelming of intakes by sediment deposition?

Freeboard

Excessive freeboard, which is excessive by following the accepted practice in design in the world, is not required as per industry practice. Rather, it is harmful, as it is against a Treaty provision that forbids artificial raising of the water level in the operating pool as it would create the feeling in the downstream riparian that more than required pondage is being built in the design.

Pondage

On the question of pondage, it is agreed that the required pondage should be there as it is required for peaking operations but when many times more is provided, the intakes are pushed further down with the result that it becomes difficult to provide surface intakes. With deeper intakes, the need of water seal arises which pushes the intake further down thus creating sediment management issues. The provision of surface intakes is the solution such that the pressure conduit starts some distance downstream of the intake mouth. The biggest advantage of this configuration is that the turbines get the least concentration of sediments and the intake is also protected from overwhelming by the progressive deposition of sediments near the intake. For surface intakes, either sediment outlets can be provided just below the intake, if un-gated spillway is provided in the design or surface gated spillway alone may suffice for sediment management. In any case, the requirement of deep orifice spillway for sediment management is squarely obviated.

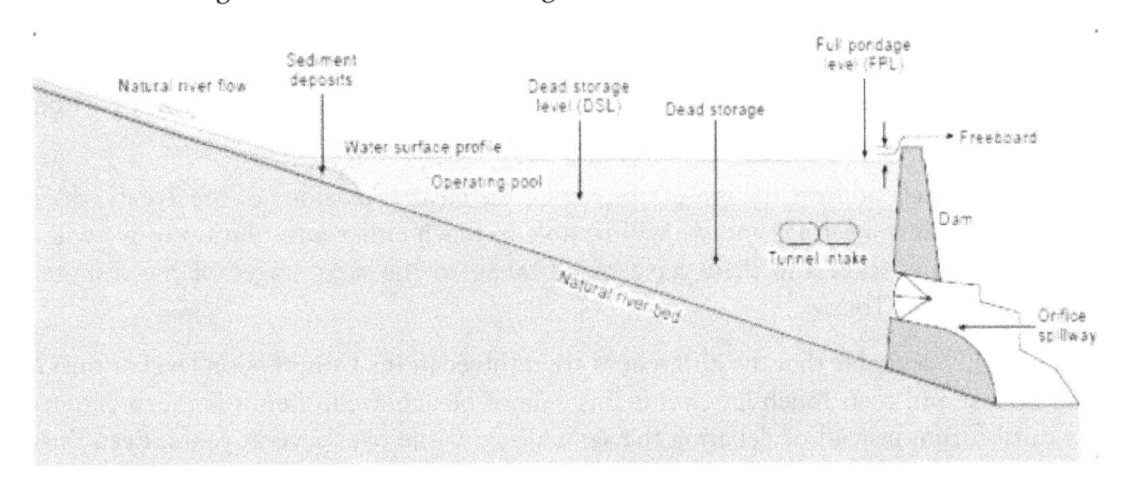

Figure 5. Schematic Drawing of Dam with Low Level Outlet

Spillways

It is very clear that un-gated spillway is the preferred choice of the Treaty. This would generally lead to the requirement of providing sediment outlets immediately below the intake which, if properly sized, would not be objectionable. It is also obvious that these would be most effective when these are placed immediately below the intake which will bring them to the highest level, thus meeting the requirement of the relevant treaty provision.

The other spillway configuration which is consistent with the Treaty is the surface gated spillways. The Treaty requires that these can be provided if necessary but with the arrangement that the bottom level of the gates, in the normal closed positions, should be located at the highest level. For various design flood situations, generally, the gates are of such depth that these provide effective protection to the intake from sediments by keeping the ultimate level of the deposited sediments in the reservoir, near the intake, much lower than the intake crest/invert level.

Design Configurations Consistent with The Treaty

There are two design configurations that are consistent with the Treaty and at the same time afford maximum benefits to the owner of the run-of-the-river hydropower plants. These are:

i) just sufficient pondage, surface intake, sediment outlets immediately below the intake with un-gated spillway; and

ii) just sufficient pondage, surface intake, surface gated spillway.

In both of these design schemes, the de-silting arrangement may be provided a short distance downstream of the surface intake ahead of the start of the pressure conduit if the sediment loads are high.

The configurations which employ excessive pondage, deep intakes, and orifice spillways not only do not comply with the Treaty but also are disadvantageous for the owner as these aggravate the sediment management problems which would require regular flushing of sediments by drawing down the reservoir below the DSL. This approach not only causes the loss precious energy during flushing operations but also enhances the risk of rapid filling of the reservoir with sediments due to a high incidence of landslides in the reservoir on account of repeated fast lowering of the water level.

The dispute resolution mechanism is very slow and takes many years in resolving the issues

It is heartening that both India and Pakistan are firmly committed to following the criteria given in the Treaty. The issues that come across are the usual issues associated with the design of the hydropower plants and though these seem complicated these can be resolved by addressing these on merit.

If both parties sincerely address the issues, respecting the clear provisions of the Treaty, the discussions would not go beyond a few meetings and we will be able to reach either a resolution or we will accept that we could not resolve the issues and these have to be taken to the next stages of the dispute resolution mechanism provided in the Treaty.

Though, it is highly desirable that the differences are resolved at the Commission level or the Government level, as it can be fast and costs much less, yet if this cannot be achieved, then it is much better to take the matter to the third forum instead of debating the same design/issue over several years. Even this process of dispute resolution, i.e., of involving a third forum, after a few such cases, would provide the required clarity to the two parties on the differences in the interpretation of the various provisions of the Treaty which would lead to a faster resolution of the future issues.

In this regard, it is important to mention the views expressed by the Court of Arbitration formulated for the Kishenganga Hydroelectric Plant case wherein in its Partial Award, the Court very clearly, took the view that the differences and disputes on the design of the Hydroelectric Plants and other works should be settled before the start of the construction work.

While it may, in precise definition, may be the spirit of the Treaty, according to which India has to provide the design of the plant six months prior to start of construction and Pakistan has the right to object on the design within three months, if in its view the design contravenes the design criteria agreed by the parties in the Indus Waters Treaty. Logically it is very clear that the remaining period of three months is for resolving these issues before starting the construction.

Improvement in Attitudes

Nothing, as mentioned above would yield results in the resolution of disputes, if attitudes are not changed of Prime importance in this case are:

(i) Disregard to the rights of the other Party to which both Parties agreed at the time of the signing of the Treaty.

(ii) Adopting a flexible attitude for achieving resolutions, i.e., realizing that if we do not adjust on our own, we will have to adjust to whatever decision comes from the Neutral Expert/Court of Arbitration.

(iii) Both the Governments should oversee the performance of their Commissioners to check that they do not adopt unrealistic rigid attitudes in dispute resolution.

CHAPTER - 38

Indian Power Plants on River Chenab

Sr. No.	Project	Location	Type	Installed Capacity	Status
1.	Dul Hasti	Near Kishtwar on Chenab River	Concrete gravity dam	390 MW	Completed
2.	Baglihar-I&II	On the Chenab Main about 147 Km U/S of Marala Headworks	Concrete gravity dam	450+450 MW	Completed
3.	Salal (I & II)	45 Miles U/S of Marala on Chenab River	Concrete gravity dam	690 MW	Completed
4.	Chinani (I&II)*	7 Km from Udhampur on the left bank of Jammu Tawi	Overflow type	14 MW –Stage-I 2 MW - Stage-II	Completed
5.	Thirot	On Thirot Nullah,, a Tributary of Chandara Bhaga River	Trench weir	4.50 MW	Completed
6.	Ranbir Canal*	Ranbir Canal off-taking from Chenab River at RD 84000	-	1.20 MW	Completed
7.	Badarwah*	On Haloon Nullah, a Sub Tributary of Chenab River	Overflow type	Pre-Treaty 0.6MW Upgraded 1.0MW	Completed
8.	Kishtwar*	Near Village Kishtwar on Chenab River	Overflow type	0.35 MW	Completed
9.	Killar	On Mahal Nullah, a Tributary of Chenab River	Weir	0.3 MW	Completed
10.	Shansha	On Shansha Nullah, a Tributary of Chenab River	Weir	0.2 MW	Completed
11.	Billing	On Billing Nullah, a Tributary of Bhaga River	Weir	0.1 MW	Completed
12.	Sissu	On Sissu Nallah, a Tributary of Chenab River	Weir	0.1 MW	Completed
13.	Rajouri*	On Darhali Nullah, a Sub Tributary of Chenab River	Overflow type	Pre-Treaty 0.65MW Upgraded 3.0MW	Completed
14.	Udhampur*	Tawi River, a Tributary of Chenab River	-	0.64 MW	Completed
15.	Nichalani Banihal*	Mangat Nullah, a Tributary of Chenab River	Overflow type	0.60 MW	Completed

INDIAN POWER PLANTS ON RIVER CHENALS UNDER CONSTRUCTION

Sr. No.	Project	Location	Type	Installed Capacity	Status
1.	Ranja-Ala Dunadi	On river upper kalnai nullah, a tributary of river Chenab	Trench Weir	15 MW	Under Construction
2.	Miyar	On Miyar Nallah a tributary of Chenab	Barrage	(3x40)=120 MW	Under Construction
3.	Lower Kalnai	On Lower Kalnai river a tributary of the Chenab	Concrete gravity dam	(2x24)=48 MW	Under Construction
4.	Ratle	On Chenab Main	Concrete gravity dam	(4x205) (1x30)=850MW	Under Construction
5.	PakalDul	On Marusadar river -right bank tributary of Chenab	Concrete faced Rock fill dam	1000 MW (ultimate 1500 MW)	Under Construction

* Pre–Treaty Hydroelectric Plants

INDIAN POWER PLANTS ON RIVER JHELUM

(COMPLETED)

Sr. No.	Project	Location	Type	Installed Capacity	Status
1.	Uri-I	Located at Uri Village about 16 miles D/S of Baramula on Jhelum River	Barrage	4x120 =480 MW	Completed
2.	Lower Jhelum	8 miles D/S Baramula on the Jhelum River	Barrage	3x35=105 MW	Completed
3.	Gandarbal*	On Sind River, a Tributary of Jhelum River	Weir	15 MW	Completed
4.	Karnah	On Quazi Nag Nullah, a Tributary of Kishenganga River	Trench Weir	1x2=2 MW	Completed
5.	Keran	On Keshar Katta Nullah, a Tributary of Kishenganga River	Trench Weir	0.35x2=0.70 MW	Completed
6.	Poonch*	On Betar Nallah, a Tributary of the Jhelum River	–	0.16 MW	Completed
7.	Bandipura*	On Madmatti Nallah, a Tributary of Jhelum River	–	0.03 MW	Completed
8.	Asthan Nallah	On Asthan Nallah, a tributary of Kishenganga River	Trench Weir	0.75 MW	Completed
9.	Upper Sind-II	On Wangat Nallah near Village Wangat, a Tributary of Sind River	Weir	35x3=105 MW	Completed
10.	Pahalgam*	Confluence of East Lidder and West Lidder, a Tributary of Jhelum River in Anantnag District	Weir	Pre-treaty 0.186 MW Upgraded 4.5 MW	Completed

Sr. No.	Project	Location	Type	Installed Capacity	Status
11.	Sumbal	Near Village Sumbal on Sind River, a Tributary of Jhelum River	Weir	22 MW	Completed
12.	Kupwara*	On Pohru River, a Tributary of Jhelum River	Weir	0.15 MW	Completed
13.	Dachigam*	On Dugwan Nallah, a Tributary of Jhelum River	–	0.04 MW	Completed
14.	Matchil	On Dudhi Nullah, a Tributary of Kishenganga River	Trench Weir	0.35 MW	Completed
15.	Parnai	On Suran River, a Tributary of Punch River	Barrage	37.50 MW	Completed
16	Mohora*	On Jhelum River	–	12 MW	Destroyed in flood
17	Uri-II	Near Village Uri on Jhelum River	Concrete Dam	4x60=240 MW	Completed

UNDER CONSTRUCTION

No.	Project	Location	Type	Installed Capacity	Status
1	Kishenganga	On Kishenganga River, a Tributary of Jhelum River	Concrete Faced Rockfill Dam	330 MW	Under Construction
2	Tangmarg	On Ferozepur Nallah, a Tributary of the Jhelum River	Weir	2x5=10 MW	Under Construction
3	Brenwar	On River Doodh-Ganga, a Tributary of Jhelum River	Weir	3x2.5=7.5 MW	Under Construction
4	Athawatto	On Madmatti Nallah, a Tributary of Jhelum River.	Weir	10 MW	Under Construction
5	Kehmil Small Plant	On Kehmil Nallah, a Tributary of Jhelum River	Trench Weir	4 MW	Under Construction
6	Boniryar Small Plant	On Hapat Khai Nallah a Tributary to the Jhelum River	Weir	2x4=8 MW	Under Construction

* Pre-Treaty Hydro Electric Project

INDIAN POWER PLANTS ON RIVER INDUS

(COMPLETED)

Sr. No.	Project	Location	Type	Installed Capacity	Status
1.	Kargil	On Suru River near Kargil a Tributary of Indus River	Weir	3.75 MW	Completed
2.	Dras	On Dras River, a Tributary of Indus River	Weir	0.075 MW	Completed
3.	Matayin	On Matayin Nallah, a Sub Tributary of Indus River	Open Trench Weir	0.12 MW	Completed
4.	Shaker Chicktan(Sanjak)	On Kinji Nala, a Tributary of Indus River	Trench Weir	1.26 MW	Completed
5.	Haftal I & II	On Haftal Nallah, a Sub Tributary of Indus River	Weir	2 MW	Completed
6.	Hunder Nobra	On Hunder Nallah, a Sub Tributary of Indus River	Weir	0.2x2=0.40 MW	Completed
7.	Sumoor Nobra	On Sumoor Nallah, a Sub Tributary of Indus River	Weir	0.10 MW	Completed
8.	Khardung	On Khardung Nallah, a Tributary of Indus River	Weir	0.30 MW	Completed
9.	Bazgo	On Bazgo Nallah, a Sub Tributary of Indus River	Weir	0.30 MW	Completed
10.	Stakna	At Stakna on Indus River Main	Trench Weir	3.24 MW	Completed
11.	Chutak	On Suru River, a Tributary of Indus River	Barrage	44 MW	Completed
12.	Nimo Bazgo	On Indus River Main near Alchi Town	Concrete Gravity Dam	45 MW	Completed

UNDER CONSTRUCTION

No.	Project	Location	Type	Installed Capacity	Status
1.	Dumkhar MHP	On Dumkhar Nallah, a Tributary of Indus River	Weir	0.50 MW	Under Construction
2	Marpachoo	On Sando Nallah, a Tributary of Indus River	Trench Weir	3x0.25=0.75 MW	Under Construction
3.	Dah Small HEP	On Dah Nallah, a Tributary of Indus River	Weir	2x3=6 MW	Under Construction
4.	Hanu Small HEP	On Hanu Nallah, a Tributary of Indus River	Weir	2x2.5=5 MW	Under Construction

CHAPTER – 39

It's Kashmir's Rivers that Pakistan Really Wants

The Economic Times, 1 April, 2005

Pakistan's obsession with Kashmir is not driven by territorial ambitions or love for the Kashmiris but rather a desire to control the rivers in Jammu and Kashmir, says a report.

"Pakistan's primary interest in Kashmir (is) to secure its water resources in order to satisfy Punjab and contain Sind (and this) is in confrontation with the interests of the people of Kashmir on both sides of the Line of Control," it says.

The report — 'The Final Settlement: Restructuring India-Pakistan Relations' — was prepared by the International Centre for Peace Initiatives, a Mumbai-based independent think tank.

"Pakistan is not interested in Kashmir alone; Pakistan wants Kashmir plus those districts of Jammu that form the catchment area of the Chenab (river)", it says. "A water war between Kashmir and Pakistan is inevitable in the future."

It says physical control over the Chenab valley would provide Pakistan an opportunity to build dams upstream and regulate river flows to Punjab and Sind. Under the bilateral Indus Waters Treaty of 1960, India can only build run-of-the-river hydroelectric stations. "If Pakistan can get control of the area, it would have no such restrictions," the report says.

It quoted Hizbul Mujahideen leader Salahuddin as having said: "Kashmir is the source from where all of Pakistan's water resources originate. If Pakistan loses its battle against India, it will become a desert."

According to the report, Pakistan's per capita water availability has declined from 5,600 cubic metres at the time of its independence in 1947 to 1,200 cubic meters in '05.

This is expected to reach the "threshold level" of 1,000 cubic metres before '10.

"There is a direct conflict between Pakistan and the people of Jammu and Kashmir. Pakistan wants the Kashmir Valley and parts of Jammu to be able to build dams to divert waters to Punjab's benefit at the cost of the Kashmiris.

As a "bright and ambitious" brigadier undergoing a course at the Royal College of Defence Studies in London, President Pervez Musharraf himself had in a dissertation said the issue of distribution of Indus river waters between India and Pakistan had the "germs of future conflict."

"The statements made by Pakistan's military officials, Kashmiri leaders and newspaper editorials describe Jammu and Kashmir as a supplier of crucial rivers, and project bloodshed there as the sacrifice made by Kashmiri youth to ensure Pakistan's water security."

"While all provinces are suffering from water shortages, there is a tendency to force Sindh to bear a disproportionately higher share of burden than Punjab. The army leadership is keen on ensuring water supply to Punjab at the cost of Sindh," it said, noting that senior officers, including Mr Musharaf, who is also army chief, have purchased land in Punjab.

The report said the construction of Mangla dam had led to resentment on both sides of the LoC — in Mirpur area of Pakistan-administered Kashmir as it has submerged large areas in the region and in the Kashmir Valley on the Indian side because the Indus Waters Treaty undermines the potential to develop hydroelectricity and irrigation projects.

CHAPTER – 40

Misusing the Indus treaty

By Asif H. Kazi (The News, Pakistan)

Prof John Briscoe of Harvard University has identified India's various unfair dealings with Pakistan in watersharing. He has said that India must not interpret the treaty with the sole objective of punishing Pakistan. There is a growing feeling in Pakistan that while India is increasingly building dams on its western rivers, it is simultaneously engaged in activities aimed at stopping Pakistan, the lower riparian, from building storage dams on Pakistani rivers. In the case of its upper riparian neighbour, Nepal, India has even deployed heavy artillery to partially destroy dams which were being constructed by the Nepalese. India's water strategy thus boils down to construction of more and more dams on cross-boundary rivers inside its own territory while obstructing dams in lower-riparian neighbours and destroying those in upper-riparian Nepal.

Pakistan's farmlands have been deprived of the uses of the waters of the three eastern rivers, Ravi, Beas and Sutlej. The flows of these rivers were allocated to India under the 1960 Indus Waters Treaty. Authorities on the subject accept that when rivers and canals in Pakistan's demarcated area were classified as Pakistan's assets under the Partition Act, 1947, it meant only one thing: that these rivers and canals were to continue to receive water in the same way as before. Under the treaty, Pakistan was to enjoy unrestricted use of the Indus, the Jhelum and the Chenab. However, exceptions were inserted as annexures which allowed India to develop and use certain specified quantities of water of the three western rivers as well. Annexure E established Indian storage limits on the western rivers, which add up to 3.6 MAF (million acre feet). If Indian dams under rapid construction since then were to impound this storage water during high flood periods, as specifically defined in the treaty, Pakistan could live with the situation. However, India deliberately followed a pattern of filling water behind Baglihar Dam constructed on the Chenab River by impounding flows in the low-flow month of September, a clear breach of the treaty which prescribes the filling period as being from June 21 to Aug 31.

Ironically, the 3.6 MAF of Indian storage share exceeds the sum total of the entire flow of the three remaining rivers entering Pakistan during the low-flow months of December, January and February. Thus the 3.6 MAF of storage creation, combined with its operational control over impounding and releases by India could mean completely drying up Pakistan's three rivers for as long as three months. The consequences of this will be disastrous. Obviously, the foregoing was not the intent of the Indus Waters Treaty. And it is precisely for this reason that Pakistan has been insisting that India adopt well-known dam design features, especially for the outlets, which can easily ensure that the reservoir operators would not be able to manipulate flows of the western rivers at their own sweet will. India is opposing this, using as an excuse the need for the prolongation of the reservoirs' lifespan through sediment flushing.

Prof Raymond Lafitte of Switzerland, the neutral expert on the Bhaglihar Dam dispute, who gave his decision in favour of India, has acted as a pure professional engineer since he is trained to look at projects in the strictest sense of their operational efficacy and economic performance. Taking it for granted that the upper riparian would not resort to immoral or unethical practices, he failed to take into account the psyches and mindsets of the litigants in the context of their historic rivalry. Had he kept these factors in view, he might have concluded that, in the absence of a spirit of cooperation, the only checks on an upper riparian to keep it from doing harm to the downstream country were constraints, as were proposed by Pakistan, in the shape of "minimum needed sizes of water outlets to be located at the highest levels" to prevent emptying and refilling of reservoirs at will. In respect of India's Kishenganga River (which takes the name of Neelum when it enters Pakistan), the treaty allows India to construct a hydroelectric project with storage within a certain limit, on a tributary of the Jhelum River. But it does not permit diversion of flows to either another tributary or to storage such as Wullar Lake on the main Jhelum. Even when the permitted storage dam is constructed on the Kishenganga River, Paragraph 21(b) of Annex E makes it obligatory to deliver a quantity of water downstream of the hydropower station into the Kishenganga during any period of seven consecutive days, which shall not be less than the volume of water received in the river upstream of the project in that period. Such elaborate provisions have been embodied with the sole purpose of causing minimum changes in the natural river flow of these rivers to protect Pakistan's interests.

In violation of these specific provisions, the proposed Kishenganga project violates the treaty in a most glaring way. Firstly, the hydroelectric plant is not located on the Kishenganga but way off the channel at the end of a long tunnel that discharges into another tributary. And, secondly, the recipient tributary ultimately outfalls upstream of the Wullar Lake, and this completely changes the patterns of the flows of both Kishenganga and Jhelum Rivers. The position taken by the Pakistani government, as reported by Khalid Mustafa in The News of June 15, will not lead us anywhere. The news item says that whichever of the two countries completed their project first will be the winner in the eyes of the Court of Arbitration that recently visited Pakistan to verify, inter alia, our project status. Such a competitive race is a confusion being created which diverts attention from the real issue, that the treaty absolutely forbids India from undertaking their project.

As regards the Wullar Barrage Project, India again cannot undertake any construction under the treaty that would develop storage for whatever purpose, under Paragraphs 7 and 9 of Annexure E, on the Jhelum Main River. The very basic provision under the treaty is to restrain India from changing the river's flow pattern (both quantity-wise and time-wise).

Several foreign experts have held the view that the highly sensitive and charged water issues between Pakistan and India have emerged out of the way the 1947 partition lines were drawn. A seemingly minor change, but one with far-reaching consequences, was introduced in the partition map, in violation of all principles laid down by the British government. It came about at the very last minute when, upon the insistence of the Indian leaders, the partition award turned over to India three vital districts that were originally allocated to Pakistan, with the sole objective of providing India with access to Kashmir. The three remaining western rivers on which Pakistan now relies upon all originate in, or pass through, Kashmir before entering Pakistan. In other words, India, after having obtained the waters of the three eastern rivers through the Indus Waters Treaty, is now trying to take control of our three western rivers as well.

CHAPTER - 41

Briscoe On The Indus Treaty: A Response

By Ramaswamy R Iyer, 15 January, 2011

John Briscoe's article ("Troubled Waters: Can a Bridge Be Built over the Indus?", EPW, 11 December 2010) on the implementation of the Indus Waters Treaty is a very one-sided presentation of the issues. Such perspectives are unhelpful in improving relations between India and Pakistan.

Some Preliminaries

John Briscoe is an old friend with whom I have had many disagreements. His article on the Indus Waters Treaty (IWT) in EPW provides one more occasion for disagreement – more serious than any in the past. Let me begin with some preliminary points.

(1) As Briscoe knows, I am unenthusiastic about big dams on the Himalayan rivers. However, the governments of India and Pakistan (and Briscoe himself) firmly believe in such "hydel" projects, and so does the state of Jammu and Kashmir; and the Indus treaty contains detailed provisions regarding such projects. That is the context for my comments.

(2) Briscoe's article seems to be a slightly muted version of an earlier more strident article which has been in circulation for some time. In this article, as in the earlier one, Briscoe adopts the Pakistani position completely on every issue between the two countries. He is free to do so. What matters is whether he has valid points to make. That is what I propose to examine.

(3) His comments (a) that Pakistani media present the Indian point of view, but there is no attempt in the Indian media to reflect the Pakistani view, and (b) that Indian reports and commentaries are all written to government dictation, are, to put it mildly, very strange indeed. (Even stranger was the statement in the earlier article that Indian intellectuals are not prepared to give unpopular advice to the government.) However, I shall leave it to others to respond to those observations if they wish to do so.

(4) There is considerable Indian nongovernmental organisation (NGO) activity in trying to build bridges between the two countries and to initiate "Track II" dialogues, and these dialogues explore possibilities of rapprochement on all issues including Kashmir. Many journalists, columnists, academics and others are involved in these attempts to promote mutual understanding and good relations. Briscoe's derisive references to Indian attitudes do less than justice to such people.

(5) Briscoe's article, doubtless well-intentioned, is a major negative contribution to the improvement of India-Pakistan relations. Some of us have been trying to dispel Pakistani misperceptions and doubts about Indian intentions on water, with a modest degree of success. Briscoe's articles throw a spanner into those efforts. In several Track II meetings in recent months, every Pakistani participant had a copy of Briscoe's earlier article ("War or Peace on the Indus", 5 April 2010, The News), and kept citing it as showing that their worst suspicions of Indian intentions were confirmed by a Harvard professor.

(6) I had written two articles on the "India-Pakistan water issue", a short one in 'The Hindu,' "Water through Pakistani Eyes", 6 August 2010, which was, I believe, well received in Pakistan, and a longer one "India-Pakistan Water: An Overview", in the South Asian Journal (No 29, July-September 2010), Lahore. The first was an attempt to draw the attention of Indian readers to Pakistan's perceptions and concerns; the second was addressed to a Pakistani readership, and tried to dispel some misunderstandings through explanations. Briscoe has either not seen them or does not think much of them.

(7) Incidentally, Briscoe carefully uses the terms "India-held Kashmir" and "Pakistan-held Kashmir", presumably to indicate his neutrality. However, that appearance of neutrality is misleading. The parallelism in terminology, in itself, implies a particular position on the dispute.

Let me now proceed to my responses to Briscoe's article.

Lower Riparian Anxiety

Lower riparian anxiety is a well-known phenomenon. India has begun to feel it vis-à-vis China over the Brahmaputra. However, while India is not protected by a Brahmaputra treaty with China, Pakistan is amply protected vis-à-vis India by the IWT. Apart from the allocation of the waters, the treaty is predominantly an instrument for the protection of Pakistan's interests. There are stringent provisions to ensure non-interference by India with water flows to Pakistan, and to protect Pakistan from the stoppage of water, reduced flows and flooding. To ensure that the treaty is properly implemented, there are institutional arrangements (the Permanent Indus Commission); and to deal with differences and disputes there is an arbitration clause, providing for a reference of "differences" to a Neutral Expert (NE) and "disputes" to a Court of Arbitration. If, after all this, there is still "lower riparian anxiety", what kind of reassurance will allay it? Is it appropriate for an "independent observer" to reinforce the Pakistani sense of insecurity?

Indian Concerns

There was genuine bewilderment and dismay in India (in both official and nonofficial circles) early in 2009 when the water issue was projected by Pakistan as a major one between the two countries, and given the same salience as Kashmir. In the past, official Pakistani criticisms about particular Indian projects, such as Baglihar, had found echoes in the media and even in civil society, but no one attributed water shortage in Pakistan to Indian wrongdoing, and no one said "India is stealing Pakistan's water". This is a new, very recent phenomenon, and it has rapidly spread and now forms the general climate of opinion in Pakistan, undoing years of patient work in both countries to promote goodwill and understanding. Hence, the profound uneasiness in India.

Briscoe, who is extremely sensitive to Pakistan's lower-riparian anxiety and insecurity, is not only thoroughly insensitive to that Indian concern, but caricatures and ridicules Indian attitudes. Is it entirely unreasonable for India to wonder whether the manufacture of a new "core issue" (potentially more powerful than Kashmir) and the building up of a sense of insecurity in Pakistan (that affects liberal civil society as well as the more rabid elements) is a deliberate strategy on the part of the army to maintain and strengthen its hold over the country, and to prevent the relations between the two countries from improving?

Baglihar and the Expert Report

Turning to the findings of the NE on the Baglihar differences, which Briscoe severely criticises, let me say first that in echoing and indeed reinforcing Pakistan's dissatisfaction with the NE's verdict, Briscoe seriously undermines the arbitration process and the functioning of the IWT. I find this deeply regrettable.

What is Briscoe's criticism of the NE's findings? He thinks that the NE reinterpreted the IWT and removed the protection that the treaty had conferred on Pakistan. Consider the charge of reinterpretation. The NE gave precise answers to the specific questions put to him, based on the existing treaty provisions. He accepted the design flood proposed by India, considered gated spillways necessary in the circumstances of the case, upheld the placement of the gates, slightly raised the placement of the water-intake, made a small reduction in the capacity of the pondage, correspondingly raised the dead storage level, and slightly reduced the freeboard. None of this involved any re-interpretation of the treaty. The charge of reinterpretation has reference to two assumptions made by the NE; one, that conformity to a treaty signed in 1960 did not mean that dams and reservoirs should be built in 2007 to the technology of 1960; and two, that an overall understanding of the treaty should take into account the positive elements in it as much as the negative and restrictive provisions. Are these unreasonable assumptions? Perhaps, Pakistan would say "yes", and evidently Briscoe would say so too. However, it is difficult to imagine a reputed engineer making recommendations on the basis that the treaty freezes everything to 1960. Besides, the treaty itself says "consistent with sound and economical design and satisfactory construction and operation"; those words cannot be ignored. To do so would amount to a reinterpretation of the treaty.

The one new element that the NE introduced (and this could be described as "reinterpretation of the treaty") was his stress on the need for periodical flushing of the reservoir for desilting purposes. The possibility of non-maintenance or inadequate maintenance must have been inconceivable to him as a professional. Briscoe thinks that this removes the protection that Pakistan had under the treaty. This is a misreading of the treaty. Where does the treaty say "protect Pakistan by abandoning maintenance"? On the contrary, it makes its prescription of "no outlets below the dead storage level" subject to the proviso "unless sediment control or other technical considerations necessitate this". It also makes all its engineering conditions and restrictions subject to sound and economical construction and satisfactory operation. In any case, how could the NE, a leading international expert, say "ignore maintenance"? (However, this issue is now being placed again by Pakistan before the Court of Arbitration in the Kishenganga case.)

Let me add a footnote to that discussion. Assuming that Briscoe is right and reservoir flushing is ruled out, what will be the consequence? The reservoir will silt up very fast and the project will soon become inoperable. No hydroelectric project can be built on that basis. To say "Don't maintain the project" is the same thing as saying "Don't build the project". This will nullify the provision in the IWT permitting India to construct hydroelectric projects on the western rivers. Would Briscoe say that that conclusion must be accepted?

Initial Filling of Baglihar

In August-October 2008, a huge controversy erupted over the initial filling of the completed Baglihar reservoir. Major deviations from the treaty provisions were alleged; the general impression was created that India had stopped the flows of the Chenab and caused serious harm to Pakistan; and mala fides on the part of India were implied if not explicitly attributed. Here again, Briscoe adopts the Pakistani position completely, including the implication of mala fides. I am referring to the language of his earlier article ("India chose to fill Baglihar exactly at the time when it would impose maximum harm on farmers in downstream Pakistan"). The EPW article makes the following reference to this episode: "From the Pakistan perspective, salt was rubbed into this raw wound when India did not (in Pakistan's view) comply with the IWT specified process for filling Baglihar". Please note the language. The "raw wound" refers to Pakistan's disappointment over the NE's findings on the Baglihar difference, discussed above. The words "salt was rubbed" seem to imply deliberate action by India. (Indeed, there is a categorical statement that India did not comply with the IWT-specified process; this is not even presented as Pakistan's point of view.) The apparent disclaimers ("from Pakistan's perspective", "in Pakistan's view") are disingenuous: Briscoe clearly thinks that Pakistan was right.

What exactly did happen in August 2008? I have explained this more than once but perhaps Briscoe has not seen my explanation. Let me repeat it.

During an initial filling of a reservoir on the Chenab, the IWT requires a minimum flow of 55,000 cusec to be maintained above Merala in Pakistan; and it requires the filling to be done between 21 June and 31 August (the monsoon period).

There is a problem in regard to the first condition. After the diversion outlets, if any, are closed, and the filling of the reservoir begins, there is bound to be a brief interruption of flows to the other side until the waters rising against the dam wall reach the outlets, ie, the spillway gates. (If, as desired by Pakistan, the gates had been placed higher, the water would have taken still longer to reach them.) However, the treaty also requires a minimum flow to be maintained during the initial filling. How are these two provisions to be reconciled? There seems to be a conundrum here. However, let us leave that aside and consider the question of compliance with the treaty.

Period: The treaty requires the filling to be done between 21 June and 31 August. The filling was completed by 28 August 2008. There was no deviation here. (Briscoe quotes Pakistani reports that the filling continued into September. Did he try to check the accuracy of those reports?)

Minimum Flow of 55,000 Cusec: (Please note that the minimum flow stipulation is for flows above Merala in Pakistan and not for releases from Baglihar.) Apart from flows through Baglihar, there are other inflows into the Chenab beyond the dam. Based on Indian calculations of those flows, it appeared that while the flows at Merala might have fallen briefly below 55,000 cusec, they might still have been around 25,000-30,000 cusec. (These are my numbers, not official ones.) Pakistan reported a lower figure. (The treaty provides no joint monitoring of flows at Merala, as exists for instance on the Ganga at Farakka.) However, I do not wish to enter into an argument on these numbers, because any flow figure below 55,000 cusec at Merala is undoubtedly a deviation from the treaty. There can be no difference of views on that point. Yes, there was a lapse, but how serious was it, and could it have been avoided?

My answers are as follows. First, this kind of one-time shortfall at the time of initial filling – for less than a day – might indeed have caused some difficulty but can hardly be described as a disaster or as a major deviation from the treaty. Second, even that brief shortfall in flows at Merala could perhaps have been avoided if the filling had been done a bit earlier, say in July, when the flows beyond the dam might have been higher, but this was not possible because the project works were still going on. The filling was done as soon as it was possible to do so, and within the period prescribed by the treaty.

When the dam was ready for filling in August 2008, the options before the Indian engineers were: to leave the completed dam unfilled (ie, abandon the project); or postpone the filling by one year; or fill it within the prescribed period but accept the likelihood of a brief shortfall in flows above Merala. They chose the last option. Again, it is for the readers to consider whether this was a deliberate violation of the treaty, and whether the brief shortfall in flows (for less than a day) amounted to the infliction of a major hardship on Pakistani farmers warranting the huge controversy created in 2008, and the strong denunciation (with a clear implication of malevolent intent) by Briscoe.

Why did Pakistan decide to raise a huge controversy over a relatively minor matter? My speculative answer is that nursing a disappointment over the NE's report, Pakistan jumped at the opportunity presented by a real deviation from the treaty provisions, however brief and minor, and decided to put India in the dock. I can understand Pakistan's action, but not Briscoe's wholesale adoption of the Pakistani view of the episode.

This is now a closed issue. At a recent meeting of the Indus Commission, Pakistan is reported to have said that it would not pursue the Baglihar filling issue any further, and India is reported to have said that it would evolve a proper consultation procedure to obviate such controversies in the future.

Kishenganga Project

This is not a "flashpoint" as mentioned by Briscoe. Pakistan has proposed the reference of some "differences" to a NE and a couple of others (regarded by Pakistan as "disputes") to a Court of Arbitration. My own view has been that these matters could have been resolved through intergovernmental discussions. However, now that the arbitration process has been initiated, it will have to run its course.

Cumulative Impact

Briscoe makes a point about India acquiring control through a significant quantum of "manipulable live storage" resulting from the cumulative effect of a large number of projects. One has also heard this point in Track II discussions. The point that is made is that even if each individual Indian project conforms to the treaty provisions, a large number of run-of-the-river projects on the western rivers might cumulatively spell trouble for Pakistan. One does not wish to dismiss this apprehension lightly. Two questions arise here: the number of projects that India is planning, and their cumulative potential for harm to the lower riparian. Some Pakistani writings talk about a hundred projects. There seems to be no basis for that number. It appears that India has in mind some 33 projects. It is not clear whether all those projects will, in fact, be undertaken, but assuming that they are, it is necessary to consider whether all of them will together give India a greater degree of control; enable large storage; make it possible for India to withhold water from Pakistan, or release stored waters and flood Pakistan. The Indian answer would be that most of these will be small projects; that all these are run-of-the-river projects; that given the restrictive provisions of the treaty, there is hardly any scope either for the retention of waters to the detriment of the lower riparian or for flooding the lower riparian. India might add that if it were to try to hold back all the waters and let nothing go through to Pakistan, such an act would be disastrous for itself. As for causing floods, Pakistan need really be concerned only with waters coming out of the last project before the border; and that is subject to limits. Assuming that India wants to harm Pakistan, it can do so only by openly violating the treaty and by harming itself and its own projects (built at great cost) first. In any case, the eastern rivers stand allocated to India, and the treaty imposes no restrictions or conditions on Indian projects on those rivers; what harm has India done to Pakistan through those rivers?

Having taken note of the positions of both sides, I would still say that the hypothetical fear of "cumulative impact" needs to be looked at, not only because of Pakistan's apprehensions, but also because of India's own concerns, ecological and other. This is roughly what I have been saying in Track II meetings, as also in my articles in 'The Hindu' and in the 'South Asia Journal'. I have also said this to the Government of India.

Reduced Flows

India is, of course, not "stealing Pakistan's water", and some sane voices in Pakistan have said so. (One wishes that Briscoe had added his voice too.) However, Pakistani participants in Track II meetings have reported observations of reduced flows in the western rivers. I have suggested that there should be a joint study of this phenomenon to establish whether, in fact, this has happened and, if so, what factors have caused it.

A Final Word

Pakistani worries about a present or impending water scarcity and the readiness to believe that India has something to do with it, and its apprehensions about the cumulative impact of planned Indian projects on the western rivers, may be well-founded or baseless, but they have the potential of causing serious strains in the relationship between the two countries at every level. India needs to dispel misperceptions, if any, reassure Pakistan that it has no intention of harming that country, and, if necessary, undertake some joint studies. Those efforts have to be made at both official and non-official levels. Initiatives on these lines are not helped by articles such as Briscoe's.

Ramaswamy R Iyer (ramaswamy.iyer@gmail.com) is with the 'Centre for Policy Research' and has written extensively on issues related to water.

CHAPTER – 42

Indus Waters: Treaty And Conflicts

By Lt. Gen. (R) Pramod Grover, 22 September, 2014

(Hindustan Times)

In a world burdened by burgeoning populations and faced by declining water resources, water is likely to trigger conflict. For India and Pakistan, too, fed as they are by the common Indus river watershed, water is a serious issue.

The Indus river, having its source in Indian Kashmir and flowing through Pakistan, is the primary freshwater source for the latter. Agriculture being the mainstay of the economy in both countries, their dependence on the Indus and its tributaries is implicit, and any problems with the flow therein can have serious consequences for both. In recent years, the water levels in the river system have been affected adversely by increasing populations, industrialisation and consequent ecological changes. The problem, posing an existential threat, apparently is more serious for Pakistan.

The Indus Water Treaty addressing the sharing of waters of the Indus between India and Pakistan, assumes a crucial role. Concluded after prolonged negotiations and facilitated under the aegis of the World Bank, it is the world's most generous water-sharing pact, both in terms of the sharing ratio as well as the total quantum of waters reserved for the lower riparian state. On September 19, the treaty signed in 1960 in Karachi, enters its 55th year, surviving hostility, conflicts, and wars between two nuclear-armed rivals.

Most Generous

Some disputes notwithstanding, the treaty is considered one of the world's most successful trans-boundary water accords, as it addresses specific water allocation issues and provides unique design requirements for run-of-the-river dams, which ensure the steady flow of water and guarantee hydroelectricity. The agreement also provides a mechanism for consultation and arbitration should questions, disagreements, or disputes arise.

The resolving of issues perceived by Pakistan regarding the construction of the Baglihar Dam and Kishanganga hydroelectric project within the framework of the deal bears ample testimony to its inherent strength.

However, for the past decade or so, Pakistan has been demanding a bigger share of water from rivers that flow from India, by objecting to the run-of-the-river hydroelectricity projects under construction on the western rivers, and by accusing India of diverting/storing water entitled to Pakistan.

Pak Objections

During the recent inconclusive talks (August 24 to 26) between the Indus Commissions at Lahore, Pakistan has raised the disputed issues under the provisions of the treaty. It has objected to design technicalities such as "deep gated spillway, excessive pondage and height of freeboard" in the construction of the Ratle (850 megawatt),

Pikkal Dul (1,000 MW), Miyar (120 MW), and Lower Kalnai (48 MW) hydroelectricity projects on the Chenab river. Pakistan has accordingly asked for changes in the design of these projects.

It has reservations, again, on our developing of Kishanganga Dam on the Neelum river, even though an international arbitrator has recognised India's right to go ahead with the project as long as the water level in the reservoir is not below minimum (dead storage level in technical terms) and the flow in the river is at least 9 cumsecs (318 cusecs).

India Adhered

In response, India has maintained that it has all along adhered to the treaty and has never deprived Pakistan of its legitimate share of water, and has no intention of doing so. However, to look at Pakistan's requirements, there will be another round of talks in New Delhi after about two months, after Pakistan has made two visits to Miyar and Kishanganga to witness first-hand the constraints and justifications put forward by India. It is clear to Pakistan that instead of going into unending and costly international arbitrations, it should find a middle path.

Must Appreciate

Pakistan must appreciate that the provisions of the treaty, while allocating the western rivers to Pakistan, permit a limited use of those by India, as they pass through the Indian territory, for drinking water, existing agriculture use, limited expansion, a storage of no more than 3.6 MAF (million acre feet), and generation of hydroelectricity through run-of-the-river projects. These permissive provisions, as per Annexure C, D and E, are hemmed in with stringent conditions and restrictions to ensure that Pakistan stands protected from the possibilities of stoppage of flows or harmful flooding. India has been trying to utilise the permissive provisions to the full, and Pakistan has been attempting to apply the restrictive provisions stringently.

Pakistan will be well advised to understand the Indian perspective and resolve issues, if any, bilaterally under the provisions of the treaty.

Fortunately, a mechanism exists under the accord to carry out consultations and research on behalf of both countries and to remove misconceptions and anxieties. Article 7 of the Indus Waters Treaty mentions 'Future Cooperation', which, inter alia, discusses efforts in the future to optimise the potential of the Indus river system jointly. Very little attention has been paid to this aspect, so far.

Simple Solution

Therefore, a simple solution is to form a joint study group of experts who should function as a part of the mechanism available within the purview of the Indus Waters Treaty on a bilateral basis.

This group should carry out consultations and research on various current issues to optimise the availability/utilisation of water for various economic purposes and to further India-Pakistan relations. The study group may also consider building hydroelectricity projects with large dams on the western rivers with assured discharge to Pakistan to offset natural calamities because of floods.

The provisions of the treaty will continue to remain the cornerstone of the watersharing between India and Pakistan; and both countries will operate in a spirit of constructive cooperation. Thus, a regional approach is required in maintaining the prosperity and dominance of the mighty Indus.

(The writer is an expert on the Indus Waters Treaty. Views expressed are his personal.)

CHAPTER – 43

Revisiting The Indus Water Treaty and Arbitration of Interstate Water Disputes

Tamar Meshel, 21 January 2014 (University of Toronto)

On 20 December 2013, the final phase in the Indus Waters Kishenganga Arbitration was completed with the rendering of a Final Award by the seven-member Court of Arbitration ("Court") tasked with resolving the latest water dispute between Pakistan and India.

The Court was constituted in 2010 following a Request for Arbitration submitted by Pakistan under its 1960 Indus Waters Treaty ("Treaty") with India. This marks the first time the arbitration mechanism provided in the Treaty has been used, as previous disputes between the parties were resolved through negotiations or the appointment of a neutral expert. The Request for Arbitration concerned India's construction of the Kishenganga Hydro-Electric Project ("KHEP"), which is designed to divert waters from a dam site on the Kishenganga/Neelum River in the Jammu and Kashmir region to another river of the Indus system. Pakistan requested the Court to determine whether this diversion breached India's obligations under the Treaty, as well as whether India was permitted to deplete or bring the reservoir level of the KHEP below the Dead Storage Level by using certain sediment control techniques in any circumstance except in the case of an unforeseen emergency.

The first decision of the Court was rendered in September 2011 following Pakistan's request for interim measures. In its decision, the Court prohibited India from constructing any permanent works on or above the Kishenganga/Neelum riverbed at the dam site that may inhibit the restoration of the full flow of the river to its natural channel. In February 2013, the Court issued a Partial Award, finding that India was permitted under the Treaty to divert water for the purpose of power generation by the KHEP. This conclusion was based, in large part, on the Court's interpretation of Article 15(iii) of the Treaty, which permits India to divert water "to the extent that the then existing Agricultural Use or hydro-electric use by Pakistan on the former Tributary would not be adversely affected". The Court interpreted the "then existing" uses of Pakistan to be essentially its hydro-electric uses, and particularly the Neelum-Jhelum Hydro-Electric Project ("NJHEP") in the Neelum Valley. The Court found that the KHEP preceded the NJHEP, and, therefore, that the NJHEP was not an "existing use" that India was required to take into account at the time the KHEP crystallized. India, therefore, had priority in right with respect to the use of the waters of the Kishenganga/Neelum River for hydro-electric power generation.

At the same time, however, the Court found that India's right to divert the waters of the Kishenganga/Neelum was not absolute, since "the premise underlying Paragraph 15(iii)—that Pakistan's existing uses are to be taken into account in the operation of India's Plants—remains a guiding principle" (Partial Award, para. 436). In addition to the Treaty, the Court found that relevant principles of the customary international law, including principles of international environmental law, also constrained India's right to divert the waters of the Kishenganga/Neelum River. Accordingly, the Court held that India was under an obligation to construct and operate the KHEP in such a way as to maintain a minimum flow of water in the Kishenganga/Neelum River, at a rate to be determined in a subsequent Final Award.

As for the second question submitted by Pakistan, the Court found that India could not employ sediment control techniques at the reservoir of the KHEP to an extent that would entail depletion of the reservoir below the Dead Storage Level. In a later decision on India's Request for Clarification or Interpretation of this finding, the Court further clarified that the prohibition on the reduction below the Dead Storage Level, except in the case of an unforeseen emergency, is of general application.

In their submissions at the final stage of the proceedings, India proposed a minimum flow of 4.25 cumecs, while Pakistan argued that a minimum flow of 80 cumecs was required in order to avoid a significant loss in energy at the NJHEP. The Court noted in the Final Award that in deciding the rate of the minimum flow, it was required to "mitigate adverse effects to Pakistan's agricultural and hydro-electric uses throughout the operation of the KHEP, while preserving India's right to operate the KHEP and maintaining the priority it acquired from having crystallized prior to the NJHEP", and to give due regard to "the customary international law requirements of avoiding or mitigating trans-boundary harm and of reconciling economic development with the protection of the environment" (para. 87).

The Court approached this task in two stages. First, it addressed the effects that the KHEP may have on Pakistan's agricultural and hydro-electric uses and on the downstream environment in the Kishenganga/Neelum River. While the Court noted that Pakistan's agricultural uses were relevant to the continuing operation of the KHEP in conformity with Paragraph 15(iii) of the Treaty, and, therefore, to the fixing of minimum flows, Pakistan had failed to submit any estimations or evidence on current or anticipated agricultural uses of the River waters and the Court, therefore, proceeded to determine the minimum flow on the basis of hydro-electric and environmental factors alone. With regard to Pakistan's hydro-electric uses, the Court noted that "the NJHEP would be affected by any prescribed minimum flow" (para. 96).

With regard to the downstream environment, the Court noted that "there is no single 'correct' approach to such environmental assessments" (para. 99) and acknowledged that "the environmental sensitivity that Pakistan urges in these proceedings does not match Pakistan's own historical practices" (para. 101). Nonetheless, the Court favored Pakistan's environmental assessment, which constituted "a holistic assessment of the interaction of a range of environmental indicators" (para. 97). On the basis of this assessment, the Court concluded that "an approach that takes an exclusive account of environmental considerations…would suggest an environmental flow of some 12 cumecs" (para. 104).

At the second stage of the analysis, the Court attempted to balance these effects of the KHEP with the priority accorded in the Partial Award to India's right to operate it effectively, finding that "India should have access to at least half of the average flow at the KHEP site during the driest months" (para. 109). This right, the Court further found, was satisfied by a minimum flow of 9 cumecs, which would maintain the natural flow regime in the most severe conditions. As in the Partial Award, in addition to India's priority in right with respect to the use of the waters of the Kishenganga/Neelum River under the Treaty, an additional factor that the Court considered in fixing the rate of the minimum flow at 9 cumecs was the customary international environmental law. Its application of this law, however, was somewhat more qualified in the Final Award.

The Court noted that its use of the customary international law was limited by Paragraph 29 of Annexure G to the Treaty, which provides that "…the law to be applied by the Court shall be this Treaty and, whenever necessary for its interpretation or application, but only to the extent necessary for that purpose, the following in the order in which they are listed: (a) International conventions establishing rules which are expressly recognized by the Parties. (b) Customary international law". While in the Partial Award, the Court emphasized that it was "incumbent upon [it] to interpret and apply this 1960 Treaty in light of the customary international principles for the protection of the environment in force today", in the Final Award the Court qualified this duty by noting that "if customary international law were applied not to circumscribe, but to negate rights expressly granted in the Treaty, this would no longer be '*interpretation or application*' of the Treaty but the substitution of customary law *in place* of the Treaty" (para. 112, emphasis in the original).

The Court also proceeded to distinguish the *Iron Rhine Arbitration*, on which it relied in the Partial Award, for the notion that "principles of international environmental law must be taken into account even when (unlike the present case) interpreting treaties concluded before the development of that body of law" (Partial Award, para. 452). The Court noted that unlike the treaty at issue in *Iron Rhine*, the Treaty in this case "expressly limits the extent to which the Court may have recourse to, and apply, sources of law beyond the Treaty itself" (para. 111). Finally, in justifying the less than ideal, from an environmental perspective, minimum flow of 9 cumecs, the Court considered that its authority "extends only to mitigating significant harm", and that it "...[did] not consider it appropriate, and certainly not 'necessary,' for it to adopt a precautionary approach and assume the role of policymaker in determining the balance between acceptable environmental change and other priorities, or to permit environmental considerations to override the balance of other rights and obligations expressly identified in the Treaty" (para. 112).

The two final issues dealt with by the Court concerned review mechanisms and monitoring. The Court considered it important not to permit the doctrine of *res judicata* to "extend the life of this Award into circumstances in which its reasoning no longer accords with reality along the Kishenganga/Neelum" (para. 118). Therefore, the Court held that "the KHEP should be completed in such a fashion as to accommodate possible future variations in the minimum flow requirement" and that "if, beginning seven years after the diversion of the Kishenganga/Neelum through the KHEP, either Party considers that a reconsideration of the Court's determination of the minimum flow is necessary, it will be entitled to seek such reconsideration through the Permanent Indus Commission and the mechanisms of the Treaty" (para. 119). In so doing, the Court both allowed for the possibility of environmental or other future developments that would justify a reconsideration of the minimum flow, and strengthened the authority of the mechanisms provided in the Treaty to undertake such reconsideration. Finally, the Court rejected Pakistan's request to establish a monitoring regime to permit the Court to evaluate India's compliance with the minimum flow fixed in the Final Award. The Court noted that such a mechanism already existed under the Treaty in the form of the Permanent Indus Commission, thereby further reinforcing its authority.

While the final rate of minimum flow fixed in the Final Award might well be criticized from a strictly environmental perspective, the Court nonetheless succeeded in reaching an effective compromise between the parties' extremely divergent positions while maintaining the viability of the Treaty and not entirely forsaking environmental considerations. It also appears that both Pakistan and India have accepted the decision, each declaring itself as the victor. Amidst growing criticism that the Treaty has become outdated and ineffective, the Kishenganga Arbitration arguably establishes the Treaty's continuous relevance to the shared Indus basin and will hopefully encourage the parties to cooperate within the framework of the Treaty so as to avoid such disputes from arising in the future. Moreover, the successful resolution of this dispute may also revive the international arbitration procedure set out in great detail in the Treaty, but never before used, and reinforce arbitration as an effective dispute resolution mechanism in other interstate disputes concerning shared water resources.

CHAPTER – 44

Defining the Geopolitics of a Thirsty world
The Parched Tiger: Indus Waters Treaty – An Unjustified Resentment Or Time To Bridge A River Divide?

(Water Politics, 12 October 2013)

Two very interesting articles on the 1960 Indus Waters Treaty which – while not perfect – represents the best that was possible in the circumstances that prevailed then and likely cannot be changed until India-Pakistan relations improve. The first, via The Hindu, suggests:

The Indus Waters Treaty must move beyond its logic of compensation and water sharing between India and Pakistan to address the energy and ecological concerns of Jammu & Kashmir.

Much of South Asia is now haunted by the spectre of hydro-electricity. At heart remains the sub-continent's unsolved riddle of trying to 'meaningfully share' its many trans-boundary rivers. Existing river development models, as all governments have learnt, are indeed a zero sum game: in which a benefit extracted from one point of the river's stem will inevitably involve a cost at another point in the flow. For all the careful wording that has gone into framing water treaties, sharing agreements or cooperation models, the overwhelming fact remains that every country in the region is energy starved, politically impatient and is compelled to tap rivers for hydropower.

CLAIM FOR 'COMPENSATION'

In April of this year, the government of Jammu and Kashmir loudly restated an earlier claim for 'compensation.' This demand for financial reimbursement was made not only upon the government of India but, in an equally emphatic tone, on Pakistan as well. And the source of this twinned nature of J&K's grief, as they dramatically point out, is the Indus Waters Treaty (IWT). Signed in 1960 between India and Pakistan, the IWT, ironically enough for J&K, continues to be celebrated as a diplomatic-legal-technical success story in the region. The consensus over the IWT, in fact, has not only held and endured wars but arguably, as well, offers one of the most substantial set of protocols for addressing disputes and disagreements that may arise over water sharing. But, clearly, this curriculum vitae of the IWT has failed to impress the J&K government, which has even gone on to hire the services of a private consultancy firm — M/S Halcrow India Limited — and tasked it to assess losses that have ostensibly been incurred by the State in the past five decades on account of the IWT.

According to one such estimate, J&K suffers an annual loss of Rs.6,000 crore; a calculation based on the perceived benefits that are denied to the State from clauses in the IWT that prevent the former from storing water (for generating electricity) and from diverting flows for irrigational needs. Jammu and Kashmir is, in fact, energy-deficit and according to the latest Economic Survey (2012-13), only 23.22 per cent of the required power was generated within the State while the rest had to be imported. As of now, J&K purchases around 1,400 MW of power from the northern grid and spends Rs. 3,600 crore annually on meeting its

493

growing demand which peaked at 2,600 MW. This, given the fact that 'potentially' it can generate 20,000 megawatts from the rivers and many cascading tributaries that run through its valleys and hills. In effect, J&K's hydro-electricity dilemmas have turned into a hard rock that the State government is now continually hurling against the IWT and battering the delicate water sharing agreement between India and Pakistan.

But if the IWT appears to be failing the people of J&K who, geographically speaking, inhabit the head-reaches of the Indus system, what does one make of the environmental mess that has come to afflict the Indus delta? Historically, the estimated total water available from the Indus catchments has been calculated at being approximately 150 Million Acre Feet (MAF) (181 billion m^3), a large portion of which then hurtled as fresh water flows into the sprawling edges of mangroves and estuarine ecologies of the delta. Over the past 60 years or so, however, the quantity of sweet water flows has been reduced below Kotri (in Sindh Province) to a peak (in the three monsoon months) of about 34.8 MAF (43 billion m^3), with barely 20 MAF reaching the mangroves. In effect, fresh water flows have been steadily slurped off in the flood plains, with diversions for agriculture and industry and reservoirs holding back volumes for power generation. Importantly as well, instead of the 400 million tonnes of nutrient-rich fine grained soil that used to annually nourish the delta, there is now barely a 100 million or so tonnes of soil washing up along the coasts.

Disastrous Implications

The long-term consequences of this water and soil squeeze on the delta are yet to be fully understood as an environmental phenomena. In fact in 2000-01, the flow downstream of Kotri (Sindh Province) was recorded as an unprecedented 'nil'. Only a few recent studies (such as A. Amjad, et al, 'Degradation of Indus Delta Mangroves' International Journal of Geology, 2007) have taken note of the potentially disastrous implications from dying fisheries, coastal erosion, mangrove destruction and an increase in sea water ingress into the coastal regions.

What does one make of this simultaneous failing and success of the IWT in the head-reaches and tail-ends respectively of the Indus system? And equally, as well, how will this perplexing developmental and environmental conundrum impact future India-Pakistan dialogue and the peace process in the region? This riddle, it could be persuasively argued, has been, paradoxically enough, constructed not only by the context of the IWT but, significantly as well, by the peculiarities of the 'knowledge regime' that has largely informed trans-boundary river management in the subcontinent.

The IWT was too simplistically (though, perhaps, appealing in its time) based on an engineering formula which 'divided' the Indus rivers (Western streams to Pakistan and Eastern branches to India), rather than treating the river system as an organic entity that was ecologically linked and environmentally viable only as a connected phenomena. Secondly, managing the IWT has been kept confined to the limited knowledge resources generated by a thin sliver of civil engineers, state managers and ideas borne out of diplomatic intrigue.

Thus, if the IWT is to be saved from a political cul de sac, as far as J&K's energy crisis is concerned and from a potential environmental collapse in the delta, the treaty and its weighty technical arrangements have to be moved beyond the zero sum logics of dividing waters. Instead, a policy architecture needs to be designed that allows and enables economic and environmental 'transactions' within the Indus system. Put differently, rather than stoking a politics of compensation based on narrower or opportunistic readings of the IWT's many clauses and annexures, the way ahead would be to craft a credible ecologically based cost-benefit model that acknowledges the Indus rivers as an organic hydraulic system made up of fluvial interconnections.

Thus, if the head waters need to be preserved to sustain ecological functions within the flood plains and the delta, a case could be made to pay-off sections in the head reaches either through the transfer of hydro-electricity or commensurate financial packages. Similarly, if the head reaches or catchments of the Indus system are recognised for the range of ecosystem services that they deliver lower down the system then the latter must be expected to be conserved as a viable environmental entity.

Excellent Case For Reward

Put differently, the government of J&K could make an excellent case for being 'rewarded' for preserving its rivers for their potential eco-system services enjoyed by downstream users rather than having to claim compensation for presumed 'lost' development benefits. The model of development, hence for the catchment, would be recognised as involving different priorities than the flood plains and the delta.

By allowing such kinds of ecologically calculated cost-benefit transactions across the Indus system, India and Pakistan can turn volatile environmental limits into both economic opportunity and political possibility. The way forward is to harness new knowledge on river ecology, de-centre the civil engineering mindset and craft fresh decision-making collectives that draw upon cultures and traditions of river management in the region.

The second, courtesy of The Third Pole, offers an additional perspective:

This is not a comment on Rohan D'Souza's very interesting article in The Hindu (September 13, 2013), but seeks to provide a somewhat different and supplementary perspective on both the Indus Waters Treaty and on the dissatisfaction with it in Jammu & Kashmir.

The most striking feature of the Indus Waters Treaty 1960 (IWT) was that it performed a drastic surgery on an integrated river system, dividing it into two segments, one for Pakistan and the other for India. There will be universal agreement that this was a bad way of dealing with a living, integral whole.

The second striking characteristic of IWT is that it is overwhelmingly an engineering document: it was a treaty between two sets of engineers. It is easy enough to criticise these features or characteristics, but in doing so we have to avoid the danger of anachronistic and ahistorical judgment.

Second best course?

Yes, there is hardly any doubt that the living, integral, organic whole ought to have been dealt with as a unity and not cut up into two segments. As a matter of fact, David Lilienthal of Tennessee Valley Authority fame, did advocate the joint management of the total system in an integrated manner, but such a course was not found practical for obvious reasons.

Given the bitterness of Partition, the horrendous bloodshed that followed, and the implacable mutual hostility in which the two new countries were locked, it would have been naïve to expect that they could jointly, constructively and harmoniously manage the Indus system as a whole. (Such a possibility might have been difficult to reconcile with the logic of Partition.) When the ideal course is not possible, we have to settle for the second best course, and that was what the treaty represented.

Once the land was partitioned in 1947, a partitioning of the waters was bound to follow, and it happened in 1960. Unfortunately, that history continues to plague us. It can hardly be said that a good, constructive, friendly relationship prevails between the two countries today, and that the IWT can now be replaced by a better and more holistic treaty.

Let me turn now to the other and more difficult point. All of us agree now that water is not a matter for engineers alone, and that it is a complex, multi-dimensional substance (avoiding the economist's language of 'resource') that demands an inter-disciplinary study. We stress hydrology, ecology, sociology, anthropology, economics, law, history, tradition, custom, culture, and so on. All this is familiar talk now and is almost becoming conventional wisdom, but it was quite unknown in the 1950s when the Indus Waters Treaty was being formulated and negotiated. From the advent of modern engineering with colonial rule up to the 1950s or even later, water was indeed regarded essentially a matter for engineers. Even the constitutional entries on water (Entry 17 in the State list and 56 in the Union List) show the strong influence of engineering thinking. Water use largely meant irrigation, irrigation meant canals, canals meant dams, barrages, weirs, gates, sluices and so on. It is therefore hardly surprising that when Partition forced the two new countries to negotiate a treaty on the Indus waters, the negotiation was largely entrusted to engineers on both sides; and it must be noted that the two opposing groups of engineers shared similar orientations, lexicons and concerns.

Besides, Pakistan was anxious not only to secure a share of the waters but also to protect itself against the twin dangers of denial of water and flooding. The IWT was thus not merely a water-sharing treaty but also a water-control treaty.

Certainly, the authors of the IWT wanted the waters used for development but 'development' then meant projects for irrigation and hydroelectric power. 'Projects' were taken to be wholly benign; Environmental Impact Assessments were unknown; the possible human and social impacts of projects were even less recognised. The idea of a 'minimum' or 'ecological' flow would have been incomprehensible.

Naturally, IWT is silent on these matters. As for climate change, that concern emerged several decades later. We must indeed go beyond IWT today and take these matters on board, but eventually IWT needs to be replaced by a very different, holistic, wise and harmonious treaty.

Unfortunately, that will have to wait for a time when the relations between the two countries have ceased to be pathological.

Let us consider now the strong resentment against the IWT in J&K. There is a widespread feeling that while negotiating the treaty with Pakistan, India failed to keep the interests of J&K in mind. At one stage, the J&K Assembly even passed a resolution demanding the scrapping of the treaty.

While one must take note of the negative feeling about the treaty in J&K, it would be unfair to say that the Indian negotiators ignored J&K's interests. Water-sharing by itself is only a small part of the treaty. The bulk of the treaty — the large and dense annexures and appendices — is about Indian projects on the western rivers, both storage and run-of-the-river. All those projects will be in J&K. Therefore, the substantial part of the negotiation was about projects to be located in J&K. How then can anyone say that J&K's interests were ignored?

True, while India proposes to build a number of hydroelectric projects on the Jhelum and the Chenab (and their tributaries) in J&K, it does not follow that J&K will necessarily benefit from those projects. J&K may well feel that the power generated in the State will be taken elsewhere for use. Other States also have similar feelings about projects in their terrain. This, however, is a matter between the J&K State and the Government of India; it has nothing to do with the Indus Treaty.

What puzzles me is the following. When J&K complains that the treaty prevents it from utilising the waters that pass through the State, it appears that it is thinking of the restrictive provisions that limit the storage that can be built and impose several stringent conditions even on run-of-the-river (RoR) projects. India has so far not built the 3.6 MAF of storage that it is allowed to build. As for RoR projects, despite all the stringent conditions, it has built, or is building, several projects, and is planning a total of 33 projects. Assuming that the treaty was less restrictive, or non-existent, India could perhaps have built many more projects in J&K, both storage and RoR. (I am not going into the question of whether they would have been built by Central or State agencies.) Is that what the State wants?

Impact on Ecology

We are talking about pristine, mountainous, seismically active, and ecologically sensitive areas.

Does the State want 50 or 60 dams and reservoirs to be built in this area? What will such a massive intervention do to the ecology of the region? Elsewhere in the country, say in Assam, Kerala, Karnataka, Odisha, and so on, there are strong movements against hydroelectric projects.

A study has been undertaken of the cumulative impacts of a large number of projects on the Ganga. The recent catastrophic floods in Uttarakhand have been partly attributed to mismanaged, mis-operated projects. In a recent case, the Supreme court has expressed concern about the cumulative impact of many projects on the Alaknanda, the Bhagirathi and on the Ganga as a whole, and has directed the MoEF as well as the State of Uttarakhand not to grant any further environmental clearance or forest clearance for any hydroelectric power project in Uttarakhand until further orders.

Is there no similar concern in J&K? Are the people of that State quite easy in their minds about as many as 33 projects being built on the Jhelum and Chenab in their State? Undoubtedly, the energy needs of the people of the State, wisely estimated, must be met. Are massive dams the only answer? Assuming that to be the mainstream view, there must be other voices; but one does not seem to hear them.

CHAPTER – 45

Justice Fazal-e-Akbar Report Indo-Pakistan Water Dispute (1946-60) and Indus Water Treaty 1960

The Partition line

By 1947, when India and Pakistan became two independent countries, the irrigation system of the Indus Basin had already become one of the most extensive and complicated in the world. However, the intricate canal system used to be operated according to a definite pattern. The partition line between Pakistan and India was drawn across the Punjab without due regard to the intricate irrigation system. The Madhopur and Ferozepur Headworks, which provided irrigation supplies to over 17 lakh acres in Pakistan, were given over to India. Apart from this, India, as the upper riparian, was placed in a position to affect the irrigation of another 40 lakh acres or so, receiving supplies from the Sutlej and the Beas

Pakistan Awards

At the time of Partition, it was made clear that the territorial division was not to affect the existing irrigation pattern. Indeed, Sir (now Lord) Cycil Radcliffe, Chairman of the Boundary Commission, stated in his award:-

> "I think I am entitled to assume with confidence that any agreements as to the sharing of waters of these channels or otherwise will be respected by whatever Government hereafter assumes jurisdiction over the Headworks concerned"

That this assumption was fully justified is explicitly borne out by the Report of Committee B of the Partition Committee which conferred that:-

> "The Committee is agreed that there is no question of varying the authorized shares of water to which the two zones and the various canals are entitled".

The Arbitral tribunal set up to resolve questions arising out of Partition handed down a decision premised on the continuance of the irrigation supplies to all the existing canals as before.

Stoppage of Water by India

On April 1, 1948, the day after the Arbitral Tribunal ceased to exist, the East Punjab cut off the supplies in every channel crossing into Pakistan. These consisted of the Control Bari Doab channels, the Dipalpur canal system, and the Bahawalpur State Distributaries. Irrigation of depth 17 lakh acres depended on these canals. Millions of human beings in Pakistan were faced with the prospect of starvation. Thousands of cattle had to be slaughtered or driven to distant areas. Of this, Sir Patrick Spens, Ex-Chairman of the Arbitral Tribunal, had this to say:-

"I remember very well suggesting whether it was not desirable that some order should be made about the continued flow of water. Neither the Attorney-General of India nor the Attorney-General of Pakistan would hear of us saying one single word about the flow of water, but we were invited by both the Attorney-Generals to come to our decision on the basis that there would be no interference whatsoever with the then existing flow of water, and the award which my colleagues made, in which I had no part, they made on that basis. Our awards were published at the end of March 1948.. I am going to say nothing more about it except that I was very much upset that almost within a day or two, there was a grave interference with the flow of water on the basis of which our awards had been made."

Early in 1951, Sir Patrick Spens wrote in the Year book of the Grotius society that:

"Awards made by the Commission for financial adjustments in respect of one new province having a larger share of canal irrigated land than the other can hardly stand unmodified if the compensated Province interferes with the flow of the water of the canals".

Interim Arrangement of 4th May 1948

Is response to Pakistan's protest over the interference with the flow of irrigation supplies, engineers of the East Punjab met with those of West Punjab. As a condition to restoring the water, the East Punjab called for the signature and notification of two draft agreements. The first of these relating to the Dipalpur Canal system provided, "This agreement will take effect from the date of its ratification by the Dominions of India and Pakistan and will be valid up to the 15th October 1948". The other relating to the Central Bari Doab canal system provided, "This agreement will take effect from the date of its ratification by the Dominions of India and Pakistan and will be valid up to the end of 1948". The Draft agreements proposed terms that could not be accepted by Pakistan, so neither agreement was ratified. Instead, representatives of West Punjab and Pakistan met in New Delhi with representatives of East Punjab and India. The result was an interim arrangement which was approved by the Finance Minister of Pakistan and the Prime Minister of India. The day after it was signed and issued, Prime Minister Nehru referred to this arrangement as "our joint statement issued yesterday regarding the dispute between East and West Punjab on canal waters."

The joint statement announced that water was being restored to the Central Bari Doab and the Dipalpur Canals, that the West Punjab was to deposit a sum of money in escrow to cover certain disputed payments and that after an examination by each side of the legal issues, further meetings would take place. In conclusion, it was stated that the Dominion Governments "expresssed the 'hope' that a friendly solution would be reached".

When the joint statement was issued and for atleast two months thereafter, India recognized that the interim arrangement, in no way, affected the rights of either side. At a meeting in July 1948, called for the purpose of working out an agreement that would affect the rights of the parties, India proposed that its contentions (which the joint statement described but expressly stated that Pakistan contested) should be embodied in a final agreement "which would take the place of all rights and liabilities which either side may have in law". No agreement was reached.

In the late summer and early fall of 1948, the Indians threatened to cut off the flow of the waters, taking the position that the arrangement described in the joint statement terminated at the time contemplated in the draft agreement presented by the East Punjab. Pakistan contended that the arrangement called for a continuance of supplies until a final agreement was arrived at. By telegram, dated October 18, India contested this view and asserted, "If there was an unreasonable delay on the part of one side, it is open to the other party to put an end to the agreement by giving a reasonable notice". In the same telegram, India, for the first time, took the position that the arrangement described in the joint announcement itself had accomplished what India in July had proposed, that is, a "final agreement, on the lines of the agreement of 4th May 1948,... to take the place of all rights and liabilities which either side might have in law."

Pakistan had, at no time, accepted the Indian view that the interim arrangement permanently affected the rights and liabilities of the parties, but it had acquiesced to the Indian view that it is open to either party to put an end to the arrangement by giving a reasonable notice. Pakistan, ultimately, gave such a notice. In 1950, when India tried to revive the joint statement, Pakistan filed a certificate with the United Nations, explaining the nature of the joint statement and certifying that it had been terminated.

Direct Negotiations

Representatives of India and Pakistan met in Karachi from 27th - 29th March 1950, to discuss the basis for a settlement of the dispute. The Indian negotiators proposed that the waters of the Sutlej be utilized wholly for the Bhakra areas, that the flow of the Beas, Ravi and Chenab be utilized for the maintenance of existing uses in Pakistan, except that (1) India would have the use of the surplus, if any, in the Beas over and above the requirements of the Sutlej Valley Canals, and (2) the supplies then used by the Central Bari Doab Canals would be used by India for extension of irrigation in Amritsar and Gurdaspur districts. It was suggested that supplies for the Central Bari Doab Canals and waters to meet the deficiencies in the Sutlej Valley Canals caused by the complete withdrawal of the Sutlej component could be met by a link from the Chenab, the entire flow of which river would be available to Pakistan. If surplus supplies in the Chenab were inadequate to meet the foregoing requirements it was proposed by India that a dam be built on the Chenab to supply these deficiencies and to provide supplies for extension of irrigation in Pakistan.

The Pakistan negotiators proposed that existing uses be met from existing sources, and that new supplies be provided from flood waters now running to sea by building dams on the Sutlej, Beas, Ravi and Chenab, the costs involved to be shared in proportion to the benefits derived. An equitable division would be made of the new supplies in the light of all relevant considerations. The negotiating committee I agreed that the engineers on both sides should study the two plans against the actual discharge figures and put up the figures in a further meeting of the Committee to be held at Delhi in May 1950.

The engineers did meet in Delhi from 15-16 May 1950, but the Indian engineers made proposals so divergent from the earlier ones that no progress could be made by the engineers. When the negotiating committee met on 29th May, the Indian negotiators, as if to avoid any chance of agreement, confirmed that they were unwilling to explore the possibility of an agreement along the lines discussed at Karachi. The Indians announced that they proposed to appropriate the entire usable flow, not only of the Sutlej, but also of the Beas and Ravi, and besides to take 10,000 cusecs from the Chenab through a tunnel at Marhu. They stated that they would proceed with projects to take this water, including a new headworks at Harike, without regard to what Pakistan offered or did. In short, India proposed to take all the water it could and leave Pakistan to supply its irrigation requirements from a mirage visible only to the Indian negotiators.

It became clear that no agreement could be reached by negotiations until the basic issue, or the international rights of Pakistan and India, was resolved. Pakistan, many times, both before and after the 1950 negotiations, formally requested India to refer this issue to the World Court for adjudication, but India always refused.

Lilienthal's Proposal

In the late spring and early summer of 1951, Mr. David Lilienthal, who had won pre-eminence in the United States as head of the seven-state Tennessee Valley Authority (TVA) and more recently as Chairman of the United States Atomic Energy Commission, made an extensive trip to the subcontinent at the invitation of the

Prime Minister of India. Hearing of his proposed trip, the Government of Pakistan urged him to inspect irrigation works in Pakistan as well. Mr. Lilientbal, after visiting both countries, recorded his observation in an article which appeared in the American magazine "Collier's" in August 1951.

Mr. Lilienthal noted that, if the matter were referred-to the World Court, it might sustain Pakistan's position. But he pointed out that a decision by the World Court would not be adequate because he recognized India's need for expanding irrigation. Mr. Lilienthal also declared that India should also recognize Pakistan's similar needs.

Drawing upon his experience in regional development work with the Tennessee Valley Authority, Mr. Lilienthal proposed that past differences be set aside and that Pakistan and India join together in the development and joint use of this truly international river basin on an engineering basis. Mr. Lilienthal expressed general optimism as to the possibilities of acceptance by both countries of a fair and equitable solution. He proposed a constructive solution, the heart of which is contained in the following quotation:-

> "...Pakistan's position, though inadequate, should be the starting point, should be accepted as a minimum, without question.
>
> The starting point should be, then, to set to rest Pakistan's fears of deprivation and a return to desert. Her present use of water should be confirmed by India, provided she works together with India (as I believe she would) in a joint use of this truly international river basin on an engineering basis that would also (as the facts make clear it can) assure India's future use as well.
>
> The urgent problem is how to store up now wasted waters, so they can be fed down and distributed by engineering works and canals, and used by both countries, rather than permitted to flow to the sea unused. This is not a religious or political problem, but a feasible engineering and business problem for which there is plenty of precedent and relevant experience."

Mr. Lilienthal noted that an engineering solution would require new engineering works. He suggested that they be jointly financed, "perhaps with World Bank help".

World Bank's Good Offices

Mr. Lilienthal's suggestion attracted the attention of Mr. Eugene R. Black, President of the International Bank for Reconstruction and Development, who, on September 6, 1951, wrote to the Prime Ministers of Pakistan and India, inquiring whether their Governments:-

> "Are disposed to look with favour upon Mr. Lilienthal's proposal to meet the requirements of both countries for expanded irrigation through the cooperative construction and operation of storage dams and other facilities bo be financed in part perhaps by this Bank.
>
> I should be most happy to recommend that the Bank lend its good offices in such directions as might be considered appropriate by the two Governments, make available qualified members of its staff and consider any financing proposals that might develop as a result of joint planning".

13th March 1952 Agreement

Both sides accepted the proffered good office. After working out the text with both Governments, Mr. Black was able to confirm, on March 13, 1958, in identical letters to the Prime Ministers of the two Countries, that:-

> "I have found common understanding as to the bases on which we can go forward under the Lilienthal proposal. We all agree that... the ultimate objective is to carry out specific engineering

measures by which the supplies effectively available to each country will be increased substantially beyond what they have ever been...

While the co-operative work continues with the participation of the Bank neither side will take any action to diminish the supplies available to the other side for existing uses"

Terms of Reference for the Co-operative work-

A working Party, consisting of the engineer representatives of the Government of Pakistan, Government of India and the World Bank, was set up for preparing a comprehensive long-range plan for the most effective utilization of the water resources of the Indus Basin for the development of the region, on the basis of the following three broad principles, which were contained in the World Bank President's letter, dated November 8, 1951:-

a) The Indus Basin water resources are sufficient to continue all existing uses and to meet the further needs of both countries for water from that source.

b) The water resources of the Indus Basin should be cooperatively developed and used in such manner as most effectively to promote the economic development of the Indus Basin viewed as a unit.

c) The problem of development and use of the Indus basin water resources should be solved on a functional and not a political plane, without relation to past negotiations and past claims and independently of political issues.

The Wording Party met ir Washington from 7th May to 18th June, 1952 and agreed upon an outline of program which provided for the collection, exchange and verification of factual data, the making of surveys and investigations, and the preparation of a comprehensive plan. During the summer and fall of 1952, each side proceeded with the collection of data and the preparation of factual studies. The Working Party met again in the sub-continent during the period from 1st December 1952, to 29th January 1953. The meeting opened in Karachi. The engineers of Pakistan, India and the World Bank then toured irrigated and un-irrigated areas in Pakistan and India and sites for dams and other engineering works and concluded their meeting in Delhi. The collection and exchange of factual material continued through the spring and summer of 1953.

Working Party's second meeting

The Working Party re-convened on 8th September 1953, at the offices of the World Bank, in Washington, for preparing an agreed Plan. The Working Party met again, in Washington, in September 1953, for the purpose of working out a comprehensive plan under the Lilienthal proposal, the ultimate objective being to provide by means of specific engineering measures supplies of irrigation water effectively available to each country substantially beyond what they had ever been. The Working Party had before it the studies containing the basic data which had been prepared separately by the engineering-designees of the two countries and exchanged in accordance with the program of studies worked out in the 1952 meetings.

In the Working Party, the engineers of Pakistan and India held divergent views about the existing uses, the uses planned before Partition and the future requirements of each country to be met from the Indus River System. The uses envisaged by the two sides could not be possibly met with the united supplies of the Indus System of Rivers even after full development. No common approach could be agreed upon. At the suggestion of the World Bank's representative, the two sides submitted to the Working Party, on 6th October 1953, their respective outline of a comprehensive plan for the development and use of the waters of the Indus River System.

Pakistan's Plan

The Pakistan's preliminary outline of the plan was based on the historical pattern of uses. The approach was first to provide supplies to protect historic irrigation uses including those uses which had been sanctioned by the Secretary of State for India or the central government before Partition, and which were still in the process of development at the time of Partition. Next, provision was made for those uses which had been jointly planned before Partition. Finally, the unused supplies remaining in the rivers were analyzed to see the extent to which these could be developed to provide new irrigation in the two countries. The supplies that could be developed for new uses, by the construction of storages, however, was not allocated to the two countries and the matter was left for negotiations.

India's Plan

In the Indian draft outline plan, the historic pattern of uses was ignored, and the objective appeared to be to transfer for use in India, fill the supplies from the Indus River System, which physically could be made available to India. The new plan provided over 23 MAP of new supplies to India, in addition to 8 MAF, that were being used by the existing canals of India. Thus, India proposed to use not only all the waters of the three Eastern Rivers but proposed to transfer about 5.6 MAF from the Chenab also, through a Tunnel connecting the Chenab and the Ravi in Himachal. The discussions held after the submission of the two plans remained inconclusive and the wide gap between the two plans could not be bridged.

Compromise Proposals

In December 1953 and January 1954, attempts were made to break the deadlock by proceeding directly to the final division of the waters. The Pakistan's representative submitted to the Bank a compromise proposal in which Pakistan's requirements for the existing uses to be met from the Sutlej, Beas and Ravi were listed after deducting the possible transfers from the Chenab. Of the balance supplies of 10.3 MAF which could be developed on the Eastern Rivers by constructing storages, Pakistan offered to India such portion as the World Bank proposed as "fair".

The Indian representative put forward his own ad hoc formula for splitting on a 50/50 basis the figure provided by the Indian and Pakistan designees for total water availability for new uses. According to this formula India was to get 21.1 MAF of usable supplies in addition to its existing use of 8.0 MAF, thus putting the entire burden of the Pakistan's Eastern River Canals on the waters of the three western Rivers.

No agreement could be reached between the Parties even on the basis of these compromise proposals.

Bank's proposal of 5th Feb 1954

To break the impasse, the World Bank's representative, on 5th February 1954, submitted a proposal of his own. The Bank, having come to the conclusion that it would be unrealistic to work out a plan on the basis of the development of the Indus Basin as one economic unit, discarded the Lilienth's approach and recommended that the irrigation system of the two countries should be developed independently. To accomplish this, the entire flow of the three Eastern Rivers was allocated for the exclusive use and benefit of India, The proposal rested on the premise that from the flow supplies of the three Western Rivers, Pakistan could meet the uses of its Eastern River canals, bring most of the Sutlej Valley canals upto allocations, and also meet the requirements of the projects in progress on the Indus.

An independent engineering appraisal of the Bank's Proposal, carried out by an American Consulting Engineer of international repute revealed that the Bank's proposal did not meet the standard of fairness recognized in International law and failed to equitably apportion the Indus Waters. It became evident that the flow supplies of the three Western Rivers would not be adequate to meet Pakistan's historic and planned uses. Realization of this fact led to a series of explanations on the part of the Bank, the net effect of which was to reduce the supplies to be made available to the projects in progress.

Acceptance of the Bank's Proposal and resumption of co-operative work

After considerable hesitation both India and Pakistan accepted the Bank proposal, with certain reservations, and tripartite talks were resumed with the objective of preparing

> "a comprehensive plan for the consideration of Governments on the basis of the Bank Proposal of February 5, 1954, taking as a starting point the division of waters envisaged therein."

It was agreed that in the event the flow supplies of the three Western Rivers were found to be inadequate to meet (i) the existing uses, (ii) bring most of the Sutlej Valley canals upto allocations, (iii) meet the requirements of Thai and Kotri Projects and (iv) meet the reasonable additional requirement of Gudu, Sukkur and the future development in the State of Jammu and Kashmir, the plan will outline the feasible means that might be adopted to meet any deficiencies. It was also agreed that "whenever the Bank deems it necessary in the process of working out the plan, the Bank will use its good offices to bring about acceptance of adjustments which the Bank shall consider reasonable in the light of all the circumstances".

Bank's Aide Memoire of May 21, 1967

The Bank engaged Messrs. TAMS of New York, a reputable firm of Engineers, to assist in the examination of the adequacy of water supplies for a plan under the Bank Proposal. After 18 months of studies in collaboration with Pakistani and Indian Engineers, the Bank reached the conclusion, contained in its Aide Memoir of 21st May 1956, that its Proposal of February 1954 needed an "adjustment", the proposed uses could not be met from the flow supplies of the three Western Rivers. In the light of the studies made by its consultants, taking certain assumed uses of projects in Pakistan, considerably less than what Pakistan had claimed and were reasonably required bythe projects, the Bank concluded that:-

"After taking into account the possibilities of the transfer of flow supplies of the Indus, Jhelum and Chenab by a system of link canals:

(i) There would be no shortages in Kharif, except for occasional 10-days periods in April and September in occasional years.

(ii) There would be consistent surpluses in Kharif, significant in quantity, duration and frequency.

(iii) There would be consistent shortages in Rabi, occasionally beginning in late September or extending into early April (see (i) above), of a degree, duration and frequency which the Bank Group could not regard as "tolerable".

The Bank, therefore, felt that:-

"An adjustment, in its proposal of February 1955 is called for. This adjustment should, in the bank's view, assure to Pakistan "timely" water, sufficient to eliminate the shortage referred to in paragraph 6(c)(iii)".

Paragraphs 8 and 9 of the Aide Memoirs, which deal with the question of the adjustment of the Bank Proposal, are self explanatory and are reproduced below:

8. (a) In the light of the conclusion at which the Bank has arrived, as set out in paras 6 and 7 above, the "Bank feels that an adjustment in its proposal of February 1954 is called for. This adjustment should in the Bank's view, assure to Pakistan "timely" water sufficient to eliminate the shortage referred to in para 6(c)(iii).

(b) The adjustment referred to in (a) above might take any of the following forms, or a combination of any two, or all of them:-

   (i) Supplies from tube-wells.

   (ii) Continued deliveries to Pakistan of "timely" water from the Eastern Rivers.

   (iii) Construction of storage on the Western Rivers.

(c) When the Bank made its proposal of February 1954, the possibility; both in India and in Pakistan, of supplementing flow by supplies from tube-wells, was realized. But this source of supply is not, in the Bank's view, an appropriate means, over the long term, of eliminating any part of the disclosed shortage. Accordingly, and if the Division of waters contemplated by the Bank Proposal is maintained, the adjustment should be in the form of storage on the Western Rivers.

9. The system of works to implement the Bank Proposal, as adjusted, should, therefore, in the Bank's view, be based on the principle that, for the purpose of meeting the "para 2 Users" the flow of the Western Rivers (Indus AS WELL AS Jhelum and Chenab) should be exploited to the maximum possible extent, and that the minimum inroads should be made on Pakistan's limited storage capacity. In the Bank's view, the cost of this system of works should be the basis of the calculation of India's financial liability".

Aide Memoire Plan

Initially, India was hesitant to accept the Aide Memoire and the co-operative work was held up. However, in September 1956, both sides accepted it unconditionally, and the-co-operative work was resumed by the parties with the object of working out, with the assistance of the Bank, a settlement of the question satisfactory to both the Governments on the basis of the Bank Proposal of February 1954 and the Aide Momoire of May 1956. Accordingly, both sides were requested by the Bunk to put in their system of works or plane. This was duly done. Pakistan's plan, worked out in consultation with a firm of engineers in U.S.A., included two links from the Indus (Tarbela-Kanshi link of 25,500 cusecs capacity and Kalabagh-Jhelum link of 14,500 cusecs capacity) and was estimated to cost $ 1,250 millions, to which was to be added the cost of operation maintenance and depreciation and also the cost of works that will eventually be required, judging from similar river developments in U.S.A., on account of changes in the regimes of the rivers (e.g. channel deterioration). Most of this cost, under the relevant principles of the Bank proposal and the Aide Memoire, was debatable to India. The Indian Plan was not disclosed to Pakistan. It is understood that the plan had not been worked out beyond the barest outline and it did not conform to the Bank Proposal and the Aide Memoire.

Bank's list of works

While estimates of the Pakistan Plan were being worked out, the Bank handed over to the Pakistan Delegation two alternative lists of works (presumably forming part of the alternative plans contemplated by them) and requested the Pakistan Delegation to estimate their cost of construction. These works were estimated to cost $937 millions and 967 millions respectively. These lists were also given to the Indians. The Bank, however, did not formally present them to the two Delegations. The Bank officials told the Pakistan's officials in informal discussions that the cost of any plan prepared in accordance with their proposals would be outside India's ability to pay. In the circumstances, it seemed to be clear that the complete division of rivers contemplated by the Bank Proposals could not be achieved.

Bank's proposal of continued deliveries from the Eastern Rivers during the period 15th September to 31st March

At this stage, the Bank informally put forward a proposal that India should continue to supply to Pakistan waters from the Eastern Rivers during the period 15th September to 31st March. During the rest of the year, the requirements of the Pakistan Eastern River Canals were to be met from the three Western Rivers. Pakistan accepted this proposal but it was rejected by India.

Heads of Agreement

It was expected that the Bank would come out with a plan of its own. Instead of their final a plan, the Bank proposed certain Heads of Agreement which included a provision that differences in regard to a plan to implement the Bank Proposal and the Mempire, should be put to arbitration on the basis of the two documents. The original response of both the countries to this suggestion vas hedged with reservations. Subsequently, Pakistan accepted the proposal for arbitration, and was, therefore, prepared to submit all points of difference to arbitration, to be decided on the basis of these documents. She also made the decision to submit the entire dispute ab initio to the jurisdiction of the International Court of Justice. India on the other hand, stated that specific questions agreed to between the two parties could be submitted to arbitration on a basis to be worked out in each case. Pakistan was of the opinion that it would be impossible for the parties to agree either as to the question to be submitted to arbitration or to the basis on which arbitration should proceed in each case and, therefore, considered that India's acceptance of the proposal was inadequate and ineffective.

Adhoc Agreements

An agreement had been reached in March 1952 providing for the maintenance of the supplies for existing uses while the co-operative work continued with the participation of the Bank. In 1954, however, India informed the Bank that it considered itself released from this agreement. Subsequently, in June, 1955, this agreement was incorporated in an ad hoc Agreement to cover the period April 1, 1955 to September 30, 1955. Similar ad hoc agreements were reached for the periods from October 1, 1955 to March 31, 1956, and April 1, 1956 to March 31, 1957. These agreements were consistent with the concept that the regime of an international river may not be changed without the consent of the interested parties, that any increased Indian withdrawals should be related to Pakistan's ability to replace and that some of the supplies transferred through Links should be utilized by Pakistan for the purpose of improving the supplies in the Sutlej Valley Project as planned before Partition. A machinery was set up under these agreements for exchange of data and inspection of works by either side.

The Bank party came out and worked in sub-continent from October to December 1957 in order to help negotiate for an ad hoc agreement for 1957-58. Negotiations were conducted in Karachi and Delhi, and eventually the Bank party considered that all points of difference, excepting one, were within the range of agreement. The negotiations broke down on India's refusal to pay for the cost of works operated in Pakistan for her benefit. The Bank team was of the opinion that India should accept this charge as Pakistan had, since 1948, paid for the cost of works operated in India for Pakistan's benefit.

Bank's Marhu Tunnel Plan

The officers of the Bank visited the subcontinent in January 1958 to explore the possibility of reducing the costs of the plan by providing for transfers from the Chenab to the Beas through a tunnel a capacity limited to 20,000 cusecs to be constructed in India at a place called Marhu, and India in return guaranteeing certain deliveries from the Eastern River contemplated by the Bank to be 3 to 4 MAF more than withdrawals at Marhu.

The Bank suggested that the two parties should consider this approach and bring their reaction to the next meeting. At the next meeting held in Rome in April and May 1958, both sides rejected the Bank's scheme. Pakistan objected to it on the ground that it departed from the fundamental concept of the Bank Proposal of February 5, 1954, by increasing Pakistan's dependence on supplies flowing from India. India objected, it appears, because, under the scheme, India was required to make available up to about 4 MAF of water from the Eastern Rivers.

In Rome, Pakistan also produced calculations and plans to show that if, instead of building the Marhu tunnel, equivalent links were built in Pakistan, the additional deliveries required from India would be of a lesser order than those required, under the Bank's Marhu tunnel scheme. Pakistan also made the offer that, if India agreed to pay the cost and make the deliveries proposed under the Bank's Marhu tunnel scheme, Pakistan would be willing to accept these as adequate, irrespective of what the real cost of works in Pakistan turned out to be. This offer, however, was not considered, as India refused to make the additional deliveries required under the Bank's Marhu tunnel plan.

London Plan

During the discussions at Rome, the outline of another plan, subsequently referred to as the London Plan, came under consideration of the Bank's team and the Pakistan delegation. By that time, the World Bank had come to recognize that Pakistan's Memoire Plan was the logical interpretation of the Proposal of February 1954 as modified by its Aide Memoire of May 1956. As visualized by the Bank's modified proposal, it achieved the maximum possible replacement of the Eastern River uses from the flows of the three Western Rivers. As Indus had a large surplus in certain important periods of the year, links of a fairly high capacity (40,000 cusecs) from the Indus became obligatory. This was one of the main factors that led to the high cost of the Aide Memoire Plan. However, India's persistent refusal to accept its obligations under the Bank's modified proposal forced the Bank to search for a comparatively cheaper plan which would meet the objectives of its modified proposal. This search led to a new concept of river operations which could result in a more efficient use of the water resources and at the same time result in considerable reduction in the cost of the plan. The concept, in brief, was to place the entire burden of Trimmu and Panjnad on the Indus and thus set free the waters of the Chenab and Jhelum for replacement of the Eastern River uses. Eventually, the Bank requested Pakistan to work out the details of the scheme on the following bases set out by the Bank:-

(1) The replacement works would be built entirely in Pakistan;

(2) Storage for replacement purposes of about 3.5 MAF on the Jhelum tributaries, reserving Mangla for reclamation;

(3) Putting the Trimmu and Panjnad requirements entirely on the Indus; and

(4) Replacement supply for the Sutlej Valley areas would be made available at Suleimanki and above.

A plan drawn up by Pakistan on the basis given by the Bank was presented at the London meeting which took place in July 1958. The Bank's original reactions were favourable. When it was explained to the Indian delegation, they requested time to assess the plan in detail. It was agreed that they should bring their comments to a meeting to be held in Washington early in December 1958.

India's Marhu Tunnel Plan

At the Washington meeting, the Indian engineers objected to the London plan on the ground that it contemplated the expenditure of more money on works at India's expense than was, in the opinion of the

Indians, necessary and that, it would take too long to implement. The Indians put forward a counterproposal, the essence of which was that India would build at Marhu a tunnel of unlimited capacity and a storage in India and deliver to Pakistan, as required, to meet historic uses the equivalent of the supplies taken through the tunnel. The Indians contended that this would involve savings in cost and time sufficient to warrant a departure from the Bank proposal and Aide Memoire.

The Pakistan engineers expressed the opinion that the cost of the Indian plan would be as great as, and, in fact, greater than, the cost of the London plan, if realistic rates were adopted and Pakistani uses to the extent already recognized in the Bank Proposal and the Aide Memoire were to be met. Apart from unrealistic estimates of cost and drastic cuts in Pakistan's uses, the Indian counter proposal contributed nothing toward reaching an agreement. A scheme for a tunnel at Marhu of limited capacity coupled with substantial deliveries of water from the Eastern Rivers having been found to be unacceptable, there was no basis for believing that an agreement could be reached on a plan providing for a tunnel of unlimited capacity and no deliveries from the Eastern Rivers. The effect of the Indian proposal would have been to give India control over a substantial flow of the Chenab, whereas the Bank Proposal provided that an assurance by India that the flow of this river will not be disturbed was essential. This, once again, led to a complete deadlock.

Bank's Plan of May 1959

The deadlock was broken through the personal efforts of Mr. Black, the World Bank's President, who visited the Sub-continent in May 1959 and resolved most of the outstanding issues through direct discussions with the Prime Minister of India and the President of Pakistan. President Black visited India first and his talks in India had primarily centered around India's financial contribution towards the cost of the plan and the length of the Transition Period. The Bank was of the view that India's main concern was with regard to these two points and that she was not concerned with the nature of works to be built in Pakistan. After successful talks in Delhi, Mr. Black visited Pakistan. At his first meeting with the President of Pakistan, which was held on 16th May 1959, Mr. Black, after relating the recent history of the Indo-Pakistan negotiations, stated that the Bank had been forced to put forward its own proposals. He gave a resume of his talks with, the Indian Prime Minister and assured Pakistan that if the Bank succeeded in its efforts, Pakistan would not have to pay anything for the construction of replacement works. He added that the Bank was optimistic about the chances of necessary finances being forthcoming. The details of the Bank's plan, or works, and the Financial Proposals were handed over to Pakistan's representatives soon after the first meeting.

Although the Bank's Plan had not been disclosed to Pakistan before Mr. Black's visit but the Pakistan Delegation had a fairly accurate idea of what this Plan was likely to be. An assessment of this "Expected Bank Plan" had been prepared with the help of engineers of the West Pakistan Government and WAPDA and submitted to the Cabinet on 15th May 1959. A brief for the talks with the Bank had been approved by the Committee of the Cabinet.

The important points, concerning the list of works, discussed with the Bank, included the following:-

"(i) <u>Storage Modification;</u> The Bank was reminded that Pakistan Engineers had always held the view that real requirements were greater; the minimum storage acceptable to Pakistan for replacement was 3.5 MAF on the Jhelum and 2.4 MAF on the Indus. If no storage was provided on the Indus and all the burden was to be thrown on the Jhelum then the additional storage required on the Jhelum would be a good deal more than 2.4 M.A.F. as losses in the long reach of the river between Mangla and Panjnad would have to be provided for. Pakistan was of the fact that the Bank engineers did not admit the accuracy of her figures and according to the Bank all tine requirements of replacement could be met from a storage of 3.4. M.A.F on the Jhelum alone. Pakistan had been anxious that this difference of opinion should be submitted to a panel of experts but this had not been possible. Pakistan had great misgivings if she was asked to accept a plan which was inadequate according to her engineers; and, therefore, if the Plan was to have her approval without reservation then Tarbela should be included in the Plan, even at the cost of Rohtas, which could then be excluded. (During the discussions, this point became involved with the points which follow).

(ii) <u>Cost of maintenance, operation and depreciation of Works</u>: On this point, Pakistan urged that those were undoubtedly India's liability and that her irrigation system could not remain economically viable if this burden was thrown on Pakistan.

Mr. Iliff eventually agreed to consider the replacement of Rohtas by Tarbela provided Pakistan agreed to waive her claims regarding these costs of maintenance, operation, and depreciation. The argument put forward was that the increase of storage capacity resulting from this modification would give Pakistan a considerable amount of additional development. The income from these factors would be used for providing depreciation and would also cover the cost of maintenance and operations. The increase in the cost of the plan on this account could thus be considered as a capitalized payment for these costs.

(iii) <u>Flexibility</u>: It was agreed that Pakistan would have the right to modify the Plan as she desired, provided it made no additional call for funds on this account and did. not seek to prolong the interim period on account of any changes which might be introduced.

(iv) <u>Sailab</u>: The Bank still held the view that water would be available for this purpose arid also pointed out that the 50 millions provided for tube-wells and drainage would go a long way towards providing replacement for Sailab.

(v) <u>Canal deterioration, Sub-soil Water Depletion and Salinity Prevention Barrage</u>: Here again, Mr. Iliff was extremely doubtful if India would agree to admit any liability on this account. He added that it was India's contention that with the signing of the Treaty, she would be free of all further liability. It was urged upon him that all that Pakistan required was a provision in the Treaty under which these matters could be taken up as and when the problems became serious. It was also pointed out that similar problems would arise in India right up to the Forozepur Headwords; and therefore, Joint planning would be the best way of overcoming these difficulties. He, however, expressed his inability to persuade India to accept any responsibility."

Amendment of the Bank's Plan

The final meeting between the President of Pakistan, members of the Committee of the Cabinet and Mr. Mueenuddin on the one side, and President Black and Vice-President Iliff on the other was held on the 18th of May 1959. The President thanked Mr. Black and expressed his willingness to go along with the proposals put forward by the Bank and drew the Bank's attention to certain outstanding matters. In response, Mr. Black thanked the President and handed over an Aide Memoire embodying the results of the discussions in Karachi. According to this Aide Memoire, it was agreed between the Government of Pakistan and the World Bank that the "amended System of Works, to be worked out by Pakistan in consultation with I.B.R.D," would include the following features:-

(a) Substitution of Tarbela Reservoir for Rohtas Reservoir.

(b) Haveli, Panjnad and Islam Systems to be fed from Indus.

(c) Revision of Link System to take account of (a) and (b) above.

Indus Basin Advisory Board (I.B.A.B)

The Government of Pakistan set up an Organization (known as IBAB), vide Resolution No.WI-19(418)/59 dated 10th June 1959, published in the Gazette of Pakistan, to prepare a firm plan for the development of the

Indus Basin supplies, in accordance with, and to implement, the Bank Proposals". The duties of the Organisation set out in the resolution were:-

(a) to review the various existing plans and to evolve the best plan for the purpose of effecting replacement from the Western Rivers of uses in Pakistan presently met from the Eastern Rivers;

(b) to integrate this plan with the needs of reclamation and development;

(c) to secure as much hydel development as is feasible within the plan.

IBAB's list of works

The IBAB, after considering the various alternative alignments of link canals and whether the burden of Islam canals should be thrown on the Indus or the tributaries, submitted its recommendations vide its Memorandum dated 18th September 1959. The IBAB decided that as availability on the Indus was greater and in the future, additions to this river from recovery of drainage were likely to be greater than on the tributaries, it was more desirable to throw the additional burden of Islam canals on the Indus.

Settlement Plan

The list of works recommended by the IBAB was approved by the government of Pakistan and communicated to the World Bank. This list of works is generally referred to as the "Settlement Plan".

Indus Waters Treaty 1960

On 19th September 1960, the Indus Waters Treaty was signed. The list of works was, however, not made a part of the Treaty. It was, however, made an annexure to the Development Fund Agreement which was executed on the same day.

Indus Basin Development Fund Agreement

The Indus Basin Development Fund Agreement between Pakistan, Australia, Canada, Germany (West), New Zealand, U.K., U.S.A., and the World Bank was signed, along with the Indus Waters Treaty 1960, on 19th September 1960, and the Treaty formed an annexure of the Fund Agreement. In the preamble of the Fund Agreement, it is inter alia, stated:-

> WHEREAS the Government of India and Pakistan have concluded (subject to exchange of ratifications), the Indus Waters Treaty 1960 (hereinafter called the Treaty, and of which a copy is annexed hereto as Annexure A) providing, interalia, for the sharing between India and Pakistan of the use of the waters of the Indus Basin;

> AND WHEREAS the effective utilization by Pakistan of the waters assigned to it by the Treaty entails the construction of a system of works a part of which will accomplish the replacement of water supplies for irrigation canals in Pakistan which hitherto have been dependent on water supplies from the waters assigned by the Treaty to India;

> AND WHEREAS by the terms of Article V of the Treaty, India has undertaken to make a payment of £62,060,000 towards the costs of the replacement part of such works, such sum to be paid to an Indus Basin Development Fund to be established and administered by the Bank;

AND WHEREAS Australia, Canada, Germany, New Zealand, the United Kingdom, the United States and the Bank, in view of the importance which they attached to a settlement of the Indus Waters problem from the point of view both of the economic development of the area and of the promotion of peace and stability therein, have agreed, as hereinafter set forth, to make a contribution towards the costs of such system of works and also to make such contribution available through the above mentioned Indus Basin Development Fund.

Works actually built

Storages and link canals actually built or being built by Pakistan are the same as included in the Indus Basin Fund Agreement except that in the case of the two storage reservoirs, the live capacity of the reservoirs is larger than the capacity indicated in the Agreement and that in the case of Kalabagh-Jhelum link, it was decided to take it off from the new Chashma barrage instead of the Kalabagh Barrage. There were also some other modifications of the proposed works which were considered essential, or, at least, highly desirable, by the technical experts.

All the works of the Settlement Plan, except for Tarbela Dam, have since been completed. The Tarbela Dam, which is under construction, is scheduled for completion by 1975.

CHAPTER – 46

Consequences Of Indus Waters Treaty 1960

1. Under the Treaty, Pakistan gave up its claim to the waters of the Three Eastern Rivers, the Ravi, the Beas and the Sutlej, and India agreed that the waters of the Indus, the Jhelum and the Chenab, except for some uses in the upper reaches, be reserved for the exclusive uses of Pakistan.

2. Along with the Treaty was signed the Indus Basin Fund Agreement which describes in its Annexure 'D' the works to be constructed. These works are also referred to as the Indus Basin Settlement Plan. Although, the primary object of this Settlement Plan, is replacement, its secondary object is to provide an element of development as distinct from replacement.

3. This Settlement Plan provides for:-

    (a) Two storage dams, one at Mangla on the Jhelum, and the second at Tarbela on the Indus, with a total live storage capacity of over 14 million acre feet.

    (b) Eight feeder canals, linking the Western Rivers between themselves and with the Eastern Rivers. These are as follows:-

      (i) Trimmu-Sidhnai linking Chanab to Ravi.

      (ii) <u>Sidlmiti</u>-Mailsi-Bahawal continuing the link No. (i) from Ravi to Mailsi and across the river Sutlej through a syphon to Bahawal Canal.

      (iii) Qadirabad-Balloki, linking Chenab with Ravi at Balloki.

      (iv) Balloki-Suleimanke, linking Ravi to Sutlej.

      (v) Chashma-Jhelum, linking Indus to Jhelum.

      (vi) Taunsa-Panjnad, linking Indus to Chenab.

    In addition to the above links, the existing Marala-Ravi and Bedian-Depalpur Links have been remodelled.

    (c) Four new barrages, at Sidhnai on the Ravi, at Qadirabad on the Chenab, at Rasul on the Jhelum and at Chaahma on the Indus, to serve along with the existing barrages, as diversion weirs for the canal system in West Pakistan.

    (d) A syphon across the Sutlej at Mailsi. The location of these works is shown in Map No, 2.

4. The two storage reservoirs are so far the most important and also the most expensive components of the project. The eight link canals are the main arteries for transporting waters from the three Western Rivers — Indus, Jhelum, and Chenab — to the irrigated areas previously supplied by the three Eastern Rivers, Ravi Beas and Sutlej.

5. Pakistan has practically completed all the works that are necessary to replenish the waters derived from the Eastern Rivers by waters taken from the Western Rivers. Tarbela Dam, which is under construction, will be completed by 1976.

6   Sind has contended that the Fund Agreement cannot be regarded as a consequence of the Treaty and that the aforesaid system of works is not a part of the Fund Agreement. The Treaty and the Indus Basin Development Fund Agreement were signed on the same day i.e. on 19th September 1960. The Treaty was also made an ;Annexure to the Fund Agreement. Reading these two documents, one comes to an unhesitating conclusion that during the transition period of 10 years, Pakistan was to complete a system of works to replace from the Western Rivers the supplies so far received from the Eastern Rivers for an effective utilization by Pakistan of the waters assigned to it by the Treaty. The Fund Agreement was not made a part of the Treaty because India would have nothing to do with the said Agreement. India's contribution for replacement works had been set at a fixed amount related to its ability to pay and was considerably less than its actual liability. Pakistan had successfully asserted that some development rather than only replacement should be included in the Agreement.

7   During the Indo-Pakistan negotiations, Pakistan insisted for reservoirs on Western Rivera to meet the replacement needs of the canals which were dependent on: the Eastern Rivers. The World Bank ultimately accepted these demands and approached the friendly Governments, United States, Canada, United Kingdom, West Germany, Australia, and New Zealand, to under-write a Water Settlement that would advance the cause of peace in the Indus Basin and ultimately succeeded in its mission. Though India had nothing to do with the Fund Agreement, still it was mentioned in Article V of the Treaty. This Treaty and the Fund Agreement were the result of a long and protracted negotiation. A perusal of the documents relating to these negotiations will leave no room for doubt that Pakistan signed the Treaty because the World Bank had agreed to a set of works demanded by Pakistan and also made arrangements to provide funds for the same. Hence, the contention of Sind, that the Fund Agreement is not a consequence of the Treaty, cannot be sustained.

Impact of Treaty on Provinces

8   Punjab, Sind and North Western Frontier Province have vied with each other in showing the injuries sustained by them by the loss of three Eastern Rivers. In accordance with the Treaty, India was allowed to divert the entire flow of the three Eastern Rivers, viz Ravi, Beas and Sutlej, from which about 24 million acre feet used to flow down to! Pakistan. In addition replacement of Eastern River's uses from the Western Rivers entailed considerable additional conveyance losses enroute. This was really a great loss to Pakistan.

9   The Indus Basin was developed, designed and operated as an integrated unit. It is, therefore, obvious that all the provinces, which had real and substantial interests in the three Eastern Rivers, suffered an irreparable loss by losing the waters of the said three rivers. Efforts, therefore, must be made to give them some relief, if possible, without quibbling as to which province was the greatest sufferer.

Settlement Plan

10 Sind has challenged the inclusion of Chashma-Jhelum Link (22,000 cusecs) and Taunsa-Panjnad Link (12,000 cusecs) in the Settlement Plan. Attempt was also made to show that these links were not at all necessary because the requirements of Haveli, Islam and Panjnad Canals could have been easily met from Mangla and the Tributary Zone, i.e., Jhelum and Chenab. Equity of placing them on Indus has also been disputed,

11 The printed records of Indus Water Dispute shows that links from Indus were mooted in 1954 and after due deliberation, the President of Pakistan approved of this arrangement. The said two links have been constructed at a cost of over one hundred crores. It is now too late after 10 years to challenge the feasibility of these links. In any event they were constructed with the approval of the President of

Pakistan, and this Committee is not competent to enter into the question of propriety or validity of his decision.

12 Some arguments have been advanced by the parties on the following issues:-

i) What level of uses of the canals dependent upon the Eastern Rivers constitute replacement need, under Article IV(1) of the Treaty; and

ii) What level of uses of the Eastern River's canals are to be met in future?

iii) Whether burden of uses to be met partly from groundwater; and

iv) to what extent Mangla and Tarbela will bear the burden of replacement?

During the negotiations of the Indus Water Dispute, Pakistan case was that deliveries to Pakistan, from the three Eastern Rivers, amounted to 24,00 MAF. The details, as to how this figure was arrived at, are summarized in the following table:-

Eastern River Supplies

River flow	Mean Annual flow (M.A.F.)
Sutlej	14
Beas	13
Ravi	6

	33
Indian canal withdrawals	9
Supply reaching Pakistan	24
Pakistan S.V.C. and C.B.C. withdrawals	11
Losses	2
Spill:-	
Below Islam	8
Below Balloki	3
	24

(Figures based on 10 years mean from 1936-37 to 1945-46)

13 Article IV(1) of the Treaty is as follows:-

Pakistan shall use its best endeavours to construct and bring into operation, with due regard to expedition and economy, that part of a system of works which will accomplish the replacement, from the Western Rivers and other sources, of water supplies for irrigation canals in Pakistan, which, on 15th August ;1947, were dependent on water supplies from the Eastern Rivers." In other words, had agreed to the replacement of 11 MAF for the irrigation canals of Pakistan which were dependent on Eastern Rivers. Out of this 11 MAF, about 8 MAF was for Kharif and 3 MAF for Rabi.

14 Relying on the word 'other sources' in Article IV(1) Sind argued that burden of uses of Eastern Rivers was to be met partly from ground water. However, from the printed record of Indo-Pakistan Water Dispute, it appears that at no stage parties ever contemplated that replacement needs should be met from groundwater. It may be mentioned that Bahawalpur State Distributary and some areas of G.B.D.C.

had prescriptive rights on the Eastern Rivers but the same could not be fed by gravity from the Western Rivers. These had, therefore, to be fed from other sources, such as lift or tubewells. In the above context, the words 'other sources' were used in Article IV(1).

15 The question as to what extent the burden of replacement should be met from the storages would be dealt in Chapter XIII.

16 The consequence of the Treaty may be summarized thus:-

(a) Flow of three Western Rivers was allocated for the exclusive use of Pakistan except for some insignificant uses in India and Jammu and Kashmir;

(b) Pakistan got a system of works, which, besides supplying irrigation water to those canals in Pakistan which had in the past depended on the flows of Eastern Rivers, also provided for substantial irrigation development in West Pakistan.

CHAPTER – 47

Indus Water Treaty

By Ahmed Rafay Alam, 07 July 2011
(The News)

Indo-Pakistan water relations are bound, limited and defined by the Indus Waters Treaty of 1960. The treaty divides the resources of the Indus Basin, one of the largest and the oldest basins on the planet, and states that India will have control over the waters of the three eastern rivers of the basin (the Ravi, the Sutlej and the Beas) and that Pakistan will have control over the waters of the three western rivers (the Indus, the Chenab and the Jhelum). The treaty then goes on to set out the rights and obligations of the riparians and, importantly, allows India to avail itself of the waters of the western rivers for domestic consumption, non-consumptive functions, limited agricultural use and for hydroelectric purposes.

So far, the treaty has held strong. However, because of a variety of factors, some voices are accusing India of stealing Pakistan's water and violating the treaty. I will not dwell upon these voices in this article because they are incorrect and, as I will try to show, they can be made irrelevant. However, some factors providing these voices their motives and reasons must be acknowledged: the mistrust that characterises Indo-Pakistan relations, gross mismanagement of water resources within Pakistan, outdated irrigation practices, poorly planned agricultural zoning, a rising population and resultant water scarcity.

What these voices are doing is choosing to ignore Pakistan's most pressing political, economic, social and environmental issues, and instead are looking for solace in the age-old chestnut: India is to blame. What else explains the reason given for having more troops deployed on its eastern border than its western, when the trouble so clearly is to ensure water security?

One of the problems in Indo-Pakistan water relations, as far as Pakistan is concerned, is that, thanks to Sir Cyril Radcliff and the outcome of English colonialism in India, Pakistan is the lower riparian. What the treaty does is set up a riparian hegemony by dividing the resources of the Indus Basin, creating an asymmetrical relationship between the two riparians and cementing India's position as the riparian hegemon. In other words, the treaty stacks the cards against Pakistan and makes it close to impossible for it to rationalise the disproportionate relative bargaining positions the treaty allocates. This is because, in practice, the more powerful riparian is loath to give up the benefits it has. There are some who suggest that, for this very reason, the treaty should be scrapped and another negotiated. To these gifted geniuses, I ask this: Very well, then, but what brilliant strategy do you have hidden away that will outmanoeuvre the riparian hegemon and get the lower riparian more than it already has under the treaty? This question is met with silence.

How can Pakistan get itself out of this situation? The answer is simple: Don't look at the Indus Waters Treaty for solutions. The treaty is based on a sort of divide-the-resource-of-the-Indus-Basin theory, which will always result in a zero-sum game for Pakistan. What we need is to look outside the "divide the resource" paradigm and look towards the opportunities afforded by the "sharing the resource" paradigm. What we need to do is see whether it is in the economic, social or political interest of both riparians to cooperate on water, rather than be antagonistic over it. What we need is a trans-boundary water opportunity analysis.

Trans-boundary analysis looks at the positive sum outcomes of sharing the resources of a water basin. The approach is unique, in that it allows the weaker riparian to offer the hegemon some additional benefit.

The idea would be to conduct a full-spectrum trans-boundary water opportunity analysis that will identify the areas where cooperation between India and Pakistan over the waters of the Indus Basin will yield economic, social or other benefits. For example, if India is building run-of-the-river dams on the western rivers, this need not be a cause of alarm in Pakistan. After all, what keeps Pakistan from purchasing the electricity from India? We are more than willing to pay an extortionately high cost for electricity from diesel-powered rental power projects when everyone knows hydroelectric power is a fraction of the cost. Selling electricity to Pakistan would also be in the economic interest of India because of the premiums it could charge. Similarly, there could be economic benefit to India if it allowed Pakistan to expand, say, its fisheries along the eastern rivers. The purpose of the trans-boundary water opportunity analysis would be to identify and quantify the all the possible positive sum outcomes of a "sharing the resource" strategy. The wider the scope of such an analysis, the more chances of identifying more and more areas of cooperation.

The analysis would involve other issues as well. One would be the identification of what sort of "green water" resources exist (as in water that falls from the sky, and distinct from "blue water", which is, essentially, surface water) and how such resources could be harnessed for the benefit of either India or Pakistan. (The study of "green water" is rare, as most hydrologists tend to ignore something they can't pipe, and government doesn't care about stuff it can't tax.) The inclusion of such things could widen the overall opportunities, at least in Pakistan, of harnessing the water resources of the country.

The economic science of sharing resources is also cutting-edge. Elinor Ostrom was awarded the Nobel Memorial Prize for Economic Sciences this year for her study of shared resources. I had the opportunity of meeting Ms Ostrum last month and to speak to her about Indo-Pakistan water relations. She hadn't studied the Indus Basin (she has studied others), but told me that, should the two countries ever decide to go down such a path, the only problems they would encounter would be working out the right profit-sharing formulas.

And, finally, in the Pakistani context, again, if Pakistan could be seen sitting down with India and doing something large-scale, without the rhetoric of Kashmir or terrorism clouding the way, it would create enormous international goodwill that, surely, Pakistan could leverage to its advantage.

On almost all counts, it is impossible to deny how attractive a proposition a trans-boundary water opportunity analysis is. It's difficult to judge how the governments of these countries would respond to the call for such an analysis. Perhaps, this is not the time for such a call and, perhaps, it isn't for the governments of the countries to conduct such an analysis. At this stage, the opportunities of sharing the resource of the Indus Basin are the perfect place for players in Track-II diplomacy to pick up the gauntlet and show their respective governments the way forward.

CHAPTER - 48

Poverty Issues In Displacement: A Sociological Study Of Baglihar Project in Jammu and Kashmir

Sudesh Kumar (ACME Internsational Journal of Multidisciplinary Research)[1]

ABSTRACT

Displacement of people due to erection of dams is a world-wide phenomenon. This displacement of people may also occur under various circumstances such as wars, racial and religion persecution, repatriation of the alien minorities and natural calamities like earthquakes, flood, great fires and famines. These circumstances, under which displacement occurs, create the problem of rehabilitation. This paper is an attempt to highlight the various poverty issues arising out of such projects. The process of rehabilitation of people displaced as a result of the erection of dams and other developmental activities is quite different from the process arising from the political and the natural calamities. The political and natural calamities are solved mostly by undertaking hurried temporary relief work before the steps for permanent rehabilitation are taken.

KEY WORDS: Displacement, Family issues, Forced Labor, Housing Problem, Joblessness, Kinship, Livestock, Morbidity, Poverty, Risks.

Introduction

The construction of a number of multipurpose dams of small, medium and big size has been undertaken in India to provide irrigation and to generate hydro-electricity. It so happens that in order to be able to irrigate vast agricultural areas, large tracts of land, commanding a vantage position, have to be used for the reservoir of water, and these tracts encompass among them habitations which have to go under water. As a result, the people inhabiting these villages or hamlets are uprooted from their hearth and home and probably fields as well. This requires the evacuation and rehabilitation of the people of a large number of villages from the submerged areas. The villages, especially the cultivators, have a deep attachment to the soil and their home. The people also desire to live among their kinsmen at the new place of rehabilitation. They are also called upon to give up their love and attachment their ancestral property, and a living possibly among to their kinsmen, and with their traditional neighbourhood relation, at the altar of the well-being of the community as a whole. The whole social and economic life is thus disturbed.

The government, no doubt, gives compensation in terms of land, site for home, and other expenses. But this economic compensation may not satisfactorily counter-balance the social and psychological disturbances. They need to be rehabilitated not only economically but socially and psychologically as well. Development

---

[1] Copyright © 2013. Sudesh Kumar. This is an open access referred article, distributed under the Creative Common Attribution License, which permits unrestricted use, distribution and reproduction in any medium, provided the original work is properly cited.

projects that displace generally give rise to social, economic and ecological and environmental problems. Family, as a system, crumbles down and its bonds by long established heritage and ancestry are scattered.

Community structure and social networks are weakened, kin groups are dispersed; coupled with this, cultural identity, traditional authority and the potential for mutual help are diminished. Family, as a system of production, ceases to exist and the nature of religions worship also gets affected. The sense of belonging to their birth place is threatened and the security of symbolic creations such as places of worship, graveyard of the ancestors, sacred mountain, trees and the deities are destroyed. It generally associates with psychological stress and results in sickness, grief and death; people are bound to live in a new atmosphere, in a new place, with a new attitude and values, which changes the entire socio-cultural lifecycle of the affected persons. The most visible offshoot of resettlement is in the form of broken families, deserted parents, quarrel for economy, increased use of liquor, gambling, stealing and so on (Dias, 2012).

Fernendes says: In Asia, a majority among those deprived of their livelihood belong to the powerless classes, and got further marginalised while planning the project and rehabilitation. For example, a substantial number of the DPs/ PAP in India are tribal, depending on the CPRs as their livelihood. But the Land Acquisition Act 1894 does not require the project authorities to compensate this loss or rehabilitate them. The CPRs are often alienated. Land owned by others is the livelihood of those who live by rendering services to the village as a community. But only the landowner is compensated. Even among those groups, women are the worst victims. But they are rarely taken into consideration while planning resettlement. (Verma, 2004).

Hari Mohan Mathur, in a recent study of projects in Rajasthan that involved resettlement, attempted to find out whether the characteristics of eight risks that make up for Crenea's impoverishment model were all present there, too. He observed that in addition to the eight fold model envisaged by Cernea, there exists one more in the form of loss of 'access to public services". It is only when the affected people move to resettlement colonies that they became aware of this loss. Even in the most isolated villages, a wide range of basic public services now exist: Schools, clinics, street lights, public tap for drinking water, village to city transport bus services, and so on.

Highlighting the pauperization aspects of the oustesd, Thukral says: "What happens to the displaced that are not relocated? It is small wonder that a substantial number among them are reduced to a rentless struggle for survival. In some cases, people who can get adjusted to new circumstances migrate to other places in search of lost livelihood. Loss of compensation money in social, cultural and religious obligations as well as liquor and gambling are the most quoted narratives. Thus, an involuntary resettlement causes a severe long-term hardship, impoverishment and environmental damage and the affected persons reach a stage of hand to mouth existence. Right from the beginning, with the inception of any development project, the impact of resettlement and rehabilitation on affected persons has not given serious consideration till date. It has often been dealt with in a haphazards ad hoc manner, as a low priority side effect of major infrastructure works. Lack of clear objectives, consistent procedures and adequate resources for addressing resettlement resulted in a serious adverse effect on the people displaced, on the host population, at relocation sites. Thukral says that dislocation and relocation in another area, unless very carefully executed, means a breakdown in community network. Since the dependence of women on men is greater, breakdown of this network creates tremendous insecurity and trauma, which the women experience more than the men who are relatively more mobile.

Over the last few decades, the magnitude of involuntary population displacement and resettlement in developing countries has increased rapidly, due to the accelerated construction of new infrastructure and growing population densities. Recent estimates indicate that every single year a co host of at least 10,000,000 people throughout the developing world enter a process of involuntary displacement and relocation, caused by a new set of development programme that, on average, is being started each year in dam construction and urban and transportation projects (Cernea, 1996).

Involuntary resettlement is often associated with projects that displace people from rural areas, the tribal people and the poorer group in particular. In fact, there are many who mistakenly believe that disruption due to displacement is only their fate, not of the people living in cities. It has been seen that persons who are uprooted from their home ground and rehabilitated in another place have to undergo an entire process of resociolisation and adjustment in an unfamiliar environment. If the host population in the new area is hostile, it only makes matters worse. The fall out in the form of alcoholism, gambling, prostitution and increased morbidity is not unknown. Displacement due to irrigation projects draws the most attention because of all development projects, it causes the largest physical dislocation, submerging vast quantities of land.

THE RISKS
Risk of Livestock

Loss of cattle is the loss of resource that is directly related to the loss of land, especially in Darmund, Baglihar and Pul Doda village in Jammu and Kashmir state, although loss of common grazing ground and loss of forest are other important related reasons. After the loss of land, those animals which are deployed on the farm are rendered superfluous. Loss of land also means less crop residue or waste as fodder to feed. Loss of forest and shrinkage of common grazing ground and the enclosure of the forest made it impossible to graze cattle. Many households do not keep cattle now; those who keep have just very few. Among the cattle, goats seem to be most preferred due to their high commercial value and because of their high survival capacity. Lack of grazing seriously affects livelihood. One grave concern after land acquisition is the unavailability of fodder and this happens also in resettlement sites where grazing land is either scarce or absent. Fuel and fodder are the two biggest problems in the new sites. Unavailability of fodder and common grazing ground means that rural people have to sell most of their cattle (bulls, cows, buffaloes, goats). Cattle are very important to the rural people. It is one of the main indicators of wealth in the society; they are a security in times of financial distress, a kind of safety net and a source of nutrition. Cattle live close to the people, often inside their houses. Children of the rural people grow up with them. They become attached to them and consider them a part of their family.

The field study showed that keeping less cattle has affected the households very hard. Nearly 80 per cent of the respondents have said that cattle made a very big contribution to the household economy. Villagers see this as a big loss in terms of security, income and a big loss in terms of nutrition.

Risk of joblessness

A very high number attribute joblessness to loss of land. Before displacement, rural people of three villages were chiefly engaged in agriculture and related activities which provided the landed as well as the landless with gainful and secure employment. Land acquisition meant loss of the most important source of employment and income. Those rendered landless or were left with uneconomic holdings had no work and no other way to earning except through wage labour. In pul doda area, it has been found that nearly about 80 per cent people were joblessness due to displacement and the government did not provide them jobs. Pul doda was the business hub of batote and Kishtwar highway and people have been running their shops and small petty business. Displacement is the main cause of joblessness of local people and now they were involved in theft, drug addiction etc for earning their livelihood.

Risk of loss of social services

Social service is important for rural people during marriages, fairs and festivals. In rural villages, people have close bonds with each other and they have maintained their own identity. But when people were displaced, they lost their social services, because people migrated from one place to other place and they have also lost kinship relations. It has been found that the host community did not accept these people due to the caste system. During a marriage ceremony, instance people face a lot of problems due to the loss of social services. Nearly 75 per cent respondents say that loss of social services is a big problem and additional pressure put on the women.

Risk of becoming forced labourers

Almost all respondents think that loss of land and livelihood had forced people to become wage labourers. Those forced into wage labour as a result of land loss bemoaned the fact that they have been reduced to being landless labourers after their displacement. They feel that they are forced to work as wage labourers in order to support their families, as they do not possess any other skill except the skill of a farmer. They have no other choice but to accept any wage labour available. This kind of labour is a form of forced labour, incompatible with a life of dignified existence which the farmers and their families enjoyed before the loss of their land. Secondary data reveal that this risk is the most common in projects that uproot indigenous people.

The field data reveal that 55 per cent respondents were becoming forced labourers due to the loss of jobs and land. They work as a wage labour every day. Before the displacement, they were doing jobs in shops; all respondents are unskilled and they have no other option for survival to earn their livelihood.

Risk of social evils

Displacement has increased the dowry demands. The girls of the affected families were sought after by the unaffected people with greed to acquire more dowries. It is found that the demands of dowry have increased due to the compensation of the ousted got. Moreover, as a consequence of displacement, there are a number of cases on the rise in social disturbances reflected by alcoholism. This increase is a social problem which is bound to affect directly the lives and status of women by way of violence inflicted on them. During the study it is found that the break up of families, weakening of kinship ties, loss of security and insurance as a fall out of displacement, the availability of cash received in compensation had led to an increase in alcohol intake by men folk resulting in violence against women.

Risk of Morbidity or health loss

Displacement is associated with psychological stress that emerges out of the fear of relocation or insecurity; also emotional stress is aggravated by a feeling of helplessness that may result in increased sickness, grief or even death. In doda village, people said that their stress has increased very much because they have to worry about their next meal because of general insecurity and children's future. Over 60 per cent respondents said that health has deteriorated in the villages. Some 17 per cent respondents said that health has improved. Over 70 per cent respondents have said that mental stress has increased. This fact was evident during interviews, including focus group discussions. People drink in order to beat their stress. Studies have indicated that the contribution of men to the household income declines due to alcoholism, further increasing the pressure on women. It also increase incidences of violence against them. Alcoholism increases risks to human health. Studies also indicated that some women were working as domestic maid workers for nurturing their children and survival for livelihood. Most of the old persons face a lot of problems due to the absence of family members. Because, due to forced migration, old persons did not get care properly, and morbidity rate will be increased gradually.

Risk Loss of kinship relation

Kinship is one of the most important relations among family. It helps a lot of people during socio-economic and financial crisis. Before displacement, people lived together and they shared each and every thing during festivals and marriage ceremonies. Social network was very strong among women. But displacement creates a lot of problems among family members due to sharing of compensation. It has been found that displaced people did not get rehabilitated properly and some families have lived on a rented basics where they have faced a lot of problems due to lack of space. One woman said that due to displacement, we have lost each and every thing: land/house/ trees etc. Every household thing depends upon market and we cannot easily afford some items which are so expensive. We have lost the whole kinship, because of migration from one place to another place. We cannot afford to visit our relatives, said another woman. When our relatives come, we find it is very difficult to treat them well. Other woman said that we face a lot of problems when our son-in law comes to our house and we can't treat him very well due to expensive things. Lack of income and lack of security after loss of land and house have affected their dignity, they said. There is also an impact on marriage, because the parents of the brides would ask: 'what is our daughter going to eat? How are you going to support her? In this way, young persons have delayed their marriage due to joblessness. It has been found that people find it difficult to find out a perfect match for marriage due to the breakdown of social network and kinship relation.

Conclusion

Displacement is the biggest consequence of development projects. It creates new poverty issues as people lose land, home, grazing land and common property resources. In the absence of a national rehabilitation and resettlement policy, the affected people will always face great challenges for the survival of life. But the policy-makers did not think about the displaced people; they have only been given monetary compensation and left behind. The data shows that displaced people become powerless due to external forces which are so strong. Development projects and R&R revolve around men and the landed. Women lose many advantages they had enjoyed in their original place of residence without receiving any tangible benefit in exchange. Most women in rural and tribal areas shoulder a tremendous burden, collecting fuel, fodder and water, and thus contributing to the household income.

References

Asthana, Roli. 1996. "Involuntary Resettlement", Survey of International Experience, Economic and Political Weekly, Vol.xxvi No. 5.

Baboo, Bal govind. 1991. "State Policies and People's Response: Lesson from Hirakud Dam". Economic and Political Weekly, Vol. 26. No, 41. PP 2373-79.

Biswal, D.N. 2000. "Forced Displacement: Illusion and Reality". New Delhi: Manak Publication.

Cernea, M.M. 1990. "Poverty Risks from Population Displacement in Water Resources Development", HIID Development Discussion paper No.355, Harvard University, Cambridge.

Fernendes, W. and Thukral, E,G. 1989. "Development, Displacement and Rehabilitation", Indian Social Institute, New Delhi. Fernandes, W. 1991. "Power and Powerless: Development Projects and Displacement of Tribals". Social Action,Vol. 41 No. 3, pp 243-270.

Fernendes, W and S. Anthony Raj. 1992. "Development. Displacement and Resettlement in the Tribal Area of Orissa, New Delhi": Indian Social Institute.

Hussain, Monirul. 2008. Interrogating Development: State, Displacement and Popular Resistance in North East India. New Delhi: Sage Publication.

Joshi, B.L. 1982. "Displacement and Rehabilitation". Parimal Prakashan, Aurangabad.

Judge, Paramjit.S. 2000. 'What Goes Wrong with Rehabilitation': A Sociological view point.

The Eastern Anthropologist, Vol.53, No. 1-2, Jan-June. PP 161-76.

Kothari, S. 1995. "Development, Displacement and Official Policies: A Critical Review", Lokayan Bulletin, March-April, Vol. 11 No.5 New Delhi.

Kumaran, K.P. 2013. "Socio-Economic Impoverishment Risks in Displacement of Tribals Under Polavaram Irrigation project". Rural Development, Vol.32 No.1 pp 33-46.

Mahapatra, L. K. 1996. "Good Intention or Policy Are Not Enough": Reducing Impoverishment Risks for the Tribals Ousted, Paper Presented in the Workshop Organised by the world Bank, NDO, March, 12-14.

Mathur, H.M. 1995. "Development, Displacement and Resettlement:" Focus on Asian Experience. Vikas Publishing, New Delhi.

Pandey, B. 1996. Impoverishment Risks: A Case study of Five Villages In Coal Mining Areas of Talcher, Orissa. Paper presented at the Workshop on Involuntary Resettlement and Impoverishment Risks, New Delhi.

Parasuraman, S. 1999. "The Development Dilemma: Displacement in India". The Hague: Macmillan and Institute of Social Studies.

Patridge, W.L. 1989 "Involuntary Resettlement in Development Project", Journal of Refugee Studies, Vol, 2 No. 3.

Sharma, Betwa. 2005. "Oustess of Indira Sagar Dam". Economic and Potical Weekly. Jan 1-7 Vol,XL. No.1.

Singh, Mirdula. 1989. "Narmada Project- Development Mines People", Main Stream, New Delhi.

Singh, Mirdula,1992. "Development Induced Displacement", New Delhi: Indian Social Institute.

Singh, Mirdula and Samantray, R.K. 1992. In E.G.Thukral (eds). "Big Dams Displaced people, River of Sorrow, River of Change", Sage Publication, New Delhi.

Singh, Satyajit. 1997. "Taming the Waters: The Political Economy of Large Dams in India". New Delhi. Oxford University Press.

Thukral, E.G. 1998. "Dam For Whose Development"? Social Action, Vol.38 No.3 pp 210- 228.

Verma, M.K. 2004. "Development, Displacement and Resettlement:" Rawat Publication, New Delhi. 98

CHAPTER – 49

Hydro-Politics, The Indus Waters Treaty and Climate Change

By Rohan D'Souza (June 2011)

DISCUSSIONS on the Indus rivers have become overwhelmingly strategic. Flows are matters of political contest, vested interests and, above all else, national security. Ironically enough, such strident noises over the division of waters have mostly avoided meaningful attempts to recall the region watershed's, often-times, troubled histories. It is, as if, the Indus Waters Treaty (IWT) of 1960 could be almost nonchalantly deployed to snip vast flowing courses into neat divisible segments and with equal ease 'rationally' allocate immense volumes between nations. That is, a mere blunt knife approach can comprehensively sever and move about a complex hydrology without so much as an afterthought about disturbing delicately poised fluvial ecologies or the implications of coarsely stirring whole river-based communities.

The IWT, with this structured 'forgetting' of the Indus basin's many pasts and varied environments, is, not unexpectedly, often seen by experts to be a 'successful' legal-technical arrangement that has suffered from frequent and exceptional political 'misperceptions'.[1] It can, however, be more convincingly argued the other way. The IWT was an unsteady political project to begin with and is now fatally failing as a legal-technical arrangement. But reversing the analytical vantage requires a sharp perceptual shift as well. A type of taproot understanding of the IWT is urgently called for, by which new facts, so to speak, must be dug up, sunned and differently seasoned in order to have one go beyond the limited simplifications of hydraulic data, official statistics, engineering opinion and statist imperative.

Between the 16th and 18th centuries, the Mughal empire held, in a single firm embrace, vast territories of what today comprises India and Pakistan. For the Mughal ruling elites, applying a regular squeeze over agricultural surpluses was the preferred route to wealth and privilege. Typically enough, given this essentially land based notion of power, the empire's numerous and intricate network of rivers were, at best, used either for navigation or as avenues to conduct easy trade. These inestimable flows, in other words, became natural outliers to the imperial governments' otherwise more onerous quest to extract revenues from soil.

It would be unfair, however, to entirely dismiss all Mughal efforts at harnessing water. Several innovative structures, for example, helped deftly steer river currents into gardens, fountains, hunting grounds and even giant reservoirs. On balance, nevertheless, comprehensive fluvial management was rarely ventured upon. It was only in the middle of the 19th century, following the steady consolidation of the British colonial rule in the subcontinent, that those big immodest engineering interventions for total hydraulic control were carried out. In particular, the vast semi-arid flood plains – sandwiched between the Indus and Gangetic river systems – became amongst the first sites the world over for implementing large-scale modern irrigation schemes.

For the sprawling Indus basin, coursed through by the fluvial fingers of the Indus, Ravi, Chenab, Beas, Sutlej and Jehlum, colonial hydraulic interventions were, in fact, both technically and politically unprecedented.[2] For the first time in the region, permanent structures in the form of barrages and weirs were thrown across river-beds. These durable headworks were equipped with a series of shutters to regulate flows by impounding water during lean seasons, to be then diverted in calibrated quantities across miles of canals. On the reverse, in times when the rivers were swollen or torrential, the shutters would be flipped open to hurriedly jettison discharge. In effect, by alternately impounding or quickening the discharge of flows, the river's variable or moody regime, it was held, could be transformed from a seasonal to a perennial irrigation possibility.[3]

Beginning with the Upper Bari Doab Canal (1859) and the Sirhind system (1882), the drive climaxed with the 'most ambitious' irrigation project of the colonial period – the Triple Canal Project (1916). These perennial canal schemes, however, were assembled not merely as channels commandeering river flows but, in the words of David Gilmartin, were crucially linked to 'political imperatives of state building.'[4] The colonial dispensation, in effect, vigorously pursued perennial irrigation and agricultural settlement as means essential for stabilizing its otherwise unsteady authority in the region. At heart, canal building was the pressing attempt to yoke the then just disbanded Sikh soldiery and a large number of non-cultivating 'predatory' herdsmen to 'permanent interests in landed property.'

The impacts of perennial irrigation, however, can also be historicized differently. Indu Agnihotri, in a seminal essay on the canal colonies in the British Punjab, argued that irrigation did not, as is widely held, simply bring water and increase agricultural productivity into hitherto desolate 'wastes'. Rather, the colonial canal colonies, of the late 19th and early 20th centuries, overwhelmed and over ran a pre-existing vibrant pastoral economy and people who, besides herding, also seasonally cultivated crops through inundation canals. This process of marginalization, if not substantial elimination, of the pastoral communities and their unique ways of living with the ecologies of the doabs continues to find only rare mention.[5]

The point here is that the introduction of modern irrigation in the semi-arid flood plains of the Indus system was enabled following intense struggles over the creation of landed property, the elimination of pastoral livelihoods and accompanied by relentless wide-ranging environmental transformations. Raising agricultural productivity through perennial irrigation, hence involved, by design or otherwise, a deafening silence about different pasts: the ignored but suffered consequences of waterlogging, soil salinization, the violence of landed property, the defeat of nomadic peoples, instabilities brought on by mono-cultures and commercial agriculture, the attrition-ridden assembling of colonial social hierarchies and inevitably, the forced 'training' of once volatile free-falling rivers into contained disciplined irrigation channels.

Profoundly intertwined with the relentless march of modern irrigation in the doabs was the life-world of the colonial civil engineer. Though often less heralded, these energetic, restless, innovative and adventurous men of empire were made steadfast with technical training in modern river management and control. Through the lens of 'imperial science', colonial environments for these engineers were not merely to be 'catalogued, studied and observed' but actively pursued for large scale manipulation, all in the name of commerce, civilization and endless improvement. In the same stride, this resolute quest to control nature was intimately tied to the equally severe project of dominating colonized populations. For the British colonial enterprise, in other words, intensely extracting from nature and exploiting subject peoples seemed almost logically to go hand in hand.

Attempting the dramatic transformation of complex and immense river systems through engineering was, however, no simple task. In aiming to physically shuffle, transfer, move or redirect vast volumes, engineers resorted to reductionist and specialized mentalities. That is, colonial engineers planned and crafted modern river control initiatives primarily through ideologies for abstractions in the form of formulas, equations, model-making, and by repeatedly fine-tuning an overwhelmingly quantitative notion of hydrology. Irrigation engineering preferred, in terms of their self image and professional training, to be defined principally by the 'mathematical sciences'.[6]

Such a notion of handling water, in effect, assumed an unequivocal trust in numbers, while simultaneously aiming to wilfully ignore and shut out local knowledge or place-specific ecological idiosyncrasies involved in harnessing flows. If anything, therefore, the ascendance of colonial hydrology meant the consolidation of the universal, expert-driven and specialized practices for river management alongside the steady marginalization of localized cultures and place-based knowledge for water management. The mighty Indus basin, in effect, was disciplined with the elegance of numbers and rational hydraulic model-building. The river systems, hence, that otherwise stood as messy miscible admixtures of flows, histories, cultures, localities and exceptional environments, were conceptually recast as straight contained channels. A once heterogeneous collection of people and places, through imperial science, cement and quantitative hydrology could be turned into homogenous spaces.

Following the hydraulic rearrangements of the 19th century, the Indus basin witnessed, in the mid-20th century, a second equally dramatic rupture – the division of waters for nation-making. In effect, scuffles over hydraulic access and rights that characterized the colonial period were transformed into bitter disagreements over clarifying issues of ownership and control of the Indus rivers. As the Radcliffe Line etched a hard border between India and Pakistan on 17 August 1947, flows had to be reconfigured as national rivers. From previously watering an uninterrupted contiguous political bloc, the Indus and its tributaries, in step with this logic of partition, had to be hastily inserted within new geographical scales and imagined as part of decolonized national biographies.

Not unexpectedly, complications over the Indus erupted as intractable hydropolitics between India and Pakistan. For a start, flows had to be instantaneously sliced and diced at multiple conceptual levels, in order to acknowledge the region's changed geopolitical realities. Stretches of the tributaries, hence, that fell within India were classified overnight as upper riparian waters while Pakistan, on the other hand, inherited downstream flows. Having been thus officially instituted as cross-border flows, the various arms of the Indus system could now only be managed through a raft of international rules and protocols. The first involved a band-aid approach, with the concluding of an immediate pact, appealingly termed the Standstill Agreement, by which all existing flow arrangements were to be maintained till 31 March 1948.

Alarmingly enough, for Pakistan, the Government of India 'suspended' supplies the very next day when the agreement officially lapsed. Though flows were eventually restored after 18 long days, the shock of being denied water not only 'seared' the Pakistani sense of entitlement to the rivers but the entire incident brutally made known to both sides that water could easily translate into severe problems of politics and power.[7] The subsequent Inter-Dominion Agreement, as a stopgap arrangement, actually ended up further amplifying the fact that sustaining a divided fluvial system, invariably, if not urgently, needed an enduring 'final settlement.'

Following a period of staggered negotiations, the IWT was finally clinched in 1960, as a trilateral deal between Pakistan, India and the World Bank. As noted by Daanish Mustafa, the IWT process substantially mirrored the political landscape of its time. A context that was defined by extreme suspicion between the two countries, their respective location in larger geopolitical strategies for the region and relationships that were repeatedly marred by political competition.

Rehearsing elements or features of the IWT, however, would not be helpful here, as they have been competently done elsewhere. What, nevertheless, needs to be marked is the fact that the IWT was overwhelmingly a legal-technical document. A notion about flows which, on the one hand, were firmly anchored in colonial legacies for water management in the region while, on the other, water agreements were crafted as legal protocols for nation-making. That is, flows were appropriated not on the basis of their ecological properties, but rather subdivided in order to enforce hard national borders.

The Indus system, in essence, was inserted into the geopolitical calculations of a troubled region and made legible primarily as statistically tabulated hydraulic data. The physical constituency of the river regime was, thus, starkly framed simply as a network of water channels, with the aspired 'normal' defined as a seasonally determined 'average volume'. Rivers, as national resources, hence, became facts without stories and quantities without qualities. That is, flows were not understood as organically interconnected and interacting elements of wetland ecologies, aquifers, lakes, marshes and the combined actions of innumerable tributary streams. Rather, as mere volumes contained in channels, rivers could be abstracted, diverted or interfered with to satisfy national priorities.

The belief that rivers are merely moving masses of water crying out to be regulated and dammed has been dramatically challenged since the 1980s by a fresh spirited theoretical turn amongst river ecologists. These ecologists have been convincingly able to demonstrate that fluvial regimes are complex geomorphologic chemical and biological processes in motion.

By recasting, in fundamental ways, the manner in which fluvial processes are understood, river ecologists are now suggesting that a fresh paradigm is required for managing and interacting with such hydraulic endowments. Centrally, what is being argued is that flows are embedded in ecological contexts and, therefore, transferring them through technological fixes can, and often do, have several unintended environmental consequences. Simple steel and concrete approaches, aimed at water abstraction, diversion and interference, in other words, must give way to an entirely new spectrum of knowledge, which will treat flows as being determined by non-linear ecological qualities. Put differently, treating rivers as mere mute volumes is flawed, both as a concept and as a water management practice.

Handling and harnessing variability and stochastic flow regimes, consequently, have become critical to shaping sustainable approaches towards river management. The entire Indus basin, in effect, is a collection of relationships between streams, floodplains, the head reaches, aquifers and, inevitably, the chaotic delta. Small wonder, then, that the so-called 'success' of the IWT has resulted in the relative ecological devastation of the Indus delta.

Historically, for the Indus basin, a rough calculation suggests that before projects for siphoning flows began in the 19th century, up to 150 million acre-feet of fresh water probably fell into the delta, along with the deposition of close to 400 million tons of nutrient rich fertilizing silt. These immense uninterrupted volumes nourished and sustained a sprawling collection of mangroves, inlets, creeks, estuaries and other wetland ecologies.

By suggesting that flow variability is central to fluvial health, river ecologists have put forward a definitive challenge to the cement-steel based water-control ideologies of the contemporary civil engineer, whose entire conceptual tool kit, as pointed out earlier, was mostly drawn up in the colonial setting of the long 19th century in the subcontinent. In a similar vein, the hitherto untroubled pre-eminence of the expertise generated by giant centralized water bureaucracies such as the Central Water Commission (India) and the Indus Waters Commission (Ministry of Water and Power, Government of Pakistan) need to, in the light of these new ecological facts, be carefully qualified and reconsidered as well.

These institutions, with their training anchored in quantitative hydraulic data, have thus far been oriented primarily towards strategizing for 'average flows'. In other words, these are technical-bureaucratic institutions that are committed to searching for, and premised entirely upon, harnessing hydraulic predictability. Significantly enough, these centralized water bureaucracies also play a crucial role in shaping national water policies and informing political processes over the building of hydraulic infrastructure in India and Pakistan, respectively. But with variability and stochasticity as the new norm for engaging with river systems, so to speak, what becomes of these legal-technical institutions and their infrastructural technologies? Put differently, if climate change is about the intensification of hydraulic unpredictability in the region, will the IWT, as a legal-technical institution, be able to respond to the new challenges.

Close to 1700 people or more perished and 1.8 million homes were damaged or destroyed in the floods that occurred in 2010 in Pakistan. In its wake, the floods also rummaged through 2.3 million hectares of standing crops and brought about a loss of US$ 5 billion to the agriculture sector and around US$ 2 billion each to the physical and social infrastructure. The flood-devastated realities of Pakistan, as Daanish Mustafa and David Wrathall argue in a recent essay, point to a far more striking conclusion: that the floods were aggravated and its impacts made even more ferocious because of vulnerability.[8]

Beginning with the dramatic hydraulic transformations in the colonial period, an independent Pakistan persevered in creating 'a mismatch between the design assumptions of the infrastructure, such as embankments and barrages, and the dynamic reality of the channels' carrying capacity.' That is, Pakistan's hydraulic and social designs were geared to 'ignore the river system's natural rhythms, in return for agricultural productivity and prosperity.' Overcoming the potential dangers in such a trade-off, for them, therefore, would require a 'better tactic', which, plainly stated, was to 'adapt to the Indus basin's hydro-meteorological regime.'

Climate change and its perceived impacts, in effect, push for an active reconsideration of the IWT framework. Instead of an overt emphases on technical, and technology based, approaches, run with the narrow expertise of engineers and state negotiators, the new compact for river management/sustainability in the region would require different social constituencies and their experiences with the Indus waters. This would involve drawing upon, and fostering cooperative dialogues between, river-front communities on both sides of the border, such as fisherfolk, irrigation dependent farmers, river ecologists, water historians, sociologists and aquatic specialists (to name a few).[10] These plural narratives can imbue the IWT with a much needed ecological sensitivity. The IWT, or another compelling version, has to be crafted to meaningfully grasp the Indus and its temperamental tributaries as qualities of flows rather than as blocs of disconnected volumes. The current reign of cement, steel and quantitative hydrology must, in other words, urgently give way to viable dialogues over fluvial relationships and ecological process.

Footnotes:

1. Ramaswamy Iyer, arguably, is the most sophisticated voice that debates the workings of the Indus Waters Treaty as being principally dogged by problems of 'political misperceptions'. His writings on the subject are too numerous to cite here. In all, however, Iyer provides some of the most valuable and informed insights on contemporary water challenges in South Asia.
2. Rohan D'Souza, 'Water in British India: The Making of a "Colonial Hydrology"', *History Compass* 4(4), May 2006, pp. 621-8.
3. Herbert M. Wilson, *Irrigation in India*. Daya Publishing House, Delhi, (first published 1903), 1989, pp. 78-81; D.G. Harris, *Irrigation in India*, H. Milford, Oxford University Press, London, 1923, pp. 5-7. For an introduction to the modern hydraulic moment in British India, see Elizabeth Whitcombe, *Agrarian Conditions in Northern India: The United Provinces Under British Rule, 1860-1900*, vol. 1. California University Press, Berkeley, 1972; *Canal Irrigation in British India: Perspectives on Technological Change in a Peasant Economy*. Cambridge University Press, Cambridge, 1985; Imran Ali, *The Punjab Under Imperialism, 1885-1947*. Oxford University Press, New Delhi, 1987; Rohan D'Souza, *Drowned and Dammed: Colonial Capitalism and Flood Control in Eastern India*. Oxford University Press, New Delhi, 2006; and David Hardiman, 'Well Irrigation in Gujarat: Systems of Use, Hierarchies of Control', *Economic and Political Weekly* 33(25), 1998, pp. 1533-44.
4. David Gilmartin, 'Scientific Empire and Imperial Science: Colonialism and Irrigation Technology in the Indus Basin', *The Journal of Asian Studies* 53(4), 1994, p. 1132. Also see David Gilmartin, 'Water and Waste: Nature, Productivity and Colonialism in the Indus Basin', *Economic and Political Weekly* 38(48), 2003, pp. 5057-65.
5. Indu Agnihotri, 'Ecology, Land Use and Colonization: The Canal Colonies of Punjab' in Mahesh Rangarajan and K. Sivaramakrishnan (eds.), *India's Environmental History: Colonialism, Modernity and the Nation*. Permanent Black, Ranikhet, 2012, pp. 37-63.
6. Benjamin Weil, 'The Rivers Comes: Colonial Flood Control and Knowledge Systems in the Indus Basin, 1840-1930s,' *Environment and History* 12(1), 2006, pp. 3-29.
7. For an excellent discussion on the politics over the Indus rivers between India and Pakistan, see Daanish Mustafa, 'Critical Hydropolitics in the Indus basin' in Terje Tvedt, Graham Chapman and Roar Hagen, *Water, Geopolitics and the New World Order*. A History of Water, Series II, Volume 3. I.B. Taurus, London, New York, 2011, pp. 374-94.
8. Daanish Mustafa, and David Wrathall, 'Indus Basin Floods of 2010: Souring of a Faustian Bargain?' *Water Alternatives* 4(1), 2011, 72-85.
9. Ibid., p. 7.
10. I draw upon this useful notion of a riverfront community from Sarandha Jain's wonderfully compelling book on the Yamuna river titled *In Search of Yamuna: Reflections on a River Lost*, New Delhi, Vitasta Publishing, 2011. The riverfront community, she suggests, refers not only to people who live by and off the river but become a 'bridge' between land and water, river and society and as 'mediators between nature and culture.'

CHAPTER - 50

Indus Water Treaty: Need For Review

By Rizwan Ullah Kokab and Adnan Nawaz, 2 May 2013
(Asia Journal of Social Sciences & Humanities)

ABSTRACT

This paper examines the history and provisions of Indus Waters Treaty (IWT) that was signed by India and Pakistan in 1960. The significance and drawbacks of the Treaty for both signatories have been highlighted and the shortcomings which were inherent in the Treaty as well as those which commenced and developed with the passage of time have been underlined. In this respect the complications arose with the planned Indian projects on the Indus Basin rivers have also been outlined. In the context of the necessities of suggested changes in the IWT such major aspects have been proposed which need to be looked out during the review of the IWT.

Introduction

Disputes between India and Pakistan over the Indus River basin began with partition in 1947. Between 1947 and 1960 the two sides addressed their differences through a number of short term agreements (Miner, 2009) but the dispute could not be settled through bilateral negotiations, and international mediation had to be sought (Sharif, 196). In 1960, after nine years of negotiations, the two sides signed the Indus Waters Treaty (IWT) (Ali, 2008, 169).

Under the Treaty, all the waters of the Eastern Rivers - Sutlej, Beas, and Ravi - were allocated to India for unrestricted use, except during the transition period of 1 April 1960 to 31 March 1970, during which water had to be supplied to Pakistan so that Pakistan might construct replacement works (two storage dams, eight inter-river link canals and six barrages) for water that was being received earlier from the Eastern Rivers. (Biswas, 1992, 208-09) (Sharif, 6) India agreed to make a fixed contribution of 62 million towards the cost of the replacement works. Pakistan received unrestricted use of the Western Rivers — Indus, Jhelum, and Chenab - which India is "under obligation to let flow" and "shall not permit any interference with these waters," except for irrigating existing areas and to develop a further 701,000 acres of irrigation from these rivers subject to certain specific conditions. Specific provisions were made for regular exchange of river and canal data between the two countries (Biswas, 1992, 208).

Needs for Modifications

Despite being a long lasting successful treaty there are some limitations within the IWT that require a review. Michel T Klare opines that it does not allow for the joint development of the Indus basin; nor does it eliminate the grounds for conflict over water distribution between India and Pakistan since it is a plan for the separate development of the basin (Feyyaz). It is also unusual among international water-sharing agreements because allocation is based on tributary locations; water is neither allocated on a quantitative basis between the parties nor managed by an operating rule. It is specific about which nation uses which tributary, but it does not create mechanisms to address issues specified in the treaty per se, such as groundwater use, changes in flow due to climate change, changing domestic demand due to population increases or rainfall variability (Miner, 2009, 211). Daanish Mustafa (2010) observes that it, by performing an amputation surgery on the basin that was much the same as the political bifurcation of the subcontinent, made matters simple and allowed the two countries to pursue their nationalist agendas without much need for more sophisticated and involved cooperation in the water field. This lack of cooperative sharing of water has considerable negative consequences for the ecology and societies of the Indus basin.

Moreover, environmental and ecological changes call for a re-consideration of the IWT. Projections of climate change on water resources have important implications for both water scarce and flood prone regions, as many indicate dry regions becoming drier and wet regions becoming wetter. (Sivakumar 2011, 545). Because of climate change, the Himalayan glaciers are melting at an alarming rate. For water resources, this means an increase in water initially due to flooding. Within the next 50 years, however, experts believe there will be a 30 to 40 percent drop in glacial melt because the glaciers will have receded. A strategy to create more storage capacity for water is the only option available. (Wasi, 2009).

In this regard, the canal withdrawals in Indus Irrigation System, which more or less, stagnated in 1979 after the construction of Tarbela Dam, have now declined to around 103 MAF, partly due to silting of the reservoirs. (Humaira, 6). This aspect has not been considered at the political level, or, at least has not gained prominence while it demands a common water vision by India and Pakistan that will be based on the realization of the importance of the shared rivers as being a natural resource that is integral to their survival. (Akhtar, 2010, 56).

Pollution control is another issue that needs consideration in the review of the IWT. Given the lack of pollution controls on industry and recent reports of hazardous industrial and chemical-rich water crossing the border into Pakistan, it could be inferred that water quality is deteriorating in the Indus. (Miner, 2009, 209). There are no provisions in any treaty on water between Pakistan and India for the control of pollution. Through the review of IWT, the issue of the pollution can also be addressed properly.

Pakistan's Federal Minister for Kashmir Affairs and Gilgit-Baltistan, Mian Manzoor Ahmad Wattoo, pointing towards another drawback of IWT, contended that the IWT was signed by a military dictator, General Ayub Khan. He observed, "Since no consultations were held or a consensus evolved, the treaty has some inherent flaws and India has been misusing it at the cost of Pakistan's interests." (The News, 2012). fresh review of the Treaty may be helpful in dissolving more differences and is, if it ever happens, likely to produce a consensus in modern times when democratic institutions are getting progress in both the states of India and Pakistan.

Thus, the IWT is a product of its time and could be fruitfully modified and renegotiated to bring it more in line with the contemporary international watercourse laws, the Helsinki rules, and emerging concerns with water quality, environmental sustainability, climate change, and principles of equitable sharing. (Mustafa, 2010).

Indian Projects

More problematic is the provision in IWT relating the use of the western rivers by India. The crux of IWT is that India was given full control of Eastern rivers and Pakistan was given full control of Western rivers. But the provision of usage of western rivers to India for non-irrigative use of western rivers has created problems afterwards. India, by virtue of the upper riparian, could always use and obstruct the waters of the Indus Basin. IWT was signed to protect the interests of Pakistan and not of India. Pakistan gave off the right of 3 eastern rivers for the sake of complete and unhindered use of western rivers. India got the benefit of the three eastern rivers in full but Pakistan's usage of the waters of three western rivers is yet on stake because India has started work on many projects at the cost of Pakistani concerns.

The challenge to the treaty came regarding the construction of the Wullar Barrage, as it is called by Pakistan, or Tulbul Navigation Project, as termed by India. There is controversy on the explanations of the specific provisions of the IWT. The 330 MW hydroelectric Kishanganaga project, that is located about 160 kilometers upstream of Muzaffarabad and involves diversion of Kishanganga or Neelum River to a tributary, Bunar Madumati Nullah of the River Jhelum through a 22-kilomtre tunnel, is another controversial water issue between the two countries which could not have been resolved under the IWT.

Located on the River Chenab in Doda district, the Baglihar hydropower project is one of the nine major hydroelectric projects identified by India on the Chenab. Pakistan protested over the design of the dam in 1992 and demanded a halt to its construction. (Wasi, 2009). Taking cue from the Bagliahr verdict of the Neutral Expert that reinterpreted the Treaty in the light of "new technical norms and new standards," "state of the art" and "best and latest practices in the field of construction and operation," the risks of increased floods associated with "climate change," it appears that the Treaty has to accommodate the new realities in the Indus basin, not only in terms of technical norms but also growing pressures on the health and viability of the Indus basin rivers. (Akhtar, 2010, 56).

The invocation of neutral expert clause has revealed another drawback in the IWT and has damaged an impression that satisfied the doubts of many Pakistanis that the World Bank was the guarantor of the IWT. It so happened that when Pakistan approached the World Bank for mediation, it clearly noted that it was "not a guarantor of the treaty," (Haq, 4). The note of World Bank, though correct legally, has raised dissatisfaction in some circles of Pakistan who always remain suspicious of Indian deception and trust only a third party that may be a guarantor in the compromises of both countries.

During 2006 to 2011, Pakistan's concerns over another controversial project, Nimoo Bazgo, near village Alchi in the district Leh in Indian held Kashmir, could not be highlighted due to the alleged negligence of its Indus Water Commissioner, Jamaat Ali Shah, against whom a probe on his alleged secret compliance with India has started in Pakistan. However, during a recent inspection, the Pakistani team learnt that more than 80 per cent of the work on the dam had been completed and the expected date of its inauguration is July 2012. (The Nation, 2012).

Notwithstanding Indian concerns over delays in the execution of projects, Pakistan's concerns for the projects are much too serious. Though India, as per the IWT, is allowed to generate power from the waters of these rivers, yet it did stop Chenab river flow on various occasions, notable being from August 19 to September 5, wherein Pakistan was deprived of 1.2 million cusecs of water at one time alone. Moreover, through IWT, Pakistan does not find immediate relief. She, through a lengthy process defined in IWT, has only the option to deliver complain to India or put the case in international tribunals that definitely require a huge amount of time and money. During the whole process, India loses nothing and Pakistan gradually loses. India often continues to start new projects day by day and Pakistan continues to complain over them. India has planned to make 62 more dams. Therefore, there is a dire need to alter the clause that allows India to use the waters of the western rivers.

Whenever India takes a decision to construct a dam, or reservoir, and the matter enters the framework of the treaty, which only provides technical specifications for building such a dam or reservoir, Islamabad invokes the jurisdiction of a neutral expert or arbitration court. During the time the case takes, the construction is completed and Pakistan, in that sense, 'loses' the case. Some observers point out that Pakistan is feeling alienated from the IWT after repeated failures to get a redress of its grievances and, hence, would like to replace it with a new treaty. But it is not easy to agree on a new pact. A pragmatic approach is required to amend and update the treaty to remove the lacuna it suffers from. (Bokhari, 2011).

It looks altogether unjust that India can use all of the rivers without restrictions but Pakistan is bound to use only western rivers even with the apprehension of Indian obstruction. The question remains unsolved what to do of the projects which India has already installed. The second issue may be this why the waters of western rivers should not be used before entering into Pakistan? For the sake of prosperity to both nations, joint projects can be initiated on the western rivers and benefits may be shared by both nations. Already initiated projects can also be shared on these grounds. But it is necessary that the clauses of the IWT must be altered in order to give Pakistan unrestricted control of the western rivers and it will be a great benefit to the energy starved nation of Pakistan.

An array of upcoming Indian projects has unfolded many challenges to the functioning of the Permanent Indus Water Commission. The institution is unable to cope with the issues which were originally not within its purview as they did not exist at that time. All above mentioned controversial projects highlight the need of mediation as well as such a new mechanism and consensus under which the issues which have risen during the implementation of IWT can be resolved. For this, an overall review and new negotiations on the water issue are the call of the hour.

There is no provision in IWT which allows India to construct a certain number of dams. Nor is there one that prohibits India from making dams beyond a certain number. Notwithstanding prescribing restrictions on the features and operations of Indian projects on the western rivers, the Treaty does not lay down any limits on the total number of projects that can be built, the height of the dams, the total power-generation capacity, etc. Ramaswamy R. Iyer (2012) thinks that the point about 'cumulative impact' needs to be considered. He, however, proposes a joint study by experts of both countries for this purpose.

Modifications' Potential Benefits to India –

India has developed disputes with three of its neighbours i.e. Pakistan, Bangladesh and Nepal. She is accused of infringing on their water rights by usurping their resources with the potential to ultimately drain their respective resources during hostilities through construction of various projects on rivers whose water is flowing downstream. (Ahmad). Siddharth Varadarajan of The Hindu says: "New Delhi needs to factor in a new reality: More than Kashmir, it is the accusation that India is stealing water that is rapidly becoming the 'core issue' in the Pakistani establishment's narrative about bilateral problems." (Bokhari, 2011).

India in pursuit of the position of regional power and on that ground desires to get the status of permanent member in the UN Security Council. In order to get international support for her case India needs an image of a cooperative country in the region. The resolution of water issues with the neighbouring states will go a long way in this regard. In the past, IWT has won a good repute for her and for Pakistan as issue resolving countries. The review of IWT will lessen the degree of conflict in South Asia, remove the doubts of South Asian countries against India and also enhance the Indian image all over the world.

India is also not satisfied with the present state of affairs and it has to bear serious economic losses because of the delays in the mechanism of IWT which have arisen due to disputes which started to arise during the last decade. Indian professionals have expressed frustrations over long delays in the approval of projects due to Pakistani objections. India argues that the IWT limits its ability to exploit the Indus's hydroelectric potential, representing an opportunity cost. (Miner, 2009, 207).

The waters of the Indus river system have a direct impact on the state of Jammu and Kashmir and are, therefore, crucial to its economic prospects. The Kashmir Valley, which is the main source of dispute between India and Pakistan, has been affected by the IWT. (Shani, 2006, 162-63). In February 1951, Prime Minister Nehru invited David E. Lilienthal, virtual founder of IWT, in order to resolve the water issue, since the core of the Kashmir problem stemmed from a "struggle over rivers, rivers with their headwaters in Kashmir, flowing through Pakistan." (Biswas, 1992, 205).

That is why, even today, the most important internal issue that strains the IWT is the view of the people in Jammu and Kashmir, who see the Treaty as exploiting their rights by both India and Pakistan and they call for its annulment as an economic liability. People of the northern areas in Pakistan are also opposed to dam projects in Pakistan like the Mangla dam. (Wasi, 2009). Likewise, the Indian government is faced with the criticism over the IWT from the Kashmiris in the Indian held Kashmir, who show concern over the division of waters. Motions were moved in the state assembly on three different occasions by the legislators asking the Indian government to review the IWT and pay compensation to the state. (Feyyaz). According to Kashmiri Separatists, IWT has deprived the state of Jammu and Kashmir to use its own water resources and became one of the reasons for the alienation of people and has severely affected the economic development in the state. (http://www.absoluteastronomy.com/topics/Indus_Waters_Treaty).

The revision of IWT and solution of water disputes can lead to the dissolution of the most important of the conflicts in the region. New ponderings on the water issue may include the concerns of the Kashmiri people and all dimensions of the water issue may be taken into consideration. This can provide India, as well as Pakistan, a fair chance towards a longstanding solution of the Kashmir issue.

The Indian government is not altogether opposed to negotiations over the IWT. It is ready to change the IWT, though under the mechanisms of the Treaty. The Indian External Affairs Minister, S. M. Krishna, told the Indian Parliament, that the Indian government "is in full compliance with the Treaty. All issues regarding implementation of the Treaty should be resolved through existing mechanisms under the IWT" (Akhtar, 2010, 13). It means that India feels the need of some progress in the IWT in the wake of new realities which have appeared during last decades.

Pakitan's Interests for Modifications in the IWT

Pakistan's groundwater resources also are being challenged. Today, groundwater contributes a mere 48% of the water available. The construction of private wells for irrigation has also been promoted through a policy of high subsidy on electricity cost. The hike in the cost of electricity in 1990s, and the development of new technologies, have led to a considerable increase in the use of diesel pumps whose numbers have grown 6 times over the last 30 years. (WWF, 3).

IWT authorized India to build hydro-electric projects not only on the eastern rivers allocated to India but also on the western rivers which are allocated to Pakistan contingent upon agreement by Pakistan. (IWT Article III Annex D). Thus India has the right to generate electricity from all six rivers while Pakistan cannot use completely the water of three eastern rivers for power generation purposes. The generation of hydro-electric power is a facility provided to India that is exceptional that is not provided to Pakistan. Pakistan, in the present condition, is power thirsty while IWT does not mention the needs of power generation for Pakistan.

Despite all the praise for IWT, it is a fact that the main emphasis of the Treaty was the balanced distribution of irrigation water. Whether it was the negligence of Pakistani rulers, or the wisdom of the Indian leaders, or the neglect of the arbitrators, Pakistan's energy needs were not at all attended in the IWT. It is a fact that the natural flow of the three eastern rivers was altogether diverted under the IWT and India had the right to change the course of these rivers altogether while India could also use the other three western rivers for its energy generating purposes. Suppose the rivers flew on their natural course; Pakistan would also have the chance and options to create energy from all of the six rivers. Pakistan, today, is confronted with energy crisis and it needs energy as well as water to fulfil its energy needs but it has options only over three rivers of the Indian Basin.

If the waters of all six rivers flew from the plains of Punjab, Pakistan could have stored the water of three rivers anywhere in Pakistan and could create power from those sources. In that case, the probability of dispute rising over power generation among the provinces of Pakistan could also be decreased. Every province would have been easily in a position to produce power in its areas.

Today, a thought in power-thirsty Pakistan can be provoked that an injustice was made to Pakistan through the IWT. For the sake of Pakistan-India relations, the compensation for the shortage of the irrigation water, that could take place in case of restrictions over rivers was provided to Pakistan, but a permanent deprivation of power generation was arranged, too. It is now essential that the IWT may be revised by statesmen; rather, such thoughts may provoke the suspicions of the people of Pakistan from international treaties as well as India.

Three inherent defects of the settlement plan as envisaged in the IWT, create problems for Pakistan. Firstly, the traditional *sailab* (flood) irrigation on the Sutlej, Beas and Ravi disappeared, because when these rivers were fully developed by India, the traditional floods decreased, or disappeared, and the *sailab* areas could not get seasonal water, which permitted cultivation. Secondly, due to the loss of regular flow in the Eastern Rivers, the channels have become silt up and floods in the channels cause great havoc in Pakistan, in addition to other environmental effects. Thirdly, the up-keep of the new link canals and storages means a very heavy additional burden on the cost of maintaining irrigation. Besides, storages are no substitute to the perpetual flow of water as the storages have a limited life.

Pakistan is increasingly confronted by an impending water crisis. As per one of the surveys of 2009, the availability of water has declined from 5000 cubic meters per capita 60 years ago to 1200 cubic meters per capita in 2009. It is also estimated that by 2020, the availability of water is estimated to fall to 800 cubic meters per capita. (Ahmad). Siddharth Varadarajan of The Hindu observes that per capita water availability is expected to fall below 700 cubic metres by 2025 — the international marker for water scarcity. (Bokhari, 2011). The water shortage in the agriculture sector has been estimated at 29% for the year 2010 and 33% for 2025. WWF – Pakistan, Report, Pakistan's Water at Risk, p.3.

A certain reasonable flow in the eastern rivers should be maintained. The eastern rivers are allocated exclusively to India, and IWT, according to Pakistani point of view, does not say anything about flows to Pakistan, but it does not follow that India is at liberty to dry up those rivers altogether and send no flows at all or drastically reduced flows to Pakistan. Pakistan argues that if current thinking can be invoked for the design of spillway gates (as the neutral expert argued in the Baglihar case), then current thinking on 'minimum flows' or 'ecological flows' must also be heeded. To Ramaswamy R. Iyer (2012) it seems a point that needs consideration in next talks on water issue.

Pakistan also has serious problems regarding the sharing of Indus waters among its four provinces. This is evident with an entrenched controversy being present in the country on every planned dam. The shortage of water has deep political, economic and social effects. For example, farmers in Sindh point their fingers at Punjabi landlords, and accuse them of 'stealing their share' of the Indus's water. The water problems within Pakistan are negated as the drawbacks of the IWT and often it is contended that they are the result largely from poor water management, but Daanish Mustafa (2010) has corroborated that the consequences of management failures are accentuated, both materially and politically, by international and sub-national hydro-politics, because a large portion of the sub-national problems in Pakistan are partially a function of the IWT, because the Sindhis perceive that Sindh compensates Punjab for water that Pakistan negotiated away to India. There is enough water in the Indus basin to provide for the livelihoods of its residents for a long time, provided that the water is managed efficiently and equitably and that additional water is made available not just through storage but, more importantly, also through higher efficiency and inter-sectoral transfers made through a review of the IWT. (Mustafa, 2010).

Conclusion ad Recommendations

Keeping in view the different dynamics of the water problem, Nausheen Wasi (2009) proposes that India and Pakistan, in good faith, should seek international support, perhaps, again, with the World Bank taking the lead to negotiate a sound water sharing and usage mechanism through an IWT II. She suggests setting up a joint organization with representatives from both countries, whose functions would entail identifying short term and long term supply capacity of the basin and its integrated development, setting up of infrastructure and coordinating activities of different technical agencies. She proposes a holistic interdisciplinary approach to understand the background and functioning of highly sophisticated irrigation systems. She stresses to harness water resources to change from being a large-scale capital and technology-intensive and environmentally degrading option to management-intensive and ecologically balanced development relying on indigenous technology. Mediation in case of water dispute resolution has worked between India and Pakistan in the past and would solve another great concern – financing the projects if India and Pakistan agree on something. (Wasi, 2009).

To cope with the next challenges, arrangements on the basis of modern techniques and methods can be included in the reviewed IWT. Arshad H Abbasi, for example, has suggested a satellite-based, real-time telemetry system in Indian Kashmir, installed at a minimum of 100 locations, for monitoring water quality and quantity would help remove mistrust on data exchange. (Express Tribune, 2012).

The Indus Waters Treaty would need to be amended to incorporate changes that have taken place since its implementation, and future projections of climate change, complemented by more efficient water use within each country. Increased energy demand by India and water demand by Pakistan amidst receding Himalayan glaciers will test the Treaty and perhaps prompt its revision. (Reddy, 2009).

To Ranjan (2010), Pakistan and India should also include the issue of water in the agenda of bilateral negotiations because it is going to be another future source of tension between these two countries. If needed, a few amendments to the Treaty can be made, but to revise, or scrap, the whole Treaty will be a blunder. As mature nation-states both of them have to understand that the need is to resolve the contending issues and establish peace between them rather than add more problems in the already existing long list of disputes.

The IWT has been a unique compromise on the distribution of river waters in the world. Both Pakistan and India have acquired benefits from the Treaty. India secured more waters from the Eastern Rivers and Pakistan got an uninterrupted supply of waters from the Western rivers. The Treaty, however, bifurcated the Indus river system and ignored some important aspects relating to the water issue. It requires to be updated according to environmental, ecological, climatic changes and requisites of safety from pollution. Controversial Indian projects have also underlined the need of reconsideration of the issues concerned to Indus Basin. While the shadows of a nuclear war are looming over South Asia and the water issue has come up as the most dangerous there is dire need not to insist on the continuation of differences or clinging to outdated solutions. It is also not expedient that all compromises be rolled back but modifications in the existing IWT are indispensable for the betterment of the people of Pakistan as well as of India.

References

Ali, S. H. (2008). Water Politics in South Asia: Technocratic Cooperation and Lasting Security in the Indus Basin and Beyond. Journal of International Affairs.

Biswas, A. (1992). Indus Water Treaty: The Negotiating Process. Water International. (17) 201-209.

Bokhari, A. (2011). Setback in the Water Dispute. Dawn, 19 September 2011.

Feyyaz, Muhammad. P-5 Members and the UN Conflict Resolution Approaches. South Asian Journal.

Haq, N. U. (ed.) (2010). Pakistan's Water Concerns. Islamabad: IPRI Publications.

Iyer, R. R. (2012). Dealing with Pakistan's Fears on Water, The Hindu, January 28.

Miner, Mary. Patankar, Gauri. Gamkhar, Shama and Eaton, David J. (2009) Water sharing between India and Pakistan: A critical evaluation of the Indus Waters Treaty. Water International. Vol: 34, No: 2, Routledge, 204-216.

Mustafa, D. (2010). Hydropolitics in Pakistan's Indus Basin. Special Report. Washington DC: United States Institute of Peace.

Ranjan, A. (2010) Water Conflicts between India and Pakistan. Daily Times.

Reddy, R. (2009). The Indus Waters Treaty: Its Persistence and Prospects. The Northwestern Journal of International Affairs, 10(I).

Shani, H. K. (2006). The Politics of Water in South Asia: The Case of the Indus Waters Treaty. SAIS Review, 16(2), 153-165 Sharif, Humaira. Inter province water distribution conflict in Pakistan. Report produced as part of the Joint Training of Pakistan-Afghanistan journalists on Conflict Reporting.

Sindhu, Abid Latif. The Pakistan-India Water War. Terminal X. [Pakistan Observer].

Verghese, B. G. (2010) Ideology Threatens Indus Waters Treaty. The South Asian Journal, 25 March.

Wasi, (2009) Harnessing the Indus Waters Perspectives from Pakistan, IPCS Issue Brief.

Daily Times (2010). 31 May.

Dawn (2010) 3 March.

Express Tribune, (2012) 12 January.

Jang (2012) 29 March

The Nation (2008) 18 October.

The Nation (2012) 21 January.

The News (2012) 31 January. WWF – Pakistan, Report, Pakistan's Water at Risk,

www.changinguppakistan.wordpress.com/2008/10/22/the-indus-water-dispute-syed-zain-ularifeen-shah

CHAPTER – 51

Reviving The Indus Treaty
The Kishenganga Arbitral Award

By Dr. K. Uprety, July 2014
(New Spot Light News Magazine)

Since the time India stated its intentions to construct the KHEP, Pakistan had been raising objections, emphasizing that the inter-tributary diversions of waters due to the KHEP were barred by the IWT, that existing Pakistani uses needed to be protected, and that the KHEP's draw-down technology to flush sediments should be prohibited.

Background: On December 20, 2013, the Permanent Court of Arbitration (PCA), constituted under the Indo-Pakistan 1960 Indus Waters Treaty (IWT), issued a landmark Award in a proceeding instituted by Pakistan on May 17, 2010 against India in connection with the construction by the latter of the Kishenganga Hydroelectric Project (KHEP).

The KHEP concerns a 330 MW hydroelectric project in India, involving a 100 km diversion of Kishenganga River (called Neelum in Pakistan) to a tributary of Jhelum (the Bunar Madumati Nullah), through a 22 km tunnel, its water to re-join Jhelum later through Wullar Lake near the town of Bandipur in Baramula district. Neelum, an important tributary of Jhelum, flows about 150 km in Pakistan controlled Kashmir before it joins the Jhelum. As a result of this diversion, it will re-join Jhelum in India controlled Kashmir. The diversion will also change the direction of the river before joining the Jhelum near Muzaffarabad, the site of Pakistan's Neelum-Jhelum Hydroelectric Project (NJHEP), which pertains to the construction of a 969 MW hydroelectric project, for which the blueprints and technical stipulations, as per Pakistan, were finalized in 1997.

Since the time India stated its intentions to construct the KHEP, Pakistan had been raising objections, emphasizing that the inter-tributary diversions of waters due to the KHEP were barred by the IWT, that existing Pakistani uses needed to be protected, and that the KHEP's draw-down technology to flush sediments should be prohibited.

The arbitral Award, which was issued in multiple segments after reviewing the details of the points of law, facts, procedures, and questions raised by the parties at different stages of the proceeding, is certain to have a significant impact on the future of water relations between not only India and Pakistan, but also amongst other countries in South Asia and beyond. In view of its significance, as well as the unusual evidentiary and treaty interpretation challenges it had posed, this article attempts to briefly introduce the dispute and the Award.

Main Questions: Pakistan had identified two questions to be central to the dispute. The first related to whether India's proposed diversion of the river Kishenganga (Neelum) into another tributary, being one central element of the KHEP, breached India's legal obligations owed to Pakistan under the IWT, as interpreted and applied in accordance with international law, including the obligations to let flow all the waters of the Western rivers, not permit any interference with those waters, and to maintain the natural channels (the First Dispute). The second related to whether India, under the IWT, could deplete or bring the reservoir level of a run-of-the-river plant below the Dead Storage Level (DSL) in any circumstance, except for an unforeseen emergency (the Second Dispute).

These Pakistani objections were based on the argument that the KHEP will significantly reduce the power generation capacity of the NJHEP, the draw-down flushing to tackle sedimentation would allow India to reduce the reservoir level of the dam below DSL, and the dam with this design would allow India to control the volume and timing of the water flow downstream.

Proceedings: Between May 2011 and May 2012, India and Pakistan made written submissions to the PCA. From 20 to 31 August 2012, a two-week hearing in The Hague was held. On 18 February 2013, the PCA issued a Partial Award and on December 20, 2013, a Final Award. Interestingly, the proceedings took less than three years after the tribunal was formed. While this timing might not mean much in normal settings, the successful resolution of a politically charged and vigorously contested interstate case of such technical complexity in three years is, as noted by scholars, a notable accomplishment.

During the very first meeting held on January 14, 2011, Pakistan informed the PCA that it had chosen to forego the immediate pursuit of an order for interim measures. However, on June 6, 2011, it applied for interim measures in the following terms: (i) India shall cease work on the KHEP until such time as the PCA renders its Award on the merits in the proceedings; (ii) India shall inform the PCA and Pakistan of any actual or imminent developments or steps in relation to the KHEP that may have a significant adverse effect upon restoring the status quo ante or that may in any other way seriously jeopardize Pakistan's rights and interests under the IWT; (iii) Any steps that India has taken or may take in respect of the KHEP are taken at its own risk and without prejudice to the possibility that the PCA may in its decision on the merits order that the works must not be continued or must be modified or dismantled; and (iv) Such further relief as the PCA considers to be necessary. In response, India requested the PCA to reject Pakistan's application entirely and to rule that the circumstances of the case did not justify interim measures.

The arguments and counter-arguments made by the Parties on the issue of interim measures revolved mainly around six themes and sub-themes, including inter alia: (i) Pakistan's original decision not to seek interim measures; (ii) the Proceed At Own Risk principle; (iii) the applicable legal standards; (iv) the urgency and irreversibility of interim measures; (v) the grounds for interim measures (for safeguarding the applicant's interests, avoiding prejudice to the final solution, and avoiding aggravation or extension of the dispute); and (vi) the different characterization of the historical records by Parties.

After analysing the numerous above points as well as India's assurances and representations, its own power to specify interim measures, and the need to avoid prejudice to the final solution, the PCA issued an Order for interim measures. It instructed that while the arbitration was pending, India could: (i) erect temporary coffer-dams and operate the by-pass tunnel it had mentioned to have completed; (ii) temporarily dry out the riverbed of the Kishenganga/Neelum at the Gurez valley; (iii) excavate the riverbed; and (iv) construct the sub-surface foundations of the dam. On the other hand, until the PCA rendered its Award, India could not construct any other permanent works on, or above, the riverbed that might inhibit the restoration of the full flow of that river to its natural channel. Furthermore, in the Order, the PCA asked the Parties to submit, by December 19, 2011, a joint report setting forth the areas of agreement and points of disagreement between them concerning the implementation of the Order.

Merits Hearing: The hearing on the merits commenced on August 20, 2012, and concluded on August 31, 2012. Upon its completion, the PCA, on February 18, 2013, was able to render a Partial Award. In relation to the First Dispute, it ruled that: (1) The KHEP constituted a Run-of-the-River Plant for the purpose of the IWT; and (2) India could divert water from the Kishenganga/Neelum for power generation by the KHEP and deliver the water released below the power station into the Bonar Nullah, contingent on constructing and operating it in such a way as to maintain a minimum flow of water in the Kishenganga/Neelum, at a rate to be determined later.

In relation to the Second Dispute, it ruled that except in the case of an unforeseen emergency, the IWT did not permit reduction of the water level in the reservoirs of the Run-of-the-River Plants on the Western Rivers below DSL. Also, the accumulation of sediment in such reservoirs did not constitute an unforeseen emergency that would permit the depletion of the reservoir below DSL for drawdown flushing purposes. Accordingly, India was not to employ drawdown flushing at the KHEP reservoir to an extent that would entail depletion of the reservoir below DSL. This prohibition, however, did not apply to the Run-of-the-River Plants that were in operation or already under construction on the date of the Partial Award, the design of which, having been duly communicated by India, had not been objected to by Pakistan.

The Partial Award, which also lifted the measures imposed by the PCA in its Order of 23 September 2011, attached no further restrictions on the construction and operation of the KHEP. However, to assist the PCA to determine the minimum flow, it asked the Parties to submit all necessary information within four months.

Search For Clarifications: Soon after the issuance of the Partial Award, India, on 20 May 2013, submitted to the PCA a Request for Clarification or Interpretation (the Indian Request) in which it took issue with the PCA's conclusion that except in the case of an unforeseen emergency, the IWT did not permit reduction (or depletion) of the water below DSL in the Run-of-the-River Plants' reservoirs on the Western Rivers. It asked the PCA to specify that such reduction or depletion depended on site-specific analyses of the feasibility of methods of sediment control other than drawdown flushing.

Upon invitation of the PCA, Pakistan submitted a Response to the Indian Request on 19 July 2013. India submitted a Reply on 2 September 2013. Pakistan presented its Rejoinder to India's Reply on 30 September 2013. The PCA considered all the submissions and issued a unanimous decision, on 20 December 2013, stating clearly that the prohibition on the reduction below DSL of the water in the reservoirs of the Run-of-the-River Plants on the Western Rivers, except in the case of an unforeseen emergency, was for general application, and not specific to KHEP only.

Fixing The Minimum Flow: In the Partial Award, the PCA had asked India and Pakistan to provide detailed information on the historical flows at the Line of Control (Loc), and at the KHEP and NJHEP dam sites. These were provided by both countries. Contrasting arguments and rebuttals occurred on the issues of hydrological data, including their reliability and integrity, methodology and analysis, flow at the different stations, effects on flow on power generation, agricultural uses and environmental impact, as well as monitoring of the minimum flow. The PCA addressed the Parties' differences, particularly regarding the hydrological data records, and the effects the KHEP was likely to have on agricultural and hydro-electric uses by Pakistan and on the downstream environment, and taking into account these effects, determined the minimum flow.

The Final Award, issued on December 20, 2013, was unanimous. It specified that, in the operation of the KHEP, India had to release a minimum flow of 9 cumec into the Kishenganga/Neelum below the KHEP at all times when the daily average flow in the Kishenganga/Neelum immediately upstream of the KHEP meets or exceeds 9 cumec. But at any time when the daily average flow in the KN River immediately upstream of the KHEP is less than 9 cumec, India had to release 100% of the daily average flow immediately upstream of the KHEP into the Kishenganga/Neelum below the KHEP. The PCA further specified that seven years after the diversion of water by the KHEP, either Party was allowed to seek reconsideration of the above specified minimum flow through the Permanent Indus Commission and the mechanisms of the IWT.

Significance: Not surprisingly, for an issue so deeplytied with geo-hydropolitics coupled with historical acrimony, the reactions about the Award had to be mixed. Indeed, there was ample joy for victory and enough sadness for defeat in both countries. In each country, there was one side which referred to the verdict as a victory, and another side, as compromising vital national interests.

The mixed reactions also indicate the Panel's efforts to take a middle path, attempting to strike a balance, on one hand, between the environmental concerns and the energy requirements of the two countries, and on the other, between the rights and duties of the parties spelled out in the IWT. Nonetheless, the Award can be considered a win-win for both: enabling India (with some significant new challenges) to proceed with developing hydropower projects on the Jhelum and Chenab, and Pakistan having its water security on the Indus, Jhelum and Chenab restored, if not redefined.

From a techno-legal perspective, for India, the Award means that it can continue to develop its hydropower projects on the Chenab and the Jhelum, but it must strictly respect the IWT-defined limits on storage, and use methods other than the construction of low gates to flush silt. The Award, having banned the use of drawdown flushing in all future projects, essentially means that all the new projects will either have to survive with shorter life or will have to use a new technology to manage the massive sedimentation load that often kills dams and reservoirs. It may be useful to recall that all the major rivers in Jammu and Kashmir and their tributaries have massively silted flows, and Chenab, the major power house of the state, has sediment load as a major crisis. Therefore, the challenge is clear and substantial for India. It will have to be more imaginative in the way in which it deals with silt management, and environmental flows. For Pakistan, the Award means that due to the construction of the KHEP, the flow of water for the NJHEP will decrease, which would reduce annual energy generation, but it will now reasonably be able to claim basic environmental flows to be restored on the Ravi and Sutlej and will not be threatened by the development of a large amount of easy-to-manipulate storage by India on the Jhelum and Chenab.

From an international legal perspective, the final Award is a landmark for the governance of shared trans-boundary water resources as the dispute had raised a multitude of important questions on the relevance of the IWT, model of development adopted by building large dams and reservoirs for hydroelectric power with environmental consequences, application of international environmental obligations, and adequacy of existing international courts and tribunals to settle complex water disputes. From an internationalist's angle, the decision is historic because it revives the Indus Waters Treaty as a central and viable instrument for cooperation on the use of the waters of the Indus Basin. Another notable point in the proceeding is the emergence of the claim to the customary status of the precautionary principle and the question of its status in international law, in connection with which the PCA emphasized that it did not consider it appropriate, and certainly not necessary, for it to adopt a precautionary approach and assume the role of a policymaker in determining the balance between acceptable environmental change and other priorities, or to permit environmental considerations to override the balance of other rights and obligations, and alluded to the contentious nature of the principle by indicating that it belongs in the realm of policy.

In the midst of the prevailing confusions, satisfactions, dissatisfactions, or interesting legal enunciations, there are some scholars who, convinced by practicality and realism, stress that to better harness the hydro-potential of the shared watercourses in the Indus basin, both countries will have to learn from world history and consider joint design and implementation of hydro- power projects that take a holistic hydrological view and maintain the environmental integrity of the entire Indus basin without compromising the developmental needs of both the riparians. Only political sagacity and sensitivity towards the legacy of common heritage, according to such scholars, can help them overcome their animosity and take an open view on shared trans-boundary Indus waters!

The Author can be reached at Kshitiz@juno.com

CHAPTER - 52

Indus Waters Treaty and Resolution of Water Conflicts between Two Nuclear Nations

ABSTRACT

This paper attempts to explore the correlation between identity and power as processes through the case study of Indus Waters Treaty (IWT) as it has played a vital role in conflict resolution on water issues between the two historical rivals, Pakistan and India and provides an insight into the evolution in the relationship between the two countries. The paper also explores the Indian hegemony and power asymmetry between the two countries in an historical context, as well as how the relationship between the two nations shaped and affected the water agreements between the two countries. The analysis focuses on discourses on both sides of the border, highlighting the issue in the post IWT. The case study of IWT will be used as an evidence to support the above assertions, and a good example of cooperation between the two nuclear neighbours, as against all odds, both countries honestly maintained this treaty in letter and spirit over the period of three full wars (in 1947, 1965 and 1971 and one limited war in 1999), but now the future and stability of this treaty is questionable due to a lack of cooperation. The new water dispute is more serious and war-threatening because of the global climate, politics and economic changes.

Introduction

"Fierce national competition over water resources has prompted fears that water issues contain the seeds of violent conflict. ...If all the world's peoples work together, a secure and sustainable water future can be ours." (Kofi Annan, World Water Day 2002)

1. Transboundary Water Conflicts:

Transboundary water resources are of two types: ground water resources and surface (rivers, lakes) water resources. It is comparatively harder to deal with water resources because water is continuously in motion; issues of control, jurisdiction and sovereignty are much more complicated as compared to static land resources and this task is even more difficult when water resources are shared by a number of political entities (Shamir and Kliot, 2001). The United National Register of International River Basins, in 1987, listed 214 international transboundary river basins in the world (UN Registry of International River Basins, 1978). In a recent inventory of transboundary river basins, 261 international rivers, covering 45.3% of the land surface of the Earth, were identified and listed (Wolf et al., 1999) while others extended the number of transboundary river basins to 280 (Green Cross, 2000 and Shamir and Kliot, 2001).

Fresh water is an integral and fundamental component of food chain, source for energy production, economic and industrial development, agricultural growth, waste disposal and human health. However, distribution of this resource is disproportionate and erratic resulting in exploitation, which has escalated the scarcity of water and conflicts in many regions of the world (Gleick, 1993). Shared water resources are geographical facts. If such resources were managed equitably and negotiated sincerely between the nations, it could lead to peacefully organised national and international treaties. Otherwise, struggle to get hold of the resource could lead to severely violent unpredictable conflicts (Ibid). Different nations have different uncertainties over shared water resources, which have increased their vulnerability to conflicts over water.

Most of the tensions appear especially in parts of southern and central Asia, central Europe and the Middle East, where the evidence of water-related conflicts extends back to 5000 years. The probability of increased water related conflicts evolving into an issue of "high politics"in these areas is soaring, because water is a scarce resource that has become increasingly important for economic and agricultural development (Gleick, 1993).

2. Water Conflicts between India and Pakistan:

Water conflicts over the distribution of Indus basin date back to the 19th century but at that time, these were intranational conflicts between the provinces of the Indian sub-continent, which were supposed to be resolved by the British India. The British India was able to resolve the first major dispute in 1935 through arbitration by the Anderson Commission. When the demand for irrigation water increased over the next few years, a new water related dispute emerged which was resolved again in 1942 by the Rao Commission. With the partition of united India, the Indus basin was also divided between India and Pakistan in 1947 (Barrett, 1994; Rehman and Kamal, 2005), which left the control of Pakistan's irrigation water in the hands of India, geographically. Therefore, water conflicts between the two nations started soon after independence in 1948, when India claimed sovereign rights over the waters passing through its territory and diverted these waters away from Pakistan. This illegitimate control of rivers threatened war when India refused Pakistan's proposal of neutral arbitration to settle down the conflict. Later on, the World Bank offered its neutral services to resolve the conflict and both India and Pakistan agreed.

The proposal of joint use and development of the Indus basin as a single water resource was refused in 1952 over the concern of national sovereignty by both, which lead to the division of the Indus and its tributaries. According to this proposal, India was offered three eastern rivers (Ravi, Beas and Sutlej), while Pakistan was offered three western rivers (Indus, Jhelum and Chenab). India was also supposed to provide monetary funds to construct canals and storage dams to replace Pakistan's irrigation supplies from the eastern rivers to the western rivers. However, India refused to pay for the construction of storage dams, which was then settled through external finance with the help of the World Bank. Since the Indus Waters Treaty (IWT) was signed In Sep 1960, many controversies have arisen over the design and construction of different projects on both sides of the basin, some of which have been resolved and others are yet to be resolved (Barrett, 1994).

From December 2001 to June 2002, India was vocally considering pulling out of the treaty as one of the steps of hitting back at Pakistan for its alleged support of terrorist outfits targeting India (Pearce, 2002), and in turn Pakistan has stated that it would be prepared to use nuclear weapons over a water crisis (Wirsing and Jasparro, 2006). A senior Pakistani diplomat, among other regional experts, confirms, "Water has become the core issue between India and Pakistan." (Wirsing and Jasparro, 2006 and Sridhar, 2005).

3. Research Aims:

The proposed research attempts to apply the Hydro-Hegemony Framework (HHF) to analyse the transboundary water conflicts between India and Pakistan since the Indus Waters Treaty. The analysis will also focus on how discourses on both sides of the border highlight the issue. This research is thus structured around two main aims:

I. To investigate the intensity of conflicts, through the hydro-hegemony framework, between the two nuclear powers.

II. To examine how India is practicing water hegemony in the region.

The findings of this research will inform the national and international policy-makers, foreign/environmental ministries and especially the Indus Waters Commission, on both sides of the border, about the importance of cooperation and the establishment of an international water law/treaty.

4. Research Questions:

This study is framed upon the following two questions:

I. How the nature and intensity of water conflicts between India and Pakistan have evolved since the Indus Waters Treaty was signed, especially after becoming nuclear powers?

II. What form of hegemony is exercised by India? How India has been able to maintain its water hegemony?

5. Methodology:

Case-study methodology is employed for the purpose of this research. By using a case-study, this research attempts to answer the original hypothesis, predicting whether the nature and intensity of water conflicts between India and Pakistan have evolved since the Indus Waters Treaty was signed especially after becoming nuclear powers. As a consequence, this paper is to evaluate the cogency of hydro-hegemony framework and the research question against the observed case-study. The proposed research will conduct the literature review on transboundary water conflicts in general and specifically water issues between the historical rivals, Pakistan and India, in the post IWT. The research itself will be an attempt to introduce the specific elements of water hegemony and power imbalances. The proposed research emphasizes the attention to the historical conflicts and rivalry between the two nations over the dispute of Kashmir and the Indus Basin.

Literature Review

1. Water Issue in General Context:s

Conflict over water has been a tendency of human behaviour throughout history though it does not tend to fit the traditional mould of full-scale wars fought purely over water. Particularly since the 20th century, water has been a significant feature of the various conflicts rather than their sole purpose (Gleick, 2006). However, now in the first decade of the 21st century, with the increasing pressures, especially from rapid population growth, urbanization and climate change, this century may, in fact, witness a birth of full-scale wars for fresh water (Gleick, 1993). Water conflicts extend back to thousands of years but this issue has been given more importance in recent years because of two major factors. Firstly, it is often mentioned in the media that the war of the next century will be fought over water for national sovereignty and security. Secondly the current water scarcity, especially in the arid and semi-arid regions, due to the global climate change and fast growing population. Much of the attention and discussions are based on war threats over transboundary water conflicts while there is little debate about cooperation over international river basins. The reason these conflicts fall short of war may have much more to do with the imbalance of power between the riparians than with a perceived cooperation between them". To take these discussions further, Zeitoun and Warner (2008, p.3) clearly argue that if there is no war over shared waters, it does not mean there would be no conflict.

2. Water as a Political Entity:

Stegner and Gleick (1993, p.9) quote, "if you get control over water, you can easily get hold of that land which depends upon it. Zeitoun and Warner (2008, p.1) state that control over shared water has taken the shape of politics because fresh water is vital for a healthy economic growth and it's not a new or much popular term among the water practitioners. Wolf and Dinar (1994, p.350) make a comparison of economics and politics in the long-term evolution of water basin development and recognise that both economics and politics play parallel roles, sometimes complementary, sometimes contradictory, but neither paradigm is autonomous.

Elhance (1999, p.10) discusses the roles of upstream and downstream riparians in the shared water resources in Asia, Africa and South America, that hydropolitics in these areas started from the concern of the downstream riparian about the actions of the upstream riparian that may reduce the quantity or quality of the water in the shared water resource. Allan (2001, p.13) and Wolf (19958, p.147) discuss the two main factors, fast growing population and economic development, which would make the water issue more political and controversial. Elhance (1999, p.9), highlighting the differences of water issue and water politics in developing and developed world, argues that, although water sometimes figures as an important issue in local or regional politics in the developing world, in the developed world it rarely plays a significant role in international politics.

3. Theory and Concept:

Before reviewing the literature regarding the interests and perspective of hydrohegemon and global water cooperation, it seems plausible to have a look at the theory and concept of hydro-hegemony which nullifies water wars. Hydro-hegemony is "hegemony at the river-basin level, achieved through water resource control strategies, such as resource capture, integration and containment" (Zeitoun and Warner, 2006: 1). The hydrohegemony framework was developed in order to evaluate and execute the presence of a hydro-hegemon and its influential role in a basin development with its co-riparians.

The concept of "hydro-hegemony" has been explored previously but has not to date been thoroughly conceptualized or theorized. The concept of hydro-hegemony distinguishes itself from earlier work in three ways. Firstly, this analysis captures and refines two approaches to water conflict prediction i.e. Yoffe's (2001) etal scale of water conflict event intensities and (b) Frey's (1993) power analytic framework into a single framework. Secondly, through the dynamics of water conflict investigation, strategies, tactics of hegemonic and counter-hegemonic behaviour and thirdly, through an alternative explanation for the absence of water wars.

The HHF can be applied to transboundary water conflicts if there is a considerable power asymmetry, control over the flow and water headworks and competition over water is stifled (Zeitoun and Warner, 2006). Power asymmetry can be determined by the domination of one riparian over the others in a river basin with regards to the three pillars of hydro-hegemony i.e. "Exploitation Potential"(capacity to build hydraulic infrastructure), "Riparian Position" (upstream, downstream i.e. geographical position), and the "Three dimensions of Power" (structural, bargaining and ideological).

Power theories of Luke (2005) are very important to understand the three dimensions of power. Structural power is referred as "power as might", in other words, the ability of a state to mobilise capabilities, including military might, economic strength, modes of production, access to knowledge as well as political support and rather more enduring features such as riparian position, size and value of territory. The second dimension of power (bargaining power) refers to control of the rules of the game (Zeitoun and Warner, 2006) i.e. the power to set the agenda, which consists of the ability of the weaker party to choose between compliance or non-compliance with the stronger party's commands (Luke, 2005:11 and Zeitoun and Warner, 2006: 8).

The third dimension of power, which is the core concept of the framework, inspired by Antonio Gramsci, is that of ideological hegemony, which can be referred as the "power to prevent people from having grievance by shaping their perceptions, cognitions and preferences in such a way that they accept their role in the existing order of things."(Luke, 2005 and Zeitoun, 2006: 76). Gramsci defines hegemony as "political power that flows from intellectual and moral leadership, authority or consensus as distinguished from armed force". (Gramsci, 1971).

Control over resources and resource capture are the main active strategies, employed through the use of tactics of compliance-producing mechanisms like military force, securitisation, sanctioned discourse, etc. (Lustick, 2002). The hegemon have access to many coercive resources by definition in greater quantity, for example the ability to mobilize funds, its preferred riparian position and relatively greater political capital. This whole dynamic is set in within a prejudiced international context, including partisanship, global political trends characterised by the absence of a universally-acknowledged international water law, which usually provides negative outcomes where the hegemon seeks acquiescence from other riparians at their expense, thereby containing and legitimising the instability that succeeds (Zeitoun and Warner, 2006: 21).

4. Interests and Perspectives of Water Hegemon:

Zeitoun and Warner (2006, p.5) argue that power asymmetry may lead to an inequitable outcome that will result in a low intensity conflict to form a positive/negative hegemony; further, the hydro-hegemon country uses different strategies like military force, coercion pressure, treaties, incentives, securitization and sanctioned discourse to form the interaction over transboundary waters that it prefers. Wolf (1998, p.6) discusses the pros and cons of up-streamer and down-streamer that they both are not in a position to wage a war over water because the upstreamer may already be in a better position by location to have control over water resources through different tactics and strategies while it would be an imprudence of the down-streamer to attack the storage or quality related projects of upstreamer which would result in a wall of water rushing back or result in an even worse quality of water than before for the down-streamer. Further, he explains that shared interests of both up-streamer and down-streamer will lead to cooperation that will result in a good quality of water and a healthy stream system, which farmers, environmentalist and beach-goers can enjoy.

On the other hand, upstreamer can build hydropower and reduce the water flow for down streamer which may affect the agriculture land of the down streamer. Additionally, Wolf (1998, p.7) and Barret (1994, p.7) mentioned the de-merits caused by the up-streamers for the down-streamers such as degradation of both surface and groundwater, change in morphology, impeded navigation, increased salinity, degraded fisheries, and danger to water supplies and public health. Zeitoun and Allan (2008, p.3) argue that in some cases even the downstreamers may enjoy the water hegemony. For example, Egypt is a downstream riparian of Nile but a water hegemon while Afghanistan, Nepal and Ethiopia are upstream riparians but are not hegemon. These examples show that being up-streamer or down-streamer may not be as important as being powerful; most of the hegemon countries are powerful, whether they are located at down-stream or up-stream.

5. Global Water Cooperation:

Cooperation over transboundary waters has a long history and achieving it is always a long and complex journey. A number of treaties, protocols and conventions have been signed from time to time for the development and protection of transboundary watercourses and related ecosystems, e.g. the 1960 Indus Waters Treaty between India and Pakistan, the 1978 Great Lakes Water Quality Agreement between US and Canada, the 1995 Agreement on the Cooperation for the Sustainable Development of the Mekong River Basin among Thailand, Laos, Cambodia and Vietnam, the 1995 Protocol on Shared Watercourse Systems in the Southern African states, the 1996 Mahakali and Ganges treaties between India and Bangladesh, and the 1959 Nile Waters Agreement between Egypt and Sudan (UN-Water, 2008).

Shlomi Dinar (2008, p.24) points out three main reasons for cooperation; firstly, the states will cooperate for their mutual benefits; secondly, the cooperating states are concerned with maximizing their benefits and will cooperate if agreements are self-enforcing or if cooperation can provide for mutual gain; and thirdly, cooperation does not depend on the hegemony, but rather on volunteer contracting among states. In addition, security and survival may play an important role for cooperation among the states and mutuality of interest, scarcity combined with the autonomous and unilateral strategies are the main incentives for cooperation.

Alam (2002, p.6) draws our attention to the fact that sometimes states cooperate to get financial support, as it happened in the case of Pakistan and India where, due to specific cooperation over the Indus water, both parties received financial support from the Indus Basin Development Fund as well as from developed countries and the World Bank. Zeitoun and Warner (2006, p.5) while explaining the cooperation from a hegemonic perspective, state that a focus on cooperation can hide the negative effects of power asymmetries.

United Nations (2006, p.24) highlights the benefits of cooperation between the riparians of shared water resources, such as better management of the basin ecosystem, water quality and biodiversity, improved management of river including increased agricultural production, energy generation, and, above all, cooperation can minimize the tension and conflict, and improve the political and economic relation between the conflicting parties. However, keeping in view the local, political, geographic, economic and cultural conditions, the nature of such benefits varies from basin to basin.

6. Indus Waters Treaty:

In August 1947, two new states, India and Pakistan, emerged on the world map. At that time Pakistan consisted of two units, West Pakistan and East Pakistan. East Pakistan gained independence in 1971 and is known as Bangladesh to the world today. Hence, the British India was broken up into three units. In the same way, the Indus Basin was due to be divided by virtue of partition of 1947 between India and West Pakistan (Husain, 2010). This great river system, the cradle of the Indus civilization, was a vital resource for the new-born state of Pakistan, which was fed by its major tributaries, five of which have their sources in Indian-held Kashmir. In addition, the irrigation canals were all in Pakistan but the headworks were in India (Ibid). Pakistan was always eager to reach a formal agreement about water sharing because of inimical relations with India.

In 1948, Pakistan's worst fears came true when India cut off the water supply to all the canals, which almost drove Pakistan to war. Following much negotiations among the two sides and intervention by the World Bank, the Indus Waters Treaty was signed in 1960. This treaty gives control of three western rivers to Pakistan and three eastern rivers to India (Husain, 2010). Since then, the Indus basin of Pakistan has been serving as a premier laboratory for water resources research and management during the second half of the 20th century. (Meadows and Meadows, 1999 and Wescoat et.al 2010).

Alam (2002, p.1) discusses the importance of the Indus Waters Treaty and provides an insight about the war rationale, that Pakistan and India should have fought a war over the Indus basin instead of negotiating the 1960 Indus waters treaty, which both countries have maintained for more than 40 years through two wars and the nuclear era. Alam (1998, p.7-12) draws our attention to two important facts; firstly, that much work had already been done in the international basins of the Middle East: the Jordan, the Nile, the Tigris and the Euphrates, while very little had been done on the Indus Basin; secondly, she senses that literature over IWT is limited.

According to the Strategic Foresight Group's[1] 2005 report, the IWT needs to be renegotiated as the treaty only offers a frail defence against heightened conflict over river resources between Pakistan and India. It is only a matter of time before water war becomes a virtually unavoidable feature of the region's political environment. Waslekar (2005) also contends that every proposal made by Pakistan through track-two diplomatic channels since 1999 has referred to water as a pivotal concern.

Indo-Pak Water Dispute and Indus Waters Treaty (IWT)

The water dispute between India and Pakistan is a long running dispute and is worsening with each passing day. Its origin lies in the creation of Pakistan and India in 1947 after the partition of the Indian subcontinent. This division led India to hold a part of the Kashmir valley, a source of six main rivers irrigating the crops of the largest province of Pakistan, The Punjab[2] (Abbot, 2010).

2 Map 1. Shows the irrigation system of Indo-Pak

Source: http://www.lead.org.pk/jw/reading_material_journalist_workshop.htm

Pakistan mainly depends on the Indus River, which passes through Jammu and Kashmir, for its survival and sustenance. The Indus River, which is 3180 Kilometres in length, originates in western Tibet, flows through China and Kashmir and then turns south into Pakistan and falls into the Arabian Sea. (Rashid, 2003).

---

[1] The Strategic Foresight Group: Indian group foresees Pak-Kashmir water war
http://www.strategicforesight.com/sfgnews_107.htm
[2] http://www.chinadaily.com.cn/cndy/2010-05/01/content_9799770.htm

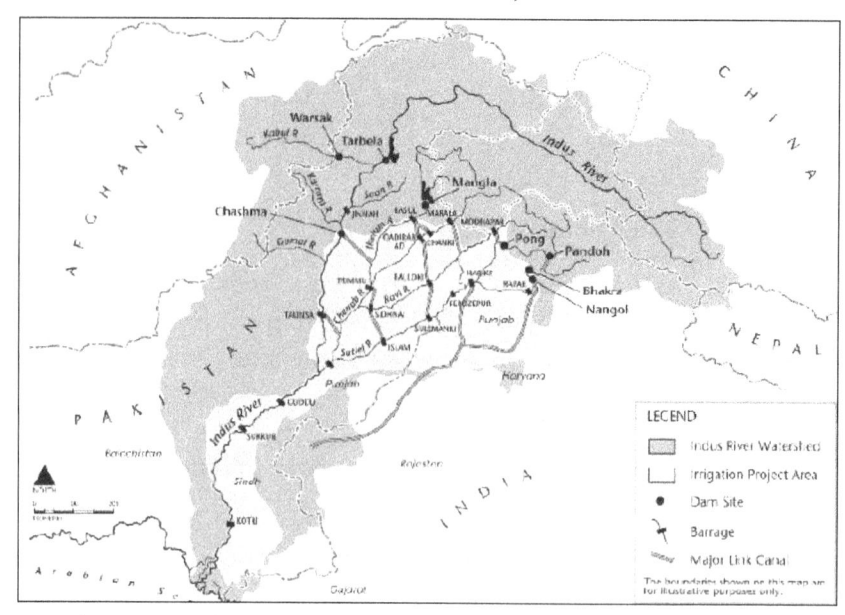

Map 2. Indus basin and its major infrastructure

Source: http://www.lead.org.pk/jw/reading_material_journalist_workshop.htm

Soon after independence in 1947 a war broke out between the two countries. Realizing the dangers of further wars, the then president of the World bank, Eugene R. Black, visited both countries and offered mediation for solving the conflict peacefully, to which both the countries agreed. Talks were held and finally a treaty was signed by Jawaharlal Nehru, then Prime Minister of India; Field Marshal Ayub Khan, then President of Pakistan; and W.A.B. Illif, then President of the World Bank, in Karachi in September 1960 (Sridhar, 2008). As mentioned earlier, under the 1960 agreement, Pakistan has the use of the three western rivers — the Indus, Jhelum and Chenab; and India, the three eastern ones — the Sutlej, Beas and Ravi. India was granted limited use of Pakistan's rivers for agricultural purposes, plus the right to build hydroelectric dams, as long as they do not store or divert large amounts of water. (Ibid).

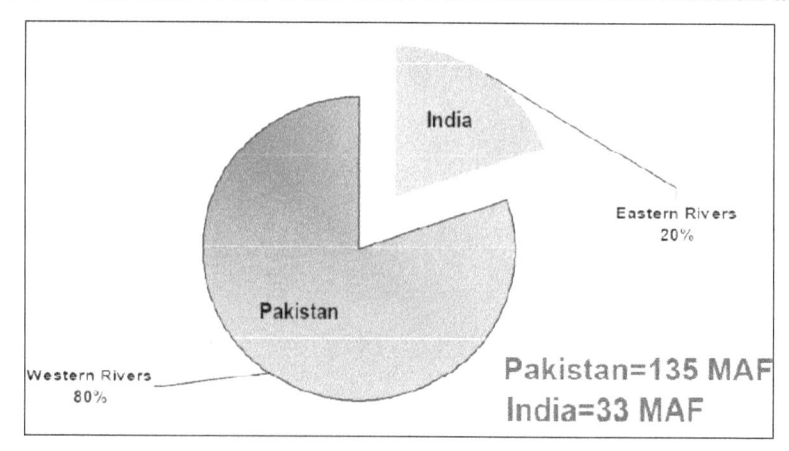

Figure 1. Pie Chart shows the water share between India and Pakistan after IWT

Source: http://www.lead.org.pk/jw/reading_material_journalist_workshop.htm

As per agreement, India started to build hydroelectric dams on the Indus basin; the structures of these dams were not acceptable to Pakistan, which caused a delay in their implementation. Pakistan has objections mainly on three projects; the Baglihar Hydro-Power Project (BHP), Tulbul Navigation Project (TNP), and Kishanganga Project.

Figure 2. The Graph shows the major projects of India over Chenab River.

Source: http://www.lead.org.pk/jw/reading_material_journalist_workshop.htm

The Baglihar project, which is a 900 MW project on the Chenab River in Doda district in Jammu, would cause downstream flow and could also be used to cause floods in the riparian areas. The Kishanganga project would affect Pakistan and Kashmir in three ways i.e. reduction of energy generation, environmental impacts on flora and fauna and the proposed heights of the gates[3]. India rejected any such possibilities with the answer that the project would release back the water into the river stream after the water was utilized for power generation. When both countries failed to resolve the dispute bilaterally, as per the IWT agreement, they referred to a third party, whereby the third party favoured the Indian stance, and, in the meantime, also recommended some changes in the project design.

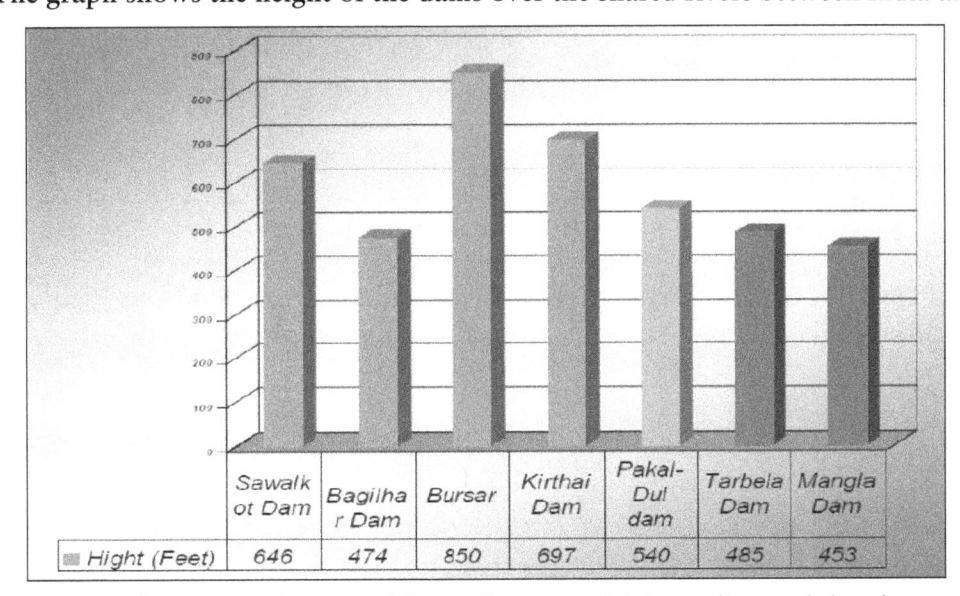

Figure 3. The graph shows the height of the dams over the shared rivers between India and Pakistan.

	Sawalkot Dam	Bagilhar Dam	Bursar	Kirthai Dam	Pakal-Dul dam	Tarbela Dam	Mangla Dam
Hight (Feet)	646	474	850	697	540	485	453

Source: http://www.lead.org.pk/jw/reading_material_journalist_workshop.htm

---

[3] "We will have to look beyond the Indus Water Treaty." Syed Jamaat Ali Shah, Pakistan's commissioner for Indus water's interview on 3rd March 2010 in the daily Dawn newspaper.

After the terrorist attacks on the Indian parliament in 2001, India openly threatened Pakistan of revoking the IWT. The Indian cabinet committee on security went to the extent to cut the major water supply of Pakistan and used it as an effective threat to stop Pakistan from helping the extremist groups in Kashmir (Rashid, 2003).

Applying the Hydro-Hegemony Framework (HHF)

1. Conflict Intensity in the Indus Basin:

The application of the hydro-hegemony framework to the Indus basin necessitates an analysis of the intensity of conflicts over the Indus waters. In view of the future water scarcity, its competitive use and Pakistan's absolute dependency upon the basin coupled with the historical disputes, including Kashmir, between India and Pakistan (Alam, 2002), it is necessary to analyse the conflict intensity and power asymmetry between the two riparians through the framework of hydro-hegemony.

2. The Water Event Intensity Scale (WEIS):

The below scale demonstrates the intensity of conflicts in two broad contexts; firstly, that each of the different levels of intensity of conflict has very different implications in terms of international relations and secondly that even the less-intense conflicts are still forms of conflicts (Zeitoun and Warner, 2006: 7).

	Scale	Event Description
Cooperation	7	Voluntary Unification into one nation
	6	Major Strategic Alliance (International Freshwater Treaty)
	5	Military, Economic or Strategic Support
	4	Non-military Economic, Technological or Industrial Agreement
	3	Cultural or Scientific Support (non-strategic)
	2	Official Verbal Support of goals, values, or regime
	1	Minor Official Exchanges, Talks or Policy Expressions
	0	Neutral or non-significant acts for the inter-nation situation
Conflict	-1	Mild Verbal Expressions displaying discord in interaction
	-2	Strong Verbal Expressions displaying hostility in interaction
	-3	Diplomatic-Economic Hostile Actions
	-4	Political-Military Hostile Actions
	-5	Small Scale Military Acts
	-6	Extensive War Acts causing deaths, dislocation or high strategic costs
	-7	Formal Declaration of War

Source: Yoffe et al. (2001: 71) and Zeitoun and Warner (2006: 7)

The WEIS attempts to exemplify the preceding paragraph in the following figure in three broad categories: no conflict, cold conflict; or 'violent conflict' (Zeitoun and Warner, 2006).

Table 2. Conflict Intensity Frame

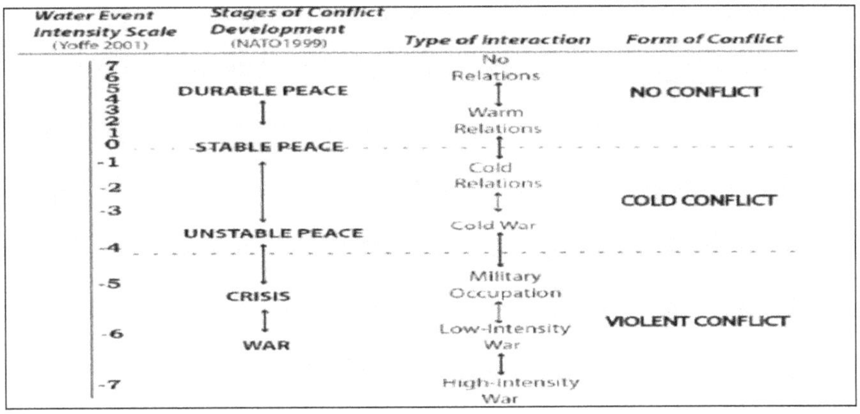

Source: Zeitoun and Warner (2006)

The Conflict Intensity Frame reveals not simply that different conflicts vary in intensity, but that the same conflict can undergo various degrees of intensity through time (Zeitoun and Warner, 2006).

3. Power asymmetry in the Indus Basin:

The HHF provides an analytic paradigm to find the impact of power asymmetries between riparians in competition for control over water resources in order to determine who is the hydro-hegemon (Zeitoun and Warner, 2006). After applying the HHF to the Nile, Jordan, Tigris and Euphrates river basin, it has been found that current hydro-hegemonic configurations tend towards the dominative form and that in each case power asymmetries influence an inequitable outcome (Zeitoun and Warner, 2006). In this part, the power of India will be analysed to show how extreme power asymmetry ensures the Indian hegemony in the Indus basin, which will be achieved through an evaluation of the three pillars of hydro-hegemony.

The hydro-hegemony's three pillars

Figure 4. The Pillars of Hydro-Hegemony

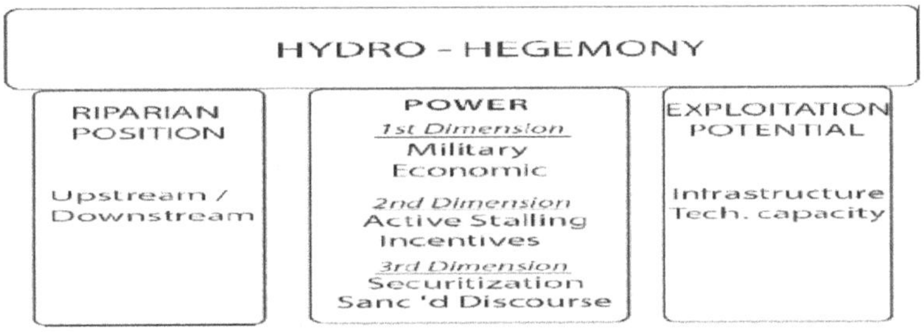

Source: Zeitoun and Warner (2006)

4. Geographical Location:

India is the upper riparian of the Indus Basin and has the capacity to turn West Punjab into a desert, which is the backbone of Pakistan's agriculture (Mandel, 1991). The power asymmetry between the riparians of Indus basin is significant. According to the 2009 report by the Woodrow Wilson International Center for scholars, Water availability in Pakistan has fallen 70% since the early 1950s to 1,500 cubic meters per capita. It is expected to reach the 1,000-cubic-meter level considered officially "scarce" by international standards in 25 years (Sharma and Wright, 2010). The 1960 Indus Waters treaty guaranteed Pakistan 55,000 cusecs of water. Yet, this year, "Pakistan has only received 13,000 cusecs during the winter and a maximum of 29,000 cusecs during summer" (Mogwai, 2009).

5. Technical Capacity

India has a greater technical capacity of making dams, which brings it to the world No. 3, with 4079 dams, after US with 6411, and China, and, it is estimated that another 2500 large dams will be required in future to achieve the ultimate storage potential to utilize it for socio-economic development (ICID, 2004). Many of these new projects have either been completed or in the process of completion on the disputed water. Pakistan's main objections are on the Baglihar Hydro Power Project (BHP) and Kishenganga Project on Chenab River in Kashmir and Tulbul Navigation Project (TNP) on the Wular Lake in Kashmir, which can disrupt the flow of water into the Jhelum River, which flows into Pakistan (Sridhar, 2008).

The Three Dimensions of Power:
(Structural, Bargaining and Ideational Power)

Structural Power: (Economic Power, Military Power and Political Support)

Kenneth Waltz and Perkovich (2010) provided a useful, colloquial definition of power as the "extent that [one] affects others more than they affect [oneself]". A state's power can thus be a combination of its capacity of military, economic and technological strength, social cohesion and mobilization, quality of governance, and diplomatic and intelligence acumen (Perkovich, 2010, Zeitoun and Warner, 2006) to influence others to behave as it wants them to and, conversely, to resist the unwelcome influence of others. Like any state, India's capacity to affect others and to resist undesired influence results from the country's various forms of hard and soft power (Perkovich, 2010).

6. Economic Strength:

A country's per capita gross domestic product (GDP) is a useful indicator of its economic strength. In 2002, India's estimated per capita GDP was $2,540 USD (Perkovich, 2010) while the GDP growth rate of India in the financial year 2009-2010 is 7.2%; on other hand, the Pakistan's overall GDP growth is 3.3%, with the decline in the agriculture sector specifically from 4.7% last year to 3% this year (DAWN, 2010). India has already achieved a fair degree of political consensus in pursuing its vision to become a developed nation and to achieve a growth rate of 8% per annum by the year 2020 (Asher and Srivastava, 2003). India has been successful in getting the world's attention by the "Incredible India" slogan coined by an advertising firm and displayed at Davos, Swtizerland a few years ago while the Pakistan's description in the international community is that of the world's "most dangerous place on Earth" because of the militant Islam, which has turned the financial world's attention away from the country (Burki, 2010).

7. Military Power:

Measuring military power of a state is more complicated than it might seem. A state's security ambitions can grow as its power potential grows. India's military security challenges are to deter or defeat Pakistani support in the state of Jammu and Kashmir (Perkovich, 2010). India raised its defence budget by 17% in the fiscal year 2003-2004 from 12% in the previous three financial years and signed at least $4 billion worth of contracts with Russia to purchase advanced military equipment. India's growing military power is mainly aimed at suppressing Pakistan and making it isolated in the international community. Pakistan military strength is very low as compared to India's. However, Perkovich (2010) penned down: "Nuclear weapons give Pakistan the capacity to stay in the game, to continue to pop up and grab India by the threat".

Country	Rnk	Land Power	Tot Qual	Tot Pop	GDP	Act Men	Mil Bud	Bud Man	AFV	Air Cmbt	Ldrs	Eqp	Exp	Spt	Mob	Trad
South Asia Nations																
India	1	2290	35	1200	$1300	1288	$30000	$23	5600	650	7	5	7	5	4	7
Pakistan	2	699	24	169	$150	619	$4600	$7	3200	380	6	4	6	4	3	7
Myanmar	3	202	12	48	$38	405	$6000	$15	600	120	5	3	5	3	1	4
Sri Lanka	4	196	25	21	$33	160	$1300	$8	330	35	7	5	8	3	3	1
Bangladesh	5	92	19	150	$70	150	$1000	$7	370	75	5	4	5	3	3	4
Nepal	6	61	10	29	$11	69	$160	$2	80	0	6	2	7	2	1	8
Afghanistan	7	27	8	31	$11	51	$200	$4	200	0	5	2	6	3	1	5

Source: Strategy Page (2010)

8. Political Strength or International support:

When India is visited by world's most powerful leaders, their main concern is to ensure the Asia's third largest economy will play in their fields while, on the other side, the when same leaders come to Pakistan, they have only one thing in their mind, that Pakistan should play its role in countering terrorism. The structural power of India is getting stronger by its central economic role and the investment from the developed world, including the recent visits by the Russian Prime Minister Vladimir Putin and the British Prime Minister David Cameron. Mr. Cameron advised the British investors to invest in India on a large scale while Mr. Putin brought in his gift with basket *"suggestions that Russia might accelerate its nuclear plant building programme in India and partner the giant democracy to produce new military equipment"*. (Burki, 2010).

9. Bargaining Power:

The bargaining power of India can be categorised in two ways. First its position as an up-streamer in the Indus basin where by different hegemonic actions it can divert, stop, or reduce the flow of water to the down-streamer and secondly its strategic relations with powerful states reinforced this bargaining power, such as the issue of Jammu and Kashmir between Pakistan and India (Ranjan, 2010). India has full support of both the US and the UK to turn the Line of Control into an internationally recognised frontier while Pakistani and Kashmiri activists are against this plan (BBC, 2010). Great vulnerability and legitimate concern of Pakistan over water scarcity made India's bargaining power more critical among water experts, such as John Briscoe, a water expert who has worked in the subcontinent for 35 years, says that India needs to be more generous on water issues with Pakistan (Gupta, 2010).

10. Ideational Power:

The use of ideational power by one state over another, to get control over shared water resources, is because of the weak International Water Law (IWL) which is only concerned with the equitable and reasonable sharing of transboundary waters and thus not addressing directly the real cause which may prevent this goal from being realised (Zeitoun and Woodhouse, 2008). India's ideational power is much linked to its bargaining power because Pakistan is totally dependent on Indus waters which pass through the disputed state of Jammu and Kashmir (BBC, 2010). New Delhi is loath to concede that claiming the 1947 accession of the Princely State of

Kashmir to India during Partition is an indisputable fact; thus it prefers to place the Kashmir related tensions within a basket of several other issues—the so-called"composite dialogue" (Fair, 2005).

Article III of the IWT binds India not to hinder the flow, or store any water or construct any storage works on the western rivers, to Pakistan, while India has started works on all these rivers mostly in Kashmir region to divert and build massive water storage dams. India as is seen, follows the "Harmon Doctrine[4]", where it gives "Absolute Territorial Sovereignty" to the upper riparian, as goes the usage of water resources passing through its lands (Tajammal, 2010).

11. Water Control Strategies and Tactics:

In every basin, both the strongest and the weakest riparians find themselves in three different situations to get control over resources; these are either (a) shared (meaning some form of cooperation exists), (b) consolidated in the stronger riparian's favour (where cooperation is minimal, and the competition is shut-down), or (c) contested (when the competition is at its fiercest) (Zeitoun and Warner, 2006). The situation of shared resource is the most stable one, where the hegemon negotiates a water sharing agreement which all the riparians perceive and thus forms a positive form of hydro-hegemony. The negative or dominative form of hydro-hegemony occurs when the hegemon seeks to attain the maximum control of water resources. This form of hydro-hegemony leads to unstable hydro-relations. To attain and consolidate the dominative form of hegemony, hydro-hegemon use different tactics to achieve three strategic outcomes i.e. resource capture, integration, or containment (Zeitoun and Warner, 2006).

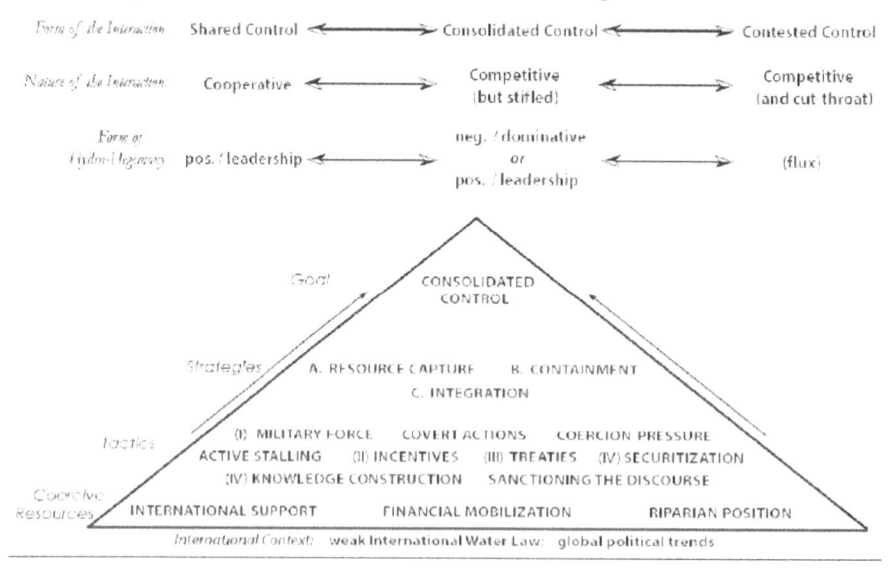

Figure 6. Water Resource Control Strategies and Tactics

12. Containment/Integration Strategy:

The conflict over Kashmir is more elemental than one realizes; one of the most important reasons among all these conflicts is the issue of fresh water resources. The Government of India and Indian politicians have been trying to turn Kashmir as a Holy land and its rivers as religious symbols, which is obvious from the

---

[4] Two sets of laws govern the water disputes; first is the Harmon Doctrine, named after Judson Harmon, who was the Attorney General of USA in 1895, when arose a dispute between Mexico and USA over the usage of "Rio Grande Waters" and second is the set of rules, called as "The Helsinki Rules", which was drafted by the ILA (International Law Association) in 1966, define the perimeters of water related disputes, in cases where the drainage of a basin is international; eleven main points/clauses govern the rights of a lower riparian.

creation of a festival called "Sindhu Darshan[5]", which casts the Indus as a Hindu river (Haug, 2010). Furthermore, India seeks to expand investment in the tourism industry by 8.5% in 2010-2011 in Indian-controlled Kashmir (Mushtaq, 2010). The containment of Kashmir, to impede Pakistan's water supply may be a direct threat to Pakistan's security, which Pakistan is desperately trying to characterize in the international community (Haug, 2010).

13. Resource Capture Strategy:

Resource capture occurs with a fall in the quality and quantity of renewable resources when a powerful group in a society shifts resource distribution in its favour leaving the poor and weaker groups of the society in a calamitous scarce environment (Homer-Dixon, 2001). The control over resources may include land acquisition, land annexation, or the construction of large scale hydraulic works, and this process is typically carried out by creating facts on ground that enable control over access to the resource (Zeitoun and Warner, 2006).

The Indian resource capture strategy in the Indus basin is the Baglihar Hydro-Power Project (BHP), Tulbul Navigation Project (TNP) and the Kishanganga Project where Pakistan has already shown its concern and objection regarding its capacity and height with the arguments that the construction of these projects would affect the flow and may cause floods downstream. The main objection from Pakistan is on the 450 MW Baglihar Dam, which is being constructed by India on the Chenab River (Masood, 2010). Pakistan fears that the construction of Baglihar Dam will give India control of an important water supply (BBC, 2005).

There are some serious technical objections from the Pakistan's side regarding the design of Baglihar Dam, that this is not confined to power generation but will, allegedly, enable India to divert over 7,000 cusecs of the Chenab water per day for irrigation purposes in violation of the 1960 Indus Basin Treaty, where India is permitted to generate electricity but it cannot divert the flow of river water. Baglihar Dam's construction is a vibrant violation of the IWT; the project allows India to store 164,000 acres feet of water and stop water for about 26 days during December, January and February (Masood, 2010).

14. Applicability of HHF to the Indus Basin:

After analysing the provisions of IWT, Hamner and Wolf (1998) state that power asymmetries exist in the articles of IWT. We, too, find that India has been using all the three forms of power, time and again, to maintain and consolidate its hydro-hegemony. India is an emerging economy in the region and, therefore, trying to invest and capture more resources to cope with energy challenges in the coming years. In this regard India has been using the resource capture strategy, via its structural power, through the deployment of a huge army in the disputed Kashmir region, while Pakistan suspects this development and views it as the holding of water resources in the region.

All the ongoing projects over the disputed waters, which is mostly funded by the World Bank and the developed world, show India's economic power in the region. India, being a big democracy, with a persuasive political set-up and a strong foreign policy, has the ability to sort out water related conflicts in its favour. It is because of its influential role in the international arena coupled with weak International Water Laws (IWL). A descriptive analysis of India's power related strategies and cooperative schemes (IWT) shows that India has fully gained its negative hydro-hegemon position. Nonetheless, cooperation exists between the two riparians in the form of IWT but the treaty itself tilts towards India. This tilt is clear from the unresolved issue of Kashmir, and the hue and cries of the Government of Pakistan on account of water shortages in its agrarian land.

---

[5] The Sindhu Darshan Festival, as the name suggests, is a celebration of River Sindhu, also known as the Indus, held every year in the month of June. It is held at Leh, in Ladakh District of Jammu & Kashmir. The main reason behind the celebration of Sindhu Darshan Festival is to endorse the Indus River (Sindhu River) as an icon of communal harmony and unity of India.

15. Limitation of the HHF:

The HHF forwards a central role of the state in transboundary water conflicts in a globalized world where a number of other powerful players, both at the international level as well as within the countries, play an important role (Sellby, 2007). These players may significantly influence powerful decision-makers in transboundary water conflicts. The assumption that the states and, as such, merely the bureaucrats are the only decision-makers, when it comes to water conflicts between two countries, is very limited and narrows down the analysis. Other key players within a state and at the international level also need to be focused while studying trans-boundary water conflicts.

Furthermore, the HHF is more applicable to situations, or between two countries, where the balance of power is tilted and may be less applicable to balanced powers regarding water hegemony. As the name suggests, there has to be hegemony as a precondition for this theory to be applied; in situations where hegemony does not exist, the theory may have limitation, in its applicability.

Discussions

1. History of Conflicts:

Pakistan and India, being two rival neighbours, have been engaged in constant rivalry since the past 63 years. They have fought wars, initiated propagandas against each other, at different international forums. Each of both has tried to make the other subordinate through one or the other way. India, being a truly democratic republic, has made development, at an enormous scale especially during the last two decades. Both are nuclear countries and are spending billions of dollars on defence budgets. On the other hand, Pakistan, after its independence, has been ruled, for most of the time, by military dictators, grabbing power through unlawful means and often putting aside democratic governments. It is not more than five years that Pakistan has again begun its journey towards democracy. Each military dictator has exploited the Indian rivalry in one way or the other. Due to its history of military coups, it is increasingly feared that the international community, lacking trust and confidence, is seeing Pakistan as a failed state.

Even in the times of elected and the so-called democratic governments, the military establishment significantly influences the international security policy of Pakistan and foreign relations, especially between India and Pakistan. For example, in the current, so-called US 'war on terror' project, it is mostly the Pakistani military establishment that takes most of the strategic decisions, which significantly influences relations between India and Pakistan. Pakistan's establishment has also been blamed for directly or indirectly supporting different Islamic extremist groups, whose most recent victim on the international level was the attack on a Mumbai hotel in India. An element of hatred against India is a common talk in Pakistan and India is blamed for almost every incident happening inside Pakistan.

Tracing the history of conflicts, it would be concluded that the very first war between the two neighbouring countries started just two months after independence when Pakistan started supporting the Muslim insurgency in Kashmir because Pakistan wanted the latter to be a part of it. The war ended on 1 January 1949 as a result of ceasefire arranged by the UN; the UN suggested referendum, which is yet to be held[6].

2. Indus Basin: Interactions and Events (1947-2010):

Gleditsch et al (2002) have tabulated armed conflicts from 1946-2001 among different nations of the world. They found out 11 major conflicts between India and Pakistan, ranging from medium to high, and to them,

---
[6] http://news.bbc.com.uk/hi/english/static/in depth/south asia/2002/india pakistan/timeline/194748.stm

the Kashmir issue remained the pivotal amongst all. In support of Gleditsch et al, Ahmed (2009) also senses Kashmir as the core issue in the dialogues between the two countries because the waters of the major rivers pass through the Indian occupied Kashmir.

Table 4. Armed conflicts between India and Pakistan

Location	Incompatibility	Opposition organization	Year	Intensity level
India – Pakistan	Territory (Kashmir)		1947-48	War
			1954	Intermediate
			1965	War
			1971	War
			1984	Intermediate
			1987	Intermediate
			1989-90	Intermediate
			1992	Intermediate
			1996-98	Intermediate
			1999	War
			2000-01	Intermediate

Source: Gleditsch et al (2002)

Mandel (1991) reveals that the water conflict intensity level between the two riparians is medium because their allies always encourage them for settlement because of the fear of the consequences of an Indo-Pakistani war precipitated around the Indus waters. Although, antagonism and differences of opinion are significant, outside mediation by the World Bank has helped to mute the existing hostility.

Treaty Title	Indus Waters Treaty
Date Signed	19th September 1960
Main Basin	Indus
Basins Involved	Indus
Signatories	Bilateral
Parties	India, Pakistan
Principal Focus	Water Supply
Non-Water Linkages	Capital
Comments on Above	£62,060,000 as replacement cost of irrigation canals in regions formerly irrigated from Eastern Rivers. Money paid to India if the 31st March 1970 expiration date is extended for upto three years.
Monitoring	Yes
Enforcement	Council
Unequal Power Relationship	Yes
Information Sharing	Yes
Conflict Resolution	Council, then a neutral third party
Method for Water Division	Complex but clear-effective division of river by tributary
Additional Comments	Engineering plans were used first, and then found lacking until political efforts could direct them. Third party negotiators (Bank) were effective.

Source: Hamner and Wolf (1998)

3. Water Conflicts and the Indus Waters Treaty:

According to the Indus Waters Treaty, the waters of the three Eastern Rivers: Sutlej, Beas and Ravi be utilized by India, while those of the three Western Rivers: Indus, Chenab and Jhelum be used by Pakistan. Impartially, the treaty has been exploited by both countries, both have benefited in the legal ways mentioned in the treaty as well as both have been trying to make the rival subordinate through different tactics. For Pakistan the tactics are employing the Mujahideens or freedom fighters that play a major role in the Kashmir conflict while for India, which, indeed, has an upper hand; better control of waters. Pakistan claims that the Indian hydro-projects are illegal in the sense that they divert water, resulting in a lesser flow to Pakistan. Pakistan has raised objections to almost all major water projects of India, where the international community ignored some, while others resulted in change of design of the projects.

The relations between the two countries have seen many ups and downs. The nature of water dispute between the two countries has changed from global (inclusion of World Bank) to local (militant groups now asking India to solve the issue as soon as possible otherwise India will face attacks)[7]. It seems that in coming years, it may turn into an issue of the street in both countries. It is quite obvious now that it is indeed India who is enjoying the hegemony on the waters between the two countries. Besides other reasons the two main factors that India has exploited well, especially in matters related to water, are its geographical location and its diplomatic relationships and image in the world community. India, as hydro-hegemon, has also been confirmed by John Briscoe (2010), who is an expert on international water-related disputes. Briscoe in an interview reveals that "both India and Pakistan have good reason to modernize the implementation of the treaty, with the ball mostly in India's court[8]".

Rather than the nuclear bomb of India, the Pakistanis seem to be concerned about the water hegemony of India. A Pakistani columnist, Rubina Rasheed, in her article on water conflicts between India and Pakistan, terms the Indian hegemony as "Water Bomb"[9] and considers the same hegemony as a very visible threat to the lower riparian Pakistan, which solely depends on the water from India for the purposes of farming and hydro-projects. To remove any possibility of war in future and for the sake of lasting peace, the bigger partner India might have to be magnanimous towards Pakistan and restrict filling up the dams during the sowing seasons. By doing that, India would have to forego some power generation for the benefit of Pakistani farmers. Pakistan could reciprocate by agreeing to the renegotiation of the treaty and allowing India to build more dams without any hassle.

But turning the above statement into reality requires a considerable amount of trust from both sides. India would, of course, like to get a grip on the jugular vein of Pakistan economy and would be hesitant to let a big bargaining tool like water go in the event of a future terror attack emanating from Pakistani soil. After all, India is fully aware of the importance of the rivers to Pakistani agriculture and hence the economy. Pakistan, on its part, would have to trust India to not violate the treaty by holding up excess water. The side-topics of Kashmir and terrorism might not but other factors could impact the issue. The overall situation today seems to be moving away from cooperation towards conflict, as mentioned earlier by Gleditsch et al (2002) and Mandel (1991), because both countries lack trust in each other, and any conflict between the two countries will be disastrous not only for them but also for the entire region keeping in view the nuclear capabilities of both countries.

4. Pakistan and IWT: The Indian Perspective:

The Indian perspective regarding IWT is that, it sees Pakistan as making it virtually impossible for them to exploit effectively the Treaty's non-consumptive uses, especially hydropower production (Verghese, 2005).

---

[7] http://www.thehindu.com/opinion/op-ed/article436582.ece
[8] Global Insider: The India-Pakistan Water Dispute, 10, June, 2010.
[9] http://un-gaid.ning.com/profiles/blogs/water-bomb-severe?threat-to

Suba Chandran, Deputy Director, Institute of Peace and Conflict Studies, New Delhi states that Pakistan is trying to fully exploit the IWT nationally, bilaterally and internationally. He argues that Pakistan internally faces severe criticism from three of its four provinces i.e. Sindh, Khyber Pakhtunkhwa and Baluchistan on the IWT because Punjab is stealing water from rest of the provinces and he further mentions it as a reason why all smaller provinces are against the controversial Kalabagh dam though Punjab is time and again insisting on the construction of this dam.

The other provinces argue that there would be exploitation of their waters by Punjab and many of their towns and cities will be inundated in case the dam is constructed; recent floods in Pakistan is a clear example of how dangerous the Kalabagh dam could be especially for the Khyber Pakhtunkhwa province. The dam is considered beneficial only for the Punjab province. Furthermore, he postulates that Kashmir has always been at the core of Pakistan's domestic and foreign policy. Realizing that the world pays less attention to the issue today, Pakistan can use water war as a strategy to bring back the attention of the international community to Kashmir.

5. India and IWT: The Pakistani Perspective:

India after partition was blessed geographically to get hold of the Indus and its tributaries and has exploited it to the fullest. Since the treaty was signed, India has aptly tried to gain control of the western rivers that belong to Pakistan, hence depriving Pakistan of its due share and that may transform the whole country into a desert land. The successive Pakistan government's perspective, regarding IWT, is that, India's retention of the right to non-consumptive uses on western rivers "presents it with the endlessly frustrating and ultimately futile task of guarding its water resources against Indian poaching." (Wirsing and Jasparro, 2006). The existing literature on Pakistani view point reveal that the construction of Uri Todiam Dam, Kishanganga Dam, Salal Dam, Wullar barrage, Tulbul Navigational Barrage, Baglihar Dam and some other dams on Pakistani rivers, shows Indian intentions to get control of Pakistani waters, because these dams can make the canal system redundant in Pakistan (Khanzada, 2008).

6. Indo Pak relations and the future of IWT:

India is third after US and China in dam building and has constructed 4365 dams. Also India is considering making 62 more hydroelectric dams on Pakistani rivers, which will enable India to close down two Pakistani rivers, Jhelum and Chenab, hence turning Pakistan barren by 2014. India is also accused of water theft by using Pakistan's share of water through tunnels. In the meantime India is also negotiating a dam on river Kabul with Afghanistan for setting up Kama hydro-electric project which will utilize 0.5 MAF of Pakistani water (Khanzada, 2008). Pakistan is of the view that India is withholding the waters and terms it a violation of the Indus Waters Treaty, while the Indians always come up with the answer that Pakistan's assumption that India is withholding its water is wrong and says that it is the flow of water that has decreased in the respective rivers causing lesser flow of water to Pakistan due to global climate change, which Pakistan calls water theft by India.

Haroon Ur Rashid, a Pakistani columnist, thinks: *"a possible tension between the two nations was feared to erupt on water sharing of the Indus Water."* Pakistan's policy towards Kashmir is deeply influenced by the water factor and it does not seem possible in the long run for Pakistan to change its policy on Kashmir. This blame game has been going on for the last 63 years and has brought no significant progress to any side, especially affecting Pakistan. What is needed now is an urgent resumption of dialogue between the two countries; the dialogue should be aimed particularly at the water dispute and both countries should try to resolve the conflict peacefully as water is the most important necessity on Earth.

The water dispute is indeed fuelling the Islamic extremists who consider India as their prime enemy and have issued warnings to India of dire consequences in case India does not follow the IWT. Danish

Mustafa,[10] a water specialist and geography professor at King's College in London, in his recent interview to the BBC, says that Pakistan exists because of the Indus, the recent horrific floods in Pakistan happened largely because of the poor management and the diversion of the Indus waters because it doesn't have the room to expand or flow, the way it used to flow. He further comments that although dams have their usefulness, river managers in Pakistan should recognise the importance of wetlands to modulate the overflow of flood water.

Pakistan will have to rethink a treaty much stronger than the IWT with India so that it could effectively and efficiently work out its plans for future dams. But again Pakistan faces several problems both at home and abroad to carry out any such projects. At home, the central Government of Pakistan must also take all the smaller provinces in confidence and should address their concerns without any further delay. And India, being an emerging economic power, needs to work on hydro-electric projects but must also listen to Pakistan so that there is no way leading to conflict as both the countries can, in no way, bear the burden of war because of the improvised conditions of the poor people.

But the question that lies in the minds of many is whether the two nuclear states will ever go to war because of the water disputes. Researchers predict that water conflicts may lead to war, but so far both states have shown flexibility and at the moment they indeed need to go beyond the IWT and sign a new agreement benefitting both of them. A war is very unlikely to break out in the near future if India reacts more generously, as so far India has been blamed on most occasions for the steps taken to stop or decrease the flow of water to Pakistan, because the source of all the rivers lies in the Indian territory.

It would be extremely unfair to hold India responsible for the water conflict, as this nation has kept upholding the treaty for more than fifty years, but, however, constant hostility between the two states is overcoming any good work done on behalf of India. The objection of Pakistan on decreased water flow is not only because of water theft but it could be caused by the increase in population of India. New strategies are direly in need of implementation between the two countries to come out of the water crisis mainly because of environmental degradation, global warming, and increasing population. It is time now that both countries set aside all hostilities and think for the betterment of the poor masses.

7. Pakistan: The Problems within:

Pakistan is not only facing regional disputes on waters; rather, it has serious internal or provincial longstanding conflicts. The most prominent one is the Kalabagh dam, which, according to its supporters would address many of the problems of the people of Pakistan; the dam is supported mainly by Punjab. While the nationalist parties of all the other three provinces have showed tough resistance, the nationalists in the Khyber Pakhtunkhwa province argue that its construction would inundate the most fertile areas of the already poor province. They have a very hard stance on the issue and it seems impossible for them to give up the position, as it is a main part of their political manifesto.

A very recent interview by the incumbent Prime Minister of Pakistan sparked immense criticism of his comments where he supported the Kalabagh dam and went to the extent to say that *"the recent floods in Pakistan would have done little harm had Kalabagh Dam been constructed."* The nationalists sent a clear message that no such project would be allowed on their land[11]. The largest province Punjab is accused of stealing 16,000 cusecs of water between Taunsa and Guddu, from 2nd to 4th Feb 2010. The Punjab

---

[10] Dr. Daanish Mustafa: Pakistan floods, why the fertile Indus River is so prone to flooding
http://www.bbc.co.uk/worldservice/news/2010/08/100818_indus_wt_sl.shtml

[11] http://www.dawn.com/wps/wcm/connect/dawn-content-library/dawn/the-newspaper/front-page/19-minister-says-kp-being-ignored-180-hh-12

government claims that system losses are to blame for the water that has disappeared. There are differences among the provinces over the respective share of water under the Indus River System Authority (IRSA) with particular reference to utilizing water.[12]

Now, by looking at the above problems, one can conclude that the way India is enjoying hegemony on the IWT, Pakistan's Punjab province is also doing the same by stealing water from other provinces, using unfair share of water, and making controversial projects, which are being rejected by other provinces. Pakistan must come out with durable solutions to internal issues otherwise with each passing day, the problems are getting severe and can even endanger the very existence of the country.

8. India's Upper Riparian Position and Manipulation of Water:

Pakistan's position is vulnerable because India, as the upper riparian, has a considerable control over the waters through different hydro-projects and dams that they are building on the western rivers, and could use these projects as different tolls, either to stop the waters from flowing to Pakistan or to store the waters and then release them which may cause floods down-stream. Pakistan always complains and accuses India of stopping and stealing water that is Pakistan's share. India's intentions of what Pakistan calls as the "drying up of Pakistan" can be classified into the 'human initiated technological disruptions' category as presented in his work by Mandel (1992). Such disruptions could result in conflicts of severe types because Pakistan being a lower riparian depends solely on the water flow from India, where its cultivable land will turn into barren, if India starts exercising its hegemony over the Indus waters.

Conclusion and Recommendations

After reviewing the available literature regarding the issue, we concluded that there are some glaring evidences, which led the two countries towards severe conflicts, which may turn into full fledge wars. Such wars will not only affect the region but the entire world keeping in view the nuclear power capabilities. Nonetheless, by the applicability of HHF, we sense that there is some sort of cooperation but mostly in the interest of India which is another proof that would lead the two countries from cold to violent conflicts because Pakistan is not ready to accept the hegemonic behaviour of India at any cost. Another reason for this is the addressing of severe intra-national conflicts among the provinces of Pakistan which puts enormous pressure on the central government to negotiate water at the national as well as the international level; however, the HHF failed to take into account this element.

The issue of waters and wars between the two neighbouring countries can be solved if the world community comes forward with the following policy recommendations:

  I. The treaty, which has survived since 1960s, needs to be renegotiated in the present scenario, where the blame game is on its fullest, coupled with climate change, increasing population and prevailing water scarcity in the region.

  II. The issue of Kashmir needs to be solved as per the wishes of Kashmiris according to the 1948 Security Council Resolution by putting pressure on both the contending countries. This will ultimately save the region from the war havoc and will settle down the water dispute between the two historical rivals.

---

[12] The water crisis and its implications, Tuesday, February 16, 2010, The News, Pakistan.

Bibliography:

Abbot, S., (2010) "Water dispute fuels tensions between India and Pakistan". Available from http://www.chinadaily.com.cn/cndy/2010-05/01/content_9799770.htm

Ahmad, T., (2009) "Water disputes between India and Pakistan- A Potential Casus Belli". Available from http://www.henryjacksonsociety.org/stories.asp?id=1230

Alam, U. Z., (1998) "Water rationality: mediating the Indus Waters Treaty". Unpublished PhD thesis. University of Durham. Available from http://www.ppl.nl/bibliographies/water/files/4613.pdf

Alam, U. Z., (2002) "Questioning the water wars rationale: a case study of the Indus Waters Treaty." The Geographical, vol. 168, no. 4, pp. 341-353.

Allan, J. A., (2001) "The Middle East Water Question – Hydropolitics and the Global Economy". I.B.Tauris, London, UK.

Asher, M.G and Srivastava, S., (2003) "India and the Asian Economic Community". Public Policy, pp. 1-24. Available from: http://www.spp.nus.edu.sg/docs/wp/wp41.pdf

Briscoe, J., (2010) "War or peace on the Indus?" Available from: http://www.countercurrents.org/briscoe050410.htm

Barrett, S., (1994) "Conflict And Cooperation In Managing International Water Resources". CSERGE Working Paper. London Business School And Centre For Social And Economic Research On The Global Environment, University College London and University of East Anglia.

Burki, S. J., (2010) "How to avoid a steep fall". The DAWN: Economic and Business. Available from http://www.dawn.com/wps/wcm/connect/dawn-content-library/dawn/inpaper-magazine/ economic-and-business/how-to-avoid-a-steep-fall-230

Elhance, A., P., (1999) "Hydropolitics In The Third World: Conflict And Cooperation In International River Basins". Volume 31, US Institute of Peace Press, 1999, Pages 309.

Fair, C., (2005) "India and Pakistan Engagement: Prospects for Breakthrough or Breakdown?" Available from: http://www.usip.org/files/resources/sr129.pdf

Frey, F., W., (1993) "The political context of conflict and cooperation over international river basins". Water International, Vol. 18(1), pp. 54–68.

Gramsci, A., (1971) "Selections from the prison notebooks of Antonio Gramsci, (edited and translated by Q. Hoare and G. N. Smith), Lawrence and Wishart, London.

Gupta, J., (2010) "China Dialogue: Boiling Point: competition over resources". Available from: http://sustainablesecurity.org/article/boiling-point

Gleditsch, N. P., Wallensteen, P., Eriksson, M., Sollenberg, M., and Håvard Strand, H., (2002) "Armed Conflict 1946 – 2001: A New Dataset". Journal of Peace Research vol. 39, no. 5, 2002, pp. 615–637.

Gleick, P. H., (1993) "Water and Conflict: Fresh Water Resources and International Security", vol. 18, no. 1, pp. 79-112.

Gleick, P.H (2006) "Water Conflict Chronology". Pacific Institute for Studies in Development, Environment and Security CA. Available from http://www.worldwater.org/chronology.html

Hamner, J. and Wolf, A. T. 1998. Patterns in International Water Resource Treaties: The Transboundary Freshwater Dispute Database. Colorado Journal of International Environmental Law and Policy. 1997 Yearbook.

Homer-Dixon, T., (2001) "Environment, Scarcity and Violence". Princeton University Press, Princeton, NJ, USA.

Haug, A. M., (2010) "Water Security in the Sub-Continent: The Implications of the Indus Treaty". The Henry Jackson Society, Project for democratic geopolitics, Available from: http://www.henryjacksonsociety.org/stories.asp?id=1360

Husain, M. Z., (2010) "The Indus Waters Treaty in Light of Climate Change". Transboundary Water Resources Spring 2010. Available from: http://www.ce.utexas.edu/prof/mckinney/ce397/Topics/Indus/Indus_2010.pdf

ICID (2004) "Appropriate Decision-Making particularly for Irrigation, Drainage and Flood Management", Government of India. Available from http://www.icid.org/tf5_paper.pdf

IWT (1960) "Indus Waters Treaty". Available from http://siteresources.worldbank.org/INTSOUTHASIA/Resources/223497-1105737253588/IndusWatersTreaty1960.pdf

Khanzada, I. A., (2008) "Chenab Water Issue: India is leaving a Bad Taste". The Daily Mail Pakistan, Available from http://www.iwmi.cgiar.org/News_Room/pdf/India_is_Leaving.pdf

Lustick, I. S., (2002) "Hegemony and the riddle of nationalism: the dialectics of nationalism and religion in the Middle East. Logos, Vol. 1(3), pp. 18–44.

Lukes, S., (2005[1974]) "Power: A Radical View". 2nd edition. Palgrave MacMillan, Hampshire, UK.

Mandel, R., (1991) "Sources of international river basin disputes" Conflict quarterly 12: 25–56. Available from http://www.lib.unb.ca/Texts/JCS/CQ/vol012_4fall1992/mandel.pdf

Masood, A., (2010) "Reservoirs of conflict". Available from: http://www.cobrapost.com/documents/Reservoirs%20of%20conflict.htm

Mogwai, R., (2009) "India and Pakistan Face Water War: Tulbul Navigation Project may cause conflict". Available from http://www.orato.com/world-affairs/india-pakistanface-water-war

Mushtaq, S., (2010) "Q+A - What's happening in troubled Kashmir?" Reuters, Srinagar, Available from http://in.reuters.com/article/idINIndia-50646920100805

Pearce, F., (2002) "Water War", New Scientist, vol.174, issue 2343, pp.18 Perkovich, G., (2010) "Is India a Major Power?" The Washington Quarterly, Vol.27(1), pp. 129-144 Available from: http://www.twq.com/04winter/docs/04winter_perkovich.pdf

Ranjan, A., (2010) "Water conflicts between India and Pakistan" Available from: http://www.dailytimes.com.pk/default.asp?page=2010\05\31\story_31-5-2010_pg3_4.

Rashid, U. H., (2003) "Possible Indo-Pak tension on Indus water sharing?" The Daily Star. Web Edition. Vol. 4, No. 80. Available from http://www.vakindia.org/pdf/indo-pakwater.pdf

Rehman, H., and Kamal, A., (2005) "Indus Basin River System – Flooding and Flood Mitigation". Ministry of Water and Power, Islamabad, Pakistan. Available from http://www.riversymposium.com/2005/index.php?element

Selby, J., (2007) "Beyond Hydro-Hegemony: Gramsci, the National, and the Trans-National" Paper presented at: Third International Workshop on Hydro-Hegemony, London School of Economics. Available from http://www.soas.ac.uk/waterissues/papers/file39697.pdf

Shamir, U., Kliot, N., and Shlomi, D., (2001) "Institutions for management of transboundary water resources: their nature, characteristics and shortcomings". Water Policy, vol. 3, pp. 229-255.

Sharma, A., and Wright, T., (2010) "India and Pakistan Feud Over Indus Waters: Fight Threatens Peace Talks as Islamabad Requests Arbitration Over New Delhi's Plans for a Hydroelectric Plant". The Wall Street journal, World, Asia NEWS. Available from: http://online.wsj.com/article/SB10001424052702304370304575151591013994592.html

Shlomi, D., (2008) "International Water Treaties: Negotiation and Cooperation Along Transboundary Rivers". Routledge, US.

Sridhar, S., (2005) "The Indus Waters Treaty". Security Research Review: Vol. 1(3). Available from: http://www.bharat-kshak.com/SRR/Volume13/sridhar.html

Sridhar, S., (2008) "The Indus Waters Treaty". Available from: http://www.bharatrakshak.com/SRR/Volume13/sridhar.html

The DAWN, (2010) "Pakistan sees 4pc GDP growth in 2010-11" Available from http://www.dawn.com/wps/wcm/connect/dawn-content-library/dawn/thenewspaper/business/pakistan-sees-4pc-gdp-growth-in-201011-740

The BBC (2005) "Pakistan team views Kashmir dam" Available from http://news.bbc.co.uk/1/hi/world/south_asia/4712303.stm

The BBC (2010) "In Depth: The future of Kashmir". Kashmir flashpoint. Available from: http://news.bbc.co.uk/1/shared/spl/hi/south_asia/03/kashmir_future/html/default.stm

Tajammal, N., (2010) "Indus Waters Treaty 1960. India Shows Complete Disrespect to International Commitments". Available from http://pakistanpal.blogspot.com/2010/04/indus-water-treaty-1960.html

United Nations (1978) "Register of international rivers", Water Supply Management, 2(1) (New York, Pergamon Press).

United Nations, (2006) "Regional Cooperation Between Countries In The Management Of Shared Water Resources: Case Studies Of Some Countries In The ESCWA Region". United Nations, New York, E/ESCWA/SDPD/2005/15. Available from: http://www.escwa.un.org/information/publications/edit/upload/sdpd-05-15.pdf

UN-Water, (2008) "Transboundary Waters: Sharing Benefits, Sharing Responsibilities". Thematic Paper, = Water for Life' 2005-2015 (UN-IDfA), Zaragoza, Spain. Available from http://www.unwater.org/downloads/UNW_TRANSBOUNDARY.pdf

Verghese, B. G., (2005) "Political Fuss over the Indus: India's Rights are set out in the Treaty," The Tribune (Chandigarh). Available from http://www.bgverghese.com/Indus.htm

Waslekar, S., (2005) "The final settlement: restructuring India-Pakistan relations". International Centre for Peace Initiatives and Strategic Foresight Group. Available from: http://www.strategicforesight.com/sfgnews_123.htm

Wescoat JR, J. L., Halvorson, S. J., Mustafa, D., (2010) "Water Management in the Indus Basin of Pakistan: A Half-century Perspective", International Journal of Water Resources Development, Volume 16, Issue 3 September 2000, pages 391 – 406.

Wolf, A. T., and Dinar, A., (1994) "Economic Potential and Political Considerations of Regional Water Trade: The Western Middle East Example", Resource and Energy Economics, vol. 16 (1994), pp. 335-356.

Wolf, A. T., Natharius, J.A Danielson, J.J Ward, B.S Pender, J.K (1999) "International River Basins of the World" International Journal of Water Resources Development, Volume 15, Issue 4, pages 387 –427

Wirsing, R.G and Jasparro, C., (2006) "Spotlight on Indus River Diplomacy: India, Pakistan, and the Baglihar Dam Dispute". Asia-Pacific Center for Security Studies. Available from: http://www.apcss.org/Publications/APSSS/IndusRiverDiplomacy.Wirsing.Jasparro.pdf

Wolf, A.T (1998) "Conflict and cooperation along international waterways". Water Policy. Vol. 1 #2, pp. 251-265.

Wolf, A. T., (1995) "The Asian Water Forum: Summary Report: Global Environmental Change". Human and Policy Dimensions. Vol. 5 (2).

Yoffe, S. B., Wolf, A. T., and Giordano, M., (2001) "Conflict and Cooperation over International Freshwater Resources: Indicators and Findings of the Basins at Risk". Journal of American Water Resources Association, Vol. 39(5), pp.1109–1126.

Zeitoun, M and Warner, J.F (2006) "Hydro-hegemony – a framework for analysis of trans-boundary water conflicts." Water Policy, vol. 8, pp. 435-460.

Zeitoun, M., and Warner, J. F., (2008) "International relations theory and water do mix: A response to Furlong's troubled waters, hydro- hegemony and international water relations", Political Geography, vol. 27, pp. 802-810.

Zeitoun, M., and Woodhouse, M., (2008) "Hydro-hegemony and international water law: grappling with the gaps of power and law", Water, vol. 2, pp. 103-119.

Zeitoun, M and Allan, J.A (2008) "Applying hegemony and power theory to transboundary water analysis." Water Policy, vol. 2, pp. 3-12.

APPENDICES

PART ONE

APP - 1

Water Wager: Kishanganga Dam And Indus Water Treaty

By Athar Parvaiz, 23 March 2011)
(China Dialogue, Third Pole Project),

India and Pakistan are once again at loggerheads over the issue of water-sharing. Pakistan is raising strong objections to India's construction of a hydropower project on the Neelum River – known as Kishanganga in India – a tributary of the Jhelum in the flashpoint territory of Kashmir. While the dispute is only the latest in a long series of such scraps, it is the first to be referred to international arbitration under the 50-year-old Indus Water Treaty (IWT), marking an escalation in the race to take control of the Indus River.

After bilateral negotiations collapsed in April last year, Pakistan took the case over the 330-megawatt Kishanganga dam to the International Court of Arbitration on the premise that India had violated the World Bank-mediated IWT, which provides a mechanism for resolution of disputes over waters originating from the Indus basin. Under the 1960 treaty, the waters of the eastern rivers of the Indus basin – Sutlej, Beas and Ravi – are allocated to India, while Pakistan has unrestricted use of the western rivers - Indus, Jhelum and Chenab.

The first meeting of the Court of Arbitration was held in January, and Islamabad is due to submit its case in April this year. But as the case drags on, India is quietly pushing ahead with dam construction, intensifying concerns in Pakistan that its government is wasting precious time in preparing its case. Recent Pakistani media reports have called for an immediate moratorium on Indian hydropower projects. The Kishanganga dispute is expected to feature prominently in the Pakistan-India secretary-level talks in New Delhi at the end of March.

This is the first case referred to international arbitration under the provisions of the IWT. Despite persistent hostilities, India and Pakistan have managed to uphold the treaty for decades. Yet, from time to time, the two south-Asian neighbours have found themselves at odds over hydropower projects, as both countries' energy and irrigation needs continue to grow.

Pakistan has raised objections to a number of controversial projects undertaken by India in Kashmir in the past, including the Baglihar project on the Chenab River and the Wullar Barrage on the Jhelum River. But the Kishanganga dispute assumes a greater significance because Pakistan is also vying to construct its own project – the Neelum-Jhelum hydro scheme – on the Pakistani side of the Neelum River. The IWT states that the country that completes its project first will secure priority rights to the river.

Adding to tensions, the Neelum River flows across the militarised Line of Control that separates the Indian and Pakistani administered parts of Jammu and Kashmir and which has witnessed the 1947-war between these two south Asian neighbours and a number of military fire-exchanges since.

The dispute over the Kishanganga project itself centres on the diversion of water from one tributary of the Indus River to another. Pakistan said this violates the IWT, while India argues the diversion is well within treaty provisions. India maintains that it will only divert the Neelum to join the Jhelum River, which also flows through Pakistan – and that therefore the water will ultimately reach Pakistan anyway.

However, Pakistan has raised strong objections, saying the diversion will turn the country's Neelum Valley into a desert. "Due to the construction of the Kishanganga project, water will be diverted from the Neelum River and a 90-kilometre long stretch of the river, that 600,000 people depend on for agriculture and fisheries, will dry up," said Arshad Abbasi, a water and power consultant, with the Sustainable Development Policy Institute (SDPI) in Islamabad.

Pakistani experts also argue that the reduced flow of the Neelum River will decrease the power generation capability of Pakistan's proposed 969-megawatt Neelum-Jhelum hydropower project by more than 20%.

Last year's floods in Pakistan forced it to halt construction of the Neelum-Jhelum project, already delayed by problems over land acquisition and failure to construct a bridge. India, on the other hand, has speeded up work on the strategically important Kishanganga project in order to finish it by 2014, well ahead of the 2016 deadline. Pakistan plans to complete the Neelum-Jhelum project by 2015.

India first developed plans for the 303-megawatt Kishanganga project in 1984, but failed to build it for a long time. Egged on by Pakistan's progress on the construction of the Neelum-Jhelum project on the other side of Line of Control, India made frantic efforts to revive the 18-year-old plan in 2008. "This project is of strategic importance to India…we have to move heaven and earth to ensure the earliest commissioning of the project," the then minister of state for power, Jairam Ramesh, told a press conference in New Delhi in 2008.

Two years later, India has reason to feel satisfied, with the Kishanganga project now in full-swing. "We have been working constantly on all fronts," said OP Thakur, general manager of the project. Arshad Abassi of Islamabad's SDPI backed up this view: "The project is far ahead of Pakistan's Neelum-Jhelum hydropower project. Technically, whoever builds first establishes the right to the river. Due to the negligence of Pakistan's water and power ministry, it is likely that we will lose the case."

Pakistan is not the only party that feels aggrieved. Kashmiri people feel "deprived" by the fact India and Pakistan use their water resources without allowing local people the benefits they deserve. "They don't share the profits and the resources generated by these rivers – which actually belong to the people of Jammu and Kashmir – with the Jammu and Kashmir state, except for the 12% royalty on power that it gets," said a Kashmiri resident, Arshad Ahmad.

Shakeel Qalandhar, president of the Kashmir Industries and Commerce Federation, said that Kashmir's economy would have greatly progressed, but for the 1960 treaty. "These three main rivers have the potential to generate 30,000 megawatts of hydropower, but we are currently generating just over 500 megawatts in the state sector and 1,600 megawatts in the central sector (and we are paying for the electricity from the central sector). This is less than 2,000 megawatts overall, whereas we require 2,500 megawatts of electricity for our own consumption – domestic and industrial."

According to Qalandhar, the Jammu and Kashmir State Power Department purchases power worth millions of dollars (from the National Hydroelectric Power Corporation) every year. "It is a tragedy that despite the potential to generate 30,000 megawatts of power, 25% of our population has no access to electricity and the remaining 75% gets only episodic electricity which is often cut off for hours in harsh winters."

In the Gurez Valley, where India is constructing the Kishanganga project, 1,300 people will be displaced. "I have been trying very hard to convince the government that they should provide displaced people with proper compensation for their land that will be submerged. But the government is adamant on giving just a paltry sum," said Nazir Gurazi, Gurez constituency member of the Jammu & Kashmir State Legislative Assembly.

"In Gurez valley, the land isn't worth much and these poor people won't be able to buy land elsewhere with the compensation they are getting. You also have to consider the fact that you are uprooting them from their culture", he added. He hopes that the government will listen to reason.

APP – 2

WANTED: BRIDGES OVER TROUBLED WATERS

Joy Deep Gupta, 8 September 2011

Editor's note: Water has always been a flash point between India and Pakistan. The two neighbours compete over use of the waters of the Indus River, the backbone of agriculture and industry in both states. As the Indian subcontinent was parted in 1947 to create the new state of Pakistan, the rivers were partitioned in 1960 through the Indus Waters Treaty (IWT). Five decades on, the radically altered landscape of Asia's water resources has put the agreement at risk.

Both India and Pakistan face a deepening water crisis, driven by population growth, industrial demand and gross mismanagement of water resources. Climate change has added fuel to the flames. Melting Himalayan glaciers are projected to reduce the flow of water in the Indus Basin, particularly for Pakistan, which is now calling for an urgent revision of the treaty. As national policymakers increasingly couch water resources in terms of national security, hard battle lines have been drawn.

In an attempt to bridge the polarised debate, third pole presents two more nuanced perspectives. Indian journalist Joydeep Gupta (below) and Pakistani academic Maaz Gardezi each offer a tentative way forward towards a more constructive cross-boundary dialogue over water resources, one that looks beyond national security and takes a more holistic ecological perspective.

As Pakistan went to the Court of Arbitration in The Hague once again in mid-August 2011, seeking an order for India to put on hold construction of the Kishanganga dam until the final decision of the court, the overwhelming response among Indian policymakers was: "Oh, not again."

The project on the Jhelum River, one of the main tributaries of the Indus, has been opposed by Pakistan since it got off the drawing board. But India has steadfastly maintained that the run-of-the-river project follows the 1960 Indus Waters Treaty between the two countries to the letter. Just about everybody in India feels that the treaty is the best basis for apportioning the waters of the giant Indus river basin, that India as the upper riparian country has stuck to the treaty through war and peace, and that Indians are unfairly blamed for Pakistan's water woes to cover up the inefficiency or worse of the water policymakers in Pakistan.

Given the near-unanimity of this view in India, and the near-constant rhetoric in Pakistan that "India is stealing our waters", there is very little space for any level-headed, rational and scientific conversation on the subject. The trust deficit is so high – especially in India since many of the country's terrorist attacks over the last three decades have been traced back to Pakistan – that anybody advocating a dialogue would be lucky not to be dubbed a spy. Anyway, Indian officials firmly hold, there is nothing to talk about: there is a treaty, India is sticking to it, that's the end of the matter. And if it is not, the officials in New Delhi add, both governments have a permanent Indus Water Commission that is meant to sort out all issues, so why is there any need for anybody else to get involved?

Expectedly, this line of argument does not go down well at all in a water-stressed country like Pakistan, especially when the average Pakistani sees in the media that India is building structures upstream that can potentially choke off a part of the river flow. Knowing the extent to which it is under international scrutiny, India has not and is unlikely to build any structure that will reduce by even one cubic metre the volume of water it is supposed to supply to Pakistan under the treaty. But thanks to the trust deficit, few Pakistanis feel reassured.

Recent projects like the Kishanganga dam have no doubt added to the worry in Pakistan, though Indians are going blue in the face assuring the Pakistanis that the hydroelectricity project will not hold back any water at all, and that the project is being carried out as per the 1960 treaty. Indian planners point out that they cannot really go any further and scrap the projects altogether – the parts of Indian-administered Kashmir through which the Indus and its western tributaries flow are chronically starved of electricity, and there are few economically viable options to meet the need other than hydropower.

It looks to be a situation where only open dialogue between India and Pakistan at every level – government, media, civil society – can clear the air. The chances of such a dialogue do not seem high at the moment, but it is nonetheless vital to keep striving for this. It is vital not only to build trust, but also because now there are two factors in the water-sharing puzzle that were not taken into account by the Indus Waters Treaty: deforestation and climate change.

The Indus and its main tributaries rise in the Tibet Autonomous Region (TAR) of China, and flow through India on their way to Pakistan and then the Arabian Sea. When the Indus Waters Treaty was signed in 1960, the volume of water was apportioned between India and Pakistan on the basis of the assumption that the flow of the water in the rivers would remain constant. This assumption is now in question due to these two factors.

While there are few official reports about the extent of deforestation in western TAR through which these rivers flow, there is plenty of anecdotal evidence that the already-sparse tree cover of the Tibetan Plateau is being rapidly denuded. Indian hydrologists have reported an increase in the silt load in the rivers as a result. They are expecting an effect on the water flow, but are uncertain of what the effect would be. The same goes for the effects of climate change. While some of the large glaciers of the Karakoram Range that feed these rivers are expanding, most of the glaciers in the western Himalayas – including the Karakoram Range – are receding due to global warming. The net effect on water flow is unpredictable, but likely to be negative, the hydrologists say.

So there is a treaty that apportions a certain amount of water between India and Pakistan. What happens to the treaty if that amount is no longer certain? How will the two countries amend the treaty – for which it does have a provision – for a fair water-sharing arrangement in the future? It requires a cool-headed, civilised dialogue to even start to answer this question. Then it requires a lot of scientific research in both countries to reduce uncertainties in the water flow projections. And it definitely requires close cooperation from the authorities in China, where the rivers originate.

Anybody advocating these steps would be considered dangerously naïve by most people in India and Pakistan today. But not to take these steps may prove even more naïve in the long run.

APP – 3

CLIMATE CHANGE: MELTING GLACIERS BRING ENERGY UNCERTAINTY

Javaid Laghari, 30 October 2013 /15 November 2013 (Nature News & comment,)

Running 2,000 kilometres from east to west and comprising more than 60,000 square kilometres of ice, the Hindu Kush–Karakoram–Himalayan glaciers are a source of water for the quarter of the global population that lives in south Asia. Glaciers are natural stores and regulators of water supply to rivers, which, in turn, provide water for domestic and industrial consumption, energy generation and irrigation.

Ice cover is decreasing in this region, as for most glaciers in the world, as a result of global warming. Between 2003 and 2009, Himalayan glaciers lost an estimated 174 gigatonnes of water, and contributed to catastrophic floods of the Indus, Ganges and Brahmaputra rivers. Pollution is accelerating the melt. An 'Asian brown cloud', formed from the 2 million tonnes of soot and dark particles released into the atmosphere every year, mostly from India and China, warms the air and surface ice.

Seasonal meltwater serves as the main source of power for an increasing number of hydroelectric dams on the rivers served by the glaciers. But hydropower faces a difficult future in south Asia because of climatic, environmental and politico-economic factors. The region is starved of energy, and power shortages of up to 20 hours a day are stunting development. Importing oil and gas from the Gulf, Iran or Tajikistan is expensive or politically difficult. So countries are turning to indigenous hydroelectric power, and to other renewable energies, such as solar and wind, for cheap, sustainable energy.

Hydroelectric power must play a part in south Asia's low-carbon energy future. But to be effective, governments around the Himalayas need to work together to measure and model glacier retreat, changing river flows and their impact on hydroelectric power generation. Political obstacles to dam construction and watershed management must also be overcome.

Glacial retreat

Glaciers feed thousands of miles of rivers in Pakistan. The largest, the river Indus, depends on glacial waters for up to half of its flow. But near the river's source, in mountains in the Indian-administered state of Jammu and Kashmir, the glaciers are thinning at an alarming rate of 0.7 metres per year. The Ganges and Brahmaputra rivers in India and Bangladesh are similarly threatened by glacial melting in the regions of their headwaters.

Modelling of glacier retreat in the Himalayas is hindered by sparse data. Field, satellite and weather records confirm that 9% of the ice area present in the early 1970s had disappeared by the early 2000s. But there has been no comprehensive assessment of current regional mass balance — the difference between the accumulation of ice and its loss.

An increased seasonal melt coupled with rains will bring more intense floods, such as those in 2010, caused by excessive monsoon rains that inundated one-fifth of Pakistan's land area for five weeks, killing 2,000 people and costing tens of billions of dollars in damage and economic impact. Sea level is rising at around 3.5 millimetres per year and the frequency of tropical cyclones is predicted to increase as a result of global warming. Because rain, rather than snow, falls on mountains in spring, river flows will peak before the main growing season. Summers will increasingly see dry streams, withered and abandoned crops, dead fish and low groundwater levels.

With the amount of electricity generated varying with the flow, the changing river patterns in south Asia will disrupt hydropower production. A 1% reduction in stream flow can reduce electricity output by roughly 3%. Generation rates will be high in the spring but lower in the summer, when energy is most needed for cooling. Greater uncertainty in the reliability of hydroelectricity will heighten disputes between the countries through which the rivers flow.

Pakistan is currently able to generate 6,700 megawatts (MW) from hydropower on Himalayan rivers, about 37% of the country's total electric-generation capacity. It has the potential to increase this to more than 25,000 MW. India has a generation capacity of around 28,000 MW (14%) from hydropower from rivers fed by the Himalayan glaciers and rainwater, and has similar plans for expansion. Nepal and Bhutan currently have 600 MW and 1,500 MW capacity from hydropower, respectively, but have the potential for much more. In 2009, India and Bhutan signed a protocol in which India will develop 10,000 MW of hydroelectric-generation capacity in Bhutan by 2020 and import surplus power into India.

For example, the proposed construction of the Kalabagh Dam on the Indus in Pakistan's Khyber Pakhtunkhwa province, which would generate more than 3,600 MW and store more than 8 trillion litres of water, has caused concern in several provinces for more than 30 years. Downstream, the Sindh province is concerned that its share of the Indus water will be cut as water stored by the dam upstream goes to irrigate farmlands in Punjab and Khyber Pakhtunkhwa. The coastal mangrove forests of Sindh could become saline deserts without the constant flow of water from the Indus to prevent seawater from encroaching. Khyber Pakhtunkhwa's concern is that large areas of the 1,700 square kilometres of Nowshera District, with a population of more than 1.4 million, would be submerged, and a wider area would suffer from waterlogging and increasing salinity, as has occurred since the building of the Tarbela Dam in the same region.

Regional action

India and Pakistan have been in dispute over India's plans to build 60 dams on the river Chenab in Jammu and Kashmir since the first, the Baglihar Dam, was completed in 2008. Pakistan is concerned that India might block off rivers feeding the Chenab — which flows through Pakistan downstream — especially in a time of war. However, India did not revoke the Indus Waters Treaty, signed with Pakistan in 1960, during any of the three subsequent Indo–Pakistani wars.

As the Himalayan glaciers melt, the lack of data for predicting how river flows will change in response is of great concern. South Asian countries urgently need to initiate joint funding and strategies, in collaboration with international, environmental and development agencies, to allow research, data collection, evaluation and monitoring of glacial and climate change to take place.

Himalayan governments and scientists need a strategy for mapping and monitoring the glaciers and deriving mass changes. Academic and scientific communities need to collaborate in research across national borders, and political leaders need to include glacier melting and the future of hydroelectric power generation in their dialogues.

The regional goal should be to maintain stability of flow by taking measures to limit black-carbon emissions, control global warming, slow glacial melting and maintain hydropower generation once its peak is reached, while simultaneously pursuing other clean-energy options, such as wind and solar, for future growth.

Modelling the changing river flows caused by glacial melting and climate change, and their impact on flooding and on power generation must begin immediately so that the future of hydroelectric power in south Asia is safeguarded.

APP – 4

WAR OVER WATER

William Wheeler, The Quietus, 27 July, 2009

Through two wars and a half-century of suspicion and resentment, the Indus Waters Treaty has governed the sharing of a strategic river between the bitter nuclear rivals eager to control and to profit from it. But will India and Pakistan's treaty survive the emerging water crisis?

Halfway between Islamabad and Peshawar, the Indus River dips beneath the smooth six-lane blacktop of Pakistan's National Highway. One day last month, I stood on the shoulder and watched the river ripple beneath the bridge. It was an olive ribbon half as wide as the riverbed, where standing puddles glinted in the afternoon sun. It looked like a creek. Or a dying river.

The Indus (the name comes from the Sanskrit for "river") is an ecological icon of the subcontinent that bears its name. Like all great rivers, it shaped the history of the ancient civilizations that appeared along its banks. Over the last century, it has grown an exoskeleton: a sprawling system of canals that has expanded into what is now the world's largest irrigation basin fed by a single river. It is a big job that's taken a heavy toll. Today, hundreds of miles downstream, the river, deprived of runoff from receding glaciers and choked by upstream diversions, no longer reaches the sea. And the sea has pushed back, intruding into the mainland, destroying millions of acres of crops and causing the evacuation of whole towns. It is a parable of human demand and its limitations.

Inevitably, the consequences are political. The river's flow has always been a source of tension between India and Pakistan, both of whom rely on it to generate hydroelectric power and to irrigate their agricultural heartland, and it springs from the heart of their most bitter dispute. The headwaters of the Indus and its tributaries flow south and west from Himalayan Kashmir, watering the rich Punjabi farmland on either side of the border, and into Pakistan where they merge and continue together toward the Arabian Sea. On a map, the waters look like a forked bolt of lightning, or a claw that reaches across a volatile divide. In 1947, the partitioning of India and Pakistan divided the Indus basin, and the river became a potential source of conflict. In the six decades since, the river system has been a cauldron of tensions that have inevitably increased as the world became warmer and more populous. But for nearly as long, a unique accord, the Indus Waters Treaty, has, if not kept the peace, at least restrained the conflict.

"The Indus treaty is one of the chapters that is taught in all universities when you talk about conflict and cooperation," says Kishor Uprety, a senior World Bank lawyer who has spent his career working on development and legal issues about rivers. It's a sign of the treaty's success, he argues, that India and Pakistan have only fought two wars since it was signed.

"Without a treaty," he says, "there would have been five or six wars between them." Today, both countries are plagued by water stress–strained by demand from booming populations and increased competition for the Indus's dwindling resources. Against the river's fickle currents, dams and large reservoirs offer a measure of control, allowing each country to produce desperately needed food and energy: The Indus's waters are a critical outlet in the quest for power to fuel India's 8-percent annual growth rate, and the water lifeline on which

Pakistan's agriculture-based economy relies, even amid the turmoil of fighting that has displaced some two million people there in recent months. And while the seven major river basins in South Asia, which are home to a quarter of the world's population, are all vulnerable to the unpredictable effects of climate change, the Indus's flow is uniquely dependent–to a startlingly unclear extent–on the seasonal runoff from rapidly shrinking Himalayan glaciers. Taken together, the incalculable impact of these factors raises questions about the future of the Indus, and the stakes for the rivals building new dams to harness its power.

"There is insufficient data to say what will happen to the Indus," says David Grey, the World Bank's senior water advisor in South Asia. "But we all have very nasty fears that the flows of the Indus could be severely, severely affected by glacier melt as a consequence of climate change," and reduced by perhaps as much as 50 percent. "Now what does that mean to a population that lives in a desert [where], without the river, there would be no life? I don't know the answer to that question," he says. "But we need to be concerned about that. Deeply, deeply concerned."

Amid tensions over a spate of Indian dams being built upstream in Kashmir, and water crisesed estabilizing both countries from within, will the region's fragile politics survive the environmental crises? Facing $4.5 billion in annual losses from environmental disaster, Pakistan formed a task force on climate change last year to investigate global warming's potential impact on the nation. The task force, says one of its cochairmen, the 76-year-old Shamsul Mulk, is now "aiming at developing the capacity to at least be able to give some estimates" of the coming change in its water patterns. "We are not the culprits of climate change–you are the culprit," he tells me, meaning the western world, over a tea tray in an office parlor in a leafy residential neighborhood of Islamabad. "And you have done nothing about it."

If Mulk is unnerved by the lack of data it is because he has spent his career tending to Pakistan's delicate hydrology, and he understands its narrow margins. His was a generation of engineers that brought a fledgling, arid nation through its environmentally challenged infancy. He also served as director at Mangla, one of the country's largest dams, which displaced more than 100,000 Kashmiri villagers when it was built under the terms of the Indus treaty. There is disagreement over the factors behind the Indus's decline–reduced glacial runoff, the heavy silt erosion typical of young mountains, and Pakistan's 6WN upstream diversions. "It's very hard to prove any causation," says Michael Kugelman, a South Asia expert at the Woodrow Wilson International Center for Scholars, "but across many different sectors of Pakistani society, there is a belief that India is responsible for water scarcity, including the fact the rivers are disappearing."

When I ask Mulk why his country is so suspicious of its upstream neighbor, he tells me a story. In the months before partition, Pakistani officials had been worried that India might turn the tap on the British-built canals under its control. "Pakistan was misled by their apparently very sincere statements. 'How could a brother stop water to a brother?' These were their exact words," Mulk tells me. On April 1, 1948, India shut the canal gates and cut off water. About 1.7 million acres of productive land went out of cultivation, he goes on, and with it almost as many jobs. India denies it was a strategic calculation, but the incident is a constant reminder in Pakistan of its vulnerability should India decide to starve or flood it–either as an act of war, or an act of espionage, or even as reckless disregard to undermine its posture in diplomatic negotiations.

Tensions were high at that time. The countries had already fought over the Muslim-majority state of Kashmir, stoking fears in diplomatic circles that a struggle for the Indus could provoke a series of intractable wars. An American named David Lilienthal traveled the region in 1951, and soon took up a role negotiating the dispute. A former head of the Tennessee Valley Authority, Lilienthal envisioned a shared management of the river basin that would rely on cooperation between technocrats, which he hoped might transcend the political problems and possibly even lead to a Kashmir settlement.

It was an engineer's solution, and was soon thwarted by politics. Only after nine frenzied years of debate, and under the firm hand of the World Bank, did a solution emerge: India would get control of the three tributaries that flow through Kashmir; Pakistan would get the Indus and the two western tributaries. There has been resentment in both countries ever since–Indians unhappy with Pakistan's 75-percent allocation of the waters and Pakistanis upset because 90 percent of the irrigated land was in India's territory. Now silt from the natural erosion of the Himalayas is clogging up Pakistan's canal system, which delivers water to other parts of the country, and there is a food shortage in many areas of Pakistan. As Mulk looks to worsening food and energy crises, he sees large dams as a necessary part of the solution. Which means the Indus. Which means that the treaty that safeguards Pakistan's interest must be honored, especially if the river falters as the planet warms.

But that will mean a renewed commitment to the spirit of the treaty, and the sacrifice it requires. "Even between a husband and a wife, as long as there is a sustained mutuality of benefits, that relationship will remain," Mulk says. "The moment it is not, then that relationship has a problem."

"We have learned to share affluence. But sharing poverty is not so easy." Mulk believes the compact should be guarded jealously: It allows for Indian hydroelectric projects upstream on Pakistan's tributaries, he concedes, but those provisions "have to be interpreted" not to allow projects that store too much water, which could then be withheld during the lean winters or crucial agricultural phases. Some Indians consider Pakistan's myriad objections to be baseless saber-rattling.

But to learn about why the country's hydro projects in Kashmir were so important, and whether Pakistan had reason to fear them, I spoke with Ashok Jaitly, former chief secretary of Jammu and Kashmir (the Indian-administered area of Kashmir) who now works for the Energy and Resources Institute in New Delhi. He called Pakistani objections "a delaying tactic."

"Every time we take up a project on any of the rivers," he says, "Pakistan objects. That's almost a given policy and we expect that." He says that India's dams upstream on Pakistan's rivers are all, in accordance with the treaty, "run of the river" dams, which use the flow of water to generate power, then release it again. "It's not reducing the flow of the water," he says. "But, yes, you do manage water for hydro-generation and therefore there is a change in the timing of the flow, which should be-acceptable."

He continues, "They are always free to look at the design and the structures and express their views on it. But at the end of the day, we also have a right to the water. We are not denying them their right." But Pakistan doesn't trust its agricultural lifeblood to Indian hands. For most of its xistence, the treaty's arbitration clause remained untried; then Pakistan, concerned about the impact of an Indian dam called Baglihar, being built upstream, invoked the measure of last resort and a neutral expert was appointed to mediate in 2005. India kept building and, two years later, the arbitrator ruled that modifications should be made to accommodate both sides. The Baglihar episode proved, says the World Bank's David Grey, that "the treaty worked–both parties accepted the ruling, and then proceeded accordingly."

But the controversy didn't end there. When India filled the dam last October, Pakistan says its water share was halved, threatening hundreds of canals, and millions of acres of crops. The Pakistani press was alive with claims of "hydrological warfare" and predictions – as well as threats of – a water war going nuclear. For some Pakistanis, the episode confirmed India's designs "to deprive Pakistan of water and render it into a desert," as an op-ed in Pakistan's Nation newspaper recently articulated it. For others, it is a reminder of their downstream susceptibility to Indian negligence or malfeasance, even as new Indian dams are being built with greater potential to disrupt Pakistani crop cycles and hydropower generation downstream.

Jaitly argues that Pakistan's objections came late in the game, and that India's project was allowed to go forward with some modifications. But John Briscoe, a former senior water advisor at the World Bank, says Indian authorities were "not fully forthcoming on either inspections or information." To him, the issues with the Baglihar dam established a worrisome precedent–to build first and inform later: that Indian authorities, in their quest to meet pressing needs, will continue to ride roughshod over Pakistani objections, provoking a dangerous feedback loop of intransigence on both sides. Until the Mumbai attacks overshadowed it last November, the dispute over planned dams with environmentally questionable impacts became the leading threat to improving relations between the countries. But the focus on big dams, says Jaitly, is part of a mentality that obscures the need to manage demand with conservation, water tariffs, and an end to destructive but politically popular practices in both countries.

"In many cases we are not doing the right things," Jaitly says. "But their policies are as bad as ours. Maybe even worse." Pakistan is too dependent on an agriculture-based economy and is plagued by inefficiency and mismanagement, he says, pointing to major diversions of rivers within Pakistan that benefit the elite upstream land barons that have triggered unrest in the country's downstream provinces. "They still have a very feudal land structure, so their water management is that much more inefficient than ours," he says.

He acknowledges that Pakistan faces the threat that Indian dams could be used to turn off the water – theoretically, at least. "If somebody on this side of the border turns off water and creates a scarcity or suddenly opens it and floods downstream, it would be so obvious," says Jaitly. "Nobody's going to be that idiotic, unless it's an act of war–which is of course a totally different ball game. But it hasn't been done so far. And hopefully it won't be done."

But life downstream is less certain. Tariq Hassan, Harvard Law School Graduate), calls the water debate "one of the most strategic issues facing the subcontinent. If there is a war here in the future," he tells me, "it will be over water."

Hassan came by his wariness naturally. His father, Sheikh Ahmad Hassan, a junior member of Pakistan's negotiating team during the debate that formed the Indus treaty, would later became the country's secretary of irrigation and power. He was an outspoken critic of the treaty for what he saw as a surrender of the eastern tributaries. ("President Ayub Khan threatened him with treason if he didn't stop talking about it," Tariq says. "My brother swears he's seen the actual letter.") The salient lesson he learned from his father: No country gives away its water rights.

The lesson came back to him during the Baglihar debate, in which Tariq Hassan played a role as an advisor to Pakistan's finance minister. Hassan says he argued that Pakistan should negotiate the dispute itself without invoking the arbitration clause, because, he figured, by the time the ruling was made, India would already have finished construction (which it did). Hassan feared that, no matter what the arbitrator believed was fair, he wouldn't rule that India should unbuild its dam. The problem, he says, is that, rather than distribute the scarcity between both parties – as would have happened in a joint-management system – the treaty made Pakistan dependent on Indian goodwill. "At the end of the day," he asks, "who's monitoring the tap? We've already lost three rivers, and it depends on how long they want to behave if we will lose the others. The treaty will hold until it becomes unbearable, and then there will be a water war. Of course," he adds, "the treaty will still be intact."

Kishor Uprety, the World Bank lawyer, says he is confident the treaty will survive. "History has told us that the Indus treaty was designed the right way. Pakistan has lost some but gained some. India has lost some and gained some. Both countries are winning," he says. It's a cautious enthusiasm shared by several of his colleagues at the World Bank, which is the treaty's guarantor and is still involved in the negotiations. But behind that optimism is the reality that "history" will be less applicable as the environment changes. And the World Bank no longer has the same influence it did when the nations were young and the politics less involved.

More relevant than whether the treaty survives is whether each side feels it is winning more than it would lose. This is a delicate balancing act that depends as much on the spirit as the letter of the law. And it will face serious pressures from the combined effect of India's planned projects, according to John Briscoe. "In the case of Baglihar," he says, "had the decision gone against India, who had already basically built the dam, there would unquestionably have been calls to abrogate the treaty." He believes that both sides are dragging their feet, creating a conflict that jeopardizes the fragile peace the treaty sustains. "I believe it will come crashing into conflict sooner rather than later," he says.

The treaty, like the river, connects both countries in a fragile political ecology. While it has not settled the Kashmir dispute, or prevented war, it represents the single thread between the countries that has never been cut, its commissioners meeting and paying their dues and preserving the singular line of communication between the nations that has remained open through wars and public calls to abrogate it.

A serious challenge will be how each country manages its resources–within and across the boundaries, and considering the wounded history between them. As a lawyer, Kishor Uprety takes heart from the treaty's potential to resolve both countries' differences. "But one has to understand," he cautions, that a treaty is "first and foremost a political instrument, and politicians will ultimately be responsible for either respecting it or disrespecting it. The future is absolutely uncertain. "Even when you build a dam," he says, "it has an age. Even a dam breaks."

APP – 5

INDIA RE-THINKING INDUS WATER TREATY

Khalid Chandyo, 27 August, 2014
Islamabad Policy Research Institute

Introduction

"Many of the wars of the 20th century were about oil, but wars of the 21st century will be over water", said Dr. Isamil Serageldin, former Vice President of the World Bank. Water is surpassing oil as the world's scarcest critical resource as water has no substitute. There's an increasing feeling in the world that everyone has a basic right to a minimum 13 gallons of water a day for basic human health. Today, the world stands divided between water haves and have-nots and Pakistan is facing critical water issues. Water management and distribution has always been an important but cumbersome process in Pakistan being a semi-arid country and its economy based mainly on agriculture and related industry.

The positive thing is that Pakistan has the largest contiguous supply-based canal irrigation system in the world. In Pakistan, the muddy plains of the Indus basin cover approximately 25 percent of the land area of Pakistan. Whereas in India, the basin includes only 9.8 percent of the total geographical area of the country. On the negative side, the aqua environment of Pakistan has been shrinking since last two decades, as the World Bank had put the country in the category of "water-stressed" in 2000. The availability of water in Pakistan has been declining over the past few decades from 5000 cubic meters per capita 60 years ago to 1200 cubic meters per capita in 2010.

Unfortunately, Pakistan's water problem is not new, as soon after independence, the country faced water problems due to blockage of its water in canals by India. Political boundary between Pakistan and India was drawn right across the Indus Basin making the country the lower riparian to India. The headwaters went to the Indian side leaving Pakistan vulnerable as India got the physical capacity to cut-off vital irrigation water. Adding insult to injury, India started demanding proprietary rights on the water of Punjab Rivers, denying Pakistan its due share as the lower riparian.

Indus Water Treaty (IWT) 1960

Negotiations commenced between Pakistan and India in 1951 under the World Bank and resultantly the famous Indus Waters Treaty (IWT) was signed on September 19, 1960. It was the partition of waters like land in 1947. Pakistan got the rights of the waters of the three western rivers, i.e., Indus, Jhelum, and Chenab, while the three eastern rivers, i.e., Beas, Sutlej, and Ravi, went in total jurisdiction of India. India was not allowed to build storages on the western rivers except to a very limited extent and also restrictions were imposed on the extension of irrigation development in India. The permanent Indus Commission was appointed for both states. International financial assistance was given to Pakistan for the development of irrigation works utilizing the waters of western rivers.

a. **Strain & Stress on IWT and Violations by India:** There is no denying the fact that the IWT survived in the midst of wars and border clashes between the two states but the Indian projects on Pakistani rivers created stress and strain as India could either reduce water flows to Pakistan or cause floods by releasing the stored-waters. There are numerous water disputes between the two, e.g., Wular Barrage, Kishanganga Project, Baglihar Dam, etc. Salal Dam was started by India without informing Pakistan, in violation of the IWT. Though an agreement was reached between the two countries, yet there is no guarantee that India would not do the same in future. Now India has got the leverage to hold water for 25-26 days which can cause an acute shortage of water for winter crops in Pakistan. This, besides causing electricity shortage, can greatly affect wheat crop in the Punjab. According to Dr John Briscoe, Professor of the Environmental Engineering and Environmental Health at Harvard University and former Senior Water Advisor to the World Bank on the Baglihar case, "In case of Baghliar, Pakistan's vulnerability was driven home when India chose to fill Baglihar exactly at the time when it would impose maximum harm on farmers in downstream Pakistan. Following Baglihar is a veritable caravan of Indian projects, i.e., Kishanganga, Sawalkot, Pakuldul, Bursar, Dal Huste, Gyspa…The cumulative live storage will be large, giving India an unquestioned capacity to have a major impact on the timing of flows."

b. **Implications for Pakistan:** Water flows in river Chenab declined to about 6000 cusecs from a 10-year-average of 10000 cusecs, mainly because of construction of over a dozen Hydro-electric Projects (HEPs) upstream by India. To fill Baglihar Dam, India had consistently obstructed River Chenab's flow. Resultantly, Pakistan received lesser water when it should have been receiving a minimum of 55,000 cusecs per day. In order to achieve the required growth targets in agriculture, Pakistan needs an estimated 277 MAF in 2025. Otherwise, the shortage of surface water will result in drought and more dependency on ground water for irrigation; hence water table will go down causing water constraints to the population. Indian water regulation capability has increased as with the completion of Salal Dam, India has enhanced its water regulation capability over river Chenab by 6-7 times. After completion of Baglihar Dam, India will be able to stop the flow of water in the river for 30-40 days as compared to previous capability of only 8-10 days. Kishanganga HEP will also enhance Indian storage capability over river Jhelum with a stoppage capability of 14 days. Also, Wullar Barrage will further enhance Indian storage capability in river Jhelum for an additional 30 days. So, depending upon the degree of water regulation capability, India can create three types of effects:

- Drying up of rivers-related canals
- Flooding of rivers
- Fluctuate discharge of rivers

c. **Possible Impacts on Global Security:** Since water security has become a principal concern for sustainable development, so availability of freshwater is one of the greatest challenges that the world is going to face in the near future. As water shortages are growing, the result could be a series of disasters and confrontations leading to regional crises. Nowhere else on Earth are the prospects of water wars more serious than in South Asia, where two of the world's greatest river systems crisscross the international boundaries of the world's largest and most densely-populated countries:

- Indus River System (IRS)
- Ganges-Brahmaputra-Meghna (GBM)

Water issues are likely to continue as a major source of conflict between India and Pakistan in coming decades as forecasted by many analysts. As populations rise, levels of economic development increase and the adverse effects of climate change become more extreme, the South Asian region will struggle to meet its growing demand while managing dwindling water supplies and the trans-boundary rivers, especially those in the IRS and GBM basins. These disputes could prove to be dangerous for world security since war over water between two nuclear armed states, i.e., Pakistan and India, would be dangerous. The possibility of such a war cannot be ruled out since water poses a survival issue and there is no substitute of this commodity.

India Re-thinking IWT

Indians consider IWT generous to Pakistan and Pakistan thinks it discriminatory right from its inception. At official levels, there is no such demand by the Govt. of India/Indus Water Commission India and so is the case with Pakistan as there is no such demand from the Govt. of Pakistan/Indus Water Commission Pakistan. But at non-governmental level, intellectuals/academia in India have started asking for re-visiting/re-thinking the IWT and probably they are making a case for the future. Brahma Chellaney, Professor of Strategic Studies at the New Delhi-based Centre for Policy Research, said that "Pakistan's reopening of the water-sharing agreement could backfire, as it might prompt India to rethink a treaty that was extremely generous to Pakistan. There was no treaty in the world which had been so generous on the part of the upper riparian to the lower riparian state. India was starving its own northern regions and reserving four-fifths of the water for Pakistan. If Pakistan played this dangerous game, they would make India review its generosity."

1. **IDSA Report:** Institute for Defence Studies and Analyses (IDSA) had published its book/task force report in 2010 titled *"Water Security for India—The External Dynamics"* in which they have given reasons and plans for re-visiting the IWT. According to the report, "...with Pakistan, given some stringent provisions in the IWT that thwart India's plans of developing projects on the western rivers, a 'modification' of the provisions of the treaty should be called for. Whether it is done through re-negotiations or through establishing an Indus-II Treaty, modifications of the provisions are crucial in case of the western rivers. Under the draft provisions of the International Law Commission 'Responsibility of States for Internationally Wrongful Acts, 2001', India can consider the abrogation of the treaty...Pakistan aids and abets terrorist actions from its soil. India should quantify the damage it has sustained over the decades because of Pakistani support to terrorism and seek as a first step suitable compensation. If Pakistan does not comply, India can possibly threaten to walk out of various bilateral agreements including the IWT." Pakistan is using water propaganda to get international attention on Kashmir so India should "talk" to Pakistan but not "negotiate". The talks should be about "water needs" and not "water rights".

2. **Five Constituencies/Point of Views in India on Re-thinking the IWT:** According to the same IDSA report, there are five constituencies that ask for revision or a re-think. "The first constituency seeks to evolve an Indus-II under the provisions of Article VII and Article XII of the IWT for an integrated or joint development of the Indus water basin. Indus-II should be fed into the current peace process as a means both for defusing current political strains over Indus-I and managing adverse impacts of climate change."

"The second constituency while understanding the merits of a new hydrologic relationship on the Indus does not see any viability of Indus-II and contends that a totally new treaty has to be negotiated. The IWT was a partitioning treaty, like the partitioning of the land. How can cooperation be built on that basis?"

"The third constituency is the domestic pressure group in [Indian occupied] Jammu & Kashmir which feels that the IWT has restricted the state's overall development by not allowing it the usage of "its" rivers, i.e., Jhelum, Chenab and Indus. It has been calling for a complete review of the treaty. The [Indian occupied] Jammu & Kashmir government has been contending that in spite of having an untapped hydro-electric potential of 15,000 MW, the state continues to suffer from an acute power shortage and related agro-economic underdevelopment."

"The fourth constituency springs into action when the political climate between India and Pakistan becomes acrimonious. While war over water is not an option, this group suggests strong-arm tactics in dealing with Pakistan and using water as a coercive tool and a bargaining instrument in the larger politico-strategic objectives of India."

"There is a fifth constituency that argues that any attempt to review the treaty can be done only after India exploits the potential already permissible under the treaty. Only a crying child, it is argued, gets the mother's milk. This constituency argues that first India should fully exploit the existing potential and then cry for more. Any attempt otherwise to review the treaty may not be seen as logical. The IWT is a product of its time and could be fruitfully modified and renegotiated to bring it more in line with contemporary international watercourse law, the Helsinki rules, and emerging concerns with water quality, environmental sustainability, climate change, and principles of equitable sharing."

Pakistan's serious projected shortages, India's trend of damming and diverting waters and global warming's expected depletion of water in the IRS are a source of increasing tensions between Pakistan and India. Based on supply and demand projections, India faces its own water scarcity, which would provide India an excuse to store or divert river water that would otherwise reach Pakistan. Water shortages would pressure the Pakistani government to increase its share of water drawn from the Indus system under the treaty as Pakistan is heavily reliant on the Indus and has few alternative water supply sources unlike India. In this environment, a renegotiation of the IWT may become an important diplomatic issue between India and Pakistan. With India, the water issue will be far more political and strategic than just water. India has also started propagating that Tibet's water is for humanity, not for China alone. But they (Indians) forget that the Indus-Ganges basins are also for humanity, not for India alone.

The Way Forward

As far as the existing treaty is concerned and keeping pros and cons in mind, there is no need to revisit/review/rethink the IWT. Due to India's continuous hegemonic attitude, Pakistan would not be in a better position to have any revision in its favour. Instead, Pakistan should continue lobbying that India has been violating the IWT and India should be compelled to abide by the IWT in its true letter and spirit. Also, Pakistan should engage with India within the context of the IWT in a comprehensive way. International lobbying should be intensified on the point, i.e., water being the "lifeline" issue for Pakistan and this could trigger war.

Pakistan should be calling for a sophisticated forecasting system, accurately estimating how much water flows into the IRS, as almost 90% of the water in the Upper Indus River Basin comes from remote glaciers of Himalaya and Karakorum mountain ranges, which border Pakistan, China and India. This region is so remote that the authorities in Pakistan do not know the exact weather conditions there. This system will also help in alleviating droughts in the country. The water forecasting system could ultimately help Pakistan in optimizing water allocation at national level by working out how much water is used for irrigation, industry, and domestic purposes.

Internally, water management in Pakistan has been poor. So, keeping in view the dwindling water resources, water must be made a part of the new "security agenda."

APP – 6

RECONSIDERING THE INDUS WATERS TREATY: THE BAGLIHAR DAM DISPUTE

Inside Index, 31 January, 2005

The Indian plan to go ahead with the Baglihar Hydropower Project on the Chenab River in the Indian state of Jammu and Kashmir (J&K) has evoked opposition from Pakistan which claims that the project puts the World Bank-brokered Indus Waters Treaty (IWT) of 1960, the only successful treaty between the two arch-rivals, at risk. While Pakistan claims the project to be in contravention of the IWT provisions, the J&K Assembly passed a resolution on 3 March 2003 asking New Delhi to reconsider the IWT to safeguard the interests of the State. The resolution stated that the IWT was discriminatory as the rights over waters of three rivers of the State - Jhelum, Chenab and Indus - were with Pakistan and India had to seek permission for any construction plans on these rivers. The failure of the recent three-day (4-6 January 2005) foreign secretary-level talks on the Baglihar project held in Islamabad led Pakistan to shoot a letter to the World Bank asking it to resolve the dispute with India. However, the World Bank responded on 19 January 2005 saying that though it is a signatory to the Treaty, it is not the guarantor for the IWT. The Bank has also said that it is for India and Pakistan to appoint a neutral expert for resolving the problem.

The Baglihar Project

Negotiations between India and Pakistan during 1951-1960 held under the supervision of the World Bank resulted in the signing of the IWT on 19 September 1960. This is the only treaty between the two arch rivals that has worked effectively for over four decades and is, at times, cited by international funding institutions, as an illustration of cooperation between the two hostile neighbours. The Indus system of rivers comprises three eastern rivers - Sutlej, Beas and Ravi - and three western rivers - Indus, Jhelum and Chenab. The Baglihar Hydropower Project (BHP) is being undertaken on the River Chenab in Doda, 160 km north of Jammu. Apart from objecting to the project design of the BHP, Pakistan has expressed opposition to the Tulbul navigation project, the Sawalkote Hydroelectric Project and the Kishanganga Hydroelectric Project, all located in J&K.

Under the IWT, the waters of the eastern rivers are allocated to India and those of the western rivers to Pakistan. The average annual flow of waters in the eastern rivers is estimated to be around 33 Million Acres Feet (MAF) whereas it is 135 MAF in the western rivers. The Pakistani contention over the BHP relates to the Article V of the IWT which relates to the compensation to be paid by India to Pakistan towards the latter's losses incurred during the construction of water drawing projects on the western rivers in lieu of water supplies for irrigation canals in Pakistan which were dependent on the water flow from the eastern rivers. The IWT allowed Pakistan to construct a system of replacement canals to carry water from the western rivers into those areas in West Pakistan that were earlier dependent for their irrigation supplies on water from the eastern rivers. The Indian contention in this regard is that since India has already paid its contribution of 62,060,000 pounds to the World Bank towards compensation to Pakistan under this clause, therefore, the Article V is no more valid. But Pakistani contention is that the IWT had imposed some restrictions on India over the usage of waters of the Indus, Jhelum and Chenab. Therefore, New Delhi cannot alter the flow of any of these rivers.

In the years after the IWT, Pakistan built the Mangla and Tarbela dams and several other storage facilities on Indus, Jhelum and Chenab. India also embarked on a series of construction projects including dams and barrages on the Ravi, Sutlej and Beas rivers. While these projects did not lead to any serious differences between the two neighbours, the BHP is opposed by Pakistan which claims that India is attempting to divert the water flow into Pakistan through this project.

J&K's Initiatives

The J&K government had sought counter-guarantees from the Centre for implementing major hydel power projects in the State. However, due to a delay in the sanctioning of such guarantees, the former Farooq Abdullah government signed a memorandum of understanding (MoU) with Jai Prakash Industries Ltd, Siemens and Hydro Vevey Ltd for completing the 450 (Megawatt) MW Baglihar hydel power project. The MoU was signed on 11 April 1999. The total cost of the project is estimated at about Rupees 3,800 crore and the project is expected to be completed by December 2004. The J&K government has already provided Rupees 150 crores for the project and work on the BHP began in May 1999. On 29 August 2003, the then Indian Prime Minister Atal Behari Vajpayee promised his government's assistance for raising Rs. 2,200 crore for the completion of the BHP. Around Rs. 1,600 crore has already been allocated for the project by the J&K government and the remaining amount would be generated with the help of the Centre and financial institutions. Vajpayee also announced the sanctioning of the Rs. 665 crore for the Sea-II power project of 120 MW capacity to be undertaken in Kashmir by the National Hydel Power Corporation (NHPC).

The BHP will tap around 7,000 cusecs of water of Chenab for irrigation purposes in the short-term and once the project is completed, electricity would also be generated for meeting the shortfalls in the State's power demands. The BHP would meet around one-third of the total power requirements of J&K. The BHP project would also provide employment to thousands of people living in the Ramban, Banihal, Doda and Gulabgarh areas. Already, the BHP has generated employment to 5000 skilled and unskilled workers. The project will have an initial installed capacity of 450 MWs which could be increased to 900 MW by an expansion programme. The Baglihar Dam will be 144 metres high and the head race tunnel two km long and 10 metres in diameter.

J&K is reported to have about 15,000 MW of power potential. In the past two decades, investments of over Rs. 4000.00 crores have already been made in the power sector. During 1997-98 to 2001-2002, investments of Rs. 1,400 crores were made which were markedly higher compared to previous years. Several debates over the BHP in the Jammu and Kashmir Assembly raised the issue that there is a growing resentment amongst the people of the State over the government's failure to harness the enormous hydroelectric power potential. This is mainly because of the provisions of the IWT which deny India the right to exploit common water resources. The Mufti Sayeed government in J&K is keen on the Baglihar project as it would help meet the power shortages in the State and contribute to generating employment as well. With the growth in the population of the State which has led to an increase in the demand for water for irrigation and other purposes, officials of the J&K government are of the view that the practical decision would be to amend, if not abrogate, the IWT.

Pakistani Opposition

Pakistan contends that the BHP would lead to a reduction in the downstream flow of water in the Indus as River Chenab is one of the important water sources for the Indus. Moreover, Pakistan is also opposed to the construction of the Wullar barrage which India is building on the River Jhelum. Both India and Pakistan are also planning to build a hydropower dam on the Neelum River (a tributary of River Jhelum). Pakistan says that the BHP would increase India's storage capacity (in J&K) to 1,64,000 acre feet which is much higher than that allowed under the IWT. The BHP will also allow India to control the flow of water to Pakistan's disadvantage. Pakistan further says that the construction of the controversial gate structure at Baglihar could deprive Pakistan of more than 7, 000 cusecs (cubic feet per second) of water a day from the Chenab. Clearly, the BHP has become a bone of contention between the two countries. Apart from the BHP, Pakistan is opposing India's other water projects on the Indus, saying that these are in contravention of the IWT.

A three-member Pakistani team of water and power experts, headed by Jamaat Ali Shah, Commissioner of the Permanent Commission on Indus Water (PCIW), had inspected the BHP in October 2003. Such annual inspections have been provided under the IWT. Following the inspection, the team presented a report to the Pakistani government, saying that India was building the dam in contravention of the IWT clauses. Moreover, they also claimed that India had not redesigned the BHP in accordance with Pakistani conditions. In its report, the team stated that the BHP would deprive Pakistan of 26 to 28 per cent water in winter season thereby affecting Pakistan's irrigation water requirements especially during the Rabi crop season [*The Nation*, 25 November 2003].

Bilateral Talks

The recent foreign secretary-level parleys held in January 2005 failed to resolve the dispute as both India and Pakistan remained stuck to their respective positions. The talks were held between a 12-member Indian team led by Secretary (Water Resources) V. K. Duggal and a Pakistani delegation headed by Secretary (Water and Power) Ashfaq Mehmood. The discussions focussed on six technical areas identified, including the pondage level, the gated spillway and the level of intake tunnels. While India stated its readiness to re-examine Pakistani objections to the design of the dam, Islamabad wants the project to be stopped, as it fears that India may eventually manipulate the flow of water, which could affect agriculture in Pakistan. Moreover, a change in the water flow table from India to Pakistan could add to the ongoing water-related tensions between Pakistani provinces. With India showing no concessions on the issue, Pakistan stepped up its campaign against the project by briefing envoys from different countries, including US and China, on 12 January 2005. However, Islamabad also assured the foreign envoys that a failure in Baglihar talks would not affect the ongoing composite dialogue process with India. The IWT provides that disagreements by the parties on the interpretation of the provisions of the Treaty are classified into three categories: questions are examined by the PCIW; differences by a Neutral Expert; and disputes by a Court of Arbitration. The fact that India and Pakistan have failed to resolve the disagreements means that it would now be referred to a 'Neutral Expert', either appointed by the two countries, or by a third party agreed upon by the two sides. In the absence of such an agreement, the appointment of the 'Neutral Expert' would be made by the World Bank, in consultation with the two countries. The decision of the Neutral Expert on all matters within his competence shall be final and binding. If the 'Neutral Expert' is of the view that the 'differences' between the two parties are to be treated as a 'dispute', then a Court of Arbitration would be established to resolve the matter.

The Way Out

The PCIW, established under the IWT, includes experts on water and power from both countries who meet annually in India and Pakistan alternately for exchanging documents relating to the sharing of common water resources of the Indus. Article IX of the IWT provides that if the two sides are unable to resolve any dispute bilaterally at the level of the PCIW, then a team of neutral experts or arbitration should be used to resolve the problem. For India, there are two options. First, India can go ahead with the project after settling the dispute with Pakistan either bilaterally or by involving the role of neutral experts for the first time in

42 years to resolve the problem. The second option for India is to go ahead with the BHP in accordance with its own designs and if met with opposition, New Delhi should walk out of the IWT. The J&K Assembly debates over the issue have reflected support for the second option. Though it is clear that the IWT's greatest achievement is that it is the only treaty that has withstood India-Pakistan hostility and also depoliticised the water issue to a large extent, the treaty needs to be amended taking into consideration the present requirements of the Indian state of J&K. The Baglihar project will significantly benefit the Kashmiri people by generating employment opportunities as well as meet the power shortages in the state. Also, the Indian leadership has reaffirmed that the project is not intended to either dam the rivers or affect the flow of waters to Pakistan. Observers therefore say that Pakistan's opposition to the project is unwarranted and indicates that Islamabad is playing with the aspirations of the Kashmiri people.

APP – 7

ACADEMIC STUDY OF INDUS WATER TREATY AND IT'S IMPACT

Parsad M. Chikshe

The river Indus was the cradle of the great Indus valley civilization of the ancient world. Historically, India has been named after this great river-Indus. The river valley and its plain had the potential to produce a large surplus because of the fertility of the soil inundated by the annual flood and the easy availability of water for irrigating the fields. The surplus production on a regular basis led to the sustenance of non-agrarian specialists like artisans, traders and rulers, who controlled and redistributed the surplus. They all lived in an area, which was away (not far enough) from the agricultural fields, gradually leading to urbanization. Historically, even after the decline of the Indus civilization, the region witnessed the emergence of the great empires of the Bactrian Greeks, the Parthians, the Turks, the Mongols, the Mughals and the British.

However, one of the common features throughout was a somewhat solo political authority in the region. The river Indus hardly became a contentious issue even under the circumstances of flanking tribal conflicts. The simple reason was that river water remained a common property, away from any centralised political control.

The Indus River System

The north-western part of the Indian subcontinent is dominated by the

Indus River and its system of upper tributaries (collectively referred to as Indus River System in this article.) Originating 17,000 feet (518 m) above sea level in a spring near Lake Manasarovar at Mt. Kailash [i], the Indus river along with the Brahmaputra [ii], Sutlej, and Karnali rivers are fed by massive Tibetan glacial waters to become a mighty river with further feeds from other glacial catchment areas in Karakoram and Zanskar ranges. The Indus then traverses a distance of 1800 miles (2900 km) through Tibet, India, Pakistan occupied Kashmir (PoK), and Pakistan before draining into the Arabian Sea south of Karachi. On its way, it is further enriched by the waters of several tributaries, the most important and discussed in this article are Beas, Sutlej, Ravi, Chenab and Jhelum rivers. The western tributaries of the Indus that include the Swat, Kurram, Gomal, Kohat, Zoab and Kabul are not discussed herein.

The great Indus river is 2900 kms. long and the length of its tributaries, as mentioned above, is 5600 kms. The river has been variously known as the *Sengge* or Lion River by the Tibetans, *Abbasseen* or Father of Rivers by the Pathans of present NWFP Pakistan, and *Mitho Dariyo* or Sweet River by the denizens of the arid Sindh.

Chenab : This 675 mile (1086 km) long river originates in the Kulu and Kangra districts of Himachal Pradesh and is fed by the tributaries Chandra and Bagha as it enters J&K near Kishtwar. After cutting across the Pir Panjal range, it enters the Sialkot district in Pakistan that built the Marala barrage across the river in 1968 with a maximum discharge of 1.1 million cusecs.

Jhelum & Kishenganga (Neelum): The Kishenganga river rises in the mountain complex west of Dras and south of Deosai plateau and is fed by a number of tiny tributaries and merges with Jhelum near Muzaffarabad in PoK. The Jhelum itself originates in the foothills of Pir Panjal near Verinag and flows through the four major cities of Anantnag, Srinagar, Sopore and Baramulla. Some important tributaries of the Jhelum are Lidar, Sind and Vishav.

Sutlej : The longest of the five tributaries, the Sutlej originates near Mt. Kailash along with the Indus and runs a course of 964 miles (1550 km) through the Panjal and Siwalik mountain ranges and enters Pakistan through the plains of Indian Punjab. The huge 740 feet (225 m) high Bhakra Dam, which Nehru called "the new temple of resurgent India," is also situated on this river. These eastern tributaries of the Indus known as Panjand combine at Mithan Kot.

Ravi: This 475 mile (764 km) long river rises in Himachal Pradesh and runs a course of 102 miles (164 km) before joining Chenab in Pakistan after flowing past Lahore. The Thien Dam (Ranjit Sagar Dam) is located on this river at the tri-section of Punjab, Himachal Pradesh and J&K States and feeds the Upper Bari Doab Canal (UBDC) which irrigates Northwestern Punjab.

Beas : This 290 mile (467 km) long river originates near Rohtang Pass in Himachal Pradesh and flows through Kulu Valley and the Siwalik Range. The Pandoh Dam is situated on this and diverts water to Sutlej through the Beas-Sutlej link.

Indus international river basin is the largest, contiguous irrigation system in the world, with a command area of about 20 million hectares and an annual irrigation capacity of over 12 million hectares. The Indus Delta covers an area of some 5,000 km^2, of which 2,000 km^2 is a protected area. The fan-shaped Delta is the sixth largest in the world and supports a population of over 130,000 people, whose livelihoods are directly or indirectly dependent on the Indus River.

According to a study made in Pakistan, the Indus river carries about 144 billion cubic yards, which is more is more than half of the total supply of water in the Indus River system.

Whereas the Jhelum and Chenab combined carry roughly one-fourth, the Ravi, Beas and the Sutlej combined constitute the remainder of the total supply of the system that is nearly one-four

Average annual flow of the rivers of the Indus system

Eastern Rivers	Western Rivers	Total
41 BCM (33 MAF)	166 BCM (135 MAF)	207 BCM (168 MAF)

British colonial rule

It was first of all under the British colonial rule that the background was prepared for future tensions in the region for the control of water flowing from the river Indus. They began huge water projects and incorporated many of the tributaries of the Indus into an integrated basin-wide management system. A network of large and small canals, connecting one branch of the river to another, was built after 1859.

Partition and its aftermath

An immediate aftermath of the partition of the Indian sub-continent and the creation of two Dominions of India and Pakistan in 1947 was that bulk of the irrigation canals developed on the Indus system went to Pakistan. Out of 26 million acres of land irrigated annually by the Indus canals, 21 million acres lay in Pakistan and only 5 million acres in India. As per the 1941 census, the population dependent on the Indus system of waters was 25 million in Pakistan and 21 million in India. Besides, India had another 35 million acres of lands crying out for irrigation from the Indus basin sources. Thus the partition gave independent India much less undeveloped area inspite of the fact that it was an upsteam country with control over Ravi, Beas, Sutlej, Jhelum and Chenab. India had not only to cater to the food requirements of 21 million people but also those millions who migrated from irrigated areas in West Punjab and Bahawalpur, now in Pakistan, all of whom were dependent on the Indus waters.

The dispute over sharing of Indus waters came to fore immediately after partition. In order to maintain and run the existing systems as before partition, two Standstill Agreements were signed on **20 December 1947** by the Chief Engineers of East Punjab and West Punjab. These interim arrangements were to expire on 31 st March 1948, after which East Punjab started asserting its rights on its waters. It was on 1 April 1948 that the East Punjab Government, in control of the head works at Madhopur on the Ravi and at Ferozpur on the Sutlej, cut off water supplies to the canals in Pakistan fed by these head works, after the Standstill agreements expired on 31 March 1948.

In fact, East Punjab had formally notified West Punjab on 29 March 1948 that the 'Standstill Agreements' would expire on 31st March, and had accordingly invited the Chief Engineers of West Punjab to Shimla for negotiating an agreement for resumption of water supplies.

According to Rushbrook Williams, the water supplies were cut because "the canal colonies in Pakistan served by these head works did not pay the standard water dues. The people incharge of the head works were applying exactly the same kind of sanction that they would have applied in undivided India - **no canal dues, no water."**

The Chief Engineers of the two Punjabs met in **Shimla and on 18 April 1948** concluded two agreements which were to take effect from the date of their ratification by the Dominions of India and Pakistan.

Finally, at the inter- Dominion Conference on 3 May 1948 at Delhi, the matter came up for discussion. It was on 4 May 1948 that an agreement was reached after a meeting at Nehru's instance between the Indian Prime Minister and Pakistan's Finance Minister, Ghulam Mohd.

By the **Delhi Agreement of 4 May 1948**, East Punjab agreed not to withhold water from West Punjab without giving the latter time to tap alternative sources. On its part, West Punjab recognized "the natural anxiety of the East Punjab." As regards the payment of seigniorage charges to East Punjab, the West Punjab government agreed to deposit immediately in the Reserve Bank of India. It may be pointed out that the British Province of Punjab recovered, before partition, from Bikaner State seigniorage charges for the supply of water to the State in addition to proportionate maintenance costs etc. of the Ferozepore headworks and of the feeder canal. East Punjab now wanted to recover a similar charge for water supplied to West Punjab.

Though this agreement was not final, it did provide some basis for dealing with the vexed problem. But soon it was found that Pakistan was unwilling to stick to the agreement, as it was seeking to use the Indus water dispute as a political tool in the battle over Kashmir being fought at the United Nations. Pakistan also sought to create anti-India hysteria in Pakistan over this issue. As such, Pakistan unilaterally abrogated the May 1948 Agreement saying that it was signed "under duress". Besides, Pakistan refused to pay the dues to India even after a year of the agreement. Pakistan now asked for a reference to the International Court of Justice for final verdict, which was objected to by India. Pakistani media and politicians launched a campaign over the issue of canal waters dispute to create a scenario of serious crisis in Indo-Pakistani relations. All along Pakistan's policy was to seek third party mediation.

The Lilienthal Proposal

It was in this atmosphere of mutual distrust and contrived tensions, that **David E. Lilienthal, formerly Chairman of the Tenessese Valley Authority and the U.S. Atomic Energy Commission** visited India and Pakistan in **February 1951** on a supposedly private visit.

Before embarking upon this visit, Lilienthal had met the then U.S. President Truman, the U.S. Secretary of State, Dean Acheson, Pakistan's Foreign Minister, M. Zafrulla Khan, and Secretary General of Pakistan's Delegation to the U.N., Muhammad Ali.

While in India, Lilienthal was the guest of Prime Minister Nehru and he also held talks with Sheikh Abdullah on Kashmir. In Pakistan, Lilienthal discussed with Prime Minster, Liaquat Ali Khan, Kashmir and the "economic warfare" between India and Pakistan. Liaquat Ali was reported to have told Lilienthal that "unless the Kashmir issue is settled, it is unreal to try to settle the issue about water or about evacuees".

On his return to America, Lilienthal wrote an article titled 'Another "Korea" in the Making', analysing the Indo-Pakistani relations. He prefaced his article with a loaded comment: "India and Pakistan are on the edge of war over which shall possess Kashmir - a fight the U.S. might be forced to enter...

The direct issue is whether the historic region of Kashmir and Jammu shall be part of India or Pakistan. On one of this disputed region's frontiers lies Red China, on another Red Tibet. Along another frontier is Soviet Russia.

Explaining the importance of the Indus waters for ensuring food security to millions of people in India and Pakistan, Lilienthal proposed that the canal waters dispute could be solved by India and Pakistan by working out a program jointly to develop and operate the Indus basin river system. He wrote: "Jointly financed perhaps with World Bank help an Indus Engineering Corporation, with representation by technical men of India, Pakistan and the World Bank, can readily work out an operating scheme for storing water wherever dams can best store it, and for diverting and distributing water".

Lilienthal, who appeared to be concerned about the presence of Communist China and Soviet Union on the borders of Kashmir, was hoping to become the head of the proposed Indus Engineering Corporation.

Whereas Lilienthal sent copies of his article to the Indian Ambassador and the Pakistani Counsel on the water dispute, he also persued the proposal with the U.S. State Department.

World Bank Initiative

Interestingly, around the same time, **Eugene R. Black,** then President of the International Bank for Reconstruction and Development, Washington World Bank and a close friend of David Lilienthal became interested in the Lilienthal proposal.

In September 1951, the World Bank formally offered its good offices to both India and Pakistan to work out a solution of the Indus waters issue on the basis of Lilienthal proposals.

The World Bank offer was conditioned by the 'essential principle' that "the problem of development and use of Indus Basin water resources should be solved on a functional and not a political plan without relations to past negotiations and past claims, and independently of political issues".

Both countries accepted the suggestion after the World Bank President, Eugene Black, personallymet both the Indian and Pakistani Prime Ministers. By May 1952, the first of the long series of conferences opened at Washington which were continued at Karachi and Delhi. But it soon became clear that Lilienthal's proposal of a joint Indus Engineering Corporation could not be realised. Instead it was found necessary to replace the existing supplies from alternative sources. So in February 1954, the World Bank officals proposed to India and Pakistan, the division of rivers.

"The three eastern rivers, Ravi, Beas and Sutlej would be available for the exclusive use and benefit of India, after a specified transitionary period. The Western rivers, Indus, Jhelum and Chenab, would be available for the exclusive use and benefit of Pakistan, except for the insignificant volume of Jhelum flow presently used in Kashmir... Each country would construct the works located on its own territories which are planned for the development of the supplies. The costs of such works would be borne by the country to be benefitted thereby".

Whereas India accepted the World Bank proposals, inspite of its sacrifices, Pakistan vacillated and accepted 'in principle' only after the Bank pressed her for a reply. In his letter of 22 March 1954 to the World Bank President, the Prime Minister of India, while conveying his general acceptance to the principles governing the Bank proposals as the basis of agreement, stressed that "the actual agreement which would be worked out with the assistance of the Bank authorities will naturally deal with a number of details including the question of the small requirements of Jammu and Kashmir."

On the other hand, Pakistan continued to ask for clarification of details and further technical studies, thereby taking several years in negotiations.

India's acceptance of the World bank proposals was based on the hope that in five years' time India would be able to make use of the waters of the eastern rivers. This was, however, frustrated by Pakistani procrastination. Pakistan was seeking a comprehensive replacement-cum-development programme in Pakistan involving high investment of about 1.12 billion US dollars.

World Bank's Financial plan

And in 1959 the World Bank USA and certain western countries became ready to foot the bill for this huge construction programme in Pakistan, so that the vexed canal waters dispute between India and Pakistan could be solved.

It was on 1 March 1960 that the World Bank made a public announcement of the financial plan it had evolved for the replacement and development works of the Indus system. It was estimated to cost about 1000 million dollars partly in foreign exchange and partly in local currencies. The Bank announced that the requisite expenditure would be contributed by Australia, Canada, New Zealand, Germany, United Kingdom, United States, the World Bank besides the contributions by India and Pakistan.

Ironically as it may sound, the bulk of this financial plan was meant to be spent in Pakistan, 691 million dollars out of 747 millions of grants and loans, with India getting only 56 million dollars as loan for the Beas Dam, as against Pakistan getting all her development underwritten by the Bank's financial plan. Besides, the World Bank press release did not mention the additional U.S. grant of 235 million dollars in local currency.

Yet, India stuck to its commitment to conclude the Indus Waters Treaty based on the World Bank proposals. And the Treaty was duly signed on 19 September 1960 at Karachi by Jawaharlal Nehru, the Prime Minister of India, President Ayub Khan of Pakistan and W.A.B. Iliff of the World Bank.

The Treaty

The main features of the Treaty are as follows :

(i) The waters of the three eastern rivers - the Ravi, the Beas and the Sutlej – would be available for unrestricted use by India, after a transition period.

(ii) The waters of the three western rivers–the Indus, the Jhelum and the Chenab – would be allowed to flow for unrestricted use by Pakistan except for some limited use such as a domestic use, b non-consumptive use, c agricultural use, d generation of hydro-electric power run-of-river-plants in Kashmir.

India's Irrigation Entitlement on Western Rivers

The Indus	Jhelum	Chenab	Total
70,000	400,000	231,000	701,000

India's Entitlement for "other" Storages

River Name	General Storage (MAF)	Power Storage (MAF)	Flood Storage (MAF)
Indus	0.25	0.15	Nil
Jhelum (Excluding Jhelum Main)	0.50	0.25	0.75
Jhelum Main	Nil	Nil	As in Paragraph 9, Annexure E
Chenab (Excluding Chenab Main)	0.50	0.60	Nil
Chenab Main	Nil	0.60	Nil

The treaty does not provide an exit clause for India per se. Article 54 of Protocol I (1977) to the Geneva Convention (1949) prohibits any measures that could result in the starvation of people. It specifically refers to water resources and irrigation works.

Abrogation is bound to incite reactions from the World Bank and the countries that were party to the treaty and have provided funds.

Why India had Sign it?

The Indus Treaty was signed by Nehru in the fervent hope of ushering all round improvement in India-Pakistan relations and resolution of all outstanding problems including Kashmir.

Perhaps, Nehru was impressed by Ayub's offer of joint defence with India made in early 1959 in the wake of deteriorating India-China relations.

Although India did not accept the concept of joint defence, it sought to improve relations with Pakistan by agreeing to substantially pay for the cost of irrigation programme in Pakistan, besides surrendering the use of three western rivers. India treated the Indus waters issue as a technical and engineering problem.

Nehru went to Karachi on 19 September 1960 to sign the Treaty hoping to begin a new chapter in the history of Indo-Pak relations.

As such Nehru's assertion in the Lok Sabha on 30 November 1960 that "we purchased a settlement, if you like; we purchased peace to that extent and it is good for both countries" was not borne out by subsequent events.

The U.N, The World Bank, The U.S. and other countries put pressure as Pakistan was a member of SEATO and CENTO, which made him susceptible to western prescriptions for regional peace and cooperation.

That Nehru himself had realised this soon after is confirmed by N.D. Gulhati, who led the Indian delegation during negotiations over Indus. Gulhati recalls: "When I called on the Prime Minister on 28th February 1961, my last day in office, in a sad tone, he said, 'Gulhati, I had hoped that this agreement would open the way to settlement on other problems, but we are where we were".

Why the World Bank and the US supported...
Pakistan was member of SEATO and CENTO.

At that time, the U.S. and its friendly western nations viewed the Communist Block - USSR and China, as a greater threat.

Pakistan succeeded in extracting a huge financial assistance of about one billion dollars from the World Bank, USA and other western countries, using the geopolitical environment in the region to its advantage.

The manner in which the Treaty was negotiated and concluded lends an impression of an external pressure group network exerting their influence since huge investments were involved in the construction of big dams and canals. It is a reflection on the functioning of the World Bank which was influenced by the Cold War politics in the region and by the interested construction lobbies.

Some Important Questions

In retrospect, it can be stated that India was too generous to Pakistan, both in terms of allowing use of waters of western rivers and by making payments of more than 62 million Pounds Sterling i.e. about 430 crores of rupees in current value to Pakistan. It is also surprising as to why the World Bank advanced such disproportionate proposals to India," particularly when the eastern rivers given to India carried 20 to 25 percent of the total flow of the Indus Basin as against the 75 to 80 percent in the three western rivers allocated to Pakistan".

Out of the total annual flow of 168.4 million acre feet (m.a.f) of water in the Indus system of rivers, the total requirement for irrigation water was 96.36 m.a.f. for the entire cultivable area of the Indus basin, thereby leaving a surplus of 72.02 m.a.f. of water which would be going to the sea.

Since the cultivable area on the three eastern rivers was 22.856 million acres, a little less than on the western rivers, 25.100 million acres, the mean annual supplies made available by the eastern rivers was only 32.8 m.a.f., that is 13.57 m.a.f. less than the actual water requirement of 46.37 m.a.f. In quite contrast to this, the mean annual flow in western rivers was 135.6 m.a.f., i.e. 85.59 m.a.f. more than its requirement of only 50.01 m.a.f. of water. It is quite intriguing as to why the Indian government delegation involved in prolonged negotiations over Indus waters, agreed to a much lower share of water available in the eastern rivers, particularly when the concerned officials were in know of the facts.

However, it appears that the Jammu and Kashmir government, particularly its irrigation and power development departments, had not done their homework to study and quantify the existing and future water requirements for irrigation, hydel power generation and other uses inside Jammu and Kashmir.

As such the Indian delegation failed to secure the necessary safeguards in the Treaty for future consumption of water for hydel power purposes, excepting by the run-of-the-river methods. Gulhati himself admits that "since no study had ever been made until then, of the development locally possible, above the rim stations, none of us had, at that time, any real idea of the quantum of future developments in the upper reaches of the Western Rivers. Nor did we have any idea of the irrigation from the Indus in Ladakh. As regards hydro-electric development, we felt that, being a non-consumptive use, it was not covered by the Bank proposal which dealt only with irrigation uses". Moreover, it is not the number of rivers but the quantum of water which was to be distributed. Besides, the World Bank did not include the Kabul river while dividing the six rivers among the two countries.

If we consider the internationally accepted Helsinki Rules framed by the International Law Association which postulate the equitable utilisation of waters of an international drainage basin taking into consideration various factors such as the extent of the drainage area, hydrology of the basin, economic and social needs of each basin state, population dependent on the waters of the basin, then India did not get a fair deal.

According to S.K. Garg, who has computed the respective entitlement of India and Pakistan on the basis of population, drainage areas, length of rivers and culturable area, India should have been given 42.8% share in the waters of the Indus Basin, as against the actual allocation of 20 to 25%, flowing in the three eastern rivers.

Impact on Jammu and Kashmir

The treaty which was carried out in the best interest of the nation has, however, deprived the Jammu and Kashmir (J&K) state to use its own water resources and thereby severely affected the development of the state.

The state's rightful riparian rights have been snatched in the so-called national interest and to benefit Punjab and that too without the state being consulted at the time of treaty or even compensated for the consequent consistent loss.

A report by IWMI-Tata Water Policy Programme has revealed that the Indus Waters Treaty signed by India and Pakistan in 1960 has put Jammu and Kashmir (J&K) behind by an estimated Rs 6,500 crore annually.

The report also says that J&K's power generation and agriculture potential has been badly hit by the treaty.

Under the treaty, J&K can use only limited waters of the Chenab and Jhelum for power generation and lift irrigation. It cannot built reservoirs or dams on these rivers without prior approval of Pakistan. Nor can it construct any barrage for irrigation.

The Irrigation and Flood Control Department of the state has proposed 12 new irrigation schemes for Baramulla, Kupwara, Anantnag and Budgam districts on the various streams which are awaiting approval.

Shaheen observes that the food grain import graph of J&K shows a sharp increase in overall imports. J&K, according to his estimates, could have increased its area under irrigation by one lakh acres had the state had the freedom to harness its available water resources. The IWMI report suggests, "One way to compensate J&K for the losses could be a favourable sharing ratio for power generated from centrally funded projects in the state."

According to the IPS News Agency, economic development in Kashimir was hindered because only 40% of the cultivatable land can be irrigated. Moreover, there is still 25% of Kashmiris living without electricity and 55% living without safe drinking.

The state's agricultural potential has also been worst hit. While in 1950-51, the state could irrigate 1.56 lakh hectares under rice cultivation, today after more than half a century, the irrigation potential has risen by an unremarkable 74 thousand hectare to 2.20 lakh hectares. Similarly, the irrigation for the area under other crops which was about 0.07 hectare in 1950-51 has come down to 0.01 hectare. There has been only a marginal increase in the irrigation infrastructure. In 1950-51, the state could irrigate 244 thousand hectare through canals, 3000 hectares by tanks, 3000 by wells and 11,000 hectares by other sources. But in 2000-01, the state irrigates only 284.25 thousand hectares by canals, 2.57 thousand by tanks, 1.42 thousand by wells and 17.73 thousand hectares by other sources.

As a result, the state has now a rationed population of 86.14 lakh people dependant on the supply by the consumer affairs and public distribution department which procures the rice from outside the state. Besides this, a good percentage of population also purchases rice from private dealers, which forms the staple food of the region.

The yield of saffron, the major and exclusive cash crop of the state, that was 2.8 to 3 kg per hectare in early nineties dipped to as low as 500 gm over the past five years. Due to the consequent non-availability of the commodity, it was the cheaper Iranian saffron which claimed the market. Besides, the absence of precipitation also brought pests and diseases to the cultivated fields.

As a result, the government has had to shell out Rs. 40 crore a month to make purchases under public distribution system from Food Corporation of India (FCI). The foodgrain imports graph of J&K state shows a sharp increase in the overall imports.

Interestingly, the productivity level of paddy, at about 40 quintals per hectare in Kashmir valley, is the highest in the country.

Hydel power potential

State government's official estimates put the total hydel power potential of the State at 15,000 MW; the Center for Monitoring Indian Economy CMIE has reported it to be at 7487 MW which constitutes about 9 per cent of the total hydel power potential of the country. The state government has to bank on more power imports from the Northern Grid and till date the arrears have touched over Rs. 1600 crore. And whenever the state is in a position to meet at least 80 per cent of the demand during spring season when the rivers remain gushing, it exports power to reduce the size of the arrears. This question has assumed significance following enormous difficulties being faced by one crore people and several thousand industrialists in the state owing to acute electricity crisis. The power shortage has been an old phenomenon, but during the past four years the state government has been forced to resort to 11 to 14 hour power shedding.

Since the Treaty has placed curbs on the construction of storage reservoirs which could ensure the provision of the requisite water flow, all power projects in the State are to be run-of-the-river type. This not only raises the construction cost of the projects but also affects adversely the cost-effectiveness of power generation from these projects. The cost of the run-of-the-river projects using small head fall is reported to be about 75 per cent higher than hydel projects using the high head fall. Thus the generating capacity of all run-of-the-river projects falls by about 65 to 75 per cent during winter because the water level in different rivers gets depleted substantially. These high cost hydel projects generate electricity much below their installed capacity. For instance, the run-of-the-river Uri Hydel Project built at a cost of more than 800 million US dollars has been producing a maximum of only 200 MW in winter as against the 480 MW installed capacity.

As such the J&K State is unable to meet its demand of about 700 MWs, even after it has been importing 230 MWs of power from the northern grid. The State accounts for only 0.9 per cent of the hydel power generated in the country.

The shortage of power in the State has not only been causing problems for domestic consumption, but has also been inhibiting the growth of industry and agriculture. During the past forty years, since the Indus Treaty was signed, there has been a sizeable increase in the State's population and standards of living. Simultaneously, the State has witnessed a big leap in demand for electricity. As such there have been fundamental changes in the ground situation, so far as the actual power requirement of the State, for domestic, agricultural and industrial uses, is concerned.

The Chenab river originates in the Indian province of Himachal Pradesh. It begins its 700 km journey as two small rivers, Chandra and Bhaga, from Baralaha Pass in Lahul Spiti district. They rejoin about 70 km later and become Chanderbhaga. This river crosses another district of Himachal Pradesh i.e. Chamba through the Pangi Valley region and enters Kashmir at its eastern end. In its 150 Km journey above, the river gathers more water and becomes a full-fledged river. Before it reaches Kashmir, it has already collected 60% of its total water flow and dropped in elevation from about 13000 feet to about 9,000 feet. In Kashmir, this river in its another 220 km journey, collects the remaining 40% water and drops another 7,000 feet elevation before it enters Sialkote area of Pakistan near Akhnur.

The above elevation drop, which the river undergoes in Kashmir, is of greatest importance to India. This, together with volume of water, is a huge energy reserve, which needs to be tapped. Hence, India has planned no less than twenty small and large projects of which Baglihar, Dul Hasti, Salal etc. are the big ones. Most of these projects are in the middle of construction or nearing completion. With the completion of the above projects, Kashmir will be significantly ahead in meeting its current and future energy needs.

Baglihar Dam

Pakistan had created a controversy over the construction of the Baglihar Dam on the Chenab river. The Rs.4000 crore Baglihar Dam project is being constructed by the Jammu and Kashmir government since the year 2000, and over Rs. 2500 crore have already been spent.

This hydel project which has an installed capacity of 450 MW and is expected to be completed by the year 2007 will go a long way in alleviating the problem of power shortage in Jammu and Kashmir. Though the Baglihar project is run-of-the river project, as provided under the Indus Waters Treaty, Pakistan sought to scuttle this project by creating a controversy over its design, pondage, height of the dam and spillways.

Pakistan disputed the Indian contention that the Bagilhar project was a run-of-the-river project and that the storage called pondage was necessary to meet the fluctuations in the discharge of the turbines and claimed that the water will ultimately go to Pakistan. Since talks over a long period remained unsuccessful, the World Bank intervened, though it made it clear that it was not a guarantor of the treaty.

A neutral expert was appointed by the World Bank. The neutral expert Professor Lafitte of Switzerland, while delivering the verdict, rejected most of Pakistan's objections but did call for minor design changes including the reduction of the dam's height by 1.5 metres. The expert did not object to the right of India to construct dams for storage purposes and did not even call the project as a dispute between the two countries but as a "difference."

Tulbul Navigation Project

Similarly, work on the construction of Tulbul Navigation Project, started by the J&K government in 1984, in order to raise the level of water in the Wullar lake for facilitating transport on river Jhelum, was stopped in 1988 after India accepted Benazir Bhutto's demands and stopped construction work at the Tulbul project.

Despite several rounds of talks held with Pakistan during the past 17 years, the issue remains unresolved. Whereas the Tulbul Project would not diminish or change the flow of water to Pakistan, it would keep the Jhelum river navigable for a considerable stretch, thereby bringing economic benefits to the people in the valley.

This project could provide a cheap mode of transport to the fruit growers in north Kashmir and thus transform the region's economy.

The existing dam in the Salal project is full of silt upto three fourths of its 400 feet height, which needs to be flushed out urgently in order to let the project run. India had earlier agreed to Pakistan-dictated terms on the Salal project, which led to very high siltation levels, affecting power generation sharply.

Various water bodies particularly the famous Dal lake, Wullar lake and other aquatic systems have shrunk, thereby causing alarm.

Timber losses

Yet another associated problem has been the revenue loss of millions of rupees to the J&K State, as a result of the floating of timber logs from Jhelum and Chenab across the LoC into Pak-occupied Kashmir. This author learnt from some responsible officials of some insurance companies operating in the J&K State, that the local timber merchants have been claiming millions of rupees of insurance compensation in lieu of their timber losses on this account.

Drinking water

Despite being endowed with plentiful water resources, Srinagar has experienced 19 droughts, extending over four to six consecutive months in a cycle of 72 years. The Kashmir Valley alone…

The acute water crisis in the Doda district of Jammu and Kashmir has added to the worries of local residents, who have been forced to face numerous problems due to it.

More than sixteen villages of the district are facing problems due to the acute shortage of water in the area.

The villagers are the major sufferer, as they have to walk for around 3 kilometers one side to fetch water for their daily chores. Women folk, children have to stand in lines for several hours to cumulate water.

Villagers have no other alternatives because there is no other source of water around 10 kilometers adjoining the village.

Villagers have even adopted different measures to preserve rainwater and in adverse conditions they even use this water for drinking purpose. Villagers have to buy water at the rate of Rs. 50 for 40 litres.

Global warming has resulted in delay of monsoon, which has further dried up major natural sources of water like rivers, streams and ground water sources like hand pumps. Consequently, harried locals are lamenting at the limited water supply.

Villagers complained that it is not a new problem for them and they have been facing this problem for the last 15 years.

What J & K people think about the Indus Water Treaty...

On 3 April 2002, the Jammu and Kashmir Legislative Assembly, cutting across party affiliations, called for a review of the Treaty. Speakers who denounced the Treaty ranged from the National Conference's G. M. Bawan to the Bhartiya Janata Party's Shiv Charan Gupta and the Communist Party of India, Marxist leader Mohammad Yusuf Tarigami.

The State government has been contending that in spite of having an untapped hydro-electric potential of 15,000 MW, the State has been suffering from an acute power deficiency due to restrictions put on the use of its rivers by the Indus Treaty.

And when the State Chief Minister, or his officials, point to the losses accrued to the State by virtue of this Treaty, they are not indulging in any rhetoric. In fact, their views that the requirements of the J&K State were not taken into account while negotiating the Treaty with Pakistan are shared largely by the intellectual, media and public circles in Jammu and Kashmir.

Not only that, some people even stretch it further, suggesting that the central government has been insensitive to the State's problems. Pakistan's action is seen to be obstructing the agro-economic development of the Jammu and Kashmir State.

The State Chief Minister Mufti Mohammad Syed and other political leaders have appealed to Pakistan to facilitate the economic growth of Jammu and Kashmir by not raising objections to hydro-power projects in the state under the Indus Treaty provisions.

Over the last few years, the state government of Jammu & Kashmir and industrial groups in the state have been demanding compensation from the central government for the losses incurred by the state because of the Indus Waters Treaty.

Dr Sheikh Showkat Hussain

Shall the state seek abrogation of IWT? Seeking abrogation can be a good political slogan but it will not work. It is as good as seeking independence. Well known political commentator, Dr Sheikh Showkat Hussain, in one of his articles in Greater Kashmir, writes: "State administration and those who moan the negative impact of Indus Water Treaty can better serve people of Kashmir by looking for protection of Kashmir interests within the ambit of the treaty rather than dreaming beyond it.

Jammu and Kashmir must pursue for its share within what India has got out of this treaty. India has managed to get exclusive rights over waters of Satluj, Beas and Ravi whereas J&K has lost its capability of exploiting waters of Chenab and Jhelum. The State of Jammu and Kashmir has not been compensated for the benefits which Punjab, Haryana and Rajasthan got out of this treaty. Infact, whole of the green revolution in India is indebted to the Indus Water Treaty. This seems to be the only positive impact of the occupation of Kashmir in favour of India.

There has been a lot of talk about monetary compensation but such compensation is unlikely to benefit masses. Most of the money, if secured, will go waste the way other financial investments in J&K have been going. Whatever aid and grant the state has been receiving from the centre has gone into the pockets of so many Chotalas of Kashmiri establishment.

Jammu and Kashmir is the recipient of 20% waters of Ravi. If we ask for exclusive rights over waters of Ravi as a compensation for losses that occurred to the state as a result of the Indus Waters Treaty, it can be a worthwhile and sustainable compensation. Ravi constitutes the border between Jammu and Kashmir and Punjab.

Exclusive right of utilisation of its water will, in a great way, enhance water resources of the state. Apart from utilizing these waters for electricity generation, they can help in complete transformation of Kathua and Jammu districts in terms of agricultural production."

Shaiq Nazir, Srinagar Based Journalist and writer

India and Pakistan have fought wars, questioned each others positions, spread discontent in each others countries and yet they have one thing common - their collective desire to exploit Kashmir's natural resources mainly water. Despite the bonhomie between the warring neighbours, it is feared that India & Pakistan are going to be more rigid on their position vis-à-vis Kashmir.

The reason is simple: they may be insecure about their water needs more than ever and obviously won't like to be exposed for one more moral crime they have committed against Kashmir in the form of the Indus Waters Treaty of 1960.

The questions both the countries have to answer are: How could they treat Punjab and J&K on the same lines? While Punjab had an international border marked and was out of any disputes between the two, Kashmir's future was as uncertain in 1960 as it is in 2006.

Also who represented Kashmir then at the table? What was the *locus standi* of the two countries to abuse waters of a region that had an independent identity till 1947 and on which they disputed each other's claim afterwards?

The fact is that Kashmiris were taken as for-granted then as they are taken now. Hence both the countries could divide waters of the region, which both had subjugated and colonized jointly.

Despite all this, it was never ensured that development in J&K remains in tune with Punjab and other regions that reaped (raped) the benefits of the Indus Waters Treaty. Nobody actually cared. When it was for the greedy needs in the form of development of both the countries, they had no problems to behave like decent neighbours and divide the water resources in an amicable way, so that the needs (greeds) of both the nations could be fulfilled leaving the poor region of Jammu and Kashmir in a lurch and also ensured that it remains in darkness (without electricity and development). The region still experiences curtailment of electricity regularly, so perfectly evolved and punctual that it has earned the name of Kashmir standard time. Predictably, the treaty has no provisions for compensating the losses to the region or share in the developmental benefits that other regions enjoy due to the treaty.

The Indian government always tries to project the state economy as tourism driven, and blames the conflict situation in J&K region since 1990, for the setback to the development. However, it does not talk about its wrongs committed against the region by its colonial policies, like gifting of its huge water resources away and depriving the region of huge earnings it could have made by them.

It has given a diplomatic edge to Pakistan and in a way strengthened its claim on J&K as it could easily argue the point that as India was never sure that it could retain its hold in J&K, it thought better not to invest in huge projects like dams and railways in the region.

Till today, there is no intra railway system in J&K, and India has only recently started some projects in this direction. Instead it opted for 'stable regions' like Punjab. Thus, in a way, it gave more credence to the Pakistan's claim on Kashmir.

Pakistan and the Indus Waters Treaty

As late as February 13 this year, many members of Pakistan National Assembly expressed great concern over the alleged violation of the Indus Waters Treaty by India in building dams across rivers meant for Pakistan and warned of a possible war between the two countries over this issue.

Even before the treaty of 1960, late Suhrawardy, as Prime Minister of Pakistan, threatened that Pakistan will go to war on the sharing of the waters of the Indus.

These threats have been repeated periodically and so regularly by people at the political, military, bureaucratic and technical levels, that these threats have lost their meaning now.

President Ayub Khan, in his broadcast to the nation on September 4, 1960, stated: "The very fact that we will have to be content with the waters of the three western rivers will underline the importance for us of having physical control on the upper reaches of these rivers to secure their maximum utilisation for the ever growing needs of West Pakistan."

Hardly a month had lapsed after Nehru's visit to Karachi, and President Ayub of Pakistan, speaking at a public meeting in Muzaffrabad, Pak-occupied-Kashmir, in early October 1960, declared that "Pakistan could not trust India until the Kashmir question was settled and that the Pak army could never afford to leave the Kashmir issue unsolved for an indefinite period."

Pakistan faces one of the severest water shortages in the world as seen in its per capita availability of water per annum fall from 5300 m^3 in 1951 to less than 1100 m^3 today. This figure is alarming given that it is below the internationally recommended level of 1500 m^3 and precariously close to the critical 1000 m^3 level. Compounded with the failure to fill the country's two largest reservoirs to capacity, declining flows in the Indus River System, elusive and contentious, the inter-provincial water accord due to mutual suspicions among provinces, and an unsustainable population growth rate of 2% do not bode well for Pakistan's water situation. Disagreements on construction of new reservoirs, declining groundwater potential, and growing number of disputes with India after a relatively uneventful period of 44 years of water-sharing will further complicate matters. In summation, the water situation in Pakistan (a country whose landscape is largely arid to semi-arid) is truly disastrous in spite of the Indus, its tributaries, and a treaty with generous concessions that has been implemented faithfully by the upper riparian, India, to date in spite of grave provocations. Pakistani farmers may be forced to change to higher yielding earlier maturing crops, modify their sowing patterns, and employ micro-irrigation in coming years to mitigate shortages–all of which will entail higher costs. Its frivolous objections to Indian projects and a general unwillingness to engage India constructively are partly to force India to amend the IWT to accommodate the emerging patterns of water use in Pakistan, such as water–sharing during periods of shortage–a situation not envisaged in the treaty.

Pakistan's primary interest in Kashmir, to secure its water resources in order to satisfy Punjab and contain Sindh, is in confrontation with the interests of the people of Kashmir on both sides of the line of Control. For the last 15 years, Kashmiri youth have been preoccupied with a conflict with India. However, a water war with Islamabad is in the offing.

Kashmir, on the Pakistani side of the Line of Control, is predominantly agriculture-based, depending on farming, livestock and related activities. **Of the total cultivated area in the region, only 10 per cent is irrigated, compared with about 80 per cent in Pakistan.**

The average farm size is only 1.2 hectares, as compared with 4.7 hectares in Pakistan.

The average annual **per capita income in Kashmir is half of the national average.**

Industry is underdeveloped, with only 930 industrial units, mostly in the private sector. There is no railway network. Road and air transport are the only means of transportation.

Per capita **electricity consumption is around 232 kWh, as compared with 325 kWh in** Pakistan.

With regard to health, as of 1999, there were 1,382 hospital beds in the province, averaging 0.46 beds per thousand persons as compared with 0.67 in Pakistan.

In Kashmir (Pakistan), 13 per cent or 172,721 hectares of land is under farming. Agriculture is an important sector of the Kashmir economy, providing livelihood to 84 per cent of the household. About 97 per cent of the farmers have less than 5 hectares of land and the farming system is based upon cereals and livestock production. The typical farmer has, on an average, 1.2 hectares land in which 60 per cent of land is either under forest or wasteland, with only 0.47 hectares constituting the farm size.

Average household size is 7-8 persons. There is an intense population pressure that is already evident in many areas. Though this region is well endowed with water resources, it is marginally irrigated. Worse, hardly any development projects have been envisaged. Apart from lack of development, the province also suffers from manipulations. Its resources are tapped, but the region is not duly compensated.

The Mangla dam, constructed in Mirpur has revolutionised agriculture in Punjab, but at the cost of Kashmir's deprivation. The Mangla dam, a major asset to the region, irrigates the canals in Punjab and also generates electricity. This dam supplies 20 per cent of the hydro-electricity needs of Pakistan. However, till early 2003, the province had not received any royalty for the electricity generated from Mangla dam. NWFP, however, has been receiving due compensation for the electricity generated from its Tarbela dam.

In late 2002, during General Musharraf's regime, it was decided to raise the height of Mangla dam by another 30 feet to 1,264 feet. This issue had long been under dispute due to objections from Kashmir. **It was feared that by raising the dam, around 44,000 persons and 8,000 households in Kashmir would be displaced, and the district of Mirpur would be submerged.**

Following the federal government's decision, Kashmiris organised several protests. Though the water authorities assured building a new city adjacent to Mirpur for the project-affected people, the locals are not inclined to trust the authorities and almost all the political parties in the province are opposed to the project.

To appease the government in Kashmir, Pakistan decided to pay royalty to the province for the electricity generated from Mangla dam. It was also decided to charge domestic consumer electricity rates, as against the prevailing bulk rates, which are considerably higher.

General Musharraf, while inaugurating the Mangla dam extension project, stated: "This raising of Mangla dam project will first be benefiting Punjab, Sindh, NWFP, Balochistan and would then accrue benefits for Azad Kashmir."

This clearly reflects Pakistan's policy towards Kashmir, an intermediate for the development of its provinces, especially Punjab. Kashmir is needed for developing water and hydropower projects that will ensure reliable supply to the provinces in Pakistan. But at the same time, Kashmir's own development needs are being neglected.

The Mangla dam project and the royalty earmarked encouraged the Kashmir (Pakistan) government to demand a share in the National Finance Commission allocations and also in the Public Sector Development Programme. Kashmir (Pakistan) has never been granted the status of being a province of Pakistan. Such demands reflect their assertion to not remaining a mere surrogate to Pakistan's interests, but also seek their share from the national exchequer.

At a seminar held by the Urdu daily *Ausaf* in early March 2003, the President of Pakistani Kashmir, Sardar Mohammad Anwar Khan, categorically demanded that the Kashmir in Pakistan be strengthened in every sense in comparison to the Kashmir in India, so as to entice the latter to join Pakistan. Similar statements are often heard from leaders in Pakistani Kashmir and these statements definitely mirror their sense of deprivation.

Unfortunately, some Indian scholars without understanding the past history of negotiations with Pakistan, have supported the idea. One of the senior analysts of India is said to have opined that "negotiating an Indus Water Treaty 2 would be a huge Confidence Building Measure as it would engage both countries in a regional economic integration process." A pious hope but an unrealistic one.

The Indus Waters Treaty is unique in one respect. Unlike many of the international agreements which are based on the equitable distribution of waters of the rivers along with other conditions, the Indus Waters Treaty is based on the distribution of the rivers and not the waters.

This unique division of rivers rather than the waters has eliminated the very hassles and conflict that would have followed had equitable distribution of water been based on current usage, historical use, past and potential use etc. People who advocate a revision of the treaty, including some influential ones in India, should realise the trap that India will be getting into.

The IWT is recognized to be a very successful treaty by experts all over the world. It has been upheld even after three wars between India and Pakistan. "Without a treaty, there would have been five or six wars between them", Kishor Uprety, Senior World Bank Lawyer. Disputes have been settled amicably and, until recently, in the case of the Baghlihar Dam, there was no need to invoke the Clause in the IWT that called for the help of a neutral expert. It was negotiated with the help and financial support from the WB in about 10 years and it seems very difficult that a more satisfactory division of water can be arranged under the present circumstances.

Indus Water Treaty: The benefits to the country to flow from the accord and efficient utilisation of water appear to be very impressive. It is estimated that about five million more acres of land can be irrigated, vastly increasing the agricultural output, including a rise of two million tons of wheat. Thus a loss of Rs. 50 million suffered by Pakistan annually would be saved. Finance Minister Sartaj Aziz estimated a gain of Rs. 20 billion to the nation annually through bringing millions of acres of land under cultivation.

Final words

Indian efforts to buy peace from Pakistan by giving concessions through the Indus Waters Treaty failed miserably. The Indus water dispute was, and is sought to be, used by Pakistan as a political tool in the Indo-Pak duel over Kashmir.

All along, Pakistan's policy has been to avoid any direct bilateral settlement with India and to seek third party intervention. The manner in which the Treaty was negotiated and concluded lends an impression of an external pressure group network exerting their influence, since huge investments were involved in the construction of big dams and canals. It is a reflection on the functioning of the World Bank which was influenced by the Cold War politics in the region and by the interested construction lobbies. It also reminds that outside mediation or arbitration in bilateral disputes between India and Pakistan, as was done by the World Bank in this case, would not lead to a lasting and positive solution based on the principles of equitability and just distribution of resources. The Treaty, which has been in force for more than 45 years, has added to the economic woes of the people of the upstream Jammu and Kashmir State by depriving them of their legitimate right to full usage of Jhelum, Chenab and Indus waters for hydro-electric generation, irrigation, navigation and other purposes. As such, there is sufficient ground for reviewing the Indus Treaty, so that it is turned into a resilient one after making necessary modifications and adjustments, which can take care of the substantial changes in the ground situation in Jammu and Kashmir.

That Pakistan has secured third party intervention, the World Bank, to resolve its dispute with India over the Baglihar hydro-project is a part of its strategy to internationalize and politicize the issue. It marks a complete deviation from the path of the "Composite Dialogue" process agreed to by both India and Pakistan to resolve all outstanding issue including Kashmir. Pakistan's objections to the construction of Baglihar dam are more political than technical in nature.

However, we argue that the Treaty has yet to provide sustainable solutions for peace- maintenance at state level, and more importantly, meaningful protection to the citizens of both countries.

The Treaty cannot be said to be a success unless it can effectively improve the living conditions of locals, who, afterall, should be the focus in a Human Security context. We suggest international inspection and close monitoring to ensure the river resources are used to their full potential. More work has to be done in ensuring the Treaty is implemented within a Human Security framework.

The treaty has engendered a vicious cycle.

Lack of trust between India and Pakistan (Improper handling of relations with Pakistan) forced the bifurcation of the Indus River Basin.

Neglect towards the future requirement of Jammu and Kashmir Lack of opportunities for the overall development of Jammu &Kashmir.

Widening the gap between Shrinager and New Delhi. As the gap between water availability and requirements widen in Pakistan, agricultural development will be affected, which, in turn, will produce a stratum of unemployed youth willing to service terrorist groups.

This, in turn, would aggravate the mistrust and hostility between the two countries.

This vicious cycle of depleting resources, spawning unemployment and fuelling terrorism, is feared to intensify in the near future.

Abrogating the Indus Waters Treaty would provide greater benefits and open up several avenues for unrestrained development of the state of Jammu & Kashmir.

It can:

- Improve hydro-electricity sector's potential as storage facilities could be developed.
- Pave the way for the industrialization of the state.
- Improve irrigation facilities which, in turn, would boost agricultural growth.
- Give rise to employment opportunities, which will indirectly keep a check on external interference in state affairs.
- Help attract private investments, propelling the state's position on India's investment map.

The opportunity to tap the Jhelum and Chenab Rivers would provide windfall gains not only to Jammu & Kashmir, but also to the neighbouring states of Punjab, Rajasthan and Haryana. The three states share the eastern rivers and are in conflict over the sharing of waters. The addition of Chenab and Jhelum would secure water availability for these states.

The Indus Waters Treaty casts a unilateral responsibility on India for compliance. It is an obligation that necessarily falls on all upper riparians. Abrogation would not be defensible on any understanding of international water laws or international humanitarian laws. Further, abrogation will necessarily have to be followed by an engineering feat that would greatly strain the Indian economy.

In any case, legally speaking, it is virtually impossible for India to abrogate the treaty. Article XII (4) states that "provisions of this treaty shall continue in force until terminated by a duly ratified treaty concluded for that purpose between the two Governments." The treaty does not provide an exit clause for India *per se*.

Abrogation is bound to incite reactions from the World Bank and the countries that were party to the treaty and have provided funds. The countries, including Australia, Canada, Germany, New Zealand, Britain and the US, are also India's major export destinations.

India is aware of the implications of the abrogation of the treaty. Therefore, despite growing protests from the Kashmiri people, no policy-maker in New Delhi is ever likely to even contemplate this move. The act of abrogation on the part of India could cause insecurity among the other countries that are lower riparians to India. India's relations with its neighbours would also be affected, as India also has water treaties with Nepal and Bangladesh. SAARC would be diluted.

In April 2008, Pakistan's Indus Water Commissioner, Jamaat Ali Shah, in a frank interview conceded that the water projects undertaken by India do not contravene the provisions of the Indus Water Treaty of 1960. He said that "in compliance with IWT, India has not so far constructed any storage dam on the Indus, the Chenab and the Jhelum rivers (rivers allotted to Pakistan for full use). The Hydro-electric projects India is developing are the run-of-the-river, projects which India is permitted to pursue according to the treaty."

There is no doubt that Pakistan will be facing increasing water shortages in the days to come leading to prolonged droughts in many of its regions. The reasons are many but some of these are Pakistan's own doing. The availability of water, even now, has reached critical proportions.

1. Global warming over a period of time has depleted the flow of water in the Indus (the major supplier) which depends mostly on glacial runoffs.

2. As in other Himalayan regions, like the Kosi in Nepal, the rivers carry very heavy sediments that result in silting the dams and barrages thus reducing the availability of water for cultivation. Proper and periodic maintenance have been lacking.

3. The canals that feed the irrigated lands are not lined resulting in seepage and loss of water.

4. There is mismanagement in use of water by using antiquated techniques and heavy cropping of water intensive varieties of farm products. Optimum crop rotations have not been done extensively as should have been done to save water.

5. No serious effort has been made to improve the storage for intensive seasons like Kharif.

6. Dwindling water flow has also been affecting power generation.

The discharge of fresh water into the Arabian sea has dwindled considerably (less than 10 MAF) which has resulted in the sea water pushing further into the estuaries and beyond, making water in those areas unfit for cultivation.

There is a larger political dimension to the whole problem of the river water distribution between Pakistan and India. To Pakistan, the Kashmir issue is irrevocably linked to the Indus Water Treaty, as the headwaters of all the rivers of Pakistan, and meant for Pakistan, flow through Kashmir, and India happens to be the upper riparian state. The fear exists that India could manipulate the waters to starve Pakistan; is that a real fear or a desire to take over Kashmir?

APP - 8

VIOLATION OF INDUS WATER TREATY

Malik Muhammad Ashraf
The News, 15 May 2015

Why can't both Pakistan and India work it out?

The World Bank backed Indus Waters Treaty between Pakistan and India has survived three wars between the two countries, but the latter has not shown any inclination to strictly abide by its obligations under the Treaty. Pakistan raised objections to the construction of Wuller Barrage, Baghliar Dam and Kishanganga Hydro-Electric Power Project, maintaining that these projects vitiated the clauses of the Treaty. The Permanent Indus Commission, created under the treaty to monitor the implementation of the provisions of the Treaty and to deal with complaints and disputes pertaining to the implementation of the agreement, failed to resolve these issues and the matter had to be referred cither to a 'Neutral Expert' or the Permanent Court of Arbitration at Hague (PAC). The verdicts in case of Wuller and Baghliar went against the position taken by Pakistan. However the decision on Kishanganga, while recognizing the Indian right to build the dam, did address Pakistan's concerns about India maintaining the level of the reservoirs below the Dead Storage Level and also recognised the concept of environmental flows in rivers to ensure that the power generating projects are operated in an environmentally sustainable manner. The final Award announced on Dec 20, 2013, specified that $9m^3/s$ of natural flow of water must be maintained in Kishanganga River at all times to maintain the environment downstream.

Pakistan being an agricultural country is totally dependent on the waters of the Indus Basin Rivers. Agriculture is the backbone of its economy with a share of 21 per cent in GDP. Nearly 45 per cent of the labour force is employed in the agriculture sector and it accounts for 80 per cent of the raw material for agro-based industries in Pakistan. Therefore the Indus River System undoubtedly constitutes the lifeline of the country. The PAC verdict on Kishanganga is viewed by experts as a win-win situation for both India and Pakistan which could usher in a new dawn for water management under the Indus Waters Treaty.

The Kishanganga Power Plant in the River Jhelum Basin, Pakistan felt, would increase the catchment area in contravention of the Treaty and also give India control over the storage and release of water. The dam is expected to be completed in 2016. But as it turns out, the Indians are still persisting with more than specified depth of the spillways of the dam in complete disregard to the Treaty and the decision of the PAC. India is also going ahead with the construction of 850 MW Ratle Hydropower Project in Jammu and Kashmir. Pakistan also has serious concerns about it. According to reliable sources, Pakistani authorities have decided to go for international arbitration and accordingly a case has been prepared for the purpose. However, it has not yet been decided whether to present it before the Neutral Expert to be selected through mutual consent or take it to the PAC. The protracted talks between the two sides on these projects have failed to produce any results.

Pakistan also has serious reservations on the designs of other projects including 1,000 MW Pakal Dul, 120 MW Miyar and 48 MW Lower Kalnai which India is building on River Chenab. Negotiations on these ventures have also reached nowhere and India remains adamant as ever to construct these facilities as per their original design. There is a permeating feeling among Pakistan authorities that looking through the past record, there seems no possibility of India showing any flexibility in this regard and Pakistan ultimately might also have to seek international arbitration on these projects as well. It is believed that the construction of the Kishanganga Dam, in contravention of the Treaty and the decision of the PAC, apart from an adverse impact on irrigation and energy producing schemes, would also profoundly affect biodiversity and ecosystems in the Neelum Valley. The volume of water in the part of the river on the Indian side is ten times than the water in the river on our side. The diversion of this water to the Jhelum basin would adversely affect the environment of the valley as well. These concerns have repeatedly been agitated with the Indian negotiators without any positive response.

It is pertinent to point out that under the Indus Waters Treaty 1960, the waters of the Eastern rivers- Sutlej, Beas, and Ravi had been allocated to India and the Western rivers Indus, Jhelum and Chenab to Pakistan, except for certain uses allowed to India, including power generation without altering the water flows. Some sources believe that India is contemplating to launch more hydropower projects with a cumulative power generating capacity of 32,000 MW on the rivers allocated to Pakistan and consequently attain the capability of regulating the water flows to Pakistan, especially reducing water flow in the river Chenab which irrigates most of the land in Punjab.

According to FAO, more than 3,600 treaties related to international water resources have been drawn up among nations sharing the waters of rivers and lakes since the 805 AD. The focus of most of these treaties was on navigational considerations. However, since 20th century, the emphasis has shifted away from navigation towards the use, development, protection and conservation of water resources and the mechanism for sharing these common resources. There are 263 trans-boundary lake and river basins in the world, covering nearly half of the land mass of the Earth. While some basins are shared by two countries, others are shared by five to eighteen nations (River Danube). The riparian nations, either through bilateral arrangements or through multilateral agreements, have been sharing these water resources in a manner that safeguards the interests of all the parties to the treaties. The UN Resolution on Law of Trans-boundary Aquifers and the UN Convention on Law of Non-Navigational Use of International Water Courses also stipulate some key guiding principles in this respect which include equitable and reasonable utilisation of international water courses, application of appropriate measures to prevent harm to other states sharing an international water course and the principle of prior notification of planned measures.

As is evident from the foregoing facts, the Indian stance and disposition towards the Indus Waters Treaty and the PAC verdict on Kisghanganga also constitute a wilful breach of international conventions and guidelines on the subject. India and Pakistan need a peaceful atmosphere for changing the fate of teeming millions on both sides of the border and, therefore, should focus more on removing irritants instead of scuttling the chances of bonhomie between the two by adopting an unreasonable position on the sharing of water resources between the two countries.

APP – 9

BAGLIHAR DAM

Usman Ahmad, May, 2006
ICE Case Studies

I. CASE BACKGROUND

1. Abstract

In the mid 1990s, India started construction on the Baglihar hydro-electric dam on the Chenab river. The dam is located in the disputed region of Kashmir. Kashmir is a region located in the southwest part of Himalayan mountains northwest of India and northeast of Pakistan. Pakistan and India have both claimed Kashmir for themselves and thus the region has experienced an on-going conflict since both countries gained independence in 1947.

There are multiple reasons why the region is so highly valued by Pakistan and India. First, there is the natural inclination of any nation-state to want to expand its territory because of self-interest. Second, Kashmir has also become an issue of national pride in both states, especially in terms of religion for Pakistan. Third, Kashmir is located in the Indus River basin area, thus contributing to the flow of several rivers in South Asia.

One of these rivers is the aforementioned Chenab river, which flows from Kashmir into Pakistan. India is able to build the Baglihar hydro-electric dam because it is located in the part of Kashmir it administers. Starting in May 1999, Pakistan asked India to suspend construction activity on the dam and engage in bilateral negotiations. The dam is controversial because Pakistan claims that the dam will impede water flow enough to disrupt agriculture and general water supply for its people. According to Pakistan, the issue is the structure of the dam which is said to violate provisions of the 1960 Indus Waters Treaty regarding ungated spillways and pondage storage capacity[1].

2. Description

Negotiations were held but resulted in no resolution to the dispute over the dam; part of the deadlock is due to continued terrorism in India allegedly supported by Pakistan. Under normal circumstances, India would have continued to fulfill its moral obligation of sharing its water with Pakistan. But unusual circumstances call for unusual action, said Jasjit Singh, former director of the Institute of Defence Studies and Analyses in New Delhi.[2] In January 2005 Pakistan, believing that India was speeding up construction of the dam, invoked article IX of the Indus Waters treaty which allowed for a neutral arbitrator to be appointed by the World Bank to resolve the conflict.

A report in New Scientist discussed the following issues for Pakistan:

- Hydrologists in Pakistan believe that a breakdown of the treaty could lead to widespread famine, and further inflame the ongoing conflict over Kashmir,

- Pakistan relies on the Indus river and its tributaries for almost half its irrigation supplies,
- Pakistan relies on the Indus river and its tributaries to generate up to half of its electricity,
- Pakistan fears that India would use the Baglihar dam as a coercive tool by causing floods in Pakistan through the release of dam waters.

Accordingly, in researching and producing a case-study analysis of this dispute, there are four main issues to be investigated. First is the explicit poverty and ecological effects construction of the dam would have in Pakistan. Second is the effects on agriculture the dam would have-according to the CIA World Factbook 21.6% of Pakistan's Gross Dometic Product is agricultural and 42% of its labor force is engaged in agriculture.[4] Third is the production and consumption of energy. This issue is as much a factor for India as it is for Pakistan. In fact, India could stand to lose substantially if construction of the dam adversely affects its plans to construct a natural gas pipeline from Iran through Pakistan. Fourth and finally is the threat that the dam could also be used as a weapon by India. Pakistani fears seem to have been confirmed in July of 2005 when India released 564,000 cubic feet per second of water into the Chenab from the Baglihar dam thus flooding portions of Pakistan.[5]

3. Duration 50+ years

4. Location

This conflict takes place in South Asia. The dam is specifically being built on the Chenab river in the Indian controlled part of Kashmir.

5. Actors

Pakistan – Population 165,803,560; Literacy total population: 48.7% male: 61.7% female: 35.2%; Gross Domestic Product $384.9 billion	India – Population 1,095,351,995 ; Literacy total population: 59.5% male: 70.2% female: 48.3%; Gross Domestic Product $3.699 trillion

II. Environment Aspects

Poverty and Ecology - The Baglihar dam is expected to further exacerbate an already dire water situation in Pakistan which is described as a water crisis by Naser I Faruqui.[6] Faruqui, in a 2004 report, discusses some key water problems in Pakistan which can be expected to be worsened by construction of the Baglihar dam:

- In 1947 there was an annual renewable water availability of 5600 m^3 per person. That has shrunk to 1000 m^3, a level Faruqui expects to induce chronic water scarcity on a scale sufficient to impede human development,
- Erosion due to deforestation has led to sediment buildup and siltation in rivers and reservoirs thus decreasing water capacity. For example, Faruqui cites a UN report which stated that water capacity at Pakistans Tarbela and Mangala dams had fallen by 4.9 million acre feet,
- Current rates of soil salinization predict that large portions of land will become unarable,
- Already, decreased water flow has caused seawater intrusion up the delta where the Indus river meets the Arabian Sea; the salinization of hitherto freshwater has forced migration of peoples to urban areas and increased dependence on other sources of water.

The loss of land to salinity build up is of agricultural concern but also general ecological concern. A report at Training Workshop on Wetlands, Biodiversity, and Water in Kushiro, Japan, confirmed that

Pakistan had not only reached the limit of its water resources, but was also utilizing all cultivable land.[7] The combination of these problems, according to the Workshop report, has led to flash floods and landslides that destroyed habitat and killed humans and animals. Again, further disruption to water flow would further exacerbate Pakistan's precarious situation.

The Water Poverty Index (WPI), as developed by Peter Lawrence, Jeremy Meigh, and Caroline Sullivan, provides a general tool which links household welfare with water availability and indicates the degree to which water scarcity impacts on human populations.[8] In this index, countries' positions are measured relative to each other in terms of 5 components: resources, access, capacity, use, and environment. Each of the five component indices is multiplied by 20 and added together for the final WPI score which ranges from 0-100. The resources category uses data regarding internal freshwater flow, external inflows, and population while the environment category uses data regarding water quality, water stress, regulation and management of environment, informational capacity, and biodiversity, based on threatened species. Pakistan scored a 57.8 with its low scores being in the categories of resources (7.3) and environment (11.5). However, data shows that India is in an even worse position; this shows that Pakistan and India are both in very similar circumstances and each has as much stake in the construction of the Baglihar dam as the other.

Summary of WPI Data			
Country	Resources Score	Environment Score	WPI Ranking
Finland	12.2	17.1	78
United States	10.3	15.3	65
Japan	8.1	11.6	64.8
Egypt	3.4	10.5	58
Pakistan	7.3	11.5	57.8
India	6.8	9.5	53.2
China	7.1	9.7	51.1
Jordan	0.4	7.3	46.3
Morocco	5.4	11.8	46.2
Nigeria	6.4	10.1	43.9
Niger	6.4	10	35.2
Haiti	6.1	5.8	35.1

Agriculture – As stated earlier, Pakistan is highly dependent on agriculture, which in turn is dependent on water. The Kushiro Training Workshop report included an assessment of Pakistan's agricultural situation. Of the 79.6 million hectares of land that makeup Pakistan, 20 million are available for agriculture. Of those 20 million hectares, 16 million are dependent on irrigation. Faruqui estimates that up to 90% of Pakistan's agriculture is dependent on irrigation.

An even more important fact is that many of Pakistan's industries are agro-based, such as the textiles industry. Thus an interruption of water supply would have broad and ranging effects. When the country suffered a drought from 1998 to 2001, there were violent riots in Karachi.

In terms of sheer ability to feed itself, Faruqui includes figures from Pakistans Water Vision for 2025 which predicts that Pakistan could be importing upto 28 million tons of wheat by 2025, an amount that Faruqui believes cannot be supported economically by the government. His belief is corroborated by Zaigham Habib in an article in Water for Food and Rural Development.[9] As of the year of publication, she calculated that 80% of Pakistan's food needs were fulfilled domestically. But she also predicted that due to degradation in land, increased salinization, and decreased water flow, that was not a sustainable mark.

Furthermore, revenue from agriculture only pays for less than 40% of the cost of irrigation. The crux of the problem, which was also identified by the Kushiro Training Workshop, is that a small portion of Pakistan's land is available for agriculture, and of that area, nearly 80% is dependent on irrigation. A summary of this situation is made in the following table taken from Habib (in Mollinga):

6. Type of Environmental Problem

Water and Land Resources of Pakistan			
Land availability and utilization		Water availability and utilization	
Gross area of Pakistan	83 million hectares	Average river inflow	138.89 million acre feet
Cropped Land	22.4 million hectares	River flow diverted for irrigation	103.36 million acre feet
Forest	3%	Rainfall below rivers main catchment	75 milion meters 460 million meters
Rain fed area	2.2 million hectares	Rainfall volume	67 million acre feet
Area with usable groundwater	65%	Rainfall in canal irrigated zone	19.38 million acre feet
Area with groundwater pumpage	65%	Daily free-surface evaporation	3 million meters-6 million meters
Percent Waterlogged	20%	Recycled Water Average Daily	37.14 million acre feet
Percent Saline	30%	Main and Secondary systems efficiency	85%
Field Efficiency	75%	Tertiary systems efficiency	75%

Energy – Obviously, the energy aspect to the construction of the Baglihar dam is of greatest concern to India. Intuitively, one knows that as one of the world's fastest growing economies, India's energy needs are also growing rapidly. Currently, the country is known for rolling blackouts and daily energy outages in some areas during certain seasons.

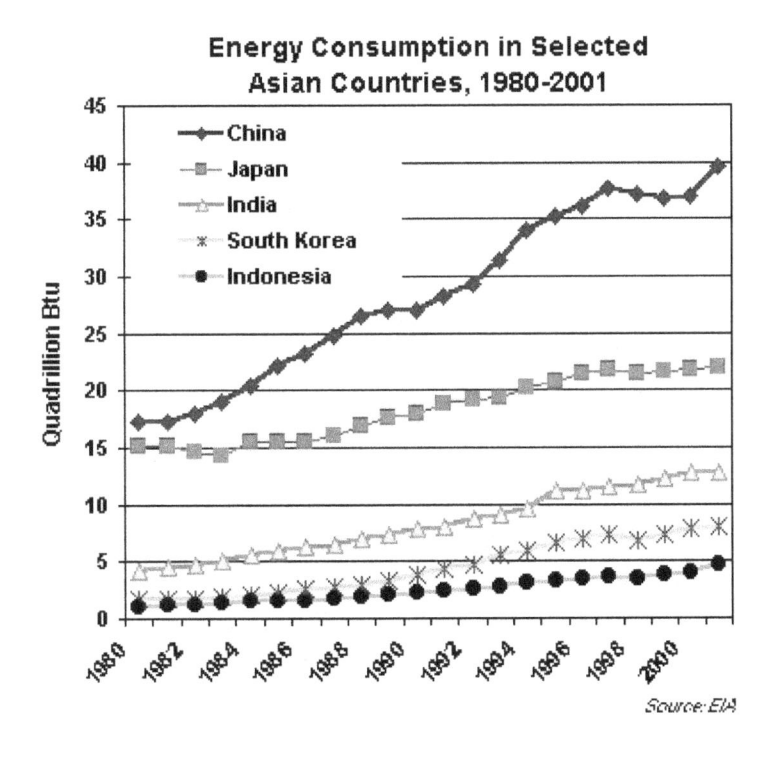

Source: EIA

It is worth noting though that it is estimated that half of Pakistan's energy comes from hydroelectricity.[10] India, on the other hand only gets 6.3% of its energy from hydo-electricity.[11] Data from a 2004 report from the Energy Information Administration (EIA) of the United States government on India shows that there is a burgeoning burden on India's energy sector. Since 1980 there has been a 208% increase in India's energy consumption. Even more alarming is that despite this growth and its massive population, it ranks below the US, Germany, and Japan in terms of consumption, indicating that its needs are not met. Thus, the Baglihar dam is a small but important part of India's energy needs.

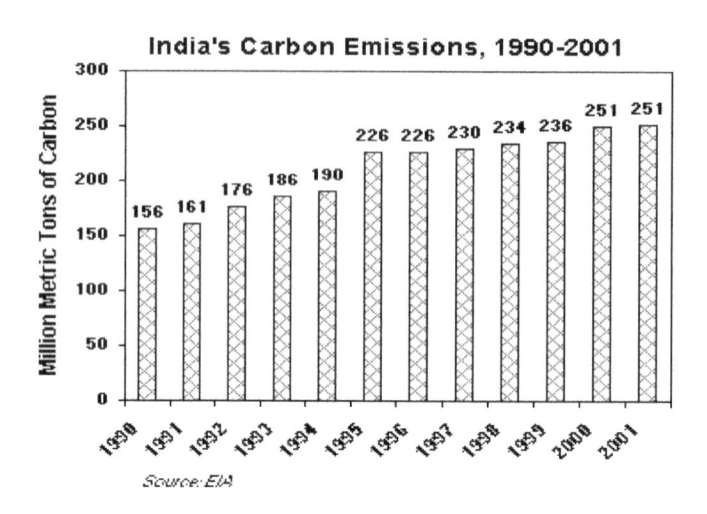

III. Environment and Conflict Overlap

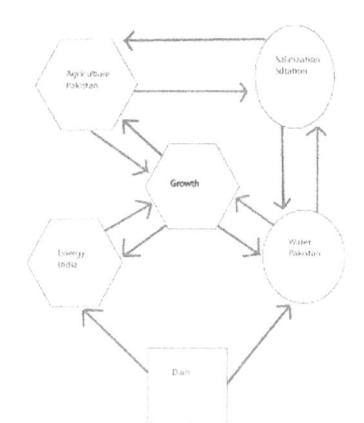

In coding the dispute over the Baglihar dam and the overarching conflict over Indus River Basin, a question to be asked under the framework of current environmental conflict theory is whether it is truly a scarcity issue. On the surface, it seems that a scarcity of water and energy is to blame for the building of, and controversy surrounding, the Baglihar dam. However, in viewing the region as a whole, it is clear that the conflict is one of surplus.

7. Environment Conflict-Link Dynamics

Prior to the division of the Indian subcontinent into India and Pakistan, there was little dispute over water rights. The partition effectively divided what had been a unified water-sharing region. In a 1950 report in the Geographical Review, FJ Fowler concludes that The boundary between India and Pakistan cuts across the hitherto unified Punjab irrigation network, giving rise to obvious difficulties. Thus this conflict should be coded as a Direct Resource conflict. The interplay of various environmental factors are illustrated in the image below. Red arrows indicate a negative relationship (ie increasing stress or decreasing the affected variable); green arrows indicate a positive (increasing) relationship with an affected variable. The hexagons represent variables of strategic interest.

8. Level of Strategic Interest

The fact that both Pakistan and India possess nuclear weapons automatically catapults this dispute to the global level of strategic interest. The causal pathways (in the image above) leading to large scale war have the potential for nuclear conflict which would have Armageddon like impacts on the world as a whole.

614

Another added complication is that in building a dam upstream of Pakistan, India will possess the ability to flood or starve Pakistan at will. This ability was witnessed in July of 2004 when India, without warning, released water into the Chenab river, flooding large portions of Pakistan.[5] The history of conflict between these two nations makes this possible use of nature as a weapon very real.

In terms of energy, India also needs to factor in the importance of their proposed gas pipeline from Iran through Pakistan. Negotiations regarding the pipeline would certianly be affected by a negative outcome in this dispute.

One important factor that makes the prospects for conflict so grim is the fact that India insists on bi-lateral negotiations only. This allows it to exercise an extra coercive force on Pakistan. However, in the case of the Baglihar dam, Pakistan has sought third party intervention, that of the WTO, to resolve the issue per the 1960 Indus Waters Treaty. Dr. Raymond Lafitte has been appointed by the WTO to act as a neutral arbitrator in the dispute. If India accepts his decision, conflict could be avoided.

9. References, Relevant Websites and Literature

1. Akhlaque, Qudssia. (November 30, 2003). Final Notice to be Served on India: Baglihar Dam Issue. Dawn.

2. Pearce, Fred. (2002). Water War. New Scientist, 174, (2343). P. 18

3. Pearce, Fred. (2002). Water War. New Scientist, 174, (2343). P. 18

4. The World Factbook. (2006). Pakistan. Central Intelligence Agency 2/2/2006

5. China Daily News Group (2005). Pakistan Issues Warning after India Releases Water into Chenab. 2/2/2006

6. Faruqui, Naser I (2004). Responding to Water Crisis in Pakistan. Water Resources Development, 20. (2) p. 177-192

7. UNITAR Hiroshima Office for Asia and the Pacific, Series on Biodiversity (2004). Training Workshop on Wetlands, Biodiversity, and Water: New Tools for the Ecosystem Management. Kushiro International Wetland Centre.

8. Lawrence et al (2002). The Water Poverty Index: An International Comparison. Keele Economics Research Papers, 19.

9. Habib, Zaigham. (2000) Resource Conservation and Civil Society: Water and Food Security in Pakistan. In Peter Mollinga (Ed.) Water for Food and Rural Development (pg. 182-196). London, UK: Sage Publications.

10. British Columbia Hydro International (1998). Snow and Ice Hydrology Project. Final Report to IDRC (Vancouver: BC Hydro).

11. EIA Country Analysis Briefs. India: Environmental Issues. Energy Information Administration (February 2004), 2/2/06- http://www.eia.doe.gov/emeu/cabs /indiaenv.html

12. Barua, Pradeep. The State at War in South Asia. Lincoln: University of Nebraska Press 2005.

APP - 10

CRUCIAL WATER ISSUES BETWEEN PAKISTAN AND INDIA: CONFIDENCE BUILDING MEASURES AND THE ROLE OF MEDIA

Muhammad Rashid Khan, June, 2013
(South Asian Studies)

ABSTRACT

This paper thrashes out the water issues between Pakistan and India and the recent developments that have taken place specifically in the year 2011. The disputes of building dams on cross - boundary rivers like the construction of Kishanganga Hydro - Electricity Project by India, Pakistan's objections to the project, decision of the International Court of Arbitration, Indian response, confidence building measures and the role of media have been analysed. The study identifies India's various unfair dealings with Pakistan in watersharing. The water issues will attain a significance greater than the Kashmir issue. Solving the Kashmir issue will lead towards solving the water issues.

Introduction

There is a growing feeling in Pakistan that while India is increasingly building dams on its western rivers, it is simultaneously engaged in activities aimed at stopping Pakistan, the lower riparian, from building storage dams on Pakistani rivers. In the case of its upper riparian neighbour, Nepal, India has even deployed heavy artillery to partially destroy dams which were being constructed by the Nepalese. India's water strategy thus boils down to construction of more and more dams on cross-boundary rivers inside its own territory while obstructing dams in lower-riparian neighbours and destroying those in upper-riparian Nepal (Kazi, 2011).

Honorary vice-president of the International Commission on Large Dams (ICOLD), Asif H. Kazi, in his column titled "Misusing the Indus Treaty" argues that: "Pakistan's farmlands have been deprived of the uses of the waters of three eastern rivers – Ravi, Beas and Sutlej. The flows of these rivers were allocated to India under the 1960 Indus Waters Treaty. Authorities on the subject accept that when rivers and canals in Pakistan's demarcated area were classified as Pakistan's assets under the Partition Act 1947, it meant only one thing: that these rivers and canals were to continue to receive water in the same way as before. Under the treaty, Pakistan was to enjoy unrestricted use of the Indus, the Jhelum and the Chenab. However, exceptions were inserted as annexures which allowed India to develop and use certain specified quantities of the waters of the three western rivers as well" (Kazi, 2011).

Annexure E established Indian storage limits on the western rivers, which add up to 3.6 MAF (million acre feet). However, India deliberately followed a pattern of filling water behind the Baglihar Dam constructed on Chenab River by impounding flows in the low-flow month of September, a clear breach of the treaty, which prescribes the filling period as being from June 21 to Aug 31 (Ibid).

Obviously, the foregoing was not the intent of the Indus Waters Treaty. And it is precisely for this reason that Pakistan has been insisting that India adopt well known dam design features, especially for the outlets, which can easily ensure that the reservoir operators would not be able to manipulate flows of the western rivers at their own sweet will. India is opposing this, using as an excuse the need for the prolongation of the reservoirs' lifespan through sediment flushing (Ibid).

Backdrop: The Indus Waters Treaty (IWT)

Analysts are of the opinion that, "the highly sensitive and charged water issues between Pakistan and India have emerged out of the way the 1947 partition lines were drawn. A seemingly minor change, but one with far-reaching consequences, was introduced in the partition map, in violation of all principles laid down by the British government. It came about at the very last minute when, upon the insistence of the Indian leaders, the partition award turned over to India three vital districts that were originally allocated to Pakistan, with the sole objective of providing India with access to Kashmir. The three remaining western rivers, on which Pakistan now relies upon, all originate in, or pass through, Kashmir before entering Pakistan. In other words, India, after having obtained the waters of the three eastern rivers through the Indus Waters Treaty, is now trying to take control of the three western rivers as well" (Kazi, 2011).

Momin Iftikhar provides further detail: "The Indus Waters Treaty (IWT), signed in Karachi on September 19, 1960, by India's Prime Minister, Jawaharlal Nehru, Pakistan's President, Muhammad Ayub Khan and Mr W.A.B. Illif of the World Bank has shown a remarkable endurance and resilience in withstanding the jolts of the Indo-Pak turbulent relations. The treaty allocates the water of the three western rivers of the Indus Basin (Indus, Jhelum and Chenab) to Pakistan, while the eastern rivers (Ravi and Sutlej) have been assigned to India for utilisation. The treaty allows India to tap the hydroelectric potential of the Pakistan specific rivers with the important proviso that generation of power should not interfere with the timings and the quantity of flow of waters into Pakistan" (Iftikhar, 2011).

In his column titled "Tackling the Kishanganga knot" Iftikhar held the view that: "If India and Pakistan had normal and trustful relations, with a credible monitoring mechanism in place, this would not have been too demanding a task to accomplish within the parameters provided by the IWT. However, with emerging water shortages for agriculture in Pakistan, and the sensitivity of timings to the flow of water in the rivers that feed the defense-oriented canals and sustains the capacity for the generation of hydroelectric power, it is easier said than done" (Ibid).

Construction of Kishanganga Hydro – Electricity Project (KHEP)

The water sharing environment in South Asia is fast deteriorating. The Pakistani frustration at Indian inflexibility was evident when it referred the matter of Baghliar Dam on River Chenab to the World Bank in January 2005. The verdict by a neutral expert, appointed by the bank, ultimately settled the issue in February 2007. The decision accommodated both the parties and each country felt that its respective stance had been addressed and vindicated. The problem did not end there; within four years, the two countries are back for arbitration over the water issue and the bone of contention this time is construction by India of the Kishanganga Storage-cum-Hydroelectric Power Project on River Neelum (Indians call it Kishanganga), which is a major tributary of River Jhelum. Iftikhar (2011) points out that: "The matter is sensitive because not only the dam will curtail the flow of water for agriculture, but Pakistan is also constructing the Neelum-Jhelum Hydroelectric Project on River Neelum, downstream of Kishanganga Project."

Pakistan's fundamental objection to Kishanganga is that it involves diverting the water of Neelum River through a 21 km long tunnel towards the Wullar Lake to generate 330 MW power. This is manifestly not allowed by the IWT. Iftikhar indicates: "This diversion is against the provisions of the IWT and has not only serious consequence for the 969 MW power generation capability of Neelum-Jhelum Hydrolectrical Project, but will also reduce the water supply for agriculture in the areas of Azad Kashmir, which are dependent on the Neelum River flow. It is estimated that the diversion of water towards Wullar Lake will reduce flow into Pakistan by 27 percent (Ibid).

According to the available data, it is estimated that, "the dry spell is likely to extend to eight months per year. The lack of water is going to have an adverse impact on agriculture in over thousands of acres in Azad Kashmir, which are dependent upon the flow of River Neelum, besides causing damage to the environmental aspects of flora and fauna nurtured by the rivers flow in the Neelum Valley" (Ibid).

Kazi (2011) supports the view that, "the proposed Kishenganga project violates the treaty in a most glaring way. Firstly, the hydroelectric plant is not located on the Kishenganga but way off the channel at the end of a long tunnel that discharges into another tributary. And, secondly, the recipient tributary ultimately outfalls upstream of the Wullar Lake, and this completely changes the patterns of the flows of both Kishenganga and Jhelum Rivers."

The International Court of Arbitration's Decision

In response to Pakistan's appeal for 'interim measures' against the dam which may inhibit the restoration of the river flow to its natural channel, "the International Court of Arbitration (ICA) barred India from any permanent works on the controversial Kishanganga hydro-electricity project (KHEP) on River Neelum at Gurez in occupied Kashmir" (Raza, 2011).

The court order said: "India shall not proceed with the construction of any permanent works on or above the Kishanganga/Neelum River bed at the Gurez site that may inhibit the restoration of the flow of the river to its natural channel. Pakistan and India shall arrange for periodic joint inspections of the dam site at Gurez in order to monitor the implementation of the court's order" (Ibid).

Irfan Raza reports that, "Islamabad had submitted its version in the World Bank's arbitration court in July (2011). The major contention was that under the law, India cannot divert the route of River Neelum. Pakistan fears that the Kishanganga dam would rob it of 15 per cent water share – a violation of the Indus Waters Treaty. Islamabad accused Delhi of trying to divert the water of Neelum river in order to harm Pakistan's Neelum-Jhelum hydro-electricity project (Ibid).

In its request, Pakistan had required: "A stop work order; an order that any steps India has taken or may take in respect of the KHEP are taken at its own risk without prejudice to the possibility that the court may order that the works may not be continued, be modified or dismantled, that India be ordered to inform the court and Pakistan of any imminent and actual developments on the Kishanganga Dam that may adversely affect the restoring of the status quo ante or that may jeopardise Pakistan's rights and interests under the treaty; any further relief the court considered necessary"... (Ibid).

Indian Response

Indian experts denied the allegations raised by the Pakistani Government on building the Kishanganga Dam. Former Secretary, Water Resources, Ramaswamy R Iyer in his column titled "Pakistan: Water on the Boil Again" writes: " So far as one knows, India has not built any storage, not even the 3.6 MAF permitted by the Treaty, nor does it intend to cause harm to Pakistan by diverting Indus waters. In any case, there is such a thing as the Permanent Indus Commission. How can India store or divert waters to the detriment of Pakistan under the watchful eyes of the Indus Commissioner for Pakistan"?

On violations of the provisions of the Indus Treaty by India, Iyer elaborates that, "the Treaty envisages and permits Indian projects on western rivers and so the projects in themselves cannot be violations of the

Treaty. They can be violations of the Treaty if they deviate from certain restrictive provisions, but that will be questioned by the Indus Commissioner for Pakistan. The questions may be resolved within the Commission, or become differences and get referred to a Neutral Expert (as happened in the Baglihar case), or may be in the nature of disputes to be referred to a Court of Arbitration (as has now happened in the Kishenganga case)."

Vibha Sharma, in a column titled "India confident of winning Kishanganga dispute", writes: "India today termed as "favourable" the International Court of Arbitration (ICA) order last week which prevents the country from undertaking permanent works above the riverbed level at the Gurez site of the Kishanganga hydropower project. The final orders are expected either in 2012-end or in early 2013." (Sharma, 2011)

Water Resources Minister, Pawan Bansal, asserted that "the stay was merely an interim legal position and in no way signified any "loss of position" for India, as was being projected by Pakistan. Bansal told The Tribune that "the neighbouring country had raised two issues–stopping the work and dismantling the construction already done–and the court did not agree to either of its two contentions." (Ibid)

"India can go ahead with construction of powerhouses, tunneling works, coffer dams, temporary bypass tunnel and concretisation under the riverbed for the dam. The only thing we cannot do is go above the surface of the river bed, which is not a problem, since we would only be able to complete these works by 2012-end and 2013 beginning, by when the court will give its final decision," Bansal said. (Ibid)

For now, India is compiling a rejoinder to emphasize its point before the International Court of Justice. "The Hague-based ICA has directed India to submit a report on environmental hazards to the ecosystem due to this project." (Ibid)

Former Secretary, Water Resources, Ramaswamy R Iyer also maintained that "the ruling was neither a win nor a loss for either country. It is just a temporary stay. India can still continue with related works except constructing the dam," he said. (Ibid)

However, taking into account political and environmental consequences of the project, Sharma is of the view that "there appears to be some amount of skepticism," with an expert saying that investments could go waste if the final award goes against India, which, in other words, also means that the power problem in Kashmir will continue."India will be taking a risk by carrying out with other works till the final ruling," said the water resources expert, who did not wish to be quoted." (Ibid)

Confidence Building Measures

Daily The Telegraph reports that: "Ahead of another round of Indo-Pak water talks scheduled in mid-September (2011), the Jammu and Kashmir government quietly abandoned the controversy-ridden plan to construct a concrete barrage where the Jhelum meets the Wullarlake in north Kashmir" (Thakur, 2011).

Thakur, Sankarshan (2011) believes that: "It's a small move with big implications: a persistent irritant in bilateral ties, the dumping of the barrage could prove a significant confidence-building measure between India and Pakistan."

Giving further details, Thakur writes that: "Work on the venture, christened the Tulbul Navigation Project by New Delhi, but better known as the Wullar barrage, was stopped two years after it commenced in 1984 upon strong objections from Pakistan which argued that the lock-cum-control barrage would not only deprive it of water but could also be used as a "natural weapon" against it". (Ibid)

The Jammu and Kashmir minister for irrigation and flood control, Taj Mohiuddin, confirmed that "the state government had resorted to alternative measures to prevent flooding in the Jhelum's upper catchments and ensure navigability in the river". (Ibid)

"We have given up the barrage project in favour of temporary rubber dams, which can work as effectively," Mohiuddin told The Telegraph. "Why should we want to erect a huge concrete structure when modern technology allows us to solve problems with more flexible methods"? (Ibid)

He did say the barrage had become "an unnecessary source of tension and suspicions" between the neighbours. "We had not been able to move on the project; it was stalled; this new rubber damming technique can probably help us a win-win way out," he said (Ibid).

Mohiuddin appeared convinced that "the new initiative would address reservations that Pakistan has had with the erection of a concrete barrage". (Ibid)

Role of Media

Zahra (2011) argues that the "Paucity of direct communication between the two states has increased the role of the media. The two nuclear neighbours are caught in a warp where the status quo in bi-lateral relations vacillates between improvement and deterioration but does not sway beyond a certain point — either way — so as to achieve anything decisive."

This part of the study glimpses at the role of the media on the water issues between Pakistan and India during 2011. Excerpts from the editorials and news reports of two leading newspapers from each country i.e. daily *Dawn* and *The Nation* from Pakistan and *The Tribune* and *The Kashmir Times* from India have been included.

Pakistani Media

An elite Pakistani newspaper, the daily *Dawn* in its editorial captioned "Controversial Project" expressed concerns on the Kishanganga hydropower project being constructed by India. The paper reads: "A series of disputes on hydropower generation projects initiated by India has given rise to concerns that New Delhi is trying to control the river water and thus `strangulate` Pakistan`s agriculture and economy. Many experts also believe that, given the situation, a future war over water between India and Pakistan cannot be ruled out". ('Controversial Projects' 2011).

Dawn extends its comments by saying that: "Repeated Indian attempts in the past to find loopholes and technical flaws in the 50-year-old water treaty that can be used to New Delhi`s advantage have hardly been helpful in easing tensions over water-sharing between the two neighbours". (Ibid)

In its course of discussion, the paper writes, "We will have primarily ourselves to blame in case of such an eventuality. Successive governments in Islamabad have failed to raise and resolve crucial water issues, including this one, that have arisen from time to time, with India to the peril of Pakistan`s agriculture and economy. While Islamabad must vigorously pursue the case at international forums to protect its economic interests, India should remember that the failure to satisfy Pakistani concerns will only delay the realisation of the dream of a prosperous South Asia whose various parts are at peace with one another". (Ibid)

Another leading English language Pakistani newspaper *The Nation* criticizes Indian policy on water sharing. In its news report *The Nation* reads, "The Treaty has, in great detail, covered a just distribution of water of rivers flowing from India to Pakistan. Under the Treaty, India in no case can hold the water or hamper the flow of water during various seasons to Pakistan." ('Pakistan likely to win', 2011)

The paper further writes, "The Kishanganga project is a part of the Indian move to build a series of water reservoirs on all the three major rivers, including river Chenab to utilize water at the upstream for the purposes of irrigation and power generation, depriving huge agricultural lands of waters which have been irrigating from these sources for centuries." (Ibid).

Commenting on the World Court of Arbitration's decision that stayed India's construction of a dam across the Neelum at Kishenganga, *The Nation* in its editorial "Kishanganga stayed" reads: "This stay order is not a final injunction, though it is the first sign that Pakistan is taking India's constant violations of the Indus Waters Treaty (IWT) with some seriousness. Earlier this year, in bilateral secretary-level talks, Pakistan had conceded acceptance of a revised Indian design of the Wuller Barrage, something which only encouraged Indian ambitions in this direction, and which furthered its ambitions to turn Pakistan into a barren wasteland, by using its illegal occupation of Kashmir to stop Pakistan's water from getting to it". ('Kishanganga stayed,' 2011)

The Nation suggests the Pakistani government to follow a two-pronged strategy. "First, to pursue this case with full vigour, and ensure that the stay is confirmed; second, to utilize this breathing space to start building irrigation-cum-generation projects on the Indus, and thus rid itself of this charge which is justified only because certain pro-Indian lobbies have been working against the Kalabagh Dam. The stay order, when confirmed, will also provide a useful precedent which will help stop Indian depredations on the Indus. However, a permanent solution will involve a settlement of the Kashmir issue. It would mean a general Indo-Pak settlement, ridding us of threat of water projects in Held Kashmir." (Ibid)

Indian Media

Daily The Tribune is published from Chandigarh. In a news report, it provides details about Pakistan's stance in the ICA. The paper writes, "Pakistan has moved the Court of Arbitration asking it to direct India to stop work at the 330 MW Kishenganga hydropower project in Jammu and Kashmir. The project is likely to be completed by 2015. A seven-judge Bench has started arbitration proceedings from January 14 this year in the Hague." ('Pakistan wants India,' 2011).

The report further reads, "Incidentally, this is the first case referred for international arbitration under the provisions of the Indus Waters Treaty, 1960. Earlier, India and Pakistan had sought the services of a neutral expert appointed by the World Bank to resolve their differences over the Baglihar Dam under construction on Chenab. The Bench – comprising Justice Stephen M Schwebel (head), Justice Sir Franklin Beman, Prof Howard S Wheater, Justice Bruno Simma, Jan Paulsson, Justice Peter Tomka and Lucius Caflisch – has three neutral umpires, including the head of the Bench, and four arbitrators nominated by India and Pakistan. Noted lawyer and an expert on International law, Shankar Das, and legal luminary, Fali s Nariman, both of whom had argued India's case in the Baglihar dam issue, are representing India." (Ibid)

Another newspaper *The Kashmir Times* from Jammu published a news report on the Nimoo-Bazgo hydropower project being built by India on the Indus River. It reads, "Pakistan wants to raise objections to the project, saying it allegedly violates the Indus Waters Treaty. The decision to approach the ICJ on the Nimoo-Bazgo project was made after Pakistani officials made their first visit to the project site and concluded it was allegedly in "total violation" of the Indus Waters Treaty of 1960, a senior unnamed member of Pakistan's Indus Waters Commission told the media. The unnamed official claimed India would be able to complete the Nimoo-Bazgo project by July 2012 and thus "suffocate" the water flow in the Indus. The design of its gated spillways and the depth of the dam allegedly breach the Indus waters treaty. The Pakistani side has raised five objections to the design of the project." (Ibid)

Conclusion

This paper identified India's various unfair dealings with Pakistan in watersharing. The important point is that water has the potential of becoming a new 'core issue' of even greater prominence than Kashmir, and calls for an urgent attention (Iyer, 2011). India-Pakistan relations in the previous decade have piercingly been affected by crucial disputes on water- sharing. A permanent solution will involve a settlement of the Kashmir issue. This concern needs to be taken seriously and should be jointly studied. Environmental concerns and climate change are post-Treaty developments and call for urgent inter-country consultations, not only at the governmental level but also at academic and expert levels. (Iyer, 2011)

References

Controversial Projects (Editorial). (2011, July 11). *Dawn*. Islamabad.

Iftikhar, Momin. (2011, October 03). Tackling the Kishanganga knot. *The Nation*. Islamabad

Iyer, Ramaswamy R. (2011, July 26). Pakistan: Water on the Boil Again. *The Hindu*. Delhi.

Kazi, Asif H. (2011, July 01). Misusing the Indus Treaty. *The News*. Islamabad.

Kishanganga stayed (Editorial). (2011, September 26). *The Nation*. Islamabad

Pak objects to project on Indus (News Report). (2011, October 10). *The Kashmir Times*. Jammu.

Pakistan likely to win Kishangaga case (News Report). (2011, August 25). *The Nation*. Islamabad: APP.

Pakistan wants India to stop work on Kishenganga Project (News Report). (2011, August 22). *The Tribune*. Chandigarh: PTI.

Raza, Syed Irfan. (2011, September 24). India told to stop work on Kishanganga dam. *Dawn*. Islamabad.

Sharma, Vibha. (2011, October 02). India confident of winning Kishanganga dispute. *The Tribune*. Chandigarh.

Thakur, Sankarshan. (2011, August 19). Wullar: Thorn Out of Indo-Pak Talks. *The Telegraph*. Calcutta.

Zahra, Farah. (2011, July 29). Sustaining the India - Pakistan Dialogue. *Daily Times*. Islamabad.

APP - 11

INDUS WATER TREATY & EMERGING WATER ISSUES

Nosheen and Toheeda Begum
(Abasin Journal of Social Sciences)

Abstract

The article introduces the Indus basin irrigation system in its historic context, and its economic impact on Pakistan's socio- economic development. The article also brings forth the problems and difficulty that emerged out of the interpretation and execution of the treaty with the passage of time. The analyses of the data focuses to provide remedies of the current problem that revolved around the treaty and its implementation.

Water is the greatest gift of nature, and the United Nations in a report has warned that global warming is causing the melting of glaciers. That will raise the issue of people migration and shortage of water. In the report, the victim countries are Pakistan and India, where glaciers are melting rapidly, and these countries are facing an increase in the problem of water shortage day by day. According to the report, water shortage will impose a war from a strong country on its neighbor, whose result will be very bad.

India having not reconciled with the creation of Pakistan created a series of problems for Pakistan soon after independence. The Indus Waters Treaty for sharing of the Indus River system waters was signed between India and Pakistan with the help of the World Bank in 1960. When the Treaty was signed, it was hoped that it would put an end to the water issue between India and Pakistan forever. However, today it appears, as if the wish was unfounded. Numerous water issues were created by India through violations of the treaty since then. All these issues remain unresolved even today. The core issue behind Pakistan's water problem is the forced annexation of Kashmir by India. The United Nations Security Council's resolution requiring plebiscite in Kashmir has still not been implemented by India and the status of Kashmir, along with control of the head reaches of the Indus River system, have still not been determined. It is feared that the ever increasing violations of the Indus Waters Treaty by India are setting the stage which may lead to the world's first water war in Asia, whose result will be terrible, as both India and Pakistan are Nuclear Powers and both have the capability of long range ballistic missile technology. (Siddiqui, 2010)

In this research report, an attempt has been made to highlight the water issue between India and Pakistan, the Indus Waters Treaty, and violation of this treaty by India.

Background of the Water Issue: The Indus river water system has been used for irrigation purposes in the Indus Basin since the beginning of civilization. In old days, availability of river water was more than the requirements, principally because the population was small and demands were less as compared to the availability of water in the rivers. When the demand grew substantially, disputes started between various water users. Upto the middle of the 19th century, the disputes were mostly between the upper and lower riparians. During British India, Sindh, which became a separate province, a lower riparian, objected to Punjab, an upper riparian, on water projects. Sindh feared that the use of water by Punjab would establish

Punjab's water rights over the Indus river water and may encroach upon Sindh's share of water. In those times these disputes were of domestic nature, as they were between provinces of the same country, the British India.

However, the nature of these disputes changed after the creation of Pakistan. These disputes which were domestic disputes, became international disputes between India and Pakistan, by virtue of creation of two independent countries, because in the partition of Punjab, Radcliffe drew the partition line right across the Punjab province, giving most of the water rich reaches of Indus Basin rivers to India. (Siddiqui, 2010).

On 1st April 1948, less than a year after the partition of the subcontinent and the creation of the separate states of India and Pakistan, Delhi stopped the flow of water from the canals on its side. India discontinued the delivery of water from the Ferozepur headworks to Dipalpur Canal and to main branches of the Upper Bari Doab Canal and denying water to some 5.5% of the sown area and almost 8% of the cultivated area. This act was criticized by Pakistan and Pakistan sent its delegation to New Delhi for negotiations on water supply. On 4th May 1948, India agreed to the Inter-Dominion Agreement with Pakistan, which allowed for the continuation of water supplies for irrigation purposes until the Pakistani side managed to develop alternative water resources. Sometime after this, then Indian Prime Minister, Jawaharlal Nehru, invited an American expert, David Lilenthal, to survey the situation, but his observations, which bolstered Pakistan's arguments, failed to get recognition from Delhi. Later, the World Bank sponsored several rounds of talks in Washington, from 1952 to 1960, eventually resulting in the signing of the Indus Waters Treaty (Gulhati,73). In 1951,when Lilienthal visited the region to write articles for Colliers magazine, he had a great interest in the subcontinent, and was warmly welcomed by both India and Pakistan. He was also briefed by the US officials, to help bridge the gap between the USA and India. During his visit, it became clear to Lilienthal that tensions between India and Pakistan were not only acute, but also unable to be erased with one sweeping gesture. In one his of articles, he wrote:-

"India and Pakistan were on the verge of war over Kashmir. There seemed to be no possibility of negotiating this issue until tensions abated. One way to reduce hostility.... would be to concentrate on other important issues where cooperation was possible. Progress in these areas would promote a sence of community between the two nations, which might, in time, lead to a Kashmir settlement. Accordingly, I proposed that India and Pakistan would work out a program jointly to develop and jointly to operate the Indus Basin river system, upon which both nations were dependent for irrigation water. With new dams and irrigation canals, the Indus and its tributaries could be made to yield the additional water each country needed for increased food production. In the article, I had suggested that the World Bank might use its good offices to bring the parties to agreement, and help in the financing of an Indus Development program." (Gulhati, 1973)

The Lilienthal plan was appreciated by the World Bank and the US government. The head of th World Bank, Eugene R. Black informed Lilienthal that his proposal "makes good since all round;" the Bank was also interested in the economic development and progress of the subcontinent and wanted to solve the water dispute between the two countries which was the main hurdle in the progress of the region. Mr. Black differentiated between the political and functional aspects of the water dispute. In correspondence with the leaders of both countries, he stressed that the water issue could be solved if the functional aspects of disagreement were negotiated apart from political aspects. He formed a group that handles the ways through which best to utilize the waters of the Indus Basin, leaving aside questions of historic rights of allocation.

Protracted talks were held, amid mounting tensions and finally the Indus Waters Treaty was signed by Jawaharlal Nehru, the Prime Minister of India, and Field Marshal Ayub Khan, the President of Pakistan, and W.A.B.III if, the President of the World Bank, in Karachi, in September 1960. This treaty provided for one of the most comprehensive dispute resolution mechanisms (Sridhar, 2008). Under the Indus Waters Treaty, India is not permitted to build dams for the purpose of water storage on the Indus, Chenab and Jhelum rivers, but it is allowed to make limited use of their water, including developing run-of-the-river hydroelectric power projects.

In 1970s, India started construction of Sallal hydro project on Chenab River and information about this project was provided to Pakistan in 1974. Pakistan objected to design, which had six low-level outlets and the over all height of spillways' gates of 40 feet, in clear violation of the treaty. After a series of meetings, the issue got resolved through agreement between the two governments in April, 1978. (Ahmed, 2012).

The alarm bells again rang in 1984, when India announced plans to build a barrage on Jhelum River at the mouth of Wullar Lake, the largest fresh water lake, near the town of Sopure, in the disputed Kashmir Valley. India called it Tu bul Navigation Project, while Pakistan referred to it as the Wullar Barrage; owing to Pakistani protests, India has stopped construction work on the project. Then in 1992, Pakistan first learned of plans for another controversial water reservoir, the Baglihar Dam on the Chenab River, which was also allotted to Pakistan by the 1960 treaty. The Indian government has kept violating the Indus Waters Treaty for many years, and over the years, India has planned construction of over a hundred large and small dams and reservoirs on western rivers. The sharing of the Indus River system is significant for India-Pakistan relations, and disputes over this issue could further complicate tensions between the two countries.

INDUS WATER TREATY (IWT) 1960

The Indus River rises in the Tibetan plateau in the vicinity of Lake Mansarovar. It flows in Tibet for about 200 miles before it enters Ladakh (part of disputed Kashmir) and then flows on towards Gilgit in Pakistan. Flowing through the north in a southerly direction along the entire length of Pakistan, it falls into the Arabian Sea near Pakistan's port city of Karachi with a total length of 3200 km. The river's estimated annual flow is approximately 207 billion m^3. Its five major tributaries are the Jhelum, Chenab, Ravi, Bias and Sutlej (also having origins in Tibetan plateau), another two tributaries of the Indus are River Kabul and River Kurram, which rise in Afghanistan. Most of the Indus basin lies in Pakistan and India. (Akhtar, 2010)

The Indus Waters Treaty is a water sharing treaty between Pakistan and India, brokered by the World Bank. The treaty was signed in Karachi on September 19, 1960 by the Indian Prime Minister Jawaharlal Nehru and the President of Pakistan Ayub Khan. The Indus Waters Treaty governs trans boundary water rights and obligations of India and Pakistan in relation to each other. It assigned full use of water of the Indus, Jhelum and Chenab rivers to Pakistan, with minor exceptions, for existing uses in Kashmir; this gave Pakistan 75% of the water of the Indus Basin system, and allowed India, under carefully specified conditions, to tap the considerable hydropower potenial of the three Western rivers before they entered Pakistan, while Ravi, Sutlej and Bias were given to India. (Tariq, 2010).

Composition of the Indus Waters Treaty:

The Indus Waters Treaty consists of three parts: the preamble, twelve articles and annexure A to H. The principal subjects covered in the treaty's annexure are: exchange of notes between the governments of India and Pakistan, India's agricultural use of certain tributaries of the Ravi, India's agricultural use of the upper reaches of the western rivers, India's generation of hydroelectric power and storage of water from western rivers, a procedure to solve disputes and differences through a commission, a neutral court of arbitration, and allocation to Pakistan of some waters from eastern rivers during the period of transition.

Principles Of Water Sharing

Before the IWT, Pakistan emphasized historical uses while India, as the upper riparian, claimed absolute rights on the Indus Basin system. The treaty tried to find a solution that was not driven by legal principles, but instead by principles of water engineering and economics. There were conflicting principles put on the table; India invoking the principle of equitable utilization, the favorite of International Law Association, while Pakistan stressing "no appreciable harm," the favorite of International Law Commission. The Treaty instead of dividing the waters of the rivers, divided the six rivers comprising the Indus Water system between India and Pakistan, which gave them independent control and regulation of supplies within their own territories. However, each country was allowed certain uses in the rivers allocated to other, subject to certain qualifications contained in separate annexures in the Treaty. Under the Treaty:

- All the waters of the Eastern Rivers shall be available for the unrestricted use of India (Article 2). Pakistan was permitted, by way of exception, to take water for domestic use, non-consumptive use and certain limited agricultural use.
- Pakistan shall receive "unrestricted use of all waters of Western Rivers" which India is under obligation to flow, (Article 3(1)) and shall not permit any interference with these waters except for domestic, non-consumptive, agriculture uses, generation of hydroelectric power and storage works. (akhtar, 2010).

Principles Of Cooperation

The Treaty lays down principles of cooperation in Article 6&7 which relate to exchange of data and future cooperation. This is intended to ensure optimum development of the rivers and cooperation and collaboration between the two countries. The data regarding the flow in, and utilization of, the waters of the rivers is to be exchanged regularly. This includes:

- Daily gauge and discharge data, relating to the flow of the rivers at all observation sites.
- Daily extraction for, or releases from, the reservoirs.
- Daily withdrawals at the heads of all canals operated by the government, or any other agency, including link canals.
- Daily escapages from all canals, including link canals.
- Daily deliveries from link canals.
- This data is to be transmitted on a monthly basis by each party to the other. (Akhtar, 2010)

Advantages Of The Treaty

- The Indus Waters Treaty was signed by India and Pakistan in 1960 and had some advantages, for example:
- With this treaty, both countries became able to operate the water supplies of the rivers of their own shares.
- The treaty made the system more reliable under seasonal variations.
- This treaty provided an opportunity to both countries for the use of water.
- This treaty also reduced the tensions between the two countries.
- Due to this treaty, a permanent Indus Commission was set up, to adjudicate any dispute in future.

Demerits Of The Treaty

- Besides the advantages, there were some drawbacks of the Indus Waters Treaty, which are:
- From Pakistan's perspective, allocation of only 75% of water, as against 90% of irrigated land violated the principle of "appreciable harm." From India's point of view, allocation of 75% of water to Pakistan violated the principle of "equitable utilization".

- Pakistan had to forego the entire perpetual flow of fresh waters of eastern rivers (24 MAF), which it historically used to receive for irrigation.

- Due to loss of regular flow in eastern rivers, silting has occurred in channels, and subsequent floods cause great destruction in Pakistan, in addition to other environmental effects.

- The traditional flood irrigation, the most ancient way of using river's waters, on Sutlaj, Bos, and, to some extent, on Ravi disappeared. As a result, no cultivation was possible in the flood plains of these rivers, thus rendering a large extent of the area barren.

- Storages are not substitutes of the perpetual flow of water, as storages have a limited life. Pakistan is already feeling the effect of silting up of its major reservoirs. (Ahmed, 2012).

Violations of the indus waters treaty by india:

Controversial Hydro projects: For almost two decades (1960s-1970s), the Indus Waters Treaty was followed by either side in its true form and spirit. Starting from the decade of 1980s, India started creating problems for Pakistan in the water sector on one or the other pretext. Since signing the treaty, India has violated it many times. Pakistan had been accommodating these for quite some time. Pakistan protested and even asked for arbitration from the World Bank, but no worthwhile results could be achieved. (Khan, 2011). The major Indian projects that have become controversial from time to time and involved issues around the compliance of the Indus Waters Treaty include Salal, Wullar Barrage/Tulbul Navigation project, Baglihar, Kishanganga, Dul Hasti, Uri II and Nimoo Bazgo and many more.

1. *Salal Hydroelectric Project*

This hydroelectric project is situated on River Chenab in occupied Kashmir. Salal was the first Indian project that became controversial between Pakistan and India. The construction of the dam was decided in 1970. India provided information about the project in 1974. Pakistan objected to the design and storage capacity of the dam. In 1976, both countries entered into a series of talks to resolve the issue. Pakistan contended that the dam would enable India either to interrupt the flow of water or to flood western Punjab. There were two rounds of intensive talks in 1976. India provided details of the project and showed flexibility by agreeing to alter the design of the dam to remove Pakistan's objection. On April 14, 1978, India and Pakistan entered into a treaty on the Salal hydroelectric project, and this was the first major dispute which was successfully resolved bilaterally under this treaty. (Siddiqui, 2010).

2. *Wullar Barrage Project*

The Wullar Barrage, which Indian refers to as the Tulbul Navigation project, was the second Indian project that became controversial and still remains unresolved. The proposed barrage is located on Jhelum in occupied Kashmir. India wants to build the barrage on the mouth of Wullar lake which is the largest fresh water lake in occupied Kashmir. India did not provide information on the project in time and started construction on the project in 1984. Pakistan learnt about the project in 1985 and raised objection and requested India to stop work on it. (Akhtar, 2010).

Under the provisions of the Indus Waters Treaty 1960, the waters of the three western rivers-Indus, Jhelum and Chenab-have been allocated to Pakistan, for unrestricted use except for certain uses by India in the areas located in the Indian Held Kashmir, and India is not allowed to build any storage on the Main Jhelum River. The matter was accordingly taken up by the Permanent Indus Commission for resolution under Article IX(1) of the treaty. However, in spite of several meetings, the Commission failed to resolve the issue and the construction work, which India had already started, continued upto September 1987, when finally it got suspended. On the request of India, bilateral negotiations started at the Secretary level. Upto 2008, as many as thirteen rounds of talks had been held but no result has so far been found. The current factual position is that although work at the site remains suspended, India still intends to restart the work. The issue is a part of the composite dialogue between Pakistan and India. (Siddiqui, 2010).

3. *Baglihar Hydroelectric Project*

Baglihar was the third Indian project that became controversial and the first one that went to the Neutral Expert for determination on technical questions raised by Pakistan. This project is in operation since October 2008. It is located on Chenab river in district Doda. The project has two stages and both are of 450 MW capacity. Pakistan raised six objections on the design of the dam and argued that the project was not in conformity with the Indus Waters Treaty. Pakistani experts also feared that India could also weaken Pakistan's defense by stopping the Chenab flow through the project's spillways, as two canals which emanate from Head Marala, Sialkot, which irrigate central Punjab and are also constructed a defense point-of-view, could be dried as and when New Delhi desires. Thus Pakistan has decided to construct the Mangla-Head Marala Link Canal to ensure water in the two canals that originate from Head Marala. (Akhtar, 2010)

In March 2009, Pakistani Minister for Water and Power informed the Parliament that Pakistan has demanded of India either to compensate for losses or provide water equal to 0.2 million acre feet. Pakistan took up this case with India and the Indus Water Commissioner, Pakistan made an urgent visit to India in this connection. India accepted the Pakistani claim of drop in Chenab flow during August and September. Two meetings were held by the Indus Water Commissioner, Pakistan with his counterpart in India, but the meetings remained inconclusive. India, as usual, stuck to its traditional obduracy and inflexibility, which is causing loss to Pakistan. Pakistan, however, is determined that India must accept the violation by it and address it in future. (Siddiqui, 2010).

4. *Kishanganga Hydroelectric Project*

After Baglihar, India and Pakistan have got locked in a dispute over the configuration of the Kishanganga hydroelectric project and the matter is now going to the Court of Arbitration for settlement. The 300 MW Kishanganga hydroelectric project is located about 160 km upstream of Muzaffarabad. Pakistan first received reports about Indian intentions to develop the Kishanganga project in 1988 but India officially confirmed it in June 1994 when it provided information regarding the storage work. Initially, Pakistan raised three objections to the project. In May 2004, amid reservations voiced by Pakistan on the construction of the Kishanganga hydroelectric project, India promised to freeze all work at the site for six months and hold a meeting with Pakistan for removing its objections. India told the meeting that it was working on the foundation of the dam and the powerhouse. Pakistan protested and said that construction work should not have begun before removing its objections. The issue was discussed in five meetings of the Commission held from November 2004 to November 2005 but differences over the project remained. Furthermore, India did not supply the data regarding the project. In May 2005, Pakistan raised six objections of which three related to the design of the dam, two of the diversion of water and one to the power generation scheme. Pakistan also accepted the Indian proposal to set 15 July as the deadline for resolving the Kishangana project issue. (Akhtar, 2010). As has been reported in the international press, the Indian cabinet has approved to go ahead with the 330 MW Kishanganga project in the Indian-held-Kashmir, in violation of the Indus Waters Treaty. It intends to complete the project by the year 2016, one year ahead of Pakistan project of diversion of Neelum river to Jhelum river. The Indian project would divert the River Neelum to Wullar Lake, upstream of the Pakistani project and would leave very little water for Pakistan's project, so Pakistan has gone to the Court of Arbitration for resolution of the issue. (Siddique, 2010)

5. Dul Hasti Hydroelectric Plant

The two-stage Dul Hasti hydropower project with an installed capacity of 390 MW is located on the main Chenab in district Doda. Pakistan believed it was not just a hydroelectric station but a full-fledged dam, aimed at storing water for irrigation needs, as seen in the case of Baglihar dam.

This project was originated in 1983 by the Indian Prime Minister, Mrs. Indra Gandhi, at a cost of Rs 34 billion. This project envisages the construction of 180.5 m long and 59.5 high concrete gravity dam upstream of Baglihar hydroelectric project on river Chenab. The construction of this dam was started in 1991. Compared to Salal and Baglihar Projects, the effect of this project on Pakistan is not grave, since the stoppage of water can be of the order of 1-2 days only. However, it is imperative to discourage India from providing under-sluices type gated spillways in the body of the dam. (Ahmed, 2012).

6. Uri-II Hydel Power Project

This hydel power project is located on Jhelum in the Baramulla district of Indian occupied-Kashmir. The project is planned immediately downstream of Uri-I and will pick up its tail water to make use of the gross head of about 130 m available in the course of the river between the Uri-I tailrace outlet. In October 2002, Pakistan asked India to supply informtion about Uri-II project. In July 2004, Pakistan again asked India to provide the said information. In March 2005, Pakistan repeated the request and India finally provided some information about the plant. In April 2006, Pakistan sent its observations to India. India did not inform Pakistan and started unilateral construction on the project in June 2007. India rejected Pakistan's demand for stopping work on the Uri-II project while Pakistan threatened to seek World Bank intervetion if India did not stop construction work. (Sharma, 2007). India remained insistent and did not stop the work. Some adjustments have been made on Uri-II, and construction work has reached its final stage and is set for completion at the end of 2011.

7. Nimoo Bazgo Hydro Project

Nimoo Bazgo Hydel project of 45 MW is a run-of-the-river scheme. It is located on the main Indus in Ladakh district. The construction work of the dam is in full swing. On March 29, 2010, in a meeting of the Indus Commissioners, India handed over construction plans and maps of the project to Pakistan. Pakistan expressed reservations on this project which showed its fear that the Indian projects might obstruct smooth supply of water to Pakistan. Pakistan has raised six objections to Nimoo Bazgo. At the July 2010 meeting of the Indus Commissioners, India expressed its inability to discuss the construction of the Nimo Bazgo hydropower project, saying it was not part of the ongoing negotiations. Pakistan has also not been allowed yet to visit the site of this project. (Akhtar, 2010)

Bursar Dam

This dam is considered as the biggest project built by India on two major rivers, Jhelum and Chenab, flowing through the state of Indian-occupied-Kashmir into Pakistan. This dam would be constructed near Hanzal village in Doda District on the Marusudar River, the main right bank tributary of the river Chenab. According to sources, it will store 2.2 MAF and generate 1020 MW of electricity and will be completed within 6-7 years at Rs. 43.78 billion. The construction of this dam would be a serious violation of the Indus Waters Treaty, as its store of the 2.2 MAF is much beyond the permissible limits. (Ahmed, 2012). The height of this dam will be 829 ft, while in comparison, the Tarbela dam's height is 485ft, and the Mangla dam's height is 453 ft. Actually, this dam will be a storage facility, which will regulate the flow of water to all downstream projects like Dul Hasti project, Baglihar dam and Salal dam.

This proposed dam violates the Indus Waters Treaty, as well as international environmental conventions. It will cause water scarcity in Pakistan, and it would also contribute towards melting of Himalayan glaciers. More than 4900 acres of thick forest would be submerged and the whole population of Hanzal village would be displaced.

According to some experts, the project is located in the Kishtwar High Altitude National Park (about 2 million acre feet) which is an environmentally protected area. Spreading over an area of 400 km, the park contains 15 mammals' species, including the musk dear and Himalayan black and brown bear and some rare birds, for which an environmental impact assessment study is necessary (Ahmed, 2012). Pakistan's Commissioner for Indus Waters has repeatedly asked his Indian counterpart to provide details of the proposed water storage and hydropower projects, including Bursar dam, but India has taken the stand that it was aware of its legal obligations and it would inform Pakistan about the project details and relevant data six months before construction activities as required under the Treaty (Ahmed, 2012).

The Court Of Arbitration Decision About Kishanganga Hydro project: Victory Or Defeat

The Court of Arbitration had granted a stay order against the construction of the Kishanganga dam structure on 25 September 2011. Both Pakistan and India initially claimed victory after the announcement of the Court of Arbitration's interim order. The court has granted the stay order against the construction of the dam structure but has allowed India to continue work on allied facilities, like the tunnel required to construct the dam. That India may not construct any permanent structures on or above the river bed is explicitly stipulated in the order. According to the order,

"Except for the sub surface foundations of the dam, India shall not proceed with the construction of any permanent works on or above the Kishanganga / Neelum riverbed at the Gurez site that may inhibit the restoration of the full flow of that river to its natural channel." (Bhutta, 2011)

While the Indian Government and Media highlighted that one clause and gave it full coverage, extrapolating that save the permanent structures, they allowed going ahead with construction. On the other side, Pakistan claimed that the decision was in its favour because that order bars India from continuing work on dam's construction. The former Indus Water Commissioner of Pakistan, Syed Jammat Ali Shah, said that the real issue was to stop India from the construction of the dam, which the court has ordered.

Kishanganga Dam: A Threat to Pakistan

The Kishanganga dam is also a big threat to Pakistan because with the construction of the dam, India would divert water from the Kishanganga river, which is known as the Neelum river when the enters into Azad Kashmir. India is constructing a 23-kilometer long tunnel, which will produce 330 MWs of power. The water will subsequently be discharged into the Wullar Lake and will ultimately flow through the Jhelum River to Muzaffarabad. If this project is completed, the dam would result in a 21% drop in Neelum River's inflow, thereby reducing the prospective energy generation from Pakistan's Neelum-Jhelum hydroelectric project by 10%. According to Pakistan's officials, India has completed 15% of the construction work on Kishanganga but according to some other sources, India has completed 43% of the work. (Bhutta, 2011)

India's Justification for using Waters of Western Rivers:

India has been betraying the international community of its foulplay on western rivers, quoting two excuses: First, Pakistan is unable to preserve its water by constructing dams and water storages in its territory, resulting into a large quantity of water flowing down to the Arabian Sea; therefore, India is securing the water while the second reason is that these water dams and storages are for the utilization of the people of Kashmir, under Indian occupation, either to produce electricity or irrigation. But both these arguments of India are baseless and without logic. India is planning to permanently deprive Pakistan from its share of water, thus converting agricultural Pakistan into desert-and-barren Pakistan. The current requirement of electricity in Kashmir is 5000 MWs and only a limited portion of the land could be irrigated by the waters of rivers because mostly the land of Kashmir is arid. So it is clear that the shifting of the waters of these rivers to the Indian territory is going through a program. Actually, India is working on these projects to produce over 43,000 MWs of electricity, which is more than the need of the people of occupied Kashmir. Than this electricity would be used for a heavy industrialization of India. While on the other side, it is true that we have not been able to build sufficient water reservoirs to preserve the surplus water, especially during the rainy season, for many reasons; nevertheless, this does not give India with enough cause to encroach over the Pakistani share of water. (Khan, 2011)

The Perceived Threat to Pakistan

During the last few years, the issue of water between India and Pakistan has gained much importance. The violation of the Indus Waters Treaty (1960) is taking place by construction of dams on western rivers, which are given to Pakistan by this treaty. Pakistan decribes India as its eternal enemy and accuses India of trying to suffocate the Pakistan's economy. Pakistani leaders blame India for acting under an internatonal conspiracy, led by America, Israel and India against Pakistan. Over the years, India has planned construction of round about 100 large and small hydroelectric projects and reservoirs on the Indus, Chenab and Jhelum.

In early 2008, an editorial in the urdu newspaper Roznama Ausaf accused India of planning a "WATER BOMB" strategy to strangle Pakistan economically, and India wants to achieve through the water bomb, what it could not achieve through the three wars waged over the past six decades. India is planning 50 dams to raid the waters of the rivers flowing into Pakistan. The IBWC warned: "If this is not foiled, Pakistan will face the worst famine and economic disaster." (Ahmed,2009)

One month after the inauguration of the first phase of the Baglihar project by the Indian Prime Minister Manmohan Singh, Jammat Ali Shah, Pakistan's Indus Water Commissioner and liaison between the countries within the framework of the treaty, warned that India plans to make Pakistan barren by 2014 by stopping its water. Within a week of the dam's inauguration, Major General Athar Abbas, a spokesman for the Pakistan Army, expressed concern over the Baglihar, describing it as a "defense security concern". He stated that a number of canals, drains and artificial distributries used for irrigation purposes are crucial during times of war. The strategic importance of Indian water projects in Kashmir is so significant that officials from the Pakistan Army headqurters attended a government meeting on the issue in February 2009 to discuss the impact of the said dams on Pakistan's water and defence interests...the Armed Forces became alarmed when they learned the projects could wreak havoc... if the same dams were to collapse or malfunction. (Ahmed, 2009). Gen.Zulfiqar Ali, former chairman of Pakistan's Water and Power Development Authority expressed that by building dams on rivers in Kashmi, India wants to make Pakistan a Somalia by stopping its water and India has achieved military, economic and political supermacy vis-à-vis Pakistan. (Ahmed, 2009).

A number of Pakistani experts and commentators warned that the water issue may incite nuclear war between the two countries. The convener of the All Parties Hurriyat Conference, Syed Yousaf Naseem, stated that Pakistan is facing a water crisis and that the Indian efforts to effect cuts in its water share from the rivers flowing into Pakistan could compel Pakistan to use unconventional weapons against India and, the Kashmir issue is cardinal to Pakistan-India relations. Unless this issue is resolved, the Damocles' sword of a nuclear clash will remain hanging over the region. Kashmir is very important for Pakistn and a delay in the resolution of this issue will jeopardize the peace of the region.

A leading Pakistani journalist, Majeed Nizami accused India of blocking water from River Chenab and further proclaimed that India wants to destroy Pakistan, saying: "Our crops are not getting water; if the situation continues, Pakistan will become Somalia and Sudan. (Ahmed, 2009)

Pakistan also fears that the cumulative live storage of these projects would have adverse impacts both in terms of causing floods and running the Chenab and the Jhelum dry in the time when Pakistan needs the water most. The sheer number of dams/schemes that India is building on the three Western rivers is massive, generating fears in Pakistan about their adverse implications for the flow of water to Pakistan. India is to build 135 big or small dams, 24 on the Indus, 77 on the Jhelum and 34 on the Chenab. Pakistan is apprehensive that even with strict compliance with the provisions of the Treaty in each case, India might taking all the projects together, acquire a measure of control over the waters of the Western rivers and might potentially be able to inflict harm on Pakistan. (Ramaswamy, 2010)

Conclusion

The Indus Waters Treaty is coming under stress due to both growing water scarcity in India and Pakistan and ecological threat to the Indus basin rivers system. The treaty was signed as a permanent solution to the water sharing problem between the two countries when water was in abundance in the Indus system. The Indus Waters Treaty provides an opportunity for future cooperation on water issue but unfortunately, since the signing of the treaty, no project has been undertaken under the provisions of "future cooperation". Due to climatic changes, water insecurity in the basin has heightened resulting in politicization of the water issue between the two countries. The growing water stress has coincided with India's ambitious plan to construct a large number of large hydropower plants, especially on the Chenab and Jhelum rivers. The fact that India has not been forthcoming in sharing information and engineering details regarding these projects as required in the Treaty has aroused Pakistan's apprehension. The projects of hydroelectric power made by India are not merely run-of-the-river structures as allowed under the treaty but their numbers and structures allow India to acquire a manipulative control that could be used to hamper water flows into Pakistan. The worst scenario for Pakistan is the Indian ability to stop water in the lean period and release it in the wet season. Further the Indian projects have adverse trans- boundary impacts, both environmental and in terms of power generation, as is evident in the case of Neelum-Jhelum project. (Akhtar,2010). All these things created a vacuum of mistrust between India and Pakistan and the water issue got much importance; now, it has got a top position in bilateral meetings between the two countries. There is a larger political dimension to the whole problem of the rivers water distribution between Pakistan and India. To Pakistan, the Kashmir issue is irrevocably linked to the Indus Waters Treaty, as the headwaters of all the rivers of Pakistan and meant for Pakistan flow through Kashmir and India happens to be the upper riparian state. The fear exists that India could manipulate the waters to starve Pakistan, so the water issue now is a core issue in Pak-India relations.

References

Ahmed, Tufail (2009, July 31) Water disputes between India and Pakistan, *Henry Jackson Society*, (online), retrieved on 22 July 2011 from http:......

Ahmad, Azhar (2012), Indus Waters Treaty, A dispassionate analysis, *MONTHLY DIGEST, 209(1), 1-14.*

Akhtar, Shaheen (2010), Emerging challenges to Indus Water Treaty, *FOCUS*, XXVIII(3),15-25.

Bhutta Zafar (2011), Kishanganga dam: is partial stay order a comprehensive victory for Pakistan?, *TRIBUNE* (online).

Gulhati niranjan D (1973), *The Indus Waters Treaty, An Exercise in International Mediation*, Bombay, Allied Publishers.

Khan, Raja Mohammad (2011 March 9), Implications of US warning for a Water War, *The Frontier Post*.

Ramaswamy R.Iyer (2010), Water through Pakistan eyes, (online), retrieved on 20 May 2011, http.......

Sattar Abdul (2007), Pakistan's Foreign Policy (1947-2005), Karachi, Oxford University Press.

Sharma, Rajeev (2007), Uri Project, Pakistan threatens to approach WB, *TRIBUNE* (online), retrieved on 20 May 2011 from http.....

Siddiqui H. Iqtidar (2010), Hydro politics and water wars in South Asia, Lahore, Vanguard Books.

Sridhar Seema (2008), Kashmir and Water: conflict and cooperation, In shahid imtiaz *Advanced Contemporary Affairs(Ed)*,Lahore: Advanced Publishers, pp 263-269.

Tabassum, shaista (2001), The role of CBM in resolving non-military issues between India and Pakistan: A case study of the Indus Waters Treaty, in Ahmer Moonis (Ed), *The challenge of confidence-building measures in South Asia*, New Delhi, Haranand Publications, p.396.

Tariq, Moh. Sardar (2009), The Indus Waters Treaty and Emerging water management issues in Pakistan, *Problems and Politics of water sharing in Pakistan*, Islamabad, Policy Research Institute, pp 87-90.

APP - 12

PAKISTAN'S WATER CRISIS

Dr Akmal Hussain
The Express Tribune, August 15, 2011

The writer is a distinguished professor of Economics at the Beaconhouse National University in Lahore.

A water crisis is emerging which could have major implications for Pakistan's economy and society. Effective management of this crisis first requires urgent mitigation and adaptation measures with close cooperation amongst Pakistan's provinces of Khyber-Pakhtunkhwa, Punjab and Sindh, on the one hand, and then between Pakistan and India on the other. If the necessary collaboration for cooperative management of the Indus basin water resources is not undertaken expeditiously, the resultant economic crisis could lead to a war with India.

The problem of water scarcity in the Indus basin is predicated partly on the inherent limitations of water supply in the Indus River System and partly on the growing water demand associated with an inefficient water use in the process of economic and population growth. Unsustainable development practices have exacerbated the problem, with the intrusion of salinity into ground water, contamination of aquifers with harmful chemicals such as fluoride and arsenic, and pollution of surface water due to the lack of an institutional framework for environmentally safe disposal of urban and industrial waste. An important dimension of the water issue in the years ahead is the phenomenon of climate change, which could take the crisis to a critical level.

Water scarcity can be measured by the availability of water compared with the generally accepted minimum per capita requirement of 1,700 cubic metres per person per year. In their book, *Freshwater Under Threat: South Asia*, Mukand S Babel and Shahriar M Wahid have estimated that the per capita availability of water in the Indus basin is 1,329 cubic metres per capita per year. This is significantly below the threshold requirement. Another interesting indicator of the water problem is the measure of development pressure on water resources, which is the percentage of available water supply relative to the total water resources. This ratio is as high as 89 per cent for the Indus basin compared to only 15 per cent for the Ganges-Brahmaputra-Meghna (GBM) basin. This indicates the relatively greater development pressure on the Indus basin.

Worse, the utilisation of water for production is also highly inefficient by global standards. Water use efficiency is measured in terms of the GDP per unit of the water used. In the case of the five top food producers in the world (Brazil, China, France, Mexico and the US) the water use efficiency is $23.8 per cubic metre. The figure is as low as $3.34 for the Indus basin.

The problem of water scarcity is expected to become more acute in the future due to the adverse impact of climate change. Dr Leena Srivastava, in a recent research paper, provides evidence to show that some of the Himalayan glaciers are melting more rapidly than the global average and this could increase the frequency of floods in the short run and increase water shortages in the long term by reducing river flows in South Asia. Furthermore, according to the UN's Intergovernmental Panel on Climate Change report, given the sensitivity of existing seeds to heat, global warming could result in a 30 per cent reduction in the yield per acre of food crops in South Asia.

Science and empirical evidence make clear that the existing water scarcity, when combined with the impact of climate change, could place a critical stress on the economy and society of Pakistan, in particular, and South Asia, in general: major food shortages, increased frequency of natural disasters, large scale dislocations of population and destabilising contention between upper and lower riparian regions.

Effective management of this crisis in Pakistan requires close cooperation with India in joint watershed management, increasing the efficiency of irrigation and water use, joint development of technologies, sustainable agriculture practices and institutional arrangements to manage food shortages as well as natural disasters. When faced with a common threat, ideology must be replaced by rationality in the conduct of governance. If we fail to do so, natural disasters could trigger the man-made catastrophe of war.

APP – 13

VICIOUS ANTI-INDIA PROPAGANDA IN PAKISTAN ON WATER ISSUES

Trithesh Nandan

Governance Now, 4 June, 2012

Pakistani politicians, officials and media are in the grip of a vicious anti-India propaganda on water issues. General Ashfaq Kayani has stated that India will remain the focus of Pakistani military doctrine so long as Pakistan has unresolved issues with India. He included water and Kashmir among the unresolved issues. In its recent strategic dialogue with the United States, Pakistan also sought to involve the US in the resolution of India-Pakistan water issue.

River Indus near Leh

The debate in Pakistan on India-Pakistan water issues has heated up. Water is being projected as an existential issue. India is being blamed for the water crisis in Pakistan. The key points of the debate are that India is violating the Indus Waters Treaty, and that it is stealing Pakistan's waters and turning Pakistan into a desert. An interesting nuance in the debate is that the water issue is even more important than the Kashmir issue. The talk of "water war" with India that could expand into a nuclear war is quite common. The following is a sampling of some recent comments made in the Pakistani media:

- *Dawn* quoted the former Foreign Minister Sardar Asif Ali as saying that "if India continues to deny Pakistan its due share, it can lead to a war between the two countries." (18 January 2010)

- In a similar vein, PML(Q) Chief Chaudhary Sujat Hussain said that the water crisis between Pakistan and India could become more serious than terrorism and can result in a war. (*Dawn*, 18 January 2010)

- Majid Nizami, Chief Editor of Nawai Waqt group of newspapers, said that "Pakistan can become a desert within the next 10 to 15 years. We should show an upright posture or otherwise prepare for a nuclear war." (*Dawn*, 18 January 2010)

- Politicians are ratcheting up the rhetoric. Members of the Punjab Assembly passed a resolution to deny India the trade transit facility until the resolution of the Kashmir dispute and issues related to water distribution. (*Dawn*, 27 January 2010)

- A member of the Punjab Assembly, Warris Khalo, said that India would "remain an enemy" until the Kashmir dispute and water issues are resolved. (*Dawn* 27 January 2010)

- Palwasha Khan, Member of National Assembly, accused India of perpetrating "water terrorism" against Pakistan and said that "experts foresee war over the water issue in the future and any war in this region would be no less than a nuclear war." (*Daily Times* 17 February 2010)

- In a recent debate in Pakistan's National Assembly, several members urged the government to impress on New Delhi "not to use" Pakistan's share of water. (*Daily Times*, 25 February 2010)

- Dr. Manzur Ejaz, a commentator, writing in *Daily Times* (3 March 2010) warned that "unless Pakistan was assured on the supply of water, it will never abandon the proxies that can keep India on its toes by destabilizing Kashmir." He further added: "For Pakistan, the territory of Kashmir may not be as important as the water issue."

At the official level too, Pakistan is raising the salience of the water issue in India-Pakistan relations. Salman Bashir, Pakistan's Foreign Secretary, was quoted by Dawn (26 February 2010) as saying that Pakistan had handed over some documents to the Indian side during the Foreign Secretary level talks with the hope that India would consider resolving the water issue within the Indus Basin Waters Treaty. He added that India had been informed about its violation of the Indus Waters Treaty, storage of water, India's plans to build more dams, the Kishanganga Hydel project, pollution in the sources of water and glacier melt. Salman Bashir said, "Water is a very important issue for us and Pakistan wants constructive engagement with India." (Dawn, 26 February 2010)

President Zardari has, in the past, raised the water issue several times. In an op-ed article in *Washington Post* (28 January 2009), he wrote that the water crisis in Pakistan was directly linked to relations with India and if this was not resolved, it could fuel extremism and terrorism. Zardari had also taken up the water issue with Prime Minister Manmohan Singh on the sidelines of the UN General Assembly in 2008 and complained that India's diversion of water from the Chenab river was causing agricultural losses in several districts in Pakistan. Pakistan, according to media reports, has demanded compensation from India for the loss of agriculture due to diversion of waters.

The notable aspect about the Pakistani debate over water is that it is highly jingoistic and uninformed. The Indus Waters Treaty of 1960 governs the sharing of waters between India and Pakistan. The Treaty, signed with the help of World Bank mediation, apportions the water between India and Pakistan. A significant feature of the Treaty was that it apportioned 80 per cent of the water of the Indus River Basin to Pakistan and only 20 per cent to India. This fact is never highlighted in the Pakistani discourse on the Indus Waters Treaty. Pakistanis also conveniently ignore the fact that the Treaty gives India the right to construct run-of-the-river dams on the Western rivers (Indus, Chenab and Jhelum) as well as construction of 3.6 Million Acre Feet (MAF) of storage facilities. India has not yet constructed any storage dam on these rivers despite the fact that the Treaty permits it. This point is also overlooked in the Pakistani media. Nor has India used the full potential of irrigation from the Western Rivers as permitted under the Treaty.

A frequent Pakistani complaint is that India is "stealing" Pakistan's water. But no evidence is given to support the allegation. Since India has not built any storage facilities, where would it store the water?

Whatever water India takes from the Western rivers is for non-consumptive use allowed under the Treaty. The Pakistani Indus Commission is regularly supplied with the data on this score.

The Pakistani side has complained of the reduced flows of water in the Western rivers. The fact that there are seasonal variations in the flow of water due to differences in monsoon and glacial melt is normally ignored in the Pakistani discourse. Jamaat Ali Shah, the Head of Pakistan's Indus River Commission, has stated in an interview that India and Pakistan should "look beyond" the Treaty to discuss such issues as the impact of climate change on water resources. Unfortunately, the Treaty, which is a technical document, does not envisage a discussion on climate change or environmental issues as these were not issues in 1960.

Undoubtedly, climate change will emerge as a major factor affecting the health of glaciers and rivers in South Asia. India and Pakistan need to discuss these issues seriously.

The Pakistani media is also dishing out ill-informed opinions on the Neutral Expert's determination on the Baglihar dam. It may be recalled that India constructed the Baglihar dam on river Chenab. The dam became operational in 2008. However, the commissioning of the dam was delayed by Pakistan as it took the issue of the dam's design to the Neutral Expert provided for in the Indus Waters Treaty. The Neutral Expert upheld the design parameters of the Baglihar dam, particularly those relating to the location of "spillways," "pondage" and height. The Neutral Expert stated clearly that sediment control, which dictated the design parameters, was crucial to dam construction. He also upheld India's view that the first objective of "pondage," to which Pakistan had objected, was to regulate the flow of the river to meet consumer demand.

The Kishanganga hydroelectric project is the next point of contention likely to sour India-Pakistan relations. The Kishanganga river is a tributary of the Jhelum. It originates in Jammu & Kashmir, enters Pakistan-occupied Kashmir (PoK) after Gurej, flows along the Line of Control (LoC) as the Neelum river and joins the Jhelum at Muzaffarabad in Pakistan-occupied Kashmir. India is planning to build a hydroelectric project on this river. It will be a run-of-the river project which will require diverting the water of the Kishanganga river through an underground tunnel. Pakistan has objected to the Kishanganga hydroelectric project. It is contemplating taking the issue to the Court of Arbitration and the Neutral Expert in accordance with the terms of the Indus Waters Treaty. India is confident that it has a valid case on the Kishanganga project.

There appears to be a deliberate attempt in Pakistan to use the water issue to inflame public opinion against India. This appears to be a part of the larger design of the Pakistani military to drive home to Western interlocutors the continued salience of India in Pakistan's security calculus. Though Pakistan is facing the prospect of destabilization due to the radicalization of its society, the Pakistan Army continues to project India as the number one threat. The water issue is being used to divert attention from 26/11 and the larger issue of terrorism, which India regards as the main issue between India and Pakistan.

Water is the driving force of all nature, said Leonardo da Vinci. But in the case of the strained India-Pakistan ties, the exact opposite is true: it has been the stalling force. With a cloud of distrust always hovering above, even the best intentions have been misconstrued and hostilities alleged.

Take the case of Tulbul navigation project (what Pakistan refers to as the Wullar barrage). In the mid-1980s, India started building a dam on the Jhelum river to help make it navigable throughout the year, but had to suspend work after Pakistan complained that the Jhelum's currents would be slowed in its territory, and that the work violated a water-sharing pact. Nine rounds of secretary-level talks have been held since the project was stalled, followed by five more meetings in 1998, 2004, 2005, 2006 and 2007 between the two countries. The latest one resumed on March 27 in New Delhi in the presence of a 13-member delegation from Pakistan led by the water and power secretary Imtiaz Kazi.

The 1960 Indus Waters Treaty governs the use of the water flowing down the rivers which course though both the countries. As per the accord, India has 'unrestricted' use of water from three rivers in the east – the

Sutlej, Beas, and Ravi. Pakistan has 'unrestricted' use of the water of the western rivers – the Indus, Chenab and Jhelum. Pakistan accuses India of violating the treaty by reducing the flow of water down the rivers it was awarded use of. Pakistan also objects to India's Baglihar hydropower and water storage project on the river Chenab. India denies any unfair diversion of Pakistan's water.

While some Indian analysts maintain that Pakistani complaints are aimed more at diverting attention within Pakistan from the internal water row, the chorus of India stealing water from the western rivers is increasing in Pakistan by the day.

In an interview with Trithesh Nandan, Pakistani water expert Arshad H Abbasi strikes a different chord. He says emphatically that India is not stealing water, and that the problem of water scarcity in Pakistan is more due to its mismanagement. Abbasi is a senior advisor, water & renewable energy, with the Islamabad-based think tank Sustainable Development Policy Institute. He says it is not terrorism, Kashmir or even boundary dispute but water and environment issues, that need an urgent attention from both the sides. To quote Mr. A. H. Abbasi:

In the last three-four years, water issues between the rival two nations have grown bigger than ever. Your comments.

Around 60-70 percent of population in Pakistan is dependent on water from Indus basin rivers. An ordinary person is least bothered about issues between India and Pakistan. But he is concerned about his own water woes. In the last few years, the flow of the Chenab is fluctuating. The issue started with the Baglihar dam on the Chenab. Pakistan protested its construction. It raised the question of design. The Indus Waters Treaty has also specifications on design. India raised (and rightly so) the issue of sedimentation. Since 1992, sedimentation has increased manifold. Because of sedimentation, India says that it changed the design.

Pakistan complained about the Baglihar dam to the World Bank and in response an independent arbitration was set up. On several counts, it rejected Pakistan's claims.

Before Pakistan went to the independent arbitrator, India gave an assurance that it will reduce the height of the dam but Pakistan refused and went to the World Bank. The verdict came in 2007, upholding only a few objections raised by Pakistan, like pondage capacity to be reduced by 13.5 percent, height of dam structure be reduced by 1.5 metres and power intake tunnels be raised by 3 metres, thereby limiting some flow control capabilities of the earlier design.

But Pakistan was not satisfied with the verdict. The decision was the best given by a neutral panel. A larger section in Pakistan still feels the other way round. It is a matter of understanding. The larger voice, which opposes the decision, does not know the subject very well. People in Pakistan say that India is stopping the flow of the western rivers by constructing more than a dozen dams. The water flow of the Chenab and Jhelum has been drastically reduced, because of a reduction in monsoon rainfall in the watershed of the Chenab. However, India should also look into why it is constructing so many dams.

So, in your view, India should not be accused of stopping the flow.

In my view, India is not stealing water. It does not have the capacity to steal water. There is certainly a reduced flow, so there is anxiety on the Pakistani side. You know we are living in a state of hostility. Accusations are the natural fallout.

There is a basic question for both the countries: why don't they take help of technology to track the water flow of the Indus basin rivers? This will help remove the mistrust between the two countries. But both the countries won't agree to the use of such technology because of a mental block. The officials sitting in the Indus Waters Treaty Commission on both the sides are so much pressurised that they can't go beyond the treaty.

The flow of the rivers reduced due to the environmental impact. The 65-year-old hostility has taken a toll on the environment, which can be seen in the Kashmir valley. Our rivers are drying. I have been advocating a serious dialogue between India and Pakistan on the environmental issues. Environmental disasters don't follow international borders.

Both the countries also need to work on joint watershed management. An environmental impact assessment is the best instrument to assess the possible negative impact that a proposed project may have on the environment, together with the water flow in the rivers.

As far as Pakistan's objection to the Kishanganga project is concerned, India argues that it will divert the water of Kishanganga (Neelum in Pakistan) to join the Jhelum river, which also flows through Pakistan – and that, therefore, the water will ultimately reach Pakistan. Due to the construction of the Kishanganga project, water will be diverted from the Neelum and a 90 km stretch of the river, that 6,00,000 people depend on for agriculture and fisheries, will dry up. But why divert water from the Neelum valley then? It will impact the whole environment. If you see studies done on the Farakka barrage (on the India-Bangladesh border), it had the worst effect on water and environment.

APP – 14

HARNESSING THE INDUS WATERS: PERSPECTIVES FROM INDIA

D. Suba Chandran
Deputy Director, IPCS
Institute of Peace and Conflict Studies, New Delhi

Invariably every comment on the Indus Waters Treaty (1960) between India and Pakistan have focussed that despite the wars of 1965, 1971 and 1999 and a border confrontation during 2001-02, India and Pakistan have not violated the Treaty. Besides, this is seen as the only success story, between India and Pakistan; hence there is a hesitancy to tinker/amend the treaty.

Few points need to be highlighted. True, the treaty has survived the four wars, a border confrontation and military stand offs; however, if the Treaty could be violated, it can be done only by one party to the contract – India. Pakistan, being a lower riparian state, cannot violate the treaty, unless it prefers to make military actions, to implement the Treaty. A radical section within Pakistan has been claiming that Islamabad should even consider the use of nuclear bombs, to protect its water rights.

Though India claims that it has not violated the treaty in principle, some of its constructions, especially relating to barrages and dams, are seen by Pakistan as against the Treaty and has been regularly complaining at international forums, including that of the Indus Water Commission. India has its own reasons to undertake those constructions, to make better use of the water systems in J&K and the surrounding region.

It is also interesting, while, on the one hand, people on both sides talk about the IWT as the most effective one (comparatively) in the last five decades, on the other hand, there have been numerous complaints on how those who actually negotiated the treaty in the 1950s, on both sides, failed to achieve the interests of their respective countries.

Finally, the Treaty was signed in 1960, almost fifty years back, in a different political, economic, demographic, ecological and energy environment. Today there has been a considerable change in all these five areas.

Should India and Pakistan take into account the contemporary issues/problems/challenges in managing the Indus Waters, or keep it aside, for the fear of not tampering something that is believed to be working smoothly? How can India and Pakistan work together to make optimum use of the Indus Waters?

How can both countries get ready to address the impending environmental, demographic, economic and political challenges, through efficient management of the Indus Waters? Finally, should India and Pakistan waste all their energies in accusing and defending, what could be done and not done legally under the IWT, or should both countries think beyond pure legal terms? In short, should the focus be "legal" interpretation of the IWT or Indus Water Governance?

Sharing The Indus Waters: Major Issues/Problems

The recent annual meeting between the Indus Water Commissioners of India and Pakistan ended with same complaints from Islamabad and almost regular defence from New Delhi. Baglihar and Kishenganga though appear to be the main reason for the complaints, there are other fault lines, internal, bilateral and multilateral, which is straining the Indus Waters Treaty (IWT). However, there are other serious issues that never get noticed in the IWT debate between the two countries. The IWT is likely to come under a larger stress in the near future; it is imperative, that people living along the Indus river understand the gravity of issues, beyond looking through their national and regional prisms.

Changed History

The IWT was signed in 1960, in a different regional and international environment – immediate pangs of partition, settlement of refugees, Kashmir in the United Nations, Cold War and Pakistan being a part of the US led pack, while India insisting on pursuing a non-alignment approach to its international affairs. Regional pulls/pressures within India and Pakistan were relatively less, if not totally non-existent; hence neither the Indian government in New Delhi nor the Pakistani government in Rawalpindi/Islamabad had to take into account the regional political demands for "their share" of water on a particular river system.

More importantly, the federal governments in India and Pakistan were strong vis-à-vis provincial governments. The latter were more dependent on the former and, in most cases, regional politics was very much controlled by the governments at the federal level. In India, the towering personality of Jawaharlal Nehru and the Congress played an important role in this process, while in Pakistan, the pressure at the national level between the military and polity, kept the regional politics at a low key level.

Today, the situation is different at the political level, in terms relations between federation and provinces/states in India and Pakistan. Regional politics and parties play a larger role at the national level, and the federal governments have to take into account the regional aspirations. On the Indus Water basin, Sindh, Balochistan, Punjab, NWFP, Northern Areas and the governments on both sides of the LoC in Srinagar/Muzaffarabad play an important role in national politics.

Clearly, the political situation in the Indus Water basin today, is not what it was fifty years back. Given the progress in the last two decades, one is likely to see more problems in the next decade. Both New Delhi and Islamabad should consider this important change, and what is likely to happen in the next decade.

On the positive side, one should also consider the positive breakthroughs that have taken place in the last one decade, despite the military and political upheavals at the bilateral levels. Both countries have matured and taken certain measures, for the first time in the last sixty years, for example opening the LoC for the movement of people and goods. Prime Minister Manmohan Singh has made a statement on making the borders irrelevant between the two countries. Despite the negative happenings, the political atmosphere today, is not how it was sixty years back. Both countries should be willing to pursue a bold political step, in terms of harnessing the Indus Waters.

Demography, Industrialization and Increased Emphasis on Water

Unlike the 1950s, both countries have grown tremendously, in terms of their population and industrialization. Despite the expansion of various sectors, agriculture still remains the primary focus of occupation for many in rural India and Pakistan. In this decade, both India and Pakistan have achieved new heights in their economic growth and have a high expectation for the next decades. Manmohan Singh has categorically stated that nine percent growth rate will be his primary emphasis – at the national and international levels; his domestic and foreign policies are likely to reflect this basic exposition.

Clearly, this has already placed an enormous stress on the effective use of water in both countries – for the purposes of irrigation and generation of electricity. Worse, these demands on the water resources for agricultural and industrial purposes are likely to expand in the coming decades. Pakistan, in particular, has been facing an energy crisis in the last couple of years; given the problems associated with energy production and the equation between the independent power producers and the government of Pakistan, one could only conclude that the energy crisis will continue. For India, to achieve and sustain a nine percent growth, as Manmohan Singh has envisaged, energy security is equally important; with the Iran-Pakistan-India gas pipeline now placed in a limbo and the Indo-US nuclear deal unlikely to produce large scale electricity in the near future, India's energy demand is no less.

Indus Waters will become an increasing bone of contention, not only between the two countries, but also between the regions/states/provinces in these two countries. In fact, there are already clear signs of an impending disaster on managing the waters at the national and bilateral levels. For J&K, on both sides of the LoC, the Indus rivers are likely to be a primary source of energy production. Invariably all the projects – Baglihar, Kishenganga, Mangla and Diamer-Basha are facing political and technological problems, in terms of creating electricity, besides the issues between the provinces and the federation, in terms of the governments of Srinagar and New Delhi, Muzaffarabad and Islamabad, and the Northern Areas administration and Pakistan. Besides the huge uncomfort that the lack of electricity creates for the ordinary people, energy insecurity also affects industrial production and any new investment and the tourism sector. Who would like to visit those hill stations, however scenic they are, if there is electricity only for a few hours every day?

Differences Within and the Disasters Without

As mentioned above, internal differences within India and Pakistan have the potential to become a major crisis, straining the IWT at the bilateral level. First, there is a clear divide between Jammu and Kashmir (J&K) and the federal government on the nature and use of IWT. The people and government of J&K, from where the Indus and most of its important tributaries flow through, are against the IWT, as they feel it is against their interests. A resolution was passed in the J&K Legislative Assembly in 2002, calling for annulling the IWT. A section inside J&K even considers the IWT as an Indo-Pak conspiracy against the Kashmiris. The Kashmiri grievances are based on emotional and economic issues; for Kashmiris, water and land have always been an emotional issue.

Second, J&K also considers the IWT as an economic liability. A majority in J&K consider that the IWT discriminates the Kashmiris by not letting them tap the potential of the Indus and its tributaries in terms of using the waters for agriculture, transport and energy. It is believed that the losses that the IWT causes to J&K are around 8000 crores annually. In recent months, there appears to be a politicization of waters, by the opposition party against the government, purely for political reasons. Mehbooba Mufti, the leader of the opposition, has been making statements on the "Loot of Water," primarily to embarrass the government. Given the fact that ethnic Kashmiris are extremely emotional about "land" and "water," this is another powder keg.

Third, the people of Northern Areas consider the IWT against their interests. The controversy over the construction of Diamer-Basha dam highlights the tensions between Northern Areas and Islamabad on sharing the Indus Waters. Many in Northern Areas feel that Islamabad has not provided any political status to the region, precisely to exploit them over the Indus Waters. They argue, had Northern Areas been a political entity, Pakistan, then, would have to share the waters and royalty. Worse, a section also believes, that while the Basha dam will submerge parts of its land and result in displacement, the royalties will go to the NWFP.

Fourth, the Pakistan occupied Kashmir has a serious problem with the rest of Pakistan on Mangala dam. Muzaffarabad feels exploited by Islamabad over the Mangala dam; the construction in Mirpur has dislocated the entire city, whereas the benefit goes to Pakistan. Islamabad is too sensitive about any water related issue involving the PoK and the Northern Areas. A government official was suspended for writing a book on Mangala dam; subsequently, all his books were banned during 2002-04 and accused of being "anti-state and an attempt to promote nationalist feelings amongst Kashmiris."

Fifth, the four provinces of Pakistan are deeply divided within, in terms of sharing the Indus waters. The controversy over the construction of Kalabagh alone will amplify internal problems relating to the water conflict. While Punjab wants to build the dam at any cost, leaders of Sindh have warned Islamabad to choose between Kalabagh and federation, meaning that construction of the dam will result in Sindh walking out of the federal structure.

Ineffective Water Governance

South Asia, as a whole, has a serious deficit relating to water governance. All countries in SAARC fail to use water judiciously; as a result, there is a huge water wastage. Besides, despite knowing that water is a precious commodity, South Asia has failed to evolve alternate modes of irrigation; canal and river irrigations are the most preferred in South Asia.

Methods like drip irrigation and crop rotation, to use the available water judiciously, are yet to be effectively evolved. South Asia, as a whole, wastes water.

Receding Glaciers & Shrinking Sources

All the above mentioned issues/demands focus on the increasing demands on the Indus Waters, based on the presumption that the supply will continue, as it has been in the past. What if there is a reduction in supply, purely for geological/environmental reasons?

Studies on the Himalayan glaciers highlight the possibility of a decline in water flow in the Indus and its tributaries. Invariably every one agrees today, that the glaciers are receding and all the major Himalayan river systems – Indus, Ganges and Brahmaputra are likely to face a shortage of water supply. Unfortunately, neither India nor Pakistan, at the governmental levels, have initiated any major studies – either independently or jointly. While the environmentalists in India and Pakistan have undertaken some excellent studies, their acceptability by the governments is yet to happen. With an expanding population and growing energy and economic needs, any decline in water flow will only increase the stress on the IWT. Given the interstate and intra-state political and emotional issues along the Indus river basin, the possibility of water scarcity resulting in water wars between the states, and within them, cannot be completely ruled out.

It is imperative, that India and Pakistan and their sub regions work together to address the growing concerns and avoid any future conflict over the sharing of waters. The IWT has an inbuilt provision to rework sections of this treaty. India, Pakistan and their sub regions should work together towards creating on Indus Waters Treaty – II, addressing the issues mentioned above. The IWT-II could very well be a conflict preventive measure relating to water issues along the Indus river basin.

II

DEBATING THE OPTIONS

What are the options available for India and Pakistan? The extremists in India have already talked about the abrogation of the Indus Waters Treaty. Nothing would harm India more than the abrogation of a treaty, which was negotiated along with the World Bank, and withstood the see-saw relations of the two countries. Besides the international ramifications, in terms of India adhering to treaties and agreements that it has signed, it would have a series of implications for similar treaties it had signed with its other neighbours.

India has similar treaties on water with Nepal (Mahakali Treaty) and Bangladesh (Ganges); any abrogation of the IWT will affect the confidence of India's neighbours on similar treaties relating to water.

Internally, it will also set a bad precedent for the states, that are fighting over sharing of water; for examples, Karnataka and Tamilnadu, with the former being the upper riparian and the latter being the lower riparian, in terms of sharing the waters of Cauvery river.

Second, a unilateral abrogation of the IWT is also unlikely to make the energy situation better in J&K. Given the level of bad governance and corruption involved in many of these projects, abrogation of the IWT is not likely to result in J&K becoming a gainer in terms of harnessing the waters.

Pakistan has been threatening to use even nuclear weapons to secure its water rights. It is a political rhetoric, aimed at local audience. Pakistan is unlikely to do anything like that, except objecting to any and every project relating to the western rivers, and, perhaps, give more support to the movement of militants. None of these options are likely to benefit Pakistan in the long term, in terms of effectively harnessing the Indus Waters. Indo-Pak history has numerous examples of where the Pakistani military exercises have led them to, ever since the IWT was signed.

It is neither in India's interests to unilaterally abrogate the IWT, nor in Pakistan's interests to wage a water war. The extremists on both sides, in the worst case scenario, may pressurize for such an option, which could be undertaken, but with no positive results. Both the above options will only hamper the water relations further and negate, whatever has been achieved so far. Clearly, the only option is to engage with each other to effectively harness the Indus Waters jointly.

III

RECOMMENDATIONS

India and Pakistan could consider the following, given the issues/problems related to the IWT, and those which are likely to arise in the next decade.

A Debate on Indus Waters Treaty – II

From New Delhi's perspective, it is important to realise that the internal political and emotional situation regarding the sharing of water in Pakistan and in J&K is likely to have a negative impact on the IWT as a whole. Experts like BG Verghese have already pitched for an Indus Waters Treaty – II, which is important from New Delhi's perspective to look into and prepare for the future. The IWT-II does not call for the abrogation of IWT, or a parallel treaty; it only aims at making the existing treaty more effective, taking into account political, economic and environmental developments in the last five decades, and those changes likely to take place in the coming decades.

A collaborative background research

Clearly, neither India nor Pakistan has a vision, in terms of what needs to be done, except for reacting to a domestic audience. There is a need for a joint, but an impartial research, that would provide alternative approaches to address the present and future challenges emanating from the Indus Waters Treaty.

Indus Waters Experts Group

As a corollary of the above exercises, there is a need to form an Indus Water Experts Group (IWEG), comprising six to ten experts, from different backgrounds, who have been working with the governmental and non-governmental sectors, like BG Verghese, Ramaswamy Iyer and Arshad Abbasi, who have undertaken some pioneering work on these issues. The IWEG should spearhead independent meetings in India, Pakistan and both sides of the LoC, with a larger group, in terms of addressing the main concerns of the stakeholders in the national and regional capitals.

Joint Study of Glaciers and Effective Use of Waters

Both India and Pakistan should jointly invest in encouraging independent scientific/environmental studies on the Himalayan glaciers and give them the necessary access. There have been numerous proposals already on converting the Siachen into a peace/science park, and monitor the developments. There is a need for such a focus on all the glaciers of the Himalayas, from which most of the perennial rivers of India and Pakistan originate.

Given the fact that countries like Nepal and Bangladesh also depend on the Himalayan source, it would be prudent to include them, along with China, which also has a stake here on the Brahmaputra system.

Reducing the Water Rhetoric

Both in Pakistan and India, along with both sides of the LoC, there is so much of political rhetoric, which is actually harming everyone, including those who are making this statement. There is a clear need to avoid "the loot of our waters," "decide the dam over federation," "we will use any weapon, including nuclear, to secure our water rights," and "abrogate the treaty, for we give them the waters, but they send terrorists." While the extremist elements are unlikely to reduce their rhetoric, nothing is stopping the moderate elements to raise their voices in favour.

APP – 15

Glossary

CORDEX	Coordinated Regional Downscaling Experiment
GAC	German Aerospace Center
ESA	European Space Agency
FAO	Food and Agriculture Organization of the United Nations
GDP	Gross Domestic Product
GIS	Geographic Information Systems
GLOF	Glacial Lake outburst Flood
GRACE	Gravity Recovery and Climate Experiment
HKH	Hindu Kush Himalaya
IBIS	Indus Basin Irrigation System
ICIMOD	International Centre for Integrated Mountain Development
IFPRI	International Food Policy Research Institute
InSAR	Interferometric synthetic Aperture Radar
IWRM	Integrated Water Resources Management
IWT	Indus Waters Treaty
IWMI	International Water Management Institute
IRB	Indus River Basin
MW	Megawatt
NASA	National Aeronautics and Space Administration
NOAA	National Oceanic and Atmospheric Administration
OECD	Organisation for Economic Cooperation and Development
UN	United Nations
UNEP	United Nations Environment Programme
UNICEF	United Nations Children's Fund
WAPDA	Pakistan Water and Power Development Authority
WHO	World Health Organization
WGMS	World Glacier Monitoring Service

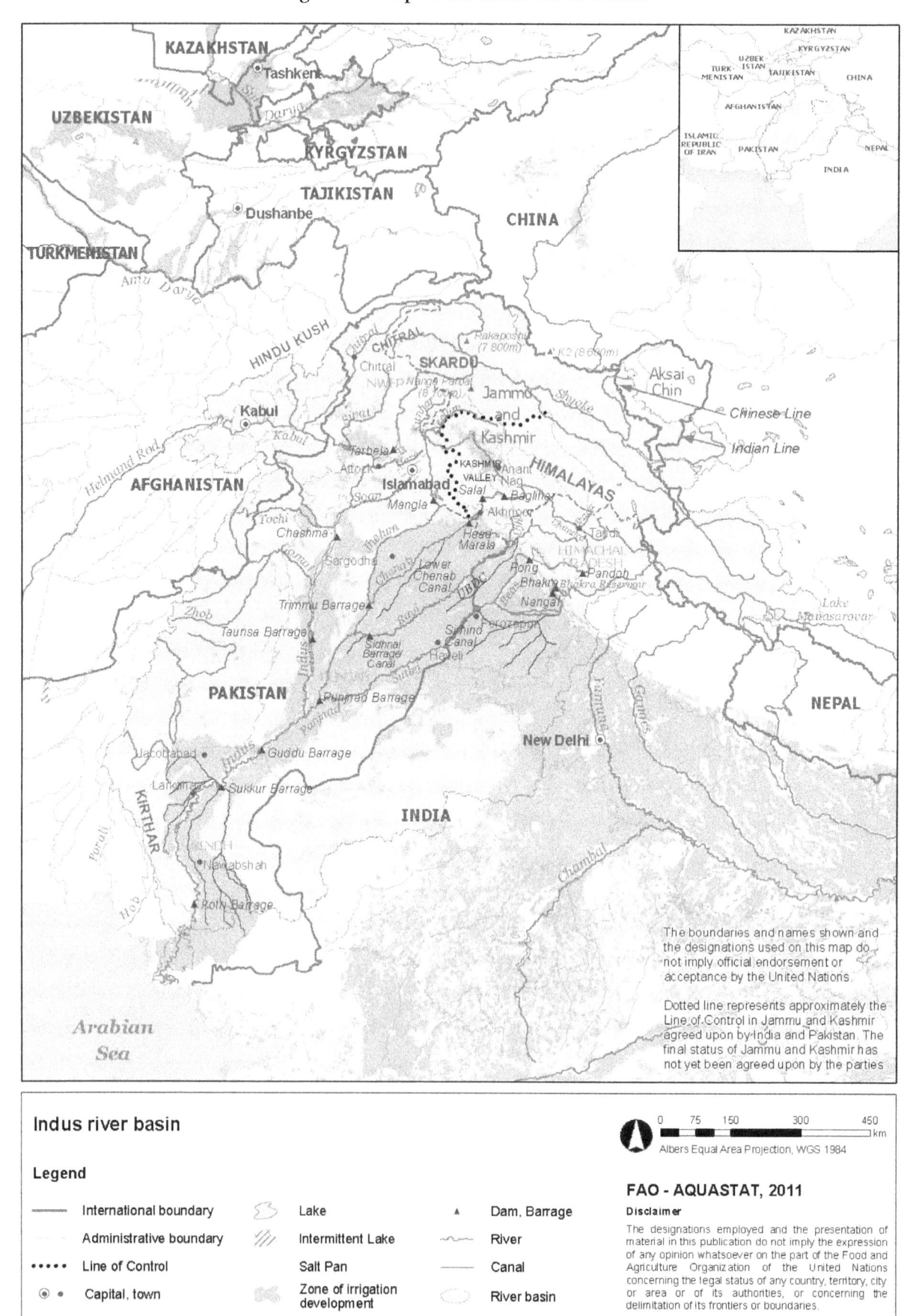

Figure 1. Map of the Indus River Basin

APP - 16

DECLASSIFIED
CONFIDENTIAL LETTERS OF THE WORLD BANK AND THE BRITISH GOVERNMENT RELATING TO INDUS WATER TREATY

BY AIR BAG
1422/221/59

SECRET

BRITISH EMBASSY,
WASHINGTON, D.C.

December 15, 1959

Dear John,

As foreshadowed in my letter 1422/218/59 of December 11 I enclose nine copies (Nos. 24 - 32) of the draft Indus Waters Treaty, with a covering Memorandum by the I.B.R.D.

2. These have been distributed to the contributors for information, to complement the draft I.B.D.F. Agreement. Iliff will no doubt give us a gloss on the present state of play with regard to the Treaty at the next Working Party meeting (now on December 22), but the wording of the Treaty itself is of course a matter to be worked out between India, Pakistan and the I.B.R.D.

3. It does not therefore seem necessary for us to consider this in any great detail. I have mentioned to Iliff the currency point arising on Article V of the Treaty; his idea is that this should be made to correspond as necessary with the I.B.D.F. Agreement, the wording of which may become firmer after the next Working Party meeting.

4. The only other point is of course that the draft Treaty is still <u>ad referendum</u> to Governments and in view of the number of detailed legal points which have been put up, particularly by the Pakistanis, the negotiation of the final wording may yet take some time. However, Iliff is still hoping to get to the point of signature during February. He hopes to be able to outline to us at the next Working Party meeting the timetable for presenting the draft I.B.D.F. Agreement to Pakistan, which is connected to the publicity question.

5. I enclose six spare copies of this letter.

Yours ever,

Harry

(H.S.H. Stanley)

J.J.B. Hunt Esq.,
Commonwealth Relations Office,
London, S.W.1.

SECRET

INDUS WATERS TREATY

DRAFT DATED DECEMBER 9, 1959

Memorandum by Bank Representative

1. The attached draft of an Indus Waters Treaty represents the measure of agreement so far reached by the Representatives of India and Pakistan during the current discussions in Washington. The draft is now for consideration by the two Governments.

2. There still remain for discussion and agreement the provisions to be included in the eight Annexures to the Treaty. With regard to Annexure H (Court of Arbitration), both Representatives are in agreement that the Annexure should contain a provision empowering the Court of Arbitration to prescribe, under certain conditions, such interim measures as, in the view of the Court, may be necessary to prevent aggravation or extension of a dispute, or prejudice to a final solution of it.

3. In the course of the current discussions it has not been possible to obtain agreement on the following point :-

Extraordinary Extension of Transition Period

During the London discussions in July and August last, Pakistan asked that a clause should be included in the Treaty providing for an extraordinary extension of the Transition Period (over and above the 3-year extension contemplated by the proposed Article II (8)) in the event that certain emergency situations should develop whose effect might be to make it impossible for Pakistan to construct the "Replacement Works" within the 13-year period contemplated. The matter was left over from the London discussions for further consideration by the two Governments and the Bank, (see Covering Memorandum by Bank Representative to Heads of Agreement dated September 15, 1959). During the current discussions in Washington the matter has been raised again.

The Bank is of the opinion that there should be some provision in the Treaty to protect Pakistan against an outbreak of international hostilities whose consequences would be to make it impossible for Pakistan to obtain, in time, equipment or materials essential for the completion of the "Replacement Works". Accordingly the Bank would recommend for the consideration of the two Governments a Treaty provision in the following sense:-

"If, at any time prior to 31st March, 1965, Pakistan should represent to the Bank that, because of the outbreak of large-scale international hostilities arising out of causes beyond the control of Pakistan,

SECRET

it is unable to obtain from abroad the materials and equipment necessary for the completion, by 31st March, 1973, of that part of the system of works referred to in Article II (5) which relates to the replacement referred to therein, (hereinafter referred to as the "replacement element") and if, after consideration of this representation in consultation with India, the Bank is of the opinion that

(a) these hostilities are on a scale of which the consequence is that Pakistan is unable to obtain in time such materials and equipment as must be procured from abroad for the completion, by 31st March, 1973, of the replacement element, and

(b) since the Effective Date, Pakistan has taken all reasonable steps to obtain the said materials and equipment and, with such resources of materials and equipment as have been available to Pakistan both from within Pakistan and from abroad, has carried forward the construction of the replacement element with due diligence and all reasonable expedition,

the Bank shall immediately notify each of the Parties accordingly. The Parties undertake that, on being so notified, they will forthwith consult together and enlist the good offices of the Bank in their consultation, with a view to reaching mutual agreement as to whether or not, in the light of all the circumstances then prevailing, any modifications of the provisions of this Treaty are appropriate and advisable and, if so, the nature and the extent of the modifications".

4. Meanwhile the Bank proposes that work should continue in Washington on the drafting of the eight Annexures to the Treaty.

(Sgd.) W.A.B. ILIFF

I.B.R.D.
Washington D.C.
December 11, 1959

Mr. Rumbold

At (1) opposite is the first draft of the Indus Waters Treaty, together with a short covering memorandum by the International Bank. Copies of both have gone to the Departments concerned.

2. Mr. Iliff has since told the Washington Working Party, at its meeting on 22nd December, that while the draft Treaty is being considered by the Indian and Pakistan Governments he is, as forecast in paragraph 4 of his memorandum of 11th December, continuing work on the Annexures to the Treaty. He has resisted Pakistan's proposal for simultaneous discussion of the two most difficult Annexures (the transitional provisions and Indian Consumptive uses), his idea being to leave the Annexure on Consumptive uses until last so that the two Governments would be faced with a clear choice between reaching agreement or wrecking the Treaty on this one point. He still thinks it reasonable to hope for signature in February.

3. Mr. Iliff has given the draft Treaty to the contributors for information and has <u>not</u> invited our comments. I must confess that I had been under the impression that our offer of a contribution was dependent upon acceptance by India and Pakistan of a <u>satisfactory</u> Water Treaty: on looking up our papers I find that this is not so. When the Secretary of State saw Mr. Black on 6th May the formula used was that we would sympathetically consider a contribution "provided the Bank's plan were accepted by India and Pakistan" and provided also that the other governments approached made suitable contributions. Similarly the Secretary of State in his letter of assurance to Mr. Black of 29th July said that our participation assumed <u>inter alia</u> that "agreement is reached between India and Pakistan on the provisions to be included in

/an

an International Water Treaty for a settlement of the Indus Waters Dispute". Nevertheless I have examined the Treaty to see if there is anything in it which should cause us difficulty and I have also sent a copy to Sir Ralph Hone so that he may consider its bearing on the Indus Basin Development Fund Agreement (of which we will be a signatory).

4. In general the draft Treaty contains few surprises. You will however wish to look particularly at:-

 (i) <u>Article V. The I.B.D.F.</u> This article will obviously require some amendment when agreement is finally reached on how our contributions should be expressed (i.e. whether in sterling or dollar equivalents) in the I.B.D.F. agreement. The footnote on page 10 makes it clear that the Bank has this point in mind.

 (ii) <u>Article VIII. The Permanent Indus Commission.</u> It is good that the Commission's functions should be spelled out. We accepted earlier that the contributors should not be members of the Commission.

 (iii) <u>Article IX. Settlement of disputes.</u> This seems satisfactory. The Executive Directors (of the I.B.D.F. agreement) are not mentioned.

 (iv) <u>Article X. General Provisions.</u> This mass of verbiage is designed to cover Mangla. Earlier Mr. Iliff had envisaged dealing with Mangla by an Exchange of Letters separate from the main Treaty. Later he consulted us about a draft article and we encouraged him to persevere with a separate exchange feeling that it might prove

/harder

harder to get agreement on a formal article for inclusion in the Treaty. Both the Pakistan and India representatives in Washington have however accepted the draft article. The formula effectively safeguards the legal claims of both countries over Kashmir. It is not altogether clear to me exactly what the position would be if Pakistan subsequently wants to do things connected with the Rivers in Azad Kashmir (e.g. raising the height of the Mangla Dam) which are outside the Bank's plan. Presumably this would be a new situation and neither side would be held to have surrendered their legal position. But this is a point which Pakistan and the Bank will no doubt have considered and there seems little point in our raising it.

JBH.
3/12 -

Mr. J. Hunt

Like you, I was under the impression that our contribution depended upon the conclusion of a satisfactory Water Treaty between India and Pakistan and although we have not made this explicit, I think that it is open to us to draw Mr. Iliff's attention to any points in this draft which we think unsatisfactory, because it is no use our making a contribution to a settlement which is in danger of not sticking. If Mr. Iliff questioned any intervention by us of this sort we could make this point to him.

/2.

2. In fact I agree with you that there is nothing serious we need quarrel with in the present draft. I notice, however, that in Article IX(3)(a) it is stated that a neutral expert "shall be appointed" but the Treaty nowhere says by whom he shall be appointed. Presumably the appointment should lie with the two Governments (or perhaps the two Commissioners) in agreement and in the event of disagreement with the International Bank.

3. The same sort of point may arise on Annexure H about the Court of Arbitration.

4. I think that we ought to put this point to Mr. Iliff.

(H.A.F. RUMBOLD)
1st January, 1960.

C.R.O.

RECORD COPY

EC. 1297/6/37

COMMONWEALTH RELATIONS OFFICE,
DOWNING STREET.

6 January, 1960.

SECRET

Mr. Reed

Enclosures (1)

In John Hunt's absence on leave I am writing to thank you for your letter of the 15th December enclosing copies of the draft Indus Waters Treaty.

We agree that the wording of the Treaty itself is a matter to be worked out between India, Pakistan and the I.B.R.D. but I think that it would be open to us to draw Iliff's attention to any points which might look to us unsatisfactory on the grounds that it is no use our contributing to a settlement which is in danger of not holding together. In the draft you sent us there seems nothing exceptional but there is one point which you might put to Iliff. In Article IX (3) (a) it is stated that a neutral expert "shall be appointed" but the draft Treaty nowhere says by whom he shall be appointed. Presumably the appointment should lie with the two Governments (or perhaps the two Commissioners) in agreement and in the event of disagreement with the International Bank. The same sort of point may arise on Annexure H about the Court of Arbitration.

(A.H. REED)

H.S.H. STANLEY, ESQ.,
WASHINGTON.

SECRET

RECORD COPY

C.R.O.

EC. 1297/6/37

COMMONWEALTH RELATIONS OFFICE,
DOWNING STREET.

6 January, 1960.

SECRET

Mr. Reed

In John Hunt's absence on leave I am writing to thank you for your letter of the 15th December enclosing copies of the draft Indus Waters Treaty.

We agree that the wording of the Treaty itself is a matter to be worked out between India, Pakistan and the I.B.R.D. but I think that it would be open to us to draw Iliff's attention to any points which might look to us unsatisfactory on the grounds that it is no use our contributing to a settlement which is in danger of not holding together. In the draft you sent us there seems nothing exceptional but there is one point which you might put to Iliff. In Article IX (3) (a) it is stated that a neutral expert "shall be appointed" but the draft Treaty nowhere says by whom he shall be appointed. Presumably the appointment should lie with the two Governments (or perhaps the two Commissioners) in agreement and in the event of disagreement with the International Bank. The same sort of point may arise on Annexure H about the Court of Arbitration.

(A.H. REED)

H.S.H. STANLEY, ESQ.,
WASHINGTON.

SECRET

SECRET

Amendments to Article V of Indus Waters Treaty proposed by Bank Representative

1. Page 10, line 29

   Delete the words "equivalent to U.S. $......"
   and substitute "of Pounds Sterling 62,500,000"

2. Page 10, line 31

   Delete the words "U.S. $......"
   and substitute "Pounds Sterling 62,500,000"

3. Page 11, lines 3 and 4

   Delete the passage in square brackets and the asterisk and substitute:

   "Pounds Sterling or in such other currency or currencies as may from time to time be agreed between India and the Bank".

4. Page 11, lines 23 to 28

   Delete second column of Table and substitute:

   Payment to India

   5% of £ stg. 62,500,000
   namely £ stg. 3,125,000

   10.25% of £ stg. 62,500,000
   namely £ stg. 6,406,250

   15.76% of £ stg. 62,500,000
   namely £ stg. 9,850,000

5. Page 11, line 29

   Renumber Paragraph (6) as Paragraph (7).

6. Insert new Paragraph (6):

   "(6) The amounts in Pounds Sterling specified in this Article shall remain unchanged irrespective of any alteration in the par value of the Pound Sterling".

7. Page 11, lines 31, 32, 33

   Delete

January 6, 1960.

BY AIR BAG
1422/8/60

BRITISH EMBASSY,
WASHINGTON, D.C.

SECRET

January 8, 1960

Dear Adrian,

Thank you for your letter EC.1297/6/37 of January 5 about the draft Indus Waters Treaty.

2. Iliff's main reason for hoping that the contributors would not chip in with detailed comments is of course that he has been having more than enough trouble negotiating the draft with the Indians and Pakistanis, whose close scrutiny of every word ought anyway to prevent loose ends. There is also the point that the present draft may well be considerably revised by the two Governments. Nevertheless he will, I am sure, appreciate your point that we cannot be expected to contribute to a scheme we think unsound. We could perhaps take an opportunity to put this point across at one of the Working Party meetings, perhaps suggesting that it might be prudent to let contributors see the final draft of the Treaty before it is signed, in case it presents any difficulties for them.

3. As regards Article IX (3) (a), I read this to mean that the neutral expert would be appointed, and "the terms of his retainer" fixed, by the Bank during the Transition Period and thereafter as in sub-section (11). I should be surprised if this was not intended, since I should expect Iliff to wish, and indeed India and Pakistan to insist, that the machinery for settling disputes could be invoked despite any obstruction by one or other party. But if the Legal Adviser considers that the section, as drafted, would not have this effect, we certainly ought to tell Iliff.

4. Could you let us know what you think about the general point in paragraph 2 and the detailed one in paragraph 3?

Yours ever,

(H.S.H. Stanley)

A. H. Reed Esq.,
Commonwealth Relations Office,
London, S.W.1.

BY AIR BAG
1422/8/60

BRITISH EMBASSY,
WASHINGTON, D.C.

SECRET

January 8, 1960

Dear Adrian,

Thank you for your letter EC.1297/6/37 of January 5 about the draft Indus Waters Treaty.

2. Iliff's main reason for hoping that the contributors would not chip in with detailed comments is of course that he has been having more than enough trouble negotiating the draft with the Indians and Pakistanis, whose close scrutiny of every word ought anyway to prevent loose ends. There is also the point that the present draft may well be considerably revised by the two Governments. Nevertheless he will, I am sure, appreciate your point that we cannot be expected to contribute to a scheme we think unsound. We could perhaps take an opportunity to put this point across at one of the Working Party meetings, perhaps suggesting that it might be prudent to let contributors see the final draft of the Treaty before it is signed, in case it presents any difficulties for them.

3. As regards Article IX (3) (a), I read this to mean that the neutral expert would be appointed, and "the terms of his retainer" fixed, by the Bank during the Transition Period and thereafter as in sub-section (ii). I should be surprised if this was not intended, since I should expect Iliff to wish, and indeed India and Pakistan to insist, that the machinery for settling disputes could be invoked despite any obstruction by one or other party. But if the Legal Adviser considers that the section, as drafted, would not have this effect, we certainly ought to tell Iliff.

4. Could you let us know what you think about the general point in paragraph 2 and the detailed one in paragraph 3 ?

Yours ever,
Harry
(H.S.H. Stanley)

A. H. Reed Esq.,
Commonwealth Relations Office,
London, S.W.1.

EC 1297/6/37

CONFIDENTIAL

COMMONWEALTH RELATIONS OFFICE
DOWNING STREET,
LONDON S.W.1.

20th January, 1960

Dear Wilson,

Will you please refer to Stanley's letter 1422/8/60 of 8th January about the Indus Water Treaty.

2. We entirely agree with the course of action suggested in his second paragraph. So long as Iliff appreciates that we can only contribute to a scheme backed by a treaty which we feel is sound, we shall be quite happy.

3. We asked the Legal Adviser to look at Article IX(3)(a), and he agrees with Stanley that the Article provides adequately for the Neutral Experts' appointment, terms of reference, etc. I am sorry that you have been troubled over this point. The Legal Adviser has however pointed out that the word "paragraph" in Article IX(3) seems incorrect and makes nonsense of the provision. The divisions of the Treaty are called Articles, and the word "Article" should be substituted in order to make sense.

Yours sincerely,

(J. J. B. HUNT)

G. M. WILSON, ESQ.,
WASHINGTON.

DRAFT LETTER

C.R.O File No. EC.1297/6/37

MR. R.G. BEER 19/1/60
MR. J.B. HUNT 19/1/

Parly U.S. of S.
Secretary of State

For Signature by: MR. HUNT

To:

G. Lee Wilson, Esq.,
B. Embassy,
Washington.

SECURITY MARKING: Confidential

Dear Wilson,

Will you please refer to Stanley's letter 1422/8/60 of 8th January about the Indus Water Treaty.

2. We entirely agree with the course of action suggested in his second paragraph. So long as Iliff appreciates that we can only contribute to a scheme backed by a treaty which we feel is sound, we shall be quite happy.

3. We asked the Legal Adviser to look at Article IX(3)(a), and he agrees with Stanley that the Article provides adequately for the Neutral Experts' appointment, terms of reference etc. He has pointed out, however, that the word "paragraph" in Article IX(3) seems incorrect and makes nonsense of the provision. The divisions of the Treaty are called Articles, and the word "Article" should be substituted in order to make sense.

Yours sincerely,

[Margin note: I am sorry that you have been troubled over this point. The Legal Adviser has however]

CONFIDENTIAL

EC 1297/6/8

COMMONWEALTH RELATIONS OFFICE,
DOWNING STREET,
LONDON S.W.1.

11th April, 1960

John Foster, Q.C., the distinguished International Lawyer who was Parliamentary Under-Secretary of State for Commonwealth Relations from 1951 to 1954 has had a telephone call from Iliff asking him to go over to Washington right away in connection with the Indus negotiations. Foster is leaving by air tomorrow.

His talk on the telephone with Iliff was necessarily brief but Iliff said that he wanted Foster's advice on a point relating to Kashmir. I explained to Foster the background to the consumptive uses and Mangla difficulties and he said that Iliff could have been referring to the latter. On the other hand he had the impression that Iliff was referring specifically to the actual signature of the Treaty and thought that a formula would have to be devised to prevent either side claiming that they were signing the Treaty on behalf of their whole territory including Kashmir.

John Foster will not be returning directly to London and I have given him your name saying that if he has any news after his talks with Iliff which he feels like passing on you will be very glad to receive it.

Needless to say, both we and the Foreign Office have impressed on Foster the great importance of doing everything possible to avoid any hitch which might prevent signature of the Treaty on 9th May.

(J. J. B. HUNT)

H. S. B. STANLEY, ESQ.

BY AIR BAG
1422/30/60

BRITISH EMBASSY,
WASHINGTON, D.C.

SECRET

January 27, 1960

Dear Mr. Hunt,

At our meeting with Iliff this afternoon on Indus Waters questions, about which I have written separately, I also spoke about the contributors' interest in the terms of the Indus Waters Treaty, on the lines of your letter to Wilson EC 1297/6/37 of January 20.

2. I fear Iliff did not at all like the idea of circulating the final draft of the Treaty to contributors before signature. He says that, as of course we know, the process of negotiation with India and Pakistan is arduous and delicate. Renegotiation at the final stages because of amendments suggested by the contributors, would therefore be impracticable. Of course he understands that the United Kingdom, and the other contributors for that matter, would not want to contribute to a scheme based on a Treaty they felt was unsound. If any of us felt really strongly we could, he supposed, decline to sign the I.B.D.F. Agreement. He would, however, obviously take a lot of persuading that a treaty acceptable to India, Pakistan and the Bank, the three parties directly concerned, could have so much wrong with it as to justify withdrawal by one of the contributors.

3. I also mentioned the drafting point in your paragraph 3. Iliff does not agree with it, because Article IX (3) deals with a "difference" whereas the sub-sections (4) (5) and (6) deal with a "dispute", the distinction between these being described in subsection (2). However, this article was going to be recast and a good deal of it put into annexures, so your point would very likely disappear anyway.

4. You may regard all this as somewhat unsatisfactory. I am sure that Iliff's attitude should not be interpreted as meaning that he will not consider any suggestions, whether of substance or of form, which we or the other contributors may have to offer on the present (incomplete) draft of the Treaty - in which he does not now expect any far-reaching changes. But we must be tactful about this. He really is having a difficult time with the Indians and Pakistanis and he hinted that if we took too much of a hand in the wording of the Treaty he might again be tempted to suggest that we took over the negotiations.

H. Stanley pp. A&R

(H.S.H. Stanley)

J.J.B. Hunt Esq.,
Commonwealth Relations Office,
London, S.W.1.

(Mr. Stanley approved this

BY AIR BAG
1422/160/60

BRITISH EMBASSY,
WASHINGTON, D.C.

SECRET

April 26, 196

Dear John,

Iliff has now circulated what he describes as "the latest draft of an Indus Waters Treaty (and of Annexures D, E, G and H) which has emerged from the current discussions in Washington, and which the Bank intends to recommend to the Government of India and the Government of Pakistan for adoption." He has also circulated a List of Amendments to the earlier draft of the Treaty (dated December 9, 1959) to facilitate comparison.

2. I enclose nine copies of all these documents, together with six copies of this letter.

3. Iliff continues "the text of the remaining Annexures (A, B, C, F and I), in whatever form they may be agreed, should not necessitate any substantive alteration in this revised text of the Treaty or of Annexures D, E, G, or H."

4. I have only just time to get these documents into the bag, so I am afraid I have been unable to look through them.

Yours ever,

(H.S.H. Stanley)

J. J. B. Hunt Esq.,
Commonwealth Relations Office,
London, S.W.1.

SECRET

APP – 17

BAGLIHAR AND KISHANGANGA: PROBLEMS OF TRUST

Alok Bansal, 13 June, 2005

During his last visit to New Delhi, renowned Pakistani journalist and Editor of *The Friday Times*, Najam Sethi, remarked that for most Pakistanis, water is a more serious issue today than the resolution of Kashmir. He also remarked that the Baglihar and Kishanganga Projects have become highly emotive issues and India must understand Pakistani sensitivities. Any accommodation here would go a long way towards creating goodwill. There is, therefore, a need to analyse these issues before India-Pakistan relations become a hostage to them.

Under the Indus Waters Treaty, the waters of the three eastern rivers (Beas, Ravi and Sutlej) were allocated to India and the western rivers (Chenab, Indus and Jhelum) to Pakistan for unrestricted use. The Treaty also provided that both countries shall have unrestricted use of the waters in each other's rivers for four purposes: domestic use, agriculture use, restricted use of hydroelectric power, through a "run-of-the river" construction and non-consumptive use. The Treaty has stood the test of time and served its purpose despite two wars and the Kargil. However, the first setback to the Treaty was in 1991, when Pakistan objected to the Wullar barrage intended to increase the depth of water in the Jhelum and facilitate navigation for transportation. India stopped the construction of the barrage pending bilateral settlement of the dispute but has failed to convince Pakistan, reinforcing the belief that Pakistan's only aim is to prevent harnessing of J&K's immense water resources.

The government also started work on various hydroelectric power projects on rivers traversing in the state to mitigate the power situation. The 430 MW Baglihar power project was conceived in 1992. Work started in 2000. The power project envisages non-consumptive use of the Chenab waters since the discharge from the power station is released into the river. All such dams need temporary storages so that power generation is uniform over short durations of time and does not fluctuate from day to day depending on the river flow. Storage of upto 50 percent and extra discharge of upto thirty percent on a daily basis are permitted under the Treaty provided the total water received and discharged over a seven day period remains constant. Pakistan has also objected to pondage on the ground that it could flood Pakistan. The fact that India has not violated the Treaty despite grave provocations has failed to convince Pakistan. It has suggested that a smaller weir should be adequate and has objected to the fact that the dam is 4.5 m above the highest water level, and could be used to store extra water. Pakistan also objects to the outlets as being too low in the wall of the dam as they could be used to flood areas downstream, whereas they are necessary for clearing silt.

The Kishanganga project envisages building a hydro-electric project on the Kishanganga River, a tributary of the Jhelum, and releases its discharge through a 22km tunnel into the Wullar Lake on the Jhelum. All of the water flows from Jhelum and goes to Pakistan; therefore, there is no consumptive use of water. Pakistan has objected to the project because it is also planning the Neelam-Jhelum hydropower project in PoK on river Neelam (as Kishanganga is called in PoK). It claims the project would deny water to the Neelam Valley and scuttle the hydropower project. However, the project will reduce the flow of water by only 27 percent and will more than meet the irrigation requirements of the Neelam Valley, though it may reduce the power generating potential of the proposed 969 MW Neelam-Jhelum hydropower project. Pakistan feels that by proposing these projects, India is trying to pit the population of J&K against the Pakistan government. Most Kashmiris feel the interests of the state were ignored while signing the Indus Waters Treaty and support the Baglihar project to alleviate power shortage in the state.

It is clear that India does not plan any consumptive use of the river waters, but the problem is the 'trust deficit' between the two countries that makes them view every step initiated by the other with suspicion. Pakistan has approached the World Bank for appointing a neutral expert in the case of Baglihar, who has has been appointed. This process will take long and his decision is unlikely to satisfy both parties. The fact of the case is that the issues involved and the differences are technical in nature. Politicizing them may derail the entire peace process. Setting up a permanent Indo-Pak commission to monitor the discharge from Baglihar could allay Pakistani fears about flooding. In the case of Kishanganga, the differences could be resolved across the table, as the project is still in its early stages.

APP – 18

BAGLIHAR HYDRO ELECTRIC PROJECT

South Asia Network
May-June 2005

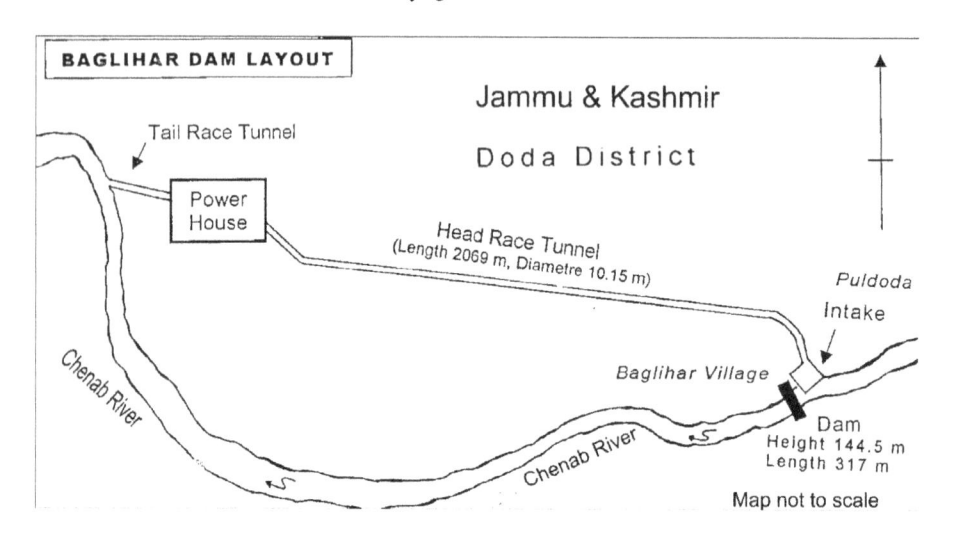

Baglihar hydropower project on Chenab River in Doda district in Jammu and Kashmir has been in news for some time now. The main reason for this 450 (3 X 150 MW) MW project to be in news is that the objections raised by Pakistan on the project has led to the project being referred to a World Bank appointed Neutral Expert. Pakistan feels that the project violates the 1960 Indus Waters Treaty, whereas India says the project does not violate the IWT. The incident of the differences being referred to a NE is happening for the first time in the 45-year history of the IWT.

According to the Indian Water Resources Ministry, Pakistan has mainly six objections on the construction of the Dam: Pondage level, Gated Spillways, Lower Weair Level, Level of Intake Tunnels, Height of Gates and Elevation of Tunnels.

Brief Background The Baglihar project, located about 120 km upstream of the Pakistan territory, has two stages each of 450 MW. The stage II powerhouse will be housed in the caverns to be formed by extending the existing caverns of Stage I. The reservoir capacity is 15 MCM and the headrace tunnels are designed to divert water to the extent of 430 cubic metres per second. An MoU was signed in April 1999 for the project by the Jaiprakash Industries, in a joint venture with the SNC-Lavalin of Canada. A 144.5 m high dam is to be constructed to deliver water through a 2.1 km long tunnel to the power station. The project was then to cost Rs. 3495 crores, to be completed in five years. In Nov. 2002 the J&K state cabinet noted with concern that the project was started without financial closure and it would cost over Rs 4600 crores, thus making the per MW installed capacity cost to be Rs 10.22 crores. In Jan. 2003, the work on Rs 1750 crores second phase of the project to generate 450 MW started, to be commissioned in Oct 2006. On March 25, 2003, the J&K Govt. indicated setting up of a Commission to probe whether the norms were observed in the allotment of Baglihar dam contracts.

The J&K State govt has said that the J&K had, the right to use the waters of its rivers.

WB The govt. of Pakistan formally sought (Jan 18, '05) the WB mediation over the dispute of the Indus Waters Treaty. Pakistan also asked India to stop construction work on the Baglihar HEP. The WB dispatched a list of three water dispute experts to Pakistan and India for their consensus. Those three experts were one each from Switzerland, Australia and Brazil.

Prof Raymond Laffitte, who has been appointed the NE by the World Bank after consulting the two counties as provided under the IWT, met the teams from the two countries for the first time in Paris on June 9-10.

Raymond Lafitte Age 70, a professor at the Swiss Federal Institute of Technology in Lausanne, chairman f the committee on governance of dam projects of the International Commission on Large Dams, a member of the advisory committee to the president of ICOLD and Dam Safety Committee of ICOLD. ICOLD essentially being a lobby in favour of large dams, it is clear that Prof Lafitte is a supporter of large dams.

As per IWT, the NE's findings will be final and binding on both the parties. If the NE feels that the points referred to him are beyond his purview or that there is a dispute (as different from "differences," as the Baglihar issue is described now), the matter will have to go to a Court of Arbitration, as per Shri Ramaswamy Iyer, former Secretary, govt. of India. (The Hindu).

Iyer goes on to say that Pakistan's concerns about Baglihar are only partly over violations of the treaty; they are more over security aspects. Pakistan is afraid that the possible water storage at Baglihar can be used as a weapon by India to the detriment of Pakistan. India's Prime Minister Dr Manmohan Singh, in fact, clarified to the visiting Pakistani editors that Pakistan has nothing to fear on that score.

RN Malik, former Engineering-in-Chief, said in his article (Daily Excelsior) that India cannot agree for a dam with an ungated spillway because the reservoir will be filled with silt in just 3 to 4 years. He said that both Jhelum and Chenab rivers are notorious for transporting a high load of silt, because of the erosion of thick mattle of sand, or the hills in the entire catchment area during the rains. Pakistan knows this fact very well because the Mangla dam reservoir, across river Jhelum in occupied Kashmir, has been heavily silted up. Indian engineers, too, know this fact very well because the 690 MW Salal project, the first one on river Chenab, got silted up within four years of its commissioning. That some of the benefits of the projects in India on the three western rivers (Chenab, Jhelum and Indus) 'given' to Pakistan under the IWT would flow to the people of Jammu and Kashmir state in India add another dimension for the differences on projects like Baglihar.

Call to stop work on Baglihar Pakistan said India wanted to resolve the matter bilaterally but Pakistan did not agree because Islamabad had exhausted all options to find a settlement through bilateral talks before approaching the WB as a last resort under the Indus Waters Treaty. However, the spokesman said, even now if India stopped work on the dam, Pakistan was willing to consider the Indian proposal for bilateral talks.

Indian PM Dr Manmohan Singh assured a group of visiting Pakistani editors that the design of the Baglihar Dam could be changed if it was found to be violating the Indus water treaty. "Nothing will be done which violates the Indus Water Basin Treaty in letter and spirit," Dr Singh stressed and said: "If weighty and credible evidence is demonstrated to us in its design, we are duty bound to rectify it."

However, India needs to worry about many aspects of the Baglihar project. Here are some of the important issues on which we need to worry.

Hydrologic viability Is the 900 MW Baglihar viable? How many days in a year can it generate power at that rate? It will require 860 cumecs of water, but the Chenab flow reduces much below that in winter. In fact, the flow in Chenab reduced to upto 50 cumecs. The authorities have not made public the hydrologic data or the projected power generation from the project. The experience of the existing 690 MW Salal project on Chenab, 480 MW Uri HEP on the adjoining basin Jhelum shows that these projects, in fact, generate much less power in winter when the need for power is maximum in J&K.

Siltation Chenab River is known to be a highly silt laden river and there are frequent events of landslides, increasing the siltation rates. Construction of so many mega projects on the same river (Salal (existing project), Baglihar, Dulhasti are under construction and Sawalkote is already being seriously considered) is also adding to the silt load of the river. In fact, as made clear by the paper on tunnelling experience at Baglihar, the rock quality at the Baglihar site ranges from poor to very poor to extremely poor. The huge silt load of the river means that the projects' useful life will be very low.

Cost As noted above, even at current cost estimates, the 450 MW installed capacity of the Baglihar project is to cost Rs 4000 crores (Rs 2700 crores have already been spent). This means that the per MW cost of the Baglihar HEP will be around Rs 8.89 crores even at current rates. This is much higher than the current cost of Rs 5-6 crores per MW installed capacity for of most such projects. The cost of electricity from the project would consequently be much higher than Rs. 5 per unit. This when the citizens of the valley are unable to pay even Rs 2 per unit charged currently. Who will pay the cost of such an expensive project and who will really benefit? There was an earlier attempt to show a lower per MW cost of the project by clubbing the two stages of the project. However, the stage II work is yet to start and it is far from clear if stage II is even feasible, particularly in view of the poor geology encountered during the construction of stage I.

As Omar Abdullah, a leader of the National Conference and a former Union Minister of State, said, there is little consultation with the local people before taking up such projects.

The project, thus, should not be interesting from the point-of-view of the questions raised in India and Pakistan. There are many questions around this project to which Indians, too, do not have clear answers.

References

1. Assessment of large dia hydraulic tunnels – Baglihar Hydroelectric project (450 MW), J&K by Ahmed Mohd. et al, presented at the International Conference on Tunneling, Asia, in Dec 2004, New Delhi, India.
2. The World Bank website www.worldbank.org
3. Website of Union Ministry of Water Resources. www.wrmin.nic.in
4. Various newspaper reports over the last four years, including the latest one in The Daily Excelsior, The Hindu.

(This was published in May-June 2005 issue of Dams, Rivers & People.)

APP – 19

PAKISTAN ASKS WORLD BANK TO APPOINT NEUTRAI EXPERT UNDER INDUS WATERS TREATY

Grish Kuber, 19 January, 2005

The World Bank, on Wednesday, received a formal request lo appoint a "neutral expert" under the Indus Waters Treaty.

Pakistan filed a petition with the Bank, asking it to intervene, to end the stand-off with India on the Baglihar hydel power project. And as a practice, the Bank has said that it will examine the request and follow the procedures laid down by the Treaty.

However, the Bank has clarified that it has "limited role" as a signatory to the Indus Waters Treaty that was signed by India and Pakistan on September 19, 1960. "The Bank is a signatory for certain specified purposes and is not a guarantor of the Treaty. Many of the purposes for which the World Bank signed the Treaty have been completed," it said.

According to the Bank, disagreements by the parties on the interpretation of the provisions of the Treaty are classified into three categories: Questions are examined by the Permanent Indus Commission; differences by a Neutral Expert; and disputes by a Court of Arbitration.

The first step under the Treaty is to resolve any "question" through the Permanent Indus Commission itself. If the "question" is not resolved there, it becomes a "difference" and is referred to a Neutral Expert, to be appointed by the two countries, or by a third party agreed upon by the two countries.

If the "difference" does not fall within the mandate of the Neutral Expert, or if the Neutral Expert rules that the "difference" should be treated as a "dispute," then a Court of Arbitration would be established.

APP – 20

BAGLIHAR CLEARED, INDIA HAS ITS WAY

Times of India, 13 February, 2007

NEW DELHI: In a vindication of India's position, the World Bank has turned down Pakistan's contention that the construction of the Baglihar Dam on the Chenab is violative of the Indus Waters Treaty, clearing the way for the project, which can help New Delhi earn popular goodwill in Jammu and Kashmir.

The verdict, which came after two years of laborious depositions, does ask India to reduce the dam's height, giving Pakistan room to derive solace. India, however, can happily live with it.

In fact, it had agreed to bring down the dam's "freeboard" by 1.5 metres during bilateral discussions. The order would be final and binding on both countries. Both India and Pakistan have promised to abide by the ruling.

Significantly, however, the World Bank has taken care to craft the verdict in a fashion that would deny Pakistan any excuse to quibble.

The Bank's Neutral Expert, Raymond Lafitte, delivered the final report on the Baglihar dispute to the diplomats of India and Pakistan in Berne, Switzerland, on Monday. Pakistan had objected to the dam's design, size and water storage capacity, and to consider other technical pursuits or modify the design.

This is the second time in recent years that India has been given a thumbs up in a dispute involving Pakistan. In 2000, Pakistan took India to the International Court of Justice for downing its surveillance aircraft Atlantique, which had crossed over to India.

The significant part of the World Bank ruling is this: India can build run-of-the-river hydro-power projects on the western rivers of the Indus.

Second, the ruling is precedent-setting in that India can build dams using modern technology to deal with sedimentation in the Himalayan rivers, technologies that were not known when the treaty was signed way back in 1960.

India's political victory is that it's a vote of confidence for its Kashmir development projects. In a statement, India said, "The three elements of design which require marginal changes, ie reductions in freeboard, pondage and increase in the height of the intakes, all arise from calculations and not from basic principles."

The ruling has been fashioned in a way so that both countries can claim a victory. Pakistani officials have been quoted as saying that three of their four objections have been upheld. On this side of the border, the J&K Power Minister, Nawang Rigzen Zora said in Jammu that the ruling was "a slap on Pakistan's face".

Former high commissioner to Pakistan, G Parthasarathy, said, "One hopes that Kashmiri separatist politicians will realise that while India spares no effort to provide development, Pakistan only seeks to delay and subvert projects benefiting Kashmiris. India should now proceed ahead with Kishenganga and Wullar barrage projects."

Technically, the most important part of the ruling was upholding India's decision to build sluice spillways on the dam. According to a government statement, "India's design of sluice spillway at Baglihar is regarded as appropriate and permissible under the Treaty... and in conformity with international practice.

APP – 21

INDIA TO MAKE PAKISTAN BARREN BY 2014

The News (Pakistan) 24 November, 2008

LAHORE: The Indus Water Commissioner, Jamaat Ali Shah, said on Sunday that India would turn Pakistan into a barren country by 2014 by blocking its waters.

Addressing a seminar at the Lahore Press Club, he said India had constructed dams on various rivers and the construction was still continuing. He said India could generate electricity but not stop Pakistan's water under the Indus Waters Treaty.

About the recent water stoppage by India, he said India claimed that it had stopped Pakistan's water from August 19 to August 28. "However, we do not accept the Indian point of view because India had stopped water till September 5 according to our estimates," he added.

He said an Indian delegation would visit Pakistan on November 29 to discuss the issue. Speaking on the occasion, representatives of various farmers organisations said India had violated the Indus Waters Treaty by constructing the Baghlihar Dam. They said if the Pakistani government remained inactive, then India would destroy Pakistan's economy and capture the country without a war.

APP - 22

INDIA VIOLATING INDUS WATER TREATY BY BUILDING DAMS

Daily Times - Pakistan, 16 February 2009

KARACHI: Indian spree of building dams on water flowing into Pakistan's territory is expected to create water scarcity in the country, said water experts on Tuesday.

Pakistan is heading towards a severe water shortage, as the Indian government has decided to build more than seven dams on rivers running into Pakistan in held Kashmir.

Pakistan has absolute rights on these rivers, as their flow is towards Pakistan and under the Indus Waters Treaty (IWT) India is violating the accord, said a senior member of the Sindh Agriculture Forum (SAF).

The SAF member said Pakistan should raise voice on international forums in order to stop the Indian government to build water reservoirs on the rivers running into Pakistan. He said Pakistan remained undecided to appoint patriotic and real water management experts to take up its case before the International Court of Arbitration against India over the construction of hydropower projects in violation of the 1960 IWT. The country is heading towards the worst water shortage in the next couple of years due to insufficient water management practices and storage capacity, he said.

Construction of Nimoo-Bazgo hydropower project, Baglihar and Kishanganga are in violation of the IWT and now it has almost completed one of the largest hydropower projects in the world on River Indus at Ladakh.

Chuttak hydroelectric project on River Suru, a tributary of the Indus in Kargil, is also near completion.

These projects would reduce the flow of Indus River, which would badly damage masses, industry and agriculture of Pakistan. Pakistan has the right to oppose these dam projects, besides opposing the Kishanganga project, because its diversion will reduce more than 20 percent of the power generation capacity of the 975 Mega Watts (MWs) Neelum-Jhelum power project on the same river downstream in Muzaffarabad, in Azad Kashmir.

In the recent past, due to the poor handling of the case with India, as well as in the International Court of Arbitration, Pakistan could not gain points in favour of its case, only because of a team of jurists, not sincere from the start.

The IWT has now become ineffective, as India has continuously been violating all clauses of the treaty and Pakistan has not been challenging them at any international forum by tacit approbation.

Under the treaty, the three western rivers, Chenab, Jehlum and Indus, are allocated to Pakistan and India is not allowed to build storages on them.

A report by the Washington DC based Woodrow Wilson Centre said Neelum-Jhelum power project, a case in the International Court of Arbitration, Pakistan would face a loss of energy of more than Rs 6 billion every year.

The IWT with India remained just on papers. India has diverted Pakistani's water and constructed more dams, which would further worsen the water situation in Pakistan. The underground water level went down from about 70-100 feet to upto 1,000 feet and has been termed as a worsening situation.

International Water Expert Engr. Bashir Malik, who has served the United Nations and the World Bank as the chief technical adviser, said the cheapest and environment-friendly solution to the water and energy crisis in Pakistan was the Kalabagh Dam, which could only be built by a patriotic and brave leader having the courage to break all barriers in the best national interest.

Malik said the 'Save Water, Save Pakistan' Forum was initiating a campaign to highlight the water and energy crisis and its solution at the national level.

Pakistan would likely face a severe water shortage if it does not plead judiciously over the controversial 330 Mega Watts (MWs) Kishanganga Hydro-Electric Power (KHEP) project in India.

It seems Indian sponsored that some politicians, nationalists, regionalists and pseudo-intellectuals are opposing the Kalabagh Dam to make Pakistan a failed state. Pakistan's Commissioner for Indus Waters, the Ministry of Water and Power, the Ministry of Environment and the Ministry of Foreign Affairs have remained tight lipped on the issue.

APP – 23

NOOR AFTAB

(The News, 27 March 2009)

A lack of operational capacity did not let Pakistan take full advantage of the Indus Waters Treaty, brokered by the World Bank, commented speakers at a seminar on 'Water Disputes & Pakistan-India Relations,' organised here, Thursday, by the Institute of Policy Studies (IPS).

"India fully utilised all its resources in terms of money and technicalities, and built dams and barrages, thus becoming the main beneficiary of the Indus Waters Treaty," they said and stressed the government that if India reclaims its right over the Western rivers, then Pakistan should also make its claim over the Eastern rivers.Speaking on the occasion, Nasrullah Mirza of the Department of Defence & Strategic Studies, Quaid-i-Azam University said Pakistan accepted the Treaty in 1960 at the stake of its very own survival and assurances from India that "it will not interfere with other rivers," but India never honoured its promises.

He underlined some of the implications of the Indus Waters Treaty, including the de facto compromise on the Kashmir dispute, the loss of legally three dams, ecological disaster and wastage of arable lands. He pointed out that there had been no water dispute at the time of partition but it was India who first violated the international norms and traditions and stopped the water flowing from occupied Kashmir to the Pakistani territory.

Dr Arshad Abbasi, former director Planning Commission, said a roadmap was prepared in 2002 to generate hydro power in Pakistan but unfortunately, even after the passage of seven years, we are hardly able to complete even a single project. He said India got water for development and Pakistan secured its share as a replacement for the Eastern rivers, so "we really felt compelled and did not move in the right direction."Masud Daher, an expert, said Pakistan is still not able to construct dams and barrages, and 135 million acres of water is flowing down the sea, which is certainly a matter of grave concern at a time when there is a huge shortfall of electricity in the country. He said India improved its technical capacity and possessed the ability to operationalise its plans in different phases.

Akram Zaki, in his concluding remarks, said whenever water flows from one country to another, different problems emerge at various points in time. He said there are different theories regarding water issues but every country presses for the one which suits its own interests. "When India stopped the water, our civil servants were inexperienced and they were not able to cope with the ongoing situation. We made mistakes and even agreed to pay for water," he said.Akram Zaki said that dictatorships weakened the state institutions because every military dictator tried to prolong his own regime, ignoring some vital national interests. He said there is a need for a composite dialogue to find out an amicable solution to the water dispute, adding that every stakeholder must support the efforts aimed at serving this purpose.

APP – 24

INDIA PLANS DAM ON RIVER CHENAB

DAWN, 22 February 2010

DAWN (a Pakistan newspaper) reported that Pakistan was still undecided when to formally seek intervention of the International Court of Arbitration against the controversial construction of Kishanganga hydropower project by India in violation of the 1960 Indus Waters Treaty. New Delhi has started preparations to build another big dam on River Chenab.

Documents available with Dawn suggest that the Government of Indian-occupied Kashmir has invited bids for a 'topographical survey of the Bursar Dam (on Chenab) for the acquisition of land and property'. New Delhi plans to begin construction by the end of the year.

The Bursar Dam is considered as the biggest project among a host of others being built by India on two major rivers – Jhelum and Chenab – flowing through the state of Jammu & Kashmir into Pakistan and assigned to Islamabad under the 1960 Indus Waters Treaty. The proposed dam would not only violate the treaty, international environmental conventions and cause water scarcity in Pakistan but would also contribute towards the melting of Himalayan glaciers.

Pakistan's previous Permanent Indus Commissioner Syed Jamaat Ali Shah had repeatedly asked his Indian counterpart to provide details of the proposed water storage and hydropower projects, including the Bursar dam. However, India has taken the stand that it was aware of its legal obligations and it would let Pakistan know about the project details and the relevant data six months before construction activities as required under the bilateral treaty, he said, adding that Pakistan could do nothing more when such projects were in the planning and investigation stage.

According to Dawn's report, responding to a question about the Kishanganga hydropower project, he said, he had already requested the government to move quickly for the constitution of an International Court of Arbitration to stop the construction of the controversial project. Pakistan, he said, had already nominated two members for the court of arbitration and had asked to do the same. He said the procedure laid down in the waters treaty required the two nations to nominate two adjudicators each of their choice and then jointly nominate three India members to complete the composition of a seven-member Court of Arbitration.

He said the procedure also required that in the case of a disagreement over the three adjudicators, the complainant nation should ask the World Bank to nominate these three members and start formal proceedings. Pakistan, he said, had even prepared the list of three joint adjudicators since India had not yet fulfilled its obligations to nominate its two members and three joint members of the court. "We have completed the entire process; it was only a matter of formal launching and only the government could do that," he said, adding that perhaps Islamabad intended to wait for the upcoming secretary level talks before triggering the legal process.

He, however, believed that these issues were of a technical nature and should be processed accordingly as provided under the Treaty.

Informed sources said that India has not only started building three other dams namely Sawalkot, Pakal-Dul and Kirthai on Chenab River, it has also completed a detail project report of the Bursar Dam site. The proposed dam would have an 829 feet height, a storage capacity of more than two million acres feet and power generation capacity of 1200MW. It should be noted that the height of Baglihar, Tarbela and Mangla Dam is 474, 485 and 453 feet, respectively.

The Bursar Dam would be constructed near the Hanzal Village (near Kishtwar) in the Doda District of Jammu & Kashmir on the 133-kilometre-long Marusudar River, the main right bank tributary of the Chenab river. Its construction would be a serious violation of the treaty, as its storage was much beyond the permissible limits. More than 4900 acres of thick forest would be submerged and the whole population of Hanzal village would be displaced.

Arshad H. Abbasi, visiting research fellow of the SDPI, said the project area fell in the Seismic Zone V and hence most vulnerable to earthquake. Two active geological faults lines — the Himalayan thrust and the Kishtwar fault — were passing through the project area, he said, adding that the worst impact of the dam would be on the glaciers of the Marusudar river basin. He said that deforestation, coupled with high altitude military activities, had already created 48 glacial lakes in the Marusudar river basin, covering an area of 225.35 sq.km, and massive construction activities in the basin would further aggravate the melting of glaciers.

He said the project was located in the Kishtwar High Altitude National Park, which was an environmentally-protected area. Spreading over an area of 400 kilometres, the park contained 15 mammal species, including the musk deer and the Himalayan black and brown bear and some rare birds, for which an environmental impact assessment study was necessary.

APP - 25

ANOTHER BLOW TO PAKISTAN'S WATER INTERESTS: INDIA STARTS BUILDING 850MS RATLE DAM ON CHENAB THE DAILY NEWS (PAKISTAN)

10 July, 2013

In an another blow to Pakistan's water interests, India has started constructing the Ratle Hydropower Dam project with a capacity to generate 850 MWs of electricity on Pakistan's Chenab River, in violation of the Indus Waters Treaty. Pakistan has already objected to this dam, which will be three times larger than the Baglihar Hydropower Dam. Mirza Asif Baig, Commissioner of Pakistan Commission of Indus Water, confirmed that India had planned to construct the Ratle Hydropower project on the Chenab, and Pakistan's side had objected to the project saying it was a sheer violation of the provisions of the Indus Waters Treaty 1960.

"We have come up with strong objections to the design of the said project in a meeting with India at the Permanent Commission of Indus Waters (PCIW) level," Baig said and vowed that in the future meeting at the PCIW level, he would continue to oppose the said project as its design violated the Indus Waters Treaty.

A Pakistani lawyer, Ms Shumaila Mehmood, in the case of Kishenganga Hydropower project, said though she was aware of the development, but it was the PCIW which dealt with the projects constructed by India on Pakistani rivers at earlier stages.

India has already carved out a plan to generate 32,000 MWs of electricity on Pakistani rivers and will be having the capacity to regulate the water flows that are destined to reach Pakistan. So far, India has built Dalhasti hydropower project of 330 MWs, Baglihar of 450 MWs and now it has started a new project named Ratle Hydropower project.

On the Neelum River that joins the Jehlum River in Pakistan, India has already completed Uri-1 and Uri-II Hydropower project and is also close to completing the Kishenganga Hydropower project. So much so, it has also built two hydropower projects on the Indus River, that include Nimmo Bazgo and Chattak hydropower project.

Former Wapda chairman Shamsul Mulk said that Pakistan needs to develop water uses in its of rivers by building water reservoirs to prevent India from constructing the hydropower project. "Once Pakistan develops its water uses, then it can argue at any international court that India cannot build its project by injuring the committed flows of Pakistan."

He said that there was a strong lobby of India in our country which did not want Pakistan to develop water uses.However, when this horrifying development surfaced, an eminent water expert Arshad Abbasi had sensitised the then Minister of Water and Power Dr Mussadik Malik, who is now the special assistant to the PM on the power sector, about this alarming development but he did not respond as expected from him. Rather, he was an advocate for the import of electricity from India.

Dr. Mussadik was asked to probe as to who had cleared this project from Pakistan's side but he didn't do so. However, Engr Safiq, who is also an eminent water expert, came down heavily on Dr. Mussadik, saying he is a dual nationality holder and is holding a much too important post and is an advocate of importing electricity from India and asked where the security agencies were. He said that Pakistan's water sector had become dysfunctional.

According to our sources, the Ratle project envisages harnessing the hydro-power potential of the river from EL 1000 m to EL 887 m. This is a concrete gravity dam at a height of 170 m, will be built across the river just downstream of the Ratle village, and an underground power house, with an installed capacity of 4X140 MWs, is proposed near Juddi village, both in Doda district. The main project will generate 2,483.37 Million Units of Electricity at the rate of Indian Rupee of only 1.22 per kWh.

After the meeting of Mr. Arshad Abbasi with Dr Mussadik Malik, a brief paper, including measures to check the enforcement of the Indus Waters Treaty in letter and spirit, was sent to Mussadik, but Musadik preferred playing his role in releasing funds for the IPPs, a more lucrative task for him.

Surprisingly, the former interim minister is an adviser to the current regime, and is only advocating importing electricity at Rs. 16 per unit. Even though he had been briefed about the 1,460 MWs Tarbela Dam Extension VI project, he still preferred to advise the government to import electricity from India.

He said that the government had planned to develop five dams so that for five times, cheaper electricity on water flows could be produced on one main river and more importantly the per capita water availability could be raised to a reasonable level, which now stands at 1,000 cubic metre per person.

About the Ratle Hydropower project, he said that the PCIW is the department which deals with such issues.

Meanwhile, in a letter addressed to the Prime Minister of Pakistan, Abbasi requested to demand an EIA (Environment Impact Assessment) report of the Ratle Hydroelectric power project. As the land proposed for this project is mostly thick conifer forests, deforestation will have a terrible impact on the river water yield in the future and the victim will be only the lower riparian i.e. Pakistan.

Islamabad Water and Power Minister, Khwaja Asif, said that, in his opinion, the Indus Waters Treaty, signed with India, does not judiciously distribute water.

Briefing the media in Islamabad along with Pakistan's Commissioner for Indus Water, Mirza Asif Baig, and Secretary Water and Power, Saifullah Chattha, Asif said that when the treaty had been signed, Pakistan had a population of 30-40 million, which had multiplied five times to 180-200 million.

The minister said Pakistan is currently contesting with India over five water projects, including Kishenganga, Ratle, Miyar, Lower Kalnai hydroelectric projects, Wullar Barrage and Tulbul Navigation project.

Terming water a life and death issue for Pakistan, Asif warned that the country could become water starved in the future.

He added that consensus on water issue is needed, so Pakistan could defend its right vigorously. He urged people to change the way they use water.

Commenting on new projects, Asif said that work on Diamer Bhasha and Dassu Dams would be started simultaneously. He added that Rs 21 billion have been spent on Bhasha Dam and land acquisition have also been completed.

Secretary Water and Power said India has been trying to get water in excess of the limits it is allowed under the Indus Basin Treaty.

The Indus Water Commissioner said the dispute regarding the proposed diversion of Neelum water by India and draw down of the dead storage level was referred to the International Court of Arbitration.

Baig informed that the final hearing was concluded on August 31, 2012 and partial award of the court has been awarded on February 18, 2013 in which the question of diversion of river water was decided in favour of India, while the question of draw down in storage level was awarded to Pakistan.

Both parties now have to submit additional data and written submissions to the Court of Arbitration and accordingly the court will decide the quantum of water to be released below the Kishenganga Hydroelectric Plant in Neelum river as environmental releases. The final award of the court is expected by December 2013.

He said Pakistan has objected on freeboard, magnitude of pondage, and placement of spillway of Ratle Hydroelectric plant of 850 Mega Watts, Miyar Hydroelectric Plant of 120 Mega Watts, Lower Kalnai plant of 48 Mega Watts and Pakal Dul Hydroelectric Plant of 1000 Mega Watts located on Chenab river.

Another disputed water project between India and Pakistan is Wullar barrage and during the sixth round of Federal Secretary level talks, was agreed that the Indian side will provide additional technical data to Pakistan.

Pakistan will examine the data to furnish its views before the next round of talks. Pakistan had objected that according to the treaty, India is not allowed to store water on main Jhelum. The work on the project is suspended since 1987 and it was last verified on May 30, 2013.

"The country of over 180 million people is going to face a huge water deficit in the next 10 to 15 years time. In the past we committed severe mistakes while protecting water rights and also showed the inability to develop water used on Pakistan's rivers."

He said that India was blocking water and hurting the country in the sowing season and it released extra water when there was no need of water, particularly during the flood time. Water and Power Secretary Saifaullah Chattha admitted that Pakistan belatedly moved its case on Kishanganga in the International Court of Arbitration.

The Minister also sided with him saying Pakistan and India were in a legal battle on Kishanganga in The Hague and in the worst scenario, the Rs. 278 billion Neelum-Jhelum hydropower was to lose 13 percent power generation and in the best scenario, the project will lose three percent, keeping in view whatsoever decision of the international Arbitration Court.

During the interaction with the media, top officials of the Pakistan Commission on Indus water were found not with the Minister and the Secretary but had the opposite views. Memon insisted that the hydropower projects that India have built so far on Pakistan's rivers are not inflicting any loss to the water interests of the lower riparian country.

Memon said that the Nimoo-Bazgo hydropower project built by India on the Indus River was justified. When his attention was drawn towards the fact that Pakistan Commission on Indus Water had helped India build the Nimoo-Bazgo project from where the Indian troops, which are at war with Pakistan at Siachen, are getting a smooth supply of electricity, Memon did not come up with a satisfactory answer and just said that the Nimmo-Bazgo project was justified. When further asked as to why the Wapda Secretary had declared the former Commissioner of Pakistan Commission of Indus Water, Syed Jamaat Ali Shah, a criminal in his preliminary report as he did not visit the site of Nimoo-Bazgo till its completion, which was clearly declared a violation of the Indus Waters Treaty, Memon opted not to answer.

Memon said that Pakistan had, so far, objected to seven projects being built by India. He said that the water flow in the Indus has slightly reduced, as India had the right to some of water on agriculture, but he insisted that water flows in the Chenab River had increased, as compared to the water flows prior to the emergence of the Indus Waters Treaty. He said that India was building 53 hydropower projects and seven dams. On the Chenab River, India managed to construct 16 projects and four were in the construction phase. He said that India was going to build the Ratle Hydropower Project of 850 MW and if its design was not changed, Pakistan will move the International Court of Arbitration.

APP - 26

WATER AS THE CARRIER OF CONCORD WITH PAKISTAN

S.V. 25 February, 2010

A Pakistani woman is seen walking back home, carrying an empty bucket, after waiting next to a hand pump, hoping for the water supply to resume after cuts, in a neighborhood of Islamabad, Pakistan, on Monday, Feb. 22, 2010. Pakistanis are facing a shortage of clean drinking water due to the low level of water in the country's dams, according to Pakistani's Meteorological Department. Photo: AP

If Islamabad can win New Delhi's trust by cracking down on terror, it could pave the way for the two sides to work together for optimum development of the Indus basin.

As India and Pakistan move towards the welcome resumption of dialogue, New Delhi needs to factor in a new reality: More than Kashmir, it is the accusation that India is stealing water that is rapidly becoming the "core issue" in the Pakistani establishment's narrative about bilateral problems.

The issue of water is emotive, touching people across Pakistan in a much more fundamental way than the demand for Kashmiri self-determination. Per capita water availability has fallen precipitously over the past few decades, thanks to rising population and poor water management, and is expected to fall below 700 cubic metres by 2025 — the international marker for water scarcity. In most years, the Indus barely makes it beyond the Kotri barrage in Sindh, leading to the ingress of sea water, the increase in soil salinity and the destruction of agriculture in deltaic districts like Thatta and Badin.

Though Pakistan's water woes predate recent hydroelectric projects, like Baglihar in Jammu and Kashmir, jihadi organizations, like the Lashkar-e-Taiba/Jamaat-ud-Dawa, have started blaming India for the growing shortage of water. Apart from inflaming public opinion against India, this propaganda helps to blunt the resentment Sindh and Balochistan have traditionally had — as the lowest riparians in the Indus river basin — against West Punjab for drawing more than its fair share of the water flowing through the provinces. The campaign also deflects criticism of Pakistan's own gross neglect of its water and sanitation sector infrastructure over the past few decades.

At the same time, the fact that river flows from India to Pakistan have slowly declined is borne out by data on both sides. Above Merala on the Chenab, for example, the average monthly flows for September have nearly halved between 1999 and 2009. India says this is because of reduced rainfall and snowmelt. Pakistan disputes this claim, preferring to link observable reductions in flows to hydroelectric projects on the Indian side. That is why, in the run-up to the February 25 meeting of the Indian and Pakistani Foreign Secretaries, Islamabad has gone out of its way to project water as the most important topic it intends to raise.

But just because water — and not terrorism — tops the Pakistani agenda today is no reason for India to refuse to discuss the subject or to treat it as important. Even as it pushes for incremental gains on terrorism, trade and CBMs, New Delhi should take a strategic view and consider two questions. First, how would a refusal to talk water play on the Pakistani political stage, where the two provinces least inclined towards jihad — Sindh and Balochistan — are also the most vulnerable to anti-India propaganda about water theft? Second, is it just possible that Islamabad could be so keen for Indian cooperation on water that it might be willing to abandon the terrorist groups it has nurtured all these years as an instrument of policy against India?

To pose the problem in this way is not to suggest a neat symmetry between two taps — that as Pakistan turns off the terrorism faucet, India can offer to turn on the water. If matters were that simple, the two neighbours would either have solved their problems by now or gone to war. Instead, the link between terror and water is more complex and it revolves around trust. Simply put, Pakistan needs to realise that a decisive action against terrorism would create an enabling environment for India to go beyond the letter of its written commitments on water and open the door for cooperation in other fields, like energy, that could also relieve some of the water pressure both countries are facing.

Though inter-provincial disputes over water-sharing were a fact of life in this region before 1947, the partition of the subcontinent introduced a further complexity. It was easy for Radcliffe to draw a line on a map and divide up the land of British India but people and water were harder to partition. The mass migration and bloodshed this triggered is well-known but the rupture to the region's hydrological system proved to be just as traumatic. The rivers which irrigated the new nation all had their origins in India. But as an upper riparian locked in a politically adversarial relationship with Pakistan, the Indian side had little or no incentive to look at the Indus basin as an integrated water system. The early years of independence saw bitter disputes, as India treated the waters of the Indus's five tributaries — Jhelum, Chenab, Ravi, Beas and Sutlej — as its own. Geography and terrain meant the Indus, itself, could not be harnessed on the Indian side of Jammu and Kashmir but intermittent, small-scale, diversions on the tributaries generated considerable tension with Pakistan. In 1960, the two countries sought to put an end to this tension by signing the Indus Waters Treaty (IWT) with the World Bank's mediation.

The IWT partitioned the six rivers of the Indus watershed on a crudely longitudinal basis. India was given exclusive use of the waters of the three eastern tributaries, the Ravi, Beas and Sutlej, and the right to "non-consumptive" use of the western rivers, namely the Indus, Jhelum and Chenab. Under the IWT, India renounced its right to block or divert the flows of the 'western' rivers and agreed to confine itself to run-of-the-river hydroelectric projects and the drawing of irrigation water for a specified acreage of farm land. This partitioning was irrational from an ecological standpoint and led to both sides incurring considerable expenses as they were forced to develop canal infrastructure drawing on "their" allocated rivers to compensate for the non-use of the other side's rivers despite that water flowing through their own territory.

Pakistani officials, from time-to-time, do accuse India of violating the 1960 treaty on the division of Indus waters. The Indian side, of course, denies this, and there is, in any case, a system of international mediation built into the IWT for binding international arbitration if the two countries cannot resolve a water-related dispute. Pakistan invoked this mechanism for Baglihar in 2005, though the arbitrator ruled in favour of the project subject to certain modifications. An earlier dispute over the Salal project was resolved in the 1970s by the two Foreign Secretaries. Today, nothing prevents Pakistan from referring any or all of the projects India proposes to build on the Chenab and Jhelum for arbitration.

Though the treaty has a mechanism to ensure compliance with the stipulated partitioning of rivers, a major weakness from Pakistan's standpoint is that it does not compel or require India to do anything on its side for the optimum development of what is, after all, an integrated water system. Inflows to Pakistan depend not just on rainfall and snowmelt in India and China (the uppermost eastern riparian) but also on the health of tributaries, streams, nullahs and aquifers as well as groundwater, soil and forest management practices. This is a classic externality problem. Costs incurred by the upper riparian on responsible watershed management will produce disproportionate benefits for the lower riparian; hence, they are not incurred.

The IWT anticipated the importance of cooperation, with Article VII stating that both parties "recognise that they have a common interest in the optimum development of the rivers, and, to that extent, they declare their intention to cooperate, by mutual agreement, to the fullest extent." o far, little has been done by either side to develop this mandate.

Since water does not figure as a stand alone topic in the Composite Dialogue framework, Pakistan's insistence on its revival is at odds with its professed priority. When the Foreign Secretaries meet, therefore, they should not allow the process to stand in the way of progress. They could, for example, discuss a framework for a standalone dialogue on water going beyond project-related disputes — for which an arbitration mechanism already exists. The focus could be on identifying short, medium and long-term steps for the optimum development of the rivers.

The Pakistani side would very quickly realise that such a dialogue, whose benefits, especially over the long-term, are tilted in its favour, can only deliver meaningful results, if there is an atmosphere of confidence and trust. If the activities of terrorists like the LeT/JuD are allowed to continue, this is unlikely to happen. But if the action Islamabad has repeatedly promised does take place, a path might open for cooperation in other areas too.

Many of the disputes that seem to be driven by fears of water scarcity are actually a reflection of another kind of scarcity: electricity. Pakistan opposes the Indian Kishenganga hydel project on the Jhelum, for example, because it will interfere with its proposed Neelum-Jhelum power plant. But if the two countries could build trust in one another, there is no reason why they cannot agree on energy swaps that could do away with the need to duplicate power projects, especially those which restrict the flow of water. Today, given the way terrorism has eroded the Indian political system's capacity and willingness to do business with Pakistan, such ideas seem hopelessly utopian. But they do offer a glimpse of the kind of future that might be possible should the terrorist menace end. Rather than refusing to talk water, India should show Pakistan how the keys to ending its aquatic insecurities lie in its own hands.

APP – 27

PAKISTAN STEPS UP WATER DISPUTE

James Lamont, March 29, 2010

Pakistani leaders have elevated a dispute over water resources to the top of Islamabad's points of contention with India, a move that could politicise a highly sensitive issue in the drought-prone region.

New Delhi fears that water from the Himalayas could emerge as a new populist dispute, on a par with the contested territory of Kashmir, between the two nuclear-armed rivals that have fought three wars over the past 63 years.

"There is a co-ordinated effort in Pakistan to create another anti-India issue that can capture the popular imagination in Pakistan," said a top Indian official. "The 'India bogey' is being created," with a scare over water shortages, said another.

Pakistan alleges that India has failed to honour a 1960 treaty brokered by the World Bank governing the use of shared river systems, claiming that Indian hydro-electric power projects are lessening the agreed flow of water into its river systems.

Indian officials insist that New Delhi has not violated the treaty and blame water shortages in Pakistan on mismanagement and inequitable sharing among the country's provinces.

"The issue of water ... is a spurious issue meant only to perpetuate animosity of the Pakistani population towards India," said K. Subrahmanyam, an Indian defence analyst. "Jihadi terrorism will seem to be more justifiable for a Pakistani on the water issue than Kashmir."

Yusuf Raza Gilani, Pakistan's Prime Minister, put water on a par with Kashmir in an interview with the Financial Times this month. "We want the world to concentrate so that with India we resolve all our core issues including Jammu and Kashmir and water," he said.

General Ashfaq Kiyani, Commander of the Pakistan Army, made similar remarks in a speech last month, and was part of a delegation to Washington that raised the issued with US officials last week.

Indian officials are particularly alarmed that leaders of militant groups, such as Lashkar-e-Taiba and its affiliate, Jamaat-ud-Dawa, have taken up the water issue.

Jamaat-ud-Dawa claims that Pakistan's Punjab and Sindh provinces are faced with desertification because of Indian dams and the diversion of water. At a farmers' rally in Lahore this month, the group accused India of declaring a water war. "India is trying to hatch a deep conspiracy of making Pakistan's agricultural lands barren and economically annihilating us," it said.

Hafiz Saeed, founder of Lashkar-e-Taiba, said: "The government must take practical steps to secure Pakistani's water. It is a matter of life and death for Pakistan."

Some analysts say that climate change justifies the modernisation of river treaties across south Asia. They warn that water stress threatens to cause conflict among populations relying on rain-fed water systems.

Already, mountain hydrologists can pinpoint where water stress will be greatest in the years to come. As the availability of water in Himalayan-fed river systems that support 1.3 bn people drops, researchers expect increased friction between India, Bangladesh and Pakistan in a battle for resources.

APP – 28

INDIA NOT STEALING PAKISTAN'S SHARE OF RIVER WATERS

Indian Express, 30 March 2010

India is not "stealing" Pakistan's share of river waters and all hydropower projects being built by the country conform to the provisions of the Indus Waters Treaty of 1960, Indus Waters Commissioner G Ranganathan said.

He made the remarks at the conclusion of three-day talks with his Pakistani counterpart Jamaat Ali Shah.

The talks, which focussed on the Nimmo-Bazgo and Chutak hydropower projects being built in Jammu and Kashmir, ended inconclusively and both sides will meet in New Delhi in May to resolve their differences.

The Indian official made it clear that his country was not "stealing" Pakistan's share of waters.

Ranganathan reiterated that India was committed to the Indus Waters Treaty and was "designing all power projects as per criteria permitted under" the pact.

He said there was "media propaganda" in Pakistan that India was stealing Pakistan's share of waters.

"Nimmo-Bazgo and Chutak dams are within the permissible limits of the Indus Waters Treaty and there is no need to change anything," he said.

Ranganathan also denied allegations that India had violated the Indus Waters Treaty. Information about India's hydropower projects was provided to Pakistan on time and there had been no delays, he said.

The Indian side had listened to Pakistan's point of view and also tried to convey its viewpoint, he said.

Pakistan's proposals and reservations will be looked into, he added.

Briefing journalists at the end of the talks here, Pakistani Indus Waters Commissioner Jamaat Ali Shah said his side had expressed concerns that the Nimmo-Bazgo and Chutak projects will affect water flows to Pakistan.

"We conveyed our concerns to India as we fear there will be a reduction of water supply in the Indus river from Indian Kashmir after the construction of the two dams," Shah said.

The Nimmo-Bazgo dam's design is aimed at maximizing "manipulatable water space", he said.

APP – 29

IS INDIA STEALING PAKISTAN'S WATER?

Indian Express, 30 March 2010

A new book separates legal facts from jingoistic fiction

Ignore the slanted media reports in Pakistan these days about how India is stealing Pakistan's Chenab River waters by building numerous dams over it for the generation of electricity. These reports ignore the fact that the Indus Waters Treaty of 1960 allows upper-riparian India to dam the rivers allocated to Pakistan, according to certain specifications, to produce electricity without any diversion of waters that belong exclusively to Pakistan.

Saiyid Ali Naqvi's *Indus Waters and Social Change: the Evolution and Transition of Agrarian Society in Pakistan* (Rs. 2,900, Oxford University Press Pakistan) looks at Indus waters and their importance to Pakistan. Anyone who wants to know the real story of each Pakistani river and its irrigation barrages should read this 796-page work from the former Asian Development Bank officer who worked on a number of water resources and rural development projects in the Philippines, Sri Lanka, Nepal, Laos, Vietnam, China, Indonesia, and Pakistan.

Pakistan is lucky as a lower riparian to have a water treaty with upper-riparian India; and the book tells us what we went through before it was finally signed in 1960.

The Inter-Dominion Agreement on the Canal Water Dispute, signed by India and Pakistan at New Delhi on May 4, 1948, restored the canal water flows that India had choked off. Through this agreement, India made clear its intent to use all of the water of the rivers in question; the agreement merely allowed Pakistan time to find alternative sources to replace the lost water.

To make matters worse for Pakistan, its West Punjab government was notified by India's East Punjab government that this agreement would be discontinued on Sept. 4, 1948. Pakistan's foreign minister appealed to the Indian prime minister, Jawaharlal Nehru, to continue water supplies to West Punjab and to the Sindh irrigation systems until the two governments could reach a final agreement. Nehru responded that supplies would be continued temporarily, and with no commitment for the future.

A few weeks later, on Oct. 24, 1948, Nehru informed the Pakistani government by telegram that the East Punjab government was under no obligation to continue the supply of water to West Punjab, and that in any future discussion of the matter, "full right of the East Punjab government to reduce the supplies at will must be recognized."

A further indication of India's intentions came when construction work began in late 1948 on the Harike Barrage, upstream of the Ferozpur Barrage, at the confluence of the Beas and Sutlej. It was clear that the Harike Barrage would make it possible for India to completely abandon the Ferozpur Barrage and shut down supplies of water to Pakistan's Sutlej Valley canals. Pakistan tried to appeal to the International Court of Justice in June 1949, but India refused to participate. Instead, India urged that the Inter-Dominion Agreement of May 4, 1948 be made permanent.

Then came the Indus Waters Treaty, leveraged with funds from the World Bank for new canals and dams for the two newly-independent but financially broke states. The Treaty said: "India shall be under obligation to let flow all waters of the western rivers, and shall not permit any interference with these waters, except for the following uses, restricted in the case of each of the river drainage basins of the Indus, Jhelum, and Chenab: (a) domestic use, (b) non-consumptive use, (c) specified agricultural use, and (d) generation of hydroelectric power."

Pakistan and India need normalization of relations, followed by free trade and territorial connectivity, to cooperate on the fast-depleting waters of South Asia. Pakistan has lost all cases of arbitration it has brought against India so far, which simply proves that the media is once again favoring war with India instead of peace. Slanted media reports about India stealing Pakistan's waters are planted to cause alarm and resultant jingoism for another war with India that Pakistan will surely lose.

APP – 30

PIPED IRRIGATION TO CHECK INDUS WATERS DISPUTE

Swaminathan S Anklesaria Aiyar, 11 April, 2010

Politicians and Islamic outfits in Pakistan accuse India of stealing upstream Indus system waters, threatening Pakistan's very existence. More sober Pakistanis complain that numerous new Indian projects on the Jhelum and Chenab will create substantial live storages even in run-of-the-river hydel dams.

This will enable India to drastically reduce flows to Pakistan during the crucial sowing season, something that actually happened for a couple of days when the Baglihar reservoir was filled by India after dam completion.

India accuses Pakistan of hysteria, saying there is really no issue, since India has always observed the Indus Waters Treaty, dividing the waters of the Indus and Punjab rivers between the two countries. Pakistan may suffer from water scarcity but so does India.

Inter-state fights over water are humungous—Punjab vs Haryana, Karnataka Vs Tamil Nadu, and Andhra Pradesh vs Maharashtra. Water raises passions, and farmers in all states claim they are being robbed of water, without going into the rather complex facts. Pakistan is no different, say Indian experts, so let's shrug aside Pakistani rhetoric.

What this debate misses is that dam-based canal irrigation is an obsolete, wasteful 19th century technology that cannot meet 21st century needs. It must be replaced by sprinkler and drip irrigation, distributed through pressurised plastic pipes. This approach has enabled Israel to irrigate the desert. It can enable India and Pakistan to triple the irrigated area with existing water resources, escaping water scarcity.

Drip and sprinkler irrigation are expensive. They use a lot of power for pumping. But they greatly improve yields too. Israeli agriculture is highly competitive.

Canals are hugely wasteful of both land and water, something well captured in Tushaar Shah's excellent book, "Taming the Anarchy." Up to 7% of the command area of a conventional irrigation project is taken up by canals, and this no longer makes sense when land is worth lakhs per acre. In the Narmada command area, farmers have refused to give up their land to build distributaries from the main Narmada canal, so only a small portion of the irrigation potential is actually used today.

Traditionally, South Asian farmers have leveled their land and flooded it with irrigation water. Rice is typically grown in standing water. This entails enormous water losses through evaporation in canals and flooded fields. This mattered little in the 19th century when land and water were relatively abundant. It matters hugely today. Piped water greatly economizes the use of both land and water.

Instead of canals, we can transport water through underground pipes that leave the land above free for cultivation. Indeed, the downhill flow of water through massive pipes can run turbines, generating electricity for pumping the water to the surface, where required.

Canal systems make farmers prisoners of the water releases decided by canal headquarters. If canal water is released to a village section, say once a month, farmers can grow only those crops suited to this irrigation schedule. This was acceptable in the 19th century when farms were large and grew the same crop, and technology and markets for unconventional crops were scarce.

But today, farmers want to diversify into a wide diversity of crops, and for this they need water on demand. This is why they have gone in a huge way for tubewell irrigation. This gives them water on demand, enabling them to grow what they like.

APP - 31

A SOUTH ASIAN TRI-AXIS: THE INDUS WATERS TREATY

(05 MAY 2010)

In 1960, an agreement over the water resources originating in Jammu - Kashmir (which, again, I will refer to as JK) was brokered by the World Bank between Pakistan and India. In the Indus Waters Treaty, uses of the waters of the Indus River and several of its principal tributaries that originate in, or pass through, the disputed JK area were divided between the two countries. Six major rivers were identified in the Indus Waters Treaty and divided categorically, to be known as the Western and Eastern Rivers. Specifically,

- the Indus River was to be controlled exclusively by Pakistan, despite its origination in southwestern China and passage through the Indian area of JK before entering the Pakistan area of JK and then Pakistan proper;

- the Jhelum River was to be controlled exclusively by Pakistan, despite its origination in the Indian area of JK and passage through the Pakistan area of JK before entering Pakistan proper and eventually merging with the Chenab River;

- the Chenab River was to be controlled exclusively by Pakistan, despite its origination in Himachal Pradesh (the northern-most province of India, outside of JK) and passage through the Indian area of JK before entering Pakistan and, eventually, joining the Indus;

- the Sutlej, Beas (tributary to the Sutlej), and Ravi, all Eastern Rivers and relatively minor in flow volume, were to be controlled exclusively by India, with a one-time financial compensation paid to

693

Pakistan for the Indian consumptive use of those waters before all three rivers pass into Pakistan and eventually join the Chenab River.

The thing is, the Treaty was meant originally to assuage Pakistani fears over the availability of water resources that originate in India or disputed regions, especially if a war between the two countries should occur. In fact, India has not revoked or violated the Treaty in three conflicts (two over JK territory) between the two countries since the Treaty was signed, even during the Indo-Pakistan War of 1965 while the Treaty was still in its specified Transition Phase. However, disputes and unilateral actions on the Western Rivers have led to continued differences between the two countries. Specifically, the Treaty allows domestic, specified agricultural and other non-consumptive use of the Western Rivers by India, including limited hydropower generation, before they cross into Pakistan. India is far more limited in its development of storage capacity on the Western Rivers, however: "Except as provided in Annexures D and E, India shall not store any water of, or construct any storage works on, the Western Rivers." (see Indus Waters Treaty, Article III, paragraph 4)

Given a Treaty that seems to be constructed heavily in Pakistan's favor as the junior riparian state (having been partitioned from greater India in 1947), does it seem reasonable to allow India as the senior riparian *some* use of the rivers that originate in or pass through its own territories? At the time of the Treaty, India maintained six existing hydropower projects on Western Rivers, only one with more than 1 MW of generation, and was already constructing eight more with three larger than 10 MW, the largest with 15 MW of power generation. Annexure D to the Treaty allowed these projects to continue as planned or already constructed and for new run-of-the-river generation plants to be constructed under specified parameters, and according to storage rules specified in Annexure E, on the mainstem Western Rivers in India's territory. On tributaries to the mainstem rivers, India had different specifications for constructing new run-of-the-river generation facilities, and on irrigation canals that originate on a mainstem Western River still other specifications. In general, these run-of-the-river facilities constituted small amounts of true storage and non-consumptive overall use.

Storage allowances stipulated in the Treaty's Annexure E are strict, limiting India to the further construction of only 1.25 Million Acre-Feet (MAF) of aggregate general storage capacity but with none allowed on the mainstems of the Jhelum and Chenab Rivers, 1.6 MAF of aggregate storage capacity for power generation but with none allowed on the mainstem of the Jhelum River, 0.75 MAF of additional capacity for flood control or other non-consumptive or domestic use but only on tributaries of the Jhelum River, and any storage determined necessary for flood control on the mainstem of the Jhelum River as long as the floodwaters are released as soon as possible after the flood event. By river, the numbers add up to 0.4 MAF of total storage on the Indus River, 1.5 MAF on tributaries to the Jhelum River but only flood control as necessary on its mainstem reaches, and 1.7 MAF on the Chenab River and its tributaries. Out of nearly 120 MAF in normal annual flow that exit the Himalaya-Karakoram Range through JK, India was allowed to retain only the smaller Eastern Rivers and approximately 3% of the Western Rivers. There are plenty of other details listed in the Treaty Annexures, including the minimum information that must be provided by India to Pakistan regarding all constructed works on the Western Rivers.

However well-regulated the sharing of Indus and tributary waters seems to be on the basis of the Treaty, differences and disputes have inevitably arisen since 1960. Most recently and publicly, India and Pakistan have pledged to improve relations overall, though the sides differ on what that really means for the agenda of renewed talks. With so much focus from the U.S. on support to Pakistan in the course of the Afghanistan conflict, India has been unwilling to resume "composite dialogue" that, despite leaving territorial claims in JK unchanged, has allowed India advancement on seemingly more important issues like bilateral trade and cross-border trust-building. India's stumbling block seems on the outside to be Pakistan's approach to reducing militant activity. In the meantime, Pakistan has recently lodged complaints against India regarding one operating hydropower project at Baglihar Dam, completed on the Chenab River in 2008, and numerous proposed hydropower projects in Indian JK. India has plans for these new projects on its frontier, while Pakistan suffers drought and diminishing water supplies for its burgeoning urban population and vast agricultural needs in Pakistani Punjab and the Indus delta, one of the largest irrigated areas in the world. Should Pakistan bring these complaints to the World Bank under the provisions stipulated in the Indus Waters Treaty, arbitration results would be legally binding for both countries, though how long it would take to reach a decision on one or more complaints, separately or in aggregate, is anyone's guess. Should Pakistan resort to measures outside of the Treaty, or bring up the possibility of renegotiating the Treaty in order to resolve the more modern issues, many feel that Pakistan would most surely lose the significant water concessions that the Treaty provides as well as anything else involved in such a confrontation.

Meanwhile, officials in the U.S. are projecting seriously mixed messages on relations between India and Pakistan. Within the past week, the Undersecretary of Defense for Policy stated that American interests in Pakistan extend "beyond Washington's security interests in the region to wide-ranging areas including support for Islamabad's key energy and water requirements." This is in direct contradiction to a sequence of diplomatic events around this most recent World Water Day: on 22 March 2010, Secretary of State Hillary Clinton delivered her remarks on the purposes of American foreign aid in the water sector:

> "Access to reliable supplies of clean water is a matter of human security. It's also a matter of national security. And that's why President Obama and I recognize that water issues are integral to the success of many of our major foreign policy initiatives...
>
> In the United States, water represents one of the great diplomatic and development opportunities of our time. It's not every day you find an issue where effective diplomacy and development will allow you to save millions of lives, feed the hungry, empower women, advance our national security interests, protect the environment, and demonstrate to billions of people that the United States cares...
>
> Water is actually a test case for preventive diplomacy. Historically, many long-term global challenges – including water – have been left to fester for years until they grew so serious that they could no longer be ignored. If we can rally the world to address the water issue now, we can take early corrective action, and get ahead of the challenges that await us. And in doing so, we can establish a positive precedent for early action to address other serious issues of global concern."

Seems earnest enough, especially as Congress slowly works out the kinks on an update and expansion to the original Paul Simon Water for the Poor Act of 2005 that just expired.

Barely two weeks after World Water Day, however, the Wall Street Journal reported that "Secretary of State Hillary Clinton has signaled that Washington isn't interested in mediating on water issues, which are covered by a bilateral treaty." The *Times of India* quoted Secretary Clinton directly:

> "We're well aware that there is a 50-year-old agreement between Pakistan and India concerning water... Where there is an agreement... with mediation techniques, arbitration built in, it would seem sensible to look to what already exists to try to resolve any of the bilateral problems between India and Pakistan... Let's see what we do to protect our aquifers. Let's see what we do to be more efficient in the use of our water. Let's see what we do to capture more rainwater; how do we actually use less of it to produce more crops? We think we have some ideas with our experts that we want to sit down and talk with your experts about and see where that goes".

First of all, Madam Secretary, you have contradicted yourself. Twice. On World Water Day you said that the U.S. "cares," then when Kashmir was an explicit aspect of the issue you said that the U.S. didn't want to get involved, and then you offered expert technical assistance to Pakistan in a direct interview with their diplomatic delegation. While I certainly agree that an exchange of technical knowledge will help build capacity in Pakistan, and might even teach us a thing or two about resource management in our own country - remember, they've been at it about 5,000 years longer than we have - that's the Lexus resolution, while we would be leaving the Olive Tree (Kashmir conflict, Pakistani militants) to it's own devices (thanks again, Tom Friedman). Setbacks in ethnic and territorial issues can quickly and easily unravel any technical and technological progress in water management and food security. The U.S. needs to form and stick to a clearer message in our approach to Pakistan's issues and helping them with *their* priorities, not just our own.

Second, the Indus Waters Treaty is held in force by the World Bank and the sheer will of the signatories, but it is entirely possible that the terms of the Treaty are outdated and need revisiting. Third, the U.S. cooperates directly with India on numerous issues and now provides significant aid (monetary and otherwise) to Pakistan. And finally, it is the U.S. that nominates the President of the World Bank and holds a plurality of the votes, with the ability to block any opposing super-majority.

In the Kashmir issue and the responsible development of the region's resources, especially water, the U.S. has leverage, vested interests, and a call for help to be answered – means, motive and opportunity if we've ever seen it. As the JK region remains at the origin of these cross-border water issues, our American commitment to self-determination and the spread of democracy comes into question when we refuse the opportunity for diplomacy between India and Pakistan, as well as the people of JK themselves who see their land and resources, including water, held in trust by the very neighbors who administer their human rights. Helping to solve the Indus waters issue, and possibly resolve the conflict over JK, may be a tough problem to wrap your brain around, but it's not as if our efforts to do so will destabilize the region any further.

APP – 32

PAKISTAN SEEKS RESOLUTION OF INDIA WATER DISPUTE

Tom Wright, and Amol Sharma
(Wall Street Journal, 20 May, 2010)

Pakistan told India it wants to begin formal arbitration proceedings over an Indian dam project in Kashmir, threatening to heighten tensions ahead of high-level bilateral talks.

Pakistan says India's planned hydropower dam on the Kishanganga River would violate a 50-year-old water-sharing treaty between the two neighbors by diverting water Pakistan needs for agriculture and power generation.

India denies its project would violate the 1960 Indus Waters Treaty. It has received Pakistan's request for arbitration and is examining it, an Indian official said.

Water disputes have become a growing point of controversy between the rivals in recent months, and could become an impediment as they seek to re-establish diplomatic ties. India cut off dialogue with Pakistan after the November 2008 Mumbai terrorist attacks, but has shown an interest in restarting talks if Pakistan cracks down on terrorists on its soil.

Indian Prime Minister Manmohan Singh and Pakistani Prime Minister Yousuf Raza Gilani met last month at a regional summit and agreed to move forward with dialogue. The countries' chief foreign-policy bureaucrats will meet in late June to prepare an agenda for mid-July, when their external affairs ministers are expected to meet in Islamabad.

In previous rounds of diplomacy, India and Pakistan have discussed issues ranging from trade to the fate of Kashmir, the disputed territory that is two-thirds controlled by India and over which the countries have fought two of their three wars.

India has said it is open to discussing all issues in the current talks, though shutting down terrorist groups and getting Pakistan to more aggressively prosecute Mumbai suspects are its core objectives.

India has said river-sharing disputes should be settled through the 1960 treaty, rather than in the bilateral talks. The accord split six Himalayan rivers between the countries, with the three Western ones going to Pakistan, the three Eastern ones to India, and each side retaining the right to the other side's resources for uses such as run-of-the-river hydropower and irrigation.

Under the treaty, the countries nominate commissioners who share data and try to resolve problems as they arise. If the commissioners can't agree, they can seek a World Bank-appointed expert to intervene, which happened in 2005 when Pakistan objected to another big dam. India was told to make minor changes to its design.

Jamaat Ali Shah, Pakistan's Indus waters commissioner, said the country is now seeking formal arbitration proceedings—a treaty mechanism that neither side has used before—because it feels India is stalling on the Kishanganga dispute.

Pakistan on Wednesday named two members that would sit on a seven-person arbitration panel. Under the treaty, India has 30 days to name its own two members, and the countries are supposed to jointly name the three other participants. If they can't agree, the World Bank would step in to name them.

Pakistani farmers and Islamist groups have staged protests against India's 330-megawatt hydroelectric project on the Kishanganga, which is a tributary to one of the rivers Pakistan was allotted under the treaty.

Water availability in Pakistan has fallen 70% since the early 1950s to 1,500 cubic meters per capita, according to a report last year by the Woodrow Wilson International Center for Scholars. India says Pakistan's poor water management is responsible for the water shortages it is experiencing in some regions.

Write to Tom Wright at tom.wright@wsj.com and Amol Sharma atamol.sharma@wsj.com

APP - 33

RHETORIC GROWS HEATED IN WATER DISPUTE BETWEEN INDIA, PAKISTAN

Karin Brulliard
Washington Post, 28 May 2010

LAHORE, PAKISTAN-- The latest standoff between India and Pakistan features familiar elements: perceived Indian injustices, calls to arms by Pakistani extremists. But this dispute centers on something different: water.

Militant organizations traditionally focused on liberating the Indian-held Kashmir have adopted water as a rallying cry, accusing India of strangling upstream rivers to desiccate downstream farms in Pakistan's dry agricultural heartland. This spring, a religious leader suspected of links to the 2008 Mumbai attacks, led a protest here of thousands of farmers driving tractors and carrying signs warning: "Water Flows or Blood." The cleric, Hafiz Sayeed, recently told worshipers that India was guilty of "water terrorism."

India and Pakistan have pledged to improve relations. But Sayeed's water rhetoric, echoed in shrill headlines on both sides of the border, encapsulates two issues that threaten those fragile peace efforts – an Indian dam project on the shared Indus River and Pakistan's reluctance to crack down on Sayeed.

It also signals the expanding ambitions of Punjab-based militant groups, such as the banned Lashkar-i-Taiba, founded by Sayeed, through an issue that touches millions who live off Pakistan's increasingly arid land.

Pakistan's water supply is dwindling because of climate change, outdated farming techniques and an exploding population. Now Pakistan says India is exacerbating its woes by violating the treaty that for 50 years has governed use of water originating in Kashmir.

India denies the charge, and its ambassador to Pakistan recently called the water theft allegations "preposterous." International water experts say that there is little evidence India is diverting water from Pakistan but that Pakistan is right to feel vulnerable because its water is downstream of India's.

Washington has pressured the two nations to settle their differences. India and Pakistan have fought three major wars, and the conflict has kept much of Pakistan's army focused eastward, not on Islamist insurgents. India wants Pakistan to target India-focused militants, and it is outraged that Sayeed – whose sermons often call for jihad against India – remains free. India blamed the Mumbai attacks on Lashkar-i-Taiba.

Yet even as the nations' civilian leaders were building bridges, Pakistan's military underscored the perceived Indian threat last month with large-scale military exercises near the border. With the Kashmir liberation struggle waning in Pakistan's public consciousness, some analysts say Sayeed's use of the water issue demonstrates his long-standing links to Pakistan's powerful security establishment, elements of which do not favor peacemaking.

"Hafiz Sayeed is trying to echo the establishment's line," said Rifaat Hussain, a professor of security studies at Quaid-i-Azam University in Islamabad. "The government is trying to shift the focus of Kashmir as part of a jihadist thing . . . to an existential issue."

Hydroelectric projects

Politics aside, experts say, Pakistan's water situation is reaching crisis proportions. As the population has grown over six decades, per-capita water availability has dropped by more than two-thirds. About 90 percent of the water is used for agriculture, making it an economic lifeline but leaving little for human consumption.

Inefficient irrigation and drainage techniques have degraded soil and worsened shortages, forcing many small farmers to pump for groundwater. A severe electricity crisis means most rely on diesel-powered pumps, but fuel prices are rising, said M. Ibrahim Mughal, head of Agri Forum, a farmers' advocacy group.

"You can't do agriculture without water," he said. "What will happen? Hunger."

The Indus Waters Treaty, which India and Pakistan signed in 1960, gave each country unfettered access to three rivers and limited rights to the other nation's rivers. A joint commission oversees the treaty, which water experts say has worked fairly well.

Cooperation has frayed as water has grown scarcer and India has stepped up new hydroelectric projects in Kashmir. Those plans have raised alarm in Pakistan, where newspapers and politicians regularly accuse India of secret designs to weaken its enemy by diverting water. Pakistan's Indus Water Commissioner, Jamaat Ali Shah, said his country believes that one proposed Indian dam on the Kishanganga, an Indus tributary, violates the treaty by making Pakistan's own plans for a hydroelectric project downstream unworkable.

"Candidness and transparency should be there. It is not," Shah said.

In a speech last month, India's ambassador to Pakistan, Sharat Sabharwal, said Pakistan has not detailed its complaints. Pakistan's water problems are attributable to factors including climatic conditions, he said, and blaming India was meant to "inflame public passions."

'Water declaration'

That is exactly what Sayeed is trying to do, according to Yahya Mujahid, a spokesman for the radical cleric's Islamic charity, Jamaat-ud-Dawa. The charity, which the United States and India call a front for Lashkar-i-Taiba, recently sponsored the farmer protest and released a "water declaration" alleging that India had "virtually declared war on Pakistan by unlawfully constructing dams and diverting Pakistani rivers."

Lashkar-i-Taiba has taken its fight against India beyond the disputed terrain of Kashmir to stage attacks in Afghanistan and work with militant organizations in Pakistan's northwest. But Sayeed has typically sought to uphold the group's Kashmir-focused reputation, making water a bit of a departure. Mujahid said Sayeed is helping desperate farmers pressure the government to solve their problems, not inciting jihad. But peace talks are unlikely to help, he said.

The dispute has hard-liners in both countries predicting war, alarming observers who say what should be a technical issue has veered into a dangerous terrain.

John Briscoe, a Harvard professor and former World Bank water specialist in Pakistan and India, said allegations of India's "water robbery" are unfounded. But because India could influence river flows into Pakistan, he said, the wisest solution would be for India to initiate talks and perhaps call for a permanent neutral party to implement the treaty.

"On the Indian side, the last thing I would want to come into India-Pakistan relations is an issue as visceral as water," Briscoe said. But, he added, "it's all about politics and political will."

APP – 34

WHOSE WATER IS IT ANYWAY?

Udit Misra and Cuckoo Paul, 20 August 2010

India's disputes with its neighbours for water will escalate in the near future unless it begins to work with them to develop joint ventures for equitable sharing

Early this year, extremists in Pakistan found a new issue to bait India with. Hafiz Saeed, founder of Jamaat-ud-Dawa, widely considered to be a front for the Lashkar-e-Toiba, rallied worshippers in Lahore, saying India was guilty of 'water terrorism'. He also led protesting farmers carrying signs that said, "Water flows or blood."

The issue managed to touch a chord among many ordinary people because Pakistan is faced with its most severe shortage of water since Independence, in spite of the recent floods that have wreaked havoc in the country. Dry spells in the past few years have seen bitter conflicts within the country: Southern Pakistan accuses the north of grabbing more than its share of water. But most in the north blame India for stealing water.

Even as India and Pakistan negotiate an equitable sharing of water, the Pakistan prime minister is having an equally tough time settling similar conflicts between the states of Sindh and Punjab. All this has led to forceful opposition to India's plans to build a hydropower project on the Kishanganga (called Neelum in Pakistan). Pakistan claims the project will violate the 1960 Indus Waters Treaty between the two countries and will lead to a 27 percent water deficit.

Around the same time Saeed was rallying farmers, another lobby group, and the Lahore Chamber of Commerce made a presentation to a delegation from the local US consulate, spelling out the scenario in the starkest terms: "It can result in confrontation between two nuclear states," one slide said. Another warned that "no water means poverty, hunger, war."

John Briscoe, professor of the practice of environmental health at Harvard School of Public Health, has spent 35 years in the World Bank studying water-related disputes around the world. He points out that large agricultural areas and most cities in the subcontinent depend heavily on groundwater, which is going down at an alarming rate. In India, the affected areas such as Punjab, Haryana, Delhi, Rajasthan, Gujarat, Maharashtra and Tamil Nadu are critical for food production.

Pakistan faces similar daunting problems. The Indus is likely to be much more seriously affected by climate change than any other river system in South Asia. Briscoe is convinced that unless there are major reforms in the way it is managed, water is likely to become a major constraint for economic growth and human well-being.

Indian policy-makers acknowledge that the situation is grim. India is already below the water stress level, which requires availability of 1,700 cubic metres of water per person. Water resources secretary U.N. Panjiar says, "After best efforts to improve water use efficiency are undertaken, India is projected to have just 1,100 cubic metres per capita by 2050."

Despite this, the government, while listing out a long list of steps planned for the future like the National Water Mission, appears to be in denial when it comes to actual water diplomacy.

In the water ministry, the focus is on managing demand by adopting best practices. The government's primary focus has been improving the water use efficiency in agriculture either through better irrigation models or with water-efficient seed and farming systems.

While Panjiar is aware that climate change is likely to have a huge impact on India's overall water availability, he says there is no quantitative assessment of the repercussions. There is also no plan to forge a partnership with neighbouring countries on water in the foreseeable future.

An example is the lack of diplomatic push in concluding projects like the High Dam on Kosi river or the Mahakali Treaty with Nepal. Though the projects would be beneficial to both countries, India has failed to sort them out even after almost two decades.

Other countries have a better record. In South America, Brazil has managed to solve long-standing water issues with Paraguay as well as Argentina. Closer home, Laos and Thailand have been able to find a sustainable solution to share waters.

Of the five SAARC (South Asian Association for Regional Cooperation) nations with whom India is sparring on water, it has resolved the problem only with Bhutan by helping the mountain kingdom develop hydro-electric power. Professor Briscoe says, "With similar maturity on both sides, arrangements can be made on generating and sharing benefits with Pakistan, Nepal, China and Bangladesh."

He says that the most critical case is Pakistan and is critical of the Indian government's handling of the situation and calls for magnanimity. "Unless both countries find ways of moving beyond mutual recriminations and tit-for-tat point-scoring, the vital Indus Waters Treaty will be under threat," he says.

There are great benefits to both countries in cooperating on the Indus. For Pakistan, this would remove a major source of insecurity for economic and human development. For India, cooperation would mean less uncertainty in financing hydropower projects in Jammu and Kashmir. And, most importantly, it would mean that extremists in Pakistan would not be able to capture the emotive issue of water. This would be of great benefit to both Pakistan and India, he says.

APP – 35

INDUS WATER TREATUY AND JAMMU & KASHMIR STATE

Suresh Thukral, January 2011

Indus Water Treaty which regulates the sharing of water between two neighboring countries India and Pakistan is a bilateral treaty which was signed in Karachi on 19 September 1960 by the then Indian Prime Minister Jawaharlal Nehru and the then President of Pakistan Field Marshal Mohammad Ayub Khan. The World Bank (then the International Bank for Reconstruction and Development) is signatory as a third party witness to the treaty.

According to the treaty, Pakistan is to enjoy exclusive use of three Western Rivers, viz., Indus, Jhehlum and Chenab, with minor exceptions, as existing irrigation canals to be continued for use of India and water required to be used for drinking purpose shall not come within the purview of this treaty; at the same time, India shall have exclusive rights for use of water on the three Eastern rivers viz. Satluj, Beas and Ravi along with water of their tributaries.

Under the provisions of this treaty, Pakistan also received financial compensation from India for the loss of water from Eastern Rivers a sum of 6,20,60,000 Pounds Sterling in ten equal installments through the medium of World Bank. The sum was supposed to be used for the development of water resources in Pakistan, but recent devastating floods in Indus Basin have shown that Pakistan have not made any effort for the regulating and development of vast water resources available to them under this treaty; rather, it has remained busy in the process of provoking public sentiments against India.

The treaty further lays down exchange of water data of rivers between the two countries with regards to gauge and discharge, data relating to flow of these rivers and formation of permanent Indus commissions with commissioners from both the countries; these two commissioners shall together form the permanent Indus Water Commission. The commissioner of each country should ordinarily be a high ranking engineer competent in the field of hydrology and water use. The purpose and function of the commission shall be to establish and maintain a cooperative arrangement for the implementation of the treaty. The commission shall determine its own procedures for functioning, meeting and to sort out day-to-day problems.

The treaty is nicely drafted with regard to water-sharing and by and large have performed well for many years; an important point is that with the ratification of this treaty, Pakistan has recognized the sovereignty of India over the state of Jammu & Kashmir and has agreed to terms and conditions with India over the sharing of water passing through the J&K State, but in aftermath, successive governments of Pakistan made it a tool to defame India over the treaty, to divert attention of their people from their country's internal problems and to suppress their democratic rights. Voices have come from Pakistan to scrap the treaty but they have failed to give any feasible alternative; this shows their malicious intention to further defame India on the international level.

Pakistan unnecessarily raised baseless objections on the Baghlihar Hydro Electric Power project constructed by India on the river Chenab to fulfill the requirement of power in the state, while the treaty does not prohibit India to exploit power potential from these rivers. Pakistan raised the issue at the international forum with the World Bank who was just a witness to the treaty and as a bank guarantor for the payment of compensation which was to be received by Pakistan from India and thereafter with the consent of both the countries, Professor Lafitte, a Swiss National Engineer and professor at the Swiss Federal Institute of Technology in Lausanne, was appointed by the World Bank on 10 May 2005 as a neutral expert to find out the differences between the two governments and to provide his expert neutral opinion under the terms and conditions of the Indus Waters Treaty agreement.

Though India was not bound for the appointment of neutral expert, yet India, with an open mind, did not object much to the appointment of the neutral expert. The neutral expert, Professor Lafitte, studied the project on the ground and also the terms and conditions of the Indus Waters Treaty. The details of findings and opinion of Prof Lafitte were announced on 12 Feb 2007 in Ben (Switzerland) in the presence of the representatives of both the countries; the opinion expressed by the Neutral Expert under the provisions of the Indus Water Treaty was that India has a legitimate right to use the water of River Chenab for hydroelectric generation.

Pakistan also raised an objection over India for the development of Tulbul Navigation Project on river Jehlum with the result that India abandoned construction work on this navigation project. While India maintained that the project was designed to improve navigation facility especially during the winter season when the water level recedes, Pakistan raised objection that the construction on Wullar barrage (Pakistan calls it a barrage) is a water storage project which will affect the flow of water to Pakistan. Work on Tulbul Navigation Project has remained at a standstill for the last many years on baseless objections. In this way, Pakistan has tried to deprive the people of Jammu & Kashmir State from the legitimate benefits of navigation facilities over river Jehlum.

The State of J&K is not affected by this treaty, as existing irrigation canals, as Ranbir Canal, Partap canal, will continue to deliver water as it is and are not within the purview of this treaty; being a hilly terrain, irrigation by big canals, taking water from rivers, is not practically feasible in J&K and irrigation by dug wells, bore wells, water from springs, streams and the traditional mode of irrigation will continue to be in operation and not affected by this treaty.

There is a vast potential of hydroelectric power project, water navigation, tourism and recreational facilities, fishing, aqua culture, mining and minerals, on these rivers, yet to be exploited, which do not come under the purview of this treaty. It is a common practice to make a hue and cry over the issue of public interest without giving a thought on it's merits and demerits; generally, merits are undermined and demerits are highlighted just to blame the authorities. Needless to say that in this context voices have also been raised in the J&K Legislative Assembly, asking the Central Government to pay compensation to the State. It is an internal issue of India and the Central Government must address it, in the same way as the water disputes of Punjab and Haryana, Tamilnado and Karnataka, since the State of Punjab is the major beneficiary to the treaty.

APP – 36

MISUSING THE INDUS TREATY
THE NEWS (PAKISTAN)

Asif H. Kazi, 1 July, 2011

Prof John Briscoe of Harvard University has identified India's various unfair dealings with Pakistan in watersharing. He has said that India must not interpret the treaty with the sole objective of punishing Pakistan.

There is a growing feeling in Pakistan that while India is increasingly building dams on its western rivers, it is simultaneously engaged in activities aimed at stopping Pakistan, the lower riparian, from building storage dams on Pakistani rivers. In the case of its upper riparian neighbour, Nepal, India has even deployed heavy artillery to partially destroy dams which were being constructed by the Nepalese. India's water strategy thus boils down to construction of more and more dams on cross-boundary rivers inside its own territory while obstructing dams in lower-riparian neighbours and destroying those in upper-riparian Nepal.

Pakistan's farmlands have been deprived of the uses of the waters of three eastern rivers, Ravi, Beas and Sutlej. The flows of these rivers were allocated to India under the 1960 Indus Waters Treaty. Authorities on the subject accept that when rivers and canals in Pakistan's demarcated area were classified as Pakistan's assets under the Partition Act, 1947, it meant only one thing: that these rivers and canals were to continue to receive water in the same way as before. Under the treaty, Pakistan was to enjoy the unrestricted use of the Indus, the Jhelum and the Chenab. However, exceptions were inserted as annexures which allowed India to develop and use certain specified quantities of water of the three western rivers as well.

Annexure E established Indian storage limits on western rivers, which add up to 3.6 MAF (million acre feet). If Indian dams under rapid construction since then were to impound this storage water during high flood periods, as specifically defined in the treaty, Pakistan could live with the situation. However, India deliberately followed a pattern of filling water behind the Baglihar Dam constructed on the Chenab River by impounding flows in the low-flow month of September, a clear breach of the treaty, which prescribes the filling period as being from June 21 to Aug 31.

Ironically, the 3.6 MAF of Indian storage share exceeds the sum total of the entire flow of the three remaining rivers entering Pakistan during the low-flow months of December, January and February. Thus the 3.6 MAF of storage creation, combined with its operational control over impounding and releases by India, could mean completely drying up Pakistan's three rivers for as long as three months. The consequences of this will be disastrous.

Obviously, the foregoing was not the intent of the Indus Waters Treaty. And it is precisely for this reason that Pakistan has been insisting that India adopt well-known dam design features, especially for the outlets, which can easily ensure that the reservoir operators would not be able to manipulate the flows of the western rivers at their own sweet will. India is opposing this using as an excuse the need for the prolongation of the reservoirs' lifespan through sediment flushing.

Prof Raymond Lafitte of Switzerland, the neutral expert on the Bhaglihar Dam dispute who gave his decision in favour of India, has acted as a pure professional engineer since he is trained to look at projects in the strictest sense of their operational efficacy and economic performance. Taking it for granted that the upper riparian would not resort to immoral or unethical practices, he failed to take into account the psyches and mindsets of the litigants in the context of their historic rivalry. Had he kept these factors in view, he might have concluded that, in the absence of a spirit of cooperation, the only checks on an upper riparian to keep it from doing harm to the downstream country were constraints, as were proposed by Pakistan, in the shape of "minimum needed sizes of water outlets to be located at the highest levels" to prevent emptying and refilling of reservoirs at will.

In respect of India's Kishenganga River (which takes the name of Neelum when it enters Pakistan), the treaty allows India to construct a hydroelectric project, with storage within a certain limit, on a tributary of the Jhelum River. But it does not permit diversion of flows to either another tributary or to a storage, such as Wullar Lake, on the main Jhelum. Even when the permitted storage dam is constructed on the Kishenganga River, Paragraph 21(b) of Annex E makes it obligatory to deliver a quantity of water downstream of the hydropower station into the Kishenganga during any period of seven consecutive days, which shall not be less than the volume of water received in the river upstream of the project in that period. Such elaborate provisions have been embodied with the sole purpose of causing minimum changes in the natural river flow of these rivers to protect Pakistan's interests.

In violation of these specific provisions, the proposed Kishenganga project violates the treaty in a most glaring way. Firstly, the hydroelectric plant is not located on the Kishenganga but way off the channel at the end of a long tunnel that discharges into another tributary. And, secondly, the recipient tributary ultimately outfalls upstream of the Wullar Lake, and this completely changes the patterns of the flows of both Kishenganga and Jhelum Rivers.

The position taken by the Pakistani government, as reported by Khalid Mustafa in The News of June 15, will not lead us anywhere. The news item says that whichever of the two countries completed their project first will be the winner in the eyes of the Court of Arbitration that recently visited Pakistan to verify, inter alia, our project status. Such a competitive race is a confusion being created which diverts attention from the real issue, that the treaty absolutely forbids India from undertaking their project.

As regards the Wullar Barrage Project, India again cannot undertake any construction under the treaty that would develop storage for whatever purpose, under Paragraphs 7 and 9 of Annexure E, on the Jhelum Main River. The very basic provision under the treaty is to restrain India from changing the river's flow pattern (both quantity-wise and time-wise).

Several foreign experts have held the view that the highly sensitive and charged water issues between Pakistan and India have emerged out of the way the 1947 partition lines were drawn. A seemingly minor change, but one with far-reaching consequences, was introduced in the partition map, in violation of all principles laid down by the British government. It came about at the very last minute when, upon the insistence of the Indian leaders, the partition award turned over to India three vital districts that were originally allocated to Pakistan, with the sole objective of providing India on access to Kashmir. The three remaining western rivers, on which Pakistan now relies upon, all originate in, or pass through, Kashmir before entering Pakistan. In other words, India, after having obtained the waters of the three eastern rivers through the Indus Waters Treaty, is now trying to take control of our three western rivers as well.

APP - 37

2007: NEUTRAL EXPERT GIVES JUDGEMENT ON BAGLIHAR DAM

DAWN — 2 July 2011

1. Summary. The World Bank-appointed neutral expert announced his ruling on February 12 regarding the controversial Baglihar dam project, which both Pakistan and India claimed as a victory. Several specifications contested by Pakistan are being addressed, but the overall design of the dam is intact and India is ready to move forward toward completion and operation in one year's time. The ruling is not only final and binding, but also establishes that India is in the clear to proceed with other projects in the region that involve waters granted to Pakistan under the 1960 Indus Waters Treaty. The Indian press praised the verdict as a victory and vindication after more than a decade of disagreement.

2. The World Bank-appointed neutral expert, Professor Raymond Lafitte, a Swiss civil engineer, released his final and binding decision on February 12 regarding the Baglihar dam to Pakistani and Indian representatives in Bern, Switzerland. Lafitte cleared the 450-MW Indian hydroelectric project on the Chenab River with only minor alterations, which India said, in a statement,"all arise from calculations and not from (conflicts with the) basic principles" of the 1960 Indus Waters Treaty. Pakistan had contended that the 4.5-meter freeboard (the vertical distance between the top of the dam and the level of the contained water supply) should be only 0.84 meters tall, but Lafitte found a 3-meter height in order. The new, shorter design will stand over 140 meters tall, total, and conform to the standards of the International Commission of Large Dams. The neutral expert ruled in India's favor that the dam could have 32.56 million cubic meters of pondage (the dam's water storage capacity), an amount lower than India's design of 37.50, but far greater than the 6.22 advocated by Pakistan. He also allowed a higher rate for the design flood than Pakistan wanted in order to account for calculation uncertainties and possible climate change. Finally, Lafitte agreed with India's approach to deal with the silt that accumulates from the sediment-rich Himalayan water. India uses an outlet method that did not exist in 1960 and will not interfere with the level of flow of the Chenab's waters, according to the neutral expert's decision and in keeping with the Indus Waters Treaty. The dam is scheduled for completion by early 2008 with a total cost of around $1 billion (estimates vary from Rs. 40 to 50 billion).

3. Many news outlets on Tuesday reflected a sense of victory and vindication for India. Multiple newspapers noted that the changes recommended by Lafitte are "marginal" and that the dam's electricity output is not expected to be affected by the verdict. The Hindu reported that India had claimed a "moral victory," and that there was "visible relief" in the Indian Water Resources Ministry. An article in The Pioneer claimed that the dam, outfitted with an anticipated second 450-MW power station, could "rejuvenate Jammu and Kashmir's economy, which is in doldrums after years of strife." The Times of India had one of the most strongly-worded articles, saying that India can "happily live with the verdict, which denies Pakistan any excuse to quibble." The article gloated, "This is the second time in recent years that India has been given a thumbs up in a dispute involving Pakistan," the earlier incident being the downing of a Pakistani surveillance aircraft by India in 1999.

4. Former High Commissioner to Pakistan G. Parathasarthy told Pol-Off on February 13 that this decision "sets a precedent for future construction of dams affected by the Indus Waters Treaty." "A lot of projects that were held up are now possible," he said. In particular, he noted that India can now proceed with its Kishenganga dam project in Jammu and Kashmir, the subject of a similar disagreement between Pakistan and India. "If the Pakistanis object, then we'll take the issue to the World Bank again," he said. "The independent expert made clear what is acceptable under the Indus Waters Treaty and what isn't." In the past, India had offered to build the Baglihar dam lower (as the verdict commands) and thus the same outcome could have been reached "15 years earlier" had Pakistan chosen to cooperate with, and not contest, India's intentions, Parathasarthy noted. He also compared the Baglihar dam project with the older Salal dam project, another dam in Jammu and Kashmir. In the case of the Salal dam, India designed and constructed the dam with Pakistani sediment-related specifications in mind. As a result, he claimed, the dam became "silted-in" in under 20 years. Given Monday's verdict, India will likely not make the same mistake twice.

5. The ruling reflected several of Pakistan's objections to the dam, as mentioned in paragraph 2. Pol-Off spoke with the Hindustan Times editor Manoj Joshi on February 13, who emphasized that the verdict has so far been well received in Pakistan. "If you can work out solutions for both capitals, then that's the way to do it," he said. Joshi finds that water is an "emotional issue" in South Asia, particularly given the current protests in Karnataka in response to the Cauvery Tribunal verdict. It would have been unproductive had the decision been India's victory alone, and disagreement over the issue would have been dragged "on and on." He summarized, "If India says one thing, the Pakistanis will disagree." That there was an international observer in this case makes the verdict palatable to the Pakistanis. Joshi pointed to the Kutch boundary tribunal of the 1960s, in which another international arbiter decided a largely technical dispute between the two nations. Although not a part of the Composite Dialogue process, Joshi believes that the Baglihar decision may have positive–though indirect–implications for other areas of contention in Indo-Pak relations.

6. Comment: The fact that both India and Pakistan are claiming victory is a positive outcome to one problem that has plagued relations for 15 years. As our Indian interlocutors frequently remind us about Indo-Pak relations, it may have been a wise decision for the U.S. not to have intervened in this issue since things very well could have transpired in a less mutually applauded way and the U.S. could have taken the blame. As it is, neither side is casting blame on Prof. Lafitte, the World Bank, the U.S., or any other third-party entity. The verdict may also mitigate India's distrust in international arbiters, allowing for their potential use in addressing other problems. Since the 450-MW hydroelectric station is expected to come on-line in one year's time, it should also provide a boon to the unmet energy needs of Jammu and Kashmir (estimated at 2000 MW) as well as India at large. That India has the green light to complete and/or build similar dams on other rivers throughout Jammu and Kashmir is a fact likely not lost on anyone in energy-starved New Delhi.

APP - 38

GOING BEYOND THE INDUS WATERS TREATY

Express Tribune, Maaz Gardezi, 15 July, 2011

A typical newspaper article on the Indus Waters Treaty (IWT) begins with explaining three or four essential elements of the treaty, pointing out a few cases in time where fingers have been pointed across the border, and then concludes on paranoid tones of a typical lower riparian. Cases such as the Baglihar and Kishanganga dams and the Wullar Barrage are cited time and time again. The end result is very monotonous, with the two nations not being able to reach an agreement. The dispute is then taken to the neutral expert and/or the Court of Arbitration. Although these issues may be important for Pakistan's sustainability, it seems that the resulting discourses have left very little, if any, potential space for cooperation.

Some might argue that the IWT has performed very well between India and Pakistan for the past 50 years. It has survived three wars. However, there is an underlying reason why this treaty has been so popular on both sides. The treaty promotes passive aggressiveness between the two nations, which is precisely what the establishment requires to maintain its status quo. It creates fear among the Pakistani population, which is based on India 'stealing our water'. The rhetoric becomes uncontrollable when it gets into the hands of non-state actors whose purpose is to depict India as having cruel intentions.

Similar to other phenomena in the world, change is the only constant in managing trans-boundary waters. Change management requires a shift in the paradigm: The way we understand the river basin, its people and their livelihood. Water is a finite, a freely flowing resource that should not be divided by geopolitical boundaries. A regional approach is required in maintaining the prosperity and dominance of the mighty Indus. Article VII of the IWT mentions 'Future Cooperation' which, inter alia, discusses efforts in the future to jointly optimise the potential of the Indus River system. Very little attention has been paid to the joint observation of discharge, seismicity etc and the potential joint engineering works to augment storage, produce power and better moderate floods.

Surely, a trust deficit exists between the two riparians. Experts suggest that advance information to the lower riparian (Pakistan) about planned interventions such as dams and barrages, and their timely filling, can bridge these issues. However, this seems hopelessly unlikely, given recent events such as the meeting on the Wullar Barrage where the Indian delegation walked out of the room in the middle of the session. We cannot depend on a few state actors to decide the fate of relations between the two countries; instead, we should work towards track-II diplomacy. One area where collaborative work should be urgently undertaken is on ground-water aquifers, especially near the border areas of Pakistan and India. The IWT only considers sharing of surface water discharge from the rivers and overlooks groundwater abstraction. A study conducted by the International Union for Conservation of Nature, using analysis from Nasa's Gravity Recovery and Climate Experiment, found that the aquifers of Pakistan are going to be affected with the disproportionate abstraction of groundwater in India. It concludes that "the issue of trans-boundary groundwater with India has to be addressed and an addendum has to be negotiated between basin states for inclusion in the IWT." The 1994 Israel-Jordan treaty can help us learn manageable ways of dealing with both ground and surface trans-boundary water.

First it was Kashmir, now it is water. The difference between Kashmir and the water issue is that the latter is an existential issue. Therefore, the consequence of bringing water to a pedestal on India-Pakistan relations can have devastating effects on regional security and prosperity. We need to work closely with our neighbours in order to share this resource, rather than divide it. I find it necessary to cite Ramaswamy Iyer's (Indian water policy expert) view on the Alternative Water Policy — he states: "The best way of avoiding conflicts is for the upper riparian (India) to adopt a cautious and minimalist approach to such interventions, undertake them where absolutely necessary, with due regard to the interests of the lower riparians (Pakistan), provide advance information to the latter about plans for intervention, consult them at all stages on possible impacts and take care to avoid significant harm or injury to them."

APP - 39

KISHANGANGA
THE NEW ARBITRATION BETWEEN
INDIA AND PAKISTAN

(The New Horizon)

India and Pakistan have yet another dispute to resolve. This time it is on a water project known as KHEP or Kishanganga Hydro-Electric Project. It is a run-of-the-river project involving a 37m tall dam to divert water through a tunnel and eventually into Wular Lake which is fed by the Jhelum River. It is similar to another project in Pakistan, known as Neelum–Jhelum Hydropower Project, that Pakistan is working on.

In 2010, Pakistan appealed to the Hague's Permanent Court of Arbitration (CoA), complaining that the Kishanganga Hydroelectric Plant violates the Indus Rivers Treaty by increasing the catchment of the Jhelum River and depriving Pakistan of its water rights. Therefore, a commission was established and the arbitration went underway. In an interim order, the court asked India, late September, to stop constructing any permanent works that would inhibit restoration of the river. While India cannot construct the dam, they can continue on the tunnel and power plant in hope that the court will allow the project.

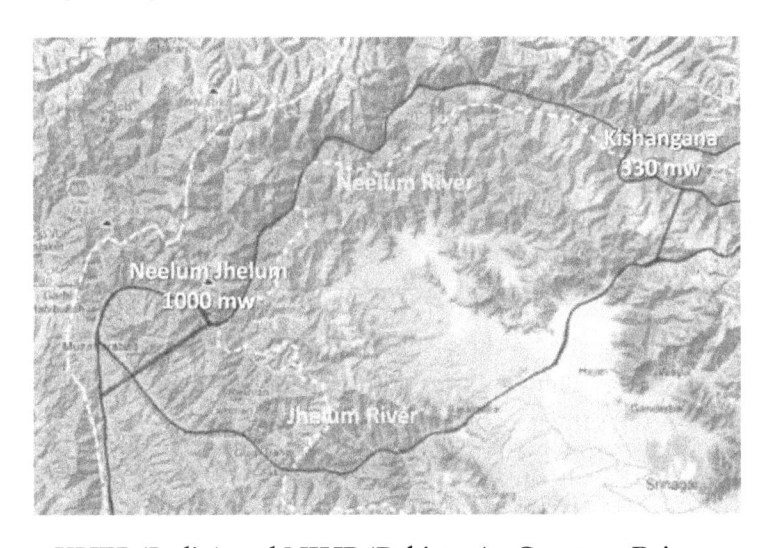

KHEP (India) and NJHP (Pakistan) - Courtesy Briscoe

The complaints of Pakistan

1. Whether India's proposed diversion of the river Kishenganga (Neelum) into another Tributary, i.e. the Bonar Madmati Nallah, being one central element of the Kishenganga Project, breaches India's legal obligations owed to Pakistan under the Treaty, as interpreted and applied in accordance with international law, including India's obligations under Article III(2) (let flow all the waters of the Western rivers and not permit any interference with those waters) and Article IV(6) (maintenance of natural channels)?

2. Whether under the Treaty, India may deplete or bring the reservoir level of a run-of-the-river Plant below the Dead Storage Level (DSL) in any circumstances except in the case of an unforeseen emergency?

The related treaty articles as mentioned by Pakistan

Article III(2): India shall be under an obligation to let flow all the waters of the Western Rivers, and shall not permit any interference with these waters, except for the following uses, restricted in the case of each of the rivers, The Indus, The Jhelum and The Chenab, to the drainage basin thereof: (a) Domestic Use; (b) Non-Consumptive Use; (c) Agricultural Use, as set out in Annexure C; and (d) Generation of hydro-electric power, as set out in Annexure D.

Article IV(6) : Each Party will use its best endeavors to maintain the natural channels of the Rivers, as on the Effective Date, in such condition as will avoid, as far as practicable, any obstruction to the flow in these channels likely to cause material damage to the other Party.

Comments – The first one above is very generic and clearly comes with exception clauses attached with it. Hence, in case India mentions something from those exception areas, Annexure C and D, this article won't be of any use. However the second one is interesting because it talks about natural channels of the rivers – something that India is not willing to maintain wholly. Interestingly, the downstream project in Pakistan is also guilty of the same offence – it's also avoiding the natural channel. However, Pakistan's obstruction won't cause material damage to India but the reverse is not true. This asymmetry puts this article in the favor of Pakistan. India may still argue that the Indian obstruction won't have a "significant" damage downstream and this is a "best effort" clause (i.e. asks the "as far as practicable"), but Pakistan can battle that vigorously. A couple of more significant factors determining the outcome of this verdict are whether Pakistan started their project first and if so, how large was it proposed initially. Pakistan cannot upscale it after knowing about the Indian project and then claim damages. The second one is what percent of river water is actually diverted – various reports suggest it to be between 10 to 33%. The court would probably have a cap on % water usage in its final verdict.

15 . Subject to the provisions of Paragraph 17, the works connected with a Plant shall be so operated that (a) the volume of water received in the river upstream of the Plant, during any period of seven consecutive days, shall be delivered into the river below the Plant during the same seven-day period, and (b) in any one period of 24 hours within that seven-day period, the volume delivered into the river below the Plant shall be not less than 30%, and not more than 130%, of the volume received in the river above the Plant during the same 24-hour period : Provided, however, that:

(i) where a Plant is located at a site on the Chenab Main below Ramban, the volume of water received in the river upstream of the Plant in any one period of 24 hours shall be delivered into the river below the Plant within the same period of 24 hours;

(ii) where a Plant is located at a site on the Chenab Main above Ramban, the volume of water delivered into the river below the Plant in any one period of 24 hours shall not be less than 50% and not more than 130% of the volume received above the Plant during the same 24-hour period; and

(iii) where a Plant is located on a Tributary of The Jhelum on which Pakistan has any Agricultural Use or Hydro-electric Use, the water released below the Plant may be delivered, if necessary, into another Tributary but only to the extent that the then existing Agricultural Use or Hydro-electric Use by Pakistan on the former Tributary would not be adversely affected.

Comments–Annexure D clearly supports water diversion using tunnels but with restrictions. As I discussed earlier, this will be enough to negate the first article proposed by Pakistan. Interestingly, the treaty specifically mentions about Agro and Hydro uses, i.e. environmental impacts won't probably affect the outcome of the case, unless the treaty is re-interpreted. Furthermore, the article (iii) scopes down to "existing" use and excludes "planned" use, favoring India. However, these are minor clauses and could be reinterpreted to maintain consistency in the treaty.

The other part of the arbitration has reference to the same old dead storage level related issue that was deemed to be the core one in Baghlihar case. The World Bank expert actually supported Indian view on that and allowed India to go ahead with sediment control spillways. This theoretically provides India with more control over the water, but also makes the dam operation consistent with current knowhow.

Related cases

I could only find one similar case between France and Spain. The summary of the case history and judgement goes like this –

"Lake Lanoux is situated in southern France near the border of Spain. The lake is fed by several streams that all originate in France. Water flows out of the lake in a single stream that joins the Carol River before crossing into Spain. In the 1950s, France began developing a plan to divert water from Lake Lanoux over a 789 meter drop to generate hydroelectric energy. Even though France promised to return the diverted water to the Carol River, Spain pressed France to arbitrate the dispute because Spain believed the plan would violate its water rights under a series of treaties signed in 1866. The arbitration tribunal issued an award in 1957, which rejected Spain's arguments because the French plan promised not to alter the volume of water entering Spain through the Carol River. Although France would not have been allowed to unilaterally promote its legitimate interests at the expense or injury of neighboring states, the tribunal did not identify a foreseeable injury to Spain. Further, the Tribunal stated that the 1866 treaties did not constitute a reason to subjugate the general rule that standing and flowing waters are subject to the sovereignty of the state where they are located."

This supports Indian position, although the treaty between India and Pakistan is different from the same between Spain and France. The facts related to injury to Spain, not altering volume of water delivered to Spain and run-of-the-river plants – all similar logic can be reapplied in this case.

Possible Outcomes

I personally think this arbitration judgement would go the same way as that of its earlier counterpart. As Baghlihar suggested, making compromises on a few technical parameters (dam height, pondage and in this case water diverted) would make India happy to settle the case with Pakistan. A less likely verdict will provide an upper hand for Pakistan and will call for an injunction on KHEP. India have to deal with a setback and prepare more thoroughly going forward.

APP - 40

WATER TREATIES & DIPLOMACY: INDIA FACES DIFFICULT CHOICES ON WATER

Brahma Chellaney, The Economics Times, 10 May 2013

With power in India shifting to the states due to an increasingly weak central government, secretary of state Hillary Clinton chose Kolkata as the first stop of her India tour to advance US foreign-policy interests.

In a televised interview before meeting with West Bengal chief minister Mamata Banerjee, Clinton pushed for India permitting foreign direct investment in multi-brand retail and for an "amicable" water-sharing arrangement with Bangladesh on the Teesta River – issues stalled by Banerjee's opposition.

The art of persuasion and co-option is central to leadership – a capability Prime Minister Manmohan Singh has failed to demonstrate, even as his politically precarious government lurches from one crisis to another.

The result has been a series of delays on critical decisions as well as policy reversals – all conveniently blamed on allies, including powerful regional satraps. This tendency to pass the buck has prompted foreign leaders to directly woo key chief ministers.

Take the water issue. The Indian Constitution has left water as a state-level subject, rather than making it a federal issue. Yet Singh's government has sought to dictate the terms of a Teesta water-sharing treaty with Bangladesh to West Bengal, although that state's interests are directly at stake.Indeed, New Delhi first negotiated the terms of the pact with Dhaka – generously loaded in Bangladesh's favour – and then sought to present West Bengal with a fait accompli.

Respect for states and their interests is the essence of federalism. Yet, this inclination to ride roughshod over states harks back to the days when the central government was exceptionally strong.Jawaharial Nehru ignored the interests of Jammu and Kashmir and, to a lesser extent, Punjab when he signed the 1960 Indus Waters Treaty, under which India big-heartedly agreed to the exclusive reservation of the largest three of the six Indus-system rivers for downstream Pakistan.

In effect, India signed an extraordinary treaty, indefinitely setting aside 80.52% of the Indus-system waters for Pakistan – the most generous water-sharing pact thus far in modern world history.In fact, the volume of waters earmarked for Pakistan from India under the Indus treaty is more than 90 times greater than what the US is required to release for Mexico under the 1944 US-Mexico Water Treaty, which stipulates a minimum transboundary delivery of 1.85 billion cubic metres of the Colorado River waters yearly.

Despite Clinton's advocacy of a Teesta treaty, the fact is that the waters of the once-mighty Colorado River are siphoned by seven American states, leaving only a trickle for Mexico.

APP – 41

PAKISTAN GIVES INDIA 'NON PAPERS' ON INDUS TREATY BREACH

Muhammad Saleh Zaafir, 9 September 2012

Pakistan has handed over "non-papers" to India on Saturday pertaining documentary evidence of serious breach of Indus Basin Water Treaty (IBWT) by New Delhi. The non-papers were delivered to visiting Indian minister for External Affairs SM Krishna here during formal talks, concluding the third round of Composite Dialogue. Highly placed diplomatic sources told The News Saturday evening that the Indian minister has been told about the relevant clauses of the treaty about water-sharing between Pakistan and India brokered by the World Bank.

The treaty was signed in Karachi on September 19, 1960, by then Indian Prime Minister Jawaharlal Nehru and President of Pakistan Field Marshal Muhammad Ayub Khan. The treaty was a result of Pakistani fear that since the Source Rivers of the Indus basin were in India, it could potentially create droughts and famines in Pakistan, especially at times of war. The Indus System of Rivers comprises three Western rivers, the Indus, the Jhelum and Chenab, and three Eastern rivers — the Sutlej, the Beas and the Ravi; and with minor exceptions, the treaty gives India exclusive use of all of the waters of the Eastern Rivers and their tributaries before the point where the rivers enter Pakistan. Similarly, Pakistan has exclusive use of the Western rivers.

The two countries agreed to exchange data and co-operate in matters related to the treaty. For this purpose, the treaty creates the Permanent Indus Commission, with a commissioner appointed by each country. The Permanent Indus Commission has survived two wars and provides an ongoing mechanism for consultation and conflict resolution through inspection, exchange of data, and visits. The Commission is required to meet regularly to discuss potential disputes as well as cooperative arrangements for the development of the basin. Either party must notify the other of plans to construct any engineering works which would affect the other party and to provide data about such works. The 'non-papers' have also given the details of correspondence between the two sides where it was mandatory for India to provide information to Pakistan according to the treaty but India failed in fulfilling its obligations. The Indian interlocutors could not offer any explanation, but they assured Pakistan that India would look into the papers and respond in the next engagement, the sources revealed. The sources said that the two sides decided not to discuss contentious issues publicly in the interest of ambiance of the talks, but the two foreign ministers discussed almost every subject yet to be resolved.

APP - 42

INDO-PAK DISPUTE OVER KISHANGANGA PROJECT

(By Zaheer-ul-Hassan, 30 October 2012)

The International Court of Arbitration (**ICA**) constituted in the matter of the Indus Waters Kishanganga Arbitration (Pakistan v. India) has concluded a two-week hearing on the merits at the Peace Palace in The Hague. Earlier, in the case of Baglihar Hdro Project, the court has asked India to redesign and carryout necessary amendments for removing three out of four technical objections raised by Pakistan. Another disputed Kishanganga Hdro-Electric Project (**KHEP**) is located on Kishanganga River, (Neelum River) near Kanzalwan. 103 M high dam will divert the water of Kishanganga to Wular Lake through a 22 km tunnel. The project would be having electricity generation capacity of 330 MW.

Pakistan and India though concluded a treaty on regulation of rivers of Indus Water Basin in 1960 but India normally shown reluctance in implementation of agreement. The water conflicts awakened again when India started constructing the hydro projects and reservoirs without the consent of Pakistan. India has planned construction of 72 water power projects of different magnitude on rivers/Nullahs of Indian Occupied Kashmir (IOK).

In doing so, it is in the process of diverting millions of acre feet of dead and live storage water from IOK to Rajistan, which will also be used to produce hydropower. She has already started of construction of a mega task "Interlinking River Project". According to the experts, the undertaking of project would likely to change the ecology of South Asia and would also cause adverse effects on the environment. Recently, Indian Supreme Court has urged that the interlinking of the rivers be accelerated and implemented by 2016. Indian Prime Minister subsequently set up of a Task Force to consider the modalities of implementing the project. Though, the interlinking of rivers has been presented by the Indian Government as a major initiative towards meeting the future water problems but overall would cause devastating effects in rivers delta of Bangladesh, India and Pakistan. Estimated to cost Rs. 5,60,00,00 million, the project envisages 30 links across Himalayan and peninsular rivers. The idea behind this is based on the fact that an enormous amount of water from rivers flows into the sea. It is envisaged that if this is prevented, and water transferred from rivers to water-deficit areas, there will be adequate supply for everyone in every part of the country.

The estimated cost is about 50 times more than the total allocation for the ongoing water resource development projects in the Tenth Plan. There are talks of opening doors to private investors; in that case traditional rights of people over water resources will be affected. The environmental and human costs of the project are going to be colossal. These will include, disturbance to pristine biodiversity rich areas, disruption of tribal lives, changes in river morphology and water quality, submergence of forests and agricultural lands etc. Connecting the Himalayan Rivers with the peninsular rivers through some 40,000 km long inland waterways will cause massive human displacement. The large network of dams and canals will also alter the natural drainage such that occasional flooding and water logging will inundate millions of hectares of agricultural land, the project may alter the geography of the country significantly. Inter linking of livers may disrupt the entire hydrological cycle by stopping the rivers from performing their ecological function before reaching the oceans. Also, given changing global climate, what seems like surplus water today, may not even be available a few years down the line. There is no provision for any mechanism to deal with matters concerning inter-basin transfers. Anyhow, regarding Indus Water Basin connecting rivers under inter river linking system and construction of hydro-electric projects constitute a violation of the IWT (Indus Water Treaty) which provides for the generation of hydropower on "run-of-the river" water only, with no live storage-not even in normal terms. Although Indian government contends that these projects are only on the "run of the river", but practically would be having full control over the water storage. In this connection, India has already attained the capability of the controlling and manipulations of water for 28 days of water of River Chennab.

Anyway, focusing on current issue of Kishanganga dispute, it would not be wrong in stating that IWT has resolved the issue of Wullar Barrage but was not able to give any way-out over Kishanganga Conflict. Pakistan had launched a complaint in the court of arbitration that Indian bid to build Kishanganga dam was violation of World Bank brokered IWT of 1960. In this connection, on September 23, 2011 the court issued an interim order, restraining India from going ahead with the controversial hydro power project over river Kishanganga in Gurez Valley of IHK. ICA was in the opinion that structure over River Neelum/Kishanganga that may affect the flow of water downstream. With the ICA's stay order, Pakistan will have the time to expedite the construction of large reservoirs so that India does not claim the right to use water Pakistan is not constructing any dams. However, Indian efforts are to make IWT ineffective and most of Indian scholars believe in re-imagining of water treaty.

Pakistan has initiated this arbitration with India under Article IX and Annexure G of the IWT, an international agreement concluded by India and Pakistan in 1960 which regulates the use by the two States of the Indus system of rivers. In these proceedings, Pakistan places two matters for determination by the Court of Arbitration: First reveals, "Whether India's proposed diversion of the river Kishanganga (Neelum) into another Tributary, i.e. the Bonar Madmati Nallah, being one central element of the Kishanganga Project, breaches India's legal obligations owed to Pakistan under the Treaty, as interpreted and applied in accordance with international law, including India's obligations under Article III(2) (let flow all the waters of the Western rivers and not permit any interference with those waters) and Article IV(6) (maintenance of natural channels)?" Second Deliberates: "Whether under the Treaty, India may deplete or bring the reservoir level of a run-of-river Plant below Dead Storage Level (DSL) in any circumstances except in the case of an unforeseen emergency?"

The primary subject of the arbitration is the Kishanganga Hydro-Electric Project (the "KHEP") currently under construction by India on the Kishanganga/Neelum River, a tributary of the Jhelum River. It is also notable here that KHEP would be in operational condition by 2016, whereas Neelum Jhelum Project would start functioning in 2017. completed Pakistan concerns and objections over KHEP are very alarming and serious in nature since completion of KHEP would reduce the flow of water into Pakistan by about 11% in summer and about 27% in winter, which would be contrary to the IWT as the Western rivers and would also damaged already constructed Neelum-Jhelum project. Moreover, Pakistan's Neelum Valley is likely to dry up and become a desert.

Another issues of would be of the management of sedimentation in the reservoir, India intends to employ drawdown flushing, a technique requiring the depletion of the level in the KHEP reservoir below Dead Storage Level (the Treaty's definition of this term is reproduced in the annex to this press release). Pakistan very rightly contended that the KHEP's planned diversion of the waters of the Kishanganga/Neelum, as well as the use of the drawdown flushing technique, both at the KHEP or at other Indian hydro-electric projects that the Treaty regulates, are impermissible under the Indus Waters Treaty. India maintains that both the design and planned mode of operation of the KHEP are fully in conformity with the Treaty.

The dam defiantly will create problems for Pakistan because it will create the shortage in Neelum River. Pakistan has, meanwhile, formalized its objections into six questions, three on the design of the project, two on the diversion of water and one on power houses. Pakistan raised the objection that about the location of the project and insisted that under the Indus Basin Water Treaty India could not divert Kishanganga water to Wuller barrage, on which it was building an 800 MW hydro-power project. India is under obligation to release as much water downstream as it stores. It is also notable here that it is going to affect the Pakistani Project too which is located 70 km downstream from Kishanganga Project.In fact, India's premise that it was already contemplating construction of a hydroelectric project on this tributary of Jhelum River at the time of signing of the treaty opens up the question of intention rather than actual plan or capability at the time. Moreover Indian argument that affect on Pakistan's Neelum-Jhelum project downstream, can be mitigated by constructing other structures seems to be speculative, preventive and requiring huge additional cost and time. Therefore Pakistan should not agreed to Indian argument is as such not agreeable. The sacristy of water (even for domestic use) will result if Indian KHEP (Kishanganga Hydro Electric Project) is allowed to be implemented. This may even of force migration/displacement of population in AJ&K damaging of agro based economy of Pakistan. In short, the amicable solution of water and territorial conflicts (including Kashmir) between two South Asian nuclear countries needs to be resolved on priority if UN, ICA and super powers are interested to save the globe from future nuclear war.

APP – 43

THE NEWS

Khalid Mustafa, 03 November 2012

A three-member committee headed by Syed Raghib Abbas Shah, chairman of the Water and Power Development Authority (Wapda), has held India responsible for building the Nimoo-Bazgo hydropower project in violation of the Indus Waters Treaty and declared Syed Jamaat Ali Shah, former commissioner of Pakistan Commission of Indus Water, as innocent, said sources on Friday.

Shah was earlier found helping and facilitating India build the project as per the preliminary report furnished by Imtiaz Tajwar, secretary Wapda, they said.

The committee was constituted to assess the criminal negligence on the part of the then commissioner of Pakistan Commission of Indus Water in the light of the report of Tajwar by the then secretary water and power Imtiaz Qazi when Naveed Qamar was the minister for water and power, said sources.

A 57-metre high Nimoo-Bazgo hydroelectric project has now been completely developed in the Leh District on the River Indus and is now operational from where the sustained and cheaper supply of electricity is being ensured to the Indian troops in Siachen.

In addition, a 42-metre high Chuttak hydroelectric project also got completed on the River Sum, a tributary of Indus, in the Kargil district of the Indian-held Kashmir, said sources.

The projects will reduce the flow of River Indus, the lifeline of Pakistan, said sources, adding that the dams can store water up to 120,000,000 cubic metres.

India has already managed to get approval of carbon credits amounting to $482,083 in seven years ($68,869 per annum) from the United Nations for two controversial projects, Nimoo-Bazgo and Chuttak hydropower, which are not in line with the Indus Waters Treaty, after showing that it has got the clearance report on trans-boundary environmental impact assessment of the projects from Pakistan.

However, the ministry could not fix the responsibility of the officials of the ministry of environment and foreign affairs involved in clearing the projects in terms of the trans-boundary environmental impact assessment except framing out of the standard operating procedures (SOPs) so that in the future, such negligence could not take place, they said.

"Yes, we have received the much-awaited inquiry report of the three-member committee, after the preliminary report of Imtiaz Tajwar, secretary Wapda, but we are shocked to read the contents of the report that has declared Jamaat Ali Shah as innocent and India has been held responsible for building the Nimoo-Bazgo project by flouting the Indus Waters Treaty," said a senior official of the ministry of water and power.

"Declaring India as responsible for building the project is just like terming the thief as a thief. The report did not fix the responsibility of PCIW at all, which is supposed to safeguard Pakistan's water interests in the upper riparian country–India." And terming PCIW's commissioner as innocent is just like to push the dirt under the carpet. When asked as to whether this report will be accepted by the ministry of water and power or not, the official said, the report is currently being analysed and a decision is yet to be made to either accept or reject the report. The ministry is analysing as to why there is a huge difference between the Raghib and Tajwar reports.

When contacted, Nargis Sethi, water and power secretary, said that she is still naive to several issues of the ministry, including the issue of Nimoo-Bazgo project, and let her see Raghib's report, then she will be able to comment on it.

Earlier, the report furnished by Tajwar revealed that Shah did not play his due role and remained silent about the Nimoo-Bazgo hydropower project that was built by India from 2002 to 2005 and between 2007, 2008 and 2009, said sources, adding that he did not raise any objections during Pakistan-India meetings at the level of Permanent Indus Commission of Indus Waters.

The most alarming aspect of the disclosure is that the PCIW team never visited the project, before and during the construction period of the project, which triggers doubts about the involvement of senior PCIW officials in facilitating India.

However, Tajwar's report said that Jamaat Ali Shah was told by India that it is going to construct the Nimoo-Bazgo project six months ago before the initiation of its construction.

Shah objected to the design of the project, terming it in negation of the provisions of the Indus Waters Treaty, said sources.

According to the Tajwar report, the Military Intelligence Directorate of the Government of Pakistan had informed on June 6, 2005 that the Indian government is planning to construct the Nimoo-Bazgo hydroelectric project and the project is likely to be completed by 2010.

The report also said that the ISI further informed on July 25, 2005 that the Indian Prime Minister Dr Manmohan Singh visited Leh, Kargil and Siachen Glacier on June 11, 2005 and laid the foundation stone of Nimoo-Bazgo and Chuttak hydroelectric power plants. Similarly, the ISI, on September 7, 2005, shared the information about the visit of the Indian prime minister to Siachen and Kargil and with reference to the deputy chief minister, it was informed that the project will be completed soon.

The report also revealed that the PCIW remained silent for three years in 2007, 2008, 2009 about the project; however, astonishingly, in 2010, Pakistan Commission of Indus Water started vigorously following the project at all levels when it was a known fact that after the completion of a project like the Nimoo-Bazgo hydroelectric project, it is impossible to change the design. At this stage, neither any court nor neutral expert may give a decision against the completed project, which is built on a huge cost for public interest. According to sources, Kamal Majidulah, special assistant to the prime minister on water, also played a pivotal role in initiating the probe against Shah. The government of Pakistan has decided to move the international court of arbitration against the Nimoo-Bazgo project, which was built by India in sheer violation of the Indus Waters Treaty.

APP – 44

INDIA AND THE INDUS WATERS TREATY

Dr. Ijaz Hussain, 24 November, 2012

Exploiting Pakistan's utter desperation to get the water supplies restored India forced Pakistan to sign the Delhi Agreement. But Pakistan had to pay the price by renouncing all rights to these waters and pledging to tap alternative sources for its needs. Then followed a series of bilateral negotiations to find a permanent solution to the issue, but due to Indian obduracy they remained inconclusive. Subsequently, the World Bank mediated the dispute which resulted in the conclusion of the Indus Waters Treaty in 1960. It allocated the Eastern Rivers (Sutlej, Ravi and Beas) to India and the Western Rivers (Chenab, Jhelum and Indus) to Pakistan, while, at the same time, allowing India the right to make "limited use" of their waters and operate run-of-the-river hydropower plants. The Treaty worked, more or less, satisfactorily over the years, even during the 1965 and 1971 wars. However, since its rise as an economic power, India has started to flex its muscle and begun abusing the Treaty by planning huge dam-like structures on the Western Rivers. It has already built one on the Chenab River called the Baglihar dam and is currently building another one on the Jhelum River called the Kishanganga dam.

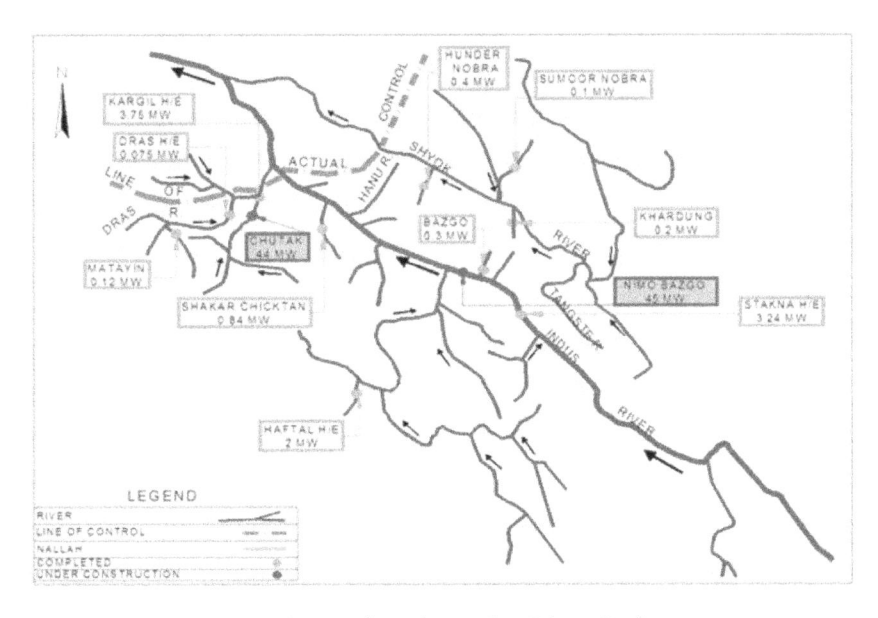

Location Of Projects On River Indus

This is, however, not the end of the story of India's dam building activity on the Western Rivers. It is now planning more than a hundred dams under the guise of hydropower projects. Pakistan believes them to be in violation of the terms of the Treaty as they are not run-of-the-river projects. Pakistan's concern about the issue is evident from the fact that according to the Strategic Foresight Group, an Indian think tank, every proposal that Pakistan has made since 1999 in the two-track diplomacy has focused on water as a matter of pivotal concern to that country. The gravity of the situation can be gauged from the fact that in March 2009, a group of more than 20 different UN bodies warned that given the rising tension over the water issue between Pakistan and India, the world could be perilously close to its first water war. India, of course, rejects Pakistan's claim by arguing that it is building hydropower projects strictly in accordance with the terms of the Treaty. It contends that Pakistan's objections are mostly political in nature and have no technical or engineering relevance. It is not prepared to engage Pakistan in order to find an amicable solution to the issue and rejects predictions of war as being alarmist.

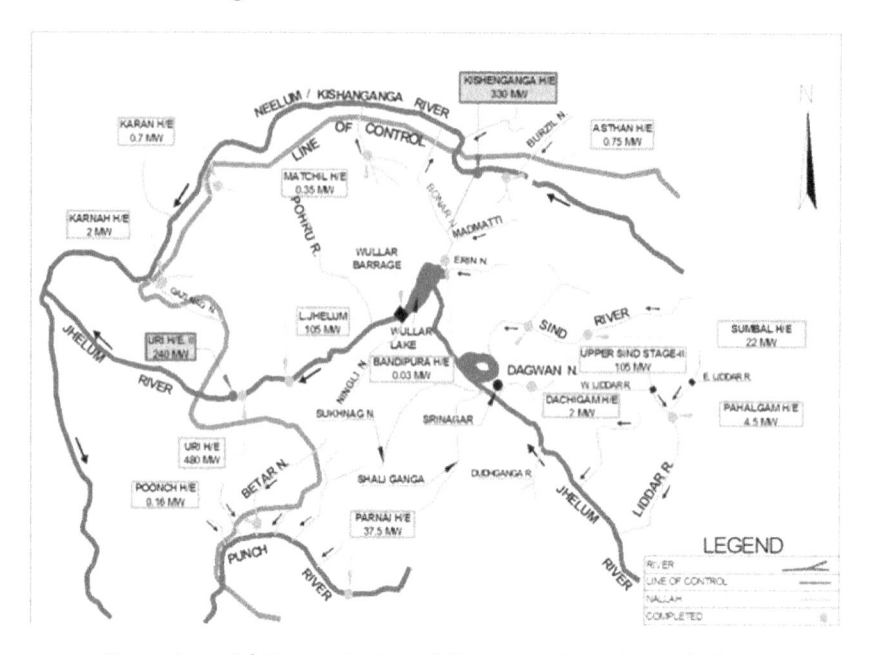

Location Of Commissioned Projects On River Jhelum

The question arises: why is India bent upon building these dams? Is it doing so merely to generate electricity or is there some hidden agenda behind it as well? From all the available evidence, it is clear that India is trying to acquire capability to control the waters of the Western Rivers in order to release them to inundate Pakistani territory or withhold them to render it dry at an opportune moment. Independent and neutral observers tend to agree with Pakistan's assessment. For example, this is what John Briscoe, Professor of Environmental Engineering at the Harvard University, who has worked on the issue for quite some time, has to say in the matter:

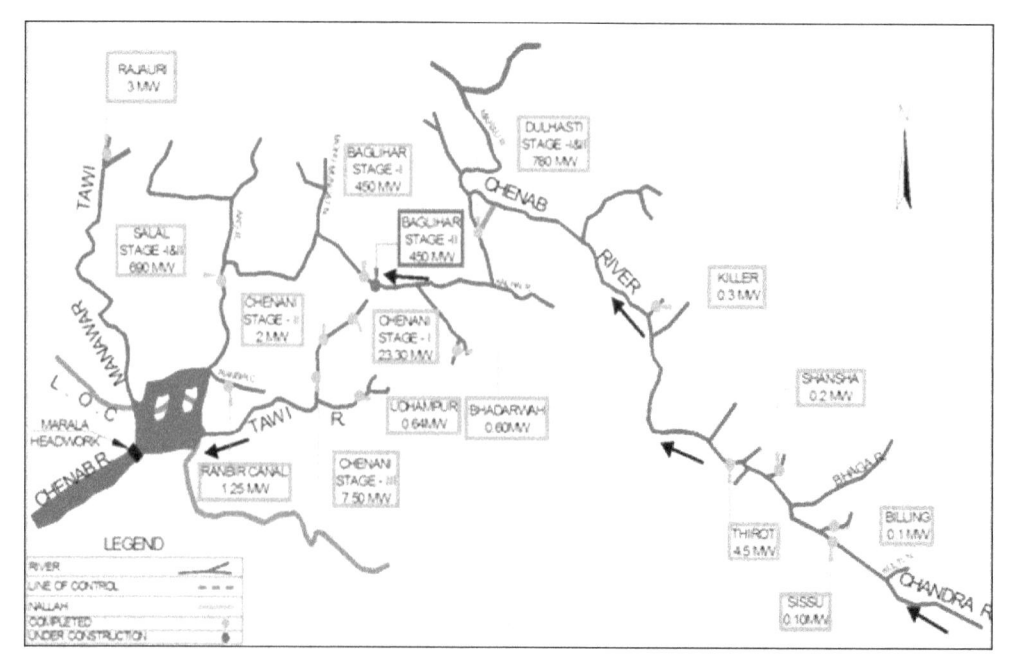

Location Of Projects On River Indus

"[There] is a veritable caravan of Indian projects-Kishanganga, Sawalkot, Pakuldul, Bursar, Dal Huste, Gypsa. The cumulative live storage would be large, giving India an unquestioned capacity to have a major impact on the timing of flows into Pakistan... [Calculations suggest] that once it has constructed all of the hydropower plants on the Chenab, India will have the ability to effect major damage on Pakistan."

Incidentally, if India is trying to control the flow of the Western Rivers, its attitude has been no different towards its other South Asian neighbours. It has succeeded in imposing unfair water treaties like the Mahakali and Tanakpur Agreements on Nepal and the Ganges Agreement of 1996 on Bangladesh. Additionally, it has plans to interlink Brahmaputra, Ganges and Meghna rivers by transferring water from surplus to deficient rivers which would hit Bangladesh hard as it would deprive the latter of water which it has historically used. In this backdrop, the Indian intentions vis-a-vis Pakistan through vast dam-building plans become clear. It is not only to steal waters which rightfully belong to Pakistan but also to use them as a weapon to reduce Pakistan to the status of Nepal or Bangladesh. India is doing so because it is a hegemonistic power which is bent upon imposing its version of the Monroe doctrine on South Asia. It is making a strategic use of water to subdue Pakistan which is the last line of resistance against India's quest for supremacy in South Asia.

APP – 45

REVIEW OF INDUS WATER TREATY (2013)

THE NEWS, PAKISTAN
(By our Correspondent, 26 March 2013)

Pakistan has raised technical objections to three hydropower projects being constructed by India on River Chenab, terming their various design parameters a violation of the Indus Waters Treaty during talks held at the platform of the Indus Water Commission with the visiting Indian delegation.

A 10-member delegation, led by the Indian Commissioner for Indus Water, Arunganathan, held talks here in the provincial metropolis with Pakistan delegation, headed by Asif Baig, Pakistan Commissioner for Indus Water.

Members of Pakistan delegation were of the view that Indian projects of 850MW Rattle, 120MW Miyar and 48MW Lower Karnai were controversial and were being constructed in sheer violation of the treaty. The main objection was building storage capacity as a component of the run-of-the-river project.

The Pakistani commissioner asked his Indian counterpart to amend the engineering design of the project in line with the provisions of the Indus Waters Treaty, otherwise Pakistan would refer the issue to the Court of Arbitration.

The Pakistani delegation observed that 48MW Kalnai Hydroelectric Project could allow India to utilize the stream flows of the Lower Kalnai River, a tributary of the Chenab River, in Kishtwar district of Jammu and Kashmir. They said India would be able to divert the water of Chenab river if the project was completed as per design. The Water of Chenab tributary was proposed to be diverted through a Water Conductor System. A Power House was proposed on the left bank of Lower Kalnai River about 200m upstream of its confluence with Chenab river.

The 850MW Rattle Hydropower plant also includes a storage element, which is not allowed as per provisions of the Indus Waters Treaty. The Miyar plant was planned on the right bank of the Chenab river near Udaipur town.

According to the Treaty, signed between Pakistan and India in 1960, Pakistan was allowed to use the Indus, Jhelum and Chenab rivers, while India was allowed to use Ravi, Sutlej and Beas.

APP - 46

WINNERS ARE LOSERS, AND VICE VERSA, IN INDUS WATER BATTLE

Shaukat Qadir, 1 April 2013

News media in India and Pakistan almost all reported February's International Court of Arbitration decision on the Kishanganga Dam issue the same way: Pakistan had "lost" another case over the 1960 Indus Waters Treaty (IWT), and India had "won."

In the Pakistan-India context, everything, from cricket to arbitration to war, is a defeat or a victory for the two nations to mourn or celebrate. Still, this seemed like a body blow to Pakistan, following as it did a 2007 decision in India's favour by a World Bank arbitrator on another IWT case, involving the Baglihar Dam.

But was this year's ruling really so bad?

At independence, the boundary left the sources of the six rivers of the Indus Basin in India. Pakistan was downstream and therefore vulnerable. The IWT was supposed to assure Pakistan of a reasonable flow of water. But now, and especially since the Baglihar Dam decision, the IWT has seemed to many in Pakistan to be one-sided in India's favour.

Kishanganga is an Indian dam project, started in 2007, to be completed in 2016. It will divert water from the Kishanganga River into the Jehlum River basin. Pakistan objects because in 2008 it began building its own dam downstream, where the Kishanganga is called the Neelam. This dam, too, is due for completion in 2016.

Pakistan's claim to the International Court of Arbitration was based on the fact that the Indian dam will cut the flow to the Pakistani one, and thus reduce the power potential there.

On the face of it, Pakistan's "loss" on Kishanganga was a foregone conclusion. An annexure to the 1960 treaty authorises actions such as India's provided that "then existing agricultural or hydroelectric use by Pakistan … would not be adversely affected."

Since construction on the Neelam-Jehlum project began after work on the Kishanganga one, many observers saw no point in Pakistan going to the international court.

Worse, a "loss" for Pakistan threatened further negative consequences. Another Indian victory, critics suggested, would only reinforce the view that India is playing by the IWT rules, while Pakistan is raising spurious objections. That view has been confirmed by much of the media reporting on the decision.

I shared that view – but only until I read the decision. That's when I learnt the underreported fact that this ruling, in fact, works in Pakistan's favour.

In dam jargon, "dead storage" is a reservoir where water is left for sediment to settle. In the Baglihar Dam case of 2007, Pakistan had claimed that excessive dead storage behind that Indian dam would give India too much control over the water flow in time of tension or war.

In taking the Kishanganga case to the court, Pakistan revived the dead storage issue as a part of its case. Needless to add, India objected to Pakistan's inclusion of an already-settled issue. But India agreed to binding arbitration on Kishanganga, probably because it was confident of winning at arbitration and assumed that the dead storage issue was already dead.

Indian officials must be regretting those assumptions now, because the ICA not only addressed the Baglihar Dam dead storage issue, but effectively reversed the decision of the World Bank-appointed arbitrator.

In the decision on Baglihar in 2007 by the international arbitrator, it appeared that India could, on the plea of "sediment flushing," raise the "live storage" (the level of water in operational use) to any level it wanted. This latest ruling reverses this, declaring that India must not increase the "live" or "dead" storage level of water beyond the level permitted by the treaty, including sediment flushing.

In the words of South African water expert John Briscoe, who appointed the original World Bank arbitrator, it now appears that with the court's Kishanganga ruling, India may have "won another battle, but lost the war."

The Kishanganga ruling will have a negative effect on power production from Pakistan's Neelam–Jehlum project. But the reduction from planned power production is not likely to exceed 25 per cent.

However, the de facto reversal of the Baglihar Dam ruling is much more important, and will go a long way towards addressing Pakistan's concerns about water security under the Indus Waters Treaty.

It is hard to believe that the Pakistani government has the subtlety required to discern in advance that it had a chance to win this reversal.

And it is surprising that so far the media have mainly ignored the implications of the arbitration court's most recent ruling. It is perhaps understandable that Indian officials should shy away from making their discomfiture public. But why isn't Pakistan's government making a point of this, particularly if this was an intended ploy?

Perhaps the answer is that this is an unexpected result that Pakistan's leadership does not yet quite comprehend.

That seems more likely, given the nature of Pakistani leadership!

APP - 47

WATER SHARING BETWEEN INDIA AND PAKISTAN: AN OPPORTUNITY FOR COOPERATION

Andrew Holland, 15 April 2013

Note from Andrew Holland: This is a guest post by Dhanasree Jayaram, a Ph.D. candidate in the Department of Geopolitics and International Relations at Manipal University, Karnataka, and an associate fellow at the Centre for Air Power Studies in New Delhi. This post gives an important view on how water resources in the Subcontinent could provide both opportunities for cooperation as well as challenges to conflict. You can see more of our work in this area in our 'Perspectives' article, "The Dams of the Himalayas"

The Letter Of The Law

In February, the International Court of Arbitration issued a partial award on the Kishanganga Dam dispute between India and Pakistan over the Indus River. This might succeed in bringing a certain sense of closure to some of the differences that exist between India and Pakistan on the sharing of the waters of the Indus Basin – but the legal and political battles are far from over. The award will allow India to establish a hydro-electric dam on the Neelum, albeit under strict conditions, that includes amendments to the design and operations of the dam.

Several factors have complicated Indo-Pakistan water sharing relations in the past and will continue to do so in the future. Under the Indus Waters Treaty (IWT) brokered by the World Bank in 1960, India was granted exclusive rights over the waters of the Eastern Rivers – the Sutlej, the Beas and the Ravi – and their tributaries before the point where the rivers enter Pakistan, while Pakistan won the rights over the waters of the Western Rivers – the Indus, the Jhelum and the Chenab – and their tributaries. Pakistan's share of the total Indus system is over 80 percent which makes India a beneficiary of less than 20 percent.

In the past decade, there have been many disputes over India and Pakistan's shared waters: the construction of Baglihar Dam on the Chenab by the Indian side was obstructed by Pakistan. When Pakistan had moved the World Bank for arbitration, the latter appointed a neutral expert, Richard Laffite, who gave green light to the project in 2007 thwarting the objections raised by the former about the structure and design of the dam.

Stresses To Current Laws

In Pakistan, there is an increasing fear of water and food insecurity, a country that is entirely dependent on the waters of the Indus (and its tributaries). Pakistan fears that India has plans to construct 155 hydropower projects on the Indus, Jhelum (74) and Chenab (56), the three rivers that were assigned to Pakistan under the IWT. This number has, however, not been confirmed by the Indian authorities. Studies show clearly that the per capita availability of water is declining in both countries due to diminishing river flows, over-exploitation of groundwater (causing salinity), low conveyance efficiency and pollution of rivers.Climate change is also exacerbating the situation, and it could only worsen in the future as the Indus is one of those rivers that have maximum dependence (151 percent) on glacial meltwater. One study states, "Based on current projections, the Indus River system is expected to fall below 2000 flow levels between 2030 and 2050. The drop-off is estimated to be most serious between 2030 and 2040, with a new equilibrium flow of 20 percent below that of 2000 reached after 2060."

On the politics side of the debate, Pervez Musharraf, former President of Pakistan, claimed in his dissertation that the Kashmir dispute was primarily based on the distribution of the waters of the Indus and its tributaries between India and Pakistan. Stressing on the fair distribution of waters, he asserts, "If one were resolved, the other would not exist." A few reports have also suggested that Pakistan would not hesitate to use its nuclear weapons against India if the latter chokes water supply to its territory.

The present treaty has also been unpopular in India, and its Government has been under constant pressure to review it and even compensate local residents for the losses (mainly agricultural) incurred on account of the treaty. The legislative council of Jammu and Kashmir passed a resolution in 2002 exhorting the Government of India to review it "in the best interests of the people of the state."
The treaty has also been lambasted in India on the grounds that India signed it without an assessment of the future availability of water in the Indus system.

Recommendations: Towards Integrated Basin Management

The Indus (and its tributaries) is the lifeline of Pakistan and the effects of environmental change are being felt on both sides of the border. Instead of revising the treaty and wrestling over riparian politics, India and Pakistan could work towards an integrated basin management, as water security is emerging as a critical issue in both countries. Water management negotiations are the biggest confidence-building measure between the two countries.At the same time, vituperative sentiments generated by certain sections of the Pakistani establishment need to be kept in check. Pakistan has time and again reiterated that the IWT is inequitable in nature and blamed India for water problems on Pakistan's soil. The facts state otherwise. The Pakistan Army's rhetoric against India that has always jeopardised the country's relations with India (the upper riparian) in the past might have lowered but the militant networks operating in Pakistan are now adding fire to fuel. For example, Hafiz Sayeed, allegedly involved in the 2008 Mumbai terror attack, openly accused India of 'water terrorism'.Finally, the Indus Waters Treaty needs to be amended to take environmental change into consideration; the focus needs to shift to Article VII that is entitled "Future Cooperation" that emphasises setting up of new hydrological and meteorological observation stations and implementing engineering works including drainage ones. Moreover, groundwater extraction close to the border areas of both countries is overlooked by the IWT (focussing on surface water recharge), an area in which India and Pakistan could cooperate.

The IWT should not be treated as 'division' of waters, as was the case during the Partition in 1947, when land was divided between the two countries. Water is an existential issue and both countries need to go beyond politics to cooperate on river water sharing.

APP - 48

THE GREAT INDIAN WATER FOLLY

Brahma Chellaney, 12 April 2013

The Indus Treaty represents the most generous water-sharing agreement in modern world history, reserving for Pakistan 80.52 per cent of the waters, or 167.2 billion cubic metres annually. No other water pact in the world comes anywhere close to this level of upper-riparian munificence. In fact, the Indus Treaty uniquely allocates entire rivers by drawing a north-south partition line to gift Pakistan the upper three Indus-system rivers, confining India's full sovereignty rights to the much-smaller three rivers to the south.

Yet, this 1960 treaty imposes more fetters on the upper-riparian state than any other water pact in the world. An elaborate series of India-specific curbs obviate any Indian control over the timing or quantum of the trans-boundary flows of the Pakistan-earmarked rivers–the Chenab and the Jhelum (which boast the largest cross-border discharge) and the main Indus stream. Indeed, the treaty remains the only interstate water agreement in the world embodying the doctrine of restricted sovereignty, which seeks to compel an upriver state to defer to the interests of a downstream state.

Pakistan, despite securing a matchless water-sharing arrangement, has repaid India's water largesse with blood by sponsoring acts of grisly terrorism here. This treaty of indefinite duration may stand out as a major folly bequeathed to future Indian generations by the Nehruvian era, yet no Indian government has ever sought to link water flows with an end to terrorism. However, the same question must haunt the Pakistani generals as Lady Macbeth in William Shakespeare's Macbeth: "Will all great Neptune's ocean wash this blood clean from my hand?"

Unfortunately for India, its already-limited sovereignty over the upper rivers is now being further crimped by a sweeping new principle defined for all future projects by the recent international arbitration award on the small Kishenganga project. The treaty permits India to build only run-of-the-river plants–a type that generates hydro-power without a reservoir by using a river's natural flow velocity and elevation drop. Because of very limited water storage, such plants experience fluctuations in power output due to seasonal flow changes, making them less cost-effective than the larger, storage-centred plants.

The arbitration award represents a triumph of Pakistan's efforts to reinterpret the treaty's terms more narrowly so as to remove whatever leeway India may have, and make the Indus regime even more lopsided. The award imposes a condition on spillway configuration that would seriously undermine the run-of-the-river plants' commercial viability by potentially allowing them to silt up, as happened with India's Salal plant in the 1980s due to design changes carried out at Pakistan's insistence. By precluding effective silt control through draw down sluicing and flushing, the award flies in the face of the common international practice to build gated spillways. Indeed, the arbiters have attempted to override–without any legal power–an international neutral expert's 2007 decision in the earlier Baglihar case that such spillway outlets were consistent with the treaty's provisions.

International arbitration–with the arbiters and high-priced lawyers collecting millions of dollars in fees from the parties–often functions on the lowest common denominator. In the Kishenganga case, the panel, while upholding the legality of the Indian project, has tilted in Pakistan's favour on the key design issue. And in an effort to further milk the two parties, the arbiters have extended the lengthy proceedings since 2010 to at least until this year-end, when they 'hope' to give their 'final award' on another issue that they have contrived–the minimum flow of water India would be required to release for Pakistan in the Kishenganga stream.

Pakistan's motive is clear: To deny the limited benefits the treaty grants Jammu and Kashmir by objecting and seeking to stall the modest-size projects that New Delhi has belatedly sought to initiate there to allay popular resentment over crippling power shortages. This motive springs from the Pakistani military's continuing strategy to foment discontent and violence there. The arbiters have unwittingly played into Pakistan's hands by going beyond the Indus Treaty's provisions on a crucial issue and seeking to effectively arm Islamabad with a veto on any Indian project's viability.

India must blame itself for reaping the bitter fruits of a remarkable lack of strategy. It concluded the treaty, as its chief negotiator admitted, without any long-term assessment. Despite a widening demand-supply water gap in its own Indus basin, India has yet to exercise some key treaty-sanctioned rights (such as on storage) but allowed Pakistan to drag it before international proceedings. How much longer can a parched but generous India remain visionless?

APP – 49

THE NEWS (PAKISTASN)

Muhammad Saleh Zaafir, 24 July 2013

Pakistan has already objected to this dam, which will be three times larger than the Baglihar Hydropower Dam. Mirza Asif Baig, Commissioner of Pakistan Commission of Indus Water, confirmed that India had planned to construct the Ratle Hydropower project on the Chenab and Pakistan's side had objected to the project saying it was a sheer violation of the provisions of the Indus Waters Treaty 1960.

"We have come up with strong objections to the design of the said project in a meeting with India at the Permanent Commission of Indus Waters (PCIW) level," Baig said and vowed that in the future meeting at the PCIW level, he would continue to oppose the said project, as its design violated the Indus Waters Treaty.

Senior Pakistani lawyer Ms Shumaila Mehmood, in the case of Kishenganga Hydropower project, said though she was aware of the development but it was the PCIW which dealt with the projects constructed by India on Pakistani rivers at earlier stages.

India has already carved out a plan to generate 32,000MWs of electricity on Pakistani rivers and will be having the capacity to regulate the water flows that are destined to reach Pakistan. So far India has built Dalhasti hydropower project of 330MWs, Baglihar of 450MWs and now it has started a new project named Ratle Hydropower project.

On the Neelum River that joins the Jehlum River in Pakistan, India has already completed Uri-1, Uri-II Hydropower project and is also close to completing the Kishenganga Hydropower project. So much so, it has also built two hydropower projects on the Indus River that include Nimmo Bazgo and Chattak hydropower project.

Sonia Gandhi, along with Prime Minister Manmohan Singh, laid the foundation stone of the 850MWs Hydro Electric Project on the Chenab River in the Kishtwar Tehsil of Doda district of the Indian-Held-Kashmir just a few days ago.

This is the first time that both leaders have jointly laid the foundation stone. The electricity to be produced from the project will be injected into the national grid of India that will then be sold to Pakistan.

Former Wapda chairman Shamsul Mulk said that Pakistan needs to develop water uses in its all rivers by building water reservoirs to prevent India from constructing the hydropower project. "Once Pakistan develops its water uses, then it can argue at any international court that India cannot build its projects by injuring committed flows of Pakistan."

According to documents available with The News, the Ratle project envisages harnessing the hydropower potential of the river from EL 1000m to EL 887m. This is a concrete gravity dam at a height of 170m, will be built across the river just downstream of the Ratle village and an underground power house with an installed capacity of 4X140 MWs is proposed near Juddi village, both in Doda district. The main project will generate 2,483.37 Million Units of Electricity at the rate of Indian Rupee of only 1.22 per KWh.

Meanwhile, in a letter addressed to the Prime Minister of Pakistan, Abbasi requested to demand EIA (environment impact assessment) report of Ratle Hydroelectric power project. As the land proposed for this project is mostly thick conifer forests, deforestation will have a terrible impact on the river water yield in the future and the victim will be only the lower riparian) i.e. Pakistan.

APP – 50

THE EXPRESS TRIBUNE (PAKISTAN)

26 October 2013

Federal Minister for Water and Power Khawaja Asif said Pakistan could face severe consequences of water scarcity in the coming few years and an Ethiopia-like situation may occur here due to the water blocked by India.

Addressing a press conference on Friday, Asif said the Indus Waters Treaty- was not in favour of Pakistan. The government would decide whether it needs to be reviewed or not.

"The water issue has become a matter of life and death for us and we will have to face a severe shortage in the coming 10 to 15 years", he said, adding that previous governments made wrong decisions causing water crisis and today the country is paying the price.

The minister said that India was blocking water and constructing dams on Pakistani rivers. He said that neighbouring countries should consider requirements of Pakistan before constructing their water reservoirs.

Asif said that to avert any unpleasant situation, the government needs to adopt water conservation methods — it will also have to control its growing population.

Pakistan has concerns regarding the Indus Waters Treaty, as under this treaty, Pakistan will get less water in the coming years. The government is seriously looking to review this treaty, Asif said.

Additional Indus water commissioner Sheraz Memon said that Pakistan had objections over seven projects of India. He said that India was using water from River Indus; therefore, the water level has reduced in the river.

He said that India was constructing 53 power projects and seven dams. It has completed 16 projects on river Chenab while another four are under construction.

Memon said India was constructing 850-megawatt Ratle project and warned that Pakistan will approach the International Court of Arbitration if India did not stop the construction of this project.

APP - 51

THE NEWS

Khalid Mustafa, 21 January 2014

In an alarming development, India plans to build another dam on the Chenab River with the name of 1,380 MW Kirthai hydropower project in Held Kashmir, breaching the 1960 Indus Waters Treaty (IWT).

The new project will not only damage water interests of Pakistan but wilt also inflict a huge blow to the environment of the lower riparian country. In a small stretch of the Chenab river basin, India is building numerous mega hydropower projects and dams to meet its energy demands.

However, in doing so, it is aggravating environmental issues in Pakistan and threatening water security. The most disturbing fact is that Pakistan's authorities cleared the said project during the caretaker regime which hit the water interests of the country which has already been declared water stressed by international initiations. India completed the Kirthai Project Design Document on September 4, 2013, and applied for the carbon credits from the UN for clean energy to be produced from the said project. The upper riparian country can apply for the carbon credits from the UN only when the lower riparian country clears the design of the project and gets satisfied that the said project will not harm its environment.

According to Arshad H Abbasi, eminent water expert associated with the SDPI, the Kirthai Dam is a blatant violation of the Indus Waters Treaty and would submerge the beautiful Paddar Valley and its agricultural land of 900 hectares and thick conifer forest land of 160 hectares. Massive deforestation would have a serious local and trans-boundary environmental impact, while the construction activities would further accelerate the melting process of the glaciers in the Chenab Basin.

The application of India in the UN seeking the carbon credits on Kirthai project shows that some unscrupulous officials during the caretaker regime cleared the project. But the sources said that the environment ministry had cleared the controversial project enabling India to claim the carbon credit.

A source in the ministry of environment insisted that India is close to geting the first installment of carbon credits from the UN. India has claimed the Carbon Credits against 1,335,828 ton of carbon at the initial level. Later, another claim for 3,390,948 ton of carbon will be claimed to make the project more economically viable.

When contacted, Commissioner of Pakistan Commission of Indus Water (PCIW), Mirza Asif Beg said he has been rendering services as the PCIW commissioner for the last one and half years; this project has never been in discussion with his counterpart in India.

Under the Treaty, India is bound to share its design with us 6 months before the construction of the project on Pakistan's rivers. However, he admitted that India can apply for carbon credits from UN agencies after the completion of the Kirthai Project Design Document.

Mr Beg said that the Ministry of Environment is the ministry concerned which clears such projects after assessing that the said project is not detrimental to Pakistan's environment. When contacted, Environment DG Asif Shuja said that his ministry has not cleared the Kirthai project.

However, India can apply for carbon credits from UN, but the validators in UN are bound to seek clearance from Pakistan as the lower riparian country as to whether the said project is harmful for the trans-boundary environment or not. "So far, the validators have not approached the CDM (clean development mechanism) cell in the ministry."

The 1380MW Kirthai Dam (Kirthai I of 390MW and Kirthai II of 990MW) stands as a stark reminder of how Pakistan failed to defend its water and energy rights. Documents available with The News show that the government of Jammu and Kashmir tried to conduct the Environmental Assessment Report in 2009, but without consulting people of the Paddar Valley.

Although the project has serious trans-boundary environmental issues that have yet to be addressed by the Indian authorities, the project even got cleared by the authorities of the lower riparian country — Pakistan.

According to the design document of the controversial project, the dam and powerhouse sites are located in the village Gulabgarh in Paddar Tehsil of Kishtwar District of Jammu and Kashmir, about 315km away from Jammu. It is approachable through a highway up till Batote, and beyond Batote up to Kishtwar. The 80km road from Kishtwar to Gulabgarh is mostly blacktopped. The elevation of the site is around 6,000 feet. The drainage area of the Chenab River up to dam site of Kirthai - I HE Project is 8530sq km, out of which 4608 sq. km are snow-fed and the rest 3922sq km are rain-fed. The basin receives precipitation round the year. During December till May, precipitation is mostly in the form of snow except in May when snowfall is confined to higher altitudes. During July to October, the precipitation is due to monsoon activity. June and November are the months of least precipitation. The mean annual precipitation over the Basin up to Kirthai dam is 750mm.

The Kirthai Dam was perceived in 1986 and detailed geological and other site investigations started in 1989 and completed in March 2005. A detailed project design and drawings were completed in December 2008. "The government of Jammu and Kashmir tried to conduct the Environmental Assessment Report in 2009, but without consulting people of the Paddar Valley. And on top of it, the project has serious trans-boundary environmental issues," the sources said.

As per glacier inventory, almost 359 glaciers spread over 1,414 square kilometres (km^2) in 1962 in the Chenab basin, but they reduced to 1,110 km in 2004, with a 21 percent reduction in the area.

According to a rough estimate, glacier areas have been reduced by 29 percent in 2010. Melting of Glaciers in the Chenab River and a decrease in snow cover area, coupled with massive deforestation, would severely impact the river yield. As a consequence, Pakistan would suffer.

APP - 52

DAMS OVER TROUBLED WATERS FOR PAKISTAN AND INDIA: VIOLATING THE INDUS WATER TREATY

Grant Atkins, 13 March 2014

The water disputes between Pakistan and India are long-standing and an often overlooked aspect of these two countries' ongoing feud. India regularly builds new dams on the Indus River and its tributaries, and Pakistan is appealing to the International Court of Arbitration for recourse over the frequent flooding and crop damage that results. Given that Pakistan's economy is heavily dependent on agriculture and on the Indus irrigation, it comes as no surprise that Pakistan doesn't take these affronts lightly.

The Indus Water Treaty (IWT)

After ten years of negotiations, and with the help of the World Bank, the Indus Water Treaty was signed on September 19, 1960 between India and Pakistan. According to the treaty, the waters of the western rivers (Jhelum, Chenab, and Indus) were awarded to Pakistan (the lower riparian country) while those of the eastern rivers (Ravi, Beas and Sutlej) were awarded to India (the upper riparian country). However, Pakistan was only given 75% of the waters in the Indus basin. Therefore, Pakistan launched the "Indus Basin Replacement Works" a project that involved the building of two major dams, five barrages and eight link canals.

According to the Treaty provisions:

- India is not allowed to establish tanks to store water for later use (storages) on Pakistani waters.

- The extension of irrigation development is restricted to both countries, but India faces stricter limitations.

- The exchange of information regarding river flows is mandatory between both countries regarding the rivers awarded to them. After observing the waters, both countries should report their findings no later than three months after their observation. Also, the annual exchange of information on agricultural use is mandatory.

- The exchange of data on project operation, extent of irrigated agriculture, and other information is mandatory.

- A permanent Indus Commission, consisting of a Commissioner for each country, is provided with the obligation for regular meetings and exchanges of visits between the two nations.

- Conflict-resolution guidelines are provided as an arbitration mechanism in case any conflict cannot be resolved by the Indus Commission or directly between the two governments.

Treaty Violations

Last September, the Ministry of Foreign Affairs informed the National Assembly that India is working on four hydropower projects, totaling a capacity of 1,716 megawatts (MW) on the Jhelum, Chenab and Indus rivers to meet its ever-growing energy demands. The projects include the Ratle Hydroelectric Plant (48MW), Miyar (120MW), Lower Kalnai (48MW) and PakulDul (1,500MW). Pakistan has objected to the construction of these dams in violation of the Treaty and has appealed to the Permanent Indus Commission. As India failed to provide information on the projects at the planning stage, the issue turned into a treaty violation. Other violations from the Indian side included insufficient design criteria in the Baglihar and Kishanganga cases, constructing projects without informing Pakistan in Chutak, and failing to abide by operational provisions in the case of the Baglihar dam.

India builds dams, Pakistan floods

Pakistan accuses India of trying to control its share of water by building dams in violation of the Indus Water Treaty of 1960. Given that the Indian side has violated the Treaty more than 10 times since 1960, Pakistan appears to have ample grounds to object.

Recently, Pakistan raised concerns over the design of the Kishanganga Dam on the Indian side of Kashmir, claiming that it would cause a shortage of water in the Neelum Valley. However, the International Court of Arbitration rejected Pakistan's objections and maintained India's right to divert water from the Kishanganga River to generate power. The disturbing truth is that the Kishanganga Dam allows India to produce nearly 300 MW of power, but it adversely affects the generation capacity of Pakistan's 969 MW Jhelum hydroelectric project by about 13%. Even more disturbing is the fact that Pakistan cannot appeal to any authority after losing the international arbitration over the Kishanganga River. Under the circumstances, it seems like Pakistan is rather pleased with being able to, at least, maintain limited rights over their river waters.

India is in the process of completing 33 new projects on Pakistan's waters, which will have an impact on the availability and timings of water flow into Pakistan. The U.S. Senate Committee on Foreign Relations released a recent report that observes:

"While studies show that no single dam along the waters controlled by the IWT will affect Pakistan's access to water, the cumulative effect of these projects could give India the ability to store enough water to limit the supply to Pakistan at crucial moments in the growing season."

This explains the massive floods that have plagued Pakistan over the previous years, with over 20 million people suffering from the effects according to the United Nations. Evidence holds India responsible for flooding in the Chenab River. According to the Pakistani government:

"India has built dams to secure itself and is releasing water into Pakistan's rivers as a part of its design to devastate Pakistan, using water as a weapon."

Bottom Line

Water wars between Pakistan and India have the potential to get out of hand. India plans to build a new dam on the Chenab River, a hydropower project of 1,380 MW. Pakistan claims that the new project is not only a new violation of the Indus Water Treaty, but it will also damage the environmental stability in the area, alongside all the previous projects that India has built in Pakistan's waters.

Sooner or later, Pakistan will strongly react against India for significantly tampering with the timing and quantity of river water flows. Disputes over water have historically cause more wars than religion, gold and women combined. And this water flow situation has a major adverse effect on Pakistan's agricultural output as well as power generation capacity and this could easily cause flare-ups in the region as things develop.

APP – 53

PAKISTAN'S WATER WOES AND INDIA BASHING

Dr. S. Chandrasekharan, 25 Apr-2014

A month ago, one of the water experts in Pakistan warned that the "most dreaded water scarcity ever" has at last hit the country. The warning came not too soon and the surprise if any is that the warning has come too late.

Unlike India, Pakistan is solely dependent on the Indus Water system and instead of meeting the water shortage, all that the Pakistan leaders at all scientific and political levels were doing was to do "India Bashing" as if India is responsible for the acute water shortage.

Increasing urbanisation, climate change, population explosion, indiscriminate usage of ground water, particularly in Punjab, and wastage of water in agricultural operations have all contributed to the shortage of water. Instead, India is being blamed day in and day out for all the ills relating to water scarcity in Pakistan.

Even one simple fact, that Pakistan, which can store up to 40 percent of its water for leaner days, has a built in capacity of storing only 7 percent of water so far, shows its lackadaisical approach towards water problems and yet India is being described as the villain in stealing the waters of the three western rivers of the Indus under the Indus Water Treaty of 1960!

The Federal Planning Development and Reforms Minister Ahsan Iqbal said on 20th March this year that Pakistan was not getting 10 million acres feet of water, its due share, due to water shortage by India.

Surely the Minister must have been aware of the division of waters of the Indus River System under the Indus Water Treaty of 1960, which envisages the division of the system with the three western rivers, Indus, Jhelum and Chenab, going fully to Pakistan and the three eastern rivers, Sutlej, Ravi and Beas, going over to India for full utilization. For the western rivers, India is allowed to construct run-of-the-river projects for power generation and a limited quantity for agricultural and other purposes. No where in the Pakistan press is there any mention that India is not fully utilizing the western waters allowed to be used for agricultural purposes and used downstream by the agriculturists of Pakistan and instead there is an unanimous uproar that India is "stealing the waters."

The Indus water treaty which has withstood the tests of times, in times of war and near war, never envisaged any division of scarcity or any generous "give and take" of water at times of crises between the two countries. It is not, therefore, clear how the Pakistan Minister could come to the conclusion that Pakistan is entitled to 10 million acres feet of water from India. It is not like the water pacts in other river systems where the waters are equitably shared between the riparian countries both during the surplus and lean seasons. The Indus water treaty is unique and given the relationship between the two countries, then and even now there could have been no better division of the river waters between the two countries India and Pakistan. Hence any call to revise the treaty, as is heard sometimes now, would only create more complications and difficulties in managing and utilising the waters of the system between the two countries. The Minister's statement mentioned in the beginning of this paper was made in a "Water Summit 2014" convened by the Ministry of Planning, Development and Reforms of Pakistan in collaboration with the

Ministry of Water, Ministry of Inter-provincial coordination and Ministry of National Food security and research for formulating the country's first National Water Policy.

It is good that Pakistan has finally woken up to the serious water crisis that was looming large in the last few years. The Minister gave some interesting statistics to highlight the impending crisis. He referred to Pakistan having 5650 cubic metre per person in 1947 and now reduced to 964 cubic metres per person. Pakistan's production per unit of water is said to be one of the lowest in the world!.Perhaps the most important and doable statement he made during the meeting was that the forum that was convened should find ways to make water "an instrument of cooperation instead of one of contention between India and Pakistan." I had in my earlier papers always suggested that the Indus Water Treaty should be implemented both in letter and spirit and that any differences, or call it disputes, should be settled between the two countries bilaterally. This spirit of cooperation has been missing all along. The Indian side has the perception that Pakistan's objections on the projects constructed in India on the western rivers in accordance with the treaty have been mainly to delay the projects and nothing else.

All along, Pakistan has been approaching the Treaty at the technical level with implementation to the letter and not the spirit of the treaty. This has only pushed Pakistan into greater scarcity than was envisaged. Pakistan went for a neutral referee in the case of Baglihar Project and to the ICJ in the case of Kishenganga Project and lost both the cases. Pakistan will be ill advised to go for a Review in the ICJ over the Kishenganga project.In going through the various articles in Pakistani media on the water crisis, the general opinion appears to veer around the view that the Indus Water Treaty should be seen and implemented in both "letter and spirit." This approach should be welcomed.Recently, Dr. Murtaza Mughal, President of PEW (Pakistan Economy Watch) made a strident observation that the "issue of water aggression (of India!) cannot be resolved through enhanced trade or negotiations." Perhaps, this is also in line with Pakistan now dragging its feet on giving India 'the most favoured nation' status in bilateral trade. If this kind of hostile approach is displayed, how can Pakistan expect India to follow the spirit of the Indus Treaty and allow more water for Pakistan at times of scarcity? How can the spirit and not the letter of the treaty be acceptable to India when the issue is also being "franchised" to jehadi groups like LET?

The Forum on the "Water Summit" should have considered these points. It is learnt that many foreign representatives were present in the meeting though none from India appears to have been invited!

There is no alternative to the Indus Water Treaty and one wishes that both sides look at the treaty both in "letter and spirit".

APP – 54

THE EXPRESS TRIBUNE

27 April 2014

The third round of talks between water experts from Pakistan and India hit an impasse on Tuesday when India refused to accept Pakistan's demands to change the design of Kishanganga dam.

An Indian delegation – led by Indus Water Commissioner (India) K Vohra – arrived in Lahore to discuss the controversial water issues between both countries that have remain unresolved for several decades. The delegation will return to India on August 28. Furthermore, it is likely that another round of talks will be held between the two delegations.

During Tuesday's session, Pakistan raised objections to the design of Kishanganga dam and four other projects.

Pakistan's Indus Water Commissioner, Mirza Asif Baig, informed the media that the talks were ineffective as both sides had failed to reach an agreement. He added that after the third round of talks ended on an inconclusive note, a dialogue report has been submitted to the government.

Asif Baig expressed dissatisfaction with the limited degree of progress made during the talks and said he was not sure when this dispute would be resolved.

A final session of talks will be held in September and October. Pakistan, according to Baig, will not allow India to put off the matter any further and a decision would be made in the final session.

After the second round of talks had failed on Monday, water experts from Pakistan had threatened to appeal to the International Court of Justice (ICJ). Baig insists that the ICJ would be in a better position to arbitrate on the issue and broker a deal. However, he is waiting for the final session of talks to end.

APP – 55

INDUS TREATY: A GOOD MODEL OF INDO-PAK CONFLICT RESOLUTION`

The News, 10 May 2014

The Indus Water Treaty between India and Pakistan that regulates the sharing of the river`s waters has provided "a fairly successful model of conflict resolution," a new study here has said.

Chronicling Pakistan's water discourse, the report says water was flagged as one of the foremost security challenges that confront the country, at par with the threat of terrorism.

The study, conducted by Islamabad-based Jinnah Institute, nevertheless says that opinion remains divided on whether the Indus Water Treaty has served to protect Pakistan's interest.

However, it said, "The treaty has provided a fairly successful model of conflict resolution, albeit its inadequacies on environmental flows and climate change may be addressed in a supplementary protocol in future."

It added that political distrust between India and Pakistan inhibits any real cooperation in the Indus Basin.

Speaking at the launch of the report here, Ahmad Alam, a co-author, said that none of the water experts that he spoke to, including the Indus Water Commissioner to an ordinary official, mentioned that India has violated the Indus water treaty. He said they came close to it but never really said it.

However, Alam said that he also came across people who blamed India for stealing water due to which they cannot take a proper bath.

The report said that many respondents also felt that India was entitled to its share of water including the building of dams under the treaty, and the impression that India was "stealing" Pakistan`s share was not based on any real empirical evidence.

It added that rapid scale of upstream construction had arguably impacted cumulative flows, and some responses flagged the "unverifiable" flow data provided by India as a source of concern.

APP - 56

INDIA ACCUSED OF VIOLATING INDUS WATER TREATY

25 August 2014

LAHORE: Pakistan expressed serious concerns on Sunday over construction of Kishanganga Dam and termed it a clear violation by India of the Indus Water Treaty (IWT).

It also said that four other proposed dams on the Chenab would be in violation of the treaty.

According to officials, the objections were raised by the Pakistani IWT commissioner during the first round of a meeting with his Indian counterpart who had arrived here to discuss disputes between the two countries.

Pakistani authorities raised objections to the diversion of Chenab water by India by constructing hydropower projects, including the 690MW Ratli Dam, 1,000MW Pikkal Dam, 1,190MW Karthai Dam and 600MW Kero Dam, and said this was a violation of the treaty, the officials said.

"Pakistan has also raised objections over design of the Kishanganga Dam that may reduce the required water discharges to Pakistan. And it will be a clear violation of the IWT," an official said.

He said the authorities had urged Indian IWT officials to change the dam's design. The officials from the two countries would discuss all issues in detail during the next round in order to resolve them amicably, he said.

APP – 57

KISHANGANGA DAM TO AFFECT ECOSYSTEM

Tariq Naqash, 28 August 2014

Apart from adverse impact to be caused by India's Kishanganga dam project on Pakistan's irrigation system and energy sector schemes, conservationists are worried about its devastating effects on biodiversity and ecosystem in Neelum Valley.

"The volume of water in the part of the river on the Indian-held side is 10 times higher than that in Azad Jammu and Kashmir territory. Therefore, its diversion will wreak havoc on the environment of the valley," said Sardar Javaid Ayub, the head of the AJK wildlife and fisheries department, on Wednesday. The problem would aggravate during winter, he added.

Mr Ayub spoke to Dawn a day after India agreed to re-examine objections raised by Pakistan over the design of Kishanganga dam on the concluding day of talks held in Lahore. The Indian team pledged to resume negotiation after two months, with a reply to the Pakistani objections.

He said that temperatures in the upper reaches of the river fell to sub-zero in winter and in case of diversion, a 20-25km stretch of the river would be frozen and all aquatic life, micro and macro organisms would become extinct.

Brown trout, a species of economic importance, and Triplophysa Kashmiriensis, another important fish, are found in the river. "When the water is frozen or regularly drawn away, it will affect the side channels serving as breeding and nursing grounds for the fish. Following reduced water flow, both varieties will be wiped out, something not just local but also of global concern," he said.

Mr. Ayub said that the diversion would also cause a devastating effect on riparian vegetation, which was also a vital area of concern for conservationists.

The Musk Deer National Park was located in the upper area of Neelum Valley and the threatened species chiefly fed on birches and shrubs growing along the banks of the river, he said.

In addition to protecting the water, riparian vegetation also provides several benefits to wildlife, such as absorption of polluted runoff.

The official said that wildlife restoration efforts depended on the presence of a healthy terrestrial ecosystem surrounding the upper part of the river.

He expressed the fear that an area of 25-30 kilometres in length and two metres in width on both sides of the river would be irreversibly affected in case of withdrawal of water, causing an adverse impact on livelihood resources of local communities and wild flora and fauna. The loss of significant amounts of plants and other green species would lead to soil erosion and a generally unstable land base, he added.

He said wild flowers blossoming in Neelum Valley promoted pollination because riparian vegetation was abode of pollinating insects. The decreased flow of water would cause decline in pollination and pollinators, subsequently affecting crops in the area.

Neelum Valley was also home to some important herbs and ferns and many water-loving trees, he said. With the change in watercourse, many medicinal plants will be eradicated.

He said that multilateral environmental laws – such as the UN Convention on Biological Diversity, Kyoto Protocol to United Nations Framework Convention on Climate Change and Ramsar Convention on Wetlands – called for preserving biodiversity and ecosystem and equitable sharing of benefits from genetic resources. "Being a signatory to the treaties and conventions, India should honour the obligations stipulated therein."

APP - 58

INDUS WATER TALKS: PAKISTAN TO SEEK ICJ INTERVENTION IF TALKS FAIL

The Express Tribune, (Pakistan) August 26, 2014

The second round of dialogue between water experts from Pakistan and India ended on a fruitless note as India refused to change the designs of its Kishanganga Dam.

Pakistan's Indus Water Commissioner, Mirza Asif Baig, said that they are currently in talks with their Indian counterparts over this issue. However, if India continues to adopt a rigid position, Pakistan would have to request the International Court of Justice (ICJ) to intervene and broker a settlement.

A 10-member Indian delegation from the Indus Water Commission in India is on a three-day visit to Lahore to discuss the prolonged water issues between the two countries.

"Our objections over the design on Kishanganga dam are logical and we have also raised serious doubts on Kishanganga project at Neelum distributory point on River Jhelum and four other points on River Chenab," Baig said. He added that the Indus Water Commission is trying its best to persuade the Indian team to accept its objections in light of the Indus Water Treaty (IWT) ratified in 1960.

Under the provision of the IWT, the western rivers – Indus, Jhelum and Chenab – were allocated to Pakistan and the eastern rivers – Sutlej, Beas and Ravi – were given to India. But only India was allowed to use the rivers to generate hydropower.

According to Baig, the second day of the meetings with the Indian team remained largely ineffective. On the contrary, both sides simply put forward their own proposals, justifications and feedback on the designs for the hydro-power project.

The talks will resume on Tuesday (today).

However, Baig insisted that Pakistan cannot wait for such a long period of time to resolve the issues through, what appear to be, a series of inconclusive dialogues.

"If these talks do not have the desired effect, we will ask the government to request ICJ to resolve the matter. We are willing to complete all the requisite procedures through our ministries just to ensure that the matter is finally dealt with," he said.

Pakistan's stance on the Indian projects was both clear and logical and authorities would try to prove this in the ICJ, he said.

APP – 59

INDIA AGREES TO RE-EXAMINE OBJECTIONS TO KISHANGANGA DAM DESIGN

Khalid Hasnain, Dawn 27 August 2014

India has agreed to re-examine Pakistan's objections over designs of Kishanganga dam and four other hydroelectric power projects on Jhelum and Chenab rivers.

During the third and concluding day of talks held here on Tuesday, a 10-member Indian team headed by the Commissioner of Indus Water Commission pledged to resume talks after two months by submitting a detailed reply/justification to the objections raised by the Pakistani Commissioner on Indus Water Commission (IWC).

"Though there is not a major breakthrough during the three-day talks, we have succeeded in explaining our objections with certain logic before the Indian team. And the team has agreed to re-examine and reply all our objections and logic deeply and restart talks again with us after two months," Pakistan's Commissioner on Indus Water Commission Mirza Asif Baig told Dawn.

"Actually some of their logics are not well-founded, which are not required to be even re-examined. And some of their justifications are required to be re-examined by us. So we will review these surely," he maintained.

While explaining the objections and justifications, the commissioner said that the Pakistani team had expressed serious concerns over the designs of Kishanganga and four other dams.

"We have objected to the spillways with deep spilling of the Kishanganga dam at the Jhelum River (Neelum distributary) and other dams at the Chenab River, as India cannot do this under the Indus Water Treaty. Similarly, we have asked them to avoid excessive water pondage and intake. Likewise, there are some other objections we have raised on the dams' designs/drawings," he explained.

Mirza Asif was of the view that if designs of these dams are not changed, India would get complete control on the western parts of the rivers which would reduce their flow. "It can destroy our agriculture sector and other sorts of water needs in the country."

He said members of the Pakistani team had categorically told their Indian counterparts that Pakistan wanted practical, acceptable, meaningful and viable conclusion of the talks after two months. "We have also told them that we will have no option but to approach the International Court of Justice (ICJ) for arbitration in case India does not change designs of its dams," he added.

APP - 60

PAKISTAN ACCUSES INDIA OF VIOLATING INDUS WATER TREATY AGREEMENT

Hindustan Times, 25 September 2014

Pakistan military's official monthly magazine has accused India of indulging in water offensive by violating Indus Water Treaty Agreement. Even as it emphasized on peaceful relations, the editor's note in the magazine 'Hilal' said the situation has the potential to ignite tensions.

"The natural flow of water is essential for Pakistan's agricultural economy. Any willful obstruction of water thereof has the potential to ignite tensions between the two states.

"Pakistan had always looked for peaceful relations with India and it is keen to resolve all outstanding issues. It is now up to India to come forward and take concrete steps to maintain peace in South Asia," the note said.

The magazine, published by the military's Inter Services Public Relations, notes that after "literally" converting river Sutlej and Ravi into "sewers", India is now eyeing other water resources of Pakistani rivers.

The editorial, titled 'Games They Play? India's Water Infringement', claims that India is in the process of building as many as 67 dams on Pakistani rivers in violation of Indus Water Treaty (IWT).

"India has built and is in process to construct big and small dams, hydropower projects and reservoirs, numbering as many as 67, on the principal rivers - Indus, Jehlum and Chenab – that were allotted to Pakistan under the IWT," it says.

It adds, "These projects include Kishanganga dam, Tulbul dam (Wullar barrage) and Uri-II hydroelectric plan on River Jhelum; Baglihar, Salal and Bursar dams on River Chinab; and Kargil dam, Nimmo Bazgo hydroelectric project on River Indus and Chutak hydroelectric plant on a tributary of Indus."

The military's September 2013 publication, Defence Day special, says India's building of dams on Pakistani rivers could cause major water shortages in Pakistan in future.

It says concerns are now growing in Pakistan that India is pursuing policies to strangulate Pakistan and is trying to exercise control over the water flows in Pakistan's rivers.

It adds, "The IWT also does not allow India to obstruct the flow of the run of the rivers by storing or diverting the water but she is doing so which is a clear violation of the treaty, and India must refrain from any such practice."

However, Pakistan's concerns don't hold water. The treaty allocates the water of the three western rivers to Pakistan, but allows India to tap the considerable hydropower potential of the Chenab and Jhelum before the rivers enter Pakistan. The treaty also allowed India to create storage on the western rivers of 3.6 MAF (million acre foot). It does not require India to deliver any assured quantities of water to Pakistan. Instead, it requires India to let flow to Pakistan the water available in these rivers, excluding the limited use permitted to India by the treaty. Also, there is a limit to the number of run-of-the-river hydropower projects India can build.

Future cooperation

Clearly, Pakistan's complaints about India building dams and drawing water out of the western rivers beyond authorisation arise out of ignorance about nuances of the treaty The questions that arise are: "What is the future of this treaty?" and "Is there a need to revisit it?" Unfortunately, there is no clause to withdraw from it unilaterally. Various sane voices from both sides have suggested that India and Pakistan should realise the strategic importance of water as an economic resource.

Fortunately, a mechanism exists under provisions of the treaty to carry out consultations and research to remove misconceptions and anxieties. Article VII of the treaty mentions 'Future cooperation' which, inter alia, discusses efforts in the future to jointly optimise the potential of the Indus river system. Very little attention has been paid to this aspect so far. Therefore, a simple solution is to form a joint study group of experts in consonance with the treaty before the water issue compounds mistrust between India and Pakistan.

APP – 61

INDIA'S WATER AGGRESSION AGAINST PAKISTAN

Sajjad Shaukat, 22 March 2015

In the modern world, there are various forms of bloodless wars like economic wars which amount to aggression. In these terms, besides supporting subversive acts including cross-bordering shelling, India has also stared water aggression against Pakistan.

In March, 2011, while speaking in diplomatic language, Indus Water Commissioner of India G. Ranganathan had refused by stating, "Indian decision to build dams on rivers has led to water shortage in Pakistan." While rejecting Islamabad's concerns regarding water-theft by New Delhi including violation of the Indus Water Treaty, he assured his counterpart, Indus Water Commissioner of Pakistan, Syed Jamaat Ali Shah, that all issues, relating to water between Pakistan and India, would be resolved through dialogue.

In international politics of today, deeds, not words, matter, so ground realties are quite different as to what G. Ranganathan indicated in his statement. In fact, India has been continuing water aggression against Pakistan.

Besides other permanent issues and especially the thorny dispute of Kashmir which has always been used by India to malign and pressurize Pakistan, water (of rivers) has become a matter of life and death for every Pakistani, as New Delhi has been employing it as a tool of terrorism to blackmail Pakistan.

In this regard, Indian decision to construct two hydro-electric projects on River Neelam, which is called Kishanganga in Indian dialect, is a new violation of the Indus Basin Water Treaty of 1960. The World Bank, itself, is the mediator and signatory for the treaty. After the partition, owing to war-like situation, New Delhi deliberately stopped the flow of Pakistan's rivers which originate from the Indian-held Kashmir. Even at that time, Indian rulers had used water as a tool of aggression against Pakistan. However, due to Indian illogical stand, Islamabad sought the help of international arbitration. The Indus Basin Treaty allocates waters of three western rivers of Indus, Jhelum and Chenab to Pakistan, while India has rights over eastern rivers of Ravi, Sutlej and Beas.

Since the settlement of the dispute, India has always violated the treaty intermittently to create economic crises in Pakistan. In 1984 a controversy arose between the two neighbouring states after India began construction of the Wullar Barrage on river Jhelum in the occupied Kashmir in violation of the Indus Basin Water Treaty.

In the past, the issue of Wullar Barrage has also been discussed in various rounds of talks, being held under the composite dialogue process between the two rivals, but Indian intransigence has continued. In the mid 1990s India started another violation by constructing the Baglihar dam on the Chenab river.

In 2005, Pakistan had again sought the World Bank's help to stop construction of the Baglihar dam. Although WB allowed India to go ahead with the project after a few modifications, yet it did not permit the interruption of the agreed quota of water flow to Pakistan.

In 2008, India suddenly reduced water flow of the Chenab river to give a greater setback to our autumnal crops. Islamabad on September 17, 2008 threatened to seek the World Bank's intervention on the plea that New Delhi had not responded to its repeated complaints on the issue appropriately. Pakistan's Commissioner to the treaty, Syed Jamaat Ali Shah had also remarked that the shortage of water in the Chenab river occurred due to the filling up of the Baglihar dam. Despite repeated pleas from Islamabad, India did nothing to address the problem.

Nevertheless, apart from intermittent violations of the Indus Water Treaty, New Delhi, in fact, has been using water as an instrument to pressurize Islamabad with a view to getting leverage in the Pak-India dialogue especially regarding Indian-held Kashmir where a new phase of protest against the Indian illegitimate occupation has accelerated. In this respect, the then Foreign Minister, Shah Mahmood Qureshi, while talking in connection with the revival of Pak-India dialogue, had said on February 8, 2010 that Pakistan's case on Kashmir and water was based on truth, and the government would fight it with full strength.

India's shrewd diplomacy of water war could also be judged from some other developments. Online reports suggest that New Delhi has secretly offered technical assistance to the Afghan government in order to construct a dam over Kabul River which is a main water contributor to Indus River.

By applying such diplomacy against Pakistan, New Delhi intends to fulfill a number of nefarious designs. India wants to keep its control on Kashmir which is located in the Indus River basin area, and which contributes to the flow of all major rivers, entering Pakistan. It is determined to bring about political, economic and social problems of grave nature in Pakistan.

In this context, China Daily News Group wrote in 2005: "Another added complication is that in building a dam upstream of Pakistan, India will possess the ability to flood or starve Pakistan at will. This ability was witnessed in July of 2004 when India, without warning, released water into the Chenab river, flooding large portions of Pakistan. The history of conflict between these two nations makes it possible for New Delhi to use nature as a real weapon against Islamabad."

According to an estimate, unlike India, Pakistan is highly dependent on agriculture, which in turn is dependent on water. Of the 79.6 million hectares of land that make up pakistan, 20 million are available for agriculture. Of those 20 million hectares, 16 million are dependent on irrigation. So, almost 80% of Pakistan's agriculture is dependent on irrigation.

It is notable that many of Pakistan's industries are agro-based such as the textiles industry. Besides, 80% of Pakistan's food needs are fulfilled domestically. Thus an interruption of water supply would have broad-ranging effects. For example, when the country suffered a drought from 1998 to 2001, there were violent riots in Karachi.

It is mentionable that half of Pakistan's energy comes from hydroelectricity, and at present, our country has been facing a severe crisis of loadshedding which is the result of power-shortage in the country. During the recent past summers, people in a number of cities like Karachi, Lahore, Multan, Faisalabad etc. lodged violent protests against loadshedding, culminating into loss of property and life.

It is of particular attention that Pakistan's Federal Minister for Water and Power Khawaja Asif warned on February 10, 2015 that although the electricity shortage in the country would be overcome within two to three years, the scarcity of water is another issue looming in the country.

While Pakistan has already been facing multiple challenges of grave nature coupled with a perennial phenomenon of terrorism like suicide attacks, bomb blasts, targetted killings etc., committed by the militants who are being backed by Indian secret agency, RAW, New Delhi also uses water as a tool by increasing its scarcity, making life too often miserable for Pakistanis with the ultimate aim of creating poverty which could produce more terrorism in turn. And, India is likely to deepen differences among Pakistan's provinces over various issues which are directly or indirectly related to water.

So, still, by employing water as an instrument of aggression, Indians continue to intensify political unrest, economic instability and social strife in Pakistan.

Surprisingly, in 2010, India started resumption of talks with Pakistan, paying a greater attention on terrorism instead of equally addressing all the issues of the composite dialogue.

Nonetheless, Islamabad must include water as a major focus of agenda in the future dialogue; otherwise, India is likely to continue its water aggression against Pakistan.

Sajjad Shaukat writes on international affairs and is author of the book: US vs Islamic Militants, Invisible Balance of Power: Dangerous Shift in International Relations.

APP – 62

PAKISTAN ASKS INDIA TO HONOUR INDUS WATERS TREATY

March 9, 2015

Pakistan today asked India to honour the historic Indus Waters Treaty, warning that it will contest at an appropriate forum if India "encroaches" upon its water rights.

"We will contest our case at an appropriate forum if India encroaches upon our water rights," Minister for Water and Power Khawaja Asif said.

Addressing a function in Lahore, Asif warned that Pakistan will face a severe drought in the next few years and wants to resolve water-related issues with India.

The Indus Waters Treaty was signed in 1960 with the support of the World Bank to settle thorny water issues, and is one of the most durable agreements between the two sides.

But with the passage of time, new issues related to sharing of water have cropped up between the two neighbours.

Pakistan earlier raised concerns over some of India's power projects in Jammu and Kashmir, saying these were being done to stop the flow of water. India rejects the allegations.

The Indus Waters Treaty stipulated that the water flow from three Western rivers – Indus, Jhelum and Chenab – will be for the exclusive use of Pakistan, while the three eastern rivers – Ravi, Sutlej and Beas – will be for India's use.

Asif said the government would resolve the issue of electricity shortage in Pakistan within the next three years but at the moment, the country was heading towards a serious water shortage, Dawn reported.

The federal minister said that construction of dams was a "matter of life and death now." He said the country faces devastating floods due to a lack of water storage facilities.

APP - 63

WATER AND POWER MINISTRY NON-SERIOUS OVER LOOMING INDIAN WATER AGGRESSION

Zeeshan Javaid, March 13, 2015

Islamabad-The non-serious attitude of one of the most important cabinet organs, Ministry of water and Power, paved the way for Indian water aggression, who is seeking full control on the western rivers of Indian Chenab in violation of Indus Water Treaty 1960.

Gearing up the water aggression against Pakistan, an Indian parliamentarian introduced a piece of legislation aimed to transfer the control of all inter-state rivers including the western rivers (Jhelum, Chenab) to central India.

The document available with "Pakistan Observer" revealed that an Indian parliamentarian Ramen Deka laid a Indian Nationalization of Inter-State River Bill, 2013] in lower house of Indian parliament (Lok Sabha), which was drafted in December 2012 seeking the nationalization of all inter-state rivers, which could restrict the rights of Pakistan on western rivers of the Indus basin allocated to Pakistan under the Indus Waters Treaty 1960.

It was also disclosed that initial expenditure would be Indian Rs. 5 billion.

Ramen Deka, the renowned politician, who represents India's largest political force, Bhartiya Janta Party (BJP) is a parliamentarian for Lok Sabha with 486,357 votes in Indian general elections 2014. He had held the same post when Mr. Manmohan Sigh was the Prime Minister of India.

Already Pakistan and India both have knocked the door of Permanent Court of Arbitration (PCA) twice over two different controversial issues including 900MW Baghliar hydropower project on the river Chenab and 330MW Kishan G Hydropower Project (KGHP) on river Jhelum; however, Indian government has drafted a plan to construct 150 run-of-the-river hydropower power plants on western rivers of which 47 projects are above the generation capacity of 50MW.

Interestingly, nobody in water and power ministry and other stake holders, including Pakistani Indus Water Commission and water and Power Development Authority (WAPDA) and the vacant office of advisor to Prime Minister for water and resources, which is no more now after the natural demise of former democratic rule, care about such a sensitive issue.

However a senior official of agricultural department privy to the development in the river system of Pakistan informed on condition not to be named, that once Indian parliament enacted the said bill as law, India would be able to have complete control over the river system, either its eastern rivers including Ravi, Satluj and Bias or the western rivers.

A list compiled by Pakistan Indus Water Commissioner's (PIWC) office revealed that India had constructed 4? projects and 12 hydropower plants were under construction, in addition to the 155 projects planned on the Western rivers.

India has completed the construction of 6 hydropower plants on River Chenab, including 450-MW Baglihar 1 and MW a Salal 2. Construction on two projects was under way, including the 450-MW Baglihar 2 and 15MW Ranja-Ala-C

Furthermore, India has planned an additional 56 hydropower projects on River Chenab, including some big project the1200-MW Sawalkot (1 and 2), 715-MW Seli, 1000-MW Pakaldul (1 and 2), 1020-MW Bursar (1 and 2), (690-MW 1 and2) and 600-MWKiru.

India has completed 15 projects on River Jhelum, including the 480-MW Uri-1,105-MW on Lower Jhelum and 10!

Six projects are under construction, including the 240-MW Uri 2 and 330-MW Kishanganga. India also plans to build projects on River Jhelum, including a few big projects such as the 165MW Sonamarg Storage.

APP - 64

'THE INDUS COMMISSION HAS NOT PLAYED AN EFFECTIVE ROLE'

Shafqat Kakakhel

The Indus Waters Treaty signed between India and Pakistan in 1960 did not envisage disputes and concerns arising in subsequent years. These include climate changes and groundwater management that were not mentioned when the treaty was being formulated. These thoughts were articulated by former deputy executive director of the United Nations Environment Programme Shafqat Kakakhel and former managing director of Wapda Khalid Mohtadullah. They were delivering a talk on 'The Indus Waters Treaty 1960: Issues and Concerns' at the Pakistan Institute of International Affairs on Friday.

Before delving into the effectiveness of the treaty and challenges in its implementation, Mr Kakakhel gave a comprehensive background of the treaty to which Mr Mohtadullah added his valuable input.

The treaty, consisting of around eight pages, had four main features, said Mr Kakakhel. "The first pertains to the division of the Indus and its five major tributaries. All the waters of the three eastern rivers — the Sutlej, Beas and Ravi — shall be available to India and Pakistan shall receive for unrestricted use all those waters of the western rivers (the Indus, Jhelum, and Chenab) which India is under obligation to let flow." He emphasised that this was not a water-sharing agreement but a water-division agreement.

The second feature, he said, was about arrangements for compensation to Pakistan for the loss of eastern rivers.

Financing was to be arranged for the building of the "replacement works" i.e. Tarbela Dam on the Indus and Mangla on the Jhelum and eight link canals which were needed to store and transport water from the western rivers to the areas which had up till now been irrigated from the eastern rivers assigned to India under the treaty. "The financing arrangements were a decisive factor in the success of the negotiations. Pakistan would not have agreed to the treaty of the three eastern rivers in the absence of funds for the construction of the dams and link canals," he said.

Other features, he explained, pertained to the establishing of an Indus Commission, led by renowned engineers, appointed by each country and the mechanism for resolving issues and disputes which were to be resolved by the commission and if they were of a technical nature then it could be referred to a neutral expert. "And if the neutral expert is unable to resolve the matter then both parties can take it to the court of arbitration," he added.

Discussing the subject in hand, he highlighted some of the key concerns and issues of the treaty. "The Indus Commission hasn't played an effective role as envisaged in the treaty. All disputes have been settled by the courts of arbitration which has been highly expensive for us," said Mr Kakakhel.

Also, there were problems with the competence of those heading the commission and its staff, he said. "There is a need to strengthen the capacity of the commission," he added.

Omissions in the treaty

When the treaty was being drafted, there were issues that were not understood and hence were not included in it. For instance, Mr Kakakhel said, it was silent on proper management of groundwater. Then it is also quiet on the issue of the quality of water being affected by pollution due to toxic industrial waste. "It does not provide for watershed management in respect of rivers whose catchment areas are located across the border. Even though the treaty permits India to use the waters of the western rivers for irrigation and hydropower projects, it does not call for an examination of the cumulative effects of a cascade of such projects."

Mr Mohtadullah later addressed the issue of groundwater in his lecture. "Pakistan's agriculture is dependent on surface and groundwater. The rate at which groundwater is depleting is alarming. It is also being polluted by saline water thus compromising the quality of groundwater."

About the treaty, he added that interpretation of the clauses led to later disputes. "I was associated with the treaty formulation as a junior officer at the time and I remember the use of hydropower was the most contentious." According to him, the treaty gave exclusive rights to India of three eastern rivers and no bar on building of hydroelectric projects on the western rivers.

Another crucial issue that was not addressed by the treaty was the impact of climate change, Mr Kakakhel said. "This include the rapid melting and recession of the Hindukush-Himalayan glaciers, disruption in monsoon pattern that replenished river flows and aquifers, increase in the number, duration, and severity of floods or droughts as well as higher temperature, and accelerated pollution of freshwater."

All these factors had also led to the net reduction in the availability of water, he said.

Mr Kakakhel thought the informal Track-II dialogue whose basis is cooperation has led to a realisation on the Indian side that these issues need to be studied. "Earlier, the Indians would argue that since such issues are not mentioned in the treaty and they are using the waters for non-consumptive purpose hence, they were unwilling to discuss those issues."

He recommended a joint monitoring of the glaciers and joint scientific studies on their change patterns as well as the pattern of the monsoons, and cooperation in predicting and coping with floods and droughts and other extreme events.

He also recommended getting in touch with third sources such as Nasa scientists, Institute of Oceanography, and Chinese experts having scientific competence on such issues who would be neutral in their stance when giving their suggestions and recommendations.

APP - 65

WATER SOLUTIONS

Javed Majid, The News (Pakistan) 22 March 2015

Pakistan has a fast growing population and uptil now no remarkable effort has been made to control this growth which is one of the highest in the world. It is estimated that Pakistan's population shall stabilise around 350 million people by the year 2035-40. Punjab alone shall have as many people living in it by 2035 as there were in Pakistan in 2005 ie 170 million people.

At present, Pakistan's wheat needs are about 20 million tons per year calculated at 120-kg per person per year and our production meets our needs as well as that of Afghanistan. However, wheat needs are expected to grow to 40 million tons when our population stabilises at 35 to 40 million people. This figure is half of what Pakistan produces today!

The basic ingredient for agriculture is water. An analysis of the water situation is important if Pakistan is to double its wheat production.

Pakistan's source of water is snow/glacier melt and rainfall. The snow melts early, that is by April, while the glaciers start melting by June. The summer monsoon starts by July 15 and ends by September 30.

The River Indus, which is our focus, flows at about 25,000 to 30,000 cusecs during the winter and starts increasing its flows from April when the River Kabul adds about 30,000 cusecs. By June, when the glaciers start melting, the River Indus starts flowing at about 150,000 to 250,000 cusecs. The Indus flows are dependent on the temperatures in the Northern Areas. Temperatures below 30°C decrease the melting while temperatures above 35°C increase the melting of the glaciers.

Rainfall has not been computed in these figures as the monsoon's contributions are not predictable. Pakistan lies in a monsoon shadow area. Summer monsoon's generated from the Indian Ocean rain over India before reaching Pakistan and a depleted monsoon reaches Pakistan.

Floods are unpredictable but generally floods occur every 6 to 8 years. The flood waters are generated below Tarbela and therefore cannot be collected. The floods contribution is devastation, silting in the area of the flood and recharging the aquifer.

The provinces of KPK, Balochistan, Sindh and 10 districts of Punjab depend upon the Indus. Their accumulated needs for irrigation are 150,000 cusecs in summer and about 100,000 cusecs in winter. Whenever irrigation supplies fall short of these figures, a hue and cry ensues from the farmers, the provinces and IRSA.

Mention must be made here about the waters of the Rivers Chenab and the Jhelum. Unfortunately there is no location in Pakistan where a dam could be built on the Chenab. Therefore, floods in the Chenab, apart from the 60,000 cusecs diverted into the canals en route, go waste to the sea. On the Jhelum River, water is stored in the Mangla Dam and excess flood waters are wasted to the sea.

The waters of the two rivers, Jhelum and the Chenab, serve 26 districts of Punjab as per the Indus Basin Treaty. The water of these rivers cannot be used in Southern Punjab, Balochistan, or Sindh as the distances are so long that 50 per cent of the water is lost to percolation and evaporation.

The three rivers of Pakistan provide sufficient water for sustainable agriculture provided that reservoirs are available to store the water generated during the summer months.

Pakistan has three options available to enhance its wheat production from 21 million tons at present to 40 million tons by 2035-40 to meet Pakistan's wheat needs to feed a population of 35 million people.

Pakistan can increase the land under irrigation thereby increasing the productive area. The projects in hand with WAPDA which will bring new areas under irrigation are the Kachi, Rainee and the Greater Thall Canals which together add 3 million acres of irrigated land. These areas will be able to produce 3 million tons of wheat or equivalent crops per season.

Water for these projects is available. However, all these projects are to obtain their irrigation supplies from the River Indus and Tarbela Dam which is silting up and losing its capacity to store water.

There are three issues related to these projects; first, that WAPDA completes them speedily as their completion has been delayed; second, ensure that a new reservoir is made on the River Indus to replace the capacity of Tarbela lost to siltation and; third, the additional requirement of wheat is 20 million tons and these projects combined provide an additional 3 million tons of wheat only.

The second option is to import wheat to meet the deficit. Unfortunately, the world population is also growing and is expected to stabilise at 9 billion as against the present world population of 7 billion.

Thus, world food needs will also grow by 2035. If there is no drastic jump in productivity, Pakistan's wheat needs will either not be met or will be extremely expensive. Pakistan might have to spend as much on the import of wheat as it spends on importing oil.

The third option is to enhance the per acre productivity. Pakistan's average wheat yields per acre are 25 maunds or one ton per acre. In comparison with the world or the Indian Punjab, these yields are extremely poor.

However, the progressive farmer in Pakistan is obtaining yields of 2.2 tons per acre with off the shelf seed, fertilizer and better agriculture practices. The difference is due to the fact that the average farmer does not have the finances and the linkages to access the available technologies and therefore is limited to a ton of production per acre for the last decade.

The most important resource that will help ensure food security is water. Due to Pakistan's peculiar climate, most of the water is generated during a period from May to September. If water generated by the River Indus is not stored, all the area irrigated by canals off taking from the River Indus shall become arid areas during the months of February to May as the flow in the River Indus decreases drastically. In these areas, wheat productivity will drop to half a ton per acre!

The Tarbela Dam was completed in 1976 with a reservoir capacity of 9 MAF. Unfortunately all dams start dying the day they are filled up. River water carries silt with it, which is deposited in the reservoir and slowly but steadily depletes its capacity to store water. The River Indus carries considerable silt in its water during the summer months as its watershed comprises high mountains which have no forests.

The Tarbela reservoir has been silting up at the rate of 1 per cent of its capacity each year. Since Tarbela was completed in 1976, it has lost 38 per cent of its capacity up to now.

As a result of the Mangla and Tarbela dams, farmers prospered, agricultural productivity was enhanced and there was inter-provincial harmony. However, by 1995, the Tarbela reservoir had lost 20 per cent of its capacity; water in the reservoir was depleting by May 15 and shortages were being felt by farmers.

To compound the problems, Pakistan entered into a dry cycle due to the La Nino effect, with water generation falling by 30 to 50 per cent during the period 1998 to 2004. These water shortages had to be shared by the provinces and canal systems were run by turn. The luxury of a lot of water was lost and farmer's resentment became evident.

The dangerous trend of provinces blaming each other and accusations of a province stealing from the other were aired in the media and the TV channels. 2005 saw the end of the dry cycle and a wet cycle started, which is still continuing. Though the Tarbela reservoir has silted up to the extent of 38 per cent by 2014 and water is depleting, by March 1, the wet cycle and the floods have helped farmers with moisture and fresh silt. Wheat production has improved, farmers have been generally satisfied and no provincial squabbles have been visible. Tension however prevails in IRSA as 20 per cent shortages exist which have to be shared between the provinces.

The government plans to construct another reservoir on the River Indus have not borne fruit as yet. Prime Minister Nawaz Sharif made a very serious effort to convince the smaller provinces to agree to the construction of the Kalabagh Dam through the Water Apportionment Accord of 1991. Unfortunately, the chief ministers did not agree.

Another attempt was made by the Musharraf regime which too could not convince the smaller provinces and as a compromise it was decided to construct the Bhasha Dam.

Bhasha is about 300 kms from Islamabad and is approached by the Karakoram Highway. It is sited at the junction of three mountain ranges ie the Himalayas, the Karakoram and the Hindukush. The Bhasha site area is crisscrossed by fault lines and has witnessed Category 4 earthquakes. Additionally, the dam is proposed to be 900 feet high, as a result about 200 kilometres of the highway will have to be reconstructed to stay above the Bhasha lake. A dam at this location will only receive snow and glacier melt as the Northern Areas do not receive the monsoons.

The exact location of the dam site has still not been finalised due to the faultlines. Seven years have passed since the Bhasha Dam was announced but Dam construction has yet to start. Even if the dam were to be started in 2015, the Bhasha dam will be completed in 12 years by WAPDA estimates ie 2027.

Since River Kabul rises in April and the River Indus rises in June, the Indus command will have insufficient water to meet the needs of KPK, Balochistan, Sindh and 10 districts of Punjab for 4 months ie from February to June each year. This will severely affect the standing crops such as sugarcane, orchards, wheat, fodder and vegetables.

Meanwhile 26 districts of Punjab, fed by the Rivers Jhelum and the Chenab, will have sufficient water as Mangla Dam's capacity has been enhanced. The stark comparison of haves and have-nots will be very evident and lead to great resentment amongst the farmers of South, economic loss, poverty, shortfall of wheat and inter-provincial disharmony. The greater the water scarcity the greater will be the inter-provincial resentments.

It is, therefore, extremely important that a dam on the River Indus is started and completed within the next five to seven years. Since the Kalabagh dam is controversial, although the most feasible, it is proposed that the Akhori Dam is initiated. Sited near Hasanabdal, this earth-filled dam will have the capacity to store 6 MAF of water which spills from the Tarbela reservoir. This 6 MAF will be released back into the Indus as required for irrigation of the KPK, Balochistan, Sindh and 10 districts of Punjab.

APP - 66

INDIA NOT RESPONSIBLE FOR WATER SHORTAGE IN PAKISTAN

The Economic Times, 12 July, 2015

India is not responsible for water shortage in Pakistan, a top official here has said while dismissing as baseless reports that India was not observing the bilateral Indus Waters Treaty.

Indus River System Authority (ISRA) Chairman Rao Irshad Ali said that reports in media about India getting more water is nothing but a propaganda.

In a meeting of the Senate Standing Committee on Water and Power chaired by Senator Iqbal Zafar Jhagra in Islamabad, Ali said India was using less than its allocated share under the Indus Waters Treaty (IWT) signed between the two countries.

The IWT is a water-sharing treaty between India and Pakistan, brokered by the World Bank (then the International Bank for Reconstruction and Development). The treaty was signed in Karachi on September 19, 1960 by the then Indian Prime Minister Jawaharlal Nehru and President of Pakistan Ayub Khan.

Ali during the meeting on Thursday dismissed media reports that India was not observing the IWT as baseless and said that India was getting less compared to their allocated share of water, The NewS reported.

Hafiz Saeed, the leader of the militant group, that carried out the 2008 attacks in Mumbai, Lashkar-e-Taiba, regularly claims that Indian "water terrorism" was responsible for the water scarcity in Pakistan.

APP – 67

INDIA FOR RESOLVING RATLE HYDRO PLANT ISSUE WITH PAKISTAN THROUGH TALKS

The Economic Times, 23 August 2015

With Pakistan expressing reservations over the under-construction Ratle Hydroelectric Power Project in Jammu and Kashmir, India has sought resolution of the issue through talks.

The Centre's response came after the Pakistani Government sent a missive to India demanding appointment of a 'neutral expert' under provisions of the Indus Waters Treaty for the 850-MW power project being constructed on the Chenab river, sources in the Union Water Resources Ministry said.

In a communication to the Indus Water Commissioner in India about 20 days ago, the sources said, Pakistan raised certain apprehensions over the project design.Pakistan has raised the issue of setting up of lower spillways for sediment management, which it apprehends could lead to flooding. Pakistan is of the view that higher spillways should be established instead of lower spillways, the sources said.

"In return, we have written to the Pakistan Government 10 days back. In our reply, we have sought to hold talks over the issue," a senior ministry official, who is privy to the development, told PTI here.Noting that the design of Ratle Hydroelectric Power Project has already been shared with Pakistan, the official said that the date for the next Indus Water Commission meeting between the two countries was yet to be decided.

Under the Indus Waters Treaty, India and Pakistan have each created a permanent post of Commissioner for Indus Waters. As per the provisions, the Commissioners may discuss questions arising under the treaty related to settlement of differences and disputes and in the case of non-resolution, take further action for resolution through a neutral expert, negotiators or Court of Arbitration.

Former Prime Minister Manmohan Singh had laid foundation of the power plant on the Chenab river in 2013. The run-of-the-river project, which is the country's first hydroelectric project that was bid out through tariff based international competitive bidding, will cost Rs 5,500 crore.The sources recalled a similar case in the past wherein Pakistan had sought appointment of a 'neutral expert' during the construction of Baglihar hydropower project in Jammu and Kashmir about a decade ago.

Later, the World Bank, which Pakistan had approached for arbitration in the issue, named a Swiss national as a neutral expert to resolve the dam issue.

Pakistan had approached the bank, which is a signatory to the 1960 Indus Waters Treaty between the two countries, for arbitration after talks between India and Pakistan had failed.

The neutral expert delivered Expert Determination on Baglihar Hydroelectric Project in 2007.

APP - 68

INDIA HAS RIGHT TO BUILD WULLAR BARRAGE: INDIAN SECRETARY

Indian secretary Dharwajay Singh said on Thursday that India has the right to build the Wullar Barrage project under all conditions but a change in its structure or design can be discussed if Pakistan agrees. Pakistan-India secretary-level talks on Wullar Barrage/Tulbul Navigational project are being held in Islamabad.

Pakistan's Water and Power secretary Javed Iqbal said that the construction of Wullar Barrage is not acceptable other than the framework of Indus Water Treaty. He also said Pakistan will not accept any project of India which may result in Indian control over the River Jhelum water.

Sources said that Pakistan has firmed up its case to challenge another project being built by India on the Indus River in violation of the 1960 Indus Water Treaty.

However, the Indian secretary said that the barrage is not in violation of the Indus Waters Treaty and will be used only for transportation.

Indian delegation, headed by Secretary Water Resources Dhruv Vijai Singh is in Islamabad from May 12 to 14 to discuss Pakistan's objection to the diversion of Jhelum River into the Wullar barrage and construction of a 439-foot long and 12-metre wide navigational lock at the barrage.

The Pakistani delegation, to be headed by Water and Power Secretary Javed Iqbal, is expected to inform the Indian team about its decision to take up with a neutral expert the building of 45MW Nimoo-Bazgo hydroelectric plant on the main Indus River.

The two countries have so far held 13 rounds of secretary-level talks, including four under the composite dialogue, on the issue lying unresolved for more than 26 years. India started constructing the Wullar barrage in 1985 but had to suspend work in 1987 after objections by Pakistan which moved to seek international court of arbitration or the neutral expert.

APP - 69

REPORT OF THE PERMANENT INDUS COMMISSION

From

    The Permanent Indus Commission

To

1. The Government of India,
   Ministry of Water Resources,
   New Delhi.

2. The Government of Pakistan,
   Ministry of Water & Power,
   Islamabad.

SUBJECT: **ANNUAL REPORT FOR THE YEAR ENDED ON 31ST MARCH 2013**

Sir,

The Commission has the honour to invite attention to Article Vlll(8) of the Indus Waters Treaty 1960 and to submit herewith its Annual Report for the year ended on 31st March 2013.

The Commission wishes to express its appreciation for the assistance received in the discharge of its functions, from the officers associated with its work.

Yours faithfully,

(G. Aranganathan)	(Sheraz Jamil Memon)
Commissioner for Indus Waters,	Pakistan Commissioner for lndus Waters,
Government of India.	Government of Pakistan

New Delhi, 31 May, 2013

ANNUAL REPORT FOR THE YEAR ENDED ON 31ˢᵗ MARCH 2013

1 INTRODUCTION

1.1 This is the Fifty Third Annual Report of the Permanent Indus Commission constituted in accordance with Article V1II(3) of the **INDUS WATERS TREATY** 1960 and relates to the work of the Commission for the year ended on 31ˢᵗ March, 2013.

1.2 During the year under report, the posts of the Commissioner for Indus Waters, Government of India, and the Commissioner for Indus Waters, Government of Pakistan, were held as follows:-

Commissioner for Indus Waters, Government of India

Shri G. Aranganathan	From 01-04- 2012 to 31- 03- 2013

Commissioner for Indus Waters, Government of Pakistan

Mr Sheraz Jamil Memon	From 01-04-2012 to 31-05-2012
Mr Mirza Asif Baig	From 01-06-2012 to 31-03-2013

2 MEETINGS OF THE COMMISSION

2.1 During the year under report, the Commission held one meeting, serially numbered as One Hundred-Eighth, in continuation of the One Hundred and Seven meetings held during the previous years. The said meeting was held in Pakistan at the place and on the dates given below:

Meeting	Venue	Dates
One Hundred-Eighth	Lahore	23ʳᵈ March to 26ᵗʰ March 2013

2.2 During One Hundred-Eighth meeting of the Permanent Indus Commission, three agenda items were discussed. The particulars regarding each of the items discussed at this meeting, including the position as on 31ˢᵗ March 2013, are given in the Annexure to this Report.

2.3 The record of One Hundred-Eighth meeting of the Permanent Indus Commission could not be signed due to shortage of time and it was agreed to finalise same by correspondence or during next meeting.

3 GENERAL TOURS OF INSPECTION

3.1 According to Article V!ll!(4)(c) of the Treaty, the Commission is required to undertake, once in every five years, a general tour of inspection of the Rivers for ascertaining the facts connected with various developments and works on the Rivers. The General Tour of Inspection to be undertaken during the five year period from 1ˢᵗ April 2010 to 31ˢᵗ March 2015 is called as the 'Eleventh General Tour. The Eleventh General Tour is to be undertaken in parts.

3.2 During the year under report, the Commission could not undertake third and fourth part of the Eleventh General Tour of Inspection in Pakistan and India as agreed during the 107ᵗʰ meeting of the Commission. Thus the total number of the General Tours of Inspection undertaken remained sixty nine.

4. SPECIAL TOURS OF INSPECTION

4.1 Under the provisions of Article VIII(4)(d) of the Treaty, the Commission is required :to undertake promptly, at the request of either Commissioner, a tour of inspection of such works or sites on the Rivers as may be considered necessary by him for ascertaining the facts connected with those works or sites". In the Annual Report of the Commission, such a tour has been referred to as 'special tour of inspection', to distinguish it from the 'general tour of inspection' in Article Vlll(4)(c) of the Treaty.

4.2 During the year under report, the Pakistan Commissioner requested for a Tour of inspection to the Tulbul Navigation Project under Article V!ll(4)(c) as well as Viil(4)(d). After exchange of correspondence, the Commissioners agreed to undertake it under the earliest possible dates under either one of these provisions; in this process, the Commission could not undertake any special tour of inspection. Thus the total number of special tours of inspection undertaken remained forty five.

5. GENERAL

The Commission expressed satisfaction over the work during the year under report and is happy that its work was marked by a spirit of goodwill, understanding and co-operation.

(G. Arangartathan)	(Sheraz Jamil pennon)
Commissioner for Indus Waters,	Pakistan Commissioner for Indus Waters,
Government of India.	Government of Pakistan.

New Delhi, 31 May 2013

ANNEXURE

PARTICULARS OF ITEMS DISCUSSED AT THE MEETINGS OF THE COMMISSION HELD DURING THE YEAR

S. No.	Items discussed	Meeting(s) at which discussed	Position as on 21st March 2013
1	Pakistan's Objections on Ratle HE Plant	One Hundred Eighth	To be discussed further
2	Pakistan's Objections on Miyar HE Plant	One Hundred Eighth	To be discussed further
3	Pakistan's Objections on Lower Kalnai HE Plant.	One Hundred Eighth	To be discussed further

APPENDICES

PART TWO

NEWSPAPER COMMENTARIES ON RECENT DEVELOPMENTS

SEPTEMBER, 2016 TO MARCH, 2017

APP – 1

RECALLING THE INDUS WATER TREATY

MUSHTAQ AHMED — 7 September 2016

The Nation -Pakistan

In a single-basin-country like Pakistan, life would be impossible even to contemplate without the Indus and its tributaries and their life giving waters. Soon after its creation in August 1947, Pakistan faced extreme and unpredictable miseries at the hands of India who claimed proprietary rights to the waters of eastern rivers passing through its territorial land and crossing Pakistan. An agreement was reached between India and Pakistan through a bilateral tribunal according to which status-quo of the flow of water in three eastern rivers Ravi, Sutlej and Beas would remain as such until 31st March 1948. On 1st April 1948, the day after the bilateral tribunal ceased to have effect India cut off the water supply in every canal crossing Pakistan. Pakistan rushed a delegation to Delhi to persuade India to refrain from such unilateral and disastrous action as its economy was a completely dependent upon these rivers. India and Pakistan signed an ad-hoc agreement on May 4th,1948 according to which India although agreed to resume water supplies to Pakistan as per sharing arrangements of pre 1947 but asserted to gradually decrease the same. Pakistan failed to obtain India's consent to submit the matter for impartial determination of rivers water flow to International Court of Justice or any other impartial tribunal. According to India it was purely a technical problem requiring nothing more than a technical solution.

In 1951 the World Bank appeared on the scene and strongly advocated a joint exploitation of waters of Indus Basin as a solution of the inflammable dispute between two riparian countries. The bank offered its good offices in finding a practical solution in 1951. The two countries accepted the suggestion on the basis that existing uses should be respected. In 1954 the World Bank made the broad proposal that the six rivers be divided between the two countries and during the transitional period, Pakistan be allowed to get water supplies from India and the cost of replacement works in Pakistan be born by India in proportion to the benefits to be derived by her for use of waters of eastern rivers historically available in Pakistan. Transition period means the period during which Pakistan will construct replacement works to compensate the loss that will occur to her because India having the exclusive right to use water of the eastern rivers. There is a provision in the treaty that the transitional period may be extended at Pakistan's request from 10 to 13 years. Originally it was thought that replacement works could involve only link canals, but detailed study established the need for storage dams. Accordingly the bank included water storages in 1956 in the replacement works projects. The same year the two countries formally accepted the bank's proposal. Afterwards financial and technical issue remained in active discussions among World Bank, Pakistan and India.

In 1957 India declared that she will stop water flowing into Pakistan by 1962. Ultimately, friendly countries came forward with offers of financial assistance and through the realistic and urgent discussions taken by new regime headed by president of Pakistan General Muhammad Ayub Khan a settlement was arrived at, popularly known as Indus Water Treaty, which divides the Indus Basin watered by six rivers into two groups of three rivers each and allows India the exclusive use of the waters of three eastern Rivers Ravi,

Sutlej, and Beas and Pakistan the use of three western rivers Indus, Jhelum, and Chenab. The drafting of the Treaty began in August 1959.

The replacement works will comprised of the following mega construction works; Mangla Dam on River Jhelum and Tarbela dam on River Indus. New barrages included: Chashma Barrage on River Indus, New Rasul Barrage on River Jhelum, New Marala Barrage on River Chenab, Qadirabad Barrage on River Chenab, Sidhni Barrage on River Ravi and Mailsi Syphon on River Sutlej. New link canals included: Chashma Jhelum Link Canal, Taunsa Punjnad Link Canal, Rasul Qadirabad Link Canal, Qadirabad Balloki Link Canal, Balloki Sulemanki Link Canal, Trimmu Sidhnai Link Canal, Sidhnai-Mailsi-Bahawal Link Canal, a well as remodeling if old link canals.

Very difficult and protracted negotiations which dragged on for 12 years between the two riparian countries ended on 19th September 1960. When Indus Water Treaty was signed at a simple yet graceful ceremony on the lush-green lawns of the President House Karachi (the then capital of Pakistan). 71 year old Pandat Jawahar Lal Nehru signed as Prime Minister of India. Tall and masculine Field Marshal Mohammad Ayub Khan signed as President of Pakistan under the auspices of the World Bank.

Indus Water Treaty is duly considered the biggest irrigation project in human history. The disadvantages were that Pakistan was made dependent on the waters of only three western rivers and would suffer considerable quantum loss to the tune of 24MAF (million acre feet) annually arising out of the giving up of her right to waters of three eastern rivers. Water would have to be brought over long distances from the western rivers to feed the areas dependent on eastern rivers involving transit losses. The Ravi of romantic associations was reduced to a nullah to be fed with water of western rivers through link canals. Lastly, these canals would expose the areas they pass through to the risk of water logging.

The advantages outweighed the drawbacks. The construction of two mega dams facilitated control of floods, provided water for irrigation and production of cheap and clean hydelpower. Pakistan became independent in matters of irrigational needs and the interlinking of rivers by canals provided more rational utilisation of waters in all six rivers. Additionally, a sum of $50 million provided for drainage channels and tube wells augmented supplies and facilitated the much needed reclamation of water-logged-areas.

APP – 2

INDIA'S REVOCATION OF INDUS WATER TREATY WILL BE CONSIDERED AN ACT OF WAR:

RIAZUL HAQ – 27 September 2016

The Express Tribune, Pakistan

Adviser to the Prime Minister on Foreign Affairs Sartaj Aziz has said any violation of Indus Waters Treaty (IWT) from India would pertain to considerable risk of war and hostilities between the two countries.

"Pakistan will not accept Indian aggression in any form and any Indian step for disrupting water flow as upper riparian will pertain to considerable risk of war and hostilities," the adviser said in the National Assembly in response to a calling attention notice on Tuesday.

The House also unanimously passed a resolution condemning "falsified Indian claim in United Nations General Assembly (UNGA) about Jammu and Kashmir being integral part of India."

The NA criticised Indian External Affairs Minister Sushma Swaraj's speech in UNGA on Monday for "drawing parallels between Jammu and Kashmir, a recognised disputed territory and Balochistan, an integral part of sovereign Pakistan."

Desperate Modi now plots to run Pakistan dry

Aziz said India was under pressure "due to our diplomatic efforts" and raising the Kashmir issue on international stage.

The adviser explained the provisions of IWT, saying as per sub provision 3 and 4 of provisions of Article 12 of IWT, the treaty could not be altered or revoked unilaterally, adding that the World Bank had facilitated the treaty and its role is defined in the treaty in case of violation by any party.

However, Pakistan Tehreek-e-Insaf MNA Shireen Mazari questioned the claim. "None of the provisions in the Treaty says the World Bank was guarantor of the treaty between the two countries, rather it was a facilitator." Aziz confirmed Mazari's assertion of the Bank's role as a facilitator.

He said the treaty would continue to be in force until modified by both the countries after an understanding. "This treaty is for an indefinite period and binding. It is not time specific or event specific."

Why things will likely be quiet on the India-Pakistan border

The adviser warned that if India tried to interrupt water flow into Pakistan as an upper riparian it would not only violate the Treaty but also set a regional state practice under which an international law can serve as precedence for others.

"Such an Indian act may also provide China with a justification to consider suspension of water of Indian river Brahmaputra."

Aziz said the Treaty survived wars of 1965 and 1971 between Pakistan and India, and was not even suspended during Kargil and Siachin conflicts. "The treaty is quoted as most successful water treaty between the two countries and its revocation can be taken as an act of war or a hostile act against Pakistan."

Answering PTI's Munaza Hassan's question as to why the government had not mentioned Indian spy Kulbhushan Yadav's arrest from Balochistan, the adviser said the government was preparing a comprehensive dossier on Yadav and Indian interference in Balochistan, as well as its operations through Afghanistan. "We will expose India at the UNSC and before the international community."

APP – 3

MODI STOPS SHORT OF ABROGATING INDUS WATER TREASTY

MARIANA BAABAR – September 27, 2016

Indian Prime Minister Narendra Modi was once again brought crashing down to earth on Monday when experts on water management counseled him that India could not afford to unilaterally walk out of and abrogate the 56-year-old Indus Waters Treaty, to send a signal to Pakistan that "blood and water cannot flow together", in reference to the Uri militant attack.

Experts cautioned Modi that abrogation of the treaty could be interpreted as a declaration of war. Modi's own analysts cautioned that "The itch to 'punish Pakistan' could have a collateral impact on the development of India's East and Northeast".

Earlier it were senior members of his security council that cautioned him against beating the war drums and any attack across the border which was tantamount to declaring a war. Chairing a meeting to review the Indus Water Treaty in the company of Foreign Secretary Jaishankar, NSA Ajit Doval, Principal Secretary Nripendra Misra, the Water Resources secretary and senior PMO officials, Modi came up with a face saving decision and leaked to the media without any official statement, "India has decided to suspend Indus water commission talks until Pakistan-sponsored terror in India ends".

In all, 112 meetings have been held by the two commissioners. Since Pakistan's Foreign Office rarely comments on media reports, New Delhi will have to wait for an official response from Pakistan, if any.

The News spoke to Ahmer Bilal Soofi, former law minister and lawyer of international repute, who responded, "Unofficial reports from India that Modi has suspended talks between the Commissioners then that is, in itself, a non-coercive act of hostility. However, more so, India is itself going down the route of threatening a water war with Pakistan by better utilizing water as an upper riparian. This will compound Pakistan's fears that India can stop water for security reasons anytime and IWT is never an iron-clad guarantee for the continuous flow of waters. Thus, in this episode, India has verified that Pakistan's fears were not ill-founded and that they are, in fact, real".

In India itself, patience appears to be in short supply as desperate measures are being taken to take attention away from the ongoing brutalities inside Indian Occupied Kashmir, which must be the only region in the world where an undeclared war has been imposed, daily seeing coffins wrapped in Pakistani flags heading towards the graveyards, which are running out of space for the dead.

Noted Indian journalist Maya Mirchandani of NDTV commented, "Talk of abrogating the Indus Waters Treaty will invite criticism/ concern over India's reliability in keeping its commitments, internationally, not to mention (the) very real possibility that China - where the Indus, Sutlej and the Brahmaputra originate - could well return the favor."

With the UNGA in session, Soofi advised Prime Minister Nawaz Sharif that since senior officials are still present in New York, Pakistan should consider bringing the threat of India to walk away from the Treaty to the notice of the United Nations (UN) Secretary General under Article 99 of the UN Charter, for such interruption of water will constitute a threat to international peace and security as mentioned in the UN Charter itself.

"Further, Pakistan can also bring this to the notice of all the permanent members of the UN Security Council, which was meant precisely to intervene whenever there is, in any region, a threat likely to endanger international peace and security.

Considering that interruption in the water flow, following revocation of the Treaty, will be an existentialist threat to the State, the situation already warrants interference by the UN as one already endangering international peace and security", he added.

Experts add that India does not have the structure nor the capacity to deal with the water in case it wants to divert it from Pakistan. Indian media quoted Shakil Ahmad Romshoo, head of the Earth Sciences Department at Kashmir University, as saying that an argument is being made that India, being upstream, can stop the flow of waters to Pakistan and bring it to its knees.

He counseled that river waters cannot be stopped or released at the turn of a switch. "Waters cannot be immediately stopped from flowing to Pakistan unless we are ready to inundate our own cities. Srinagar, Jammu and every other city in the state and in Punjab would get flooded if we somehow were able to prevent the waters from flowing into Pakistan," he said.

Soofi, a firm believer in legal diplomacy, advocated that Indian threats to revoke the Indus Waters Treaty (IWT/Treaty) are clearly against international law because international law does not allow the unilateral suspension of a treaty.

"In fact, the provisions are to the contrary, as states have an obligation to honour the treaties in good faith. Further, there are no provisions for India to unilaterally walk away from the Treaty. If it tries to do so, it will be viewed as a breach of said treaty", he added.

Soofi appeared worried that the developments over the last day or two on the Indian side have now given Pakistan the ability to take the position that the IWT is inadequate to allay Pakistan's fear of the lack of guarantee of water flow and that the IWT is deficient in providing a mechanism to address this issue. "Therefore, this matter can rightly be taken up as an independent agenda of bilateral talks outside the IWT framework. Thus, this incident has, thankfully, freed Pakistan's elbows to raise this issue in the UN and any other international forum, including bilaterally", he said.

If India ever thinks that it can walk away from the IWT it would be in reality contemplating stopping or interrupting the water flow of the rivers into Pakistan. "This can be viewed as a hostile act because preventing the flow of waters will result in threatening the right to life of the people of Pakistan, destroying the agriculture and crushing their reliance on hydro-electricity. This will, in turn, equip Pakistan with the right to retaliate under the international law principles of the Law of Reprisal which permit a state to carry out a retaliatory measure against an unlawful act", he pointed out.

It is also a principle of law that when an international treaty or a contract has been substantially performed, it cannot be revoked; particularly when Pakistan has already incurred the sufferings under the provisions of the Treaty by having denied itself the waters of Ravi, Sutlej and Beas (which have been dried up), in consideration of the continuation of the uninterrupted flow of water in the three Western Rivers.

Ashok Malik, a senior Indian analyst cautioned, "There are suggestions in some quarters — including in cloud cuckoo land and news television studios, which are now interchangeable domains — that India should unilaterally tear up this treaty.

India is a candidate for the Nuclear Suppliers' Group (NSG), one of the international system's foremost rule-setting bodies. If India abrogates a long-standing treaty at this point, it will only give India skeptics at the NSG a handle to ask if New Delhi is ready for a global governance role".

Meanwhile according to PTI, the Indian Supreme Court in Delhi Monday refused to grant an urgent hearing on a PIL seeking declaration of the India-Pakistan Indus Water Treaty as unconstitutional. "There is no urgency in the matter. It will come up for hearing in due course," a bench comprising Chief Justice T S Thakur and Justice A M Khanwilkar said. Advocate M L Sharma, who filed the PIL in his personal capacity on the issue, sought urgent hearing of the matter saying the treaty was unconstitutional as it was not signed as per the constitutional scheme and hence should be declared "void ab initio." "Keep politics aside. The matter will come in due course," the bench said when the lawyer insisted on an urgent hearing.

Meanwhile according to PTI, the Indian Supreme Court in Delhi Monday refused to grant an urgent hearing on a PIL seeking declaration of the India-Pakistan Indus Water Treaty as unconstitutional.

"There is no urgency in the matter. It will come up for hearing in due course," a bench comprising Chief Justice T S Thakur and Justice A M Khanwilkar said. Advocate M L Sharma, who filed the PIL in his personal capacity on the issue, sought urgent hearing of the matter saying the treaty was unconstitutional as it was not signed as per the constitutional scheme and hence should be declared "void ab initio." "Keep politics aside. The matter will come in due course," the bench said when the lawyer insisted on an urgent hearing.

APP – 4

DESPERATE MODI NOW PLOTS TO RUN PAKISTASN DRY

Zafar Bhutta September 27, 2016

The Express Tribune, Pakistan

Experts say India cannot walk out of Indus Waters Treaty unilaterally,

Indian Prime Minister Narendra Modi's reaction post-Uri assault has been full of flip-flops. First, he rattled his sabres — only to back off later. Then, he talked about mounting a global campaign to 'isolate Pakistan diplomatically'. And now he is threatening to undo the only achievement that has withstood periods of tensions and conflict between the two arch foes.

Modi conferred with his senior aides on Monday to reconfigure the Indus Waters Treaty of 1960 — a World Bank-brokered agreement that governs the distribution of water of six rivers between Pakistan and India. "Blood and water cannot flow together," he was quoted by *Times of India* newspaper as telling his aides.

Indian prime minister reviews Indus Waters Treaty

At the huddle it was decided that India would 'exploit to the maximum' the water of the Indus, the Chenab and the Jhelum by fast-tracking its building of new hydropower plants along the three Pakistani rivers.

Modi's threat to run Pakistani rivers dry shows his utter desperation and naivety. International law experts say it is not possible for either country to just walk out of the Indus Waters Treaty. "There is no provision in the Indus Waters Treaty to scrap the agreement unilaterally. If India does so, it'll violate international law," *BBC Urdu* cited Ahmer Bilal Soofi as saying.

"There is no precedent where a country has reneged on an international agreement. Such agreements are not between governments but between states — and states are bound to honour them," he added. About India's threat to review the Indus Waters Treaty, Soofi said, "If India scraps the treaty, then it will be considered an aggressive step which could jeopardise regional peace and security."

Soofi believes the UN secretary general could take suo motu notice, if the Indian threat materialises.

Jamaat Ali Shah, the former Indus waters commissioner, agrees with Soofi. "India cannot walk out of the agreement unilaterally, though the two countries can make changes in the agreement with mutual consensus," he told *The Express Tribune*.

Congress tells Modi to bring own house in order before advising Pakistan

Shah believes Modi's threat is a political gimmick aimed at pressuring Pakistan following the Sept 18 deadly attack on a military base in Uri sector of Indian occupied Kashmir.

He said Pakistan had surrendered 26 million acre feet water of Beas, Sutlaj and Ravi rivers to secure a right over the water of the Indus, Jhelum and Chenab rivers. "The government should take up the Indian threat with the World Bank, which was instrumental in brokering the Indus Waters Treaty," he added.

A former Pakistani prime minister's adviser on water and agriculture resources says India is desperate after losing the case on Kishanganga hydroelectric plant in the International Court of Arbitration. "The court had ruled that India was violating the Indus Waters Treaty by building the Kishanganga plant," Kamal Majeedullah told *The Express Tribune*.

The Indus Waters Treaty was signed in 1960 in a bid to resolve disputes, but India's ambitious irrigation plans and construction of thousands of upstream dams has continued to annoy Pakistan, which depends on snow-fed Himalayan rivers for everything from drinking water to agriculture.

Modi threatens to 'isolate' Pakistan globally

The World Bank – then called the International Bank for Reconstruction and Development – had brokered the treaty which was signed 56 years ago by Jawaharlal Nehru and Ayub Khan. According to the agreement, India got a right over water of the rivers Beas, Ravi and Sutlej, while the rivers Indus, Chenab and Jhelum came under Pakistan's control.

Majeedullah said India was already stealing water from Pakistan's rivers. "The International Telemetry System should be installed to monitor the flow of water from India," he added. "Pakistan should not allow a revision of the treaty which was brokered by the World Bank."

A senior government official, however, laments that the water issue doesn't figure anywhere on the priority list of Pakistani policymakers. "We had an acting Indus water commissioner who had been working on an ad-hoc basis since 2012," he said. "This is the situation of the body that is assigned to sort out contentious water issues with India."

APP – 5

INDUS WATERS TREATY RIDES OUT LATEST CRISIS

Athar Parvaiz, – September 29, 2016

Dawn (Pakistan)

The 1960 World Bank-mediated Indus Waters Treaty between India and Pakistan is considered one of the great success stories of water diplomacy, especially as it has survived the India-Pakistan wars of 1965, 1971, 1999 and much bad blood during and after the wars. Tension between the two countries is again at a peak following a terrorist strike in Kashmir, and some Indian commentators are speaking of reneging on the treaty as a non-military option to pressure Pakistan.

On September 18, 2016 an attack was carried out on an army base in the garrison town of Uri, 75 kilometres north-west of Kashmir's summer capital Srinagar, near the Line of Control (LoC) that effectively divides Kashmir between India and Pakistan. Eighteen Indian army personnel and four terrorists were killed in the attack, and India has blamed the attack on militants from Pakistan.

India and Pakistan have long been embroiled in diplomatic face-offs over Kashmir and have fought three wars, but have so far managed to uphold the treaty that provides mechanisms for resolving disputes over water-sharing.

Under the treaty, Pakistan received exclusive use of waters from the Indus and its westward flowing tributaries, the Jhelum and Chenab, while the Ravi, Beas and Sutlej rivers were allocated for India's use.

Using water as weapon

Just two days before the Uri attack, an Indian author on water disputes, Brahma Chellaney, wrote that, "India should hold out a credible threat of dissolving the Indus Water Treaty, drawing a clear linkage between Pakistan's right to unlimited water inflows and its responsibility not to cause harm to its upper riparian." Other commentators, too, such as Yashwant Sinha, who has served as both foreign minister and finance minister in a previous government, have suggested that the treaty be abrogated.

Officially the Indian government has said little. In response to a question, the spokesperson of India's Ministry for External Affairs, Vikas Swarup, merely said, "For any such treaty to work, it is important that there must be mutual cooperation and trust between both the sides." He avoided going into details.

The mediator

The World Bank – which negotiated the treaty and sets up an adjudicator in case of disputes – has not made an official statement either. Speaking to thethirdpole.net, a World Bank spokesperson said, "The World Bank's role in the Indus Waters Treaty is limited and strictly procedural."

Putting this in perspective, Ashok Swain, who teaches at Department of Peace and Conflict Research, Uppsala University, Sweden, said that World Bank is co-signatory for certain provisions of the Indus Waters Treaty and its role is limited to a dispute regarding the implementation of the treaty, not its abrogation. At most the World Bank would step into, as per the treaty, to appoint a "neutral expert", or help set up a Court of Arbitration, in case of a dispute.

On whether India can create any problem for Pakistan by stopping water, Swain said that India does not have the enough storage facility to create a supply problem immediately for Pakistan.

"It has to raise its dam structures and that will take time. There is also another angle to it. India, even if it wants to, cannot take the water out of Kashmir Valley. So, the water of the three rivers (Indus, Jhelum and Chenab) will remain in their basin and India cannot divert that to other areas due to geographical reasons. India can stop the supply for some time, but cannot divert it."

Acting within the treaty

Uttam Sinha, a research fellow at New Delhi based Institute for Defence Studies and Analyses (IDSA) also disagreed with those asking for scrapping the treaty.

"For sending a message to Pakistan, we don't necessarily need to go to the extent of scrapping the Indus Waters Treaty. We can even send a strong message to Pakistan by using the waters of western rivers of Indus basin for irrigation, electricity and storage of up to 3.6 Million Acre Feet (MAF), well within the norms laid down in the treaty," Sinha told thethirdpole.net.

"Scrapping the treaty would rather act against our own interests and international standing as it would cause anxiety among our other neighbours like Bangladesh and Nepal with which we have water-sharing treaties, apart from earning us a bad image in the global community."

Azeem Ali Shah, a Lahore based researcher with the International Water Management Institute (IWMI), told thethirdpole.net, "A unilateral withdrawal from the Treaty will bring World Bank into the dispute. It will also incite further anxiety among Pakistani people and might lead to violence."

Despite a huge debate generated in the media, the silence of the principal parties, whether it is the Indian government or the World Bank, seems to indicate that the treaty is safe for the time being. The former chief minister of the Indian state of Jammu & Kashmir, Omar Abdullah, tweeted, "Will stick my neck out and say that nothing will happen to Indus Waters Treaty. It survived four wars and a J&K assembly unanimous resolution." Jammu & Kashmir Assembly had passed a resolution in 2003 asking India and Pakistan to review the treaty which had not considered the developmental needs of the state, which mostly hosts the three rivers allocated to Pakistan.

"Such statements in favour of scrapping the treaty can only be treated as mere propaganda, not a diplomatic option," Medha Bisht, who teaches International Relations at South Asian University, told thethirdpole.net. One major reason for this is that India is itself a middle riparian country for two of the six rivers mentioned in the treaty. The Indus and the Sutlej flow from Tibet, and there is no treaty between China and India to manage the relationship. One senior Indian commentator has even claimed that China has indicated it would act to divert waters from Indiaif India decided to divert waters from Pakistan. Such a scenario, though, would lead to flooding and huge damages to all three countries. This highlights that, more than anything else, such treaties survive not just because of trust or goodwill, but because they serve the interests of all the nations involved.

APP - 6

WORLD BANK NOT GUARANTOR OF INDUS WATER TREATY,

Fawad Yousafzai –September 30, 2016

The Nation (Pakistan)

ISLAMABAD - A parliamentary committee was informed yesterday that the World Bank had just brokered the Indus Water Treaty, but was not a guarantor of it.

"It is incorrect that the World Bank was a guarantor of the Indus Water Treaty. The bank had brokered the treaty and facilitated negotiations between Pakistan and India," Indus Water Commission Additional Commissioner Sheraz Memon told the Senate Standing Committee here. The World Bank was not a guarantor of the water treaty except its two provisions, he added. The World Bank's role was just limited to the accord's two articles which relate to appointment of neutral experts and the Court of Arbitration chairman," he maintained.

The Senate Standing Committee on Water and Power, chaired by Senator Sardar Yaqoob Khan Nasir, discussed the Indus Water Treaty in the backdrop of the statements of Indian leadership regarding unilateral revocation of the treaty, its repercussions, Pakistan's stance and preparedness to combat a war-like situation. The Senate had referred the matter to the standing committee for consideration and report till October 3, 2016.

The committee asked the Water and Power Ministry to make an alternative strategy to counter Pakistan's water, blocking threats of India. The ministry was further directed to devise an alternative plan to cope with the situation if India revoked the Indus Waters Treaty.

Minister of State Abid Sher Ali informed the committee that the World Bank had also offered to broker a deal with Afghanistan on the River Kabul. He further stated that Pakistan needed to develop reservoirs to stop water from going into the sea from downstream Kotri.

Sheraz Memon informed the committee that the treaty was signed in 1960 between India and Pakistan. According to the Treaty, Pakistan is entitled to unrestricted use of all those waters of the western rivers which India is under obligation to allow its flow under the provisions of paragraph 2 of the treaty. "India shall be under an obligation to let all the waters of the western rivers and shall not permit any interference with these waters while India shall not store any water or construct any storage works on the western rivers. Under the treaty, the water of three western rivers will be given to Pakistan whereas the waters of three eastern rivers will be for India. Pakistan can only irrigate 45,000 acres of land with the water of the River Ravi. Both the countries were free to use their allocated rivers.

"Eastern rivers (Sutlej, Beas and Ravi) allocated to India (33 MAF), except domestic and agricultural uses, Western Rivers (Indus, Jhelum, Chenab) allocated to Pakistan (137 MAF), except domestic, agricultural, non-consumptive and hydroelectric uses," he added. Out of the total 33 MAF water flow of eastern rivers, Pakistan was using 24 MAF water.

The additional commissioner said setting up of run-of-the river hydroelectric projects by India with reservoirs creates issues.

The committee, however, raised concerns that if India takes 2 MAF water for agriculture purposes in addition to already agreed 2.85 MAF water, it will be around 5 MAF. India can irrigate 1.339 million acres of land with the water of rivers allocated to Pakistan.

Today, India can manipulate 94,309 acres feet water of the Chanab out of a total 20.25 million acres feet water of the river. However, New Delhi may be able to control Pakistani share of water after some years, particularly of the River Chenab, the officials of the ministry, Indus River System Authority (IRSA) and Indus Water Commission told the Senate SPECIAL COMMittee on Water and Power. On the River Jhelum, India is constructing 14 hydropower plants, including two big projects. On the Chenab, it has constructed 17 hydro projects, the additional commissioner added. As per the agreement, India has to get its design approved from Pakistan before the execution of the hydro projects, he asserted.

There is no guarantor of the treaty, but in case of violation, a mechanism has been provided in the Article 9 of the treaty, Memon explained.

Senator Nisar Muhammad said a full-house committee should be constituted to formulate a long-term policy on water issues.

APP – 7

TREATY IN TROUBLE

Sikander Ahmed Shah | Uzair J. Kayani – October 03, 2016

Dawn (Pakistan)

In the wake of the Uri incident, India has launched a campaign to 'punish' Pakistan. The Indian offensive has proceeded swiftly on the diplomatic, political, economic and, as of this writing, militaristic fronts. An early salvo is India's aggressive stance on the Indus Waters Treaty (IWT) of 1960. Last week, India said it would increase its water withdrawals from three rivers that flow through India to Pakistan to the maximum levels permitted under the treaty. India is also considering building dams on the Jhelum which flows through the Kashmir Valley before entering Pakistan. Both measures threaten serious economic and humanitarian harm for Pakistan.

India has further claimed it will cease participating in meetings of the Permanent Indus Commission, set up under the IWT, until "terror comes to an end". It has decided to indefinitely suspend the regular meetings of the Indus water commissioners of India and Pakistan. Each of these measures is a potential breach of the treaty, and Pakistan should prepare its case for the Permanent Court of Arbitration, should any of these materialise. The basic elements of such a case are straightforward. First, the IWT does not permit India to unilaterally abrogate its obligations. Such an abrogation would be a material breach, since the treaty has no termination date. Treaties of this kind exist in perpetuity unless rescinded or modified by both parties through mutual consent. Second, Pakistan has approached the World Bank (a party to the treaty) — so there is an ongoing dispute or controversy. In the Nicaragua case, the US was not allowed to retract its consent to the International Court of Justice's jurisdiction once a dispute arose and was being entertained by the court. This was so even though, unlike the IWT, the treaty at issue there allowed the US to withdraw its consent to ICJ jurisdiction.

There is some suggestion that India might justify a breach of the IWT or other actions in bad faith by claiming it is 'retaliating' to some supposed misstep by Pakistan. As a threshold matter, there has been no independent inquiry of any such accusation, and curiously, no interest on India's part in allowing one. However, even assuming, for argument's sake, that such claims were tenable, they would not justify the type of collateral 'retaliation' India seems to contemplate. Put simply, two wrongs would not make a right. International law has parallel obligations, and treaties such as the IWT are self-contained. The breach of one treaty or obligation does not allow the aggrieved state to respond by breaching a different treaty, or other international law principles. But if India jettisoned the law, it would still need to consider the political and economic fallout. First, the IWT was based on negotiations and compromise. India should realise that if the IWT were to go away, Pakistan's claim to the rivers that were given to India (Beas, Ravi and Sutlej) would be revived. Absent the treaty, Pakistan, as a lower riparian state, would have strong rights on these waters.

Second, the IWT does not exist in a vacuum. By breaching it, India would also likely breach the Shimla Agreement, by going against its 'guiding principles'. At a minimum, it would be working against its spirit. A breach of the Shimla pact will likely be costlier for India than Pakistan. It could lead to a chain reaction, with tit-for-tat withdrawals by both countries from operational arrangements and security agreements. Given these states' nuclear capabilities, such an unravelling would pose a significant threat to international peace and security.Third, aside from Pakistan's reaction, India should carefully consider its reputational costs in the international community. India has a number of similar treaties with other countries, like Myanmar and Bangladesh. The international community will rightly be concerned by India's cavalier treatment of its international law obligations.Albatrosses notwithstanding, India continues to escalate. It pulled out of the now cancelled Saarc summit and has convened a meeting to discuss stripping Pakistan of its Most Favoured Nation trade status. Modi and External Affairs Minister, Sushma Swaraj have also given back-to-back inflammatory speeches labelling Pakistan a "terror state" or "state sponsor of terrorism." It is hard to imagine what sort of endgame such cowboy posturing is meant to achieve.

One possibility is that by 'retaliating' through planned IWT violations, India is creating a pretext for undermining CPEC. Critical Chinese investments in Gilgit-Baltistan and AJK depend on the river water India now threatens. A salient example is the Neelum–Jhelum hydropower plant. If such a pretext is at play, then India must consider not only Pakistan's reaction, but Chinese concerns as well. Just as India is an upper riparian state to Pakistan, China is an upper riparian to India. Any sabotage of the One Belt, One Road project can trigger a reaction from China.India has also claimed having undertaken "surgical strikes" inside Pakistan. This is a deeply troubling development, and raises the possibility that India could use restricted water supply as a preparatory step for further hostile action. This context adds another dimension of international law. The waters awarded to Pakistan under the IWT are its natural resource. Stopping them or diverting them is a direct breach of Article 2(4) of the UN Charter by India, because it violates the territorial integrity and political independence of Pakistan. Targeting a state's natural resources, installations, assets, or citizens extraterritorially is a serious violation of international law. Numerous aggrieved states have responded to such violations with force.

A breach of Article 2(4) would trigger Pakistan's inherent right to self-defence. Pakistan should make good-faith diplomatic and legal efforts to dissuade India from such a course. However, as a last resort, and complying with the requirements of necessity and proportionality under the law of self-defence, Pakistan would be within its rights to use not only "necessary countermeasures", but also force, to remove any headworks, dams, or other diversionary installations in India-held Kashmir that illegally restrict the flow of these rivers into its territory.

APP - 8

INDUS WATERS TREATY MODEL OF PEACEFUL COOPERATION

ANWAR IQBAL – October 03, 2016

Dawn (Pakistan)

The United States has urged India and Pakistan to adhere to the Indus Waters Treaty (IWT), calling it a model for peaceful cooperation.

The Indian media reported this weekend that India was seriously considering a proposal to scrap the treaty to force Pakistan to change its Kashmir policy.

"The Indus Waters Treaty has served as a model for peaceful cooperation between India and Pakistan for over 50 years," a spokesperson for the US State Department told Dawn.

"We hope and encourage India and Pakistan to resolve any differences through bilateral dialogue," the US official added.

The IWT is a water-distribution agreement between India and Pakistan, brokered by the World Bank and signed in Karachi on Sept 19, 1960, by then president Ayub Khan and then prime minister Jawaharlal Nehru.

The treaty gives India waters of the Ravi, Sutlej and Beas rivers and Indus, Jhelum and Chenab to Pakistan, with limited allowance to India over the three western rivers for power generation, etc.

But after the Sept 18 militant attack on an Indian military facility at Uri in held Kashmir, New Delhi suspended biannual talks with Pakistan — as mandated in the treaty — to discuss water distribution.

Last week, Indian Prime Minister Narendra Modi held a meeting to review the 56-year-old treaty, which decided to "exploit to the maximum" the water dispute as a foreign policy tool.

Pakistan reminded India that international laws prevented upper riparian states from stopping the flow of water to those down the river. Pakistan also warned India that stopping the rivers was an act of war.

On Sept 27, a Pakistani delegation met senior World Bank officials in Washington and urged them to prevent India from making illegal constructions on the Neelum and Chenab rivers.

The delegation reminded the officials that the treaty authorised the bank to establish a court of arbitration and appoint three judges to the court. India and Pakistan each appoint two arbitrators.

Diplomatic sources in Washington told Dawn that the review meeting in New Delhi discussed three options: scrapping the treaty, recommencing work on one of the dams and suspending biannual talks.

The sources said that all three options were still on the table, forcing Pakistan to take the matter to the World Bank.

The construction on the dam, called Wullar Barrage in Pakistan and Tulbul Project in India, started in 1987 but stopped when Pakistan objected. The review committee has now decided to resume it.

A senior Pakistani diplomat, while pointing to the US description of the treaty as "a model of cooperation", said that "India may find it difficult to scrap the treaty as it will irk the international community, but it may continue working on the other two options".

The Pakistani team that met World Bank officials in Washington reminded them that the Kishanganga project was also a violation of the Indus Waters Treaty.

The Indians, however, argue that the World Bank can only establish a court of arbitration when the biannual talks fail. Since the talks have only been suspended, not scrapped, the bank cannot set up a court yet.

"The Pakistanis are saying that they have exhausted all efforts at the bilateral level. And earlier this year, the Indus Water Commission also declared it a dispute. So now is the time for the World Bank to play its role," said an official aware of the proceedings.

Pakistanis are believed to have told the bank that they consider the resumption of disputed projects a "very serious violation" of the treaty and an example of "India's high-handedness".

The Pakistani team informed the World Bank officials that "the three rivers are their lifeline as they are an agrarian nation", said the official who spoke to Dawn.

On Saturday, China blocked a tributary of the Brahmaputra river as part of a major hydroelectric project, which also strengthened Pakistan's case.

In Washington, the step is seen as a warning to New Delhi against using water as a foreign policy tool.

APP – 9

IMPLICATIONS OF THE LATEST INDIAN MOVES ON THE INDUS WATERS TREATY

Shafqat Kakakhel – October 3, 2016

The Express Tribune

Pakistan should respond to India's latest moves on the Indus Waters Treaty (IWT) in a responsible manner aimed at achieving its core concerns over the shared water resources of the Indus Basin, its sole source of fresh water. In this regard, an analysis of the decisions taken by a high-level meeting convened by Prime Minister Modi on September 26 is called for. In the absence of an official statement, we have to rely on the summary of the outcome of the meeting carried by *The Hindu* on September 27.

Happily, India has decided to neither seek a review of, nor abrogate, the IWT amid speculations in the Indian media on the likely renunciation of the agreement that has survived three wars and recurring tension between India and Pakistan since it was signed in 1960.

India's decision to utilise "to the fullest possible extent" its share of waters under the Treaty is unexceptionable but innocuous. The IWT gives India the three eastern rivers for unrestricted use and permitted it to use the flows in the three western rivers (the Indus, Chenab and Jhelum) for limited irrigation, domestic consumption and run-of- the-river (ROR) projects for electricity generation, irrigation and domestic consumption. Pakistan has never questioned India's entitlements and need not do so now. However, a decrease in the water flows of the western rivers has occurred perhaps due to long periods of drought in the catchment areas of the rivers and the effects of climate change. In order to prevent the declining flows from causing tension in their relations, India and Pakistan should jointly probe the quantum of reduction in the flows and the factors responsible for it. India should also share the findings of its hydrometric and telemetric systems for monitoring the flows in the western rivers with Pakistan as a confidence-building measure.

The New Delhi meeting is reported to have decided to "suspend the Indus Waters Commission until the ending of (Pakistan-supported) terror". The suspension of the Commission is likely to adversely affect India more than Pakistan. The Commission is the conduit of communication on all aspects of the implementation of the IWT, including settlement of objections raised by Pakistan to the Indian hydro-electric projects on the western rivers. In fact, the time and energies of the Commission have been expended largely on the Indian hydro projects. Pakistan has reportedly objected to five Indian hydro power projects, in addition to the three decades old dispute over the Wullar Barrage/Tulbul Navigation Project which must be settled before India can start or resume work on them .The disabling of the Commission will prolong the delays in the completion of the Indian projects.

Another decision referred to "a review of the 1987 suspension of the Tulbul Navigation Project at the mouth of the Wullar like where the Jhelum originates. Pakistan had opposed the project contending that the proposed barrage violated the IWT, rejecting India's claims that it was a navigation project meant to facilitate transportation linking several Kashmiri towns. Discussions at several high-level meetings have failed to resolve the differences and the dispute is included in the agenda of the bilateral composite dialogue. We do not know what the proposed review holds for this project but India should refrain from resumption of work on the project.

Another decision taken at the Delhi meeting mentions the intention "to build more run-of- the-river projects on the western rivers to exploit their full potential". This is a curious move since India has tried to exploit the full potential of the flows of the western rivers for producing electricity, the only impediments being lack of money and Pakistan's objections to projects it considers impermissible under the IWT. The decisions taken by Prime Minister Modi also include the resolve to "expedite" construction of the Pakal Dul, Sawalkot and Bursar dams on the Chenab in Jammu and Kashmir. Pakistan has reportedly objected to one of these projects, namely the Pak Dul project and India should not start work on it pending a settlement of Pakistan's reservations.

Yet another decision taken by India mentions the "full use of the 20% of the water allowed to it by the IWT in order to benefit farmers in Jammu and Kashmir". The so-called 20% of the Indus Basin's water given to India probably refers to the flows of the three eastern rivers, totalling 33 MAF representing one-fifth of the Basin's waters. India has fully exploited its share.

In short, the decisions taken by India on September 26, especially its renewed adherence to the IWT are inconsequential and do not justify the angry outbursts of our Senators against the Treaty. Pakistan should respond to the Indian moves by not only reiterating support for the full implementation, in letter and in spirit, of the Treaty but also express readiness to discuss measures to ensure more expeditious processing of Indian hydro projects. We should also propose a comprehensive dialogue on all aspects of the looming water crisis facing the Indus Basin, including climate-change impacts. The proposed dialogue should consider issues related to the Indus Basin which were not anticipated or fully understood when the IWT was negotiated — nearly half a century ago. These issues have been jointly identified by Indo-Pak Track 2 dialogue in recent years, including joint studies on the adverse impacts of climate change and cooperation in mitigating them; protection of the watershed of the rivers; preserving the sustainability of transboundary aquifers being over-exploited on both sides of the Indo-Pak divide; agreeing a procedure for dealing with any notable decrease in the water flows so as to preclude any misunderstanding ; the desirability of ensuring environmental flows in the eastern rivers; and, above all, broader cooperation in promoting integrated water resource management. Let the Indus, which had nourished the shared and glorious Indus Valley Civilisation, serve to foster peace and amity in our subcontinent.

APP - 10

RIVER DIPLOMACY ON TEST

Nimmi Kurian –October 4, 2016

The Indian Express

Blood and water can't flow together. Prime Minister Narendra Modi's comment on the river Indus, with the dark hint of retribution, sends out a chilling signal to Pakistan. It also disturbingly hyphenates the link between terrorism and water. This is reinforced by the frenzied talk of avenging Uri by revoking the 56-year-old Indus Water Treaty. To what extent has India's political signaling on the Indus taken into account the possible payoffs?

International experience on using water as a weapon to stop terrorism is a sobering one. Turkey used water as a weapon to punish Syria for its alleged role in supporting the terrorist activities of the Kurdistan Workers' Party (PKK) directed against it. In 2014, Turkey completely cut off water from the Euphrates leaving seven million downstream Syrians without access to fresh water. By doing so, Turkey reneged on a 1994 international agreement to guarantee a minimum share of the waters of the Euphrates to Syria and Iraq. Earlier this year, Israel stopped water supply to several Palestinian towns and cities for weeks. Each of these instances brought serious collateral damage to civilian populations and proved to be a cure worse than the problem.

Advocates of a similar strategy on the Indus would do well to remember that it could only end up worsening future distributional conflicts over water in the sub-region. Given that nearly 65 per cent of its territory is part of the Indus basin, Pakistan's dependence on its flows cannot be overstated. If downstream communities hold the upper riparian state responsible for their livelihood setbacks, can India's public diplomacy afford to ignore their sentiments? Article 54 of Protocol I to the Geneva Convention prohibits actions targeting civilian populations that may result in "inadequate food or water as to cause its starvation".

India would also do well to remember that its actions as an upper riparian country run the risk of seriously undermining its position as a lower riparian state vis-à-vis China. On the Brahmaputra, India has stakes in institutionalising norms of first-user rights, joint management and consultative processes. India's plan to build 168 mega dams in Arunachal Pradesh and the moves to expedite hydroelectric projects on the sub-basins of the Siang, Lohit and Subansiri rivers are part of its attempts to establish user rights. If it chooses to renege on its own international obligations, how realistic are India's chances of getting China to invest in process-oriented, institutionalised norms in a transboundary basin?

How would a planned move to abrogate international obligations be read in Dhaka, Kathmandu or Thimphu? Is it likely to inspire confidence in India's credentials as a leader with an inclination to design regional norms of benefit-sharing? Or would it further reinforce the perception that India has a strong unilateralist streak? What is worse, contradictory political signalling can result in a high degree of uncertainty. For instance, on the one hand, India provides flood-forecasting data to Pakistan and Bangladesh free of cost but on the other, it has not been averse to occasionally flexing its muscles as an upper riparian country.

It will also be in India's interest that the exercise of its power as an upper riparian state is seen as legitimate and credible. International experience validates this quite clearly. Be it Brazil's binding agreements with Paraguay on the Parana or the US-Mexico freshwater treaty on the Colorado, hegemonic upper riparian states have found it worth their while to invest in the creation of regional public goods.

Political signalling is a game all nations play. Some just happen to play it better than others. But signalling almost always involves costs, especially in fraught situations of international conflict. A review of the Indus Water Treaty could prove to be a double-edged sword for India. Pakistan could just as well use it to signal that the Indus framework is increasingly inadequate, call to question India's intentions and demand additional international guarantees to ensure uninterrupted flows. The non-military option on the Indus is hardly the silver bullet solution it is being bandied to be and India could end up shooting in the foot.

APP - 11

WHEN MODI PROPOSED AND VAJPAYEE DISPOSED

Charu Sudan Kasturi – 4 October, 2016

The Telegraph (India)

The Indus Waters Treaty was not serving two barren Indian districts though it could, Narendra Modi thought. He called a meeting of senior officials in his government, who endorsed the view, and set in motion a process aimed at changing India's use of the pact.

It was May 2002, and the proposal was shot down by then Prime Minister Atal Bihari Vajpayee.

Last week, Modi, now the Prime Minister, ordered a review of India's use of the bilateral treaty with Pakistan as part of New Delhi's diplomatic response to the Uri terror attack that left 19 soldiers dead.

Modi's desire to take a re-look at the pact's use by India dates back at least 14 years. Then, as Gujarat chief minister, he had formally asked Vajpayee to divert Indus basin waters to the state, three officials familiar with that request have independently confirmed to **The Telegraph**.

The written representation had sought diversion of some water from the basin to the districts of Banaskantha and Kutch, claiming Gujarat's entitlement as a part of the Indus basin, the officials recalled. Days later, the then Gujarat cabinet had also declared its support for Modi's move.

But Vajpayee turned down Modi's proposal, after diplomats and water resources ministry officials concluded that Gujarat wasn't part of the Indus basin under the 1960 pact the World Bank brokered between India and Pakistan.

After months of back and forth between New Delhi and Gandhinagar, the Vajpayee government had made its rejection public, in Parliament.

"Government of Gujarat has submitted proposals for allocation of the waters of the Western rivers of the Indus basin to the Kutch region of Gujarat on the plea that it is a part of the basin," Arjun Charan Sethi, water resources minister in Vajpayee's government, told the Rajya Sabha on April 8, 2003, according to Parliament records accessed by this newspaper. "It is not permissible to allocate Indus waters to the Kutch region of Gujarat according to the existing Indus Waters Treaty as no part of the state of Gujarat lies in the Indus basin."

Sethi, who was responding to questions from BJP MP A.K. Patel and Congress MP Alka Balram Kshatriya, also made it clear that "presently there is no proposal" for a revision of the Indus Waters Treaty.

As Prime Minister, Modi's motivations for reviewing the Indus Waters Treaty are rooted in India's attempts to leverage all diplomatic tools available to it in cornering Pakistan into agreeing to curb terror from its soil.

Modi, at the meeting on September 26 with national security adviser Ajit Doval, foreign secretary S. Jaishankar and water resources secretary Shashi Shekhar, decided to suspend for now all meetings of the bilateral commission that monitors the implementation of the treaty. The meetings - typically held twice a year - will now be held only when there is an "atmosphere free of terror", said a senior official.

"Blood and water cannot flow together," Modi said at the meeting, two officials said.

India's decision to review its use of the treaty has triggered a diplomatic response from Pakistan, which approached the World Bank in Washington last week through a delegation led by the country's attorney general, Ashtar Ausaf Ali. Pakistan has sought the formation of a court of arbitration by the World Bank to resolve differences between India and Pakistan over the implementation of the pact.

"In the meeting with the Pakistani delegation, the World Bank committed itself to (the) timely fulfilling (of) its obligations under the treaty while remaining neutral," the Pakistan embassy in Washington said in a statement.

World Bank officials have since told this newspaper they are preparing a proposal for a court of arbitration, but could realistically go ahead with Pakistan's demand only if India also agreed to arbitration. The World Bank's role, both in 1960 and now, is merely that of a facilitator, the group's officials said.

An all-party meeting in Pakistan, chaired by Prime Minister Nawaz Sharif today, condemned "the stated intent by India to use water as a weapon against the people, not just of Pakistan but of the region".

India is not proposing, for the moment, any abrogation of the Indus Waters Treaty or even a unilateral violation, officials here have insisted. Instead, a task force formed to review India's use of the pact will only look at ways to maximise the gains the country can glean from the treaty - within the rights granted currently.

But some aspects of the treaty under review bear a resemblance to Modi's 2002 proposal for the diversion of water from the Indus basin for irrigation in Gujarat.

Then, the Gujarat government had argued that Kutch in particular falls within the basin of the western rivers - the Indus, Jhelum and Chenab - from which Pakistan has rights to 80 per cent of the water under the Indus treaty.

The Gujarat proposal, though dismissed by New Delhi then, had included a suggestion that the water from the Indus, Jhelum and Chenab be routed to the eastern rivers - the Ravi, Beas and the Sutlej. India has rights to all the water from the eastern rivers under the Indus Waters Treaty.

The water could then be funnelled to Gujarat by extending the Indira Gandhi canal in Rajasthan, which receives water from the eastern rivers, the state government had proposed.

Now, the central government - with Modi as its chief executive - has concluded that India is not utilising water from the western rivers adequately for irrigation.

India is allowed, under the treaty, to irrigate up to 9.1 lakh acres of land using water from the western rivers, with an additional 4.3 lakh acres allowed if New Delhi shares more water than it is required to. But currently, officials said, India uses these rivers to irrigate only 8 lakh acres.

APP – 12

CHALLENGES BEFORE INDIA

Syamal Kumar Sarkar – October 05, 2016

Deccan Herald (India)

INDUS WATERS TREATY

The recent media reports on leveraging the flexibility in The Indus Waters Treaty 1960 (IWT) to India's advantage and suspending the talks at the Permanent Indus Commission-le-vel, seen in the background of Uri attack, have brought into sharp focus the functioning of the treaty. Since 1960, the oper-ation of the IWT has witnessed ups and downs in dealing with transboundary water issues between India and Pakistan. The treaty allocates waters of eastern rivers of the Indus (Ravi, Beas, Sutlej and their tributaries) to India, to the extent of about 33 million acre feet (MAF) while allocating those of the western rivers (Indus, Jhelum, Chenab and their tributaries) largely to Pakistan to the extent of about 135 MAF. India is, however, permitted to use water of western rivers for domestic, non-consumptive and agriculture use, besides for power generation.

India is also allowed to construct 3.6 MAF storage of water on the western river system. There also exists under the Treaty, a dispute settlement mechanism such as setting up of a Permanent Indus Commission (consisting of two Commissioners for Indus Waters, one from each country), and a recourse to neutral experts as well as to court of arbitration, if required. Such mechanism has been used by both the parties over many water related issues. he Commission is the basic institutional mechanism for implementation of the IWT, the members of which may undertake tours to ascertain facts (more than 100 tours undertaken so far), meet at least once a year (more than 100 meetings taken place so far), supply monthly flow data (for 280 sites by India and for 345 by Pakistan), make available annual village/tehsil level statistics for irrigated crop areas (pertaining to western rivers, to Pakistan by India, and for the same in respect of the eastern rivers, to India by Pakistan), and finally, resolve the disputes in a manner as specified under the Treaty.

The role of third parties, such as the World Bank and others, are also recognised under the treaty during selection of neutral experts or members of the court of arbitration. Ever since IWT's existence, out of eastern rivers, India allocated water to Punjab, Haryana, Rajasthan, and Delhi; constructed various dams such as Bhakra, Pong, Thein, Pandoh; established network of links such as Beas-Sutlej, Sutlej-Yamuna and also substantially developed various command areas such as Bhakra canal command, and Indira canal command.

In respect of the western rivers, the IWT allowed India to withdraw water over and above what existed in 1960, for an additional irrigated cropped areas (ICA) of about 7 lakh acres. This effectively implies that India can have about 13.4 lakh acres ICA in the drainage areas of the western rivers. Against this, till 2011-12, India was able to achieve a capacity of 8 lakh acre ICA, suggesting a big opportunity for India to further harness the water use. Regarding hydel power, the estimated potential is about 18,000 MW, against which the completed/under construction capacity is only about 4,000 MW. Several projects on eastern rivers such as Ujh multipurpose project, second Ravi Beas link, Sahapurkandi projects are pending completion, while on the western rivers, Bursar and Gyspa storage projects are also delayed.

For Pakistan, the Indus is the main river contributing about 64% of water supplies, with Jhelum giving 17% and Chenab 19%. Thanks to the IWT, the country built a series of link canals to divert water from western rivers to provide the same to southern Punjab. It also constructed a huge reservoir capacity to cater to the country's needs during periods of scarcity. The financial support received by Pakistan under the IWT helped build many dams, and undertake massive tube well programme in addition to building power transmission system, making the country self sufficient in food production by 1970. Both India and Pakistan used the basic institution, Permanent Indus Commission (PIC), and others to move forward in resolving many water-related issues during the course of implementation of the treaty. For example, Salal hydro electric project (690 MW) was resolved at the foreign minister's level, the Buglihar project at the level of neutral expert, Kishanganga project (330 MW) at the level of court of arbitration, while Uri-II and Chetak hydroelectric projects were resolved at the level of the PIC.

Tulbul project

In the case of Nimoo Bazgo hydro electric project (45 MW), Pakistan has given notice for taking recourse to neutral expert, and also requested for discussion in the case of lower Kalnai, Miyar, Ratle, and Pakal Dul hydro electric projects after raising objections on various issues. The Tulbul project, essentially meant for navigation from Anantanag to Baramulla, and suspended since 1987, is yet to be resolved as Pakistan has raised several objections.

This analysis clearly shows that India can significantly harness the ICA potential as well as hydro power potential under the IWT framework. However, past experience also leads one to believe that any attempt to construct storage or harness hydro power potential will generate legal challenges under the garb of violating the treaty by using the dispute settlement mechanism. India has to move deftly to handle this likely scenario in case it seeks to maximise the advantage flowing out of the IWT. The other challenges are domestic. They include speedy clearance of project proposals by various authorities in India, reconciliation of states concerned over sharing of water, speedy resolution to legal cases pending before the Indian courts, allocation of substantial financial resources to build projects, acceptability of projects by local residents etc. With India's recent thinking on maximising the advantages under the treaty, these issues call for a time-bound resolution.

One external challenge, however, may emerge: China's support to Pakistan in the present political scenario, inter alia, through possible interruption of flows of rivers in which it controls the upper riparian section.

APP – 13

INDIA COMPLETES KISHANGANGA HYDROPOWER PROJECT WITHOUT RESOLVING DIFFERENCES

Munawar Hasan – October 6, 2016

The News (Paksitan)

LAHORE: India has completed its 330-megawatt Kishanganga hydropower project on the western waters in the Indian-occupied Kashmir, while Pakistan is still constructing 969MW run-of-river Neelum-Jhelum power plant downstream at the same tributary.

The News learnt from reliable sources that India succeeded in constructing the project before the commencement of the dispute resolution mechanism presently being persuaded by Pakistan for ensuring adherence to the provisions under the Indus Waters Treaty.

Indian Indus Waters Commissioner PK Saxena told his Pakistani counterpart about the completion of Kishanganga hydropower project.

"As estimated by the project authorities, the initial filling below the dead storage level of the Kishanganga hydroelectric project is proposed to be carried out from 14 August to 20 August 2016 under the provision of Paragraph 18 of Annexure E of the Treaty," the Indian official said in a letter.

Experts believe it is not a good omen that India completed the hydropower plant without Pakistan's consent. They attributed the apathy of the federal ministry of water and power and Pakistan Commission for Indus Waters to this fiasco.

Interestingly, Pakistan Commissioner for Indus Waters Mirza Asif Baig and power ministry has yet to make this fact public.

Baig did not respond to the calls and text messages from this scribe to know about the developments.

The development has neither been shared with other stakeholders, like Indus River System Authority (Irsa), Punjab Irrigation Department (main user of Jhelum water) and Water and Power Development Authority.

Even Rao Irshad Ali, chairman of Irsa, when contacted, expressed ignorance over the development, saying his department was not aware.

Being a prime water regulator, Ali said the Irsa should have been informed about every development regarding the construction of infrastructure on the western rivers.

A senior official at the Punjab Irrigation Department also expressed shock over the report.

"It is a standard operating procedure that any development regarding building of infrastructure on the western rivers has to be communicated with my department," the official said.

An ex-ministry official said all the relevant departments should have shared information about the filling of Kishanganga hydropower project with all the stakeholders.

"We should proactively deal with the water-related issues with India," the official said. "It is the right of India to fill the lake of the hydropower project, if it is following the provisions of the treaty."

However, he added, at least an exercise of damage control should be done.

Jamaat Ali Shah, ex-commissioner at Indus Waters also supported the idea of sharing this important development with all the concerned departments. "India should also have been asked about the construction, which was in violation of the treaty and its construction must have been stopped," Shah said.

First time, India provided the Kishanganga hydropower project's design to the Pakistani authorities back in 1996. The country, however, could not fully take up the issue to the relevant forums. Its attempt to thwart the Indian move by resorting to the Hague-based International Court of Arbitration also met with a little success.Sources said Pakistan now wants to again raise this issue internationally. They said Indus Waters Commissioner is working on ad-hoc basis and his stay at the commission is already overdue by around two years.

The sources accused the secretary water and power for overlooking the administrative snags. They alleged that the secretary only focused on the power sector projects, which would be completed before 2018.A spokesman at the power ministry did not deny the fact that India completed the construction of Kishanganga hydropower project. He, however, said the hypothesis about the response of the departments is not correct. "None of the officials purposely ignored any such matter," he added.

All the information and actions are being taken after due consultations and keeping national interest supreme, said the spokesman.

He said the Indus Waters Commission will provide the technical details about the project's completion. "We should not mix it with self-concocted hypothesis and half-truths to twist the facts against any office or official," he said.

APP – 14

THE INDUS WATERS TREATY

Hussain H. Zaidi – October 08, 2016

The News (Pakistan)

Amid the nosedive in Islamabad-New Delhi relations in the wake of the Uri attack, apprehensions are rife that India may terminate the Indus Waters Treaty (IWT) to penalise Pakistan. The Indian prime minister has also consulted his aides on having the treaty revised. For Islamabad, denunciation of the agreement by New Delhi will amount to a declaration of war.

Why is the IWT in the limelight? Can India unilaterally walk out of the treaty? The answer to such questions entails looking at the text of the treaty, which has been effective since April 1, 1960.

As stated in the preamble of the treaty, the IWT aims at fixing and de-limiting the rights and obligations of each party about the use of the waters of the Indus system of rivers comprising three western rivers – Indus, Jhelum and Chenab – and the three eastern rivers – Ravi, Sutlej and Beas. The last mentioned river does not enter Pakistan but joins the Sutlej before the country's territory starts.

Article II provides that the waters of the eastern rivers shall be available for unrestricted use by India. However, domestic and non-consumptive use by Pakistan is allowed. Domestic use, under Article I, includes drinking, washing, sanitary and use of water for industrial purposes.

The same article specifically mentions that domestic consumption does not include agricultural use or generation of hydro-electric power. Non-consumptive use is for purposes such as navigation, fishing and flood control. Again, non-consumptive use precludes use for agriculture or hydro-electric power generation.

Article II also provides for a transition period beginning on April 1, 1960 and terminating on March 31, 1970 during which Pakistan was to have unrestricted use of the waters of the eastern rivers. Pakistan's claim on the eastern rivers ended after expiry of the transition period.

Article III entitles Pakistan to unrestricted use of the three western rivers, albeit with some exceptions. In addition to domestic and non-consumptive uses, as in the case of the eastern rivers, the exceptions also included agricultural use and use for hydro-electric power generation. However, the treaty restricts the resort to these exceptions. India is also prohibited from storing water or building any storage on the western rivers.

Under Article IV, Pakistan undertook to replace the canals fed by the eastern rivers with western rivers. The same article also provides that non-consumptive use by any party shall not materially change water flow in any channel.

Article V requires both Pakistan and India to exchange data, on a monthly basis, about the flow in and utilisation of the waters of the six rivers. Article VII stipulates that in case either Pakistan or India plans to construct any engineering work which would interfere with the waters of any of the rivers in such a manner as would affect the other country materially, it shall notify its plans as well as provide the relevant data to the latter.

Article VIII sets up a Permanent Indus Commission comprising one commissioner for the Indus waters from each country. The commission serves as the regular channel of communication on all matters pertaining to the implementation of the treaty. The commission is required to meet annually.

Article IX puts in place an elaborate mechanism with regard to the interpretation or application of any provision of the IWT or settlement of any dispute that may arise about the rights and obligations of either country. The dispute settlement consists of three levels. The first level is the Permanent Indus Commission. In case the commission fails to sort the issue out, the next level is bilateral consultations between the two governments. In case the consultations also fail, the matter shall be referred to a neutral expert or a court of arbitration. The latter is to comprise three members or umpires

It was under Article IX of the IWT that Pakistan took India to arbitration on the Kishenganga (on the Neelum River, which meets River Jhelum at Muzaffarabad) and Ratle (on River Chenab) hydroelectric projects.

Under Article XII, the IWT may be amended with mutual consent. Unless amended, the treaty shall remain in force in the current form. The IWT does not have a sunset clause – that is to say, neither country can opt out of the treaty on its own.

The waters-sharing treaty has been a watershed in the history of the otherwise estranged Pak-India ties. The agreement has remained intact notwithstanding high tensions, even wars, between the two South Asian neighbours.

The major reason for that is that neither country can unilaterally amend, suspend or terminate the treaty. Therefore, in case India decides to opt out of the IWT or insists on having it modified without Pakistan's consent, it will violate its international obligations. Not only that, pacta sunt servanda, one of the fundamental principles of international law, stipulates that every treaty is binding upon the parties signatory to it and that treaty obligations must be honoured in good faith.

Pakistan is a low riparian country and the rivers of the Indus system enter Pakistan through Indian territory. Like Kashmir, the issue of the distribution of the waters of the Indus system of rivers between Pakistan and India had its origins in the partition of India scheme. Under the scheme, the Punjab was bifurcated into West (Pakistan) and East (Indian) Punjab. The important headworks of Ferozepur and Madhpur were given to Indian Punjab. Those headworks irrigated about 1.7 million acres in the West Punjab.

The idea was to give the two new states joint control of the water channels. A standstill agreement was made to preserve the status quo till March 31, 1948. However, within 24 hours of the expiry of the agreement, India blocked the vital supplies to Pakistan from the Ferozepur and Madhpur headworks.

River Indus and its tributaries are the life-blood of Pakistan. Therefore, any attempt by India to denounce the IWT will cause tremendous economic loss to Pakistan. It seems New Delhi wants to use the waters-sharing pact to pressurise Pakistan into toning down its Kashmir stance.

The writer is a graduate from a western European university.

APP - 15

THE INDUS WATERS TREATY IS HERE TO STAY

Rajeshwari Krishnamurthy – October 10, 2016

The Diplomat (India)

India cannot easily and will not abrogate the Indus Waters Treaty.

In the wake of the deplorable attacks against the Indian Army in Uri, Jammu & Kashmir, tensions in the New Delhi-Islamabad bilateral, which were already running high over the preceding weeks, escalated further. In addition to pursuing Islamabad's diplomatic isolation within the region, India indicated that it will review Pakistan's Most Favored Nation (MFN) status, granted to Pakistan under its World Trade Organization (WTO) obligations. Surprisingly, India also indicated that it will 'review' the Indus Waters Treaty (IWT), the one bilateral treaty between the two countries that has stood the test of time – even through the most difficult of times in the relationship.

Reviewing the IWT does not automatically imply its abrogation. Yet, it would be pertinent to assess two factors: Are there any downsides to withdrawing the MFN status or abrogating the IWT, for India? If yes, what are they? Are they manageable?

While there appears to be a high degree of public support in India for withdrawing the MFN status and rescinding the IWT, one could expect New Delhi to not abrogate the IWT.

Enjoying this article? Click here to subscribe for full access. Just $5 a month.

Withdrawing the MFN and the IWT

MFN status is a trade related matter and, given how both India and Pakistan are bound by WTO rules, legally, India is well within its rights to withdraw the MFN status it has granted to Pakistan. The legality of doing so was already assessed as far back as the early 2000s. Withdrawing the MFN status is possible via the provisions of Article XXI(b) of the WTO's General Agreement on Tariffs and Trade [GATT] – the very provision Pakistan has cited to justify its refusal to grant MFN status to India. The implications of withdrawing MFN status are likely to be a zero sum outcome; and, as retired Ambassador VP Haran recently wrote, "on the economic front, the scores may be even; but on political terms, India would have scored a point." The more important issue here is that of the IWT. The IWT is a bilateral water sharing treaty between India and Pakistan that has been in force since September 19, 1960. Perhaps the knowledge that India has the legal right to withdraw the MFN status might have something to do with the leadership's increased confidence regarding 'reviewing' the IWT as well.

However, unlike in the case of the MFN status, any unilateral change to the IWT could potentially be harmful to Indian interests. Pakistan is signatory to the 1969 Vienna Convention on the Law of Treaties albeit it has still not ratified it. India is not signatory to the Convention. The rules of the Convention are not binding on New Delhi. There may be scope for India to wiggle an interpretation that might allow it to abrogate the Indus

Waters Treaty unilaterally. However, although there might be a chance – albeit bleak – to pull this off, New Delhi will not do so because, fundamentally, India is not an irresponsible country. Moreover, the legal, political, and economic consequences — both domestic and international — of doing so would be tremendous. If New Delhi or Islamabad abrogate the treaty unilaterally, the troubles for the instigator would have just begun. All treaties and agreements, bilateral or multilateral, are signed on the basis of the *Pacta Sunt Servanda* principle, i.e. "agreements must be kept" – which means employing good faith. By extension, it means that all modifications to, or suspensions and terminations of, the treaty should be carried out as per the provisions agreed to in that treaty. The IWT does not contain a provision for either party to unilaterally suspend/terminate the contents of the treaty. It has a provision for establishing a Permanent Indus Commission to settle differences and disputes. It also contains provisions for modalities of mediation and arbitration, as well as for referring matters to a Neutral Expert. Moreover, Article XII(4) of the Indus Waters Treaty provides that

The provisions of this Treaty, or, the provisions of this Treaty as modified under the provisions of Paragraph (3), shall continue in force until terminated by a duly ratified treaty **concluded for that purpose between the two Governments**. [Emphasis added]

Therefore, from a technical point of view, neither India nor Pakistan can unilaterally abrogate or modify the treaty. Yet, if one side so wishes, it can abrogate it despite this. However, doing so would automatically mean losing credibility and being deemed rogue on the international front. Since Pakistan is dependent on the water supplied via this treaty, it will not want to abrogate it because it is not in its interest to do so. For India, unilaterally abrogating or modifying the terms of the treaty would set an extremely dangerous precedent for itself, given how India too is a lower riparian state to important rivers that originate in China. Additionally, if India still does so, it will be in a tricky position while challenging Pakistan's ceasefire violations via the *Pacta Sunt Servanda* route. New Delhi is aware of these conundrums.

Multiple Contexts of the IWT

- *Strategic implication:* From an Indian perspective, such an action with humanitarian consequences towards a water-stressed, lower-riparian state such as Pakistan runs the risk of causing China – Pakistan's "all weather friend" to use it to its advantage. Major rivers – including the Indus and the Brahmaputra – that flow into India originate in Tibet. Beijing's construction of dams on the rivers originating from the Tibetan plateau has already caused unease in New Delhi and Dhaka.

- *Geopolitical aspect:* Although the IWT was facilitated by the World Bank, it was the United States that had midwifed it. The treaty was drafted such that there would be no easily exploitable loose ends. The endurance of the IWT through wars and other conflicts has been the United States' only true success story in South Asia – and Washington will try everything possible in both New Delhi and Islamabad to prevent it from breaking down.

- *Diplomatic aspect*: India will not cut off water supply to Pakistan and earn the risk of losing its credibility as a responsible rising power on the international area. Even indicating that it could do so makes India come across as a bully – and that is counterproductive for New Delhi.

- *Practical aspect:* A prerequisite for cutting off water supply of such a large measure is the capacity to store it so that it does cause not damage to Indian territory and property. At present, the infrastructure is insufficient to match this requirement.

Looking Ahead

Anyone who believes that India will attempt something incredibly silly would be mistaken. Yet, it will be useful to remember that on a fundamental level, humanitarian reasons are a strong but secondary motivator for upholding this treaty. The sections above list few among the many reasons why the IWT has managed to survive for as long as it has; and therefore, in the long term, unless these factors or circumstances change dramatically, chances are, the treaty will not be unilaterally abrogated or modified, at least by India. The real issue here is that with this incident, strategists in Pakistan have gotten a high potential opportunity to alter their waning international image. It would be wise if New Delhi does not walk into Islamabad's trap. At the moment, this whole episode is working in Pakistan's favor in the eyes of international entities. The belligerent-sounding rhetoric coming out of Indian public discourse – even if it is mere signaling – makes New Delhi look like a regional bully and Islamabad, the victim (even though this is not the case in reality). The international tide is currently not entirely in India's favor. New Delhi would do well to address this issue smartly and not blindside itself.

Surely, there are other ways to exert pressure on an adversary without damaging one's own hard-earned credibility or legitimacy. The IWT itself may have answers.

Views expressed are the author's own and do not necessarily reflect those of the organizations to which she is affiliated.

Rajeshwari Krishnamurthy is Assistant Director at Institute for Peace and Conflict Studies (IPCS), New Delhi. A version of this piece originally appeared at South Asian Voices, an online platform for strategic analysis and debate hosted by the Stimson Center.

APP – 16

LAW OF THE INDUS

A. G Noorani – October 15, 2016

Dawn (Pakitan)

"The upstream users of an international river are no longer entitled to the unrestricted use of (the waters) of such a river, and are bound, when taking decisions concerning its use, to take reasonable account of the interests of other users in downstream areas." On Sept 25, 1997, the ICJ gave its imprimatur on the rule in a case between Hungary and Slovakia (concerning the Gabcíkovo-Nagymaros Project), putting it beyond dispute.

Thus, even if the Indus Waters Treaty did not exist, India would not be able to take any of the diversionary measures that official leaks in the media threaten. It reflects legal incompetence, contempt for international morality, and a barbaric outlook.

The court followed an earlier ruling of its predecessor, the Permanent Court of International Justice, in 1929 with regard to the River Oder, which said "the community of interest in a navigable river becomes the basis of common legal right, the essential features of which are the perfect equality of all riparian states in the use of the whole course of the river and the exclusion of any preferential privilege of any one riparian state in relation to the others".

Therefore, in its judgement, the ICJ pointedly stated: "Modern development of international law has strengthened this principle for non-navigational uses of international watercourses as well, as evidenced by the adoption of the convention of 21 May 1997 on the Law of the Non-Navigational Uses of International Watercourses by the United Nations General Assembly. The court considers that Czechoslovakia, by unilaterally assuming control of a shared resource, and thereby depriving Hungary of its right to an equitable and reasonable share of the natural resources of the Danube [...] failed to respect the proportionality which is required by international law."

The law mandates equitable and reasonable shares for all the countries through which an international river runs. In 1895, US attorney general Judson Harmon was asked for an opinion on the rights of the US and Mexico over their shared river, the Rio Grande. US farmers had increasingly begun to divert its waters, significantly reducing its flow to Mexico.

He responded: "The fundamental principle of international law is the absolute sovereignty of every nation as against all others, within its own territory." He conceded that he had found in support of his view "no precedent or authority which has a direct bearing" and the "case presented is a novel one". The Harmon Doctrine of absolute territorial sovereignty, which privileged the upper riparian state, died swiftly and was buried by the US supreme court.

East Punjab was therefore ill advised to cut off the water supplies in every canal crossing into Pakistan in April 1948, which ran contrary to the agreement reached by Committee B (one of the committees set up to deal with issues arising from Punjab's partition) when it stated: "There is no question of varying the authorised shares of water to which the two zones and the various canals are entitled." Cyril Radcliffe expected that "any agreements [...] as to the sharing of waters from these canals will be respected".

It is unnecessary to trace the tortuous course of events that followed this standstill agreement of May 1948 until the signing of the Indus Waters Treaty in Karachi, on September 1960, by Jawaharlal Nehru, Ayub Khan and W.A.B. Iliff (representing the World Bank) — albeit for specified purposes. As judge Richard Baxter, an expert on international waterways law, noted, the World Bank was not a disinterested presence but one of the parties to what were actually tripartite negotiations. It was, therefore, not a bilateral treaty but a multilateral one — for yet another reason.

On the same day and place, two other agreements were also signed: the Indus Basin Development Fund Agreement by representatives of Pakistan, the US, the UK, Australia, Canada, Germany, New Zealand and the World Bank, and a loan agreement between Pakistan and the World Bank. Enormous sums of money were spent and expensive irrigation works construction was undertaken.

The treaty says that it can be terminated only by another treaty. Article 63 of the Vienna Convention on the Law of Treaties (1980) says: "The severance of diplomatic or consular relations between parties to a treaty does not affect the legal relations between them by the treaty except in so far as the existence of diplomatic or consular relations is indispensable for the application of the treaty." Even severance of diplomatic relations does not affect the treaty.

To obstruct the Permanent Indus Commission is to trigger the formation of a court of arbitration (Article IX). The treaty is not a weapon to be used for political ends; it has a long history and is entrenched in international law.

APP - 17

ASSESSING INDIA'S WATER THREAT

Fahim Zaman | Syed Muhammad Abubakar – October 10, 2016

Dawn (Paksitan)

Blood and water can't flow together," declared a belligerent Indian Prime Minister Narendra Modi on September 26, 2016 in the wake of 19 Indian soldiers dying in a militant attack on Uri military base, just inside Indian-administered Kashmir. Holding Pakistan responsible for the violence, Modi promised to unshackle India's policy of "restraint" — implying that India was now going to hurt Pakistan by choking its water supply.

For the people of Pakistan, a nation dependent upon agriculture for its survival, the Indus rivers are their lifeline. As it is, Pakistan is ranked second, after China, in the Water Shortage Index, highlighting the vulnerability of the Pakistani population to frequent water shortages. Modi's proclamation generated lots of nationalistic hyperbole in the two nuclear-armed twins but also inflicted some damage: many on this side of the border are perturbed about Modi making good on his threat and stopping water supply to Pakistan.

Can Modi turn the taps off immediately?

The Indus Waters Treaty of 1960, which governs water sharing arrangements between India and Pakistan, outlines a framework for how either country can exploit water potential and how they can't. While the Indus Waters Treaty is upheld, India cannot turn the taps off — in fact, it does not have the capacity at the moment to do so either — but it can definitely delay the release of water flows. And historically, India hasn't been averse to using this tactic when relations with Pakistan turn sour. This time has been no different.

In a story printed in the October 12 edition of Dawn, irrigation department officials warned of a record reduction of water levels at Head Marala in the Chenab. The fear is that water shortage in the river and two of its canals, Marala-Ravi Link Canal and Upper Chenab Canal, can adversely affect the sowing of crops particularly in Sialkot, Gujrat, Gujranwala and Sheikhupura districts. The situation has worsened at the time of this report going into print.

The cultivation cycle in the subcontinent is divided into two seasons: khareef (monsoon) and rabi (winter). Khareef sowing starts in July or even June while the sowing of rabi crops begins in September and October, depending upon glacial melts and the amount of rains. The water flows in the Indus system varies exponentially in different months. Up to 90 per cent of flows can be accounted for during July to September.

For rabi crops such as wheat, pulses, onions, tomatoes and potatoes, timing is crucial. With October at an end, the record reduction of Chenab water flows can translate into delayed rabi sowing, which in turn will adversely impact produce for local consumption in the coming season and lead to price inflation.

In practical terms, consider this: tomatoes are being sold in the market at 25 rupees per kilo today; expect this price to rise manifold in the coming year. This is besides the food and income insecurity that thousands of growers in Punjab and Sindh will be pushed into.

A crisis is certainly brewing.

Beyond hyperbole and nationalistic fervour, the two South Asian giants need to be at the negotiating table. Normally a dispute like the one reported by Dawn on October 12 could have been resolved at a meeting of the Indus water commissioners, mandated by the Indus Waters Treaty to be held once a year. But the Indian assertion that these meetings will resume only once "an atmosphere free of terror is established" spells disaster for our farmers. The only safeguard that the Indus Waters Treaty offered Pakistan was through the Permanent Indus Commission whose meetings India has been routinely flouting under one pretext or the other. If the situation persists, Pakistan will have no option but to take the matter through the cumbersome route of World Bank and international arbitration. All through this period, India will enjoy undue exploitation of water resources at the expense of the people of Pakistan.

What can India not do?

Caught in nationalistic fervour, hawks in the Indian media have been blaming their previous governments for failing to exercise a water offensive like the one PM Modi is intent on implementing.

Indeed, India can hypothetically terminate the Indus Waters Treaty and restrict even the rivers flowing into Pakistan through the diversion of Indus rivers waters. But when it comes to practice, this position remains untenable.

The waters of the Indus rivers flow through deep gorges of the Karakoram and Himalayan mountains. The only way to divert water from here is to tunnel through hundreds of kilometres of the world's highest and toughest mountains.

Granted that all technical problems have technical solutions. However such an undertaking would be financially prohibitive, technically extremely challenging, and with minimal cost-benefit ratios. The longest tunnel dug in the world is the Gotthard Base Tunnel to facilitate rail travel. Although it is being drilled for the last 22 years through the Swiss Alps, it is merely 57 kilometres long and has already incurred an estimated cost of 12 billion US dollars. For India to divert waters of the western Indus basin rivers for meaningful use, it will have to dig up to 300 kilometres of tunnels.

As such, diverting the water going into western rivers which feed Pakistan is not a feasible option.

In addition, India has remained part of the Non-Aligned Movement and prides itself in having contributed towards drafting many international conventions including the UN Convention on the Law of the Non-navigational Uses of International Watercourses 1997, Helsinki Rules 1966 and their Berlin Revisions of 2004. Politically, an attempt to scrap the Indus Waters Treaty would bring massive international condemnation to India.

India's planned infrastructure projects: how can they affect Pakistan?

While India may not have the capacity to turn off the taps immediately or divert the waters of the rivers flowing into Pakistan, it is undertaking a number of projects that could have an adverse impact on Pakistan's water availability in the future.

The Indus Waters Treaty handed Pakistan the right to unrestricted use of the three western rivers — Indus, Chenab and Jhelum. The eastern rivers — Sutlej, Beas and Ravi — went to India. While the treaty allowed India to divert the waters of the eastern rivers, it could only tap into 3.6 MAF of water from the western rivers for irrigation, transport and power generation.

Experts at the Indus River System Authority (IRSA) complain that India has been constructing huge water storages on all six Indus basin rivers, not just on the three under its full control. For example, Baglihar and Salal on Chenab are already generating 450 MW/h and 690 MW/h respectively while the planned Bursar and Pakal hydroelectric projects also on the Chenab will produce 1020MW and 1000 MW/h respectively. The size of the energy outputs is an indication of the size of the projects. Pakistan's Mangla, for comparison, generates 1000MW/h.

In all, India is in different phases of planning or construction of some 60 storages of varying capacity over the six Indus rivers, though analysis of satellite imagery obtained by Dawn suggests the number may be more [see map]. Technical experts in Pakistan worry that such storages will provide India ultimate strategic leverage of increasing or decreasing river flows during tensions between the two countries, even if it cannot legally divert the waters for its own use.

Sheraz Memon, additional commissioner of the Indus Water Commission, argues that India does not have sufficient capacity to withhold the water of the western rivers nor it can divert them. "But they may keep the implementation of the treaty at a snail's pace, for example through delaying the meetings of the Permanent Indus Commission and not providing data or information about their new hydroelectric plants," he warns.

There is also talk of expediting the construction of the Pakal Dul, Sawalkot, and Bursar dams, also in Jammu and Kashmir. Indian media reports claim that the Indian government might also resume work on the Tulbul Navigational Project — also known as Wullar Barrage — work on which began in 1985 but stopped soon after Pakistan lodged a formal complaint against its construction. Pakistan opposed the project at the time since it would have allowed India to store, control and divert River Jhelum, which was a clear violation of the Indus Waters Treaty. If completed, Tulbul will adversely affect the water storage potential of Mangla Dam.

Original sins

During 1956, Pakistani negotiators were warned by their irrigation officials and technical experts not to accede to Indian delegation chief ND Gulhati's demand — also supported by the World Bank — to allow India to build small storages over the western rivers.

Until the signing of the treaty, the Indian predicament was that while Customary International Law and conventions gave them a legitimate right over 33 MAF or 21 percent of the six Indus rivers water — corresponding to 21 per cent of the Indus basin being in Indian territory — India had little room to utilise this water within the basin. The Indus Waters Treaty gave them an opportunity to divert water towards Rajasthan for irrigating over 700,000 acres of land which was previously bare sand dunes.

Before the Treaty, the waters of the Ravi, Beas and Sutlej were utilised for the cultivation of lands as far south as Bahawalpur State. Suddenly there was no water for thousands of farmers on this side of the border until Tarbela Dam was finally opened in 1976.

But Pakistani negotiators at the time acquiesced, on the pretext that this shared water would also benefit their Muslim brethren in Kashmir. Pakistani negotiators did not even bother to specify the size of the so-called small storages but agreed to India officially withdrawing up to 3.6 MAF of water for local use. In comparison, the current storage capacity of Mangla Dam, after expansion, is about 7.4 MAF.

Given the pliancy of Pakistani negotiators at the time, the Indus Waters Treaty emerged as a treatise that was skewed in favour of India. Perhaps it is for this reason that PM Modi announced that while India will not review or abrogate the Indus Waters Treaty, it will exploit water under its share to the fullest. It will, for example, build more run-of-the-river hydropower projects on the western rivers and irrigate over 400,000 acres in Jammu and Kashmir.

One thing seems certain: India will continue to build additional storages on the Indus rivers to store more than its allowed quota of up to 3.6 MAF of water. This will also provide hawks the option of delaying khareef crops in Pakistan from time to time. If the winters' torment is harsh, delay in summers sowing would be a national crisis.

Looking within: what Pakistan needs to do

There is a real danger that current Indian antics will push Pakistan towards construction of very large dams at Diamer and Kalabagh, displacing more people and adversely impacting our environment which is already in a poor state.

"India is employing pressure tactics on Pakistan by announcing it will speed up dam construction," argues Dr Pervaiz Amir, director of the Pakistan Water Partnership. "Pakistan must address its own internal water security and create sufficient storage. India has 200 projects in hand. Saving water is a planned response by India, and Pakistan should follow suit."

But increasing storage capacity is not the same as storage capacity from large dams, which in any case is not the panacea that it is made out to be.

During the last 69 years, Pakistan has developed three major water storages at Tarbela, Mangla and Chashma with a cumulative storage capacity of 12.1 MAF against average water flows of 133 MAF annually through the three Indus rivers. There have been little or no independent studies to either assess or address the issues of resettlement, the massive loss to the environment and overall economic cost due to construction of large dams. In addition, issues of climate change —which have only recently come to the fore — raise questions about the risks posed to and by large dams. Freak weather conditions, such as unusually intense cloudbursts, are becoming more common and have already resulted in threats to people living downstream of large dams.

To add insult to injury, we have been ruthlessly pumping out underground water through tubewells. Such pumping is severely affecting the underground water levels in the country and often being replaced by saline water, adversely affecting agricultural output. The number of tubewells in Pakistan has risen from 2,400 to over 600,000 since 1960.

While we could continue to curse the World Bank bureaucracy, American interests in the region and Indian cunning for having deprived the country of its water share, we must also look at our own wasteful attitudes towards utilisation of available water resources as well as the politics around available water.

Pakistan loses almost half of its existing available water through seepage in the irrigation system [see table]. This is a prime cause of waterlogging and salinity which are turning large areas of fertile land barren. Surely lining of water canals and water courses should be the first priority in saving the water we have at our disposal, rather than the construction of large dams.

According to WAPDA's published figures, average cereal production in Pakistan against a metre cube of water is mere 0.13 kg. In India, the same amount of water yields 0.39 kg, yield in China is estimated at 0.82 kg, in the US 1.56 kg and in Canada 8.2 kg [see table]. Clearly better management of water resources, efficient crop yields and serious efforts towards population control will be much more advantageous than building additional dams and storages that will ultimately result in catastrophic environmental issues and human resettlement crises as being faced in India and China.

The issue of water supply does not simply concern the two nuclear-armed neighbours. Tahir Rasheed, CEO of the South Punjab Forest Company (SPFC) and a senior environmentalist, warns that if the Indo-Pak water crisis spirals out of control, the friction can engulf other countries of the region as well, especially Afghanistan.

"Afghanistan is [currently] utilising 1.8 MAF of water [from the Kabul River which feeds into the Indus], which is estimated to rise to 3.6 MAF in the future," says Rasheed. "Pakistan currently does not have any water sharing accord with its northwestern neighbor. But the projected increase of water use by Afghanistan can affect the lower riparian, Pakistan."

In conclusion

The Indus Waters Commissioners of Pakistan and India have met every year since the Indus Waters Treaty came into force. The wars of 1965 and 1971, the Siachen and Kargil conflicts and the Mumbai attacks weren't able to dent it. In standing the test of time, the treaty has shown that it generates the least conflict and more cooperation between the South Asian neighbours.

The chances of India scrapping the treaty altogether and diverting the western rivers are negligible to none. But one must not put past India its flouting the spirit of the treaty and manipulating water flows to turn the screws on Pakistan.

Pakistan's response, however, should not be as cavalier as when it negotiated the treaty, ignoring sound technical advice and short-changing itself in the bargain. It needs to put its own house in order on an urgent basis — by better utilising its existing water resources. Pakistan's protestations against India's perfidy will then carry far more weight.

APP – 18

REVIEW INDUS WATERS TREATY

Priyanka Mallick – November 03, 2016

Deccan Herald (India)

This is a good time for New Delhi to review the Treaty and re-sign it given the nature of hostility with Pakistan.

Prime Minister Narendra Modi's decision to review the Indus Waters Treaty (IWT) suggests a strategic shift in the policy towards Pakistan.

Modi stated that "Water and blood cannot flow simultaneously." For the first time, New Delhi has decided to explore the possibility of river water as a strategic weapon vis-a-vis Islamabad.

The IWT was negotiated over nine years between India and Pakistan and was signed on Sept 19, 1960. It is a unique treaty simply because it is based on sharing rivers between two countries – not their waters. According to the IWT, three western rivers – Indus, Chenab and Jhelum – are allocated to Pakistan while the three eastern rivers – Sutlej, Beas and Ravi – flow into India. The IWT also permits India to the restricted use of western rivers for domestic, non-consumptive and hydro-electric with minimal storage purposes. While 80% of the waters of the Indus river system benefits Pakistan, only 20% flows into India.

Under the Treaty, disagreements by the parties on the int-erpretation of the provisions are classified into three categories: Firstly, all questions will be decided by the Permanent Indus Commission. Secondly, differences will be decided by a neutral expert. Thirdly, disputes will be decided by a Permanent Co-urt of Arbitration at The Hague. The popular perception is that the IWT represents a superb slice of success in India-Pakistan relations. But the only positive of the IWT is simply that it has survived the three India-Pakistan conflicts of 1965 and 1999 over Kashmir, besides 1971 related to East Pakistan. The Treaty is not free from controversies. In reality, there are differences over several issues that have not been sorted out despite prolonged bilateral talks.

Pakistan has opposed the Tulbul Navigation Project and Kishanganga Hydro-Electric Project (KHEP) on Jhelum River Basin and DulHasti and Baglihar Hydro-Electric Project on the Chenab river basin. The fact that Pakistan perceives several problems over the IWT with India makes one really wonder ab-out the success of this World Ba-nk mediated treaty. Despite the fact that India is legally entitled to construct dams on the western rivers with minimum water storage, Pakistan has raised objections on these projects. Islamabad strongly feels that the allocation of river water and India's construction of dams do not follow the criteria specified in the IWT and diversion of water would disturb the flow of western rivers into Pakistan. However, India says that all its dam projects are completely in compliance with the terms of the Treaty. Yet Pakistan has taken the KHEP to the Permanent Court of Arbitration. In the case of Baglihar dam, which India started to build in 1999 and completed in 2008, Pakistan objected to its height and storage capacity. Eventually in the Baglihar Dam case, neutral expert Raymond Laffite gave his final award in 2007 with only some minor changes on the project design but Pakistan expressed her dissatisfaction on the matter.

In principle, Pakistan said that the Indian riverine projects or dams do not follow the criteria specified in the IWT. Islamabad holds the position that unlimited proliferation of dams and diversion of water would badly disturb flow of the western rivers into Pakistan. However, India says that all Indian projects are fully in compliance with the Treaty.

Diverting water

In the Kishanganga case, the Permanent Court of Arbitration allows India to divert water for power generation with a minimum flow 318 cusecs into the Kishanganga river below the KHEP throughout the year. In this case also, the decision did not favour Pakistan, though in both the cases, Islamabad raised the issue for third party mediation. While the Indus river is critical for Pakistan's existence, it holds equal importance for the India's northern border state of Jammu & Kashmir, especially the western rivers which are allocated to Pakistan under the Treaty.

Today, J&K suffers from acute power deficiency due to the IWT's restrictions on its use of rivers. The northern border state still has untapped hydro-power potential of over 25,000 MW. Recently, J&K Chief Minister Mehbooba Mufti said that "There have been so many wars, but the IWT was not touched because both the countries benefited from our resources, even as J&K suffered losses."

Considering that J&K is an integral part of India, the prevalent socio-economic situation there assumes greater significance rather than its hostile western neighbour Pakistan. New Delhi could diplomatically leverage the IWT to dilute the anti-India sentiment among the Kashmiri people in the border state. Importantly, the adverse impact of climate change is clearly visible in our water resources sector. The change in rainfall pa-ttern and retreat of glaciers has resulted in an acute water shortage across the country. Can India afford to be so liberal about sharing the waters of the Indus river system with Pakistan?

Therefore, this is the right time for New Delhi to review the Treaty and re-sign, given the nature of relations with Pakistan characterised by hostility. Also, J&K should be treated as a stakeholder in the revised IWT which should be re-worked keeping the interests of the northern border state in mind.

APP – 19

PAKISTAN WARNS INDIA AGAINST BREACH OF INDUS WATER TREATY

Zafar Bhutta : November 8, 2016

The Express Tribune, PAKISTAN

Islamabad has warned New Delhi that Pakistan will respond with full force if India shows open aggression by breaching the World Bank-sponsored Indus Waters Treaty (IWT)."India will be responded [to] if it shows aggression by unilaterally breaking the treaty," Water and Power Secretary Younis Dagha told the Senate Standing Committee on Water and Power on Monday.The committee had met to reconsider the report regarding an adjournment motion moved in the upper house of parliament by Senator Sherry Rehman on September 27. Rehman had moved the motion in the backdrop of Indian threats to unilaterally revoke the IWT.

The PPP senator had sought details about the possible repercussions of the move and Pakistan's stance and preparedness to combat such a warlike situation.Talking with reference to the Indian threats, Dagha told the panel that there are some more conventions in place in addition to the IWT to safeguard Pakistan's water rights."If India shows aggression then there are some other options," he added. "India cannot stop more water from Neelum River. It can stop water only temporarily for using it."Dagha said the government had started work on the National Water Policy 2016 and consultations would be completed in the next one to two months. Later, the parliamentary panel formed a subcommittee, comprising members National Assembly, Water and Power Ministry officials and experts on water to review the IWT.Rehman expressed concerns over violation of the IWT and said Indian Prime Minister Narendra Modi had threatened to end the treaty unilaterally."According to a report of the Water and Power Development Authority (Wapda), India has no authority to break the IWT unilaterally," she said, adding that India has taken advantage due to past mistakes of different governments in Pakistan.Rehman lamented that India built several dams on various rivers but Pakistan could do nothing to stop it. "India has built Kishanganga dam and Baglihar dam. Our Mangla dam will be adversely affected due to more dams being built by India," she said.She said the IWT should be reviewed with mutual consultations, adding that India is blocking Pakistan's water and government should think over the solutions.

Wapda officials informed the committee that 584 appointments were made in the authority during the last one year. As many as 516 appointments were made on contract while 68 on daily wages.

APP - 20

FARMERS WILL GET EVERY DROP, MODI ON INDUS WATER TREATY

DECCAN CHRONICLE 25 November, 2016.

'The fields of our farmers must have adequate water, it cannot go to Pakistan' said Modi.

Prime Minister Narendra Modi on Friday raked up the Indus Water Treaty and said 'water that belongs to India cannot be allowed to go to Pakistan'. "The fields of our farmers must have adequate water. Water that belongs to India cannot be allowed to go to Pakistan," Modi said at a rally in Bhatinda. "My farmers have the right over the water that flows through Indus, will strive to get that water back," he added.

Modi said his government has formed a task force on Indus water treaty to ensure farmers of Punjab and other states get each drop of water due to them."There is no reason that we cannot use our rights (over our waters) and let our farmers suffer," he said, adding, "I need your blessings in order to fulfill your requirements for watering your fields."

The solution for the problems of water could be found out through common dialogue, he said. Criticising the previous governments at the Centre, Modi said, "Waters kept flowing to Pakistan, but successive governments kept sleeping on this issue and my farmer kept crying for the want of water." "If Punjab farmers get sufficient amount of water, they could produce 'gold' from the soil and could fill the coffers of the country," he said."Our government is committed to work in tandem with the Badal government in Punjab to get farmers their rights and address their concerns," he said.His remarks come two days after Pakistan warned India against "use of water as an instrument of coercion". "The international community must assume a responsibility to develop, nurture and protect normative frameworks, at multilateral and bilateral levels, to ensure that states remain willing to resolve water issues cooperatively,"

Pakistan's Ambassador to the UN, Maleeha Lodhi said in her address to the UN Security Council during an open debate on water, peace and security on Wednesday.

Modi attacked Pakistan in his speech and said that it should concentrate on fighting terrorism and corruption.

"When school in Peshawar was attacked every Indian was sad. People of Pakistan should tell their rulers to fight corruption, fake notes," said Modi.

APP – 21

PAKISTAN PRE-EMPTS INDIAN WATER THREATS

Mariana Baabar – November 26, 2016

The News (Pakistan)

Pakistan had preempted Indian threats that it was now going to use water as the new weapon of war, and had in time warned world capitals that they "must assume a responsibility to develop, nurture and protect normative frameworks, at multilateral and bilateral levels, to ensure that states remain willing to resolve water issues cooperatively."

Prime Minister Modi on Friday while speaking to a rally in Punjab threatened, "Under the Indus Water Treaty, India has the right over water of Satluj, Beas and Ravi rivers. It rightfully belongs to our farmers, but this water is not reaching the farmer's field, instead the water is flowing to Pakistan and eventually going to the sea. Governments came and went in Delhi, but farmers kept suffering as water continued to flow to Pakistan. Not any-more, I will ensure that farmers get what is rightfully theirs".

It is not uncommon to hear Indian leaders hit out at Pakistan whenever they are in election mode, whether they are campaigning in Kashmir, Punjab or any other part of India. Under great pressure at home, after having failed to deliver and now his de-monetization policy playing havoc with the lives of ordinary Indians, with the Indian rupee hitting a record low, Modi is using the guise of water wars to win domestic sympathy and support.

The situation in Indian Occupied Kashmir (IoK) is one for which New Delhi has no answers, and as questions are being raised in important world capitals behind closed doors, Modi has now tried to provoke Pakistan and draw attention on an issue which is life or death for lower riparian.

"This water is neither being utilized by Pakistan nor does it come in Indian farmers destiny. I have set-up a task force. I'm committed to ensure that every single drop of water, which is rightfully ours, under the Indus Water Treaty, is brought to the farmers in Punjab, Jammu and Kashmir, and other parts of the country," Modi pointed out.

Unlike many other bilateral treaties and understandings between the two neighbors, the 1960 World Bank-mediated Indus Waters Treaty between India and Pakistan has survived till date despite of wars between the two sides.

Till Modi's latest threats, this treaty has ensured that water of six rivers — Beas, Ravi, Sutlej, Indus, Chenab and Jhelum — are to be shared between the two countries.

Earlier Advisor on Foreign Policy Sartaj Aziz had tried to send a subtle message to New Delhi that if it tries to interrupt water flow into Pakistan, it will not only violate the Indus Waters Treaty, but also set a regional state practice under which international law can be served as a precedent. "It will provide China, for example, a justification to consider suspension of waters of the Brahmaputra river," he had commented.

In fact China had not too long back, blocked a tributary of the Brahmaputra River in Tibet as part of the construction of its "most expensive" hydro project, which at any time could have a severe impact on all lower riparian countries.

Earlier this week, Pakistan's Ambassador to the UN, Maleeha Lodhi said in her address to the UN Security Council during an open debate on water, peace and security, that the Indus Water Treaty of 1960, between Pakistan and India, with the World Bank as guarantor, as "a model of what can be achieved through bilateral agreements".

"Access to water is a fundamental right that must be protected at all times. We will respect and protect our existing understandings and build where they are yet to be reached. The international community must remain vigilant to any sign of unwillingness to maintain cooperation and be willing act to avert any conflict," she said.

Lodhi emphasized that it was the Security Council's responsibility to resolve international conflicts and disputes, especially longstanding, prolonged conflicts, in particular in Asia and Africa. "Unburdened by conflicts of the past, new challenges can then be addressed cooperatively and comprehensively", she advised.

APP - 22

THE GREAT WATER FOLLY

Brahma Chellaney – December 13, 2016

The Hindustan Times

The Indus Water Treaty with Pakistan symbolises India's enduring strategic naivete and negligence, writers Brahma Chellaney

The linkages between water stress, sharing disputes and environmental degradation threaten to trap Asia in a vicious cycle. In a continent where China's unilateralism stands out as a destabilizing factor, only four of the 57 transnational river basins have a treaty on water sharing or institutionalized cooperation. Indeed, the only Asian treaties incorporating specific sharing formulas are between India and its downriver neighbours, Pakistan and Bangladesh.

When Pakistan was carved out of India as the first Islamic republic of the post-colonial era, the partition left the Indus headwaters in India, arming it with formidable water leverage over the newly-created country. Yet India ultimately agreed under World Bank and US pressure in 1960 to what still ranks as the world's most generous (and lopsided) water-sharing pact.

The Indus Waters Treaty (IWT) reserved for Pakistan the largest three rivers that make up more than four-fifths of the Indus-system waters, leaving for India just 19.48% of the total waters. After gifting the lion's share of the waters to the congenitally hostile Pakistan, India also contributed $173.63 million for dam and other projects there. The Great Water Folly — one of the major strategic problems bequeathed to future Indian generations by the Nehruvian era — began exacting serious costs within a few years.

Far from mollifying an implacable foe, the IWT whetted Pakistan's territorial revisionism, prompting its 1965 military attack on India's Jammu and Kashmir. The attack was aimed at gaining political control of the land through which the three largest rivers reserved for Pakistani use flowed, although only one of them originates in J&K. The 1965 attack was essentially a water war.

India's naïve assumption that it traded water munificence for peace in 1960 has backfired, saddling it with an iniquitous treaty of indefinite duration and keeping water as a core issue in its relations with Pakistan. As for Pakistan, after failing to achieve its water designs militarily in 1965, it has continued to wage a water war against India by other means, including diplomacy and terrorism. Put simply, 56 years after the IWT was signed, Pakistan's covetous, water-driven claim to India's J&K remains intact.

Pakistan has cleverly employed the IWT to have its cake and eat it too. While receiving the largest quantum of waters reserved by any treaty for a downstream state, it uses the IWT to sustain its conflict and tensions with India. Worse still, this scofflaw nation repays the upper riparian's unparalleled water largesse with blood by waging an undeclared, terrorism-centred war, with the Nagrota attack the latest example.

Pakistan has recently succeeded — for the second time in this decade — in persuading a partisan World Bank to initiate international arbitral proceedings against India. Seeking international intercession is part of

Pakistan's 'water war' strategy against India, yet it is the World Bank's ugly role in the latest instance that sticks out. This should surprise few.

After all, it was the World Bank's murky role that spawned the inherently unequal IWT. Whereas the British colonial government was the instrument in India's 1947 land partition, the Bank served as the agent to partition the Indus-system rivers, floating the river-partitioning proposal and ramming it down India's throat. India's full sovereignty rights were limited to the smallest three of the six rivers, with the Bank uniquely signing a binational treaty as its guarantor.

Since then, World Bank support enabled Pakistan not only to complete mega-dams but also to sustain its 'water war' strategy against India by seeking to invoke international intercession repeatedly. Now, in response to Pakistan's complaint over the design features of two midsized Indian hydropower projects, the World Bank has sought to initiate two concurrent processes that mock the IWT's provisions for resolving any 'questions', 'differences' or 'disputes' between the parties: It is appointing both a court of arbitration (as sought by Pakistan) and a neutral expert (as suggested by India), while admitting that "pursuing two concurrent processes under the treaty could make it unworkable over time".

India says it "cannot be party to actions" by the World Bank that breach the IWT's terms, implying that it might not accept the arbitral tribunal. India's bark, however, has always been worse than its bite. While protesting the Bank's "legally untenable" move in the latest case, India has shown little inclination to respond through punitive counter-measures.

Had China been in India's place, it would have sought to discipline the Bank and Pakistan. Indeed, it is unthinkable that China would have countenanced such an egregiously inequitable treaty. While mouthing empty rhetoric, India still allows Pakistan to draw the IWT's full benefits even as Pakistan bleeds it by exporting terrorists. The truth is this: The IWT symbolizes India's enduring strategic naiveté and negligence. Despite water shortages triggering bitter feuds between Punjab and some other states, India has failed to tap even the allocated 19.48% share of the Indus Basin resources.

For example, the waters of the three India-earmarked rivers not utilized by India aggregate to 10.37 billion cubic metres (BCM) yearly according to Pakistan, and 11.1 BCM according to the UN. These bonus outflows to Pakistan alone amount to six times Mexico's total water share under its treaty with the US, and are many times greater than the total volumes spelled out in the Israel-Jordan water arrangements. Although the IWT permits India to store 4.4 BCM of waters from the Pakistan-reserved rivers, a careless India has built no storage. And despite the treaty allowing India to build hydropower plants with no dam reservoir, its total installed generating capacity in J&K currently does not equal the size of a single new dam in Pakistan like the 4,500-megawatt Diamer-Bhasha, whose financing for construction was approved last week.

APP - 23

WORLD BANK DECLARES PAUSE TO PROTECT INDUS WATERS TREATY

Shahbaz Rana – 13 December, 2016

The Express Tribune (Pakistan)

The World Bank Group on Monday announced a pause in the separate processes initiated by India and Pakistan under the Indus Waters Treaty to allow the two countries to consider alternative ways to resolve their disagreements. According to a press release issued by the World Bank, the announcement temporarily halts the appointment of a neutral expert, as requested by India, and the chairman of the Court of Arbitration as requested by Pakistan, to resolve issues regarding two hydroelectric power plants under construction by India along the Indus rivers system. Both processes initiated by the respective countries were advancing at the same time, creating a risk of contradictory outcomes that could potentially endanger the Treaty. "We are announcing this pause to protect the Indus Waters Treaty and to help India and Pakistan consider alternative approaches to resolving conflicting interests under the Treaty and its application to two hydroelectric power plants," said World Bank Group President Jim Yong Kim.

"This is an opportunity for the two countries to begin to resolve the issue in an amicable manner and in line with the spirit of the treaty rather than pursuing concurrent processes that could make the treaty unworkable over time. I would hope that the two countries will come to an agreement by the end of January," Kim added. The pause was announced by Kim in letters to the finance ministers of India and Pakistan, stressing that the Bank was acting to safeguard the treaty. Pausing the process for now, the Bank would hold off from appointing the chairman for the Court of Arbitration or the neutral expert – appointments that had been expected on December 12 as earlier communicated by the Bank. The current processes under the treaty concern the Kishenganga (330 megawatts) and Ratle (850 megawatts) hydroelectric power plants. The power plants are being built by India on, respectively, the Kishenganga and Chenab Rivers. Neither of the two plants are being financed by the World Bank Group. The Indus Waters Treaty 1960 is seen as one of the most successful international treaties and has withstood frequent tensions between India and Pakistan, including conflict. The treaty sets out a mechanism for cooperation and information exchange between the two countries regarding their use of the rivers, known as the Permanent Indus Commission which includes a commissioner from each of the two countries. It also sets out a process for resolving so-called "questions", "differences" and "disputes" that may arise between the parties.

APP – 24

WATER DISPUTES: WORLD BANK HALTS INDO – PAK ARBITRATION

Shahbaz Rana – December 14, 2016

The Express Tribune, Pakistan

The World Bank has temporarily stopped playing the role of arbitrator in the India-Pakistan water disputes – a development interpreted by an expert as accepting the position of New Delhi that is increasingly seeking bilateral resolution to all disputes with Islamabad.

"The World Bank Group today announced a pause in the separate processes initiated by India and Pakistan under the Indus Waters Treaty (IWT) to allow the two countries to consider alternative ways to resolve their disagreements," said an official handout issued by the local office of the Washington-based lending agency.

Adviser to Prime Minister on Foreign Affairs Sartaj Aziz said Pakistan's foreign office would issue a statement after reviewing the World Bank's press release. Pakistan's Indus Water Commissioner Asif Baig also declined to comment.

The global lender said the announcement temporarily halts the appointment of a neutral expert, as requested by India, and the Chairman of the Court of Arbitration, as requested by Pakistan, to resolve issues regarding two hydroelectric power plants under construction by India along the Indus rivers system.

Both processes initiated by the respective countries were advancing at the same time, creating a risk of contradictory outcomes that could potentially endanger the treaty, said the handout.

Pakistan had disputed India's move to construct two power plants – the 330-megawatt Kishanganga hydropower plant and 850-megawatt Ratle hydroelectric power plant. The power plants are being built by India on the Kishanganga and Chenab rivers respectively.

It is for the first time since the IWT became operational some 56 years ago that the WB has halted the arbitration process. The WB has earlier played the role of mediator in case of Kishganga project when Pakistan raised the legal issues and Baglihar project.

India has recently raised temperatures after it revealed its intentions to block waters flowing into Pakistan. Islamabad has taken an exception to the Indian designs, saying any such move will be taken as open aggression.

"We are announcing this pause to protect the IWT and to help India and Pakistan consider alternative approaches to resolving conflicting interests under the treaty and its application to two hydroelectric power plants," said World Bank Group President Jim Yong Kim.

He said this was an opportunity for the two countries to begin to resolve the issues in an amicable manner and in line with the spirit of the treaty rather than pursuing concurrent processes that could make the treaty unworkable over time.

"I would hope that the two countries will come to an agreement by the end of January," said the group president. The WB announced the pause the day it was supposed to appoint the Chairman for the Court of Arbitration or the Neutral Expert.

"The WB took the decision under pressure of India and Pakistan has been trapped into it," said Jamat Ali Shah, former Indus Commissioner of Pakistan. He said the WB paused the process only after Pakistan explicitly gave an understanding of following other mechanisms to resolve the disputes.

Shah said Pakistan had first applied to the WB for appointment of Chairman of the Court of Arbitration, therefore, the WB should not have accepted India's request for appointment of neutral expert.

"The WB's decision to follow two parallel processes in a single dispute is a bizarre move, which subsequently allowed India to denounce that it would not accept court of arbitration," Shah said.

He said that under the 1960 Indus Basin Treaty, the only other option was taking up the matter at the Permanent Indus Commission level. Both the countries have already exhausted this option and availing it again would not resolve the disputes, said the former official.

He said during this time India would make significant progress on both the projects.

In November this year, India had refused to take part in the Court of Arbitration established by World Bank to solve the Kishanganga dispute with Pakistan, stating that it was legally untenable to set up two parallel dispute mechanisms. The Ministry of External Affairs spokesperson Vikas Swarup had said India could not be party to actions which were not in accordance with the IWT.

The WB said the IWT 1960 is seen as one of the most successful international treaties and has withstood frequent tensions between India and Pakistan, including conflicts.

The treaty sets out a mechanism for cooperation and information exchange between the two countries regarding their use of the rivers, known as the Permanent Indus Commission, which includes a commissioner from each of the two countries.

"As an international financial cooperative that has the mandate to act in the interests of all its shareholders, the bank will always remain supportive of the development goals of both countries," said the WB's Washington-based spokesman Alexander Ferguson.

He was responding to a question whether WB has accepted India's position by pausing the process. Ferguson did not give a clear answer to another question about future line of action if both the countries do not reach to an agreement by January.

"The announcement is consistent with the WB's historic role as a neutral, pragmatic and proactive partner to both countries and is without prejudice to the processes initiated by [them]," he said.

APP – 25

PAKISTAN AND INDIA TO CONSIDER ALTERNATIVE WAYS ON DISPUTE

Munawar Hasan, 14 December, 2016

The News (Pakistan)

LAHORE: The World Bank Group has announced a pause in the separate processes initiated by Pakistan and India under the Indus Waters Treaty on two controversial power projects being built in Indian held Kashmir to allow the two countries to consider alternative ways to resolve their disagreements. The bank has temporarily halts the appointment of a neutral expert, as requested by India, and the chairman of the Court of Arbitration, as requested by Pakistan, to resolve issues regarding two hydroelectric power plants under construction by India along the Indus rivers system. Both processes initiated by the respective countries were advancing at the same time, creating a risk of contradictory outcomes that could potentially endanger the treaty.

"We are announcing this pause to protect the Indus Waters Treaty and to help India and Pakistan consider alternative approaches to resolving conflicting interests under the treaty and its application to two hydroelectric power plants," said World Bank Group President Jim Yong Kim. "This is an opportunity for the two countries to begin to resolve the issue in an amicable manner and in line with the spirit of the treaty rather than pursuing concurrent processes that could make the treaty unworkable over time. Kim said the bank hoped that the two countries will come to an agreement by the end of January." The pause was announced by the bank's president in letters to the finance ministers of India and Pakistan and emphasised that the bank was acting to safeguard the treaty. "Pausing the process for now, the bank would hold off from appointing the chairman for the Court of Arbitration or the neutral expert – appointments that had been expected on December 12 as earlier communicated by the bank," it said in a statement. The current processes under the treaty concern the Kishenganga (330 megawatts) and Ratle (850 megawatts) hydroelectric power plants. The power plants are being built by India on, respectively, the Kishenganga and Chenab Rivers. Neither of the two plants are being financed by the World Bank Group.

The Indus Waters Treaty 1960 is seen as one of the most successful international treaties and has withstood frequent tensions between India and Pakistan, including conflict. The Treaty sets out a mechanism for cooperation and information exchange between the two countries regarding their use of the rivers, known as the Permanent Indus Commission which includes a commissioner from each of the two countries. It also sets out a process for resolving so-called "questions", "differences" and "disputes" that may arise between the parties.

APP – 26

INDUS WATER TREATY: GOVERNMENT SETS UP TASK FORCE TO LOOK AT FULL USE OF WATER SHARE

Amitabh Sinha - 15 December, 2016

The Indian Express

The Indus Water Treaty of 1960 allocates the waters of three rivers of the Indus basin to India and of the other three to Pakistan.

India has constituted a high-level task force under Principal Secretary to Prime Minister Nripendra Mishra to decide on measures to be taken to ensure full utilisation of its share of river waters under the Indus Water Treaty. This comes amid a fresh round of bickering with Pakistan over an old issue relating to a hydroelectric project in Jammu and Kashmir.

Government sources told The Indian Express that India was not considering the option of walking out of the Indus Water Treaty in the near future, but was keen to ensure that all the water it was entitled to was fully utilised for development.

The Indus Water Treaty of 1960 allocates the waters of three rivers of the Indus basin to India and of the other three to Pakistan. All the six rivers flow from India to Pakistan. India has full rights over the so-called eastern rivers — Sutlej, Beas and Ravi — while it must allow the three western rivers — Indus, Chenab and Jhelum — to flow unrestricted to Pakistan.

India can utilise water of western rivers for "non-consumptive" uses, in the manner prescribed in the treaty, but has not done so. Even the waters of the eastern rivers have not been exploited to their full capacities.

Following the Uri attack, the government had decided to take a hard look at the treaty, with Prime Minister *Narendra Modi* declaring that "blood and water could not flow together".

The formation of the task force is another step by the government to assert its rights on the river waters in the Indus basin. The task force has NSA Ajit Doval, Foreign Secretary S Jaishankar and Finance Secretary Ashok Lavasa among its members. It is expected to hold its first meeting next week to review all projects and other ongoing activities on the six rivers on the Indian side.

The task force already has an emerging crisis to deal with. Pakistan has lodged a fresh complaint with World Bank over a run-of-the-river project on Kishanganga river in Jammu and Kashmir. It has also raised a dispute over construction of Ratle Dam over Chenab river. The World Bank, which brokered the Indus Water Treaty in 1960, acts as mediator in such disputes. Pakistan has complained that the Kishanganga project violates the treaty and demanded setting up of a Court of Arbitration.

India has opposed the need for a Court of Arbitration and has filed a separate request with World Bank, asking only for the appointment of a neutral expert to assess whether the design of the project conformed to provisions of the treaty.

The World Bank had earlier said it would initiate both proceedings but, following India's objection, it announced Wednesday that it was declaring a 'pause' to allow the two countries to "consider alternative ways to resolve their disagreements".

APP – 27

INDIA SIGNALS PEACE ON INDUS WATER ISSUE

Suhasini Haider, 15 December, 2016

The Hindu (India)

Conciliatory statement comes after World Bank paused arbitration process

Signalling a step back from tensions in the past month over the Indus Water Treaty with Pakistan, India said there was "no reason" the two countries could not sort out their differences as they have in the past.

"Given the will to address these matters through the appropriate mechanisms provided for in the Indus Waters Treaty, there is no reason why the technical design parameters on which Pakistan has raised objections cannot be sorted out by professional, technical experts from both sides," Ministry of External Affairs spokesperson Vikas Swarup said on Thursday.

WB concession

India's statement comes after the World Bank acceded to its wishes and halted the two processes for mediation and arbitration that it had put into place over Pakistan's objections to 'design features' in the Kishanganga and Ratle hydroelectric power projects in Jammu and Kashmir.

"It is a matter of satisfaction that [India's] point has now been recognised by the World Bank. We believe that these consultations should be given adequate time," the spokesperson said.

India had objected to the World Bank's earlier decision as it said the acceptance of Pakistan's appeal for an arbitration process under article IX was "illegal", accusing the World Bank of "favouring Pakistan". The strong language of the statement appeared to have weighed with the World Bank, and on December 12, the day its President Jim Yong Kim was due to announce the names chosen for the arbitration panel and as mediator, he instead said he was suspending the entire process at least till the end of January 2017.

"We are announcing this pause to protect the Indus Waters Treaty and to help India and Pakistan consider alternative approaches to resolving conflicting interests under the Treaty and its application to two hydroelectric power plants," Mr. Kim said in letters addressed to the Finance Ministers of both countries.

The World Bank plans to send an expert, Ian Solomon to New Delhi and Islamabad in the next few weeks to discuss the issues for both governments and help restart talks between them.

Pakistan did not comment on the World Bank decision against its proposal to bypass the bilateral process. The Foreign Ministry spokesperson said on Thursday that "inter-departmental consultations are on" to discuss the letter received from Mr. Kim.

Water use panel

Meanwhile, the Centre is putting in place a special panel to look at ways to utilise India's share of the five rivers in the Indus system better, the Water Ministry said this week. The panel follows Prime Minister Narendra Modi's promise made on the campaign trail in Punjab that "each drop of water" of the Sutlej, Beas and Ravi rivers allocated to India would be used and not allowed to go "waste" into Pakistan. The PM's speech had received a sharp retort from Pakistan, who said there was no question of "stopping waters", and that India couldn't abrogate the treat unilaterally.

Officials say India has "no intention" of abrogating the 1960 Indus Water treaty, but would not allow Pakistan's unreasonable objections to legitimate water projects. In September, after the Uri attacks, India also decided to suspend talks with Pakistan on the two projects under the Permanent Indus Commission.

'Will stick to treaty'

Striking a more conciliatory note, Minister of State for External Affairs V.K. Singh said only a "full utilisation of India's rights under the Treaty" were being pursued, making it clear India's actions remained within the ambit of the treaty.

"India has always strictly adhered to the letter and the spirit of the Treaty and expects Pakistan to abide by the Treaty and not impede realisation of the full potential of the development of Indus and its rivers," Mr. Singh on Thursday told the Rajya Sabha in response to a question on the possibility of abrogating the treaty.

APP - 28

PAKISTAN NOT TO ACCEPT ALTERATION IN INDUS WATERS TREATY

Anwar Iqbal – December 17, 2016

Dawn (Pakistan)

WASHINGTON: Fearing that India is buying time to complete its two disputed water projects, Pakistan made it clear that it would not accept any modifications or changes to the Indus Waters Treaty (IWT) after New Delhi said on Friday it was ready to bilaterally resolve its differences with Islamabad over the implementation of the treaty.

The treaty, signed in 1960, gives India control over the three eastern rivers of the Indus basin — the Beas, the Ravi and the Sutlej— while Pakistan has the three western rivers— the Indus, the Chenab and the Jhelum.

The IWT also sets up a mechanism, the Permanent Indus Commission, which includes a commissioner from each country.

Talking to Dawn here on Friday, Special Assistant to PM Tariq Fatemi said: "Pakistan will not accept any modifications or changes to the provisions of the Indus Waters Treaty. Our position is based on the principles enshrined in the treaty. And the treaty must be honoured in...letter and spirit".

Earlier, a spokesman for the Indian Ministry of Foreign Affairs, Vikas Swarup, told reporters in New Delhi that the resolution process required more time.

"India has always believed that the implementation of the Indus Waters Treaty, which includes the redressal of the technical questions and differences, should be done bilaterally between India and Pakistan," he said. "We believe that these consultations should be given adequate time."

India's request for more time, however, alarmed Pakistan. Islamabad argued that India used the same strategy on previous occasions, completing a project during the dispute and then insisting that since the project was already complete, it could not be modified.

The current dispute revolves around the Kishanganga (330 megawatts) and Ratle (850 megawatts) hydroelectric plants. India is building the plants on the Kishanganga and Chenab Rivers, which Pakistan says violate the IWT.

Tensions over the water dispute increased late last month when Indian Prime Minister Narendra Modi threatened to block the flow of water into Pakistan. International experts fear that the threat, if implemented, could lead to armed clashes between the two sides.

New Delhi sought the appointment of a 'neutral expert' while Islamabad asked the World Bank to appoint the chairman of the Court of Arbitration. The IWT recognises the World Bank as an arbitrator.

Pakistan's fear that India was buying time to complete the disputed projects was backed by independent experts Dawn spoke to. They noted that both sides had already completed the process proposed in the IWT and approached the World Bank only after the commission declared it "a dispute," as required. "Dragging it through an already exhausted process will not help," said one expert.

Pakistan was seeking a court of arbitration because only the proposed court had the authority to consider both legal and technical aspects of the dispute. A neutral expert could only consider the technical aspects.

Pakistanis argue that the designs of the two Indian projects violate both legal and technical provisions of the treaty. India, however, opposes Pakistan's effort for setting up a court of arbitration.

The disagreement persuaded the World Bank to announce earlier this week that it was temporarily 'pausing' its arbitration and it was doing so to protect the treaty.

The next step was to go to the UN Secretary General who, under the treaty, has the authority to appoint a chairman for the proposed court.

APP – 29

PAKISTAN HAS ITSELF TO BLAME FOR WORLD BANK DECISION

Zafar Bhutta, 17 December, 2016

The Express Tribune, (Pakistan)

The Indus Waters Treaty (IWT) is considered one of the most successful water-sharing endeavours in the world. But it is at stake today. Reason: The World Bank, which had brokered the treaty between Pakistan and India in 1960, has apparently buckled under New Delhi's pressure.

On December 13, the World Bank announced a pause in the separate processes initiated by India and Pakistan under the treaty to allow the two countries to consider alternative ways to resolve their disagreements. The current processes under the treaty concern the 330-megawatt Kishanganga and 850-megawatt Ratle hydroelectric power projects being built by India on the Kishanganga and Chenab rivers.

Officials and experts say the World Bank has no mandate to ask Islamabad and New Delhi to resolve their water-related issue bilaterally. At the same time, they say Pakistan has itself to blame for the dilemma it faces today.

"The World Bank's role is limited to facilitating the appointment of chairman court of arbitration," Kamal Majidullah, the prime minister's former special assistant on water resources, told *The Express Tribune*.

However, Majidullah said it was a wrong decision by the incumbent government to approach the World Bank. "Pakistan should have knocked at the door of International Court of Arbitration," he added. "India preferred the World Bank because it had won a favourbale decision from a neutral expert nominated by the bank on the Baglihar hydroelectric power project built by India on the Chenab river."

He said the United Nations secretary general and the World Bank had a mandate to appoint a chairman court of arbitration. "In the case of Kishanganga, the UN secretary general had already appointed a chairman court of arbitration," he added.

Officials say the non-serious attitude of the Pakistan government has led to the situation where Pakistan has again been forced to hold talks with India even though Premier Narendra Modi has repeatedly threatened to run Pakistan dry.

They cite the change in Pakistan's stance at the World Bank as a reason for the IWT guarantor to give in to the Indian pressure. Premier Nawaz Sharif's predecessor had approved a summary in 2009 to petition the World Bank to act as a neutral expert over the design of Kishanganga dam. "However, the incumbent government withdrew that plea and instead sought the World Bank help to set up a court of arbitration on Kishanganga's design," one official told *The Express Tribune*. India, in the meanwhile, requested the World Bank to act as a neutral expert rather than establishing court. Interestingly, the World Bank had granted Pakistan's request of establishing a court of arbitration but the case was not pursued.

"This was the reason that the World Bank came under Indian pressure," another official said. "When Pakistan's request for setting up a court of arbitration had been accepted by the World Bank, there was no reason to hear India's plea to act as neutral expert."

Pakistan's former Indus Waters Commissioner Jamaat Ali Shah agrees that the slow response from the Pakistan government was the main reason for the World Bank buckling under India's pressure. "The World Bank has asked the two countries to find out a solution, but a bilateral arrangement might not be possible given the hostility between the two neighbours," Shah added. The Indus waters commissioner is mandated to pursue cases involving water issues with India or any other country. But officials say it is regrettable that Pakistan doesn't have a permanent Indus waters commissioner. Asif Baig, who is currently working as Indus waters commissioner, is an employee of the consultant firm NESPAK and has been holding the position since 2012. "In such a situation, how any country can safeguard its water interests," a third official told *The Express Tribune*.

Ahmer Bilal Soofi, president of the Research Society of International Law, says the World Bank should decide the case instead of asking the two states to resolve it bilaterally.

"It will be difficult for India and Pakistan to find a mutually acceptable solution," he told *The Express Tribune*. "If India uses water as weapon, then Pakistan approach international forums like the UN secretary general outside the mechanism in the IWT."

Experts and officials say India would press the World Bank to appoint a neutral expert rather than going to the international court. Appointment of a neutral expert by the World Bank may entail the same consequences that Pakistan had faced in the case of Baglihar dam, they believe. Pakistan should go to the International Court of Arbitration rather than relying on the World Bank.

APP – 30

INDIA AND PAKISTAN NURSE MYTHS ON INDUS TREATY, SAYS PROFESSOR

Peerzada Ashiq – 18 Dcember, 2016

The Hindu (India)

As India and Pakistan continue to exchange barbs over the 56-year-old Indus Water Treaty (IWT), Shakil Ahmad Romshoo, an ecological engineering and climatology expert, says both countries "nurse many myths" around the treaty.

While Pakistan keeps complaining about a "deliberate slowdown of discharge" from the Jhelum, Indus and Chenab rivers in Jammu & Kashmir, Professor Romshoo, Head of the Earth Sciences Department at Kashmir University, attributes it to climate change and a fast-changing discharge pattern. "India is not stealing waters as Pakistan tends to believe. Pakistan is right about water discharge coming down but the reason lies somewhere else — it is the melting of glaciers and global warming," Mr. Romshoo told *The Hindu*.

Post-1995 fall in discharge

He said that from the 1960s to 1995, water discharge had steadily increased by around 30 per cent, leading up to the highest estimate of 159 million acre feet (one acre foot is enough water to cover an acre of land one foot deep) in the three rivers. "After 1995, water discharge started coming down to 117 million acre feet. This worried Pakistan, but the fact remains that it continues to get sufficient water as per the treaty," Mr. Romshoo said.

Against the beliefs in Pakistan of a significant decrease in supply, Mr. Romshoo said India could still retain 10 million acre feet, which could irrigate large tracts of around seven lakh hectares in the State. "The fact is that water remains under-utilised in J&K. The State has no resources to fund major hydroprojects," he added.

Of late, Prime Minister Narendra Modi has evolved a fresh narrative around the treaty, describing it as "discriminatory" and planning "to retain waters of six rivers", including three in Punjab, within India only.

'It's impossible'

"One has to be a country like North Korea to think of stopping water flow into Pakistan. It's impossible. For example, the Kashmir Valley is a flat land and stopping the Jhelum means flooding the land. Even connecting the J&K's three rivers is almost next to impossible and may incur incalculable costs," Mr. Romshoo said.

Describing the IWT as the "best treaty" for the two countries, Mr. Romshoo warned against scrapping it. "It's difficult to scrap the treaty unless an alternative treaty is in place. This kind of treaty is not unique to

India and Pakistan. Europe has the Helsinki Rules on the Uses of the Waters of International Rivers, where riparian rights are shared between States."

"Two, scrapping the treaty means fuelling anger in 95 per cent of the population of Pakistan, whose water needs are fulfilled by these rivers," he added.

'Common concerns'

In J&K, both the ruling Peoples Democratic Party (PDP) and the opposition National Conference (NC) have called for a re-negotiation of the treaty to make it more "pro-J&K", and have sought compensation from the Centre for the losses incurred due to the treaty.

But Mr. Romshoo said the futuristic approach for both the countries would be to have joint hydropower projects on a river such as the Indus. "There is needed to rebuild cooperation and synergise common concerns within the scope of the treaty, and outside it through mutual agreement," he added.

APP – 31

WORLD BANK MOVE JEOPARDISES PAKISTAN'S WATER RIGHTS

Shahbaz Rana – 25 Decemberl, 2016

The Express Tribune, (Pakistan)

Pakistan on Saturday said the World Bank's (WB) decision to temporarily halt mediation on the implementation of the Indus Waters Treaty seriously jeopardises the country's interests and water rights.

Finance Minister Ishaq Dar, in a letter to WB Group President Jim Yong Kim, urged the lender to immediately appoint the chairman of the Court of Arbitration, suggesting Islamabad would not like to resolve the issue with India bilaterally as suggested by the international financial institution. "In our assessment, a pause in the process of empanelment of the Court of Arbitration will seriously prejudice Pakistan's interests and rights under the Indus Waters Treaty, 1960," Dar said in what was the first official response by Pakistani authorities to WB's decision to stop playing mediator between Islamabad and New Delhi. The government took almost two weeks to respond to the Washington-based lender's move, which experts believe was made under Indian lobbying pressure. "The WB's decision to pause the process would not contemporaneously pause the construction of the two hydroelectric plants whose designs are the subject matter of the present dispute," Dar wrote in his letter, stressing that the pause would merely prevent Pakistan from promptly approaching a competent forum and having its grievances addressed. Islamabad has disputed Delhi's move to construct the Kishanganga Ratle hydropower plants on the Kishanganga and Chenab rivers, respectively. The minister pointed out that the treaty does not provide for a situation where a party can stop performing its obligations under the pact. He stressed that as the World Bank had earlier acknowledged, the lender has "a well-defined role, which should remain consistent with the provisions of the treaty."

"The lives of millions of people and the ecology of the Indus Basin depend on the flow of the western rivers," he said, adding that "through the treaty, the Bank owes a duty of care to the people and the environment in which they live."

APP - 32

THE INDUS WATER TREATY AND THE WORLD BANK

Malik Muhammad Ashraf - 28 December, 2016

Pakistan Today

Water, water everywhere

Pakistan and India have been involved in intractable discussions to resolve the dispute regarding construction of two hydro electric power plants namely Kishenganga and Ralte being built by the latter in violation of the provisions of the Indus Water Treaty. So in view of the stalemate on the issue Pakistan requested the World Bank which had brokered the accord and also assumed the role of guarantor of the Treaty, to establish a court of Arbitration to resolve the differences between the two countries. India simultaneously requested the World Bank for the appointment of a neutral expert. The World Bank initially agreed to set up both the Arbitration Court and the appointment of the neutral expert. However in response to the Indian objection on two parallel processes which it maintained was not legally tenable, the World Bank decided to announce a 'pause' and asking both the parties to resolve the issue through bilateral avenues. Giving the reason for this action the President of the Bank in a letter written to finance ministers of both the countries said " We are announcing this pause to protect the Indus Water Treaty and to help India and Pakistan to consider alternative approaches to resolving conflicting interests under the treaty and its application to two hydro electric power plants. This is an opportunity for the two countries to begin to resolve the issue in an amicable manner and in line with the spirit of the treaty rather than pursuing concurrent processes that could make the treaty unworkable over time. I would hope that the two countries will come to an agreement by the end of January,"

The position taken by the World Bank is regrettably akin to what India had argued. It is tantamount to shirking the responsibility as a guarantor of the accord charged with the responsibility, as per the Treaty itself, to ensure that both parties stick to the provisions of the accord and in case of failure of the two sides to sort out their differences on any issue related to the treaty, appoint a court of Arbitration. The Indian government has welcomed the 'pause' announced by the World Bank. A spokesman of the Indian Ministry of External Affairs has said "By temporarily halting both processes now, World Bank has confirmed that pursuing two concurrent processes can render the treaty unworkable over time. Indian remains fully conscious of her international obligations and is ready to engage in further consulting on the matter of resolving current differences regarding the two projects"

It is pertinent to mention that Pakistan had approached the World Bank after being frustrated to find a solution to the dispute through permanent Indus Water Commission, a body set up under the Treaty to settle disputes through mutual consultations. The arbitration was even more necessary in view of the latest threats by Modi government to control the flow of water of the western rivers into Pakistan. Reacting to the World Bank decision, Finance Minister in his letter to the President of the World Bank has rightly maintained that under the Treaty no party can 'pause' performance of the obligations under the Treaty and the position taken by the Bank would only prevent Pakistan from approaching a competent forum and having its grievances addressed. It is hard to contest the points made by Ishaq Dar as under the Treaty it was the World Bank which could set up a Court of Arbitration when there was a stalemate on a dispute. The bilateral arrangement had failed to produce the desired results. It was why Pakistan had approached the guarantor to fulfill its obligations under the Treaty.Reportedly India held a meeting of the inter-ministerial task force last week which has been tasked to enhance storage of western rivers waters, which is a very alarming development. Under the circumstances, the World Bank avoiding to take a position in line with its obligations under the Treaty amounts to almost giving up on its own brokered agreement. The hope expressed by the World Bank that both sides would be able to resolve their differences, represents lack of understanding of the prevailing situation. India is actually trying to build pressure on Pakistan to back off from the position taken by her on the Kashmir issue, particularly in regards to current uprising in the valley. It is not a technical issue. India has been threatening to review the Indus Water Treaty in the backdrop of Uri attack which it blamed on Pakistan. In an atmosphere loaded with tensions between the two countries, expecting them to show goodwill in resolving the issue is hoping against hope. The World Bank has a role to play as per the Treaty and it should not try to avoid it. Under the Indus Water Treaty, the waters of the Eastern rivers Sutlej, Beas, and Ravi had been allocated to India and the Western rivers Indus, Jhelum and Chenab to Pakistan except for certain uses allowed to India including power generation without altering the water flows. According to reliable sources India is contemplating to launch more hydropower projects with a cumulative power generating capacity of 32,000 MW on the rivers allocated to Pakistan and consequently attain the capability of regulating the water flows to Pakistan, especially reducing water flow in the river Chenab which irrigates most of the land in Punjab. Such a situation could lead to serious consequences and may even threaten peace and security in the region in the event of armed conflict over the issue between the two countries. It is pertinent to point out that the case of Kishanganga has already been considered by the Permanent Court of Arbitration at Hague which in its final award on the dispute while recognizing the Indian right to build the Dam did address Pakistan's concerns about India keeping the level of reservoirs below the Dead Storage Level and also recognized the concept of environmental flows in rivers to ensure that the power generating projects were operated in an environmentally sustainable manner. The Award announced on 20 December 2013 specified that natural flow of water must be maintained in Kishanganga river at all times to maintain environment downstream. But India is not even abiding by the award of the Permanent Arbitration Commission.Pakistan is not asking for something beyond the treaty obligations of the World Bank. The World Bank must revisit its decision and set up a court of arbitration as requested by Pakistan, because there was no hope of resolving of this issue through bilateral arrangement as suggested by the previous Indian behavior on issues which ultimately had to be referred for arbitration.

APP - 33

PAKISTAN'S WATER SECURITY MADE PART OF CPEC FRAMEWORK

Shahbaz Rana – 30 December, 2016

The Express Tribune, (Pakistan)

Pakistan and China on Thursday decided to make water security a part of the China-Pakistan Economic Corridor (CPEC) framework amid threats by India to review its position on the 1960 Indus Waters Treaty.

The decision to exploit full hydel potential of Pakistan was taken during the sixth meeting of the Joint Cooperation Committee (JCC) of the CPEC which was held in Beijing. The JCC is the highest policy making forum of the CPEC.

The JCC also decided, in principle, to make the mass transit projects of all four provinces part of the CPEC. These projects will be formally made part of the CPEC after their financial and technical vetting by Working Group on Transport in February next year.

For development of hydroelectric projects on the Indus River, particularly construction of the Diamer-Bhasha dam, the JCC on Thursday constituted a group, said Planning and Development Minister Ahsan Iqbal after the meeting. The planning ministry released the video of his statement.

"Pakistan may face a very severe water crisis and for economic and food security of the country, the immediate construction of Diamer-Bhasha is crucial," he said. If the Diamer-Bhasha dam becomes part of the CPEC, it will be a landmark achievement, he added.

For more than two decades, Pakistan has been trying to construct the Diamer-Bhasha dam that has an estimated cost of $14 billion. Due to opposition by India, both the World Bank and the Asian Development Bank have refused to lend money under one pretext or another.

After the rise in tensions along the Line of Control (LoC) in recent months, India's Prime Minister Narendra Modi had threatened to cut Pakistan's water supply. He has managed to influence the WB that recently paused the process of playing mediator, which it is bound to play under the 1960 Indus Waters Treaty, according to experts on the accord. Chinese help to secure Pakistan's water rights will be seen as a major development, according to them.

The Indus River is a source of more than 17 gigawatts of hydropower capacity in India and Pakistan and feeds the Indus Basin Irrigation System, the largest contiguous irrigation network in the world. Pakistan is particularly dependent on the Indus, as more than 90% of its agricultural production comes from this basin.

Ahsan Iqbal said that the sixth JCC has taken the CPEC to the next level, which will ensure Pakistan's industrialisation and inclusion of all the provinces.

The minister said that the JCC approved to make mass transit projects of four provinces part of the

CPEC framework. He said that these projects are Orange Line metro project Lahore, Karachi Circular Railway, Peshawar Greater Circular Railway and Quetta Circular Railway.

Their inclusion in the CPEC will ensure huge tax exemptions and availability of finances for execution. The inclusion of these projects into CPEC is a gift for the people of provincial capitals, said the planning minister.

The planning minister said that the JCC approved to construct one industrial park in each province, Islamabad Capital Territory and in special areas of the country. He said that the Chinese experts would visit Pakistan in February to review their feasibility. The JCC also approved to make three more infrastructure projects part of the CPEC. These are Dera Ismail Kha-Zhob road project, Baseema-Khuzdar road project and a missing link of the Karakoram Highway project.

The minister said the JCC also decided to start construction work on Matiari-Lahore Transmission Line project. He said the new projects that the provinces had proposed for inclusion into the CPEC have been recommended to the respective working groups for their financial and technical evaluations.

He said it has also been agreed that the Gwadar City Master plan will be completed within one year. The minister said that China also agreed to transfer knowledge in five areas, including water resources management, urban development, small and medium sized industries and climate change.

The Peshawar circular rail project has been accepted as part of the CPEC and the working group will approve it in next meeting, said K-P Chief Minister Pervaiz Khattak after the JCC meeting. Khattak went to Beijing to attend the meeting. He said that K-P's projects would be approved in February next year. He added that the JCC approved to make one industrial park part of the CPEC while two more will be approved next year.

APP – 34

PAKISTAN SEEKS U.S. BACKING ON WATER ROW WITH INDIA

Shahbaz Rana – 31 December, 2016

The Express Tribune, (Pakistan)

Irked by the World Bank pause in mediation, Pakistan has sought US support on the implementation of the Indus Waters Treaty (IWT) with India, as Secretary of State John Kerry urged New Delhi and Islamabad to amicably resolve the row.

Kerry made a phone call to Finance Minister Ishaq Dar on Thursday night and discussed the row over the IWT implementation and the role of the World Bank (WB), which had brokered the treaty in 1960.

After Kerry's call, US Ambassador to Pakistan David Hale also met Dar at Q-Block – the seat of the finance ministry. The back-to-back contacts highlight the importance of the water issue, which can potentially endanger regional stability if the situation slips out of control, according to finance ministry sources.

"The US would like to see an amicable solution to this [water] issue," a finance ministry handout quoted Kerry as saying. Kerry told Dar that the WB president had informed him about Pakistan's complaint against India on the IWT.

The water dispute has catapulted the US back into Pakistan's economic picture. The American civilian and military assistance to Pakistan has drastically come down in recent months and its implications on Pakistan's fiscal situation have started emerging in the shape of a larger-than-anticipated budget deficit.

Independent analysts argue that Washington may not play an effective role in resolving the water dispute, as the Obama administration is preparing to hand over the White House to Donald Trump next month.

"Senator Dar indicated that the US support on the principles and legal position of Pakistan will be greatly appreciated," stated the finance ministry. Early this month, the WB had announced a pause in playing its legally binding role of mediator in the IWT implementation. In October, Pakistan had approached the WB seeking appointment of the Chairman of Court of Arbitration to resolve a dispute over construction of two mega hydropower projects by India in violation of the IWT.

However, the WB announced a pause in mediation – much to the dismay of Islamabad. The bank urged the two countries to resolve the issue at a bilateral forum even though the two sides had already exhausted that option.

The finance minister told Kerry that the IWT was an international commitment and it was the WB's responsibility to make sure India honoured the treaty and the water rights of hundreds of millions of Pakistani people were protected, said the finance ministry.

Dar added that the Court of Arbitration was the legal requirement, and the World Bank must fulfill the commitment to appointing the Chairman of the Court of Arbitration.

India's repeated threats to run Pakistan dry pose a real threat to Pakistan's food and economic security. The civil and military leadership has already announced that materialisation of India's threat would be considered 'open aggression' and a blatant 'act of war'.

Pakistan and China on Thursday decided to make water security a part of the China-Pakistan Economic Corridor (CPEC) framework aimed at preparing a plan against any adverse impact of any such Indian move on Pakistan's economic security.

Dar informed Kerry that the WB president had been in touch with him during the current month. Sources, however, said the WB has yet not made a formal commitment that the mediation process would be started immediately.

The finance ministry said Kerry has also appreciated the improvement in Pakistan's economic indicators. Dar shared the latest developments in the economy and the Pakistan Stock Exchange and said all economic indicators had improved over the last three years. He added that the government after having achieved macro-economic stability was now focused on achieving higher sustainable and inclusive economic growth.

The finance minister and Ambassador Hale discussed the current status of trade and economic ties between Pakistan and the US. The ambassador said the United States valued its longstanding ties with Pakistan and considered Pakistan an important partner. He acknowledged the economic turnaround Pakistan has achieved over the last three years.

APP - 35

PAKISTAN, INDIA AND THE INDUS WATER TREATY

Kuldip Nayyar – 9 January, 2017

Pakistan Today

Islamabad has asked the World Bank to honour the Indus Water Treaty executed between India and Pakistan in 1960. This is in response to Prime Minister Narendra Modi's remark that India is free to use the water which flows into the sea. This is not correct because according to the treaty India cannot use more than 20 percent of the Indus water.

The World Bank spent many years to persuade New Delhi and Islamabad to reach an agreement. I recall that afterwards Prime Minister Jawaharlal Nehru and Martial Law Administrator General Mohammad Ayub travelled in the same car Mian Iftakharuddin suggested if they could sign an agreement on Kashmir in the same spirit, both remained silent. Iftakharuddin was then the top Muslim League leader who had joined it after being a Congressman for many years. According to the treaty, India could draw water from the Ravi, the Beas and the Sutlej while Pakistan from the Indus, the Chenab and Jehlum. Even though both countries felt that they could utilise the water which was flowing through their country, they refrained from doing so because of the treaty. In fact, the Indus Water Treaty is an example before the world that it held the ground even when the two countries went to war.

Modi's off-the-cuff remark has created consternation in Pakistan, forcing it to appeal to the World Bank to "fulfill its obligation" relating to the treaty. In a letter to World Bank President Jim Yong Kim, Pakistan Finance Minister Ishaq Dar has said the treaty did not provide for a situation wherein a party can 'pause' performance of its obligations and this attitude of the World Bank would prejudice Pakistan's interests and rights under the treaty. I think that the fear of Pakistan is exaggerated. The country does not want any alteration in the treaty. In its reaction, the World Bank has said that it has paused its arbitration in the water dispute between India and Pakistan, saying it is doing so to protect the Indus Water Treaty. India would take no unilateral step to stop the water going unused into the Arabian Sea. However, there is a case where the two countries should sit and hammer out another treaty because the old one is outdated. Then it was thought that the water given to Rajasthan would be utilised by the rest of the country because the state, part of the desert would not be able to do so. But this has turned out to be wrong. The state has utilised the water allotted to it and wants more. When Prime Minister Modi wants to have good relations with Pakistan and has wished his counterpart Nawaz Sharif on this birthday last week, Modi would not take any step which would harm Pakistan. There were enough of provocations from Islamabad like the attacks on Pathankot and Uri that killed many civilians to act unilaterally. Even otherwise, it is in the interest of both countries that peace should prevail in the region. Both would benefit.

Kashmir is the problem which divides the two countries. Representatives of both countries should sit across the table sort it out. Nawaz Sharif unnecessarily harangued Kashmir on the Pakistan television networks that Kashmir belonged to Pakistan and there would be no peace in the region until it became part of his country. This irresponsible statement, coming as it does from a country's Prime Minister, has affected the tourist season in the valley still further. So much so that even Syed Shah Geelani, the pro-Pakistan Hurriyat leader, joined a procession to appeal to the tourists to return to the valley. Both he and Yasin Malik, who wants the valley to be independent, were part of the procession. They were particular that the message should reach New Delhi so that it takes steps to see that the tourists return to Kashmir.

The separatists in the valley do not realise that the tourists flocked to the valley as if they were visiting part of India. The demand of independence or the threat of disturbance has scared them. They have picked up some other hill resorts in India which may not be as beautiful as the valley but compares favourably with it. They would wait and see whether the peace had really returned before drawing up their itinerary for the next year.

It is in the interest of Kashmiris not to disturb the status quo until they can have something better. This is possible if the three parties, India, Pakistan and the people in Kashmir, come together for a dialogue. New Delhi is not prepared for that because Islamabad has gone back on its promise not to allow its territory to be used by terrorists. This was also agreed upon when Pakistan was under General Musharraf s rule. He went to Agra and almost signed an agreement with Prime Minster Atal Behari Vajpayee, until news had leaked, that India's then Information Minister Sushma Swaraj changed the draft agreement omitting Kashmir from the text. Since then the two countries have stayed distant. Mushraff s misadventure at Kargil only aggravated the matter further. It must be said to the credit of Vajpayee that he took a bus to Lahore. I was sitting behind him when he showed me New Delhi's telegram which said that several Hindus had been killed near Jammu. He said he did not know how the country would react about his trip to Lahore but he was determined to pick up the thread with Nawaz Sharif. The rest is history.

The Indus Water Treaty can be replaced with another treaty but the consent of Pakistan is necessary. When it has not been willing to allow getting electricity from the run of the river it is difficult to imagine that it would agree to the use of rivers in the Indus system even though water from them is pouring into the Arabian Sea without being used for either irrigation or hydroelectric projects. There is a tendency in Pakistan to link everything with Kashmir, which is a complicated problem and it would take many years to solve. The revision of Indus Water Treaty, which can satisfy both the countries, would add to the peace prospects. Let the treaty be discussed separately. The rest can follow. The only point to be taken into account is how the two countries can come closer to each other.

APP – 36

VIOLATION OF INDUS WATER TREATY?

Babar Khan Bozdar – 30 January, 2017

Pakistan Observers

THE most liberal water-sharing pact known as Indus-Water Treaty was signed by Pakistani President Ayub Khan and Indian Prime Minister Jawaharlal Nehru on September 19, 1960, in Karachi and the water of six rivers-Beas, Ravi, Sutlej, Indus, Chenab and Jhelum was shared between two countries. This landmark pact was brokered by World Bank. Since this agreement, India and Pakistan had fought three major wars and there was a constant strain in their diplomatic relations but treaty survived despite severe nature of relations between both countries. Recently, Indian Premier Narendra Modi stated that "Blood and Water can't flow simultaneously" but in fact, this Indian move will flow blood over water simultaneously. Historically, the partition of Sub-continent created a conflict over the water of Indus Basin. The newly born states were unable to share water and manage an essential and cohesive network of irrigation. Moreover, during partition, the tributaries of Indus basin were given to India and Pakistan felt its livelihood threatened by the possibility of Indian control over the tributaries that bolstered water into the Pakistani portion of Indus Basin. The IW system of rivers comprises of three Eastern Rivers, the Sutlej, the Beas and the Ravi while three western rivers are the Indus, the Jhelum, and the Chenab. As per arrangements, Ravi, Beas, and Sutlej which constitute eastern system are exclusively allocated to India, Similarly Pakistan had allowed exclusive use of western rivers and India was bound to supply water to Pakistan for 10 years, Until Pakistan will be able to construct canal system for the utilisation of water of Indus, Jhelum, and Chenab. The accord was meant for the permanent solution of water between India and Pakistan but none of them was eager to trade off their particular positions and arrangements achieved a stalemate. Pakistan attempted to take the matter to the International court of Justice (ICJ) for the peaceful settlement of dispute but India refused to argue that it will be resolved bilaterally. The treaty has placed limitations on design and operation of hydroelectric plants, storage works and other river works that are to be constructed by India on the western rivers. India is bound to provide information relating to these works in advance while Pakistan has right to communicate its objection with India. Indus water treaty was meant for resolving their issues bilaterally, but now water dispute is intensely politicised in India because hawks in India publically demanding for abrogating the treaty without realising the side effects or rationality of their demand. Indeed, their demand is an attempt of pushing both countries to the brink of war. The legal instrument had so far sustained and delivered despite ups and downs in Indo-Pak relations, but it is the first time that Modi's government called for abrogating IWT. The possible reason behind this statement is that Modi government lost his credibility and capability in delivering good governance. It also lost his support within. Hence, it came down to terrorist activities likes abrogating IWT. In this way, Modi's statement is an attempt to divert the mind of people and gain anti-Pakistan sympathy. It is not so easy to scrape Indus water treaty because World Bank is the Mediator while certain restrictions are implemented on both Parties in case of violating treaty. The article nine of IWT provide its better explanation and restrict both countries from violating Indus water treaty. Simultaneously treaty couldn't be scraped unilaterally. Without consultation with Pakistan Indian move will be treated as an act of war and again it might trigger conflict between hostile neighbours over water which has serious consequences for both countries. Pakistan is an agricultural country and water is the source of survival. Similarly, Indian robbery over water will never be accepted from Pakistan side. In fact, it is the matter 180 million lives. In this situation, Indian ambition of scraping Indus water treaty will be dangerous. Linking water with security, I think it is a narrow minded approach because there is no connection war and wide. So, such policies will not only suffer India and Pakistan but region too. In this situation, leaders should come up with durable solutions rather than triggering hostility.

APP – 37

PAKISTAN'S NEGLECT BEHIND LINGERING OF WATER DISPUTE WITH INDIA: UNDP

Amin Ahmed, 2 February, 2017

Dawn (Pakistan)

The United Nations Development Programme (UNDP) says that Pakistan's negligence in conducting a sound analysis of trans-boundary water issues and delays in presenting the cases of dispute with India to the Indus Water Commission or the World Bank on the issues related to the Indus Waters Treaty have caused the issues to linger on and remain unaddressed.

Focusing on water security situation in Pakistan which is the most critical development challenge for the country, a UNDP report points out that awareness about trans-boundary water issues is a recent phenomenon and systematic studies are needed in this regard.

The report titled "Development Advocate Pakistan" was released by the UN global development network on Wednesday.

According to it, an increase in water stress in the basin states since the early 90s has brought the treaty under strain. In fact, its survival appears weak, although there is no exit clause. The treaty fails to address two issues: the division of shortages in dry years between India and Pakistan, when flows are almost half as compared to wet years, and the cumulative impact of storages on the flows of the River Chenab into Pakistan.

The Wular Barrage and Kishenganga project on the Jhelum and Neelum rivers present a similar problem whereby water storage during the Rabi season is critical as flows are almost one-fifth of the Kharif season.

The report says that Pakistan has gone as far as calling the treaty an inefficient forum for resolving water issues, elevating the water issue to a "core issue" and including it in the composite dialogue. But India has refused to include the issue in the composite dialogue because it is not ready to discard the treaty.

The treaty permits India to create storages on the western rivers of 1.25, 1.60 and 0.75 million acre feet (MAF) for general, power and flood storages, respectively, amounting to a total permissible storage of 3.6 MAF.

The report says: "A clear ambiguity in the treaty occurs in its permission to be interpreted differently, thereby creating conflicts between Pakistan and India. The treaty also fails to clearly address India's share of shortages in relation to storage dams on the western rivers, an issue of major concern."

As a consequence of climate change, shrinking glaciers and changing precipitation patterns render the need to address issues of water scarcity and resources, it says. During floods, for example, majority of the water runs into the rivers of Indus-Pakistan which leaves the province of Sindh flooded. Such negative setbacks on the economy will eventually have dire consequences if not addressed, the report warns.

It says that with control of the River Chenab through the Salal dam, India has several plans under way for development of hydropower with enhanced water storage on the western river. Pakistan continues to face reduced flows from the Chenab owing to the recent storage of water in the Baglihar dam.

According to the report, annual flows in the Chenab during wet years have continued to decline since 1958-59 with an increase in droughts since 1937-38. Same is the case with the River Jhelum being controlled by India. Since the river is a major source of irrigation and hydropower for Pakistan, it will pose dire impacts for the country if India chooses to close the gates of the barrage.Although the treaty does not allow Pakistan to prohibit construction of hydropower dams by India, it grants it right to voice issues regarding Indian developing strategy on water storage during dry periods.Although Pakistan benefits from international legal frameworks for water resources management, it is largely dependent upon the treaty for resolving transboundary water conflicts with India, it points out.

Trust deficit among provinces

In its conclusion, the report says that water has been a highly politicised issue in Pakistan and there is an extreme deficit of trust among the provinces. The trust deficit is largely due to a lack of access to data and information. It suggests that popular papers should be prepared along with posters and stickers for creating mass awareness. Without awareness, water cannot be made a 'business for everyone'.It says that past efforts to create a single central data repository have been unsuccessful owing to data collection being conducted by a mix of several agencies in the federation and provinces. The solution lies in developing a decentralised database by different agencies, followed by centralising the database by feeding the data into one single central data repository. The federal statistics division will be the pertinent authority to take charge of coordination and networking in this regard.With an increase in the demand and variety of water uses, its quality is now a growing concern, the report says. Therefore, standards for water quality need to be developed for all subsectors of water use. There is a need to develop an inventory of water quality for surface and groundwater to represent all the major ecosystems and environments, ranging from wet mountains to the Indus basin, barani lands, deserts and the coast.

APP - 38

SURVIVAL OF INDUS WATERS PACT WEAK: UN REPORT

Press Trust of India, 3 February, 2017

Hindustan Times (India)

The 40-year-old Indus Waters Treaty between India and Pakistan has been an outstanding example of conflict resolution but scarcity of water in the basin states since the early 1990s has brought the agreement under strain and its "survival appears weak", according to a UN report.

"The treaty fails to address two issues: the division of shortages in dry years between India and Pakistan, when flows are almost half as compared to wet years, and the cumulative impact of storages on the flows of the River Chenab into Pakistan," said the UNDP report, 'Development Advocate Pakistan'.

Wular Barrage and Kishenganga project on the Jhelum and Neelum rivers present a similar problem whereby water storage during the Rabi season is critical as flows are almost one-fifth of the Kharif season, according the report, which was released on Wednesday. "For over 40 years, the Indus Waters Treaty has proved to be an outstanding example of conflict resolution. An increase in water stress in the basin states since the early 90s has brought the Treaty under strain, In fact, its survival appears weak, although there is no exit clause," it said.

The report said that Pakistan has gone as far as calling the treaty an inefficient forum for resolving water issues, elevating the water issue to a "core issue" and including it in the composite dialogue. But India has refused to include the issue in the composite dialogue because it is not ready to discard the treaty.

The treaty permitted India to create storages on the western rivers of 1.25, 1.60 and 0.75 million acre feet (MAF) for general, power and flood storages, respectively, amounting to a permissible storage of 3.6 MAF.

"A clear ambiguity in the treaty occurs in its permission to be interpreted differently, thereby creating conflicts between Pakistan and India. The treaty also fails to clearly address India's share of shortages in relation to storage dams on the western rivers, an issue of major concern," the report said.

As a result of climate change, shrinking glaciers and changing precipitation patterns render the need to address issues of water scarcity and resources. "During floods, for example, majority of the water runs into the rivers of Indus-Pakistan which leaves the province of Sindh flooded. Such negative setbacks on the economy will eventually have dire consequences if not addressed," the report said.

It said that with control of the River Chenab through the Salal dam, India has several plans under way for development of hydropower with enhanced water storage on the western river. Pakistan continues to face reduced flows from the Chenab owing to the recent storage of water in the Baglihar dam.

Awareness on trans-boundary water issues is a recent phenomenon and systematic studies are needed, the report said.

APP - 39

INDIA TO LOSE IF IT BREACHES WATER TREATY

Sehrish Wasif, 9 February, 2017

The Express Tribune, (Pakistan)

Urging the Modi government to stop politicising the water issue with Pakistan, Minister of State for Information, Broadcasting and National Heritage Marriyum Aurangzeb said on Wednesday that India will be a net loser if it violated the treaty.

Speaking at a national consultation on 'Pakistan's Water Challenges', she said that the government was formulating a comprehensive strategy to deal with challenges facing the Indus Waters Treaty. "India itself will suffer if it violates the Indus Water Treaty ... Instead of politicising the issue, it must adopt a policy of dialogue," she said.

The treaty was brokered by the World Bank in 1960, which survived three wars and many bouts of tensions between the two neighbors. It governs the distribution of water from six rivers between Pakistan and India. The treaty's fate is uncertain ever since Indian Prime Minister Narendra Modi threatened to 'review' it in the wake of simmering tensions between the two countries. Pakistan, however, is adamant that India cannot unilaterally revoke the water accord.

Recently, the head of WB visited both Pakistan and India to ensure that the situation did not deteriorate. The minister of state said that the government believed in reaching out to its neighbors, including India. "We want amicable solution to all problems with India," she said, adding that despite Indian belligerence, Pakistan was showing restraint and acting in a responsible manner. Aurangzeb pointed out that both countries' economic progress was linked with the treaty.

She said that Prime Minister Nawaz Sharif believed in politics of consultation and reconciliation. "Therefore, he will consult with all political parties on water issues," she said.

After 17 years, she said, the government had decided to carry out census this year because it was crucial for assessing population and devising strategies to overcome challenges.

APP - 40

INDIA TO ATTEND LAHORE MEETING ON INDUS WATERS TREATY

Suhasini Haidar 3 March, 2017

The Hindu

World Bank officials play mediator in two months of diplomatic negotiations.

Signalling a major shift in its position on talks with Pakistan on the Indus Waters Treaty (IWT), India has accepted an invitation to attend a meeting of the Permanent Indus Commission (PIC) to be held in Lahore in March, various sources confirmed to *The Hindu*.

According to officials privy to the development, the move came after two months of diplomatic negotiations, with World Bank officials playing the mediator in encouraging Pakistan to extend an invitation and for India to accept it.

The news closely follows the visit of World Bank Chief Executive Officer Kristalina Georgieva to New Delhi, where she met with Union Finance Minister Arun Jaitley, weeks after her visit in January to Islamabad, where she met Prime Minister Nawaz Sharif.

Officials acknowledged that the holding of the next annual round of the PIC, which was last held in July 2016, was a "positive" sign, given that India had announced it was "suspending" the talks after the Uri attacks in September.

According to senior government officials at the time, the decision to suspend the talks was taken when Prime Minister Narendra Modi held a meeting with key officials, including National Security Adviser Ajit Doval and Foreign Secretary S. Jaishankar, to "review" the IWT.

At the time, tensions with Pakistan were high, as the government considered all retaliatory measures after the Army camp attack, in which 19 soldiers were killed.

"Meetings can only take place in an atmosphere free of terror," a senior official briefing the press about the suspension of the Indus talks had said.

Asked if the scheduling of the talks now in March despite the previous decision meant a climbdown in India's position or whether terror attacks had in fact decreased in the past few months, the Ministry of External Affairs did not offer an official comment.

"It is a regular bilateral meeting of the Permanent Indus Commission, which implements the Indus Waters Treaty," a senior official told *The Hindu*, denying that there was any "shift" in India's position.

In November, another controversy erupted over the World Bank decision to constitute a Court of Arbitration to look into complaints from Pakistan over India's construction of Kishenganga and Ratle river water projects. India said the World Bank decision was biased in Pakistan's favour, threatening to "take steps" against it.

Eventually the matter was resolved after it was taken up at the highest levels between the World Bank President Jim Yong Kim, who also spoke over the telephone to Mr. Jaitley and to his Pakistan counterpart Ishaq Dar. This was followed by visits to India and Pakistan by World Bank expert Ian Solomon and then Ms. Georgieva.

Ms. Georgieva discussed the impasse over the IWT at length with Mr. Jaitley during her visit to Delhi, and even suggested putting some of the key issues on Kishenganga and Ratle hydel projects on the agenda for the Lahore meeting, sources said.

APP - 41

INDIA SOFTENS STANCE ON INDUS WATER TREATY AND AGREES TO MEETING

Nayanima Basu – 3 March, 2017

The Hindu

The Permanent Indus Commission looks at everyday operations and implementation of the Indus Water Treaty. The Permanent Indus Commission will be meeting end of this month in Lahore to discuss the Indus Water Treaty even as the government had decided to suspend the commissioners meeting in the wake of the terrorist attacks on the army base at Uri last September.

"It is Pakistan's turn to host its next meeting and the Indian Commissioner has accepted his counterpart's invitation for the meeting to take place in the second half of March," a top official said requesting anonymity. The Permanent Indus Commission is a bipartisan body that looks at everyday operation and implementation of the Indus Waters Treaty. It is mandated to meet at least once a year for stock taking purposes. The meetings are held alternately in India and Pakistan. The official also said that the government and commission are different.

"The commission meeting is not talks between governments, as is mentioned earlier. Government and commission are different. The commission is not concerned with political aspect and only deals with technical matters," the official said. The Ministries of External Affairs (MEA) and Water Resources, which deal with the political aspect of it, are not concerned with when commission meets and what it discusses, according to sources. Meeting of the Permanent Indus Commission assumes huge significance as it demonstrates softening of India's stance. Last year Prime Minister Narendra Modi had called for suspending the regular meetings of the commission post the alleged role of Pakistani based militant outfits in carrying out the terror attack in Uri.

He had categorically stated: "Blood and water cannot flow together."

Modi had also said at that time Pakistan cannot be allowed to enjoy the benefits of the treaty and that the meeting of the commission can only take place when the atmosphere "free of terror". The commission, which comprises of Indus Commissioners from both sides, basically discusses technical matters related to implementation of the treaty. Since the inception of the treaty in 1960, it has met 112 times. Mutually convenient dates and mutually agreeable agenda are worked out directly by the commissioners themselves and the government has no role in this regard. Regular meetings of the Commission deal with technical matters concerned with implementation of the treaty, sources said.

APP - 42

INDIA AGREES TO REVIVE INDUS WATERS COMMISSION LEVEL TALKS

Munawar Hasan, 4 March, 2017

The News (Pakistan)

India has agreed to revive Indus Waters Commission level talks for discussing water issues, saying the official delegation will participate in the meeting later this month in Lahore, an official said on Friday.

A senior official of Pakistan Indus Waters Commission told this scribe that India last month wrote a letter to convey its willingness for attending bilateral moot in Lahore in the second half of the month. The letter in this connection was sent by the Indian Indus Water commissioner to his Pakistani counterpart, asking to propose dates for the parleys, said the official.

India wanted to hold talks preferably around mid-March, the official further said and adding senior officials of both the countries are nowadays engaged in correspondence for finalising date, agenda and other modalities of the upcoming talks on the water issues.

He added that India tried to defer these talks till mid-March, keeping in view the issues relating to its internal politics in a bid to avoid giving any impression during the ongoing states elections.

By showing willingness to resume activities of Permanent Indus Commission, India has virtually ended boycott of the negotiation process at Commissioner level after about one and half year of impasse, said the sources. The last meeting of the commission was held in 2015. India has also started exchanging water flow and agriculture use data with Pakistan, they added.

A senior official said India shared crucial data of agriculture water usage of Western rivers to Pakistan in January this year. The sharing of such data is a routine but assumes immense importance as far as implementation of the Indus Waters Treaty is concerned, official said.

The official said Pakistan did not want to discuss objections raised on the two Indian projects in the upcoming meeting of Indus Water Commission. As far as resumption of talks on contentious water issues is concerned, the official said only routine issues would be discussed.

"We want to follow separate process under the supervision of the World Bank for negotiation on Kishanganga and Ratle hydropower projects," he said. Last year, Pakistan submitted case for the establishment of court of arbitration for discussing objections to 330 megawatts-Kishanganga hydropower project and 850mw-Ratle hydropower projects, being built by India in sheer violation of the Indus Waters Treaty.

The Official said the talks on both these controversial projects have not seen any tangible headway, saying that it was solely due to India's stubbornness as it always avoided negotiated progress on objections raised by Pakistan at difference forums.

In fact, he added, India had intentionally slowed down implementation of the Indus Waters Treaty. No routine meetings of the commission are regularly held. The exchange of water data was also not being shared in letter and spirit as per stipulated period. Moreover, he said, inspection of various water infrastructure was also suspended for the last several years. Even, mandatory inspection of Kishanganga has not taken place yet, he added.

APP – 43

PAKISTAN AND INDIA TO DISCUSS INDUS WATERS TREATY

Munawar Hasan, 8 March, 2017

The News (Pakistan)

Pakistan has formally conveyed a message about a two-day meeting of the Indus Waters Commission scheduled to start from March 20 to India to discuss the bilateral water issues, officials said on Tuesday.

"We are expecting a confirmation from the Indian Indus Waters Commission today (Tuesday)," a senior official told The News. The official added that the Indian delegation, led by its Indus Waters Commissioner, is expected to arrive in Lahore on March 19 for the two-day talks on various aspects of the Indus Waters Treaty and will leave on March 22.

The annual meeting of Indian and Pakistani delegations is mandatory at least once in a year. However, it could not be held for around one-and-half year in the wake of a terrorist attack in Uri in held Kashmir.

It is expected that around 10-member delegation from the Indian side will take part during the meeting of the permanent Indus Commission. On the meeting agenda, the official said there will be a discussion on the hydropower projects, such as Pakal Dul, Lower Kalnai and Miyar, which are being built by India on the Chenab River.

Pakistan has raised objections over the designs and other features of the projects. However, these issues could not be discussed earlier owing to a lack of regular meetings, he added. "Now, we plan to raise these objections in detail."

There will also be a discussion on the modalities of a proposed visit to the site of Kishanganga hydropower project. The official said visits are important because they help in getting on-the-ground information about the physical progress of a certain project as per its design. However, there will be no discussion on Ratle and Kishanganga hydropower projects being constructed in the held Kashmir in violation of Indus Waters Treaty, added the official. Pakistan has already lodged its protest over the two power projects with the World Bank, but these cases would separately be pursued. The official said the meeting will also discuss the issues related to the data exchange. "We will stress on regular data exchange as smooth sharing of information about water use and flows are indispensable for the implementation of Indus Waters Treaty." Moreover, Pakistan will also emphasise the implementation of a tour of inspection for regular visits of various under-construction and completed sites.

APP – 44

REVISITING THE TREATY

Tariq Husain, 14 March, 2017

The News (Pakistan)

The proposed dialogue about Kishanganga and Ratle offers Pakistan and India a golden opportunity to optimise the resources of the Indus Basin. The Greek historian, Herodotus, described Egypt as the "gift of the Nile".

That description applies more aptly to River Indus and its tributaries which contribute to the fertility of the alluvial plains of Pakistan and large parts of India. The rivers – Indus, Ganges, Brahmaputra – originating in the Himalayas, provide food, fuel and employment to more than one and a half billion people of India and Pakistan. In our culture, this water-fed land is referred to as 'the motherland'.

Mountain sources of run-off in these rivers have become vulnerable to climate change. Concerns about the impact of climate change on the run-offs of Indus and the other South Asian rivers have given rise to expectations of drastic decreases in flows and displacements of their timings. So far, these concerns are derived from global studies in which temperature increases are producing extreme effects on the climate and these effects are expected to magnify over time.

The specific effects of climate change on glaciers and on river flows in the Western Himalaya-Karakoram-Hindukush are less studied. There are conflicting views – not firmly based on scientific studies – among engineers and scientists that have serious implications for sustainable water management in Pakistan and India. In addition, we have an adversarial geo-political situation directly impacting the utilisation of water resources in both India and Pakistan.

Optimising the utilisation of water resources in our joint basin is also a necessity for our socio-economic wellbeing. This requires us to evaluate options from a 30-50-year perspective as our populations increase but the water supply remains fixed – or decreases. The Indus Basin is already experiencing 'water scarcity'. A 2010 estimate for Pakistan puts water availability at below 1,000 cubic metres per capita. For India, the situation is similar .The UN medium population projection puts Pakistan's population at 246 million and 335 million for 2025 and 2050 respectively. This translates to water availability of 711 and 522 cubic metres per capita for 2025 and 2050 respectively.

Expressed simply, the population in Pakistan will continue to increase by about 4 million every year. This means that the Indus Basin will need to produce adequate food and fuel supply against the backdrop of declining per capita availability of water. Recent World Bank studies (Briscoe and Qamar 2007) have suggested that, "There are no feasible interventions which would enable Pakistan to mobilise appreciably more water than it now uses. On the other hand there are significant possibilities for lower water availability due to reallocation of flows….."

This scenario also applies to our friends on the other side of the border and this is the challenge both nations will face when discussing the issue on March 20, 2017. With the experience of 56 years with the Indus Waters Treaty, we can create a contemporary basis for the dialogue in the light of this hard constraint. The gains from this approach are larger, and the sharing of both benefits and costs more equitable.

The Indus Waters Treaty was designed to regulate the technical specifications of individual projects. Our current process is thus to discuss individual projects as they are initiated by either side. To incorporate the experience, we could ask how we would have developed the Indus Basin if the border were not there. The portfolio of development projects proposed under such a scenario would be different from what is being discussed and for optimisation, the evaluation metrics would be holistic.

The concerns of the lower riparian – pondage, sediment effects, operating rules, volume and timing of flows – would be treated differently. For example, there are many vulnerable ecosystems within the Indus Basin, including wetlands, floodplains and riparian areas, which are affected from upstream interventions. The most serious concern is the limited flow of freshwater to the Indus delta. Lower Indus has seen significant seawater intrusion – up to 100 km upstream – with drastic effects on lower riparian livelihoods, loss of biodiversity, degradation of mangrove systems, declining fish population and loss of agriculture.

From a holistic and sustainable viewpoint, there is a clear need to incorporate these effects in the economic calculations of an upstream intervention. The intra-Pakistan Water Accord 1991 recognised the need for a minimum flow to the delta of 10 million acre feet. The Revised Action Programme 1979 had recommended an area of 20 million acre feet for this use. Sustainable management of the basin would also require conjunctive utilisation of ground and river water and the export of salt and chemicals in the irrigation effluent.

The hydrology of glaciers in the Upper Indus Basin (UIB) would also be treated differently. The mountain ranges encircling the Tibetan Plateau are a complex highland lowland hydrological system involving a range of water supply and use environments. The contribution of mountains to the total flow of the major rivers of South East Asia and the sources of run-off within individual mountain catchment basins vary throughout the region. Recent concerns (IPCC 2007) arising from climate change, retreating eastern Himalayan glaciers and the role played by these glaciers in the rivers of Asia have highlighted how little the scientific community understands the role of the mountain headwaters (glacier melt, snow, rain) to the Asian rivers.

Much of the present understanding of the climate, hydrology and glaciers of these mountains is based on a few analyses of a limited data base. In an area of over 160,000 sq km above the Tarbela reservoir, there are only five hydrometric stations in the main stem of River Indus and fewer than 20 manual climate stations. This density is significantly less than World Meterological Organisation's recommendations of one gauge per 250 sq km. Credible recent mass balance data is available only for a few glaciers in the Karakoram. The hydrometeorology and glaciers of the Upper Indus Basin (UIB) are not understood due to the orographic complexity of the three-dimensional mosaic of topoclimate within the extreme terrain of the UIB – some of the glaciers are retreating while others are advancing.

Under the current rules of the Indus Waters Treaty, the two parties are expected to evaluate the projects sequentially. This is not optimal since options close with time and thus the utilisation of the basin's water is sub-optimised. Implementing the treaty without a contemporary understanding of the cumulative impacts and operating rules is appropriate from a legal and engineering perspective, but is sub-optimal from the perspective of water utilisation for the basin as a whole – a situation which both parties should find less than satisfactory.

In 2017, both countries may wish to reconsider the way the treaty is to be implemented – project by project or holistically. There is international experience with the modification and reaffirmation of trans-boundary water sharing (or other complex) treaties. A two-pronged approach may be considered: continuation of negotiations of Kishanganga and Ratle for a resolution via a basin-wide optimisation metric and a parallel effort to create the knowledge base to optimise the basin development.

While the current legal role of the World Bank is limited, its role as a friend and financier is considerable. As was the case for the original Indus Waters Treaty, the analysis and negotiations will be done by Indian and Pakistani scientists and engineers. But the bank may be able to play a substantial role similar to what it played in the 1950s. It can do this by facilitating the development of a shared knowledge base: science-based understanding of the cumulative effects of project cascades and the necessary adjustments (due to the effects of climate change on volume and composition of Indus flows). It can also identify and possibly finance the infrastructure investments including the ones needed for an improved understanding of the hydrology of Himalayan glaciers.

The World Bank can explore potential institutional mechanisms to implement and monitor basin development, including the role of the Permanent Indus Commission, and that of third party technical resources. It can also develop a detailed plan to monitor the basin development under alternative infrastructural cascades with associated operating rules.

This two-pronged approach will not only optimise basin development, but may also positively impact the inter-country relations between India and Pakistan through joint scientific and investigative work.

The writer is a former senior adviser of the World Bank.

APP – 45

INDIA WANTS TO BY PASS WORLD BANK IN WATER TALKS

Munawar Hasan, 18 March, 2017

The News (Pakistan)

India insists on discussing Pakistan's objection to Khishanganga and Ratle hydropower projects at the platform of Permanent Indus Waters Commission, bypassing ongoing World Bank-driven dispute resolution mechanism, it is learnt here on Friday.

"I may like to renew my request to discuss your objections on design of Kishenganga and Ratle Hydroelectric projects to make an attempt for an amicable solution of the issues connected with the design of these projects," stated PK Saxena, Indian Commissioner for Indus Waters while communicating agenda of the upcoming meeting in a letter addressed to his Pakistani counterpart, Mirza Asif Baig, confirming participation of his delegation in the 113th meeting of PIWC scheduled for March 20-21 in Islamabad. Hence, Saxena added, "I propose discussion on the Pakistan's objections on Kishenganga, Ratle, Miyar, Lower Kalnai and Pakal Dul Hydroelectric projects in the forthcoming meeting." However, Pakistan while corresponding to India did not include discussion on Kishenganga and Ratle Hydroelectric projects in the agenda and wanted to pursue its case lodged with the World Bank over constitution of Court of Arbitration. Instead, Pakistan stressed holding concluding discussion on the Pakistan's objections on Miyar, Lower Kalnai and Pakal Dul Hydroelectrict plants in the 113th meeting of PIWC.

Both sides nevertheless agreed on discussing arrangements regarding communication of advance information of flood flows during the flood season 2017. Pakistan also wants to discuss programme of tours of inspection, including programme for visit of India Commissioner for Indus Waters and his two advisers or assistants to Pakistan.

Ten-member delegation each of both Pakistan and India, headed by Mirza Asif Baig and PK Saxena respectively, will participate in the meeting. The coming meeting of the Commission was overdue and could not be held last year. In his letter to Indian counterpart, Pakistan's Commissioner for Indus Waters had said: "As you know, Pakistan's commissioner wrote to his Indian counterpart, it is mandatory for the Commission to meet at least once a year and also when requested by either Commissioner under the provisions of Indus Waters Treaty. The last meeting of the Commission was held in New Dehli from 30th to 31st May, 2015. This too was a short meeting and dealt with only finalization of the Annual Report and record of 111th meeting of the Commission. In any case, if the Commission does not hold a meeting before 31st March, 2017, it shall be violating the mandatory provisions of the Treaty and I am sure you do not want it to be so."

APP - 46

PAKISTAN KEEN TO SET UP CLIMATE CHANGE MONITORING SYSTEM FOR INDUS RIVERS

Munawar Hasan, 19 March, 2017

The News (Pakistan)

Pakistan will put forward an advice of deploying a monitoring mechanism to assess the adverse affects of climate change on the water flows of Indus rivers system during a meeting, scheduled on March 19, with an Indian delegation, officials said on Saturday.

As per the fourth point of agenda of the 113th meeting of Permanent Indus Waters Commission, Pakistan has communicated to India that discussion would be held on the monitoring of the parameters relevant to the climate change for the Indus system rivers, a senior official confirmed with The News.

"As climate change would influence the flow of the rivers, so it cannot be excluded from the treaty framework," the official of Pakistan's Indus Waters Commission said. "Further, Paragraph 29 of Annexure G of Indus Waters Treaty mentions the international conventions and customary international law. Under these, the environment and climate change cannot be excluded."

The treaty states except as the Parties may otherwise agree, "The law to be applied by the court shall be this treaty."

The Indus Waters Treaty gives option to the parties to resolve the issues. Pakistan and India signed the treaty after hectic negotiations in Karachi on September 19, 1960. It consists of 12 articles and 8 appendices.

A 10-member delegation of Indian Indus Waters Commission would arrive in Pakistan today (Sunday) for taking part at the two-day annual meeting of the commission.

India agreed to revive Indus waters commission-level talks for discussing water issues after having virtually ended boycott of the negotiation process after around one and half year of impasse. The last meeting of the commission was held in 2015. India has also started exchanging water flow and agriculture use data with Pakistan.

Another official said there is dire need to have a joint monitoring of Indus basin to deal with such a burning issue.

Global warming is going to greatly affect the river flows, the official added.

"Therefore, we can never ignore the importance of having such a monitoring mechanism."

Watershed management is another tool that could help in making water flows smooth. Both countries should develop a mechanism in this regard and also ensure real time exchange of data related to river flows.

The official said both the countries should immediately take steps under the guiding principles of treaty to effectively mitigate adverse effects of climate change.

He said Pakistan is already a victim of flow restriction on the eastern rivers. Even, India was not releasing flows in Ravi and Sutlej rivers to reduce environmental degradation. Due to a loss of regular flow in the eastern rivers, the riverbed has accumulated sand dunes, which are causing havoc to the fragile ecology of the area.

A senior official said India insisted on discussing the objections of Pakistan on Kishanganga and Rattle hydroelectric projects at the platform of Pakistan Indus Waters Commission instead of World Bank-driven process. Pakistan has refused this.

"We have responded to that and our response is that these will not be discussed as the process of discussion has been completed and gone to the forward stages."

APP – 47

PAK-INDIA WATER TALKS RESUME

Muhammad Saleh Zaafir, 20 March, 2017

The News (Pakistan)

Pakistan on Sunday said it believed that continuation of purposeful talks with sincere efforts from both sides would lead to resolution of the matters at the Permanent Indus Commission level in accordance with the provisions of the Indus Waters Treaty which was a symbol of peaceful management of trans-boundary resources.

The press statement was issued in connection with the 113th Meeting of Permanent Indus Commission, which begins today (Monday).

It said Pakistan would continue making efforts for resolution of the matters according to the Indus Waters Treaty provisions and "expects that our goodwill will be reciprocated by the Indian side".

The official statement appreciated India's decision to resume the regular talks and welcomed the Indian delegation to Islamabad.

The two-day meeting is taking place after almost two years, with the last round held in May 2015. The long pause occurred after Pakistan's Indus Waters Commissioner announced the failure of the talks after protracted discussions at commission level in 111th meeting of PIC in Jan-Feb 2015 on the design aspects of Kishanganga and Ratle hydroelectric plants that India is constructing on Kishanganga/ Neelum River (a tributary of Jhelum River) and Chenab River respectively.

Though India had offered to continue discussing the matters at the commission level, Pakistan could not afford delay in the resolution process as construction of the two projects was in progress.

After a two-day meeting between the secretary water and power and the Indian secretary for water resources in New Delhi on July last year, the two disputed matters have been referred for third party resolution through the World Bank. Pakistan has been pursuing the matter of regular meetings of the Permanent Indus Commission with India to bring the other remaining issues under discussion.

Despite various media statements causing speculations, Pakistan showed restraint and kept on making efforts for resumption of commission level talks.

The agenda of the two-day talks includes discussions on the design aspects of Pakal Dul, Lower Kalnai and Miyar hydroelectric plants, flood data supply by India and the tour programme of inspection and meetings by Pakistan and India to the sites of their interest in the Indus Basin, the statement concluded.

Our correspondent adds from Lahore: Earlier, a 10-member delegation of Indian Indus Waters Commission led by PK Saxena arrived through the Wagah border to take part in the meeting. Later, the delegation members and their host left for federal capital soon after their arrival on Sunday.

During the talks, both sides will also discuss arrangements regarding communication of advance information of water flow during the coming flood season.

Moreover, Pakistan will put forward a proposal of deploying a monitoring mechanism to assess the adverse affects of climate change on the water flows of Indus rivers system during the meeting.

As per the fourth point of agenda of the 113th meeting of Permanent Indus Waters Commission, Pakistan has communicated to India that discussion would be held on the monitoring of the parameters relevant to the climate change for the Indus system's rivers.

"As climate change would influence the flow of the rivers, so it cannot be excluded from the treaty framework," said a senior official of Pakistan's Indus Waters Commission.

"Furthermore, Paragraph 29 of Annexure G of Indus Waters Treaty mentions the international conventions and customary international law. Under these, the environment and climate change cannot be excluded," he added.

APP - 48

DAM ISSUE LIKELY TO FIGURE IN INDIA - PAK TALKS

Moushumi Das Gupta and Jayanth Jacobn, 19 March, 2017

Hindustan Times (Pakistan)

The differences over five hydroelectric projects will likely be the key areas of discussion when Indus water commissioners of India and Pakistan meet in Islamabad on March 21 and March 22, signalling a possible respite from their tussle over water issues.

Prodded by World Bank, which brokered the Indus Water Treaty (IWT) of 1960, the two sides seem to be again leaving it to their experts to discuss the technical issues related to water-sharing which often get tangled in their mutual hostility.For India, the main aim will be to resolve differences over Kishenganga and Ratle hydro power projects which are being constructed on the Jhelum and Chenab rivers, respectively.

Objecting to the design of the 330MW Kishenganga project, Pakistan maintains it would result in 40% reduction in water flow into the country which according to the neighbour is against the provisions of IWT, a charge denied by India.For the 850 MW Ratle power plant, Pakistan wants the planned storage capacity of the project to be reduced from 24 million cubic metres to eight million cubic metres. It also wants the height of the dams to be further reduced. But India maintains it never reduced the water flow to Pakistan and the project is run of the river. Pakistan is set to raise issues related to three dams — 1,000 MW Pakuldul on Chenab, 120 MW Miyar located across Miyar Nalla, a right bank main tributary of River Chenab and 43 MW Lower Kalnai hydro project on Lower Kalnai Nalla, tributary to river Chenab in Doda." Pakistan has listed these three projects in their agenda for discussion," said a source.Under the provision of the Indus Waters Treaty 1960, the waters of the eastern rivers Sutlej, Beas and Ravi have been allocated to India and the western rivers Indus, Jhelum and Chenab have been allocated to Pakistan except for certain purposes allowed to India which include generation of hydro power through run of the river plants.Pakistan had raised objections to the construction of these three projects earlier also on the ground that the dams will result in diversion of Pakistan's share of water from the western river Chenab. After the terrorist attack in Uri last year, India had decided to exercise its rights to use its share of water permissible under the IWT, for meeting its power and agricultural requirement.

In the past three months, viability appraisal of about half-adozen hydropower projects on the Chenab river in Jammu and Kashmir has been completed.

APP – 49

INDIAN TEAM ARRIVES TO DISCUSS WATER PROJECTS

Khaleeq Kiani and Khalid Hasan, 20 March, 2017

Dawn (Pakistan)

Marking the revival of bilateral engagement at the institutional level after two years, a 10-member Indian delegation led by Indian Indus Water Commissioner P.P.

Saxena arrived on Sunday for two-day talks on the designs, disputed by Pakistan, of three controversial water projects being built on river Chenab.

The water experts of the two sides at the level of Permanent Indus Commission last met in May 2015 in New Delhi and could not hold mandatory annual meetings since then despite repeated requests by Islamabad.

The two sides would not discuss the controversial Kishanganga and Ratle hydropower projects on which Pakistan is seeking international court of arbitration (ICA) through the World Bank, a senior official told Dawn. He explained that the World Bank was at the advanced stage of appointing an ICA, hence not on the bilateral agenda.

The teams led by Mr Saxena and Pakistan's Indus Water Commissioner Mirza Asif Beg would open formal talks on Monday before leaving for Lahore in the evening where the talks would conclude on Tuesday. The visiting delegation would leave for New Delhi the same day.

The officials said that Pakistan had raised objections to the designs of three projects on Chenab it considered being built by India in violation of the 1960 Indus Waters Treaty. These include Pakul Dal of 1,000MW, Miyar of 120MW and Lower Kalnai of 48MW.

The two sides will exchange data on river flows and try to finalise the schedule of future meetings and tours of inspections by Pakistani water engineering experts to the various rivers and project sides across the Line of Control. An official said that Pakistan's objections to the three projects led the Indian side to agree on putting them on the agenda of the meeting. He said Pakul Dal, a mega project with a proposed generation capacity of 1,000MW, would be built on Chenab and would be able to store nearly one million acres feet of water. The project design envisaged its filling every monsoon season between mid-June and end-August.

Pakistan would seek details of the project and engineering designs and raise specific questions and objections and expect the visiting delegation to satisfy the hosts with envisaged changes.

Officials said the two sides had previously scheduled their annual meeting in September last year with systematic delays caused by New Delhi when Prime Minister Modi declared unilateral suspension of talks and announced speeding up hydropower projects on Pakistani rivers.

An official said India was entitled to store about 3.6m acres feet on Pakistani rivers and almost one-fourth of that quantity could be exploited through Pakul Dal.

In addition, Pakistan has also objected to the design of the 120MW Miyar hydropower project on Miyar Nullah — a major tributary of Chenab on its right bank. The project involves a barrage, head race tunnel, surge shaft, penstocks and tail race channel.

The Miyar project has the capacity to discharge about 61.35 cusecs of water.

Islamabad's objections on the project relate to the barrage height, intake height, head and tail race channels and discharge levels.

Likewise, the 48MW Lower Kalnai project would also be located on river Chenab and impact Pakistan's water rights, an official said.

Under the provisions of the Indus Waters Treaty 1960, waters of the eastern rivers — Sutlej, Beas and Ravi — had been allocated to India and the western rivers — Indus, Jhelum and Chenab — to Pakistan, except for certain non-consumptive uses for India.

APP - 50

INDUS COMMISSIONERS TALKS: FIRST STEP TO COMPOSITE DIALOGUE?

Mirza Khurram Shahzad, 20 March, 2017

Dawn (Pakistan)

After months of tensions, India and Pakistan have finally agreed to resume talks of Indus Water Commission, which were threatened by the hawkish Indian Prime Minister Narendra Modi's aggressive policies towards Pakistan.

Though Indian authorities have publically downplayed the talks taking place on March 20-21 in Islamabad, saying these are just a regular meeting of the Indus Water Commission, the Pakistani officials concerned have termed it of 'much importance'.

The significance emanates from a letter by Indian Indus Water Commissioner P.K. Saxena in which he proposed to discuss highly important disputes such as the construction of Kishanganga and Ratle hydro projects on Jhelum and Chenab rivers by India.

Pakistan, however, has rejected this proposal as the matter has already been taken to the World Bank for dispute resolution.

The Indus Water Commission was set up following the Indus Waters Treaty signed by the two countries in 1960 after the World Bank succeeded in getting them reach an agreement on a water-sharing formula.

The commission has to meet at least once every year, alternately in India and Pakistan, and is responsible for the implementation of the treaty.

"These talks are important because India has come back to the table to discuss the issues after refusing for more than a year," said Mirza Asif Baig, Pakistan's Indus Water Commissioner.

"They were talking about suspension of the waters treaty but now they have come out of that paradigm," he said, adding that the Indian commissioner wrote to him to include the Ratle and Kishanganga projects in these talks but Pakistan declined the proposal.

The last meeting of the commission took place in New Delhi in May 2015. The officials of the two countries could not meet for the annual meeting in 2016 because of heightened tensions between the two governments as Premier Modi threatened to suspend the treaty, saying 'blood and water cannot flow together', following an attack on an Indian military base in held Kashmir.

"The agenda of talks includes projects such as Miyar, Lower Kalnai and Pakal Dul, exchange of data (about flow of water, floods, etc), inspection tours and meetings," Mr Baig said.

Syed Jamaat Ali Shah, Pakistan's former commissioner, termed this meeting a 'step forward' from the former position but said it also showed Pakistan's helplessness on the issue.

"Though it's a routine meeting and India is trying to use it to drag back the issues already taken to the World Bank for arbitration, it has highlighted the reactionary policy of Pakistan government," Mr Shah said.

"It's like we say yes when India says yes, and when they say no, we have no option but to say no. We should have a proactive policy and not the reactive."

"In my view, Modi is successful in his strategy. They have stalled Pakistan's arbitration efforts at the international level and have started six mega hydro projects on a war footing," he said.

"On the other hand, we are doing nothing. Our government is struggling for stability and is stuck in Panama issue; they have not devised any strategy to win these water disputes."

Pakistan's former High Commissioner to India Aziz Ahmed Khan differs.

"It's not verified that Modi has ever said to suspend the Indus Waters Treaty. Some Indian officials categorically denied this statement to me. So I think these Indus water talks are a regular feature and continuation of an ongoing process," he said.

Mr Khan said that linking this meeting to the resumption of higher level talks between the two countries was inappropriate. He, however, viewed that some other move can be expected by the Indian prime minister to take the process forward.

"Electioneering is over in India and Modi may take any other dramatic step to normalise the relations, but we should not link this water commissioners' meeting to the resumption of high-level talks," he said.

Pakistan's foreign ministry takes this development as a bilateral initiative like other departments.

"It's like our DGMOs (Director General Military Operations) talk to each other as and when required," says Nafees Zakaria, spokesman for the Foreign Office.

"Recently Indian parliamentarians were here to participate in an Asian parliamentary conference. Earlier the parliamentarians of both countries were together in Dubai for a conference organised by Pildat, so it's not an indication that this meeting will pave the way for foreign secretary-level talks," he said, adding that the foreign secretary-level talks are a totally different ball game.

"For that India has to agree to discuss Kashmir and they are not showing willingness to talk about this issue so far," Mr Zakaria said.

As the state elections are over in India, the subcontinent may finally see a chance for peace talks but some analysts believe that the landslide victory by the Indian ruling party BJP (Bharatiya Janata Party) may worsen situation as the Indian leadership will become over-confident.

APP – 51

PAK-INDIA INDUS WATERS TREATY TALKS

20 March, 2017. The News (Pakistan)

Pakistan on Monday hailed Indian decision to take part in talks on Indus Waters Treaty (IWT) and hoped that the meeting would help resolve the standing issues between the two countries.

Taking to media, Federal Minister for Water and Power Khawaja Asif said all the matters would be discussed with the Indian delegation. Pakistan is insisting on implementing decision of Court of Arbitration on Kishanganga Project, which India is constructing despite our reservations, the minister added.

Pakistan on Sunday said it believed that continuation of purposeful talks with sincere efforts from both sides would lead to resolution of the matters at the Permanent Indus Commission level in accordance with the provisions of the IWT which was a symbol of peaceful management of trans-boundary resources.

The press statement was issued in connection with the 113th Meeting of Permanent Indus Commission, which commenced today.

It said Pakistan would continue making efforts for resolution of the matters according to the Indus Waters Treaty provisions and "expects that our goodwill will be reciprocated by the Indian side".

The official statement appreciated India's decision to resume the regular talks and welcomed the Indian delegation to Islamabad.

The two-day meeting is taking place after almost two years, with the last round held in May 2015. The long pause occurred after Pakistan's Indus Waters Commissioner announced the failure of the talks after protracted discussions at commission level in 111th meeting of PIC in Jan-Feb 2015 on the design aspects of Kishanganga and Ratle hydroelectric plants that India is constructing on Kishanganga/ Neelum River (a tributary of Jhelum River) and Chenab River respectively.

Though India had offered to continue discussing the matters at the commission level, Pakistan could not afford delay in the resolution process as construction of the two projects was in progress.

After a two-day meeting between the secretary water and power and the Indian secretary for water resources in New Delhi on July last year, the two disputed matters have been referred for third party resolution through the World Bank. Pakistan has been pursuing the matter of regular meetings of the Permanent Indus Commission with India to bring the other remaining issues under discussion.

Despite various media statements causing speculations, Pakistan showed restraint and kept on making efforts for resumption of commission level talks.

The agenda of the two-day talks includes discussions on the design aspects of Pakal Dul, Lower Kalnai and Miyar hydroelectric plants, flood data supply by India and the tour programme of inspection and meetings by Pakistan and India to the sites of their interest in the Indus Basin, the statement concluded.

A 10-member delegation of Indian Indus Waters Commission led by PK Saxena arrived through the Wagah border to take part in the meeting. Later, the delegation members and their host left for federal capital soon after their arrival on Sunday.

During the talks, both sides will also discuss arrangements regarding communication of advance information of water flow during the coming flood season.

Moreover, Pakistan will put forward a proposal of deploying a monitoring mechanism to assess the adverse affects of climate change on the water flows of Indus rivers system during the meeting.

As per the fourth point of agenda of the 113th meeting of Permanent Indus Waters Commission, Pakistan has communicated to India that discussion would be held on the monitoring of the parameters relevant to the climate change for the Indus system's rivers.

"As climate change would influence the flow of the rivers, so it cannot be excluded from the treaty framework," said a senior official of Pakistan's Indus Waters Commission.

"Furthermore, Paragraph 29 of Annexure G of Indus Waters Treaty mentions the international conventions and customary international law. Under these, the environment and climate change cannot be excluded," he added.

APP – 52

SHED THE INDUS ALBATROSS: INDUS WATERS TREATY OFFERS ONE-SIDED BENEFITS TO PAKISTAN

Brahma Chellaney, The Times of India

20 March, 2017

At a time when India is haunted by a deepening water crisis, the Indus Waters Treaty (IWT) hangs like the proverbial albatross from its neck. In 1960, in the naïve hope that water largesse would yield peace, India entered into a treaty that gave away the Indus system's largest rivers as gifts to Pakistan.

Since then that congenitally hostile neighbour, while drawing the full benefits from the treaty, has waged overt or covert aggression almost continuously and is now using the IWT itself as a stick to beat India with, including by contriving water disputes and internationalising them.

A partisan World Bank, meanwhile, has compounded matters further. Breaching IWT's terms under which an arbitral tribunal cannot be established while the parties' disagreement "is being dealt with by a neutral expert", the Bank proceeded in November to appoint both a court of arbitration (as demanded by Pakistan) and a neutral expert (as suggested by India). It did so while admitting that the two concurrent processes could make the treaty "unworkable over time".

World Bank partisanship, however, is not new: IWT was the product of the Bank's activism, with US government support, in making India embrace an unparalleled treaty that parcelled out the largest three of the six rivers to Pakistan and made the Bank effectively a guarantor in the treaty's initial phase.

With much of its meat in its voluminous annexes this is an exhaustive, book-length treaty with a patently neo-colonial structure that limits India's sovereignty to the basin of the three smaller rivers.

The Bank's recent decision was made more bizarre by the fact that while the treaty explicitly permits either party to seek a neutral expert's appointment, it specifies no such unilateral right for a court of arbitration. In 2010, such an arbitral tribunal was appointed with both parties' consent. The neutral expert, however, is empowered to refer the parties' disagreement, if need be, to a court of arbitration.

The uproar that followed the World Bank's initiation of the dual processes forced it to "pause", but not terminate, its legally untenable decision.

Stuck with a mess of its own making, it is now prodding India to bail it out by compromising with Pakistan over the two moderate-sized Indian hydropower projects. But what Pakistan wants are design changes of the type it enforced years ago in the Salal project, resulting in that plant silting up. It is threatening to target other Indian projects as well.

Yet Indian policy appears adrift. Indeed, India is backsliding even on its tentative moves to deter Pakistani terrorism. For example, after last September's Uri attack, it suspended the Permanent Indus Commission (PIC) with Pakistan. Now the suspension has been lifted, allowing the PIC to meet in the aftermath of the state elections.

In truth the suspension was just a charade, with the PIC missing no meeting. Prime Minister Narendra Modi reversed course in time for PIC, which meets at least once every financial year, to meet before the current year ended on March 31 in order to prepare its annual report by the treaty-stipulated June 1 deadline. But while the suspension was widely publicised for political ends, the reversal happened quietly.

Much of the media also fell for another charade that Modi sought to play to the hilt in Punjab elections: He promised to end Punjab's water stress by utilising India's full IWT-allocated share of the waters.

His government, however, has initiated not a single new project to correct India's abysmal failure to tap its meagre 19.48% share of the Indus waters.Instead, Modi has engaged in little more than eyewash: He has appointed a committee of secretaries, not to find ways to fashion the Indus card to reform Pakistan's conduct, but farcically to examine India's own rights under IWT over 56 years after it was signed.The answer to India's serious under-utilisation of its share, which has resulted in Pakistan getting more than 10 billion cubic metres (BCM) yearly in bonus waters on top of its staggering 167.2 BCM allocation, is not a bureaucratic rigmarole but political direction to speedily build storage and other structures.

Despite Modi's declaration that "blood and water cannot flow together", India is reluctant to hold Pakistan to account by linking IWT's future to that renegade state's cessation of its unconventional war. It is past time India shed its reticence.Pakistan's interest lies in sustaining a unique treaty that incorporates water generosity to the lower riparian on a scale unmatched by any other pact in the world. Yet it is undermining its own interest by dredging up disputes with India and running down IWT as ineffective for resolving them.

By insisting that India must not ask what it is getting in return but bear only IWT's burdens, even as it suffers Pakistan's proxy war, Islamabad itself highlights the treaty's one-sided character.In effect, Pakistan is offering India a significant opening to remake the terms of the Indus engagement. This is an opportunity that India should not let go. The Indus potentially represents the most potent instrument in India's arsenal – more powerful than the nuclear option, which essentially is for deterrence.

APP – 53

WHAT IS INDUS WATER TREATY?

Adrija Roy Chowdhury 20 March, 2017

The Indian Express

Internationally, the Indus Water Treaty is seen as one of the most successful cases of conflict resolution especially considering the fact that it has stayed in place despite the two countries having been engaged in four wars.

Indian and Pakistani officials are currently in the midst of a two day meeting of the Permanent Indus Commission, starting Monday. The meeting is likely to address the conflict between the two countries over the construction of the Kishenganga and Ratle hydroelectric plants on Kishenganga and Chenab rivers respectively. Signed in 1960, the IWT is an agreement that was signed by former Prime Minister Jawaharlal Nehru and the then President of Pakistan, Ayub Khan, marking out control over the six rivers running across the Indus basin following partition of the subcontinent.

Internationally, the IWT is seen as one of the most successful cases of conflict resolution especially considering the fact that it has stayed in place despite the two countries having been engaged in four wars. However, between the two countries, it has seeded dissatisfaction and conflicts regarding its interpretation and implementation. As the two countries look forward to engaging in discussion over the current dispute, here's a look at the historical background and nature of the treaty and the conflicts it has given rise to.

What is the Indus Water Treaty (IWT)?

The six rivers of the Indus basin originate in Tibet and flow across the Himalayan ranges to end in the Arabian sea south of Karachi. Preceding partition, it was one common network for both India and Pakistan. However, while partition managed to draw terrestrial borders, the question of how to divide the Indus waters was something that needed to be worked out. Since the rivers flowed from India to Pakistan, the latter was unsurprisingly threatened by the prospect of being fed by the former.

Initially, the issue of water sharing was sorted out by the Inter-Dominion accord of May 4, 1948 that laid out that India would release enough waters to Pakistan in return for annual payments from the latter. The problems of this arrangement was soon realised and it was considered necessary to find an alternative solution.

Eventually, in 1960, the two countries reached a decisive step with the intervention of the World Bank wherein precise details were laid out regarding the way in which the waters would be distributed. The components of the treaty were fairly simple. The three western rivers (Jhelum, Chenab and Indus) were allocated to Pakistan while India was given control over the three eastern rivers (Ravi, Beas and Sutlej). While India could use the western rivers for consumption purpose, restrictions were placed on building of storage systems. The treaty states that aside of certain specific cases, no storage and irrigation systems can be built by India on the western rivers.

From the Indian point of view, the basic dissatisfaction with the treaty arises from the fact that it prevents the country from building any storage systems on the western rivers. Even though the treaty lays out that under certain exceptional circumstances storage systems can be built, the complaint raised by India is that Pakistan deliberately stops any such effort due to the political rivalry it shares with India. The matter is further aggravated by the fact that the western rivers lie in the disputed region of Jammu and Kashmir, which has been a subject of tussle between the two countries since independence. Since the treaty's conception in 1960, the two countries have been embroiled in conflicts over a number of projects including the Salal hydroelectric project on the Chenab, the Tulbul project, the Kishenganga and Ratle hydroelectric plants.

While the tense political relations between the two countries have to a large extent resulted in conflicts over the treaty, to a large extent it is the framing of the treaty itself that has led to grievances. Water policy expert, Ramaswamy R. Iyer writes the following in his work "Indus treaty: A different view":

One can immediately see how differences arise. One party can claim to be in full conformity with the criteria laid down in the treaty, and the other party can say that this is not the case.

In the first place, as pointed out by Iyer, the treaty is highly technical leading to far ranging divergences between the two countries in terms of interpretations. For instance, while the treaty says that storage systems can be built but to a limited extent, the technical details makes it increasingly difficult to conclude under what circumstances projects can be carried out.Added to this inherent limitation within the treaty is the political situation between the two countries. As per the writings of Iyer, while India on the one hand tries to make maximum use of the breathing space provided by the treaty to build projects on the western rivers, Pakistan on account of its suspicions towards India keeps an extra keen eye on every technical aspect of the project and tries its absolute best to get it suspended.

What is the ongoing conflict about?

The current conflict is over the Kishenganga dam project and the Ratle hydroelectric project. The Kishenganga hydroelectric plant is a $864 million worth of project that was initiated in 2007 and was projected to be completed by 2016. Pakistan took the project to the Court of Arbitration in 2010 raising six issues that they say violate the treaty. In 2013, the Court of Arbitration ruled India to go ahead with the project under the condition that a minimum water flow to Pakistan of 9 cubic metres per second is maintained. On several other issues however, no agreement between the two countries could be reached.

APP – 54

PRESS RELEASE BY PAKISTAN INDUS WATER COMMISSION ABOUT PIC'S 113ᵀᴴ MEETING HELD AT ISLAMASBAD

20ᵗʰ – 21ˢᵗ March, 2017

113ᵗʰ meeting of Permanent Indus Commission was held on 20/21 March, 2017 at Islamabad. In the meeting discussions were focussed on India's proposed Miyar, Lower Kalnai and Pakal Dul hydropower projects as well as on matters pertaining to exchange of data and conducting tours and meetings of Indus Commission.

On Miyar hydropower project, India has withdrawn its design after Pakistan had raised objections to it in the previous meetings of the commission. On the other two projects discussions took place on Pakistan's prior objections relating to poundage and freeboard of Lower Kalnai and freeboard and spillway of Pakal Dul Hydropower projects. Indian delegation agreed to re-consider Pakistan's observations on these projects and will respond in the next meeting of the Commission.

India delegation also agreed to arrange inspection tour of Pakistan's Indus Commission which is expected to be arranged before August 2017. Pakistan's IWC demanded from India to provide the outflows from Baglihar and Salal dams (on Chenab river) during flood season to issue early flood warnings. Indian delegation has agreed to consider Pakistan's request and it is expected that India would start providing the required data starting from the coming flood season.

APP - 55

HIGH LEVEL 'WATER TALKS' WITH INDIA FROM NEXT MONTH

Khaleeq Kiani – March 2017

The Dawn (Pakistan)

India has decided to return to the negotiating table with Pakistan over its disputed hydropower projects in April, following the intervention of the US and the World Bank.

Water and Power Minister Khawaja Mohammad Asif said on Monday that the two nations would hold three-day secretary-level talks on the Kishanganga and Ratle hydropower projects, under the aegis of the World Bank, in Washington from April 11.

Speaking on the sidelines of the two-day talks between Indus water commissioners from both sides, the minister, who also holds the portfolio for defence, welcomed the Indian decision to resume negotiations under the 1960 Indus Waters Treaty on the proposed Pakul Dal, Miyar and Lower Kalnai hydropower projects, disputed by Pakistan.

"The US has intervened at the highest level to help both countries resolve the issue. There will be secretary-level talks on the Ratle and Kishanganga hydropower projects in Washington on April 11, 12 and 13," he said at a press conference.

"We are happy that India has finally agreed to resume talks at the commission level. We welcome this decision and the visit of the Indian delegation," he added.

The 10-member Indian delegation currently in Islamabad is led by Indian Indus Water Commissioner P.K. Saxena.

Khawaja Asif said Pakistan would be in a position to protect its rights on Ratle hydroelectric project, adding that the country's stance had not been negated at any level. He refused to speculate whether or not the water talks could ultimately lead to the resumption of composite dialogue.

"We want that India should share the design of the three proposed projects, and if they hurt Pakistan's interests, then objections will be raised at the appropriate forum; this is our right. Since the treaty was signed, 116 project inspection visits have been undertaken," he said.

Pakistan has been protesting over the design and construction of the two projects — the 330MW Kishanganga hydroelectric project and the 850MW Ratle hydroelectric project in India-held Jammu and Kashmir. Islamabad has been demanding international arbitration through the World Bank — the so-called guarantor of the 1960 treaty.

The minister said Pakistan had decided to seek international arbitration following the failure of secretary-level talks on Ratle on July 14-15 in New Delhi.

Pakistan, he said, had objection over the project design. The minister claimed that the World Bank-sponsored International Court of Arbitration had given its verdict in Pakistan's favour over the Kishanganga project and Islamabad was now demanding that it be implemented.

A former water and power secretary, however, disagreed. He was of the opinion that Islamabad's main objection over the diversion of the river waters by India was not entertained by the International Court of Arbitration because authorities could not establish through evidence its water uses from the Line of Control to Muzaffarabad.

The minister, however, conceded that Kishanganga would affect the generation capacity of the 969MW Neelum-Jhelum Hydropower plant, which is located downstream of the proposed Indian project, by about 10pc.

The minister said the two-day talks on 1,000MW Pakul Dal, 120MW Miyar and 48MW Lower Kalnai projects would be led from the Pakistani side by Mirza Asif Beg, Pakistan's Indus Water Commissioner.

He said India had not shared the design of these projects with Pakistan, as required under the treaty, adding that Islamabad had serious reservations over these projects and believed they would give India the capacity to impede water flows to Pakistan.

He said Pakistan always believed the accord was one of the few international treaties capable of resolving serious disputes over water reservoirs through peaceful means and sanctity of the treaty and resolutions of dispute though this was in the interest of the two nations.

In July 2016, a high-level delegation headed by the water and power secretary had visited New Delhi to discuss these projects, but India's inflexible attitude resulted in their failure to reach a conclusion. After this, Pakistan decided to approach the Permanent Court of Arbitration against India.

Last September, Pakistan approached the World Bank when Indian Prime Minister Narendra Modi threatened to revoke the 56-year-old treaty following the Uri attack.

Under the treaty, the World Bank has an important role in establishment of the Court of Arbitration.

APP - 56

INDIA YET TO DECIDE ON WORLD BANK PROPOSED WATER TALKS WITH PAKISTAN

Moushumi Das Gupta and Imtiaz Ahmed- 22 Marach, 2017

Hindustan Times

New Delhi is yet to take a call on the World Bank's proposal for a meeting between the water secretaries of India and Pakistan in Washington next month to resolve differences over the Kishanganga and Ratle hydropower projects.

Pakistan's water and power minister Khawaja Asif told a news conference in Islamabad on Monday that Indian and Pakistani officials are set to meet in Washington during April 11-13 for talks brokered by the World Bank.(wb). Asif was speaking on the margins of a meeting between the Indus water commissioners.

An Indian government source told Hindustan Times, "As of now, we have not decided anything. We will take a call after the 10-member team headed by Indus water commissioner PK Saxena returns from Islamabad."

The World Bank, which brokered the Indus Waters Treaty of 1960 and has a key role in helping resolve differences, said it is prepared to facilitate the meet. "We continue to work with both countries to resolve the issue in an amicable manner and in line with the spirit of the treaty. We would hope that the two countries will come to an agreement soon," said Alexander Anthony Ferguson, World Bank's senior manager communications (South Asia).

APP – 57

NO INDIAN WORD TO HALT WORK ON CONTROVERSIAL WATER PROJECTS

Khaleeq Kiani – 22 March, 2017

The Dawn

Two-day Pakistan-India Permanent Indus Commission (PIC) talks concluded here on Tuesday on a positive note as India withdrew the design of a smaller hydropower project and agreed to reconsider Pakistan's observations on two others.

There was, however, no commitment from the visiting side to halt construction work on the controversial projects, indicating India's traditional time-gaining approach to project development. This was evident from the fact that a senior member of the Pakistani team confirmed that construction work on the Lower Kalnai project was in progress while that on the Pakul Dal project was yet to start. Both projects are on two different tributaries of the Chenab River. When asked by Dawn if India had given any assurance to stop constructions, the official requesting anonymity said he would not talk beyond an official statement.

A former water and power secretary said it was a pattern from all the previous controversial projects like Baglihar and Kishanganga that New Delhi engaged Islamabad in technicalities and kept civil and side works moving for years until reaching a fait accompli stage when challenged in international forums.

The Pakistani side was led by Indus Waters Commissioner Mirza Asif Baig while his counterpart P.K. Saxena led the Indian delegation.

A statement issued by the water and power ministry at the conclusion of the talks said India had withdrawn its design on the Miyar hydropower project after Pakistan raised objections to it at the commission's previous meetings. It said the 113th meeting of the PIC held discussions on India's proposed Miyar, Lower Kalnai and Pakal Dal hydropower projects as well as matters relating to exchange of data and conducting tours and meetings of the commission.

On the other two projects discussions were held on Pakistan's prior objections to pondage and freeboard of Lower Kalnai and freeboard and spillway of Pakal Dul hydropower projects.

"The Indian side has agreed to reconsider Pakistan's observations on these projects and will respond in the next meeting of the commission," the statement said.

The Indian side also agreed to inspection tour by the Pakistan's Indus Commission which is expected to be arranged before August. The Pakistani side asked India to provide data of outflows of Baglihar and Salal dams (on the Chenab) during the flood season so that it could issue early flood warnings.

"The Indian side has agreed to consider Pakistan's request and it is expected that India would start providing the required data starting from the coming flood season," the statement said.

Insiders said Pakistan had already withdrawn its objections to freeboard of the 1000MW Pakal Dul project located on the Marusadar River — a right bank tributary of the Chenab. Pakistan has raised objections to its pondage, spillway and filling criteria.

It is a storage-cum-power project and can have gross storage of about 108,000 acre feet of water. The project design envisaged its filling every monsoon season between mid-June and end-August.

Pakistan is of the opinion that the tunnel spillway of Pakal Dul should be raised closer to the dead storage level because its placement 40 metres below the dead storage level could allow drawdown flushing not permitted to India under the 1960 waters treaty.

On the 48MW Lower Kalnai project, Pakistan has raised objections to its freeboard, pondage and intake. Islamabad is of the view that depth of bridge girder and provision of freeboard should be close to one metre and considers two-metre freeboard as 'excessive'.

Pakistan has also challenged the discharge series of river Lower Kalnai at Dunadi for winter months and estimated permissible pondage of 0.38 cubic megametres compared to Indian design pondage of 2.74 cubic megametres.

The Lower Kalnai project is on a left bank tributary of Chenab and can have gross storage of about 1,508 acre feet of water.

Pakistan has also raised objections to freeboard, pondage, spillway and intake of the 120MW Miyar hydroelectric project on the right bank Miyar tributary of Chenab. It is also a run-of-the-river project but the barrage type structure could have gross storage of about 1,298 acre feet of water.

Under the provisions of the Indus Water Treaty 1960, waters of the eastern rivers — Sutlej, Beas and Ravi — had been allocated to India and the western rivers — the Indus, Jhelum and Chenab — to Pakistan, except for certain non-consumptive uses for India.

APP - 58

INDIA DENIES REPORT ON MIYAR POWER PROJECT

Mariana Babar - 23 March, 2017

The News Internastional

India has vehemently denied reports in the Pakistan media that it had agreed to either scrap its Miyar (120MW) power project or alter its design on the request of Pakistan.

India has also dropped hints that it might not attend the secretary level talks next month in Washington. "India has never agreed either to halt work on the Miyar power project or redesign it because of demands from Pakistan. These reports are factually incorrect.

India had before this meeting in Islamabad faced some issues because of the topology in the area where the Miyar power project was being set up", an Indian official in New Delhi told The News.

When asked, the officials did not have the details of the topology of the region and why it affected the old design of the Miyar power project. The decision by Indian experts was taken much before the Islamabad meeting.

It was for this reason that experts were now busy redesigning the Miyar power project and this information was passed on to the Pakistan side in the two-day meeting which concluded on Tuesday in Islamabad.

It appears simply to earn some brownie points someone from the Pakistan side gave a spin to this 'redesigning,' to appear as if the change in design of Miyar was because of concerns shown by Pakistan.

In the past Pakistan has been flagging concern over designs of India's five hydroelectricity projects -- Pakal Dul (1,000MW), Ratle (850MW), Kishanganga (330MW), Miyar (120MW) and Lower Kalnai (48MW) -- being built/planned in the Indus river basin, contending these violate the treaty.

According to Indian media reports three projects, being built on tributaries of the Chenab River, are in the pre-construction/under-construction stages. Pakal Dul and Lower Kalnai are being built in Jammu and Kashmir at cost of Rs7,464 crore (November 2008 price level) and Rs396 crore respectively.

Miyar hydroelectricity project, located in Himachal Pradesh's Lahaul Spiti district, is estimated to cost Rs1,125 crore. Meanwhile, the Hindustan Times now reports that there could be "confrontation" between the two countries over the Indus Water Treaty as Indian officials now say that there is no need to meet at the secretary level in Washington which was proposed by the World Bank, for next month, because it finds this proposed meeting against the "spirit of the pact".

"India believes that there is no need to look for another mechanism to break the deadlock since the treaty already had a dispute resolution system built in", an unnamed official commented.

The report explained that "India also believes the WB which brokered the pact in 1960 has lately been "biased" in following the treaty provisions." It said India could not be party to any meeting "which is against the provisions of the Indus Water Treaty".

"New Delhi feels the World Bank continues to work against the spirit of the pact by initiating two separate dispute resolution mechanisms," said the Indian newspaper. Minister for Water and Power Khawaja Asif said on Tuesday that Secretary level talks on Ratle Hydroelectric plant will begin on April 12, in Washington between the two countries.

APP – 59

INDIA MAY WALK OUT OF INDUS WATER TALKS WITH PAKISTAN

Jayanth Jacob and Moushumi Das Gupta - 23 March, 2017

Hindustan Times

New Delhi finds the US meeting against 'spirt of the pact' and believes World Bank has been 'biased' in following provisions.

India and Pakistan are set for another showdown over the Indus waters treaty with New Delhi finding the World Bank's proposal of a secretary level meeting in Washington next month against the 'spirit of the pact'.

Earlier this week, Pakistan water and power minister Khwaja Asif announced that the two countries would hold a "three-day 'way forward'" meeting on the Ratle and Kishenganga projects in April in Washington. Sources say India believes that there is no need to look for another mechanism to break the deadlock since the treaty already had a dispute resolution system built in it.

India also believes the World Bank which brokered the pact in 1960 has lately been "biased" in following the treaty provisions. Sources indicated that India cannot be party to any meeting "which is against the provisions of the Indus waters treaty", putting the Washington meet under a cloud.

These sources maintain that World Bank is playing the role of a 'mediator' whereas it should be a 'facilitator' between India and Pakistan to resolve the issues "in accordance with the provisions of the Indus waters treaty". The World Bank had suggested the meeting of water resources secretaries for three days in April.

Sources familiar with the developments told HT that the World Bank proposal for the water resources secretaries meeting in Washington goes against the 'spirit of the treaty'. New Delhi feels the World Bank continues to work against the spirit of the pact by initiating two separate dispute resolution mechanisms.

In the dispute of Kishenganga project, India wanted the neutral experts mechanism to solve the issue but Pakistan favoured arbitration. The World Bank had kicked in the two mechanisms at the same time, much to the anger of India last year.

Indian and Pakistani officials of the Indus water commission who met in Islamabad on March 21 and 22 could not make much progress on the issues. Indus water commissioner P.K. Saxena led the Indian delegation while the Pakistani side which was headed by Mirza Asif Saeed.

For the Indian side, the main issue now is resolving differences the over Kishenganga and Ratle hydro power projects.

The two projects are being constructed on the Jhelum and Chenab rivers respectively. Pakistan while objecting to the design of the 330 MW Kishenganga project maintains it would result in a 40% reduction of water flowing into the country, which it says is against the provisions of IWT. India refutes that charge.

For the 850 MW Ratle power plant, Pakistan wants the planned storage capacity of the project reduced from 24 million cubic metres to eight million cubic metres. Pakistan also wants the height of the dams to be reduced.

But India maintains it never reduced the water flow to Pakistan.

Pakistan is set to raise issues related to three dams — 1000 MW Pakuldul on Chenab, 120 MW Miyar across Miyar Nalla which is a major tributary of the Chenab and the 43 MW Lower Kalnai hydro project — on Lower Kalnai Nalla, a tributary of the Chenab. "Pakistan has listed these three projects in their agenda for discussion," said a source.

APP - 60

NEXT ROUND OF WATER TALKS WITH INDIA IN JEOPARDY

Anwar Iqbal – 23 March, 2017

The Dawn

WASHINGTON: The next round of India-Pakistan water talks — that the World Bank offered to hold in Washington next month — may be delayed or cancelled because of India's refusal to accept arbitration.

Pakistan not only wants the talks to be held as scheduled but is also seeking the World Bank's arbitration as the guarantor of the Indus Waters Treaty.

But Indian officials told reporters in New Delhi on Wednesday that India was against such arbitration and preferred negotiations within the framework of the treaty.

Pakistan too recognises the treaty's pivotal role but disagrees with the Indian interpretation, which seeks to minimise arbitration.

ADVERTISEMENT

The proposed talks will focus on two controversial hydropower projects — Kishanganga and Ratle — over which Pakistan is seeking International Court of Arbitration through the World Bank.

Indian and Pakistani officials met in Islamabad and Lahore this week to discuss three Indian projects on the Chenab River that Pakistan fears would decrease the flow of water into its territory.

After the meetings, Water and Power Minister Khawaja Asif told reporters that talks on the Kishanganga and Ratle hydroelectric schemes would be held in Washington next month, with the World Bank as the mediator.

But officials in New Delhi told the Indian media that they had not received any formal communication about the Washington meeting. They also said that India opposed Pakistan's proposal for the bank's mediation or arbitration and would prefer a neutral expert to review the two projects and give his or her opinion.

Pakistan says it wants a decision that is legally binding on both India and Pakistan and such a decision can only come from a court of arbitration and not from a neutral expert.

Late last year, New Delhi suspended talks on the treaty, which distributes the eastern tributaries of the Indus — Sutlej, Beas and Ravi to India and the western tributaries — Jhelum, Indus and Chenab — to Pakistan.

In September 2016, Indian Prime Minister Narendra Modi threatened to scrap the treaty after a terrorist attack killed 19 Indian soldiers. Pakistan warned that any such move would be a "declaration of war".

Pakistan has repeatedly accused India of violating the treaty by building dams on the western rivers. India says that the treaty unduly favours Pakistan by giving it a greater share of water.

"Pakistan wants the World Bank to continue to play its role as the guarantor of the treaty," an official source told Dawn in Washington. "The Pakistanis fear that India is trying to undermine the bank's role as the repository of this treaty."

The World Bank first seemed interested in Pakistan's proposal for arbitration over Kishanganga and Ratle projects "but may opt out under India's pressure", the source added.

Pakistan has also said that it wants a resolution "through the provisions of the treaty, in their letter and spirit", and "not through India's interpretation of the agreement".

A similar meeting, held in November 2016, made little progress as India rejected the World Bank's terms of reference because, it claimed, the terms favoured Pakistan's demand for arbitration.

APP - 61

ISLAMABAD BELIEVES IN PEACEFUL RESOLUTION

Mian SaifurRehman - 23 March, 2017

The News International

Despite the pressure from local administrations inside Pakistan's Punjab and Indian Punjab, in the past, to assert claims to national territory right up to the boundary and to take forcible control of canal headworks on the border, higher authorities instead opted for flexible working arrangements and mutual accommodation.

This has been stated by the author of the Indus Divided: India, Pakistan and the River Basin Dispute, historian Daniel Haines in one of his latest write-ups.

Haines goes further to appreciate the restraint exercised by both the Pakistani and Indian armies as he says, "Both armies were wise enough not to risk escalation over patches of land that had little strategic value."

"Already, small-scale armed conflicts between civilians and border police, especially over seasonal river islands, had dragged both sides into shooting matches."

Moving forward from Haines' appreciation of both armies on Indo-Pak water disputes, it can be further asserted on the basis of Pakistan's overall conduct and good diplomacy that Pakistani authorities in particular have always shown extraordinary care about resolving disputes of any nature, especially the issues arising out of construction of dams on western rivers whose water, according to the Indus Waters Treaty, is to be used exclusively by Pakistan.

And, in this area, Pakistan's armed establishment and political governments have remained on the same page, aiming at getting our due water rights through negotiations and mediation instead of escalation although India's plans for hydropower projects in Kashmir at Baglihar and Kishenganga and elsewhere have remained a constant source of tension. Pakistan has been protesting against these plans that simply meant breaking the Indus Waters Treaty.

The present negotiations between the two sides, however, augur well and now it is being inferred from the other day's Indo-Pak experts' parleys that India would not ignore Pakistan's concerns anymore.

Haines also appreciates good environmental diplomacy on water issues. According to him, "Since 1960, the Indus Waters Treaty has governed relations over the rivers. The treaty is widely known in the world of environmental diplomacy as a good example of peaceful water-sharing. It was negotiated without bloodshed, and has survived three wars between India and Pakistan.

Yet readers in South Asia hardly need to be reminded of the scale of recent conflict over rivers. Following a militant attack on an Indian Army camp at Uri in September last year, which many Indians blamed on Pakistan, Indian hawks called on Prime Minister Narendra Modi to cut off Pakistan's water supply.

It may be recalled that Narendra Modi did follow the hawks' advice and acted as the biggest anti-Pakistan hawk by publicly issuing a warning in an unbearably aggressive tone that Pakistan's water supply would be cut off.

Haines also gives benefit of doubt, rather a clean chit to Pakistan by saying, "Journalists and scholars have long assumed that the water dispute was really about Kashmir, or that the Kashmir dispute was actually about water. But there is little hard evidence for such theories.

For example, some historians have speculated that Pakistan's formal entry into the Kashmir conflict in 1948 was partly intended to capture the headwaters of the River Chenab. While researching, I found that the historical evidence had not been systematically examined. What I found was not a simple cause-and-effect relationship between the two disputes, but a complex, overlapping and shifting set of insecurities. Kashmir and river water represented two of the key problems in how theleaderships of bothnations imagined their own sovereigntlyu".

APP – 62

PAK-INDIA SHOWDOWN OVER INDUS TREATY LIKELY

Monitoring Desk - 24 March 2017

The News International

NEW DELHI: India and Pakistan are set for another showdown over the Indus waters treaty with New Delhi finding the World Bank's proposal of a secretary level meeting in Washington next month against the 'spirit of the pact', reports foreign media.

Earlier this week, Water and Power Minister Kh Asif announced that the two countries would hold a "three-day 'way forward'" meeting on the Ratle and Kishenganga projects in April in Washington. Sources say India believes that there is no need to look for another mechanism to break the deadlock since the treaty already had a dispute resolution system built in it.

India also believes the World Bank which brokered the pact in 1960 has lately been "biased" in following the treaty provisions. Sources indicated that India cannot be party to any meeting "which is against the provisions of the Indus waters treaty", putting the Washington meet under a cloud.

These sources maintain that World Bank is playing the role of a 'mediator' whereas it should be a 'facilitator' between India and Pakistan to resolve the issues "in accordance with the provisions of the Indus Water Treaty". The World Bank had suggested the meeting of water resources secretaries for three days in April.

Sources familiar with the developments told the foreign media that the World Bank proposal for the water resources secretaries meeting in Washington goes against the 'spirit of the treaty'. New Delhi feels the World Bank continues to work against the spirit of the pact by initiating two separate dispute resolution mechanisms.

In the dispute of Kishenganga project, India wanted the neutral experts mechanism to solve the issue but Pakistan favoured arbitration. The World Bank had kicked in the two mechanisms at the same time, much to the anger of India last year.

Indian and Pakistani officials of the Indus water commission who met in Islamabad on March 21 and 22 could not make much progress on the issues. Indus water commissioner P.K. Saxena led the Indian delegation while the Pakistani side which was headed by Mirza Asif Saeed.

For the Indian side, the main issue now is resolving differences the over Kishenganga and Ratle hydro power projects. The two projects are being constructed on the Jhelum and Chenab rivers respectively. Pakistan while objecting to the design of the 330 MW Kishenganga project maintains it would result in a 40 percent reduction of water flowing into the country, which it says is against the provisions of IWT. India refutes that charge.

For the 850 MW Ratle power plant, Pakistan wants the planned storage capacity of the project reduced from 24 million cubic metres to eight million cubic metres. Pakistan also wants the height of the dams to be reduced.

Pakistan is set to raise issues related to three dams — 1000 MW Pakuldul on Chenab, 120 MW Miyar across Miyar Nalla which is a major tributary of the Chenab and the 43 MW Lower Kalnai hydro project — on Lower Kalnai Nalla, a tributary of the Chenab.

APP - 63

INDIAN GOVERNMENT TO CHANGE IT'S STAND ON INDUS WATER TREATY

The Hindu 24 March, 2017

Gopal Baglay, Spokesperson ofIndian Minisstry of External Affairs says the India will continue to meet Pakistan on the issue .The Ministry of External Affairs on Friday said the government has not changed its position on the Indus Water Treaty even as India is assessing the outcome of the last meeting of the Indus Water Commission, held in Pakistan on March 20-21.

The meeting of the commission after almost two years did not seem to have concluded on a positive note with both sides singing different tunes.

"They (Indus Water Commissioners) had detailed technical discussions.

"Our team has since returned and the deliberations and discussions at the meeting are being assessed. Let me categorically tell you that there has been no change in our previous position on any of the matters discussed at the meeting," said Gopal Baglay, Spokesperson, Ministry of External Affairs (MEA).However, Pakistan has said that both sides will have a high-level meeting on the issue in the US on April 11-13.

"As I have mentioned earlier, the meeting of the permanent Indus Water Commission on March 20-21 in Pakistan is a mandatory Treaty requirement. So long as we are a party to it, to fulfil our obligations, we attend the Treaty-mandated meetings held at least once every financial year. The Commission is a bilateral body of engineers and technical experts," he added.

Baglay also hinted at a possible resumption of dialogue between both sides but in an environment that will be "free from terror."

This, he said, was mentioned in a letter sent by Prime Minister Narendra Modi to his Pakistani counterpart Nawaz Sharif on the occasion of their National Day.

"Pakistan has to walk away from terror and we would like it to be effectively addressed by Pakistan," he said.

APP - 64

FIVE HYDEL PROJECTS UNDERWAY DESPITE PAKISTAN'S OBJECTIONS

The News (Pakistan) 30 March, 2017

NEW DELHI: Five Indian hydropower projects being built on tributaries of the Indus, over which Pakistan has raised objections, are at various stages of implementation in the Indus river basin, the Lok Sabha was informed Wednesday as reported by foreign media.

Minister of State for External Affairs Singh V K Singh made a statement in this connection, days after media in Pakistan claimed that India had agreed to halt work on Miyar Nallah during Permanent Indus Commission's meeting held in Lahore earlier this month.

"...Projects such as Miyar Nallah, Lower Kalnai, Pakal Dul, Kishenganga and Ratle are at different stages of implementation," Singh told the Lower House. Work on two other hydroelectricity projects – Bhakra Nangal (on Sutlej River) and Pong Dam (Beas River) has been successfully executed, he added.

APP – 65

PAKISTAN'S WATER DIPLOMACY

Ali Tauqeer Sheikh - 25 March, 2017

Dawn (Pakistan)

FOR no other known reason but to avoid being seen as violating the Indus Waters Treaty (IWT), India sent a 10-member delegation to Pakistan from March 20 to 21, for the 113th meeting of the Permanent Indus Waters Commission. India had practically declined these mandatory annual meetings since May 2015. It is a positive development, even if the result was predictably inconclusive.

India and Pakistan are pursuing two diametrically opposed approaches: India is implementing a long-term plan of constructing a chain of hydropower projects while occasionally sharing drawings and sometimes even agreeing to revise them. Pakistan has no plan. It has instead relegated negotiations to water engineers who can only raise technical objections. The policy is devoid of a long-term vision and needs a new, strategic push. Pakistan is apprehensive that the Indian infrastructure will diminish water quantities over time, whereas the real threat is that it will dissipate the Indus ecosystem as we know it.

Islamabad's regional water strategy needs to be two-pronged: i) make some strategic moves to win friends for Pakistan's case and ii) integrate external diplomacy with domestic water sector investments.

Presently, our water diplomacy is overly Indus Waters Treaty centric, and begs for an integrated view. While the IWT is a strategic asset that both India and Pakistan must strive to protect and constantly enrich, for Pakistan it is a lifeline that drives livelihoods for the poor and lifestyles for the rich.

Pakistan gets about 127 million acre feet water under the treaty. But, as mentioned above, its water policy has become too IWT centric, often at the cost of other strategic assets: almost 70 per cent of water in our rivers flows from the glaciers; groundwater is the source of over 60pc of water used in our agriculture; and almost all of our rainwater, particularly during the monsoon, is neither harvested nor stored or productively used. Additionally, the Indus River system gets more than 15pc of its water from the Kabul River, but no agreement with Afghanistan exists to secure or regulate these flows. Our regional water diplomacy must concurrently respond to these challenges. Having a water policy that ignores non-IWT sources of water is perilous for Pakistan's security and economy.

This country's water diplomacy in the region must be based on four cardinal principles:

First, water for Pakistan is not only a bilateral matter with India — and Pakistan is not the only country with which India has unresolved water issues. In fact, India has unresolved water disputes with almost all its neighbours, from Bangladesh to China. India's water neighbours can benefit from Pakistan's experience. Pakistan should therefore elevate transboundary waters to bilateral discussions with all of India's water neighbours — particularly Bangladesh and China, but also with increasingly more assertive Bhutan and Nepal.

Pakistan's regional diplomacy should seek to proactively respond to India's efforts to keep a lid on water as a bilateral matter and deal with each neighbour separately. India's water policy can use better consistency in dealing with her neighbours, and they in turn sure can learn from each other.

Second, transboundary water is not only about diplomatic negotiations, but also an issue of upstream investments for downstream economic needs. Pakistan has not made adequate investments to secure water for its future use. Upstream investments in Bhutan by India have resulted in three hydel power projects of 1,416MW, and three more of 2,129MW are under construction. Afghanistan-Pakistan geography and topography is ideally suited for benefit sharing from Kabul River. Pakistan needs to consider similar upstream investments in Afghanistan, where the construction of 13 smaller dams is under consideration. Pakistan can fully or partially fund the construction of one or two smaller dams in Afghanistan. In return, Pakistan can secure both energy and water to lift its tribal areas and parts of Khyber Pakhtunkhwa out of water and energy deficits. A clear proposition by Pakistan can help Islamabad forge common ground with Afghanistan and, ideally, with the World Bank. Prolonged inaction by Islamabad will inevitably result in a void that can be too tempting for extra regional actors.

Upstream water investments in Afghanistan are in Pakistan's strategic interest: increased agricultural productivity and livelihood options can help curtail migration from Afghanistan to Pakistan for economic opportunities between Peshawar and Karachi. This can also lay the foundation for regional water markets. Much like the proposed South Asian energy corridors, the time for regional water markets is fast approaching.

Third, water for Pakistan is more than about precipitation during the monsoon. Climate change is creating a similar set of challenges for regional countries in the Himalayan-Hindu Kush regions, and from the Bay of Bengal to the Arabian Sea. It is posing serious threats to food security, increasing migration and extreme events, including floods, droughts and heatwaves. Cloudbursts in Jammu inundated Sialkot, much as Nowshera became a victim of flooding in the Kabul River. Transboundary flooding risks are attributable to climate change and are engulfing the entire South Asian region. Transboundary water management needs to be ramped up by Pakistan to a higher regional and international security plateau, and employed as an instrument to enhance regional trade and economic cooperation.

Fourth, for success in regional water diplomacy, Pakistan must invest in institutional infrastructure. How could a country that depends so much on transboundary water supplies not have a full-fledged water ministry and departments at the federal and provincial levels? How could Pakistan afford not to have national and provincial water policies? Or water pricing? In order to bury the ad-hocism of regional water diplomacy, a National Commission on Transboundary Waters needs to be established with a constitutional status comparable to the Election Commission, mandated to manage all transboundary water issues dealing with the Upper Indus Basin, Afghanistan and, of course India and the IWT's Permanent Commission.

Finally, we are notorious for using water wastefully and have extremely poor drop-to-crop ratios. We need to make investments and upscale our infrastructure, augment storage capacities and improve our agricultural system efficiencies. Getting our due share under IWT is only half the game. The other half is how efficiently and judiciously we use the water we get from various sources.

APP – 66

INDIA CANNOT SKIP WORLD BANK-MEDIATED PROCESS ON WATER ISSUE

Munawar Hasan – 25 March, 2017

The News (Pakistan)

LAHORE: India can never skip the proposed World Bank-mediated negotiation process as such parleys are very much part and parcel of mechanism defined under the Indus Waters Treaty, said a senior official on Thursday.

The notion given by India through media leaks during last couple of days that only bilateral talks are possible for discussing Pakistan's objections over Kishanganga and Ratle hydropower projects being built in Indian Held Kashmir, and a meeting being hosted by World Bank on April 11 would not be attended is factually not correct, an official of Ministry of Water & Power said.

India is wary of any trilateral discussion on different subjects with Pakistan, particularly on Kashmir and water issues. Despite such obvious insistence, India had filed an application last year with the World Bank to appoint a Neutral Expert for solving dispute with Pakistan over Kishanganga and Ratle hydropower projects.

Before this move, Pakistan did file its case with the World Bank for setting up Court of Arbitration for the same purposes under the provision of Indus Waters Treaty, the official said, adding India wanted to nullify Pakistan's case by asserting different type of dispute resolution mechanism.

The next month meeting was convened by the World Bank to find headway about the future course of action regarding mechanism of dispute resolution, the official said. Hence, this meeting is part of a serial of trilateral negotiation process.

Commenting on Indian media's reports in which India vehemently denying participation in the World Bank mediated negotiation, he said it may be an official line given to the media as part of a tactic before entering into negotiations. It is very much similar to past Indian tactics, official observed.

As India had to abandon their earlier propaganda line of successive suspension of meetings of the Permanent Indus Waters Commission (PIWC) and inspection tours, they would ultimately abandon their latest posture as well, he opined.

Talking about the April 11 meeting, a senior official said let the Indians retract from the line they had expressed through media. "I expect the meeting would certainly happen, though there could be some delay. We had already opposed Indian effort of discussing objections on Kishanganga and Ratle hydropower projects in the recent meeting of Indus Commission as both the countries already exhausted this option," he added.

Pakistan's latest response was over New Delhi notion that World Bank's proposal of a secretary level meeting in Washington next month was against the spirit of the pact.

India reportedly believes that there is no need to look for another mechanism to break the deadlock since the treaty already had a dispute resolution system built in it.

Contrary to this, Pakistan expressed the opinion that such system was already exercised by the both countries on contentious issue of Kishanganga and Ratle hydropower projects.

APPENDICES

PART THREE

NEWSPAPER COMMENTARIES ON RECENT DEVELOPMENTS

April, 2017 to December, 2018

APP - 1

LEGAL BINDINGS: 'PRIOR DISPUTE RESOLUTION KEY TO ALL INDUS PROJECTS'

The Express Tribune (Pakistan) 7 April, 2017

Legal interpretations by the International Court of Arbitration bars the construction of any Indus Water Treaty project without prior dispute resolution and this elucidation of international law are binding upon both Pakistan and India, signatories to the treaty. These views were expressed by Shamila Mahmood, an international law and development expert, at the session titled 'Kishanganga and Ratle Projects: Deliberating on IWT's Dispute Resolution Mechanism and the Way Forward', held at the Institute of Policy Studies (IPS) here on Wednesday. Other speakers at the session included Ashfaq Mahmood, water and energy expert and former federal secretary for water and power and Mirza Hamid Hassan, another former secretary water and power and member of the IPS-National Academic Council.

Shamila Mahmood said that India always raised objections on projects in the disputed territory, claiming that they required NOCs (No-Objection Certificates). The World Bank, she said, had always supported India's version. "When Pakistan raises similar questions over Indian projects, one of the responses it always gets is that the project will not affect Pakistan. This, however, is incorrect because such projects do affect Pakistan because it is a lower riparian (country)."

According to her, it was also essential to keep within parameters set by the treaty itself. "When the World Bank does not allow Pakistan funding for any such project over India's objections, the case should be taken up against the World Bank because it is not in accordance with human rights." She said that even in the case of the Ratle project, India was ignoring an international decision. "India has to honour the arbitration determination," she said. "Its own domestic laws stress on honouring the arbitration determination, but it deliberately ignores this to suit its interest." Shamila believed that Pakistan should take a firm stand, exerting pressure on the World Bank to remain within its mandate and pursue and resolve the matter without any delay.

Ashfaq Mehmood said that Pakistan's biggest failing regarding water issues with India were that "we did not strategise well". "We didn't (learn) from our past failures and did not lobby our points effectively at international level." India, he said, had strategically halted the process at the Indus Water Commission level while Pakistan had not been proactive by denying India time for construction. The commission, he said, was not able to move forward on both Kishanganga and Ratle projects. "Pakistan has been passive against the Indian violations of the Treaty," he said.

APP – 2

PAK-INDIA SECRETARY-LEVEL TALKS LIKELY IN US BY END OF APRIL

Khalid Mustafa. The News (Pakistan). 11 April, 2017

In a new development, Pakistan and India secretary-level talks for developing a consensus in the light of Indus Waters Treaty (IWT) on the mechanism for resolution of 'faulty designs' of 300MW Kishenganga and 850MW Ratle hydropower projects may now be held either by end of the current month or in the first week of next month in Washington, a senior official told The News.

Minister for Water and Power Khawaja Asif on March 20, while addressing a news conference, had given breaking news, saying that Indo-Pak secretary-level talks were going to take place in Washington from April 11-13, not knowing that the World Bank had just proposed the dates for talks which were yet to be finalised with India and Pakistan. Pakistan was already prepared for the talks, but India was not ready on the dates proposed by the World Bank. However, talks on the two projects on the said dates are not being held as consultations between Pakistan and India with the help of World Bank are still underway to finalise the dates. "And we are hopeful that belated talks will take place by the end of current month," the official said.

The official said the World Bank's repute is at stake and it is trying its best to arrange the talks between the two nuclear states of India and Pakistan over selection of a mechanism for resolution of the dispute of both the projects being built on Chenab and Jhelum rivers.

The World Bank wants both the countries to develop a consensus either on mechanism of neutral expert or of court of arbitration mentioned in the treaty for the resolution of issues pertaining to the said projects. And in case of failure, both the countries need to develop an agreement on the middle way to resolve the issues.

In case of secretary of water and power level meeting held between both the countries, one of the top men of the World Bank would also be the part of the meeting and they would try to persuade both the parties to reach consensus to any of the mechanisms or find out the middle way.

Pakistan wants the World Bank to constitute court of arbitration to resolve the disputes, but India wants the solution through the mechanism of neutral experts, which is why the World Bank announced a 'pause' on December 12, 2016 till the agreement on procedure or mechanism between the parties to the dispute. India is also keen to resolve the issue through out-of-court settlement.

APP – 3

PAKISTAN'S INDIA OBSESSION HIDES ITS REAL WATER CHALLENGES

Hassaan F Khan. Dawn (Pakistan) 27 April, 2017

Over the past few months, with the deterioration of relations between Pakistan and India, there has been a renewed interest in the Indus Waters Treaty (IWT). Statements made from India seem to indicate a shift in approach regarding water sharing in the Indus basin. There has been extensive discussion and speculation on the implications of India's 'new policy' and what it means for Pakistan's water resources. However, a proper sense of perspective of this problem relative to Pakistan's water resources seems to be lacking in much of these discussions and commentaries.

Not only has the media coverage been disproportionately directed towards this issue, it has often been hyperbolic and misleading. Take for example, the coverage of a speech where Indian Prime Minister Narendra Modi said, "The fields of our farmers must have adequate water. Water that belongs to India cannot be allowed to go to Pakistan... The government will do everything to provide enough water to our farmers." This statement was portrayed in Pakistan as an aggressive threat by India to 'divert' or 'stop' water flow to Pakistan.

Setting aside the fact that India doesn't have the infrastructure to have any appreciable impact on water flows entering Pakistan, nor will it in the near future, what most of the coverage failed to acknowledge was that Modi was talking about utilising the flows on the eastern rivers that have anyway been apportioned to India under the IWT. It is also important to remember that he was making these statements in the run-up to important elections (South Asian politicians using water issues to garner votes is nothing new).

What was essentially electioneering was made out to be a threat to the sanctity of the IWT by many in Pakistan.

APP – 4

WB OFFICIAL IN DELHI TO BREAK WATER TREATY STALEMATE

Anwar Iqbal. Dawn (Pakistan) 28 April, 2017

WASHINGTON: The World Bank's vice president for the South Asia region, Annette Dixon, is now in New Delhi for talks aimed at breaking the stalemate over a water dispute between India and Pakistan, official sources told Dawn. They said Ms Dixon went to India on Tuesday, but the Indians did not publicise the visit as they discourage international mediation in their disputes with Pakistan. The World Bank, however, is recognised as an arbitrator in the 1960 Indus Water Treaty (IWT) that distributes waters of the Indus and its tributaries between India and Pakistan.

The latest dispute concerns two hydroelectric projects — Ratle and Kishanganga — that India is building over one of the tributaries. Pakistan views these projects as a violation of the treaty and wants the World Bank to appoint a court of arbitration. India opposes the proposal and has asked the bank to depute neutral experts to further probe the matter. Pakistan sees the Indian approach as aimed at buying time to complete the two projects and argues that since a neutral expert has no legal authority, the expert's decision is not legally binding. As the two sides stick to their positions, the World Bank finds itself in a tight spot and is softly urging both sides to resolve the dispute through talks as it has the potential to undermine the water treaty. Pakistan fears that India wants to go beyond the treaty by bringing in neutral observers. "We do not want to encourage any process outside the IWT, even showing an inclination to consider that option could hurt the treaty," said a senior Pakistani official while explaining why Islamabad is reluctant to accept the Indian demand. Sources in Washington say the World Bank also is against wasting more time and is trying to persuade both sides to start negotiations on the matter. The decision to send Ms Dixon to New Delhi also shows the importance the bank attaches to the issue. Her assignment at the bank includes promoting poverty reduction projects in South Asia. She oversees lending operations and bank-funded projects worth more than $10 billion a year. Pakistan and India were scheduled to hold three-day talks on the 850MW Ratle and 330MW Kishanganga hydroelectric projects at the World Bank headquarters in Washington on April 12, but India refused to send its delegation. Pakistan, however, had informed the bank that it would attend the talks, if held as scheduled. Initially, the World Bank wanted to host secretary-level talks between Pakistan and India in Dubai, but Pakistan proposed that the venue be changed to Washington. Pakistani authorities had announced that Annette Dixon would personally attend the talks and facilitate both countries in resolution of disputes on run-of-the-river hydroelectric projects being constructed in India-held Kashmir. The Indus water commissioners of both countries met in Islamabad last month to discuss the designs of three proposed hydroelectric projects — Pakal Dul, Lower Kalnai and Miya — in held Kashmir and flood supply data. Pakistan says India has not shared the designs of the three projects.

The Ratle hydroelectric project is in initial stage and Pakistan has objections to its design. The Obama administration also played a supporting role in encouraging the talks, but so far the Trump administration has not indicated its approach.

APP - 5

INDUS WATER TREATY: FARMERS SAY INDIAN POLICIES LEAVING PAKISTAN HIGH AND DRY

The Express Tribune – 8 May 2017

LAHORE: Terming it vital for the survival of growers and the country, farmers have urged the United Nations (UN), the US and the World Bank to ensure nonstop supply of water to Pakistan under the Indus Waters Treaty (IWT). Addressing a news conference at the Lahore Press Club on Sunday, Central leaders of the Pakistan Mutahidda Kissan Mehaz (PMKM), underscored that fair distribution of water between India and Pakistan had immense importance not only for the survival and livelihood of people, but also peace in this region. Construction of several water and power projects on Indus, Jhelum and Chenab rivers by India were a serious threat to river flows towards Pakistan, a lower riparian state.

They said farmers from across the country would gather in Islamabad on October 19 to lodge their protest on what they called the Indian failure to comply with the Indus Waters Treaty. Farmer leaders said growers would be left with no option but to amass in the diplomatic enclave in the federal capital to present a memorandum to representatives of the UN, the USA and the World Bank. They were of the view that Indian hegemonic policies in South Asia had resulted in squeezing water supplies to Pakistan from western rivers. They said it was unfortunate that India had openly threatened to stop flow of the rivers and a series of dams and hydropower projects had been planned or already constructed on Western rivers that were allotted to Pakistan under the Indus Waters Treaty.

The farmers stated such a huge infrastructure can be manipulated to restrict flows of river towards Pakistan. The stance of the Indian leadership is aggressive as far as the flow of western rivers was concerned, PMKM leaders observed. They noted that Indian designs were obvious in this regard, adding the instances of IWT's violation were testimony to this fact. During negotiation over designs of several projects, they said it emerged that India tried to increase storage capacity of certain projects on western rivers. "Unfortunately, some of these violations were allowed against the spirit and provisions of the treaty." With the support of 18 farmer organisations, they said thousands of growers from all the provinces would attend a demonstration in the federal capital. He said the rally would be held on the 57th anniversary of IWT. The PMKM leaders also asked the federal and provincial governments to take immediate steps to increase water storage capacity so that the issue of scarcity could be resolved. They also stressed the need for early completion of Kachhi Canal project. After a lapse of 12 years, work on the first phase of Kachhi Canal could not be completed, which was sheer injustice with the people of Balochistan, they concluded.

APP – 6

PAK – INDIA DEADLOCK ON RATLE, KISHENGANGA PROJECTS PERSISTS

Khalid Mustafa. The News (Pakistan), 6 July, 2017

Almost over seven months have elapsed, yet the stalemate continues between two nuclear states India and Pakistan on how to advance and develop consensus in the light of Indus Waters Treaty 1960 on the mechanism for resolution of 'faulty designs' of 300 MW Kishenganga and 850 MW Ratle hydro power projects. However, the ice is hoped to melt in the ongoing current month of July as World Bank is striving from pillar to post to help develop the consensus mechanism between the parties to the dispute, a senior official at Ministry of Water and Power told The News. The credibility of World Bank that brokered the Indus Waters Treaty in 1960 is at stake and keeping in view the incessant endeavours of the Bank to persuade India to have talks with Pakistan for consensus on mechanism to proceed on the resolution of the disputed projects, it is being hoped that the progress to this effect may be made sometime in the current month.

There are signals emanating from the other side of the border that India has accelerated the pace of construction work on the Kishenganga and 850 MW Ratle hydro power projects which is very alarming development, the official disclosed and argued: "Pakistan had moved World Bank about a year ago to constitute court of arbitration to bar India from constructing the said projects with faulty designs which are the blatant negation of the Indus Waters Treaty, so India is not supposed to continue the construction work on the said projects."

The impasse had emerged in the wake stance taken by Pakistan and India as former wanted the resolution of the disputed projects, being constructed on Jehlum and Chenab rivers by India, at the level of Court of Arbitration, whereas latter desired the decision by Neutral Expert. This had compelled World Bank to announce 'pause' on December 12, 2016 till the agreement on procedure or mechanism between the parties to the dispute – Pakistan and India. World Bank now wants both the countries to develop consensus either on mechanism of Neutral Expert or of Court of Arbitration mentioned in the Treaty for the resolution of the issues pertaining to the said projects. And in case of failure, both the countries need to develop agreement on the middle way to resolve the issues.

Both the countries were to hold the talks on April 11-12, 2017 at secretary level in Washington in the presence of the top official of the World Bank, but the meeting could not take place at the eleventh hour because of the India's evasive attitude and since then the World Bank is in the process of persuading India to come on the table for talks on how to proceed on the resolution of the disputed projects. Under the Indus Waters Treaty 1960, World Bank, the broker of the Treaty, is not allowed to pick up any procedure of the two enshrined in the Treaty on its own to resolve issue or dispute unless parties to the dispute agree on one mechanism of the two that include the constitution of Neutral Expert and Court of Arbitration.

The top mandarins of Ministry of Water and Power told The News that if 850 MW Ratle Hydropower Project on Chenab river gets constructed under its existing objectionable design, then the water flow of Chenab river at Head Marala will be reduced by 40 percent which will be very detrimental to the irrigation in central Punjab of Pakistan. India has awarded the contract of the Rattle project to a private company that will run the project on BOT (build, operate and transfer) basis for 35 years and then it would hand over the project to India. This dam will be three times larger than the Baglihar hydropower dam. India has already carved out the plan to generate 32,000MW of electricity on Pakistan's rivers that will enable New Delhi to regulate the water flows that are destined to reach Pakistan.

The revenants officials disclosed that Pakistan has raised the three objections on Kishanganga project's design saying that the pondage of the project is 7.5 million cubic meter which is excessive and it should be one million cubic meter. Pakistan also wants India to raise intake by up to 4 meters and also raise spillways up to 9 meters high. And on the issue of Ratle Hydropower plant, Islamabad raised 4 objections. Pakistan wants India to maintain free board at 1 meter whereas India wants to keep it at 2 meters. In addition India wants to keep the pondage of 24 million cubic meters but Pakistan wants the pondage of 8 million cubic meters. Pakistan also wants the intake of the project should be raised by up to 8.8 meters and it spillways should be raised by up to 20 meters.

APP – 7

IWT VIOLATION: INDIA NOT SHARING FLOOD INFORMATION WITH PAKISTAN SINCE 1999

Sehrish Wasif. The Express Tribune, 10 July, 2017

There may be multiple reasons for floods in the country, but Pakistan's archrival India has also played a major role in aggravating Pakistan's problems.

Official sources say New Delhi – despite being bound by the Indus Waters Treaty (IWT) – has not shared with Islamabad details about water outflow from its rivers since 1999, causing major floods in Pakistan.

During all these years, Pakistan has repeatedly requested India for provision of information with regard to rains and floods but India has been reluctant to share timely information.

Due to the absence of this vital information, Pakistan is unable to get accurate and timely preparation for the monsoon and remains at risk of heavy flooding. In last 15 years, Pakistan has to endure at least five major floods that have caused huge human and financial losses.

According to a senior government official, Pakistan has raised this issue several times at various international conferences and meetings, but the Indian government has turned a dead ear.

"Earlier there was some possibility of convincing India but as the tension between the two countries is mounting it seems very difficult to get the required information from the hostile neighbour," he told this correspondent.

In a high-level meeting held recently, Chairman National Disaster Management Authority (NDMA) Lt Gen Omar Mehmood Hayat also urged 'upper riparian neighbour' India to cooperate by giving timely information on water outflow from its rivers and actual rainfall recorded as stipulated in the IWT.

The NDMA chief observed that along with the flood hazards from heavy rainfall in catchment areas and glacial melt, release of waters from across the borders in eastern and western rivers like Kabul, Chenab, Jhelum and Indus was the major vulnerability.

He also urged the Pakistan Commission for Indus Water (PCIW) to enhance coordination mechanism of early warning arrangements for release of water, especially from the eastern rivers so that timely and effective response for flood mitigation may be initiated by relevant stakeholders.

APP – 8

PAKISTAN-INDIA WATER TALKS NEXT WEEK

Anwar Iqbal, Dawn (Pakistan), 27 July, 2017

WASHINGTON: Pakistan and India seem all set to finally hold the much-delayed water talks in the US capital next week, hoping to avoid further tensions over an issue that has far-reaching consequences for both.

Official sources told Dawn that Minister for Water and Power Khawaja Mohammad Asif is likely to lead the Pakistani delegation at these talks that would be held at the World Bank headquarters in Washington. The delegation will include Secretary Water and Power Yousaf Naseem Khokhar and several other senior officials.

Secretary Ministry of Water Resources Dr Amarjit Singh is likely to lead the Indian delegation.

The last round of the World Bank-supervised talks was held in November 2016, and the World Bank had indicated that it intended to hold another round in April this year but could not do so, as India refused to accept the third-party arbitration.

Pakistan not only wanted the talks to be held as scheduled but also sought the World Bank's arbitration as the guarantor of the Indus Waters Treaty (IWT). But India rejected arbitration, saying it preferred negotiations within the framework of the treaty.

Pakistan too recognises the treaty's pivotal role but disagrees with the Indian interpretation, which seeks to minimise arbitration.

The talks will focus on two controversial hydropower projects — Kishanganga and Ratle — over which Pakistan sought International Court of Arbitration through the World Bank.

Pakistan believes India has been using delaying tactics to complete the controversial hydel projects it is building on western rivers in held Kashmir.

"We are ready to hold talks with India under World Bank and the US guidance. But we will not withdraw our case against Ratle and Kishanganga projects," a Pakistani official said, adding that India had also refused earlier to respond to Pakistan's call for inspection of Pakul Dal and other dams it's constructing in the occupied area.

APP – 9

PAKISTAN, INDIA CONCLUDE WATER TALKS IN WASHINGTON

Anwar Iqbal. Dawn (Pakistan), 2 August, 2017

Pakistan and India concluded the much-delayed water talks in the US capital on Tuesday, raising hopes that they would avoid further tensions over an issue that has far-reaching consequences for both. Secretary Water and Power Yousaf Naseem Khokhar led the Pakistani delegation, which included technical experts from his ministry. Ambassador Aizaz Ahmed Chaudhary also attended the two-day talks held at the World Bank headquarters in Washington. Secretary Ministry of Water Resources Dr Amarjit Singh headed the Indian delegation, which also included representatives of the Ministry for Foreign Affairs. The Washington meeting was part of the World Bank's efforts to resolve a dispute over Kishanganga and Ratle hydroelectricity projects that India is building in the occupied Kashmir. Pakistan opposes the two projects, saying that the plans violate the 1960 Indus Water Treaty that distributes waters of the river Indus and its tributaries between India and Pakistan.

The negotiations are part of World Bank's efforts to resolve a dispute between the two countries over India's hydroelectricity projects in Kashmir. The two countries last held talks over the two projects in March this year during the meeting of Permanent Indus Commission in Pakistan. The last round of the World Bank-supervised talks was held in November 2016, and the World Bank intended to hold another round in April this year but could not do so, as India refused to accept its arbitration. Since 2013, India had been refusing to hold direct talks with Pakistan and also rejected Islamabad's efforts to restart the dialogue. Earlier this week, an Indian official in New Delhi told journalists that the Indian position had not changed and "talks under the Indus Water Treaty do not amount to bilateral talks". Indian Prime Minister Narendra Modi said last year that India would not share the Indus water with Pakistan until Islamabad prevented militants from launching attacks inside India. Pakistan rejected the Indian charge, saying that it never allowed any group to carry out cross-border attacks and the uprising in Kashmir was indigenous and independent. Pakistan approached the World Bank last year, raising concerns over the designs of the two projects after India indicated that it wanted to review the Indus Water Treaty, linking it to the situation in Kashmir. The projects will allow India to use water of three Indus tributaries to irrigate 912,000 acres of land, up from 800,000 acres, and to produce 18,600MW of electricity. Pakistan argues that the two projects would lessen its share granted in the treaty and urges the World Bank to play a mediatory role between the two countries, as laid out in the 57-year-old water distribution pact. While the Pakistani side has so far not held any briefing for the media, the Indian Embassy in Washington shared with the Indian media a statement from a senior World Bank official, assuring New Delhi that it will continue to "be a neutral and impartial" player in helping the two countries find an "amicable way forward". In a letter to India's Ambassador to the US, Navtej Sarna, senior World Bank official Annette Dixon said: "We are pleased both parties have confirmed their participation in the meeting hosted by the World Bank in Washington, DC". "The World Bank welcomes the spirit of goodwill and cooperation," she said, and assured Ambassador Sarna of its "continued neutrality and impartiality in helping the parties find an amicable way forward".

APP - 10

INDUS WATER TREATY: INDIA – PAKISTAN TALKS HELD IN SPIRIT OF GOODWILL, COOPERATION, SAYS WORLD BANK

Indian Express, 2 August, 2017

The World Bank asserted that India and Pakistan have agreed to reconvene in September in Washington for continued discussions over the Indus Water Treaty, 57-year-old water distribution pact.

The talks between Indian and Pakistani officials over the Indus Water Treaty took place in a spirit of goodwill and cooperation, the World Bank has said asserting that the two parties have agreed to reconvene in September here for continued discussions over the issue. "The parties have agreed to continue discussions and reconvene in September in Washington, DC," the World Bank said in a brief statement issued at the conclusion of the Indus Water Treaty (IWT). The World Bank said that the secretary-level discussions between India and Pakistan on the technical issues over the IWT took place this week in a spirit of "goodwill and cooperation". However, it did not provide any other details.

Earlier, in a letter dated July 25, the World Bank had assured Indian Ambassador to the US Navtej Sarna its "continued neutrality and impartiality in helping the parties to find and amicable way forward." The two countries last held talks over the two projects in March this year during the meeting of the Permanent Indus Commission (PIC) in Pakistan.

Pakistan had approached the World Bank last year, raising concerns over the designs of two hydroelectricity projects located in Jammu and Kashmir. It had demanded that the World Bank, which is the mediator between the two countries under the 57-year-old water distribution pact, set up a court of arbitration to look into its concerns. On the other hand, India had asked for the appointment of a neutral expert to look into the issues, contending the concerns Pakistan raised were "technical" ones. Following this, the international lender had in November 2016 initiated two simultaneous processes — for appointing neutral expert and establishment of court of arbitration to look into technical differences between the two countries in connection with the projects.

The simultaneous processes, however, were halted after India objected to it. After that, representatives of the World Bank held talks with India and Pakistan to find a way out separately.

APP – 11

PAKISTAN, INDIA TO MEET AGAIN NEXT MONTH FOR WATER TALKS: WORLD BANK

Anwar Iqbal, Dawn (Pakistan), 3 August, 2017

Pakistan and India displayed goodwill and cooperation in the latest round of talks on a water dispute and have agreed to meet again next month, the World Bank said. The World Bank hosted the two-day talks, which concluded on Tuesday, and the next round of talks will also be held at the bank's headquarters in Washington. "The secretary-level discussions between India and Pakistan on the technical issues of the Indus Waters Treaty took place this week in a spirit of goodwill and cooperation," said a brief statement issued after the talks. "The parties have agreed to continue discussions and reconvene in September in Washington," the bank added. The bank also released a brief description of the dispute and of its efforts to resolve it, along with a short background of the Indus Waters Treaty (IWT), signed in 1960.

India and Pakistan disagree about the construction of the Kishenganga (330MW) and Ratle (850MW) hydroelectric power plants being built by India. The bank clarified that it was not financing the disputed projects. India and Pakistan disagree over whether the technical design features of the two hydroelectric plants contravene the treaty. The plants are being built on a tributary of the Jhelum and the Chenab rivers. The bank notes that the treaty "designates these two rivers as well as the Indus as the western rivers to which Pakistan has unrestricted use".

But the bank also points out that India is permitted to construct hydroelectric power facilities on these rivers subject to constraints specified in annexure to the treaty. Pakistan has asked the World Bank to facilitate the setting up of a court of arbitration to look into its concerns about the designs of the two hydroelectric power projects. India asked for the appointment of a neutral expert for the same purpose. The requests followed a series of bilateral talks that failed to resolve the dispute. The bank says that it sought to fulfil its procedural obligations with respect to both the court of arbitration and the neutral expert but the treaty does not empower the World Bank to choose whether one procedure should take precedence over the other. The treaty vests the determination of jurisdictional competence on each of the two mechanisms. "At the same time, the World Bank actively encouraged both countries to agree amicably on a mechanism to address the issues," the statement said. On Dec 12, 2016, World Bank Group President Jim Yong Kim announced that the bank would pause before taking further steps in each of the two processes requested by the parties. It said that since December 2016, the bank had worked towards an amicable resolution of the matter and to safeguard the treaty. Mr Kim spoke several times with the finance ministers of both countries. World Bank Chief Executive Officer Kristalina Georgieva travelled to both countries for high-level meetings. The World Bank Vice President for the South Asia Region, Annette Dixon, visited both countries twice. Mr Kim's adviser, Ian Solomon, made multiple visits to the region.

The bank explained that locally-based World Bank teams had convened dozens of meetings with different stakeholders. "A variety of proposals have been discussed."

APP – 12

POSITIVE ATTITUDE RAISES HOPES FOR RESOLUTION OF PAKISTAN-INDIA WATER DISPUTE

Anwar Iqbal. Dawn (Pakistan), 10 August, 2017

WASHINGTON: A constructive engagement between Pakistan and India during the recently held water talks in Washington has raised hopes for an amicable resolution of this dispute, according to diplomatic sources. The World Bank, which hosted the talks at its headquarters two weeks ago, also noticed this positive change and mentioned it in a press release on Aug 1, noting that the "meetings ... were held in a spirit of goodwill and cooperation". Islamabad and New Delhi disagree over construction of the Kishenganga (330MW) and Ratle (850MW) hydroelectric power plants being built by India. (The World Bank is not financing either project). Islamabad contends that the technical design features of the two plants contravene the Indus Waters Treaty.

The plants are on a tributary of the Jhelum and Chenab rivers, respectively. An international expert, who closely monitors the Pakistan-India water talks, told Dawn this was the first time in many years that delegates "held a constructive discussion, instead of merely stating their official positions". The expert said in previous talks "sometimes the two sides did not even exchange formal greetings". They would "just read the statements they brought with them and leave, but this time it was different," he added. Both sides have now returned to their capitals to consult their governments on the ideas discussed at Washington. The negotiation concluded at the World Bank headquarters on Aug 1. The Indus Waters Treaty was signed in 1960 after nine years of negotiations between Pakistan and India with the help of the World Bank, which is a signatory. Seen as one of the most successful international treaties, it has survived frequent tensions, including conflict, and has provided a framework for irrigation and hydropower development for more than half a century.

Former US president Dwight Eisenhower described it as "one bright spot ... in a very depressing world picture that we see so often". But recent tensions also affected the water talks as India expressed its intention to use water as a tool to influence Islamabad's Kashmir policy. Islamabad rejected New Delhi's charge of supporting militants, but vowed to continue supporting the Kashmiri movement for self-determination. That's why the spirit of cooperation displayed during the last meeting was welcomed in Washington. Careful not to hurt this rare opportunity for a positive engagement between the two neighbours, the World Bank decided not to publicise the talks.

However, it did issue a brief statement on Aug 1, announcing that the talks had ended and the two sides had agreed to meet again next month. The bank also issued a fact-sheet with the statement, giving a brief description of the dispute and the efforts it had made to resolve it. One paragraph stated that under the Indus Waters Treaty, "among other uses, India is permitted to construct hydroelectric power facilities on these rivers subject to constraints specified in annexure to the treaty". This paragraph was interpreted by the Indian media as an endorsement of New Delhi's position, causing the World Bank to issue a clarification. "The 1960 Indus Waters Treaty does not bar India from constructing hydroelectric power projects on tributaries of the Jhelum and Chenab rivers with certain restrictions, the World Bank says in its fact sheet on the treaty," the Indian media reported. The bank, however, rejected this conclusion as "erroneous" and reminded all parties that "discussions between India and Pakistan about the Kishenganga and Ratle hydroelectric power plants are ongoing". A reference in the Pakistani media to former US secretary of state John Kerry's call to Finance Minister Ishaq Dar in January also caused some unease as the Indian side apparently believed that Pakistan was trying to create an impression that the United States was playing a mediatory role, which it was not.

The disagreement

The treaty designates the Jhelum and Chenab Rivers as well as the Indus as "western rivers", to which Pakistan has unrestricted use. Among other uses, the agreement permits India to construct hydroelectric power facilities on these rivers subject to constraints specified in annexure to the treaty. Pakistan asked the World Bank to facilitate the setting up of a "court of arbitration" to look into its concerns about designs of the Kishenganga and Ratle projects. India asked for the appointment of a neutral expert for the same purpose. These requests came after the Permanent Indus Commission, which is part of the treaty's resolution mechanism, failed to resolve the dispute.

APP – 13

KHAWAJA ASIF ACCUSES INDIA OF VIOLATING INDUS WATERS TREATY, URGES WORLD BANK TO INTERVENE

Naveed Siddiqui. Dawn (Pakistan), 29 August, 2017

Foreign Minister Khawaja Muhammad Asif on Tuesday alleged that India was not fulfilling its commitments regarding the Indus Waters Treaty and urged the World Bank (WB) to play its role in ensuring the implementation of the accord.

Addressing a seminar in the federal capital, the foreign minister highlighted the importance of building water resources following the recent climatic changes.

"Pakistan has raised reservations over the designs of India's dams," Asif told the audience.

The matter of Indus Waters Treaty is an important issue between the two sovereign countries, [but] India is not cooperating in the implementation of the accord, the defence minister said.

Commenting on the local issues regarding water distribution, Asif said that the government is only able to recover 80 per cent of the money spent on distribution of water locally. "We [Pakistanis] use water in a manner as if we have unlimited resources," he added. "If we continue to waste water like this, we will have to face some serious issues in the near future."

The previous governments had taken no initiatives to address this grave concern, complained Asif, adding that the incumbent government realized the issue and formed a separate ministry for this.

APP – 14

INDIA, PAKISTAN RESUME TALKS TO RESOLVE WATER DISPUTE

Anwar Iqbal. Dawn (Pakistan), 14 September, 2017

India and Pakistan resume talks on a longstanding water dispute on Thursday amidst renewed hopes for a peaceful resolution of this potentially dangerous issue. The last round of these talks, held at the World Bank headquarters in Washington, concluded on Aug 1, with the bank praising both Pakistan and India for displaying a new spirit of "goodwill and cooperation". The two parties agreed to hold the second round, also in Washington, on Sept 14 and 15. The World Bank will supervise the talks. The Pakistani delegation, headed by Secretary of Water Resources Division Arif Ahmed Khan, reached Washington on Tuesday, when the Indian delegation also arrived. The Pakistani delegation includes Secretary of Water and Power Yousuf Naseem Khokhar, High Commissioner of Indus Waters Treaty Mirza Asif Baig and Joint Secretary of Water Syed Mehar Ali Shah.

The dispute concerns the 330MW Kishanganga hydroelectric plant that India is building on the Neelum river and the 850MW Ratle hydroelectric plant on the Chenab river. Pakistan argues that their designs violate the 1960 Indus Waters Treaty between the two countries. The World Bank played a key role in concluding the treaty and is recognised by both parties as an arbiter. The treaty gives Pakistan the right of unrestricted use of water from the two rivers and the Indus. Islamabad believes that the two projects, if completed, would stop adequate flow of water to its side. India is also building several electricity projects, such as the 1,000MW Pakal Dul, 120MW Miyar and 48MW Lower Kalnai on Chenab's tributaries.

In previous discussions, both sides merely stated their official positions but the last round was more productive as they exchanged several substantive proposals as well. Both delegations also said that they needed to discuss the proposals with their governments and requested the World Bank to give them more time for consultations. "The fact that both parties have come back, indicates a degree of sincerity, at least with regard to the proposals being discussed," said an official source familiar with the talks. The bank too had mentioned this in its concluding statement after the last round, saying: "The secretary-level discussions between India and Pakistan on the technical issues of the Indus Waters Treaty took place in a spirit of goodwill and cooperation." In a brief description of the dispute and of its efforts to resolve it, the World Bank clarified that it was not financing the disputed projects.

India and Pakistan disagree over whether the technical design features of the disputed hydroelectric plants contravene the treaty. The bank notes that the treaty "designates these two rivers as well as the Indus as the western rivers to which Pakistan has unrestricted use". But the bank also points out that India is permitted to construct hydroelectric power facilities on these rivers subject to constraints specified in annexure to the treaty.

APP – 15

PAKISTAN'S WATER TALKS WITH INDIA IN WASHINGTON

Dawn (Pakistan) / Anwar Iqbal / 14 September, 2017

Pakistan and India concluded the first day of their two-day talks on Thursday on a long-standing water dispute — maintaining a spirit of goodwill demonstrated in the last round.

The talks are held at the World Bank headquarters, as the 1960 Indus Waters Treaty for the distribution of water between the two neighbouring states recognises the bank as an arbiter.

An Indian official told reporters in New Delhi on Thursday that Union Water Resources Secretary Amarjit Singh is leading a multi-disciplinary delegation at the talks, which includes representatives from the ministry of external affairs, power, India's Indus Water Commissioner and Central Water Commission. The second round of talks on Ratle and Kishanganga hydroelectric projects "are focusing on technical issues," the official added. Second round of dialogue is focused on Ratle and Kishanganga hydroelectric projects

Secretary Water Resources Division Arif Ahmed Khan is leading the Pakistani delegation, which includes Secretary of Water and Power Yousuf Naseem Khokhar, High Commissioner of Indus Waters Treaty Mirza Asif Baig and Joint Secretary of Water Syed Mehar Ali Shah.

After the last round, which concluded on Aug 1, the two delegations returned to their respective capitals for consultations on the proposals that each had brought with them. In the second round, they will focus on the responses and may seek more consultations with their political leadership before making any commitment, official sources said. "This will be a long process and we should not expect an early result," said a technical expert who has worked on India-Pakistan water disputes in the past. "But this is already an improvement, as in the past they often returned home after re-stating their official positions."

In a statement issued after the last round, the World Bank too appreciated this "spirit of goodwill and cooperation" demonstrated during the talks and announced that the two teams had agreed to meet again in September for the second round. The World Bank observed that the Indus Water Treaty allows India to construct hydroelectric power facilities on tributaries of the Jhelum and Chenab rivers but with certain restrictions. Pakistan contends that the designs of two hydropower projects located in Jammu and Kashmir violate the treaty and approached the World Bank for mediation.

In August, the World Bank also issued a factsheet, which India interpreted as an endorsement of its position on building hydroelectric facilities on the shared rivers. Pakistan rejected the Indian interpretation, but agreed to continue the talks.

Pakistan first approached the World Bank last year, raising concerns over the designs of Ratle (850MW) and Kishanganga (330MW) hydroelectricity projects.

It demanded that the World Bank, which is the mediator between the two countries under the 57-year-old treaty, set up a court of arbitration to look into its concerns. India rejected the Pakistani proposal and asked for the appointment of a neutral expert to look at the issues, contending the concerns Pakistan raised were "technical" ones. Consequently, the World Bank initiated two simultaneous processes in November 2016 — for appointing neutral expert and establishment of court of arbitration — to review. The simultaneous processes, however, were halted after India's objection.

The World Bank then held separate talks with both India and Pakistan to find a way out. The current talks are part of the same process.

APP – 16

INDIA PAKISTAN BEGIN HIGH-LEVEL TALKS ON INDUS WATER TREATY IN WASHINGTON

Hindustan Times - 15 September, 2017

The World Bank IN AUGUST had said under the Indus Waters Treaty, India is permitted to construct hydroelectric power facilities on tributaries of the Jhelum and Chenab rivers with certain restrictions.

India and Pakistan in Washington started high-level talks on technical issues of the Indus Waters Treaty on Thursday night, a senior World Bank official said.

"These meetings are a continuation of a discussion on how to safeguard the Treaty for the benefit of the people in both countries," a World Bank spokesperson told PTI.

The meetings between India and Pakistan on the technical issues of the Indus Waters Treaty (IWT) are taking place in Washington on September 14-15, the spokesperson added.

The World Bank in August had said under the IWT, India is permitted to construct hydroelectric power facilities on tributaries of the Jhelum and Chenab rivers with certain restrictions.

Pakistan opposes the construction of the Kishanganga (330 megawatts) and Ratle (850 megawatts) hydroelectric power plants being built by India, it had said in a fact sheet issued at the conclusion of secretary-level talks between the two countries over the IWT.

The IWT was signed in 1960 after nine years of negotiations between India and Pakistan with the help of the World Bank, which is also a signatory.

The World Bank's role in relation to "differences" and "disputes" is limited to the designation of people to fulfil certain roles when requested by either or both of the parties, the fact sheet said.

APP – 17

NO AGREEMENT REACHED AT INDUS WATER TREATY TALKS

The Times of India – 16 September, 2017

WASHINGTON: The latest round of talks between India and Pakistan on Indus Water Treaty concluded without reaching an agreement, the World Bank has said even as it assured that both countries will continue to work to resolve the issues in an amicable manner.

"While an agreement has not been reached at the conclusion of the meetings, the World Bank will continue to work with both countries to resolve the issues in an amicable manner and in line with the Treaty provisions, "the World Bank said in a student.

"Both countries and the World Bank appreciated the discussions and reconfirmed their commitment to the preservation of the Treaty, "the World Bank said after the conclusion of the Secretary-level discussions between the two South Asian neighbours on the technical issues of the Kishenganga and Ratle hydroelectric power plants within the framework of the Indus Waters Treaty (IWT).

The two-day discussion took place at the World Bank headquarters on September 14-15.

"The World Bank remains committed to act in good faith and with complete impartiality and transparency in fulfilling its responsibilities under the Treaty, while continuing to assist the countries, "the bank said in its statement.

The IWT was signed in 1960 after nine years of negotiations between India and Pakistan with the help of the World Bank, which is also a signatory.

The World Bank's role in relation to "differences" and "disputes" is limited to the designation of people to fulfill certain roles when requested by either or both of the parties.

The Indian delegation was led by the Union Water Resources Secretary Amarjit Singh. It also had representatives from Ministry of External Affairs, Power, India's Indus Water Commissioner and Central Water Commission.

APP – 18

INDO-PAK TALKS TO SAFEGUARD BENEFITS OF INDUS WATERS TREATY, SAYS WORLD BANK

Dawn / Anwar Iqbal / 16 September, 2017

As Pakistan And India Concluded Their Two-Day Water Talks Here On Friday, The World Bank, Which Is Mediating The Talks, Said The Meetings Were Part Of A Process To Safeguard Benefits Of The 57-Year-Old Indus Waters Treaty.

The World Bank Hosted The Two Latest Rounds At Its Headquarters In Washington On July 31-Aug 1 And Sept 14-15. Concluded In 1960 With The World Bank's Support, The Indus Waters Treaty recognises The Bank as a mediator. It Is Also Acclaimed As One Of The Most Successful International Agreements For Peacefully Resolving Previous Water Disputes Between India And Pakistan.

"These Meetings Are A Continuation Of A Discussion On How To Safeguard The Treaty For The Benefit Of The People In Both Countries," Said World Bank Spokesperson Elena Karaban When Asked For Comments.

She Also Said That The Sept 14-15 Meetings In Washington Focused On "The Technical Issues Of The Treaty" And The Bank Will Provide More Information About The Talks When Available.

In A Previous Statement, The Bank Praised "The Spirit Of Goodwill And Cooperation" That Both India And Pakistan Demonstrated In The Last Meeting And Hoped That They Would Maintain This Spirit To Peacefully Settle The Current Dispute As Well.

The Indian Express Newspaper Reported On Friday That New Delhi Dropped Its Earlier Objections To Holding Water Talks With Pakistan To Participate "In A Bank-Brokered Dialogue" And This Decision "Surprised All Sides".

Bimal Patel, A Member Of India's National Security Advisory Board (NSAB) And Law Commission, Told The Newspaper That He "Doesn't Know What The Government's Intention Is, But It Is Uncalled For To Participate In Such Meetings To Perpetuate A Third Party Role".

APP – 19

PAK INDIA SECRETARY LEVEL TALKS ON INDUS WATER TREATY END WITHOUT AGREEMENT

The News – 16 September, 2017

Pakistan and India on Saturday failed to reach an agreement during the latest round of talks on Indus Water Treaty.

"While an agreement has not been reached at the conclusion of the meetings, the World Bank will continue to work with both countries to resolve the issues in an amicable manner and in line with the Treaty provisions," the World Bank said in a statement.

"Both countries and the World Bank appreciated the discussions and reconfirmed their commitment to the preservation of the Treaty," the World Bank said after the conclusion of the Secretary-level discussions between the two South Asian neighbours on the technical issues of the Kishenganga and Ratle hydroelectric power plants within the framework of the Indus Waters Treaty (IWT).

The two-day discussion took place in Washington at the World bank headquarters on September 14-15.

"The World Bank remains committed to act in good faith and with complete impartiality and transparency in fulfilling its responsibilities under the Treaty, while continuing to assist the countries," the bank said in its statement.

The Pakistani delegation was led by Secretary Water Resources Division Arif Ahmed Khan along with Secretary of Water and Power Yousuf Naseem Khokhar, High Commissioner of Indus Waters Treaty Mirza Asif Baig and Joint Secretary of Water Syed Mehar Ali Shah.

The Indian delegation was led by the Union Water Resources Secretary Amarjit Singh. It also had representatives from Ministry of External Affairs, Power, India's Indus Water Commissioner and Central Water Commission.

The Indus Water Treaty was signed in 1960 after nine years of negotiations between India and Pakistan with the help of the World Bank.

APP – 20

TALKS ON INDUS WATER TREATY END WITHOUT AGREEMENT

The Nation / 16 September, 2017

Pakistan and India were unsuccessful in reaching an agreement during the latest round of talks on Indus Water Treaty.

"While an agreement has not been reached at the conclusion of the meetings, the World Bank will continue to work with both countries to resolve the issues in an amicable manner and in line with the Treaty provisions," the World Bank said in a statement.

"Both countries and the World Bank appreciated the discussions and reconfirmed their commitment to the preservation of the Treaty," the World Bank said after talks concluded between the two South Asian neighbours on the technical issues of the Kishenganga and Ratle hydroelectric power plants within the framework of the Indus Waters Treaty (IWT).

The two-day discussion took place in Washington at the World bank headquarters on September 14-15.

"The World Bank remains committed to act in good faith and with complete impartiality and transparency in fulfilling its responsibilities under the Treaty, while continuing to assist the countries," the bank said in its statement.

The Pakistani delegation was led by Secretary Water Resources Division Arif Ahmed Khan along with Secretary of Water and Power Yousuf Naseem Khokhar, High Commissioner of Indus Waters Treaty Mirza Asif Baig and Joint Secretary of Water Syed Mehar Ali Shah.

The Indian delegation was led by the Union Water Resources Secretary Amarjit Singh. It also had representatives from Ministry of External Affairs, Power, India's Indus Water Commissioner and Central Water Commission.

The Indus Water Treaty was signed in 1960 after nine years of negotiations between India and Pakistan with the help of the World Bank.

APP - 21

PAKISTAN SEEKS ARBITRATION COURT AS WATER TALKS FAIL

Dawn / Anwar Iqbal / 17 September, 2017

Pakistan has asked the World Bank to constitute a court of arbitration to settle its water dispute with India after the latest round of talks ended without an agreement.

Dawn has learned that India and Pakistan failed to break the impasse on choice of a forum for settling the dispute. "India not only refused to accept any of the amendments proposed by Pakistan but also refused to agree to any of the dispute settlement options proposed by the World Bank," an official source told Dawn.

"While acknowledging the Bank's continued efforts, Pakistan has now requested the World Bank to fulfil its duties under the (Indus Waters) Treaty by empanelling the Court of Arbitration," the source added.

The World Bank, which was hosting the talks, issued a statement on Saturday, which underlines its commitment to help find a solution.

"While an agreement has not been reached at the conclusion of the meetings, the bank will continue to work with both countries to resolve the issue in an amicable manner and in line with the Treaty provisions," the bank said.

The World Bank noted that both countries "reconfirmed their commitment to the preservation of the Treaty".

The bank "remains committed to act in good faith and with complete impartiality and transparency in fulfilling its responsibilities under the Treaty, while continuing to assist the countries", the statement added.

The secretary-level talks took place on Sept 14-15 at the World Bank headquarters in Washington, within the framework of the Indus Waters Treaty (IWT). Concluded in 1960 with the World Bank's support, the treaty recognises the bank as a mediator.

In the last two months, the World Bank hosted two rounds of IWT talks. In the first round, which concluded on Aug 1, India and Pakistan exchanged proposals.

They returned to Washington this week for the second round, which focused on the technical issues of two hydroelectric plants — Kishanganga and Ratle — that India is building on the tributaries of the Jhelum and Chenab rivers.

APP - 22

PAK NEEDS TO PURSUE IWT AT WORLD FORUMS MORE VEHEMENTLY

Pakistan Observer / Rayyan Baig / 13 October, 2017

The countries surrounding India are faced with a neighbor who acts like a "bee in the bonnet". There is not a single Indian neighbor who didn't suffer in the hands of this belligerent. Since its creation India has not accepted the ground realities and failed to live like a responsible neighbor. In addition to interfering in their internal affairs, India has spatial and water related disputes with almost all her neighbors. As for water is concerned her thirst has found no bounds, not only the lower riparian rather few poor upper riparian have also been suffering, if given a choice India would like to gulp all the resources of her neighbors. Unfortunately, at the time of partition the Hindus and British Indian administration conspired and drew political boundary between Pakistan and India right across the Indus Basin, thus intentionally making Pakistan lower riparian of India. The headwaters were given to India, making Pakistan vulnerable as India was given physical control to cut off supply of water to Pakistan at will. Just after the petition, India stopped the supply of water to Pakistan from every canal flowing from India to Pakistan. These were later restored temporarily through an interim agreement, however to find a permanent solution Pakistan approached the World Bank in 1952 to settle the issue once for all. After long exhaustible negotiations for almost nine years, with India and Pakistan, the World Bank came up with a water distribution treaty, known as "Indus Waters Treaty (IWT)". The sanctity of this treaty can be judged from the fact that it was personally signed by Prime Minister of India Jawaharlal Nehru, President of Pakistan Ayub Khan and Senior Vice President of the World Bank, W.A.B. Liff.

The treaty withstood testing times two major of 1965 and 1971 and is cited as a success story of international riparian engagement. As per the treaty all the waters of the Eastern Rivers were made available for the unrestricted use to India and Pakistan received all those waters of the Western Rivers for unrestricted use. The Western Rivers were to flow unrestricted without interference from India except for, domestic use, non-consumptive use and agricultural use and for limited hydro-electric power etc. the treaty fared well since its conclusion; however, the first dispute emerged in 1985 when India, without informing Pakistan and in complete violation of IWT, floated a tender to construct Wullar Barrage. Then in 1999 India started constructing Baglihar Dam on Chenab River in 2007 India started work on Kishanganga – Ratle Project designed to divert water from the Kishanganga/Neelam River to Jhelum River. Pakistan went to the international court of arbitration against these projects, as these violated IWT and would allow India to store, control, and divert the water of these rivers, but Pakistan lost these cases due to slackness/biased judgments. Earlier, India violated the treaty and started constructing Salal Dam on River Chenab in 1978, though an agreement was reached between the two countries but India didn't abide by the same as well. India is also working on/ constructing 1856 MW Sawalkot Dam, 1000 MW Pakuldul Dam, 1200 MW and 829 feet high Bursar Dam with the storage capacity of more than two million acres feet of water and 260 MW Gyspa Dam, with about 1 million-acre feet of storage capacity and many more smaller/bigger dams and hydroelectric projects on Chenab and other western rivers. The availability of water in Pakistan has already dropped from 5,000 cubic meters per capita, around 60 years ago, to 1017 cubic meters. This figure is expected of time. For the last many years, the average water flow in river Chenab has drastically declined. With the present dams and hydroelectric power projects on western rivers, India has got the capacity to hold water for 25-26 days thus being able to cause acute shortage of water for winter crops in Pakistan. With the completion of all proposed projects there is a fear of Pakistan getting fully starved/flooded by India, as her cumulative live storage capacity will have major impact on the timing of flows. India can utilize the same capability to drown Pakistan or use it against Pakistan Army in case of war. Mr. John Briscoe, a water resources expert, former World Bank senior water expert and a professor at Harvard University, recognized Pakistan's unhappy position in the following words: "This is a very uneven playing field. The regional hegemon is the upper riparian and has all the cards in its hands. "It's not only Pakistan rather all the low riparian states have been raising concerns over India's tendency to use water of common rivers unilaterally without considering its human, social, economic and ecological implications on the lower riparians. Whenever Pakistan raised objection on Indian violation of IWT, through Indus Water Commission, India entangled Pakistan in unnecessary discussion with a view to gain maximum time to complete larger part of the controversial work. Frustrated from Indian attitude whenever Pakistan approached the Court of Arbitration or a Neutral Expert to protest, the time gained by India in mutual discussions enabled her to have substantial on-ground evidence needed to prove her stakes in front of mediators for the continuation of its projects, thus gaining undue concessions against the will of Pakistan. India has made the IWC ineffective by delaying its meetings or by evading to participate in its meetings. India has not been sharing necessary data about constructions, storage capacity and water flow etc. and also denying tours/inspection asked by Pakistan, to be arranged on a prompt basis as allowed in the Treaty. The favors given to India, so for, by the Neutral Experts/Arbitrators, about the gated structures and the height of dams, are on the environmental hazards "of the day" confronting Pakistan should have also been considered before giving decision, and the Eastern Rivers should also be reopened as per the "international norms of the day" about sharing common rivers. The World Bank/Arbitrators must weigh the survival of over 20 million people over technical norms. History has proved that whenever India acquired a capability it fully utilized it to her advantage disregarding the international norms and ethics. After building Farakha Barrage on Ganges River Indra Gandhi sought permission from Sheikh Mujeeb to fill the dam just for once to check its technical efficacy, thereafter India never let the water of Ganges go to Bangladesh and dried it causing environmental havoc in Bangladesh. It's impossible to think that after acquiring the capability to hold water, India would not exercise it to harm Pakistan. The environmental havoc which diversion of Western rivers have caused in Pakistan are already overwhelming, the water tables have gone down and sub-surface water has turned poisonous resulting into rampant water borne diseases in Pakistanis. Pakistan needs to raise this issue at international forums more vehemently, terming it a nuclear flashpoint between two nuclear rivals and a humanitarian crisis in making. Pakistan must take all Indian violations of IWT to the World Bank without wasting time in mutual discussions. We cannot afford any further slackness in pursing our cases in arbitration courts, there is a need to have skilled and dedicated panel of law experts who can successfully fight Pakistan's case. In the backdrop of water shortage and the challenges arising from Indian violations of IWT there is also a need that we manage our water resources and adopt modern techniques of irrigation and agriculture. The time is running out fast, as a nation we need to wake up and demand from our leadership to save us from fast approaching drought. In the larger interest of the nation we need to shun our differences and build all the dams, declared fit by our technical experts on war footing.

APP – 23

INDIA COMPLETES KISHENGANGA PROJECT WITH FAULTY DESIGN

The News / Khalid Mustafa / 28 November, 2017

India has managed to complete 330 MW Kishenganga hydropower project with the faulty design in negation of Indus Waters Treaty 1960. Though World Bank is in process of mediation between the two nuclear states on how to advance and develop consensus in the light of Indus Waters Treaty 1960 on the mechanism for resolution of 'faulty designs' of 300 MW Kishenganga and 850 MW Ratle hydro power projects and there is still a statement even after the lapse of 11 months since the Bank announced the pause on December 12, 2016, but India on the other hand has managed to complete its controversial project against what Pakistan has moved World Bank, a top senior official told The News.

"Yes, India has unfortunately completed the project while we are engaged in talks under World Bank's umbrella and now we have proposed some modifications to be introduced in the Kishenganga project's design without hurting the project's ability to generate electricity, ensuring no damage to Pakistan's water interests. We have asked the World Bank to constitute the Court of Arbitration as soon as possible," Mirza Asif Baig, Pakistan Commissioner of Indus Waters told The News. "However, the response of the World Bank is still awaited." As far as construction of 850 MW Ratle Hydropower project is concerned, the top official said that there are reports that the contractor of the project has run away and Indian authorities are in the process of hiring new contractor.

Pakistan and India last held talks in Washington at secretary level talks on 14-15 September 2017 which ended with no headway. World Bank wanted both the countries to develop consensus either on mechanism of Neutral Expert or of Court of Arbitration mentioned in the Treaty for the resolution of the issues pertaining to the said projects. And in case of failure, both the countries need to develop agreement on the middle way to resolve the issues. Both the countries held many talks at secretary level in Washington in the presence of the top official of the World Bank, but the meaningful meeting could not take place at the eleventh hour because of the India's evasive attitude and since then the World Bank is in the process of persuading India to come on the table for talks on how to proceed on the resolution of the disputed projects. Pakistan had raised objections on the technical designs of both the projects being built by India; one on Chenab and other one on Jehlum rivers arguing the designs are not in line with the provisions of the Indus Water Treaty and both projects with the existing designs are detrimental to water interest of Pakistan.

The top mandarins of Ministry of Water and Power told The News that the 850 MW Ratle Hydropower Project on Chenabr river if gets constructed under its existing objectionable design, then the water flow of Chenab river at Head Marala will reduce by 40 percent which will be very detrimental to the irrigation in central Punjab of Pakistan. India has awarded the contract of the Rattle project to a private company that will run the project on BOT (build, operate and transfer) basis for 35 years and then it would hand over the project to India. This dam will be three times larger than the Baglihar hydropower dam. India has already carved out the plan to generate 32,000MW of electricity on Pakistan's rivers that will enable New Delhi to regulate the water flows that are destined to reach Pakistan. India has also begun electricity projects including the 1,000 MW Pakal Dul, 120 MW Miyar and 48 MW Lower Kalnai projects on River Chenab's tributaries. Pakistan planned to raise its reservations over these projects too. The last secretary-level talks between the two countries were held in the last week of July in Washington. Pakistan and India share the waters of Indus River Basin which has been a major source of contention between the two states since independence.

APP – 24

INDIAN GOVT. MOVES TO TAP SHARE OF INDUS TO STRIKE BACK AT PAKISTAN

The Times of India / Vishwa Mohan / 30 Dec, 2017

In keeping with its decision to review utilisation of Indus waters+ as part of its signalling that Pakistan cannot expect past voluntary concessions to continue as long as it exports terror to India, the government has moved further on a project to store water in Jammu and Kashmir's Kathua district. Looking to fast-track utilisation of India's rights under the Indus Waters Treaty (IWT), the Central Water Commission (CWC) has finalised a detailed report on Ujh multi-purpose project and the government made it clear the proposal aims to harness water that was flowing untapped across the border. The project report has been submitted to the J&K government for evaluation so that construction may begin at an early date. The project, which is to come up in Kathua district, will store around 0.65 million acre feet (MAF) of water from Ujh (a tributary of Ravi) to irrigate 30,000 hectares and produce over 200 MW of power. The government decided to take a relook at the implementation of the Indus treaty after PM Narendra Modi decided to do so following the attack by Pakistan-backed terrorists on the Army camp at Uri in 2016+. An inter-ministerial task force with Nripendra Mishra, principal secretary to the PM, and national security adviser Ajit Doval was formed to examine the IWT with Pakistan. Under the IWT, signed with Pakistan in 1960, waters of Ravi are allocated to India. It, however, took the CWC 16 years to complete the process of detailed project report (DPR) after getting a formal nod to do so in 2001, following a political prompt from the current government. The task force was set up after India decided it will explore all options for utilising the maximum waters of the Indus system that is legally given to it under the treaty.

APP – 25

INDUS WATERS TREATY: DON'T LOSE THE GAME

The News / Ahmad Rafay Alam / 25 January, 2018

India and Pakistan have reached an impasse over issues of the Kishenganga and Ratle power plants. Their last meeting in the "good offices" of the World Bank last August and September yielded no progress and there has been no movement on the Indus Waters Treaty since. There are two opposing points of view regarding the forum to resolve concerns regarding the design of the two power plants. Pakistan has moved to establish an international court of arbitration (CoA) while India argues that the matters must be heard by a neutral expert. Reports indicate that India has refused four different options of forums presented by the Bank. The impasse has persisted since July 2016, when it was discussed at the secretary-level talks. A better understanding has been made difficult by the deterioration in bilateral relations following the Uri attack on September 18, 2016. India had accused Pakistan of masterminding the attack near the Line of Control. A week later, Indian Prime Minister Narendra Modi commented that "blood and water cannot flow together" while cancelling, for several months, scheduled meetings of the Indus Water Commission. Some reports indicated that India was even reconsidering their participation in the treaty.

What is clear is that the treaty is being dragged into the broader Indo-Pak relationship. It is necessary to understand the tactics that are being used against Pakistan and how we can overcome them.

Pakistan faced a setback with the decision of the neutral expert appointed in the Baglihar case in 2007. It had claimed that the Baglihar plant did not conform with the criteria prescribed in the treaty and, more crucially, that gated spillways in the design would allow India to control the flow of River Kishenganga, by way of drawdown flushing, in violation of India's obligation to "let flow" the waters of the western river. Rejecting Pakistan's arguments, the neutral expert determined that the conditions of the site, including the hydrology, sediment yield, topography, geology and seismicity, required a gated spillway.

However, in the Kishenganga arbitration case (2013), the ICA observed that the treaty gave no indication that a neutral expert's determination had precedential value beyond the scope of the particular issue before it. On the other hand, it clarified that its own decisions would be binding with respect to the questions presented before it. In doing so, the ICA restricted the impacts of the Baglihar determination to the facts of the case and averted, in the words of Ijaz Hussain, an "enormous catastrophe" for Pakistan.

In Kishenganga, the COA was called to determine the "ultimately legal" nature of the drawdown flushing for sediment control. It held that "the issue of drawdown flushing at the [Kishenganga Dam] would in all probability not comply with the flow restrictions of…the treaty" and "identified at least one operative provision that prohibits the depletion of dead storage for drawdown flushing". By recalling that "flushing is… one of a number of techniques available for sediment control", the ICA elaborated "that India's right to generate hydroelectric power on the western rivers can meaningfully be exercised without drawdown flushing extends beyond the specifics of the [Kishenganga Dam] to other, future, run-of-river plants".

The Kishenganga Award has also clarified that requests for the appointment of a neutral expert cannot not serve to impose procedural hurdles in accessing the CoA. The court held that nothing in the treaty requires questions to be solely decided by a neutral expert first, and that it could also consider such questions.

The Kishenganga Award effectively blocks India from benefitting from the determination in the Baglihar case by restricting all future dam designs. The intransigent Indian position in the current impasse can, therefore, be seen as a desperate attempt to force an adjudication by a neutral expert instead of a CoA, as the forum of the neutral expert is the only place within the treaty where India can possibly expect a favourable outcome on the drawdown flushing design of its future dams.

The impasse must also be seen in light of the deterioration of Indo-Pak relations following the Uri attack in September 2016. India immediately blamed Pakistan for the attack. But it did not respond to Pakistan's earlier formal request to establish a CoA for the Kishenganga and Ratle disputes until October 2016 when it responded by requesting that a neutral expert be appointed instead.

On November 10, 2016, India criticised the Bank "for its decision to favour Pakistan" in relation to the establishment of the CoA. The Bank has a limited procedural role in relation to the treaty, but was now, nonetheless, caught up in the imbroglio.

A week later at a political rally on the banks of the Ravi, Modi declared that he would not let a drop of the waters of River Ravi to flow into Pakistan. The waters of the Ravi are already allocated to India under the treaty and the elections in Indian Punjab – in which a BJP alliance lagged behind a resurgent Congress Party – were on the horizon. On December 10, the Bank called for a "pause" in the treaty proceedings as "both processes initiated by the respective countries create[d] a risk of contradictory outcomes that could potentially endanger the treaty". On March 8, 2017, the Indian National Investigation Agency found the two accused "Pakistani boys" had accidentally wandered across the borders and were not, in fact, involved in any terrorist activity. During the same week, the Congress Party trounced the BJP alliance in the Punjab election and India announced that it would resume treaty talks with Pakistan. In this context, it can be seen that the Indian government used the Uri attack as a political distraction to prevent Pakistan from approaching the COA. Its ratcheting up the rhetoric on the treaty by cancelling scheduled talks and calling the Bank biased can also been seen as a failed attempt to rouse political support in the Punjab election. Pakistan must resist the forces attempting to draw the treaty – a technical document best left untouched by politicians – into the broader Indo-Pak relationship.

The country must see through the ruse of India's insistence that only a neutral expert should be appointed for the Kishenganga and Ratle disputes. Its stance that the disputes should be adjudicated by the ICA rests on firm legal foundations. Drawdown flushing is against the terms of the treaty.

Pakistan must not be distracted from its negotiation position through India's political strategy or the Bank's response to it. The Bank already has considerable investments – and influence – in the country, which should not be allowed to influence our position. By keeping the Bank's role limited to its procedural mandate, Pakistan can reduce the risk of the international body employing its influence to determine the course or outcome of future treaty negotiations.

This article is an abridged version of a policy brief written for the Jinnah Institute. The writer is a lawyer.

APP - 26

JHELUM WATER INFLOW DECLINES ALARMINGLY

The News / Khalid Mustafa / 20 February, 2018

After 52 years, Pakistan has experienced mammoth reduction in the Jhelum water inflows from 8,000 cusecs to 1,900 cusecs on Sunday (Feb19) but on Monday it slightly scaled up to 2,000 cusecs, raising the eyebrows of many in the country as all other rivers have normal flows. However, a senior official of Pakistan's Permanent Commission of Indus Waters (PCIW) attributed the decline in water inflows in Jhelum River to less rainfall, below average snowfall and low temperatures in the catchment area which is situated in Indian Held Kashmir.

Asked if India is in process of filling the reservoir of the just-completed Kishenganga hydropower project, he said that it depends upon the rise in temperature in the catchment area and the water flows are not gaining the momentum at the moment. However, water experts apprehended that the massive dip in water inflows may be the result of filling of Kishenganga Dam by Indians as other rivers have normal flows. IRSA spokesman Khalid Idrees Rana said that historically water flows in Jhelum river stay at 7,000-8,000 cusecs per day in these days, but now they have dropped down to an alarmingly level of just 2,000 cusecs. However, the data shows during peak winter season water flows hovered in the range of 7,000-8,000 cusecs and specifically on December 26, 2017, the water flows stayed at 7,900 cusecs, but in January 2018, the flows dropped massively to be in the range of 4600 to 4,000 cusecs. By mid- February, when spring season starts approaches, the water flows drastically went down raising many a eyebrows. This means that India had started the process of filling of dam from January, 2018.

However, PCIW is totally unaware of the filling of the dam by India as it has failed to get information of any existing and future projects being erected on Pakistan's rivers in the last four years particularly after Pakistan going to World Bank asking for the constitution of the court of arbitration (CoA) on the designs of Kishenganga and Ratle hydropower projects. The World Bank has failed to constitute the court of arbitration on account of India's opposition as New Delhi is insisting that the matter should be resolved at the forum of Neutral Expert. Since then, Modi government is keeping Pakistan in the dark about the design of the future projects on eastern rivers. So Pakistan is not in a position to verify if India is filling the Kishenganga Dam.

APP – 27

INDIA PLANS SIX NEW 6,322MW PROJECTS ON CHENAB RIVER

The News / Khalid Mustafa / 23 February, 2018

India has stepped up its water war against Pakistan and to this effect, New Dehli has strategised a plan to maximise the usage of Indus waters under which six new projects will not only to be built to generate 6,322MW electricity on the Chenab River but also have huge capacity to store water that is destined to reach low riparian country--Pakistan. This has been disclosed in a letter written on January 2018 by the High Commission for Pakistan in New Delhi to the Ministry of Water Resources. The letter in possession of this correspondent arranged from the ministry also divulges that most of the new projects are in the detailed project report stage. These projects are being expedited by the government of India, and, to this effect, the government has issued the grants to cover funding for completing the three projects, including Pakal Dal, Kwar and Kiru by 2022-23 and has pledged the Held Kashmir government that it will fund the rest of the projects.

The six projects that are being planned to be constructed include Sawalkot (1,856MW), Kirthai-1 (390MW, Kirthai II (930MW), Pakal Dal (1,000MW), Kwar(540MW), Kiru (624MW) and Bursar (800MW) in the Chenab basin and Ujh project (212MW) in the Ravi basin. The upcoming projects like the Swalkote, Kirthai-I and Kirthai-II, Pakal Dal, Kwar, Kiru and Bursar are on the Chenab basin. Apart from them, India had already completed the projects on the Chenab River that include Baghlihar-I and II and Daul Hasti. The combined capacity of 6,323MW is projected to be around double the current installed generation capacity of 3,220MW in Held Kashmir from the projects built over several decades, this has been communicated by High Commission for Pakistan in New Delhi to the Ministry of Water Resources in a letter dated January 2018. Mentioning about the Sawalkot (1,856 MW), the document says, there has been a controversy over clearance of project being built in Ramban district in Held Kashmir. Experts contend that environmental impact assessment (EIA) report about the project was misleading. In 2016, a group of eminent experts from across India had written a report raising these concerns.

The EIA in India claims that Sawalkote is a run of the river scheme, but this claim appears misleading considering that it involves 192.5 metre high, 1159 hectare reservoir with 530 million cubic metres of storage capacity and a massive power house. About 800MW Bursur hydro-electric power projects, the document unfolds that the said project has got the clearance. The said project is being constructed on the Marusudar--one of the major tributaries of the Chenab River--will be a major hydropower and storage project in Held Kashmir. The project will be having the construction of a 265 metre high concrete gravity dam with water storage of 618 million cubic metres. The document also says that a total of 1,779 hectare is required for the project out of which 1,149 hectares is forecast land. The project will reportedly incur a cost of $2.5 billion.

APP – 28

IRSA ASKS PCIW TO TAKE UP ISSUE OF REDUCED JHELUM WATER INFLOWS WITH INDIA

The News / Khalid Mustafa / 25 February, 2018

In a new development, the Indus River System Authority (IRSA) has asked the Pakistan Commission of Indus Water (PCIW) to take up with Indian counterpart organisation the issue of 82 percent reduced water inflows in the Jhelum River. The water regulator has asked the PCIW to probe into the massive tumbling in water inflows apart from visiting the Indian sites to know the reality if India is involved in the filling any dam on the Jhelum River. The letter that IRSA wrote to the PCIW on February 22, 2018, with headline "Drastic reduction in the Jhelum River inflows at Mangla" also addressed to the Ministry of Water Resources, secretary, Wapda Member, secretaries of provincial irrigation departments and Chief Engineer (Mangla) Wapda has asked for an emergent visit of the Jhelum River flowing in Indian side may also be conducted remaining with the ambit of Indus Waters Treaty 1960.

The letter of which a copy is also in the procession of The News unfolds, while mentioning the Jhelum River inflows data that during the period from February 11, 2018, to February 22, 2018, the average water supplies were 2,863 cusecs against the last 10 years average of 16,175 cusecs showing the mammoth deficit in water inflows up to 82 percent. The phenomenon of, the letter says, tumbling of river inflows has also been seen in all rivers, but a major deviation is observed in the Jhelum River inflows. Earlier, the Punjab government has also sensitised the PCIW about the 82 percent reduction in the Jhelum River and asked for taking up the issue with Indian authorities concerned. "We are too much perturbed over the lowest ever water flows in the Jhelum River and has sensitised the Pakistan Commissioner of Permanent Commission Indus Water (PCIW), Syed Mehr Ali Shah about the mammoth dip in the Jhelum River and asked him to take up the issue with Indian counterpart organisation seeking the details and the visit of the sites of the projects of rubber dam and Kishenganga project." Mr Siddiqui said that there are reports that India is filling the rubber dam with 0.3 million acre feet (MAF) of water at Wullar Barrage and water shifting to Wullar lake through tunnel from Kishanganga dam.

Meanwhile, the Indus River System Authority (IRSA) has issued the letter two major federating units-- Punjab and Sindh asking for experiencing the 36 percent water shortage as both Punjab and Sindh have been provided the shortages of 30 percent and 32 percent respectively during the ongoing Rabi season 2017-18 from October 01 to February 20, 2018. However, according to water inflows data of Thursday shows that in the Mangla dam, the inflows have started improving and increased to 6,700 cusecs from 2,100 cusecs which is a welcoming sign for Punjab.

APP - 29

WATER SHORTAGE SWELLS TO 60PC

The News / Khalid Mustafa / 27 February, 2018

The water shortage for two federating units, Punjab and Sindh, the food baskets of the country, have increased to alarmingly level of 60 percent from now onward to March 10 as the inflows in Pakistan Rivers are not improving up to the mark.

This phenomenon will adversely impact the maturity of standing wheat crops both in central and southern parts of the Punjab, Senior Adviser to Punjab Irrigation Department M H Siddiqi told The News adding: "Only nature can help out by increasing the temperature in catchment areas of rivers."

IRSA had earlier worked out the water deficit of 36 percent for the country, however, during the short period but very crucial for maturing of crops starting from today (February 26 up to March 10), the water scarcity has increased up to 60 percent.

In the said period, two factors are very important which include the water availability that has already drastically gone down and maturity of crops. "Now, we are banking on the rise in temperature for relief in water shortages."

Meanwhile, Sindh is opposing the opening of the Chashma-Jhelum Link canal which IRSA has opened to provide water from the Indus. Sindh says that C-J Link canal can not be operational, but Punjab says that C-J link canal was constructed as a result of Indus Waters Treaty.

The Punjab also says that Tarbela and Mangla dam structures were also erected as a result of Waters Treaty 1960. Punjab also argued saying that it has its share in Indus and has the right to withdraw the water share from any outlet. This exchange of these arguments was taken place in the crucial meeting held on February 08, 2018, at the IRSA office, Islamabad. In that particular meeting, the decision to open C-J link canal was approved in IRSA meeting with 3:1 majority.

Mr Siddidi said that the Punjab province has already suffered 82 percent reduction in water flows of the Jhelum River during the period from February 11, 2018, to February 22 as the average water flows were at 2,863 cusecs against the last 10 years average of 16,175 cusecs.

The water flowing data of Monday shows that inflows in Tarbela were at 21,700 cusecs per day; whereas, the outflows stood at 35,000 cusecs.

APP - 30

WATER POLICY DRAFT TO BE TABLED IN CCI

The News / Khalid Mustafa / 19 March, 2018

The four federating units are all set to take up the Pakistan's first ever national water policy (NWP) on March 21 in the meeting of Council of Common Interests (CCI) as the cabinet has already given a go-ahead for presentation of the policy draft before supreme decision making body.

According to the official agenda for the meeting, CCI headed by Prime Minister Shahid Khan Abbasi will take up the draft of the policy which was finally prepared by the Planning Commission (PC) after taking inputs from stakeholders for approval. In case of approval by CCI, this will be the first ever Pakistan's NWP.

Provencal chief ministers have been invited to attend the meeting. Apart from the NWP, the CCI will also take up a report of the oversight committee of senators for five percent validation exercise of census results.

The PC deputy chairman briefed the cabinet meeting on March 13 about the issues relating to water management and the water policy that aims at the introduction of integrated water management for addressing water-related challenges.

The policy addresses issues relating to enhancing water storage capacity, conservation, research and development, capacity building of existing administrative departments, allocation of financial resources and establishment of the institutional set-up at provincial levels. In case the CCI approves the NWP, provinces will carve out their own water implementation policies.

APP - 31

INDIA, PAKISTAN TO HOLD PERMANENT INDUS COMMISSION MEET FROM MARCH 29

The Times of India / PTI / 27 March, 2018

- The meeting will take place in the backdrop of the continuing tension between the two countries over a host of issues, including the alleged harassment of diplomats.
- The IWT covers the water distribution and sharing rights of six rivers -- Beas, Ravi, Sutlej, Indus, Chenab and Jhelum.

The Indus Water Treaty covers the water distribution and sharing rights of six rivers -- Beas, Ravi, Sutlej, I... Read More

NEW DELHI: India and Pakistan will hold a two-day meeting of the Permanent Indus Commission here from Thursday to discuss various issues under the Indus Waters Treaty, sources said on Tuesday. This will be the 114th meeting of the Permanent Indus Commission (PIC), which should meet at least once a year as per the Indus Waters Treaty (IWT), they said. India's Indus water commissioner PK Saxena, technical experts and a representative of the Ministry of External Affairs (MEA) will be part of the Indian delegation for the annual meeting. Pakistan's six-member delegation will be led by Syed Muhammad Mehar Ali Shah. The meeting will take place in the backdrop of the continuing tension between the two countries over a host of issues, including the alleged harassment of diplomats. "The meeting will be held on March 29 and March 30," a government source told PTI. According to the sources, the issues relating to India's Ratle hydroelectricity, Pakul Dul and Lower Kalnai projects, located in Jammu and Kashmir, may come up for discussion during the meeting. Pakistan contends that Ratle (850 MW), Pakal Dul (1000 MW) and Lower Kalnai (48 MW) projects -- located in the Chenab basin -- were violating the IWT, signed in 1960. "But India is very clear that designs of the projects are in accordance with the treaty," a sources said. The sources said that the issues concerning the 340 MW Kishanganga hydroelectric project, located on river Jhelum's tributary in Bandipora district of Jammu and Kashmir, may not figure during the meeting since the project has already been commissioned.

The PIC had last met in March 2017 in Islamabad. The meeting of the PIC is held alternately in India and Pakistan every year.

APP – 32

INDIA, PAKISTAN TO DISCUSS INDUS WATERS TREATY ISSUES DURING 2-DAY MEET IN DELHI

Hindustan Times / Press Trust of India / 28 March, 2018

The 113th meeting of the Permanent Indus Commission was held in Pakistan in March last year. The 114th meeting in New Delhi will cover technical grounds

Pakistan's objections over the designs of some of India's hydropower projects along with other issues related to the Indus Waters Treaty are likely to be discussed during the two-day meeting of the Permanent Indus Commission here starting Thursday, sources said. India's Indus water commissioner P K Saxena, technical experts and a representative of the Ministry of External Affairs (MEA) will be part of the Indian delegation for the annual meeting. Pakistan's six-member delegation, led by Syed Muhammad Mehar Ali Shah, has already arrived here for the Commission's 114th meeting, which will take place in the backdrop of the continuing tension between the two countries over a host of issues, including the alleged harassment of diplomats.

The PIC is an established mechanism under the IWT, which mandates it to establish and maintain cooperative arrangements for the implementation of the water distribution pact and to promote cooperation between the two sides in the development of the Indus water systems. "Pakistan has objections over designs of some of India's projects. Their objections have been there since 2012. These issues may come up for discussion. There will also be routine exchange of information between the two countries," an official source told PTI. According to the sources, Pakistan has been expressing concerns over India's Ratle (850 MW), Pakal Dul (1000 MW) and Lower Kalnai (48 MW) projects -- located in the Chenab basin – contending that they violate the IWT, signed in 1960.

India continues to maintain its position that designs of the projects are very much in accordance with the treaty, the source said. The sources said that the issues concerning the 340 MW Kishanganga hydroelectric project, located on river Jhelum's tributary in Bandipora district of Jammu and Kashmir, may not figure during the meeting since the project has already been commissioned. The IWT covers the water distribution and sharing rights of six rivers -- Beas, Ravi, Sutlej, Indus, Chenab and Jhelum. The treaty specifies that waters from the three western rivers -- Indus, Jhelum and Chenab -- are reserved for Pakistan, while waters from eastern rivers -- Ravi, Sutlej and Beas -- are for reserved for India. The PIC had last met in March 2017 in Islamabad. The meeting of the PIC is held alternately in India and Pakistan at least once every year as mandated by the treaty.

APP – 33

PAKISTAN TO DOUBLE ITS WATER STORAGE CAPACITY

The News / Khalid Mustafa / 28 March, 2018

Pakistan will double its water storage capacity to at least 28 million acre feet (MAF) of water from existing 14 MAF increasing the storage capacity from 10 to 20 percent of total water flows, reveals the draft document of National Water Policy (NWP) prepared during last 7 decades and tabled in Common Council of Interests (CCI) that met with Prime Minister Shahid Khaqan Abbasi in the chair here on Tuesday. Though the CCI attended by three chief ministers of Sindh, KP, Balochistan and Finance Minister of Punjab deliberated the draft of the National Water Policy in detail and decided that the said draft with more inputs from federating units be brought in next meeting for approval. However, as per the copy of draft of the policy, in procession of this scribe, the authorities in Pakistan will also carve out the plan of reduction of 33 percent in 46 million cares feet river flows that are lost in conveyance. The decision makers will also come up with the plan to increase at least 30 percent in the efficiency of water use by produce more crop per drop ensuring g the gradual replacement and refurbishing of irrigation system.

Mentioning about the agriculture sector, the NWP draft point outs saying that the strategies and action plans shall be prepared to ensure food security of people of Pakistan focusing the concept of 'More Crop per Drop' that will be pursued with full determination. Apart from it, irrigation system will be modernized. Irrigation facilities will be extended to new cultivable command areas for growing low delta high value crops. And to make the water availability sustainable, the water charges will be increased to realistic extent. In addition special measures for rain-fed agriculture will be taken such as solar pumping, rainwater harvesting and less intensive crops.

Dilating upon the institutional framework, the water policy divulges that other than revitalization of WAPDA, new and vibrant institutions such as National Water Council will be established headed by Prime Minister to oversee the implementation of national water policy. Besides Provincial Water Authorities will be set up with the capacity to design and construct the small and medium dams. Ground Water Authority will also be established to issue, establish, and enforce standards for development and utilization of ground water. In the policy, it has been mentioned saying that the investment of 2.891 trillion in water sector is required, meaning by that Rs1.6 trillion to build Diamer-Bhasha and Mohmand Munda Dam, Rs800 billion for water conservation, Rs150 billion for drainage, Rs12 billion for flood control, Rs300 billion for rehabilitation of barrages, head works and canals and Rs29 billion for research purposes.

Touching the issue of impact of climate change, the policy measures related to water resources will be adopted in line with provisions of National Climate Change Policy (2012). Adoptive measures, short and long terms, will be worked out to mitigate impacts of climate change. And to better understand how rainfall patterns will shift, local climate model will be prepared and to this effect collaboration will be worked out with international agencies and organizations in weather simulation and modeling. On the issue of drinking water and sanitation, plans and strategies will be undertaken to progressively provide access to clean and safe drinking water. Full financial sustainability will be aimed at for the Urban Water Supply and Sanitation Systems.

APP - 34

PERMANENT INDUS COMMISSION MEET BEGINS IN DELHI

The Hindu / Special Correspondent / 28 March, 2018

The last such meeting was held in Islamabad in March 2017, a significant move at the time as it came after the "surgical strikes" by India across LOC.

India and Pakistan went ahead with talks on the Indus Waters Treaty (IWT) on Thursday despite an upsurge in tensions over LoC crossfire and allegations of harassment of diplomats in Delhi and Islamabad. On Wednesday, sources in the Ministry of External Affairs sources said, "According to the treaty provisions, the 114th meeting of the Permanent Indus Commission (PIC) will take place in India on March 29-30, 2018 in New Delhi to hold technical deliberations on various issues." India's Indus water commissioner P.K. Saxena, technical experts and a representative of the Ministry of External Affairs are meeting a six-member delegation from Pakistan, led by Syed Muhammad Mehar Ali Shah.

The last PIC meeting was held in Islamabad in March 2017, a significant move at the time as it came after the "surgical strikes" by India across the Line of Control, and the government's announcement that it would reconsider its position on the 1960 treaty with Pakistan after terrorist attacks in Uri. While the government kept its treaty commitments to meet, it has been exploring ways to utilise its share of the Indus waters more efficiently and to the maximum permissible. Ahead of the Thursday meeting, Minister for Water resources Nitin Gadkari announced that three dams would be built in Uttarakhand to further that effort. "Water from our [share of] rivers was going into Pakistan. We are making detailed project reports to stop that from happening and water will be given to Punjab, Rajasthan, Delhi and Haryana," Gadkari said in Rohtak.

APP – 35

INDUS WATER TALKS BEGIN AMID POLITICAL TENSIONS

Dawn / The Newspaper's Correspondent / 30 March, 2018

An annual two-day meeting of the Permanent Indus Commission (PIC) began on Thursday amid political tensions in which the pact frequently gets framed as a pawn. This is the 114th meeting of the PIC that looks into the sharing of the waters of the Indus since the treaty — brokered by the World Bank — was signed by Pakistan and India in 1960. Pakistan's six-member delegation for the meeting is being led by Syed Muhammad Mehar Ali Shah. The Indian delegation for the annual meeting comprises country's Indus Water Commissioner P. K. Saxena, a representative of the Ministry of External Affairs (MEA) and technical experts, sources said. The meeting comes in the backdrop of continuing tension between the two countries over a host of issues, including the alleged harassment of diplomats. The PIC is an established mechanism under the Indus Water Treaty (IWT), which mandates it to establish and maintain cooperative arrangements for the implementation of the water distribution pact and to promote cooperation between India and Pakistan in the development of the Indus water systems.

Commissioners are representatives of their respective governments for all matters arising out of this treaty. The meeting will continue on Friday when Islamabad's objections on designs of some of India's hydropower projects and other related will be taken up. Pakistan has been expressing concerns over India's Ratle (850MW), Pakal Dul (1,000MW) and Lower Kalnai (48MW) projects — located in the Chenab basin — contending they violated the IWT, The Economic Times said. India, however, has been maintaining that designs of these projects are very much in accordance with the treaty. Islamabad has also been expressing its concerns at Kishanganga dam and Wullar Barrage on the Jhelum river.

During Thursday's proceedings, both sides shared information on flood data and administrative matters, the sources said. The IWT covers the water distribution and sharing rights of six rivers — Beas, Ravi, Sutlej, Indus, Chenab and Jhelum. The treaty specifies that waters from the three western rivers — Indus, Jhelum and Chenab — are reserved for Pakistan, while waters from eastern rivers — Ravi, Sutlej and Beas — are reserved for India. The PIC had last met in March 2017 in Islamabad. The meeting of the PIC is held alternately in India and Pakistan at least once every year as mandated by the treaty.

APP – 36

PAKISTAN APPROACHES WORLD BANK AFTER INDIA BUILDS KISHANGANGA ON NEELUM

Dawn / Khaleeq Kiani / 5 April, 2018

Having confirmed that India has completed the controversial Kishanganga hydropower project, Pakistan has asked the World Bank to recognise its responsibility under the Indus Waters Treaty of 1960 to address its concerns over two disputed projects. A government official told *Dawn* that power division of the energy ministry sent a fresh communiqué early this week to the bank's vice president urging the international organisation to "recognise its responsibility" and play its role to ensure that India abided by the provisions of the 1960 treaty while building the projects. The official said there was no doubt that India had completed the 330MW Kishanganga project during the period the World Bank "paused" the process for constitution of a Court of Arbitration (COA) as requested by Pakistan in early 2016. The Pakistani request was countered by India by calling for a neutral expert.

Pakistan had called for resolution of disputes over Kishanganga project on the Neelum river and 850MW Ratle hydropower project on the Chenab. The official said the letter had reached the bank's head office in Washington and had been delivered to its vice president concerned as confirmed by Pakistan's director to the bank. When asked what the government expected now that India had completed the Kishanganga project, the official said the authorities could not just sit back and had to take the matter to its logical conclusion. Islamabad had received reports in August of 2017 that New Delhi had completed the Kishanganga project as per the design that had been objected to by the former. The new letter was sent to the World Bank after a Pakistani delegation of the Indus Waters Commission was not allowed to visit various controversial projects in India, including Kishanganga and Ratle schemes. In December 2016, the bank had announced that it had "paused" the process for either appointing a COA or a neutral expert and started mediation between the two countries on how to advance and develop consensus in the light of the treaty on the mechanism for resolution of faulty designs of the two projects.

Since then the bank has arranged two rounds of talks between the two sides but the Indians kept on building the project. On completion of the scheme, Pakistan proposed some modifications to partially address its concerns over the Kishanganga project's design for water storage without affecting its power generation capacity, but in vain. The last round of bank-facilitated and secretary-level talks between India and Pakistan were held in Washington in September that ended in disappointment for the latter. In view of the inability of the parties to agree on whether a COA or a neutral expert is the way forward, the World Bank is reported to have called another round of discussions to minimise the differences but failed to bring New Delhi to the negotiating table. Pakistan had raised a number of objections over the design of the two projects at the level of Permanent Indus Waters Commission almost eight years ago followed by secretary-level talks and then requests for arbitration through the World Bank.

Under the treaty, in case the parties fail to resolve disputes through bilateral means the aggrieved party has the option to invoke the jurisdiction of the International Court of Arbitration or the neutral expert under the auspices of the World Bank. The jurisdiction of the court could be invoked either jointly by the two parties or by any party as envisaged under Article IX (5), (b) or (c) of the treaty for constitution of a seven-member arbitration panel. Pakistan's experience with both the international forums — neutral expert and CoA — has not been satisfactory for varying reasons and outcomes, partially due to domestic weaknesses including delayed decision-making. Pakistan first challenged the Baglihar hydroelectric project before the neutral expert and then the Kishanganga and Wuller Barrage projects before the CoA. Islamabad has been under criticism at home for losing its rights through legal battles instead of building diplomatic pressure in world capitals to stop India from carrying out "water aggression". Pakistan felt its water rights were being violated by India on two rivers, the Chenab and Jhelum, through faulty designs of Ratle and Kishanganga projects, respectively.

An official said the government had originally decided to take up the matter at the international forums provided for in the 1960 treaty back in December 2015 but the process was delayed for unknown reasons. Pakistan believed that Kishanganga's pondage should be a maximum of one million cubic metres instead of 7.5 million cubic metres, intake should be up to four metres and spillways should be raised to nine metres. About the Ratle project, Pakistan had four objections. Freeboard should be one metre instead of two metres, pondage should be a maximum of eight million cubic metres instead of 24 million, intake level should be at 8.8 metres and spillways at the height of 20 metres. It believes the Indian design of Ratle project would reduce Chenab flows by 40 per cent at Head Marala and cause considerable irrigation loss to crops. The Ratle dam is believed to be three times larger than the Baglihar dam. Under the provisions of the Indus Water Treaty, the waters of the eastern rivers — the Sutlej, Beas and Ravi — had been allocated to India and that of the western rivers — the Indus, Jhelum and Chenab — to Pakistan except for certain non-consumptive uses.

APP – 37

WORKING WITH INDIA, PAKISTAN TO SETTLE DAM CONTROVERSY, SAYS WORLD BANK

Dawn / Anwar Iqbal / 6 April, 2018

The World Bank confirmed on Thursday that it had received Pakistan's complaint on the completion of the Kishanganga hydropower plant by India and was working with Islamabad and New Delhi for an amicable resolution of the dispute. "We confirm receiving the letter from Pakistan earlier this week regarding the Indus Waters Treaty," a spokesperson for the bank told *Dawn* in Washington. "The World Bank continues to work with both countries to resolve the most recent disagreement in an amicable manner and to safeguard the Treaty."

Pakistan complained that India has violated a World Bank-mandated pause, placed in 2016, by completing the controversial Kishanganga project. Pakistan believes that both Kishanganga (330 megawatts) and Ratle (850 megawatts) contravene the Indus Water Treaty's restrictions on the construction of run-of-the-river plants. The plants are respectively on a tributary of the Jhelum and the Chenab rivers. A World Bank fact-sheet notes that the two countries disagree over whether the technical design features of the two plants violate the treaty. The bank acknowledges that "the treaty designates these two rivers as well as the Indus as the Western Rivers' to which Pakistan has unrestricted use".

But in the same fact-sheet, the bank also says that "India is permitted to construct hydroelectric power facilities on these rivers subject to constraints specified in annexures to the Treaty". The annexures require that the design of any new run-of-river plant shall not raise the water level in the operating pool above the full pondage level specified in the design. It shall also take due account of the requirements of surcharge storage and of secondary power.

APP - 38

NON-FICTION: REVISITING THE INDUS WATERS TREATY

Dawn / Erum Sattar / 15 April, 2018

Ijaz Hussain, former dean of Social Sciences and chairman of the International Relations Department, Quaid-i-Azam University (QAU), Islamabad, has accomplished a monumental undertaking with the publication of Indus Waters Treaty: Political and Legal Dimensions. The book is timely because although Pakistan and India signed the Indus Waters Treaty (IWT) in 1960, its operation is becoming increasingly complex — a complexity that is only added to by the continuing role of the World Bank in the treaty's dispute settlement administration.

Hussain notes that pursuant to the treaty, the World Bank acknowledged that the proposed allocation and diversion to India of the so-called three Eastern rivers of the Indus would involve the transfer of freshwater on an unprecedented scale — nearly twice as much as Egypt had hoped to get from the High Aswan Dam. He evaluates other relevant studies on the issue (he counts seven) from both the Pakistani and Indian perspectives but, as he acknowledges, in the final analysis it is nearly impossible to approach the study of 'facts' from a neutral perspective. And as professional and dispassionate as his book is, ultimately it is a book written from a Pakistani perspective. It is refreshing to see this healthy self-reflection on the very emotive issue of water-sharing and for that candour alone, this book, with its particular focus on the political and legal aspects of the treaty, needs to be read widely.

The scope of the book is immense and the author builds on other excellent work that has been done in the field. For present purposes, the book begins with the pre-Partition colonial-era origins of the Indus waters' dispute in which British administrators undertook canal building at an unprecedented scale. As Imran Ali's exceptional book The Punjab Under Imperialism, 1885-1947 has shown, the goals were to increase food production and settle 'new' lands profitably, thereby aiming both to pacify the region after conquest and to tie the region's new settlers to the state and its provision of canal waters for the production of their livelihoods and social power. This is important history to cover as it is too easily lost and forgotten in official present-day planning and development efforts, which ahistorically treat the operation of the current irrigation system as having somehow transcended and become free of these colonial-era objectives. As Hussain's work reflects — and as I too have argued in my dissertation 'Water as Power: The Law and Politics of Federalism in the Indus Basin' — the colonial-era canal construction scheme continues to shape and affect the upstream-downstream water rivalry between Pakistan's main canal-irrigated provinces, respectively Punjab and Sindh in the context of Pakistan's federal institutional structure. If the country's planners hope to overcome this long-contested history, they must first acknowledge and understand it and Hussain's book is a rich source for that potential understanding.

The first runner-up in the Karachi Literature Festival-German Peace Prize is a critical and timely contribution to literature on the hotly debated India-Pakistan treaty. After laying out the origin of the water dispute between what became upstream India and downstream Pakistan after Partition, Hussain then considers the World Bank's entry into the canal waters dispute. As he explains, this intervention took the form of a unique and unprecedented mediatory role that the bank adopted to bring the parties, particularly Pakistan, to the treaty's signing table. Through some fortuitous finds and excellent detective work tracing clues in the World Bank's archives, Hussain shares valuable insights into how Pakistan was moved towards an agreement of what had been India's initial plan to divide the rivers. He further explores the unique role of David Lilienthal who, in the context of Cold War politics and development, applied his long leadership experience as head of the United States' Tennessee Valley Authority to the India-Pakistan water rivalry, and suggested that the basin be jointly developed and managed. Even though it became clear to the parties fairly early in the long treaty negotiations that, given the mutual mistrust and hostility, this proposal of co-management had very little prospect of success, Hussain rightly wonders whether there may still come a time when joint management of the Indus would be both wise and politically feasible.

Given Hussain's analysis — which takes the reader on a rollercoaster ride through the effects of climate change, glacial melt, federal and trans-boundary geopolitics, the complexity of the international dispute-settlement mechanisms that the treaty sets up, and India's continuing construction-related pressure in the Kashmiri territory it controls in the form of dams, hydropower generation and a cascade of run-of-the river projects — his conclusion is cautionary. In 2011, the US State Department, in a report under the chairmanship of then Senator John Kerry, concluded that the "cumulative effects of these projects could give India the ability to store enough water to limit supply to Pakistan at crucial moments in the growing season." But since we began this present chapter of the IWT nearly 60 years ago with a similar problem resulting from the effects of Partition, the report's finding begs the question of how far we have advanced to settle the dispute after all. Hussain leaves unanswered the as-yet untested question of the "causal relationship between water and wars." All those who desire a more peaceful and prosperous future for the region must undertake some clear-headed study of the long history of water-sharing and development in the Indus basin. To that end, this book is a critical contribution.

In addition to being a superb work, Hussain has also overcome actual but needless and unfortunate hurdles as an archival historian. We should acknowledge his immense commitment in undertaking the vast archival research necessary to his inquiry at the World Bank's headquarters in Washington DC. After requests for funding to his former institution QAU, Pakistan's Higher Education Commission and the Fulbright programme failed to materialise, Hussain used his own funds and relied on the hospitality of friends in the American capital. This book is a testament to his desire to undertake his research with crucial primary documents in the archives and we can only hope that there is a lesson in here somewhere for both educational and research institutions who may be more generous in supporting the work of future researchers. In addition to these logistical hurdles, Hussain very soon hit the wall of classification which researchers working on water in the South Asian region invariably have to face. Given the norm of declassification after 25 years, the fact that he could only access documents the Bank classifies as belonging to it and failed — again, after repeated requests — to access documents the Bank holds while classifying them as belonging to the respective governments, should be of concern to decision-makers as well as researchers. Why, in its fifth decade, are the treaty's negotiating materials still classified by both governments? Given the reliance of the region on the waters of the Indus in the face of greater climate uncertainty, rising populations and increasing demands for economic development, we may legitimately ask whether continuing classification of the treaty's negotiating documents in fact hampers productive policy-making going forward. Perhaps the richness of Hussain's book, albeit from its limited sources, may encourage some soul-searching in relevant quarters to rethink policies that may have outlived their usefulness.

The reviewer is a Visiting Fellow at the Islamic Legal Studies Programme: Law and Social Change, at Harvard Law School

APP – 39

WORLD BANK URGED TO SCHEDULE TALKS ON WATER DISPUTE WITH INDIA

Dawn / Anwar Iqbal / 26 April, 2018

Islamabad has asked the World Bank to schedule a meeting with a Pakistani team in Washington later this month for talks on water dispute with India, official sources told Dawn on Wednesday. Early this month, Pakistan asked the World Bank to address its concerns over India's two hydropower projects — the 330-megawatt Kishanganga and 850MW Ratle plants. Islamabad believes that both plants violate the Indus Water Treaty that distributes water of Indus River and its tributaries between India and Pakistan.

The Kishanganga plant is on the Neelum River and Ratle is on the Chenab and the treaty gives Pakistan exclusive rights over both. The treaty, however, also gives India the right to build hydropower plants over these tributaries if they do not violate specifications included in the agreement. Pakistan complains that both plants violate specifications and also that India has completed the Kishanganga plant despite a World Bank pause on such constructions, enforced in December 2016. While confirming to Dawn that it has received Pakistan's complaint, a World Bank spokesperson said earlier this week it's working with both Islamabad and New Delhi for an amicable resolution to the dispute. This week, the bank sent its envoy, Ian Solomon, to India to familiarise itself with the Indian position on this issue. Last week, Pakistan's Adviser on Finance Miftah Ismail met Managing Director of World Bank Kristalina Georgieva in Washington and urged her to help resolve the dispute.

Since the meeting also covered other issues, Pakistan has now asked the bank to schedule an exclusive meeting on the water dispute, in Washington, to enable Pakistani experts to explain Islamabad's views on this issue. Mr Solomon, who was appointed a World Bank envoy in December 2016 for talks with both India and Pakistan on the water dispute, may also visit Islamabad soon. Since December 2016, the World Bank has arranged two rounds of talks between India and Pakistan but failed to stop the Indian authorities from continuing to build the plants.

APP - 40

PAKISTAN TO PURSUE WITH WORLD BANK 'VIOLATIONS' OF INDUS WATERS TREATY BY INDIA

Hindustan Times / Imtiaz Ahmad / 3 May, 2018

The last round of talks on Indus Water Treaty between India and Pakistan was facilitated by the World Bank in Washington in September.

Pakistan's top security body with representation from the civilian and military leadership has directed authorities to pursue what it described as India's "violations" of the Indus Waters Treaty with the World Bank, which is the guarantor for the most durable pact between the two countries. A meeting of the National Security Committee on Wednesday was briefed on a new water policy and a water charter by the deputy chairman of the Planning Commission. "The Committee also directed the Water Resources Division to forcefully pursue the violations of the Indus Waters Treaty by India with the World Bank," said an official statement issued after the meeting. It did not give details.

The meeting, chaired by Prime Minister Shahid Khaqan Abbasi, was attended by interior minister Ahsan Iqbal, the chairman of the Joint Chiefs of Staff Committee, Gen Zubair Hayat, army chief Gen Qamar Bajwa, navy chief Admiral Zafar Mahmood Abbasi, air force chief Mujahid Khan, Inter-Services Intelligence chief Lt Gen Naveed Mukhtar and National Security Advisor Nasser Janjua. The committee hailed the water policy approved by the Council of Common Interests and the water charter signed by the prime minister and four chief ministers. The committee said the approval of the water policy was "a very significant achievement and if properly implemented could prove instrumental in averting the water crisis that was seriously threatening Pakistan". Following the completion of the Kishanganga hydropower project by India, Pakistan had asked the World Bank to recognise its responsibility under the Indus Waters Treaty of 1960 and address its concerns over the project on the Neelum river and the Ratle hydropower project on the Chenab. The committee, while reviewing Pakistan's economic performance, asked the government to address "potentially destabilising factors".

APP – 41

PAKISTAN EXPRESSES CONCERNS OVER INAUGURATION OF KISHANGANGA DAM PROJECT BY INDIA

Dawn / Naveed Siddiqui / 18 May, 2018

Pakistan on Friday expressed "serious concerns" over the inauguration of the controversial Kishanganga hydropower project by India and termed it a "violation of the Indus Waters Treaty".

A statement issued by the Foreign Office said, "Pakistan believes that the inauguration of the project without the resolution of the dispute is tantamount to violation of the Indus Waters Treaty (IWT)."

Despite several rounds of bilateral negotiations as well mediations by the World Bank, India continued with the construction of the project, the Foreign Office said, adding that "this intransigence on part of India clearly threatens the sanctity of the Treaty".

The Foreign Office reiterated that as the custodian of the treaty, the World Bank must urge India to address Pakistan's reservations on the Kishanganga project.

Advertisement

Pakistan maintains that India had completed the 330MW project during the period the World Bank "paused" the process for constitution of a Court of Arbitration (COA) as requested by Pakistan in early 2016. The Pakistani request was countered by India by calling for a neutral expert.

Pakistan had called for the resolution of disputes over the Kishanganga project on the Neelum river and 850MW Ratle hydropower project on the Chenab.

APP – 42

PAKISTAN TO DISCUSS INDIA'S VIOLATION OF INDUS WATER TREATY WITH WB PRESIDENT

The Express Tribune / News Desk / 20 May, 2018

Ambassador to the United States Aizaz Ahmed Chaudhry has stated Pakistan will discuss India's violation of the Indus Water Treaty with the president of World Bank, *Radio Pakistan* reported.

Speaking to media on Saturday, Chaudhry revealed a four-member delegation led by Attorney General of Pakistan (AGP) Ashtar Ausaf Ali had arrived in Washington to hold the talks. He added that the issue of construction of the Kishanganga Dam on River Neelam will be discussed in the meeting.

The move comes in light of Indian Prime Minister Narendra Modi inaugurating a hydroelectric power plant in the Indian Occupied Kashmir (IoK) amid protests from Islamabad as the project will disrupt water supply to the country.

Pakistan has maintained that the dam violates a World Bank-mediated treaty on the sharing of the Indus River and its tributaries upon which 80 per cent of its irrigated agriculture depends.

"Pakistan is seriously concerned about the inauguration (of the Kishanganga plant)," the Foreign Office said in a statement on Friday. "Pakistan believes that the inauguration of the project without the resolution of the dispute is tantamount to violation of the Indus Waters Treaty (IWT)."

APP - 43

WHAT IS THE KISHANGANGA WATER DISPUTE

Dawn / Anwar Iqbal / 20 May, 2018

The dispute revolves around a hydroelectric power plant on the Kishanganga River, which is a tributary of the Jhelum and is known as the Neelum in Pakistan. On Saturday, Indian Prime Minister Narendra Modi inaugurated the project — which includes a dam on the tributary — barely metres away from the Line of Control in the disputed Kashmir region. The project will generate 1,713 million units of electricity per year. The dam will divert Jhelum waters to an underground power house. To do so, it will transfer the water from the Gurez Valley back into mainland Kashmir, instead of allowing it to flow into Pakistan. The Kishanganga River flows through the regions of Neelum in AJK and Astore before entering the India-held region of Gurez. The dam will give India control over a river that flows from Pakistan into India-held Kashmir and then re-enters Pakistan.

What is Pakistan's position?

Islamabad argues that the 1960 Indus Waters Treaty (IWT) gives Pakistan control over the waters of the Indus, Chenab and Jhelum Rivers. The treaty gives India control over three eastern rivers — Beas, Ravi and Sutlej. India may also use the waters of the western rivers in "non-consumptive" ways. It interprets this as a permission to build "run-of-the-river" hydel projects that do not change the course of the river and do not deplete the water level downstream. Pakistan argues that the Kishanganga project violates both conditions by changing the course of the river and depleting the water level.

What steps did Pakistan take to stop India from building the Kishanganga dam?

India started work on the project in 2007. In 2010, Pakistan took the matter to the Permanent Court of Arbitration at The Hague, which stayed the project for three years. But in 2013, the court ruled that the Kishanganga was "a run-of-the-river plant within the meaning of the Indus Waters Treaty and that India may accordingly divert water from the Kishanganga (Neelum River) for power generation".

Room for Pakistan

The court also ruled that India was under an obligation to "construct and operate" the Kishanganga dam in such a way that it "maintains a minimum flow of water in the river". The minimum flow was fixed at 9cumecs, a unit of flow equal to one cubic metre of water per second. India declared that it was lowering the height of the dam from the planned 98m to 37m and resumed construction at full swing. Pakistan, however, collected evidence to prove that India was violating the treaty as well as the court's verdict.

Pakistan seeks World Bank's arbitration

In August 2016, Pakistan asked the World Bank to appoint a court of arbitration to review the designs of Kishanganga and another project on the Chenab, called Ratle. India rejected the suggestion, saying that Pakistan's objections were technical in nature and that the matter should be decided by a neutral expert. Pakistan disagreed, arguing that a decision by a technical expert was non-binding and India would be under no obligation to implement the expert's recommendation. The World Bank set in motion both processes but paused them when India and Pakistan refused to withdraw their proposals. After the pause, the bank held several rounds of talks — the last of which took place in September 2017 — but failed to resolve the dispute.

Pakistan's latest move

After India announced last month that it was commissioning all three units at Kishanganga, Pakistan wrote to the World Bank demanding that it ensured India abided by the treaty. It is now sending a high-level delegation to the United States for talks with the World Bank. The delegation, led by Attorney General Ashtar Ausaf, will reiterate Pakistan's demand to constitute an international court of arbitration.

Neelum-Jhelum project

Unable to stop India, Pakistan countered Indian aggression by building its project on the Neelum River and last month Prime Minister Shahid Khaqan Abbasi inaugurated the first unit of the Neelum-Jhelum Hydroelectric Project.

Zojila Pass

Mr Modi is also inaugurating the 11,578-foot-high Zojila Pass tunnel, which will allow India to monitor the China-Pakistan Economic Corridor.

APP - 44

WORLD BANK LISTENS TO PAK'S GRIEVANCES ON INDUS WATERS TREATY

The Hindu / Press Trust of India / 22 May, 2018

A Pakistani delegation raised the issue of India's alleged violation of the Indus Waters Treaty with the World Bank which discussed opportunities within the treaty to seek an amicable resolution, officials said today. Monday's meeting took place days after Prime Minister Narendra Modi inaugurated the 330 MW Kishanganga hydroelectric project in Jammu and Kashmir, amid protests from Pakistan which claims that the project on a river flowing into Pakistan will disrupt water supplies. Pakistan's Foreign Office had, on Friday, voiced concern over the inauguration of the hydroelectric project, saying inauguration without resolution of dispute between the two countries will tantamount to violation of the Indus Waters 1960 that regulates the use of waters in the shared rivers.

The discussions are scheduled to continue today. The Pakistani delegation is led by Attorney General, Ashtar Ausaf Ali. Islamabad had been raising objections over the design of the hydel project, saying it is not in line with the criteria laid down under the Indus Waters Treaty (IWT) between the two countries. The project was started in 2007, located at Bandipore in North Kashmir, envisages diversion of water of Kishan Ganga river to underground power house through a 23.25-km-long head race tunnel to generate 1713 million units per annum. On May 17, 2010, Pakistan moved for international arbitration against India under the provisions of the Indus Waters Treaty.

The Hague-based International Court of Arbitration allowed India in 2013 to go ahead with construction of the project in North Kashmir and upheld Indias right under the bilateral Indus Waters Treaty to divert waters from the Kishanganga for power generation in Jammu and Kashmir. The international court, however, decided that India shall release a minimum flow of nine cubic metres per second into the Kishanganga river (known as Neelam in Pakistan) at all times to maintain environmental flows.

Pakistan is building a 969 MW Neelum-Jhelum hydroelectric project downstream. The Pak Foreign Office in a statement in Islamabad last week said it was seriously concerned about the inauguration of the hydroelectric project. "Pakistan believes that the inauguration of the project without the resolution of the dispute is tantamount to violation of the Indus Waters Treaty (IWT)," it said. "Pakistan reiterates that as the custodian of the Treaty, World Bank must urge India to address to Pakistan's reservations on Kishenganga Hydroelectric Project (KHEP)," the statement said.

APP - 45

WB SAYS IT'S SEEKING AMICABLE SOLUTION TO PAKISTAN-INDIA WATER DISPUTE

Dawn / Anwar Iqbal / 23 May, 2018

The World Bank said on Tuesday that it was holding talks with a Pakistani delegation to seek an amicable resolution of its water dispute with India. A Pakistani delegation, headed by Attorney General Ashtar Ausaf Ali, arrived in Washington on Sunday, a day after Indian Prime Minister Narendra Modi inaugurated a controversial dam in India-held Kashmir, which Pakistan fears will reduce its share in the waters of the Indus and its tributaries.

The Indus system of rivers comprises three western rivers — the Indus, Jhelum and Chenab — and three eastern rivers — the Sutlej, Beas and Ravi. The controversial Kishanganga dam is built on the Neelum river, which is a tributary of the Jhelum river. "Senior World Bank officials are meeting on Monday and Tuesday with a Pakistan delegation at their request to discuss issues concerning the Indus Waters Treaty," a World Bank spokesperson, Elena Karaban, told Dawn. The 1960 Indus Waters Treaty gives Pakistan exclusive use of the western rivers, the Jhelum, Chenab and Indus, while the eastern rivers — Ravi, Beas and Sutlej — go to India.

"The meetings are discussing concerns raised by the Pakistan delegation and opportunities within the treaty to seek an amicable resolution," Ms Karaban said. The World Bank supervised the talks that led to the treaty, which gives it a key role in settling water disputes between India and Pakistan. But in a recently updated factsheet, the bank says that its role in relation to "differences" and "disputes" is limited to the designation of people to fulfil certain roles when requested by either or both of the parties. The bank, however, considers the treaty a major achievement, which has successfully prevented water wars between South Asia's two nuclear-armed nations. "The Indus Waters Treaty is a profoundly important international agreement that provides an essential cooperative framework for India and Pakistan to address current and future challenges of effective water management to meet human needs and achieve development goals," said Ms Karaban while explaining why the bank considered the treaty one of its major achievements.

Both Pakistan and India have stayed engaged with the World Bank over the last 70 years, seeking its assistance whenever they had a dispute over the interpretation of the treaty. In August 2016, Pakistan asked the World Bank to appoint a court of arbitration to review the designs of Kishanganga and another project on the Chenab, called Ratle. India rejected the suggestion, saying that Pakistan's objections were technical in nature and that the matter should be decided by a neutral expert. Pakistan disagreed, arguing that a decision by a technical expert was non-binding and India would be under no obligation to implement the expert's recommendation.

In December 2016, World Bank President Jim Yong Kim paused the process of negotiation to help India and Pakistan consider alternative approaches to resolve their dispute over the two hydroelectric plants. "We are announcing this pause to protect the Indus Waters Treaty," he said. The World Bank said that this week's meetings were also being held on Pakistan's request. While explaining why it was important to protect the treaty, the World Bank said it had "survived frequent tensions, including conflict, and has provided a framework for irrigation and hydropower development for more than half a century". The bank's factsheet also referred to a statement by former US president Dwight Eisenhower, who described the treaty as "one bright spot... in a very depressing world picture". Under the treaty, India is permitted to construct hydroelectric power facilities on the rivers concerned, subject to constraints specified in annexures to the treaty.

APP - 46

WATER TALKS FAILED TO PRODUCE AGREEMENT IN PAKISTAN'S WATER DISPUTE WITH INDIA: WB

Dawn / Anwar Iqbal / 24 May, 2018

The World Bank on Wednesday announced that two days of talks with a Pakistani delegation did not lead to an agreement on the way forward in Pakistan's water dispute with India. A four-member Pakistani delegation arrived in Washington on Sunday, a day after Indian Prime Minister Narendra Modi inaugurated a controversial dam in India-held Kashmir, for talks with senior World Bank officials. Pakistan fears the dam will reduce its share in the waters of the Indus and its tributaries and will also damage the ecosystem of the Neelum and Jhelum rivers. The World Bank said that senior bank officials met the Pakistani team, at their request, on May 21-22 and discussed issues regarding the Indus Waters Treaty and opportunities within the treaty to seek an amicable solution to the India-Pakistan water dispute. The Pakistani agenda for the talks included four key points: the height of the dam built on the Kishanganga River, its capacity to hold water, Pakistan's demand for setting up a court of arbitration to settle the dispute and India's counter-demand for an international expert, instead of the court. In a statement issued after the talks on Wednesday evening, the bank said the Pakistani delegation also shared with it their concerns about the recent inauguration of the Kishanganga hydroelectric plant. "Several procedural options for resolving the disagreement over the interpretation of the Treaty's provisions were discussed," the World Bank said. "While an agreement on the way forward was not reached at the conclusion of the meetings, the World Bank will continue to work with both countries to resolve the issues in an amicable manner and in line with the treaty provisions." As in a previous statement, the bank insisted that the Indus Waters Treaty was a profoundly important international agreement that provides an essential cooperative framework for India and Pakistan to "address current and future challenges of effective water management to meet human needs and achieve development goals". The World Bank said that the treaty only gives it a "limited and procedural" role in resolving India-Pakistan water disputes, although the bank supervised the negotiations for the treaty and is recognised as an arbitrator by both countries. In particular, the role in relation to 'differences' and 'disputes' was "limited to the designation of people to fulfil certain roles when requested by either or both parties," the bank said. The World Bank assured India and Pakistan that it "remains committed to act in good faith and with complete impartiality and transparency in fulfilling its responsibilities under the Treaty, while continuing to assist the countries". The Indus system of rivers comprises three western rivers — the Indus, Jhelum and Chenab — and three eastern rivers — the Sutlej, Beas and Ravi. The controversial Kishanganga dam is built on Neelum, which is a tributary of the Jhelum River. The 1960 Indus Waters Treaty gives Pakistan exclusive use of the western rivers, the Jhelum, Chenab and Indus, while the eastern rivers — Ravi, Beas and Sutlej — go to India. Although the World Bank issued a comprehensive statement on the two-day talks, the Pakistani team, which was led by Attorney General Ashtar Awsaf Ali, has remained silent. It's not clear if the delegation will also meet US officials and seek their help in seeking a peaceful end to its water disputes with India. In the past, Pakistan maintained a close liaison with the United States over such issues and Washington did play an effective role in easing tensions between South Asia's two nuclear neighbours.

APP – 47

INDUS TREATY IN JEOPARDY

Dawn / Shamila Mahmood / 8 June, 2018

The writer was legal counsel for the Pakistan government in the Kishenganga arbitration at the Permanent Court of Arbitration, The Hague.

THE failure to resolve issues concerning the Kishenganga Hydro Electric Plant became apparent when Indian Prime Minister Narendra Modi inaugurated KHEP on May 19, 2018, in India-held Kashmir. The move prompted Pakistani officials to rush to the World Bank headquarters in Washington to register their protest against India's completion of the project without resolving technical issues pertaining to restrictions on low-level orifice spillways and plant operations. The World Bank 'paused' the process for appointment of a chairman, court of arbitration, requested by Pakistan and a neutral expert requested by India in December 2016, ostensibly to "protect the [Indus Waters Treaty] in the interest of both countries" and to allow the parties an opportunity to resolve issues concerning the KHEP and the Ratle Hydro Electric Plant amicably. In the interim India, taking advantage of the gap in the process and the ensuing postponement in breaking the deadlock succeeded in completing the project without making changes in design, thus exacerbating the dispute.

The general misconception that the bank is guarantor of the treaty is erroneous as the bank has no treaty-related defined role except for the limited procedural function of appointing a neutral expert or for the bank president to appoint a chairman, court of arbitration in the event that the parties are unable to reach an agreement. The debacle presented by the parties in their differing choices regarding the mechanism for dispute settlement is difficult to comprehend in light of the fact that this very question was discussed and settled by the court of arbitration in the Kishenganga Partial Award. India's position on the applicable mechanism on issues raised by Pakistan has been circuitous. It has ranged from refusing to accept that the technical issues fall under the competence of a neutral expert at the Permanent Indus Commission level as, according to India, KHEP was consistent with the parameters defined by the treaty, to stating that the question of drawdown flushing (a technique to manage sedimentation) is non-admissible before a court of arbitration as it comes under the technical questions to be determined by a neutral expert. In its partial award, the court states, "having consistently maintained in the Commission that no difference between the parties existed, India cannot now assert that the second dispute is, in fact, a difference after all…"

India is obligated to design and operate its plants in a manner so as not to cause injury to Pakistan. The parties' adversarial relationship was taken into account when drafting the treaty, thus the preamble emphasises the need to make "provision for the settlement, in a cooperative spirit, of all such questions as may hereafter arise in regard to the interpretation or application of the provisions agreed upon herein". Towards this objective, the treaty provides a comprehensive framework for the resolution of disagreements, avoiding pathological clauses to ensure swiftness in process. Both dispute-settlement mechanisms are scrupulously discussed and the court finds no treaty bar for a court of arbitration to consider questions technical in nature. India's request for the appointment of a neutral expert at such a late stage when the process of establishing a court of arbitration is nearly concluded can be construed as an attempt to disable that process by placing a procedural hurdle.

More importantly Article IX(1) of the treaty unambiguously provides that a duly constituted court of arbitration can consider any question "concerning the interpretation or application of the treaty or the existence of any fact which, if established, might constitute a breach of this treaty". The World Bank may have been well meaning, but its conduct in this particular instance has certainly imperilled the process and the efficacy of the treaty. Moreover, there can be no justification or sagacity in maintaining the hiatus for almost 18 months without a commitment from India that it would stop work on the project until all issues were resolved. KHEP involves the diversion of the waters of the Kishenganga/Neelum river through a 23.24-kilometre tunnel into another tributary and eventually into the Jhelum river. Pakistan will receive this water when it crosses the Line of Control at Chakotthi although the timing and quantity of flows may be affected by this and other Indian projects along the Jhelum. However, the main victims of the diversion are the environment and people of the Neelum valley. The economic well-being and development of the people of the valley is dependent on the river that will now be unable to support sustainable economic development. Degradation of this natural resource will lead to widening inequality, undermine poverty alleviation and create conflict. From news reports it appears that there is similar apprehension and dissatisfaction on the other side of the LoC as 88 per cent of the power generated will go to the national grid.

Although not considered to be economically viable by Indian experts, KHEP is of strategic importance to India as it is an assertion by India over the territory and resources of Jammu and Kashmir. Whatever the motive and irrespective of how ethical and moral it may be India is obligated under international law to design and operate its plants in a manner so as not to damage or cause injury to Pakistan. Pakistan may be responsible for not taking timely action, but cannot be accused of overreacting as India's dams on the western rivers impound significantly large volumes of water. The overarching territorial dispute is intricately enmeshed in the bilateral relationship, obstructing comprehensive agreement on treaty issues, therefore, it becomes imperative for external stakeholders to make a genuine effort to steer the two countries towards cooperation. Never before has there been a greater need for both parties to demonstrate a firm commitment to the goals set out in the treaty's preamble. Extreme weather events and water shortages threaten livelihoods and the social and economic development of the peoples of the two countries. The forces of nature are now intervening to compel the two neighbours to consider peace as they will need to work together if they are to avert the catastrophe presented by climate change. The bank may well be perceived to be partisan; ranked seventh by voting power in World Bank institutions, India wields political influence in policy and decision-making with the US that ranks as number one. The bank must look beyond the personal associations of its staff, political alignments and its broader business interests to identify a solution to end the predicament lest it be remembered for this uncomfortable legacy.

APP – 48

TARBELA, MANGLA DAMS FACE 45PC WATER STORING DEFICIT

The News / Khalid Mustafa / 4 August, 2018

Pakistan alarmingly, so far, braves 45 per cent deficit in the water stored in both the Tarbela and Mangla dams as the said reservoirs currently have 6.3 million acres feet (MAF) in them as against 11.7MAF water deposited in the same period last year.

Though water level in Tarbela and Mangla dams has slightly improved, but still the critical situation is not averted, top sources in Water Ministry told The News arguing : "We are expecting another monsoon starting from coming Sunday which may help improve the water situation in the country and but again it depends upon the intensity of the next spell."

Last year monsoon ended by August 15 and if the current situation continues to hover, they said, then Punjab and Sindh will have to face 50-60 per cent water shortage during the Rabi season as the available water in the dams will be consumed for maturity of Khraif crops.

Under the scenario when the country has appalling water situation, water losses have surged up to 10.4MAF against the estimated loss of 08MAF. The officials disclosed that provinces--Punjab and Sindh--have reported the water loss of 10.4MAF which is more than the live storage capacity of Diamer-Bhasha and Mohmand dams.

In Pakistan Rivers, normal flows in these days usually stand at 70.3 MAF, but this time by July 31, flows in rivers stood at 52.7MAF showing the massive dip in flows by 25 per cent. The official said the ever minimum flows in rivers are registered at 50.5 MAF which is close to the 52.7 MAF flows recorded on July 31, 2018.

To a question, they said that average water level in Tarbela dam stands at 1519 feet and the same level the reservoirs currently has. However, Mangla has 1,150 feet water level against its average level of 1,207 feet.

This means that Punjab will sustain the huge hit as in Chenab-Jhelum zone, 13 million acre feet of water will not be available for the province which is the food basket of the whole country. "For Rabi season (winter season), they argued, there will be mammoth shortage of water for Punjab province.

When asked if the authorities will be able to have some carryover in dams for Rabi season, they said it depends upon the next spell of monsoon.

APP - 49

MINISTER SUSPECTS FOREIGN INVOLVEMENT IN OPPOSITION TO KALABAGH DAM

Dawn / Khaleeq Kiani / 7 August, 2018

Caretaker Minister for Water Resources Ali Zafar suspects foreign involvement in the opposition to the construction of the Kalabagh Dam (KBD) and has asked the incoming government to work on building a consensus on it. Speaking at a news conference, the minister said India was watching Pakistan's inaction over the construction of the KBD — as well as other dams — and was violating river rights. He said the anti-KBD conferences arranged abroad were better organized and seemed far better funded than the seminars held in Pakistan.

He said India constructed the Kishanganga Hydropower Project in violation of the 1960 Indus Water Treaty (IWT) and then even went on to alter the project design after sharing it with Pakistan. The minister said that New Delhi was also planning to begin working on the Ratle Hydropower project as well as other dams, violating the treaty. Zafar says following Indus Waters Treaty, India built 400 dams while Pakistan could not make KBD. He said he had studied the Ratle Hydropower Project and Pakistan's case against its construction was strong. Pakistan wanted the World Bank to constitute an arbitration court on the issue and it would be an important challenge for the incoming government to compel the WB to fulfil its responsibility. In response to a question, the minister said the reversal of the IWT was neither possible nor in the interest of Pakistan but good news is that China, Turkey, Russia and many other nations understand Pakistan's case against India and the World Bank would have to constitute a court of arbitration. Mr Zafar said that following the IWT, India had managed to build about 400 dams and reservoirs on the eastern rivers — Sutlej, Bias and Ravi — while Pakistan had not even managed to build the KBD. Even the 15.1 million acre feet (MAF) storage from Tarbela and Mangla dams dropped to 13MAF. He said it was strange that the KBD, which was part of the 1960 plan, had not been built so far due to lack of consensus among the provinces and disagreements that kept on increasing over the time. But it is bizarre and extremely unfortunate that we haven't even been able to construct other such reservoirs and dams.

"It (KBD) is very important. It is life — and it should be built as a priority," the caretaker minister said, adding Pakistan had been declared a 'water scarce country' because its per capita water availability had dropped to 1,000 cubic metres. He said the caretaker government had considered advice from international experts, and after discussions with various domestic departments, finalised a 10-point reform package for Pakistan's water priorities. He said lining of the canals could save up to 6.5MAF — that is almost equal to any of the two existing dams, and that is much cheaper than building one. Mr Zafar deplored that Pakistan was still employing 200-year-old agriculture techniques including mechanisms to manage flooding. The minister said it was ironic that nations were irrigating their deserts with modern techniques, while Pakistan was wasting even clean drinking water. He said that the top priority for the new government for the water sector reforms should be the construction of the Kalabagh, Diamer-Bhasha and Mohmand dams. He said that efforts must be made to resolve critical issues such as compensation, resettlement and the demarcation of the power house of the Diamer-Basha dam.

APP – 50

INDIA, PAKISTAN TO RESUME TALKS ON INDUS WATERS TREATY IN LAHORE ON WEDNESDAY

The Hindu / Press Trust of India / 27 August, 2018

Pakistan is to raise concerns over 1000MW Pakal Dul and 48MW Lower Kalnai hydroelectric projects on the Chenab river. India and Pakistan will resume their talks on various aspects of the Indus Waters Treaty in Lahore on Wednesday, the first bilateral engagement since Prime Minister Imran Khan took office.India's Indus Water Commissioner P.K. Saxena is expected to reach here on Monday to begin the two-day discussions with his Pakistani counterpart Syed Mehr Ali Shah on Wednesday, *Dawn* quoted a government official as saying. The last meeting of the Pakistan-India Permanent Indus Commission was held in New Delhi in March during which both the sides had shared details of the water flow and the quantum of water being used under the 1960 Indus Waters Treaty.

Water-sharing concerns

The Pakistani side will reiterate its objections over two water storage and hydropower projects being built by India, during the two-day talks scheduled for August 29-30. The official said Pakistan would raise its concerns over 1000MW Pakal Dul and 48MW Lower Kalnai hydroelectric projects on the Chenab river. The official said that the two sides would also finalise the schedule of future meetings of the Permanent Indus Commission and visits of the teams of the Indus commissioners. He said that the water commissioners of Pakistan and India were required to meet twice a year and arrange technical visits to projects' sites and critical river head works, but Pakistan had been facing a lot of problems in timely meetings and visits. The two-day session is also expected to discuss ways and means for timely and smooth sharing of hydrological data on shared rivers.

First official engagement for Imran Khan

The talks will be the first official engagement between India and Pakistan since Mr. Khan became prime minister on August 18.In a letter to Mr. Khan on the day he was sworn in as Pakistan's 22nd prime minister, Prime Minister Narendra Modi expressed India's resolve to build good neighbourly relations between the two countries. On July 30, Mr. Modi telephoned Mr. Khan to congratulate him on his Pakistan Tehreek-e-Insaaf party's victory in the general elections and expressed hope that both countries will work to open a new chapter in bilateral ties. The 1960 Indus Waters Treaty, brokered by the World Bank and signed by then prime minister Jawaharlal Nehru and Pakistan's president Ayub Khan, administers how the water of the Indus river and its tributaries that flow in both the countries will be utilised. Under the provisions of the Indus Waters Treaty 1960, waters of the eastern rivers — Sutlej, Beas and Ravi — had been allocated to India and the western rivers — the Indus, Jhelum and Chenab — to Pakistan, except for certain non-consumptive uses for India.

APP - 51

INDIAN DELEGATION TO ARRIVE ON AUG 28 FOR WATER TALKS

The Express Tribune / Asif Mehmood / 27 August, 2018

An Indian delegation will arrive in Pakistan on August 28 to discuss the construction of two Indian power projects under the ambit of the Indus Water Treaty.

The nine-member delegation will be led by Indian Commissioner PK Saxena and caretaker commissioner Syed Mehar Ali Shah and his delegation will represent Pakistan.

The two-day moot will focus on Indian hydropower projects at Lower Kalnai and Pakal Dul which will have installed capacity of 48 and 1,000 megawatts respectively. As a result of these projects, India will be able to control 108,000 acre-feet of water from river Chenab.

The earlier venue for the two-day huddle was Lahore, which was later changed to Islamabad by the water and power minister.

In 2012, Pakistan objected over Pakal Dul's design for violating the Sindh Taas Agreement. On the occasion, Pakistani officials demanded that the freeboard height should be reduced from seven-feet to two-feet and that the installation of the seal way gates should be done with an additional 40 metres in order to bring it to 1620 metres and align it with sea level.

Despite Pakistan repeatedly dissenting the storage of water in the dam and the provision of data in regards to its operation, Indian Prime Minister Narendra Modi inaugurated the projects in May.

Following this development, a statement issued by the Foreign Office said that despite several rounds of bilateral negotiations as well as mediation under the auspices of the World Bank, India continued with the construction of the project.

Both the projects constitute a violation of the Indus Water Treaty 1960. The treaty allotted the waters of three eastern rivers namely Ravi, Beas and Sutlej exclusively to India while that of Western rivers namely Indus, Chenab and Jhelum to Pakistan. However, India has some rights on Western rivers which include unrestricted rights to develop hydroelectric power within the specified parameters of the design.

Permanent Indus Commission, formed under the treaty signed between India and Pakistan in 1960 comprises of Indus commissioners for both the countries. The treaty provides for both the commissioners to meet at least once every year, alternately in India and Pakistan.

APP – 52

9-MEMBER INDIAN DELEGATION REACHES LAHORE FOR TWO-DAY WATER TALKS WITH PAKISTAN

Dawn / Ali Waqar / 28 August, 2018

A nine-member Indian delegation arrived in Lahore on Tuesday for two-day Pakistan-India Permanent Indus Commission talks scheduled for August 29-30. Led by Indian Water Commissioner P K Saxena, the delegation reached the provincial capital through Wagah border for the talks starting tomorrow. Pakistan Water Commissioner Syed Mehr Ali Shah, who welcomed the Indian delegation at the border, will lead his side during the discussions that will take place at the Lahore headquarters of the National Engineering Services of Pakistan (Nespak).

During the two-day talks, Pakistan will reiterate its serious objections over two controversial water storage and hydropower projects being built by India, _Dawn reported on Monday_. A government official said Pakistan will raise its concerns over the construction of 1000MW Pakal Dul and 48MW Lower Kalnai hydroelectric projects on River Chenab despite Islamabad's serious objections over their designs. Pakistan has been raising reservations over the designs of the two projects and would like India to either modify the designs to make them compliant to the 1960 Indus Waters Treaty or put the projects on hold until Delhi satisfies Islamabad. The two sides will also finalise the schedule of future meetings of the Permanent Indus Commission and visits of the teams of the Indus commissioners. The water commissioners of Pakistan and India are required to meet twice a year and arrange technical visits to projects' sites and critical river head works, but Pakistan has been facing a lot of problems in timely meetings and visits, the official told _Dawn_. The two-day session is also expected to discuss ways and means for timely and smooth sharing of hydrological data on shared rivers.

Pakistan's concerns

Both projects — Pakal Dul and Lower Kalnai — are on two different tributaries of Chenab river. India had promised in March last year to modify the designs of the two projects and address Pakistan's concerns but in vain. Instead, Prime Minister Narendra Modi laid the foundation stone of 1000MW Pakal Dul project in May this year to kickstart the project, without addressing Islamabad's reservations. According to Indian media reports, the project's completion is targeted within 66 months with a commitment to provide 12 per cent free of cost electricity to India-held Jammu and Kashmir. A former water sector official said it was typical Indian style to build projects in violation of the 1960 treaty as was evident from all previous controversial projects like Baglihar and Kishanganga. During execution of these projects, New Delhi engaged Islamabad in technicalities, but kept civil and side works moving for years until reaching the fait accompli stage, when challenged at international forums. Pakistan has objections to the pondage and freeboard of Lower Kalnai and pondage, filling criteria and spillway of Pakal Dul hydropower projects on Marusadar River — a right bank tributary of the Chenab. Pakal Dul is a storage-cum-power project and can have gross storage of about 108,000 acre feet of water. The project design envisages its filling every monsoon season between mid-June and end-August.

Pakistan is of the opinion that the tunnel spillway of Pakal Dul should be raised closer to the dead storage level because its placement 40 metres below the dead storage level could allow drawdown flushing not permitted to India under the 1960 water treaty. Pakal Dul dam-cum-hydropower project is three times larger than Kishanganga Hydroelectric Project that Pakistan believes has been built in violation of the treaty. Islamabad is seeking international arbitration <u>without success</u> at the level of intransigent World Bank administration. On the 48MW Lower Kalnai project, Pakistan has raised objections to its freeboard, pondage and intake and is of the view that the depth of bridge girder and provision of freeboard should be close to one metre and considers two-metre freeboard as 'excessive'.

Pakistan has also challenged the discharge series of River Lower Kalnai at Dunadi for winter months and estimated permissible pondage of 0.38 cubic megametres compared to Indian design pondage of 2.74 cubic megametres. The Lower Kalnai project is on a left bank tributary of Chenab and can have gross storage of about 1,508 acre feet of water. Under the provisions of the Indus Waters Treaty 1960, waters of the eastern rivers — Sutlej, Beas and Ravi — had been allocated to India and the western rivers — the Indus, Jhelum and Chenab — to Pakistan, except for certain non-consumptive uses for India.

APP – 53

INDUS WATER TREATY PROVIDED FRAMEWORK FOR RESOLVING DISPUTES ON WATER USE: UN

The New Indian Express / Press Trust of India / 28 August, 2018

UN Deputy Secretary-General Amina Mohammed, addressing the High-Level Panel on Water Diplomacy in Stockholm yesterday, said that water can represent a source of cooperation, shared growth.

UNITED NATIONS: The 1960 Indus Water Treaty between India and Pakistan has survived disputes between the two countries and provided a framework for resolving disagreements over water use, a top UN official has said. UN Deputy Secretary-General Amina Mohammed, addressing the High-Level Panel on Water Diplomacy in Stockholm yesterday, said that water can represent a source of cooperation, shared growth and mutual support.

She, however, warned that getting caught up in 'water-war' rhetoric will be a mistake for the international community. "When we examine history, we see that cooperation over water can prevail over conflict over water. Through water diplomacy, sometimes known as 'hydrodiplomacy', neighbouring states can be reminded of the benefits of cooperating around water resources," she said, adding that water, if fairly shared, can become a confidence-building measure. Such confidence-building measures are urgently needed in many of the current conflict areas, Mohammed said. The 1960 Indus Water Treaty between India and Pakistan has survived disputes between the two countries, providing a framework for resolving disagreements over water use. "In the Middle East, water use has been an area where cooperation has been possible between some countries. In Central Asia, the United Nations is collaborating closely with the International Fund for Saving the Aral Sea," she said. Mohammed said that by 2050, the world population is projected to rise to 9 billion, who will be sharing a finite resource water. "One-third of the world's population already lives in countries with water stress. As the impacts of climate change grow, so too will the prospects of further stress," she said. She stressed that water security encapsulates complex and interconnected challenges and highlights water's centrality for achieving a larger sense of security, sustainability, development and human well-being. Many factors contribute to water security, ranging from biophysical to infrastructural, institutional, political, social and financial many of which lie outside the water realm, the UN official added. India and Pakistan, nuclear-armed arch rivals in south Asia, signed the Indus Waters Treaty in 1960 after nine years of negotiations, with the World Bank also being a signatory. The Treaty sets out a mechanism for cooperation and information exchange between the two countries regarding their use of the rivers. However, there have been disagreements and differences between India and Pakistan over the treaty.

While the World Bank has said India is allowed to construct hydroelectric power facilities on tributaries of the Jhelum and Chenab rivers with certain restrictions under the 1960 Indus Waters Treaty, Pakistan opposes the construction of the Kishanganga (330 megawatts) and Ratle (850 megawatts) hydroelectric power plants being built by India.

APP – 54

INDIAN DELEGATION DISCUSSING INDUS WATER TREATY TO ARRIVE IN LAHORE TODAY

The News / 8 June, 2018

In first interaction with the new government, India has sent a delegation to hold talks on the Pakal Dul and lower Kalnai projects, which will arrive in Lahore today (Tuesday).

The nine-member delegation, headed by Indian Water Commissioner Pradeep Kumar Saxena, will arrive via Wagah border. The dialogues will discuss Indus Waters Treaty and other issues over the course of two days. The Pakistani delegation will be headed by Pakistani Commissioner for Indus Waters Syed Meher Ali Shah. Pakistan believes India's construction of dams on western rivers with an intention of increasing its holding capacity at a time when there is chronic water scarcity in the country has breached the treaty.

As per earlier reports, the delegation was to visit Pakistan in July but could not because of elections in the country. Officials confirmed that India wanted to place spillway of 1,000 megawatts of Pakal Dul Dam on Chenab River in Indian Kashmir, about 15 meters down against the permissible limit, which will give the country undue leverage of holding 11,000 acres of feet water in addition to allowed volume of water storage.

APP – 55

PAK-INDIA WATER TALKS COMMENCE IN ISLAMABAD

The Express Tribune / Asif Mehmood / 29 August, 2018

Talks between Pakistan and India commenced on Wednesday to discuss the pressing issue of water distribution and construction of two dams on the Indian side of river Chenab under the ambit of the Indus Water Treaty of 1960. The first round of the two-day moot is being held at National Engineering Services Pakistan (NESPAK). The Indian delegation is led by Commissioner PK Saxena whereas interim commissioner Syed Mehar Ali Shah and his delegation are representing Pakistan. Authorities from both countries shall raise their concerns on the matter.

The focus of the discussions will include Indian hydropower projects at Lower Kalnai and Pakal Dul which will have installed capacity of 48 and 1,000 megawatts respectively. As a result of these projects, India will be able to control 108,000 acre-feet of water from river Chenab. Both the projects constitute a violation of the Indus Water Treaty 1960. The treaty allotted the waters of three eastern rivers namely Ravi, Beas and Sutlej exclusively to India while that of Western rivers namely Indus, Chenab and Jhelum to Pakistan. However, India has some rights on Western rivers which include unrestricted rights to develop hydroelectric power within the specified parameters of the design. The earlier venue for the two-day huddle was Lahore, which was later changed to Islamabad by the water and power minister.

APP - 56

INDO-PAK TALKS ON INDUS WATERS TREATY COMMENCE, JOINT NOTIFICATION LIKELY

Hindustan Times / Press Trust of India / 30 August, 2018

India and Pakistan commenced crucial talks on Wednesday on various aspects of the Indus Waters Treaty here, the first bilateral engagement since Pakistan Prime Minister Imran Khan took office. The first round of the two-day meeting is being held at the National Engineering Services, Pakistan. The water commissioners of Pakistan and India are required to meet twice a year and arrange technical visits to project sites and critical river head works, but Pakistan had been facing a lot of problems in timely meetings and visits, a source said. The Indian side is being represented by a delegation of the Indian Water Commission led by Commissioner PK Saxena whereas Pakistan Commissioner for Indus Waters Syed Meher Ali Shah and his delegation are representing Pakistan, it said. Both the countries are expected to present their reports during the talks. After the meeting, a joint notification would be issued. On Tuesday, Shah and additional commissioner Sheraz Jamil received the nine-member Indian delegation led by Saxena on its arrival here via Wagah border. The talks will be the first official engagement between India and Pakistan since Khan became prime minister on August 18. The last meeting of the Pakistan-India Permanent Indus Commission was held in New Delhi in March during which both the sides had shared details of the water flow and the quantum of water being used under the 1960 Indus Waters Treaty. India and Pakistan signed the treaty in 1960 after nine years of negotiations, with the World Bank being a signatory. The treaty sets out a mechanism for cooperation and information exchange between the two countries regarding their use of the rivers. However, there have been disagreements and differences between India and Pakistan over the treaty. Shah on Tuesday said Pakistan has raised objections on 1000MW Pakal Dul and 48MW Lower Kalnai hydroelectric projects on River Chenab and a detailed discussion will be held during the talks. "We had also raised concerns over construction of dams on Pakistani rivers and India did not bother about it and continued doing the same," Shah said, adding India will reply to Pakistan's queries on controversial water projects. Former Pakistan Indus Water Commissioner Syed Jamaat Ali Shah told PTI that the successive Pakistani governments had given much importance to its water disputes with India. "India does not bother Pakistan in this regard. It begins work on building hydro power projects on the Pakistani rivers and the Pakistani government raises objections afterwards. Unless the Pakistani government seriously takes up these matters with India it will not get relief," he said and added that Pakistan also needs to plead its case in the World Bank. According to an official of the Pakistan Water Commission, Pakistan has been raising reservations over the designs of the two projects —1000MW Pakal Dul and 48MW Lower Kalnai hydroelectric projects on River Chenab — and would like India to either modify the designs to make them compliant to 1960 Indus Waters Treaty or put the projects on hold until Delhi satisfies Islamabad. "The two sides will in talks also finalise the schedule of future meetings of the Permanent Indus Commission and visits of the teams of the Indus commissioners," the official said. Pakistan has also challenged the discharge series of River Lower Kalnai at Dunadi for winter months and estimated permissible pondage of 0.38 cubic megametres compared to Indian design pondage of 2.74 cubic megametres. The Lower Kalnai project is on a left bank tributary of Chenab and can have gross storage of about 1,508 acre feet of water.

APP – 57

PAKISTANI EXPERTS TO INSPECT TWO INDIAN HYDROPOWER PROJECT SITES

Dawn / Khalid Hasnain / 31 August, 2018

India agreed on Thursday to get sites of its two hydropower projects — 1,000MW Pakal Dul and 48MW Lower Kalnal — inspected by Pakistani experts by the end of next month. It also assured Pakistan of taking up its objections/concerns over the two projects seriously by resolving them amicably in the light of technical memorandums to be prepared and exchanged by the two countries in the next meeting to be held in New Delhi. "The major breakthrough of the two-day talks held in Lahore is that India has agreed to get the projects' sites visited by our experts. Therefore, our team comprising experts will visit the sites in India by the end of next month," Water Resource Secretary Shamail Ahmad Khawaja told Dawn. "During the visit, our experts will minutely examine the sites, construction in the light of the provisions of Indus Water Treaty (IWT) and the objections raised by Pakistan to the aforementioned projects being executed by India over the Chenab River," he added. Both delegations headed by Pakistani and Indian commissioners for Indus waters resumed talks on day two, reiterating their stance over construction of the projects. The Indian side led by Pradeep Kumar Saxena reviewed Pakistan's objections minutely. It also presented its point of view amid justification in response to the objections. Agreement reached in two-day water talks held in Lahore.

The Pakistani side led by Commissioner for Indus Water Syed Mohammad Mehr Ali Shah continued defending its stance, requesting the Indian delegation to address the issues as sought. However, it was mutually decided that both countries would separately prepare technical memorandums based on their point of view and possible solutions. "We think that we have succeeded in convincing India to address our issues since we don't want to see any disruption in the flows of our rivers by anyone under the IWT. "That is why they (Indians) have seriously reviewed our objections once again. And finally during the second round of the two-day talks, which concluded in Lahore on Thursday, it has been decided that both the countries would prepare technical memorandums separately on the issue and exchange the same with each other during the next meeting to be held within next three to four months," Mr Khawaja, who is supposed to oversee the country's water-related issues and projects, including the IWT, explained.

He claimed that the next round of the talks — which would be held in India between the two countries — would be the final and conclusive in connection with discussions over Pakistan's concerns. "Resumption of talks between Pakistan and India — which have been suspended since 2014 — in March and August indicates some positive things. We hope that India would surely respect the IWT by considering our objections through an amicable solution in the next meeting," he believed. According to an official privy to the meeting, the two countries stick to their stances on the issue. Both the countries reiterated their stance in the meeting. However, the Indian delegation finally responded to Pakistan's demand for looking into this issue in the next meeting, he told Dawn. The official said the Joint Commissioner for Indus Waters also raised objections over heading the Pakistani side by Commissioner Mehr Ali Shah on the very first day before commencement of the talks. "Actually Joint Commissioner Sheraz Jameel Memon was of the view that he should lead the Pakistan side while conducting the meeting with the Indian delegation since Mr Shah was heading the department on additional charge for a period of three months. But when Mr Memon reached there to head the Pakistani team, he came to know that Mr Shah succeeded in getting extension in his additional charge of office. So he returned to office," the official explained.

He said Pakistan's demands included reduction of the height of Pakal Dul's reservoir up to five metres, maintenance of 40-metre height above sea level while making spillways' gates of the Pakal Dul project, besides clarifying the pattern and mechanism for the water storage and releases and some technical concerns over design of the Lower Kalnal hydropower project. Earlier, both the Pakistani and Indian sides avoided the media gathered since morning outside the head office of Nespak in Lahore. Though the media tried to convince the staff for access to the talks, the officials didn't agree. "We inform you all that we would neither brief you nor issue a joint statement regarding the talks," an official told journalists. At this, the media persons protested over the officials' attitude, asking the authorities to reveal the outcome of the talks to the nation. On the other hand, former commissioner for Indus water Syed Jamat Ali Shah expressed reservations over the behavior of Pakistani and Indian sides. "They should have briefed the media since there is no secret. Our nation must know the facts," he said.

APP – 58

INDIA AGREES TO ALLOW PAKISTAN TO INSPECT KISHANGANGA PROJECT

Dawn / Khalid Hasnain / 4 September, 2018

India has agreed to allow Pakistan to inspect the projects in the Jhelum basin, including Kishanganga hydroelectric project, in the near future and Islamabad will allow New Delhi to carry out inspection of the Kotri barrage over the Indus under Article VIII (4) (c) of the Indus Waters Treaty (IWT), it has been learnt.

According to the minutes of the 115th meeting of the Permanent Indus Commission held between the two countries from Aug 29 to 30 in Lahore, "Pakistan also urged India to arrange for the Special Tour of Inspection of the projects in Jhelum basin including Kishanganga HEP which is pending since 2014, on which ICIW (India's Commissioner for Indus Waters) gave his assurance to arrange the same promptly."

During the meeting, the Pakistani and Indian authorities were unanimous about strengthening the role of the Permanent Indus Commission. Islamabad also highlighted the need and asked New Delhi to share the information about potential projects at the planning stage for examination. "In this way any objections (if raised by Pakistan) can be addressed in the design at the early stage of planning instead of debating with India at belated stage when practically incorporating the requisite changes becomes a challenge."

Decision also reached in recent water talks to let Indian team visit Kotri barrage on Indus

In order to converge on the objections raised by Pakistan, both sides reiterated their stance and endeavoured to resolve the issues. In this regard both sides agreed to exchange the detailed basis of adopting various design parameters for both 48MW Lower Kalnai and 1000MW Pakal Dul HEPs at the Chenab River. "During the meeting both the sides agreed to conduct the General Tours of Inspection which could not be conducted since 2014.

"In this regard first PCIW (Pakistani Commissioner for Indus Waters) will visit the Chenab basin in the last week of September 2018 followed by the tour of ICIW to the Kotri barrage in the Lower Indus, according to Article VIII (4) (c)," the document reveals.

In the meeting, which was held under Article VIII (5) of the IWT, both sides also agreed to arrange the next meeting of the commission soon after the tour of inspection on both sides to discuss and endeavour to address Pakistan's objections on Lower Kalnai and Pakal Dul.

Pakistan has already approached the World Bank and sought referring the case to International Court of Arbitration (ICA). However, India, on the other hand, wants the dispute decided by the neutral experts. In June, this year, World Bank had reportedly asked Pakistan to accept India's demand of a 'neutral expert' and stand down from pursuing its stand of referring the dispute to the ICA. Pakistan had also raised concerns over the inauguration of the Kishanganga hydropower plant by India during talks with the World Bank in Washington.

"Since the talks between the two countries have been restored, Pakistani team may inspect the Kishanganga project on the eve of the next meeting of the permanent commission for the Indus waters in India or before this," a senior official told Dawn on Monday.

In reply to a question, he said India had no objection on the Kotri barrage in the lower Indus. "Their (Indian experts) visit to Pakistan will be after ending our experts' inspection of the Lower Kalnai and Pakal Dul projects scheduled by end of this month," the official said. "The Indian experts' visit / inspection of the Kotri barrage is sort of routine one, as they have no objection or concerns in this regard. It is a part of the compilation and exchange of the data by the two countries related to rivers' flow, water storage, releases, etc," he added.

APP – 59

PAKISTAN ASKS INDIA TO SHARE KISHANGANGA WATER DATA

Dawn / Khalid Hasnain / 5 October, 2018

Pakistan has asked India to immediately share the data showing inflow and discharge of water at the Kishanganga dam and water flows in different rivers.

It has also sought dates for inspection of the 330MW hydroelectric project that India had agreed to during a two-day meeting held in August in Lahore between Indus water commissioners of the two countries.

"We recently asked Indian authorities for Indus waters in writing to give us dates for inspection of the Kishanganga dam as soon as possible. Through the letter, we have also pressed Indian authorities to immediately share the data concerning flows of water at the river and releases/discharges, in/outflows at the dam with us under the relevant provisions of the Indus Water Treaty," Pakistan's Commissioner for Indus Waters Syed Muhammad Mehr Ali Shah told Dawn on Thursday.

Dates for inspection of 330MW power project also sought

"We are receiving water at Jhelum basin in our territory, but to ascertain our need or requirement we need data India is obligated to share with us time to time," he said.

During the 115th meeting of the Permanent Commission for Indus Waters, India had agreed to allow Pakistan to inspect the projects built on the Jhelum basin, including Kishanganga hydroelectric project, in the near future.

Similarly, Islamabad had agreed to allow New Delhi to carry out inspection of the Kotri barrage over the Indus under Article VIII (4) (c) of the Indus Waters Treaty (IWT). Besides Kishanganga, India had also agreed to let Pakistani experts inspect sites of two hydropower projects — 1,000MW Pakal Dul and 48MW Lower Kalnal at Chenab basin — by the end of September.

However, Indian authorities later confirmed on Oct 7 to 11 for tour/inspection of the projects by a three-member Pakistani team, headed by the Indus water commissioner. But finally it postponed the inspection on the pretext of local elections in held Kashmir.

Mr Shah said that Pakistani authorities wanted to have a detailed tour of the Kishanganga project since Pakistan had already raised various objections on its design and construction.

Pakistan has already approached the World Bank, demanding constitution of a seven-member court of arbitration to address its concerns. On the other hand, India wants a neutral expert over the issue.

However in June this year, the World Bank reportedly requested Pakistan to stand down from pursuing its stand of referring to the Kishanganga dam dispute to the court of arbitration and instead accept India's offer of appointing a neutral expert, but Pakistan didn't do so and stuck to its stance to date.

"Our stance is still the same as it was before. Under the treaty, it is our right to select the way that suits us. And that is the court of arbitration. Similarly, the World Bank, under the treaty, could not proceed further until willingness of both the parties at a mutually agreed stance. Recently, the WB president reportedly assured our foreign minister to make another effort to address Pakistan's concerns on the project," the commissioner explained.

In reply to a question about the fate or status of Pakistan's objections since the project has already been completed by India, Mr Shah said that it did not matter.

"Technically, Pakistan's objection can be addressed even now, as our concerns are related to design and legally, under the IWT, if any project facing objections by either party could not be recognised," he maintained.

Under the treaty, he said, if the decision came after completion of any project facing objections raised by either party, the relevant portions of such schemes would be demolished.

"Under the same provisions, the neutral expert had got demolished the upper side of the Baglihar dam in India," Mr Shah said.

He said that Pakistan had also written a letter to Indian authorities to give dates for inspection of Pakal Dul and Lower Kalnal projects at Chenab basin.

APP - 60

WB MAY BE APPROACHED OVER INDIAN HYDEL PROJECTS

Dawn / Khalid Hasnain / 8 December, 2018

Pakistan may approach the World Bank under Article 9 of the Indus Water Treaty (IWT) to press India to fulfil commitment it had made in August of getting its two hydropower projects — 1,000MW Pakal Dul and 48MW Lower Kalnal — inspected by Pakistani experts.

"We still hope that India will fulfil its commitment it had made with us during a high-level two-day meeting of the Permanent Commission for Indus Waters (PCIW) held in Lahore during last week of August. However, we (in case of complete refusal by India) may invoke the IWT's Article 9 that empowers the two countries to approach the WB for the appointment of neutral expert or constitution of a court of arbitration for resolving any issue if it proves to be the breach of treaty," Pakistan's Commissioner for IWT Mehr Ali Shah told Dawn on Friday.

During the PCIW's 115th meeting held between the two countries from Aug 29 to 30 in Lahore, India had agreed to allow Pakistani experts to inspect the projects at Chenab basin by the end of September. It had also promised to schedule visit of Pakistani experts for inspection of the Kishanganga project at Jhelum basin at a later stage. Similarly, Islamabad, too, had agreed to allow New Delhi to carry out inspection of Kotri Barrage over the Indus after September. As a result, India had finally scheduled inspection of the projects at Chenab basin by Pakistani experts from Oct 7 to 11. But later, it postponed the same on the pretext of local bodies' elections in the respective areas.

During the last week of October, the Pakistan's Indus water commissioner telephoned his counterpart Pradeep Kumar Saxena and urged him to give a schedule for the tour of experts. However, Mr Saxena said it wouldn't be possible during first or second week of December due to local Punchayat elections in the state where these projects are located.

"We will once again contact the Indian commission for Indus waters through hotline on Monday or Tuesday, urging it to fulfil the commitment as soon as possible. And we will continue requesting it to do so," Mr Shah said. "And if the commission finally refuses, we will have no option but to invoke the treaty's Article 9. We have already told them that the treaty empowers us to approach the WB in case any issue remains unresolved at the commission level."

Pakistan had written the last letter (third reminder) on Nov 24 to India and sought scheduling of the inspection soon after conclusion of the Punchayat elections. However, India is yet to reply.

"As the Punchayat elections would probably end on Dec 11, we still hope that they would schedule our visit during third or last week of this month. We also hope that India wouldn't force us to invoke Article 9," Mr Shah said.

APP – 61

POST-SCRIPT

As this book was entering the final phase of its preparation in 2017-18, three books saw the day light and their thereby stole march on the exasperated editors and the patient publisher of this compilation of most valuable contributions made by the World Bank experts and eminent scholars of three counties- India, Pakistan and the U.S. These three books are as follows.

1. The Indus Water Treaty (Issues and Options) compiled by Dr. Nadeem Shafiq Malik, Fiction House, Lahore; 2017

2. Indus Divided (India, Pakistan and the River Basin Dispute. By Daniel Haines, Penguin/Viking (London)

3. Indus Water Treaty (Political and Legal Dimensions) by Dr. Ijaz Hussain. Oxford University press (Karachi) 2017.

On page 6 of this commendable and readable book Dr. Hussain says; " There are in total only seven full fledged studies which have been undertake so far."

The first one is The Indus River: A study of the effects of partition by A.A Michel(1967)

The second study is by N.D Gulirot. Indus Water Treaty; An exercise in International Mediation

The third study is entitled Water Rationality: Mediating the Indus Water Treaty by Uzala Lam (Doctoral dissertation, Department of Geography, University of Durham, 1998.)

The Fourth study is entitled "The Indus Water Treaty in Retrospect by Bashir Malik (2005)

The fifth study is entitled "The Indus Water Treaty "by R.K Arora (2007).

The sixth study is in Urdu- How did we lose three rivers by R.A Malik (Malik,2008)

The seventh study is; Indus Water and social Change by S.A Naqvi

APP - 62

INTRODUCTION TO THE EDITORS AND PAKISTAN ACADEMY OF LAW AND SOCIAL SCIENCES

Naseem Ahmed Bajwa (Editor)

Born 15 December, 1936 in Hamirpur (Punjab in British India and now Hamachal Pradesh); M.A in Political Science (Punjab University, 1960); Undergraduate student of law in London (1975-80); LLM from University of Nottingham (1992); Called to the Bar of England and Wales as a member of Gray's Inn (2012); Broadcaster with the BBC (1970-74); Taught Social Sciences at Aitchison College Lahore (1964) Lahore and at various colleges in England (1967-78); Publisher/Editor of People's Voice since 2010; Secretary, Movement for Radical Reforms and People's Participation in Pakistan since 1982 (Lord Eric Avebury was the President until he passed away in February 2016); Director, Pakistan Academy of Law and Social Sciences; President, British Pakistani Lawyers Forum since 2004; Visiting lecturer in various Colleges and Universities in Asia and Africa; Writes weekly column for Daily Dunya (Pakistan); Drove an old van (carrying wife and six young children and plenty of rations) from Manchester in north of England to Lahore in Pakistan and back (1974-75); Has practised law in England and Pakistan since 1992; Married to Yasmeen (Taught Economics in colleges in Pakistan and England for 10 years and obtained another M.A. from the University of Bradford) since 1962; Father of six children and grandfather of six; Still plays cricket and plans to do so for more years, hopefully, one day, as a member of Peter Osborne's team touring Chitral in the Himalayas.

naseemahmadbajwa@gmail.com

Uzair Ashraf (Assistant Editor)

Born in Ireland on 26th November, 1988, of Pakistani parents; father is a medical consultant; grandfather (maternal) was a college lecturer; he obtained the degree of LL.B from a London University in 2012; worked in a London-based firm of solicitors for three years; awarded LL.M (International Trade Law and Policy) by University of Barcelona (Spain) practising as a legal consultant in International Trade Law in Lahore (Pakistan).

Maryum Amir (Assistant Editor)

Born in Islamabad Pakistan on 26 August, 1983; obtained Bachelor's Degree in telecommunications engineering (improbable for a female in Pakistan) from Hamdard University (Islamabad) in 2002; pursued academic studies in the UK in 2007 and was awarded MBA (Strategic Management) by the University of Wales, Cardiff, in 2011; working in administrative/managerial positions in England for the last 8 years.

This is the fourth book sponsored by Pakistan Academy of Law and Social Sciences (P.A.L.S.S.)

Open invitation to all to join as an active member to undertake research, translation of articles/books into Urdu, to participate in academic seminars, to be engaged in giving free lectures in universities in Pakistan (plus India and Bangladesh) and to make contribution towards a better understanding of Law and Social Sciences in the three neighbouring countries of South Asia and to promote intellectual friendship between their intelligentsia.

<u>London Office</u>

Oakfield
36 Southend Crescent
London
SE9 2SB
Tel: +44 (0)7867 786562
Email: naseemahmadbajwa@gmail.com

Year of publication: 2020

Other titles edited by Naseem Ahmed Bajwa

Indian Independence and British Parliament (1947): Volume 1
ISBN 978-1-78148-937-6

Indian Independence and British Parliament (1946): Volume II
ISBN 978-1-78623-553-4

Declassified British Secret Documents: Diplomatic Communications Relating to Pakistan (1980)
ISBN 978-1-78623-526-8

Available for purchase online from all major international book retailers, including Amazon, or from the office address of P.A.L.S.S. given above.